The
OLD ROSE
ADVISOR

PLATE 1. 'Princess May', 'Mme Abel Chatenay', 'Ben Cant', 'Bardou Job', 'Lady Moyra Beauclerc', 'Lady Roberts'

The
OLD ROSE
ADVISOR

by

Brent C. Dickerson

— ✳ —

*"These roses sing, 'I have kept the faith,
I have fought a good fight.' "* [ARA40]

— ✳ —

TIMBER PRESS
Portland, Oregon

ISBN 0-88192-216-1
Printed in Hong Kong

TIMBER PRESS, INC.
9999 S.W. Wilshire, Suite 124
Portland, Oregon 97225

Library of Congress Cataloging-in-Publication Data

Dickerson, Brent C.
    The old rose advisor / by Brent C. Dickerson.
        p. cm.
    Includes bibliographical references and index.
    ISBN 0-88192-216-1
    1. Old roses.   2. Old roses — Varieties.   I. Title.
SB411.65.O55D53 1992
635.9'33372 — dc20

91-29686
CIP

"He who would have beautiful Roses in his garden
must have beautiful Roses *in his heart*." [H]

CONTENTS

Color plates follow page 192

AUTHORIAL TESTIMONY

"On appearing before the tribunal of public opinion, every author who has not cherished an unreasonable estimate of his own qualifications, must necessarily be impressed with considerable anxiety respecting the probable reception of his work. . . . The present work is the first of the kind that has ever been attempted. . . . Owing to the indispensable nature of this work, it makes no positive claim to the character of an original composition, in the strict acceptation of that term." [D]

I have received the anxious and ready assistance of a number of rosarians and non-rosarians the world over, without whose friendly cooperation this project would have turned out very differently indeed. The great rosariums of L'Haÿ and Sangerhausen have been particularly generous in their help, for which I can only give my inadequate but warmest thanks. Among libraries, special recognition must go to the Libraries of the University of California at Berkeley, whence came the illustrations for this work, and the Library of the U.S. Department of Agriculture, as well as to the Bibliothèque Nationale, the Société d'Horticulture d'Angers et du Département de Maine-et-Loire, and the Société Nationale d'Horticulture. The Tuna Club in enchanting Avalon, California, provided unique assistance, as did Les Amis de Vieux l'Haÿ in France. Mrs. Paul Gardner and Mr. George C. Thomas IV were most gracious and helpful with my researches on Capt. Thomas. The Conard-Pyle Co., at the forefront of American rose commerce for lo! these many years, provided with the greatest generosity research materials of the highest importance to my effort to clarify the American side of things. Mr. Brad Bunnin, of Berkeley, California, provided not only needed legal advice but also a cool head at a critical juncture. The ever-helpful and efficient staff members of the Inter-Library Loan desk at California State University, Long Beach, Cathrine Lewis-Ida and Sharlene Laforge, two of the most long-suffering individuals in this whole process, obtained for me whole shoals of books I had imagined unobtainable; the length of the "works consulted" listing is, to a great degree, a monument to their efforts. The able and important overseas assistance I have received from Mme Christiane Delacour and, particularly, the indefatigable Monsieur Georges Massiot — a true *débrouillard* — in negotiating Gallic intricacies as well as in helping me to obtain copies of valuable, rare material is not only deeply appreciated by myself, but is also yet another example of the generosity and spirit shown by the French throughout these pages. It will be one of the greater rewards of my work if the good will which I have received so abundantly from so many is adequately reflected in the information and pleasure which this book provides.

I must acknowledge in advance the kind assistance rendered by those who write to me, care of the publisher, correcting some error or misreading made when weary eyelids dropped *too* low, apprising me of the veritable existence of a cultivar thought extinct, or informing me of remarkable characteristics hitherto unrecorded of this cultivar or that. There are still mysterious names to be explained, obscure genealogies to be supplied or unraveled, and reclusive facts to be coaxed from their hermitages. Background information on several figures, most notably Vibert and Laffay, has been most difficult to come by; more would be welcome on these as well as on the other horticulturalists mentioned in these pages. Moreau-Robert, bearing the heritage of Descemet and Vibert, suddenly disappears without a word in the early years of this century: Did the firm have any successor (I understand that the site of the Vibertian nurseries in Angers is now covered by apartments!)? Any and all such data would be of interest to readers of future editions. A work of this nature is built on the cooperative vigilance of all, and it is by running such efforts through the mill of disseminated information and human experience that we may grind it into something more perfect and more useful.

The debt which I, and we all, owe to Vibert, Laffay, Sisley, Lacharme, Rivers, the Pauls, Buist, Ellwanger, Capt. Thomas — indeed, to all who are listed and unlisted in the Bibliography and Index — is unpayable, just as the real camaraderie I have felt working with these my *silent* partners is undeniable. If some readers are moved to take a closer look at *their* work — their writings, their roses, their thoughts — perhaps then some of this debt will have been repaid, and one of my goals met.

"The number of varieties has become so considerable that it is difficult if not impossible for the amateur to deal with the interminable list of names that breeders old or new have given their introductions. It became necessary to have a guide, a special work which contained, methodically arranged, all the necessary information. . . . This work . . . gives a true-to-life presentation of the most popular roses . . . it is not necessary to demonstrate the utility of this *Dictionary*: It is incontestable. . . . The *Dictionary of Roses* may, in a word, be considered as the Rosarian's complete library.

"In presenting the description of six thousand roses [**The Old Rose Advisor**, *not covering the old European cultivars in this edition, provides two thousand three hundred and thirty-two*], will I be able to satisfy everyone? No! In giving my readers a *précis* of everything that appeared in the rose world up to 1885, will I have a complete work? No! In making known each book published till now, will I satisfy my readers? No! And do I therefore lose my nerve, and decide not to publish my *Dictionary of Roses*? No! Critics, hear me: I have listened to the comments of able men, I have followed the counsels of capable persons — and I laugh at those who nit-pick or complain simply for the pleasure of nit-picking or complaining. I publish this book with the wish of providing a needed service. Will I bring it off? I hope so!" [S]

9

Chapter One
PRELIMINARY

Prefatory

"How shall I dare to tread upon the territory of the Rosarian? For nothing so exasperates the specialist as when the mere amateur comes along and blithers bright nonsense about his own particular pet subject on which he has accumulated the wisdom of years. Therefore go I very daintily, for fear of the pruning knives of the National Rose Society banded unanimously against me." [Fa]

"When it is considered, that almost everybody of note, engaged in the propagation and sale of the Rose, has, more or less, written upon the subject of its culture, and that amateurs of some experience have added their share to the Rose literature of the age, it cannot be anticipated that much can be offered that has not, in some form or other, been given to the public." [Gl]

Taking these observations to heart, I have gathered in this work the comments and observations of those who have written on the Rose, concentrating on material written since 1790. As valuable as the notes of any individual author are, or could be, it has always seemed to me that what was required was the broader view. Because one author cries "Horrible . . . horrible" when confronted with a variety which has somehow managed to provoke his particular ire, and his book is the one a gardener happens to read, that gardener may become alienated from a rose which is perfectly suited to his climate or taste.

One purpose of this book, then, is to give the reader a perspective on these cultivars, a perspective taking advantage of the many years they have been in cultivation, so that he may choose wisely for his own garden having been able to compare the various opinions of a century and more of experts and fanciers. "For comparisons are not odious. It is only those who have good reason for dreading them who forged the silly lie that they are; comparisons are the very sole basis of all judgement, of all moral and religious ideas that the world has ever conceived, or ever will, or ever could." [Fa]

Like the cultivars themselves, these "old" opinions are valuable and should not be neglected in the mistaken notion that "new" is intrinsically good. I have concentrated upon the opinions offered between 1790 and 1920 because that is when most of these roses were widely grown, because works of this period are more difficult for most gardeners to obtain and consult, and because—the newer ones are still under copyright. Even these newer and newest books, however modern, scholarly, pretty, dignified, likable, or valuable they may be—and most are indeed all of the above—do not cover all of the available material. Nowhere could one find a *complete* list of the extant varieties for any of the classes. I have made every attempt to list all of the cultivars which still exist, though sharply—in some cases, completely—curtailing the descriptions of the more modern Polyanthas and Hybrid Teas, classes which have persevered beyond the "old" category.

Despite my efforts to provide listings of all extant cultivars, however, specimens of some varieties thought extinct will doubtless come to light; for example, reports of the death of 'Hume's Blush', 'Parks' Yellow', 'Slater's Crimson', 'Pâquerette', and a number of others have fortunately been greatly exaggerated, as they are again available. Consequently, I have also included in the listings, but in square brackets, some of those which, though now seemingly extinct, I either suspect or blindly hope will be rediscovered. Others, many of them very desirable cultivars indeed, lead a twilight existence in botanical gardens in one place or another, notably France's Roseraie de l'Haÿ or Germany's Sangerhausen. Those of most limited availability or most rarefied interest are listed primarily in the chapter supplements, and easily double the number of "old" roses usually considered extant.

These cultivars—all of them—have their value in the horticultural world on both the æsthetic and breeding levels. The Hybrid Perpetuals, Damask Perpetuals, and Hybrid Chinas solve the "what roses for my cold-winter conditions?" problem, while the Teas, Chinas, and Noisettes deserve to reclaim ground from Hibiscuses, Oleanders, and Bougainvilleas in the subtropical regions. Furthermore, complicated as they are, the rather purer genetic lines of the older roses make them more desirable breeding material than are the infinitely more miscellaneous and complex modern hybrids. Moreover, these lines deserve further work in their own right as garden subjects; their possibilities have by no means been exhausted. The problem, of course, for non-European rosarians is that many of these cultivars are only available from overseas sources, and then usually undergo periods of quarantine or other such trials so that one has to be something more than obsessed to persevere. It would be desirable if—particularly now that the Rose is the national flower of the United States—American devotees of these various cultivars would turn their efforts to establishing and coordinating pools of these roses in the U.S. to enable those interested to obtain them easily. Perhaps a *complete* national collection of old roses in some favored location is not too much to hope for. . . .

The genealogies of some of these roses, particularly those developed in the early years, were often the product of after-the-fact guesswork by the breeders—not that these were simply pulled out of thin air, as the number of sorts good for breeding was limited, and the characteristics of each were well known by the hybridists. These earliest genealogies, then, should be regarded in many cases as earnest attempts and educated guesses rather than as received doctrine. Even as careful a worker as Lambert was evidently undecided as to whether his 'Kaiserin Auguste Viktoria' was derived from 'Perle des Jardins' × 'Belle Lyonnaise' or to 'Coquette de Lyon' × 'Lady Mary Fitzwilliam'. Both were quoted in periodicals which he read; and, though he was given to correcting the Press's errors, he never wrote in to correct either attribution. Either seems likely; in such cases, I give both.

I have pared down the quotations in the main entries to a minimum to make room for the greatest amount of diversity with the least amount of *needless* repetition. Modern writers have sometimes made comments which I have not been able to resist including; I have made sparing use of these with the much appreciated permission of the writer and/or publisher. The key to the citations, both modern and "old," is located in the Bibliography.

The order followed in each entry varies with the nature of the remarks available. I wish that I had had for every cultivar the resources I had for 'Gloire de Dijon'! I have made no attempt to follow a chronological order; time is an empty distinction in this connection, as in so many others. I am not overly fond of the word "old" as applied to these roses; it suggests an arcanum which unfortunately alienates as many people as it attracts. I have known people to wrinkle up their noses and say "Old rose? Who would want an *old* rose?" as if we were talking about an old sheep or an old sandwich. These roses are not old in that way, decrepit, decaying. They were simply *developed* "of old," and specimens now on the market are as young and vigorous as the specimens of last year's all-America selection at the local nursery. The breeding which produced them could have taken place in 1990 as easily as in 1890 — but the eye which selected them as being desirable material was an eye trained in the æsthetics of another time. This, however, should be no barrier to appreciation. Ramifications of the same æsthetic are admired today when we listen to Offenbach or Puccini, read Dickens or Conan Doyle, or, most particularly, when we appreciate the visual artists of the era — the designers, the architects, the *artists* — because horticulture and plant-breeding are also popular *Arts*, much as novels, clothes-design, and theater-arts are and were. Those who appreciate the finer things are still delighted today by the beautiful in horticulture just as they cherish man's productions in any of the other arts. The special cachet of Vibert or Lacharme stamps their work no less than the spirit of Renoir, Atget, or Nijinsky infuses *theirs*. Yes, these are "old" roses, but as we do not distinguish other works of the time as "old," the distinction seems rather unfair. Nothing should be dismissed because of the historical accident of its having been developed at one particular time or another; everything bears its special quality as a gift to us. We need only make the effort to reach out and accept it.

Research holds many rewards, so it was always with the greatest pleasure that I would find myself on some wintry morning turning the pages of the *Journal des Roses,* the *American Rose Annual,* or any of the other hundred and more materials which stand behind this work. Though the romance of our tale seems to diminish — as romance will — as we approach the present, the research has nevertheless held very exotic, very exciting tales even as it has also much of the homey and even more of the very human! More than once, armies — Napoleonic, Prussian, Allied — have marched over the rosefields before my eyes; I have taken the cure at Vichy with Mons Lévêque; stood, eagle-eyed, with Mme Béluze in the maison Béluze window; attended Mons Desprez at his death-bed; looked with young Rivers one fine morning in June over his first bed of seedlings; even found a memorable use for an ill-starred stray cat. I hope that I have been able to communicate to the reader some of the excitement, pleasure, and life which I have experienced in preparing these pages; and that, by the time he turns the last page, he will have a fuller understanding not only of the cultivars but also of their milieu.

"The little work which follows took much time and effort. Perhaps it could be said that one's leisure time could be better employed by writing more useful things: the questions of nomenclature and of horticultural history are only of moderate interest to the present generation of amateur growers! One may respond to those of this inclination [*presumably with a shrug*] that, very well, such is their opinion; but as for me, in wishing to learn these things for myself, I like to hope at the same time that such a historical outline as this would be interesting and useful to others as well. Finally, I cannot conceal the hope that, apart from the pure chimeras which seem to have guided these researches, perhaps the admonishing spirits — the professional rose-breeders — who know to read between the lines, will find there something of profit." [JR31/128]

Poetical

"Of all the flowers with which Nature embellished our gardens, the Rose is that which unites the brilliance of the most beautiful blossoms with the most agreeable fragrance. In the farthest ages, in the homes of the ancients as well as the moderns, it always occupied the premier place. Is that so strange? This amiable flower appeals to and at the same time charms all the senses; it is attractive to all ages: the young girl, the fortunate lover — the happy couple seek it out and gather it eagerly; it becomes for them the troth or prize of their amours. And when we have come to be old, it awakens in us the remembrance of the pleasures of youth; and when finally life's winter deadens all our senses, it is the sweet perfume of a rose that brings them back again for a moment." [V1]

"And then, in the cyclones of snow and ice, begins the spring. . . . And on the dead rose-bushes hang a thousand buds, like withered moths, dark amid the whirling snowflakes. The Japanese cherish their gift of condensing a whole aspect of nature or emotion into one tiny phrase: listen:

> *Furu-dera ya;*
> *Kane-mono iwazu*
> *Sakura chiru.*

For here is the crystallized loneliness of spirit:

> *Ancient temple;*
> *Voiceless bells;*
> *Falling cherry petals.*

What could be more delicately and more completely pictorial? And, like all pungent and memorable portraits of human emotion, direct and simple and naked. But if we of the West desire . . . to condense into a phrase the blankest and lowest hour of winter, I, at least, cannot better express it to myself than by that picture of all the little blackened wasted rose-buds, standing stiff on their dead boughs in a snowstorm. —Bah, let them quickly be pruned away—hideous reminders of bygone beauty." [Fa]

Historical

"The culture of the Rose, handed down from antiquity, has never ceased in Europe; but it was the Moors in Spain who were the first, among modern peoples, to give particular attention to their culture. The fine plains of Valencia, the gardens of Cordova and of Granada were the true rose-beds—which are not to be found today." [JF]

"The Rose was, for quite some time, neglected, unlike certain other flowers: Anemones, Hyacinths, Carnations, and Tulips, which were the object of extreme enthusiasm in the 18th and 19th Centuries, sometimes beyond all reason. Because of their brightness—as well as their suckers—some specimens of a small number of species and varieties persisted in cultivation, among which were the Gallicas, the Damasks, and the Centifolias—the most popular. But if indeed someone were to plant many roses, it would only be for the various uses of pharmacists or perfumers.

"The Dutch were the first to propagate Roses by seed. They particularly favored the Gallicas. It wasn't long before they had cornered the Rose market.

"At that time, France didn't have the specialized rose-breeding of the establishments of Dupont and Vilmorin, of Paris; Godefroy, of Ville-d'Avray; Descemet, of Saint-Denis; and Vibert, of Chennevières-sur-Marne." [F]

"Among those in our country [France] who have increased our pleasures, Mons Descemet without a doubt takes a place of honor. Because of his numerous seedlings developed over more than a dozen years, produced methodically, his wonderful results, his acute observations, as well as the more than two hundred interesting varieties due to him, he merits such a place. Fanciers and others who set a great price on the progress of the Rose will regret always those events of 1814 and 1815 which forced him to take his knowledge and efforts elsewhere [Russia]. I [Vibert] was fortunate enough to be able to save his large and interesting collection from being dispersed. His breeding material, his plants being studied, and more than ten thousand seedlings of all ages passed into my hands. Mons Descemet had amassed a great many notes on his seedlings; the origins of a part of his seedlings were contained in those notes. This precious work, which gave us valuable notions on the tricks of Nature and on which varieties are the best to sow, was destroyed as a consequence of that war; a small part, which was fortunately saved, makes me regret all the more the remainder lost, which would have spared me much time and effort." [V1]

"The trade of cultivating Roses in France is in the hands of many individuals; and to visit that country with the view of forming a collection is (I speak from experience) a laborious undertaking. As far as my powers of observation serve me, I should think the establishments where they are grown for sale, in the neighbourhood of Paris, vary in extent from one to five acres; and there are others, situate in various parts of France, nearly all of like extent. It is thus that English amateurs, who may chance to visit any of them, are usually disappointed, owing to the contrast of their Rose Gardens with those of England, which are much more extensive. The most splendid collection in France [*as of 1848, that is*] is that in the Jardin du Luxembourg in Paris, which is under the supervision of Monsieur Hardy. Most of the plants there are of some age, and flower most profusely in the season. It is true that they look rather drawn; but when we consider their proximity to the heart of the city, it is surprising that they flourish so well." [P]

"The most well-known collection was that of Malmaison, formed for the Empress Josephine by Dupont; and those of the Luxembourg, under the direction of Hardy. About three hundred varieties could be named, mostly Gallicas, before they were added to, rather later, by Hardy, Prévost of Rouen, Vibert, Desprez, Laffay, etc. Along with the Gallicas, the classes of Centifolias, Mosses, Damasks, and Portlands were being formed. . . .

"Meanwhile, the China and Tea-Scented Roses were brought onto the scene between 1798 and 1810, along with Noisettes and Bourbons a few years later. Of these early varieties, however, few other than the common China [presumably 'Parsons' Pink'] are still with us.

"The seedlings increased, and, in 1828, the number of old varieties quintupled, over and above the nearly 300 varieties of Chinas, Bourbons, Teas, and Noisettes. . . .

"Jacques, gardener at the Neuilly estate of the Duc d'Orléans (who became King Louis-Philippe I), developed the Sempervirens class, in which is 'Félicité et Perpétue', then Vibert, Laffay, Béluze, Hardy, and other breeders gave us, up through the middle of the 19th Century, such varieties as the following: 'Aimée Vibert', 'Lamarque', 'Mme Hardy', 'Mrs. Bosanquet', 'Cramoisi Supérieur', 'Persian Yellow', 'Safrano', 'Hermosa', 'Triomphe du Luxembourg', 'Ophirie',

'Céline Forestier', 'Chromatella', 'Solfatare', 'Souvenir de la Malmaison', 'Niphetos', 'Souvenir d'Un Ami', '[Mlle de] Sombreuil'. Meanwhile, the race of Hybrid Perpetuals was being developed with: 'Duchesse de Sutherland', 'Baronne Prévost', 'Ernestine de Barante', 'Géant des Batailles', 'Lion des Combats', 'La Reine'—enough! The others are well known.

"The appearance of these beautiful remontant varieties, which are much the greater part of our modern collections, brought about the neglect of the old sorts, the Gallicas, Damasks, Centifolias, etc.; their decline and fall came quickly." [F]

With the appearance of the Hybrid Perpetuals came, at length, the development of the Rose Show, a factor of great, though largely untold, significance; their rise signals the decline of the rose as a garden plant considered as such, making way for the rose considered as a blossom with its plant as a mere appendage. These rose shows, first *notably* organized in 1865 by Camille Bernardin, "to whom much of the success of the Exhibition is due," [R-H65] did rosedom the great favor of stimulating the imaginations and efforts of the hybridists of the day. Rose shows have also played their part in standardizing—for better or worse—our ideas of what a rose should look like; the "bigger is better" mystique was, and still is, bolstered by the nature of competition in such exhibitions; and this, in turn, lies behind the common notions of how a rose plant should be pruned. Bernardin's "special rose exposition" at Brie-Comte-Robert in 1865 was, in its way, the quiet revolution making modern rosedom what it is today.

"I sometimes fear that the passion for large, well-formed blossoms, and the desire for novelty, will make some of the dear old Roses of our childhood pass into entire neglect." [Br]

Practical

"Cultivate none but the best, and cultivate them thoroughly." [FP]

"It is suggested that roses in the different classes should be grown where they are best adapted to the various climates." [Th2] "At all times of the year roses need constant and watchful care; and the amateur—especially if a woman, hampered with tiresome petticoats—must have space in which to move, in order to pick off caterpillars, cut the flowers whether alive or dead, and see to all the various needs of the plants, such as weeding, watering, manuring and pruning." [K2]

"The object in pruning a Rose is to give it a suitable form, and to rejuvenate the branches as much as possible for the best flowering. It is difficult to be specific, but pruning ought to be done according to the vigor of the variety, the exposure, and particular culture followed. The general rules one might state are: For varieties of feeble growth which are very floriferous, prune to 2 or three eyes; for those of varying growth, 4 or 5 eyes; for strong-growing or climbing, 6–15 eyes.

"Roses are pruned during the first days of March [in St.-Sulpice, Tarn, France; *I* on the other hand do it the week after Christmas here in Southern California]. Pruning consists of cutting out the dead or weak branches, eliminating competition between branches so that they do not cross, and in rejuvenating the plant as much as possible by cutting out the secondary branches." [LR]

"*Do not* choose the varieties for your garden from exhibits at shows. The blossoms there I know are fine, and the temptation is great to have some of the novelties sent on to you. Do not yield to it. The exhibition specimen may be the special effort of a variety which for garden decoration may be practically worthless." [Bk]

"Unfortunately descriptions are sometimes rather fantastic, but everyone will allow how extremely difficult it is to describe any rose . . . the beauties of the rose are difficult to translate [from sight to words]; entire pages must be devoted to the description of each variety if one would give an exact picture of the rose described." [G&B]

Explanatory

Cultivars are listed by the names under which they were originally introduced—when determinable—or, where there is any doubt as to synonymy, under the name with which they enjoyed the widest distribution. The ritual of "release to commerce" being the deciding factor, the names introducers provided are preferred to those bestowed by the breeder. I heed the "earnest desire" of one breeder/introducer, and prefer 'Panachée d'Angers' to the earlier name 'Commandant Beaurepaire', particularly as 'Commandant Beaurepaire' was a name intended for a non-remontant form. The date for the cultivar is that of the year in which it was released to commerce, with, for instance, a rose originally announced in late 1885 as being for the "1885–1886 season" being listed here as an 1885 rose.

Main entries in [square brackets] refer to those roses which are, or seem to be, extinct, but which are nevertheless important or interesting enough that to leave them out of this account would be a disservice. Names in (round brackets or parentheses) are synonyms or translations. It is worth remembering that a "synonym," in this connection, is not a word or name of equal merit to be used interchangeably with the "original" name; it is an appellation which is "incorrect" for some reason, which has however been used at some point, and which should be kept in mind should it pop up in research material or on a label in some rosarium.

The next element in an entry is the name of the breeder and/or introducer, followed by the date of introduction. In the item "Laxton/G. Paul, 1876," Laxton is the breeder and G. Paul the introducer, which will be the order followed throughout. A solitary name indicates the introducer.

The parentages, as discussed above, are always open to question, and yet are never to be regarded as intentional or sinister mis-statements by those from whom I have culled the information. The *fact* in many cases being unascertainable, the *conjecture* of an expert — usually the breeder — surely weighs in as important evidence.

Following the parentages are the quotations, arranged in whatever order their content suggested, but generally beginning with remarks on color and other characteristics of the blossom, continuing with characteristics of the leaves and plant in general, and ending with such cultural and/or historical data as is available and relevant. Each quotation is followed by a code designation indicating the work from which it came, which designation is "translated" for would-be researchers in the reference key located in the Bibliography.

The illustrations for *The Old Rose Advisor* come from the copy of the 1877–1914 *Journal des Roses* in the collection of the library of the University of California at Berkeley. I would like to take this opportunity to express my appreciation again to that library in general, and to its photo lab in particular, for making these illustrations available to me in such a fine form. This institution is a model of what a library should be in responsible service and high quality.

The plate captions provide what is intended to be the full, "official," name of each cultivar. In a number of cases, the artist of the original illustration includes within the plate a variant of one sort of another. I have arranged the plates within each group according to the date that the pictured cultivar was introduced. This was done in the hope that such an arrangement, at least in the more profusely illustrated groups, would provide the reader with a sense of how the cultivar "stacked up" against its contemporaries, as well as to demonstrate the progress and changing ideals in each group to those who survey the general sweep of the plates.

Many of the original artists of the lithographs display an elegance, accuracy, and whimsy in their work which is, in my opinion, at least equal to the work of Redouté. Such opinions are, of course, a matter of taste. Let us hope, however, that along with the "Raphael of Flowers," æsthetic rosarians also remember, for one, Lina Schmidt-Michel, whose delightful pictures seem to me to capture not only the beauty of the roses, but also the spirit of their time.

My guiding principle in choosing the format and arrangement of this book has been primarily to serve the needs of the "rank and file" gardener, who is the backbone of all horticulture, and then, secondarily, to provide for the special needs of the enthusiast and the researcher. Because of this, I have avoided some of the more abstruse flights of botanical fancy in favor of the conventions of horticulture, which are clearer and more familiar to the majority of those using this book. "We will not list [the cultivars] in the scholarly style, as Lindley, de Pronville, Prévost, and others, have done, but will instead use the commercial nomenclature, the best indeed to use with nurserymen." [Pq] Otherwise — "Is human Writing, then, the art of burying Heroisms and highest Facts in chaos; so that no man shall henceforth contemplate them without horror and aversion . . . ? What does [the writer] consider that he was born for; that paper and ink were made for?" [Cy2]

What indeed!

Chapter Two
DAMASK PERPETUALS

"What is the rose called 'des Quatre Saisons'? Where did it originate? No one can say! . . . Is a person able to establish common characteristics to form a more or less homogeneous group? No! One finds here many roses classified as 'Portlands' which are very different from the type — for example, 'Rose du Roi', 'Julie Krudner', 'Célina Dubos' — varieties which, by their bearing and growth, have little in common with the 'Quatre Saisons' rose with which they are classed." [JR9/56-57]

And so we are left with a rather heterogeneous collection tied together by their relationship to the original Damask Perpetual, the pink-flowered entity known variously as *Rosa damascena bifera*, *R. damascena semperflorens*, the Autumn Damask, the Rose of Castile, as well as any number of other *ad hoc* names. This, the 'Bifera', originated quite early, in ancient times, evidently through a natural cross of *R. gallica* and *R. moschata*.

The next, and most problematical, step in the story of Damask Perpetuals occurred some 2,000 years later, evidently for La Quintinye, Louis XIV's chief horticulturalist based at the Trianon palace. In a list of the 14 cultivars of roses cultivated in France in his time, he includes "The Tous-les-Mois ["Year-Round"] Rose, which is a sort of red Musk Rose bearing its blossoms in clusters, the rose called 'Grande', and finally the Damask or Musk Rose." [LaQ] One notes that La Quintinye feels the 'Year-Round Rose' to be new or unfamiliar enough to need a description; one also notes that, conversely, the Musk Rose, *R. moschata*, seems to have been known well enough to serve as an object of comparison and definition.

What, then, was this 'Tous-les-Mois', this "sort of red Musk Rose"? Obviously not the old pink 'Bifera'. It certainly seems to have been considered as belonging to the Damask tribe; it was apparently what Rivers has in mind when differentiating "our very old Damask Rose, the Red Monthly," from "the comparatively new rose, 'Rose à Quatre Saisons' of the French." [R8] To continue with seemings: this "old Damask Rose, the Red Monthly," seems to be the cultivar referred to when we learn that "there was, some time ago, a new type of Perpetuals going by the name of 'Trianon' because the Red Damask was particularly noted in that area." [JDR54/30] "I was at Rouen in September 1829, at the home of an English plantsman [*probably London-based Calvert*] whose garden had been left to itself for awhile, and noticed there, among the seedlings, a semi-double rose blooming, which, aside from its remontant qualities, showed characteristics I hadn't seen in other species [*or* 'sorts']. Some [growth-] buds of this rose were given to me, and, as the place had the name 'Trianon', that is what I named the rose.

"Having sown the seed of this rose for 8 or 9 years without having gotten more than one good variety, I sowed instead the seed of some flesh-colored semi-doubles with foliage which was different [from that of their ancestor, this 'Trianon' from Rouen]; after having done the same for three or four years, I was able to raise a white, and the seeds of *this* were what I subsequently sowed, for the most part. The greater part of my seed-bearers are in their 5th or 6th generation, and it is really quite extraordinary to see such diversity among plants springing from the same Type. . . .

"The number of such Roses descending from my Perpetual 'Trianon', doubles and semi-doubles, has surpassed 40, and I am sure to add many to the number of doubles before too many years have passed. Many of these roses bloom in clusters of 50 to 60 blossoms; their diameter varies from 3−8 cm [ca. 1−3 in]; most waft an elegant perfume. From purest white to light purple, all shades are found. But, above all, it is in the details of their appearance that Nature has exercised freedom: wood, leaves, thorns, manner of growth — all vary. . . .

"Such, then, are the reasons I have set up a new division of Perpetuals. . . .

"Let me add an important observation: Within this set of roses are plants which bloom the first year from seed, which does not ordinarily happen with Chinas, Noisettes, or Bourbons; last year, 10 or 12 young plants bloomed in July.

"All of these Roses coming from this 'Trianon' seem to me to be very receptive to pollination from other varieties — or perhaps it is because of their own inherent qualities that they show so much variation, which seems to me to be the more likely explanation [signed: Vibert, Angers, June 28, 1846]." [dH47/282]

"The Musk Rose lives on in the 'Trianons' and 'Portlands' under the names 'Sapho', 'Blanche Vibert', 'Delphine Gay' [Vibert, ca. 1821, pale red], 'La Candeur' [Vibert, 1849, flesh], etc." [JDR54/42] But how do the Portlands fit into this?

In 1775, Weston lists the 'Portland Crimson Monthly Rose', already "to be readily found," separately from the 'Tous-les-Mois' group; by 1785, as we learn from Buc'hoz, it had entered France, though evidently not making much of a splash, as Fillassier does not mention it in 1791; in 1805, Andrews reports that it is "said" that the rose was named "in compliment to the late Duchess" — second Duchess of Portland, who died in 1785. But as to its origin, the nearest we can come is second-hand information recorded in 1882 by a writer who *seems* to have a first-hand account at his elbow as he writes: "At the end of the last century or the beginning of this one . . . was found at Portland, England, a rosebush quite dis-similar to *R. damascena bifera*, from which came the seed, a seed which was in most probability a hybrid with *R. gallica* because the new acquisition showed certain resemblances to both species. It had semi-double flowers, scarlet-purple, successively until frost. It was called the 'Portland Damask'. . . . Some years later, perhaps about 1820, Godefroy, nurseryman at Ville d'Avray (Seine-et-Oise) [*and, perhaps significantly, sometime colleague of Vibert; as detailed in M-V49/102, the two were, about this same time (1820), putting their heads together to identify the Centifolia 'Foliacée'],* developed a sub-variety of 'Portland' dis-similar enough to its progenitor to begin a new race by the name of 'Perpetual Rose'. Its foliage was light green; its flowers pink, semi-double, in clusters, and remontant until November." [JR6/153] "In 1815, remontant roses were still rare; one can only find two in the Portland series, the biferas 'Palmyre' and 'Venusta'. In the month of August in that same year, 'Rose du Roi' was developed from seedlings grown in 1814 . . . [at] Sèvres, near St. Cloud . . . " [JF] (but see under 'Rose du Roi'). "Jacques, the King's gardener at Neuilly, developed from the Portland the hybrid 'Athalin', a variety which, like 'Malton', is an excellent seed-bearer. 'Athalin', crossed with 'Rose du Roi', would later give remontant roses having the Portland character — a short and stiff flower-stem, with the blossom nestling among the leaves — which distinguished the first descendants of 'Athalin', varieties of feeble growth and weak remontancy. Rosarians gave these Portland-derived varieties the name Hybrid Portlands to distinguish them from other remontant hybrids." [JF]

"[In the *Hybrid* Perpetuals,] the leaves are completely glabrous, and smooth in youth; however, in age, they thicken a little, becoming stiff and slightly rugose; it is this which distinguishes these *hybrids* from *true Portlands*, which have soft, slender, downy leaves." [I'H51/121]

"As the culture of this class of roses is at present but imperfectly understood, I shall give the result of my experience as to their cultivation, with suggestions to be acted upon according to circumstances. One peculiar feature they nearly all possess — a reluctance to root when layered; consequently, Perpetual [Damask] Roses, on their own roots, will always be scarce: when procurable, they will be found to succeed much better on dry poor soils than the budded plants, which require a rich soil. Perpetual Roses, as a general rule however, require a superabundant quantity of food: it is therefore perfectly ridiculous to plant them on arid lawns, and to suffer the grass to grow close up to their stems, without giving them a particle of manure for years. Under these circumstances, the best varieties, even the 'Rose du Roi', will scarcely ever give a second series of flowers. To remedy the inimical nature of arid soils to this class of roses, an annual application of manure on the surface of the earth is quite necessary. . . . I have said that this treatment is applicable to dry poor soils; but even in good rose soils it is almost indispensible; as it imparts such increased vigor, and such a prolongation of the flowering season, as to amply repay the labor bestowed. If the soil is prepared as directed, the plants will twice in the year require pruning: in November, when the beds are dressed, and again a short time before the first flowering in June. At the November pruning, cut off from every shoot of the preceding summer's growth about two-thirds; if the shoots are crowded, remove some of them entirely. If this autumnal pruning is attended to, there will be at the end of May, or early in June, the following summer, a vast number of luxuriant shoots, each crowned with a cluster of buds. Now, as June roses are always abundant a little sacrifice must be made to insure a fine autumnal bloom; therefore, leave only half the number of shoots to bring forth their summer flowers, and shorten the remainder to about half their length. Each shortened branch will soon put forth buds; and in August and September the plants will again be covered with flowers. In cultivating Perpetual Roses, the faded flowers ought immediately to be removed; for in autumn the petals do not fall off readily, but lose their colour and remain on the plant, to the injury of forthcoming buds." [WRP]

"This nearly extinct class of roses should find in the heart of the rosarian a warm corner, because of their splendour when planted in masses, for they are in truth genuine bedding roses, and bloom superbly from July to October; their colours rich, their odour spicy and refreshing." [Hd] "The neglect of them is a patent instance of good things lost sight of from the caprice of fashion, or want of knowledge by the moderns of their existence." [WD]

ARTHUR DE SANSAL
Listed as a Hybrid Perpetual.

[BELLE FABERT]
('Belle Favert', 'Grand Perpetual')
Unknown, Pre-1825?

"Deep pink." [V4] "Full, flat, very large, beautiful." [LF] "Bright rosy crimson, sometimes tinted with purple, very large and full; form, globular. Very sweet." [P] "Brilliant." [Hstl:308] "Handsome carmine-pink often tinted with maroon." [S] "Large, deep pink, full d'ble, convex." [WRP] "Very large, very double, attaining 5 in[ches] in diameter [ca. 1.25 dm], pink, not very regular." [Go] "Very sweet-scented." [M'l] "A true Perpetual rose of great excellence, requiring a rich soil and good culture to bloom in perfection. It has one great fault — the flowers produced in July are so large that they almost invariably burst; its autumnal flowers are much more symmetrical." [WRP]

BIFERA
(*R. damascena bifera, R. damascena semperflorens,* 'Rose of Pæstum', 'Rose of Castile', 'Quatre Saisons', 'Autumn Damask')
Ancient Introduction
Probably *R. gallica* × *R. moschata.*

"Growth very vigorous; canes pretty strong, branching; bark light green, with numerous brown thorns which are very sharp and nearly straight. Foliage ample, handsome green, slightly rugose, 5–7 oval, rounded, finely dentate leaflets; petiole strong, thick, armed with 4–5 little prickles. Flowers to 3 in [ca. 8 cm] or so, nearly full, cupped, solitary on the branchlets, more often in clusters in which the number of blossoms varies according to the vigor of the cane; color, delicate pink, brighter in the center, petal edges paler; peduncle short, glandular. Calyx tubular; sepals leaf-like. The 'Quatre-Saisons' rose is the most fragrant of all roses, and is much besought for its perfume; but its name is unjustified, as it is not very remontant; pretty hardy, it nevertheless suffers in the coldest winters." [JF] "When the plant is left to itself, it blooms but little, often only once, and indeed perhaps not at all. . . . Plant the specimen in a pot and prune all the canes short enough to produce shoots which terminate in a blossom. After the bloom, it is necessary to withhold water from the plants in such a way as to stop growth and make them shed their leaves; then prune them and water them again The new shoots don't wait to grow, and, in their turn, produce their blossoms. If this travail is repeated in just the right way, one is able, in a year, to get four bloom periods, justifying the 'Quatre Saisons' appellation. . . . The 'Rosier des Quatre-Saisons', after having been cultivated on the grand scale — in pots for the flower markets, as well as for industrial uses, perfume is on the point of disappearing . . . . It will rejoin its many kinsmen, 'Gloire des Perpétuelles', 'Lodoïska', 'Antinoüs', 'La Magnanime', 'Palmyre', 'Mme Ferray', 'Joséphine Antoinette', which are said to belong to the same clan, and for which one today may similarly search in vain." [R-H85] The pre-1811 white sport

of 'Bifera' — 'Bifera Alba' — has been rediscovered recently in South Africa.

BLANCHE-VIBERT
('Blanc de Vibert')
Vibert, 1847

"White, tinged with flesh, large, very full, flat form; often comes with green center." [EL] "Flowers yellowish when first opening, changing to white, of medium size, full." [P] "One of the purest whites." [HstXXX:45] "Cupped flowers opening flat . . . Scented . . . 3 × 2 [ft; ca. 9 × 6 dm]." [B] "Flower 6–7 cm [ca. 3 in], full, matte white, yellowish when opening, crested at the center. Flower very beautiful and quite unique in its genre." [M-L 46/271] "Blooms well in the autumn." [FP] "Light green foliage." [G] "Vigorous, branches upright and short." [S]

As for Vibert himself: "Mons Vibert . . . has devoted all of his attentions since 1810 to growing Roses." [L-D] *Mons J.-P. Vibert,* [was a] member of the Horticultural Society of St. Denis (Seine) . . . winter of 1833-34. *For more than twenty years, Mons Vibert has given himself up exclusively to raising roses, and has done so with passion and discernment. His establishment serves as a model to others which have sprung up since, and though his success continues and grows, Mons Vibert announces in this catalog which is to be published that he will quit business in 1835, and sell at that time all his roses, greenhouses, frames, and acreage together or separately, depending upon the wishes of the buyers. It is distressing that Mons Vibert is retiring! However, the fruit of his long experience will not be forgotten; he has published many highly regarded papers, and it seems that there will be no shortage of people requesting such information."* [R-H33] Many of the rose-breeders with whom we are concerned have left us as earthly biography little more than their mute living proxies, their roses. While a person can with relative ease garner rough sketches of the lives of some of the better-known *rosiéristes,* the lives of the two greatest fathers of modern rose-breeding — Vibert and Laffay — have remained quite as mysterious as those of the least significant. It is only with the very greatest difficulty that the researcher has been able to come up with even the given name of either of the two, and, as to such basic biographical facts as birth-dates and death-dates — !

The importance of these two men to rose-advancement — Vibert's development or at least distribution of 'Gloire des Rosomanes' [B] and his series of Damask Perpetuals providing basic building materials, and Laffay leading the way in progressive breeding — mandates interest in them as human beings. We thus take great pleasure in offering to the reader the following on Vibert (and, later, some words on Laffay), the most important facts of which were gained through the assistance of the indefatigable Mons Massiot:

Jean-Pierre Vibert was born on January 31, 1777, in Paris, to Robert Vibert, and Aimée Françoise (Leiris) Vibert. [V5] His parents, who had five children in all, [ADE] were of the "small businessman" class in society. His father was a hosier, and other relations were haberdashers or hosiery makers.

To grow up in Paris as the decay of aristocracy — and of the monarchy itself! — began to fill the nostrils of the French; to be age 12 when the Bastille fell; to have a king guillotined 10 days before his 16th birthday, war declared on England a few days after; to see a "Reign of Terror" surround his 17th birthday; to see Napoleon, a few months later, restore a sort of order by main force; blood, battle, death on all sides; *this* was the youth of our Vibert. His grandson tells us (in *The Century* magazine, vol. 51, p. 79) *not* of a quiet, shy horticulturalist in the making, shunning violence, finding inner peace in rustic solitude in some out-of-the-way corner; *au contraire,* he tells of "Jean-Pierre Vibert, a soldier of the First Republic and of Napoleon, who, compelled by his many wounds to leave the army, became a gardener because he loved flowers." We do not know how much he was incapacitated by these "many wounds," but in due course he began to work as a salesman at a hardware store at 178 rue du Four in Paris, [MCN, ECS] between the Seine and the Palais du Luxembourg in the St.-Germain quarter of Paris, where we find him on July 20, 1804, taking out a ten-year loan [MCN] in the amount of 28,000 francs (in present terms, about $100,000) at a rate of 5.1%, the lender being one Mme Pezé, widow of a hardware dealer — presumably his former boss — and the collateral being the mortgage on a house which his father and mother owned at 38 rue des Moulins in Paris, on the other side of the Seine. With this loan, he bought a hardware store of his own at 30 rue du Four — a long street, and a good one for business — near the church St. Germain des Prés. By 1805, we find him married to the former Adélaïde Charlotte Heu.

As a hardware store owner, he would have sold gardening tools in particular, because there were still at that time numerous gardens in Paris, particularly in the southern quarters where the Revolution had dispossessed numerous religious houses. Thus it is that a few hundred yards from Vibert's store could be found, in the rue St.-Jacques, the garden of one Mons Dupont, a great rose fancier and breeder patronized by the Empress Joséphine, who, in this "jardin de Ste.-Marie," had brought together all of the roses then known to Europeans, indeed constituting a sort of "school of roses." [SHP36/140–141, L-D]

Perhaps through professional relations, or perhaps only out of initial curiosity, Jean-Pierre began a friendship with Mons Dupont, which developed his taste for roses and their culture. Vibert himself put together a small collection of roses in 1810 in a Parisian garden near the then city limits, on the Boulevard Mont-Parnasse, [SHP36] an area then rather out in the countryside. Thus began his career as a Rosiériste.

Though the term of his loan was ten years, falling due in 1815, Jean-Pierre had reserved the right to make occasional payments against the debt, a provision which he made use of, repaying 8,000 francs November 5, 1808, and another 10,000 the 5th of March in 1812, all of which would seem to indicate that he was prospering. But, about 1811 or 1812, he sold his hardware store and left Paris with his wife and three children, Théodore, Aimée, and Adélaïde, for the village of Soisy-sous-Etioles, along the Seine, some thirty kilometers from Paris. [MCN] This town was the cradle of his mother's family. [ECS] His father, now retired from business, was the mayor, and two of his own sisters lived there. [MCN, ECS] Jean-Pierre seems to have stayed only a short time in Soisy. Having doubtless found better ground for his roses, in 1813 he went north to Chennevières-sur-Marne where he would stay until 1827. The third and final payment on the loan was made on the due date in 1815, the mortgage on the collateral being released on the 18th of August.

That same year, the respected Mons Descemet, who had bred roses for more than twelve years in St. Denis, near Paris, [V1] was obliged to flee the country in the aftermath of the allied English, Prussian, and Russian invasion following Napoleon's loss at Waterloo June 18. Descemet's nursery was evidently sacked by the invading armies, and requests for indemnification from the government went unheeded. [Go] Vibert thereupon purchased from a no-doubt anxious Descemet his nursery stock and, evidently, other "movables" at the site, including in particular those of Descemet's breeding notes which were not destroyed in the invasion, as well as ten thousand rose seedlings of all ages, comprising the progeny of perhaps 250 individual species and varieties. During a season unfavorable for such an undertaking, on August 3, 1815, Vibert moved all of these young plants to his nursery at Chennevières. Nearly all of the stock survived and bloomed in the following years, providing more than a hundred new varieties "which later proved of consequence in the culture of this plant [*i.e., the Rose*]." [SHP29/146]

"What luck!" one would be tempted to say; *"These must have been happy, prosperous years for Vibert and his family!"* But Fate would have it otherwise. Just a month later came the death of his five-year-old daughter Adélaïde, on September 4, 1815, at the house of her grandparents at Soisy, [ECS] staying there no doubt while Jean-Pierre and Adèle were trying to accommodate Descemet's material at what must now have been a very crowded nursery. [SHP29/146, L-D] A few months later, on February 17, 1816, occurred the sad death of his young wife (age 30), [ADVM, ADY] leaving him to raise his two remaining young children alone. Later that year, in the pages of Vibert's first catalog [SHP29/150] could be found a new Gallica rose — 'Adèle Heu'.

Oddly enough, in that busy year of 1815 he had requested and obtained the post of tax-collector at Chennevières for that community and for two others nearby — doubtless to supplement his income. This sort of job, however, was not very time-consuming, and did not affect his horticultural work or the publication of his catalogs. He retained this office for some twelve years. [ADY, ADVM, ADE, SHP29]

In 1820, his useful and interesting essay *Observations sur la Nomenclature et le Classement des Roses* was published, followed in 1826 by his equally meritorious *Essai sur les Roses*. Meanwhile, in 1825, he began selling the important 'Gloire des Rosomanes', one of the most influential roses of all. Enlarged by several purchases over the years, his nursery had by now attained the size of about 4 hectares, almost entirely devoted to roses, though he also grew fruit trees as something of a fancier. [SHP29/147] Also in 1825, he introduced into France the new yellow Tea ('Parks' Yellow Tea-Scented China', called by Vibert 'Thé Jaunâtre') from England, [SHP29/149] a plant which was at length to be of the greatest importance to French — and general — rose progress. He also introduced into France at this time the yellow Banksia and the Microphylla (*R. roxburghii*). [SHP29/149]

Plagued by insects (cockchafers) and their depredations at Chennevières, he moved operations to St. Denis in January of 1827, choosing the site with care, though it was indeed slightly smaller than his grounds at Chennevières. [SHP29/147, SHP36/142] It was also in this year that he became a founding member of the Société d'Horticulture de Paris, the first of its sort in France. [SHP27]

Two years later, he happened to be visiting the abandoned garden of an Englishman in Rouen, when he found there a valuable Damask Perpetual, parent of his special 'Trianon' line of DP's which was developed by him and his successors for some 50 years, [dH47/282] plants not only important in the beauty they brought — and bring — to gardens, but also of immense importance in their position as parents, with the Bourbons and Hybrid Chinas, of the original Hybrid Perpetuals.

In January, 1835, evidently intending to retire, as we gather from the above excerpt from *Revue-Horticole*, he sold his property at St. Denis and moved to Longjumeau, just south of Paris, taking with him not only his roses but also 267 fruit trees and numerous grape-vines. [SHP36/143] Soon, however, his plans of retirement changed. In 1836, he wrote, "My firm, which I founded in 1815 and where only roses are cultivated for sale, is the first of its sort which has existed in France. Thirty years of practice in this specialty, numerous and repeated experiences with all adjuncts of rose-culture, and longstanding habits of scrutiny, study, and comparison of the products of this beautiful family — such at least are the claims which I have on the public's confidence. I quite know that the long and sustained welcome which Science, Fanciers, and Commerce have been so kind as to honor me with imposes obligations on me, and thus it is that I have decided to respond to these marks of favor by putting off retirement [*Vibert was 59*].

"To cover the costs of my garden and, above all, to husband my time — these are my goals. Without seeking to extend my [commercial] relations, I will with pleasure accept orders from those people who understand what it costs these days in time, care, and money to obtain truly distinct novelties. . . .

"I will always continue with my seedlings — I will never abandon them; I will propagate them, and the greater part of my material will be from them.

"Forced to accommodate the demands of business, I have deleted from my stock, over several years, many roses which are in small demand. . . . My goal is to grow, for sale, only the most interesting roses of each group — those in which the characteristics are the most distinct. Thus it is that, wanting to break up the uniformity of color — sometimes too frequent in our single-colored roses — I have for a long time devoted myself to marbled roses, striped roses, dotted roses, and the like. If, with such Roses so worthy of interest, I have any success, it would perhaps only be the due of my long perseverance. . . .

"This year's catalog, though it contains about 150 thoroughly new, undistributed, good roses, is far from showing all those which I grow. I have seen, for several years, so many grave errors committed by those who hurry to propagate [_unknown varieties_] from untrue descriptions or faulty observations that I can hardly believe my eyes. A propagator who buys [_new material_] too cheaply and too fast is the failing of the day; making a sale is the prime interest of certain people who don't even know the names of the roses they send out! . . .

"My 'school' [_demonstration garden_], which takes in more than 1,300 specimens, nearly all own-root, will always be kept up with great care in a manner which will leave no doubt as to the true identity of the species or varieties which make it up. These specimens, which will not be sold, are just the thing to help fanciers make their choice. No other such school . . . exists in Paris or anywhere thereabouts." [V4]

Vibert's old enemies the cockchafer grubs proved daunting at Longjumeau, and in a mere three years, in 1839, he left and went to Angers, far from his long-accustomed Parisian environs, and much to the distress of Parisian rose-fanciers: "The largest and most complete rose nursery — that of Mons Vibert — is being moved from Longjumeau to Angers. Fanciers regret this move . . . but [_let us_] hope that, in imitating this Dean of Rosarians, they are able to come up with worthy successors who have not only his knowledge but also his integrity." [R-H39]

He had entered into good commercial relations with horticulturalists in the region of Angers, France, a region which boasted rosarians both numerous and qualified. He knew as well that the Angevin sun seemed less favorable to the growth and spread of vermin. [V8] Another reason could have been the agriculture in the valley of the Loire and the proverbial mild conditions of the region. Vibert, always interested in roses, was interested in grape-vines as well. At St. Denis as well as at Longjumeau he had grown grape-vines to produce raisins; but the Parisian region was not sunny enough, and the raisin, if it ripened at all, did not usually have a high enough sugar content. He thus left Longjumeau in 1839 to set up in the suburbs of Angers.

In Angers, he seems to have kept up his industriousness and his contacts, indeed visiting England at some point, [L-D] no doubt visiting the then-young William Paul and Thomas Rivers, the latter of whom he received one day at his premises: "In the month of July, 1842, I [_Rivers_] was at Angers, and looking over the gardens of Mons Vibert, when his foreman brought me a bouquet of yellow Roses, some in bud and some about half expanded. I had never in my life-time seen anything so beautiful [_as the soon-to-be released 'Chromatella'_]." [C]

From the end of 1843, he added to each of his rose catalogs a catalog of raisin-vines, and at the same time mingled articles on the Vine with those on the Rose. Always full of energy, in 1845, at the age of 68, he moved once again to enlarge his premises, staying however in the conurbation of Angers.

Finally, in 1851, at the age of 74, he sold the Angers business to his gardener, Mons Robert — possibly the aforementioned foreman — and retired to the countryside — back to the environs of Paris — to Montfort l'Amaury, which, as Mons Massiot advises, is calm, picturesque, and surrounded by forests. Here, at his ease, finally able to have his time to himself, he wrote occasional articles and letters for various publications, and no doubt tended his personal collection of roses, keeping up these activities for some fifteen years. Around the end of 1865, he wrote an article on irregularities in roses for the journal of the Société Nationale d'Horticulture, "and more recently wrote the Société several letters with some interesting facts." [V7] "Some days before his death," reports his grandson (again in the pages of vol. 51 of _The Century_ magazine), "while arranging his daily bouquet in a vase, he said to his grandson: 'See, my child, a man knows truly what he has loved best on earth only when in his last days he finds it still in his heart. Like the rest of the world, I have thought that I adored and detested many men and many things. In reality I have loved only Napoleon and roses. Today, after nearly a century of rebellion against all the unjust things I have seen and all the evils from which I have suffered, there remain to me only two objects of profound hatred: the English, who overthrew my idol, and the white worms that have destroyed my roses.'" Soon after, on January 27, 1866, four days before his 89th birthday, he died "about two in the morning in his home," [V5] "without suffering." [V7]

Of miscellaneous information, we have the following. "Mons Vibert is not only an excellent horticulturalist; he is also an enlightened writer." [SNP29/149] And indeed, in addition to the works mentioned above, he also provided us with many detailed and professional articles on various aspects of horticulture, such as on the artificial cross-breeding of roses in the 1831 _Annales de la Société d'Horticulture de Paris_ (pp. 68–71), on the acclimation of plants, [SHP37/129–134] on grape-vines (in the 1850 edition of _Mémoires de la Société Centrale d'Agriculture_, two on his nemesis, the cockchafer grub (1827 and 1863), various articles on physiological effects of grafting and budding roses or grape-vines (1846, 1851, two in 1865), and, in 1827, a long and masterly counter-attack to certain hazy assertions of Mons Pirolle, another horticulturalist of the day.

His spirited grandson — son of Théodore — _Jehan_ Georges Vibert, of Paris, the very successful "artiste-peintre" (September 30, 1840–July 28, 1902), was a witness at the recording of J.-P. Vibert's death, which was also witnessed by Charles E. Souhaité, "age 34, friend of the deceased." [V5] In 1867, Moreau-Robert back in Angers dedicated a Moss Rose to him, 'Souvenir de Pierre Vibert', a cultivar which is still extant. The name Vibert, one finds, is a form of "Guibert" or "Gilbert," which is a Teutonic name meaning "War-Bright," or (prosaically) "he who is illustrious in combat."

Thus it was with Jean-Pierre Vibert. "We should wreathe his tomb with our homage and our respect." [V6]

CELINA DUBOS
('Céline Dubois', 'Cœlina Dubos', 'Sélima Dubos', 'Rose du Roi à Fleurs Blanches')
Dubos, 1849
Sport of 'Rose du Roi'(DP).

"We are unable to resist the pleasure of noting . . . a new variety which is both perpetual and very remontant called 'Célina Dubos'." [R-H49] "White, or nearly white . . . worthy of attention, both from its origin and quality . . . its flowers are well shaped, very durable, and highly fragrant." [R8] "Medium-sized, full, lightly blushed white." [BJ] "Grayish white." [S] "The new white Damask Perpetual 'Célina Dubos', with very pale blush center, though believed to be a sport from 'Rose du Roi', is very constant, and is the nearest approach to white amongst the Perpetuals." [HstX:398]

COMTE DE CHAMBORD
Robert & Moreau, ca. 1860

There is confusion between this variety and 'Mme Boll', which see. "Bright pink fading to lilac-mauve . . . a plump plant . . . fragrant." [G] "Vigorous erect bush . . . very fragrant pinkish lilac, full, flat flowers . . . continuously. Outstanding . . . 3 × 3 [ft; ca. 1 × 1 m]." [B] "Feeble growth; branches with bumps, dingy green, somewhat spiny; flower of moderate size, somewhat full; color, pale flesh." [S] This last comment is the only contemporary quote I have found on 'Comte de Chambord', and leads me to believe that the material presently known as 'Comte de Chambord' is actually 'Mme Boll'.

DELAMBRE
Robert & Moreau, 1863

"Carmine." [LS] "Double, deep reddish pink flowers freely produced on a compact plant with good foliage . . . 3 × 2 [ft; ca. 9 × 6 dm]." [B]

DOMBROWSKII
Listed as a Hybrid Bourbon.

DUCHESS OF PORTLAND
Listed as the 'Portland Rose'.

JACQUES CARTIER
Moreau-Robert, 1868
There is confusion between this variety and 'Marquise de Boccella', which see.

"About 100 mm across [ca. 4 in] . . . clear rich pink . . . fading to paler pink . . . quartered, have button eyes . . . fragrant." [G] "Full, flat . . . clear pink. Recurrent . . . a strong scent . . . 4 × 3 [ft; ca. 1.25 m x 9 dm]." [B] "Vigorous; light pink, center darker; flower large, full." [S]

MARBRÉE
Robert & Moreau, 1858

"Very large, full; bright rose-pink, marbled white." [S] "A many petalled, sizable rose of clear, rose pink, marbled white. Little or no fragrance . . . 4 × 2 [ft; ca. 1.25 × .6 m]." [B]

MARQUISE DE BOCCELLA
Desprez/Cochet, 1840

"Rich rosy blush, distinct, perfect." [WRP] "Pink, large." [HoBoIV/319] "Medium-sized, full, flesh with darker center." [Pq] "Delicate flesh, a decided acquisition among a class of Roses the prevailing colours of which are purple and crimson." [P2] "Circumference almost blush, large and full; form compact. Habit, erect; growth, robust. A beautiful Rose, and very sweet; the petals small in comparison with others of the group, but more numerous." [P] "Very fragrant; very pretty exhibition rose; handsome light green foliage." [S] "The most abundant bloomer." [HstXI:224] "Very double with a 'button' center; . . . 3–5 [ft; ca. 9 dm to 1.5 m]. Continuous . . . very excellent." [Lg] "This rose was raised at Yèbles . . . by Mons Desprez, one of the great hybridists of our time. . . . [It] is one of the remontant hybrids of unknown provenance, or Portlands, under the same heading as 'Rose du Roi'. One can reproach such varieties for hiding their light under a bushel basket, as it were, by bearing their flowers down in the foliage. . . . It is trying that we cannot obtain Portlands which are perfectly remontant and of a color other than a more or less dark pink. . . . It has been available to the public since 1840, and up till now has not been surpassed; what is more, it doesn't even have any serious rivals. . . . Leafy branches furnished with numerous prickles or short harmless bristles; leaves of 5–7 leaflets, curled, irregularly dentate, rugose, oval-elongate, sometimes rounded; petiole usually bristling with stiff bristles; stipules with narrow 'wings,' smooth, ciliate, attached to the petiole at nearly a right angle, an arrangement forming two auricles or acute 'teeth' at the base of the leaf; flower stalks very short, bristling with red bristles; ovary glabrous, elongate; sepals foliaceous, rugose; blossom surrounded by foliage, ordinarily opening one or two buds." [PIB]

MIRANDA
De Sansal, 1869

Not to be confused with the white China, nor with the purpled-red Gallica. "Flower large, full; color, delicate pink." [S] "3.2 in [ca. 8 cm] across, semi-double, fragrant, recurrent; growth upright, medium." [Kr]

MME BOLL
Listed as a Hybrid Perpetual.

MME KNORR
Listed as a Hybrid Perpetual.

MOGADOR
('Rose du Roi à Fleurs Pourpres')
Varangot, 1844
Sport of 'Rose du Roi'.

"Brilliant crimson, often shaded with rich purple, large and full; form, cupped. Habit, branching; growth, moderate. A superb kind." [P] "Large, semi-double flowers of red with purple shadings . . . to 4 [ft; ca. 1.25 m]." [HRG] "Flowers medium-sized." [S] "Cupped and elegant: its flowers are, perhaps, a little more double than are those of its parent; and its habit is more robust." [R8] "Evidently a more constant bloomer at Mons Varangot's [than 'Rose du Roi'], but reverts to the type in many areas." [R-H46] "Branches with red bristles; thorns very small; foliage light green with a yellow tint; flower to 4 in [ca. 1 dm], full; center petals recurved, dark red, often violet-purple." [R-H44] "Thorns . . . thick, closely-set. Foliage . . . 5–7 leaflets of medium size, pointed, regularly dentate; flower stem strong, upright, reddish, also bristling with thick bristles, as is the ovary, which is long and covered with glandular hairs; calyx very long, slightly leaf-like [sepals]." [dH45/278] "Very beautiful . . . 3 × 3 [ft; ca. 1 × 1 m]." [B]

PANACHÉE DE LYON

('Striped Crimson Perpetual', 'Rose du Roi Panachée')
Dubreuil, 1895
Sport of 'Rose du Roi'.

Synonyms listed above are for a probably identical variety listed by Prince in 1846. "Very pretty and regular striping of the flowers. The ground color is a uniform China pink with regular brilliant purple-red 'flames.' The form and perfume are those of 'Rose du Roi'." [JR19/148] "Pink striped red." [LS] "Rose, purple, red; vigorous." [TW] " 'inconstant' . . . usually pale flesh color, striped with crimson, but some flowers lose the stripe entirely." [WRP]

PERGOLÈSE

Robert & Moreau, 1860
"Amaranth." [LS] "Medium-sized, full, crimson." [S] "Carmine, medium-sized, full." [N]

PORTLAND ROSE

('Portlandica', 'Duchess of Portland')
Unknown, ca. 1770
"Flowers deep rose, tinted with purple, large and semidouble; form, cupped. A pretty colour, and most abundant summer bloomer." [P] "Flowers semi-double, sparkling maroon." [No] "Clear pink col. red, single, with conspicuous anthers . . . 4 × 3 [ft; ca. 1.25 × 1 m]." [B] "Vivid red, single flowers completely covering the compact plant, 3 × 3 [ft; ca. 1 × 1 m]." [HRG] "One of the most striking by the brightness of its color, and its precious quality of blooming from spring to fall. The leaves are oval. The thorns which cover the wood are both long and short all mixed together, hooked, flesh-color on the young wood. The flower buds are pointed and crowned with lacinated leaflets formed by the elongated sepals. This rose, which is only semi-double, is very flashy; its color is a handsome red which makes it distinct and noticeable among all other sorts, especially in the fall, when no others of that color are to be found. This rose, grafted on the briar, forms a good head, and is easily contained by pruning." [C-T] For matters historical, see the headnote to this chapter.

QUATRE SAISONS

(trans., 'Four Seasons')
This name has been used as a synonym for both 'Bifera' and 'Tous les Mois', both of which see.

QUATRE SAISONS BLANC MOUSSEUX

('Perpetual White Moss')
Laffay, ca. 1835
Said to be a sport from 'Bifera'.
"White, buds handsome and well mossed, flowers good size and tolerably double, blooming in clusters." [JC] "White, of medium size, double; form, expanded, blooming in large trusses, very mossy, but produced sparingly in the autumn." [P] "Well endowed with brownish-green moss on both stems and buds . . . 4 × 3 [ft;

ca. 1.25 × .9 m]." [B] "Still an excellent variety; its white blossoms, in tight clusters, make it perhaps the most interesting of the group." [R-H63]

ROSE DE RESCHT

Original introducer and date unknown
"Fragrant bright fuchsia-red long blooming . . . very double . . . 60 mm [ca. 2 in] across." [G] "Deep rose-red, very double blooms . . . 3 × 3 [ft; ca. 1 × 1 m]." [HRG] "Pompom-like. Scented. Abundant foliage. Remontant." [B] "Shrub upright, compact; leaves large, particularly for the size of the plant, dark green, attractive, not much affected by mildew. Blossoms fade rather quickly to a slatey shade, and do not last long; the fallen petals reveal the white nub. Fragrance delicious. Vigorous, but dwarf." [BCD] Rescht is a provincial capital in Persia, to which this rose was possibly brought during the French rapprochement circa 1807. It is possibly the red 'Tous-les-Mois'.

[ROSE DE TRIANON]

Vibert, ca. 1830
"Semi-double . . . pink." [V4] "Bright pink, blooming in large clusters; the plant is of dwarf habit." [WRP] "Flowers rose, of medium size, double; form, cupped." [P] "Full; color, flesh pink; vigorous." [S] 'Adèle Mauzé', listed in the Supplement, was known also as 'Rose de Trianon Double'.

ROSE DU ROI

('Rose Lelieur', 'Lee's Crimson Perpetual')
Écoffay, Souchet, Lelieur, 1819
"One of the most beautiful and remontant varieties. It is the first to appear in our markets, and the last to give a blossom in our gardens. From the beginning of spring until frost, the 'Rose du Roi' is, for all intents and purposes, constantly bearing graceful, ravishing flowers, from which escape an agreeable aroma which gladdens the mind and calms our perturbed senses. It was discovered not by Comte Le Lieur [sic], former director of the Royal Gardens, as is generally believed; rather, it was Mons Écoffay, old gardener of the florist of Sèvres [Mons Souchet], who raised it in 1819 from seedlings he had sprouted in 1816. [*But seedlings of **what**, Monsieur?*] Its appearance was greeted with enthusiasm because, at that time, perpetual or quatre-saisons roses were uncommon. To raise so perfect a rose was a veritable triumph; one can see why Comte Le Lieur . . . or the florist of Sèvres would pose as the father of 'Rose du Roi'." [PIB] "Struck by the plant's constant bloom, Souchet took it to Count Lelieur . . . and the mother-plant, carefully tended, flowered beautifully in 1816. It bore at first the name 'Comte Le Lieur', then afterwards took on the name 'Rose du Roi' because of Louis XVIII's regard for it. It is perfectly remontant, and its merit cannot be denied." [JF]

"Bright red, of perfect form, with the fragrance of the old Damask rose, and is a new constant and profuse bloomer." [WRP] "Bright crimson, large, double, very fragrant; occasionally blooms in autumn." [EL] "Red and violet . . . 3 × 3 [ft; ca. 1 × 1 m]." [B] "Flowers, middle-sized, bright red, often more vivid at the second flowering than in the spring. Remarkable from its calyx, which has often six sepals." [Go] "Outer petals large, obovate, the others smaller and smaller as they approach the center; flower stem short, with numerous glandular hairs. Calyx tubular, slightly constricted at the top, having (like the flower stem) numerous glandular hairs; sepals leaf-like." [JF] "Seeds abundantly . . . the seedlings will bloom in three years." [Bu] "Very vigorous; branches of medium size and upright; bark light green, reddish where the sun strikes, bristling with very numerous little prickles, unequal and very sharp; foliage light green, slightly bullate, of 5–7 oblong finely-toothed leaflets; leafstalk slender and elongated, pubescent and lacking prickles; flower, about 2.5 in [ca. 6 cm] across, well held, upright, open, usually solitary; color, a handsome bright carmine red with violet reflections. Much recommended, very remontant, and very fragrant." [S]

"Evokes the memory of all of a tragic [French] past: 1812 — the Russian campaign, the decline of the Empire; many French hearts beating for the return of the Bourbons, and it was this hope which was entrusted to a beautiful rose of an intense red — the color of the blood shed since 1789." [JR31/92] "It is about thirty years since this famous rose was grown from seed in the gardens of one of the royal palaces near Paris, remaining comparatively obscure, and was considered a rare article in England in 1831, where I first saw it growing, carefully surrounded by rods to keep its admirers at a distance. In 1832 or 3 I imported it as the gem of the day, and it is still admitted to be the king of Perpetuals, blooming profusely and perfectly from June till Christmas; the colour is bright red, (not crimson,) a perfectly formed flower, with all the fragrance of a Damask Rose, and without any extra pruning never fails to bloom the whole season — richly deserving a place in every garden." [Bu] "I have met with a remark of Mons Desprez', the celebrated Rose amateur at Yèbles, that he has sown thousands of seeds of 'du Roi' . . . , and never yet obtained a Perpetual rose. In all, the characters of *Rosa gallica* are visible. But we must remember this variety partakes largely of the nature of the Gallica." [P] "The boundary between Gallica and Portland is not as easy to draw as one might think." [JR12/170]

[SAPHO]
('Perpétuelle Sapho')
Vibert, 1847

Not to be confused with 'Thé Sapho', a synonym for 'Mrs. Bosanquet', [B] nor with the circa 1846 Setigera 'Sappho', nor with the 1889 Tea. "Flower 5 cm [ca. 2 in], a lightly fleshed white, full." [M-L46/271] "Flower of medium size, full; color, white, shaded flesh pink." [S] "Blooms in corymbs, blossoms medium to large, double, white." [JR9/88]

SYDONIE   PLATE 2
('Sidonie')
Vibert, 1847
Seedling of 'Belle de Trianon'.

"Rosy blush, very delicate, and very sweet." [HstVIII:381] "Large flowers of a rose or bright salmon . . . blooms profusely." [FP] "Soft pink." [JR2/60] "Flesh." [LS] "8 cm [ca. 3 in], full, pink, superb flower." [M-L47/361] "Blooms four times a year." [JR6/43] "Rose color, medium size, very full, quartered form very free blooming, very hardy; five to seven leaflets, red thorns. Its poor shape destroys its usefulness." [EL] "Free-flowering, shorter growing variety. Fully double, clear pink with frilled edges . . . scented . . . 3 × 2 [ft; ca. 9 × 6 dm]." [B] "Habit, erect." [P] "Blooms in a cluster having 4–10 blossoms, depending upon the plant's vigor. One notes as well the delicious Damask fragrance. Its flowers, big to very big, a little flat when fully open, have a slightly muddled center. The color is a brilliant soft pink, well-held, remontant until heavy frost, vigorous bush, quite hardy, and very floriferous." [JR6/153–154]

[TOUS-LES-MOIS]
('Year-Round Rose', 'Quatre Saisons')
La Quintinye, ca. 1680

"A sort of red Musk Rose bearing its flowers in clusters." [LaQ] "It doesn't grow more than 3 ft [ca. 1 m] high; its name comes from its characteristic of blooming nearly all year when one encourages new growth by pruning after each bloom. Its blossom, a beautiful red, though double is less so than the Centifolia's — but the perfume is more intense. It has three varieties: flesh-colored, white-flowered, and very pale pink. All make numerous clusters of flowers." [Fr] "Notable because of its ovary, which is pear-shaped at first, fusiform when the flower is open, and oval after being fertilized; flower medium-sized, semi-double, light pink." [S] *Red Tous Mois of Gardeners.* The ordinary red 'Tous Mois', grown by all gardeners, has wood a little less prickly [than that of the Damask], and does not grow as vigorously. Usually, it bears six to ten blossoms on the same petiole. *White Tous Mois.* Also much grown by gardeners, this has the same characteristics as the foregoing; it is a little less common, and more delicate in growth . . . *Tous Mois.* Color, gray [!], crowned with double flowers. Wood and leaves like the 'Tous Mois' [above], less prickly, glaucous green or ashen. Calyx very long, as is that of the type. Bud round, distinctly tipped by prettily lacinated sepals, which accompany the blossom, projecting beyond it. This one is quite as double as a Centifolia, of a pretty and delicate pink, and blooming around June 10. It should give rise to a number of pretty varieties." [C-T] The 'Red Tous Mois', "grown by all gardeners," was evidently one of the parents of the Bourbon race.

YOLANDE D'ARAGON
('Iolande')
Vibert, 1843

"Flowers deep pink, their margin lilac blush, large and full; form, cupped. Habit, erect; growth, robust. The flowers of this variety are produced in immense clusters in summer." [P] "Of a rosy blush color, full double and beautiful." [WRP] "Deep-pink flowers, and is an abundant autumn bloomer." [FP] "Lilac-rose, flat form, straggling habit; worthless." [EL] "Sumptuous flowers of over 75 mm [ca. 3 in] . . . very double and very fragrant . . . bright pink towards the centre . . . tall to about 1.5 metres [ca. 5 ft] . . . luxuriant light green foliage." [G] "Globular flowers of considerable size. Bright, rich pink in colour. Scented. Growth upright . . . 4 × 3 [ft; ca. 1.25 × 1 m]." [B] Yolande d'Aragon, wife of Louis II of Anjou and the Two Sicilies.

Supplement

[ADÈLE MAUZÉ]
('Rose de Trianon Double')
Vibert, 1847

"Flowers rose, large and full; curious foliage." [P] "Flower 6–7 cm [ca. 2.5 in], double, pink. Wood and foliage unique."

[M-L46/271] "Flower medium-sized, full; color, light pink; growth vigorous." [S]

[BELLE DE TRIANON]
Prévost, pre-1826
"Pale pink." [LS]

BERNARD

('Mme Ferray', 'Perpetual Pompon')
Unknown, 1836
Sport or seedling of 'Rose du Roi'.

"Delicate pink, full, flat, medium-sized, superb." [LF] "Pink." [V4] "Bright salmon-pink, flowers double, small, and beautiful, quite a gem, habit dwarf." [JC] "Flowers salmon, of medium size, full; form, cupped. A beautiful little rose." [P] "A most beautiful new rose, with rather small flowers, but they are very double and finely shaped, of a delicate carmine color: this is a true Perpetual, and a most desirable rose." [WRP] Bernard, stage name of the French actor/comedian Wolf, fl. 1830's.

DUCHESSE DE ROHAN

R. Lévêque, 1847

"Lilac pink." [LS] "Growth very vigorous; leaves dark green, often touched black; flower large, full, opening with difficulty; more to be recommended for its buds than for its blossom; color, bright pink bordered very delicate pink." [S] "Canes large and vigorous, with small, numerous, recurved, yellowish-brown thorns; leaves comprised of 5 medium-sized leaflets, fairly frequently bullate, regularly and finely dentate, fresh green, borne on an upright, strong stalk; blooms in a bouquet of 3 or 5, ovary medium-sized, nearly turbinate, without constriction; sepals longly foliaceous. Flowers 8–10 cm across [to 4 in], very full, plump, beautiful bright red nuanced dark violet. The first rows of petals are a paler pink, making it look like one of our beautiful Gallicas." [An47/19]

[FÉLICITÉ HARDY]

Hardy, ca. 1831

"Hybrid of Portland and Damask . . . dedicated to Mme Hardy. A very vigorous bush with long, erect canes which are light green and armed with numerous un-equal thorns, long and straight for the most part; the leaves are large, smooth, nearly all with 7 leaflets which are regularly dentate, a handsome green above and slightly pubescent beneath. One notes that here, as with many other roses, the lower leaves have oval-rounded leaflets, while the higher leaves are oval-elliptical. The leafstalk is hispid and slightly prickly. The blossoms are a very pure white, full, flat above, 3.75 in across [ca. 8 cm], centifolia perfume, in corymbs on long and strong thorny stems; bud, large, round, pink outside; ovary oval, hispid; some sepals become foliaceous at the top and pinnatifid on the sides. This rose is one of the best introductions in a long time." [R-H32]

JACQUES AMYOT

Varangot, 1844

"Lilac-pink." [LS] "Deep rose, fine." [FP] "Short canes." [JDR54/45] "Vigorous, climbing, practically thornless." [S] "Canes reddish at first, later changing to dark green, with occasional small thorns, canes very noticeable due to the young buds, which are violet or reddish. Leaves composed of 5 leaflets, sometimes 7, oval-pointed, beautiful dark green, finely and regularly dentate; stem big and thick, long, reddish, covered with glandular bristles which are close-set; sepals elongated and foliaceous. Flower very full, from 7–9 cm across [to ca. 4 in], beautiful purplish red, double; the central petals are for the most part split in bud [*fendus en bouton*]. This flower resembles a beautiful purple Ranunculus." [dH45/279] "Seed-bearing by this new variety is almost out of the question. The blossom looks ordinary enough, but all of the stamens have become petaloid; the pistil, for its part, has developed a sort of pink crater at its tip where may be found scaly petaloids, and nectar from each of the young ovules." [R-H51] Jacques Amyot, Bishop of Auxerre and translator, 1513–1593.

JEUNE HENRY

(trans., 'Young Henry')
Descemet, before 1815

Not to be confused with Vibert's Centifolia, which was bright pink. "Velvety red." [LS] "Red, medium size, full, tall." [Sn] "Branches, tinged with purple. Flowers, full, purplish, of a deep vivid red." [Go]

JOASINE HANET

('Johasine Hanet')
Vibert, 1847

"Flower 5–6 cm across [ca. 2.25 in], full, purple-red." [M-L 46/274] "Vigorous; flower medium-sized, full, growing in clusters, very floriferous; color, bright grenadine." [S]

JULIE DE KRUDNER

Laffay, 1847

"Pale flesh; form, compact." [P] "Remontant." [JR20/149] "Growth very vigorous; flower medium-sized, full; flesh pink." [S]

LAURENT HEISTER

Moreau-Robert, 1859

"Slatey carmine." [LS] "Blazing carmine." [Y̆]

[LOUIS-PHILIPPE I]

('Louis Philippe')
C. Duval, 1832
Seedling of 'Rose du Roi'.
Not to be confused with the China.

"Carmine." [LS] "Crimson, shaded with dark purple; form, expanded; colours rich and fine. A good seed-bearer." [P] "Very large, full flowers, deep violet, elegant fragrance." [An32/312] "A true Perpetual." [WRP]

MARIE DE ST.-JEAN

Damaizin, 1869

"Growth pretty vigorous; canes medium-sized, slightly thin, upright; bark light green, with numerous dark gray, fine, straight, unequal thorns. Leaves, glaucous green, strongly nerved, divided into 3 or 5 oval-rounded, finely dentate leaflets; leafstalk slender, armed with some small prickles. Flowers about 2.25 in across [ca. 6 cm], very full, plump, nearly always solitary; color, pure white; outer petals fairly large, center petals smaller and muddled; pretty bud, white shaded carmine; flower stalk short and glandulose. Calyx tubular; sepals leaf-like. This variety has the look of 'Rose du Roi', and is very remontant and very fragrant; hardy." [JF]

MARIE ROBERT

Moreau-Robert, ca. 1860?
Not to be confused with the Noisette.

"Frosty pink." [LS] "Lilac pink." [Y̆]

MME SOUVETON

Pernet père, 1874

"Medium growth; bloom abundant and continuous; flower medium-sized, fairly full, cupped, delicate pink touched with white." [S]

[PALMYRE]
Vibert, 1817

"Lilac nuanced pink, full, flat, medium sized, beautiful." [LF] "Blush, with rosy pink centre, of medium size, full; form, compact." [P] "Canes long and vertical; flower medium-sized, double, regular; pale pink becoming flesh." [S] "Following, except in point of colour, the 'Rose du Roi'." [P2] "[Resembles 'Marquise de Boccella'.]" [VPt46/83]

[PRÉSIDENT DUTAILLY]   PLATE 3
Dubreuil, 1888

"It sprang from seeds culled from a group of Gallica roses which had not been artificially pollinated. These seeds were sown in 1882. The original plant bloomed for the first time in 1885. The size of its blossoms, its penetrating scent, and its perfect form all attracted the attention of fanciers from the beginning. But when joined with its happy faculty of reblooming, of flowering in the fall, like the HP's . . . I could not wait to propagate it, and classed it in a new category, that of Reblooming Gallicas, which, I hope, will be enriched later with other varieties of different colors. Here is its description: Vigorous, with strong canes, erect, covered with numerous small thorns mixed with stiff bristles. Foliage ample, luxuriant, matte green above, glaucescent beneath. Flowers upright, borne on stiff stems which carry 3 or 4 blossoms at the end of the cane; perfectly cupped; buds globular; petals numerous, gracefully arranged; beautiful crimson red with carmine reflections towards the center, velvety maroon amaranth towards the outside. Elegant and penetrating scent." [JR12/169–170]

QUATRE SAISONS D'ITALIE
('Rosier de la Malmaison')
Dupont, before 1815

"Vermilion, striped sometimes." [Y̆] "Received from Florence by Dupont, who had it propagated." [Gx] Vibert lists, in 1820, a non-remonant Quatre Saisons 'Rose d'Italie'. Evidently reintroduced by V. Verdier in 1865.

REMBRANDT
Moreau-Robert, 1883

"Growth very vigorous, very floriferous; flower very large, full; color, vermilion red shaded carmine, sometimes striped white; flower stalk long and strong." [S] "Blooms continuously over a long season. Good foliage well retained. Flowers of cutting value." [Capt28]

ROBERT PERPÉTUEL
Robert, 1856

"Violet pink, medium size, full, medium height." [Sn]

[VENUSTA]
(trans., 'Charming'; syn., 'Bifera Venusta')
Descemet, pre-1814

"A new French variety, yet very rare; the flower is of a delicate rosy hue, and very double." [WRP] "Flower medium-sized, full; delicate pink." [S] "Calyx, having frequently six sepals. Flowers, middle-sized, full, of a very light pink." [Go]

Chapter Three
CHINAS

"*Rosa chinensis*, Jacq. . . . Introduced in 1768. Brought from China to England by Captain Ekeberg, who visited Canton in 1766 and 1767. Later propagated in France under the names '*Bengale Guenille*' and '*Rose Bichonne*' [*Gore gives us neither introducer nor date, but does provide synonyms* ('Nasturtium-Scented China Rose', 'Raspberry-Scented China Rose') *and description* ('Shrub, delicate and very small. Flowers, middle-sized or small, double; of a purple-crimson, fragrant, with concave petals')]. . . .

"*Rosa semperflorens*, Curt. . . . Introduced in 1789. Introduced in England in 1789 by William Kerr, then by Slater, and in France in 1798 by Barbier, surgeon from Val-de-Grâce. Blooms constantly, and propagates and hybridizes with ease." [ExRé]

"This charming race of Roses was discovered in China by Gustave Ekeberg, Swedish Captain of the Admiralty, in one of his many trips to the Celestial Empire, whence he furthermore brought a Tea tree [*Thea sinensis*], which he introduced into his Scandinavian homeland in 1763. The original of this wonderful class . . . was described and named by Jacquin in his *Observationes Botanicæ*, Vienna, 1764–1771. Ph. Miller, in his *Dictionnaire des Jardiniers* . . . , Paris, 1785, also gives a description of this rose, taken from plants growing in England. One goes on to read that live specimens of the typical form were re-introduced into England ten or fewer years later. According to Lindley, the original plant was a little bush of delicate growth and constitution, with semi-double flowers which were crimson, and which it bore only once a year. The *Botanical History of Roses*, London, 1820, tells us that English gardens of the time already had many magnificent semi-double crimson varieties of *R. chinensis*, but that we, the French, evidently had some much more beautiful which, at that time, were not in the rosaries of our cross-channel neighbors. These varieties just mentioned were mainly cultivated at the Trianon by Mons Barrier, a distinguished fancier and caretaker of that château; and it was in the city of Rennes where they first saw the light of day, though the name of their fortunate breeder has been forgotten." [JR7/119]

"At the name of a rose so interesting that all its qualities are cherished, which already is responsible for such a great number of varieties, and which, moreover, is so rich in promise, there arises in one a natural curiosity as to who first introduced it to Europe. One finds — not without surprise — that the name of such a man is nearly unknown here [France] as well as in England, and that all of my enquiries on the subject seemed to have proven fruitless, when Mr. Sabine, secretary of the London Horticultural Society . . . let me know the name of the gentleman in question. He bore the name 'Ker,' and took this rose from Canton in China to the garden of the King [*Kew, presumably*] around 1780. It seems that, about the same time, another gentleman by the name of Slater introduced a second variety of dark color, which I alas do not otherwise know. . . . The Chinas . . . have alone received from Nature the ability to bloom without interruption; cold, certainly, stops their growth in winter; but, in their home ground, growth is *not* suspended, and the example of specimens grown here under glass leaves no doubt in that regard. They differ from those roses which we designate 'Perpetuals' [i.e., Damask Perpetuals] in that their branches, without exception, are fully floriferous, while with these others they are only partially so. This advantage, so invaluable and unique, does not seem to have excited the same admiration upon introduction to France that it does nowadays. . . . Returning to the origin of its cultivation in France, we find that the first specimen was given to the Jardin des Plantes around 1800, probably by an Englishman — but by whom in particular it is impossible to say. Dr. Cartier, a distinguished fancier, was the second to cultivate it, and it was he who obtained from sowings in 1804 the full-flowered variety. The introduction of the China to France, and, later, that of the Noisette, have had the very greatest influence on the Rose, an influence well worth noting. . . . 'Sanguinea', the 'Autumn Pompon', 'Atro-Purpurea', and, one might say, the greater portion, have, by all pertinent reports, a resemblance in the particulars of their growth to the Common China; a number of them, however, diverge singularly, it is reported, in their ovary and in their internal structure. Let us moreover note that the fruits of 'Sanguinea' as well as those of all the maroon-colored ones very much resemble those of the Gallica. . . . Up to the present [1826], white was pretty much the only color not to be found in the Chinas — but that difficulty has now, for the most part, been overcome. I have among my seedlings a very beautiful variety of which all the branches bear blossoms of the purest white, without any tinge of pink or flesh; this rose, somewhat green at the center, is quite double (70–75 petals on grafted specimens); unfortunately, it doesn't set seed. If perhaps this rose can't be classified with the Chinas, it is at least a variety intermediate between them and the Noisettes." [V2]

"That which bears the name 'China Rose' and is hawked about the streets as such was raised in the Museum's temperate house, and it was only in 1804 that commerce brought it into the amateur's greenhouse, where it was raised as something marvelous. . . . It was a distinguished Parisian doctor, a great rose fancier, who — the first in France — procured for himself the Common China; he presented it to the venerable A. Thouin, who had only expected to see a Centifolia with the look of a China. Dr. Cartier made numerous sowings of this rose, and, in 1818, obtained the common China which is so well known in our gardens." [JF]

"We cannot recommend too highly to flower lovers the roses called 'Chinas'; they bloom continuously in our climate, they are richly colored, the plants are hardy, and the perfume is elegant." [JR34/171] "From the first days of spring until the frosts of autumn, these charming bushes are covered in flowers. . . . The varieties belonging to this section are quite numerous, and, over many years of seed-sowing, some very curious colors have been obtained. However, in spite of such meritorious novelties, one should not neglect such great old varieties as 'Cramoisi Supérieur', 'Ducher', 'Impératrice Eugénie' [*not the* 1855 HB from Béluze, *nor* the slatey HP from Delhommeau, but rather a China with 'flower semi-double, silvery-pink in color,' [JR23/104] 'Sanglant', 'Prince Eugène de Beauharnais', 'Ordinaire' ['Common China' or 'Parsons' Pink'], 'Louis Philippe', etc., which are always much sought after." [JR23/24–25]

"So many factors contribute to vary the colors of Roses that it is impossible to satisfactorily classify them in this way. . . . Everyone knows that most of the white Chinas are sometimes pink, and the 'Le Vésuve', 'Le Camélia' [*but probably* '*Caméléon*' *is meant*], and the full-flowered China, though ordinarily pink, are often maroon. . . . The Chinas are very much more variable, by report, than are the other species." [V2]

"The China Rose, and all the short-jointed, smooth-barked kinds that are like them in habit, will strike [*root*], bud, graft, grow, and bloom, any month in the year." [GI] "They are all fairly hardy, and bloom very freely during summer and autumn when grown in beds or borders of rich, well-drained soil, and in a sunny position. They are not suitable for heavy cold soils or sunless positions. China roses always produce the best effect when grown by themselves." [TW]

The Chinas may conveniently be divided into three sections: (1) That which developed from 'Parsons' Pink China', usually having "gay green foliage, plain green on top, ashy green beneath, and little or no purple on the fully-developed [leaflet-] tips." [JR23/104] (2) That which developed from 'Slater's Crimson China', usually having "mutable foliage, leaflets sometimes short, sometimes longly oval-lanceolate, sometimes indeed acuminate, depending upon the branch; [leaflets] dark green bordered purple brown within, and, around the edges, dark green more or less washed purple. Wood slender or fairly slender, nearly upright, making small thick bushes." [JR23/104] (3) "Another group, completely different from the preceding . . . was obtained by crossing 'Rival de Pæstum' [*a China × Tea hybrid which we list with the Teas*] with 'Mme Falcot'(T), making a special sort which, crossed again with 'Falcot' gave this series extra floriferousness and attractiveness; and we define it as follows: vigorous, bushy, numerous stems of an upright nature, smooth; sparsely thorned, with slightly recurved thorns of a medium size; flexuous, fairly long flower stem; round calyx, surmounted by long sepals; foliage dark purplish green; leaflets pretty large, lanceolate, dentate, with sharp prickles beneath the leafstalk; flower medium to large, double, lightly perfumed; color varies from China rose to Indian pink, more or less dark; the most characteristic varieties are: 'Mme Laurette Messimy', 'Aurore', 'Irène Watts', 'Mme Eugène Résal', 'Souvenir de J.-B. Guillot', and 'Comtesse du Caÿla'; less characteristic . . . [is] 'Souvenir de Catherine Guillot'." [JR33/137–139]

Thus we see that China × Tea hybrids, and Teas with characteristics making them more of the "decorative" class than of the "exhibition" class (less double, less well-formed, smaller blossoms, blooming in clusters) tend to be bumped into the China class. In many classes, "classness" is a concept rooted in *appearance* and/or *behavior*—entirely appropriate in such a pragmatic art as horticulture.

"Well! Ker and Gilbert Slater have endowed Europe with our most beautiful Oriental Roses, and yet no one has given a thought to remembering them by bestowing either one or the other's name on any of these most beautiful roses." [PIB]

ARCHIDUC CHARLES

('Archduke Charles')
Laffay, 1825(?)
Seedling of *R. chinensis* 'Parsons' Pink'.

"Pink, changing to crimson, full, flat, superb." [LF] "Deep red, double and well formed." [Dr] "Rose, . . . margin almost white when newly expanded, gradually changing to rich crimson, from which peculiarity the plant bears flowers of various tints at the same time; very large and full; form expanded." [P1] "Sometimes one-half of the flower is white, the other crimson red." [HstXXX:142] "A noble variety . . . ; the points of the petals are frequently tipped with bright red." [Bu] "I have seen them in France nearly black." [R8] "Very fine show flower." [HstIV:478] "I find it fascinating and delightful, the opening blossoms often being extremely well formed, and laden with a subtle musty banana scent; 2 to 4 in across; often in clusters; profuse; sometimes nodding when fully expanded. Plant compact and leafy with good foliage, large and handsome on the strongest shoots, rich green, some mildew (easily controlled); very decorative with numerous chalky pink, rich pink, glowing rose, and deep crimson blossoms studding the bush. Sets seed rarely, usually in the fall, though all floral parts appear well and functional throughout the year; ovary oval, characteristic of the Chinas. Most charming and rewarding." [BCD] "Bush of ordinary growth, with upright branches which are smooth, armed with a small number of reddish, curved thorns which are enlarged at the base. Leaves composed of three and more often five slightly lanceolate leaflets of a dark green with regular reddish serrations. Flowers numerous, double, of medium size, in a cluster, regular in form, like a cup. The petals are very intense, brilliant pink. The ovary is glabrous, while the peduncle has small glandular bristles. This charming China ['*Bengale*'] . . . blooms a lot and has a very charming appearance." [An35/373] "We believe it was introduced into England about ten years since [making 1840] . . . this and several of the Indicas we do not recommend to be grown on their own roots, their habit being, when thus grown, to throw up unwieldy suckers, greatly to the detriment of the rest of the plant." [C] "A profuse bloomer, moderate grower. One of the best changeable Roses. Unique." [HstVI:368] "4 × 3 [ft; ca. 1.25 × .9 m]." [HRG] Archduke Charles of Austria, 1771–1847.

ARETHUSA

W. Paul, 1903

"Clear yellow, apricot shading. Foliage very good. Growth fair." [Th2] "Flower medium-sized, full, light yellow tinted apricot yellow. Of the 'Queen Mab' sort." [JR30/186] "Creamy yellow tinted orange and shaded with pink on a 3 × 3 [ft; ca. 1 × 1 m] plant." [HRG] "Rather ragged petals . . . [blooms] in clusters. Foliage shiny but somewhat sparse." [B1] "Very floriferous; vigorous." [Cx] Arethusa, a celebrated spring or fountain near Syracuse, Sicily, as well as its naiad.

BEAUTY OF ROSEMAWR   PLATE 12
Van Fleet/Conard & Jones, 1903

"Carmine, with bright red in depths of the rose. Incessant bloomer." [Dr] "Carmine and crimson." [LS] "Fairly dense, upright-growing . . . fragrant, loosely formed, soft carmine . . . paler veining . . . 3 × 2 [ft; ca. 9 × 6 dm]." [B] "Rather short of foliage for my taste." [B1] "Fairly vigorous, hardy, very floriferous, giving large flowers, full, fragrant, of a handsome carmine pink veined vermilion and white. Certain catalogs class 'Beauty of Rosemawr' as a China, others as a Tea; it is simply a hybrid of the two." [JR32/141] "We take pleasure in recommending this Grand New Rose, because we feel sure it will please all who want fine Hardy Ever-Blooming Roses. It was selected from among our choicest hybridized seedlings as combining more good qualities for general planting than almost any rose we know. It has stood for five years entirely unprotected in the open ground and never failed to bloom continuously every season. We are so confident of its value that we have named it after our place — 'Beauty of Rosemawr'. . . . It is a healthy, vigorous grower, making a strong, handsome bush, entirely hardy, needs no protection, begins to bloom very quickly and continues blooming the whole season until stopped by hard frost. The flowers are large and perfectly double, with fine overlapping petals and raised centre. The color is a lovely shade of rich carmine rose, exquisitely veined with fine crimson and white markings, exceedingly beautiful and delightfully fragrant. [C&Js03]

BENGALE CENTFEUILLES
("Bengale Œillet"?, "Bengale à Grandes Feuilles"?)
Noisette, 1804

"Pink bordered deep wine." [LS] "Intense pink, middle-sized, full." [N] "Middle-sized, hemispherical, almost full; varying from lilac-pink to light claret." [Go] "[of 'Grandes Feuilles':] vigorous, with smooth, upright branches armed with numerous thorns which are violet, large at the base, and hooked; leaflets elongate, flat, slightly toothed, quite large and of a dark green; the flowers are in clusters of 3 to 5 at the ends of the branches, double, light pink when opening, then carmine, then finally dark maroon." [S]

CELS MULTIFLORA
Listed as a Tea.

COMTESSE DU CAŸLA
P. Guillot, 1902
From crossing a seedling of 'Rival de Pæstum' (T) and 'Mme Falcot' (T) back with 'Mme Falcot' (T).

"Orange-red . . . salmon-pink with age . . . loose . . . fragrant." [Hk] "Flower large, full, fragrant, varying from carmine nasturtium red, tinted orange on the reverse of the petals, to coppery orange yellow, shaded carmine; very pretty." [JR26/131] "Flower large, fairly full, cupped; very floriferous; vigorous." [Cx] "It does not bloom freely enough to warrant its being planted for effect in the garden." [OM] "Very free flowering . . . 3 × 3 [ft; ca. 1 × 1 m]." [B] "Small, semi-double, flat, fragrant; . . . Continuous bloom. Compact growth: 2–3 [ft; ca. 6 dm to 1 m]." [Lg] "Highly scented." [B1] "Tea and sweet-pea scent." [T3] "Beautiful plant with fine canes and small foliage and the coppery orange flowers which are different." [ARA29/50] "Rather sparse, bronzy-green foliage . . . harmonizes very well with its flowers . . . of a very branching and straggling habit of growth . . . flowers freely and with wonderful persistency . . . we may at times find all mixtures of red, pink, and orange, in varying proportions and inextricably mixed, but the colour is always striking and attractive. Unlike most of the

Chinas, which are not particularly fragrant, 'Comtesse du Caÿla' is decidedly sweet-scented, with the perfume of the Tea Rose . . . without full sunshine it does not seem nearly so floriferous, nor are the flowers so noticeable . . . on the whole very free from mildew and other diseases." [NRS/12] "Personal preference for best China." [Th]

CRAMOISI SUPÉRIEUR   PLATE 5
('Agrippina', 'Queen of Scarlet')
Coquereau/Audiot/Vibert, 1835
Seedling of *R. chinensis* 'Slater's Crimson'.

"The following letter, addressed to Mons Scipion Cochet, came our way: *July 24, 1883. Mon Cher Mons S. Cochet, The rose 'Cramoisi Supérieur' was raised in 1832 by Mons Coquereau, a fancier at la Maître École, near Angers (Dept. Maine-et-Loire), who presented it to another fancier of that area, Mons Audiot. This latter took it to Mons Vibert, then at Longjumeau, who released it to commerce in 1835. Sincerely yours, Petrus Rosina.*" [JR7/120] "Unequalled crimson." [Ed] "Velvety crimson." [HoBoIV/320] "Flowers are so finely formed, and its crimson tints so rich." [R8] "Intense maroon; flower medium-sized; cupped; very floriferous; vigorous." [Cx] "Bright carmine." [R-H35] "Blood-red. Rich velvety texture. Free and constant." [Dr] "Though an old rose, this is still one of the best and most popular of its class . . . it is cupped, beautifully formed, and of a rich, brilliant crimson, with a delicate white stripe in the center of each petal. It is one of the most hardy and desirable of the old China Roses." [SBP] "Perhaps no rose gives so great a succession of flowers . . . which are of the richest scarlet crimson, very glowing. The rose being pendulous, the edges reflex most gracefully, to exhibit more fully as it were the extreme richness and velvety scarlet of their inner sides. . . . Nothing can exceed the richness and beauty of a large head of 'Cramoisi Supérieur' on a low stem convered with its graceful flowers in constant succession." [C] "Perfect globular shape." [HstXI:225] "Semi-double, cupped . . . only slightly scented . . . 3 × 3 [ft; ca. 1 × 1 m]." [B] "Continuous supply of flowers." [L] "Universally admired for its brilliant crimson cup formed flowers, perfectly double; it is a strong grower, and should be in every collection." [Bu] "Growth moderate." [P1] "Good foliage. Medium growth. The climbing sport is better" [Th2] (the "climbing sport" referred to is 'Mme Couturier-Mention', not a sport but rather a climbing seedling). "Thin stems . . . small leaves." [Hk] "Weak and straggling growth." [K2] "Sturdy and free-blooming, free from disease and insect attacks." [UB28] "A good bedding variety." [EL] "Fairly vigorous; branches slender and nodding; bark light reddish green; prickles red, narrow, elongated, straightish, and quite sharp; leaves smooth, dark green, shiny, somewhat reddish, 5–7 oval leaflets , pointed, red-tinted along the fine serration; leaf-stalks narrow, armed with numerous prickles; flower about 2 in across, globular, a little quilled, solitary on the branchlets, or in clusters on the more vigorous branches; color, bright crimson; flower stalk, large enough, but thin and bending under the weight of the blossom; pretty buds." [S] "Calyx glabrous and rounded." [JF] "Especially valued for its fine buds . . . the best of the [China] class." [EL]

DUCHER   PLATE 7
('Bengale Ducher')
Ducher, 1869
Not to be confused with Ducher's yellow/salmon-pink/red Tea of 1874.

"Mid-sized double blooms of creamy-white . . . constant bloom, vigorous to 4 [ft; ca. 1.25 m]." [HRG] "Pure white, of

28

medium size and fine form, full. Promising as a free and continuous white bedding Rose." [P1] "Double but flat. Good white decorative. . . . Foliage, good to very good." [Th] "One is tempted to guess that 'Ducher' has Tea heritage . . . vigorous, with slender branches, sometimes large, branching, smooth bark of light green, furnished with reddish, long thorns which are somewhat numerous. The foliage is glossy, light green, and divided into 3–5 narrow leaflets, elongated and pointed. The flowers, which reach about 4 in across [ca. 1 dm], are full, well-formed, and either solitary or, on vigorous branches, in clusters. The outer petals are large, the inner ones petite and folded. The bud is quite pretty. This variety is very remontant. It is the only really vigorous white China." [JR8/89] "Of moderate vigor; blooms in panicles; flower medium-sized, full, fragrant, in a reflexing cup; pure white; very floriferous." [S] "[The thorns are] long, reddish, substantial, slightly hooked, and very sharp . . . flower-stem slender and slightly nodding. Calyx ovoid." [JF] "Dislikes frost." [S]

Born at Lyon in 1820, "Claude Ducher died the 24th of this month [January, 1874] . . . Claude Ducher was 54 years old. He was a devoted rosarian, honest, intelligent, and hard-working, esteemed by all his colleagues. He developed quite a number of good Roses which shine in our collections, particularly in the Tea class." [R-H74]

DUCHESS OF KENT
('Duchesse de Kent')
Laffay?*, 1840
Not to be confused with the 1968 Floribunda of the same name.

"Creamy white, sometimes beautifully edged with rose, then very pretty and distinct, small and full; form, cupped." [P] "Large, full, well-formed, light pink." [R-H42] "A neat pale rose, of a dwarf habit, and rather small sized flower." [Bu] "Has given way to new and superior varieties." [WRP] *"Mons Laffay, who has developed many novelties, always dedicates them to English princes." [PIB]

DUKE OF YORK
W. Paul, 1894

"Rosy-pink and white. Distinct." [H] "Variable between rosy-red and white, sometimes pale with deep red centres, sometimes white edged and tipped with carmine in the way of 'Homère' [T]." [P1] "Deep pink, shading to white, bordered and touched pink; flower large, full, quartered; floriferous; vigorous." [Cx] "Semi-double blooms on a bushy plant to 3 [ft; ca. 1 m]." [HRG] "Branching habit . . . 3 × 2 [ft]." [B] "Dark shiny foliage." [B1] "A good and very floriferous variety." [JR19/53]

EUGÈNE DE BEAUHARNAIS
('Prince Eugène')
Hardy, 1837
Not to be confused with the cupped HP from Moreau-Robert, 1865.

"Amaranth, the buds beautiful when first unfolding, sometimes dying off blackish crimson, large and very double; form cupped." [P1] "Beautiful bright lake, a free bloomer through the summer and autumn . . . free grower . . . A charming variety." [HstVI:368] "Large full double fragrant flowers in purple and crimson on a small bushy plant to 2 [ft; ca. 6 dm]." [HRG] "Deep purple, very double; intensely fragrant. Excellent repeat bloom . . . 1–3 [ft; ca. 3–9 dm] . . . excellent . . . does mildew." [Lg] "Of moderate growth." [S] "Bush of ordinary growth, with upright branches; [*thorns*] equal, reddish; leaflets of a glaucous green, purplish at the edges; flowers numerous, medium-sized, in a cluster, full, well-formed, with petals of a beautiful violet red. One of the

most beautiful Bengals existing." [An37/25] "By way of preamble to my botanical description, let me say that I don't want you to conclude that the China 'Eugène Beauharnais' is quite without spines or thorns; *au contraire*, it is part of a group of heavily thorned varieties. But the thorns are quite rare in the vicinity of the flowers . . . so rare indeed that one can ordinarily cut a blossom with a branch several decimeters long without having a single thorn on the cutting. I must concede that, beneath the leafstalk, there are two or three small, sharp, recurved prickles. As for the bush, it is very vigorous, with shiny wood, slightly brown, very glabrous, and, as previously stated, having occasional thorns which are flat or flared and rusty brown. The leaves are small, with five oval leaflets, very much elongated, somber green beneath . . . they are regularly and finely dentate like a saw, and have a purplish edge of the shade found on the underside of the leaves, the glow of which seems to have penetrated the dentation. The stipules are short; the young shoots of this rose are an intense purple. . . . The flowers are borne on a stem 1.5–2 in long [ca. 3–5 cm], which is not strong enough to hold the flower upright; it nods like Zeus with a grace and imposing majesty, even (I would say) with respect. The ovary is short, glabrous, green; the five sepals are entire, sometimes green, most often as purplish as the leaves, always bordered with a short whitish down which is not readily apparant. The corolla is a perfect miniature: its diameter is about 2 in [5 cm], sometimes 2.75 in [7 cm]. The very numerous petals are cupped within, and in a rosette without; they are imbricated in the most perfect manner towards the center, where they are very small, and leave a little gap which nevertheless does not allow the stamens to spoil the picture. The line of the exterior petals is slightly reflexed. This gives the blossom a graceful convexity, above all when seen from the side. The color! — oh, the color is the sparklingest brightest that we have ever seen in a red rose. The outer petals are intense carmine; those of the center are browner, one might say of maroon velvet. The scent is very elegant and sweet." [PIB] " 'Prince Eugène' is a very rich crimson rose, being in colour between 'Cramoisi Supérieur', and 'Roi des Cramoisis' [*see below for this latter cultivar*]; perfectly double and hardy . . . 'Roi des Cramoisis' was brought by me, in 1839, from Paris, where I saw the original plant, around which there was a regularly beaten path made by its admirers, of which I was one, never before having seen a dark rich crimson rose with so much odour; the flowers too were large, fully double, and cup formed; the plant three or four ft high [ca. 1 m], and fully loaded with its gorgeous blossoms. It has since appeared in several collections, having been imported under the name of 'Eugène Beauharnais' . . . it grows freely, and is well worth cultivating." [Bu] "A good sort, but inferior to 'Agrippina' ['Cramoisi Supérieur']." [EL] Prince Eugène de Beauharnais, Duke of Leuchtenberg and Prince of Eichstädt; Empress Josephine's brother; lived 1781–1824. The interesting cactus *Leuchtenbergia principis* is also named after Eugéne de Beauharnais.

FABVIER
('Général Fabvier')
Laffay, 1832

"Dazzling crimson with white stripe." [H] "Scarlet, semi-double." [HoBoIV/320] "Rosy-crimson." [EL] "Crimson scarlet, of medium size, semi-double; form expanded. One of the most brilliant of Roses, very showy." [P1] "Deep crimson . . . here and there a petal streaked with white, the glorious colour heightened by the golden stamens of the expanded blooms, is most charming. . . . 'Fabvier' is always gay, no matter how wet the weather." [JP] "Fiery crimson; velvety." [Go] "Sparkling bright red." [Pq] "Occasional white flecks. Healthy and free-flowering. Well foliated . . . 2 × 2 [ft; ca. 6 × 6 dm]." [B] "Spreading growth . . . twiggy branches." [G] "The bright red flowers are poised on strong, erect stems, and make a first-rate display." [OM] "Small dark green foliage and an erect yet compact habit of growth. . . . The flowers are of medium or rather small size for a China, and of excellent colour—light crimson to crimson scarlet, with a well marked white eye. They have little beauty of form, but produce a good effect in the bed, though the petals are rather thin . . . a sweet and clean little perfume . . . quite free from disease . . . inclined to resent too hard pruning. . . . He [Mr. Easlea] considers that, next to the old Pink China ['Parsons' Pink'], 'Fabvier' is the very best of the tribe." [NRS/12] "Placed in a bed with other Chinas, 'Général Fabvier' can be picked out at a great distance. Slender bearing, vigorous branches, very productive flower clusters, and magnificent appearance are its principal obvious characteristics, to which we will add the following: Bark green, smooth, furnished with very long thorns which are quite slender, hooked, and sharp, and of a light purple. Leaves somber green, of 5–7 leaflets, with the leafstalk and main vein of the leaflets furnished with prickles and glandular hairs which are more or less strong depending upon where they are. The leaflets are sometimes heart-shaped, but most often a pointed and very long oval, always finely and elegantly toothed; the stipules, ciliated with notable finesse and symmetry, are glabrous, narrow, long, drawn up above the petiole, and terminating in two long points. The tip of the young growth is a very delicate purple. Flowers of a very dark poppy red, sometimes a bright carmine, large to about 2.5 in across [ca. 6 cm], somewhat full, carried on stiff, upright stems, holding the blossom perfectly. This rose was raised by Mons Laffay at Bellevue . . . who dedicated it to one of our most distinguished generals. This was the brave general who had the courage, in the bosom of our House of Peers . . . to protest against the many extortions made by the public administration as well as against the importunate entreaties which, all too often, took advantage of the members of the two Houses of the French parliament." [PIB]

FELLEMBERG
Listed as a Noisette.

FIMBRIATA À PÉTALES FRANGÉS
('Serratipetala', 'Rose-Œillet de Saint-Arquey', 'Œillet de Saint-Arquey')
Jacques, 1831

"Bright red." [HoBoIV:318] "Serrated . . . like a damaged carnation." [G] "Mean with its blooms, gaunt in growth." [Hk] "Somewhat vigorous; branches weak; flower medium-sized, full, flat; color, bright red, exterior petals crinkled." [S] "Mons Vilfroy, chief gardener [of the Abby St. Nicholas-au-Bois], made, in 1911, some cuttings of a horticultural form of Jacquin's *R. chinensis*; the slips were placed in a cold frame also containing slips of carnations. Mme Faure, manageress of the château, and Mons Vilfroy both noted with stupefaction in 1912 that, by a strange coincidence, many of the rose cuttings bore flowers which could easily be mistaken for carnations!! The cuttings were carefully tended. Mme Faure did us the honor of asking our opinion of the value of the rose, and we must deem it the most curious rose to be developed in a long time. . . . The 'Rose de St.-Arquey', propagated through our efforts, will be released to commerce probably in the fall of 1915, to the joy of fanciers of new roses and of plant oddities. Nothing similar to this exists; it is a true novelty." [JR37/182–183] "This curious rose which saw the light of day in 1911 at the Abby St. Nicholas-au-Bois, in the Département de l'Aisne, is certainly one of the most interesting novelties to come along in quite some time. . . . [It] resembles a carnation to such a degree that, placed on the stem of a carnation plant which has blossoms of the same shade, it can't be distinguished from them. . . . As for the rest of the plant, the branches and foliage are typical *R. chinensis*, whence it came. We presented the 'Rose de St.-Arquey' at a meeting of the French National Horticultural Society last August 28th [1913] in the name of its happy discoverer Mme Faure; it excited the curiosity of both amateur and professional." [JR37/149] "Mons Huguier-Truelle, the distinguished rose fancier from Troyes . . . proposed the name . . . 'Rose-Œillet de Saint-Arquey'." [JR38/21] "The rose may be . . . 'Fimbriata' . . . raised by Mons Jacques in 1831. . . . For unknown reasons, the rose had degenerated and lost its carnation type, which, however, being innate, became again apparent in the frame." [K]

GLOIRE DES ROSOMANES
Listed as a Bourbon.

HENRY'S CRIMSON CHINA
(*R. chinensis spontanea*)
A. Henry, 1885

"Four to twenty ft in height [ca. 1.25–6 m], . . . crimson, pink or white." [Hk]

HERMOSA
Listed as a Bourbon.

HUME'S BLUSH TEA-SCENTED CHINA
Listed as a Tea.

IRÈNE WATTS   PLATE 10
P. Guillot, 1895
Seedling of 'Mme Laurette Messimy' (Ch).

"Salmon; flower very large, full, quartered; very floriferous." [Cx] "White tinted pale pink . . . 2 × 2 [ft; ca. 6 × 6 dm]." [B] "Salmon-white in bud, changing to salmon-rose; long buds, very free and good." [P1] "Dark green foliage margined with purple." [B1] "Vigorous, very floriferous, with numerous branches, bushy; leaves purplish green; bud elongated, salmon-white; flower large, full, well-formed, varying from pinkish salmon-white to a very delicate China pink." [JR19/147] "A neat compact grower, and continuous bloomer all summer and fall." [C&Js99]

[LAFFAY]
Laffay, ca. 1825

"Flower medium-sized, full, bright cerise red." [S]

As for Mons Laffay: *"Catalog of Roses cultivated by Mons Laffai* [sic]*, rue Rousselet-Saint-Germain, P N° 17, Paris.* Mons Laffai having been especially devoted to the culture of Roses, and loving them warmly, it is natural that his collection is the most complete in having both the most and the newest. Let it be stated of him that his trips to England, Belgium, and Holland as well as his correspondents in Italy have not let him miss a single beautiful rose nor fail to make any sacrifice to obtain it. He furthermore has often bred his own varieties from seed, and his industry has been such that it would be difficult to find a good rose that was *not* stocked on his premises on Rue Rousselet." [R-H36] "Since I [*Laffay*] began cultivating roses, I have devoted myself to growing seedlings of this beautiful family: In the beginning, the pretty varieties which I thus obtained encouraged me to renew those first attempts which were so lucky; but Nature is occasionally capricious! As we know few of her secrets, the several years which followed didn't always produce the results which I had obtained in my first tries. My perseverence, however, in continuing made me certain that with new combinations she would reward me with her treasures. And so, over a number of years, I have developed some wonderful roses in that precious group of *hybrids with constant bloom*, and am occupied, at the present time, with propagating them so that I can offer them to the fanciers who are looking for them as soon as possible; thus they will be able to enjoy varieties of elegant fragrance, rich color, and (above all) hardiness—like those they are already used to, but over the *whole* season. Despite the preference which I seem to give to this new sort of roses, I am nevertheless always involved with other sorts. I must, however, admit that the Noisettes, Chinas, and Teas are occasionally neglected in budding because I have decided to grow only the most meritorious, and those only as potted plants [*i.e., as 'own-root' plants in pots, not as budded 'standards' (tree-roses) or budded 'dwarfs' (bush-roses)*]. These varieties, exotic by nature, are too risky to attract those nurserymen who otherwise would grow them." [LF] "M. Laffay wrote to me [W. Paul] last autumn [1847] . . . :'It is my intention to cease cultivating the Rose, in a commercial sense. My project was to do so this autumn, and to install myself in the south of France, in the land of oranges and palm-trees; but my father, who is very aged, wished that we should not quit Paris this winter. This rather alters our plans of emigration, although they are only retarded. But it is very possible that I may yet offer you some good roses, especially of the Hybrid Moss, for I intend to make a sowing of several thousands of seeds of these varieties. Thus I presume that my seed-plot will be worth visiting for some years to come. I am persuaded that in future we shall see many beautiful Roses, which will efface all those that we admire now. The Mosses will soon play a grand part in Horticulture'." [P] "My first recollection of Roses is of the occasion when I [George Paul] went as a lad to Paris with my father to see the first great French Exhibition in 1855, and visited Mr. Laffay, who had retired to a house and garden amongst the woods of the Paris suburb of Belleville [*sic*], taking with him his seedling Roses." [NRS17/101] "The Société Centrale d'Horticulture de France lost, in 1878, . . . Laffay, the celebrated rose-breeder who has given our gardens so many magnificent varieties." [SNH/24] "Report to the Council of Administration, in the name of the Floricultural Committee, on How to Use the Gift of Mme Laffay. By Mons Eugène Delamarre, Secretary of the Committee. Sirs, You have charged the Committee of Floriculture to find the best way of using the sum donated by Mme Laffay in memory of Mons Laffay, her husband, the late member of the Society, who was one of the devotees of *methodical* breeding of the Rose, and who developed many good varieties of Roses, among which I will mention only 'La Reine', which everybody knows, and which will for a long time stand at the head of the remontant hybrids. A special Commission composed of Messrs. Margottin père, Jamain, C. Verdier, Lévêque fils, Millet fils, Hérivaux, Bergman, Leprieur, Dutitre, Bachoux, and Delamarre, named by the Committee, after having considered the remarks of Mons Eugène Verdier, who represented Mme Laffay, herewith renders you the following proposals, which the Committee has approved: The Commission believes it just and equitable to convert Mme Laffay's generous gift into medals which will be awarded to the Lyonnais specialists who are the flower of French breeders and who have truly brought rosiculture forward as a result of their great number of very good varieties. These able Lyonnais horticulturalists don't have the same opportunity as the Parisian to get the rewards which they so justly merit. The Commission thus believes it appropriate to recommend to you that Mme Laffay's gift be used to strike three medals, two in gold for Messers Lacharme and Guillot fils, and one of silver gilt for Widow Ducher [*representing both herself and the late Mons Ducher*], all three Lyonnais horticulturalists, for their outstanding obtentions, in particular 'Captain Christy', 'La France', and 'Mlle [*sic*] Marie Van Houtte'." [SNH/272–273]

One tries, with meager results, to put together a time-line for Jean Laffay, who is—like Vibert—curiously obscure for being a leader in his field acknowledged as such in his own lifetime. *Sic transit gloria mundi!* After the very greatest efforts of, in particular, my inestimable colleague Mons Massiot, we may offer the following: Born at Paris August 17, 1794, to Jean Laffay (who died at about 90 on July 14, 1852) and his wife Jeanne (Fagotay), [LF1] by 1825 he has set up for himself at Auteuil, having formerly been "head gardener" to the nurseryman Ternaux of that community, with whom, no doubt, he released his first introductions around 1815—perhaps as early as 1810; [LS, Jg] is still there in 1829 [R-H29]—an important year in his life, as his marriage contract is dated February 28 of that year. In 1835, he imported from England the remontant Pimpinellifolia 'Stanwell Perpetual'. [SHP35/125] By 1836, we see him in Paris at 17 rue Rousselet-St. Germain; [R-H36] by 1837, he is established in Bellevue-Meudon, [An40] where, rather well-to-do, he remains—at first in business, and then retired—at least until 1855 [NRS17/101] or so, during which period he achieved his great pioneering triumphs in the development of the Hybrid Perpetual. His first HP, from 1837, "was a superb purple Rose, which he called 'Princesse Hélène', and of which he spoke with all the enthusiasm of his good and generous nature." [R-H63/294–295] The area of Bellevue was the home of the Marquise de Pompadour, mistress of Louis XV, who bought it for her in 1757; sold as "national goods" at the Revolution, the château and grounds were preserved intact up to 1819, when they were bought by one Guillaume, who demolished the château and sold the grounds bit by bit in large parcels. The Laffays bought at least two of these plots, in February and in August of 1837, thereafter reselling at least four smaller portions of this land. It is possible that they had purchased the property by way of speculation, as this desirable location overlooking one part of Paris could be expected to increase rapidly in value. At length, Laffay put into effect his 1847 plans to remove to the South—*but* with a difference. The Bellevue-Meudon voting lists for 1857 bear a small notation next to his crossed-out name: *Parti en Afrique*—"Left for Africa"!

The year 1859 found him at Kouba in Algeria, a community above Algiers where one has a good panorama of the city and its harbor, and which has good air and few frosts. At length, however, in 1877, we find him back in France, an honorary member of the Société Nationale d'Horticulture — he had been, like Vibert, a founding member in 1827 of its predecessor the Société d'Horticulture de Paris — living at his Villa Apollonie at Cros Vieil, Cannes, where he died April 15, 1878. [LF1] Mme Laffay's name was Apollonie (Fournier). [LF1] Both were buried on the "Allée du Silence" in the Cannes cemetary. We find no indication of offspring. Mons Massiot adds some etymological information, knowing my mania for miscellanea: *Laffay* is the name of the region of Lyon and le Massif Central (Clermont-Ferrand). Written also "Lafay," it means *hêtraie* or Beech Grove, and is perhaps more familiar in its diminuative form, "Lafayette."

Always in the forefront of breeding, whether with the "new" Noisettes, Teas, and Chinas in 1820, the "new" Hybrid Perpetuals in the middle of his career, or the "new" Hybrid Mosses and who knows what in Africa at the end, Jean Laffay has as his lasting monument the great and distinguished influence his work has had on rose progress.

LE VÉSUVE [PLATE 4]
('Lemesle')
Laffay, 1825

"Intense carmine shading to pink; many colors on the same specimen; flower very large, very full; very vigorous; very floriferous." [Cx] "Flower medium-sized, full, shining red tinted pink." [LR] "Handsome, intense red." [No] "Bears some flowers rich crimson and some rosy pink." [K2] "Wine red with buff center." [Capt28] "Shapely, pointed buds opening loose and blowsy, silvery pink with deeper shadings . . . 3 × 3 [ft; ca. 1 × 1 m]." [B] " . . . double, large; pink, turning to flame-colour." [Go] "['Lemesle':] Flower large, full, camellia-form; color, bright pink." [S] "['Vésuve':] . . . double, large, pink passing to fiery red. Calyx tube narrow, long, claviform, narrowing imperceptibly into the peduncle." [S] "The most perfectly formed rose that I have seen. It is as regularly imbricated as a Camellia; quite large, and of a lovely bright pink color." [HstXV:29] "Delicious soft tea-scent." [T3] " 'Flower, of medium size, not singly borne, varying from pink to crimson red. The part of the petals which is covered by others is ordinarily flesh, and the part not covered is fiery cerise or crimson red' [—*from Prévost's 1829 catalog*]. All the descriptions of this variety which we have found seem to us to have been taken from Prévost's catalog as they are completely similar. The China 'Le Vésuve' forms a pretty, bushy small shrub, vigorous, very floriferous, and having nice shiny green foliage. Bedded, or in a group, it produces a fine effect." [JR15/72–73]

L'OUCHE
Buatois, 1901

"Light pink shaded yellow." [LS] "Pale rosy flesh reflexed with yellow; large, full, fine conical buds; growth vigorous." [P1] "Double pink flowers of old fashion form on bushy plant." [HRG] "Fairly dark, thick foliage." [B1] "4 × 3 [ft; ca. 1.25 × 1 m]." [B] "Vigorous, with strong-growing wood, well-branched. Foliage ample, bronze-green. Flower large, full; bud conical and of a pretty flesh pink, yellow at the nub." [JR26/3] Named after a Dijonnais river.

LOUIS-PHILIPPE [PLATE 6]
('Président d'Olbecque' [?], 'Crown', 'Purple')
Guérin, 1834

"Velvety crimson, full, cupped, large." [LF] "Dark crimson, the edges of the centre petals almost white, of medium size, full; form, globular." [P1] "Fragrant; bright red. Excellent repeat bloom . . . 3–4 [ft; ca. 1–1.25 m] . . . excellent." [Lg] "Deep purplish red. Bushy . . . 3 × 2 [ft; ca. 9 × 6 dm]." [B] "Fimbriated petals." [ARA40/37] "Stimulating fragrance of spices." [ARA39/48] "Of moderate vigor, giving very pretty flowers, full, globular, and deep maroon. This description is in our opinion the only one which is quite exact." [JR23/25] "Crimson; an inferior 'Agrippina' ['Cramoisi Supérieur']." [EL] "Small double red flowers and shiny, green foliage . . . a great favorite as a hedge rose." [SHj] "Vigorous, twiggy plant, 3 × 3 [ft; ca. 1 × 1 m]." [HRG] "Has done so

well in Florida that it is called the 'Florida Rose'." [ARA25/112] "Has not an equal for growth, in good soils frequently making a shoot six ft long [ca. 1.75 m] in one season; the flowers are large, perfectly double, of a globular form; the circumference of the bloom is of a dark crimson colour, the centre a pale blush, making it altogether perfectly distinct." [Bu]

LOUIS XIV
Listed as an HP.

[MME DESPREZ]
Desprez, ca. 1835
Not to be confused with the important Bourbon of the same name.

"Pure white, double, cupped, large, beautiful." [LF] "Very fine white." [CC] "White tinged with lemon, large and very double; form, cupped." [P] "A facsimile of a Double White Camellia, with the most agreeable fragrance." [Bu] "Foliage smooth; numerous clusters; flowers pretty full, large (3 in [ca. 7.5 cm]), pure white." [R-H35]

MME EUGÈNE RÉSAL [PLATE 9]
P. Guillot, 1894
Seedling of 'Mme Laurette Messimy' (Ch).

"Coppery rose; vigorous." [J] "Bicolored, nankeen-yellow shaded intense pink; flower large, semi-double, cupped, fragrant; floriferous; very vigorous." [Cx] "Variable, ranging from coppery-red to bright china-rose on an orange ground, exceedingly rich and effective, large and double, with fine petals. Splendid for massing." [P1] "This rose is not one of the first flowers in spring, but it is one of the last flowers in fall, which makes it precious. It seems to contradict the appellation 'Monthly Rose', as it tends to bloom continously from spring to fall . . . foliage of a dark green." [JR23/41] "From seed gathered from the China 'Mme Laurette Messimy', and sown in 1887 by Mons Pierre Guillot. . . . It is a vigorous bush, compact and blooming abundantly until frost. The blossoms are large, double, or full; the buds, elongated, of two colors, nasturtium-red shading to orange yellow at the base; varies from, upon opening, nasturtium-red to a very bright China pink, with a ground of orange-yellow changing to coppery-pink. But with its vigor, its luxuriant foliage both 'purple' and glossy, its buds and flowers looking like big variegated Nasturtiums, I think that, when planted in groups or beds, this will prove to be one of the happiest acquisitions for such purposes." [JR19/56]

MME LAURETTE MESSIMY
Guillot et fils, 1887
From crossing an un-named seedling of 'Rival de Pæstum' (T) and 'Mme Falcot' (T) with 'Mme Falcot' (T).

"Coppery yellow brightened by flame and shaded intense pink; flower large, full, fragrant; very floriferous; vigorous." [Cx] "Medium size, not well filled, Chinese pink, ground colour bright saffron yellow. Very free-flowering, soon over, but very effective; continuous till autumn." [Hn] "Graceful flowers . . . salmon-rose tints." [E] "Very vigorous; flower large or moderate, double or full, well formed, tapered bud; beautiful sparkling China pink, very bright coppery yellow at the base." [JR11/149] "Fair degree of perfection [in cool seasons]." [L] "Very free . . . vigorous for its type . . . 4 × 3 [ft; ca. 1.25 × 1 m]." [B] "Ample glossy leaves of grayish green." [B1]

MONTHLY ROSE
Listed as 'Parsons' Pink China'.

MRS. BOSANQUET
Listed as a Bourbon.

MUTABILIS
('Tipo Idéale'?)
Introducer and date unknown.
Not to be confused with 'Lutescens mutabilis', which was "full," [S] with the very double Ayrshire, nor with da Costa's double Tea.
"Honey-yellow to orange and red." [B] "Spreading . . . to 8 [ft; ca. 2.5 m] . . . soft yellow changing to pink then crimson, excellent rebloom." [HRG] "Large single flowers." [Hk] "Beautiful clusters . . . stems and leaves . . . are red." [DP] "Of Oriental grace, with chiffoned petals poised delicately as if about to flutter away. It shares with many of the Sasanqua Camellias their sort of artless elegance." [BCD] "May be partly derived from the Tea Rose." [T3] Oddly enough, gets touches of rust (which seem to do no harm)—most unusual in either Chinas or Teas; does *not* get mildew—which Chinas often do get; has small, few-seeded hips, which set only in the fall for me; and generally marches to the beat of a different drummer in all things. Could it be something on the order of Tea × *R. moschata*, or . . . ? Its recorded history is on the scant side, but it seems to have gone from China to Réunion (the Bourbon Isle) to Italy before being generally distributed (see W.J. Bean, *Trees and Shrubs Hardy in the British Isles*, 8th ed. revised). Phillips & Rix report that one Prince Ghilberto Borromeo gave it to Henri Correvon of Geneva in 1896.

NAPOLÉON
Laffay, ca. 1835
"Blush." [M'l] "Yellow, tinted crimson." [LS] "Flower large, full, flared; pale pink touched crimson." [S] "Blush, mottled with pink, large and double; form cupped." [P1]

NÉMÉSIS
Bizard, 1836
"Crimson, later quite dark." [N] "Flowers full or semi-full, colored deep red." [JR23/104] "Flower small, full, velvety dark crimson; petals muddled." [S] "Crimson, changing blackish, larger and more robust in habit than [other 'fairy roses']." [P] "Dainty small leaves on a dwarf twiggy bush. The flowers are double, quite small, of rich plum crimson with coppery shadings, borne in small clusters early in the summer and in great heads on the strong shoots later. Not much scent. 2 to 3 ft [ca. 6–9 dm]." [T3] We learn from *Les Amis des Roses* nº 215 (page 5) that Mons Bizard was Angers' advisor to the royal court, and that Mons Millet, first president of the Angers Horticultural Society (and, at least in the 1840's, president of the *Comice Horticole de Maine et Loire*), said that Bizard was to some degree responsible for the rose-growing predilections of Angers, being the first person in town to put together a collection of roses.

ŒILLET DE SAINT-ARQUEY
Listed as 'Fimbriata à Pétales Frangés'.

OLD BLUSH
Listed as 'Parsons' Pink China'.

OLD CRIMSON
Listed as 'Slater's Crimson China'.

PARKS' YELLOW TEA-SCENTED CHINA
Listed as a Tea.

PARSONS' PINK CHINA
('Old Blush', 'Monthly Rose', 'Common China')
Parsons, 1793
I give above the traditional attribution for this cultivar. The headnote to this chapter provides its recorded history—such as it is—and whether we owe it all to Peter Osbeck of Sweden in 1752, his countryman Capt. Ekeberg's 1763 introduction, to Mr. Ker, or Keer, or Kerr, "around 1780," to a misreading by Vibert of Sabine's handwriting, making "Ker" out of "Kew," or to anything or everything else, is problematical. "I [*Loiseleur-Deslongchamps*] saw in 1798, in the greenhouses of Mons Barbier, chief surgeon of Val-de-Grâce and distinguished amateur botanist, the first China Rose ['*Rosier de Bengale*'] which he had gotten from England, where it had been received from China via India in 1789—say some—in 1780 or indeed 1771 say others." [L-D] The likelihood is that the original pale pink China was "introduced" a number of times from China by all and sundry, and that the person originally responsible is quite undiscernible by now.

Whether or not Dr. Cartier's "full-flowered" China seedling is indeed the 'Common China' "which is so well known in our gardens" is another questions to ponder. Clearly, the early introductions were not single; extant dried botanical specimens from then indicates some degree of doubleness. Just as clearly, today's 'Parsons' Pink' is not what we or anyone would describe as "full-flowered," being rather on the semi-double side. In his catalog of 1820, Vibert distinguished the "common" China from both the "single pink" and the "full flowered," indicating that the common China of his catalog was semi-double. Considering this, Jamain & Forney's 1873 statement about Dr. Cartier's "well-known" variety seems to be derived from a misreading of Vibert, whose book seems to have been at Jamain & Forney's respective elbows as they wrote.

At any rate, it would seem that 'Parsons' Pink' has met all comers for two hundred years, and has prevailed. Here is why:
"One of the oldest China Roses, but one of the very best. There can be nothing more perfect than its half-expanded bud, of a light crimson, inclining to blush. It commences blooming among the earliest, and, if the old seed-vessels are picked off, will continue to bloom abundantly through the summer and autumn, even after severe frosts. It is one of the hardiest of the class." [SBP] "The flower is of a dark blush or rose colour, and about three in[ches] in diameter [ca. 7.5 cm]; it grows very strong, frequently making shoots five ft long [ca. 1.5 m] in one season in rich sandy soil." [Bu] "Pretty clear pink colouring . . . dainty scent and neat foliage . . . compact, low." [J] "Blush pink aging darker pink . . . twiggy . . . to 3 [ft; ca. 9 dm]." [HRG] "Perpetual silvery pink with a crimson flush. Upright . . . 5 × 4 [ft; ca. 1.5 × 1.25 m]." [B] "Small, semi-double, and freely produced." [Hk] "Constant and free bloomer." [ARA31/31] "Of vigorous habit, and there are in some gardens bushy plants eight ft high [ca. 2.25 m] . . . [the blossoms are] showy from their profusion, and appear well when in bud." [WRP] "The wood

is stout, of a glaucous green, bearing brown hooked prickles . . . vigorous in growth, flowering successively, and the fruit is ovate in form and scarlet." [JP]

PINK PET
Listed as a Polyantha.

POMPON DE PARIS
Miniature China.
"Flower small, pretty full; pink." [JR4/21] "1 × 1 [ft; ca. 3 × 3 dm]. [B1]

PRINCESSE DE SAGAN   PLATE 8
Dubreuil, 1887
Affiliated with the progeny of 'Souvenir de David d'Angers' (T).
"Deep cherry-red, shaded maroon." [H] "Velvety crimson shaded with blackish purple and reflexed with amaranth; of medium size, full, growth vigorous." [P1] "A dark red, rather single, rose. Very small, but numberless blooms. I have often done the whole dinner-table with this rose. Useful for cutting." [HmC] "Of moderate dimensions in growth, but vigorous and robust; branches armed with many very strong and hooked thorns; leaves of 5 bright leaflets, beautiful green above, paler beneath. Buds very long in the spring, shorter in summer, longer than the sepals, which are long and foliaceous, whereas the ovary is short and squat. Flowers solitary, medium-sized, with long stems, upright at the ends of the branches; widely cupped, with many petals perfectly imbricated in the outer rows, somewhat concave, and slightly wavy ." [JR11/183] Jeanne-Alexandrine-Marguerite Seillière, Princesse de Sagan; died 1905.

PURPUREA
Chenault, 1930
"Rich, glowing, purplish crimson colour . . . 18 in [ca. 4.5 dm]." [T3]

QUEEN MAB
W. Paul, 1896
"Apricot, reddish suffusion, dwarf, compact habit." [Wr] "Peach, center orange." [LS] "Soft rosy apricot, centre of flower shaded with orange and the outside tinted with rose and violet. It blooms with wonderful freedom, and is one of our best roses for garden decoration, especially in the late summer and autumn, when the beautiful colours of the flowers are intensified by the lengthening nights." [P1] "Very delicate and beautiful, with HT form. Small grower." [Th2] "Flower large, semi-double, moderate vigor." [Cx] "Coppery young foliage, wiry growth to over a metre [ca. a yard] . . . very double, flat . . . , quartered and 60 mm [ca. 2.25 in] . . . soft apricot which deepens." [G] "This variety is quite different from its forbears, and is superior to them by reason of the vigor of its growth, and the texture of its petals, the quality of which permits the blossom to last a long time, cupped at one point, certainly longer than other roses we know." [JR20/67] "This variety is a good example of those of the boutonnière class, like 'Ma Capucine' and 'Mme Laurette Messimy'. Nevertheless, it differs from these two roses as well as all others by the strength and regularity of its growth, as well as by the substance of its petals, which are very strong, allowing it to last a long time as a cut flower — longer, indeed, than any other rose known." [JR20/164] *See also* 'Morning Glow' (T) in the Teas chapter supplement.

RIVAL DE PÆSTUM
Listed as a Tea.

ROSA CHINENSIS SPONTANEA
Listed as 'Henry's Crimson China'.

ROULETII
Correvon, 1815
"Almost evergreen, the tiny shrub is bushy and well endowed with small thorns. Fully double, clear pink flowers, borne in upright clusters . . . 6 × 6 in [ca. 1.5 × 1.5 dm]." [B1]

SERRATIPETALA
Listed as 'Fimbriata à Pétales Frangés'.

SLATER'S CRIMSON CHINA
('Old Crimson', 'Semperflorens')
Slater, 1790
"Semi-double light crimson blooms produced constantly on a vigorous plant to 4 [ft; ca. 1.25 m]." [HRG] "A rather velvety crimson red, double rose, 2.5 to 3 in [ca. 6.5–7.5 cm], growing on a thin stem singly and in clusters; it is truly everblooming . . . branching, almost twiggy, as the branches are wiry, of 3 to 4-ft height [ca. 1–1.25 m], with foliage of a deep lustrous green, showing purple or deep red in the young leaflets." [ARA33/70] "Centre petals sometimes slightly streaked with white." [B1] "A constant daily bloomer. The bright red roses are small and nearly single, the bush dwarf and spindling, with nothing to indicate its well-known strength and longevity." [Dr] "Perfectly double, cup shaped, of a rich crimson colour . . . though of humble growth gives a profusion of bloom throughout the entire season." [Bu] "Brilliantly coloured flowers, and is quite one of the showiest roses; it makes quick progress when planted against a south wall . . . freer flowering [than 'Cramoisi Supérieur']." [OM] "Its branches are slender; wood dark green; leaves shiny, tinted more or less with purple; growth short and bushy; flowers, produced singly, of a deep crimson, and the fruit is quite round." [JP]

SOPHIE'S PERPETUAL
Listed as a Bourbon.

VIRIDIFLORA   PLATE 12
('The Green Rose')
Bambridge & Harrison, 1855
Sport of *R. chinensis* 'Parsons' Pink'.
"Dark green; flowers medium-sized, full; very floriferous; very vigorous; a curiosity." [Cx] "Green flowers, of no beauty whatsoever." [EL] "An engaging monstrosity . . . very easy to grow." [Hk] "Flowers . . . light green, in clusters of 10–20." [I'H55/54] "[Its blossom has the scent of] pepper." [JR33/101] "This monstrous rose has parts which are identical with those of all other roses; . . . each petal is transformed into a veritable leaf identical in texture and form to one of the stem leaves, only one is not able to see the dentation without a lens." [S] "The Green Rose was seen in all its glory; Mons Eugène Verdier exhibited many specimens . . . Poor Green Rose! Just a few more years, and it will cease to be! But that's all it's capable of. Inconstant as the nuns of another reign, like them, loving admiration, they know that their finery is too simple to be attractive, and that it is necessary to take on brighter, livelier colors to secure admirers. A young botanist, Mons Alphonse Lavallée, showed us this year, to good effect, blossoms strongly tinted poppy red in which the central petals had metamorphosed into stamens and pistils. It is thought, and for good reason, that this supposed species with green flowers, originating in Japan, is nothing other than a sport which will revert

to the type after a few years of growth. . . . The flowers shown by Mons Verdier were totally green." [I'H58/61–62] "4 × 3 [ft; ca. 1.25 × 1 m]." [B]

"It is so ugly that it is worth nothing, except as a curiosity; and if it ceased to be a curiosity, it would be quite valueless. It is a green rose. I got a small plant from Baltimore, in America, some years ago, and I find it perfectly hardy. It blooms very freely, and all through the summer; the bud is a perfect Rose bud in appearance, but the open flower shows that the Rose is of monstrous and not natural growth; the petals are, it seems to me, no real petals at all, but an expansion of the green heart, which often appears in Roses, and which has here been so cultivated as to take the place of the natural Rose. The petals are coarse and irregular, and have serrated edges, with a very faint scent." [Br] " 'I received "Viridiflora" from Charleston, from which it was sent me . . . perhaps 35 years ago [*ca. 1854*] . . . it was from the same source [Mons Andrea Gray of Charleston?] that I also received . . . "Isabella Gray" . . . [signed:] Eugène Verdier fils, 1889.' . . . Despite further re-searches, we have yet to determine the exact origin of 'Bengale à Fleurs Vertes'." [JR13/114–115] " 'It is a sport from ['Parsons' Pink']. . . . It was caught in Charleston, S.C., about 1833, and came to Baltimore through Mr. R. Halliday, from whom I obtained it, and presented two plants to my old friend Thomas Rivers in 1837.' " [Buist being quoted second-hand in Br.] 'Viridiflora' was evidently held a number of years before being *commercially* released. Why?: "More appropriate to the collection of the celebrated Barnum than to any serious horticultural exhibition." [R-H 55]

WHITE HERMOSA

Not a sport of 'Hermosa' (which is a B).
Listed as 'Marie Lambert' (T).

WHITE PET

Listed as a Polyantha.

Supplement

ALICE HAMILTON

Nabonnand, 1903
From 'Bengale Nabonnand' (Ch) × 'Parsons' Pink China'.

"Flower very large, semi-full, well formed, large petals, light and sweet perfume; color, brilliant velvety crimson red, madder reflections; pretty, long bud, nearly always solitary; very beautiful, compact, dark green foliage; very vigorous, very floriferous." [JR27/164]

ALICE HOFFMANN

Hoffman, 1897
"Pink, touched cherry." [LS] Alice Hoffmann, daughter of Albert Hoffmann, first rosarian of the Sangerhausen Rosarium.

[ANTOINETTE CUILLERAT]

Buatois, 1897
"Flower semi-double, electric white on a bright coppery sulphur yellow ground, petals' edges lightly colored violet carmine; vigorous bush forming a compact plant constantly covered with bloom." [JR21/147] "Beautifully formed flowers" [C&Js99]

AURORE

Widow Schwartz, 1897
Seedling of 'Mme Laurette Messimy' (Ch).
"Vigorous, delicate foliage tinted purple; flower large, full, ground color golden yellow fading to cream tinted dawn gold and carmine pink. Very beautiful variety." [JR21/148]

BEAUTY OF GLENHURST

Morley, 19–?
Seedling of 'Parsons' Pink China'.
Pink, single.

BÉBÉ FLEURI

Dubreuil, 1906
"Medium growth, dark foliage, very floriferous. Blooms in clusters of three to five flowers, China pink varying to currant red, sometimes striped white. Very dwarf, but vigorous." [JR30/150]

BELLE DE MONZA

(='Belle de Florence'?)
Villaresi/Noisette, ca. 1825
"Maroon-violet." [LS] "Pale cherry, produced in elegant clusters, of medium size, semi-double; form cupped. A showy rose." [P1] ["Florence":] "Light carmine, blooms in large clusters." [FP] "Branches, erect. Tube of calyx, smooth, oval-turbinated. Flowers, almost full, middle-sized; of a very pale purple, often marbled with a deeper shade. Petals, those of the centre, narrow and wrinkled. This beautiful rose is one of more than twenty varieties of the Bengal or China rose created by Signor Villaresi, superintendant of the Archducal gardens at Monza, in the Milanese." [Go] Evidently re-introduced by Vibert in 1840.

BENGALE ANIMÉE

('Animating', 'Bengale Animée des Anglais')
Laffay, 1832
Has also been attributed to Mons Boursault. Possibly both Laffay and Boursault imported it from England.

"Crimson." [Y̆] "Purplish pink." [LS] "Flower small, full; color, pale lilac." [S] "Branches often long; in which case bearing leaves with seven leaflets. Flowerstalks, hispid, glandulous. Tube of calyx, smooth, bulging at the base, narrow, and long-throated. Flowers, full, middle-sized, fragrant; of a purple-red or pale lilac; often irregular." [Go]

BENGALE D'AUTOMNE

Laffay, 1825
"Variable red." [Y̆]

[BENGALE NABONNAND]

Nabonnand, 1886
"Of exceptional vigor; flower large, full, imbricated, erect; large foliage, glossy dark green; very dark velvety purplish red, coppery, shaded yellow. The most beautiful China, and one of the most profuse. Unique." [JR10/170] A parent of "Alice Hamilton" (Ch).

BENGALE POMPON
Introducer unknown, before 1820
Grown by Vibert. This name encompasses a series of cultivars.

"Growth of moderate vigor; branches slender and twiggy, divergent; bark smooth, green, and reddish on the young growths; thorns the same color, slender, long, slightly hooked, very sharp; leaves small, dark green; leafstalks slender, dark green, slightly reddish beneath; flower small, to perhaps an inch across [ca. 2.5 cm], nearly full, usually cupped; solitary, or in clusters on the vigorous branches; color, light pink or red, depending upon the variety." [S] "Shrub, from one to two ft high [ca. 3–6 dm]. Leaflets . . . never tinged with purple. Tube of calyx, oval, smooth. Flowers, semi-double, light pink." [Go]

BENGALE POURPRE
Listed as 'Pourpre'.

BENGALE SANGUINAIRE
Desprez, 1838

"Flowers crimson, small and very double." [P] "Growth weak, sprawling; branches, leaves, and flower stalks very purple; blossom medium size, slightly globular, very double; velvety, very bright crimson purple; petals concave, having a white nub; twenty to thirty-five styles." [S]

BENGALI
Nonin, 1913

"Dark pink, medium size, full, light scent, tall." [Sn]

CATHERINE II
Laffay, 1832
A 'Catherine II' is also listed by Vibert, in 1829.

"Medium, full; color, flesh; very beautiful." [S] "Leaflets, large. Flowerstalks, curved. Tube of calyx, long and thick. Flowers, large, full, hemispherical; flesh-coloured, sometimes inclining to lilac." [Go] Catherine II, called "the Great," empress of Russia; lived 1729–1796.

[CHARLOTTE KLEMM]
('Sirene', 'Sirena', 'Sisena')
Türke, 1905
From 'Alfred Colomb' (HP) × 'Cramoisi Supérieur' (Ch).

"Fiery red. — Moderately vigorous. — Garden. — A fine China." [Cat12] "Growth dwarf; flower large, full, flat, sparkling scarlet red." [JR30/25] NRS12/70 indicates that 'Charlotte Klemm' is less compact and less erect than 'Fabvier' (Ch), being on the other hand more "showy in the autumn garden." "For those who wish a bed of Roses something after this colour [*that of 'Gruss an Teplitz'* (B)] I should be inclined to recommend either 'Petrus Donzel' [*'Mons Petrus Donzel', Ch, A. Schwartz, 1903*], very like a dwarfer 'Gruss an Teplitz', or better still, 'Charlotte Klemm'." [NRS12/95] Charlotte Klemm, probably daughter or wife of the Klemm of Hoyer & Klemm, "rose-growers of Dresden." [JR37/10]

CROWN
In the main listings as 'Louis-Philippe' (Ch).

DARIUS
Laffay, 1827

"Lilac-purple, fell, flat, large, beautiful." [LF] "Calyx tube conical, oblong, often slightly gibbose on one side at the base; flower large or medium large, very double, light violet or lilac, sometimes slightly fragrant." [S] "Tall." [Sn] Darius the Great, King of Persia, lived ca. 558–486 BC.

DESGACHES
Desgaches, 1840

"Carmine." [Ў] "Not very vigorous; branches weak, few thorns, but amply furnished with bright deep green foliage; flower large, full, in a cluster; delicate pink." [S]

[DOUGLAS]
V. Verdier, 1848

"Deep, rich cherry red; large full flowers; very sweet, constant and profuse bloomer." [C&Js02] "Very vigorous bush; branches short, bright green, not very thorny; beautiful bright dark green foliage; flower large, full, globular; color, delicate pink. Much to be recommended for borders and bedding." [S]

ELYSE FLORY
('Elise Fleury')
Guillot père, 1852

"Fine rose, large and full." [FP] "Bright pink." [S] "Pink, shaded." [LS] "Ordinary pink at the center, paling along the edges, resembling the Bourbon 'Triomphe de la Duchère' [Béluze, 1846, delicate pink]." [l'H52/148] "Growth vigorous; flowers medium or large, full, nuanced pink; strong stem." [l'H56/198]

GÉNÉRAL LABUTÈRE
Introducer and date unknown.

"Bright pink." [LS]

GRANATE
Dot, 1948

"Crimson red." [Ў]

HÉBÉ
Introducer and date unknown.

"Pink." [LS] Hebe, the cup-bearer of the Olympian gods.

INSTITUTRICE MOULINS
Charreton, 1893

"Carmine pink." [Ў]

JEAN BACH SISLEY
Dubreuil, 1898

"Opening delicate silvery-rose, outer petals salmon-rose lined and veined with carmine, large for its class, and very sweet; a beautiful and distinct variety." [P1] "Pale pink and white, blushing deep rose . . . 4 × 3 [ft; ca. 1.25 × 1 m]." [HRG] "Bright foliage; floriferous. Flowers solitary, or in threes at the end of vigorous branches; of notable form in opening. . . . Flower well-held, erect on its stem." [JR22/163]

[LAURE DE BROGLIE]
Dubreuil, 1910
From 'Baronne Piston de St.-Cyr' (Ch. Dubreuil, 1901, light incarnate; parentage unknown) × 'G. Nabonnand' (T).

"Bush of good growth, shrubby, branching, robust, blooming in large clusters on the strongest canes or solitarily on others, long stems. Bud very long on strong peduncle, blush ivory-white. Flowers large, full, perfect form, white shaded bright incarnadine. Very fetching and novel coloration. Extremely decorative, blooms without pause from May to November. Just the thing for bedding and pot-culture." [JR34/168]

[LUCULLUS]
Guinoisseau-Flon, 1854

"Flowers medium-sized, in clusters, very full, opening well, velvety black-purple." [I'H54/34] "Very vigorous . . . color bright purple at first, then after fully open velvety deep purple. This China is one of the most recommendable." [S] "The Black Rose; splendid large rich crimson, extra full and fragrant, very double and a constant and profuse bloomer. Excellent for bedding and garden culture." [C&Js02] Parent of 'Pink Soupert' (Pol). Lucius Licinius Lucullus, fl. first century B.C.; successful Roman military man who, following the temporary ingratitude of the Roman people, did some notable gardening in Rome.

[MADDALENA SCALARANDIS]
Scalarandis, 1901

"Both buds and flowers are extra large and exceedingly beautiful, and its productiveness is truly astonishing, the whole bed being a perfect blaze of bloom for weeks and months; color, dark rich rose on deep yellow ground elegantly flamed with scarlet and crimson." [C&Js06] "This grand and beautiful Rose attracted wide attention in our Rose Exhibit at the Saint Louis World's Fair last year, and was one of the leading varieties in group 108 for which we were awarded a Grand Prize." [C&Js05]

MARÉCHAL DE VILLARS
Introducer and date unknown.

"Flower large, full; color, bright crimson nuanced violet." [S]

MARQUISETTE
Ducher, 1872

"Pink with some salmon." [Ÿ]

MISS LOWE'S VARIETY
Lowe, 1887

"Single crimson." [P1]

PAPILLON
(trans., 'Butterfly')
Dubourg, ca. 1826
Not to be confused with the climber by Nabonnand.

"Purple." [LS] "Rose red, medium size, full, dwarf." [Sn]

POURPRE
('Bengale Pourpre')
Vibert, 1827

"Moderate growth; flower medium sized, deep purple." [S] "Tube of calyx, long and narrow in the throat. Sepals, simple. Flowers, small or middle-sized, single; of a purple-crimson. Petals, spatulated. Styles, six to fifteen." [Go] "Dwarf." [Sn]

PRÉSIDENT D'OLBECQUE
(='Louis Philippe'?)
Guérin, 1834

"Cerise, often changing to crimson; pretty and distinct." [JC] "Cherry red; form, cupped." [P]

PRIMROSE QUEEN
Lippiat, before 1918
Sport of 'Arethusa' (Ch).

"Light yellow, medium size, full, moderate height." [Sn] "Primrose yellow. Vigorous. Winter flowerer." [Au]

PUMILA
Colville, ca. 1806
Not to be confused with Hardy's dwarf Noisette 'Pumila Alba'.

"Flower medium sized, nearly full; virginal white." [S] "Small, double, almost star-like flowers usually borne singly on a short, slightly spreading, miniature plant with long (for size of plant) thin mid-green leaves . . . 1 × 1 [ft; ca. 3 × 3 dm]." [B1]

PURPLE
In the main listings as 'Louis-Philippe'.

[RED PET]
('New Red Pet')
Parker/G. Paul, 1888

"A very pretty miniature Rose, low bushy growth, constant and profuse bloomer, small, round, very double flowers, color deep rich red, blooms all the time; fine for borders and edging, also for pot culture." [C&Js98] 'Old Red Pet' would be 'Lucullus'.

ROSADA
Dot, 1950
From 'Perla de Alcañada' (Min Ch; parentage: 'Perle des Rouges' [Pol] × 'Rouletii' [Min Ch]) × 'Rouletii' (Min Ch).

"Peach pink." [Ÿ]

ROSE DE BENGALE
('Sanguinea')
Introducer and date unknown.

"Bright red single deepening with age to crimson. Twiggy, angular growth . . . 4 × 3 [ft; ca. 1.25 × 1 m]." [B] "Interesting quilled petals." [Hk] "Continually in flower . . . about a metre [ca. 3 ft]." [G] "Stouter wood and larger, darker flowers than 'Miss Lowe'." [T3]

ROSE DE L'INDE
Jacquin, date unknown

"Dark pink." [Ÿ]

SANGLANT
Cherpin/Liabaud, 1873

"Flower full, variable light red." [JR23/104] "Growth vigorous; flower varying from light pink to dark pink depending upon the sun." [S]

SANGUINEA
Listed as 'Rose de Bengale'.

SIRENE
Listed as 'Charlotte Klemm'.

SOUVENIR D'AIMÉE TERREL DES CHÊNES
Widow Schwartz, 1897
Seedling of 'Mme Laurette Messimy'.

"Dwarf; elegant, handsome purple tinted foliage. Bud elongated, of many shades from golden yellow to orange apricot yellow. The open blossom is small, well formed, beautiful coppery pink nuanced carmine." [JR21/148] "A handsome new bedding rose of Tulip form, large full flowers, lovely creamy white, beautifully edged and flushed with rose crimson. A strong healthy grower, producing lovely buds and flowers the whole growing season." [C&Js05]

SOUVENIR DE CATHERINE GUILLOT   **PLATE 11**
P. Guillot, 1895

"Darkest orange-red." [ARA27/19] "Very floriferous, branches and foliage purplish, buds long, nasturtium red mixed with carmine towards the tip. Flower large, full, well-formed, varying from carmine nasturtium red on an orange yellow ground to carmine Indian yellow; very fragrant." [JR19/147] "Coppery carmine, centre shaded with orange; an exceedingly rich-coloured Rose of great excellence; growth fairly vigorous." [P1] "Decorative; hard to establish; remarkably fine color." [ARA28/104] "May be taken as the best . . . of several button-hole Roses issued within the last few years, which have quite small flowers, often only semi-double, but exceedingly rich in brilliant combinations of colours." [F-M2]

SOUVENIR DE J.-B. GUILLOT
('Rose d'Herbeys')
P. Guillot, 1897

"Crimson, shaded bright coppery-red. A fine buttonhole variety." [H] "Orange and crimson." [LS] "Flowers are large, full and very sweet." [C&Js99] "Very floriferous; flower large or medium-sized, varying from nasturtium-red nuanced crimson to light nasturtium red, depending upon the temperature. Very brilliant, novel coloration." [JR21/147] "Very rich and effective; growth vigorous." [P1]

ST. PRIEST DE BREUZE
Desprez, 1838

"Bright crimson, pink towards the center." [S] "Rich deep crimson, their centre rose, of medium size, full; form, globular." [P] — Or a Bourbon?

UNERMÜDLICHE
(trans., 'Indefatigable')
Lambert, 1904
From 'Mlle la Comtesse de Leusse' (T) × 'Mme Caroline Testout' (HT).

"Maroon, center white." [LS]

Chapter Four
TEAS

"We have . . . a numerous family separated from the China roses, solely by their scent, which the French, with their usual nicety of perception, have compared very appropriately to Green Tea." [C] "They bewilder the susceptible rosarian by their exquisite elegance of form, delicacy of colour, and peculiarly refreshing fragrance, which, though likened to that of a newly-opened sample of the choicest tea, is really distinct, and, we will venture to say, unlike all other odours, whether of flowers or leaves, and the most refined and blessed fragrance obtainable in the garden of the world." [Hd]

"The tea-rose is the spoilt child of the family. Natives of China, they seem to keep in their heart all the wealth of which they had a glimpse there in the far East. Their colors, so rich, so warm, so pure, so true and tender, are of infinite variety. From nankeen yellow to dark yellow, pale, pure white, salmon pink, bright red and carmine, every shade that the heavens give us at the rising and setting of the sun live again in these flowers. They are highly esteemed in the gardens of the aristocracy, and dear to the brush of the artist." [G&B]

"From the earliest to the latest, nothing in the history of the rose has been of greater importance than the creation of the Tea. Its introduction to the Occident ranks with the bountiful best gifts of the nineteenth century." [Dr] Having originated, it is speculated, in natural or man-induced crosses between forms of *R. chinensis* and *R. gigantea*, "the [blush] Tea Rose was introduced directly from China to England in 1789; recommended by London to the Empress Josephine in 1810, it entered into cultivation around 1816." [JF] "The yellow variety was obtained from China in 1824, and, even now, after so many fine varieties have been raised, is surpassed but by few in the size and beauty of its flowers, although they are but semi-double. It has only a very slight tea-like odour. . . . Both the Chinese varieties referred to were introduced to our country [the U.S.A.] by the late William Prince, the father of the author, many years before any other persons made similar importations, and the first considerable importation of varieties originated from these 2 Chinese parents ['Hume's Blush' and 'Parks' Yellow'], was made from Loddiges & Sons of London, by the author himself." [WRP] "Nearly 300 varieties of Tea Roses have been catalogued [by 1845], and 40 or 50 are still cultivated." [PIB]

"The roses of this section are, for the most part, of refined growth; the branches are generally slender, nodding, and slightly thorny; the bark is smooth; the leaves, divided into three, five, rarely seven leaflets, are shiny, and often more elongated than with the other sorts; the flowers, though of varying color, are generally pale, more commonly whitish or yellowish, rarely red, and wafting a light tea scent; they are nearly always solitary at the ends of the branches, and supported by feeble stems which often reflex under the weight of the blossom; the tube of the calyx (ovary) is short and rounded . . . when the plant is vigorous, it produces very strong branches, on which the flowers, in a cluster, vary in number according to the variety and vigor of the particular specimen." [BJ]

"The short-branched [*that is, non-climbing*] varieties divide into three sorts which are quite distinct from one another in their respective characters. . . .

"Certainly, such normal-looking varieties as 'Catherine Mermet', 'Bougère', 'Mme Cusin', 'Maman Cochet', [and] 'Souvenir d'Un Ami', would, after scrutiny, be classed as Hybrids or Tea Hybrids. Their reproductive organs are generally incomplete, the hips which they produce but rarely fertile; the varieties which come down to us are more or less fixed sports with the characteristics of the type—the same growth, flower form and doubleness, but varying in color from deep pink to white, or, rarely, yellow.

"Those which sport fairly frequently are quite interesting, one of the above varieties, 'Catherine Mermet', producing seven sports: 'Bridesmaid', 'Mme Joseph Laperrière' [Laperrière, 1899, "pink with silvery reflections" [LS]], 'Maid of Honour', 'Muriel Grahame', 'The Bride', 'Waban', [and] 'White Catherine Mermet' [Forrest, 1887, white]. . . .

"Alongside those varieties are others which are particularly fecund, such as 'Alphonse Karr', 'Anna Olivier', 'Mme Lambard', 'Marie Van Houtte', etc., which very easily produce a multitude of hips, and the offspring of which vary according to the parent such that it is plausible to consider them [*the parents, we presume*] types, or at least sub-types. . . .

"The variety 'Safrano' may be considered as the primordial type; all the varieties which one might name are surely related to it. Two, however—'Adam' and 'Caroline'—are particularly different: in their growth and foliage, which are somewhat scanty; in the form of the 'Caroline'-type flowers, which are medium-sized; in the arrangement of the petals, which are reflexed, crumpled, and incurved upon the calyx, covering the pistils—not æsthetically, nor offering the beauty found in the 'Adam' and 'Safrano' types in which the buds and the flowers are larger and more elongated, with well-developed petals—important things, of consequence to the grace of the blossom. The characteristic of the groups formed by 'Adam' and 'Caroline' is that all their varieties are pink, varying from dark to light, without a true yellow.

"It is of the greatest importance that we not apply these remarks to the varieties which were the first to come out. We find the typical elements necessary to form our groups only in the modern varieties. . . . Between 1825 and 1840, we lost the old race, and thus take as the foundation of our three groups the varieties already mentioned. . . .

" 'Caroline' is a very old variety offered by Guérin in 1835. Growth moderate, somewhat diffuse; stems slightly upright, smooth; prickles moderately abundant; foliage of medium size, leaflets oval-ish, lanceolate, light green; abundant bloom, in clusters; bud short; flowers moderately full such that the petals incurve upon the pistils; stem short, weak; calyx small, widening at the top; color, intense pink with a light coppery tint at the base; fragrant. Through its descendants it has produced three distinct sorts: 'Souvenir de David d'Angers' . . . , 'Comtesse de Labarthe' . . . , and 'Mme Damaizin'. . . .

" 'Souvenir de David d'Angers' and most of its varieties are characterized by growth which tends to droop, while the other 2 groups tend to be upright. Their characteristic color varies from intense red to dark crimson to wine-lee red. Its best varieties are 'Belle Panachée' [Gamon, 1902, "crimson striped pink" [LS]], 'Chevalier Angelo Ferrario' [Bernaix, 1894, "purple-crimson" [LS]], 'Colonel Juffé' [Liabaud, 1893, "blackish purple" [LS]], 'Francis Dubreuil', 'Général Billot' [Dubreuil, 1896, "amaranth and purple" [LS]], 'Princesse de Sagan' [_which we list as a China_], 'Professeur Ganiviat', [and] 'Souvenir de François Gaulain'.

" 'Mme Damaizin' is characterized by very ample foliage, large flowers which are very full and fragrant — not the case with the other two — a very long calyx in the form of a cone enlarged at the top at maturity; color, salmon pink with the same characteristics to be found in 'Jeanne Abel' [Guillot fils, 1882, "delicate pink" [LS]], 'J.-B. Varrone', 'Mme Angèle Jacquier' [Guillot fils, 1879, "pink and yellow" [LS]], 'Mme Joseph Godier' [Pernet-Ducher, 1887, "pink and yellow" [LS]], 'Marquise de Querhoënt', [and] 'Souvenir de Jeanne Cabaud'.

" 'Comtesse de Labarthe' is the only one which preserves the primitive ['Caroline'] characteristics, and which passes them on to its varieties, such as 'Comtesse Riza du Parc', 'Mme Charles Franchet' [Liabaud, 1894, "pink and yellow" [LS]], 'Mme Joseph Schwartz', 'Souvenir du Général Charreton' [Reboul, 1887, "white and red" [LS]], etc.

"The second group takes in those varieties descended from 'Adam', offered by Adam in 1833 [_1838, I rather think_]. All rosarians have doubtless noted the differences between this group and that of 'Safrano'. The growth of these is bushy, and the canes are often slender with medium-sized thorns, which are somewhat numerous, and hooked; the wood is smooth; the foliage is slightly scanty, with oblong and denticulate leaflets, which are also leathery, slightly rugose, and with sharp prickles beneath the leafstalk; fairly long nodding flower stem; bud rounded, slightly pointed; flower large, full, fragrant; interior petals short and narrow, outer petals large; blossom quite full, cupped; color, a pretty salmon pink of a light shade; calyx round, surmounted with sepals, quite obvious being much inflated at maturity. Its varieties maintain the form of the calyx and cupped flower, with slight variations in the growth, which is sometimes more upright with larger foliage; 'Archiduchesse Marie Immaculata' [Soupert & Notting, 1886, "chamois and vermilion" [LS]], 'Catherine Mermet', 'Ernest Metz', 'Goubault', 'Devoniensis', 'Jules Finger', 'Mme Cusin', 'Mme de Vatry', 'Mme de Watteville', 'Mme Pauline Labonté', 'Mme Pierre Guillot', 'Maréchal Bugeaud' [introducer unknown, 1843, "pink and chamois" [LS]], 'Souvenir d'Un Ami', '[Mlle de] Sombreuil', etc.

"The third group is headed by 'Safrano', offered by Beauregard in 1839. Its absolutely typical characteristics make it the variety to adopt as the type. Due to its fertility, it is the basis of a great number of varieties with individual characteristics, which it is better to list below classed in sub-groups according to such characteristics. Growth both abundant and tall, purplish foliage composed of elongated leaflets which are dentate and furnished with sharp prickles beneath; wood smooth, reddish; thorns fairly sturdy, recurved, fairly numerous; flower stem long, slightly flexuous; calyx pretty large, pyriform, much enlarged at maturity; bud very long; flower fragrant, large, full, very elegant, with large petals nicely packed in; color, a pretty saffron yellow; makes a shrub of the first order, worthy of a place in every rosery. We find in this group the yellow for which we have previously sought in vain: 'Beauté Inconstante', 'Comtesse de Frigneuse', 'Dr. Grill', 'Étoile de Lyon', 'Jean Pernet' [Pernet père, 1867, yellow], 'Luciole', 'Mme Charles', 'Mme Chédane-Guinoisseau', 'Mme Falcot', 'Mme Honoré Defresne', 'Mme Margottin', 'Mlle Jeanne Philippe', 'Perle de Lyon' [Ducher, 1872, "deep yellow" [LS]], 'Perle des Jardins', 'Reine Emma des Pays-Bas', 'Sunset', etc. . . .

"The varieties which differ [only] by their coloration are 'Anna Olivier', 'Dr. Félix Guyon', '[Mlle] Franziska Krüger', 'G. Nabonnand', 'Honourable Edith Gifford', 'Innocente Pirola', 'Louis Richard', 'Mme Edouard Helfenbein' [P. Guillot, 1893, chamois], 'Mme Hoste', 'Mme Jacques Charreton', 'Mme Lambard', 'Marie Van Houtte', 'Meta', 'Peace' [Piper, 1902, "pale lemon yellow" [LS]], 'Perle de Feu', 'Souvenir de Pierre Notting', and many others it would be easy to name.

"While we are on this group . . . there are certain varieties which, by their particular qualities, engage our attention. One of the principal ones is 'Red Safrano', offered by Oger in 1867. It is at the root of a series of hybrids with flowers of intense pink to red to a greater or lesser degree, in which the petals are, at their bases, yellow or coppery, or with yellow reflections throughout the blossom — though less than in the type . . . 'Comtesse Festetics Hamilton', 'Charles de Legrady', 'Garden Robinson' [Nabonnand, 1900, "red with a lighter center" [LS]], 'Général Galliéni', 'Général Schablikine', 'Mrs. B. R. Cant', 'Mons Tillier', 'Princesse Hohenzollern' [_more properly,_ 'S.A.R. Madame la Princesse de Hohenzollern, Infante de Portugal', Nabonnand, 1886, "sparkling bright red" [JR10/169]], '[Mme la Princesse [de] Radziwill' [Nabonnand, 1886, carmine], 'Souvenir d'Auguste Legros', 'Souvenir de Mr. William Robinson' [Bernaix, 1899, "pink fading to chamois" [LS]].

"Another similar group, doubtless mixed somewhat with the Chinas, has a complexion intermediate between that of the Chinas and that of the Teas, and a different look from the above varieties; their characteristics are: upright branches which are rigid and smooth; sparse but fairly strong thorns; flower-stem medium-length, rather strong; calyx ovoid, growing into a funnel shape; foliage stiffish and of a shiny dark green with large oblong leaflets; prickles evident beneath the leafstalk; flowers large, full, fairly scentless; petals large and rounded; color varying from shaded white to intense red, lit with yellow at the base of the petals: 'Duchess of Edinburgh', 'Baronne M. de Tornaco' [Soupert & Notting, 1896, "whitish pink and yellow" [LS]], 'Fiametta Nabonnand' [Nabonnand, 1894, "white, pink, and yellow" [LS]], 'Isaac Demole' [Nabonnand, 1895, "carmine bordered white" [LS]], 'Papa Gontier', 'Professeur d'André' [Nabonnand, 1902, "deep pink marbled white" [LS]], 'Rainbow'." [JR33/136–139]   "One might note that, in general, the Teas with flowers in clusters and with which the ovary is fusiform are from various hybridizations of Tea and China. 'Baronne Henriette de Loew' (Nabonnand, 1888) would be an example, as would 'Souvenir d'Espagne' (Pries, 1888), 'Souvenir du Père Lalanne' (Nabonnand, 1895 ['carmine with a golden center' [LS]]), [and] '[Mlle] Marie-Thérèse Molinier' (Widow Schwartz, 1896 ['pink on a yellow ground' [LS]]), from 'Mme Chédane-Guinoisseau' [T] × '[Mme] Laurette Messimy' [Ch]." [JR24/44]

"It is curious to look back on one's childhood and recall the awe with which Tea Roses were regarded—things too delicate and precious for any place but the conservatory." [K1] "They appear to have been designed by nature to furnish the highest test of skill and patience in rose culture, and to afford constant evidence of the fact that the cultivation of roses does not consist in merely buying the plants and sticking them in the ground, and then pruning them with a knife and fork." [Hd] "The less they are pruned the better." [OM]

"The confusion arising from the misleading term 'hybrid perpetual' has effectively concealed the fact that the true perpetual bloomers are the Tea Roses, so keeping the noblest of all Roses out of gardens even in the southern counties." [Ro] "Southern gardens can have no flowers of any strain as prolific, constant, hardy, beautiful, and fragrant as the Tea and kindred roses. . . . Where sweet violets blow and honeysuckles, heliotropes, jasmines, myrtles and spicy carnations exhale perfume upon the air, the Tea rose blends and completes the bouquet." [Dr] "In the Lower South we can grow the . . . Teas and Noisettes so easily that we can almost flout the rules. Common sense would tell us that we cannot grow them in soil where the drainage is positively bad. Nor can we expect to starve the bushes and still gather a profusion of bloom. I recommend the Teas because they are climatically adapted to the Lower South, require less attention than other kinds, and at least a portion of them are far better cut flower varieties than is generally believed. . . . I think that all of us appreciate vigorous and hardy shrubs that do not have to be coddled. Tea roses come in that category. Perhaps I came easily into an appreciation of what is hardy and dependable. My father loved Tea roses, and like them he was rugged, hardy, and dependable. It seemed that like Teas he could flout climatic conditions. Although the modern Danes are a highly cultured people, and he was of that stock, they are descendants of the Vikings. Whenever the weather was cold and rainy, my father liked to walk around in it, calmly smoking his pipe turned upside down. The elements could throw whatever they liked at him; he laughed at them through a life that lasted 86 years. The Teas take whatever is thrown at them by the elements or the enemies of the rose. . . . If you follow the rules for rose culture, plant any kind of roses you please. If you aren't going to the trouble, then plant Teas, and perhaps you will have roses anyhow." [SHj]

"In California, and nearly all States south of Richmond, the Tea Rose requires no winter protection, and is there seen in the greatest perfection." [pH] "Perhaps it is because Tea roses may be grown in the South with so little effort that they are passed by for other roses, many of which are disappointing in Southern gardens. Here, in Georgia, Tea roses are among the loveliest and most useful of garden roses. They are unsurpassed when planted in beds. There are varieties which can be used as specimen plants, for low hedges, for pillars, or for growing on trellises or arbors. What more could be expected of roses?" [SHj]

"Many breeders have neglected the Tea Rose for a long time to devote themselves to Hybrid Teas." [JR29/135] "There is a great opportunity awaiting the man who may be successful in raising new Teas—superior Teas—which will have the welcome they deserve when they do come to us." [NRS13/41] "While the Hybrid Teas and the Pernetianas have displaced the Teas in England, . . . the latter are much better adapted to our Southern, Interior-Southern, and Southwestern Zones than the first 2 classes, for not only do they retain their foliage wonderfully, but most of them are more lasting in form and color than the majority of the other 2 types. . . . Teas in the Southwestern, Interior-Southern, and the Southeastern Zones grow to prodigious size, and the best do splendidly on their own roots. The faults of the Teas in our Southern Zones are that the lighter kinds discolor in rain or heavy, damp, or very hot winds; that many have weak stems for cutting . . . , and a few tightly rolled varieties ball and discolor in wet ocean winds. . . . Unquestionably, Teas are the best roses for our heated sections with long growing seasons . . . they last exceedingly well, and the lighter-toned varieties hold their color better than the Hybrid Teas." [Th2]

"If there are Teas among the Roses the beds will be beautiful from the first break of growth in spring. It is one of the supreme joys of the Rose-grower to watch the bed break gently, almost imperceptibly, into a tender film of bronze, which presently deepens, thickens, and darkens. The first leaves are slender, shimmery, almost intangible things. They hover over the earth like a tinted cloud. The first glimmer of the shoots is like the faint radiance of a distant firmament at dawn. There is life, there is brightness, there is interest in the bed long before the first flower appears." [Wr]

"The roses grouped under this heading may be said to represent the crème de la crème of the rose family. Exquisite in the delicacy, variety and superb loveliness of the tints of their beautiful blooms; unspeakably delicious in their fragrance; invaluable for the freedom with which they flower, and for the long duration of their flowering period, they are unquestionably the finest class of roses we have in cultivation at the present day." [TW]

ADAM

Adam, 1838

Possibly from 'Hume's Blush' (T) × 'Rose Edouard' (B).

"Salmon and fawn, large, sweet and fine, none better, quite distinct." [HstXXX:142–143] "Blush-rose, very sweet, very large and full." [FP] "Lilac-pink." [EER] "Beautiful delicate pink; flower large, cupped, fragrant; moderate vigor." [Cx] "Rosy blush, very large and magnificent, with beautiful Camellia-like petals, blooms freely, moderate grower, rather tender. . . . Very fine." [HstVI:368] "Handsome light carmine-pink." [JR2/141] "One of the very largest roses in this family: its flowers are not so regularly shaped . . . ; color, rose, very fragrant, and showy." [WRP] "One of the finest tea-scented roses. Its flowers are . . . of perfect form." [SBP] "Large double flowers of peachy-pink in clusters of threes or singly. . . . Scented . . . 8 × 6 [ft; ca. 2.25 × 1.75 m]." [B] "A globular bud . . . many short rosy-salmon petals." [Hk] "The flowers . . . not very abundantly produced." [P2] "Of poor growth and small reputation. The blooms are large, globular and very sweet, but loose and untrustworthy, and the sort is of little value as a free-flowerer or autumnal." [F-M3] "Buds ovoid-elongate. . . . This variety was raised around 1837 by Mons Adam, gardener at Rheims, and is one of the most beautiful and elegant of the Teas . . . has hooked, nearly purple thorns . . . the flowers ordinarily reflect a coppery pink around the center. These characteristics closely approach those of the rose 'Souvenir d'Un Ami', which is easily distinguished by its flower stalk bristling with glandular hairs." [PIB] "Large dark green leaves." [B1] "Pretty vigorous; branches slender and nodding; wood smooth, light green, with flat red thorns which are hooked, enlarged at the base, and very sharp. Leaves shiny, of a slightly yellowish green, divided into 3 or 5 pointed and finely dentate leaflets, bristling with sharp, hooked prickles of varying size. Flower 3.25–3.5 in across [ca. 8 cm], full, widely cupped, usually solitary; color, a handsome light pink, more intense in the center; petals of the circumference large, slightly concave, those of the center rumpled; flower-stem glabrous, short, fairly thick, and nodding. Ovary urn-shaped, green with a 'bloom'; sepals leaf-like, long and narrow, green without, whitish within. This rose wafts a light tea scent; its bud is very pretty." [JF] "Flower large, expanded, magnificently held and well borne; color, bright rose; exquisite scent; bush fairly vigorous; . . . leafstalk reddish, bristling with little stickers of varying size, stickers which are hooked and very sharp. Very tender." [S] "Still rare and little-known. Wood strong with purplish-green canes having large, hooked, purplish-pink thorns. Leaves large, 2 pairs of leaflets with the odd one, petiole purplish crimson, prickly beneath; leaflets large, oval, serrated, wavy, fresh green, glossy above, paler beneath, rachis purplish. Blossoms solitary or in twos; peduncle glabrous, large, strong, purplish green, 4–5 cm [ca. 2 in], bearing at the base 2 small purplish-green bracts. Calyx round, sepals oval with a point, green bordered purple. Flower full, big, 7–8 cm [ca. 3 in], outer petals large, round, reflexing back; center petals more muddled, reflexing inwardly; all petals delicately colored flesh, darker at the nub in the open blossom, flesh pink in the just-opening stage. A very beautiful rose." [An41/12–13] "One of the finest." [FP]

ADÈLE PRADEL

Listed as 'Mme Bravy'.

AIMÉ PLANTIER

Listed as 'Safrano'.

ALBA ROSEA

Listed as 'Mme Bravy'.

ALEXANDER HILL GRAY

('Yellow Maman Cochet')

A. Dickson, 1911

"Of deep lemon-yellow colouring and perfect form. The growth is vigorous. Unfortunately, the blooms have weak stalks, and therefore droop." [OM] "Soft yellow; fragrant; double." [ARA29/95] "Vigorous, erect; all the branches end in a bud which gives birth to a blossom which is very large, full, of perfect form, high-centered, very fragrant—strong Tea scent—lemon yellow upon opening. It is the best and most beautiful Tea rose known till now; a superb plant, and to be recommended . . . particularly fine in the autumn." [JR36/72] "Good foliage and form; growth fair; blooming qualities good." [ARA18/110] "Long-pointed bud; large, full flowers; lasts very well; tea fragrance. Splendid foliage, seldom diseased and holds well. Fine spreading growth; long stem, sometimes weak." [Th2] "A very attractive, upright bush with large, lemon-yellow blooms. A good worker throughout the season." [ARA29/88]

ANNA OLIVIER

Ducher, 1872

Affiliated with 'Safrano' (T).

"Yellowish flesh shaded pink; flower large, full, cupped; vigorous." [Cx] "Buff, shaded with rose." [EL] "Lively creamy blush." [C&Js05] "Colour varies from terra-cotta." [F-M2] "To obtain that lovely terra-cotta shade the soil must be naturally impregnated with iron." [FRB] "Flowers large and full, fine form, creamy buff, flushed with rose; charming in bud; vigorous growth." [W/Hn] "Rosy-flesh; base of petals, dark; a large, beautifully-formed flower." [DO] "Flowers tolerably large, smooth and beautiful; habit moderate." [JC] "Reverse of petals rose." [P1] "Shapely and well perfumed . . . 4 × 3 [ft; ca. 1.25 × 1 m]." [B] "Easily damaged by wet." [J] "Had credit for avoiding damage from rain." [Hk] "Very vigorous and variable over the season; the autumn flowering is perfect—distinct in form and color from the spring blossoms. The first buds are urn-shaped, and the reverse of the petals is flesh-pink passing to red. As the season advances, the flowers produced on the present year's wood are globular, and salmon." [JR12/180] "Lovely buds." [Dr] "One of the best of the Tea roses for garden display; it blooms very freely and continuously. The small blooms, of good form, are pale rose and buff shades. Growth is vigorous. A fine rose for all purposes." [OM] "Extreme freedom of bloom . . . vigor of growth, and fair amount of hardiness." [F-M2] "Somewhat dwarf and upright, foliage a nice green." [JR9/70] "Good grower with bright foliage." [F-M] "Resistant to mildew." [JR33/37] "Foliage very good and lasting. Vigorous growth in Southern Zones." [Th2] "One of the best and most distinct." [H] "Always beautiful." [NRS/13]

ARCHIDUC JOSEPH   PLATE 55

Nabonnand, 1892

Seedling of 'Mme Lambard' (T).

"Coppery pink." [LS] "Clear shining red, with pale pink tint." [Dr] "Pale white tinted copper." [JR20/7] "Large shapely deep rose-shaded purple buds open to a very full flat bloom in shades of rose-flushed purple and pink with orange and cream in the centre intensifying with age. Very variable with weather conditions, more purple and orange with moist moderate temperatures, more rose and pink in dry hot conditions." [HRG] "A mixture of pinks, purple and orange with a paler centre . . . very vigorous . . . 4 × 4 [ft; ca. 1.25 × 1.25 m]." [B] "Very large, very full, cupped, perfectly poised; bud conical, pure carmine, lighter towards the tip; wood brownish red; very handsome dark ashy-green foliage; thorns sharp; color, violet-pink, center bright copper, petal edges paler. Very vigorous, splendid variety, and very floriferous." [JR16/166] "Blooms abundantly, above all through fall. . . . The foliage of dark ashy-green gives the plant an appearance both original and unique." [JR24/56]

BARONNE HENRIETTE SNOY
('Baronne Henriette de Snoy')
Bernaix, 1897
From 'Gloire de Dijon' (N) × 'Mme Lambard' (T).

"Solid light peach-flesh. Globular." [Capt27] "Petals carnation inside, outside carmine pink." [K2] "Flesh pink with deeper reverse, shapely . . . 3 × 3 [ft; ca. 9 × 9 dm]." [B] "Large double flowers on stiff stems . . . this variety grew as rank as 'Mme Lambard' . . . but produced larger flowers in the spring and summer." [SHj] "Strong plant to 4 [ft; ca. 1.25 m]." [HRG] "Of good vigor, with bronzy green foliage, purple above and below in the young growth, flower very pretty, very large, and perfectly double; petals elegantly spaced, soft, sweetly rounded, and recurved towards the tip and sides. Color flesh-pink within, with a yellow nub; carmine China pink outside, making a charming combination. Lovely." [JR21/148] "Somewhat mildewy, like 'Gloire de Dijon' during a humid season — but does not shake it off like that stalwart. The buds are wonderful, particularly on a strong shoot, but open to show a green eye. It seems as if it should be pruned back in the manner of Hybrid Teas — which is to say that the twiggy growth tends to come to nothing. Distressing at its worst, beautiful at its best, trial is merited." [BCD]

BLUMENSCHMIDT
J.-C. Schmidt, 1905
Sport of 'Mlle Franziska Krüger' (T).

"Citron-yellow flowers. Very fine garden rose. Blooms constantly." [Dr] "Large flower, full, lemon-yellow, the outer petals blushing." [JR31/105] "The flower, of a clear [or 'light'] yellow shaded carmine at the edges of the petals, is very resistant, and blooms in the fall." [JR29/152] "Flower very large, full, fragrant; primrose yellow to pale pink. . . . Repeats bloom well." [Lg] "Green pip in center, outer petals blush rose-pink." [HRG] "Low, compact, hardy; foliage plentiful, healthy; bloom plentiful, continuous." [ARA18/124] "Vigorous, very floriferous in autumn." [JR34/24]

BON SILÈNE
('Goubault'?)
Hardy, 1835

"Cerise red." [V4] "Red marbled with crimson, full, cupped, large, superb." [LF] "Bright rose, very large and double; form expanded. The young buds of this Rose are of the most elegant form, shewing of a rich deep crimson as the sepals part. Very sweet." [P] "Superb red." [Sx] "Flower large, double, fragrant; deep pink with white streaks." [Lg] "Very free flowering . . . shapely . . . rich rosy crimson. Scented . . . 3 × 3 [ft; ca. 1 × 1 m]." [B] "Deep salmon-rose, illumined with carmine, medium size, semi-double, highly scented, very free-flowering. This is only desirable in the bud state." [EL] "A very beautiful tea-scented rose, cupped, very double, and fragrant. Its color is rose, shaded with crimson, and the plant is hardy and of luxuriant growth." [SBP] "Valued for its beautiful rose-coloured, fawn-shaded buds, and vigorous growth." [Dr] "Extremely large petals; though not so double as some, yet it amply compensates for this deficiency in the size of the flowers which are of a bright rose, changing to cherry red,

with an agreeable fragrance." [Bu] "Flower large, full, flat; bright rose-colored, saffron at the center." [S] "Very variable in color, and often described differently under different circumstances; the plant is robust and hardy, and will grow in any situation." [WRP] "Surpassing sweetness and brilliancy of tint, with substance of petal. The color is a clear brilliant flesh colored rose, centre paler blush slightly tinged with yellow, outer petals of great substance, beautifully cupped and of a deeper color. . . . Of all Tea roses, this is our favorite for fragrance . . . a sweeter and more fruit-like scent [than has 'Devoniensis'], peculiarly delightful." [C] "Raspberry-scented." [JR33/101] "Low-growing, spreading . . . foliage sufficient, healthy; bloom moderate, continuous." [ARA18/124] "Seeds freely." [Bu] "Sprang from a bird- or wind-sown seed, in a cleft at the base of a stone monument." [Dr] "Is very much admired." [FP] "Your correspondent Mons Schultheis is also in error as to identifying 'Goubault' with 'Bon Silène'; there is, perhaps, some slight resemblance between the two, but the latter is a shade darker, has better form and stronger scent, and is certainly a better variety to grow. [*signed*] H.B. Ellwanger." [JR5/45] A *striped* version of 'Bon Silène', should it turn up anywhere, would be 'American Banner' (Cartwright, 1877) or 'Flag of the Union' (Hallock & Thorpe, date uncertain).

[BOUGÈRE]
('Clotilde')
Bougère, 1832

"Flowers deep salmon colour, very large and full; form, cupped. Growth, vigorous. A superb Pot or Forcing Rose, with thick petals." [P] "Salmon and fawn, flowers very large and full; a good rose of vigorous habit." [JC] "Floriferous, pretty hardy; flower large, full, cupped, Hydrangea pink." [S] "A singular and splendid rose; the buds and flowers are very large, full double, perfectly cup shaped, of a fine roseate hue, shaded with bronze; the plant is of vigorous growth, blooms abundantly, and is one of the most hardy." [WRP]

BRIDESMAID
('The Hughes', *not* 'Thé Hughes')
Moore, 1893
Sport of 'Catherine Mermet' (T).

"Clear bright pink." [H] "Deep silvery pink. Mildews." [ARA27/20] "An American sport of 'Catherine Mermet', with much higher and better colour — a clear pink. This makes it a decided improvement on the original, whose one fault is weakness of colour. In all other respects it is identical, save that it seems to me that the outer petals do not reflex and open so readily as in the type." [F-M 2] "Moderately vigorous." [J]

[CAROLINE]
('Caroline de Rosny')
Guérin, 1829

"Light pink, center yellowish, beautiful." [LF] "Rosy-flesh, deeper towards centre; prettily formed buds." [EL] "Blossom medium sized, full, bright pink." [S] "Blush, suffused with deep pink, large and full; form, cupped. Grows and flowers freely." [P] "A pretty rose, with flowers very double, of a bright rose color, and very perfect in their shape." [WRP] "Pale rosy-pink; a very good, hardy, free growing rose." [JC] "This is a Tea, very close to the China hybrids. . . . Wood smooth, thorns very rare, short, light red, recurved at the tip; young branches purplish; leaves a handsome green, with five or sometimes seven leaflets which are large, oval, elongated, slightly stalked, very finely dentate, and a glaucous green or at least shiny; stipules very small, glabrous, ciliate; leafstalk usually feeble, furnished beneath with some small prickles, and above with stiff, short, glandular hairs; flower stem long, about an inch and a half [ca. 3.5 cm], purplish, with transparent epidermis with stiff, short hairs; ovary glabrous, inflated, short; sepals short, entire, shiny, slightly ciliate with unequal red hairs, sometimes with rust-colored pubescence; bud very firm, red, ovoid; flower medium sized, intense flesh, often with a green pip at the center. This Rose is quite pretty . . . it resists seven or eight degrees of frost fairly well, being one of the few somewhat hardy Teas." [PlB] "Raised at Rosny in 1829. It makes a stocky bush, sending its canes straight up and forming a good head. Its branches are jointed, and reddish in the sun, being also armed with fairly straight small prickles; foliage with leaflets which are oval-rounded, small with the lower leaflets oval-elliptical and larger than the upper leaflets, regularly dentate like a saw. Corymbs of 3–15 delicately lilac-pink blossoms, quite full, of moderate size, well formed; flower-stalk lightly hispid; ovary turbinate, short, glabrous; sepals short, feathery. Centifolia perfume." [R-H32] We learn from *Les Amis des Roses* nº 215 (page 5) that "Caroline" was the name of a very pretty woman of Angers.

CATHERINE MERMET
Guillot fils, 1869
Affiliated with 'Adam' (T).

"Pale pink; moderately vigorous . . . perfectly formed flowers." [J] "A dull and dirty sort of cream." [F-M2] "One of the very finest varieties we have . . . large, of the finest form, constant and floriferous. . . . Though the blossoms vary more or less in depth of color, the prevailing tint is flesh-colored rose, with a dash of yellowish buff." [HstXXX:318] "Lilac-pink, very delicate flesh; flower large, full, globular, imbricated, very fragrant, moderate vigor." [Cx] "Flesh color, with the same silvery lustre seen in 'La France'; large, full, well-formed; not very productive, yet not a shy bloomer; very beautiful in the bud; when the flowers expand they exhale a delightful perfume. The finest of all the Teas." [EL] "A shy bloomer." [Dr] "Profuse bloomer; of splendid growth in Southern Zones; also, stands shade in Pacific South-West, with growth of large size; wilts in great heat." [Th2] "Keep the buds dry . . . the colour is more fleeting than the shape . . . liable to mildew . . . moderate growth . . . not strong foliage . . . easily injured by rain . . . cannot be called hardy or of strong constitution, particularly free in bloom, a good autumnal, or able to do anywhere." [F-M2] "Generally, the flowers are borne solitary and are nearly always nodding, as are the branches which bear them. This weakness, a great fault, is amply compensated by the perfection and beauty of the buds, of a nice size, and a beautiful delicate satin pink . . . about four in across [ca. 1 dm], slightly flat, very full, muddled in the center; satin pink exterior; within, flesh pink, shaded lightly with pale yellow or salmon principally towards the base of the central petals." [S] "Branches green and armed with hooked red thorns." [JR10/92] "Low, moderately spreading, not vigorous; foliage sufficient, healthy; bloom moderate . . . more in July and August than later." [ARA18/124] "4 × 4 [ft; ca. 1.25 × 1.25 m]." [B] "Practically useless in the open garden." [OM] "A glorious flower, truly the Queen of the Teas." [FRB]

CELS MULTIFLORE
('Cels Multiflora')
Hardy/Cels, 1836

"Flesh color, very free-blooming." [EL] "White, shaded with pink, and flowers very freely." [FP] "Blush, pink centre; a very profuse bloomer." [HstXI:225] "Flower medium-sized, charmingly colored pink with marbling; the bush blooms constantly and abundantly. These three roses [*among which is 'Cels Multiflore'*],

children of the Luxembourg, are being propagated in the establishment of the Cels brothers." [An36/96] "Flesh, large, full, flat, very floriferous, superb." [LF] "Among the best of the blush roses; indeed, for profusion of bloom it has not a rival; every flower perfect, fully double, and cup shaped, growing freely in almost any soil or situation, and is an excellent variety to force into early bloom." [Bu] "Of moderate vigor." [S] "Very hardy." [P2] As for Cels: "*Catalog . . . of Mons F. Cels, Chaussée du Maine, Nº 55; at Paris, 1832. . . .* It soon will have been a century that the name Cels has been renowned in Europe, and it occupies a distinguished place among those responsible for the developement of horticultural taste in France. J.-M. Cels, the father of the present owner of the concern, was a man of much merit who, through his wide knowledge, his spirit, and his contacts, contributed strongly to the encouragement of the taste for Horticulture among the notables of his day." [R-H32] "The First Prize for the collection containing the most rare and beautiful plants was awarded to that exhibited by Mons Cels, nurseryman." [R-H32]

CHARLES DINGEE
Listed as 'William R. Smith'.

CLEMENTINA CARBONIERI
Bonfiglioli & Figlio, 1913
From 'Kaiserin Auguste Viktoria' (HT) × 'Souvenir de Catherine Guillot' (Ch).

"Very floriferous and vigorous; of pretty form, light violet pink; long bud of a superb shining reddish-nankeen; exterior petals nuanced violet pink, with the nubs saffron yellow." [JR38/88] "Yellow, orange, pink and salmon . . . very lovely rose with good foliage . . . 3 × 2 [ft; ca. 9 × 6 dm]." [B]

COMTE DE SEMBUI
Listed as 'Jean Ducher'.

COMTESSE DE LABARTHE
('Duchesse de Brabant')
Bernède, 1857
Affiliated with 'Caroline' (T).

"Salmon pink, very pretty, but not full; habit free." [JC] "Shrimp-pink." [JR30/183] "Pink, shaded with carmine-rose, very pretty in the bud." [EL] "Light silvery pink. Small." [Capt27] "Cupped blooms of pearly shell pink, pale gold coloring at base of petals, bushy." [HRG] "Clear, bright pink, blooming in clusters. . . . Buds exquisite, but open roses, not double." [Dr] "Peachy pink, very fragrant, a great bloomer, forces well, a choice rose and hard to beat." [HstXXX:142143] "Soft rose pink . . . with long buds like tulips . . . confused short petals inside." [Hk] "Very double . . . clear pink to rose. Shapely, cupped and free flowering with a spreading habit . . . 3 × 3 [ft; ca. 1 × 1 m]." [B] "Growth vigorous; flower of medium size, pretty full, globular; color, delicate flesh pink." [S] "The cupped flower is nearly totally imbricated, the petals concave, quite mucronate at the tip, partly emarginate at the center—does it not recall a China, of which 'Comtesse de Labarthe' is thus a hybrid?." [JR24/42] "Continuous supply of flowers." [L] "Small growth; shy blooming qualities." [ARA18/115] "The freest bloomer in our state [California]. It is usually loaded with flowers nearly the entire year." [ARA19/133] "Distills the sweetest perfume." [ARA32/21] "A pink cup brimming with fragrance." [ARA36/16] "Moderately tall, compact, vigorous, hardy; foliage plentiful, healthy." [ARA18/124] "Perfect foliage." [Th2] "Makes a stocky bush with beautiful foliage that will be attacked, but not seriously, by black-spot." [ARA39/48] "This rose grows to six ft [ca. 1.75 m], and perhaps four ft across [ca. 1.25

m], and is very profuse, a bush of this size bearing 150 blossoms and buds." [JR6/43] "Needs little care, growing to ten ft [ca. 3 m]." [ARA40/31] "Very good [in Bermuda]." [UB28] "A well-shaped, pleasing plant." [ARA29/88]

COMTESSE RIZA DU PARC   PLATE 20
Schwartz, 1876
Seedling of 'Comtesse de Labarthe' (T).

"Clear rose, salmon tinge, coppery yellow ground. Slightly cupped." [Capt27] "Beautiful metallic rose, changing to pink, large and full, form globular, growth vigorous." [JC] "Bronzed rose, with a carmine tint; medium size, moderately full, highly perfumed." [EL] "Attractive flower of distinct color and medium size" [Capt 28] "Of really strong growth, with good foliage. This Rose is very faulty in form, and a good shaped one is rare indeed. It is not large, a free bloomer, or a good autumnal, and it is only noticeable for its colour, which is a charming shade of pink, with an indefinable sensation of yellow pervading it, especially at the base of the petals." [F-M3] "Persistent and vigorous, but of uneven growth." [JR9/70] "Good growth; fair foliage, well-held." [Capt28] "Very vigorous, with branches quite reddish, smooth, with prickles lightly hooked and occasional, brownish red. Foliage is ample, comprised of 5–7 oval-elliptical leaflets, serrated, handsome somber green on top, light green beneath, taking on a purple tinge as they develop. The flower stem is long, firm, and dark, and the blossoms come singly. The flower is large, full, well held, having petals both long and wide, numerous, and of a pretty China pink with carmine reflections, shaded pinkish yellow at the base, on a copper ground." [JR4/25] "Branches erect and divergent." [S] "A distinct, effective, and most floriferous variety." [P1]

DANZILLE
Listed as 'Mme Bravy'.

DEVONIENSIS
('Magnolia Rose')
Foster, 1838
From 'Parks' Yellow' (T) × 'Smith's Yellow' (T).

"Still unrivalled: its creamy white flowers, with their delicate rose tint, are always beautiful." [R8] "Creamy-white . . . centres sometimes buff sometimes yellowish, very large and full; form cupped. A splendid Rose." [P1] "Creamy-white, sometimes tinged with blush, very large, almost full; one of the most delightfully scented. Either this or the climbing variety should be in every collection; though neither is very productive." [EL] "Of high quality in its line of colour—ivory-white, with a yellowish fawn centre. In shape its flower is somewhat like that of 'Malmaison', with which favorite kind it has marked affinities. . . . We believe that it is worthy of notice that neither of these has produced seed." [WD] "A very beautiful rose, of immense size . . . sometimes a shy bloomer when young." [SBP] "Gorgeous . . . nearly four in[ches] in diameter [ca. 1 dm]." [Ed] "Perfectly unique in form, in color, and in sweetness, for no other rose has the same scent." [R1/203] "Moderate in growth." [DO] "Another new rose; though at first represented as being a fine sulphur-yellow . . . it proves to be a creamy-white, but when just open, in cloudy weather, is of a canary colour; when well cultivated it produces flowers of immense size, and in clusters; it grows freely, with dark green foliage, possesses a delightful fragrance far surpassing the ancient Tea Rose, and is a very valuable variety." [Bu] " 'Petals thick and Camellia-like, very large and powerfully scented.' On this splendid English Rose it is hardly possible to bestow too much praise. . . . Not only is it the most powerfully scented and the largest of its family, but

its petals are so thick and waxy, its foliage so magnificent (even to the thorns which are of brilliant crimson), as to render it in every respect perfect. . . . The fortunate raiser of this Rose was the late George Foster, Esq., of Oatland, near Devonport, whose brother Edward W. Foster has kindly favored us with the following information as to its parentage. . . . 'His opinion was that it was produced from the Yellow China by an impregnation of the Yellow Noisette "Smithii" which was growing alongside it.' . . . Delighting in a fertile moist soil, the 'Devoniensis', perhaps more than any other rose, amply recompenses the cultivator for all the assiduity he bestows on it." [C] "Beautiful now as then [in Rivers' time]." [K1]

DR. GRILL   PLATE 33
Bonnaire, 1886
From 'Ophirie' (N) × 'Souvenir de Victor Hugo' (T).

"Rose with coppery shading . . . free." [H] "Deep, clear yellow. An extra fine rose in every respect." [Dr] "Rosy fawn." [E] "Clear rose, coppery center. Loose." [Capt27] "Large, full, regular form, erect, coppery-yellow, with bright pink lustre." [Hn] "Good growth; well-held foliage . . . coppery red bud; flower double; aurora with outer petals sometimes splashed carmine . . . usually with good stem, but usually somewhat flat." [Capt28] "Shapely." [HRG] "Not as universally cultivated as it should be. Perfect in shape, prolific in flowers of a delicious mixture of pale copper shaded with tender pink and China-rose, it is deliciously fragrant and lasts well in water." [K1] "Hay-scented." [JR33/101] "Rather moderate in growth, a button-hole Rose only valuable in the bud, small, but free-flowering and distinct and attractive in colour." [F-M3] "A branching plant . . . 3 × 3 [ft; ca. 1 × 1 m]." [B] "Sown in 1883 by Mons J. Bonnaire, . . . the seeds, which were very numerous (about 200) didn't sprout more than a small quantity (5 or 6 or so) . . . only one was found to be vigorous and worthy of the attention of the breeder, who studied it several years before releasing it to commerce, not at first having found any satisfactorily large blossoms. . . . It is a pity that 'Dr. Grill' was not propagated [right away], because last summer we did not see any [other] so pretty, so floriferous, and so vigorous, without being a climber, that we do not hesitate for an instant to say that this is one of the best new roses . . . in many years. Its extreme floriferousness and great brightness of the blossoms make one overlook the flower's lack of fulness." [JR15/40–41] "Dedicated to Dr. Grill, a flower-lover." [JR34/16]

DUCHESSE DE BRABANT
Listed as 'Comtesse de Labarthe'.

ÉTOILE DE LYON   PLATE 23
(trans., 'Star of Lyon')
Guillot fils, 1881
Seedling of 'Mme Charles' (T).

"Deep yellow." [EL] "Large, double blooms of gold." [ARA29/95] "Fine saffron yellow, brighter in centres; large, full, and of superb form and habit; requires a hot season." [P1] "Medium size, double; medium yellow, fading lighter. Repeats bloom." [Lg] "Deep lemon, very rarely exhibited, as it must have hot, dry weather." [FRB] "Quite superior in vigor and flowering, its blossoms are cupped . . . very bright yellow." [JR10/45] "Unites excellent flowers with great vigor; the flowers are large, globular, full, well formed, brilliant yellow with a darker center." [JR7/157] "Could be more double . . . well-held, vigorous, floriferous, and persistent [of leaf]." [JR9/70] "The largest and most sumptuous of all yellow roses is 'Étoile de Lyon', but it must be admitted that this rose is capricious, and only opens well in warm soil." [JR12/179] "A good yellow tea rose . . . with proper care will bloom the year around." [BSA] "Twiggy . . . rich golden-yellow flowers, each with a . . . weak neck. Highly scented . . . 2 × 2 [ft; ca. 6 × 6 dm]." [B] "Strong good growth and foliage, but is a very disappointing Rose out of doors, having been much over-praised. The blooms come generally badly, of confused and queer shapes, and require as a rule very dry warm weather . . . globular shape . . . outer petals being short, and kept well up to the bloom. . . . Rather liable to mildew, of good lasting qualities when dry." [F-M3] "Very low, compact, not vigorous; foliage sufficient, healthy; bloom, sparse, mostly early and late." [ARA18/125] "Long, pointed buds and elegant roses. Delicious Tea odor. Fine habit. Free flowering." [Dr] "Small growth; blooms undersized." [ARA18/115] "This variety preserves many of the principal characteristics of its mother, but detracts from 'Mme Charles' by way of its own vigor, floriferousness, and rich coloration . . . a vigorous and handsome bush with upright branches, bearing superb young foliage of a dark red which passes to intense green." [JR11/122–123] "Branches . . . purplish-red in color. The leaf is comprised of 5 leaflets, purplish-red becoming dark green. The blossoms are scented, very large, very full, and with central petals which are narrow and muddled, surrounded by 5 or 6 rows, imbricated. The color is a bright sulphur yellow, whitish-yellow on the reverse. —One of the finest yellows yet produced." [JR5/116] "Bushy plant with soft foliage." [HRG] "Fine double flower, which needs heat to mature . . . a fine decorative in the Pacific South-West." [Th2] "This is undoubtedly the best Pure Yellow Rose for garden planting yet introduced." [C&Js05]

FRANCIS DUBREUIL
('François Dubreuil')
Dubreuil, 1894
Affiliated with 'Souvenir de David d'Angers' (T).

"Velvety purple-red, one of the darkest of the Teas; flower large, full, cupped; very floriferous; vigorous." [Cx] "Deep crimson flower of velvety texture." [Dr] "Ox-blood red. Balls in dampness." [Capt27] "Perhaps the darkest Tea; it grows vigorously with strong stems, and gives a harvest of roses for bouquets in the fall." [JR32/34] "Crimson, almost double . . . fine, pointed bud . . . slightly spreading, twiggy. . . . Scented . . . 2 × 2 [ft; ca. 6 × 6 dm]." [B] "Beautifully formed buds." [P1] "Robust and very remontant; flower very full, of admirable form, erect on a rigid stem at the extremity of the branch; thick petals, very regularly rounded, shapely, opening with great ease; an absolutely new color in tea roses, velvety purplish crimson-red, with intense amaranthine-cerise reflections; bud long-ovoid, and of great beauty. Considering the perfection of its form and the intensity of its purple and amaranthine tones, this variety constitutes the most beautiful red Tea Rose known." [JR18/149] "A very prettily shaped flower, but . . . the colour was too dull a red to be really attractive, and it was retained only as a curiosity." [NRS21/115]

FREIHERR VON MARSCHALL
Lambert, 1903
From 'Princesse Alice de Monaco' (T) × 'Rose d'Evian' (T).

"Dark carmine; fine foliage, often tea-colored." [Th] "Purple-rose and cochineal. Varies." [Capt27] "The color of 'Red Radiance' is much superior in every way." [ARA40/31] "Bright red. Vigorous. Blooms profusely through the entire season." [Dr] "Buds long and pointed; flowers large, full and of perfect imbricated form." [C&Js09] "Growth good, but variable in hardiness. Form and color not of the best." [ARA18/115] "Growth is good, and its buds are well formed, and of good color; it blues, however, somewhat

when open." [ARA29/89] "Pointed flowers of rich carmine-red. Attractive, red foliage. Vigorous . . . 4 × 3 [ft; ca. 1.25 × 1 m]." [B]

GÉNÉRAL GALLIÉNI
Nabonnand, 1899
From 'Souvenir de Thérèse Levet' (T) × 'Reine Emma des Pays-Bas' (T).

"Maroon shaded violet poppy-red toned salmon — strange and bizarre." [JR36/160] "Poppy red on a white ground with coppery-pink reflections; flower large, full, cupped; very floriferous; very vigorous." [Cx] "Flower . . . well-held. . . . Very warm color, exterior petals poppy red tinted blood red; pretty bud; very handsome foliage; bush branched, very vigorous, very floriferous." [JR23/179] "Marvelous in foliage and flower; one of the rare dark-flowered autumnals, it is prettier at that season than during the summer . . . ; flower . . . with a golden center."[JR36/187] "Bright cerise, base of petals coppery orange, reflexed bright red. Pointed buds. A profuse bloomer." [P1] "Large well-filled flowers, fine rich brownish red, very sweet; a healthy, vigorous grower and constant and abundant bloomer." [C&Js05] "Fair growth; not a profuse bloomer." [ARA18/115] "3 × 2 [ft; ca. 9 × 6 dm]." [B] "Foliage persistent, despite snow and rime; color bizarre and handsome." [JR38/48]

GÉNÉRAL SCHABLIKINE
Nabonnand, 1878
Affiliated with 'Safrano à Fleurs Rouges' (T).

"Coppery-rose. Very free, good bedder." [H] "A free-flowering variety for the garden, having salmon-red blooms, lacking in ideal form. It grows freely, and makes a good display." [OM] "Quartered." [Hk] "Vigorous, with occasional large thorns, and reddish wood; the blossoms are large, full, cupped, and of good form. The color is brilliant copper-red, with purple reverse." [JR3/9] "Double . . . coppery-red and cherry . . . compact plant . . . 3 × 2 [ft; ca. 9 × 6 dm]." [B] "Its abundant flowers . . . are never wanting throughout the season — I cut a handful on November 11, last Autumn — and with its good foliage made it admirable in a group." [K1] "Resistant to mildew." [JR33/37] "Weak; winterkills." [ARA18/115] "Vigorous . . . beautiful plum-colored shoots and elegant leaves . . . five ft [ca. 1.5 m] or so." [T2] "If a law was passed that one man should cultivate but one variety of rose, I should without hesitation choose 'Général Schablikine'; for general utility it is without rival, flowering continuously from October to summer, flowers of a fine shape and wonderful evenness; a hundred blooms could be gathered off one plant, and every one exactly resembling its neighbour; the flower-stalk has a peculiar curve, which identifies it from other sorts. . . . This of all roses serves us the most faithfully and generously." [B&V]

[GIGANTESQUE]
('Thé à Fleur Gigantesque')
Hardy/Sylvain-Péan, 1835
Seedling of 'Parks' Yellow' (T).
Not to be confused with Odier's 1849 HT.

"Its pale fleshy coloured flowers are very showy." [Bu] "Flowers of the largest size, but not very perfect in form, of a pale incarnate hue, and very showy." [WRP] "Very well formed." [S] "Flesh colour, shaded with rose, very large and full. Growth, vigorous. Coarse." [P] "Deep rose, sometimes mottled; often fine, but apt to come malformed or somewhat coarse." [EL] "The blossoms of this rose are very abundant, of a deep clear pink, paler at the edges." [JR6/178] "This rose, from the Yellow Tea, maintains several characteristics of its parent. It is vigorous, with branches which spread out horizontally, armed with strong but not very numerous thorns, which are equal, very much enlarged at the base, and reddish. The leaflets are a glossy green, and some are oval while others are heart-shaped. The blossom is of very large size (about five in across [ca. 1.25 dm], irregular in form, with the petals placed very close together; delicate pink within, and paler at the tip; they are borne on a strong, upright, glabrous stem." [An35/146] Parent of 'Mlle de Sombreuil' (Cl. T).

GOUBAULT
Listed as 'Bon Silène'.

GRAND DUC HÉRITIER DE LUXEMBOURG
Listed as 'Mlle Franziska Krüger'.

HARRY KIRK
A. Dickson, 1907
"Lemon." [LS] "Flower large, full, well-formed; petals regular, deep sulphur-yellow." [JR35/15] "Deep sulphur yellow, passing to a lighter shade at edge of petals. The flowers are large, full, of perfect form and great substance. Buds are long and elegant. A splendid free-flowering Rose and much the best of its color." [C&Js10] "Color clear; very good in growth, foliage, and hardiness; form almost perfect in bud, not so good in open flower; fairly good bloomer." [ARA18/111] "In growth this Rose more nearly approaches the Hybrid Teas than a pure Tea; its chief feature is its colour, a good deep yellow — sulphur almost in the centre of the flower, fading to white at the edges of the petals. The flowers so far have not come so large as one would like — it is free rather than vigorous in growth — has not been exhibited very much up to the present. . . . It will require shading and high culture." [F-M]

HOMÈRE
Robert & Moreau, 1858
Possibly a seedling of 'David Pradel' (T).
"Pink, center flesh shaded whitish; flower medium-sized, full, cupped, ruffled, fragrant, very floriferous; very vigorous." [Cx] "Salmon-rose, often richly mottled; a free bloomer, moderately hardy, best in the open air; the buds are very beautiful, even though of variable shades. Certainly one of the most useful tea roses." [EL] "Variable, sometimes flecked with purple." [Hn] "A peculiar and beautiful rose when in bud. Its color is rose, tipped with red, and with a salmon center." [SBP] "Striped pinkish-white and purple." [JR20/6] "Gives single flowers [in Havana]." [JR6/44] "Vigorous, floriferous, pretty hardy; flower large, full, globular; color rose pink with flesh-white salmon center; one of the best for the open ground. In 2 or three seasons, the plant makes a little spreading shrub of perhaps thirty in [ca. 9 dm] in height. The branches end in a bud, rarely two, of moderate size; the fully expanded blossom is rather globular-elongate; barely open on its firm stem, it remains thus for several days if the temperatures are not too high. Though rainy periods are unfavorable to other varieties, 'Homère' blooms prettily right through them. Its scent resembles that of *R. semperflorens* ['Slater's Crimson China']." [S] "3 × 3 [ft; ca. 1 × 1 m]." [B] "Twiggy . . . dark foliage." [B1] "Of very strong growth, with fair foliage, but more suited for a pillar than a wall, and best as a big bush. It has a sturdy branching habit, quite distinct from the characteristic growth of the pure Teas, and is no doubt a cross of some sort, though born long before Hybrid Teas were thought of: it is perfectly hardy, very vigorous and of strong constitution, and I wonder we have had no seedlings from it. It is not liable to mildew and but little injured by rain, does well as a dwarf, is a free bloomer and capital in

the autumn, pretty in colour, with a crimpled edge, but small in size. It is hard to prove a negative, and I will not say 'Homère' never comes perfectly shaped, because I have heard of one or 2 though I have not seen them. Its bad manners is this respect are the more aggravating, because each bloom has the promise of a beautiful shape but marred by a malformation. As often happens, the strongest blooms are the most imperfect, and the buds should be cut small before their promise is spoiled. . . . A capital cottage garden Rose which should not be closely pruned, doing well anywhere." [F-M] "So well known as to hardly need description." [FRB]

HUGO ROLLER
PLATE 73
W. Paul, 1907
"Light canary yellow with claret, sometimes reddish lilac shading — varies. Low growth. Very distinct in color. . . . Foliage, very good." [Th] "A very dainty flower; lemon-yellow, tinged with rose. It is a poor grower, though possibly worth including in one's collection for the sake of a few of the very pretty blooms." [OM] "Most attractive and distinct color; very good form; low growth; not hardy." [ARA18/111] "The seeds from which it came were sown in mixture, and the cross from which it resulted is thus not recorded; but the traits of the plant would indicate that the variety owes its origin to a cross of a Tea Rose with a Hybrid Tea, or vice-versa. The color of the blossom is a rich and handsome crimson on a ground of light yellow; the contrast of these shades loses nothing of its brilliance in the heat of summer, and approaches the cool nights of fall changing only by developing a deeper shade of red. Of a largish medium-size or so, the blossoms are of good form, held on upright stems, and produces abundantly — qualities making a variety of the first merit for garden and bedding." [JR32/168–169]

HUME'S BLUSH TEA-SCENTED CHINA
Banks/Hume/Colville, 1810
Supposedly of *R. chinensis* × *R. gigantea* ancestry.
"Flesh-pink, full, flat, very large, beautiful." [LF] "Blush, centre rose, large and full." [FP] "Creamy-white, their centre salmon-buff, large and full; form, expanded. Growth, vigorous." [P] "Flowers, large, semi-double; of a pale pink or flesh-colour, almost white. Petals, concave, of a pale yellow at the base. Styles, filiform, straight, and salient." [Go] "Carmine, fading to blush, large flowers, somewhat loose but good in the bud; one of the most fragrant. The larger number of the Teas are descendants of this sort." [EL] "Vigorous . . . Globular, double . . . 6 × 4 [ft; ca. 1.75 × 1.25 m]." [B] "Few or none of the family possess the peculiar fragrance of this delightful rose; its large rosy blush flower buds will ever be admired; when full blown it is not so attractive as others, but will always be desirable for its agreeable odour, though perhaps one of the most difficult of the family to grow well. A liberal portion of leaf mould and sand appears to suit it." [Bu] "Strong green luxuriant shoots, with flowers varying in color from pure white to crimson." [WRP] "Semi-double variety, of ever-blooming habit, discovered by an agent of the British East India Company, who obtained plants in 1808 from the Fan Tee Nurseries at Canton, and dispatched them to Sir Abraham Hume, of Wortlebury, who received them in 1810, and bestowed on them the name 'Hume's Blush', in honour of his wife, the Lady Amelia Hume . . . pale pink flowers, on half evergreen foliage consisting of 5 or 7 foliate leaves, borne on long sarmentose branches, armed with scattered, hooked prickles. The leaflets were responsible for the perfume after which the Teas were named, for the flowers varied considerably in odour (as do those of the mdern H.T'.s) and some had no perfume at all." [EER] "Taken from China to England by Joseph

Banks in 1809, this rose flowered for the first time in the nursery of Mr. Colville, who mentioned it as a variety in which the flower had the aroma of tea, which, Redouté says, is not quite the case." [Gx]

ISABELLA SPRUNT
('Isabelle Sprungh')
Sprunt/Buchanan, 1865
Sport of 'Safrano' (T).

"Pale fawn yellow." [ARA40/31] "Lemon-yellow. Beautiful pointed bud." [H] "Brilliant yellow . . . large to medium . . . vigorous; needs a southern exposure . . . about 104 blooms per season." [ARA21/90–91] "Sulphur-yellow." [P1] "Light canary-yellow flowers." [FRB] "Flower large, semi-full; very floriferous." [S] "High-centered, medium . . . , double; soft-pale yellow, fading lighter . . . 2–3 [ft; ca. 6–9 dm]." [Lg] "Flowers in clusters, soon over. Exquisite when half-open." [Hn] "The many buds open without trouble; plant stays green; blooms early to late." [JR9/70] "Flowers moderately well formed." [JC] "Moderately tall, compact, hardy; foliage plentiful, healthy; bloom free, continuous." [ARA18/125] "Hardy, but not a strong grower." [F-M2] "On a west aspect quickly covers a wall 15-ft. high [ca. 4.5 m]." [NRS/17] "Growth not good. No distinguishing characteristics." [ARA18/116] "Well known as one of the most useful kinds." [EL]

JEAN DUCHER
('Comte de Sembui', 'Ruby Gold')
Widow Ducher, 1874

"Yellow, shaded salmon and red in the center; very good grower; fine foliage, flowers large and full; very fine." [HstXXX:236] "Bronzed-rose, large, very full, globular form; not to be depended upon, but very beautiful when well grown." [EL] "Lemon to salmon-yellow, centres shaded with peach; large and full; form globular; growth vigorous. One of the best." [P1] "Buff bordered cream." [JR11/50] "A blossom beyond description, of good form and substance." [JR12/180] "Perhaps the most sensitive of all Roses to wet or rain . . . when a fine bloom does come at last it is grand in shape, petal, centre, size, colour, and lasting qualities . . . a free-bloomer . . . colour is variable . . . very decorative at a distance." [F-M2] "Very vigorous, well held, not long-lasting, and too double." [JR9/70] "A magnificent tea, but it absolutely requires a dry hot season . . . impatient of wet." [FRB] "Strong stout stiff growth, with good foliage . . . not liable to mildew." [F-M2]

JEANETTE HELLER
Listed as 'William R. Smith'.

LADY HILLINGDON
Lowe & Shawyer, 1910
From 'Papa Gontier' (T) × 'Mme Hoste' (T).

"Deep apricot yellow, . . . fading . . . lighter . . . long-pointed buds open to flat, semi-double, fragrant, flowers . . . continuous profusion . . . 3–4 [ft; ca. 1–1.25 m]." [Lg] "A handsome orange-vermilion." [JR35/183] "Of remarkable orange yellow colour, and possessing long, shapely buds . . . satisfactory in the garden." [OM] "With better growth would be one of the best yellows." [Th] "The vigorous shrub has pretty foliage, and strong, upright shoots covered with attractive full blossoms which have large petals and are of a handsome light yellow which is sometimes shaded." [JR34/118] "Flowers not full, but elongated and handsome." [Hk] "Does not open well and droops in heat; odor slight." [ARA26/94] "Delicious fragrance." [T2] "Gives wonderful color in Pacific South-West, if grown in shade, under which conditions

it does not bleach for several days, petals seems to increase in substance, and stem is longer and stronger. . . . Prune sparingly." [Th2] "Very vigorous in warm climates, to 6 [ft; ca. 1.75 m]." [HRG] "Rather a weak grower [in Bermuda]." [UB28] "3 × 2 [ft; ca. 9 × 6 dm]." [B] "Height and compactness medium, rather weak, not very hardy; foliage sufficient, almost free from black-spot; bloom moderate, almost continuous." [ARA18/126] "Always on the job." [PS] "most attractive Rose not only for the beauty of its flowers, but also on account of the decorative effect of flower and foliage . . . bright fawn yellow, suffused orange. . . . The flowers are carried well . . . though usually somewhat bent over . . . certainly grows extremely well. Its stems are smooth and the young foliage is a beautiful ruby bronze, this tint being retained, though diminishing and merging into green while the leaves last. The flowers are thin but a beautiful shape, with deep shell-shaped petals. It does not suffer much from mildew. The principal defect of this Rose is that in cold weather many of the flowers — sometimes nearly half of them — are apt to come of a pale washed-out apricot, when much of their beauty and distinction is lost. Its strength lies in the grace and beauty of flower and foliage." [NRS/13] "Far outsells all others combined [of yellows and apricots in Houston, Texas]." [ET]

LADY PLYMOUTH
A. Dickson, 1914

"Deep ivory-cream (sometimes yellow). Balls in wet weather." [Capt27] "The best of the light yellow type found among the Teas." [Th] "A meritorious Rose, of the 'Souvenir de Pierre Notting' type, whose pearly cream petals are very faintly flushed, giving it a most piquant finish. Delicately tea-perfumed." [C&Js16] "Lovely. . . . Ivory white flushed cream and blush on a dense plant. Slightly fragrant . . . 3 × 3 [ft; ca. 1 × 1 m]." [B] "Well-formed, semi-double." [HRG] "Good in color, form, and lasting qualities; foliage especially fine . . . fair in blooming." [ARA18/111] "A good addition to the Teas — spiral or conical shape with a nice recurved outer petal. Colour, deep cream with almost yolk of egg centre. Foliage a good contrast; a good grower and fragrant; a very beautiful Rose." [NRS/14] "Mild perfume . . . growth bushy, with good number of canes, but not exceptionally tall. A good rose." [ARA17/25]

LADY ROBERTS   PLATE 1
F. Cant, 1902
Sport of 'Anna Olivier' (T).

"Rich apricot, base of petals coppery red, edges of petals shaded orange, long pointed bud and large full flowers." [P1] "Cream and orange." [JR34/10] "Orange-apricot to fawn. Weak stems." [Capt27] "Its pretty flowers of reddish apricot shaded salmon, its petals often bordered with orange, with coppery-red nubs and metallic reflections, and a pretty pointed bud, make this a rose of the first merit. The plant is vigorous and very floriferous." [JR37/13] "Small, of good form. . . . One of the best Tea roses." [OM] "Flowers large and perfect in shape, with long, pointed buds; colour variable." [Hn] "Does not spoil in rain or ball in damp winds, but becomes smaller in heat. Foliage very fine and lasts well." [Th2] "An apricot-coloured sport from 'Anna Olivier', which Rose it resembles in habit . . . a fair amount of glossy olive green foliage. The carriage of the flowers is good, and as a rule erect, but big flowers will sometimes droop. The blossoms are as a rule medium sized, having an apricot centre with coppery base to the petals, the edges becoming pale yellow, but the colour varies a good deal. . . . It is not much affected by mildew . . . exceptional continuity of its flowers." [NRS/13] "A quite pretty rose, having leaves and flowers in abundance during the fall." [JR36/188]

LA SYLPHIDE

Vibert's yellowish-flesh Tea of this name (1838) is probably extinct; Boyau's flesh and lilac Tea of this name (1842) is listed in the supplement; the pink-bordered-white Gallica 'Sylphide' is outside the scope of these lucubrations; and W. Paul's 1895 Tea 'Sylph' is listed under that name, below.

LORRAINE LEE

A. Clark, 1924

From 'Jessy Clark' (Gigantea, A. Clark, 1924, pink; *R. gigantea* × 'Mme Martignier' [Cl. T] × 'Capitaine Millet' [T]).

"Terra-cotta tint . . . a length of petal that bears comparison with anything seen elsewhere . . . freedom of flower . . . long buds, rich tea scent, . . . disease resistant . . . semi-double." [TS] "Bud long-pointed; flower medium size, double, open, cupped, lasting; warm rosy-apricot-pink; moderate fragrance. Foliage disease-resistant. Vigorous, upright; continuous bloomer." [ARA24/176] "Foliage rich green and glossy. . . . Needs extra care . . . 2 × 2 [ft; ca. 6 × 6 dm]." [B] "I hear of 'Lorraine Lee' as a spectacular hedge-plant in Australia." [T2]

MAMAN COCHET   PLATE 57

S. Cochet, 1892

From 'Marie Van Houtte' (T) × 'Mme Lambard' (T).

"The admirable Tea Rose 'Catherine Mermet' . . . is surpassed in size, poise, form, and vivacity of color by a pretty hybrid which Mons Scipion Cochet has bred, and will offer to commerce this fall [1889]. This remarkable introduction . . . : 'Maman Cochet', which is dedicated to the mother and grandmother of the rose-breeders in Suisnes of that name . . . the widow of Pierre Cochet, in her 87th year . . . it is a very vigorous shrub, though not 'climbing,' giving an abundance of flowers which are large or very large for the sort, of flesh-pink washed with a more-or-less light carmine, with salmon nankeen-yellow mixed in . . . very full; the outer petals are large and do not reflex like those of 'Catherine Mermet'; those of the center are sometimes formed into a rosette, or 'quartered.' It is nearly always held upright on its stem despite its size and fulness if it isn't on smaller branches or branchlets. . . . Among the best of its sort." [JR13/137] "Pink shaded lemon-yellow." [H] "Rose." [E] "Flesh-coloured rose shaded with carmine and salmon yellow, large and full, fine large bud. A magnificent rose of vigorous growth." [P1] "Carmine rose to cream and fawn. Balls in dampness." [Capt27] "Beautiful blooms that . . . never ball [in Bermuda]." [UB28] "Large, well-filled, tulip-like form, flesh-coloured pink, changing to copper colour. Growth strong, flowers solitary, very fine." [Hn] "Very recommendable as an autumnal, giving enormous blossoms lasting, cupped, 8–10 days without fading or discoloring." [JR16/179] "Blooms are very large, stout and lasting . . . well shaped, but have often some little imperfection . . . the colours . . . in fine hot weather sometimes beautiful but often undecided and weak." [F-M2] "'Maman Cochet' and 'White Maman Cochet' are, without question, the best garden roses for southern Kansas . . . perfect blooms which are never malformed or blighted." [ARA21/171] "Only an occasional perfect bloom." [PS] "Lacks quality in the flower." [ARA25/105] "Large shapely blooms . . . to 4 [ft; ca. 1.25 m]." [B] "The flower . . . measures nearly four in [ca. 1 dm], and is thus one of the largest blossoms in the Teas." [JR17/103] "Most attractive in form and color; lasts well; good growth and foliage; a shy bloomer." [ARA18/112] "A heavy constant bloomer, with long fine buds of a pearl-pink." [BSA] "Fragrant. Vigorous with few thorns . . . 3 × 3 [ft; ca. 1 × 1 m]." [B] "Tall, compact, vigorous, hardy; foliage plentiful, black-spots somewhat." [ARA18/126] "Growth is very strong . . . foliage is good, but has . . . attacks of

. . . 'silver-leaf.' " [F-M2] "Resistant to mildew." [JR33/37] "Succeeds best in rather poor soil." [OM] "As good a border rose as one can find. It was in flower here last year from June to mid-October, its enormous blossoms the admiration of all who saw it." [K1] "One of the best Tea roses offered for many years." [JR22/107] "A variety to study and to recommend." [JR17/149]

MARIE D'ORLÉANS

Nabonnand, 1883

"Rich coppery red, with pink centre." [CA93] "Bright rose shaded, large and full." [P1] "Brick-red washed pink; . . . fragrant; very floriferous; very vigorous." [Cx] "At the center of the blossom, . . . the 'muddled' ['*etroites lanières*'] form." [JR23/118] "Continuous bloom; flower very large, full, flat, very well formed, well held; color, bright pink, shaded." [S] "Very pretty." [JR22/81] "Hardy and free." [TW] "A 'top of the line' variety." [JR7/184]

MARIE LAMBERT

('Snowflake', 'White Hermosa', 'Priscilla')

E. Lambert, 1886

Sport of 'Mme Bravy' (T).

"Medium-sized, full, pure white." [LR] "Beautiful pale flesh color, passing to rich, creamy white; large, regular flowers, full and well formed buds, delightfully perfumed." [CA90] "Has the vigor of its parent 'Mme Bravy'. Color, pure white; flower of medium size; this variety takes well to pot culture. A very beautiful variety." [JR10/171] "Habit of growth, free; flower, globular." [TW] "Tall, bushy, hardy; foliage very plentiful, healthy; bloom free, continuous." [ARA18/126] "Without a doubt an excellent acquisition . . . pretty." [JR25/65]

MARIE VAN HOUTTE   PLATE 18

('The Gem')

Ducher, 1871

From 'Mme de Tartas' (T) × 'Mme Falcot' (T).

"Light yellow edged with pink, an universal favorite, and a magnificent grower. . . . It is a very fine exhibition variety, particularly in moist weather." [FRB] "Yellow canary, deeper center, border of petals tipped with bright rose. An old favorite." [Th] "White slightly tinted with yellow, often edged with rose; large, full, and good; growth vigorous." [P1] "Medium-sized or large, slightly quilled, of perfect form and poise, particularly while opening; additionally, it is of a superb shade of light yellow at the center, which enhances an ample border of rose-pink which appears only on the outer petals, where also may be seen patches of milk-white." [S] "The consensus of opinion among professional gardeners is that this is the most valuable white rose for garden growth anywhere." [Dr] "Cream flesh to light peach, edged rose. Balls easily." [Capt27] "Large, very double . . . of gold and cream, suffused with carmine-pink and fragrant." [HRG] "White slightly tinted with yellow, border of the petals tinted with rose, flowers quite full and well formed." [JC] "Blooms from May to frost. The flower is large, full, globular, lightly fragrant. . . . In southern climes, we have sometimes seen blossoms which were nearly white, and in the Lyon area, when positioned in full sun, it takes on a pink tint which is very delicate and bewitching; other times, it is a dull porcelain white." [JR16/141] "Bright pink tinged orange and cream. Fragrant. Rich, green foliage . . . sprawling habit . . . 3 × 3 [ft; ca. 1 × 1 m]." [B] "Of a reversed bell shape (like a bell as the ringer jerks it upward for a good peal of joy) . . . a supremely lovely flower, with the faintest suggestion of a tulip in it, and a breath of quite peculiar sweetness." [HstXXX:288] "Noteworthy in color and lasting qualities; growth and form good;

quite a bloomer." [ARA18/113] "The flowers droop, it is true, but very gracefully . . . free from mildew and other diseases." [NRS/13] "The white, waxy buds are exquisite and open better than most Teas, and although the open flower is rather flat, its full petalage and peach-colored center make up for that fault. It is the most vigorous of my Teas . . . more upright than most of its class, with a zigzagging, slantwise growth that never permits the blossoms to trail in the dust, like 'Maman Cochet'. It has a distinct perfume, good foliage, and superb stems." [ARA29/70] "Constantly in bloom. One year a three-year-old bush here displayed sixty-two well-shaped blossoms in the middle of October." [K1]

" 'Marie Van Houtte' is quite one of the freest, prettiest 'Teas' in cultivation. A small plant, which only came to me last April (a gift from Mr. Bennett, of Salisbury), is now just finishing a second crop of flowers, and growing away in all directions for another efflorescence." [R3/329] "Almost tall, compact, vigorous, hardy; foliage very plentiful, healthy; bloom free through summer, moderate in fall, almost continuous." [ARA18/126] "A free bloomer which does fine work after cool weather comes . . . vigorous and healthy but inclined to sprawl." [ARA29/88] "In the splendid line of Tea Roses, that which is dedicated to Mlle Marie Van Houtte, of Ghent (Belgium), is assuredly one of the most beautiful . . . very vigorous, strong, and upright branches, with hooked thorns. The ample foliage, composed of five to seven leaflets, is of a light bright green; the stem is strong. The flowers are very large, full, and well formed, in cluster of 2 or three at the ends of the branches, though sometimes they are solitary . . . yellowish-white edged bright pink, aging to a light pink throughout . . . very fragrant." [JR4/57] "Fine growth and production . . . best for interior South." [Capt28] "Developed into a huge plant [in Brazil], always in bloom." [PS] "Needs light pruning." [DO] "Of good habit, and in every respect a most charming sort. The finest of all Teas for out-door culture." [EL] "One of the strongest and best . . . at all times a beautiful flower . . . first-class autumnal . . . no one should be without." [F-M2]

MATHILDE
Listed as 'Niphetos'.

MÉLANIE WILLERMOZ
Listed as 'Mme Mélanie Willermoz'.

MINNIE FRANCIS
Noisette/Griffing, 1905

"This is a new Tea rose, originating on the Noisette farm at Charleston. . . . It is the best-growing Tea rose we have ever seen, making a very large strong bush in one season, and in two or three years will make a spread of from 4 to 6 ft [ca. 1.25–1.75 m]. Flowers are extra large and full; buds long and pointed; color fine chamois-red, richly shaded with velvety crimson; very sweet and a constant bloomer. . . . " [quoted from the 1905 Griffing catalog] [ARA26/212] "Open flowers." [G] "[Good in Florida] . . . like an improved and somewhat darker 'Mme Lambard'. It grows to considerable height . . . , and is apparently of much value." [ARA24/85]

MLLE FRANZISKA KRÜGER   PLATE 21
('Grand Duc Héritier de Luxembourg')
Nabonnand, 1879
From 'Catherine Mermet' (T) × 'Général Schablikine' (T).

"Peachy pink with soft shades of sunset and twilight lavender." [ARA36/19] "Exterior petals are white bordered with flesh and fawn; the inner ones change from yellow to pink." [JR12/180] "Coppery

yellow, shaded peach." [H] "Cream flesh to apricot-copper. Balls easily; mildews." [Capt27] "Very double, large blooms of coppery yellow with pink, green pip in center, fragrant." [HRG] "Often very perfect in form . . . good growth and foliage, not much liable to mildew . . . anything but robust." [F-M2] "An extremely attractive bloom, either in bud or fully open." [ARA29/88] "Handsome green foliage which lasts and is very resistant to disease. The blossoms are large, very full, well formed." [JR12/24] "Bush vigorous, as is the growth; . . . very free; color, coppery flesh-white shaded yellow and pink, fading into pink reflections and washed with the shades already mentioned; planted at the foot of a banked wall, it promptly grows to perhaps five ft in height [ca. 1.75 m], and its blossoms take on a coloration impossible to describe, but of great charm . . . the flower stems . . . nod under the weight of the blossoms." [S] "Moderate height, compact, hardy; foliage plentiful, healthy; bloom profuse and continuous till September, after that liberal and continuous." [ARA18/125] "Foliage of a leathery texture. Low to medium height, spreading . . . 25 to 54 blooms per season." [ARA21/92] "A good hot weather rose." [L] "Much appreciated in the North." [JR5/21] "Should be in every collection. Very showy." [Dr] "An excellent Tea in every way." [FRB]

MME ANTOINE MARI   PLATE 70
Mari/Jupeau, 1901

"Rose-pink to flesh. Loose." [Capt27] "The flowers are numerous, open well, of a rich pink often tinted with white; the bud is large and elongated." [JR28/30] "Blush-white; moderate, bushy." [ARA17/31] "Ground colour rose, freely washed and shaded with white; very handsome buds which open well; growth extra vigorous and free from mildew." [P1] "Pink on a ground of white; flower large, full, cupped; very floriferous, very vigorous." [Cx] "Pretty bud of a lightly blushing white, carmine at the edge. In winter, this rose is nearly white, and in form resembles a camellia." [JR24/113] "Nice shape, but small flowers; balls and discolors in damp winds. Foliage nearly evergreen, without disease. Growth very good, stem weak." [Th2] "Fine dark green foliage, . . . though almost crimson when it first starts into growth. The flowers are a pale rose, shaded white, of a very creamy appearance, and most delicate colouring. . . . The carriage of the flowers is rather drooping, but not objectionally so, unless they get much rain upon them . . . good free growth. . . . Flowers well and continuously . . . practically free from mildew . . . a tendency to produce rather too many weak side branches." [NRS/13] "[One of] those which approach more nearly in habit of growth to the Chinas." [NRS/14] "It is, as a bedding Rose, the most nearly perfect Tea Rose in my garden. Whether we regard its hardiness, its habit of growth, its beautiful foliage, its distinctive pink buds, its shapely flowers and the creamy texture of its petals, or the delicacy of its varying tints of flesh pink colouring, it is alike excellent . . . from 2-ft. to 2-ft. 6-in high [ca. 6–7.5 dm]. The flowers are pointed and freely borne, of fair substance, but not full enough for exhibition, nor to give any sense of heaviness." [NRS/11] "Beautiful Camellia, immortal plant, always blooming." [JR37/172] "Never so nice as in this [fall] season; it is, what is more, a Camellia which celebrates a new spring every six months; the bud and half-open flower are pretty. . . . Never sick, never moribund." [JR36/187] "Mons Mari has grown this superb rose for some six years [i.e., since 1895]." [JR24/146] "I adore it, and want always to possess it." [JR38/48]

MME BERKELEY
Bernaix fils, 1898

"Salmon washed, pink shaded; flower large, full, imbricated; very floriferous; moderate vigor." [Cx] "Salmon-white, fine petals, semi-double, but very good; growth robust." [P1] "Salmon-pink with gold base to petals, tea fragrance, free bloom. Vigorous to 4 [ft; ca. 1.25 m].” [HRG] “Foliage sumptuous, branches of moderate size, bud very elongate-ovoid, gradually narrowing from the base to the tip. Exterior color, pale blush washed violet pink. Flower large, flesh, salmon at the center, washed pink, pale violet on the exterior petals, which are notable for their size.” [JR22/162] “Foliage dark green, handsome, pert, healthy; plant bushy, compact; the blossoms, in form and color, remind me of a smaller, more intensely-colored ‘Gloire de Dijon’, and last a long time. In sustained shade, the blossoms open a very pale fawn with yearnings for chartreuse; sun brings out a rather more attractive coloration. Profuse; tendentially in rather far-flung clusters at first. References to its being a good parent seem unjustified, as very few hips have formed on my specimen.” [BCD]

MME BRAVY

(‘Alba Rosea’, ‘Adèle Pradel’, ‘Danzille’, ‘Isidore Malton’, ‘Mme Denis’, ‘Mme de Sertot’, ‘Mme Maurin’)
Guillot père, 1845

“White, pink centre, a beautiful tea, quite distinct in form to any other tea variety.” [FRB] “Full, creamy-white with pink markings, fragrant.” [HRG] “Cream, centre blush, exquisitely formed; in dry weather, superb.” [JC] “Large, full, of very symmetrical form and great fragrance; one of the most beautiful and useful in the class.” [EL] “Form, cupped.” [P] “Globular, not very regular in form . . . short outer petals.” [Hk] “Pretty white buds. Full blown flowers lacking in substance.” [Dr] “Blooms come very well . . . globular . . . almost like an incurved chrysanthemum. Blooms . . . pendant.” [F-M2] “Strong fragrance . . . 3 × 3 [ft; ca. 1 × 1 m].” [B] “Raspberry-scented.” [JR33/101] “Free-flowering. Growth moderate.” [Hn] “Growth vigorous.” [P1] “Average growth and fair foliage.” [F-M2] “The best of white Teas known.” [S] Phillips & Rix report that ‘Mme Bravy’ was “raised by Guillot of Pont Cherin in 1846 and introduced by Guillot of Lyon in 1848” (attribution unspecified); however, we find from the *Catalogue et Choix des Plus Belles Roses Remontants* . . . of Chez Étienne Armand, “Propriétaire Horticulteur à Ecully-lez-Lyon,” that it is already being offered to the public in 1845; Jean Sisley, one of the most significant *rosiéristes* of the last two-thirds of the 1800’s, reports that ‘Mme Bravy’ was raised “from seed by Mons Guillot, gardener at the Château d’Azelles, and delivered into commerce by Guillot père.” [JR3/53] Let us, at any rate, also remember her husband, “G. Bravy, of the Société d’Horticulture de l’Hérault.” [I'H64/75]

MME DENIS

Listed as ‘Mme Bravy’.

MME DE SERTOT

Listed as ‘Mme Bravy’.

MME DE TARTAS

Bernède, 1859

“Intense pink; flower large, full, cupped; very vigorous.” [Cx] “Blossom moderate in size, pretty full; color, light pink.” [S] “Bright rose, large, full, and produced abundantly; growth moderate.” [P1] “Blowsy pink blooms.” [Hk] “Blush pink . . . scented . . . sprawly in habit . . . 3 × 3 [ft; ca. 1 × 1 m].” [B] “Coarse in growth.” [Hk] Seemingly of the ‘Comtesse de Labarthe’ tribe.

MME DE WATTEVILLE

Guillot fils, 1883
Affiliated with ‘Adam’ (T).

“Cream bordered rose. Distinct, tender, fragrant.” [H] “Lovely coral pink and canary.” [Dr] “Very distinct pale lemon, with distinct margin of pink; large, full, and free.” [DO] “Vigorous; large flowers, full, well-formed, very fragrant, well held; buds are long; color is white with some salmon, each petal fairly well edged pink. This wonderful variety is quite notable for the shading of the blossoms, resembling a tulip.” [JR7/158] “Requires dry weather.” [FRB] “Needs careful disbudding.” [DO] “Has never been wholly satisfactory with me: but where the buds have been well thinned . . . I by no means despise a bunch of its lovely blossoms on long stalks.” [K1] “Liable to mildew . . . weak.” [F-M] “Branching habit of growth.” [B] “Growth fair; not distinct.” [ARA18/116]

[MME FALCOT]   PLATE 14

Guillot fils, 1858
Seedling of ‘Safrano’ (T).

“Buff yellow.” [SBP] “Deep rich orange-yellow, petals large and of good substance, flowers not full, buds exquisitely beautiful, rich dark foliage; habit free.” [JC] “Exterior of the outer petals having often the most charming combinations of red and yellow, the inner petals being of a beautiful self-yellow. A good autumnal.” [F-M2] “Flower medium or large, double, sometimes full; color, nankeen yellow fading to lighter yellow. Plant vigorous.” [I'H58/98] “Deep apricot; resembles [‘Safrano’], but is somewhat larger, more double, of deeper shade, less productive.” [EL] “A word in passing on the subject of ‘Mme Falcot’; one errs considerably if one judges according to the young plant; the blossoms bear a great resemblance to ‘Safrano’, while the plant is less productive; but this is not the case after 3, 4, 5, or 6 years; it blooms at that point quite as much as ‘Safrano’ and is much more brilliant and double. Fortunate shrubs! Age only increases their beauty!” [JR2/5] “Beautiful fawn-color . . . a charming variety.” [R8] “Medium to large in size, nankeen yellow, darker in the centre; beautiful tulip-like form. Free-flowering with moderate growth. The most perfect flowers appear in autumn.” [Hn] “Loose.” [Capt27] “Rich saffron-yellow, large and very double; petals large and thick; growth moderate. In the way of ‘Safrano’, but of a higher colour. . . . Introduced in 1858 and still one of the best.” [P1] “It has all the Tea-rose characteristics except that of having its young growths a maroon-red color. Its blossom of 2–3 in [ca. 5–7.5 cm] doesn’t have any — or has very little — scent, and opens very quickly; its colors are nankeen yellow fading to plain yellow . . . when completely open, the flower is flat and a disgrace.” [JR20/60]

“Fair growth and foliage.” [F-M2] “Vigorous; reddish branches; hooked thorns, numerous and large; foliage of 5–7 lanceolate, finely toothed, shiny green leaflets; good autumn bloom; . . . color, moroccan yellow fading to light yellow.” [S] “Pretty vigorous; branches slender and nodding; bark smooth, reddish with similarly colored thorns which are straight and pointed. The young growth is a handsome maroon red. Leaves of medium size, pale green . . . borne on a reddish leafstalk armed with a number of slightly hooked prickles. Flowers about 2.5 in across [ca. 6 cm], fairly full, cupped, solitary; . . . outer petals large, those of the center folded and rumpled; flower stem glabrous, reddish, slender, and nodding. Calyx rounded . . . the bud is long and well formed.” [JF] “More feeble [than ‘Safrano’].” [EL] “I planted many specimens of ‘Safrano’, of which variety I would take many cuttings, because I knew they would give good seeds. That same year I gathered fiftyish of such seeds, which I planted. Many didn’t germinate. Nevertheless, among the resulting seedlings I noticed one which had semi-double blossoms of a nankeen yellow, new for that time.” [JR4/88-89]

[MME HOSTE]   PLATE 40
Guillot & fils, 1887
Seedling of 'Victor Pulliat' (T).
Not to be confused with the flesh-white Gonod HP of 1865.

"Creamy color." [OM] "Flushed with rose." [C&Js00] "An exceedingly beautiful Rose; extra large, full, flowers of excellent substance; color fine canary yellow, deepening at center to rich golden yellow. Grand for forcing." [CA93] "Fragrant." [Cx] "Vigorous; flower very large, full, very well formed, with large, thick, imbricated petals; well held." [JR11/149] "Of good growth and fine foliage. . . . The flowers are rather thin, and though they stand a long time in the advanced bud stage, when once they open they soon go, showing a weak centre. They are, however, very large and of very fine shape, and produced in great abundance, often very fine in the autumn . . . the stems are stiff and straight and the buds long and clean." [F-M2] "After serious study, the fortunate raiser of this beautiful introduction, recognizing what was, by all reports, an excellent plant, released it to commerce in fall, 1887. Dedicated to the wife of a Lyonnais horticulturalist well known for his work with dahlias, chrysanthemums, pelargoniums, etc. . . . it is propagated on a large scale, notably in North America, where it is in great demand because of its cupped flowers. It is a vigorous plant, blooming very well, and giving an abundance of very pretty, very large blossoms, which are imbricated, and yellowish-white on a ground washed dark yellow. The large buds are long and borne on very firm stems. The plant is excellent as a garden rose." [JR17/9]

MME JOSEPH SCHWARTZ   PLATE 22
('White Duchesse de Brabant')
Schwartz, 1880
Sport of 'Comtesse de Labarthe' (T).

"Blush, the edge of the petals tinged with carmine." [EL] "Flesh." [LS] "Lightly blushed white; flower cupped, medium-sized; vigorous." [Cx] "A new rose; flower of medium size, full, well formed, white washed flesh-pink fading to pale flesh, from the Tea 'Comtesse de Labarthe', a plant of the highest merit." [JR4/165] "Deliciously sweet." [CA90] "Double; white, tinged with pink in cool weather. Continuous . . . 2–3 [ft; ca. 6–9 dm]. Supposedly a seedling of ['Comtesse de Labarthe']; evidence proves rather that it is definitely a color sport." [Lg] "Low growing, moderately compact and hardy; foliage plentiful, healthy; bloom free, almost continuous." [ARA18/126]

MME LAMBARD
('Mme Lombard', 'Mme Lambart')
Lacharme, 1877
Supposed to be a product of a cross between 'Mme de Tartas' (T) and something in the 'Safrano' (T) line.

"Salmon, shaded rose . . . variable in colour." [H] "Flower large, full, intense red. Very fragrant." [LR] "Rich cream and gold, flushed with rose-pink, very double and vigorous to 5 [ft; ca. 1.5 m]]." [HRG] "Large, double, fragrant; flesh pink with salmon center. Repeats . . . 2–3 [ft; ca. 6–9 dm]." [Lg] "Very vigorous; large flowers, beautiful bright red at the first bloom, more pale at the last." [JR1/12/13] "A pink rose that deepens on opening fully." [ARA39/48] "A somewhat coppery pink; flower large, full, cupped." [Cx] "Long considered the best all-around Tea . . . at its best in the fall. Whereas the flowers are light salmon-pink in the spring and summer, in the fall they deepen into carmine, almost red, and bloom right on in a mild winter until stopped by heavy frosts." [SHj] "Salmon-pink, shaded with rose and yellow, sometimes the pink and sometimes the yellow colour predominating; . . . globular, perfect in shape, and petals fine." [P1] "Good both

early and late, and is not too full to open in bad weather. The flowers are very variable in colour; I think a typical blossom may be described as a deep coral pink with a tinge of copper, but some may be found almost salmon, and others light rosy buff; quite a fair number of them come of good form, and the plant is very free, flowering almost continuously through the season." [NRS/11]

"As to red Tea Roses we have travelled far and fast since I first saw 'Mme Lambard' at the Paris Exhibition of 1878. It had appeared the year before, and was described as the 'finest deep-red Tea Rose in cultivation'. I shall not soon forget the excitement she created. Doubtless her colour in France is deeper than in England; for even here one sees the difference sun and warmth make to her, the first blooms in July being much darker in colour than the charming, rather pale blossoms I see from the window on an early October day. Few Teas, whether old or new, surpass her; strong, hardy, always in flower, she is hard to beat. But of course for deep vivid colour she cannot now compare with some of her modern rivals." [K1] "Scentless. The best and hardiest of the light red Teas." [S] "Large double flowers on stiff stems." [SHj] "Stems only fair." [Capt27] "Showy pink . . . rather round buds." [BSA] "Such a free bloomer that it adds much to the appearance of a garden." [ARA29/88] "Nearly perpetual through the season, always blooming some, and staying green till winter." [JR9/69] "Free bloomer of good growth [in Bermuda]." [UB28] "3 × 2 [ft; ca. 9 × 6 dm]." [B] "Small plants; winterkills." [ARA18/116] "Tall, compact, hardy; foliage very plentiful, black-spots slightly." [ARA18/126] "Liable to mildew . . . a cool season rose." [F-M2] "Foliage is well retained." [Th2] "A truly magnificent variety." [FRB]

MME MAURIN
Listed as 'Mme Bravy'.

MME MÉLANIE WILLERMOZ
Lacharme, 1845

"Creamy-white, centre tinted with fawn, petals very thick and finely formed, handsome large foliage, and moderately robust." [JC] "Vigorous; flower large, full, white shaded salmon at the center; one of the oldest and most esteemed Tea Roses." [S] "Of very sturdy stout growth with splendid foliage: an old Rose, formerly of considerable repute, but getting fast superseded by those of better manners . . . generally sadly lacking in the production of handsomely shaped useful blooms. . . . The petals are very fine but the form is not good . . . a well-defined point in the centre being often absent. . . . On rare occasions it does open well in hot weather with a good point in the centre, and is then very fine. It does well as a dwarf, the stiff upright character of the wood being well suited to this form of culture. It cannot be called a free-bloomer or good autumnal." [F-M3] "Wood, strong, big, glaucous green tinted violet, long internodes. . . . Foliage, ample, rather long-stemmed . . . somber green, glossy above, glaucous green beneath. Flower stems long, strong, with two, three, or four foliaceous stipules around the point of attachment to the branch. . . . Color, delicate pink at the center, white around the edges; the petal-edge is often marbled pink. Blossom very large (to four in [ca. 1 dm]), full, rounded, cupped, deep, regular, perfect, sexual organs evident, always opens easily. Scent, very weak. . . . This rose grows rapidly and energetically . . . one of the hardiest of this delicate section. The large and beautiful flowers of 'Mélanie Willermoz' appear abundantly throughout its period of active growth on its robust branches, and stand out elegantly by their delicate shading against the bright and lustrous green of the handsome foliage." [PIB] "An excellent sort for out-of-door culture." [EL]

MME SCIPION COCHET   PLATE 36

Bernaix, 1886

From 'Anna Olivier' (T) × 'Comtesse de Labarthe' (T).

Not to be confused with S. Cochet's red edged-white 1872 HP of the same name.

"Pale pink shaded white on a ground of yellow, center canary; flower large, full, cupped, fragrant; very floriferous; very vigorous." [Cx] "Beautiful creamy rose with deep crimson center; flowers large, somewhat tulip shaped, quite full, and very sweet; a good, constant bloomer." [CA90] "Thick, glossy foliage. . . . Bush grows to about 2.5 ft [ca. 7.5 dm], branching from the base . . . branches not of the climbing sort, reddish, furnished top to bottom with doughty thorns. . . . Leaves numerous, thick, of 3–5–7 leaflets . . . somber green, shiny, like those of a Camellia above, lighter beneath. Flower solitary, erect at the summit of the stem . . . very double; bud ovoid, abruptly more slender towards the tip . . . ; exterior petals regularly concave lengthwise, perfectly imbricated, pale pink with hints of flat white and, towards the base, light yellow; center petals more irregular, apricot/canary yellow, with touches of deep pink." [JR10/138] "A strong healthy grower and constant and profuse bloomer." [C&Js05] "A plant of the first rank." [JR14/93]

MME TIXIER

Listed as 'Souvenir d'Un Ami'.

MOLLY SHARMAN-CRAWFORD

A. Dickson, 1908

"A beautiful rose . . . large, with a good centre . . . a pleasing shade of white, with a slight suggestion of eau de nil." [F-M] "Very double, greenish white, fading to white . . . 2–3 [ft; ca. 6–9 dm]. Repeats." [Lg] "Bridal white. Large and full, with high, pointed centre. Broad, smooth petals. Delightful perfume. Very free and constant. A rose of entrancing loveliness." [Dr] "Good color; only fair in other qualities." [ARA18/117] "Medium to large . . . little perfume. Blooms all the year. Foliage well held; slight mildew in dampness on young foliage. Good growth. Distinct." [Capt28] "Low-growing, slim, hardy; foliage sufficient, healthy; bloom moderate to free, almost continuous." [ARA18/127] "Beautiful foliage and a rather upright habit of growth, holding its head well, and always giving a shapely flower." [NRS/11] "Sometimes ill-shaped." [Capt27] "Its foliage is a fine ruddy colour when young, and this tint is more or less preserved for some time. Its flowers are charming, large and full, and produced in quantity from one end of the season to the other. They are well formed and nearly white, but have a little cream colour with the faintest tinge of pale green. It is customary to call them 'Eau-de-nil white', but from my recollection of the time when I took an interest in ladies' ball dresses, I should say the colour eau-de-nil has a considerable amount of blue in it, and this, I think, 'Molly Sharman-Crawford' has not got. The contrast between the flowers and foliage is very effective and pleasing. The blossoms are carried very erect for a Tea Rose . . . not free from mildew, but suffers very little from this trouble." [NRS/13] "The prettiest white rose on Earth." [JR32/56]

MONSIEUR TILLIER   PLATE 54

Bernaix, 1891

Affiliated with 'Safrano à Fleurs Rouges' (T).

"A handsome carmine-red shaded brick, passing to violet-shaded red." [JR15/106] "Blood-red, with violet markings . . . 4 × 4 [ft; ca. 1.25 × 1.25 m]." [B] "Large, very double, with quartered center . . . dark pink to carmine red. Free, continuous bloom. . . . Leathery gray-green foliage . . . lovely blooms are produced to profusion on a very tough plant. Easy to grow."

[Lg] "An absolutely thrilling sight. This thoroughly novel color among roses makes it easy to distinguish from others. . . . The bush is vigorous, thick, pretty hardy, and, above all, floriferous." [JR22/24–25] "It is a rare dark rose among the autumn roses which are pretty nearly always light." [JR36/187] "The tints resemble those of 'Mlle Franziska Krüger'. Beautiful." [JR16/21] "Flower large, flat; good bedder." [Cx] "Seems to be a full-blooded Tea, but with small, double red blooms." [SHj] As with most (if not all) "red" Tea Roses, the sun will scorch the blossoms; some shade is desirable (BCD). "Bush not climbing, very floriferous, of moderate size, with bright brownish-green leaves. The blossom is quite double, with numerous petals, often imbricated in the Camellia fashion." [JR15/150] "Looked as if its sturdy flowers would go on till Christmas." [K1] "But why is not that beautiful Rose, 'Monsieur Tillier', . . . seen oftener here? . . . It is simply invaluable for cutting, never out of bloom from June to November, and bearing heads of medium-sized flowers in such abundance, that a group of two or three plants makes a vivid splash of colour right across my garden. I first saw it at the Paris Exhibition of 1900, and have planted it freely ever since with great success, as it is quite hardy and even more effective than a China Rose, and lasts for many days in water." [K1] "L. Tillier, former head of the National School of Horticulture in Versailles." [JR11/158] "The bookstore *Octave Doin* is going to publish a charming work by Mons L. Tillier, the title of which is *L'Année Horticole*. It's a review of the novelties released to commerce in 1892." [JR17/63]

MRS. B. R. CANT

B. R. Cant, 1901

Affiliated with 'Safrano à Fleurs Rouges' (T).

"Deep rose on the outer petals, and in the Autumn frequently a rich red, inner petals soft silvery rose suffused with buff at the base, of good substance and symmetrical in form; a hardy variety and a vigorous grower." [P1] "Sparkling pink, brighter than the usual Tea." [ARA29/95] "Deep rose fading to light rose." [JR32/139] "Beautiful . . . with silvery inner petals suffused with buff . . . worthy of a place in the front rank of the many pink and salmon Tea Roses." [K1] "A good rose. Unique color; excellent foliage; blooms very well; growth good." [ARA18/113] "Perfume mild . . . best of the red Teas." [ARA17/24] "Grows vigorously all season and blooms continuously. Not so much character but gives fine big blooms of typical rose color; also blooms well in the fall when most of the roses are off duty." [ARA29/88] "Most beautiful in the fall." [SHj] "A very free-flowering Tea, with rose-red blooms that make a good display in the garden, but have few claims to fine form." [OM] "Flowers full and globular." [W/Hn] "Form varies, being flat in the East, yet without open center and is of good size. Does not ball and holds its color well, even in heat. Has beautiful foliage and long stems. Of splendid growth, and blooms constantly." [Th2] "Medium height, compact, fairly hardy; foliage plentiful, healthy; bloom moderate, intermittent." [ARA18/127] "Resistant to mildew." [JR33/37] *Not* resistant to mildew, *I* say (BCD). "To 4 [ft; ca. 1.25 m]." [HRG] "Seems in vigour, hardiness, freedom of flower . . . sweetness, colour, fulness and shape to be . . . a most valuable introduction." [F-M2]

MRS. CAMPBELL HALL

Hall/A. Dickson, 1914

"Delicate creamy buff, edged or suffused rosy carmine. Of fair hardiness in Central Zone, but of small growth there. Valuable for its color. A collector's rose, and suggested for the South-East Zone only." [Th2] "The center of the bloom is warm cerise-coral-fawn. . . . Deliciously tea-perfumed." [C&Js15] "Very fine . . . of excellent constitution; habit similar to 'Maman Cochet'; very free-flowering . . . of exquisite shape and colour." [F-M] "Large and high-centred in bud, opening full and somewhat blowsy. Dark, leathery foliage on a vigorous bush . . . 4 × 3 [ft; ca. 1.25 m × 9 dm]." [B1]

MRS. DUDLEY CROSS
W. Paul, 1907

"Chamois-yellow, blushing pink in cool weather." [HRG] "Colors in warm weather and is hidden with blushes." [ET] "Flower very large, light chamois yellow, pink and crimson in the fall. A very beautiful variety." [JR35/14] "Improved 'Marie Van Houtte'. Good growth, form, and color, although not of best; fair bloomer." [ARA18/113] "A superb light yellow rose. Large, full, and of elegant form." [Dr] "A fascinating rose, producing large double flowers on stiff, absolutely thornless stems. When used as a cut flower it is first light yellow, then becomes two-tone, and finally all pink." [SHj] "Good growth and stem, but foliage mildews badly. Flower lasts well, and is fine for cutting. Especially adapted to dry southern climates." [Th2]

MRS. HERBERT STEVENS
Listed as a Hybrid Tea.

NILES COCHET
('Red Maman Cochet')
California Nursery Company, 1911
Sport of 'Maman Cochet' (T).

"Red on edge of petals, pink at base. . . . Thorough tests have demonstrated that it is unquestionably far superior to any of the other Cochet varieties, being a much better bloomer and of finer color and substance." [CA11] "Deep claret to cream. Balls in dampness." [Capt27] "A variegated rather than a solid red." [Capt28] "Large, double, sometimes irregularly shaped; cherry-red with lighter center." [Lg] "Form almost identical with its parent, but claimed to be a trifle smaller and with better stems; slight fragrance. Fine foliage, and otherwise like its parent." [Th2]

NIPHETOS
(trans., 'Snowy'; syn., 'Mathilde')
Bougère, 1841 (*or before*)

"Of a pale lemon, turning to snow-white." [FP] "White, centre pale straw, long handsome buds, large Magnolia-like petals; in dry weather superb." [JC] "Suffers much from rain; the blossoms open poorly . . . in essence, it is a greenhouse rose." [JR7/3] "Large, full, tulip-like form, pure white; buds long, tapering, drooping. A delightful rose." [Hn] "Very large, very floriferous, large petals." [R-H42] "No white Tea can beat it for purity of colour." [FRB] "Large, globular, fragrant white. Repeats . . . 2–3 [ft; ca. 6–9 dm]." [Lg] "Frequently malformed." [F-M] "Delicate long-pointed buds . . . not very strong in growth." [BSA] "Remarkable for its large taper formed flower bud, and till it is fully open is very splendid . . . when fully expanded, it is not at all attractive; the wood is strong." [Bu] "Flower of medium size, full; color, pure white; form, pointed; the most tender of white roses . . . the leaves are light green, rather dense, sufficient unto the blossom, which itself is just the thing to cut a fine figure in the open garden, but it is primarily cultivated under glass, giving excellent results." [S] "The bush is small, stocky, with light green serrated leaflets. The young wood is green, and is sometimes covered with rust-colored spots. The thorns are solitary, much recurved, and very thick. The marvelous buds are greenish-white; their stem is long; long sepals; when the blossom opens, its petals are pure white, reflexing to the

stem *à la* 'Maréchal Niel'; this characteristic keeps the flower in an attractive bell-like form from first to last. As the final petals unfurl, they take on a tint of pale pink intermingled with little lines." [JR4/174]

"Created as great a sensation as any rose that ever appeared. The peculiar elongated, oval, pure white bud had not been seen among roses." [Dr] "It occurred in the sixties [i.e., 1860's] that 'Niphetos' was entirely lost to culture. The most diligent search failed to recover a single 'Niphetos' rose-bush. It was universally regretted. Accidentally, a Northern tourist came across a garden of the Blue Ridge, Virginia, that had in it a rose-bush full of unmistakeable elongated, oval, snow-white 'Niphetos' buds. The prize was secured and taken to Philadelphia. 'Niphetos' was restored to its own." [Dr] "Represents, among roses, a perfect distinction, a supreme elegance, finesse, and, finally, nobility." [JR13/152]

PAPA GONTIER   PLATE 25
Nabonnand, 1882
Seedling of 'Duchess of Edinburgh' (T).

"Intense pink; reverse, carmine-red; flower large, imbricated; very floriferous; fairly vigorous." [Cx] "Rosy crimson, pointed bud, free." [H] "Rich pink rose of striking color for a Tea." [ARA29/95] "Vigorous, very large thorns, . . . large flower, semi-double, well-formed, bright pink at the center, shaded yellow, the reverse of the petals being purplish red; winter-flowering." [JR6/186] "Lovely color." [Capt28] "Red flowers during the regular season, giving blossoms which are more pale but more profuse in the fall." [JR16/179] "An old favourite Tea rose, with lovely rose-crimson buds that too soon become full-blown flowers. It is only fairly strong growing, though it blooms freely." [OM] "Somewhat thin petals, and not very many of them." [F-M2] "Splendid buds and good habits." [BSA] "Buds long, clean, and handsome; not double enough for a show Rose, but excellent for cutting." [P1] "Very pretty in color and foliage, but subject to malformation; also, sometimes it lets fall its leaves, proving Bourbon descent . . . no scent." [JR13/92] "Resistant to mildew." [JR33/37] "Beautiful bud, but opens loose, with scanty petalage in heat; fine substance; fragrant; does not ball or discolor in heavy winds, but bleaches somewhat in heat. Has fine foliage and blooms constantly . . . beautiful bush in the garden." [Th2] "Free-flowering, especially on loamy soil." [Hn] "Without rival in its class. . . . The bud . . . is a splendid floral marvel; it grows to about 2.25 in [ca. 5.25 cm], and more, in length; its elongated, elegant form is always graceful . . . color, very bright deep rose, quite extraordinary, sumptuously shaded carmine; it is hardly possible to imagine anything more attractive . . . does not 'blue' . . . of great vigor . . . wood, somber red or bronze green depending upon its age, large and robust; amply furnished with thorns both large and small, fairly upright. Its foliage is a handsome somber green, quite shiny, and is large and full . . . it is nearly inexhaustibly floriferous, comparable to the noble 'Safrano' in this regard." [JR14/72–73] "4 × 3 [ft; ca. 1.25 × 1 m]." [B]

"One of the most remarkable of the many varieties which flourish in the Riviera. The flat filbert shaped bud, produced at the extremity of an unusually long and strong stem, is of clear carmine rose; as such and until half expanded is beautiful in the extreme, nothing in the rose-world can well be superior; with greater maturity alas! this excellence of form and colour vanishes. The flower when fully expanded is large and loose, in very short time owing to the flaccidity of its petals is deprived of all elegance of appearance; the colour, truly splendid in the earlier stage of flowering, degenerates into a mixture of mauve and purple, a false and unpleasant tint. Cut flowers allowed to open indoors are very superior to those which have been exposed to the sun. When planted in a strong rich loam it flourishes and grows in a manner truly surprising, two or three years suffice to turn a single little plant into a large tree or bush." [B&V] "So tremendous a philanthropist is 'Papa Gontier' that it seems almost disrespectful to name him with such familiar brevity. Anyhow, he loves the north as he loves the warm land of his raising; and rejoices in our [British] green summers and rain as much as ever in the sun-baked slopes and torrid seasons of Golfe Juan [*Nabonnand territory*]; always, everywhere, of a temper that you can absolutely rely on, and a beauty that no poor words of yours can ever hope to realise or express." [Fa]

"While visiting the wonderful nurseries of Mons Gontier père, greenhouse produce expert [*'primeuriste'*], on the Orléans road at Montrouge, one can be convinced that Horticulture is a science requiring intelligence to succeed. Mons Gontier is indeed one of our most able horticulturalists. And for Mons Gontier, there are no Seasons — he is able to produce in winter what nature gives us in summer. . . . Mons. Gontier's establishment has become a sort of horticultural laboratory in which he can create, at will, the most delicious fruits. . . . In seeing his establishment run so intelligently, in recalling the services rendered, I can only ask myself why this able horticulturalist has not yet received the high honors which have already been given to many of his associates. His work, so knowledgeably undertaken, so replete with judicious observation, is above all praise. . . . It is hard to understand how the Société impériale d'horticulture of Paris, which for several years has had several chevalierships in the Legion of Honor at its disposal, has been able to forget one of our celebrated horticulturalists; we hope that it will quickly repair this omission." [l'H59/219]

PAPILLON
Listed as a Climber. Also see the China supplement.

PARKS' YELLOW TEA-SCENTED CHINA
('Old Yellow Tea', *'R. odorata ochroleuca'*, 'Flavescens', 'Lutescens Flavescens', 'Lutescens flavescens jaune yellow')
Parks, 1824

"By the bye, I have had a Tea Rose in blossom in the vinery — of a sort I rarely see, and of which I really do not know the proper name. It used to grow over a cottage in Hertfordshire, which I knew many years ago, and the Hertfordshire nurseryman, from whom I got my standard, call it 'the old yellow China'. Is this the right name, and is the Rose more common than I imagine? Its petals are loose and thin, and of a pale primrose colour, and before it is fully out is at its best. Its leaves are large and handsome, and of glossy green. Its blossom has a certain half-bitter scent of Tea about it, to which the scent of no other Tea Rose can at all compare — it is so strong and aromatic." [Br] "The original Tea Rose. Pale yellow, double . . . 6 × 4 [ft; ca. 1.75 × 1.25 m]." [B] "Pale straw colour, extremely large bold petals; it is very splendid when half expanded, but when full blown is loose and not fully double; it bears an abundance of seed, but we have never produced a good rose from it. . . . In fresh sandy rich soil it grows very strong, and flowers profusely, but does not thrive in heavy soils." [Bu] "Light yellow, long, fine buds, fragrant. This has been the parent of many of our finest yellow Teas." [EL] "Vigorous; strong branches; large flower, full, globular; bud, remarkably handsome, elongated; same shade as 'Maréchal Niel'; color, bright yellow bordered sulphur; one of the best old Tea roses." [S] "Smooth glossy leaves and faint Tea-odour sufficiently show its affinity." [WRP] "Many of these lovely Roses very distinctly show the effect of the old Yellow Tea Rose upon the race, in the golden and sulphur base which adds such richness of tone to their countless

shades of white, pink, crimson and copper." [K1] "In France the Yellow Tea Rose is exceedingly popular, and in the summer and autumnal months hundreds of plants are sold in the flower markets of Paris, principally worked on little stems or 'demi-tiges'. They are brought to market in pots, with their heads partially enveloped in coloured paper in such an elegant and effective mode that it is scarcely possible to avoid being tempted to give two or three francs for such a pretty object." [R8] "Brought to England by John Dampier Parks in 1824, who was then collecting for the Royal Horticultural Society in China and Java." [EER] "My [*Buist's*] late partner, Mr. Hibbert, introduced this rose and the *White China* into this country [the U.S.A.] in 1828, and the first plants that were sold of them was in 1830; they are are found in thousands over every part of the United States." [Bu] "For delicacy of color, delightful fragrance and beauty of bud, has scarcely a peer, and, in my judgment, has never been excelled." [HstXXX:143]

PERLE DES JARDINS   PLATE 19
(trans., 'Garden-Pearl')
Levet, 1874
Seedling of 'Mme Falcot' (T).

"Bright straw-color, uncertain in form." [H] "Apricot suffused light buff." [Capt27] "Canary yellow, centres orange yellow, large and full. . . . One of the best." [P1] "Full . . . much copper and a little pink in the center." [ARA36/19] "Said to be of the highest merit; the flowers are very large, full, and well formed; it is vigorous in growth, color varying from pale yellow to deep canary-yellow. This will be a formidable rival to 'Maréchal Niel' because of its rich color and the continuous manner in which its flowers are produced." [HstXXX:236] "Flower large, full, globular, high-centered, opening well, coppery chrome yellow, with the petals' exteriors fading to cream yellow." [JR38/41] "Fragrant, shapely, sulphur to buff . . . wiry plant . . . 3 × 2 [ft; ca. 9 × 6 dm]." [B] "Canary-yellow, large or very large, full, well formed, stiff stems, very free; the leaflets are five to seven in number, deeply serrated, very dark and glaucous . . . fine . . . in open air." [EL] "Shows a high production of blooms . . . , but until a few weeks ago I had never seen a perfect one. The outer petals have always shriveled before the buds were ready to cut." [ARA25/99] "Fades too easily." [ARA25/105] "Needs warmth." [HRG] "As a rule balls in wet and damp." [Capt28] "Sometimes opening badly in centre." [DO] "A rose of shocking bad manners." [F-M2] "Very vigorous and persistent, and very good in a warmer climate, but a little too double for here [England]." [JR9/70] "Growth small; superseded by better roses." [ARA18/117] "Growth moderate; very fragrant." [Hn] "Tall, bushy, hardy; foliage very plentiful, black-spots slightly; bloom abundant in June, moderate in July, none later." [ARA18/127] "Exquisite tea-fragrance; a free-grower and bloomer . . . excellent in the open ground." [SBP] "Valuable for winter blooming." [Dr] "Foliage attractive and good. Stem fairly good . . . there seems to be a general opinion that it is better to grow the climbing sport rather than the bush form of this rose. Is found useful in Gulf Coast regions, but balls in damp winds." [Th2] "The most elegant and cherished rose for bouquets, it blooms the whole year [in Havana] without being pruned." [JR6/43]

PRESIDENT
Listed as 'Adam'.

QUEEN VICTORIA
Listed as 'Souvenir d'Un Ami'.

RAINBOW

Sievers, 1889

Sport of 'Papa Gontier' (T).

"The color of this lovely rose is a deep Mermet pink, striped and splashed in the most fanciful way with rich Gontier shades, just sufficient to add greatly to its beauty; the base of the petals is of a rich amber. The flowers are well carried on long stiff stems of the same general character as those of the 'Papa Gontier', but are most decidedly larger, sweeter, of greater substance, and produced much more freely." [CA93] "Semi-double pale pink blooms striped with carmine-red." [HRG] "Rosy flesh, splashed crimson. Distinct and free." [H] "Originated in California, and resembles its parent in all features, even in color, which is a light yellow at the base, shading upwards to a bright red, while on the exterior of the petals there are silvery stripes." [JR16/38] "Has a resemblance to 'Mme de Tartas'." [JR28/183] "Pretty; growth vigorous." [P1] "Though delicate, very nice." [JR36/188] Not to be confused with 'Improved Rainbow' (see supplement).

RED MAMAN COCHET

Listed as 'Niles Cochet'.

RIVAL DE PÆSTUM

Béluze, 1841

Considered a hybrid of China and Tea.

"Yellowish white, large, superb." [WRP] "Flower medium, full; floriferous; moderate vigor." [Cx] "Flower small, full." [S] "Beautiful, the flowers abundant, not full, but of charming purity and form." [Ro] "Bud tinged pink . . . white with blush and ivory base. Foliage dark . . . 3 × 2 [ft; ca. 9 × 6 dm]." [B] "Young shoots, thorns, and leaves rich glaucous plum colour. Long creamy buds are borne erect, but nod to open into loose, semi-double, ivory-white blooms. Gracious and floriferous. Slight tea-scent. 4 ft [ca. 1.25 m]." [T3]

ROSETTE DELIZY

P. Nabonnand, 1922

From 'Général Galliéni' (T) × 'Comtesse Bardi' (T).

"Yellow blooms with petals blushing pink to chestnut red as they open, pronounced tea fragrance." [HRG] "Flower large, full, well-formed; cadmium-yellow, with apricot reflexes, outer petals dark carmine. Very vigorous; profuse bloomer." [ARA23/152] "Although called yellow by its introducer, this nice little rose reminded us very much of 'Mrs. B. R. Cant', with much exaggerated light shadings." [ARA27/143] "Rose-pink, buff and apricot . . . deeper colouring on the outside . . . vigorous . . . 4 × 3 [ft; ca. 1.25 × 9 dm]." [B] "Perfect foliage, immune to mildew . . . strongly recommended." [Capt28] "The combination of colors (yellow, buff, gold, coral, pink, rose) and form often attain a singular perfection of beauty, particularly during the cooler months when the coloration is more delicate. The blossoms unfurl slowly, meanwhile wafting a delicious 'tropical fruit punch' perfume. The flower stems are strong and hold the blossoms upright if not beaten down by the rain. The plant blooms abundantly, in bursts, and grows vigorously, quickly reaching six ft or so [ca. 1.75 m]." [BCD]

RUBENS

Robert & Moreau, 1859

Not to be confused with Laffay's amaranthine HP of 1859, nor with Verdier's "pansy-colored" HP of 1864.

"Creamy-white with pale gold base, very double . . . blushing pink on edge." [HRG] "Rosy-flesh, deeper at centre, large, full, well formed, fine in the bud. An excellent variety." [EL] "White,

shaded with rose, centres bronzy yellow, large and full; form cupped, fine; growth vigorous. A good and distinct sort." [P1] "Fragrant; moderate vigor." [Cx] "White shaded rose . . . and if it can be grown with that delicate shade of pink it is magnificent. A red sandstone loam suits this variety best." [FRB] "Resembles ['Souvenir de la Malmaison'] a little in form, but its color is white washed with pink and not flesh." [JR20/44] "Of elegant bearing, very remontant, and delicately colored." [JF] "A good grower, producing strong clean shoots with very fine foliage, and quite capable as a short standard of covering the wall of a one-storied building. It is not liable to mildew, and the blooms, which are slightly pendant, can stand a little rain. They can be generally relied on to come of good shape, but the petals are thin and the form fleeting. The fine half-open buds are well supported by grand foliage, but the flowers are difficult to exhibit well, as they look weak and unsubstantial when shown with other Teas. It is pretty hardy, best as a standard and in cool weather: capital, early and late, against a dwarf wall: very free blooming and a good autumnal, thriving well on lightish soil." [F-M2] "Vigorous, with slender, nodding branches; bark smooth, light green; prickles reddish, elongated, compressed, enlarged at the base, upright, pointed; foliage shiny, of a handsome green, of 3–5 rounded-acuminate, finely dentate leaflets; leafstalk green, armed with several very fine little prickles; flower, to 3.5 in across [ca. 8 cm], full, globular, solitary, sometimes in twos or threes on vigorous branches . . . petals large, those of the center small and folded; flower stalk smooth, green, slender and nodding; very remontant; tender." [S] "Old but still pretty, and almost certain to give the first blossom of the season." [JR12/180]

RUBY GOLD

Listed as 'Jean Ducher'.

SAFRANO   PLATE 13

('Aimé Plantier')

Beauregard, 1839

Supposedly From 'Parks' Yellow' (T) × 'Mme Desprez' (B).

"Apricot yellow. Very free." [H] "Bright fawn." [HoBoIV/320] "When the bud opens in the morning, [it] is a fine saffron or dark orange colour, and is beautiful; in the forenoon it is blush, and in the afternoon a very poor white not worth notice." [Bu] "Large, double, dark yellow, copper towards the center." [JR1/2/8] "A fresh butter-yellow, washed carmine; flower large, imbricated, fragrant; very floriferous; vigorous." [Cx] "Pale apricot-buff with peach." [HRG] "Pointed flowers, semi-double . . . 4 × 3 [ft; ca. 1.25 × .9 m]." [B] "Lovely buds of sunset coloring." [ARA29/95] "Saffron to apricot in the bud, changing to pale buff, large and double; form cupped. A pretty and hardy variety, worthy of a place in every collection; growth vigorous." [P1] "Scarcely excelled by any [other] rose. Its half-opened bud is very beautiful, and of a rich, deep fawn color. When open, its form is poor, and its color a much lighter fawn. These fawn-colored roses have peculiar charms for us; and of them all, there are none more beautiful or richer than 'Safrano'." [SBP] "The action of light on the buds at an early stage is very remarkable in this Rose; frequently giving to the backs of half unfolded petals a perfectly rosy hue, distinctly defined by the expansion of the overlapping ones." [C] "Opens pale, with a poor centre of short petals." [Hk] "Does not last." [Capt27] "Carnation-scented." [JR33/101] "The seed organs are better developed than in almost any other kind." [EL] "Continuous supply of flowers." [L] "Never ceases blooming till the frosts." [K1] "Useful as a low decorative. Good growth and foliage; color pretty, not of best; excellent blooming qualities." [ARA18/114] "Foliage mildews, but it is a profuse and constant bloomer in Southern Zones." [Th2]

"Bronze foliage." [ARA40/36] "Good, early, vigorous — but less good late in the season; it loses its leaves." [JR9/70]

"It is to a devoted rose amateur, Mons de Beauregard, reserve officer, chevalier in the Legion of Honor, that we owe the development of the beautiful Tea rose 'Safrano'. . . . This variety, precious to florists, dates to 1839, and came most probably, according to particular information, from the seed of ['Parks' Yellow'], the one rose which, at that time, set seed." [JF] "Suffice it to say that 'Safrano', raised at Angers by Mons de Beauregard in 1837, is one of the prettiest yellow varieties known; it came from our old Yellow Tea, and was entered into commerce in the autuch hoopla; the journals of the time don't mention it [— *so true!*]. . . . Branches smooth, furnished with occasional thorns which are short and purple; very ample foliage, dark green above, glaucous beneath, on the old wood, and a very elegant purple — quite bright — on the young branches, particularly beneath. Leaves with five leaflets, elliptical, very slightly dentate, slightly stalked; stipules smooth, narrow, finely and delicately ciliate; leafstalk articulated at the second pair of leaflets, and furnished beneath with two or three prickles as well as numerous stiff hairs. Flower stem feeble, light red, bristling with glandular hairs, long, nearly 2 in [ca. 6 cm], but its position on an aborted branch adds as much again to its length . . . the ovary is short, inflated, smooth, purplish; the sepals short, often entire, or with only two very small projections like long teeth; they are slightly rugose, ciliate, lanate within; bud elongate, ovoid. Bush vigorous, easily recognized in the spring by the purple of its young foliage. The beauty, the delicious scent, the elegant bearing of the Tea Rose 'Safrano' assure it a foremost place in all collections." [PIB]

SNOWBIRD
Listed as a Hybrid Tea.

SOUVENIR D'ELISA VARDON
('Souvenir d'Elise Vardon')
Marest, 1854

"Outer petals cream, centre salmon and fawn, petals large, flowers full and generally perfect, though occasionally producing a hard centre; a most superb rose." [JC] "High centre . . . pale rosy salmon, more cream inside." [Hk] "Medium-sized, full, well-formed, soft salmon-pink." [JR2/142] "Yellowish-rose centre; very large and globular; foliage copper-coloured. Although at times difficult to grow, this beautiful rose should not be left out." [DO] "Fragrant, coppery-yellow overlaid with cream . . . 3 × 3 [ft; ca. 1 × 1 m]." [B] "Flesh color, shaded with rosy salmon, large, full; highly esteemed in England, but we have never admired it; refinement is lacking in the flower." [EL] "The petals are shell-shaped, of notable substance; its form is wonderful, and lasts in good condition for a long time. . . . Its color is a very light straw-yellow with yellowish-white, a little darker at the center, and lightly tinted pink around the edges of the young flowers. This variety has only moderate growth, but each bud formed will produce a pretty flower." [JR15/120] "Cream with rosy tint, a magnificent tea, if it is grown well. Unfortunately, it lacks vigor." [FRB] "Of great substance; the flowers are usually few but fine." [P2] "Not perpetual enough." [JR9/70] "Massive roses. Heavy foliage." [Dr] "Not liable to mildew, but easily injured by rain . . . when fine, the finest and best of all show roses . . . not for general cultivation." [F-M 2] "Seems to be very hardy." [I'H55/31] "Wood big, strong; long internodes. The smooth epidermis is, when young, reddish purple and covered with a 'bloom.' . . . Thorns, fairly numerous. . . . Leaves, pretty ample . . . smooth and a slightly yellowish light green, glossy, when growing frequently tinted purple above; beneath, whitish green, having a cottony appearance. . . . Flower stems large, long, strong, firmly supporting the blossoms. . . . Buds, fairly large, long, usually solitary at the branch-ends, flesh-pink and maroon-red when the sepals open. . . . Flowers large (about 3.5 in [ca. 8 cm]), very full, quite regular; outer petals very large, thick, compressed slightly, concave, reflexing strongly however at the tip, containing numerous smaller petals, crowded, also concave, but only with difficulty reflexing at the tip, giving the blossom a lightness, the form of an elegant cup, the edges of which are recurved; always opens well, whatever the weather; color, delicate flesh-pink shaded chamois-yellow, becoming a nearly white flesh around the edges; center, a pronounced coppery pink; the petal tips are often a brighter purplish-pink than the petal reverse. Scent, the usual tea-scent, but weaker. . . . The growth of this rose, which is vigorous and easy, assures it a flowering both abundant and prolonged. . . . Placed under the protection of the name of a young girl, 'Souvenir d'Elisa Vardon' offers a touching and symbolic reminder of grace and charm, qualities which it so effectively brings to mind." [PIB] "Exquisite." [H]

SOUVENIR DE PIERRE NOTTING   PLATE 71
Soupert & Notting, 1902
From 'Maréchal Niel' (N) × 'Maman Cochet' (T).

"Beautiful apricot yellow; flower very large, very full, quartered; very floriferous; very vigorous." [Cx] "Dark yellow to apricot. Discolors in wet weather." [Capt27] "Large, very double, high centered; pale yellow tipped pinkish and red. Profuse, continuous bloom . . . 2–4 [ft; ca. 6 dm–1.25 m]." [Lg] "Fragrant, double, orange-copper." [ARA29/95] "Often with lilac splashes near edges; form full. . . . Foliage generally well retained and immune from mildew under worst conditions." [Th2] "Small and delicate; delicious Tea odor. Bush slim." [ARA26/96] "Large, finely formed buds and flowers. . . . Good foliage. Strong bushy grower. Averages 50 blooms per season." [ARA21/92] "The shrub is compact with shiny foliage, and produces and abundance of flowers of a thrilling beauty. The bud is much bigger and longer than that of 'Maman Cochet'." [JR22/181] "The buds . . . are long and shapely, and of apricot-yellow colouring, though they are none too double, and in hot weather quickly open to full flowers. It grows well, and is quite a good Tea rose for the garden." [OM] "Weak outside petal . . . free flowering." [F-M] "The cross was made in May, 1894, and yielded 26 seeds which were sown November 17 of the same year. Of those, 12 successfully sprouted in March and April, 1895. One of these plants bloomed at the end of April, and was noted down as 'bud and flower very elongated' in the way of 'Maman Cochet'. Four open-air stocks were grafted from this mother plant, and bloomed magnificently in August, 1895. Ravishing in the beauty of their blossoms, we referred to them by the name 'Yellow Maman Cochet'. The plant is of great vigor without being 'climbing'; the wood is reddish, the foliage large and of a pretty somber green, and isn't attacked by 'silver-leaf' or mildew. The blossoms, of exceptional size, are full, of an admirable elongated form, and well-held. . . . I might add to the distinction of this flower by mentioning that it is of quite long duration, ordinarily 10–15 days. . . . The color is a very delicate China pink strongly tinted saffron, the center pure golden yellow. . . . In floriferousness it surpasses all the varieties which might be mentioned . . . [under glass] the exterior petals do not fall — they dry up, and the inner petals grow and renew the blossom. . . . Sometimes neither pistils nor stamens but rather small petals are found in the center of the blossom. These develop slowly, and thus help the duration of the flower." [JR23/109] "Excellent in every way." [K2]

SOUVENIR D'UN AMI

(trans., 'In Remembrance of a Friend'; syn., 'Mme Tixier', 'Queen Victoria')

Bélot-Défougère, 1846

Affiliated with 'Adam' (T).

"We have just received from Mons Bélot-Défougère, horticultor at Moulins, some samples of his magnificent Tea Rose 'Souvenir d'Un Ami'; it is a wonderful introduction, considering its form and size, its typical Tea Rose fragrance, and its color, a beautiful dark delicate pink. I believe it to be the most beautiful Tea yet, with its abundant and lasting bloom-period. . . . This rose, as with all Teas, gives better blossoms in September than during its first flowering in June." [R-H46] "Variable somewhat as to colour, but usually a pale or a deep rose; large, well-formed, and free." [DO] "One of the largest . . . a clear pale flesh, and may be termed of robust habit." [WHoIII] "Large, double, cupped, fragrant; pale rose-pink with salmon tints. Repeats bloom . . . 2–3 [ft; ca. 6–9 dm]." [Lg] "Moderately full, globular, delicate pink, flowers drooping on long stalks. Growth regular; fragrant." [Hn] "Very full; fine handsome foliage; a most superb rose for forcing or out of doors." [JC] "The queen of the tea-scented roses, and will rank the very first among them. Its habit is good, it blooms freely, and its large and beautifully imbricated flowers, when open, much resemble in form those of 'Souvenir de la Malmaison'. Its color is a delicate salmon, shaded with rose, and its general character highly recommends it as first-rate in every respect." [SBP] "Petals of the circumference are large, those of the center muddled and folded; flower stem pretty big; brown. Calyx rounded. Much recommended; one of the most vigorous of the Teas; flowers well formed; very beautiful bud; very attractive tea scent." [JF] "Flower soon loses colour and is apt to look dirty." [F-M2] "Vigorous; branches slender and flexuous; bark reddish green, primarily where the sun strikes; thorns brownish-red, very clinging, hooked, and very sharp; leaves olive green, lustrous, of 3–5 oval, rounded, pointed leaflets; leafstalks reddish, long, flexible, armed with a few sharp, hooked prickles; flower to three in across [ca. 7.5 cm], globular, concave, often solitary; color, light flesh-pink." [S] "Constitution is hardy, the foliage fine." [P2]

"One of the roses for memory. Bright pink, sweet-scented, hopeful, and as constant as the summer days, equally as interesting as its claims to beauty, life, and strength, is its tender history . . . not a line of prose or poetry has ever revealed the secret of its name. . . . Motives of delicacy seem to have prompted withholding the name of the friend. Was it death or estrangement? Was it a name under political ban? The name of the remembered friend folded forever in the heart of the rose; by whom and for whom named a mystery." [Dr] "The rose in question is still new. . . . It was two months ago or more that this Rose was added to our catalog of species and varieties in our trial garden. . . . We have been able to judge and predict for this rose the success which it merits. It is an introduction raised at Moulins . . . by an amateur, and which was sold to Mons Bélot-Défougère, who brought it into commerce. The name of the plant alludes to the friend who negotiated the deal. . . . A superb flower of the most beautiful intense flesh that one could hope to see. Petals numerous, imbricated and in a rosette as with the Centifolia, substantial, one could nearly call it immortal, giving this pretty rose a charm and a perfect form . . . flower stem brown, thick, strong. Ovary short, green; sepals entire, elongated, ciliated with small glandular hairs. . . . In 'Souvenir d'Un Ami', the delicacy of the tints and the brilliant sparkle of the nuances last as long as the blossom, and thus prolong the spring-like charms up to the hoarfrost of winter." [PIB] "One of the wonders and delights of my childhood was a fine plant . . . which grew up a pillar in the conservatory in Fir Grove near by. And when once the dear owners bestowed one of its flowers upon me, I think there was not a happier little girl in all Hampshire. . . . I determined it should be the first Tea Rose I planted when I made my garden here. . . . It never gets any special attention. . . . But each year its great bell-shaped fragrant flowers on their long slender stems show grandly against the Rhododendrons." [K1] "One of the brightest and most refreshing of the Teas." [Wr] "Mons Bélot-Défougère, having sold his nursery, has kept his seed business." [I'H52/188] "A distinguished horticulturalist, Mons Belot-Désfougères [*sic*], died January 13 [1868] at Moulins (Allier), where he had a horticultural establishment. He was 69 years old. Mons Belot-Désfougères had retired a long time since, and had turned over his form to Mons Marie, who still maintains the premises." [R-H68]

SUSAN LOUISE

Adams/Stocking, 1929

Seedling of 'Belle Portugaise' (Gigantea).

"Bud medium size, long-pointed, deep pink; flower medium size, semi-double, open, fairly lasting, slightly fragrant, flesh-pink, borne singly on average-length and strength stem. Foliage sufficient, disease-resistant. Growth very vigorous (4 to 5 ft. [ca. 1.25–1.5 m]), upright, bushy; profuse blooms (40–50), intermittent bloomer (about every six weeks)." [ARA30/220] "Blooms from the time of the first bloom until freezing weather . . . never without buds or blossoms." [ARA34/213] "A strong grower and free bloomer, with slight mildew . . . attractive bronzy foliage . . . very long buds and flowers of dainty coloring." [ARA36/216–217] "In a bad year, a good deal of mildew . . . it has been a real joy at Breeze Hill for several years; its long bud reminds the Editor of its distinctive parent 'Belle of Portugal'." [ARA35/204] "Blooms mid-winter in warm areas." [Lg] "A joy to all who have grown it." [ARA31/208]

SYLPH

W. Paul, 1895

Not to be confused with Vibert's yellowish-flesh Tea of 1838, 'La Sylphide'; nor with Boyau's flesh and lilac Tea of 1842, 'La Sylphide'; nor with the pink-bordered-white Gallica 'Sylphide'.

"Ivory white tinted with peach colour, centre creamy pink, a very lovely blending of colours; large, high-centred, and deep stiff petals; habit erect, a magnificent exhibition Rose, also good for garden decoration; hardy and vigorous." [P1] "Large and very free-flowering." [DO] "Free blooming, requiring fine weather and liberal treatment . . . large, of good pointed shape . . . white, tinted with pink and in some cases . . . violet . . . many do not come good . . . fair growth and habit with stiff wood." [F-M2]

THE BRIDE

May, 1885

Sport of 'Catherine Mermet' (T).

"White, suffused with lemon, a magnificent tea . . . sometimes the flowers have a slight pink shade at the extremity of the petals, which has a charming effect . . . a moderate grower." [FRB] "An ever blooming pure white Tea Rose, of large size and most perfect form. The buds are pointed and the ends of the petals are slightly curved back. It is a very free blooming variety and has the most delicious tea fragrance." [CA88] "Large, well-filled, cupped, creamy-white with a greenish-yellow high centre, the outer petals often tinted with pink. Growth moderately strong. A charming rose." [Hn] "This novelty is without a doubt the most beautiful white rose ever offered to the public. It is a sport of 'Catherine Mermet', which it resembles except in color, which is pure white.

The blossoms are beautiful and strong, and have the advantage of staying fresh, once cut, longer than any other variety. It is more floriferous than its mother" [May being quoted in JR10/71.] "The flowers are equal in quality to those of the parent rose, and are carried well above the foliage. In all respects a first-class Rose." [P1] "Better form [than 'Catherine Mermet']."[Hk] "Very fragant; very floriferous."[Cx] "Weak-growing, tender." [ARA18/124] "The plant is vigorous and very pretty when left to develop its natural form."[JR20/57] "Foliage slightly liable to mildew." [Th2] "The best import from America . . . it surpasses 'Niphetos' easily."[JR16/37] "Of great value. It speedily took a high rank, and gained a great reputation quite equal to that of the type, and is generally acknowledged as being one of the best half-dozen. In manners and customs it is similar to 'C. Mermet', but, like its sister sports, 'Bridesmaid' and 'Muriel Grahame', differs from it a little in form as well as colour. The true form of 'The Bride' is perhaps the nearest approach to globular, yet with a point, that we have . . . white with occasionally in a young bloom a greenish lemon tinge at the base of the petals. There are very few, if any, white Roses which are more lovely than a perfect flower of 'The Bride'."[F-M2]

THE HUGHES
Listed as 'Bridesmaid'.

TRIOMPHE DU LUXEMBOURG
('Triomphe de Luxembourg')
Hardy/Sylvain-Péan, 1835
"Salmon-pink blooms changing to buff-pink."[HRG] "Fire-red."[RR] "Flower full, having a coppery-red color." [R-H35] "Flesh colour, tinged with fawn and rose, very large and full; form, globular. Growth, vigorous. A beautiful Rose, and very sweet." [P] "Rosy blush." [Sx] "Buff-rose, large, good in the bud, of healthy habit; a desirable sort."[EL] "Fiery dawn red; flower very large, full; very vigorous."[Cx] "Bronzed rose."[JC] "Rosy pink, with fawn shading. Remarkably fine, handsome buds. Without a fault except that it is not a profuse bloomer. Popular since 1836. Magnificent form of growth. Abundant dark, leathery foliage."[Dr] "The flowers are often six in [ca. 1.5 dm] in diameter, of peculiar rosy-buff colour, and may be frequently seen of a yellowish-white or deep rose, according to season and situation; its growth is remarkably strong, in some soils producing shoots five ft long [ca. 1.5 m] in one season, flowering freely and perfectly, and is possessed of considerable fragrance."[Bu] "This very large and imposing flower has probably attracted more attention and been more extensively disseminated during the ten years of its existence, than any other of the Perpetual flowering classes, and at first it was sold as high as thirty to forty francs at Paris; the bud and flower are very large and distinct, the latter often five in [ca. 1.25 dm] or more in diameter, of globular form, fragrant, usually of aurora hue shaded with pink, but varying somewhat."[WRP] "Shrub vigorous with horizontal branches which are violet in the new growth; thorns equal, not numerous, wider at the base; leaves of three cordiform leaflets, glossy, margined reddish, pretty regularly dentate; flowers pretty numerous, well formed, in a cluster, often solitary, four in across [ca. 1 dm], borne on a strong, upright, glabrous stem; petals large, fawn mixed with pink, very nice scent. The calyx-tube is very short and bears some glandular hairs at its base. This superb variety, born at the Luxembourg Palace, is one of the most beautiful teas known."[An35/51] Alexandre Hardy, 1787–1876. Chief horticulturalist of the Luxembourg Palace in Paris: "M. Hardy is no stranger in the Rose world: One of his varieties alone ('Mme Hardy' [Damask]) would have sufficed to render his name popular; but he has been fortunate enough to raise

many others of first-rate properties, some bearing the after appellation of 'Du Luxembourg'. And how could it be otherwise, when he has devoted so many years to the cultivation of his flowers, and raised so many thousands of seedlings? He has never practised selling his Roses, but exchanges them with his friends for other plants. The Roses in the Gardens of the Luxembourg are seen from the public promenades; and M. Hardy is very courteous to foreigners. It is necessary to visit him early in the morning during the Rose season."[P]

WHITE DUCHESSE DE BRABANT
Listed as 'Mme Joseph Schwartz'.

WHITE MAMAN COCHET   PLATE 63
Cook, 1896
Sport of 'Maman Cochet' (T).
"Cream white, lightly pink at the edge of the petals; flower large, full, globular, fragrant; very floriferous; vigorous."[Cx] "Light lemon to cream-flesh, edged rose. Weak stems."[Capt27] "Large double flowers on stiff stems."[SHj] "White blushing pink in cool weather."[HRG] "A beautiful rose, nearly hardy, not always opening well. Affected by rain, when it looks bad, getting eaten into . . . it breaks off at the stem."[JR37/171] "It opens its flowers easily."[JR24/102] "Wonderful vigor . . . beautiful blooms that . . . never ball [in Bermuda]."[UB28] " 'Maman Cochet' and 'White Maman Cochet' are, without question, the best garden roses for southern Kansas . . . perfect blooms which are never malformed or blighted."[ARA21/171] "Of growth free and vigorous . . . the habit of the plant is very spreading, but often unequally balanced. . . . The foliage is dark green, glossy and good, free from mildew, but some of my friends have found it suffer from black spot. . . . The flowers are a grand pointed shape, and most beautiful when perfect, but rather too liable to come with a split centre . . . The petals are of fine lasting substance, very pale lemon with rose on the edges of the outer petals . . . if the weather be wet they rot wholesale in a woeful fashion. They have a slight Tea fragrance."[NRS/10] "Has the advantage over its mother of opening more easily even during rainy periods."[JR22/19] "Medium height, spreading, almost hardy; foliage very plentiful, black-spots somewhat; bloom almost abundant, continuous." [ARA18/128] "Does not fade easily, being one of the best of its color in this respect . . . does well on 'Mme Plantier' [HN] stock, and does not ball."[Th2] "The half-open buds are particularly lovely."[Hn] "Lacks quality in the flower."[ARA25/105] "Must be lightly pruned."[DO] "Quite the finest and best white Tea Rose of the pure pointed shape we have at present."[F-M2]

WILLIAM R. SMITH
('Charles Dingee', 'Jeanette Heller')
Bagg, 1908
From 'Maman Cochet' (T) × 'Mme Hoste' (T).
"Silver-flesh to cream-peach edged lilac. Balls in cold and dampness."[Capt27] "Rich creamy-white flushed with buff, full double blooms, compact plant."[HRG] "Exceedingly promising . . . excellent growth and habit . . . creamy white, the outside petals of the younger flowers being tinged a delicate pink . . . good shape and size . . . develops a split."[F-M] "Blooms medium to large, full, of excellent form, lasting five to seven days; . . . strong enduring fragrance. Excellent foliage . . . vigorous. . . . Averages 36 blooms per season. Very fine autumn bloomer. Hardy."[ARA21/91] "Large double flowers on stiff stems."[SHj] "Form lovely; fine size; lasting quality is almost perfect. Stem strong; growth good. Hardy for a Tea. . . . Immune from mildew

under worst conditions." [Th2] "The plant is spreading in growth, the foliage is exceptionally fine, a deep olive-green in color, it is thick and leathery and exceptionally free from disease. The buds and blooms are simply perfect in the fall." [C-Ps28] "Its growth is pretty much the same as 'Kaiserin Auguste Viktoria'; its solitary buds are long; its double flowers are of good size and a nice pale pink. It has the same foliage as 'Maman Cochet'." [JR32/22] "It grows well, and gives freely of good blooms. One of the best new Teas. The bloom is liable to come divided." [OM] "An extra fine late summer and autumn rose." [Dr] "Most attractive in color and form; growth and foliage good; lacks in blooming qualities." [ARA18/114] "Whether you live East, West, North or South, whether you wish one Rose or 1000, *here is a Rose which has our unqualified endorsement.* It will thrive abundantly in almost any reasonable location. The flowers are large, full and double and most exquisitely formed. The petals are so firm they look like wax, softly curled, colored cream with flesh tint tips, buff yellow base and the center a heart of pink. Perfect buds. The flowers are borne on long, strong stems, just right for making bouquets. Fragrance is delightful. You will admire the foliage too, deep green leaves on red stems and the new growth of rich garnet; the plant will grow for you vigorously, is among the hardiest in this class and blooms abundantly. TRY A ROSE BED FULL OF THIS ONE KIND." [C&Js10] "3 × 3 [ft; ca. 9 × 9 dm]." [B]

"Very likely it would interest you and others to know exactly how the rose 'William R. Smith' was produced. It happened years ago in my greenhouses, in Bridgeton, N.J. One morning, late in September or early in October, I noticed among a few roses in pots a 'Maman Cochet' in bloom, with fewer petals than usual but a perfect set of pistils. This was an opportunity that had never occurred before, or since for that matter, so I immediately began a search for pollen, and was quite provoked because the only rose with pollen to be found was a 'Mme Hoste', so I used that. When the hip was ripe the seeds were planted; five or six germinated and grew; one went ahead of all the rest and soon produced a fine little double flower. The rest of the plants were about half the size of this one, and had little, single, pink flowers. *This little double one*

was afterwards named 'William R. Smith'. That fall I moved to Philadelphia and kept it in the greenhouse of a friend. It would not do anything as a winter rose, so I lost a good bit of my interest in it. Afterwards I was told by a reliable party that my friend sold it for $500, but he never paid me a cent of it. . . . Mr. John Shellem, at a dinner party, sold the rose 'William R. Smith' to E.G. Hill for $500. The trouble with me was, that I lost my property in Bridgeton. I had to get work somewhere and struck it with Mr. Shellem. I went there in the fall and took two or three little seedling roses with me, and he let me plant them on a bench where some of his roses had died out. . . . Yes, I know that 'William R. Smith' has been renamed by several. One of the names is 'Charles Dingee'. Just a swindle! Why cannot people deal square? Sincerely yours, Richard Bagg." [ARA30/206] "Mr. John Shellum, of Philadelphia, never claimed to have originated the variety named 'William R. Smith', but I could never get from him the information as to who did originate the rose. . . . I bought the variety . . . with the understanding that I was to have all stock of the said rose. I had understood that Mr. Robert Craig had a few plants of the variety on trial, but these and all other plants of the same were to be given into my possession on the payment of $500, and as Mr. Shellum was being hard pressed for money at the time, I advanced him the amount ($500) in good faith, and he later sent me a considerable number of plants which, I supposed, were all of the variety, but I afterward found that he had let out plants on trial to five or six other parties. . . . The rose was christened at a dinner party in Philadelphia, by blooms furnished by Mr. Shellum. Mr. [Robert] Craig, I believe, was the principal mover in the affair, and thought it would be nice for it to bear the name of his old Scotch friend, William R. Smith. . . . We found that other parties had this rose and we never exploited it as a novelty. Very truly yours, E. G. Hill." [ARA30/207]

YELLOW MAMAN COCHET

Listed as 'Alexander Hill Gray'. See also 'Souvenir de Pierre Notting' and 'Souvenir de Jeanne Cabaud'.

Supplement

[A. BOUQUET]
('A. Boquet')
Liabaud, 1873

"White, striped." [LS] "Not very vigorous; flowers in a cluster; large, full, whitish pink." [S] "Coppery red." [CA90]

[ABBÉ GARROUTE]
Bonnaire, 1902

"Very vigorous well-branched bush. Flower very large, very full, always opening well. Color, coppery yellow within with carmine pink, petal edges golden china pink on a yellow ground. This beautiful variety, blooming singly, is extremely floriferous." [JR26/162] "Flowers very large and fragrant." [C&Js06]

ABRICOTÉE
('Fanny Dupuis')
Dupuis, 1843

"A large rose of a bright rosy fawn color, with a deeper centre, and superb." [WRP] "Yellow." [LS] "Apricot colour . . . margins

flesh . . . large and double; form cupped; growth moderate. A beautiful Rose." [P1] "Flower large, full, cupped; color, coppery yellow, and at the center apricot pink with yellow reflections. Growth vigorous; floriferous." [S] "Colour of flowers is as near as may be to that of the fruit from which this variety is named, of moderate size, not full, and rather untidy form, free-flowering; grows low with branching habit. Much resembles 'Mme Falcot'." [B&V] "Much esteemed." [M'I]

[ADÈLE DE BELLABRE]
Ducher fils, 1888

"Coppery pink." [LS] "Flowers reddish peach, shaded with carmine and yellow, large and full; growth vigorous." [CA93] "Dwarf." [JR12/166]

[ADÈLE JOUGANT]
Listed as 'Mlle Adèle Jougant'.

ALBERT HOFFMANN
Welter, 1904
From 'Souvenir de Catherine Guillot' (Ch) × 'Maman Cochet' (T).

"Pretty yellow bordered pink." [LS] Albert Hoffmann was the first official rosarian at Sangerhausen.

[ALBERT STOPFORD]
Nabonnand, 1898
From 'Général Schablikine' (T) × 'Papa Gontier' (T).

"An improved 'Bon Silène', color dark crimson rose, very vigorous and free blooming." [C&Js02] "Flower very large, full, solitary, with large sepals, very large thick petals; color, brilliant deep carmine pink, center coppery; exterior petals deep carmine, recurved elegantly; bud long; very well formed; borne on a long stem; large foliage; very strong wood and thorns; very vigorous bush; very floriferous; fragrant." [JR22/165]

ALEXANDRA
Listed as 'The Alexandra'.

[ALINE SISLEY]
Guillot fils, 1874

"Color varying from red to purplish rose." [CA88] "Large double and sweet; fine violet crimson; beautiful. 15 cts each." [C&Jf97] "Vigorous; foliage yellowish green; flower of the first rank, first in all votes; large, full, centifolia-form; color, deep purple mixed with red and deep violet." [S] "An 1869 seedling of Guillot fils, who released it to commerce in 1874. Vigorous and 'climbing,' as Mons Clarke says, it can be used on a fence . . . this variety is very good for forcing, and should be cut back to 4 to 6 eyes. It freezes at 10." [JR10/12]

ALIX ROUSSEL
Gamon, 1908
Yellow with a salmon center; large, full.

ALLIANCE FRANCO-RUSSE
Goinard, 1899

"Vigorous, floriferous and remontant, forming a bush which can attain 3–4 ft [ca. 1–1.25 m]. The young branches are upright, Russian-copper red, with slightly hooked thorns of the same color. The foliage looks rather like that of 'Perle des Jardins'. The leaves, composed of five leaflets, are large, regularly serrated, bright green, dark above, paler beneath, with a lightly colored midvein. The stem is strong and rigid, the same color as the young stems, and bearing . . . a long bud. The flower holds this form when just opening, but then becomes progressively flatter, finally reaching a diameter of about 3.5 in [ca. 8 cm]. The outermost petals are large, and fold back; the others are muddled. The Tea-yellow shade usually grades to salmon towards the center." [JR23/33] "An elegant bedder." [C&Js03]

[ALPHONSE KARR]
Nabonnand, 1878
Seedling of 'Duchess of Edinburgh' (T), and a parent of 'Mme Antoine Rébé' (T).
Not to be confused with the flesh HP of 1847.

"Rosy crimson." [EL] "Vigorous, a child of 'Duchess of Edinburgh', but even more vigorous; flower large, full, well-formed, imbricated, an illuminated crimson-maroon red, lighter at the center; floriferous. A wonderful variety." [JR3/9] "A valuable and

very beautiful tea rose; fine, large buds and flowers, full and double; color bright violet crimson, deeply shaded with purplish red; center brilliant carmine, strong grower and free bloomer." [CA88] "The *Journal des Roses* has lost one of its first collaborators in the person of Alphonse Karr, who died September 22 [1890] . . . at the age of 82. A most distinguished writer, Mons Karr not only provided a literary point of view, but also had a great reputation as a horticultural publicist. Born in Paris in 1808, Karr at first turned to teaching, and became a very young professor at the Lycée Bourbon. But his vocation was literature, which he was unable to resist, and before long was a great success at it. Having tried his hand, unsuccessfully, at politics, Mons Karr then devoted himself to horticulture, and retired to Nice around 1852, where he took the title of Gardener. . . . Upon the annexation of Nice, Mons Karr went to Saint-Raphaël, where he built his home 'Maison-Close,' in the garden of which he planted a rich collection of all sorts of flowers, and in the middle of which he whiled away many peaceful moments over the many years." [JR14/161] "It is to Alphonse Karr . . . that we owe the first tentative steps towards the commercial culture of the Rose. In 1870, he created, in his garden in Nice, the first set-up for growing and marketing the cut flowers. Since then, that branch of horticultural agriculture has undergone enormous development." [JR34/41] And let us not forget "the celebrated dog of Mons Alphonse Karr, 'Freschutz.' " [VPt46/84]

AMAZONE
Ducher, 1872
Seedling of 'Safrano'.

"Deep yellow, reverse of petals veined pink." [JR12/172] "Sulphur white." [JR1/7/6] "Golden yellow. Best in bud." [H] "Its color is fairly pure, while being veined, rather obviously, salmon-pink; its blossoms are very well formed." [JR10/45] "Very beautiful flower, much to be recommended, very floriferous; flowers in 3's or 4's at the ends of vigorous branches; very well formed; about 3.5 in across [ca. 8 cm], full, opens well; outer petals deep yellow, bordered pink." [S] "Of rather poor slender growth, with long pointed buds of a good deep yellow, a colour which is still much wanted in this class . . . very loose and wanting in centre, of no value as a free bloomer or autumnal, and can be no means be reckoned among the best." [F-M3] "A charming Tea Rose with yellow flowers; one of the most beautiful obtained by the late Mons Ducher of Lyon." [VH75/167]

[AMERICAN BANNER]
Cartwright, 1877
Sport of 'Bon Silène' (T).

"Flower medium-sized, semi-full; whitish pink striped lilac; exquisite perfume; dwarf bush; floriferous." [S]

ANDRÉ SCHWARTZ
Schwartz/Rolker, 1882

"Brilliant glowing scarlet, very bright and striking." [C&Js99] "Medium-sized or large, full, well-formed, deep crimson-red fading to cherry-red, sometimes striped white. This is the brightest color among Teas." [JR6/116] "Vigorous, well-branched, branches armed with occasional reddish, hooked thorns; the wood in smooth, without glands or bristles; it grows to perhaps a yard or so high [ca. 1 m]. . . . The leaves are numerous, remote, of 35 leaflets of which the upper pair is larger and the lower smaller; the leaflets are oblong or elliptical, glabrous, shiny above, pale and sometimes glaucous beneath, sharply toothed; stipules lacy, subulate; the color of the leaves and wood is reddish bronze when young, changing to a bronzy dark green in age. The flower is large-ish, well-formed, petals numerous, color varying from dark crimson red, striped white within, to cerise shaded carmine, the reverse of the petals being yellowish pink. As for blooming, it is very floriferous; from May until frost it is constantly in bloom." [JR10/73]

ANNA JUNG
Nabonnand, 1903
From 'Marie Van Houtte' × 'Général Schablikine'.

"Very large, semi-double, large petals, perfectly held; color, bright pink with some salmon, tinted madder; center coppery; bud long, on a strong stem, coppery carmine . . . extremely vigorous, making a strong bush; very large fairly dark foliage; very floriferous; fresh scent." [JR27/164]

[ANNIE COOK]
J. Cook, 1888
Seedling of 'Bon Silène'.

"Delicate shade of pink; a new American rose of great promise." [CA90] "Beautiful pink to white; what is more, it is a vigorous and abundant variety." [JR16/38]

[ANTOINE WEBER]
Weber, 1899

"Soft, rosy flesh, edge of petals bright rose, centre of flowers pale creamy yellow, sometimes tinted with salmon and fawn; large, full and double; makes strong, healthy bushes with fine foliage. An early and abundant bloomer, producing beautiful buds and large, handsome flowers through all the growing season." [C&Js02]

[ANTOINETTE DURIEU]
Godard, 1890
Seedling of 'Mme Caro' (T).

"Deep yellow." [LS] "Chrome yellow." [Jg]

AUGUSTE COMTE   PLATE 60
Soupert & Notting, 1895
From 'Marie Van Houtte' × 'Mme Lambard'.

"Very vigorous, flower large, magnificent 'Maman Cochet' form; color, madder pink, outer petals carmine red with a large darker border, center waxy flesh pink; barely open buds are extraordinarily handsome and of long duration. Very floriferous." [JR19/148] "Well branched; the beautiful dark green foliage is never attacked by mildew or the like . . . strong stem. . . . As an autumnal, it is one of the best." [JR24/8] "Constant and abundant bloomer." [C&Js98]

[AUREUS]
('Aurea')
Ducher, 1873

"Not very vigorous; branches upright, with irregular thorns, sometimes hooked, sometimes straight; flower medium-sized, full; coppery yellow." [S]

[BARON DE ST.-TRIVIERS]
Nabonnand, 1882
Seedling of 'Isabelle Nabonnand'.

"A delicate flesh-coloured rose shaded to copper, half-full, free-flowering and pretty." [B&V] "Soft rose, full and good shape; fragrant." [CA88] "Very vigorous, few thorns . . . ; flower very large, semi-full, very well formed, colored delicate flesh pink; very large petals; blooms in the winter." [JR6/186]

[BARONNE ADA]
Soupert & Notting, 1897
From 'Mme Lambard' (T) × 'Rêve d'Or' (N).

"Vigorous bush, flower very large, full, globular; color, cream white, the center magnificently chrome yellow; outer petals large, inner ones narrower. The buds are enormous. . . . Very fragrant and floriferous." [JR21/146]

[BARONNE HENRIETTE DE LOEW]
('Therese Welter')
Nabonnand, 1888
Said to come from a T × Ch cross.

"Large, full, beautiful pale pink, shaded with golden yellow in the center, pink outside; free flowering." [Hn] "One of the best white Tea roses for cutting." [JR16/179] "Not very full . . . floriferous, vigorous, having extra strong thorns, good habit, and with a dark green polished foliage which is very pretty and distinct. Especially fine as a standard, making when grown on its own roots a strong stem." [B&V] "Quite vigorous, forming wonderful thickets; wood short; blossom medium-sized, in a cluster, very full, elegantly perfumed; color, delicate pink nuanced golden yellow at the center; reverse of petals brighter pink. Top of the line for bedding; very floriferous, and good for the North." [JR12/147]

BAXTER BEAUTY
A. Clark, after 1936?
Hybrid Gigantea
Apricot-yellow sport of 'Lorraine Lee'.

BEAUTÉ INCONSTANTE
Listed as a Climber.

[BELLA]
California Nursery Co.?, 1890

"Yellowish white." [LS] "Pure white; good form; splendid large pointed buds." [CA90]

BERYL
A. Dickson, 1898

"Deep golden yellow; rather small but pretty buds." [P1] "Long bud." [JR28/31]

[BETTY BERKELEY]
Bernaix fils, 1903

"Bright red shading to crimson scarlet, buds very long, flowers medium size; robust habit of growth; distinct and beautiful." [C&Js08] "Growth robust, with moderately thick, bright somber green foliage. Buds solitary, elegantly upright on their stiff stems, ovoid, long, uniformly intense English red, with cochineal crimson and blood red. Blossom just the same color, with moderate size and fullness. Notable for the intensity and solidity of the uncommon shade." [JR27/147]

BLANCHE NABONNAND
Nabonnand, 1882

"Vigorous, semi-dwarf, flower very large, full, well-formed, imbricated, pure white, continuous . . . good for the North." [JR6/186]

[BOADICEA]
W. Paul, 1901
"Rich creamy pink edged with rose." [C&Js03] "Very pale peach delicately tinted pink and violet, the center being very rich pink. The ensemble of these different colors is charming and agreeable to the eye. The flower is large with a slightly high center, long; petals large and pretty thick. . . . Very hardy, elegant deportment, very pleasant fragrance. A good exhibition variety and at the same time a magnificent garden variety. The growth is vigorous and it gives flowers profusely in summer and fall." [JR25/85]

BURBANK
Burbank/Burpee, 1900
From 'Hermosa' (B) × a seedling of 'Bon Silène' (T); *or* from a seedling of 'Hermosa' × 'Bon Silène'.
"Light pink and crimson." [LS] "This grand Ever-blooming Rose comes from California, and has proved one of the hardiest and best ever-bloomers for garden planting, flowers 3 to 3.5 in across [ca. 89 cm], very double and sweet bright rose-pink shading to silver-rose. 15 cts." [C&Js05] "Bushy growth; blooms not distinctive or attractive." [ARA18/115] "Very superior in color to those [flowers] of the 'Hermosa', and the foliage of the plants is glossy and brilliant . . . a merit surpassing all the rest, is the power of resistance of the Burbank rose . . . to those ever-present foes . . . mildew and rust." [Lu]

[CAMILLE ROUX]
('Camille Raoux')
Nabonnand, 1885
"Very vigorous bush; thorns large and occasional; very floriferous; flower large, full, well formed, globular; color, bright red towards the center, pinkish at the petal edges." [JR9/166] "Fine large flowers, well filled out, very double and highly scented; color bright carmine rose, with fiery red centre [*sic*]; very striking and handsome." [CA93]

[CANADIAN BELLE]
Conard & Jones, 1907
"Rich creamy-buff with deep apricot centre finely shaded with rose and amber, delightfully perfumed." [C&Js07]

[CANARI]
Guillot père, 1852
"Canary yellow, beautiful little buds, delicate habit." [EL] "Clear pale yellow, beautiful only in the bud, free habit." [JC] "Full." [S] "Well doubled, silky bright yellow; to good effect as a bud." [I'H52/148] "A yellow flimsy thing according to modern notions." [F-M2] "Vigorous bush; flowers medium-sized, in clusters, canary yellow; very floriferous and pretty good as a bud." [I'H56/200]

[CAPITAINE LEFORT]
Bonnaire, 1888
From 'Socrate' × 'Catherine Mermet'.
"Purplish rose, reverse of petals paler; very large; buds long and large." [CA93] "Very vigorous, canes erect; . . . flower very large, beautiful purple pink, petals' reverse China pink. The flower sometimes reaches 12–14 cm across [ca. 5–5.5 in]." [JR12/146] "Rich violet crimson, good grower and bloomer." [C&Js98]

[CAPITAINE MILLET]
Ketten Bros., 1901
From 'Général Schablikine' × 'Mme A. Étienne' (T).
"Bright copper-red, dark carmine reverse." [RR] "Blossom light nasturtium red, deep carmine at the edges, gold ground, large, full, fragrant, bud long, opens well, stem strong. Growth vigorous, very floriferous." [JR25/146]

CAPTAIN PHILIP GREEN
Nabonnand, 1899
From 'Marie Van Houtte' × 'Devoniensis'.
"Cream with carmine." [LS] "Carmine pink." [Y̆] "Large, full, erect; large petals. Color, cream of the 'Marie Van Houtte' sort; beautiful long bud, solitary, carmine straw yellow, long stem. Handsome foliage, strong wood, strong thorns. Very vigorous, very floriferous. Fragrant." [JR23/179]

[CHAMOÏS]
Ducher, 1869
"Flower medium-sized, semi-full; color, fawn yellow sometimes changing to coppery yellow." [S] "Buds deep apricot, when fully opened nankeen colour, distinct, flowers small; habit moderate." [JC] " 'Chamois' . . . a *Noisette* in the form of its blossom and in its coloration, and a *Tea* in branching and foliage." [JR23/166]

[CHARLES DE FRANCIOSI]
Soupert & Notting, 1890
From 'Sylphide' × 'Mme Crombez'.
"Vigorous; buds long, well formed, and red-orange in color. Flower large, full, rosette-form; color, chrome yellow nuanced delicate salmon yellow; outer petals lightly tinted pink. This novelty is uni-flowered on upright canes; it is much to be recommended for forcing in winter." [JR14/147] "Mons Charles de Franciosi, president of the regional Société d'Horticulture du Nord de la France." [JR13/120]

CHARLES DE LEGRADY   PLATE 28
Pernet-Ducher, 1884
"This splendid rose is almost unexcelled for general planting; color fine chamois red, richly shaded with violet crimson; very sweet, and a constant bloomer; extra fine." [CA93] "Very vigorous, flower large, full, very well formed, of a beautiful coloration: carmine red passing to very dark China pink; the petal edges are somewhat silvery; the plant is very floriferous." [JR8/152] "Grows stout and bushy with fine foliage, and an early and constant bloomer; makes beautiful buds and large handsome flowers, very fragrant and highly valued for garden planting. Color fine chamois-red, passing to violet-crimson; a great bearer, covered with buds and bloom all through the growing season." [C&Js02] "Dedicated to Mons Charles de Legrady, Councilor of Royal Commerce, member of the municipality and Chamber of Commerce and Industry of Budapest." [JR11/105]

[CHARLES ROVOLLI]
('Charles Rovelli', 'Rovolli Charles')
Pernet père, 1876
"Large globular flowers, very full and double, delightfully fragrant; color, a lovely shade of brilliant carmine, changing to silver rose; center and base of petals clear, golden yellow; very beautiful." [CA88] "Bush straggling, nearly always late; this rose, despite its weakness . . . seems to us to be due some recognition because of its elegant buds, which are unrivalled in color; these buds are quite perfect; despite the feeble growth, one sees it produce large

or perhaps medium-sized buds which are long, solitary on the stem, of the most perfect form, and most elegantly held; their color is a superb delicate pink, darkening slightly and gradually to the petal-tips; these buds become a rose which is nearly large, full, well-formed, and delicate pink with a brighter center according to Mons Petit-Coq [*alias* Scipion Cochet]." [S]

[CHÂTEAU DES BERGERIES]
Widow Lédéchaux, 1886

"Vigorous with erect branches, which are reddish; thorns fairly numerous, large, slightly recurved, brown; leaves composed of 5 oval leaflets of a handsome light green, unequally and somewhat shallowly toothed; flowers large, globular, very full, pale canary yellow, darker at the center. The bud is large and well-formed." [JR10/171]

[CLAUDIUS LEVET]
Levet, 1886

"Velvety pink." [LS] "Carmine rose, salmon center; large and full." [CA90]

[COMTE AMÉDÉ DE FORAS]   PLATE 69
Gamon, 1900
From 'Luciole' (T) × 'G. Nabonnand' (T).

"China pink shaded saffron." [JR32/139] "This is a very charming new hardy Tea Rose, never before offered in this country [U.S.A.]. It is a perfectly lovely hardy ever-bloomer, makes large, elegantly-formed buds and extra fine full double flowers, with broad, thick petals, very durable and lasting. Color rich peachy pink or buff rose, with orange and fawn shading, a good healthy grower and a most constant and abundant bloomer, deliciously sweet." [C&Js05]

[COMTE CHANDON]
Soupert & Notting, 1894
From 'Lutea Flora' (T) × 'Coquette de Lyon' (T).

"Vigorous, hardy, flower large, full, outer petals light yellow lake, center ones shining chrome lemon yellow; one of the brightest of its class." [JR18/147] Parent of 'Gustav Sobry' (HT, Welter, 1902, yellow).

[COMTESSE ALBAN DE VILLENEUVE]
Nabonnand, 1881

"Vigorous; flower full, very well formed, erect; petals large and thick, coppery pink, nuanced, brightened with red at the center, shaded scarlet red. Novel coloration." [JR5/148]

[COMTESSE ANNA THUN]
Soupert & Notting, 1887
From 'Sylphide' × 'Mme Camille'.

"Flower large, full; exterior petals large; cupped; color, golden orange yellow nuanced saffron. Very fragrant. Vigorous." [JR11/152]

[COMTESSE BARDI]
Soupert & Notting, 1895
From 'Rêve d'Or' (N) × 'Mme Lambard' (T).
Not to be confused with "Comtesse de Bardi," Soupert & Notting's 1899 Tea, which was much the same color, but with a fawn center.

"Vigorous, flower large, full, petals large, beautiful form, light reddish coppery yellow, center coral red with golden reflections, sometimes yellow shaded reddish. Mignonette scent." [JR19/148]

COMTESSE DE CASERTA
Listed as 'Mme la Comtesse de Caserta'.

[COMTESSE DE FRIGNEUSE]
Guillot & fils, 1885
Seedling of 'Mme Damaizin'.

"Vigorous and very floriferous; flower large, full, well-formed; color, beautiful shining canary yellow; the elongated buds produce a beautiful effect. Of the first merit." [JR9/165] "More full than 'Mme Chédane-Guinoisseau', and the bud is longer." [JR10/184] "Beautifully colored foliage; buds like those of 'Niphetos', long and of good form, canary yellow, more delicate within. . . . A great rose for bedding, and blooms well in the autumn." [JR11/18] A parent of 'Mme Albert Bernardin' (T).

[COMTESSE DE LEUSSE]
Listed as 'Mlle la Comtesse de Leusse'.

COMTESSE DE NOGHERA
Nabonnand, 1902
From 'Reine Emma des Pays-Bas' (T) × 'Paul Nabonnand' (T).

"Pink and salmon." [LS] "Delicate salmon pink." [JR32/139]

[COMTESSE DE VITZTHUM]
('Comtesse de Vitzthun')
Soupert & Notting, 1890
From 'Mlle Adèle Jougant' × 'Perle des Jardins'.

"Vigorous; flower large, full, good form, exterior petals light yellow, center bright Naples yellow; extremely floriferous; particularly to be recommended for bedding." [JR14/147]

[COMTESSE DE WORONZOFF]
Listed as 'Regulus'.

[COMTESSE DUSY]
Soupert & Notting, 1893
From 'Innocente Pirola' (T) × 'Anna Olivier' (T).

"Vigorous, bushy, blossom large, full, well formed, imbricated; color, magnificent white; bud long and nicely shaped; very floriferous and long-lasting. Excellent for forcing. Fragrant." [JR17/147] "Long buds of an immaculate white." [JR23/41]

COMTESSE EMMELINE DE GUIGNÉ
Nabonnand, 1903
From 'Papa Gontier' (T) × 'Comtesse Festetics Hamilton' (T).

"Delicate flesh-pink." [LS] "Flower very large, full, perfect form, fragrant, large thick petals which recurve slightly, strong stem; color, brilliant carmine red tinted crimson, center coppery, warm tones; beautiful long elegant ovoid bud, coppery carmine; bushy, very vigorous, very floriferous; handsome dark green foliage." [JR27/164]

[COMTESSE EVA STARHEMBERG]
Soupert & Notting, 1890
From 'Étendard de Jeanne d'Arc' (N) × 'Sylphide' (T).

"Vigorous; good hold; flower large, full, good form; bud long; petals large and strong; color, cream yellow, center chrome-ochre; edge of outer petals lightly tinted pink. Of the first merit." [JR14/147]

COMTESSE FESTETICS HAMILTON
Nabonnand, 1892

"Flower large, full, well formed; petals flaring; nearly always solitary; bud long, very elegant; wood reddish; leaves very large, wavy, dark green; thorns numerous and very strong. Color, brilliant carmine red, coppery reflections in the center; exterior petals darker, ruddy at the edge. Very vigorous, very floriferous." [JR16/166]

[COMTESSE JULIE HUNYADY]   PLATE 43
('Comtesse Julie Hunyadi')
Soupert & Notting, 1888
From 'Mme Lambard' × 'Socrate'.

"Flower large, full; beautiful form and good hold; color, Naples yellow shaded greenish canary yellow; petals' edges lake pink. This beautiful variety sometimes produces red flowers and yellow flowers on the same plant. The blossoms obtained through forcing in a hot-house or frame, in winter, are always purest yellow." [JR12/147]

[COMTESSE LILY KINSKY]
Soupert & Notting, 1895
From 'Marie Van Houtte' (T) × 'Victor Pulliat' (T).

"Very vigorous bush; flower large, quite full, of good form; color, pearly white with a yellowish glow, the center a light waxy yellow sometimes nuanced flesh." [JR19/148] "Very sweet and pretty." [C&Js98]

[COMTESSE SOPHIE TORBY]
Nabonnand, 1902
From 'Reine Emma des Pays-Bas' (T) × 'Archiduc Joseph' (T).

"Flowers rich peachy-red with orange shading, highly perfumed; a strong grower and free bloomer." [C&Js07]

[COQUETTE DE LYON]
Ducher, 1871

"Pale yellow; medium, or small size; pretty in bud, and useful for bedding." [EL] "Canary-yellow, flowers tolerably full, buds pretty and clustering, habit moderate." [JC] "Well-formed." [JR3/28] "Growth vigorous." [CA88] "Medium growth; flower medium-sized, full; color, silky yellow." [S] "Well shaped flowers of moderate fulness, canary yellow of rather distinct a shade. A very charming and graceful rose flowering and flourishing well under glass; outside it prefers a shady situation. Rather delicate, which may be the reason why it is but seldom seen in England." [B&V]

CORALLINA
W. Paul, 1900

"Deep crimson pink." [JR30/15] "Deep rosy-crimson. Specially good in the bud and for autumn flowering." [H] "Crimson and deep vermilion, shaded vivid pink." [RR] "Almost single-flowered." [NRS10/55] "Deep rosy crimson, shaded with coral red; large petals, especially beautiful in the bud state. Growth vigorous. . . . A splendid autumnal bloomer. As free as the old pink Monthly Rose." [P1] "Small growth; very little bloom." [ARA18/115]

[CORINNA]
W. Paul, 1893

"Beautiful flesh-color shaded with rose and tinted with coppery-gold. The flowers are of large size, excellent shape and very freely produced." [C&Js98] "Has been compared to 'Luciole' in stature and flower color, but much more hardy; forms a very floriferous, vigorous bush. The flowers, borne on an upright firm stem, are more medium-sized than large, pink mixed with coppery yellow at the base of the petals. . . . The very long bud will be much besought for bouquets." [JR17/85]

[CORNELIA COOK]
('Mlle Denise de Reverseau')
A. Cook, 1855
Seedling of 'Devoniensis'.

"Flower white, generally tinted pale yellow; remarkably large and quite full. This blossom exhales the exquisite perfume of its mother, which is responsible for the favor it enjoys. For a great many years, this rose has been cultivated in great quantity in frames; it is only with the recent appearance of 'The Bride' that its culture under glass has diminished." [JR16/36] "Splendid long pointed buds, pure creamy-white sometimes tinged with pale rose. Excellent substance and very sweet." [C&Js02] "Medium vigor, flowers white tinted flesh, large and very full . . . not opening very well, but magnificent when well grown." [JR4/61] "Canes twiggy, green at the base, slightly reddish towards the tip; thorns pretty straight, red, remote; leaves of 5 or indeed 7 leaflets (but then the last pair is very small), oval-lanceolate, tinged red at the edge; petiole red; stipules large and ciliate; peduncle long, stiff; flower 8–9 cm across [nearly 4 in], white washed yellow, globular, outer petals shell-like; sepals long and lacy at the tip; ovary green and spherical. Unfortunately, the blossom sometimes has difficulty in opening, and pulls itself apart. . . . Prune short." [JR10/186]

DAVID PRADEL
Pradel, 1851

"Pale rose and lavender, mottled, a peculiar flower, often of an enormous size, habit free and tolerably hardy." [JC] "Rose, large and full." [FP] "Large, purplish, superb." [JR3/28] "Plant pretty vigorous; flowers large, full, lilac pink maculated purple. Good variety grafted and own-root." [I'H53/223] "Moderate growth; flower large, full, globular; color, light pink marbled lilac, yellow nubs." [S] "This is a grand rose for the garden and lawn and sure to give satisfaction. It is a clean, handsome grower and an early and profuse bloomer, both buds and flowers are extra large and beautiful; color rich rosy red, elegantly shaded. Very fragrant." [C&Js05] "A distinct, old, clear lilac-rose Tea of cutting value with good foliage. Unknown in this country and strongly recommended for southern climates." [ARA28/101] Possibly the parent of 'Homère' (T).

DR. FÉLIX GUYON
Mari/Jupeau, 1901

"Dark yellow, center lighter." [LS] "Deep orange, centre shaded with apricot. Very large, opens well, fine buds, and very sweet. Growth vigorous." [P1] "A yellow Tea . . . foliage immune to mildew and flower opens . . . easily. Distinctly good in southern seacoast climates." [ARA28/101] "Pretty deep green foliage and large handsome buds and flowers." [C&Js04] "Vigorous, bushy, good wood, nearly thornless, handsome foliage, beautiful buds, flowers very large, opening well; exterior color deep orange, interior shaded apricot; very fragrant, very floriferous." [JR24/147]

DR. GRANDVILLIERS   PLATE 53
Perny, 1891
From 'Isabelle Nabonnand' (T) × 'Aureus' (T).

"Reddish fawn." [LS] "Vigorous with upright branches having much foliage and thorns both numerous and hooked. The flower is medium-sized, full, of most graceful form, and of a shade of dark buff yellow; petals pretty large, sometimes tinted on the inside with the exterior crimson. The buds, which are very long, and usually solitary, are held flirtatiously on their stems, and grow in clusters, making a most charming sight." [JR15/146] "Dr. Grandvilliers, a well-known medical man who, for reasons of health, left Paris for Nice." [JR16/120]

[DR. POULEUR]   PLATE 64
('Dr. Poleur')
Ketten Bros., 1897
From 'Lady Zoë Brougham' (T) × 'Alphonse Karr' (T).

"Carmine-aurora, and copper-red. Globular."[ARA27/19] "Flower dawn gold, center coppery red, exterior petals striped reddish pink, medium to large, full, fragrant. Vigorous bush." [JR21/135136]

[DUC DE MAGENTA]
Margottin, 1859

"Pale flesh delicately tinted with fawn, petals large and of a fine waxy substance, flowers large, double and exquisitely formed, handsome dark foliage and good habit." [JC] "Flower medium-sized, very full and very well formed, notable because of its beautiful coloration of pink and salmon nuanced white; this variety scores highly in different polls." [S] "Rose coloured, shaded to salmon. When grown in a situation and under circumstances congenial to its taste, it nearly approaches a floral wonder. Does equally well as a bush, standard or climber, and grows to great size. I have seen a stem as big as a man's arm, and defended by enormous thorns. It produces an abundance of flowers of good size and regularity." [B&V]

[DUCHESS OF EDINBURGH]
('Prince Wasiltchikoff')
Nabonnand/Veitch, 1874
Seedling of 'Souvenir de David d'Angers' (T).
Not to be confused with the silvery pink HP by Bennett, also from 1874.

"Light red." [JR1/7/6] "Red carmine. This rose of moderate size flowers very abundantly, has a good effect when the flowers are half or three quarters expanded; when full after exposure to the sun, they lose colour, become limp and are distinctly vulgar." [B&V] "Flowers of good substance." [CA88] "Its flower, held erectly but not stiffly, attains the greatest size on the vigorous shoots. The blossom is well-formed, imbricated, and slightly cupped, with pretty concave petals . . . some rosarians find China characteristics in this variety." [JR9/55] "A Bengal with Tea blood. Crimson, turning lighter as the bud expands; of good size, moderately full." [EL] "The 'Duchess of Edinburgh' Rose, which was sent out some five or six years ago as a 'Crimson Tea'. The misleading name of 'Tea' induced hundreds of florists to attempt its growth under the same conditions as the 'Safrano' or 'Bon Silène' class, and the consequence was in every case almost complete failure. This type evidently partakes more of the Hybrid Perpetual than of the Tea class, and as they are hardy and deciduous, refuse to bloom in midwinter unless given the rest that their nature demands." [pH] "Vigorous with purple branches having a 'bloom,' and armed with dark and formidable thorns; leaves glaucous; flower cupped, well formed, very elegant, particularly before expansion; petals concave, well disposed, carmine red, whitish on the edge; enjoys much favor in England, where it is considered as being of the first merit; doubtless the foggy climate of Great Britain is more to its liking than is ours [of sunny France], as here it grows very little . . . but for that fault, it would pass as a good rose of some merit, above all because of the well-formed buds." [S]

DUCHESSE DE VALLOMBROSA
Nabonnand, 1879
Not to be confused with Schwartz's pink HP.

"Coppery red, distinct." [EL] "Coppery pink." [Y̆] "Very vigorous, flower very large, full, well formed, blooms in clusters, dark brick red with copper." [JR3/179] "Very floriferous; a new coloration." [S]

[DUCHESSE MARIE SALVIATI]
Soupert & Notting, 1889
From 'Mme Lambard' (T) × 'Mme Maurice Kuppenheim' (T).

"Growth vigorous, flower large, full, magnificent long buds, which open well; ground color orange, shaded and touched delicate flesh pink, center peachy red. Sometimes unshaded saffron yellow blossoms are produced. Much to be prized due to its scent of violets." [JR13/147]

[EDMOND DE BIAUZAT]
Levet, 1885
"Peach color, tinted with salmon; large and full." [CA93]

[EDMOND SABLAYROLLES]   PLATE 44
Bonnaire, 1888
From 'Souvenir de Victor Hugo' (T) × 'Mme Cusin' (T).

"Very vigorous with upright canes; pretty bronzy foliage; flower medium to large; edge of the blossom beautiful hydrangea pink, interior peach yellow with nasturtium reflections, passing to very bright carmine pink. This variety has such variable flowers that one might be inclined to think that several different varieties had been budded together on the same stock . . . constant bloom." [JR12/146]

[EDOUARD GAUTIER]
('Edouard Gauthier')
Pernet-Ducher, 1883
Seedling of 'Devoniensis'.

"Vigorous, looking like 'Jean Pernet'; flower large, full, globular, very well formed, of good hold; outer petals white, slightly pink on the reverse; interior buff yellow with light pink reflections." [JR7/160]

[ELISA FUGIER]   PLATE 48
('Eliza Fugier')
Bonnaire, 1890
From an unnamed Tea × 'Niphetos'.

"Very vigorous, canes upright though not very erect, looking much like 'Niphetos'. The bearing of the plant itself, however, is much better, not defoliating like 'Niphetos'; its foliage is more abundant, and is always green; bud very long; flower very large, very full, pure white lightly tinted soft yellow at the center, good for cut flowers and very hardy." [JR14/146] "Of moderate growth, highly spoken of at first, but at present not sustaining its reputation. Of nice pointed form, but not likely to prove first-class." [F-M3]

[ELISE HEYMANN]
Strassheim, 1891
From 'Mme Lambard' (T) × 'Mont Rosa' (T).

"Vigorous, flower very large, full, petals large, of very beautiful form; color, coppery yellow nuanced nankeen yellow, center peach-pink, reverse of the petals chrome yellow, touched light pink." [JR15/150] "Has the foliage, hold, doubleness, and scent of its mother 'Mme Lambard'; it is distinct only in its color, which is coppery yellow nuanced nankeen yellow; the center of the flower is somewhat peach-pink, while the exterior petals are chrome yellow nuanced light pink. 'Elise Heymann' is, above all, very good for pot culture and for cutting." [JR17/85]

[ELISE SAUVAGE]
Miellez, 1838

"Straw yellow." [LS] "Orange-yellow, medium size, full." [EL] "Pale yellow, centre orange, in dry weather very beautiful, but the most tender and delicate of all roses." [JC] "Flowers pale yellow, their centre sometimes inclining to buff, sometimes to orange, large and full; form, globular. One of the most beautiful, but of a rather delicate habit." [P] "Another of that description of colour [*'creamy yellow before it is deprived of that hue by the sun,' description applied to the early Tea 'Duchesse de Mecklenbourg'*]; though very different in growth [from 'Mecklenbourg'], which is not so strong, yet the flowers are very large, and make a splendid appearance when forced." [Bu] "A profuse bloomer." [CA88] *"Rivers* — 'Pale yellow — orange centre — superb', *Lane* — 'Fine deep straw — splendid,' *Wood* — 'Yellow — orange centre — superb' . . . *Curtis* — 'centre petals pale yellow — superb orange centre — globular and pendulous.' It lacks, we are well aware, that great desideratum, substance of petal, but in the greenhouse this hardly appears a disadvantage, for with its fine pendulous blossoms and distinct orange yellow centre, its graceful appearance can scarcely be exceeded. It was raised, we are informed, by Mons Mi[e]llez, a florist at Lisle, about ten years since. . . . We have had most success in blooming 'Elise', on worked plants against walls; when, planted in buds or borders, unless the situation be warm and well sheltered, we would advise that it be protected in winter." [C] "Branches slender, purplish green; thorns long, pointed, not much recurved, dark red; leaves comprised of three or five small, oval-pointed leaflets of a nice dark fresh green, paler beneath; rachis purplish; petiole purplish, prickly. Flower stalk glabrous, green, with two small bracts at the base. Calyx round, sepals entire, long, pointed. Flowers full, 6 cm [ca. 2 1/2 inches]; petals large, rounded, ragged in the center, yellowish white, darker at the nub." [An41/15] Parent of 'Princess of Wales' (T).

ÉMILIE CHARRIN
Listed as 'Mme Émilie Charrin'.

[ÉMILIE GONIN]
('Chameleon')
P. Guillot, 1896

"This is a beautiful ever-blooming rose; ivory white, delicately tinted with orange and fawn; each petal broadly edged with bright carmine red; very large and full; quite new and scarce." [C&Js99] "Vigorous bush with a very large, full, well-formed flower, white tinted orange yellow on a darker ground, each petal much bordered bright carmine. Fragrant." [JR20/147]

[EMPEREUR NICOLAS II]
Lévêque, 1903

"Handsome foliage and splendid large buds; dark rich crimson, flamed with brilliant scarlet." [C&Js07] "Very vigorous bush; beautiful dark green folige; flowers very large, full; very beautiful long buds; superbly colored aniline madder, very bright; always in bloom." [JR27/165]

[EMPRESS ALEXANDRA OF RUSSIA]
W. Paul, 1897

"Carmine red lightly tinted a nice shade of orange and tipped fiery red. It is large, globular, has vigorous growth and looks good whether as a plant or a cut flower." [JR21/50] "The flowers are large and double with full center and broad, thick petals. The buds are dark violet red, and the open flowers rich purplish lake deepening at centre to fiery crimson, large, full, and globular; a strong, vigorous grower, early and constant bloomer, very fragrant and desirable, quite hardy." [C&Js02]

ENCHANTRESS
W. Paul, 1896

"Cream white, fawn center; very large, globular, petals slightly folded at the edge; vigorous; abundant bloomer." [JR20/164] "For garden decoration this Rose is almost unequalled. The plant produces and continuous supply of strong growths crowned with fine trusses of lovely cream white, buff shaded blooms; large, full, and globular form. For winter blooming it stands unrivalled." [P1] "Small growth; winterkilled." [ARA18/115] "Was the product of a cross between a Tea and a China." [JR21/66] *See also* 'Morning Glow' (T).

[ENFANT DE LYON]
('Sweet Anise Rose')
Avoux & Crozy, 1858

"Beautiful creamy rose, delicately shaded with rich coppery yellow, and having the delightful fragrance of sweet anise, which is truly delicious and quite remarkable. It is a very pretty Rose, a constant bloomer and much admired." [C&Js02] "Very vigorous bush, beautiful foliage, flower large, flat, full, beautiful yellow fading to straw yellow." [JDR58/37]

[ERNEST METZ]
Guillot & fils, 1888

"Satiny pink. Shaded rose, very sweet." [C&Js98] "Vigorous bush; flower very large, quite full, opening well, very well formed, solitary; stem firm; bud long; color, very delicate carmine pink, center brighter, reverse of petals darker." [JR12/146]

ERZHERZOG FRANZ FERDINAND   PLATE 59
('Louis Lévêque')
Soupert & Notting, 1892
From 'Mlle Adèle Jougant' (T) × 'Adrienne Christophle' (N).

"Vigorous, flower large, full, cupped, outer petals large, peach red on a yellow ground, interior petals peony formation, beautiful dawn gold, the center being carmine lake with golden reflections; reverse often striped magenta red like 'Luciole' [T]. Very fragrant." [JR16/139] "Fair growth and form; not a profuse bloomer." [ARA18/115] Archduke Franz Ferdinand, 1863–1914; nephew of Emperor Franz Josef I of Austria; his assassination in Sarajevo sparked World War I.

[ESTHER PRADEL]
('Estelle Pradel')
Pradel, 1860

"Bush vigorous; leaves large, dark green, shiny; flower medium-sized, full; color, chamois, nub darker, passing to salmon." [S] "Lovely pure white buds; flowers medium size, full and sweet; profuse bloomer." [CA93] "Low bushy grower." [C&Js05]

[ETHEL BROWNLOW]
('Miss Ethel Brownlow')
A. Dickson, 1887

"Salmon pink." [LS] "Of robust nature, with rich glossy foliage, blooming very freely and abundantly. Flowers large, of strong substance, opening well, and perfectly formed; petals very thick, long, round, and very smooth. Color, bright salmon red shaded yellow at the base of the petals." [JR11/93] "Not a very strong grower, but in this and other respects it seems to have decidedly improved, for it was by no means a general success with amateurs for the first three or four years. Now it is fast rising in reputation, and it was plain, when first shown, that it was the best example of the imbricated form among Teas, if not among all Roses. The blooms come generally regular, and the well-formed point in the centre of good perfectly imbricated petals, which is the typical form but unfortunately seldom attained by the full-sized flowers, makes it a great favorite with those to whom shape is the first thing. It has very good lasting qualities in form, but the freshness of the first colour is very difficult to maintain and shading will destroy it. Rather late, and best as a standard, it requires fine hot weather, and needs protection against rain. Very free-flowering, the buds must be well thinned to get exhibition blooms, but are charming half-open in themselves." [F-M3] "Dedicated to the well-known English novelist." [JR17/177]

[EXADELPHÉ]
Nabonnand, 1885

"Very vigorous, branching, big-wooded, very floriferous; flower very large, very full, very well formed; color, quite yellow; extremely fragrant." [JR9/166] "A good strong grower and free bloomer; large, full, well-formed flowers, quite double and fragrant; color, fine canary yellow, passing to rich creamy white, faintly tinged with pale lemon; very sweet." [CA90]

[F. L. SEGERS]
Ketten Bros., 1898
From 'Safrano' (T) × 'Adam' (T).

"Carminey scarlet nuanced yellowish pink, creamy white around the edge, touched mauve pink; large, very full, fragrant; bud long, opening well, strong peduncle. Vigorous bush." [JR22/132] "Extra large flowers, fine cupped form, full and deep, lovely soft rosy-pink, very sweet and handsome." [C&Js02]

[FLAVIEN BUDILLON]
Nabonnand, 1885

"Broad, thick petals; delicate pale flesh; highly perfumed." [CA90] "Very vigorous, very remontant, with big wood and long thorns; flower very large, very full, globular, imbricated, cupped; color, delicate pink." [JR9/166]

[FORTUNA]
('The New Riviera Rose')
W. Paul, 1902

"Flower of large size; color apricot nuanced chamois, outer petals lightly tinted red." [JR26/87] "A distinguished beauty." [C&Js07]

[FRANCES E. WILLARD]
('President Cleveland')
Good & Reese/Conard & Jones, 1899
From 'Marie Guillot' (T) × 'Coquette de Lyon' (T).

"Greenish-white." [Jg] "Pure white." [CA10] "Tall, almost climbing, many strong shoots; foliage plentiful, healthy; bloom free, almost continuous." [ARA18/125] "Named in honor of the noble life and work of Frances E. Willard, The Great Apostle of Temperance and Purity, and the Late Venerated President of the W.C.T.U. The 'White Rose' being the Emblem of this Society, it seems eminently fitting that the most beautiful of all White Roses should be named in commemoration of one who has given her life for the cause she loved, and the memory of whose good works will always live in the hearts of her country women. This beautiful rose is a strong vigorous grower and true ever-bloomer, making handsome bushes. The buds and flowers are of the very largest size — pure snow white and so full and perfect they resemble a Camellia. The fragrance is delicious, and it is claimed to be by far the grandest of all Pure White Ever-Blooming Roses." [C&Js01]

[FRANCISCA PRIES]
Pries/Ketten Bros., 1888

"Pink striped salmon." [LS] "One of the most robust growing among the Teas, not climbing, but making long, sturdy shoots. Flowers medium size, creamy white, shaded with amber; exceedingly free flowering." [CA93] "Flower blush white, center coppery saffron, outer petals washed pink; pretty large, full, cupped fragrant. Vigorous growth; floriferous." [JR12/181]

[FRAU GEHEIMRAT VON BOCH]
('Mme Von Boch')
Lambert, 1898
From 'Princesse Alice de Monaco' (T) × 'Duchesse Marie Salviati' (T).

"Very vigorous growth, very floriferous, with very sturdy flowers; blooms from June to November. The flowers are large, strong, quite full, of beautiful form, opening well with large petals; the buds are large indeed and long, on long stems. The color is cream with carmine on the back of the exterior petals. The perfume is of the most penetrating, and most agreeable to the nose. Equally good as garden plant or exhibition variety, outside or in. Dedicated to the wife of a minister of commerce and the interior." [JR21/51]

FÜRSTIN INFANTIN VON HOHENZOLLERN
('Fürstin Hohenzollern')
Bräuer/Ketten Bros., 1898
From 'Mlle la Comtesse de Leusse' (T) × 'Marie Van Houtte' (T).

"Lilac pink on an ochre yellow ground, large, full, fragrant. Vigorous, floriferous, often blooming in clusters." [JR22/133] "Exquisite lilac rose, on ochre ground; a fascinating combination seldom seen; has a delightful delicate fragrance. A vigorous grower and good bloomer." [C&Js05]

G. NABONNAND   PLATE 45
Nabonnand, 1888

"Pale rose shaded with yellow; very large petals and handsome buds. Exceedingly free." [P1] "Pale flesh, shaded rose. Long-pointed flower." [H] "Perfect form . . . strong stem, very long branches, extraordinarily profuse." [JR31/119] "Very vigorous; wood a handsome bronze-green; handsome foliage; bud very long, well held, flesh pink, gold reflections; flower very large, full; very large petals, which are erect; color, delicate pink shaded with yellow, a very fine color; very floriferous, quite a marvel, and excellent for winter flowers." [JR12/147] "Some say this is the best tea-rose of all, a little like 'Gloire de Dijon', but gentler and a better colour. It is very strong, never suffers from mildew, and grows high." [HmC] "Very large flowers, light rose shaded to yellow, not very full with extra large petals, erect. The bud is elongated, big, and of a clear rose colour, very vigorous, grows to a great size and most floriferous. After 'Paul Neyron', I know of no other rose producing blooms of such magnitude, but those in question possess the additional charm of being of good shape and delicate. Magnificent, hardy, and easy to cultivate, this rose deserves a conspicuous place in every garden, but strange to say it is by no means well-known or generally grown." [B&V]

[GÉNÉRAL D. MERTCHANSKY]
Nabonnand, 1890

"Exquisite rosy flesh; of good large size, fine full form; petals somewhat imbricated; a good grower and constant bloomer." [CA96] "Rose to a tender scarlet, with bright centre. The bud very attractive." [B&V] "Very vigorous; flower large, full, erect, very elegant, perfect in hold and form. Pretty semi-long bud, which opens well. Wood reddish; medium thorns. Color, beautiful delicate flesh pink, center more intense. Superb; very floriferous." [JR14/165]

[GENERAL ROBERT E. LEE]
Good & Reese, 1896

"A beautiful new tea rose originated in the South; color, soft apricot yellow, delicately tinted with rose." [C&Js98]

[GÉNÉRAL TARTAS]
('Général De Tartas')
Bernède, 1860

"Dark rose, large and full." [FP] "Brilliant carmine, shaded with violet purple; large and fragrant." [CA88] "Bush vigorous; canes long, very flexile, bright green touched violet on the sunny side; thorns flattened, hooked; leaves deep bright yellowish green; blossom medium-sized, full, very well formed; color, bright crimson; very remontant and blooming abundantly until frost." [S]

[GEORGES FARBER]
Bernaix, 1889

"Shrub medium-sized, very vigorous; beautiful bright green foliage; buds longly oval, conical, elegantly formed; flower borne on a long, strong stem; flower pretty large, with strong thick petals uniquely pointed, outer petals velvety purple, veined and reticulated with somber fiery red, center petals cochineal red passing to light carminey cerise red on the obverse, paler pink on the reverse, making an agreeable contrast." [JR13/162]

[GEORGES SCHWARTZ]
Widow Schwartz, 1899
From 'Kaiserin Auguste Viktoria' (HT) × 'Souvenir de Mme Levet' (T).

"Growth very vigorous; foliage deep green tinted purple; bud long, deep chrome yellow; flower large, full, perfect form, borne on a long, strong stem, keeping until fully open its magnificent deep canary yellow color. Very floriferous, scent good and penetrating, novel coloration. Much to be recommended for bedding." [JR23/178]

GLOIRE DE DEVENTER
Soupert & Notting, 1896
From 'Devoniensis' (T) × 'Distinction' (HT).

"Very vigorous, handsome foliage, long bud; flower large, full, opens well, cupped, well held; cream white, reverse blush pink, center darker. The contrast between these colors, and the graceful poise of the blossom, gives it its own distinctive look. Very fragrant." [JR20/148]

[GOLDEN GATE]
Jones/Dingee & Conard, 1892
From 'Safrano' × 'Cornelia Cook'.

"Cream and orange." [LS] "The flowers are extra large, very full and finely formed; the buds are long and of the most desirable form; the color is a rich creamy white, beautifully tinged with fine golden yellow." [CA93] "Most remarkable . . . its flowers are very large and quite double; the buds are long and pointed, showing the magnificent 'Niphetos' form; its color is a rich creamy white with the heart and petal bases delicate golden yellow frequently tinted light pink; it blooms very freely." [JR15/89] "Of only fair growth, with habit and foliage somewhat similar to 'Niphetos'. A Rose for exhibitors, capable of producing very large, finely shaped, creamy white blooms, but not vigorous or free-flowering enough for general purposes. The name, of course, is taken from the harbour of San Francisco: but English gardeners are naturally apt to expect it to be yellow: whereas it is certainly not golden, any more than it is like a gate." [F-M2] "Insufficiently known." [JR16/38]

[GOLDEN ORIOLE]
('Shepherd's Oriole')
Shepherd, 1905
Sport of 'William Allen Richardson' (N).

"Deep saffron-yellow to deep cream; blooms are small but very double; in heat retains its color and keeps a high center; gives many blooms at one time; of decorative value only. Foliage perfect and well retained. Grows to 5 ft, with sturdy habit . . . while showing some Noisette characteristics of wood and foliage, is not a climber and blooms singly. Distinct and beautiful." [Th2]

[GRAND-DUC PIERRE DE RUSSIE]   PLATE 61
Perny/S. Cochet, 1895

"Rich rose, passing to salmon shades, a strong vigorous grower and good bloomer." [C&Js98] "Enormous flowers and buds of perfect form opening well. Color, pale pink veined darker pink. Charming." [JR19/165]

GRAZIELLA
Dubreuil, 1893

"Vigorous, plant nicely shaped, leaves large, thick, brilliant. Flower very large, expands slowly, petals satiny, brilliant, cream white tinted blush, like 'Souvenir de la Malmaison'." [JR17/166]

[GROSSHERZOGIN MATHILDE]
('Grand Duchess Hilda')
Vogler, 1869
Seedling of 'Bougère'.

"Vigorous; flower large, nearly full; very floriferous; color, greenish white, like lily green." [S] "Moderate in growth, but vigorous enough to produce nice flowering wood; flowers have large outer petals. The color is nankeen yellow with ochre center." [CA96]

[H. PLANTAGENET COMTE D'ANJOU]
Tesnier, 1892

"Brilliant China rose in color, with deeper shadings. A moderately good grower, producing an abundance of nicely formed flowers." [CA95]

[HELEN GOOD]
Good & Reese, 1906
Sport of 'Maman Cochet'.

"Soft light pink, darker shadings. Varies." [ARA27/20] "A rose that has all the good points of the Cochets. The buds are of exquisite form; color is a delicate yellow, suffused with pink, with deeper edge." [CA10] "Has good form, size, and stem, and is lasting. Foliage very good." [Th2] "Good in growth, foliage and form; color pleasing, not of the best; fair in blooming." [ARA18/11] "Moderate height, rather compact; foliage sufficient to plentiful, healthy; bloom moderate, intermittent in flower three-fourths of the time." [ARA18/125]

HELVETIA
(='Louis Richard'?)
Ducher, 1873

"Coppery salmon." [LS] "Pink, tinged with fawn." [EL] "Growth vigorous; flower large, full, globular; color, salmon pink with peach pink center." [S] "Small growth; not a bloomer." [ARA18/116]

HENRY BENNETT
Levet, 1872

"Growth moderately vigorous; flower medium-sized, full, very fragrant; color, light pink with a yellow deep sulphur center." [S]

[HENRY M. STANLEY]
Dingee & Conard, 1891
From 'Mme Lambard' × 'Comtesse Riza du Parc'.

"Deep chamois rose, delicately tinged with fine apricot yellow petals, bordered with bright carmine red." [C&Js02] "Pink and apricot." [LS] "Its color is a rare shade of pink-amber of the most delicate from the middle out, shaded with apricot yellow. Very full and fragrant." [JR16/38] "Makes a beautiful contrast to 'Golden Gate' . . . edged and bordered with rich carmine; deliciously scented." [CA93] "Vigorous and healthy, of elegant, neat growth; flowers of good size, quite regular, quite full, and very fragrant; light pink, sometimes nuanced salmon. This is a very freely blooming rose producing magnificent buds; presumably forcing conditions will give the best results." [JR15/88] "Low-growing, rather compact, reasonably hardy; foliage plentiful, healthy; bloom moderate, intermittent, in flower about one-half the time, scattered well through season." [ARA18/125]

[HERMANCE LOUISA DE LA RIVE]
Nabonnand, 1882

"Vigorous; flower large, full, well formed, imbricated; color, beautiful flesh white, pinker towards the center, perfect form; a magnificent variety, one of the most beautiful of the genre. Blooms in winter and continuously." [JR6/186] "Large, full and imbricated." [B&V]

[HONOURABLE EDITH GIFFORD]
('Miss Edidth Gifford')
Guillot fils, 1882
From 'Mme Falcot' × 'Perle des Jardins'.

"Very perfect white, with sometimes a pale pink centre. A very free bloomer, and a rose no garden can do without. Strong habits, and bushy but not high." [HmC] "Creamy white with centre of flesh, large, full and well formed flowers, free, thoroughly reliable and considered excellent for exhibition purposes, good growth, fine foliage, rather liable to mildew, in other respects giving little trouble and thrives well." [B&V] "Vigorous, of good stature, blossoms large or very large, full, very well formed; superb

long buds; color, flesh white, light yellow ground, center salmon pink fading to white; very floriferous." [S] "Of good stout stiff but not long growth, with fine foliage, liable to mildew in the autumn, and requiring protection from rain. A very good Tea Rose indeed, an unusually large proportion of the blooms coming good, of fine shape, petal, centre and size. It is thoroughly reliable, an excellent show Rose, one of the earliest, very free blooming, a good autumnal and does excellently as a dwarf. A good Rose, and a 'good doer,' giving little trouble and ample returns." [F-M3] Parent of 'Mme Jenny Gillemot' (HT).

[HORTENISA]
(trans., 'Hydrangea'; *not* = 'Hortense')
Ducher, 1870

"[Growth:] free. . . . Rose color, back of petals a washed-out pink; a coarse, poor sort." [EL] "Moderate growth; flower large, very full; color, pink with yellowish reflections." [S] Parent of 'Mama Looymans' (HT).

HOVYN DE TRONCHÈRE
Puyravaud, 1899
Seedling of 'Regulus' (T).

"Coppery red, petals' edges silvery pink, ground of golden yellow, borne on strong stem, large, full, plump, fragrant; growth vigorous, very bushy, slightly thorny, beautiful green foliage. Very floriferous . . . dedicated to a rose fancier from Guîtres." [JR22/133]

[IMPÉRATRICE MARIA FÉODOROWNA DE RUSSIE]
('Empress Marie of Russia')
Nabonnand, 1883

"Fine, stately flowers, extra large, very full, and delightfully sweet; color, fine canary yellow, passing to white, delicately tinged with pale lemon; very beautiful." [CA90] "Very vigorous, with large thorns; flower very large, imbricated, with very large petals, full, well formed; color, yellowish white, marbled pink, nuanced, picoteed." [JR7/183]

[IMPROVED RAINBOW]
Burbank?, by 1896

"Entirely distinct in its markings. The 'Improved Rainbow' instead of being broadly marked like its parent, the 'Rainbow', is penciled with brightest 'Gontier' color, every petal in every flower, and base of petals of bright amber color, making a very distinct and charming flower." [CA96] "Just what the old 'Rainbow' ought to have been but never was. The color is a lovely shade of deep coral pink elegantly striped and mottled with intense shining crimson; finely colored at center with rich glowing amber, makes beautiful buds, and the flowers are extra large, very sweet and of greatest depth and substance." [C&Js98] "Fair growth and good foliage; distinct color." [ARA18/118]

[INNOCENTE PIROLA]
Widow Ducher, 1878

"A very perfect-shaped white rose. A little liable to mildew, and it likes a rich soil." [HmC] "Clouded white, medium size, full, well-formed buds. In the style of 'Niphetos' [T], but is inferior to it in all respects save mere vigor of growth." [EL] "Only fair in growth and foliage; requires rich soil and in many places does not do well as a dwarf; rather liable to mildew, but for a white Tea Rose little injured by rain. The blooms come well, and the typical shape is unique, one of the most perfect we have, something like the whorl of a shell. Fairly free in bloom, and lasting, but not often very large till overblown. A first-class Rose, fine in petal and centre, it should be a great favorite with those purists (with whom I have much sympathy) who insist upon regularity and perfection of shape as the one thing desirable above all others." [F-M3] "Growth very vigorous; canes short and upright, perfectly held; blossom very large, full, well formed, with big long buds; color, pure white, sometimes lightly blushing. Considering its vigor and abundance, replaces 'Niphetos'." [JR2/167]

[ISABELLE NABONNAND]
Nabonnand, 1873

"Its blush-centred white blooms are fairly double, and yet open freely through the winter." [J] "Flower of chamois leather tinge with darker centre, large, half full and very sweet. A very pretty and popular rose." [B&V] "Growth extremely vigorous, large and abundant foliage, large fawn-pink roses, darker at the center, delicious fragrance." [JR5/21] A parent of 'Dr. Grandvilliers' (T).

[IVORY]
('White Golden Gate')
Durfee/American Rose Co., 1901
Sport of 'Golden Gate'.

"Large pure white flowers." [CA02] "Perfect form; ivory white, which keeps until the blossom is done; irreproachable hold and quite full." [JR25/65] "The beautiful 'Golden Gate' Rose is now so well known that to say ' 'Ivory' is exactly like it, only different in color,' is all the recommendation that it needed to place it in the front rank of our most beautiful Ever-blooming Roses. It is an exceedingly free bloomer, sure to be covered with buds and flowers as long as the bush is kept in growing condition. The flowers are large, full and sweet, clear ivory white, and highly valued for cutting and all kinds of florists' work." [C&Js03]

[J.-B. VARONNE]
('J.-B. Waronne')
Guillot & fils, 1889

"Vigorous bush; flowers large, full, well formed; color varies from deep China pink to very bright carmine, with a coppery yellow center." [JR13/181] "Fine long buds." [CA93] "This fine rose always shows up well. The flowers are large, full and round, very double and sweet. Color, a very pleasing shade of soft, rosy crimson. It is a vigorous grower and constant bloomer, and makes beautiful buds for cutting." [C&Js02]

JEAN ANDRÉ   PLATE 58
Pelletier, 1894
From 'William Allen Richardson' (N) × 'Ma Capucine' (T).

"This pleasing variety of nearly continuous bloom was developed in 1894. . . . It makes a shrub of good vigor for a Noisette, canes semi-climbing, flowers solitary . . . medium size . . . full and fragrant, orange yellow with a darker center." [JR31/173]

[JOSEPH MÉTRAL]
Bernaix, 1888

"Extra vigorous; buds ovoid with reddish sepals tipped with a foliaceous appendage. Flower very double, opening well; form, slightly flattened; petals numerous, undulate and curled under at the edges, creped and chiffoned at the center; color, somber magenta red passing to cherry red nuanced purple; bloom abundant and continuous. Excellent for bedding." [JR12/164] "A strong, healthy grower." [CA93]

[JOSEPH PAQUET]
Ketten Bros., 1905
From 'G. Nabonnand' (T) × 'Margherita di Simone' (T).

"Rose on yellow ground. Loose." [ARA27/20] "China pink tinted lake red, petal bases light yellow; large, full, fragrant; bud very long. Very floriferous." [JR29/166]

[JULES FINGER]
Widow Ducher, 1879
From 'Catherine Mermet' (T) × 'Mme de Tartas' (T).

"Red, with a silvery lustre; a promising sort." [EL] "Very large, full, fine form, splendid bright salmon-pink to red." [Hn] "Bush very vigorous, with strong and upright canes; thorns rare, recurved, red; beautiful large dark green foliage composed of 5 leaflets. Flower very large, full, very well formed, outer petals large, more muddled towards the center; color, beautiful bright red fading to nuanced light red, shaded silvery; reverse of petals darker; very floriferous." [JR3/164] "Of good growth with fair foliage; does well as a dwarf but better as a standard, not liable to mildew and can stand a shower. The blooms generally come well, but the shape is not a refined one, the centre petals being generally incurved, whereas we expect the more elegant pointed form in a Tea Rose. Pretty good as a free-bloomer and autumnal, not very large, and aggravating in colour. This is fairly good and pure when the flower first opens, but it will not hold when cut, and if kept too long, for it has a lasting shape, it turns to a livid hue, which almost tempts one to use the word 'ugly'." [F-M3]

JULIUS FABIANICS DE MISEFA
Geschwindt, 1902
From 'Bardou Job' (B) × 'Souvenir du Dr. Passot' (T).

"Carmine and crimson shaded fire-red." [RR]

[KONINGIN WILHELMINA]
Verschuren, 1904
Either sport of 'Dr. Grill' (T), or from 'Dr. Grill' × HT seedling.

"Coppery salmon." [LS] "Color, rose pink. Flowers said to resemble a Dahlia." [C&Js11]

[LA NANKEEN]
Ducher, 1871

"Coppery-yellow, outer petals paler, large, full, and of tolerably good form." [JC] "Highly valued for its magnificent buds, which are deep orange yellow at base and rich creamy white at the point; exceedingly beautiful, and different from all others; very fragrant." [CA90] "Vigorous; canes thin and reflexing; bark pale green, with reddish brown, upright, flattened thorns which are wider at the base; leaves smooth, light green, of 3 or 5, rarely 7, oval-pointed, finely dentate leaflets; leafstalk slender, armed with some small prickles; flower 67 cm across [ca. 3 in], very full, expanded form; color, nankeen yellow, lighter at the center; outer petals long and rounded at the edge. Buds much in demand for making bouquets. Very tender." [S]

[LA PRINCESSE VERA]
Nabonnand, 1877

"White on a coppery ground." [LS] "White, with yellow tint; very full; fine form." [CA88] "Very vigorous; flowers large, very full, yellowish coppery white on a very bright reticulated ground; big-wooded, few thorns." [JR1/12/1314]

LA SYLPHIDE
Boyau, 1842

"Outer petals cream, tinted with pale carmine, centre fawn, very large and full; a beautiful free blooming rose for outdoor culture." [JC] "Blush, very large and double." [P] "Yellow flesh-colour; vigorous, grows to a big size and sweet scented. In bud or half-open stage no rose in cultivation can excel it in beauty, shape, or delicacy. Filbert shaped with petals folded one on the other with remarkable regularity, the edges slightly re-curved as in the 'La France' group. Flourishes to great advantage under the protection of glass, its flowers being very delicate, wind, or rain or too much sun are detrimental to the perfect opening of its flowers. Beautiful foliage of the same shade as that of 'Maréchal Niel'. Not a common rose, but one well deserving more attention and notoriety. Unfortunately a great favorite with the Rose Bug." [B&V]

[LA TULIPE]
Ducher, 1868

"Creamy white, tinted with pale carmine, handsome in the bud, but only semi-double, moderate habit." [JC] "Moderate growth; flower large, full; color, white tinted pink." [S] "For many years, having paused often enough before 'La Tulipe' . . . , I was inclined to think that I had before me a hybrid of Tea × Noisette. I took some cuttings in order to have own-root specimens to observe, and the most vigorous of them was planted in a plot which was always under one's eye. For three or four years, the specimen would stay pretty spindly, with no differences from the plant from which it was cut. But then, at the next bourgeoning of Spring, I noted, shooting out obliquely from the specimen, long canes which were slightly undulate, with matte green foliage, at the tips of which beautiful self-yellow roses opened, a yellow comparable to that of '[Mme la] Duchesse d'Auerstädt', which grew alongside. While the blossoms were just opening, lateral canes began to develop in profusion from the upper two-thirds of the cane in a direction noticeably perpendicular to the position of the axes from which they grew, an arrangement which I understand to be characteristic of the Noisettes. The young canes — and first the uppermost — would begin to bloom when cold and snow suddenly brought an end to all other growth. The effect of the frost on the plant was rather curious. The typical 'La Tulipe' branches were completely untouched, while the long anomalous canes were severely hurt. Due to all this, I would of course be inclined to lay the sporting of roses to the account of Hybridity. There are two strains in the Hybrid, and the characteristics of growth results from their close mixing. When a difficulty crops up in the mix for any reason, it is outwardly reflected in a change in growth." [JR24/43] Parent of 'Mme Emile Metz' (HT), which was the parent of 'Florence Haswell Veitch' (Cl. HT).

[LADY CASTLEREAGH]
A. Dickson, 1888

"A pure Tea producing many branches which are short and strong, with particularly bushy and beautiful foliation; blooms abundantly and very late. The flowers are of good form, large and lush, always opening well; the petals are thick, round, and smooth. Their color is of a very delicate shade, pink with yellow, the pink predominating around the outer edges. This magnificent rose hasn't the least tendency to mildew, and what is more is very robust outside without protection, never suffering from cold . . . it blooms with astonishing profusion." [JR12/106] "Foliage large and leathery." [CA93]

LADY MARY CORRY
A. Dickson, 1900

"Deep golden yellow; flower erect." [JR30/15] "Of good size, perfect form; freely produced." [P1] "An exquisite decorative Tea Rose, growth vigorous and erect branching habit, fine large bold flowers of perfect build . . . delightfully tea-scented." [C&Js02]

[LADY STANLEY]
Nabonnand, 1886

"Very vigorous; flower very large, very full, globular, imbricated, of perfect form; color, lilac on a ground of yellow, petal edges purple. Very floriferous." [JR10/169] Not to be confused with Dubos's pink Bourbon of 1849.

[LADY ZOË BROUGHAM]
('M. H. Graire')
Nabonnand, 1886
Seedling of 'Isabelle Nabonnand' (T).

"Very vigorous bush . . . flower large, full, imbricated, of beautiful form; color, extraordinarily bright chamois yellow, darker at the petal edges; bud quite long. Unique." [JR10/169] "Yellow to chamois-leather colour, edges of petals rather darker, good elongated bud, vigorous, floriferous and grows to a large size. Does not like the sun, which very rapidly sucks all colour from the blooms; it does better in every respect when the sky is clouded. Have seen some very fine examples of this rose which were flowered at Wimbledon, superior in colour and texture to what we can grow here [on the French Riviera]." [B&V]

[LE PACTOLE]
('Mme de Chalonges')
Miellez, pre-1841

"Silky yellow, full, large." [LF] "Flowers cream, their centres yellow, large and full; form, cupped. Growth, moderate. A beautiful Rose." [P] "Creamy white to pale yellow. Low growing, is quite a desirable variety, with especially beautiful buds." [B&V] The Pactolus, in Lydia, Asia Minor, was the river in which Midas immersed himself in order to *lose* his ability to turn things to gold; in ancient times — indeed, up until the Christian era — gold could be found in the river's bed. The Pactolus's modern name is "Sarabat."

[LENA]
A. Dickson, 1906

"Glowing apricot. The flowers are freely produced, frequently showing sprays of from seven to nine perfect blooms. An exquisite garden rose." [C&Js08]

[LÉON XIII]
Soupert & Notting, 1892
From 'Anna Olivier' (T) × 'Earl of Eldon' (N).

"Very vigorous, foliage large and beautiful; flower large, full; petals large and well rounded; bud long like that of 'Niphetos'; color white, lightly shaded straw yellow, the center light ochre." [JR16/139] Pope Leo (or Léon) XIII; lived 1810–1903.

[LÉON DE BRUYN]
Soupert & Notting, 1895
From 'Maréchal Robert' (T) × 'Rubens' (T).

"Plant bushy, like 'Perle de Lyon'; flower large, full, Centifolia-form; exterior petals large; color, light straw yellow, center Naples yellow. Very floriferous." [JR19/148] "Highest in the center with petals over-lapping like shingles on a roof . . . very free and fragrant." [C&Js98]

[LÉONIE OSTERRIETH]
('Léonie Oesterreith', etc.)
Soupert & Notting, 1892
From 'Sylphide' (T) × 'Mme Bravy' (T).

"Vigorous; foliage light green; flower large, full; blooms in clusters of 5–6 blossoms, cupped; color, bright porcelain white nuanced very delicate yellow towards the center. Fragrant and very floriferous." [JR16/139] "In freedom of bloom this variety rivals a Polyantha." [CA95]

[LETTY COLES]
Keynes/Coles, 1876
Sport of 'Mme Mélanie Willermoz' (T).

"Still regarded as one of the finest roses of its color; soft rosy pink, shaded with intense crimson; extra large, full, globular form; very double; exceedingly sweet tea fragrance." [CA88] "Very vigorous; flower large, full; color, beautiful delicate pink." [JR1/6/10] "An abundant bloomer, too; large, double flowers of a deep, globular form, and borne on strong, stiff stems; in fact, one of the strongest and finest growing roses in its class." [C&Js02] "Low-growing, bushy, not very hardy; foliage sufficient, healthy; bloom sparse, occasional during midsummer." [ARA18/126]

LOUIS LÉVÊQUE
Listed as 'Erzherzog Franz Ferdinand'.

LOUIS RICHARD
(='Helvetia'?)
Widow Ducher, 1877

"Vigorous, flower large, full, coppery pink with a dark red center." [JR1/12/12] "This is a grand bedding rose, extra large, full and double, and richly tea scented. Color clear rosy flesh, passing to creamy pink; a tremendous bloomer, very handsome and desirable in every way." [C&Js04]

[LOUISE DE SAVOIE]
Ducher, 1854

"Pale canary yellow." [CA90] "Plant vigorous; foliage glaucous green; flower very large, quite full; color, sulphur yellow, sometimes light yellow, taking on a buff tint. Tender." [S] "Clear pale yellow, very large and full, fine shape, habit vigorous; does not always open freely out of doors, but under glass it is superb." [JC]

[LUCIE FAURE]
('Louis Faure')
Nabonnand, 1898
From 'Mme Léon Février' (T) × 'Niphetos' (T).

"Flower large, full, solitary, exquisite form, outer petals larger, recurving gracefully; color, ivory white on an amber ground; pretty long bud, perfectly held; long stem; vigorous bush; very floriferous." [JR22/165] "A neat compact grower, pretty buds and round full flowers, pure French white sometimes tinted with salmon and pink; profuse bloomer all Summer and Fall, hardy and good." [C&Js02]

[LUCIOLE]   PLATE 34
Guillot & fils, 1886
Seedling of 'Safrano à Fleurs Rouges' (T).

"Large, full, well-formed; bud long; color, china pink with carmine, very intense, tinted saffron yellow, on a ground of coppery yellow; reverse of petals bronze. Very fragrant." [JR10/123] "A button-hole Tea Rose of very poor growth, with good long buds most charmingly tinted." [F-M2] "A large long bud. Strong rose, with red stiff stalk . . . The books call it a buttonhole rose, and I do not agree with them!" [HmC]

[LUTEA FLORA]
Touvais, 1874

"Moderate growth; flower large, full; color, brilliant yellow fading to white." [S] A parent of 'Comte Chandon' (T).

[MA CAPUCINE]   PLATE 17
(trans., 'My Nasturtium')
Levet, 1871
From 'Ophirie' (N) × *R. fœtida*.

"Bronzy yellow, shaded red. Distinct and beautiful in bud." [H] "Flower medium-sized, nearly full, coppery nasturtium yellow." [S] "Moderate vigor, and very floriferous; it produces very pretty pointed buds. The blossoms are large, full, nasturtium yellow when opening, fading to white when fully open." [JR28/125] "Beautiful buds; a very distinct rose, which, from its delicate habit, is useless for ordinary cultivators to attempt growing." [EL] "Another weakly growing buttonhole Tea Rose, most charming in colour. The buds are quite small, and not particularly long or pointed, but sure to attract notice." [F-M2]

[MADELEINE GUILLAUMEZ]   PLATE 56
Bonnaire, 1892
From a cross of an unnamed Tea × 'Mlle de Sombreuil' (Cl. T).

"Vigorous with upright canes; flower medium-sized or large; stiff stem; form globular, beautiful white with a salmony center, nuanced orange yellow. Very beautiful plant; very floriferous." [JR16/152]

[MADISON]
Brandt-Hentz, 1912
From 'Perle des Jaunes' (T) × a seedling of 'The Bride' (T) and 'The Meteor' (HT).

"The flower is large, perfectly double and fragrant. Color is rich creamy white." [C&Js14] "Low, weak-growing, winterkills some; foliage plentiful; bloom moderate, best spring and fall." [ARA18/126] Madison, the city in New Jersey where the Brandt-Hentz Co. was headquartered.

[MAID OF HONOUR]
Hofmeister, 1899
Sport of 'Catherine Mermet' (T).

"The petals are extra large, full regular form and very sweet, petals thick and of good substance, color soft rosy pink or delicate flesh-color; a splendid variety, first-class in every way." [C&Js02]

[MARÉCHAL ROBERT]
Widow Ducher, 1875

"Flower very large, full, well formed, globular; color, yellow within, blushing slightly along the edges." [S]

[MARGHERITA DI SIMONE]
P. Guillot, 1898

"Vigorous bush, very floriferous, bud very elegant, carmine orange yellow; flower large, full, well formed, varying from bright China pink to carmine nuanced with deep yellow, reverse of petals orange yellow flamed with gold-pink on a more or less deep carmine ground, depending upon the temperature and the exposure; very fragrant; of the 'Luciole' sort. To be recommended for bedding." [JR22/179]

[MARGUERITE GIGANDET]

Nabonnand, 1902

From 'Mlle Franziska Krüger' (T) × 'Reine Emma des Pays-Bas' (T).

"Reddish coppery yellow, passing to golden yellow." [C&Js06] "Flower very large, very full; color, coppery yellow with grenadine reflections or tints; center a sparkling mélange; bud well formed, coppery yellow tinted blood red while opening; very beautiful foliage; shrub very vigorous, very floriferous. Fragrant." [JR26/148]

[MARGUERITE KETTEN]

Ketten Bros., 1897

From 'Mme Caro' (T) × 'Georges Farber' (T).

"Flower yellowish peach red, petal edges tinted icy pink; golden reflections; large, full, fragrant. Bush medium-sized and vigorous; floriferous." [JR21/136] "A fine, large, beautifully formed rose; makes elegent buds, deliciously sweet . . . constant and profuse bloomer." [C&Js99]

MARIA STAR

Pery-Gravereaux, 1913

From 'Mme Gustave Henry' (T) × 'Mme Jules Gravereaux' (Cl. T).

Salmon-gold.

[MARIE GUILLOT]

Guillot fils, 1874

"Greenish white." [LS] "A pure, snowy-white rose . . . constant bloomer." [C&Js05] "Vigorous bush; flower large, very full, imbricated; white, tinted yellowish." [S]

MARIE SEGOND

('Marie Legonde')

Nabonnand, 1902

From 'Mme la Comtesse de Leusse' (T) × 'Mlle Lazarine Poizeau' (T).

"Flower medium sized, full, well formed; warm coloration, light or bright pink tinted flame, nub brilliant coppery carmine without, golden within; center flame; pretty elongated bud, coppery tinted carmine; very pretty foliage; very vigorous and bushy, constantly in bloom. Fragrant." [JR26/148]

[MARIE SISLEY]

Guillot fils, 1868

"Cream, deeply margined and shaded with rosy-salmon, flowers full size and very fragrant; a distinct and good rose, habit free." [JC] "Large and double flowers, delicious tea scent; color exquisite shade of pale yellow, broadly margined with bright rose." [CA93] "Bush vigorous; flower large, full, globular." [S]

[MARIE SOLEAU]

Nabonnand, 1895

Seedling of 'Mlle Suzanne Blanchet' (T).

"Blossom large, full, admirably formed, elegantly held; color, ravishing silvery pink; pretty bud; elegant foliage. Very vigorous bush; extremely floriferous." [JR19/180] "Very sweet." [C&Js98]

[MARION DINGEE]

J. Cook, 1889

Two parentages given: (1) 'Mme la Comtesse de Caserta' (T) × 'Duchess of Edinburgh' (T); or, (2) 'Mme la Comtesse de Caserta' × a seedling of 'Général Jacqueminot' (HP) × 'Safrano' (T).

"Bright carmine." [LS] "Deep rich crimson, one of the darkest colored ever-blooming roses we have." [C&Jf97] "Beautiful cup-shaped flowers, quite full and fragrant and borne in great profusion all through the growing season; excellent for garden planting." [C&Js98] "A splendid red Rose, and one of the finest additions to our list of bedding Roses we have had in many years; flowers of good size, nicely cup-shaped, and borne in wonderful profusion all through the growing season. Color, deep crimson, changing to carmine in the matured flowers." [CA96]

[MARQUISE DE QUERHOËNT]

Godard, 1901

From 'G. Nabonnand' (T) × 'Mme Laurette Messimy' (Ch).

"Coppery China pink on a golden yellow ground." [JR32/139] "Carmine on flesh or yellow ground." [CA17] "Salmon red to saffron. Decorative; mildews badly." [ABA27/20] "Persistent bloomer, bloom of good size, prime substance, full and sweet; color, beautiful china rose, salmon, copper and golden yellow. A combination rarely seen." [C&Js13] "Medium height, bushy, hardy, foliage very plentiful, healthy; bloom moderate; almost continuous." [ARA18/126]

[MARQUISE DE VIVENS]   PLATE 30

Dubreuil, 1885

"Pale rose, centres shaded with yellow; semi-double." [P1] "Carmine and pink." [LS] "Novel shade of violet crimson, with center and base of petals creamy yellow; large, full flowers; a constant and profuse bloomer." [CA90] "Not climbing, with hooked thorns; large leaves with 5–7 leaflets which are bright, glossy, dark green; bud very long; flower large, bicolored, fading in age; calyx with long glabrous sepals, dark green without, whitish and chalky within; petals rounded-obovate, cuneate, gracefully rolled . . . ; upper surface bright carmine along the edge, attenuating to China pink at the middle and finally to straw yellow at the nub; lower surface flesh white nuanced sulphur." [JR9/166]

[MAUD LITTLE]

Dingee & Conard, 1891

From 'Pierre de St.-Cyr' (B) × 'Comtesse de Labarthe' (T).

"Of moderate growth, satisfactory stature, medium culture; flowers beautiful and full; color, China pink, delicate with a distinctly bright tint; distinctive and notably beautiful." [JR15/88]

[MAURICE ROUVIER]

Nabonnand, 1890

"Of remarkable vigor making an enormous bush; flower very large, very full, enormous, of perfect form; bud long, opens very well, firmly held; wood reddish brown; thorns medium; foliage light green. Bloom continuous and very abundant. Color, beautiful delicate pink, very lightly veined red, pale on the outer edge." [JR14/165]

[MEDEA]

W. Paul, 1890

"Light canary-yellow; large, of good form. Vigorous grower in Southern zones and especially adapted to warm weather." [Th2] "Lemon yellow with a silk-yellow center, and light, bright tintings; large, very full, buds somewhat disposed to proliferity, but blossoms opening in a ball; a vigorous hybrid. It is a magnificent Tea rose." [JR15/87] "High centers; foliage dark and thick." [CA96] "Of stout stiff growth, but tender against frost, not very free-blooming, a fine Rose for exhibition, but not well suited for general cultivation. The blooms are particularly full, with the rounded centres which require a hot season or situation for their full development. They are sometimes very large, and in perfect blooms the outer petals reflex well, making a very fine shape." [F-M2]

[META]
A. Dickson, 1898

"Strawberry red touched saffron yellow." [JR32/139] "Crushed strawberry to coppery yellow. Poor growth." [ARA27/20] "Small growth; winterkilled." [ARA18/117]

[MEVROUW BOREEL VAN HOGELANDER]
Leenders, 1918
From 'Mme Léon Pain' (HT) × 'Mme Antoine Mari' (T).

"Fine growth, good foliage, and nice double. Flesh, shaded carmine and pink." [ARA28/102] "Bud medium size, globular; flower medium size, globular, borne several together, on average-length stems; very lasting; strong fragrance. Color rosy white and carmine. Foliage abundant, medium size, leathery, dark green. A vigorous grower of bushy habit and a profuse bloomer." [ARA20/135]

MISS AGNES C. SHERMAN
Nabonnand, 1901
From 'Paul Nabonnand' (T) × 'Catherine Mermet' (T).

"Peach." [LS] "Soft rose, centre brighter rose tinted with salmon red, large and full, perfect shape; growth vigorous." [P1]

MISS ALICE DE ROTHSCHILD
A. Dickson, 1910

"Canary to citron-yellow. Mildews." [ARA27/19] "Fine, double, canary-yellow Tea. Large flower with good stem, lasting. Growth fair and foliage mildews in dampness. Best for interior South." [ARA28/102] "Delicious fragrance ('Maréchal Niel' perfume)." [C&Js12] "Evidently the best yellow garden rose since 'Maréchal Niel'. Its color is a rich lemon yellow becoming darker as the blossom expands. The growth is very vigorous; floriferous; long-lasting, large, full, perfectly formed blossoms, with a scent quite as delicate as that of 'Maréchal Niel', in rigid stems. The very erect bud is pointed and opens easily outside as well as under glass." [JR34/103] "Beautiful color; growth and foliage only fair; hardiness varies; form good; blooming fairly good. Needs time to become established." [ARA18/113]

[MISS MARSTON]   PLATE 49
Pries/Ketten Bros., 1889

"Pink and yellow." [LS] "A light-colored Tea. Should be grown through Southern zones." [ARA28/102] "Flower yellowish blushy white, bordered very deep pink, center yellow peach red; large, full, delicious violet scent; bush of moderate vigor; extremely floriferous. A distinct variety and of the first merit. Superb!" JR13/147. "Bushy growth; not a profuse bloomer." [ARA18/117]

[MISS WENN]
Guillot & fils, 1890

"Vigorous; flower large, full, well formed, beautiful China pink; beautiful and very floriferous." [JR14/146] "Moderate growth." [CA96]

[MLLE ANNA CHARRON]
('Mlle Anna Chartron')
Widow Schwartz, 1896
From 'Kaiserin Auguste Viktoria' (HT) × 'Luciole' (T).

"Cream and crimson." [LS] "Cream-yellow, washed lilac-rose. Loose." [ARA27/20] "Vigorous bush, very floriferous, foliage somber green edged purple; flower large, full, well formed, borne on a long, strong stem, usually solitary. The large petals are folded back into a point, giving the flower a starry look; cream tinted and edged bright carmine, center very delicate pink. The very long bud, which is very graceful, shows darker shades of the open blossom. Quite distinct, very good for cutting." [JR20/163]

MLLE BLANCHE DURRSCHMIDT
Guillot fils, 1878
Seedling of 'Mme Falcot' (T).

"Flesh colour, of medium size, double, free flowering and effective; growth vigorous." [P1] "Very vigorous, flowers large or medium, double or full, well formed; color, flesh white, tinted salmon pink fading to white; blooms in clusters or solitary . . . very pretty for bedding." [JR1/12/14] "Semi-double, worthless." [EL] "Canes olive green tinted red, lower sections with violet tints; thorns hooked, not very numerous; flat; leaves of 3–5 glossy green, finely dentate leaflets." [S]

MLLE BLANCHE MARTIGNAT   PLATE 72
Gamon, 1902
Possibly a seedling of 'Marie Van Houtte' (T).

"Salmon-yellow, with pink glow. Globular." [Capt27] "Salmon nuanced dawn-pink." [LS] "Vigorous without being 'climbing,' giving at the end of every sufficiently strong branch long buds producing very large creped blossoms with dawn-gold centers, outermost petals salmon pink, sometimes completely pink . . . very fragrant." [JR32/77]

[MLLE CHRISTINE DE NOUÉ]
Guillot & fils, 1890

"Carmine-lake shaded salmon. Mildews slightly." [ARA27/19] "An elegant deep red rose of fine texture and size." [CA95] "In form, conical; in appearance, hazy. The plant is strong and floriferous." [JR20/58] "Flower very large, full, well formed and of good hold; outer petals imbricated, deep maroon purple-red; center petals more muddled, lake pink and light purple, nuanced icy silvery white; fragrant; very beautiful variety." [JR14/146]

[MLLE CLAUDINE PERREAU]   PLATE 35
('Mlle Claudine Perreault')
E. Lambert, 1886
Seedling of 'Souvenir d'Un Ami' (T).

"Extra large, full, perfectly double flowers; color, rosy flesh on white ground, with rich crimson center; free bloomer." [CA90] "From 'Souvenir d'Un Ami', but much more vigorous without being 'climbing.' Color, very bright pink, sometimes delicate pink; canes upright, peduncle very strong. Of premier merit." [JR10/171]

MLLE EMMA VERCELLONE
Schwartz, 1901
From 'Chamoïs' (T) × 'Mme Laurette Messimy' (Ch).

"Vigorous, bushy, foliage purple red, long bud, flower large, full, bright coppery red on a golden yellow ground fading to coppery salmon pink nuanced dawn-gold. Beautiful; very floriferous." [JR25/163] "Small growth; no special merit." [ARA18/116]

MLLE JEANNE GUILLAUMEZ   PLATE 46
Bonnaire, 1889

"Very vigorous, with erect branches; foliage . . . evergreen; flower large, full, well formed; beautiful long buds, of a pretty dark rose color. When partially open, this rose is brick red, with much salmon and metallic red in the interior, on a ground of dark straw yellow after opening. A superb variety of novel coloration." [JR13/162]

MLLE JEANNE PHILIPPE   PLATE 67
('Jeanne Philippe', 'Mme J. Phillips')
Godard, 1898

"Nankeen, bordered carmine. Mildews slightly." [ARA27/20] "Very vigorous and compact, with upright, strong branches; foliage bronzy red, wood smooth and nearly thornless; flowers very large, full, beautiful nankeen yellow with chamois reflections, petal edges lightly touched carmine." [JR23/2] "The buds are long and open quite well . . . perfectly formed flowers . . . moderate vigor . . . blooms abundantly from late frosts to fall." [JR27/119] "Weak; winterkills." [ARA18/116]

MLLE LA COMTESSE DE LEUSSE
Nabonnand, 1878

"Very vigorous, flowers large, semi-double, cupped, very large imbricated petals. Color, delicate pink with saffron reflections at the center; bud, bright pink." [JR3/9]

[MLLE LAZARINE POIZEAU]
Levet, 1876

"Fine orange-yellow, of medium size, full, fine form, growth vigorous, free bloomer." [JC] "Vigorous Tea rose, flower medium-sized, full, well formed, and well held; color, beautiful orange-yellow. Very floriferous." [JR1/1/7] "Small size, very pretty in the bud." [EL] "Branches dusky reddish green; few thorns; leaves glossy, olive green; young leaves reddish." [S]

[MLLE MARIE-LOUISE OGER]
Lévêque, 1895

"Vigorous bush; flower very large, beautiful dark green foliage; beautiful milk white, shaded — very lightly — yellowish. Very beautiful. *Note:* This rose is dedicated to the daughter of a businessman from La Fère." [JR19/163] "Abundant bloomer." [C&Js98]

[MLLE MARIE MOREAU]
('Mme Marie Moreau')
Nabonnand, 1879

"Pale silvery white, elegantly flushed with crimson and yellow; petals margined with rich carmine; large, finely formed flowers; full and sweet." [CA88] "Vigorous bush; compact growth, well formed; flower medium-sized, full, well formed; color, bright pink, shaded, lighter at the center; bloom abundant and very early; good for making wonderful beds." [S]

[MLLE SUZANNE BLANCHET]
Nabonnand, 1885

"Rose tinted with flesh color; large and of fine form; very fragrant." [CA90] "Very vigorous, big-wooded, thorns rare; flower very large, very full, imbricated, erect, cupped; splendid coloration: A novel flesh pink; bloom continuous; very fragrant." [JR9/166]

[MME A. ÉTIENNE]
Bernaix, 1886

"Bright rosy flesh." [CA93] "Wine-pink." [LS] "Wine-red and paler red, with white centre." [RR] "Of moderate vigor; long bud; calyx with long, pointed sepals; flower large, full, well-formed, cupped, fragrant; color, vinous pink at the petals' edges, passing gradually through pale pink to white at the center; center petals smaller, muddled before the flower is completely open; fresh and intense pink which, by its brightness, sets off the paler pink of the outer petals. A very fetching coloration." [JR10/172]

MME ACHILLE FOULD
Lévêque, 1903

"Very vigorous, leaves dark green, flowers very large, well formed, globular, yellow nuanced bright carmine pink, shaded red-copper and salmon, sometimes light salmon pink throughout, or carmine pink nuanced yellow, magnificent colors, superb." [JR27/165]

[MME ADA CARMODY]
W. Paul, 1898

"Ivory white bordered with pink tints, center of the blossom a little yellowish as with 'Cleopatra'. The flower is large and full, with very long buds. Without being extremely vigorous, the bush grows well and blooms abundantly." [JR22/56]

MME ADOLPHE DOHAIR
('Mme Adolphe Dahair')
Puyravaud, 1900
From 'Général Schablinkine' (T) × 'Mlle Lazarine Poizeau' (T).

"Flower white lightly nuanced cream, large, full, satiny, plump center, cupped, fragrant, staying in bloom a long time. Growth vigorous, exhibiting the blossom well on a rigid stem; very floriferous . . . dedicated to the wife of a Niort horticulturalist." [JR24/135]

[MME AGATHE NABONNAND]
Nabonnand, 1886

"Rosy flesh, bathed in golden amber; immense buds, broad, shell-like petals, and large, full flowers." [CA90] "Carmine-magenta." [LS] "Flesh-coloured flowers of great size, slightly margined with a darker shade; buds are egg-shaped, very large and heavy, easily affected by damp; vigorous, grows to large size and very floriferous, a really magnificent rose, but very difficult to obtain from it perfect flowers; the plant seems unequal to the task of opening these great fleshy buds." [B&V] "Very vigorous, continuously covered with flowers; flower very large, full, splendid." [JR10/169] "Attractive color; fairly good in growth, foliage, and blooming." [ARA18/112]

MME ALBERT BERNARDIN
Mari/Jupeau, 1904
From 'Comtesse de Frigneuse' (T) × 'Marie Van Houtte' (T).

"Vigorous, slender branches, wood smooth, small thorns, flower medium or large, center canary yellow, exterior white washed bright carmine, very well formed, like a beautiful Camellia." [JR28/168]

MME ANTOINE RÉBÉ
Laperrière, 1900
From 'Alphonse Karr' (T) × 'Princesse de Sagan' (Ch).

"Dwarf and stocky, of good vigor. Buds quite long, opening easily. Flower bright sparkling red . . . of the first order for bedding." [JR25/5]

MME AZÉLIE IMBERT   PLATE 16
Levet, 1870
Seedling of 'Mme Falcot' (T).

"Pale yellow." [EL] "The English consider it good for exhibitions because of the size and beauty of the blossom; the growth is very vigorous, and the flowers large, full, well formed, and beautifully colored salmon yellow." [JR7/104]

[MME BARTHÉLEMY LEVET]
Levet, 1879
Seedling of 'Gloire de Dijon' (N).

"Very vigorous; foliage of 5–7 brilliant green leaflets; flower medium sized to large, full, well-formed, with rounded petals; color, a handsome canary yellow; very remontant, very beautiful." [JR3/165] "Semi-climbing." [JR10/44] "Pretty in color, but too small." [JR13/43]

MME C. LIGER
('Mme C. Ligier')
Berland/Chauvry, 1899

"Semi-climbing; bud round and very large; flower large, very full, well formed, cupped, varying form delicate pink to deep pink, center dark red; penetrating fragrance." [JR24/2]

[MME C. P. STRASSHEIM]   PLATE 65
Soupert & Notting, 1897
From 'Mlle Adèle Jougant' (T) × 'Mme la Princesse de Bessaraba de Brancovan' (T).

"Very vigorous without being 'climbing'; the abundant coppery red glossy foliage gives a good look to the plant. The bud is held upright on a pretty strong stem. . . . The blossom is medium to large, full, yellowish-white in the summer bloom period, sulphur-yellow passing to chamois in the second blossoming . . . very fragrant." [JR24/72] "A good hardy grower and very free bloomer; excellent for bedding and borders." [C&Js99] C. P. Strassheim was the editor of the German periodical *Rosen-Zeitung.*

MME CAMILLE
Guillot fils, 1871

"Delicate rose, violet shade, flowers veined, very large and full . . . habit free." [JC] "Salmon-pink, large and full; form cupped; growth vigorous." [P1] "Vigorous; flower large, full, well formed; delicate pink with dawn gold, veined, whitish reflections." [S] "Mushroom-color, large, coarse flowers; not worthy of cultivation." [EL] "A magnificent rose; extra large size; very double and full; immense buds; color delicate rosy flesh, changing to salmon rose, elegantly shaded and suffused with deep carmine." [CA88] "A splendid garden Rose, extra large, full and sweet; clear, rosy-flesh, passing to salmon pink; good, free bloomer, very handsome and one of the Roses you can always depend upon." [C&Js11]

[MME CARO]
Levet, 1880
Seedling of 'Gloire de Dijon' (N).

"Growth very weak; foliage dark green, purple beneath; thorns occasional; blossom well formed, very full, medium size, salmon-yellow." [S] "Shrub with strong wood." [JR4/167] Parent of 'Antoinette Durieu' (T).

MME CAROLINE KÜSTER
Pernet, 1872
Seedling of 'Le Pactole' (T).

"Pale yellow, often mottled with rose; a free blooming, excellent shrub rose, one of the best bedding kinds." [EL] "Very vigorous, with upright canes; flower globular, full, large, beautiful orange yellow." [JR3/29] "Centre canary yellow, outer petals pale lemon, flowers large . . . a very beautiful rose." [JC] "Lemon-yellow fading to white." [S] "Not of climbing growth . . . strong good growth . . . small foliage; the blooms sometimes come divided, especially the strongest ones, and they are weak in colour, but good in petal, shape, fulness, lasting qualities, and size. This is an accommodating Rose; a strong established plant in good soil may be cultivated . . . as a most useful bush to 'cut and come again.' . . . It is very free blooming and a good autumnal." [F-M 2] "Vigorous with green wood armed with red thorns; leaves of five leaflets, glossy, oval, much serrated; leafstalk very prickly; flower stalk green or reddish, bristly, ovary cylindrical; flower very beautiful; very remontant; blooms in clusters. . . . Mme Caroline Küster is a native of Germany. Being in Lyon, she visited the premises of Mons Pernet, and was so ravished by this new rose that Mons Pernet was pleased to give it her name." [JR10/78]

[MME CÉLINE NOIREY]
Guillot fils, 1868

"Salmon-rose, flowers large and double; very beautiful." [JC] "A fine large rose, very double, full and sweet; color, soft rosy blush, beautifully shaded with deep purplish red; one of the best." [CA88] "Bush vigorous; flower large, full, well formed; color, salmon-pink; reverse of petals purple red." [S] "From Guillot fils' 1865 seedlings, released to commerce in 1868. Very curious in its delicate salmony pink color, with purple red on the petal-backs. The growth is vigorous, but the canes are weak, flexile, and bending under the weight of the blossom, which is full, well formed, solitary or in a cluster, and able to be 6–7 cm across [ca. 3 in]; the leaves, composed of 3 or 5 oval-acuminate leaflets are a light shiny green; petiole reddish and prickly; peduncle long and purplish. This beautiful variety was obtained by open-pollination; its origin is unknown. . . . Can't withstand more than 8° or 10° of frost. Prune short." [JR10/93]

MME CHARLES
Damaizin, 1864
Seedling of 'Mme Damaizin' (T).

"Flowers sulphur or yellow, their centre salmon; large, full, of good form, and very abundant; growth vigorous." [FP] "Deep orange-yellow or apricot; beautiful colour and handsome in bud." [JC] "Very pretty flowers of a pure color, a lightly coppery nankeen yellow; vigorous." [JR10/46] "Medium growth, floriferous . . . flower large, nearly full, semi-globular." [S] "Very well-clothed with leaves, dwarfish, blooms abundantly." [JR9/70] "Brown foliage, and one I do not disbud." [HmC] "An improved strain of 'Safrano'." [F-M2]

[MME CHARLES SINGER]
Nabonnand, 1916

"Flower large, double, erect, garnet on opening, dark velvety purple-garnet when expanded, keeps a long time; very vigorous." [ARA18/108] "Fine medium-sized red with nice form; good stem; immune foliage; medium growth." [CaRoll/3/2] "Flowers come singly on a strong stem. . . . Valuable in the southern seacoast districts because it does not ball or mildew, and worth growing in heated areas because of its lasting qualities." [ARA28/103]

MME CHÉDANE-GUINOISSEAU
Chédane-Guinoisseau/Lévêque, 1880
Variously described as a seedling or sport of 'Safrano' (T).

"Extremely floriferous, and its beautiful silky yellow flowers are well formed." [JR8/156] "Canary. Fair growth." [ARA27/20] "Moderate growth. The buds are pointed and well shaped, and the colour is bright yellow." [F-M2] "Very vigorous; foliage a handsome shiny glaucous green; flower large, full, very well formed, sulphurous canary yellow; buds long, like 'Mme Falcot' or 'Safrano', but larger." [JR4/164]

[MME CLAIRE JAUBERT]   PLATE 39
Nabonnand, 1887

"Very vigorous, with big wood; flower very large, semi-double, in a cluster, with very large petals, imbricated, erect; color, brick yellow, nuanced, novel. . . . Very floriferous." [JR11/165] "Yellow brick colour shaded to a fine rose-pink. Vigorous, grows to a great size, very free flowering, the blooms being of large size, good form and showing great uniformity. A splendid thing." [B&V]

MME CLÉMENCE MARCHIX
Bernaix fils, 1899

"Crimson and light pink." [LS] "Cochineal red tinted with rose, handsome deep cherry red buds; growth vigorous." [P1] "Very remontant, branches bearing 1–5 blossoms at their tips. Bud ovoid, pretty form, matte cerise red, very vigorous. Flower cupped." [JR23/168]

MME CONSTANT SOUPERT
Soupert & Notting, 1905
From 'Souvenir de Pierre Notting' (T) × 'Duchesse Marie Salviati' (T).

"Deep yellow shaded peach. . . . Vigorous; best in Autumn." [Au] "Yellow tinted red." [LS] "The best and most beautiful Tea put into commerce over the past ten years. Many breeders have neglected the Tea Rose for a long time to devote themselves to HT's. . . . 'Mme Constant Soupert' proves that there are yet pearls of rare beauty to be had from Teas . . . vigorous and stocky; foliage dark green and much serrated; the long bud is pointed and upright on a long, erect stem; its color is a deep golden yellow strongly tinted and touched peach pink; the large blossom is very full, opens slowly, and is beautiful pinkish yellow when fully open." [JR29/135] "Slender buds, opening to large, full flowers; odor slight. Bush small and weak. 13 blooms." [ARA26/94] "Attractive color; growth and blooming qualities not good. Being tested on 'Gloire des Rosomanes' stock, where it seems to be improving." [ARA18/112]

[MME CROMBEZ]
Nabonnand, 1882

"Vigorous bush, dwarf, very large flower, very full, very well formed, imbricated, perfectly held; color, yellow slightly nuanced coppery. This magnificent variety is one of the most beautiful nuanced yellow roses known till now." [JR6/186] "A large, finely formed rose, very fragrant; double and full, petals prettily imbricated; color, rich rosy buff, dashed and tinged with bronze and pale blush." [CA90] "A pure yellow, good sized flower, full, imbricated with outside petals reflexed after the manner of 'La France'. When well done this is one of the most beautiful of all roses; it seems to be capricious, hence not too popular among the growers; satisfactory for cutting, as it lives in perfect condition a long time in water. One of our greatest favorites." [B&V]

[MME CUSIN]   PLATE 24
Guillot fils, 1881

"Crimson, with light center, slightly tinted with yellowish white; medium size, good form and quite distinct." [CA90] "Violet rose, base of petals of a yellow tint, free-flowering, very distinct, has large flowers, full and the form very perfect. Of moderate growth and good habit. Very desirable." [B&V] "Vigorous, of pretty deportment with upright, light green canes; leaves light green, composed of 5 leaflets; flowers large or medium, well formed, well held; color, purplish pink on a slightly yellowish white ground, sometimes a beautiful violet red; superb, very floriferous, novel coloration." [JR5/116] "Of short, thick, and often weak growth, with distinct wood and small foliage. It is rather liable to mildew and requires hot dry weather. . . . The blooms almost always come well, though they are often undersized, and the shape is unique and very good, with a fine point in the centre, and the petals arranged in imbricated form, but standing well apart from one another. This is the true form, but large flowers sometimes do not show it. . . . Very free-flowering: it must be well thinned for the production of exhibition blooms, but even the small flowers are lovely and of good lasting quality. A fine colour sometimes, but this is not often very lasting." [F-M3] "L. Cusin, Secretary of the Société d'Horticulture pratique du Rhône." [JR5/118]

MME DAMAIZIN
Damaizin, 1858
Probably the result of a cross between 'Caroline' (T) and 'Safrano' (T).

"Buff with salmon tint, outer petals cream; a distinct and very beautiful rose; habit vigorous." [JC] "Creamy-white, shaded salmon, very large, double; not well formed." [EL] "Called a perfected 'Safrano'. Such perfection, however, is not to be had without hybridization, as is abundantly shown by the manner of branching, the globular form of the flower, the concave form of the petals, and the nearly white shade of yellow." [JR24/42] "Very remontant, growth very vigorous; handsome foliage; flower large, full, pretty form; color salmon-flesh; abudant bloom." [S] "Very vigorous; foliage thick; flower globular, flesh nuanced salmon, abundant bloom." [I'H58/128] "Mons Frédéric Damaizin began raising roses in 1854 . . . [and] was the first in Lyon to undertake forcing roses." [JR3/55] It seems that Damaizin sold his business to one Mons Charton in 1876. [JR3/56]

[MME DAVID]   PLATE 31
Pernet père, 1885

"A beautiful and promising sort; full, medium size; somewhat flat form; very double and finely scented; color, soft pale flesh, deepest in center; petals elegantly margined with silver rose." [CA90] "Vigorous bush, with smooth wood and upright canes; flower very large, nearly full; stem upright and strong; color, delicate pink edged white, sometimes salmon pink." [JR9/148]

[MME DE ST.-JOSEPH]
Introducer unknown, 1846

"Pale salmon tinted with pink . . . nearly unique in colour; but its flowers are often very irregular in their shape." [R8] "Fawn, shaded with salmon, large and beautiful." [JC] "Very sweet." [FP] "Not well formed." [EL] "Pale pink, with deeper centre, sometimes dying off apricot colour, very large and double; form, expanded. Growth, vigorous." [P] An ancestor of 'Gloire de Deventer' (T).

[MME DE VATRY]
('Mme de Vitry')
Guérin, 1855

"Deep rose, large and full." [FP] "Centre bright pink slightly tinted, outer petals paler, full, of good size, and free habit; an excellent hardy rose." [JC] "A splendid rose; large full form; very double and sweet; color rich crimson scarlet; very bright." [CA88] "A good healthy grower and makes a fine supply of lovely buds and large fragrant flowers the whole season." [C&Js02] "Vigorous bush; flower large, full, fragrant. According to Mons Petit-Coq [*alias* Scipion Cochet], this rose, with robust canes, growing quite as large as 'Malmaison', is nevertheless stocky in habit. No matter what the site or exposure, you'll see it prosper; it resists frost better than other teas. Its wood is pretty big, with thorns here and there. Its dull green leaves, well-filled by leaflets of a good size, [clothe nicely] the plant which bears them; its upright flowers, on pretty long, thick, and usually uni-flowered stems, are large or robustly medium-sized, slightly cupped, full, deep pink, slightly paler at the center, and fragrant. We recommend it because of its robustness, its elegant stature, its bloom which is prolonged and gives very beautiful flowers up to heavy frost, and, finally, for its bud, which may be used in making bouquets." [S]

[MME DEREPAS-MATRAT]
('Yellow Maman Cochet')
Buatois, 1897
From 'Mme Hoste' (T) × 'Marie Van Houtte' (T).

"A new and beautiful Hardy Tea Rose, throwing up fine strong stems bearing large solitary buds of grand size, and beautiful sulphur-yellow; flowers perfectly double, splendid form and freely borne." [C&Js05] "Flower solitary, borne on a long peduncle, very large, very full, opening well; color, sulphur yellow, center darker, lightly nuanced carmine while opening; growth vigorous, nearly thornless." [JR21/148]

[MME DEVOUCOUX]
('Mme Devacoux', 'Mme Devacourt')
Widow Ducher, 1874

"A magnificent rose; beautiful, clear canary yellow; delicious tea fragrance; large, very double and full; beautiful in bud and flower." [CA90] "Flower medium-sized, full, very well formed; color, bright yellow; vigorous." [S]

[MME DR. JÜTTÉ]
Levet, 1872
Seedling of 'Ophirie' (N).

"Flower grenadine yellow, very fragrant." [S] "Salmon, orange, and copper, very peculiar color, flowers rather loose." [JC]

[MME DUBROCA]
('Mme Dubrocca')
Nabonnand, 1882

"Very vigorous; flower large, full, well formed, perfect hold; color, delicate pink brightened with pink at the base of the petals. Novel coloration, constant bloom." [JR6/186] "A splendid rose; extra large, full flowers and finely formed buds; color clear salmon, delicately tinted and shaded with rich carmine; very beautiful." [CA90]

[MME ELIE LAMBERT]
E. Lambert, 1890
From 'Anna Olivier' (T) × 'Souvenir de Paul Neyron' (T).

"Flowers extra large, fine globular form, very full and well built up. Color a rich creamy white, faintly tinted with pale golden yellow, and exquisitely bordered with soft rosy flesh." [CA96] "In clusters of 4–7 blossoms." [JR13/120] "Extremely floriferous and of uncommon vigor, though of moderate height. Buds elegantly borne on upright, rigid stems; flower cupped, globular, of a rare perfection, absolutely novel in color, having a center of the most beautiful blush pink, in which the flirtatious and delicate sweetness is further enhanced by the pure white found nuanced in the outer petals. The so-delicate tints of this rose, so distinct, as well as its perfection of form, will make it much besought by all fanciers." [JR14/163]

MME EMILIE CHARRIN   PLATE 62
('Mme Emilie Charron')
Perrier, 1895

"Released to commerce in 1895 by its Lyonnais breeder, Mons Perrier. It appeared in a group of pink flowered Teas, among the most beautiful varieties . . . moderate vigor, grows pretty well, and gives many easily-opening blossoms of medium size, very double, China pink shading to bright blush." [JR32/46]

MME ERNEST PERRIN
Widow Schwartz, 1900

"Large flower, coppery yellow, base of petals creamy white, shaded with yellow and mauve. Fine in a hot season." [P1] "Vigorous, foliage cheerful green edged purple; enormous bud; flower very large, ground color apricot nuanced yellow; petals largely tinted creamy blush, bordered mauve and peachblossom pink. A magnificent variety because of its many tints." [JR24/163]

[MME ERNESTINE VERDIER]
Perny/Aschery, 1894

"Mauve-rose, shaded salmon. Medium size." [ARA27/20] "Extra vigorous, with thorny, upright canes; the very large flower, possibly the largest of this sort [Teas?], is very full, and opens with great ease. The form is very graceful, and the erect hold perfect. The wonderful buds are a pretty nuanced pink shade, varying according to exposure and season. As for the blossom's color, it is a mixture of pink, white, and red which is not easy to describe." [JR18/3–4]

MME ERRERA
Soupert & Notting, 1899
From 'Mme Lambard' (T) × 'Luciole' (T).

"Variable, base of petals coppery orange, outer petals flushed and veined with rose, large and full." [P1] "Very great vigor, handsome foliage, beautifully formed bud; flower large, full, well-held; color, salmon yellow, sometimes bright cerise nuanced light yellow. . . . Floriferous and very fragrant." [JR23/170]

[MME EUGÈNE VERDIER]
Levet, 1882
From 'Gloire de Dijon' (N), possibly hybridized with "Mme Barthélemy Levet' (T).

"Branches strong, very handsome icy-green foliage, flower large and well formed, surpassing all others of the 'Gloire de Dijon' sort; thorns straight and light; deep fawn color, very fragrant; a novel coloration." [JR6/149]

[MME F. BRASSAC]
Nabonnand/Brassac, 1883

"Flowers and buds extra large, very double and full; color, a novel shade of bronze red, delicately tinted with coppery yellow; entirely distinct, and justly considered a very excellent rose." [CA90] "Very vigorous; flower large, full, well formed, very large petals; novel coloration, bright red, splendid for this genre. Will be much besought for its unique color." [JR7/184] "Prune to 5–7 eyes. Mme Brassac is the wife of the distinguished Toulouse horticulturalist." [JR10/61]

MME FANNY PAUWELS
Soupert & Notting, 1884

"Flower medium sized, full, bright yellow shaded light yellow, yolk-yellow in the center, sometimes reddish gold. This magnificent rose is one of the most floriferous." [JR8/164] "Growth vigorous and bushy, flower medium-sized or small, light yellow." [JR10/154]

MME GAMON
Gamon, 1905

"Vigorous, bushy, flower large, full; long bud; apricot, nuanced dawn, on a golden yellow ground; very floriferous and fragrant." [JR30/24] "Apricot yellow. Mildews." [ARA27/20] "Very graceful globular form." [JR31/73]

[MME GUSTAVE HENRY]
Buatois, 1899

"Bright pink with orange nubs." [LS] "Vigorous, bushy, flower very large, bud well formed; color, bright coppery pink, nubs golden yellow, extra floriferous." [JR23/169] Parent of 'Maria Star' (T).

[MME HENRI GRAIRE]
Lévêque, 1895

"Bright rose shaded vermilion, tinted bronze, large, full and sweet." [C&Js98] "Vigorous bush; very beautiful, ample, dark green leaves; superbly colored chamois yellow shaded with pink, and with light carmine; often the center is deep peach." [JR19/163]

MME HONORÉ DEFRESNE   PLATE 37
C. Levet, 1886
Seedling of 'Mme Falcot' (T).

"Sparkling yellow." [LS] "Vigorous, seemingly from 'Mme Falcot'; flowers large, full, very well formed; color, beautiful dark yellow with coppery reflections; superb." [JR10/182] "Petals elegantly reflexed. A strong, vigorous grower, with thick foliage." [CA90] "Floriferous. . . . Dedicated to the wife of the great French nurseryman." [JR28/157]

[MME JACQUES CHARRETON]   PLATE 66
Bonnaire, 1897

"Very vigorous and floriferous bush with strong canes holding large or very large flowers with oval long buds pointed at the tip; flowers very beautiful half-open. The exterior petals are milky white, center petals beautiful coppery salmon; very distinct and curious." [JR22/147]

MME JEAN DUPUY
Lambert, 1901

"Yellowish rose with reddish golden yellow centres, outer petals edged with rose. Large and full, opening well; growth vigorous; almost thornless." [P1] "Deep yellow-fawn, edged rose. Mildews." [ARA27/20] "Dedicated to the wife of the sympatico French minister of Agriculture . . . vigorous, well covered with beautiful foliage, and its branches are paratially thornless. . . . Its deportment is that of 'Maman Cochet' or 'Franziska Krüger'. Its buds are long and solitary, and develop at the ends of the long branches, and are more or less erect. The blossoms are large and well formed, coppery red without and pinkish yellow within . . . freely remontant . . . delicious perfume." [JR25/170] "A good healthy grower. Makes a neat compact bush." [C&Js04]

MME JOSÉPHINE MÜHLE
Listed as 'Safrano à Fleurs Rouges'.

[MME JULES CAMBON]
Bernaix, 1888

"Flesh color, reverse of petals magenta; of medium size, full; growth moderate." [CA93] "Moderate vigor. Elegant flower with firm petals, mostly oval; color, fresh incarnate pink with the petal edges carmine with magenta reflections grading insensibly into the straw yellow nub. . . . This variety exhibits, at the same time, stronger or weaker coloration, giving it a mutable character which is quite striking." [JR12/164]

[MME LA BARONNE BERGE]
('Baronne Berge')
Pernet père, 1892

"Beautiful light rose, shaded with cream and yellow. Very free and constant bloomer." [CA95] "Vigorous, shooting out upright canes; flower large or medium-sized; petal edges bright pink, center light yellow, very fragrant; variety notable due to its coloration and good growth. Bloom is continuous." [JR16/154] "A most lovely rose, large full flowers, very double and sweet, color bright rosy red, with clear golden-yellow centre, very full and continuous bloomer, plants begin to bloom while very young; grand for bedding; very bright and sweetly scented." [C&Js98]

MME LA COMTESSE DE CASERTA
Nabonnand, 1877

"A pretty cherry-pink, veined red." [JR5/21] "Large and very beautiful flowers; fine full form, very double and fragrant; color dark purplish red, elegantly clouded with a pale coppery yellow." [CA93] "Flower large, petals thick, not very full, showy, imbricated, coppery red; heavy, vigorous wood with large thorns. A quite new sort." [JR1/12/14] "Vigorous; branches greenish red; thorns hooked, occasional, pretty large . . . effective, very fragrant." [S]

[MME LA PRINCESSE DE BESSARABA DE BRANCOVAN]   PLATE 50
Bernaix, 1890

"Pink and yellow." [LS] "Growth moderate in size, branching, vigorous, very floriferous, bud subglobular to slightly ovoid; flower of middle size and fulness; in color, changeable, very fresh carmine, shading to blush at the edge, irradiated with canary yellow to pale chrome when opening." [JR14/163] Parent of 'Mme C. P. Strassheim' (T).

MME LAURENT SIMONS
Lévêque, 1894

"Very vigorous, foliage ample, glossy green; flowers very large, full, handsome long bud; color, coppery pinkish yellow nuanced chrome red and tinted blush pink. Sometimes the same plant will bear coppery red blossoms shaded yellow." [JR18/150]

[MME LÉON FÉVRIER]
Nabonnand, 1882

"A pretty and desirable variety; color a rare shade of silver rose, beautifully clouded with rich ruby crimson; flowers large, moderately full, very regular in form and exceedingly sweet." [CA90] "Very vigorous; flower very large, semi-double, perfect bud, superb hold; flesh-white, blooms in winter." [JR6/186]

[MME MARGOTTIN]
Guillot fils, 1866

"Rich citron-red, shaded apricot; large, full flowers; profuse bloomer." [C&Js98] "Flowers large or medium-sized, very full, slightly globular, a beautiful deep citron yellow with a peach pink center, petal edges white." [I'H66/318] "Vigorous bush . . . the fairly long and feeble peduncle lets the flower nod a little too much — but this is not always the case." [S]

[MME MARTHE DU BOURG]
Bernaix, 1889

"Large, nearly double, nicely pointed centre; creamy white with carmine on the edges; very pretty." [CA93] "Fine cup shaped roses with prettily crimped petals, creamy pink with rose center." [C&Js98] "Of good vigor, covered continuously with flowers during the height of the season. Flower pretty big, well formed, with thick petals; outer petals very large, recurved, spread out in back; center petals stiff and concave; color, white washed violet-carmine with a blush border — at first — then passing upon expansion of the blossom to pale chrome yellow washed blush. Very fresh color." [JR13/162]

[MME MAURICE KUPPENHEIM]
Widow Ducher, 1877

"Pale yellow, shaded with apricot." [EL] "Vigorous; flower large, full, salmon yellow, sometimes light pink." [JR1/12/12] "A remarkably pretty rose; flowers of elegant form, large, full and double; color pale canary yellow, faintly tinged with pink, shaded with coppery rose, sometimes soft rosy flesh; very sweet." [CA90]

[MME NABONNAND]
Nabonnand, 1877

"Blossom very large, full, well formed, flesh white shaded pink, canes upright and big, perfect 'hold.' " [JR1/12/14] "White, shaded to light carmine, free-flowering and very attractive when in good condition and well grown. Grows more tall than bushy, and cannot boast of a strong constitution." [B&V] "Bush able, in two or three years, to make a plant a yard high [ca. 1 m], having pretty numerous sub-branches divided into flowering branchlets, sometimes multifloral, but usually terminating in one blossom nodding slightly on its stem." [S]

[MME OLGA]
Lévêque, 1889

"Beautiful large buds and flowers, cream white, shaded carmine, very sweet." [C&Js98] "Vigorous bush; foliage ample, dark green; flower large, full, very well formed, held well and firmly; beautifully colored white very finely and delicately shaded yellow nuanced greenish. Very distinct and beautiful." [JR13/164]

[MME PAUL VARIN-BERNIER]
Soupert & Notting, 1906

From 'Mme C. P. Strassheim' (T) × 'Mme Dr. Jütté' (T).

"Melon color in the different shadings; good size and perfect form." [C&Js10] "The plant is of a healthy vigor and bears dark foliage. The flower is lightly double and large. The bud is completely charming and resembles . . . [that of] 'Richmond'. One could call 'Mme Paul Varin-Bernier' a 'Richmond with Yellow Flowers'. It forces easily, easily producing solitary buds held proudly just as it does outside. . . . No matter what the season, [the buds] open well; bloom doesn't abate until frost; it blooms in bouquets late in the season. The color is melon in the various shades; center and buds are dark yellow, petal edges light silvery yellow. . . . Captivating perfume." [JR30/152]

[MME PAULINE LABONTÉ]   PLATE 15
Pradel, 1852

"Salmon rose; large, full and good in the bud; an excellent sort." [CA88] "Vigorous bush; flower large, full, fragrant; color, salmony pink." [S] "Outer petals flesh tinted with cream, centre deep salmon-buff, very large and full, sometimes peculiarly mottled [*reminding one of 'David Pradel'*]; a superb and distinct rose." [JC]

[MME PELISSON]
(='Mme Pellissier'?)

Brosse, 1891

"This new variety . . . is distinguished by its abundant and continuous bloom; the bush is vigorous and compact; the blossom is colored light citron with exterior petals being white on the outside; always growing and always covered with flowers until frost comes to destroy them; it's the first rose to open, and the last to come out; in a cluster of six to twelve double blossoms, they are of sparkling beauty. Delicious perfume; flower of medium size; having a pretty long stem which allows one to cull them without cutting the whole group." [JR15/179] "Fine tulip form, very sweet." [C&Js98]

[MME PHILÉMON COCHET]   PLATE 41
S. Cochet, 1887

Seedling of 'Sylphide' (T).

"Bright, rich, rosy pink, beautiful buds and large, well-filled flowers, very fragrant and constant bloomer." [C&Js99] "Bush of good vigor, with thick fairly upright canes of a pale purple brown, having somewhat triangular occasional or paired thorns. Leaves of 5–7 leaflets, of medium size, bright green staying purple for a long time beneath. Peduncle very thick and smooth. The solitary bud is of good size, being however not very conical but rather truncated-obtuse at the tip, very light flesh pink in color; some petal-bases are sometimes tinted a lightly carmined pink. Flowers medium-sized or large, of a slightly hollowed cup-shape, outer petals relatively large, extremely light pink, often marked exteriorly with large blotches of a lightly salmoned pink. The base of this blossom is light pink nuanced pale salmon with a *soupçon* of bluish violet which gains in intensity around the petal-tips. . . . This rose, of beautiful form, is also fragrant . . . issued in 1884 from 'Sylphide', and has the wonderful trait of being extremely floriferous even towards the end of the season." [JR11/167]

[MME PHILIPPE KUNTZ]   PLATE 47
Bernaix, 1889

"Large, full, bright pink or China rose, finely formed and fragrant; free bloomer." [CA93] "Vigorous; beautiful brilliant green foliage. Flowers borne on thick stems, cupped, with large outer petals held out strongly; color, cerise red fading to delicate blush. This variety is notable for the contrast of colors in the flower which, delicate salmon pink upon opening, very rapidly becomes velvety crimson [*thereafter fading to blush pink*]." [JR13/162]

[MME PIERRE GUILLOT]
Guillot & fils, 1888

"Vigorous; flower large, quite full, opening well, very well formed, nearly always solitary; stem strong; color, a ground of coppery orange yellow grading insensibly to a lighter shade at the top; petals bordered and tipped distinctly with carmine pink, with a yellowish white reverse; fragrant; unique coloration; extra beautiful." [JR12/146] "Free bloomer." [CA93]

MME PIERRE PERNY
Nabonnand, 1879

"Saffron-yellow. Beautiful bud." [H] "Moderate vigor, nearly thornless, with semi-double flowers, well-formed, with a saffron-yellow elongated bud." [JR5/21]

[MME REMOND]
E. Lambert, 1882
From 'Comtesse de Labarthe' (T) × 'Anna Olivier' (T).

"A charming and valuable new rose, very double and full, fragrant, color pale sulphur yellow; petals broadly margined with bright red; very striking and remarkably beautiful." [CA88] "Vigorous, having medium-sized, full flowers which are yellow with the petal edges nasturtium; canes green, nearly thornless." [JR6/163]

[MME THÉRÈSE DESCHAMPS]
Nabonnand, 1888

"Flowers red, reverse of petals whitish; large, semi-double; growth vigorous." [CA93] "Very vigorous; big-wooded; small thorns; foliage very thick, matte bronze-green; flower large, erect, in clusters of 5–6; color, a veined red with white reflections towards the petal edges." [JR12/148] "Growth spreading, branching, with canes horizontal or indeed pendulous. Wood—old, greenish brown striped grayish; new, brownish green on the sunny side, paler on the shaded. Thorns occasional, some of them small; decurrent sometimes, to a lesser degree than they are high; hooked, the upper edge convex; grayish on the old wood, brown on the lower part of the [*present-season's*] branch, pink above. Foliage plain matte green, the reverse a little purplish at the head; leaves somewhat spaced. Short rachis supplied beneath with hooked prickles, and, on the sides, with very rare glandular hairs, branched or reflexed at the summit. Leaflets five or seven, the side ones neatly petiolate; all longly oval-lanceolate, often acuminate; toothed, the dentations slanting somewhat. Inflorescence few-flowered—2, 3, or 4 blossoms—the secondary floral axes extremely short, growing from the axil; either with one simple bract and one leaf of three leaflets; or with one simple bract, one foliaceous bract, and one leaf of three leaflets. Peduncle long, smooth or pubescent, obscurely articulate, rather abruptly inflated into a conical-cylindrical calyx-tube. Calyx segments barely longer than the bud; outer edges with filiform auricles; reflexing. Bud crimson; imbricated with, at the center, obscure bundles of petals. Flower semi-double, very bright pink; petals striped on the upper surface with carmine lines along the nerves;

yellowish white on the reverse. Styles numerous, long, pubescent, pink. Stigmata yellowish." [JR23/162–163] Author of the immediately previous quotation places 'Mme Thérèse Deschamps' in the Noisette camp; could there be confusion with 'Deschamps', *alias* 'Longworth Rambler', the Noisette offered by Mons Deschamps in 1877?

[MME THERESE ROSWELL]
('Mme Rathswell,' 'Rathswell'?)
California Nursery Co.?, by 1906

"Rose-colored; small bloom; good growth; perfect and retained foliage; thornless." [CaRoll/3/2] "Bud carmine, opening rose, with deeper shadings, somewhat short; open flower double and holds center well; though small, often of value as cut-flower. A climber or semi-climber with perfect foliage, which stands the dampest conditions without mildew. Blooms practically the whole year in Pacific South-West. Most valuable because it neither balls in dampness nor opens too quickly in heat and retains color well." [Th2] "A most valuable light red Tea for seacoast areas." [ARA28/103] It is by sheer conjecture that we connect the mysterious 'Rathswell' of Capt. Thomas to the equally mysterious 'Mme Therese Roswell' of the California Nursery Co.

MME V. MORRELL
Listed as 'V. Viviand-Morel'.

[MME VERMOREL]
Mari/Jupeau, 1901

"Apricot yellow." [LS] "Dark, coppery yellow with bronze center; double; good size; lasting; fine cutting rose, with long stem; will ball in wet; splendid foliage." [CaRoll/3/3] "Attractive in color; form of rose varies; good growth and foliage; fair bloomer. Does well in hot weather." [ARA18/112]

[MME VICTOR CAILLET]
Bernaix, 1891

"Bush very floriferous and of good vigor. Blossom rather large than medium, pretty double. Exterior petals concave, cupped, thick, separate, inner petals raged and muddled, all of a peony pink with carmine reflections nuanced salmon. Novel coloration, notable, having the singular quality of fading to white in age, and thus showing on the same plant both red and white flowers." [JR15/150]

[MME VON SIEMENS]
Nabonnand, 1895
Seedling of 'Mme Nabonnand' (T).

"Perfect form, fine rosy flesh color, beautifully shaded, very sweet, constant and abundant bloomer." [C&Js98] "Flower very large, full, perfect hold; color, flesh pink; very beautiful long bud; very pretty foliage. Very vigorous bush, very floriferous, very beautiful variety." [JR19/180]

[MME WELCHE]
('Mme Welch')
Widow Ducher/Bennett, 1876
From 'Devoniensis' (T) × 'Souvenir d'Un Ami' (T).

"Pale yellow, deep orange center, often shaded with reddish copper; flowers large, well formed and very double." [CA88] "Large, full globular flowers, and long, finely pointed buds; color soft peachy yellow, delicately clouded with pale rose; very sweet and handsome; blooms freely during the whole season." [C&Js98] "Vigorous bush; floriferous; flower large, full, flat, very fragrant;

color, coppery orange yellow within; outer petals pale yellow." [S] "Height and compactness medium, hardy; foliage sufficient to plentiful, healthy; bloom moderate, almost continuous spring and fall, about half time in July and August." [ARA18/126] "The ownership of the beautiful Tea Rose bearing the name of Mme Welche, the wife of the prefect of Lyon . . . was sold to Mr. Henry Bennett." [JR1/1/8]

[MONSIEUR CHARLES DE THÉZILLAT]
Nabonnand, 1888

"Flowers creamy yellow, centres chamois; very large, full, globular form." [CA93] "Very vigorous; flower very large, very full, globular, imbricated, erect, a true Tea, large petals; splendid color of creamy yellow, with a center of nuanced buff." [JR12/148]

[MONSIEUR EDOUARD LITTAYE]
Bernaix, 1891

"Buds large, long, and of very fine shape; full and double when open; color rosy carmine, tinted light pink, often shaded with violet pink." [CA95] "Non-climbing; flowers abundant, of good hold; buds wonderful in form, conical-ovoid; color, carmine pink tinted amaranth during expansion, paler pink when the flower is open, the center being violet red. Very remontant." [JR15/150]

[MONT ROSA]
('Montrosa')
Ducher, 1872

"Dawn gold." [LS] "Vigorous; flower medium-sized, full; flesh pink." [S] An ancestor of 'Oscar Chauvry' (N).

[MORNING GLOW]
W. Paul, 1902

"Rose glow, deepening towards center." [CA06] "Carmine and orange." [LS] "Flower large, full; petals thick; color, bright crimson pink tinted orange and maroon." [JR26/87] "These varieties [of which 'Morning Glow' is one], say the breeders, are a selection of our seedlings from [the] Riviera[,] born from the Tea-scented and China sorts grown in quantity in the south of Europe for cutting. They continue the beautiful series which we began several years ago with the now well-known roses 'Enchantress' and 'Queen Mab'." [JR26/86]

[MRS. ALICE BROOMHALL]
A. Schwartz, 1910
From 'Dr. Grill' (T) × 'G. Nabonnand' (T).

"Vigorous bush; flower large, double; opens well; bud long; color, salmon apricot nuanced and tinted coppery orange yellow fading to pale pink tinted cream, pretty coloration, very elegant bud, very floriferous." [JR34/169] "A nice Tea, much like 'Souvenir of Stella Gray', with better stem and good foliage." [ARA28/100]

[MRS. EDWARD MAWLEY]
A. Dickson, 1899

"Bright rich pink, shading to tender rose or flesh color, very large and full, long plump buds on very long stems; a superb garden rose of grand size and substance, a vigorous grower, abundant bloomer, and quite hardy." [C&Js02] "Pink, tinted carmine.—Moderately vigorous . . . One of the best exhibition Teas. Fragrant." [Cat12]

MRS. FOLEY-HOBBS
A. Dickson, 1910

"Ivory white." [Bk] "Purely an exhibition variety, in creamy white with some variable pink at the tips. It has magnificent flower form and substance, more than the stems can hold upright." [Hk] "Good in color and growth; blooming below the average." [ARA18/117] "Vigorous and very robust, each branch developing a bud which matures into a magnificent, enormous blossom." [JR34/103]

MRS. HERBERT HAWKSWORTH
A. Dickson, 1912

"Deeply zoned, delicate ecru on milk white. With us, something on the order of 'Kaiserin Auguste Viktoria'. Practically no disbudding." [Th] "Very pretty, globular, very large, velvety petals, numerous and gracefully arranged . . . the growth is very vigorous, extremely floriferous. . . . The color is, at first, dull white; then, as the rose opens, it becomes silvery white . . . delicious Tea scent." [JR36/91] "Growth good, hardy; good foliage and stem; medium to large size, lasts well . . . thirty blooms in 1915." [ARA16/20] "Low-growing, moderately compact, hardy; foliage sufficient, black-spots; bloom moderate, almost continuous." [ARA18/127] "Perfume mild; thirty-four blooms throughout the season; growth average. A fair rose for all purposes." [ARA17/22]

MRS. HUBERT TAYLOR
A. Dickson, 1910

"Shell-pink, the edges of the petals being ivory-white; a really superb Rose, of perfect formation and finish. Distinct and fine." [C&Js14] "A beautiful Tea, with a flower . . . nearly white in colour." [F-M] "Good grower and bloomer; color fair; foliage susceptible to mildew. Without these faults would be a good fall decorative." [ARA18/117]

[MRS. J. PIERPONT MORGAN]
May/Dingee & Conard, 1895
Sport of 'Mme Cusin' (T).

"A sport from 'Mme Cusin'; in every way much superior to that variety. The flowers are much larger and very double, petals are broad and massive; prolific bloomer; color intensely bright cerise or rose pink. Considered one of the finest and most beautiful in form, color, and substance ever produced." [CA95]

[MRS. JAMES WILSON]
A. Dickson, 1889

"Pale yellow tipped with rose pink." [CA93] "In form, this beautiful novelty resembles the superb 'Catherine Mermet'. The flowers are a deep lemon yellow. The petals are edged pink. They are very large, full, of perfect form, and delicious perfume; petals thick and smooth. The growth is vigorous, putting forth many canes, and the blossoms which are produced profusely all season are borne on upright stems, which shows off the blossom's good [high] point and keeps it in good condition for an extremely long time. Splendid for exhibition." [JR13/90] "Of good growth when established, and fair foliage. The habit is peculiar, in that the centre or crown bud is quite overwhelmed and starved out by the growth of the side flower buds unless these be thinned out at once; and even when this is done, the bud does not grow proportionately to the thickness of the shoot, and the blooms are rather undersized and disappointing. The petals are good and the shape nicely pointed: it is late in blooming, and not many flowers come to perfection on one plant. A pretty colour, sometimes a little like that of 'Marie Van Houtte'." [F-M3]

[MRS. JESSIE FREMONT]
Dingee & Conard, 1891
Seedling of 'Comtesse de Labarthe' (T).

"A seedling of 'Duchesse de Brabant' [*alias* 'Comtesse de Labarthe'], its buds are not quite as big, but they are more double and more substantial; the color is white, passing to deep flesh pink, sometimes nuanced coppery red of a very delicate appearance; this is a vigorous hybrid which blooms very freely." [JR15/88] "Often taking on nuances of coppery red or of old rose." [JR16/38]

MRS. MYLES KENNEDY
A. Dickson, 1906

"Silver-white, shaded light peach-buff. Mildews." [ARA27/20] "Surpasses 'Souvenir d'Elise [*sic*] Vardon', favored in its time, because this new variety is more vigorous. The color is beautiful silvery white with chamois shading." [JR31/73] "Deeper pink in centre with back edge of petals a slightly deeper shade of pink." [C&Js08] "Fair growth; very shy bloomer." [ARA18/117] "Flowers of great size. Colour silvery white, with a delicate picotee edging to the petal. It is purely an exhibitor's Rose, and requries high culture. A fairly vigorous grower for this class." [F-M]

[MRS. OLIVER AMES]
R. Montgomery, 1898
Sport of 'Mme Cusin' (T).

"Delicate pink, the petals edged deep pink at their tips while being nearly white at their base." [JR26/5] "Creamy yellow and soft glowing rose." [C&Js03] "Round full flowers with lovely shell shaped petals, elegantly ruffled. . . . The plant is a neat bushy grower, and a most constant and abundant bloomer, particularly fine for bedding, as it is a strong robust grower, and a tremendous bloomer, the buds are very beautiful and borne in great profusion all through the Summer and Fall. Delightfully fragrant." [C&Js05]

MRS. REYNOLDS HOLE
Nabonnand, 1900
From 'Archiduc Joseph' (T) × 'André Schwartz' (T).

"Blossom very large, very full; color, deep purplish pink, interior tinted crimson; very handsome solitary bud borne on a long stem; growth very vigorous, wood thorny, bronze-red; very pretty foliage; very floriferous. Fragrant." [JR25/4]

MRS. S.T. WRIGHT
A. Dickson, 1914
Sport of 'Harry Kirk' (T).

"Cadmium yellow." [Ÿ] "The guard petals are delicate old-gold; the center petals have a delicate and charming suffusion of delightful pure rose-pink on orange-chrome. The uniquely colored blooms have a deliciously pervading perfume. It is very floriferous." [C&Js16] "Good color; lacks in growth and blooming." [ARA18/117]

[MURIEL GRAHAME]
('Yellow Mermet')
A. Dickson, 1898
Sport of 'Catherine Mermet' (T).

"Pale cream." [Cat12] "Similar in shape to 'Catherine Mermet'; fine canary yellow, tipped with rosy pink. A healthy vigorous grower and abundant bloomer. Flowers are among the very largest in the ever-blooming class." [C&Js06]

MYSTÈRE
Nabonnand, 1877

"Vigorous, flowers very large, full, well-formed, upright, cupped, pink veined and marbled darker. Unique in color." [JR1/12/14]

[NAMENLOSE SCHÖNE]
(trans., 'Nameless Beauty')
Deegen, 1886

"Upon presenting a number of cut flowers [of 'Namenlöse Schöne'], I asked the first convention of the society of German rose hobbyists in Darmstadt — on June 19, 1885 — for an identification of this valuable cultivar . . . and myself told them, 'About 33 years ago, we received among other rose shipments this rose as a single specimen without name and number; because it was unlabeled, it was ignored at first and the shipper was not noted. Later, however, because of its bloom, advantages, and beauty, it caught our attention. It is a Noisette-Tea, extraordinarily rich in bloom and very regularly remontant, such that a person can easily and readily have it quickly and perpetually in bloom. The bud and blossom are of high quality, pleasingly formed and double, blooming in exquisite pure white, only occasionally tinted a slight flesh-red in the open air. With less light outside, it is softly imbued with sulphur yellow of the finest hue. The blossom changes, in its further development, from the loveliest double closed form to, finally, the open bowl of the rose 'Souvenir de la Malmaison', and nearly the same size. The flower has a remarkably strong but nevertheless sweet and mild fragrance, and is not likely to be surpassed by any other sort of rose in that. The blossom is perched upon a slender stem, and is surrounded by many buds. On the leafstalks of the plant are five elongated, elegantly-formed leaves of a vivid green coloration. Never is a flower scorched, even in the most intense heat of the sun; indeed, the more intense the sun's rays on this rose, the more flawlessly pure white it is, the more rapidly it reblooms, the more aromatic the pleasant fragrance, and the more splendid the bud and flower form. Its inexhaustible bloom, both ready and early, even from the smallest plants, is not even surpassed by 'Hermosa'. As is well known, we have managed large, extensive, rose collections for about 33 years, but neither I nor the local rosarians Franz Deegen jr. and Ernst Herger — nor the foreign rose concerns — have gotten to know this rose, except from this one, now old, specimen. Further, no one anywhere else has come across it. To be sure, however, its high value has become recognized by the above-mentioned experts as well as by the nurseries. The old plant is still in my possession, recently propagated; but, because it was nameless, starts of it have not yet been distributed.'" [RZ86/23–24] "Held in high consideration by German growers. It is white, tinged with sulphur yellow; very fragrant; buds and flowers large and well formed; very free blooming." [CA90]

[NARCISSE]
Avoux & Crozy, 1858

"Pale lemon yellow, tinged with salmon rose; medium size, full and double; very fragrant." [CA90] "Flower large, full, beautiful yellow fading to straw yellow; much to be recommended." [S] "Fine pale yellow, habit of a Noisette; a beautiful abundant blooming rose, moderate in habit, and tolerably hardy." [JC] "A small bush much in the way of 'Narcisse' and '[Le] Pactole'." [l'H57/98] There is confusion between this cultivar and the 1845 Noisette 'Narcisse' of Mansais.

[NELLY JOHNSTONE]
G. Paul, 1906
Seedling of 'Mme Berkeley' (T).

"Pure rose pink often shot with light pale violet on the outside; blooms fairly double with fine light petals. Free flowering and deliciously fragrant." [C&Js08] "Vigorous bush, beautiful long bud, flower large, full; color, carnation pink, sometimes tinted violet on the outside." [JR33/184–185]

[NITA WELDON]
A. Dickson, 1908

"Ivory-white with each petal edged light pink; perfect." [C&Js12] "White, tinted blush. — Vigorous. — [For the] garden." [Cat12]

[PALO ALTO]
Conard & Jones, 1898

"This is a splendid new rose from California. It is large, full and very sweet; the color is a lovely chamois rose, delicately tinged at centre with golden-yellow and creamy white. The bush is a strong healthy grower, and constant and abundant bloomer; it is a rose sure to please and give satisfaction in every way; bears beautiful large sweet roses all through the season." [C&Js98] Possibly originated by Luther Burbank. Palo Alto, city in California.

PAUL NABONNAND
Nabonnand, 1877

"Satiny-rose." [EL] "Bright rose." [ARA27/20] "Pure rose colour, large and full, beautiful bud, vigorous, free-flowering and fine. It is very popular with the nurserymen who cultivate its flowers largely for export." [B&V] "Very vigorous; flower very large, very full, form and 'hold' perfect." [JR1/12/14] "Large growth; very fine foliage, well held; no mildew. Flowers of medium size, double, opens well, light rose to strawberry in the center. Good on seacoast. Decorative." [ARA28/103] "Vigorous, with dark green branches touched with red; thorns hooked, often flat, pretty big; leaves olive green, finely dentate; flower very large, very full, Hydrangea pink. This variety is wonderful by all reports, and should not be left out of any collection." [S]

[PEACH BLOSSOM]
Conard & Jones, 1898

"A superb new Tea Rose introduced from California; the flowers are of exquisite form, with broad deep petals of excellent substance, and deliciously sweet; the color is a rich shade of golden rose or peach blossom; very rare and beautiful. All we have seen of this rose leads us to believe it is a variety of the very first quality." [C&Js98] Possibly originated by Luther Burbank.

[PEARL RIVERS]
Dingee & Conard, 1890

"Obtained by crossing 'Devoniensis' [T] and 'Mme [de] Watteville' [T], this variety partakes of the distinctive characteristics of these two varieties, but the stature of its growth is better and its blossoms open more freely. Its color is an ivory white delicately nuanced and bordered light pink; very fragrant and of an exquisite beauty." [JR15/88] "The flowers are large and full with peachy-red buds . . . very beautiful and deliciously sweet." [C&Js98]

PENELOPE
J. Williams, 1906
Red with an ivory center.

PERFECTION DE MONPLAISIR
('Perfection de Montplaisir')
Levet, 1871
Seedling of 'Canari' (T).

"Clear lemon, form of the flowers similar to [that of 'Parks' Yellow Tea-Scented China'], very pretty, habit moderate." [JC] "Flower medium-sized, full, fragrant; color, bright canary yellow." [S] "A good Tea, which may be described as an improved 'Canari'; like that sort it is delicate." [EL] "[Of 'Perfection de Monplaisir', 'Jean Pernet', and 'Perle des Jardins',] 'Perfection de Montplaisir' [*sic*] has the lightest color." [JR10/45] Monplaisir was Levet's home community.

[PERLE DE FEU]
(trans., 'Fire-Pearl')
Dubreuil, 1893
From 'Mme Falcot' (T) × 'Claire Carnot' (N).

"Chinese-yellow. Small." [ARA27/20] "Bushy plant, very vigorous and very floriferous; medium-sized flower; graceful, pretty form; a most remarkable color . . . copper-red nuanced nankeen yellow, with purplish chamois reflections. Sometimes in the spring it is incarnadine with chamois reflections." [JR17/166] "This is a perfect little gem; flowers are only of medium size, but the buds are large in proportion and of beautiful, perfect form, and the color is so intense that its name, 'The Fire Pearl', is a better description than any we can write." [C&Js99]

PERLE DES JAUNES
Reymond, 1903

"Deep orange yellow, tinted salmon." [K2] "Very vigorous, with twiggy growth, handsome foliage, large and full flowers; superbly colored dark golden yellow, with orange and carmine. Remarkable for the pretty shade of yellow, and for the flowers, which are just as large as those of 'Mme Falcot', but fuller. This rose forms a bush which is compact, a quality which will make it much desired for bedding; very floriferous." [JR27/131] "Fair growth; no special distinction." [ARA18/117]

PRIMROSE
Dingee & Conard, 1908
Light yellow. "Poor growth and foliage; shy bloomer." [ARA18/117]

PRINCE WASILTCHIKOFF
Listed as 'Duchess of Edinburgh'.

[PRINCESS BONNIE]
Dingee & Conard, 1896
From 'Bon Silène' (T) × 'William Francis Bennett' (HT).

"Rich vivid crimson, large, semi-double with fine petals, exceedingly fragrant, beautiful long buds." [CA97] "The flowers are extra large and full, perfectly double, and deliciously sweet; the color is solid rich crimson, exquisitely shaded; a constant and abundant bloomer, loaded with flowers the whole season; a hardy vigorous grower, and one of the sweetest and most beautiful everblooming roses you can possibly have." [C&Js98] "This rose would seem to be of very abundant bloom, nearly continuous. The flowers are borne on upright, strong stems; they are large, pretty full, and a beautiful crimson which is more pronounced than that of 'William Francis Bennett'. The reverse of the petals has the same color as those of 'Général Jacqueminot', while the interior is lightly striped white. The perfume is penetrating and sweet though not as strong as that of the HP's." [JR20/98] "Moderately high and compact, fairly hardy; foliage sufficient, black-spots somewhat; bloom free, continuous." [ARA18/127]

[PRINCESS OF WALES]
Bennett, 1882
From 'Adam' (T) × 'Elise Sauvage' (T).

"Moderate vigor; flower large, well formed; exterior petals pink yellow; those of the center, deep rich waxy yellow; distinct; opens well; buds long and pointed. . . . Very floriferous, and well held." [S] "Well cupped handsome flower of good size and form. In habit this rose resembles 'Comtesse de Nadaillac' [T, Guillot fils, 1871, coppery-flesh]." [B&V] "Of small dwarf growth and foliage, requiring fine weather. . . . A small stem will sometimes grow, stiffen, and swell for a long time without opening the bud, which when it does come will be a great and probably a good Rose, while a much stronger shoot of three times its length perhaps remains pliable, opens quickly, and produces a much inferior bloom. The shape of the smaller flowers is weak and undecided, but there is no doubt about its beauty in form and every other quality when it does come good, though it is seldom very large. It is variable in colour, and is somewhat capricious, doing well in some soils and badly in others, but generally best as a standard." [F-M3]

[PRINCESSE ALICE DE MONACO]
Weber, 1893

"Blush pink." [JR20/7] "Creamy yellow edged with rose, centre peach colour, handsome buds; very free and effective; one of the most beautiful decorative Tea Roses." [P1]

PRINCESSE DE BESSARABA DE BRANCOVAN
Listed as 'Mme la Princesse de Bessaraba de Brancovan'.

PRINCESSE DE VENOSA
Dubreuil, 1895

"Non-climbing, wood dark, foliage very bright, bud a beautiful long ovoid form, white tinted blush nuanced yellow upon opening. Flower . . . well formed, opens well, very fragrant, golden nankeen yellow nuanced carmine with amethyst violet glimmerings." [JR19/147]

PRINCESSE ÉTIENNE DE CROY   PLATE 68
Ketten Bros., 1898
From 'Comtesse de Labarthe' (T) × 'Mme Eugène Verdier' (T).

"Lilac peach carmine, tinted China pink, on a ground of pale orange, very large, very full, opens well, erect, firm stem. Vigorous and floriferous." [JR22/133]

PRINCESSE HOHENZOLLERN
Listed as 'S.A.R. Mme la Princesse de Hohenzollern, Infante de Portugal'.

PRINCIPESSA DI NAPOLI
Bonfiglioli, 1898; or Brauer/Ketten Bros., 1898
From 'Duc de Magenta' (T) × 'Safrano' (T).

"Fresh pink with lilac." [Ÿ] "Pale rose, base of petals cream colour, fine long buds; hardy and free, vigorous." [P1] "Flower pale pink on a cream ground, large, full, solitary, long stem, scent of 'Maréchal Niel'. Bush floriferous and vigorous." [JR22/133]

PROFESSEUR GANIVIAT   PLATE 51
Perrier, 1890

"Shaded fire-red." [RR] "Dark red." [LS] "Fair growth; good foliage. Medium sized wine-color blooms with orange glow in center; has cutting value." [ARA28/103] "Seems to be very floriferous; the flower is medium-sized, very full, a pretty color of cherry-red, and the bud is well formed." [JR14/166] "Growth very vigorous,

very floriferous, flower well formed, large, full, stem firm, color poppy-red, shaded, not as dark as 'Souvenir de Thérèse Levet'." [JR14/164]

RATHSWELL
Listed as 'Mme Therese Roswell'.

[RECUERDO DI ANTONIO PELUFFO]   PLATE 74
Soupert & Notting, 1910
From 'Mélanie Soupert' (N) × 'Mme Constant Soupert' (T).

"Diaphanous light yellow, washed delicate pink along the edges. Flowers extremely large, of perfect form, produced continuously until late in the autumn. . . . The plant is vigorous with quite decorative foliage; it produces long and elegant buds." [JR34/183] "An old Tea which rivals the best of the Hybrid Teas in size and cutting value. Variegated light yellow and pink. Strongly recommended for all southern climates." [ARA28/103] "Medium growth." [CaRoII/3/3]

RED SAFRANO
Listed as 'Safrano à Fleurs Rouges'.

REGULUS
('Comtesse de Woronzoff')
Moreau-Robert, 1860

"Bright rose, shaded with copper, large and full." [FP] "Bright copper and rose; pretty, habit vigorous." [JC] "Large regularly formed solid flowers, borne in great abundance on stout hardy bushes all through the growing season; color, clear rosy pink, very fragrant and desirable. A fine garden rose." [C&Js06] "Growth very vigorous; flower medium-sized, full, flat; petals fluted; very fragrant; color, intense coppery-pink, center darker." [S] Marcus Atilius Regulus, flourished 240 BC, Roman consul and general.

[REICHSGRAF E. VON KESSELSTATT]
Lambert, 1898
From 'Princesse Alice de Monaco' (T) × 'Duchesse Marie Salviati' (T).

"Flowers extra large and quite full, petals broad and nicely arched, color brilliant carmine, passing to rose-pink on pure white ground; petals edged with rich crimson, very fragrant. The bush is a handsome erect grower and abundant bloomer." [C&Js99]

[REINE EMMA DES PAYS-BAS]
Nabonnand, 1879

"Yellow, shaded with reddish salmon." [EL] "Yellow, orange, red—looking just like a sunrise. It is large, full, very well formed, and well held." [JR3/156] "Its medium-sized flowers are semi-double, and divided into two parts; its color is sharp." [JR10/46] "Vigorous, nice foliage; flower very large, full, imbricated, perfect form, measuring as much as five in across [ca. 1.25 dm]; color, gold tinted salmon with dawn-gold reflections, singularly beautiful; same coloration as 'Fortune's Double Yellow', but bigger and fuller." [S] "Reverse of petals almost flame-coloured, free growing, full size, vigorous and floriferous. Although quite distinct the metallic blush of its flowers is remindful of 'L'Idéal' [N, Nabonnand, 1887, yellow/carmine]. A valuable and most desirable variety." [B&V]

[REINE OLGA]

('Queen Olga of Greece')

Nabonnand, 1885

"Soft rosy pink, shaded with golden yellow; edge of petals silver rose." [C&Js07] "Full flowers; an exceedingly free bloomer." [C&Js11] "Very vigorous bush, with not very thorny big wood; flower large, full, imbricated, perfect form; color, nuanced coppery red; novel coloration; very fragrant." [JR9/166]

RHODOLOGUE JULES GRAVEREAUX

Dr. Fontes, 1908

From 'Marie Van Houtte' (T) × 'Mme Abel Chatenay' (HT).

"Yellowish pink, medium size, very full, light scent, moderate height." [Sn]

ROI DE SIAM

Laffay, 1825

"Pinkish-yellow." [EER] "Ovary ovoid; flower large, semi-double, pale pink; lower petals muddled and rolled at the edge." [S] "Tall growth, not bushy; very shy bloomer." [ARA18/116]

[ROSA MUNDI]

Conard & Jones, 1898

"Deep rich crimson, large cupped form, very free bloomer. A splendid rose that ought to be better known. Scarce and rare." [C&Js98]

[ROSALIE]

('Reine des Fées')

Ellwanger & Barry, 1884

Seedling of 'Marie Van Houtte' (T).

"Medium sized flowers, very full and regular; color clear, bright pink; deliciously scented; a profuse bloomer." [CA90] "Moderate growth, but very healthy. Its flowers are small, it is true, but of luxuriant bloom and well-scented. Carnation pink." [JR16/36] "Canes thin but vigorous; flower small but a little larger than 'Paquer-Lambard' [*? — evidently an early Polyantha cross; 'Paquerette' (Pol) and 'Mme Lambard' (T)*]. In bud, it is very pretty; once open, it is robust and lasts a long time with a very elegant scent. One of its precious qualities is that it blooms well outside, and that each branch bears a flower. We regard it, say its breeders, as a charming rose in miniature, which, moreover, can be forced." [JR8/29–30]

[ROSE D'EVIAN]

Bernaix, 1894

"Pink, carmine center." [LS] "Long buds of a beautiful magenta red before expansion. Flower very large, quite double, cupped; petals numerous, thick, beautiful China pink, blush on the reverse, carmine-y on the obverse. Very fresh coloration." [JR18/163–164] "Stout stems and thick glossy green leaves. The flowers are large and handsome, somewhat cup-shaped, but well filled and very sweet. The color is deep rich rosy red, reverse of petals pale amaranth; makes extra long pointed buds, and blooms abundantly all through the Summer and Fall. 15 cts." [C&Js99] "D'Evian" refers to a French town in Haute-Saone which had a yearly rose festival (those interested may see JR28/89, etc.).

ROSE NABONNAND

Nabonnand, 1882

"Large and beautiful; flowers quite full and regular; color, soft satiny rose, changing to salmon, elegantly tinted with amber and pale yellow; very pretty and highly scented." [CA90] "Very vigorous bush, big-wooded; thorns rare, but protrusive; flower very large, very full, imbricated; color, delicate pink towards the center . . . very floriferous; good variety for the North." [JR6/186]

ROSOMANE NARCISSE THOMAS

Bernaix fils, 1908

"Crimson to burnt orange. Small." [ARA27/19] "Fine variegated copper, orange and red blooms. Very prolific. Most valuable for southern zones." [ARA28/104] "Wonderful color; good growth, foliage, and blooming qualities; flowers small, most attractive in bud-form." [ARA18/114] "Vigorous, beautiful brilliant foliage, bud develops an unusual intensity of color. Flower medium, scarlet, with dawn copper red upon opening, large nub of apricot yellow. Outermost petals colored reddish violet at the tip. This variety has quite novel tintings; a thoroughly curious coloration." [JR32/135]

[S.A.R. MME LA PRINCESSE DE HOHENZOLLERN, IN-FANTE DE PORTUGAL]

('Princesse Hohenzollern')

Nabonnand, 1886

"Extra large, perfectly formed flowers, very full and double; color, a handsome shade of bright peachy red, passing to rich crimson." [CA90] "Very vigorous; flower very large, full, of perfect form; color, bright red, sparkling, outer petals darker than the central ones. . . . Flower very fragrant, very floriferous." [JR10/169] "Noted for strong vigorous growth and beautiful dark green foliage . . . [flowers] often borne in clusters." [C&Js03] "S.A.R." = "Son Altesse Royal" *alias* "Her Royal Highness."

[SAFRANO À FLEURS ROUGES]

('Red Safrano', 'Mme Joséphine Mühle')

Oger, 1867

Seemingly a sport of 'Safrano'.

"Saffron yellow, shaded with coppery red, semi-double; a peculiar scent, not pleasing." [EL] "Medium growth; flower medium-sized, fairly full; color, shining red nuanced copper-yellow. Cultivated in America on a grand scale for its attractive bud which wafts a delicious aroma." [S]

SANTA ROSA

Burbank, 1899

From 'Hermosa' (B) × a seedling of 'Bon Silène' (T); *or* from a seedling of 'Hermosa' × 'Bon Silène'.

"Shell pink, inclining to crimson." [CA02] "An elegant new Tea Rose from California. It somewhat resembles 'Hermosa', but is larger and more beautiful. The flowers are large, round, full and sweet; the color is rich rosy pink, shading to coppery red. It is a constant and abundant bloomer and quite hardy." [C&Js99] "Another exceptional quality . . . is the power of resistance . . . to those ever-present foes of the rose family, mildew and rust." [Lu]

[SAPPHO]

W. Paul, 1889

Not to be confused with the DP.

"Large, full and globular flowers; rich apricot yellow, delicately tinged with fawn and pale rose; strong and vigorous grower." [CA93] "Buds peacock [*sic*] in color, with a pink nuance; flowers open with a shade of yellow and hazel-buff-yellow, large and full; this pretty and distinctive rose is of strong build, stronger than 'Homère'; it produces its flowers with a profusion which is extraordinary for a Tea; petals large and of good substance, and we know of no other variety which keeps so long in a good state, as well on the plant as when cut . . . 'beautiful, very full and thick blossoms of an apricot-yellow, with a delicious "Gloire de Dijon" scent.' " [JR13/70–71]

[SÉNATEUR LOUBET]

('Sénateur Laubet')
Reboul, 1891

"Dwarf, but vigorous; very large, finely formed flowers. Outer petals light tender rose; center, metal yellow color, heightening sometimes to crimson." [CA96] "Very floriferous; flowers large, very full, center petals finely serrated, [serration] gradually enlarging around the exterior edges; petal color delicate pink, on a ground of metallic yellow towards the center, changing to poppy red when fully open. Novel coloration." [JR15/165–166]

[SENATOR MCNAUGHTON]

California Nursery Co.?, by 1895

"A sport of 'Perle des Jardins', to which it is similar in every respect excepting color; rich glossy foliage, sturdy habit of growth, and extremely free-flowering. The flowers are very large and full, with excellent shaped buds. Color, a delicate creamy white." [CA95]

[SHIRLEY HIBBERD]

Levet, 1874
Seedling of 'Mme Falcot' (T).

"Moderate growth, floriferous; blossom medium-sized, full; color, buff nankeen yellow." [S]

[SIMONE THOMAS]

Introducer unknown, by 1927

"Carmine to coppery red. Mildews." [ARA27/19] Otherwise unknown. Probably "Margherita di *Simone*" grown by Capt. *Thomas*.

[SMITH'S YELLOW CHINA]

('Smithii', 'Jaune of Smith')
Smith, 1834
From 'Blush Noisette' (N) × 'Parks' Yellow Tea-Scented China' (T).

"Sulphur yellow, full, cupped, large, beautiful." [LF] "Fine straw-color; a beautiful rose." [HstI:308] "White, center yellow." [R-H56] "Lemon, center yellow, large and very full, a superb rose, but often disfigured by a green centre; only fit for forcing." [JC] "Pale straw colour, large and full; form, globular. A fine forcing Rose, but seldom opens well out of doors." [P] "Growing freely . . . opening in great profusion, except in time of rain . . . pale lemon-yellow before the sun destroys it . . . delightfully fragrant." [Bu] "Vigorous; branches green, touched with violet where the sun hits them; flower . . . sulphur yellow." [S] "Vigorous bush; wood brownish with deep purple thorns which are remote, big, short, and upright; leaves petiolate, alternate, with five oval, nearly rounded leaflets, which are dentate, which terminate in a more or less sharp point, and which are a fresh green. Purplish bracts. Blossoms well formed, lemon yellow, very full and fragrant, 130–160 short petals which are slightly rolled and well arranged. We received from England last month this rose under the name 'Noisette Jaune', a name we believe should be kept for it, despite certain persons who claim that it comes from the Bengals. These people base their belief on the fact that, previously, it hadn't bloomed

in a cluster. Hopefully, the weak specimen I have received will show that particular characteristic in due course. Furthermore, the doubleness of the blossom is such that we haven't been able to tell if the stamens' filaments are free or united. Whatever the case, should there be an error in its classification, we won't fail to put it right once we have a chance to study it more closely. Putting aside such matters, this rose, which blooms all year, is a precious introduction, and will certainly pique the curiosity of fanciers. We think that it will endure the winter out in the open; however, as it is indeed a rarity, we advise its possessors to let it spend that season in a greenhouse or frame. Propagated by graft, budding, and layering." [An33/19–20]

SOCRATE

('Baronne G. Chandon', 'Princesse Marie Dagmar')
Robert & Moreau, 1858

"Pink, center peach." [LS] "Large, full, deep pink, apricot at the center." [JR3/28] "Dark rose with an apricot yellow heart." [JR10/47] "Deep rose, tinged with fawn, large or medium size, double or full. Quite a good Tea." [EL] "Vigorous; flower large, full, flat, very pronounced peach scent." [S] "Bright salmon and fawn, large and full, habit free; a most distinct and beautiful rose." [JC]

SOUVENIR D'AUGUSTE LEGROS

Bonnaire, 1889

"Growth very vigorous, somewhat bushy, of the 'Souvenir de Thérèse Levet' sort, but developing larger, erect branches; foliage glossy green; flower handsome fiery red mixed with dark crimson; blossom very large; beautiful elongated bud, one of the largest among the Teas. Flower stem strong." [JR13/162]

[SOUVENIR D'ESPAGNE]

Pries/Ketten Bros., 1888

"Yellow, pink, and white." [LS] "A grand new Tea Rose; color coppery yellow and rose beautifully blended; very fine in bud; a strong grower and free bloomer." [CA93] "Flower reddish orange on a yellow orange ground; petals edged with a large border of pinkish carmine; reverse of petals blush white; medium-sized or large; pretty full, cupped, very fragrant, opening well. Moderate bush with very rich and continuous bloom. Coloration novel and ravishing." [JR12/181] "Hybrid of Tea and China." [JR24/44]

SOUVENIR DE CATHERINE GUILLOT

Listed as a China.

[SOUVENIR DE CLAIRVAUX]

E. Verdier, 1890

"Bush of good vigor with strong, erect canes; leaves composed of five undulate leaflets which are glossy, deep green, reddish in youth, and irregularly but fairly deeply toothed; thorns not very numerous, strong, hooked, blackish; flowers medium to large, quite full, well formed, borne on a strong and rigid stem; color, very fresh, a beautiful China pink shade, petal bases apricot yellow washed nankeen and tinted carmine; excellent variety, very floriferous, very nice scent." [JR14/163] "Color of '[Souvenir de] Thérèse Levet'." [CA96]

[SOUVENIR DE DAVID D'ANGERS]
Moreau-Robert, 1856
Reputedly descended From 'Caroline' (T).

"Glistening dark red, shaded maroon." [RR] "Rosy-salmon, fine petal, flowers very large and double; a most deliciously fragrant rose, and very beautiful." [JC] "Bright cherry-color, distinct and good." [FP] "Double, bright cerise, in clusters." [JDR56/41] "Flower large, full, well-formed; color, dark red nuanced maroon and violet. Growth moderate." [S] Pierre Jean David d'Angers, sculptor; 1788–1856.

SOUVENIR DE FRANÇOIS GAULAIN
Guillot & fils, 1889

"Vigorous growth; flowers large, full, well-formed; varies from magenta red nuanced violet to dark violet shaded crimson." [JR13/181]

[SOUVENIR DE GABRIELLE DREVET]   PLATE 29
Guillot & fils, 1884

"A rare shade of salmon, red, or terra cotta, delicately toned with violet crimson; a very striking and novel color; deliciously fragrant and very beautiful." [CA90] "Vigorous, flowers large, full, well formed and well held; color, whitish salmon, center bright pink, on a ground of coppery yellow, passing to light salmon; very fragrant." [JR8/133] "Fair form and very sweet." [B&V]

SOUVENIR DE GENEVIÈVE GODARD
Godard, 1893

"China pink." [Y̆]

[SOUVENIR DE GEORGE SAND]
Widow Ducher, 1876

"Very vigorous, short canes, flower very large, full, very well formed, tulip-form; color, salmony yellow, reverse of petals ribboned lilac." [JR1/1/8] "Fine, large full flowers; bright carmine buds, changing when open to reddish amber, veined with brilliant crimson; very fragrant." [CA90] "Flower large, full, tulip-formed; color, salmon pink, sometimes light coppery pink; much to be recommended for forcing; the bud is generally used like that of 'Safrano' for making bouquets." [S]

SOUVENIR DE GERMAIN DE SAINT-PIERRE
Nabonnand, 1882

"Very vigorous, blooms in clusters, flower very large, semi-double, with very large petals of purple-red, unique in the sort. Constant bloom, at least as abundant as 'Safrano'. This wonderful rose for winter bloom is named in memory of our late collaborator [on the *Journal des Roses*]." [JR6/186] "Very showy and attractive . . . large, full and sweet." [CA90] "Germain de Saint-Pierre, Commandeur de l'Ordeur Impérial de la Rose. President (1870–1872) of the Société Botanique de France." [JR2/40]

SOUVENIR DE GILBERT NABONNAND
P. Nabonnand, 1920

"Fire-red to apricot-yellow. Shy bloomer in late fall." [ARA27/19] "Variegated copper and pink, fine growth; foliage immune to mildew; good cutting value; continuous and prolific bloomer; holds foliage tenaciously. Entirely distinct, and strongly recommended for southern seacoast climates." [ARA28/104] "Gilbert Nabonnand, who died at Golfe-Juan last January 6 [1902] in his 76th year. Born at Grézolles, near Roanne (Loire) May 20, 1829, he worked in the fields as a laborer until he was 16. The love of

flowers which he had made him enter into a two-year apprenticeship at Vienne (Isère) at a nursery where he began his horticultural education. After two more years at a tree-farm in Lyon, he was 20, and entered the establishment of Mons Guillot. . . . After completing his education at various other firms, he was at the age at which it is necessary to decide upon which road to take in life. He established himself at Sorgues (Vaucluse), where he grew fruit-trees, conifers, and shrubs. Then, in 1858, he moved to Avignon, where he took up roses exclusively. Finally, in 1864, having been tempted by the luxuriant vegetation and enchanting venues offered by the coastal Mediterranean area, he fixed on Golfe-Juan, in the Alpes-Maritimes, where he created a horticultural establishment of the first rank." [JR27/23]

SOUVENIR DE J.-B. GUILLOT
Listed as a China.

[SOUVENIR DE JEANNE CABAUD]
('Yellow Maman Cochet')
P. Guillot, 1896

"A grand new rose, producing in the greatest profusion extra large fully double flowers, beautiful coppery yellow, finely tinted with apricot and rosy carmine, exceedingly beautiful and a good healthy grower; quite hardy." [C&Js06] "Vigorous bush; flower large, full, well formed; exterior petals coppery yellow, center petals carminey apricot yellow. Fragrant, very beautiful." [JR20/147]

[SOUVENIR DE L'AMIRAL COURBET]
Pernet père, 1885

"Round, globular flowers, very solid and compact, and borne in large clusters; color, bright fiery red, very lively and striking; highly scented." [CA90] "Moderately vigorous, with strong and upright canes; flower medium-sized, nearly full, bright red; flower-stem upright and strong; abundant bloom. This variety will be of much merit for borders and bedding as well as pot culture; at first bloom, average stems bear 20–25 buds on the same shoot — better than the Polyanthas." [JR9/148]

[SOUVENIR DE LADY ASHBURTON]
C. Verdier, 1890

"A fine shade of rich coppery red, delicately suffused with pale orange yellow; highly scented with true Tea Rose odor." [CA96] "Flower very variable, coppery red, salmon yellow, sometimes red, sometimes bright red, light yellow, showing all shades, sometimes separate, sometimes mixed, depending upon the stage of bloom." [JR16/156]

SOUVENIR DE LAURENT GUILLOT
Bonnaire, 1894

"Very vigorous, beautiful bronze-green foliage; thorns pink; flower large, very full, beautiful China pink with a peach yellow center, petal edges carmine. Very pretty." [JR18/130]

[SOUVENIR DE MME LAMBARD]
California Nursery Co.?, by 1890
A sport of 'Mme Lambard', we would conjecture.

"Large canary colored flowers, exquisitely shaded and tinted with salmon rose; a fine vigorous grower and free bloomer." [CA90]

[SOUVENIR DE MME LEVET]

E. Levet, 1891

From 'Mme Carot' (T) × 'Mme Eugène Verdier' (T).

"Vigorous bush, blossom large, full, well formed, opening very well, stem very strong; color, beautiful deep orange yellow; very fragrant; petals very thick, keeping their tints well. Heavy wood, few thorns, growing to 4–5 dm [ca. 1.5 ft]; its beautiful dark green foliage attracts notice because of its shade and good poise. The plant is extra floriferous." [JR15/164] Parent of 'Georges Schwartz' (T).

SOUVENIR DE MME SABLAYROLLES   PLATE 52

Bonnaire, 1890

From 'Devoniensis' (T) × 'Souvenir d'Elisa Vardon' (T).

"Growth very vigorous, with erect branches having handsome somber green foliage; flower stem very strong, flower large, full, beautiful globular form, nearly always solitary; color, apricot pink nuanced yellow, the edge of the petals bordered carmine fading to cream white." [JR14/146]

[SOUVENIR DE PAUL NEYRON]

Levet, 1871

Two parentages are given: (1) From 'Devoniensis' (T) × 'Souvenir de la Malmaison' (B); (2) Seedling of 'Ophirie' (N).

"White, with rose and buff tint, flowers large, full, and very distinct; a first-rate rose, habit free." [JC] "An elegant sort; color white, beautifully tinged with clear golden yellow, each petal edged with bright rosy crimson; very distinct and fine; the flowers are of medium size, very full and double, with delicious tea scent; a profuse bloomer." [CA88] "Very vigorous, very floriferous . . . Flower large, full, semi-globular, very fragrant; color, salmon yellow bordered pink." [S] "Of rather weak growth with small foliage, though occasionally a plant will grow pretty well. . . . It is a good autumnal where it will grow sufficiently, and very free-flowering in the season, every wood bud all over the plant trying to grow as soon as the flower buds are formed." [F-M3]

SOUVENIR DE THÉRÈSE LEVET

Levet, 1882

From 'Adam' (T) × ? "Safrano à Fleurs Rouges" (T).

"Crimson-maroon. Medium size." [ARA27/19] "A magnificent variety with large pink blossoms." [JR8/146] "Crimson, shaded pink at the center, beautiful in bud." [JR11/50] "Wood strong; foliage dark green; large, hooked thorns; flower large, poppy red, shaded." [S] "Pretty good growth and foliage . . . late in blooming and fairly hardy . . . remarkable for its colour, which is a deep, dull, and sometimes blotchy crimson, forming a great contrast to the bright light colours common to the rest of this section. The blooms do not often come perfect, but are fine when they do, and very lasting. If the colour were bright, pure, and velvety, it would be much better, but as it is it does not show well against the pure whites, pinks, and yellows of its sisters in a stand of Teas. Perhaps it ought to be more cultivated, but most fanciers of Tea Roses seem half ashamed of it, as if it had no business to be dark red; and it is not in general highly esteemed in this country, but does much better in hot climates, being very popular in Australia. 'François Dubreuil' [*sic*] . . . is very like this Rose, and perhaps in some respects a little improvement on it." [F-M2]

SOUVENIR DE VICTOR HUGO   PLATE 32

Bonnaire, 1885

From 'Comtesse de Labarthe' (T) × 'Regulus' (T).

"Vigorous with upright branches; flower-stem strong; flower large, full, very well formed, beautiful intense sparkling China pink, center nasturtium yellow; reverse of petals silvery, bright carmine red at the edge." [JR9/136]

[SOUVENIR DE WILLIAM ROBINSON]

Bernaix fils, 1899

"Salmon-carmine to nankeen. Mildews." [ARA27/20] "Very graceful ovoid bud, middle chamois to the base, and pale blush yellow in the outer two rows, like 'William Allen Richardson'. Flower well formed, variegated, nearly quadri-colored, peony-pink — very freshly so, or with salmon — partly cream white, and apricot yellow with violet veins." [JR23/168] "Vigorous. . . . This variety often varies in its shadings." [JR25/10]

[SOUVENIR DU DR. PASSOT]

Godard, 1889

"Velvet carmine." [RR] "Vigorous growth; flowers large, full; color, velvety crimson red fading lighter." [JR13/181] A parent of 'Julius Fabianics de Misefa' (T).

SOUVENIR DU ROSIÉRISTE RAMBAUX   PLATE 26

Rambaux/Dubreuil, 1883

Seedling of 'Bon Silène' (T).

"This graceful gem should be a part of every collection, possessing as it does everything that one could wish for, beautiful form and color, straw yellow, heavily bordered bright rose, tints which, together, are very effective. Its tea scent is very pronounced and elegant." [JR10/46] "Very vigorous and floriferous; leaves medium sized, glossy above, glaucous beneath; buds ovoid; flower erect, cupped; petals streamlined, concave at the base, folding back elegantly at the tip; carmine pink within, with a large straw yellow nub; exterior bordered bright pink on a ground of pale canary yellow. Very engaging because of its fresh appearance, and the contrast of its colors, a unique feature; very fragrant." [JR7/169] "Makes a handsome bush." [JR8/24]

[SOUVENIR OF STELLA GRAY]

A. Dickson, 1907

"Light to deep orange, beautifully variegated by apricot and crimson shadings; buds and open flower short, loose, and of only fair size; fragrant. Foliage very fine." [Th2] "Flower medium-sized, very full, perfect form, deep orange veined yellow-apricot-salmon and crimson. Very beautiful variety; lacks something in the way of vigor, but remarkable due to its rich coloration." [JR35/14] "Hard to establish." [ARA27/19]

[SULPHUREA]

W. Paul, 1900

"Bright sulphur yellow, fine buds and large full flowers. Very fragrant; a good bloomer." [C&Js07]

[SUNRISE]

Piper, 1899

Sport of 'Sunset' (T).

"Salmon-rose, center yellow, salmon, and orange." [ARA27/20] "This is a sport of smaller size from 'Sunset' . . . a button-hole Rose of most varied and beautiful colours when grown under glass. It appears to be even more tender than the variety from which it sported, and a worse grower, and I fear it may be apt to give disappointment out of doors." [F-M4] "The flowers are extra large, perfectly double, and of excellent form and texture. The foliage is thick and glossy, and the new growth is the darkest and most beautiful found among roses. The buds are long and pointed, beautifully colored with scarlet and yellow. The flowers are large and full, with broad shell-shaped petals, and delightfully sweet. The color is dark coppery-red, beautifully shaded with rich orange, exceedingly beautiful. The bush is a strong, healthy grower, and most abundant bloomer." [C&Js02] "Pretty color; lacks in growth." [ARA18/118]

SUNSET   PLATES 19, 27
Henderson, 1883

"One of the most fragrant and beautiful roses in cultivation. The flowers are extra large size, fine full form, and delightfully perfumed; color rich, coppery yellow or real old gold, elegantly clouded with dark, ruddy crimson, true sunset tints; robust and vigorous, and a constant bloomer." [C&Js00] "A sport from 'Perle des Jardins', of the same colour as 'Rêve d'Or': a handsome, useful, strong-growing Rose, with foliage of a beautiful red colour in the spring. It comes a little better than its progenitor, and is a very good autumnal, but the blooms are always small compared with the size and stoutness of the shoots, the plant is tender to frost, and like the parent variety this tenderness is shown by the summer blooms coming malformed when the plant is grown out of doors. Like the original, it does well and is much esteemed in Australia." [F-M2] "Orange." [LS] "Apricot, shaded yellow. Good in autumn; bronzy foliage." [H] "In all ways it is like its parent, except in color, which is, instead of canary yellow, saffron orange, like 'Mme Falcot', only darker. It also differs in its leaves, which when young are a dark crimson which contrasts nicely with the flowers." [JR7/172] "A yellow tawny rose. In some places it grows yellower than in others; perhaps it fades a little in the sun. It is always covered with bloom and is very strong." [HmC] "Fairly vigorous, giving lots of flowers, more often medium-sized than large, and wafting a delicious Tea-rose scent." [JR17/40–41] "Moderate growth; branches not very vigorous, green touched sometimes with violet." [S] "Weak growth; winterkills." [ARA18/118]

SWEET LITTLE QUEEN
Listed as 'The Sweet Little Queen of Holland'.

SYLPHIDE
Listed as 'La Sylphide'.

THE ALEXANDRA
W. Paul, 1900

"Beautiful rosy buff flowers." [C&Js02] "Pale buff with orange yellow centres shaded with apricot and bronze; very beautifully shaped, exceedingly attractive." [P1] "Flower large, full, and very well formed." [JR30/15] "Small growth; winterkills." [ARA18/115] Queen Alexandra of England, wife of Edward VII; lived 1844–1925. *The* Alexandra', not *Thé* Alexandra'.

[THE QUEEN]
('Souvenir de S.A. Prince')
Dingee & Conard, 1889
Sport of 'Souvenir d'Un Ami' (T).

"White, of peculiar delicacy; good sized flowers of perfect globular form. Most attractive and of extreme elegance." [B&V] "Good pointed form. . . . I cannot get the blooms to come as large as those of the type." [F-M3] "A pure white kind of 'Souvenir d'Un Ami', well formed, vigorous plant, always in bloom. It gives a large amount of buds and flowers the whole season; buds, well-formed; petals, strong and of good substance. It opens well and keeps well." [JR13/71] "A vigorous, healthy grower, and one of the heaviest and most continuous bloomers we know. The flowers

are large, full and well filled; color, pure snow white and very sweet. A remarkably early forcer; makes fine buds; opens well, has plenty of substance, and is a good keeper." [CA91] "Can't be recommended as a nursery flower, but as a garden flower it is splendid." [JR16/38]

[THE SWEET LITTLE QUEEN OF HOLLAND]
Soupert & Notting, 1897
From 'Céline Forestier' (N) × 'Mme Hoste' (T).

"A very dainty and attractive Rose, grows neat and compact, and is a quick and most abundant bloomer, scarcely ever without flowers during the whole season, makes elegant buds, and the flowers are large, full and double. Color, bright rich golden yellow, centre shaded with orange and blush, very sweet and a really charming rose." [C&Js02] "Vigorous bush, beautiful glaucous green foliage, long bud, flower very large, full, good form, outer petals large, center petals narrower; color, shining daffodil yellow, the center ochre yellow mixed with pink and bright orange yellow. The petals are pointed like those of the Chrysanthemum, giving the blossom a look all its own. Very fragrant and floriferous. Color and form novel among Teas. Excellent for forcing." [JR22/20]

[THÉRÈSE LAMBERT]
Soupert & Notting, 1887
From 'Mme Lambard' (T) × 'Socrate' (T).

"Elegant and very handsome in color and form; delicate rose, base of petals finely tinged with old gold, center pale silvery salmon; very large and full." [CA93] "Good hold; color, delicate pink on a yellowish red ground; center silvery salmon gold. Very fragrant." [JR11/152]

THERESE WELTER
Listed as 'Baronne Henriette de Loew'.

[TRIOMPHE DE MILAN]
Widow Ducher, 1877

"White, suffused with pale yellow, without fragrance; a fine rose, similar, but inferior, to 'Marie Guillot'." [EL] "Flower large, full, well-formed; color, white with a deep yellow center. Good exhibition rose, and recommendable for bouquets, particularly before expansion; bush vigorous, with short, upright branches." [S]

[TRUE FRIEND]
California Nursery Co.?, by 1905
"Light yellow." [CA05]

[UNCLE JOHN]
Thorpe, 1904
Sport of 'Golden Gate' (T).

"Blush white." [LS] "Creamy yellow." [CA07] "A very pleasing constant blooming rose; never out of bloom during the whole growing season, pretty buff yellow flowers shading to white and pink, large full and fragrant; a strong bushy grower, splendid for garden planting." [C&Js06]

[V. VIVIAND-MOREL]　　　　　　　PLATE 42
('Mme V. Morrell')
Bernaix, 1887
Seedling of 'Red Safrano' (T).

　　"Bright cherry pink, shaded salmon, very large and double, long plump buds on strong stems; a fine garden rose, and a strong healthy grower and free bloomer." [C&Js06] "Bush with thick canes, upright, robust, purplish; leaves spread-out; leaflets leathery, glossy above, glaucescent and reddish beneath; stems long, strong, and very rigid, holding the blossom vertical without bending, 5–7 cm long [ca. 2.5 in], measuring from the base of the last leaflet to the base of the ovary; calyx and ovary nearly smooth; bud long before expansion; petals thick, firm, veined, reticulated with flattened anastomical stripes; exterior petals very large, revolute; inner petals wedge-shaped, large, rounded at the tip; flower crimson red, nuanced oriental matte grenadine while opening; very large completely open; moderately double; shimmering, passing from crimson to poppy-red, lightening gradually to carmine nuanced saffron red." [JR11/151]

[V. VIVO É HIJOS]
Bernaix, 1894

　　"A new coloration, quite double, exterior petals large, carmine pink, paler at the center and base, middle petals numerous, ragged, bright dawn yellow with salmon, apricot, and often tinted incarnadine." [JR18/163–164] "Medium size." [CaRoll/3/3] "Carmine-salmon and apricot-yellow. Medium growth." [ARA27/20] "A variegated pink Tea, verging on salmon and apricot. Good growth; very floriferous; perfect foliage. Strongly recommended for southern zones." [ARA28/104]

[VALLÉE DE CHAMONIX]
Ducher, 1872
Affiliated with the Noisettes in JR23/163.

　　"Copper, afterwards yellow and rose, very variable." [JC] "Bud pink [and] orange pink. Flower semi-double. Color, pinkish yellow, lightly coppery at the center." [JR23/163] "A very beautiful rose; good size, very double, full and sweet; color coppery yellow, elegantly shaded and tinged with rosy blush." [CA90] "Vigorous; flower medium-sized, full, flat." [S]

[VICOMTESSE DE BERNIS]
Nabonnand, 1883

　　"Striped pink." [LS] "Fine, large, full flowers; very fragrant; color rich coppery rose, passing to fawn and deep salmon; showy and handsome." [CA90] "Very vigorous; flower very large, full, imbricated, with very large petals, perfect form, good hold; color, delicate pink towards the edge, bright pink towards the center." [JR7/184]

[VICOMTESSE DE WAUTHIER]　　　　PLATE 38
('Vicomtesse de Vautier')
Bernaix, 1886

　　"Bright carmine red; center and reverse of petals silver rose." [CA90] "Pretty vigorous; long bud; flower large, full, pretty well formed; beautifully colored pink tinted yellowish on the exterior of the petals and blush white within. The blush white is often striped pink. The flower's middle is a very deep pink, which produces a superb effect. Novel coloration." [JR10/172]

[VICTOR PULLIAT]
Ducher, 1870
Seedling of 'Mme Mélanie Willermoz' (T).

　　"Yellowish-white, large, full and clustering; habit moderate." [JC] "Flower medium-sized, full, flat." [S] "Pale yellow, long buds, quite a good Tea." [EL] "Victor Pulliat, the vinologist known to all grape-vine growers." [JR22/160]

VICTOR VELIDAN

One runs across this name here and there, and it is, I think, a mishearing, mispronunciation, or misremembrance of some other variety, perhaps 'Victor Waddilove', McGredy's 1925 Pernetiana HT which didn't generate very much enthusiasm. 'Waddilove' varied in color from pink to yellow much as the blossoms of many Teas do.

[VIRGINIA]
Dingee & Conard, 1894
From 'Safrano' × 'Maréchal Niel' (N).

　　"A very beautiful Tea Rose, pure deep yellow, both buds and flowers, are very handsome and borne in great profusion all through the season; richly tea scented." [C&Js98] Also attributed to Nanz & Neuner, 1896.

[WABAN]
Wood, 1891

　　"Originated at the Waban Conservatories, Massachusetts, from whence it takes its name. It is a sport from that excellent old rose, 'Catherine Mermet', and identical with it in every characteristic except color, which is a rich, deep bright pink, much brighter and more durable than 'Mermet', but has the same beauty of form, and is a more abundant bloomer." [CA93] "In foliage and vigor, 'Waban' takes after its parents [sic]; the flowers are borne on long, strong stems, and the petals are a little larger and more numerous than those of 'Catherine Mermet'. Its color is carmine pink . . . plumed with fiery madder red, brightly nuanced on the outer petals." [JR15/88] "Does not often come good." [F-M3]

[WHITE BON SILÈNE]
Morrat, 1884
Presumably a sport of 'Bon Silène' (T).

　　"Flower medium sized, full; color, virginal white. Much to be recommended for its good bloom." [S] "This elegant new variety is valued particularly for its splendid buds, which are remarkably large and handsome; the color is pale lemon yellow, passing to rich creamy white; very beautiful." [CA90] "Its color is not perfectly white, which is why it isn't much liked as a nursery rose; nevertheless, its fragrance is exquisite, making it perfectly precious as a garden plant, where it surpasses all other white roses." [JR16/38]

[WHITE PEARL]
Ritter/Nanz & Neuner, 1889
Sport of 'Perle des Jardins' (T).

　　"A white product of 'Perle des Jardins', of very vigorous growth, blooming easily under glass, and profusely. Not recommendable as a nursery rose." [JR16/38] "Blooms in great abundance; stems quite upright, buds very pretty, foliage large and very well formed. Excellent for pot culture and for open air where Teas will grow [or 'develop']." [JR13/71] "Low-growing, compact, winterkills some; foliage sufficient to plentiful; bloom moderate, almost continuous." [ARA18/128]

[WINNIE DAVIS]

Little, 1892

From 'Devoniensis' (T) × 'Mme de Watteville' (T).

"Flesh pink, outer petals silvery blush." [CA17] "Growth seems quite fair, blooms of good size and nice color." [ARA18/114] "Named in honor of the daughter of the Confederacy. The buds are long, heavy, and splendidly formed. Color is apricot-pink, shading to flesh tint at the base of petals." [C&Js07]

[WINTER GEM]

Childs, 1898

"Lovely creamy pink and a tremendous bloomer." [C&Js03] "This is a very beautiful Winter-blooming Rose, a perfectly wonderful bloomer, continuing covered with lovely buds and flowers as long as kept in growing condition. The blossoms are borne on long graceful stems, and are large, full and double. . . . Very sweet and beautiful. It is a strong rapid grower, and blooms nearly all the time, particularly in Winter." [C&Jf03] "Very low-growing, moderately compact, winterkills some; foliage plentiful, healthy; bloom free, almost continuous." [ARA18/128]

[ZEPHYR]

W. Paul, 1895

"A beautiful sulphur yellow with beautiful white reflections; the flowers are large, full, and cupped, and open very well. The bush grows vigorously, and is very floriferous. Much to be recommended for cut-flowers." [JR19/67] "A truly elegant rose of vigorous growth and good habit. Extra large flowers of beautiful cupped form; pale sulphur yellow passing to creamy white; large broad petals; very deep and deliciously tea scented." [C&Js98]

Chapter Five

BOURBONS

"It is now about thirty years since a beautiful semi-double rose, with brilliant rose-coloured flowers, prominent buds, and nearly evergreen foliage, made its appearance in this country [England] under the name of 'L'Ile de Bourbon Rose', said to have been imported from the Mauritius to France, in 1822, by Mons Noisette. It attracted attention by its peculiar habit, but more particularly by its abundant autumnal flowering; still, such was the lukewarmness of English rose amateurs, that no attempts were made to improve this pretty imperfect rose, by raising seedlings from it, although it bore seed in large quantities. This pleasing task was left to our rose-loving neighbours the French, who have been very industrious, and, as a matter of course, have originated some very beautiful and striking varieties, and also, as usual in such cases, have given us rather too many distinct and fine-sounding names attached to flowers without distinctive characters. In a little time we shall be able to rectify this very common floricultural error.

"Many fables have been told by the French respecting the origin of this rose. The most generally received version of one of these is, that a French naval officer was requested by the widow of a Monsieur Edouard, residing in the island, to find, on his voyage to India, some rare rose, and that, on his return to l'Île de Bourbon, he brought with him this rose, which she planted on her husband's grave: It was then called 'Rose Edouard', and sent to France as 'Rose de l'Île Bourbon'. This is pretty enough, but entirely devoid of truth. Monsieur Breon, a French botanist, gives the following account, for the truth of which he vouches:— 'At the Isle of Bourbon, the inhabitants generally enclose their land with hedges made of two rows of roses, one row of the common China Rose [presumably 'Parsons' Pink'], the other of the Red Four-Seasons [presumably the red 'Tous-les-Mois']. Monsieur Perichon, a proprietor at Saint Benoist, in the Isle, in planting one of these hedges, found among his young plants one very different from the others in its shoots and foliage. This induced him to plant it in his garden. It flowered the following year; and, as he anticipated, proved to be quite a new race, and differing much from the above two roses, which, at the time, were the only two sorts known in the island.' Monsieur Breon arrived at Bourbon in 1817, as botanical traveller for the government of France, and curator of the Botanical and Naturalization Garden there. He propagated this rose very largely, and sent plants and seeds of it, in 1822, to Monsieur Jacques, gardener at the Château de Neuilly, near Paris, who distributed them among the rose cultivators of France. (Whence the name often given to the Common Bourbon Rose of 'Bourbon Jacques'.) Mons Breon named it 'Rose de l'Île de Bourbon'; and is convinced that it is a hybrid from one of the above roses, and a native of the island." [R8]

"In October or November 1819, I [Mons Jacques] received from the Île-Bourbon a large collection of seeds of trees and shrubs; they were sent to me by Mons Breon, then chief gardener of the isle's royal possessions, and one of my good friends. In the number were found five rose-hips without any name other than that of 'Rosier de l'Île Bourbon'. At the end of November, I sowed all the seeds in hot-beds, and, along with the others, the roses. Come spring, five individuals came up and, after having been pricked out, raised in pots, and having passed the winter in a cold-frame, two bloomed and rebloomed well enough in the spring of 1821; one had semi-double flowers of a brilliant pink, and served that same year as a model for Redouté's picture, and was then propagated under the name 'Rosier de Bourbon'; the other was also propagated, but wasn't drawn." [JR17/158] "It was introduced first, in 1819, in the form of seeds sent to Mons Jacques . . . ; second, in 1821, by Mons Neumann, in the form of cuttings from this same 'Rose Edouard'. It was distributed, soon after this last introduction, under the name 'Rose Neumann' and 'Rose Dubreuil'." [JR25/137] "It was Mons Grandidier who brought it to Europe." [Hd] "It was introduced to this country [the U.S.A.], in 1828, by the late Mr. Thomas Hibbert, whose name will always be associated in the memory of many with rose culture." [Bu]

"Whatever the case, the new rose attracted attention by its vigor as well as by the novelty of its characteristics; its bright pink flowers of a shade all its own . . . its long wood which could be distinguished by the strong thorns which armed it. Its arrival was much celebrated, and it was grown by practically everyone—and then it was removed from the gardens because it took up too much room. This rose gave a great quantity of seed, giving rise to many seedlings—which at first were not so good: The plants arising from them were single, or perhaps too full, always aborting as with the Bourbon 'Neumann', for example, from which one had to content one's self with gathering buds only . . . the future looked bleak." [VH51/77–78]

"In 1831, Mons Desprez, amateur from Yèbles . . . indefatigable hybridist, raised two plants from the original type. They were two varieties which, by their good qualities, still hold a place in the catalogs. I speak of the Bourbons 'Charles Desprez' ["Rose colour. Worthless." [P] "Delicate pink, full, medium sized, beautiful" [LF]] and 'Mme Desprez', which had, particularly the latter, an immense vogue which was well-deserved. By this, then, the future of the class was decided." [JR23/125]

"Owing to the original being a hybrid, the roses of this family vary much in their characters." [WRP] "The Roses of this section are, in general, vigorous; the branches, often short and ordinarily stouter than those of the Tes or Chinas, terminate in one sole bloom; but when growing vigorously, it will attain a great length and end in a more or less great number of flowers per cluster; the bark is very smooth; the thorns, short, strong, and enlarged at the base, are curved at the tip, and are occasional; the leaflets, oval-rounded, toothed, shiny somber green, are in 3's, 5's, or 7's; the ovary is rounded, often short, and inflated." [BJ] "The Bourbon roses have one feature that is seldom found in another class—the opalescence or translucence of the

94

petals—the hues seem to shimmer around according to the angle from which you look at it." [K]

"This class does not possess the hardiness of the Remontants, nor the free blooming properties of the Bengales, Teas, and Noisettes, and therefore can never compete with the former for the North, nor with the latter for the South. In it, however, are varieties like 'Hermosa', 'Souvenir de la Malmaison', and others, which are scarcely surpassed in any class. The Bourbon Rose has also qualities which make many varieties favorites. These qualities are its greater hardiness than the Tea Rose, its very thick, leathery foliage, its luxuriant growth, its more constant bloom than the Remontants, and its thick, velvety petals, of a consistency to endure the summer's sun." [SBP]

ADAM MESSERICH
Lambert, 1920
From 'Frau Oberhofgärtner Singer' (HT, Lambert, 1908, pink edged white [itself from 'Jules Margottin' (HP) × 'Mme Eugénie Boullet' (HT, Pernet-Ducher, 1897, pink; parentage unknown)]) × an unnamed seedling (parentage: a seedling of 'Louise Odier' [B] × 'Louis Philippe' [Ch]).

"Bright pink to rosy red . . . 5 × 4 [ft; ca. 1.5 × 1.25 m]." [B] "Rich raspberry fragrance." [T3] "Bud ovoid, rose-red; flower medium size, semi-double, clear rose-red . . . ; open cupped, borne singly or several together . . . lasting. Very vigorous; trailing; bushy; blooms abundantly and continuously from May to October." [ARA21/163]

APOLLINE
V. Verdier, 1848
Seedling of 'Pierre de St.-Cyr' (B).

"Flower large, intensely shaded delicate pink. This variety was developed from seed gathered from 'Pierre de St.-Cyr', which it resembles in its growth." [R-H48] "A beautiful and glossy rose colour." [R8] "The most valuable [of Bourbons] . . . large cup-shaped blossoms of rosy-carmine that are very attractive." [EL] "Large flower, full; delicate pink shaded bright rose." [S] "A most lovely fall rose, growing in good ground from ten to fifteen ft [ca. 3–4.5 m], and glorious from September to November. It blooms profusely during the summer, but as the fall advances its color is of the most vivid pink." [HstXXVIII:193–194] "A beautiful rose, and a good weeper; pillar or wall rose." [JC]

BARDOU JOB   PLATES 1, 82
Nabonnand, 1887
From 'Gloire des Rosomanes' (B) × 'Général Jacqueminot' (HP).

"Deep scarlet shaded to yellow, reverse of petals a darker hue, surface of velvety down, beautiful in the extreme. This rose is impatient of the sun, when well grown and protected from its direct rays, every shade from dark beetroot to golden yellow may be observed on its lovely petals; the flowers greatly vary, some being so much darker than others, that surprise is felt that all could be attached to the same growth. Semi-double, indeed almost a single rose, centre brilliant yellow, generally bearing an excessive quantity of pollen. Likes to climb, is most attractive." [B&V] "Very vigorous; flower large, semi-double, of perfect form, erect; bud conical, elongated, perfect; large leaves of a splendid dark green; color, velvety scarlet on a ground of black, reverse of petals darkly velvety. . . . Very fragrant . . . always in bloom." [JR11/164] "Of good growth requiring but little pruning. This is almost, if not quite, a single Rose. . . . I do not know of one to beat it for size of petal, freedom of flower, and brightness of crimson colour." [F-M2]

BELLE DIJONNAISE
Listed as 'Zéphirine Drouhin'.

BENGALE CENTFEUILLES
Listed as a China.

BOULE DE NEIGE   PLATE 79
(trans., 'Snowball')
Lacharme, 1867
From 'Mlle Blanche Laffitte' (B) × 'Sapho' (DP).

"Pure white, centre delicately shaded with cream, flowers medium size, beautifully imbricated and very perfect; habit vigorous." [JC] "Full, cupped. Flowers white, tinted with greenish-yellow. Blooms freely in clusters. A good autumnal rose." [Hn] "Imbricated, perfect rosettes . . . charmingly shaped." [F-M2] "Flower about two in across [ca. 5 cm], full, globular, well formed, pure white; the blossom tends to nod . . . incontestibly one of the best roses for the garden as it is very floriferous and remontant." [JR10/59] "Petals large, quite convex, those of the center being smaller . . . not entirely hardy." [S] "Petals of great substance . . . good habit, hardy and free; growth vigorous. One of the best." [P1] "Perhaps the most floriferous of all the whites; undoubtedly, not the most beautiful, but it blooms through the fall nearly to winter." [JR32/34] "Elegant upright shrub, 4 × 3 [ft; ca. 1.25 m × 9 dm]." [HRG] "Glossy foliage . . . strong fragrance . . . 5 × 4 [ft; ca. 1.5 × 1.25 m]." [B] "8–10 [ft; ca. 2.25–3 m]. Attractive dark foliage." [Lg] "Should not be . . . pruned closely." [F-M2] "From the work of Lacharme, the able and fortunate Lyonnaise breeder whom all the horticultural world knows and who fills our gardens with wonderful introductions. This one is of the highest merit; its growth is perhaps to 4.5 or so ft [ca. 1.3 m]. Its blossoms are pure white, but the exterior petals are sometimes tinted pink; it makes numerous clusters of blossoms . . . not an exhibition rose, but in the garden it deserves a place among the best . . . the abundance of its handsome shiny green foliage . . . sorts well with the snowy white of the flowers." [JR18/136] "Pretty vigorous; canes of moderate size, sometimes slightly slender, branching; bark smooth, pale green, with numerous reddish, hooked, sharp thorns. The wavy leaves are light green, sometimes bordered red, divided into five or seven nearly round leaflets which are acuminate and finely dentate; leafstalk, slender and nodding. Flower about 2.5 in across [ca. 6.5 cm], full, globular, very well formed, often solitary; color, pure white; petals large, scalloped, those of the center smaller; flower stalk slender, reflexing under the weight of the blossom. Calyx rounded, pear-shaped; sepals leaf-like . . . one of the most beautiful white roses in the HP's [*that is, if one were to consider it as being in the HP's*]." [JF] "It is said this rose cannot be propagated from cuttings." [B&V] "Very much in vogue in England where it is considered as one of the best Hybrid Noisettes [*but we consider this sort of 'Hybrid Noisette' to be a Bourbon*]." [JR27/152]

BOURBON QUEEN
Listed as 'Reine des Île-Bourbons'.

CATHERINE GUILLOT
('Michel Bonnet')
Guillot fils, 1861
Seedling of 'Louise Odier' (B).

"Flower large, perfect form, purplish pink." [JR1/2/7] "Carmine-rose, beautiful even smooth petal, flowers large and beautifully formed . . . vigorous." [JC] "Intense purple illuminated by carmine . . . fragrant."[Cx] "Beautiful rosy-peach, large, full, and of fine form; blooms freely. . . . Growth vigorous."[P1] "The bud doesn't open [in Havana]."[JR6/44] "Crimson . . . to about 2 metres [ca. 6 ft] . . . quartered and fragrant."[G] "From seedlings grown in 1857 . . . vigorous, of the 'Louise Odier' sort, whence it sprang."[JR10/91]

CHAMPION OF THE WORLD
Woodhouse, 1894
From 'Hermosa' (B) × 'Magna Charta' (HP).
"Pale pink with lilac."[T1] "Deep rose-pink, double . . . scented . . . 4 × 3 [ft; ca. 1.25 × 1 m]."[B] "Dark red."[LS] "Ever free and constant blooming. . . . One of the finest roses an amateur can have, blooming when quite young, it continues for years; the older the bush, the more and better the roses. The colour is bright pink; the roses large and double."[Dr] "Dainty bearing . . . small, light green, neat leaves."[T1] "The plant is vigorous and thrifty, and produces flowers abundantly all through the growing season."[C&Js98] Conard & Jones, as well as, more recently, Phillips & Rix, equate this cultivar with 'Mrs. Degraw', an HB put out by Burgess in *1885*.

CHARLES BONNET
Listed as 'Zéphirine Drouhin'.

CHARLES LAWSON
Listed as a Hybrid Bourbon.

COMMANDANT BEAUREPAIRE
Listed, as earnestly desired by its originator, as 'Panachée d'Angers', among the HP's.

COQUETTE DES ALPES
Lacharme, 1867
From 'Mlle Blanche Laffitte' (B) × 'Sapho' (DP).
"White, centre rose shaded, of medium size, full, form fine; growth vigorous."[P1] "Moderate vigor; flower . . . full, demiglobular."[S] "White, tinged with blush; size, medium to large; semi-cupped form, the wood is long-jointed. A very desirable white rose."[EL] "Fragrant, medium stem. Good foliage, sufficient. Growth tall; hardy."[ARA23/159] "Clustering . . . habit free."[JC] "Profuse and constant. Iron-clad in constitution."[Dr]

COQUETTE DES BLANCHES   PLATE 78
Lacharme, 1865
From 'Mlle Blanche Laffitte' (B) × 'Sapho' (DP).
"Pure white with greenish reflections."[S] "White lightly washed pink; flower medium-sized, full, cupped, fragrant; vigorous, with erect branches."[Cx] "Pure white, large and globular; growth vigorous. One of the best."[P1] "Flowers freely in trusses."[Hn] "Very full, somewhat flat, but pretty; growth bushy. An improvement on . . . 'Mme Alfred de Rougemont'."[EL] "Free growth. Elegant foliage. Symmetrical bush. Beautiful cemetary rose."[Dr] "Of a robust constitution . . . it quickly forms a fine bush . . . on which are borne quantities of Centifolia-form flowers, medium to large in size, well held, and of a sparkling white sorting well with the handsome green foliage."[JR9/88–89] "Always green, consequently blooming continually. Its foliage is a very beautiful green, and its wood vigorous, presenting nothing to speak of in the way of thorns. The poise of the blossoms is perfect; they are of medium size, and borne gracefully on long stems . . . beautiful shaded pearly white, lightly tinted at the center with pink when they open in the sun . . . Today, February 25th [in Havana], our specimens of 'Coquette' are covered with a multitude

of flowers, veritable snowballs . . . the semi-open buds somewhat resemble a white Camellia. . . . 'Coquette des Blanches' is not sufficiently known; it is lost in a crowd of novelties."[JR10/57–58]

COUPE D'HÉBÉ
Listed as a Hybrid Bourbon.

EUGÈNE E. MARLITT
Listed as 'Mme Eugène E. Marlitt'.

FELLEMBERG
Listed as a Noisette.

GLOIRE DES ROSOMANES
(trans., 'Glory of the Rose-Maniacs'; syn., 'Ragged Robin', 'Red Robin')
Plantier/Vibert, 1825
"Single, dark crimson, and very sweet-scented . . . the foliage is not dense, and it straggles."[BSA] "Brilliant crimson, semi-double."[EL] "Intense red with a white nub; flowers large, full."[Cx] "Purpling in heat."[Th2] "Hard, almost unpleasant color."[Capt28] "A most brilliant and beautiful variety . . . deficient in fullness . . . they fade very quickly in hot weather; it is only in the cool cloudy days of autumn, when their flowers never fully expand, that they are seen in perfection."[R8] "We find in our archives the following description of this old and beautiful rose: 'Nº 109.—Gloire des Rosomanes (Hybrid Remontant), Vibert 1825, flower nearly single, brilliant intense red.' Such is the description of its introducer. —But we hasten to add that this plant is assuredly a China hybrid."[JR31/69] "Unlike the Bourbon rose in everything."[Sx] "Vigorous; flower large, semi-double, widely cupped; very floriferous; blooms up to winter."[S] "Never flowerless."[J] "The only stock at the Knoxville station which blooms in both the spring and the fall."[ARA30/73] "For profusion of bloom from June till severe frost, has not an equal; the flowers are nearly bright scarlet, produced in large clusters, but are not fully double, of rampant growth . . . clothed with large foliage from bottom to top."[Bu] "A hybrid of most remarkable habits. Its large foliage, luxuriant growth, and showy semi-double crimson flowers, make it one of the most desirable of this division [Bourbons]. . . . I cannot imagine any thing more imposing in floriculture than a pillar, from twelve to fifteen ft high [ca. 3.5–4.5 m] covered with the splendid flowers of this rose from June till October."[WRP] "This variety is above all notable for its dark green foliage; the canes are armed with strong thorns, the blossoms are very large, flat, of a vermilion red, and nearly single. This variety, of moderate growth in our climate, blooms well enough, but prefers warmer regions. In le Midi, where it may grow ten to fifteen ft high [ca. 3–4.5 m], it is much sought out as a beautiful and profuse bloomer, flowering once in the year."[JR2/44] "Continuous supply of flowers."[L] "Does well everywhere."[Capt28]
"Glory isn't lacking in the world of Roses. Open any commercial catalog of consequence, and you will see *Gloire de Guérin, Gloire des Hellenes, Gloire de Paris, Gloire d'Auteuil, Gloire des Perpétuelles, Gloire de France, Gloire de Colmar, Gloire d'Un Parterre, Gloire de Pelay, Gloire des Lawrenceanas, Gloire d'Angers, Gloire de la Guillotière,* and a thousand other Glories; but you will not always find *Gloire des Rosomanes.* It is not that the rose is mediocre—far from it; it is only that it is old. . . . 'Gloire des Rosomanes' was raised at Lyon about fifteen years ago by Mons Plantier, who had the good sense to give it a name it deserves so well, as it is the glory of the fanciers who possess it. It

appeared in a section of mixed remontant hybrids. . . . Branches long, of notable vigor, 'climbing,' bark smooth, glaucous green; thorns occasional, of a flesh-shaded yellow, very strong, elongated, hooked, very sharp, pretty regularly distributed two-by-two at the base of the leaves, which are themselves composed of seven large leaflets, rounded, curled pretty much like those of the Elm, with long much-tapered dentations, and hints of purple, a shade infusing the leaf as a whole; the leafstalk is lightly pubescent above, and furnished beneath with 6–10 prickles of the sort found on the branches, but shorter and smaller. The blossoms come in clusters at the ends of the canes; they are borne on long stalks of 1–1.5 in [ca. 2.5–3 cm], bristling with purplish glandular hairs, as are the ovary and sepals, which have the distinctive characteristic of having cottony pubescence, and are much tapered, sometimes extending into smaller divisions, making them lyrate-filiform. The ovary is small, and narrowed at the summit. The flower is 'hollow,' or single, in common parlance; but, to be exact, it is double, because it is composed of two rows of petals instead of the one found in single blossoms. . . . Its fragrance is delicious, and its color a sparkling maroon, at the center of which one sees its numerous sulphur-yellow stamens. Examining the separate petals, one notes that they are whitish at the nub, violet-red beneath and velvety maroon above. They are cordiform and number about five rows." [PIB]

GREAT WESTERN
Listed as a Hybrid Bourbon.

GRUSS AN TEPLITZ   PLATE 85
(trans., 'Greetings to Teplitz'; syn., 'Virginia R. Coxe')
Geschwindt/Lambert, 1897
From an unnamed seedling (parentage: 'Sir Joseph Paxton' [HB] × 'Fellemberg' [N]) × another unnamed seedling (parentage: 'Papa Gontier' [T] × 'Gloire des Rosomanes' [B]).
  "Brilliant cinnabar scarlet shaded with velvety fiery red. . . . Very vigorous." [P1] "Iron red; flower medium-sized, cupped, fragrant." [Cx] "Flowers fairly large, some solitary, some in small clusters, bright orange-scarlet cherry-red . . . often flowers well in autumn." [Hn] "Crimson . . . deepening with age . . . strong spicy scent . . . 6 × 4'." [B] "Unequalled as a free-flowering . . . rose." [J] "Little or no rebloom in fall." [JR33/93] "A favorite variety, with semi-double, bright crimson blooms that are especially freely produced in autumn." [OM] "Foliage is dark." [W] "Leaves . . . small." [Hk] "For . . . districts without dampness . . . mildews." [Capt28] "Foliage, immune from mildew; slightly susceptible to [black-]spot." [Th] "Growth perfect." [ARA17/24] "Moderate height, rather stocky, vigorous, hardy; foliage very abundant." [ARA18/125] "It is absolutely the best rose for hedge purposes." [Th] "Semi-climbing. . . . Its clusters of well-shaped flowers and pointed buds borne at the end of long shoots, its luxuriant green foliage edged with red, its abundance of bloom and delicious fragrance, make it one of the most valuable roses of the last ten years. . . . From June to November it is always in flower here." [K1] "It thrives splendidly when not trained in any way, and it is especially valuable because it comes into flower rather late, and in September is at its best. The blooms are in big loose bunches, chiefly on the upper part of the stems; they are only semi-double, but of vivid crimson-red colouring, and most fragrant. . . . It thrives with me in a half-shady corner, and there flowers quite freely, though it is certainly worth a place in the sunshine." [OM] "Ornamented with large, shiny, coppery foliage. . . . One of the great advantages of this flower is that it doesn't blue after being cut, and lasts a long time in a vase." [JR23/138] "This Rose has good and attractive foliage and a strong semi-climbing habit, growing readily into a good symmetrical,

rather upright bush. . . . The flowers, which are produced in loose clusters, are semi-double and not well shaped, but very brilliant in the garden. The colour is normally a bright crimson, occasionally tending towards maroon. They are not well carried, and much inclined to hang their heads. They are produced in considerable quantity and very continuously, the autumn crop being specially good. The flowers are fragrant, and the plants have a magnificent constitution." [NRS/12] "Blooms early and has all the Tea and Hybrid Tea characteristics. The shrub is quite large, with brilliant foliage, and very leathery leaves; the young growths are very distinctly a bronzy reddish-green. The large blossoms, nearly always solitary, are sometimes in clusters of two or three, and are upright and cupped; the color is a rusty cinnabar illumined with fiery red and brown. The flower has no bluish tone. The scent is of an incomparable sweetness. This variety is of easy culture, blooms abundantly both early and late, and maybe in winter as well!" [JR21/67] "Happy, cheery, and most friendly of all roses! A great big lusty fellow, always nodding 'howdy-do' with bunches of red posies." [C-Ps27]

GYPSY BOY
Listed as 'Ziguenerknabe' among the Hybrid Bourbons.

HERMOSA
(trans., 'Beautiful'; syns., 'Mélanie Lemaire', 'Armosa')
Marcheseau/Rousseau, 1834
  "Deep pink, of medium size, full. Growth, moderate. A most abundant bloomer." [P] "Well formed, intense flesh." [R-H42] "Lilac pink, fragrant." [G] "Bright rose . . . constantly in flower, bushy habit." [EL] "Delicate pale pink cupped blooms . . . 3 × 2 [ft; ca. 9 × 6 dm]." [B] "Sweet, small, full, China-pink rose beloved by everyone who knows it." [ARA36/19] "Fades in heat." [Th2] "Has been cultivated these ten years, and is still a favorite; the flowers are of the most exquisite form, perfectly cupped; though under the medium size, the deficiency is made up in the profusion of pale rose coloured flowers. It is a dwarf grower." [Bu] "Its beauty of form and color strongly recommend its being in every collection, independently of its profuseness of autumnal flowering and perfect hardihood . . . will bloom abundantly where China Roses, to which it bears a strong resemblance, will scarcely exist." [C] "Has China growth characteristics, and Bourbon floral characteristics; it is a hybrid of China ['Parsons' Pink'?] and Bourbon ['Mme Desprez'?]." [JR23/56] "Quite ordinary and unexciting, but liberal in yield." [ARA20/16] "A distinctive and free bloomer." [ARA31/31] "Truly a jewel; always in bloom [in Brazil]." [PS] "Good decorative rose. . . . Foliage, very good." [Th] "Leaves, greyish-green." [B1] "Requires little or no pruning." [JP] "Vigorous; branches thin and divergent . . . bark, dark green, glabrous, armed with the occasional brownish thorn, perhaps a little reddish; smooth foliage is a handsome green; flower, about 2.5 in across [ca. 6.25 cm], globular, slightly cupped." [S] "Branches thin, boding a sickly constitution, but nevertheless growing with vigor, glabrous, shiny, olive green; armed with some remote, abruptly narrowed thorns, sharp, composed of five or rarely three unequal leaflets which are glabrous, smooth, shiny, fairly strongly dentate, dark olive green above, paler and glaucescent beneath. . . . Flowers ordinarily solitary at the ends of the branches, loosely full, very well formed in a rosette, of medium size, a pretty pale pink, darker at the edge. Flower stalk to two in [ca. 5 dm], glandular-pilose, somewhat flexile. . . . Calyx with glaucous green tube, glabrous, hemispherical, slightly elongated, not contracted at the mouth. . . . Bud ovoid, pointed, intense pink, ordinarily with five darker lines. Petals obovate, spoon-shaped, nearly white at the base; outer ones large,

drawn up, well imbricated; outer petals pink to the base on the reverse; those of the center folded or weakly curled, showing some anthers. . . . 'Hermosa' is a very graceful rose, even stylish, and of a delicate color. Its bud opens easily and with perfect regularity, giving birth to a flower which is exactly in the form of a cup during the first moments of opening, after which the outer petals reflex, drawn aside as if by design; at that point, their brilliant color begins to lose its freshness, and indeed the delicate pink which it had takes on a flat tint which foretells the end of this ephemeral beauty. This variety was raised by Mons Marcheseau. . . . During recent years, it has again been released to commerce under the name 'Mélanie Lemarie' [*sic*]." [PIB] "Calyx nearly pear-shaped, glabrous; sepals narrow." [JF] "An old variety, but still one of the very best of this group." [SBP]

HOFGÄRTNER KALB
Felberg-Leclerc, 1913
From 'Souvenir de Mme Eugène Verdier' (HT) × 'Gruss an Teplitz' (B).

"Semi-double, delicate pink, very floriferous." [JR38/30] "Growth vigorous, bushy, upright, about three ft in height [ca. 9 dm]; foliage copper-colored. Very full, large blossoms, fragrant, of good form. The color is brilliant carmine, with a yellow center; the exterior petals are somber carmine, sprinkled with brilliant red. 'Hofgärtner Kalb' blooms up to frost without interruption, giving 20–25 blossoms on each stem. This novelty, by its homogeneous height and flowers of notable color, is just the thing for bedding." [JR37/137] "Balls and mildews badly. Vigorous. [Best in] Interior South." [Th2]

HONORINE DE BRABANT
Introducer and date unknown.

"Double blush-pink, mottled and striped with violet and mauve. To 4 [ft; ca. 1.25 m]." [HRG] "Loose . . . well scented." [G] "Large, full, cupped, fragrant; lilac-pink striped crimson and red. . . . Repeats . . . common, but excellent." [Lg] "Main crop at midsummer." [T1] "Especially good in Autumn . . . 5 × 4 [ft; ca. 1.5 × 2.5 m]." [B] "Mid-green foliage on a vigorous plant." [G]

INGEGNOLI PREDILETTA
Listed as 'Zéphirine Drouhin'

KATHLEEN HARROP
A. Dickson, 1919
Sport of 'Zéphirine Drouhin' (B).

"Delicate pink." [Cw] "Soft shell-pink . . . 6 × 5 [ft; ca. 1.75 × 1.5 m]." [B] "Not so vigorous [as 'Zéphirine Drouhin'], but makes a very pleasing bush with flowers of bright, light pink, the petals being much darker on the reverse . . . beautifully marked with transparent veins." [T1] "Bud large; flower large, semi-double; moderate fragrance." [ARA20/128] "An effective hedge background." [ARA33/18]

KRONPRINZESSIN VIKTORIA VON PREUSSEN
Volvert/Spæth, 1888
Sport of 'Souvenir de la Malmaison' (B).

"Milk white, tinted with sulphur-yellow. Good." [P1] "Of all the new roses introduced to commerce in 1888, the present subject is certainly one of the best, and when it becomes well known, it will take a place in the forefront of cultivated varieties for its abundant bloom . . . originated in Germany . . . a sport of 'Souvenir de la Malmaison', and has the same bearing and growth. . . . As for the

flower, it is quite beautiful; the bud is slightly oval and is a handsome pure white; once open, the edges of the petals remain white while the center of the blossom has shadings of pale yellow. The flowers have the precious advantage of staying open a long time, and take on the appearance of a pretty Camellia." [JR15/6] "Over the entire summer and autumn, it never stops bearing flowers abundantly." [JR32/34] "Very vigorous, with branches usually short and erect, furnished with unequal thorns, few in number; the leaves are soft green and oval; the blossoms, large rather than medium in size, are about four in across [ca. 1 dm], full, with large, rounded petals around the circumference, those of the center being shorter and more narrow; cupped, ruffled, perfect and graceful; very delicate sulphur-white, even throughout; strong Alba fragrance . . . very floriferous and remontant, as the short Bourbons tend to be; opens well from a tapered bud." [JR12/120] "Good vigor, upright branches; leaves of a handsome dark green, sometimes brushed on the edges with light pink. . . . The bud is of good oval form and lasts a long time ." [JR11/166]

LA FRANCE
Should be here, but we bow to tradition and pretend it is a Hybrid Tea.

LAS-CASES
Listed as a Hybrid Bourbon.

LE BIENHEUREAUX DE LA SALLE
Listed as 'Mme Isaac Pereire'. Our best wishes to anyone who ever used this synonym.

LEVESON-GOWER
('Leweson Gower', 'Malmaison Rose')
Béluze, 1846

Confusion exists between this variety and 'Malmasion Rouge'. Part of the problem is yet further confusion between 'Leveson-Gower', the deep pink Bourbon, and 'Souvenir de Leveson-Gower', a "deep purple." [HP] The Bourbon 'Leveson-Gower' was never stated to be a sport of 'Souvenir de la Malmaison', and, considering their respective dates of introduction, 'Gower' could perhaps be a sibling, or, more likely, a related cross. 'Malmaison Rouge', from nearly forty years later, was indeed a sport of 'Souvenir de la Malmaison'.

"Deep rose, tinged with salmon, the flowers are of the same character as 'Malmaison'." [EL] "Fresh satiny pink." [JR9/12] "Blossom very large; color, violet pink." [S] "Large, full, beautiful pink. Fragrant." [LR] "Rosy salmon." [TW] "Purplish pink." [Cw] "Bright pink to red . . . 4 × 3 [ft; ca. 1.25 × 1 m]." [R] "Rose, shaded with salmon, very large and full; form, cupped. Growth, robust. Partakes of the nature of the Tea-scented." [P] "Something of a hybrid tea." [JR2/104] George Granville Leveson-Gower, 1773–1846, 1st Earl Granville, Ambassador at Paris. "W. [*sic*] Leveson Gower, Esq,. whose Roses at Titsey, near Godstone, are well known for their beauty." [P]

LOUISE D'ARZENS
Lacharme, 1861

"Creamy-white, beautifully cupped and well formed, flowers rather too small, though distinct, and very pretty; habit moderate." [JC] "White with yellowish reflections." [JR1/2/8] "Pure white, medium size, full, and of fine form; growth moderate; one of the best." [P1] "Quite a gem, producing its pure white exquisitely formed flowers in great abundance; it might almost be called a perpetual 'Mme Hardy' [D]." [P2] "One of the best for massing."

[FP] "Of moderate vigor, floriferous . . . one of the prettiest white roses." [S] Parentage consisting of 'Mlle Blanche Laffitte' (B) × 'Sapho' (DP) may be suspected.

LOUISE ODIER   PLATE 76
('Mme de Stella')
Margottin, 1851
Seedling of an unnamed seedling of 'Émile Courtier' (B).

"A bright rose-color, of a beautiful cupped form . . . it has a tendency to bloom in clusters." [FP] "Very double, full; bright soft pink with lavender shadings. Repeats. . . . Excellent soft green foliage . . . 6–10 [ft; ca. 1.75–3 m]." [Lg] "Camellia-like . . . vigorous and perpetual . . . 4 × 4 [ft; ca. 1.25 × 1.25 m]." [B] "Almost equal to 'Coupe d'Hébé' in the shape of its bright rose-coloured flowers." [R8] "Good centifolia form." [Hn] "Very floriferous." [Cx] "Branches vigorous, somewhat thin, olive green. . . . Leaves generally of five leaflets tinted brownish red when young, later turning a beautiful olive green above and pale green beneath. . . . Flowers large, very full, perfectly formed, beautiful intense pink, solitary or in twos or threes at the end of the cane. Bud rounded-oval, handsome red. Flower stem glandular, thick, fairly long, very stiff, holding the blossom well. . . . Exterior petals wider than long, upright, well imbricated, nubless, shell-like, rounded at the outer edge; center petals narrower or ragged and folded." [PIB] "Calyx pear-shaped and quite glabrous." [JF] "Branches fairly slender and divergent; bark, a somewhat yellowish green, armed with occasional maroon thorns, hooked and quite large; leaves smooth, olive green, in three to five acuminate irregularly dentate oval leaflets; strong leafstalks, furnished with four to five little prickles; flower, about 2.5 in across [ca. 6.25 cm], very full, cupped, solitary on the smaller branches . . . one of the best Bourbons; hardy." [S] "Very beautiful variety both grafted and own-root; its only problem is that it grows a little too high." [I'H53/224] "A free growing and beautiful rose." [JC]

MALMAISON ROSE
(trans., 'Pink Malmaison')
Listed as 'Leveson-Gower'.

[MALMAISON ROUGE]
('Red Malmaison')
Gonod, 1882
Sport of 'Souvenir de la Malmaison' (B).
Confusion exists between this variety and 'Leveson-Gower', which see.

"Flower medium sized, full, beautiful velvety dark red. Fragrant." [LR] "Large flowers, beautifully imbricated; very full, perfect form; color bright, glowing crimson, very vivid, rich, and velvety; highly scented, and a very promising variety." [CA88] "Sport of 'Souvenir de la Malmaison'. This variety has the thorns of its parent; the foliage is of five leaflets which are very dark green; it blooms just like 'Malmaison'; the blossom is of moderate size, and a dark velvety red. It is quite valuable for bouquets due to its cupped flowers. It produces a charming effect when bedded with 'Malmaison'." [JR6/149–150]

MARTHA
Sport of 'Zéphirine Drouhin' (B).
Knudsen/Zeiner-Lassen & Dithmer, 1912
Not to be confused with Lambert's coppery pink Polyantha of 1905.

"Double deep pink fragrant flowers of medium size." [G] "Unusual mauve-pink shapely flowers, very free-flowering on a vigorous shrub, 5 × 4 [ft; ca. 1.5 × 1.25 m]." [HRG] "Vigorous. . . .

The blossom is of an irregular form, intense pink on a yellow ground, brilliant. Very floriferous, this variety blooms until frost. Foliage, dark green with metallic reflections. Resistant to all maladies and insensible to cold, 'Martha' is, because of its many good points, an excellent introduction for bedding." [JR37/25] 'Martha' is said to be a sport of 'Charles Bonnet', a statement which can be interpreted as above — 'Charles Bonnet' being a synonym of 'Zéphirine Drouhin' — or, alternatively, as referring to the *HP* 'Charles Bonnet', listed in the HP supplement.

MÉLANIE LEMAIRE
Listed as 'Hermosa'.

MICHEL BONNET
Listed as 'Catherine Guillot'.

MME ALFRED DE ROUGEMONT
Lacharme, 1862
From 'Mlle Blanche Laffitte' (B) × 'Sapho' (DP).

"Pure white, lightly and delicately shaded with rose and carmine, large and full, shape of the Cabbage Rose; one of the best." [FP] "My most favorite [of this race]. It is small, and at first pure white, then blushing pink at the edges of the petals. It blooms early and easily." [JR18/38] "Cupped, fragrant." [Cx] "Beautifully formed flower." [P2] "Of medium growth, floriferous, blooming in clusters; flower large, full, centifolia-form; color, white shaded pink and bordered carmine." [S] "Surpassed by 'Coquette des Blanches'." [EL] "A perfect little gem . . . covered with its delicate and lovely roses. The wood and foliage are of a light green, the growth moderately stout, and with a free and graceful habit. The roses are small in size, quite double and full; when newly opened they are most handsomely cupped, white with a delicate tint of flesh color, deeper towards the centre. It is a most abundant bloomer, and though by no means showy, is yet exceedingly attractive in its modest loveliness." [HstXXVIII:165]

MME DE STELLA
Listed as 'Louise Odier'.

MME DESPREZ
Desprez, 1831
Seedling of 'Rose Edouard' (B).
Not to be confused with the white China of the same name.

"Deep pink." [V4] "Violet pink, full, flat, large, superb." [LF] "Rose and lilac shaded, produced in large clusters, large and full; form cupped; growth vigorous." [P1] "This fine and robust rose blooms beautifully; its large clusters of very splendid lilac roseate flowers are indeed superb." [WRP] "It is eleven years since I first imported this rose, together with 'Aimée Vibert', 'Lamarque', 'Jaune Desprez', and some others of equal celebrity. . . . This rose originated with Monsieur Desprez . . . it is considerably hybridized with the Noisette, and like that rose produces its bright rose coloured flowers in immense clusters; from thirty to seventy bloom in each when the plant is fully established; the foliage is a rich green, strong and handsome." [Bu] "The secondary branches come only at the ends of the canes. The shrub is branched, but not intricately." [JR23/115–116] "Vigorous . . . leaves purplish green passing to very dark glaucous green; flowers very full, open well, three in across [ca. 7.5 cm], well formed, intense pink at first, then violet pink, finally lilac, such that, as it is floriferous, one can see four different shades of flowers all at once in perfect condition. This variety has won the support of the many fanciers who have seen it." [R-H33] The influence of 'Mme Desprez' should not be overlooked, for she is partially responsible for such notables as 'Safrano' and 'Souvenir de la Malmaison', and it is her lilac-pink gene carried by 'Safrano' and 'Mme Falcot' which popped up again in 'La France'—all names to conjure with. Further, she served as nurturing mother quite anonymously to many of the early Hybrid Bourbons and Hybrid Perpetuals, being a notoriously fecund remontant variety just when such was needed for breeding. The vital importance of 'Mme Desprez' to the progress of the Bourbons has already been noted in the headnote to this chapter. Important to Teas, HT's, HP's, Hybrid Bourbons, Bourbons—'Mme Desprez' was certainly no slouch, and I am glad to note that a few specimens remain in European hands; it would be most unfortunate for such an important variety to become extinct.

MME DUBOST
Pernet père, 1890
Not to be confused with Pernet's 1891 HP 'Mlle Dubost' of much the same color.

"Flesh, center pink." [LS] "Vigorous, of good growth, well branched, with branches upright and strong; blooms in clusters; flowers of medium size or larger, pretty full, white blushing at the edge and bright pink at the center; well held; very floriferous; opens easily; quite remontant." [JR14/164]

MME ERNST CALVAT
Widow Schwartz, 1888
Sport of 'Mme Isaac Pereire' (B).

"Flower very large, full, of perfect form, variable, changing from China pink to intense pink; petal nub yellowish. Very fragrant." [LR] "Ruffled." [Cx] "Many yellow anthers." [GAS] "Very vigorous, 'climbing'-type canes, somber green foliage, reddish beneath; flower . . . variably tinted, fading from China pink to bright pink or lilac-pink . . . quite remontant." [JR12/163] "6 × 4 [ft; ca. 1.75 × 1.25 m]." [B] Ernest Calvat, died 1910; manufacturer (glover) and amateur horticulturalist, particularly interested in Chrysanthemum hybridization [—from R-HC].

MME EUGÈNE E. MARLITT
Geschwindt, 1900

"Carmine-red [and listed as giving between 100 and 200 blossoms annually]." [ARA20/84] "Vigorous, practically continuous blooming, very fragrant." [ARA25/112] "A beautiful rose and almost thornless; flowers large, very double and full, bright rich carmine red, does not fade or bleach so quickly as others, but continues bright and beautiful a long time, a strong healthy grower, constant and abundant bloomer; quite hardy and delightfully fragrant, makes plenty of buds and flowers for cutting all Summer and Fall." [C&Js06] "Blooms are large, full, globular, crimson shaded with scarlet on an almost thornless plant, 4 [ft; ca. 1.25 m]." [HRG]

MME GUSTAVE BONNET
Listed as 'Zéphirine Drouhin'.

MME ISAAC PEREIRE   PLATE 81
('Le Bienheureaux de la Salle')
Garçon/Margottin, 1880

"Carmine-red, very large, full, free blooming." [EL] "Rosy-carmine, extra large and full; form expanded; growth vigorous." [P1] "Revolting in colour." [Hk] "Of a pretty color of lilac-rose, and the blossoms are well formed." [JR7/157] "Weak in centre." [F-M2] "Flower enormous, full; color, bright carmine-red; imbricated; very well formed." [S] "Light carmine. Good in autumn." [H] "Huge shaggy blooms of purple crimson . . . free . . . 6 × 4

[ft; ca. 1.75 × 1.25 m]." [B] "Of good growth. A splendid rose, with a wonderful blooming record all reason." [ARA18/112] "Long branches clad with dull foliage, nasty little thorns, and mildew." [Hk] "For our part, we believe that it is not a pure Bourbon. A simple examination suffices to show that it is strongly hybrid . . . we retain the classification which was given it by its introducer, which is to say that we place it with the Hybrid Bourbons [*no we don't*], of which it is certainly one of the prettiest, if not indeed the prettiest, variety . . . it is always an excellent sort, making such a vigorous bush that one would sometimes be able to call it a climber; its numerous blossoms, in bid clusters, rarely solitary, are very large, full, well-formed, imbricated, very pretty bright carmine-red, and exhaling an exquisite perfume. It is furthermore an excellent seed-bearer." [JR17/52–53]

MME LAURIOL DE BARNEY
Listed as a Hybrid Bourbon.

MME MOSER
Listed in the Hybrid Tea chapter supplement.

MME PIERRE OGER   PLATE 80
Oger/C. Verdier, 1878
Sport of 'Reine Victoria' (B).
Not to be confused with the 1899 Letellier HP, which was bright pink.

"Creamy-white; petals blotched and bordered delicate lilac-pink; a new coloration." [JR2/187] "Medium size, cupped, beautiful loose form, pale pink, gradually becoming redder in colour; a particularly charming, delicately-scented rose. Vigorous growth, good in autumn." [Hn] "White, edged with lilac, distinct and pretty." [P1] "Blush, the exterior of the petals tinged with rosy lilac, cupped form, not a free bloomer." [EL] "Petals rigid, porcelain-like; very floriferous; very vigorous." [Cx] "Very pale silvery pink. Translucent cupped flowers . . . 4 × 4 [ft; ca. 1.25 × 1.25 m]." [B] "Makes a vigorous shrub with upright branches; its abundant foliage is light green; its abundant blossoms are medium to large, full, globular, and well formed. The color is creamy-white on opening, with the outer edges of the petals taking on a nice coppery lilac-pink with age . . . a rose of the first order." [JR9/104]

MRS. BOSANQUET
('Mistress Bosanquet', 'Thé Sapho', 'Pauline Bonaparte')
Laffay, 1832

"Very soft pink flower of much charm." [E] "Rosy flesh, very productive." [EL] "White, their centres delicate flesh, large and full; form cupped; growth vigorous. A beautiful Rose, sweet, and an abundant bloomer." [P1] "Very delicate and beautiful, at the same time large and double." [FP] "Flat in the form of a camellia; color, white shaded peach-pink." [JR26/57] "Globular." [Cx] "Medium size, full, cupped, white tinted with pink, fragrant, flowering till autumn. An old charming Rose of moderate growth and established merit." [Hn] "One of the very best of the pale roses . . . perfectly double, of cup form; colour waxy blush; the growth is strong, nearly approaching the Bourbon roses, to which it is related." [Bu] "This rose appears intermediate between the Chinese and what are called Bourbons. . . . If possible, more unique and beautiful than any other variety. A truly splendid Rose." [HstVI:368] "Very vigorous, blooms with abandon up to frost . . . salmon-white." [S] "One of the most desirable of the old China roses, and there are few in any other class that are superior to it. Its growth is luxuriant, and its superb cupped, wax-like flowers are of a delicate flesh-color, and are produced in the greatest abundance." [SBP] "Yet unrivalled." [R8] "The next collection which demands our notice is that at Broxbournebury, the seat of George J. Bosanquet, Esq., where there are at the present time a great number of very fine specimens. . . . I believe this to be the best private collection of Roses in England." [P]

MRS. PAUL
G. Paul, 1891
Seedling of 'Mme Isaac Pereire' (B).

"Blush white, shaded rosy peach; large open flower like a Camellia. Distinct and handsome." [P1] "Soft, pale pink to white . . . ample, although somewhat coarse, foliage . . . 5 × 4 [ft; ca. 1.5 × 1.25 m]." [B] "Flowers white with carmine, tinted peach-blossom pink." [JR17/166] "Petals thick. . . . Strong-growing, free-flowering, well into the autumn." [Hn] "Poor autumnal . . . colour blotchy." [F-M2] "A charming Bourbon rose; the blossom is exquisite in form and structure, the petals are large, imbricated, and recurved. The shade is a delicate pink, blanched at the center of the old petals. The tender shade contrasts nicely with those of other roses." [JR14/174–175] "Growth very strong, foliage . . . not liable to mildew." [F-M2] "Mr. George Paul [*cousin, incidentally, of William Paul*] . . . who for many years has mainly been interested in raising roses from seed had the idea of breeding varieties with the great vigor and remontancy of 'Mme Isaac Periere', thus profiting from all the good qualities found in that variety. He turned his hand to that task, and got seeds from 'Mme Isaac Periere', hoping to get seedlings which kept the magnificent bearing and growth of their mother, yet producing flowers which were more perfect and of a more beautiful color. The hope was translated into reality in one of the seedlings . . . the plant inherited the vigorous habit and handsome foliage of the parent, as well as its remontancy. . . . The exterior petals, which form a 'guard of honor,' are large and of a form without parallel, giving it a very distinctive character, while meantime the pearl-white color, sometimes with shadings of peach, makes it very intriguing . . . will play a very important role in rosiculture during this fin-de-siècle." [JR17/116–117]

PANACHÉE D'ANGERS
Listed as an HP.

PARKZIERDE
Listed as a Hybrid Bourbon.

PAULINE BONAPARTE
Listed as 'Mrs. Bosanquet'.

PERLE DES BLANCHES
(trans., 'Pearl of the Whites')
Lacharme, 1872
From 'Mlle Blanche Laffitte' (B) × 'Sapho' (DP).

"Creamy-white, changing to pure white, foliage of 'Boule de Neige', and flowers somewhat similar; vigorous habit." [JC] "Pure white, medium-sized, full, quite globular, blooming sumptuously in clusters, growth strong, elegant habit, a very beautiful rose." [N] "Globular, full, deep, double roses. Buds hard and round. Very hardy. Free and constant. A very fine, old, pure white rose." [Dr] "Inferior to others of the type." [EL] "Very fragrant." [LR] "To five metres [ca. 15 ft] with handsome foliage." [G]

PRINCE CHARLES
Listed as a Hybrid Bourbon.

QUEEN OF BEDDERS
Standish & Noble, 1877
Seedling of 'Sir Joseph Paxton' (B).

"Rich crimson. Few recent roses have been so highly praised as this; evidently a useful free-blooming sort." [SBP] "Vigorous, full, cherry-red, very floriferous." [JR1/12/13] "Flower full, large, dark cerise-red . . . blooms up to the fall; resembles 'Charles Lefebvre' [HP]." [S] "Medium size, very full; a free flowering sort. The color is not very durable." [EL] "Short growing, compact . . . shapely carmine flowers produced freely . . . 3 × 2 [ft; ca. 9 × 6 dm]." [B] "Moderate growers, like 'Queen of the Bedders', require their strongest shoots to be shortened to three or four in [ca. 8 cm–1 dm], and the weaker ones to one or two in [ca. 2.5–5 cm]." [TW]

QUEEN OF BOURBONS
Listed as 'Reine des Île-Bourbons'.

RED MALMAISON
Listed as 'Malmaison Rouge'.

REINE DES ÎLE-BOURBONS
('Queen of the Bourbons')
Mauget, 1834

"Fawn and rose, medium or small size, fragrant, very free; of delicate habit." [EL] "Moderately full, a very fresh carmine pink." [JR1/2/7] "White with a hint of flesh." [JR8/26] "Salmon carmine pink; flower large, full; very floriferous; very vigorous." [Cx] "Semi-double magenta and pink flowers, mainly in June. Crinkled and veined." [T1] "Medium or large, full, very delicate flesh color." [R-H42] "Its petals are arranged with a beautiful regularity." [SBP] "Delicate salmon-flesh, often tinged with buff, large and very double; form cupped, fine; growth moderate. An abundant bloomer, sweet, and of fine habit." [P1] "At first it was thought to be a Bengal, the same as 'Madam [*sic*] Bosanquet'. . . . The colour is a beautiful waxy blush, with petals perfectly formed, bold, and cup-shaped; a half-blown rose from this plant is loveliness itself . . . dwarf in habit." [Bu] "Peculiar compact habit of growth." [Fl] "Vigorous . . . 6 × 4 [ft; ca. 1.75 × 1.25 m]." [B] "Continual and copious bloom." [WD] "Large fruit in the autumn." [G] "Vigorous, with short fecund branches; wood green, furnished with rust-colored prickles which are short but big; leaves of three to five rounded, dentate leaflets; numerous buds; flower semi-double or nearly full, of a salmon-carmine pink, blooming over many months." [S] "Quite unique in their colouring, and well worthy of cultivation." [R8] "A charming hardy rose of proved merit." [Hn]

REINE VICTORIA
Labruyère/Schwartz, 1872

"Beautiful bright pink." [I'H72/261] "Flower large, full, very well formed, of a handsome rose-color. A very beautiful variety." [JR26/57] "Very vigorous; flower medium-sized or large, full; color, bright pink. Reblooms very well and flowers until winter." [S] "Damask fragrance intense." [W] "5 × 3 [ft; ca. 1.5 × 1 m]." [B] "Extremely sparse recurrence for me. Long willowy branches which hang and bend forlornly with the weight of the spring bloom, made all the worse by rain, when the beauty of the globular blossoms becomes discernible to none but observant lizards and æsthetically-inclined ants. Susceptible to attacks of mildew, suffering much. The blossoms are a smoky lilac-rose, and are overly tenacious of petal — the plant must be 'dead-headed.' Does not set seed. In good weather, it makes a handsome specimen; and, despite its weaknesses, is in such ideal conditions something to admire in full bloom." [BCD]

REV. H. D'OMBRAIN
Margottin, 1863

"Large flower, full, silvery carmine red." [JR1/2/7] "Bright pink, carmine center . . . very beautiful." [N] "Vigorous . . . color, very brilliant carmine." [S] "Well-formed, cupped." [JR3/29] "Fragrant and opens flat . . . to 1.5 metres [ca. 4 ft]." [G] "Matt green foliage rather prone to mildew but the bush is of quite tidy habit." [B1]

ROSE EDOUARD
('Rose Neumann', 'Rose Dubreuil')
Perichon/Neumann, 1821

From the red 'Tous-les-Mois' (DP) × *R. chinensis* 'Parsons' Pink'. There is confusion between 'Rose Edouard', 'Rosier de l'Île Bourbon', and anything else called anything like 'Rose-' or 'Rosier de Bourbon'. Properly, 'Rose Edouard' is the plant, or clones of the plant, found by Mons Perichon among his hedgelings that fateful day on the Isle Bourbon. Cuttings of this were imported to France by Mons Neumann. The 'Rose-' or 'Rosier de Bourbon' designation, as well as 'Bourbon Jacques' or 'Rose Jacques', should refer to one (or the other!) of two seedlings which Mons Jacques sprouted from seed sent to him by Mons Breon, and which was subsequently illustrated by Redouté. 'Rosier de l'Île Bourbon' is an ill-advised additional name given to 'Rose Edouard' by certain of the Bourbon islanders; and, worse and worse, early seedlings of any of these might also find themselves called either of the '— Bourbon' names; at length, it seems that any of these varieties would have been likely to have been called any of these names.

"Bright pink, shaded." [LS] "It is everblooming, and bears double blossoms of a charming pinkish color; Mons Richard says that he never saw single blossoms." [JR19/9] "['Souvenir de la Malmaison'] is not distinct from 'Rose Edouard', except in its flowers, which are whiter, more double, and blushing a little in the center; in other characteristics, they are the same." [JR19/9] "One might perhaps be able to consider it the type of the class . . . this new rose attracted attention by its vigor and the novelty of its characateristics: its bright pink blossoms of a particular shade, sparkling and brilliant, its long shoots notable for strong thorns. . . . This rose gave a great many seeds, instigating many sowings which, at first, did not meet with good fortune. The specimens brought forth had single flowers, or very double blossoms which aborted." [JR23/125] "The name 'Rose Edouard' (in remembrance of Mons Edouard Perichon, late settler)." [JR25/137]

ROSIER DE BOURBON
('Bourbon Jacques', 'Rose Jacques')
Breon/Jacques, 1821
Seedling of 'Rose Edouard' (B).

"Flower medium-sized, full, expanded form; bright lilac." [S] "Branches, long and divergent. Thorns, very crooked; glandular at the base. Leaflets, large, oval, cordiform at the base. Tube of calyx, oval-oblong, glaucous and smooth at the summit. Flowers, middle-sized, cup-shaped, semi-double or double; of a brilliant deep pink." [Go] "Its peculiar habit and profusion of brilliant bright rose coloured flowers, blooming in June, with a slight tendency to flower again in autumn; not being fully double, it produced an abundance of seed, from which varieties were obtained that bloomed freely the whole season." [Bu]

SOUVENIR DE LA MALMAISON   PLATE 75
(trans., 'In Remembrance of Malmaison')
Béluze, 1843
From 'Mme Desprez' (B) × 'A Tea Rose' (possibly 'Devoniensis').

"Malmaison" was the palace to which the Empress Josephine retired after her divorce from Napoleon. On the grounds, she created the world's most complete collection of roses, unsurpassed until the advent of Sangerhausen and L'Haÿ two or three generations later. The collection was evidently dispersed shortly after her death in 1814, with first attempts at reconstitution not taking place until *circa* 1900.

"Mons Béluze, horticulturalist at Vaise, a suburb of Lyon, has found among his seedlings a new Bourbon rose which, as a fancier from Lyon [*Plantier, no doubt*] tells us, is very beautiful. Basically flesh, the blossom, tinted violet upon opening, is full, large to about four in [ca. 1 dm], and the bush is quite remontant, like 'Mme Desprez'. This rose, 'Souvenir de la Malmaison', will be available . . . at the beginning of June." [R-H42] "It was in 1840 that Mons Béluze Sr., rose-breeder in Lyon, sowed the seeds which produced the splendid and magnificent rose I now place before the reader. Two years later, in 1842, the breeder affirmed that he had produced a rose which was out-of-the-ordinary, though without having been able, up to that time, to get more than one sole blossom, which was on the one stem of the original plant, that stem having reached a foot [ca. 3 dm] or so in height. The situation was judged by Mons Plantier, distinguished rosarian, who declared on sight that this was one of the most fortunate obtentions of the time. . . . The great question to be resolved concerned which variety produced the seeds from which 'Malmasion' sprang. Over and again the Société d'Horticulture Pratique du Rhône hoped to resolve the question in its meetings. . . . [The Société determined] that in all probability 'Souvenir de la Malmaison' came from the Bourbon 'Mme Desprez', the opinion of Béluze, which was indeed shared by Plantier. In support of this, it is a fact that the seeds collected and sown were for the most part from 'Mme Desprez'. Upon close scrutiny, one notes a great similarity between the stature and foliage of the two varieties. . . . The original specimen of 'Malmaison' still exists at Lyon [in 1879], where it continues to bloom so well that it originates offspring, despite being in a less than favorable position — a southern exposure." [JR3/73] "The blossoms . . . were taken to the markets of Lyon, whence they were quickly borne off, and Béluze was not of a mind to release this wonderful variety [*wanting to maintain his 'monopoly' on its appearance in the florist trade*] . . . Béluze was so happy in the possession of this jewel that, whenever someone would enter his yard, he would place that person under the strictest surveillance, believing that otherwise the person would take many cuttings. The story also goes on to say that Mme Béluze would stand, watching, in one of the windows of the house. As for Béluze himself, he would be lost in watching the visitor from head to toe." [JR19/9–10] "Béluze . . . released it to commerce in June, 1843, when specimens of it sold at the price of 25 francs. It bloomed for the first time [*that is, off Béluze's premises*] at Paris in 1844. . . . When Mons Béluze announced his rose, he described it as 'ground, flesh, lightly violet when opening, full, large to 3.5 in [ca. 8 cm]'. In effect, the rose is white. . . . As to the form, it is equally variable. If the plant is somewhat vigorous, the blossom is flat, ruffled in the center, and nearly completely white; the petals, instead of assuming a graceful round form, imbricate, resembling the scales of a pine cone. . . . The variety is vigorous, grafted on good stock; the blossom is symmetrical; its stem is long and somewhat flexible, and the flower nods gracefully . . . examined closely, it is composed of rounded petals, imbricated, diminishing from the circumference to the center; taken together, they form a veritable Legion of Honor officer's medal." [PIB]

"A grand flesh-colored rose, of vigorous growth." [JP] "Creamy-white, fine." [Sx] "Soft pearly flesh-pink, large, quite flat, quartered in form, strong on its stem." [ARA36/19] "A large and splendid rose of pale incarnate hue, slightly tinged with fawn, very double, and of fine form; it is deemed one of the richest acquisitions of this class of roses." [WRP] "Unsurpassed among roses. It is very large, and beautifully formed. It is of a light, transparent flesh-color." [FP] "Satiny white flower." [Hn] "Flesh-colour . . . margins almost white, very large and full; form compact; growth vigorous. A magnificent Rose, with large thick petals." [P1] "Blush centre, disk circular in outline, perfectly double, though flattish. Its tendency is to bloom in corymbs, and its habit, when upon its own roots, is rather robust and straggling. The perfume is delicious, and its flowers average nearly five in[ches] in diameter [ca. 1.25 dm]. The purity and exquisite loveliness of this old variety is unsurpassed." [WD] "Grown upon its own roots, and well mulched through the winter, it gives us, early in summer and late in autumn, the flowers so exquisite in the eve of their full development." [R1/159] "The grand old rose 'Souvenir de la Malmaison' is never so beautiful in summer as in autumn, so that it is quite worth while to sacrifice the summer blooms, and let it bloom in autumn only." [GG] "Injured by rain." [F-M2] "The petals of kid-like texture are smoothly folded back from the centre, forming a broad, flat rose like no other except the Hybrid Perpetual 'Mme Charles Wood'." [Dr] "Superlatively beautiful buds, blush-white with rose-pink flirtings, open slowly into fascinating blossoms which look like circlets of rumpled blush-colored satin. Dream-like sweet yeasty aroma. Has an affinity for mildew (no rust), but takes spraying well. Blooms in bursts rather than continuously." [BCD] "Magnificent foliage — very large and distinct — a superb rose . . . of very robust growth. . . . The flowers are frequently *immensely* large, borne on erect stout footstalks, with broad and beautiful foliage deeply serrated, giving to the whole plant a remarkably noble appearance." [C] "Altogether the most perfect and superb rose of this or any other class. . . . Its flowers are cupped, and of very perfect form, very double, with thick velvety petals; they are of the largest size, often four to five in[ches] in diameter [ca. 1–1.25 dm], and their color delicate blush, with a rich tint of cream. Its large and very luxuriant foliage, compact habit, and flowers of exceeding beauty, render this one of the very finest roses known." [SBP] "Foliage very good, holds well. Vigorous growth in Southern Zones." [Th2] "Bear in mind that vigorous growers like 'Souvenir de la Malmaison' must not be pruned too closely. Simply shorten the strongest shoots one-third and the weakest two-thirds." [TW] "Vigorous; branches pretty strong, divergent, the young growth being reddest; bark a handsome green, with slightly reddish thorns, which are short, upright, and very sharp; foliage of 3–7 leaflets, which are slightly rounded at the base, acuminate at the tip, and finely toothed; the leafstalks are narrow, and armed with a few little prickles; the flower is about 3.5 in across [ca. 9 dm], very full, cupped, flat, solitary on the branchlets, clustered on the more vigorous branches; color, salmon-white, and towards the center bright light pink with violet-pink reflections; the bud is well formed, and the color is a more pronounced flesh-pink; the outer petals are large and concave; those of the center are more petite, rumpled, and very numerous, making a 'muddled' center; the flower stalks are short, and nod under the weight of the blossom. This variety is without rival for late bloom. Does not like harsh winters." [S] "Calyx short, rounded, and glabrous." [JF] "We believe that it is worthy of notice that neither of these ['Devoniensis' and 'Malmaison'] have produced seed." [WD] "Has never given me seeds." [JR26/101] "Sported 'Kronprinzessin Viktoria' (Volvert, 1888 [milk-white]); 'Mme Cornélissen' (Cornélissen, 1865 [yellowish pink]); 'Mlle Berthe Clavel' (Chauvry, 1891 [yellow and pink]); 'Mlle Marie-Thérèse de la Devansaye' (Chédane-Guinoisseau, 1895 [pure white]) . . . [*not to forget* 'Malmaison Rouge' (Gonod, 1882; red); 'Climbing

Souvenir de la Malmaison' (Bennett, 1893); 'Capitaine Dyel, de Graville' (Boutigny, 1905; pink); and 'Souvenir de St. Anne's' (Thomas, 1950; semi-double)]." [JR26/106]

One sees occasionally an interesting saga about the naming of this rose involving a Russian nobleman obtaining cuttings of this cultivar — from no less a place than Malmaison itself! — and, in the best romantic tradition, going into such transports of nostalgia that said nobleman demanded that the name of the cultivar be none other than . . . 'Souvenir de la Malmaison'. As Rivers says in another connection, this is pretty enough, but entirely devoid of truth. As we have seen, Béluze jealously guarded his cultivar prior to introduction — no cuttings to Russian noblemen, and certainly none to a Malmaisonian garden which had been in decay for some thirty years and was not due to be reconstituted for another sixty years. Finally, *even prior to introduction* the name of the rose was 'Souvenir de la Malmaison', evidenced by the announcement in the 1842 *Revue-Horticole* which we offer above. We have not, however, investigated the possibility that Béluze himself was the Russian nobleman, *incognito*. "Inimitable." [JR20/23] "Like water lilies upon a dark pond." [Hk] "Always beautiful, always ravishing." [JR25/3] "Its beauty suggests a blending of the finest sculpture and the loveliest feminine complexion." [HstIII:61] "As yet unrivalled in its noble flowers, so delicate in colour and so truly beautiful." [R8] "Pale beauty and peculiar fragrance — we have nothing like it among the modern roses." [ARA29/50] "Imperial Malmaison . . . your memory is always alive in me." [JR38/49]

SOUVENIR DE MME AUGUSTE CHARLES
(' — Charlet')
Moreau-Robert, 1866

"Salmon-flesh." [LS] "Light pink tinged salmon, medium sized, full, well formed, petals rolled." [N] "Not . . . very vigorous." [G]

SOUVENIR DE MONSIEUR BRUEL
(*not* ' — Mme Bruel')
Levet, 1889

"Light red." [LS] "Growth vigorous, flower large, full, well-formed, brilliant light red, large thorns, heavy wood, handsome dark green foliage, very floriferous." [JR13/147]

SOUVENIR DE ST. ANNE'S
G. S. Thomas/Hilling, 1950
Sport of 'Souvenir de la Malmaison' (B).

Blush. "Rich quality in [the flower's] delicate tints and beautiful sculptured shapes." [T1] "Semi-double . . . very attractive . . . 4 × 3 [ft; ca. 1.25 × 1 m]." [B] The sport, according to one report, occurred in the garden of Lady Ardilaun at St. Anne's, Clontarf, Ireland; according to Graham Stuart Thomas, however (*v. The Garden* of August, 1989), the sport, having occurred prior to 1916, was *preserved* by Lady Moore.

THÉ SAPHO
Listed as 'Mrs. Bosanquet'.

VARIEGATA DI BOLOGNA
Lodi/Bonfiglioli, 1909

"Very pronounced stripes of purple on a creamy white background . . . tall . . . a bit sparse in foliage . . . 5 × 4 [ft; ca. 1.5 × 1.25 m]." [B] "Very fragrant." [G] "Not profuse in the least for me — three blossoms in two years — and very subject to mildew and rust. The canes on mine exceeded eight ft in length [ca. 2.25 m]." [BCD]

VIRGINIA R. COXE
Listed as 'Gruss an Teplitz'.

VIVID
Listed as a Hybrid Bourbon.

ZÉPHIRINE DROUHIN
('Belle Dijonnaise', 'Charles Bonnet', 'Ingegnoli Prediletta', 'Mme Gustave Bonnet')
Bizot, 1868
    "Cerise-pink, semi-double . . . 10 × 8 [ft; ca. 3.2 × 2.25 m]."
[B] "Brilliant crimson red; flower large, full." [Cx] "Finely shaped double . . . of sparkling pink . . . true, rich, rose scent." [ARA29/98] "Beautiful soft pink . . . a fragrance all its own . . . a healthy plant which blooms for several weeks." [ARA29/50] "Long, pointed buds." [W] "Fair growth; beautiful color; good form; very occasional flowers in summer and fall." [ARA18/121] "This variety is well known for adorning walls and making arbors. In my opinion, few varieties surpass it; very vigorous and very floriferous, it is not perhaps remontant enough, but the first bloom is so abundant that it is prolonged late into the season." [JR13/33–34] "Pinkish, bronzy foliage . . . practically evergreen." [ARA29/101] "Lusty shrub to 10 [ft; ca. 3 m]." [HRG] "An effective hedge background." [ARA33/18]

"Makes an excellent bush, and its lovely, fragrant blooms of soft rose-colour, that are freely produced for weeks together, are most welcome. . . . The smooth, vigorous stems, richly coloured young leaves and the profusion of fragrant flowers of a most exquisite shade of rose pink, constitute its chief attractions; considered together with its accommodating nature and ease of cultivation, they should ensure its *entrée* into every rose garden worthy of the name." [OM] "Evidently does best in seacoast climates." [Th2] "The climbing and reblooming rose 'Zéphirine Drouhin' is very vigorous, of unfailing hardiness. . . . It presents another advantage—that of being thornless. This variety is one with very persistent foliage, is hardy, vigorous, very floriferous, and particularly remontant . . . the many buds expand from May until late into the fall . . . dedicated . . . to Mme Zéphirine Drouhin, the wife of an amateur horticulturalist residing at Semur, on the Côte d'Or." [JR27/151–152]

ZIGEUNERKNABE
Listed as a Hybrid Bourbon.

Supplement

ACIDALIE
Rousseau/V. Verdier, 1837
    "White, center flesh, full, medium-sized, beautiful." [LF] "White, in dry weather beautifully tinted; a very good white rose, suitable for a pillar, wall, or tall standard." [JC] "Who that has seen this beautiful rose in fine calm weather in September, has been able to withhold intense admiration? Its large globular finely-shaped flowers of the purest white, delicately tinted with purplish rose, seem always to be drooping with beauty. Yes, it is indeed unique and charming." [R8] "Has been in cultivation several years, but is only now coming into notice for its distinct pale rose-white colour; the flower is perfect in form, large, and a little fragrant; the plant is quite hardy, and grows well." [Bu] "Vigorous, with long, robust canes of a violet maroon green on the sunny side; thorns somewhat numerous, large, short, enlarged at the base and strongly recurved; leaves somber green, slightly dentate; flower large, full; bowl-shaped; color, white shaded light pink; very fragrant. Of the first order." [S] "Canes big, green, thorny; thorns close, large at the base, pointed, purplish, nearly straight. Leaves comprised of five or seven medium-sized, oval, dentate, fresh green leaflets, petiole prickly, wider at the base; young growths purplish yellowish green. Blossom solitary, 7 cm across [ca. 2.5 in], petals large, twisted, and rounded, flesh at first, then pure white, then pink at the edge, rolled; light scent." [An41/14–15] "A beautiful Rose in fine weather. Very sweet." [P1]

ADRIENNE DE CARDOVILLE
Guillot père, 1864
    "Flowers delicate rose." [FP] "Flower medium sized, perfect form, very full, opening well, delicate pink." [I'H64/328] "Not very vigorous; canes weak, green; thorns occasional, slightly hooked, nearly straight; leaves distinctly pointed, dark green." [S]

ALEXANDRE CHOMER
Listed as an HP.

ALEXANDRE PELLETIER
Listed as 'Monsieur Alexandre Pelletier'.

AMÉDÉE DE LANGLOIS
Vigneron, 1871
    "Flower medium-sized, full, growing in a cluster; dark velvety purple." [S]

BARON G.-B. GONELLA
('Baron J.-B. Gonella', 'Baron J.-G. Gonella')
Guillot père, 1859
Seedling of 'Louise Odier' (B).
    "Pink and lilac shaded, large, full, and fine." [FP] "Bright cherry-coloured . . . blooms in large corymbs, and is distinct and beautiful." [R8] "Bronzed rose, well formed, fragrant; non-autumnal." [EL] "Very vigorous, flower large, full, beautiful form, reverse of petals violet pink, white in the center." [JDR59/28] "Bright cerise, with a fine bronzy hue, petals large, smooth, thick, and beautifully disposed; flowers large, double, and exquisitely formed; a superb rose of free habit." [JC] "Growth moderate." [P1] "Growth pretty vigorous; canes of medium vigor, upright or branching; bark smooth, somber green, with some reddish thorns which are unequal, much compressed, and somewhat hooked. Leaves somber green, divided into 3 or 5 rounded and finely dentate leaflets; leafstalk pretty strong, no prickles. Blossoms about three in across [ca. 7.5 cm], full, cupped, well formed, solitary or in a cluster of two or three on the stronger branches; color, light pink, center silvery; reverse of petals violet pink; outer petals convex and very thick, center petals ruffled; flower stalk strong, upright, holding the blossom well. Calyx globular. A variety of the first order, well poised and very remontant, but with little fragrance; it is proof against such winters as Paris has." [JF]

BARONNE DE MAYNARD
Lacharme, 1865
From 'Mlle Blanche Laffitte' (B) × 'Sapho' (DP).
    "French white, beautifully cupped." [FP] "Very beautiful blossom, much to be recommended, very floriferous, bearing flowers until October; flower medium-sized, full, in a cluster; color, virginal white; growth vigorous." [S]

BARONNE DE NOIRMONT
Granger, 1861

"Pale, shaded rose, compact and good." [FP] "Flower medium-sized, full, cupped, very bright purplish-pink, blooming in clusters of five or six." [JR1/2/7] "Rose, large, full, and very sweet; form cupped, fine; growth moderate." [P1] "Fresh rosy-pink, petals of good substance, flowers large, full, and beautifully formed; with a delicious violet scent; a very fine rose, habit robust." [JC] "Very vigorous; canes upright, furnished with flat thorns which are straight and violet green; blossom medium sized, full, very beautiful in form; color, delicate but very bright pink." [S]

BÉATRIX
Cherpin, 1865
From 'Louise Odier' (B).

"Flower large, full, centifolia form; bright carmine red." [S] *"Béatrix* is the name of the beloved of Dante to whom a statue is going to be raised in Florence. It is a felicitous appellation. . . . The bush is vigorous and remontant, with upright, smooth stems, nearly thornless; foliage elegant, blossoms solitary, sometimes in twos or threes. The blossom is upright on its stem; it is of the globular [*'pommée'*] form, medium to large depending upon the exposure. The exterior is a whitish pink. Upon opening, it takes on carmine tints deep within. It has neither stamens nor pistils. All of its short petals are arranged like steps to the interior, forming a cup. This cup opens little by little, but without breaking." [RJC65/155] "The rose propagators . . . of Paris sold, this spring, an old rose named 'Gulino' [*'Louis Gulino', Guillot père, 1859, HP; seedling of 'Général Jacqueminot'*] as the new variety 'Béatrix'. There is all the difference between the two varieties that there is between an oak and a fir tree! The first has big wood and a big flower; the second, a Bourbon hybrid from 'Louise Odier', has long canes completely or nearly thornless. — The blossom, rather small than medium, opens like a Centifolia, like which it has the form and coloration." [RJC66/159–160]

BEAUTÉ DE VERSAILLES
Listed as 'Georges Cuvier'.

BELLE NANON
Lartay, 1872
"Carmine." [Ÿ]

BIJOU DE ROYAT-LES-BAINS
Veysset, 1891
Seedling of 'Hermosa' (B).

" 'Hermosa' marbled carmine pink." [JR16/21] "Flower silvery pink, exterior and interior striped bright pink and bright carmine; medium-sized, well-formed; vigorous; very bushy and floriferous." [JR15/149]

BLANCHE LAFFITTE
Listed as 'Mlle Blanche Laffitte'.

BOUQUET DE FLORE
(trans., 'Flora's Bouquet'; syn., 'Bouquet des Fleurs')
Bizard, 1839

"Bright light red, full, superb." [LF] "Light carmine." [HoBoIV] "Bright rosy carmine." [FP] "A great favorite . . . the flowers are very large, perfectly double, with large round firm petals, blooming very profusely; it possesses considerable fragrance, is a strong grower, and quite hardy." [Bu] "Canes amply furnished with handsome dark green foliage; flower large, full, cupped; bright carmine

pink." [S] "Light glossy carmine, very large and double; form, cupped, exquisite. Growth, vigorous. Foliage and petals particularly elegant. Flowers, sweet. Forms a fine Standard or Pillar; good also for Pot-culture. A good seed-bearer." [P]

CAPITAINE DYEL, DE GRAVILLE
(*the comma is part of the name!*)
Boutigny, 1905
Sport of 'Souvenir de la Malmaison' (B).

"Flower very large, very full, a fresh beautiful pink with a darker center; well-held, very remontant, opens perfectly. . . . Dedicated to a valiant captain of [the Franco-Prussian War in] 1870." [JR30/153]

CAPITAINE SISOLET
Introducer unknown, before 1846

"Flower large, full, flaring; bright pink." [S] "A magnificent rich fulgent rosy lilac, and distinct." [WRP] "Rose-red, large, full, tall." [Sn] "Flowers beautiful rose, large and very double; form, cupped. Habit, branching, fine; growth, vigorous. A very showy Rose. A good seed bearer." [P] As it was also called a Hybrid Bourbon, weak remontancy is to be expected.

CLAIRE TRUFFAUT
Listed as 'Mlle Claire Truffaut'.

COMICE DE TARN ET GARONNE
Pradel, 1852

"Cherry-color." [FP] "Carmine-red, well formed." [EL] "Color, very brilliant red." [S] "Moderate vigor; flowers medium-sized, full, intense brilliant deep pink." [I'H56/198]

COMTESSE DE BARBANTANE   PLATE 77
Guillot père, 1858
Seedling of 'Reine des Île-Bourbons' (B).

"Blush, shaded with rose." [EL] "Flesh colour, large and full; form cupped; growth vigorous. A good useful Rose." [P1] "Moderate vigor . . . flesh white shaded pink." [JR26/137] "Flowers of medium size . . . blooms in clusters. Of the 'Louise Odier' sort." [S] "Very floriferous." [JR3/28]

COMTESSE DE ROCQUIGNY
Vaurin, 1874

"White; tinted with rosy salmon, beautiful." [P1] "Flower medium-sized, full, globular." [S]

DEUIL DU DR. RAYNAUD
Pradel, 1862

"Crimson, shaded." [Ÿ] "Vigorous; flower large, nearly full; velvety crimson black." [S]

DEUIL DU DUC D'ORLÉANS
Lacharme, 1845

"Flowers clouded purple, large and very double; form, expanded. Growth, vigorous." [P] "Very vigorous; branches 'climbing,' nearly thornless; leaves dark green lightly touched yellowish green; flower large, full, very well formed; color, deep purple." [S]

DR. BRIÈRE
Vigneron, 1860
"Cerise." [Ÿ]

DR. LEPRESTRE
('Dr. Leprêtre')
Oger, 1852

"Bright purplish-red, shaded." [FP] "Very vigorous; foliage olive green; flower large, full, well formed; quite remontant; velvety purple." [S] "Moderate vigor; flower medium-sized, full, very intense velvety purple red; superb." [I'H56/198]

DUC DE CRILLON
('Duc de Grillon')
Moreau-Robert, 1860

"Brilliant red, changing to bright rose, large and full."[FP] "Vigorous; flower large, full, flat; fiery red passing to bright pink."[S]

[DUCHESSE DE THURINGE]
Guillot père, 1847

"Flower large, full, growing in cluster; color, blush white, tinged lilac." [S]

DUNKELROTE HERMOSA
(trans., 'Deep Red Hermosa')
Geissler, 1899
From 'Reine Marie Henriette' (Cl. HT) × 'Hermosa' (B).

"Cerise red." [JR25/177] "Dark carmine." [LS] "Has the vigor of growth and profuse blooming habit of the well-known 'Hermosa' Rose, with bright glossy green foliage and beautiful vinous crimson flowers; a beautiful new variety which must soon become very popular, as it is quite hardy and a constant bloomer." [C&Js02]

EDITH DE MURAT
Ducher, 1858

"Flesh-color, changing to white, of fine form." [FP] "Good form, medium-sized, white lightly tinted pink." [I'H58/128] "Growth vigorous; flower medium-sized, full, well formed; color, a lightly blushing white." [S] "Palest pink double blooms with rather fringed petals, tidy upright shrub to 4 [ft]." [HRG87]

[EMILE COURTIER]
('Emilie Courtier')
Portemer, 1837

"Lilac-pink or sometimes light red . . . very good seed-bearer." [PIB] "Medium sized, full, well-formed, light red, shaded." [R-H42] "Pale rose, large." [HoBoIV] "Form, compact. Growth, moderate. A free flowerer, of fine habit, often splendid in the autumn. Excellent for a Standard." [P] "Wood vigorous, canes large, green, thorny; thorns short, wide at the base, red, pointed. Leaves comprised of five oval-pointed leaflets which are deeply toothed, dark green, and borne on a prickly leafstalk. Blooms in a bouquet of four or five, stem thick, green, glabrous, with short, lacinate, purplish bracts at the base. Calyx rounded, sepals short, entire, pointed. Bud round. Blossom flat, full, large to 6 or 7 cm [ca. 2.5 in], outer petals round, inner ones ragged, lilac pink." [An41/13–14]

[EMOTION]
Guillot père, 1862
Not to be confused with Fontaine's salmony Bourbon of 1879 of the same name.

"Pinkish-white." [BJ] "White, here and there touched light pink, beautiful virginal pink." [JR3/28] "Flower medium-sized, full; light flesh, with silvery white reflections." [S] "Delicate shaded blush, compact and good." [FP] "Vigorous growth." [I'H62/276]

FRAU DR. SCHRICKER
Felberg-Leclerc, 1927
From 'Gruss an Teplitz' (B) × 'Souvenir de Mme Eugène Verdier' (HT).

"Flower large, double, full, very fragrant, bright fiery crimson and coppery red. Foliage dark green. Growth vigorous, upright; very free-flowering." [ARA28/242] "The Bengale blood in this Rose gives it greater hardiness than the Hybrid Teas, so this recommends it to people in the North who want a continuous-flowering Rose that is hardy. The luminous, carmine-red flowers are of medium size but well formed. They come abundantly throughout the entire season. Fragrance also noteworthy." [C-P31]

FRAU O. PLEGG
(*cf.* 'Frau Oberbürgermeister Piecq', HT, Jacobs, 1911, yellow)
P. Nabonnand, 1909

"Deep red, medium size, full, very fragrant, tall." [Sn]

GARIBALDI
Pradel, 1860
Not to be confused with Damaizin's lilac-pink HP of 1859.

"Flower large, full, cerise red nuanced lilac." [S] Giuseppe Garibaldi, 1807–1882; promoted the unification of Italy.

GEORGES CUVIER
('Beauté de Versailles')
Souchet, 1842

"Bright cerise, shaded pink." [S] "4–6 cm [ca. 2 in], outer petals concave." [dH44/334] "Bright rose, fine form, large and full." [FP] "Vigorous; canes weak, deep olive green, violet on the sunny side; thorns straight, flattened at the base; leaves very dark intense green; flower full, cupped; carmine pink." [S] "Rosy cherry, beautifully tinted with light purple, large and full; form, compact. Growth, moderate. A splendid Autumn Rose. Habit and foliage fine." [P]

GLOIRE D'OLIVET
Vigneron, 1886
Seedling of 'Monsieur Dubost' (B).

"Vigorous, upright, pretty numerous chestnut-colored thorns; flower large, full, globular, beautiful delicate lilac-flesh; perfectly poised; beautiful long bud. Very floriferous." [JR10/147] Olivet was Vigneron's community in the department of Loiret.

GOURDAULT
Guillot père, 1859
Seedling of 'Souvenir de l'Exposition de Londres' (B).

"Rich purple, fine form, full." [FP] "Flower medium-sized or large; deep purple." [S] "Very vigorous bush; flower medium-sized, full, deep purple to good effect." [I'H59/108]

HÉROÏNE DE VAUCLUSE
Moreau-Robert, 1863
Not to be confused with Cherpin/Guillot's 1844 Tea, which was pink marbled white.

"Velvety pink." [Ÿ] "Vigorous, blooming in clusters; flower large, full, globular; color, bright pink, sometimes washed with carmine." [S] We are advised by my colleague Mons Massiot that the Heroine of Vaucluse was Laure de Noves of the town of Vaucluse near Avignon, the object of Petrarch's love from afar, who however remained true — alas! (but so much the better) — to her husband.

J. B. M. CAMM
G. Paul, 1900
From 'Mme Gabriel Luizet' (HP) × 'Mrs. Paul' (B).
   "Opaque salmon pink." [LS] "Light pink, large, very full, medium scent, medium height." [Sn] "Resembles the hardy perpetuals in foliage and habit of growth. . . . Flowers very large and remarkably full, perfectly double and delightfully sweet, color soft flesh pink; a fine out-door rose, entirely hardy." [C&Js02]

JEAN RAMEAU
Darclanne/Turbat, 1918
   "Pink, large, full, tall." [Sn] "Sport of 'Mme Isaac Pereire' [B], and a great improvement over it in color. Long, full bud of tender pink; flower double, the reverse of petals rose Nilson, interior iridescent rose. Very hardy." [ARA19/100]

JOSEPH GOURDON
('Joseph Gourdeau')
Listed as a Hybrid Bourbon.

LADY EMILY PEEL
Lacharme, 1862
From 'Mlle Blanche Laffitte' (B) × 'Sapho' (DP).
   "White tinged with blush." [EL] "Shaded French white." [FP] "White, slightly shaded with rose, large and full; growth vigorous." [P1] "Vigorous, blooming in large clusters; flower medium-sized, full; color, white edged with carmine; floriferous. One of the most beautiful white roses developed up till now." [S]

LE ROITELET
Soupert & Notting, 1868
   "Flower small, full; color, silky pink; growth moderately vigorous." [S]

MADELEINE DE VAUZELLES
Listed as 'Mlle Madeleine de Vauzelles'.

MARÉCHAL DU PALAIS
Béluze, 1846
   "Delicate rosy blush, large; form, cupped." [P] "Flower large, full, flared; color, pale pink." [S] "A delicate pink, plump, full, large." [dH46/258]

MARIE DERMAR
Geschwindt, 1889
Seedling of 'Louise d'Arzens' (B).
   "Cream and flesh." [LS] "Yellowish white, medium size, full, medium scent, tall." [Sn]

MARQUIS DE BALBIANO
Lacharme, 1855
   "Rose, tinged with silver, full, fine form, distinct." [FP] "Tinged with lilac, large and full; form cupped, fine; growth vigorous, well furnished with handsome foliage." [P1] "Flower medium-sized, full, very beautiful form; color, crimson nuanced satiny pink." [S] "Growth vigorous, looking much like a hybrid; flower full, well formed, carmine pink nuanced silvery." [I'H56/2]

MLLE ALICE MARCHAND
Vigneron, 1891
Seedling (or sport?) from 'Reine Victoria' (B).
   "Very vigorous and floriferous, blossom medium to large, full, globular, perfectly held, beautifully colored very delicate pink shading to blush white at the petal edges; very pretty variety." [JR15/148]

MLLE ANDRÉE WORTH
Lévêque, 1890
   "Very vigorous, flower large, full, extremely well formed, light pinkish white or washed pure carmine, very delicately nuanced, vigorous, quite remontant; foliage ample, glaucous green." [JR14/179]

MLLE BERGER
Pernet père, 1884
   "Moderately vigorous, canes upright, well intermingled, thorns protrusive and numerous, handsome somber green foliage, flower medium-sized or large, full, beautiful delicate pink, autumn bloom much brighter, very well held, quite remontant, always opens well." [JR8/151]

MLLE BLANCHE LAFFITTE
('Blanche Lafitte')
Pradel, 1851
   "Faintly tinged with flesh-color." [FP] "Vigorous, blooms in clusters; blossom medium-sized, full; color, flesh-white. A pretty, very floriferous variety both grafted and own-root." [I'H53/224] "Autumn-blooming." [S]

MLLE CLAIRE TRUFFAUT
E. Verdier, 1887
   "Vigorous, short-wooded; continuously in bloom; thorns hooked, pink; leaves composed of 3–5 leaflets of a delicate green, with shallow and irregular pink dentation; flowers medium-sized, full, very elegant and fetching in form; charming silvery pink, very delicate and fresh." [JR11/167]

MLLE FAVART
Lévêque, 1869
   "Bright pink." [Y̆] "A charming rose of perfect form; very light satiny pink lightly edged white . . . very floriferous." [I'H70/125] "Flower medium-sized, full; color, silky flesh pink." [S] Pierette-Maria Pingaud, stage name "Mlle Favart." [1833–1899]

MLLE JOSÉPHINE GUYET
('Mlle Joséphine Guyot')
Touvais, 1863
   "Deep red." [FP] "Flower medium-sized, full; color, bright velvety red." [S] "Red, exterior petals deep red." [S] "Rich violet-crimson, petals smooth, shell-shaped, flowers globular, large, full, and exquisitely formed; habit moderate." [JC]

MLLE MADELEINE DE VAUZELLES
Vigneron, 1881
   "Very vigorous, with upright canes, few thorns, light green foliage, flower large, full, beautiful delicate pink, center brighter, perfect form, well held, quite remontant, of the first merit." [JR5/185]

MLLE MARIE DAUVESSE
Listed as an HP.

MLLE MARIE DRIVON
Widow Schwartz, 1887
Seedling of 'Apolline' (B).
  "Poppy-pink." [Ÿ] "Very vigorous, leaves cheerful green, of 3–5 twisted leaflets. Flower medium-sized, perfect form, very full, petals large and rounded at the edge, arranged around a muddled center of pointed and seemingly ligulate petals. The color varies from bright pink nuanced peachblossom, marbled, spotted carmine or lilac pink . . . extremely floriferous and freely remontant." [JR11/150]

MME ADÉLAÏDE RISTORI
Pradel, 1861
  "Flower full; color, deep cerise red with coppery reflections." [S]

MME ARTHUR OGER
Oger, 1899
Seedling of 'Mme Isaac Pereire' (B).
  "Pink tinted salmon." [LS] "Bright red." [Ÿ]

MME CHARLES BALTET
E. Verdier, 1865
  "Flowers large, in clusters of 4–6, imbricated, beautiful delicate pink." [I'H65/338] "Vigorous . . . very full, delicate pink." [S] "Charming in color and imbrication, like 'Louise Odier', whence it comes." [I'H67/54]

MME CHEVALIER
Pernet père, 1886
  "Moderately vigorous, growing with upright canes; flower large, fairly full, opens well, beautiful bright pink; bloom continuous and abundant." [JR10/183]

MME CORNÉLISSEN
Cornélissen, 1865
Sport of 'Souvenir de la Malmaison' (B).
  "Yellowish pink." [Ÿ] " 'Souvenir de la Malmaison' with white flowers plumed pink; smaller, poorly formed, and often inconstant." [JR12/173] "Of medium growth; flower large, nearly full, flat, looking like 'Souvenir de la Malmaison', but of a less pretty form; white, with blush-pink and yellow center." [S]

MME D'ENFERT
Widow Vilin & fils, 1904
From 'Mme Ernst Calvat' (B) × 'Mme la Duchesse d'Auerstädt' (N).
  "Vigorous, very floriferous, canes upright, thorns not much hooked, remote; foliage delicate green; bud virginal white; flower pretty, full, very pale blushing flesh white, a little pinker towards the center." [JR28/157]

MME DE SÉVIGNÉ
Moreau-Robert, 1874
  "Vigorous; flower large, full, growing in clusters; color, pale pink, brighter towards the center, petal edges blush white." [S]

MME DORÉ
Fontaine, 1863
  "Vigorous; flower large, full; color, light pink." [S]

MME EDMOND LAPORTE
Boutigny, 1893
  "Very vigorous, dark green canes, leaves of 5 leaflets, very glossy dark green, flower very large, semi-globular, full, slivery white within, very fresh pink without, very remontant." [JR17/147]

[MME FANNY DE FOREST]
Schwartz, 1882
  "Pure white constant bloomer, handsome and desirable." [C&Js99] "Vigorous bush with upright canes, foliage dark green; flower large, well held, of a size surpassing all others of this series [i.e., the line begun by Lacharme comprising in the main—if not entirely—progeny of crossing 'Mlle Blanche Laffitte' (B) and 'Sapho' (DP): 'Lady Emily Peel', 'Mme Alfred de Rougemont', 'Baronne de Maynard', 'Coquette des Blanches', 'Boule de Neige', 'Coquette des Alpes', 'Perle des Blanches', 'Mme François Pittet', etc.], full, well formed, salmony white upon opening, fading to white lightly tinted pink." [JR6/148]

MME FRANÇOIS PITTET
Lacharme, 1877
Seedling of 'Mlle Blanche Laffitte' (B).
  "White, small, and very double; growth vigorous. A very effective garden Rose." [P1] "Vigorous, flower medium, extremely well formed, very beautiful white, globular . . . the most beautiful of miniatures. Not to be forgotten!" [JR1/12/13]

MME GABRIEL LUIZET
Liabaud, 1867
Not to be, or indeed perhaps to be, confused with Liabaud's 1877 HP of the same name.
  "Carmine." [Ÿ]

MME JOSÉPHINE GUYET
Listed as 'Mlle Joséphine Guyet'.

MME LÉTUVÉE DE COLNET
Vigneron, 1887
Seedling of 'Mme Dubost' (B).
  "Vigorous, firm and upright canes, beautiful dark green foliage, thorns chestnut brown and fairly numerous; flower very large for the class, full, beautifully colored lilac within, petal edges silvery, perfectly poised, a splendid, very floriferous variety." [JR11/152]

MME MASSOT
Lacharme, 1856
  "Medium-sized, full, white, center flesh." [S] "Much like 'Blanche La[f]fitte', but with smaller flowers." [JDR56/41]

MME MOSER
Listed as an HT.

MME NÉRARD
Nérard, 1838
Seedling of 'Rose Edouard' (B).
  "Silvery-blush, centre pink." [FP] "Delicate blush, large." [HoBolV] "Vigorous; flower . . . very full, flaring, very good fragrance, very good seed-bearer; delicate pink shaded bright pink." [S] "Form, cupped, fine. A beautiful Rose, of moderate growth." [P] "Flower large, flat, flesh, nearly full. . . . This new variety has been very fecund, giving birth to a great number of other varieties." [JDR59/32]

MME NOBÉCOURT
PLATE 83

Moreau-Robert, 1893

Seedling of 'Mme Isaac Pereire' (B).

"Very vigorous, wood strong and robust, beautiful light green foliage, bud very large and long, flower extra large, cupped, beautiful light satiny pink, in clusters, very fragrant." [JR17/164]

MME OLYMPE TÉRESTCHENKO

Lévêque, 1882

Sport of 'Louise Odier' (B).

"Very vigorous; beautiful dark green foliage; flower large, full, extremely well formed, cupped; a lightly blushed white, or perhaps washed and marbled carmine pink; very elegant color of rare beauty." [JR6/148]

MME THIERS

Pradel, 1873

"Vigorous; flower medium-sized, full; pink, center brighter, edged violet." [S]

MONSIEUR ALEXANDRE PELLETIER

H. Duval, 1879

"Velvety pink." [Y̆] "A rose of the 'Louise Odier' sort, vigorous, medium-sized flowers, full, very abundant, bright pink." [JR3/182]

MONSIEUR A. MAILLÉ

Moreau-Robert, 1889

"Bright carmine red, changing to deeper red; very large and full." [P1] "The formation of the petals is nearly the same as is the case with 'Charles Lefebvre', and one is indeed able to conceive of this as 'Lefebvre' in carmine; strange to say, they both have the same penetrating perfume. The growth is the same as that of 'Mme Isaac Pereire', but the foliage is more like that of the usual Bourbon. . . . The most suitable training for 'Monsieur A. Maillé' is most certainly as a climber." [JR23/19] "Very vigorous, big-wooded and robust, with recurved thorns, beautiful very dark green foliage, flower very large, very full, always opens well, a model in form, sparkling carmine red while opening, passing to a darker red; blooms in clusters, very floriferous, quite as much as 'Souvenir de la Malmaison', and, contrary to the usual habit of Bourbons, very fragrant . . . dedicated to the honorable Monsieur A. Maillé, former mayor of Angers, former deputé." [JR13/100]

MONSIEUR CORDEAU

Moreau-Robert, 1892

"Violet pink." [Y̆] "Very vigorous, big-wooded with thorns; flower very large, full, opens well, globular; color, bright carmine red shaded vermilion, very fragrant and floriferous." [JR16/153]

[MONSIEUR DUBOST]

Vigneron, 1864

"Very light salmon." [LS]

OLGA MARIX

Schwartz, 1873

"Rosy-flesh, changing to white; inferior." [EL] "Flesh coloured, changing to pure white, of medium size, full; growth vigorous." [P1]

OMER-PACHA

Pradel, 1854

"Purple." [JDR55/19] "Brilliant red, large, full, and good form." [FP] "Flower medium-sized, full; delicate pink." [S] "Flower imbricated, velvety bluish purple tinted slaty; upright stem; very floriferous." [I'H55/33]

PAULINE BONAPARTE

Listed as 'Mistress Bosanquet' in the main section.

PERLE D'ANGERS

Moreau-Robert, 1879

"Extraordinarily vigorous, flower large, very full, opens perfectly, very well imbricated, very delicate frosty flesh-pink, nearly white, blooms frequently and in clusters." [JR3/167] "Blush." [EL]

PHILÉMON COCHET
PLATE 84

('Philémon')

Cochet, 1895

Seedling of 'Mme Isaac Pereire' (B).

"Extremely vigorous, semi-climbing; wood heavy, dark green; thorns slightly recurved, reddish; foliage handsome, 5 leaflets, dark green above, light green beneath; very floriferous. Flower very large, very full, often solitary, held upright, well formed, somewhat globular, beautiful deep bright pink." [JR19/164]

[PIERRE DE ST.-CYR]

Plantier, 1838

"Pale rose, robust." [HoBoIV/319] "Pink, large and full." [FP] "Light pink, free flowering, a fine pillar rose." [JC] "Vigorous; flower large, full, flaring, very remontant, very good seed-bearer; silvery flesh-pink." [S] "Pale glossy pink, very large and very double; form, cupped, fine. Growth, vigorous. A distinct and beautiful variety, blooming and seeding freely. Grown as a Weeping Rose, it forms a beautiful umbrageous tree, laden with its elegantly-cupped flowers throughout the summer and autumn." [P]

PRÉSIDENT DE LA ROCHETERIE

Vigneron, 1891

Sport of 'Baron G.-B. Gonella' (B).

"Vigorous and very floriferous, flower very large, full, cupped, perfect poise, beautifully colored bright red, center lightly shaded purple, fragrant, a magnificent variety." [JR15/148]

PRÉSIDENT GAUSEN

Pradel, 1862

"Flower large, full, bright carmine red." [S]

PRINCE ALBERT

Fontaine/A. Paul, 1852

Seedling of 'Comice de Seine-et-Marne' (B, Desprez, 1842, scarlet; parentage unknown).

Not to be confused with Laffay's pink to dark violet HP of 1837.

"Brilliant crimson-scarlet . . . its autumn bloom is abundant." [FP] "Growth vigorous; canes very long, nearly lacking thorns; flower medium-sized, full; very well formed; color, deep scarlet; beautiful exhibition rose." [S] "Vigorous bush; medium sized flowers in a cluster; deep intense cerise, shaded darker; very floriferous." [I'H56/247] "The plant is described as pretty stocky, with very robust shoots, and well clothed with large foliage of a very rich green. Its habit is to produce its blossoms in large bouquets; but, instead of ramping in the sun like 'Mme Desprez', it has short, stocky canes, like 'Comice de Seine-et-Marne' . . . only more robust, larger in its proportions, brighter in color, and more double. Its dwarfish habit joined with the length of its bloom (from June to November) recommends it for bedding . . . the autumn flowers are darker but less brilliant." [VH52/158]

PRINCE DE JOINVILLE
Listed as an HP.

PRINCE NAPOLÉON
Pernet père, 1864

"Flowers bright rose; very large and very double; growth vigorous; very effective." [FP] "Abundant bloom; flower . . . nearly full; bright pink." [S]

PROSERPINE
Mondeville/V. Verdier, 1841

"Velvety crimson flame, full, flat, medium sized, superb." [LF] "Crimson to purplish crimson, variable, sometimes velvety, beautiful, of medium size, full; form, compact, fine. A free bloomer and good seed-bearer, of dwarf growth." [P] "Grown from seed by Count Mondeville at Saint-Radégonde, near Mennecy . . . now owned exclusively by Victor Verdier. . . . It seems to be a Bourbon of the 'Emile Courtier' sort, having all of that variety's characteristics as far as wood and foliage go, partaking equally of the Bengal so as to look intermediate between *Rosa bengalensis* Pers. (*R. semperflorens* Lindl. [*we call it R. chinensis*]) and *R. borboniana* Desp. (*R. canina burboniana* Thory [or *R. × borboniana*]. The bush is vigorous and seems very hardy; its canes are green, glabrous, and armed with strong, hooked, pale red thorns. Its leaves are comprised of 3 or 5 leaflets which are oval-elongate, pointed, cordiform at the base, serrate, deep green above, paler beneath, and glabrous. It bears, at the tip of the cane, flowers in threes or fours on a more or less long stem of a purplish green which bears, at nearly the half-way point, a leaf-like bract, incised at the tip; calyx glabrous, glaucous green; bud round. Flower very full, 8–9 cm across [ca. 3–3.5 in], slightly plump; petals large, oval, rounded at the edge, smaller towards the center, uniformly colored a very dark and velvety crimson — quite beautiful. This rose, borne horizontally on its stem, is very showy, and will take a high place among the Bourbons because of its coloration. It reblooms freely, its first bloom occurring in June." [An40/281–282] Proserpine or Proserpina, mythological daughter of Ceres and wife of Pluto.

REINE DES VIERGES
(trans., 'Queen of the Virgins')
Béluze, 1844

"Flower medium-sized, sometimes large, semi-full; rarely grown out-of-doors; color pale pink, flesh towards the center. Very good under glass." [S] "Growth, robust. A good Forcing Rose, whose flowers do not always open out of doors." [P] "This rose surpasses 'Souvenir de la Malmaison' in form and beauty." [dH45/395]

REVEIL
Guillot père, 1852

"Cherry red tinted velvety deep shaded violet, resembling 'George IV' [HCh]." [I'H52/148] "Flower large, full." [S]

REYNOLDS HOLE
Standish & Noble, 1862
Not to be confused with W. Paul's maroon HP of 1872.

"Lively pink, increasing in brilliancy as the flowers advance in age, large, not very full." [FP] "Medium size, very fragrant, medium height." [Sn]

ROBUSTA
Soupert & Notting, 1877

"Vigorous, flower large, full, in clusters, fiery velvety red passing to purple." [JR1/12/12] "Foliage large and superb; not very remontant." [S] "A fine Pillar Rose." [P1]

ROUGE MARBRÉE
(trans., 'Marbled Red')
Introducer and date unknown.

"Red and violet." [Ÿ]

SCIPION COCHET
S. Cochet, 1850

"Vigorous plant; flowers medium-sized, nearly full, sparkling red." [I'H53/202] "Very vigorous; flower large, full, very floriferous; color, bright pink, sometimes deep grenadine." [S] Scipion Cochet, one of the founders of the 1877–1914 *Journal des Roses*, a publication so important to rose research. "Born at Suisnes the first of October, 1833, Scipion Cochet had not reached the age of 63 when death came. . . . His ancestors were gardeners. His grandfather and father were horticulturalist-nurserymen. . . . The vast works which he directed at Suisnes . . . were created in 1799 by Christophe Cochet, encouraged and advised by Admiral Count Bougainville, for whom he was chief gardener." [JR20/82–83]

SIR JOSEPH PAXTON
Listed as an HB.

SOPHIE'S PERPETUAL
Introducer unknown, pre-1928

"Fragrant, shapely, double flowers of silvery pink, petal edges blushing deep rose." [HRG] "Cupped . . . 8 × 4 [ft; ca. 2.25 × 1.25 m]." [B] Sophie, Countess Beckendorf.

SOUCHET
Souchet, 1842
Not to be confused with 'Charles Souchet', the deep carmine B of 1843.

"Deep crimson-purple, vivid, superb." [FP] "Deep crimson, large and full." [HoBoIV/319] "Blossom 7 cm across [ca. 3 in] . . . full, carmine-purple." [dH44/335] "Flower large, full, very tightly filled, very fragrant; color, bright grenadine." [S] "Purple-red . . . medium height." [Sn] "Flowers bright rosy purple, sometimes brilliant crimson, glossy, very large and full; form, compact. Growth, moderate. A superb Rose, and sweet. Raised by Mons Souchet in the vicinity of Paris. Introduced in 1843 [*we beg to differ concerning that date — BCD*]." [P] "Canes vigorous, light green, with large, hooked, red thorns; leaves with five leaflets, glossy green above, a more glaucous green beneath, finely and regularly dentate. Peduncle upright, strong; ovary smooth, short, and round; flower 10–11 cm in size [ca. 4 in], with large petals around the circumference, more muddled towards the center, a pretty bright purple, seeming more somber than it is by the clarity of the violet shade on the backs of the petals. It is very full." [An42/337] "Mons Souchet, gardener-florist in Bagnolet [in 1840]." [An42/210]

SOUVENIR D'ADÈLE LAUNAY
Moreau-Robert, 1872

"Light red." [Ÿ] "Flower large, full, opens well; color, bright pink." [S] "Pale rose, globular; a pretty well formed flower, with good foliage and vigorous habit; a good pillar or wall rose." [JC]

[SOUVENIR DE L'EXPOSITION DE LONDRES]
Guillot père, 1851

"Flower medium-sized or large, depending upon the season and the vigor of the plant; full; color, rich velvety poppy." [VH51/112] "Plant moderately vigorous; flowers medium-sized, full; velvety bright red. Pretty both grafted and own-root." [l'H53/224] Parent of 'Gourdault' (B).

SOUVENIR DE LOUIS GAUDIN
Trouillard, 1864

"Reddish-purple, shaded with black, fine form, full, abundant bloomer." [FP] "Flower medium-sized, full, purple shaded black; very floriferous, very remontant." [S]

SOUVENIR DE NÉMOURS
Listed as a Hybrid Bourbon.

SOUVENIR DE VICTOR LANDEAU
Moreau-Robert, 1890

"Very vigorous, handsome dark green foliage; heavy upright robust growth, thorny, flower extra large, full, cupped, bright red nuanced carmine, in clusters, very strong and numerous." [JR14/148]

SOUVENIR DU LIEUTENANT BUJON
Moreau-Robert, 1891

"Very vigorous shrub, beautiful dark green foliage, big-wooded, thus bearing the enormous bud perfectly upright; blossom extra large, full, opening well, cupped; color, light red passing to carmine, very floriferous and very fragrant. A top of the line variety." [JR15/148–149]

SOUVENIR DU PRÉSIDENT LINCOLN
Moreau-Robert, 1865

"Very vigorous; flower medium-sized, full; color, crimson red nuanced black." [S]

TOUSSAINT-LOUVERTURE
Miellez, 1849

"Flower medium-sized, full, well-formed; color, deep violet red." [S] Pierre Dominique Toussaint-Louverture, 1743–1803; Haitian liberator.

TRIOMPHE DE LA DUCHÈRE
Béluze, 1846

"Rosy-blush, large and full." [FP] "Pale rose, produced in large clusters, of medium size, full; form, cupped." [P] "Well formed; color, delicate pink; branches 'climbing'; blooms in clusters." [S] "An abundant bloomer, and a good pillar or climbing rose." [JC]

VELOUTÉ D'ORLÉANS
Dauvesse, 1852

"Flower large, full; light purple." [S]

VICOMTE FRITZ DE CUSSY
Margottin, 1845

"Lively red." [FP] "Cherry colour, tinged with purple, large and very double; form, compact. Growth, moderate." [P] "Very remontant, flower well-formed, prettily colored bright pink." [An47/209] "Branches vigorous, light green; thorns large, slightly hooked, light red; leaves of 5 dark green leaflets, deeply toothed; flower stem strong, long, upright; ovary smooth, slightly rounded; sepals narrow and long; flower 7–8 cm across [ca. 3 in], full, well-formed, beautiful bright cerise-red; blooms easily. Grown from seed by Monsieur Margottin in 1844." [dH46/270]

VICTOR-EMMANUEL
Listed as an HP.

ZIGEUNERBLUT
(trans., 'Gypsy Blood')
Geschwindt, 1889
From *R. alpina* × a Bourbon. Could be classed as a Boursault.

"Purple-red, large, full, tall." [Sn] "Viigorous growth, with large cup-shaped flowers of deep crimson, tinged with purple." [GAS]

Chapter Six
HYBRID BOURBONS, HYBRID CHINAS,
and
HYBRID NOISETTES

"The roses of this class form a series of varieties developed from 1820 to 1840. . . . They are also the founders of the HP's." [JF] "This section owes its origin to the Bourbon, China, and Tea-Scented Noisette, crossed with the French, Provence, and other summer roses, and also to the latter crossed with the former. The varieties first obtained by this crossing arose by accident. . . . Many of the flowers in this section combine all the properties desired in the rose — viz., size, form, fulness, and exquisite colouring. *Hybrid Bourbon*. . . . This very splendid family of roses owes its origin to the Bourbon rose, which is itself a hybrid. 'Coupe d'Hébé' may be given as a specimen of this family, which for the disposition and regularity of its petals is quite unique. They differ from the hybrid Chinas in the greater substance of their flowers and foliage, but, like them, are remarkable for the abundance and beauty of their flowers." [M'I] "Our Hybrid Chinas . . . bear fruit but rarely." [V2]

Many Gallicas lie under heavy suspicion of being Hybrid Chinas or Hybrid Bourbons, and rightly so, we believe. It seems likely that non-remontant offspring generated in HP breeding would, if they were of high quality, be offered to the public now and then under the banner of a familiar class — Gallicas — particularly if the breeder, in his indiscriminate sowing of unmarked seed from miscellaneous sources — the normal practice for many breeders — had no idea of the seedling's genetic heritage. As we, too, have no idea of the background of varieties with veiled pasts, it is difficult for us to point out a plant and declare that "This is certainly [or certainly not] a Hybrid China," unless we make rash behavior a way of life; the differences are relative and subtle: "The Hybrid Chinese differ from the French Roses in their growth, which is more diffuse; in their foliage, which is usually smooth, shining more or less, and retained on the tree later in the year; in their thorns, which are larger, and usually more numerous; and in their flowers, which are produced in larger clusters, whose petals are less flaccid, and which remain in a perfect state a longer time after expansion." [P] Consequently, we dart a quick glance at some of these varieties on which contemporaries were themselves ambiguous, and promise fuller treatment in the future when we come to consider the old European roses and the miscellaneous classes.

"The Hybrid Bourbon Roses . . . are less diffuse and more robust in growth than the Hybrid Chinese, being readily distinguished from them by their broad stout foliage, the leaflets of which are more obtuse. The *tout ensemble* of these Roses is particularly fine: some are compact growers, many are abundant bloomers, and the flowers are in general large and handsome." [P]

"Being certain to bloom only once in the season, [most Hybrid Chinas] are scarcely worthy of cultivation, compared with the Remontants." [SBP] "The superior varieties of this fine division give a combination of all that is or can be beautiful in summer roses; for, not only are their flowers of the most elegant forms and colours, their foliage of extreme luxuriance, but their branches are so vigorous and graceful, that perhaps no plant presents such a mass of beauty as a fine-grown hybrid China rose in full bloom." [R8]

[ATHALIN]
('Général Athalin')
Jacques, 1830
Hybrid Bourbon
Not to be confused with the striped Gallica 'Athelin'.

"Cerise." [LS] "Bright red, double, large, cupped." [LF] "Rosy crimson, sometimes spotted with white, lively, of medium size, double; form, cupped. Habit, branching; growth, robust. A distinct and showy Rose, of a fine habit, blooming most abundantly: requires but little pruning. A good seed-bearer, and the parent, on one side, of many of the Hybrid Perpetual Roses." [P] " 'Athalin' crossed with 'Rose du Roi' later gave remontant roses having the Portland character . . . distinct from the first seedlings from 'Athalin', varieties feeble in growth and poorly remontant." [JF] "Divergent branches; thorns somewhat numerous, unequal, nearly straight; leaves comprised of 3–5 oval leaflets, light green, slightly shiny, distinctly and irregularly dentate; flower large, double, regular, bright cerise red." [S] "Sprang from the Bourbon rose." [JR31/130]

BELLE DE CRÉCY
Hardy/Rœser, 1829

Hybrid China; usually construed a Gallica

"Flower medium-sized, very full, purple-black." [S] "Flowers red, shaded with velvety p[e]uce, changing to dark slate soon after opening, exhibiting flowers of different characters on the plant at the same time, of medium size, full; form, expanded. Habit, erect; growth, moderate, branches covered with small black spines. An abundant bloomer, and showy, but often faulty, from exhibiting a green eye in the center." [P] "Shrub pretty vigorous. Branches slender, armed with numerous thorns, slightly hooked; of a dark brown. Leaflets, seven in number; long; irregularly and very deeply toothed. Flowers numerous, in clusters, full, middle-sized. Petals, violet; shaded and velvety, irregularly sloped at the summit, symmetrically arranged at the circumference, rolled in the centre." [Go]

BRENNUS
('St. Brennus', 'Brutus', 'Queen Victoria')
Laffay, 1830
Hybrid Bourbon

"Light poppy, large, full, flat, superb." [LF] "Deep carmine; a handsome old variety." [JC] "Purplish-crimson." [Hstl:307] "Cup., brilliant crimson, very large." [CC] "Globular, vivid red." [Go]

"Cupped, crimson-maroon." [JR9/162] "Light carmine, large and full . . . habit branching; growth vigorous; foliage fine." [P1] "Superb; the flowers are extra large, of a glowing red, perfectly double; it makes fine shoots, and is an excellent pillar plant." [Bu] "Finer . . . as a pillar rose . . . than as a bush; its luxuriant shoots must not be shortened too much in winter pruning, as it is then apt to produce an abundance of wood, and but very few flowers. This rose often puts forth branches in one season from eight to ten ft in length [ca. 2.25–3 m]." [R8] "Well-clothed plant of 4 [ft; ca. 1.25 m]." [HRG] "One of the most beautiful of the non-remontant hybrids." [JF] Brennus, the 4th century B.C. Gallic chieftan whose forces overran Rome.

CARDINAL DE RICHELIEU   PLATE 87
Laffay, 1840

Hybrid China; usually construed a Gallica

"Flower medium-sized, full; color, very deep violet, becoming blackish Parma [violet]; petal edges carmine." [S] "Vigorous, bushy, giving a great quantity of medium sized blossoms of a very dark violet in spring, the petals lightly bordered carmine." [JR29/170] Armand Jean du Plessis, Duc — and Cardinal — de Richelieu; minister of Louis XIII; lived 1585–1642.

[CÉLINE]
Laffay, ca. 1835

Hybrid Bourbon

"Bright pink, double, very large, cupped." [LF] "Flowers pale rose, very large and double; form, cupped. Habit, branching; growth vigorous; the flowers produced in large clusters. A loose Rose. A good seed bearer." [P]

[CHARLES DUVAL]
C. Duval, 1841

Hybrid Bourbon

"Flesh pink, cupped, large, beautiful." [LF] "Rose, large, double." [HoBoIV] "Very large, full, light red, pretty form." [R-H42] "Light pink." [Pq] "Deep pink . . . form, cupped. Habit, erect, fine; growth, vigorous; the shoots clothed with beautiful foliage. A good rose, either for a pot or pillar; forms also a very handsome tree. A good seed bearer." [P]

CHARLES LAWSON
Lawson, 1853

Hybrid Bourbon

"Bright pink, very large, full and perfect, a noble rose, with large handsome foliage." [JC] "Flowers vivid rose shaded . . . form compact; growth vigorous." [P1] "Large and beautiful roses." [R1/251] "Highly scented." [Wr] "A brilliant crimson pillar rose . . . not easily surpassed . . . flowers are borne in immense quantities." [K2] "Branches dark green; thorns unequal, numerous, bristling, the larger ones being hooked; flower large, full, very well formed; delicate pink shaded rose." [S] "Rather ungainly habit . . . 6 × 4 [ft; ca. 1.75 × 1.25 m]." [B1] "Another old favorite too rarely seen nowadays." [K1] "Considered by amateurs fortunate enough to possess it as one of the finest climbing roses in the world." [GAS] "Introduced in Scotland." [GAS] "Lawson and Son, Messrs., Nurserymen, Edinburgh, N.B. [*among P's subscribers*]." [P]

COUPE D'HÉBÉ
(trans., 'Hebe's Cup')

Laffay, 1840

Hybrid Bourbon

"Delicate pink lightly touched saffron, full, large, cupped, superb." [LF] "Delicate rosy-flesh, large and double; one of the most beautiful of all summer roses." [JC] "Sometimes recurrent." [W] "Good full pink colour." [J] "It is of a beautiful shaded blush, and the form and arrangement of its petals are all that can be desired. It has, however, from the very delicacy of its shade, a great tendency to fade. It should, therefore, be grown where the full power of a July sun will not be brought to bear upon it." [Ed] "Deep pink, medium or large size, cup-form; seven leaflets. A fine distinct sort." [EL] "Globular, soft pink . . . lush pale green foliage, free-flowering . . . to 6 × 4 [ft; ca. 1.75–1.25 m]." [HRG] "Vigorous, fairly 'climbing'; foliage, blackish-green . . . delicate pink shaded cerise." [S] "Rich deep pink, exquisite in colour, large and very double . . . habit erect. . . . A good seed bearer." [P1] "A delicate blush when fully expanded . . . a fine grower and profuse bloomer, with large glossy green foliage." [Bu] "Remarkable both for the perfection of its cup-like form, and for the delicate rose-color of its petals. Its growth is very vigorous; and, like most of its kindred, it is perfectly hardy." [FP] "The gem of this family . . . a beautiful wax-like pink, and in the disposition and regularity of its petals it is quite unique . . . soon forms a large bush." [R8] "Growth is luxuriant, and adapted for pillars." [SBP] "Foliage glossy, sub-evergreen, and abundant." [WRP] "Mildew if precautions are not taken in time." [B1] "Wonderful variety." [JR9/164] Hebe, goddess of youth and cup-bearer to the Olympian gods.

DEMBROWSKI
('Dombrowski')

Vibert, 1840

Hybrid Bourbon

"Crimson shaded dark violet." [S] "Medium-sized, more or less floriferous, dark scarlet." [R-H42] "A beautiful flower, of a deep brilliant red hue, approaching to scarlet, well worthy of a place in the [HB] group." [WRP] "Flowers full, 8 cm across [ca. 3.5 in], deep violet crimson; sport, fixed by graft," [M-V49/234] where listed as a "Portland." "8–9 cm, full, purplish crimson violet, still the only one of its color in its class, from a sport of the Damask 'Pope' [from Laffay, ca. 1844; *WRP reports: 'Large and distinct, crimson purple, and inclines to bloom in autumn'*] which I [Vibert] enfixed." [M-L48/427] "Flowers deep scarlet, often shaded with purple, of medium size, very double; form, cupped. Habit, branching yet compact; growth, moderate. A very abundant bloomer, producing a fine effect on the tree. A good seed bearer." [P] "A medium, vigorous plant. Scented . . . 4 × 3 [ft; ca. 1.25 m *times* 9 dm]." [B]

DUCHESSE DE MONTEBELLO
Laffay, by 1829

Hybrid China; usually construed a Gallica

"Flowers rosy pink changing to flesh pink, of medium size, full; form, compact. Habit, erect; growth, moderate. Almost a French Rose." [P] "Tube of calyx smooth, oval or globular. Flowers, full, middle-sized; flesh-coloured." [Go]

[EDWARD JESSE]
('Edouard Jesse')

Laffay, ca. 1840

Hybrid Bourbon (or Hybrid Perpetual?)

"Deep purple nuanced crimson, full, large." [LF] "Deep rose, small, double." [EL] "Dark purple, shaded." [HoBoIV:319] "Rich purplish crimson, often shaded with blackish purple, of medium size, double; form, cupped. Habit, branching; growth, moderate.

A good seed bearer." [P] "Vigorous; branches very limber, bearing the blossom with difficulty at the end of the cane." [S] "The well known naturalist and popular author of *Gleanings in Natural History,* Mr. Edward Jesse." [C]

FULGENS
Listed as 'Malton'.

GEORGE IV
('Rivers' George IV')
Rivers, 1820
Hybrid China
"Deep velvety crimson and purple, full, cupped, large, beautiful." [LF] "Superb crimson." [Sx] "Dark rose." [Hstl:307] "Glob., deep velvety crimson." [CC] "Large, full, cupped, reddish crimson with touches of dark maroon." [JR9/163] "Semi-double or double; no longer of any value." [EL] "An old rose . . . but is still one of the most desirable of this class. Its flowers are of a dark crimson, and its young shoots have a purple tinge. Its very luxuriant habit makes it suitable for a pillar." [SBP] "Growth feeble; branches thin, with short, flat thorns; leaves dark green, rounded; flower large, full, flat." [S] "In clusters on a lax but healthy plant. Scented. 3 × 2 [ft; ca. 9 × 6 dm]." [B] "An old but splendid variety, of the richest crimson colour, always perfect and fully double, of cupped form, a free grower in rich soils. . . . Mr. Rivers, of England, a celebrated rose grower, raised this variety from seed . . . according to his own history of the plant, it came up in a bed of seedlings, unexpected, and without any act on his part to produce it." [Bu] "As this came by accident, its origin is not so well ascertained." [R8] "Even now I have not forgotten the pleasure the discovery of this rose gave me. One morning in June I was looking over the first bed of roses I had ever raised from seed, and searching for something new among them with all the ardour of youth, when my attention was attracted to a rose in the centre of the bed, not in bloom, but growing with great vigour, its shoots offering a remarkable contrast to the plants by which it was surrounded, in their crimson purple tinge . . . shoots more than ten ft [ca. 3 m] in length in one season." [R8] "A death which is a blow to horticulture, arboriculture in particular, is that of Mr. Thomas Rivers, nurseryman of Sawbridgeworth, England, which happened last October 17 [1877]. . . . He was 69." [R-H77] George IV of England, lived 1762–1830.

GREAT WESTERN
Laffay, 1838
Hybrid Bourbon
"Magenta-crimson, flushed with purple." [T1] "Deep crimson, very fine." [Hstl:307] "Red shaded crimson, double, fragrant; poor." [EL] "Bright reddish crimson, beautiful." [FP] "Large, full, globular; color, ashen, marbled reddish-violet." [S] "Quartered, followed by red fruit." [G] "Not a delicate but a *grand* rose, of the habit of 'Céline', but more robust, and makes shoots 6 to 8 ft in length [ca. 1.75–2.25 m], of the diameter of a moderate sized cane. The leaves are enormous, often nine in [ca. 2.25 dm] from base to tip, leaflets three and a half by two in [ca. 9 × 5 cm]; its large clusters of flowers comprise ten to fifteen in each, but as these are frequently too much crowded to expand properly, it is better to thin out each cluster by removing about half of the buds; the color is a peculiar deep rich red, sometimes tinted with purple, variable according to the season." [WRP] "Varying exceedingly, sometimes brilliant, sometimes dark and beautiful, produced in great clusters, very large and double; form, globular. Habit, branching, fine; growth, robust. An extraordinary Rose, forming an immense tree, producing a splendid effect when in flower. A good seed

bearer. Requires but little pruning." [P] *Great Western,* a notable American steamship.

GYPSY BOY
Listed as 'Zigeunerknabe'.

HOFGÄRTNER KALB
Listed as a Bourbon.

LAS-CASES
('Las Casas')
Vibert, 1828
Hybrid Bourbon
"Purplish pink, full, flat, large, beautiful." [LF] "Rose, very large." [HoBoIV/318] "Carmine, shaded. Non-remontant." [LS] "flowers rosy pink, sometimes deep rose colour, edged with crimson, very large and full; form, cupped. Habit, branching, fine; growth, robust; the foliage particularly good. A splendid Rose in warm seasons." [P] "Something over 1.5 m [ca. 5 ft]." [G] "Of the most robust habit, producing very large flowers of a deep shaded rosy hue, nearly of the color and shape of the old Cabbage Provence rose." [WRP] "Branches very 'climbing,' too feeble to hold the blossoms, which nod under their weight. Frequently used as a weeping standard budded on the briar; flower of medium size, very full, expanded form; color, carmine marbled grenadine." [S] "Much esteemed." [M'l] Emmanuel, Comte de Las-Cases; 1766–1842; historian, companion of Napoleon's on St. Helena. *Not* Bartolomé de Las Casas; 1474–1566; interesting if occasionally misguided Spanish prelate, companion of Columbus; in his humane attempts to protect the Indians and their liberty, he alas helped found the African slave trade; chronicled the Spanish discoveries of 1492–1520.

MALTON   PLATE 86
('Fulgens')
Guérin, 1829
Hybrid China
"Vermilion red, full, cupped, medium-sized, beautiful." [LF] "Crimson velvet, cupped." [HoBoIV/318] "Cerise; flower large, full; very floriferous; very vigorous." [Cx] "A very old, but almost forgotten rose . . . its color is almost scarlet, and a charming peculiarity is that of its petals having a shell-like bloom outside, while their inside is that of a glowing red." [R8] "Almost double . . . bright cerise-crimson . . . upright . . . good foliage . . . 5 × 3 [ft; ca. 1.5 × 1 m]." [B] "A bushy compact plant, 4 × 3 [ft; ca. 1.25 × 1 m] . . . Reblooms in California." [HRG] "Very decorative, will climb to ten ft in height [ca. 3 m]. The blossoms, clustered in small close groups, are very numerous, of medium size, quite full, a little concave, well held, of a cherry carmine red which does not fade up to the time the petals fall. It is a plant of the first order, without rival in its color. This very fine climber was obtained from a sowing made at Angers about 1830 by Mons Guérin, who, error has it, dedicated it to his niece; however, the truth of the matter is that he dedicated it to Mons Malton, his brother-in-law." [JR8/126] "And so, the fortunate Guérin proclaims not only his victory, but also that of his town, in naming two of his Hybrid Chinas (which are of the greatest beauty) 'Triomphe de Guérin' and 'Triomphe d'Angers'. Another rose, probably by Mons Guérin, with less Glory than these other two, has received the modest name of 'Malton'." [R-H29/358] "Shrub, having straight, strong, numerous branches; the bark green, variegated with dark purple." [Go] "The shoots must not be pruned very close, for in that case it will not show a bloom." [Bu] "An excellent seed-bearer." [JF] "Played a large part in the creation of the first HP's." [JR12/45]

"Certainly one of the most brilliant and beautiful . . . the entire plant is also worthy of admiration, independent of its magnificent globular scarlet flowers, as its foliage is so abundant, and so finely tinted with red; its branches so vigorous, and yet spreading so gracefully, that it forms one of the very finest of standard roses." [WRP]

MME LAURIOL DE BARNEY
Trouillard, 1868
Hybrid Bourbon; has been called a Hybrid Arvensis

"Light silvery pink. Most beautiful." [T1] "Quite large and fully double . . . quartered." [G] "Very flat . . . unusual fragrance . . . 5 × 4 [ft; ca. 1.5 × 1.25 m]." [B] "Branches 'climbing,' used for covering rocks and for forming alleés." [S]

MME PLANTIER
Plantier, 1835
Hybrid Noisette; has been called an Alba

"Flowers creamy white when newly opened, changing to pure white, of medium size, full; form, compact. Habit, branching; growth, vigorous; shoots, slender; foliage of a light green. An immense bloomer, and a beautiful Rose, forming a large bush or tree, producing a sheet of white blossom, and lasting a long time in flower." [P] "A Hybrid Noisette, of vigorous growth, producing pure white full double flowers of extreme beauty and in great profusion." [WRP] All of Plantier's other introductions were either Bourbons, Hybrid Chinas, Hybrid Perpetuals, or Teas; would he suddenly, uniquely, switch gears and cross Albas and Noisettes, or Albas and *R. moschata*? Not likely! This is no doubt a genetic throwback of "mainstream" parentage; Plantier was meantime about pioneering with HP's ('Reine de la Guillotière', Plantier, 1835, light pink).

PARKZIERDE
Geschwindt/Lambert, 1909
Hybrid Bourbon

"Very floriferous for a short period in early summer . . . scarlet-crimson . . . long stems . . . 4 × 4 [ft; ca. 1.25 × 1.25 m]." [B] "Growth not especially good; blooms fade quickly." [ARA18/122] "Foliage dark green." [B1]

PAUL RICAULT
Portemer, 1845
Hybrid Bourbon

"Flowers rosy-crimson, large and full." [P1] "Carmine-crimson, medium size, fine globular form; one of the most beautiful summer roses." [EL] "Bright rose pink. Superb flattish sometimes quartered flowers . . . good perfume. Vigorous upright . . . 4 × 3 [ft; ca. 1.25 × 1 m]." [B] "A most desirable variety in colour; one of the most brilliant of the group." [R8] "Outer petals reflexed, inner ones recurved." [Kr] "Magnificent in its form, size, and in the rich crimson of its hue . . . of moderate growth." [Ed] "Brilliant carmine, often shaded with velvety-purple, flowers large and exquisitely formed, habit free, though not vigorous; one of the most beautiful roses in cultivation, and a superb show rose." [JC]

PAXTON
Listed as 'Sir Joseph Paxton'.

PRINCE CHARLES
Hardy, ca. 1842
Hybrid Bourbon

"A fine new light crimson variety, very perfect in form, and, as well as many others of similar good qualities, is an offspring of the Luxembourg Gardens." [Bu] "Brilliant carmine, superb." [HstIV:478] "Large and globular, of a fine rosy-red." [WRP] "Bright cherry, very double." [FP] "Brilliant crimson, often suffused with light purple, of medium size, full; form cupped." [P1] "Flower of medium size, full, expanded; color, brilliant carmine bordered light purple." [S] "Scented . . . 4 × 3 [ft; ca. 1.25 × 1 m]." [B] "Noticeable veining in maroon to lilac, double . . . early summer only . . . to 5 [ft; ca. 1.5 m]." [HRG]

RIVERS' GEORGE IV
Listed as 'George IV'.

SIR JOSEPH PAXTON
('Paxton')
Laffay, 1852
Hybrid Bourbon

"Bright rose shaded with crimson, large and full; form expanded; growth vigorous . . . handsome foliage." [P1] "Lilac pink." [Y̆] "Flowers medium-sized, full, in clusters, intense nuanced pink; effective." [I'H56/200] "Deep red, slightly tinged with violet, medium size, well formed, non-autumnal." [EL] "Very vigorous; flower large, full, bright pink nuanced flame. Branches 'climbing'; flowers occasionally dark red." [JR28/18]

VIVID
A. Paul, 1853
Hybrid Bourbon

"Bright carmine." [LS] "Brilliant crimson, very showy." [P1] "Very bright . . . magenta pink. Vigorous and rather prickly. Scented . . . 4 × 3 [ft; ca. 1.25 × 1 m]." [B] "Light grenadine towards the center." [S] "Its flowers are not large, but they are of the most vivid crimson; and the vigorous habit of the plant makes it very suitable either for a pillar or a trellis." [FP]

[WILLIAM JESSE]
Laffay, 1838
Hybrid Bourbon

It is a good guess that 'Mme Desprez' is the Bourbon parent of 'William Jesse', while the other parent is something on the order of 'Brennus'. 'William Jesse' is particularly significant as being the supposititious — and altogether likely — parent of 'La Reine'.

"Vermilion, full, flat, very large, superb." [LF] "Very large flower of a beautiful purplish pink, nearly full. Very handsome foliage. Doesn't seem to repeat very freely." [An42/335] "Crimson, tinged with lilac, superb, very large and double." [FP] "Crimson, black tinged." [HoBoIV:319] "Red, suffused with violet, in the way of 'Pius IX'. An undesirable sort." [EL] "Very well formed." [S] "Light crimson, tinged with purple, very large, and very double; form, cupped. Habit, erect; growth, moderate. A magnificent Rose, but an uncertain autumn bloomer. A good seed bearer." [P] *Rivers*, 'Light crimson — lilac tinge — very large — beautiful and cupped,' *Paul*, 'Crimson — tinged with lilac — superb — very large and double,' *Wood*, 'Bright rose — very large and highly scented — one of the finest' . . . *Curtis*, ' — the king of perpetuals — light crimson — backs of the petals pale lilac — magnificent in size — most beautifully cupped shape and highly fragrant.' This truly noble rose was raised by Mons Laffay, and named in honor of his friend Mr. Jesse, of London; brother to the well known

_____

naturalist and popular author of *Gleanings in Natural History,* Mr. Edward Jesse. 'William Jesse' was sent out as a hybrid china rose, in 1838, but after being cultivated a few seasons in the country, it commenced blooming in the autumn, and has continued to do so ever since. It has now stood the test of years, and may fairly be ranked as one of our largest and most striking show roses, a model of shape as well as size. In colour it is a light crimson with pale backs to the petals, which are very large, beautifully cupped, and exquisitely scented. Under the poorest cultivation it is a large rose, but grown under the most favourable circumstances, we have measured specimens seventeen in[ches] in circumference [ca. 4.25 dm]. Its growth is vigorous and flexible, it makes a good half pillar rose, and is also fine for the greenhouse and for forcing. 'William Jesse' is one of our freest seed-bearing roses, yielding hips of great size, but unless they are very carefully hybridized, they are not worth sowing. We speak thus confidently from experience, having raised thousands of seedlings without producing one really better than the parent rose." [C]

ZIGEUNERKNABE

('Gypsy Boy')
Geschwindt?/Lambert, 1909
Hybrid Bourbon
Two parentages have been advanced: (1) seedling of 'Russelliana' (Multiflora Rambler, Russell, 1900, red); or, (2) seedling of an unnamed "Russelliana" seedling × an unnamed Rugosa seedling.

"A great bush bearing hundreds of rich purple roses at midsummer." [T1] "Light fragrance . . . vivid crimson-purple." [G] "Medium double . . . deep crimson, almost purple to black . . . 5 × 3; [ca. 1.5 × 1 m]." [B]

Supplement

ANAÏSE

(*not* 'Anaïs')
Introducer and date unknown
Hybrid Bourbon
Not to be confused with the lilac Gallica.
"Pink, medium size, full, moderately tall." [Sn]

BELMONT

Vibert, 1846
Hybrid China
See also 'Fun Jwan Lo' in our chapter on Noisettes and Climbers.
"Flesh, tinted pink." [Ў]

CAPITAINE SISOLET

Listed as a Bourbon.

CATHERINE BONNARD

Guillot fils, 1871
Hybrid China
"Vermilion." [Ў] "Cerise, flowers moderate size, full and well formed; will make a good pillar rose." [JC] "Very vigorous; wood quite prickly; foliage dull green, slightly scanty, but its large, full blossom, well formed and well held, can be picked out among all others because of its rich scarlet-crimson color, which is very brilliant." [S] "Note that I call this a non-remontant hybrid, which means that this variety is little known to those finicky amateurs who won't buy such a thing as a rose which won't rebloom. This is a pity, because it is worthy of a place in all collections. It is a very vigorous plant . . . its canes are armed with numerous thorns, its blossom is very large, well-formed, very well held, and of a superb sparkling carmine red. It is a product of open pollination. It is supposed that it descends from 'Jules Margottin' or one of its tribe, but its raiser himself did not feel any confidence in making an attribution." [JR10/91]

CHARLES LOUIS Nº 1

Foulard/V. Verdier, 1840
Hybrid China
Not to be confused with the "small, of ranunculus form, rich roseate blush" (WRP) 'Charles Louis Nº 2'.
"Large, a bright deep cherry color, exceedingly splendid." [WRP] "Globose." [WRP] "Flowers rosy carmine, large and full;

form, cupped. Habit, branching; growth, moderate. Sometimes fine, but produces too often a green bud in the centre of the flower." [P] "Medium scent, tall." [Sn] "Vigorous bush, with slightly purplish green canes; thorns thin, very pointed, purplish; flowers rounded, very regular, slightly plump, very full; petals well imbricated, erect, smaller at the center than around the edges of the blossom; the four or five last rows of petals are a pale pink, while the others are a bright purplish pink. This rose has an elegant fragrance, and is charming in effect. Its leaves are comprised of two or three pairs of leaflets with an odd one, an attractive fresh green in color, purplish when young. Mons Verdier, who has grown it for three years, received it from Mons Foulard, a fancier in Mans. The bud is round, the sepals long, foliaceous, and fringed at the edge. The peduncle is strong and bears several blossoms." [An40/246] Sangerhausen has a note connecting it with Guinoisseau; perhaps it was collected for Sangerhausen from the Guinoisseau breeding-grounds.

CHÉNÉDOLÉ

Thierry, ca. 1840
Hybrid China
"Bright carmine." [LS] "Very large, very double, cupped, light vermilion." [JR9/163] "So called from a member of the Chamber of Deputies for Calvados, a district in Normandy, where this fine rose was raised. It has often been asserted that no rose could compete with 'Brennus' in size and beauty; but I feel no hesitation in saying, that in superior brilliancy of color, and size of flower, this variety is superior; the foliage and habit of the plant are also much more elegant and striking; in color its flowers are of a peculiar glowing vivid crimson, discernable at a great distance: it is indeed an admirable rose, and cannot be too much cultivated." [WRP]

CHÉVRIER

('Miralda', 'Miralba')
Laffay, ca. 1825
Hybrid China
"Purple violet." [V4] "Vigorous growth; flower small, very full; color, very deep violet, striped carmine." [S] "Not a large rose, but decidedly one of the most brilliant and beautiful dark crimson roses we possess." [WRP] "Medium height." [Sn] "Shrub, small, not vigorous. Stems, straight, armed with very small thorns, crooked and uneven. Leafstalks, unarmed. Leaflets, near together;

some oval, some oblong, regularly toothed. Flowers, small, full, regular; of a purple-black." [Go]

COCCINÉE SUPERBE
Listed as 'Le Vingt-Neuf Juillet'.

COMTESSE DE LACÉPÈDE
C. Duval/V. Verdier, 1840
Hybrid China
"Grown from seeds by Mons Duval of Montmorency. Growth vigorous, with green canes bearing close-set red thorns which are slender and of varying lengths. Beautiful green leaves in two or three pairs with an odd one, bordered purple when young. Flower round, very full, flat, white with some flesh; outer petals very large, inner ones smaller. Buds round, sepals large and pointed with small foliaceous processes at the base. The bud, while opening, resembles that of the Tea; its exterior petals are very flesh-colored; and, indeed, when first opening, the blossom's center shows a very pronounced flesh tint. Lightly scented, very profuse." [An40/246–247] "Growth vigorous; branches weak, slightly upright, nearly thornless; flower large, full, flesh pink." [S] "Silvery blush, their centre sometimes rosy flesh, large and full; form, cupped, delicately beautiful. Habit, branching; growth, moderate. A good rose, partaking somewhat of the nature of the Hybrid French." [P] "A most abundant bloomer and a charming rose." [JC]

DR. JAMAIN
Listed as an HP.

ENFANT D'AJACCIO
Listed as 'Souvenir d'Anselme'.

FRANCES BLOXAM
G. Paul, 1892
Hybrid China
"Salmon pink." [Ў]

[FRANCIS B. HAYES]
May, 1892
Hybrid Bourbon
"Scarlet" [CA 6]

FRÉDÉRIC II DE PRUSSE
V. Verdier, 1847
Hybrid Bourbon
"Rich crimson-purple, large and double." [FP] "Violet-purple and crimson, large, handsome and distinct; a good rose of vigorous habit." [JC] "Medium scent, tall." [Sn] Friedrich II of Prussia, called Frederick the Great; lived 1712–1786.

[GÉNÉRAL ALLARD]
Laffay, ca. 1835
Hybrid Bourbon
"Bright pink, full, medium sized, globular, superb." [LF] "Fine deep rose, very double." [FP] "Not very vigorous; branches very feeble; flower medium-sized, semi-double, globular; color, carmine pink." [S] "Flowers rosy carmine, of medium size, usually very double, but varies as to fulness; form, globular, exquisite. Habit, branching; growth, small. A distinct and beautiful Rose, blooming occasionally in the autumn. . . . A tolerably good seed bearer." [P] Parent of 'Mme Laffay' (HP).

GIULETTA
Listed as an HP.

GLOIRE DES HÉLLÈNES
Listed as 'La Nubienne'.

IMPÉRATRICE EUGÉNIE   PLATE 88
('Marguerite Lartay')
Béluze, 1855
Hybrid Bourbon
Not to be confused with the lilac pink Delhommeau/Plantier Bourbon of 1854, nor with Oger's white Bourbon of 1858.
"Large rose-coloured flowers." [R8] "Growth vigorous; floriferous; flower large, full, delicate silvery pink." [S] "Silvery-rose, medium size, full, fragrant; a good variety, and would be very useful had we not 'La France'. Subject to mildew; shows Bourbon character." [EL] "Vigorous canes bestrewn with occasional flat, very sharp, hooked, purple-red thorns; leaves lush, composed of 3 or 5 unequal, oval, diminishing, pointed, dentate, smooth, glossy leaves, dark green above, whitish-lanate beneath. Flowers on a pretty long stem, large to 7–8 cm [ca. 3.75 in], cupped at first, then flattening, very full, purplish pink at the edge, carmine pink at the center." [I'H56/49] Empress Eugénie; lived 1826–1920; wife of Louis Napoleon.

JOSEPH GOURDON
('Joseph Gordeau')
Robert, 1851
Hybrid Bourbon
"Flower from 6–7 cm [ca. 3 in]; full, globular, incarnate red, beautiful form." [VH51/112]

JULES JÜRGENSEN
Schwartz, 1879
Hybrid Bourbon
"Magenta-rose." [EL] "Very vigorous, with strong and branching canes; foliage olive green; flower large, full, well formed, magenta pink, interior violet carmine with slatey reflections, reverse of petals pale pink; very beautiful; fragrant." [JR3/165]

L'ADMIRATION
Robert, 1856
Hybrid China
"Light pink." [LS] "Pink, medium size, single, medium height." [Sn]

LA NUBIENNE
('Gloire des Héllènes')
Laffay, 1825
Hybrid China
"Wine-lee." [V4] "Deep velvety purple, globular, full, beautiful." [LF] "Flowers slatey purple, of medium size, full; form, cupped. Habit, branching; growth, moderate." [P] "Very vigorous; flower large, full, widely cupped; color, bright carmine, and, at the second bloom, amaranth red marbled reddish lilac." [S] *Tube of calyx,* hemispherical, smooth. *Flowers,* full, convex, regular; of a slate-coloured purple, often dark." [Go]

LE VINGT-NEUF JUILLET
('Coccinée Superbe')
Introducer unknown, before 1836
Hybrid China

"Deep purple." [V4] "Velvety carmine, full, flat, medium-sized, superb." [LF] "Alike beautiful in its flowers and foliage; in early spring its leaves and shoots are of a most vivid red, and this appearance they retain the greater part of the summer; its flowers are brilliant in the extreme, crimson purple shaded with scarlet: the shoots of this rose must be left at nearly their full length." [WRP] "Very vigorous shrub; robust canes of a beautiful green; very 'climbing'; flower large, full, well formed; color, deep crimson, center scarlet." [S] *Not* by Vibert or Laffay, as neither claims it in his respective catalog. My colleague Mons Massiot advises that 'Le Vingt-Neuf Juillet' refers in most probability to July 29, 1830, the capper of the three "glorious" days of revolution which eventuated in the replacement on the French throne of Charles X by Louis-Philippe, the "Citizen King"; the day also saw Lafayette chosen to replace the white flag of the Bourbons with the Tricolor in the City Hall of Paris.

MARGUERITE LARTAY
Listed as 'Impératrice Eugénie'.

MIRALDA
Listed as 'Chévrier'.

MME AUGUSTE RODRIGUES
Chauvry, 1897
Hybrid Bourbon
From 'Souvenir de Nemours' (HB) × 'Max Singer' (HPol, Lacharme, 1885, ruby-red; parentage: 'Polyantha sarmentosa' × 'Général Jacqueminot' [HP]).

"Vigorous, upright, 'climbing'; foliage dark green; round very large buds; blooms in clusters, sometimes solitary; blossom very large, very full, globular; the petals flare back in a Camellia form; very pretty color, pure frosty pink, reverse silvery; the flowers last 8–10 days on the bush; fragrant . . . blooms up to the middle of July." [JR21/149]

MME GALLI-MARIÉ
E. Verdier, 1876
Hybrid China

"Very vigorous, flower medium size, full, well-formed, beautiful bright pink; very pretty." [JR1/6/11] "Dull green canes; flower . . . in a cluster." [S]

MME JEANNINE JOUBERT
Margottin fils, 1877
Hybrid Bourbon

"Bright cerise." [Y̆] "Red, medium size, non-autumnal." [EL] "Vigorous, flower large, full, beautiful carmine red, very beautiful imbricated form." [JR1/12/12]

[MRS. DEGRAW]
Burgess, 1885
Hybrid Bourbon

"Bright coral pink." [CA96] "Flowers are borne in clusters; very handsome and recommended as a free and constant bloomer; a good, healthy grower, quite hardy, and not troubled with insects." [C&Js98]

NUBIENNE
Listed as 'La Nubienne'.

PAUL PERRAS
Levet, 1870
Hybrid Bourbon

"A fine, very large rose, of the most luxuriant growth . . . in colour it is of a fine bright rose." [R8] "Beautiful pale rose, large and very double; form compact; growth vigorous. . . . An abundant seed bearer." [P1] "Foliage glossy dark green . . . a true exhibition variety." [S]

PURITY
Cooling, 1899
Hybrid Bourbon
Parentage said to be 'Devoniensis' (T) × 'Mme Bravy' (T).

"Pure white. Very free and early, good Pillar Rose." [H] "Absolutely distinct from all others in its class . . . pure white with a lightly rosy center; the petals are firm and very regular. The medium sized blossom is of perfect form and extremely early . . . semi-climbing." [JR22/68] "Flowers . . . freely cover the plant. It is of very strong growth, not so much an actual climber as a suitable Rose to form a large bush, or to clothe a short pillar." [F-M2]

RICHELIEU
V. Verdier, 1845
Hybrid China

"Beautiful delicate pink, full, cupped, superb." [LF] "Lilac-rose, large and full; form, compact, perfect. Habit, branching; growth, vigorous. A fine Pillar Rose." [P] Not to be confused with 'Cardinal de Richelieu'.

RIÉGO
Vibert, 1831
Hybrid China (introduced as a *Rubiginosa* hybrid)

"Bright pink, full, cupped, large, beautiful." [LF] "Rose, raspberry odor." [WRP] "Very vigorous bush; canes strong; foliage thick, dark green; flower large, full, globular, very fragrant; color, bright carmine." [S] "Flowers light carmine, the colour clear and beautiful, large and double, very sweet; form, globular. Habit, branching; growth, robust, forming an immense bush or tree with fine dark foliage. A little hybridized with the sweet-briar, but retains more of the features of this group [Hybrid Chinas] than of any other seed-bearer." [P] "Partakes of the sweet briar, might be made the parent of some beautiful briar-like roses by planting it with the 'Splendid Sweet Briar'." [WRP] Rafael del Riego y Nuñez, Spanish revolutionary, 1785–1823.

ROXELANE
('Roxelana')
Prévost, ca. 1825
Hybrid China; often construed a Gallica

"Shrub, very floriferous. Branches, slender and vine-like. Flowers, small, cup-shaped, double; pink, the interior petals often marked with a white line." [Go] Given in V3 as a "Hybrid of China and Noisette."

SOUVENIR D'ANSELME
('Enfant d'Ajaccio')
Introducer and date unknown
Hybrid Bourbon

"Growth very vigorous; foliage thick, making a magnificent cover, dark green; young growth chocolate mixed with red; flower large, full, cupped; bright cherry red." [S]

SOUVENIR DE MÈRE FONTAINE
Fontaine, 1874
Hybrid China
   "Growth vigorous; flower very large, full; bright red, nuanced carmine, carmine-lake towards the center." [S]

SOUVENIR DE NÉMOURS
Hervé, 1859
Hybrid Bourbon
   "Bright fresh rose-coloured, reverse of petals being somewhat darker, flowers large and full." [B&V] "Growth very vigorous; flower large, full; color, delicate pink." [S]

SOUVENIR DE PAUL DUPUY
('Souvenir de Pierre Dupuy')
Levet, 1876
Hybrid Bourbon
Seedling of 'Général Jacqueminot' (HP).
   "Red, large, globular flowers, well formed, fragrant." [EL] "Fine deep velvety red, enormous size, growth very vigorous, extra fine." [JC] "Growth vigorous; branches olive green armed with irregular thorns of a dark yellow red; flower very large, full, beautifully held . . . it should be considered non-remontant." [S]

SOUVENIR DE PIERRE DUPUY
Listed as 'Souvenir de Paul Dupuy'.

TRIOMPHE DE LAFFAY
Laffay, ca. 1830
Hybrid Noisette
   "Pure white, full, globular, superb." [LF] "Flower large, full, regularly formed with imbricated petals; greenish white fading to pure white." [S] "A beautiful rose, not of a pure white, but rather what is called French white, the outer petals inclined to rose-color." [WRP] "Flowers delicate flesh when newly opened, changing to white, large and very double; form, expanded. Habit, pendulous; growth, moderate. A showy Rose." [P] The only other Hybrid Noisette cultivar likely to be encountered is 'Mme Plantier'.

Chapter Seven
HYBRID PERPETUALS

"This class is like Moses' serpent, it swallows up all the rest." [Hd]

"The first HP's were developed around 1837; before that date, the Portlands were the only cultivated Roses which rebloomed." [JR25/139] "Guérin obtained [in 1833] the dwarf variety 'Gloire de Guérin' [*listed in the chapter supplement*] from the rose 'Malton', a variety which, for that era, was a precious introduction. Up to 1835, the catalogs contained only the hybrid *non*-remontant series; soon, however, these hybrids underwent a notable physiological change. Little by little, the seedlings of these hybrids took on the characteristics of the Oriental roses, while preserving the bearing of the European roses . . . [*Meanwhile, in 1834, Victor Verdier released his HP 'Perpétuelle de Neuilly', bred from the HB 'Athalin'; see under the entry for the HP 'Victor Verdier', as well as the entry for 'Perpétuelle de Neuilly' in the chapter supplement*]. In 1835, one would have been able to mention an HP unknown to us, 'Sisley' [*listed in the chapter supplement; we might also mention Plantier's 1835 HP, 'Reine de la Guillotière'*], developed by Mons Sisley of Paris; however, it is to Mons Laffay, horticulturalist of Auteuil, then at Bellevue, that we must allow the honor of having actually created the race of Hybrid Perpetuals." [JF] "It was in 1837 that Mons Laffay . . . sent to Mr. William Paul, his friend, the first cross-bred hybrid from the old Damasks, then so much in fashion." [R-H63] "My [i.e., William Paul's] friend Mons Laffay once told me that he raised many of his splendid Hybrid Perpetual Roses from 'Athalin' and 'Céline' [HB's], crossing them with the free-flowering varieties of Damask Perpetual and Bourbon." [P] "Some of this class owe their descent to the Damask Perpetual, crossed with the China or Bourbon; others, to the latter roses, crossed with the Hybrid China and Hybrid Bourbon. In many cases it is difficult to trace their true genealogy. But whatever their descent may be, their value is undisputed." [Ed] "[Laffay] developed, in 1837, 'Prince Albert' and 'Princesse Hélène'; then, in 1839, 'Comte de Paris', 'Mme Laffay', and 'Louis Bonaparte'; in 1840, 'Duchesse de Sutherland' and 'Mistress Eliot'; finally, in 1843, that superb rose 'La Reine', his triumph. Several rosarians, going the same route, successfully developed worthwhile varieties. . . . Finally given this impetus, this beautiful race of roses took the foremost place in our gardens." [JF]

"Certainly, a more beautiful and interesting class of roses does not exist; their flowers are large, very double, most fragrant, and produced till the end of autumn. Their habit is robust and vigorous in a remarkable degree, and, above all, they are perfectly hardy." [WRP] "We would advise you to plant Perpetuals instead of 'June Roses,' as they have all the beauty, size, color, and fragrance of the June roses, with the advantage of blooming several times in the season." [HstV:247] "Now, the class of roses called 'Hybrid Perpetual,' or 'Remontants,' is not exactly rightly named — that is, they do not bloom perpetually, but only at intervals. They bloom full in June, and then give a few scattering blooms along during the summer, and a good display again in September, doing better or worse, according as they are illy or liberally treated." [HstXXVI:187]

"As we look upon them, we survey a gorgeous chaos. Here are innumerable varieties of foliage and flower, perplexing us in our search for genealogies and relationships. . . . All require rich culture and good pruning. When an abundant autumn bloom is required, a portion of the June bloom must be sacrificed by cutting back about half the flower-stems to three or four eyes as soon as the flower-buds form. When the flowers fade, these also should be cut off with the stems that bear them, in a similar manner. The formation of seed-vessels, by employing the vitality of the plant, tends greatly to diminish its autumn bloom. Give additional manure every year, and keep the ground open and free of weeds. If rank, strong shoots, full of redundant sap, form in summer, check their disproportioned growth by cutting off their tops." [FP] "And when you are advised to let the shoots grow long and then to peg them down, do not yield; it does not answer. For a year or two, it may look well, but it spoils the plants and is a mistake." [HmC]

A note on the name of the class may not be out of place. "Hybrid Perpetuals" refers to "Hybrid *Damask* Perpetuals" — which is to some degree just what the first HP's were, as we have seen: Damask Perpetuals hybridized with Bourbons, Hybrid Bourbons, Hybrid Chinas, and the like. At length, these differing ancestries enabled fanciers to split the HP's into groups (the following adapted from Cx, Ellwanger, JR25/12–15, and JR25/22–25):

Group A, 'La Reine' Type. The roses of this group are vigorous and hardy; canes upright, slightly rigid with small to medium-sized prickles; foliage ample, serrated, light green; leaflets rounded, slightly glandular; flowers profuse, globular or cupped, very large, very full, fragrant, varying in color from delicate to intense pink; petals recurved on interior of the calyx; calyx very long and widely spreading at the tip, glandular, deep pink and cerise at maturity. They sucker with the stems arising at some distance as is the case with the Gallicas, which they much resemble in their growth. Some examples: 'La Reine', 'Anna de Diesbach', 'François Michelon', 'Mrs. John Laing', 'Paul Neyron', 'Ulrich Brunner fils', 'Alice Dureau', 'Antoine Mouton', 'Archiduchesse Elisabeth d'Autriche'. The 1901 Congress of Rosarians at Paris discerned a 'Louise Peyronny' sub-group which includes those varieties lacking any tint of lilac, which was found endemic, from delicate lilac to deep lilac pink, to the *true* 'La Reine' group. Some of the varieties thus split off to form the 'Louise Peyronny' *non-lilac* subgroup are: 'Louise Peyronny', 'Anna de Diesbach', 'Mme Eugène Verdier', 'Mme Montel', 'Mrs. John Laing', 'Paul Neyron'.

Group B, 'Baronne Prévost' Type. It is generally believed that the roses of this group are only sports of the type, an old hybrid of Gallica × Bourbon extraction. They form handsome bushes of a longevity uncommon in the HP's. Their principal characteristics are: strong, slender branches which are spreading in growth, armed with numerous strong, slender thorns; foliage ample; flower flat, full, resembling those of the Centifolia, varying from pink to deep pink; bearing little fruit. 'Baronne Prévost', 'Caroline De Sansal', 'Duchesse de Sutherland', 'Dr. Hurta', 'Louis Noisette', 'Mme Charles Verdier', 'Mme Desirée Giraud', 'Orderic Vital', 'Triomphe d'Alençon'.

Group C, 'Géant des Batailles' Type. Bush vigorous, hardy, floriferous, and very remontant, with brown, upright but not rigid canes; thorns numerous, strong; foliage small, not very ample, very subject to the fungal disorders; leaflets medium-sized, lanceolate, dentate, crowded on the leafstalk; flower flat or cupped, small to medium-sized, sparkling flame red to scarlet or dark red; petals short; fruit small to medium-sized, ovoid or cupped, grading into the stem. 'Géant des Batailles', 'Empereur du Maroc', 'Abbé Berlèze', 'Abbé Bramerel', 'Cardinal Patrizzi', 'Claude Jacquet', 'Eugène Appert', 'Napoléon III', 'Souvenir du 'Président Lincoln'.

Group D, 'Victor Verdier' Type. The varieties of this group are homogeneous, different from the ordinary HP's, and are very close indeed to the Hybrid Teas. They are notable for their pretty growth and their abundant bloom. Bushes vigorous; canes upright, large, short, smooth, green; thorns not very numerous, fairly large, recurved, enlarged at the base; foliage beautiful, ample, purplish green, elegant; leaflets elongate, dentate, glossy; flower very large, cupped; petals large, pink nuanced intense carmine; calyx round, with long, dentate sepals which themselves cover the round bud which gradually lengthens until becoming magnificent as the blossom just opens; little or no perfume. 'Victor Verdier', 'Comtesse d'Oxford', 'Hippolyte Jamain', 'Eugénie Verdier', 'Lyonnais', 'Marie Finger', 'Pride of Reigate', 'Pride of Waltham', 'Suzanne-Marie Rodocanachi'.

Group E, 'Général Jacqueminot' Type. The roses forming this group, the most important of all, are hardy, bushy plants of vigorous growth, very floriferous, and bearing much fruit. Canes long, flexile, and generally slender; thorns very numerous, sharp, hooked, variable in size and shape depending upon the cultivar; foliage dark green; leaflets oval, dentate, slightly bullate; usually blooms in clusters; flower large, full, very fragrant, cupped or ruffled, sometimes globular; color, light red to blackish maroon; fruit abundant, fairly rounded, red at maturity. 'Général Jacqueminot', 'Abel Carrière', 'Baron Girod de l'Ain', 'Éclair', 'Eugene Fürst', 'Fisher-Holmes', 'Jean Liabaud', 'Monsieur Bonçenne', 'Prince Camille de Rohan', 'Prosper Laugier', 'Roger Lambelin', 'Alfred K. Williams', 'Duc de Montpensier', 'Gloire de Bourg-la-Reine', 'Jules Chrétien', 'Princesse de Béarn', 'Souvenir de William Wood'.

Group F, 'Jules Margottin' Type. Bushes of unusual vigor without being "climbing," very resistant to cold. Canes upright, armed with numerous large, strong, sharp, hooked thorns; foliage ample, stiff, slightly bullate; leaflets oblong, denticulate, dark green; bloom abundant, most often in clusters; the bud surrounded with foliaceous long, green, toothed sepals; sepals inserted at the tip of the calyx; mature calyx takes on the color of the flower; flowers large, full, perfectly imbricated, varying from pink to bright red, without the dark shades; very fragrant; fruit very elongated, resembling that of the Damasks, from which this group was probably developed. 'Jules Margottin', 'Heinrich Schultheis', 'Mme Gabriel Luizet', 'Magna Charta', 'Berthe Baron', 'Catherine Soupert', 'Clio', 'Duchesse de Vallombrosa', 'Mme Renard'. The 1901 Congress of Rosarians at Paris splits off a less vigorous, smaller-flowered subgroup, the thorns of which are, for the most part, replaced by "rugosities" or medium-sized thorns: 'Comtesse de Serenye', 'Heinrich Schultheis', 'Mme Gabriel Luizet', 'Mme Lacharme', 'Violette Bouyer', 'Margaret Dickson'.

Group G, 'Mme Récamier' Type. Bushes not terribly vigorous, but very floriferous; branches more upright than branching, resembling those of 'Général Jacqueminot'; very numerous thorns; foliage dense, glaucous green; leaflets oblong, dentate, rugose; flower pretty big, cupped or nearly globular, not very fragrant, white to blush white; fruit short, small, slightly conical, tinted pink at maturity, not very abundant. 'Mme Récamier', 'Elisa Boëlle'.

Group H, 'Triomphe de l'Exposition' Type. The roses of this group are very vigorous, hardy, and fairly floriferous. Canes long, sometimes "climbing," with extended internodes, glandulose; thorns not very numerous, variable in form and size; foliage ample, dark brownish green, purple when young; leaflets spaced out, dentate, rounded at the base and pointed at the tip; flower large, very full, generally flat, sometimes bulging, fragrant, often tripartite, varying from red to dark red to velvety crimson or violet; fruit variable in form, generally round or ovoid, colored carmine cherry red at maturity. Its descendants are somewhat variable, though not enough so to form any subgroups. 'Triomphe de l'Exposition', 'Captain Hayward', 'Achille Gonod', 'Clémence Joigneaux', 'Comte Adrien de Germiny', 'Duhamel-Dumonceau', 'Eclaireur', 'Jean Goujon'.

Group I, 'Mme Victor Verdier' Type. This group is much like Group J, in that the constituent roses are like 'Général Jacqueminot', but with smoother wood, and longer and more flexile canes; thorns often wider at the base and colored purple on a ground of greenish brown at the tip; the plants are very vigorous, very floriferous, hardy, bushier than is the case with Group J, and quite remontant. Branches smooth, green; thorns small and rare; foliage green, medium sized; flower large, globular or cupped, full, well-formed, well-held, very fragrant, and blooming most often in clusters of 3–12, depending upon the vigor of the plant's growth; the calyx more ovoid than those in Group J, sometimes takes on the form of an elongated cone at maturity; the bud is round, well-formed, and opens easily; most of the varieties in this group are characterized by the habit their axillary growth-buds have of sprouting very quickly, sometimes making it difficult to find buds for propagating with certain varieties; here one finds the greatest variety of colors, from pink to blackish maroon. 'Mme Victor Verdier', 'Dupuy-Jamain', 'Victor Hugo', 'Alfred Colomb', 'André Leroy d'Angers', 'Bernard Verlot', 'Beauty of Waltham', 'Countess of

Rosebery', 'Duchesse de Galliera', 'Duke of Edinburgh', 'Duke of Teck', 'Earl of Dufferin', 'Eugène Verdier', 'Général Duc d'Aumale', 'Louis Van Houtte', 'Paul de la Meilleraye', 'Reynolds Hole', 'Crimson Bedder', 'Souvenir de Spa'.

Group J, 'Charles Lefebvre' Type. As mentioned above, the roses of this group are much like the preceding. The plant is vigorous and hardy; canes pretty strong, long, not very branching, brownish or purplish-green, smooth; thorns large, sharp, hooked, pretty strong, and rare; foliage, ample; leaves very large; leaflets oval, dentate, deep purple-green; flower large, full, very well formed, globular, cupped, or imbricated, darkly colored from red to blackish red, occasionally pink; calyx small, round, inflated at maturity; sepals long, covering the bud, which is short, pretty big, and conical; the inflorescence is of 3–7 flowers, depending upon the plant's vigor. 'Charles Lefebvre', 'Dr. Andry', 'Aurore Boréale', 'Capitaine Peillon', 'Colonel Félix Breton', 'Duchess of Fife', 'Emperor', 'Florence Paul', 'Horace Vernet', 'Lord Bacon', 'Miller-Hayes', 'Président Schlachter', 'Salamander', 'Souvenir de Laffay', 'Souvenir du Dr. Jamain'.

Group K, 'Souvenir de la Reine d'Angleterre' Type. This group is very close to the "La Reine" group. Plants very vigorous; canes very long, very strong, thick; thorns large, short, hooked, and close together; internodes very short; foliage ample, stiff; leaflets long, dentate, dark green; blossom solitary, cupped, quite full; color, fresh or light pink, except in the sports when it is white or blush-white; flower scentless; the form of the calyx resembles that in the 'La Reine' group, but is shorter. Some of the varieties diverge from the above in having short canes, and a flower on a very short stem. 'Baronne Adolphe de Rothschild', 'Mabel Morrison', 'Merveille de Lyon', 'Souvenir de la Reine d'Angleterre', 'Spenser'.

Group L, Miscellaneous HP's. Includes both those not fitting into the other classes, and those not yet classed. 'Comtesse Cécile de Chabrillant', 'Denis Hélye', 'Frau Karl Druschki', 'Gloire de Chédane-Guinoisseau', 'Gloire de Ducher', 'Her Majesty', 'Hugh Dickson', 'Mme Laffay' (characteristics between those of the 'La Reine' group and those of the 'Jules Margottin' group), 'Mme Scipion Cochet', 'Marchioness of Londonderry', 'Oskar Cordel', 'Paul's Early Blush', etc.

"The French cultivators have carried this division into 'groups' to excess." [R8]

"The gradual decline of the Hybrid Perpetuals . . . is very apparent." [NRS/14] "The decline of the Hybrid Perpetual may be traced to the advent of the Hybrid Tea, and few new Hybrid Perpetuals are being introduced at present. . . . Their greatest fault, with few exceptions . . . is that they have but one short blooming period. Further, the plant becomes ungainly in the long summers of the Southeastern and the Interior Southern Zones by reason of its habit of losing foliage. Many of the Hybrid Perpetuals blue easily and are discolored by rain. . . . The history of the Hybrid Perpetual makes it evident that great hardiness and everblooming characteristics were sacrificed abroad for more perfect beauty of flower for exhibition. Many really valuable kinds have been lost sight of in the steady advance of widely heralded new varieties." [Th2] "No rose, however queenly and however lovely, that blooms but once or even twice a year is worthy of cultivation in gardens where everblooming kinds can be induced to grow." [Dr]

"I cannot refrain from protesting against the neglect this really wonderful class is being subjected to. When all is said, it is of the easiest culture and the only hybrid rose that is safely hardy and naturally permanent without winter protection north of the Mason and Dixon line, and if given half the attention required by the Hybrid Tea, it would give great satisfaction. Some people object to its scarcity of bloom after the June outburst, but even if none was forthcoming for the rest of the season those beautiful massive blooms repay us well for having waited a year and given the plants the little attention they require. Who would think of discarding the lilacs, peonies, or iris because they bloom but once! . . . Let us be fair to the most beautiful if not 'fancy' rose and the least exacting — the Hybrid Perpetual." [K]

ABEL CARRIÈRE PLATE 120
E. Verdier, 1875
Seedling of 'Baron de Bonstetten' (HP).

"Rich velvety maroon, shaded with violet, large, full and finely shaped. One of the best." [P1] "A dark crimson red which does not blush; flower large, full, flat; floriferous; vigorous." [Cx] "One of the good roses; the blossom, despite tints of blackish maroon, is pretty sun-proof." [S] "Blooms often 'come' bad . . . malformed . . . beautiful colour, one of the really dark ones . . . in some seasons the petals will burn." [F-M2] "The bush is adequately vigorous and very floriferous. . . . 'Abel Carrière's' advantage is that the blossoms are fairly resistant to damage by the sun's rays during hot periods while others of the same sort get quite burnt." [JR31/60] "Velvety crimson, with fiery centre; large, full flowers, fragrant; short wood, sharp red spines; shows traces of Bourbon blood. . . . Shy in autumn." [EL] "Fine, dark maroon, imbricated; wood very thorny; rather inclined to mildew." [DO] "Refuses to grow strongly in the spring. Foliage second-rate . . . liable to mildew and orange fungus . . . should only be grown by exhibitors." [F-M2] "Upright, wood green, armed with light pink thorns; foliage of three to five leaflets irregularly serrated; blossom about four in across [ca. 1 dm], very pretty and of good form, ordinarily in a cluster of three

to five." [JR10/10] "It is not recommended as a reliable variety for the garden." [OM] "We had wished to complete our notes on 'Abel Carrière' by giving a few words on its origin — but such is not possible. Its breeder, Mons E. Verdier, picks out each year a considerable number of seedlings (perhaps twenty or thirty thousand), and plants them all mixed together as those which seem, comparatively, the best." [R-H75] "Carrière (Elie-Abel). - – Editor in Chief of *Revue Horticole*. Born at May-en-Multien (Seine-et-Marne) in 1818, died at Montreuil (Seine) in 1896. In charge of the breeding-grounds at the Museum. Published various works, among which was *Traité Général des Conifères*." [R-HC] "Carrière was always a simple man, but of boundless devotion to those he honored with the title 'friend.' He quitted this Earth after a long and sad illness at the age of 79." [JR20/144]

ALFRED COLOMB PLATE 104
Lacharme, 1865
Seedling of 'Général Jacqueminot' (HP).
Not to be confused with the Cherpin/Ducher HP of 1852, which was red, and had "dingy" foliage.

"Strawberry red, reflexes crimson carmine . . . 4 × 3 [ft; ca. 1.25 × 1 m]." [B] "Bright fiery red, large and full; form globular and excellent; very effective; one of the best; growth vigorous." [P1] "One of the few perfect roses which is *toujours gai*. In colour, a rich carmine, with a crimson glow on it; in style, large, globular, symmetrical." [R1/159] "Has a certain look of 'Charles Lefebvre'; moderate vigor; . . . pink, with an underlying and handsome fiery red." [S] "Sometimes it is hardly distinguishable from 'Marie Baumann'. Very fragrant." [DO] "Bears the name of a great Lyonnais rose fancier . . . esteemed by amateurs, it is of moderate vigor, but the flowers, which have the expanded Centifolia form, are large, full, well-formed, pink on the underside of the petals, which above are of a handsome fiery red. Nothing has been forgotten in the color and form of this beautiful and good HP." [JR2/72] " 'Semiglobular, high centre': very good in petal, centre, size, lasting qualities, fragrance, and colour." [F-M2] "Late-flowering; vigorous, and fragrant." [J] "Blooms well in the fall." [JR10/11] "Needs heavy soil." [Th2] "Of fine growth and foliage in good soil but not on poor or light land. Seldom attacked by mildew and can stand some rain." [F-M2] "Green wood, with occasional pale green thorns, the foliage large and handsome. A grand rose." [EL]

ALFRED K. WILLIAMS
Schwartz, 1877
Sport of 'Général Jacqueminot' (HP).

"Carmine red, changing to magenta; large, full, and expanded." [P1] "Magenta-red, shaded with crimson; large, full flowers, partly imbricated . . . very beautiful . . . but . . . not constant and reliable." [EL] "Blooms nearly always come perfect . . . not a good bloom to last, or of the largest size . . . bright colour." [F-M2] "Early flowering . . . moderate growth . . . one of the most perfect in form." [J] "Free-flowering, especially towards autumn." [Hn] "Constitution is weak. Thorny, with good foliage, and will stand some rain. . . . Plants not hardy or long-lived." [F-M2] "Does not appear to like removal, so when it is possible it should be budded where it is to remain." [DO] "A perfect bloom, of bright red colour, but the growth is weak. Indispensible to exhibitors, but of little value for garden display." [OM]

AMERICAN BEAUTY
Cook/Bancroft/Field, 1886

" 'Mme Ferdinand Jamin' and 'American Beauty' are, in many ways, similar in color, but not in the form of the flower. The foliage of the latter is more stiff than is that of the former, and the young stalks of the American are more upright than are those of the other." [JR11/97]

"Large, double, rich rose-pink blooms of exquisite fragrance." [ARA29/96] "Deep even rosy carmine, with very fine petals, large and full; form cupped; very sweet." [P1] "Rich rosy red, very large, fragrant, long stemmed, solitary, and well held. The bush is vigorous enough, and blooms abundantly"." [JR10/39–40] "A majestic blossom of very nice color, fragrance, and growth, but not blooming with much abundance, and often giving imperfect blossoms." [JR13/92] "Free bloomer in autumn." [SBP] "Imperial pink to deep rose; remarkably fine form, very large, full, cupped; rich fragrance. . . . Has been a disappointment as a outdoor rose in the East wherever tried, but in the arid regions of the Interior South has proved to be most valuable, blooming for a long-continued season . . . subject to mildew." [Th2] "Large, globular, of a dark rose shaded with carmine, with an exquisite perfume. The mystery of its origin hangs over it." [JR16/37] "The daughter of our distinguished historian, Mr. George Bancroft, first saw the rose in bloom in the rose nursery of Mr. Anthony Cook, of Baltimore. She purchased the plant and had it transplanted to her father's rose garden in Washington City. Mr. Cook is very positive that it is one of nine hundred seedling roses that he raised. Mr. Field, the well-known florist of Washington City, obtained cuttings from Mr. Bancroft's plant. He propagated a large number of plants. . . . The colour is difficult to describe. The unusual shade of carmine-crimson, with a brilliant underglow, has over it a soft violet tinge, as if a film of bluish smoke hovered over the red velvety petals." [Dr] "The year 1916 has seen the decline of the old favorite, 'American Beauty' . . . our much worshipped 'Beauty' is slowly being pushed aside." [ARA17/111]

ANNA ALEXIEFF   PLATE 96
Margottin, 1858

"Rose, tinted with pink, large, full, and produced in great abundance; form cupped." [P1] "Beautiful . . . large, full, and somewhat flat." [JR28/140] "Very vigorous; flowers full, in a tight cluster, beautiful light salmon pink." [JDR58/36] "Fresh rosy-pink, superb colour, flowers very large, well formed, habit vigorous; a fine and most abundant blooming rose." [JC]

ANNA DE DIESBACH   PLATE 97
('Anna von Diesbach')
Lacharme, 1858
Seedling of 'La Reine' (HP).

"Brilliant glossy pink, colour exquisite and lasting, flowers unusually large, full, and cupped; petals broad and smooth; a fine rose of moderate habit." [JC] "Flowers large, full, beautiful carmine pink with reflections." [I'H58/128] "The most lovely shade of carmine; very large and thick; deeply cupped; growth vigorous." [P1] "Semi-globular, fragrant light crimson flowers . . . sometimes a few in the fall." [ARA34/78] "Carmine-pink, tinted silvery." [JR1/2/7] "Tall, very fragrant . . . deep, rose pink with deeper shadings . . . 4 × 3 [ft; ca. 1.25 × 1 m]." [B] "Petals few and far between." [P2] "Large vulgar flowers, loose and uneven, of a vivid rose." [B&V] "Of very strong hardy growth, but has the . . . fault of general looseness and unevenness in the blooms. They are of the largest size and more or less of the true cupped shape, but a perfect one is a rarity." [F-M3] "Giving [in autumn] fewer than before, but of an exquisite freshness." [JR16/179] "Free in autumn." [Th2] "Vigorous, upright branches armed with numerous prickles ordinarily quite small; foliage ample, thick petioles . . . flower stalk firm . . . flower of about three or so in [ca. 7.5 cm] . . . of such freshness that one wonders if it isn't artificial; petals around the circumference straight and elevated, those of the center ruffled." [JR10/13] "Canes fairly large, upright; bark light green, with occasional small, hooked, sharp prickles. Leaves glaucous green, divided into three to five leaflets which are oval-elongated and pointed; leafstalk an even glaucous green, strong and long. Flowers about 4.5 in across [ca. 1–1.25 dm], full, widely cupped, solitary or in clusters of two or three on the most vigorous branches. . . . Calyx tubular; sepals leaf-like. A variety of the first order, one of the biggest and most beautiful of roses." [JF] "[Lacharme] dedicated it to the daughter of the Countess of Diesbach, amateur rosarian of Fribourg, Switzerland. This estimable variety developed from seed from 'La Reine' produced by Mons Lacharme in 1849; he grew it for nearly ten years to study it well, and having developed an appreciation of its merits, he released it to commerce in November, 1858. . . . Not overly productive of its wonderful blossoms, perhaps, it *is* very vigorous, lasts well, and the flowers are quite large, well formed, and of a handsome carmine pink tinted silver." [JR2/58] "Though old is always one of the best, as much for the size of the blossom as for its color." [JR17/101]

ANTOINE DUCHER
Ducher, 1866
Seedling from 'Mme Domage' (HP, Margottin, 1853, crimson, "centifolia form; very fragrant." [S] Progenitor unknown).

"Bright purplish red, very large, full, and fine; growth robust." [P1] "Rich dark crimson, flowers globular, large, full, and deep; a distinct and beautiful rose; habit moderate." [JC] "Cupped, bright orange [!]." [I'H66/369] "Violet-red; large, well shaped flowers, fragrant; wood very thorny. The color is very fleeting." [EL] "Very vigorous hybrid; flowers upright, cupped, extra-large, full and very well formed, bright red. . . . [In comparison with 'Mme Domage',] flowers prettier, darker in color; very good for forcing." [RJC66/209] This variety is the unlikely co-founder, with *R. fœtida persiana,* of the Pernetiana class, a class which, crossed with the old Hybrid Teas, initiated the modern Hybrid Teas.

ARCHIDUCHESSE ELIZABETH D'AUTRICHE
Moreau-Robert, 1881

"Extra-vigorous, nearly thornless, with handsome dark green foliage; the blossom is very large, full, and opens well; the color is beautiful light satiny pink, shaded, the reverse lighter; extremely floriferous." [JR5/172] "Well formed, of a delightful color." [JR7/157] Archduchess Elizabeth, daughter of Emperor Franz-Josef of Austria.

ARDOISÉE DE LYON
(trans., 'The Slatey One of Lyon')
Plantier/Damaizin, 1858

"Violet rose, a poor color." [EL] "Bright red with blue reflections." [JR2/59] "Flower very large, full; color, slate-violet with red-violet reflections; center, lively brilliant red. The blossoms may grow over four in [ca. 1 dm] across." [S] "An extraordinarily large rose, of a very deep purple color, and will, I have no doubt, prove a splendid rose." [HstXV:426] "Fully double, quartered, flowers of rich deep pink with violet and purple shadings. Sweetly scented . . . 4 × 3 [ft; ca. 1.25 × 1 m]." [B] "Vigorous, branches upright, beautiful dark green foliage, flower four or so in across [ca. 1 dm+], quite slatey, center bright shining red." [JDR58/36] Another slate-colored cultivar by the name of 'Impératrice Eugénie' was exhibited by Delhommeau of Mans in 1854: "The blossom is red when it has just opened; it takes on a slatey tint — or, more precisely, a violet tint — when fading. Mons Delhommeau must certainly take us to be children of Mother Goose, or perhaps he hasn't seen any rose other than his own before. We must advise him, before he propagates this wonderful novelty, to observe the various stages a rose-blossom goes through, in particular those of 'Géant des Batailles'; we, at least, understand what he, it would seem, ignores — that turning violet or 'slatey' is a fault and not a virtue in a rose." [I'H54/131]

ARRILLAGA
Schœner, 1929
From an unnamed seedling (a Centifolia × 'Mrs. John Laing' [HP]) × 'Frau Karl Druschki' (HP).

"Bud large, glowing pink; flower very large, double (35 petals), unusually lasting, intensely fragrant, vivid pink, golden glow at base of petals, borne on long, stout stem. Foliage handsome and healthy. Growth very vigorous (8 to 10-ft. canes [ca. 2.25–3 m] in season); profuse bloomer in summer, scant in autumn." [ARA31/226] "Enormous blooms of excellent quality nearly five in [ca. 1.25 dm] in diameter and 3 in [ca. 7.5 cm] deep, very double. . . . At Breeze Hill the plants grew fairly well and produced ordinary pink flowers." [ARA32/175] "Immense, very double flowers and a really outstanding variety." [ARA31/208]

ARTHUR DE SANSAL
Cochet père/Cochet Brothers, 1855
Seedling of 'Géant des Batailles' (HP).

"Blackish maroon with fiery shadings." [BJ] "Dark velvet crimson; superb." [HstXIII:225] "4 × 4 [ft; ca. 1.25 × 1.25 m] with flowers of rich crimson-purple." [HRG] "Highly scented." [B] "Upright, compact plant. . . . Light green foliage." [G] "Vigorous; foliage very dark and velvety; flower of medium size, very full, opening with difficulty; the buds are much sought for bouquets." [S] "It is a seedling of the *Giant*, from which it takes its deportment and imbrication . . . it is to 'Géant des Batailles' what 'Mogador' is to 'Rose du Roi'." [I'H55/207] One sees the name "Cartier" mentioned as this variety's breeder, but: "[It was a] seedling of Mons Pierre Cochet's, Suisnes rosarian, sold in 1855 by his two sons Philémon and Scipion." [JR10/20] Dedicated to Mons Desprez's son-in-law: "Before his marriage [to Caroline Desprez] he lived at Combs-la-Ville, afterwards going to stay at Dammarie-les-Lys, near Melun." [JR10/77] "Our readers doubtless know that for nearly his whole life Mons De Sansal was occupied with horticulture, and we who have had the opportunity to study his notable collection of conifers and other plants, Cucurbitaceæ in particular, at his property in Farcy-les-Lys, near Melun (Seine-et-Marne), are particularly able to say so. But it was the rose which he held in special esteem, and he had a large and rich collection of them. He was never content to do like the simple amateur and plant merely the varieties available through commerce; he sowed many rose seeds, and horticulture is indebted to him for many beautiful varieties from which he never made any money." [R-H75]

BARBAROSSA
Welter, 1906
From an unnamed seedling (parentage: 'Frau Karl Druschki' [HP] × 'Captain Hayward' [HP]) × 'Princesse de Béarn' (HP).

"Pure carmine red; a red 'Frau Karl Druschki'; vigorous and floriferous." [JR34/25] "A superb red-flowered variety dedicated to Barbarossa, which was the well-known surname given to the Holy Roman Emperor Frederick I [1123?–1190; drowned while on a crusade]. If one can believe the German horticultural press, this introduction will have exactly the same growth, floriferousness, and bearing as 'Frau Karl Druschki', from which it differs only in its carmine-red color. What is more, it also has a delicate perfume — not, unfortunately, the case with 'Druschki'. . . . Peter Lambert . . . eminent rosarian, protests vigorously against the boasts made about the qualities of this new introduction, which in his opinion it doesn't merit." [JR31/26] "The plant is a vigorous grower with shining dark foliage, entirely hardy and best of all it is very free flowering." [C&Js09]

BARON DE BONSTETTEN   PLATE 115
Liabaud, 1871
From 'Général Jacqueminot' (HP) × 'Géant des Batailles' (HP).

"Velvety maroon, shaded with deep crimson, somewhat lighter in shade than 'Prince Camille [de Rohan]', and rather smaller in size, but with a little more substance; shy in autumn, but a grand rose." [EL] "Rich velvety-purple, very dark, liable to burn in hot weather; a superb rose when newly opened; habit robust." [JC] "Red, black, and crimson, large, full, and good." [P1] "A bad rose." [K1] "A fine Rose, flat, but double." [WD] "Very double . . . 4 × 3 [ft; ca. 1.25 × 1 m]." [B] "A color of the darkest, it blooms in abundance, and the blossoms bear the rays of the summer sun with ease. . . . The flowers of 'Baron de Bonstetten' seem to us larger and of richer color than those of 'Monsieur Bonçenne'. . . .

We believe that this rose . . . is the product of seeds obtained from 'Monsieur Bonçenne' . . . vigorous and pretty hardy; the numerous, very large, and well formed blossoms are full, fragrant, and of a magnificent color of velvety-black crimson red. Much recommended." [JR17/23] "Vigorous, strong branches armed with numerous hooked prickles; foliage sparse and rough to the touch. . . . Mons le Baron de Bonstetten is a wealthy Swiss estate owner, and is a great fancier of roses." [JR10/22]

BARON GIROD DE L'AIN   PLATE 163
('Baron Giraud de l'Ain')
Reverchon, 1897
Sport of 'Eugène Fürst' (HP).

"Bright red with white edging . . . fragrant and healthy . . . 4 × 3 [ft; ca. 1.25 × 1 m]." [B] "Large, full; color, varying from crimson red to bright carmine; petals scalloped, largely blotched and bordered white, giving the blossom the aspect of a Flemish carnation." [JR21/113] "[As compared to 'Roger Lambelin',] 'Baron Girod de l'Ain' is certainly equal, if not superior, in beauty. . . . First of all, the flowers are larger . . . the white piping at the edge of the petals is larger. The shrub is very vigorous." [JR30/45]

BARONESS ROTHSCHILD
Listed as 'Baronne Adolphe de Rothschild'.

BARONNE ADOLPHE DE ROTHSCHILD   PLATE 110
('Baroness Rothschild')
Pernet père, 1868
Sport of 'Souvenir de la Reine d'Angleterre' (HP).
Not to be confused with Lacharme's HP of 1862, 'Baron Adolphe de Rothschild', which was a "shaded purple" (LS).

"Fresh pink, petals' edges silvery; flower very large, very full, cupped." [Cx] "Pale rose." [ARA17/28] "Bright flesh pink, shaded white. . . . Vigorous, erect, hardy; blooms early; the color is very clear." [S] "Light pink, large but not quite full flowers of perfectly cupped form. Robust with a fine erect habit, one of the most charming of pink roses, though without any scent. Useless to us [on the French Riviera] as it seldom flowers till the second week in May; a very distinct variety." [B&V] "She robes herself in glossiest satin, and draws around her the drapery of ample folds dyed with richest, yet most delicate, peach-blow tints. The stout shoots, armed with ivory-like spines, have an air of matronly dignity . . . it bears the fierce heat of our July sun uncommonly well." [HstXXVIII:166] "Light colored blooms of ideal shape with a silvery sheen, and scentless, but with age a few blooms can be expected in autumn." [ARA34/77] "Flowers freely in autumn, but in unfortunately scentless; cannot be done without." [DO] "Blooms . . . late . . . [the blossoms] generally come well, of globular shape, and a beautiful pink colour . . . very large . . . come again well in the autumn . . . quite scentless." [F-M2] "Highly scented . . . upright, tidy plant with ample foliage . . . 4 × 3 [ft; ca. 1.25 × 1 m]." [B] "One of the largest roses." [SBP] "One of the most beautiful, and, so far as I have tested it, one of the most reliable of our light-coloured roses, for though short in limb, she is strong and sturdy in constitution . . . one meets with strange antitheses. Of this very rose, and only the other day, a rosarian said to me, 'Ah, yes—isn't she lovely!' and then added, with a tender pensiveness, 'I do believe that I've given the Baroness more than double her share of—pig manure!.'" [R1/159] "The wood is short-jointed, thick, light green, armed with occasional light green thorns. . . . A very distinct, beautiful rose, free blooming, and greatly valued, both as an exhibition and a garden sort." [EL] "Growth . . . 'robust' . . . short, thick, stumpy, stiff, upright wood, with grand foliage

right up to the blooms." [F-M2] "Upright sturdy plant, 6 × 3 [ft; ca. 1.75 × 1 m]." [HRG] "Calyx small, pear-shaped; sepals leaflike." [JF] "This was considered last year in England as *the rose* of the year, and it is pleasant to learn that the experience of the present season has more than confirmed all that has been said in its favor." [HstXXIV:284–285] "One of the first of roses." [HRH]

BARONNE PRÉVOST   PLATE 89
Desprez/Cochet, 1842
"Bright rose color, a very large flower, strong, vigorous, free grower, blooming freely from June till November. Always opens its blooms well. . . . A most magnificent Rose." [HstVI:367] "Large, full, bright pink." [R-H43] "The prince of perpetuals—bright rose color—immensely large and magnificent. . . . Few roses give so striking and grand an effect as this; producing in such abundance, flowers of so immense a size, frequently measuring with moderately good culture, five or six in in diameter [ca. 1.25–1.5 dm]." [C] "Flattish . . . deep, rose pink. Upright and vigorous . . . ample foliage . . . 4 × 3 [ft; ca. 1.25 × 1 m]." [B] "Pale rose, sweet." [P2] "Fragrant, very hardy. The shoots are stout and stiff." [EL] "Very vigorous, forming a handsome bush which is long-lived, rare enough among HP's! . . . The foliage is ample and well-distributed, and is of a pretty green. The blossom, despite its size and fulness, is held well, is of a perfect form, and is carmine-pink, unshaded, perhaps with some lilac, and is very fragrant." [JR3/152] "Flower about four in across [ca. 1 dm], flat, the center petals ruffled, perfectly held." [JR10/34–35] "One of the very best of its class, blooming freely in autumn. . . . It is also of luxuriant growth, and large, rich foliage." [SBP] "This is the first time that this rose has bloomed at Mons Verdier's; it seems to rebloom very freely. The blossom is large, and pretty full; the petals are large, a pretty pink with a touch of lilac; the bush is vigorous, with strong canes having very sharp reddish thorns; the canes are topped by a bouquet of five to six flowers which bloom successively; the leaves have seven leaflets which are finely dentate, fresh green, undulate, and bullate; the perfume is elegant." [An42/332] "Canes fairly large and branching; bark a pretty green, with numerous prickles which are reddish and unequal, though generally short. Foliage very elegant, a handsome gay green, divided into 5–7 leaflets which are somewhat rugose, as well as oval-rounded, barely acuminate, and quite dentate. The leafstalk is fairly slender, nodding, armed with a number of small prickles. Flower, 3.5–4 in across [ca. 1 dm], full, rounded, solitary or in a cluster of 3–5 on the vigorous canes; color, a handsome fresh pink; outer petals large, those of the center smaller and inter-folded; flower stem pretty long, glandular, strong, supporting the blossom well. Calyx tubular; sepals leaf-like. A variety of great merit." [JF] "Dedicated to the sister of his [Desprez's] friend Mons Guenou[x], fancier and breeder of Dahlias at Voisenon, near Melun. On July 27, 1841, Desprez relinquished ownership of this variety to Mons Cochet Sr. for about a hundred francs. Cochet released it to commerce in fall, 1842." [JR3/152] "It is reliable everywhere for an abundance of its large, fresh, blushing roses." [R1/203]

BLACK PRINCE
W. Paul, 1866
Seedling of 'Pierre Notting' (HP).
Not to be confused with 'Prince Noir' (HP).
"Dark crimson shaded with black, cupped, large, full, and of fine form; growth vigorous." [P1] "Glowing crimson shaded with purple, flowers large, full and globular, fine imbricated form; a distinct and first-rate rose, habit robust." [JC] "Very dark maroon, good climber." [FP] "Gives . . . quite a good dark bloom . . . rarely." [F-M2] "Fragrant, large, cupped . . . rich crimson shaded

almost black. Vigorous . . . 4 × 3 [ft; ca. 1.25 × 1 m]." [B] "Fair growth and fine foliage." [F-M2] "Very vigorous; branches upright, short, amply furnished with flat thorns." [S] "Not considered a reliable sort, occasionally it is very fine." [EL]

BOULE DE NEIGE
Listed as a Bourbon.

CAMILLE BERNARDIN   PLATE 105
Gautreau, 1865
Seedling of 'Général Jacqueminot' (HP).

"Light crimson, paler on the edges. A very certain Rose; fragrant." [H] "Bright red, large, full, and of fine form, blooms freely, very sweet." [P1] "Flower large, full, well formed, cerise red bordered white." [JR1/2/7] "Medium size, semi-cupped form, fragrant; does not bloom until late in the season, and then the flowers fade easily; never very productive." [EL] "Light crimson, shaded, flowers very large and full; a well formed good rose, habit vigorous." [JC] "Camille Bernardin died at Brie-Comte-Robert last December 5th [1894] in his 64th year. . . . Having studied with an eye towards the legal profession for quite some time, but at length preferring the country life to that of the Bar, Bernardin settled early in life at Brie-Comte-Robert, and devoted himself entirely to the interests of the Briard populace, who never referred to him by any name other than the familiar one of 'Monsieur Camille.' . . . For many months, a cruel malady had sapped his strength. . . . 'He was the friend of the common man, and of Democracy. . . . ' . . . Around 1860, he took up the Rose. . . . He organized, at Brie, the first special Rose Exhibitions which have subsequently echoed throughout the entire world." [JR19/1–2]

CANDEUR LYONNAISE
Croibier, 1913
Seedling of 'Frau Karl Druschki' (HP).

"White, sometimes shaded yellow." [NRS/15] "The blooms are large and of fine form, but they are of palest sulphur colour." [OM] "Surpasses ['Frau Karl Druschki'] in substance and size, and if it were not tinted pale yellow, it would at times outclass it as an exhibition rose. It naturally produces its flowers on long, strong stems, a great many singly, but not as freely as 'Druschki'." [ARA34/76] "Of great vigor, very hardy, with upright canes branching somewhat; foliage somber green; prickles fine and not very numerous; pretty ovoid bud, usually solitary, borne on a very rigid stem; flower or extraordinary size, having attained 6.5 in [ca. 1.5 dm] across. Color, a handsome pure white, sometimes lightly tinted very light sulphur yellow. . . . The main ways in which 'Candeur Lyonnaise' differs from its mother are that this rose is very full, that it 'keeps' until fully open without showing its stamens and pistil, which are hidden in the petals in the center of the blossom, and that it surpasses 'Druschki' in dimensions." [JR37/151]

CAPTAIN HAYWARD
Bennett, 1893
Seedling of 'Triomphe de l'Exposition' (HP).

"Brilliant carmine-crimson; flowers very full, cupped, fragrant; very, very floriferous; very vigorous." [Cx] "Not very full . . . fine petals of great substance." [J] "Of perfect form; very sweet and opening well. An early bloomer." [P1] "Flowers long, pointed, beautiful form, scarlet-crimson, fragrant; likes partially shaded places." [Hn] "Well-formed long petals; needs to be well done [i.e., given liberal treatment with fertilizer and water] if to give of its best. Very free-flowering, somewhat inclined to be thin." [DO] "The flowers, which are none too full, are of scarlet-crimson shade. . . . An easy rose to grow, and one that gives a few blooms

in autumn." [OM] "At its very best, grown as strongly as possible, in a cool season, it is with its pointed form and long smooth petals . . . as magnificent an example of the bright red H.P.'s as we have . . . petals are rather thin and few in number . . . opens very quickly." [F-M2] "Fragrant, light crimson, high-centred, double . . . excellent orange hips . . . 6 × 4 [ft; ca. 1.75 × 1.25 m]." [B] "Nearly all the flowers come out at the same time . . . twice in the year . . . ablaze with its bright coloured, well formed blossoms, which are carried on stiff stalks, bolt upright. In between times and after the autumn flowering we get a few blooms, but not enough to be of much value." [NRS/13] "Perfect form when grown under cool, moist conditions; fragrant. . . . Poor in hot weather." [Th2] "Extra vigorous growth with very fine foliage . . . not much liable to fungoid pests or to come malformed." [F-M2] "An admirable Rose in all ways and very sweetly scented." [K1]

CAROLINE DE SANSAL
Desprez/Jamain, 1849
Seedling of 'Baronne Prévost' (HP).

"Flesh color, deepening towards the centre; large, full flowers, flat form, often indented; subject to mildew; very hardy. An unreliable sort, but beautiful when in perfection; generally it is of better quality in September than in June." [EL] "Clear flesh colour with blush edges . . . a fair-weather rose only." [P2] "Very free, strong grower. The foliage is large and luxuriant. The flowers are very large, double, and cupped like the old Centifolias. The color is a pale silvery blush, with a fleshy tinge in the center, resembling very much . . . 'Souvenir de la Malmaison'." [HstIX:492] "Nearly as large and fine as 'La Reine' . . . decidedly the best light colored one we have yet seen." [WHoII] "A blush 'Baronne Prévost'. . . . This is a very desirable variety from its hardiness, size, and fine habit." [C] "A robust growing and most excellent rose, though in cold damp conditions it does not open freely." [JC] "Very vigorous, with red-tinged branches lightly bethorned; foliage dark green sometimes touched with yellow; flower large, full, well-formed, imbricated, well-held . . . it bears the name of . . . the daughter of Mons Desprez, married to Mons Arthur De Sansal." [JR10/77] "Mons Hippolyte Jamain has, among a crowd of the most precious introductions, two roses bred by Mons Desprez, whose death threatened to deny to horticulture . . . 'Berthe De Sansal' [HP, 1849, bright pink] and 'Caroline De Sansal'. . . . Very vigorous, with slightly reddish bark which has brown, upright, and unequal thorns; leaves, 5–7 large leaflets of a dark green above, oval-oblong, sharply toothed, the upper leaflets larger and rounded; the blooming and blossom form resemble that of 'Baronne Prévost' . . . the flower stems are erect, to 1.5 in long [ca. 3.75 cm], covered with rust-colored glandular bristles; the blossoms are solitary, or in a cluster of 3–5 at the tip of the cane; the calyx tube is funnel-shaped, not contracted at the mouth, bristly-glandular like the flower-stem; the blossom is 4–4.5 in across [ca. 1 dm], with rounded, imbricated petals." [R-H49] "Does very well grafted as well as own-root." [I'H53/172] "Hard to beat." [HstXXVI:331] "Always bonnie, always bountiful." [R1/203]

CHAMPION OF THE WORLD
Listed as a Bourbon.

CHARLES GATER
G. Paul, 1893
"Brownish crimson." [LS] "Carmine brown." [JR20/6] "Deep crimson brown. Flower globular. Exhibition rose." [JR19/36] "Deep crimson; vigorous; good, late." [TW] "Brownish red; vigorous and hardy." [P1] "Clear red, globular blooms . . . good foliage

. . . 4 × 3 [ft; ca. 1.25 × 1 m]." [B] "A grand rose; extra large size, fine full form, dark rich crimson, exquisitely shaded; very fragrant and handsome. A good healthy grower and free bloomer." [C&Js99] "My [George Paul's] old friend and foreman, the late Mr. Charles Gater." [NRS17/103] "Charles Gater, of Cheshunt, and his brother William, of Slough . . . were probably the best growers of pot Roses the world has seen." [NRS20/26]

CHARLES LEFEBVRE

('Paul Jamain')

Lacharme, 1861

From 'Général Jacqueminot' (HP) × 'Victor Verdier' (HP).

"Bright crimson, with purplish centres, large, very double, and of fine form." [P1] "Velvety scarlet, smooth and thick petals, flowers evenly and beautifully formed, a very fragrant and most superb rose, habit moderate." [JC] "Flower about 3.5 in across [ca. 8 cm], cupped, full, well-formed, very fragrant, bright red with touches of maroon. Magnificent flowering. . . . Mons. Charles Lefebvre is the son of a great lover of roses from Autun." [JR10/139] "A superb dark crimson, indescribably rich. . . . This stands almost alone for its vigorous strong wood and large leathery foliage, that possesses almost the substance of the leaves of a camellia. It is excellent for all purposes." [WD] "Fine in petals, centre and size, lovely in colour, very fragrant and beautifully round and smooth . . . open and semi-imbricated . . . not a good form to last . . . free in bloom and a good autumnal . . . the G.O.M. ['Grand Old Man'] of the dark crimson roses." [F-M2] "Has the form of a ranunculus, expanded." [HstXXIV:253] "Fades quickly and blues under heat." [Th2] "Few roses are as beautiful when it is at its best." [J] "One of the sweetest in scent." [E] "Beautiful in both flower and leaf." [EIC] "A few thorns of light red; the wood and foliage are of light reddish-green. A splendid rose." [EL] "Of strong growth, with stout stiff smooth wood and fine foliage, requiring strong soil . . . more liable to orange fungus than to mildew . . . can stand rain." [F-M2] "Very floriferous." [JR3/26] "Flower stalks pretty long, slender, strong, supporting the blossom well; petals of the circumference large, those of the center smaller. Calyx pear-shaped, nearly globular. A very pretty variety of the 'Jacqueminot' sort." [JF] "4 × 4 [ft; ca. 1.25 × 1.25 m]." [B] "Vigorous upright growth to 5 [ft; ca. 1.5 m]." [HRG] "In good soil makes shoots eight to ten ft [ca. 2.25–3 m] in a season." [WD] "A marvelous production by a well-known breeder." [VH62/102] "A magnificent rose." [DO]

CHARLES MARGOTTIN   PLATE 102

Margottin, 1863

Seedling of 'Jules Margottin' (HP).

"Brilliant carmine . . . centres fiery red, very large, full, and sweet; growth vigorous." [P1] "Rich in nuance and size." [l'H67/54] "Form fine; outer petals large and round." [FP] "Retains the color well; smooth, reddish wood armed with occasional red spines; foliage slightly crimpled. An excellent, distinct rose, quite unlike the parent in habit. It doubtless comes from a natural cross of some dark sort like 'Charles Lefebvre' on 'Jules Margottin'." [EL] "This notable variety was developed . . . in 1859 . . . very vigorous, with large well-formed flowers of a beautiful sparkling carmine red, intense flame in the center. Grafted, this variety boasts luxuriant growth, while on its own roots it is feeble." [JR3/29] "Branches dark green, slightly reddish, with small upright

red thorns; leaves of five leaflets, oval-lanceolate; flower stem bristling with hairs; sepals long, two or three of them leaf-like; blossom about three in across [ca. 7.5 cm], full, fragrant, charming, slightly cupped, very bright carmine red, center scarlet red . . . bears the name of . . . the son of its raiser." [JR10/140]

CLIO   PLATE 158

W. Paul, 1894

"Flesh colour, shaded in centre with rosy pink, very large; fine globular form, and freely produced . . . splendid . . . unsurpassed in the beauty of its flowers and their effect in the garden." [P1] "A beautiful color of pink-tinted cream; it is very vigorous with long stems." [JR32/34] "Almost globular shape . . . very pale pink . . . practically white on the outside . . . by no means first-class in form or colour . . . rain soon spoils it." [F-M2] "They open well outside in the open air." [JR18/66] "The numerous blossoms are of pretty form, the bud is very large, and when the flower has opened the color is a beautiful rose-pink." [JR32/13] "Slight fragrance; needs thinning. . . . Balls badly in damp weather." [Th2] "Imbricated." [Cx] "A very vigorous variety; the shoots are so strong that they should be pegged down instead of being cut back at pruning time. The flowers . . . come in thick clusters, but they are not very attractive." [OM] "Hardy, strong, almost rank grower, with large foliage and thorns . . . not much liable to mildew." [F-M2] "Healthy plant . . . 4 × 3 [ft; ca. 1.25 × 1 m]." [B] "A vigorous and good all-round Rose." [DO] Clio, the Greek Muse of History.

COMTESSE CÉCILE DE CHABRILLANT

Marest, 1858

Seedling of 'Jules Margottin' (HP).

"Pink with a paler reverse." [JR2/59] "Medium size, very good habit and very full, silky flesh-coloured. Vigorous growth, erect. Very fragrant." [Hn] "Satiny-pink, never above medium size, full, fragrant; of perfect, globular form; numerous dark thorns of small size; foliage dark and tough. A lovely rose." [EL] "When in its best state, it is of matchless beauty." [P2] "A perfect model of symmetry, though scarcely large enough to satisfy the craving for monstrosity, which is the failing of the public taste among rosarians at the present day; in all other respects it is perfect." [WD] "Shell-like petals, so beautifully set in cup-like form, and so sweetly tinted with shaded pinks . . . each rose is so perfect, not crowded in a cluster so close that none can get room to unfold in perfection, but singly, borne on the point of each strong shoot." [HstXXVIII:167] "Bright rose colour, surface of petals like satin, reverse having a silvery tinge, large and full flower; grows vigorously; foliage very much polished; good and valuable variety. Very fragrant; altogether a lovely rose." [B&V] "Very vigorous shrub with stocky, fat canes growing no longer than 40 cm [ca. 16 in], and forming a well rounded head; the thorns, which are rather numerous, are small, thin, slightly hooked, very unequal, and intermixed with glandular bristles. The foliage is ample, and composed of leaves with 5 or 7 oval-elliptic leaflets which are slightly stalked, nearly obtuse, unequally dentate — lower dentation glandulose — bright green above, paler beneath; rachis nearly straight, glandulose, creased into channels above, glabrous and armed with some small prickles beneath. The blossoms, a fetching bright icy pink with silvery reflections, are globular, very full, perfectly formed, and regularly imbricated in the outer rows of petals, which are mostly obovate, pure pink above, and silvery beneath. The peduncle is strong, very glandulose, and flaring at the tip into a glabrous calyx tube which is funnel-shaped, and not contracted at the throat; the sepals are slightly glandular, the two outer ones being somewhat foliaceous, while the three inner ones are simple and very pointed.

This new rose was developed by Mons Marest, rue d'Enfer, Paris. It is very remontant and blooms very abundantly. We have been watching it bloom since spring, and have satisfied ourselves that the last blossoms are quite as beautiful as the first." [I'H58/97–98] "Vigorous, forming a bushy, somewhat tall, shrub; branches with green bark, fairly upright, armed with small unequal red prickles intermingled with bristles; leaves of 3–5 leaflets, oval-elliptical, of a soft green; petiole glandular; flower 2 to 2.5 in in diameter [ca. 5–6 cm], full, globular, well-held, beautifully symmetrical; silvery pink fading to lilac; fragrant; strong stems covered with bristles." [JR10/184–185] "Good perfume. Good, strong foliage . . . 4 × 3 [ft; ca. 1.25 × 1 m]." [B] "What a name! . . . a superb rose, without a doubt." [HstXV:426]

COMTESSE D'OXFORD   PLATE 111
Guillot père, 1869
Seedling of 'Victor Verdier' (HP).

"Carmine with soft violet shades; velvety, flowers large, full, and cupped; petals smooth and well formed." [JC] "Vermilion red." [Cx] "Of the largest size . . . good in petal and centre . . . shape . . . open . . . fairly lasting . . . colour soon gets dull." [F-M2] "Fades quickly . . . subject to mildew." [EL] "Good foliage which is most lovely in the early spring . . . does not suffer much from mildew . . . especially liable to . . . rust." [F-M2] "Very vigorous with upright branches. Its foliage is very handsome. As for the blossom, it is very large and supported on a firm stem, very double and of good form. Its rish color is a bright, dazzling carmine-red." [JR4/101] "Branches large, with green bark; foliage of 2 to 5 leaflets of a dark green on top, more pale beneath; thick; much serrated; leafstalk thick; flower stalk upright and strong; the blossom is of a rare elegance being 4–4.5 in across [ca. 1 dm], somewhat flat, somewhat fragrant . . . very vigorous and remontant. . . . It bears the name of the English countess Eliza Nugent, daughter of the Marquess of Westmeath, Countess of Oxford; it was found desirable to 'frenchify' the name of the rose." [JR10/185] "A reliable Rose when well treated." [DO] "A fine showy Rose, the best type of its style." [WD]

CROWN PRINCE
W. Paul, 1880
Seedling of 'Duke of Edinburgh' (HP).

"Bright purple, centres shaded with lurid crimson, very large and double, petals fine, very floriferous, and of excellent growth and habit; a most effective garden Rose, yielding large quantities of fine flowers." [P1] "Globular in form, deep crimson; early and free." [W/Hn] "Charmingly scented." [S]

DENIS HÉLYE
Gautreau/Portemer fils, 1864

"Brilliant rosy-carmine; lovely color; very large and full; very effective; growth vigorous." [FP] "In clusters, purplish violet red, red on the reverse." [S] "Quite floriferous." [I'H67/54] "Intense carmine; flower very large, cupped, fragrant; pretty vigorous." [Cx] "Our much esteemed comrade Denis Hélye was born on the Rue de la Clef in Paris on June 7, 1827. He signed on with the Jardin des Plantes at the age of ten after the death of his father, having thus become the only means of support for his aged and infirm mother, receiving as an apprentice there only sixty centîmes a day, a sum indeed too small to meet his needs. This, however, did not defeat him. After work, he went to his night job as a stevedore. His taste for gardens and horticulture grew as he grew; the layouts he designed showed much intelligence, and his merit was noted by both amateurs and his superiors. At length, he was named Chief

Horticulturalist at the Natural History Museum at the age of 20. Whenever offered more lucrative positions elsewhere, he would refuse them in order to retain his old post, which he indeed kept until his death last March 29 [1884] at the age of 57." [JR8/67]

DOMBROWSKII
Listed as a Hybrid Bourbon.

DR. ANDRY
E. Verdier, 1864
Seedling of 'Victor Verdier' (HP).

"Flowers dark bright-red; very large, full, and perfectly imbricated." [FP] "Rosy-crimson, large, semi-cupped flowers, double; sometimes full, fades badly; foliage large and glossy; wood moderately smooth; thorns large and red. A better rose in England than in this country [U.S.A.]." [EL] "Blooms . . . apt to be divided . . . sometimes irregular . . . fair in size, good in petal and centre, and very bright at first in colour . . . very free flowering . . . not good in autumn." [F-M2] "Very vigorous, flowers full, 12 cm across [ca. 4.25 in], very intense dark carmine red." [I'H64/327] "Vigorous; wood smooth; flower large, full, cupped; color, bright crimson shaded grenadine. In the style of 'Charles Lefebvre'; good autumnal." [S] "Double, crimson flowers flushed deep pink opening cupped, upright vigorous growth . . . 4 × 3 [ft; ca. 1.25 × 1 m]." [B] "Of perfect form. . . . Very fragrant." [DO] "Fine smooth petals . . . robust." [JC] "Excellent for pillars; pegs down well." [WD] "Capital growth and foliage, hardy and of strong constitution . . . early . . . not much subject to mildew or orange fungus . . . standing rain. . . . A useful and thoroughly reliable Rose." [F-M2]

DUC DE WELLINGTON
('Duke of Wellington')
Granger/C. Verdier, 1864
Seedling of 'Lord Macaulay' (HP).
Not to be confused with Calvert's violet-purple China.

"Bright crimson, full, of fine form and free." [DO] "Flower large, 10–12 cm across [ca. 4 in], intense velvety red shaded blackish and brightened with intense flame towards the center." [I'H64/327] "The pointed form . . . capital in petals and fullness, grand in dark crimson colour and lasting qualities . . . of fair average size." [F-M2] "Bright velvety red, shaded with blackish maroon; large and very effective; growth moderate." [P1] "Centre fiery-red; large and full; growth vigorous." [FP] "Good size, cupped and well up in the centre." [JC] "Shapely flowers. . . . Scented . . . 4 × 3 [ft; ca. 1.25 × 1 m]." [B] "Fair in vigour and foliage . . . not very liable to mildew or much injured by rain, a free bloomer and quite a good autumnal." [F-M2] Arthur Wellesley, 1st Duke of Wellington; lived 1769–1852.

DUCHESSE DE SUTHERLAND
('Duchess of Sutherland')
Laffay, 1839

"Bright glossy pink, changing to pale rose; an old and very beautiful rose." [JC] "Medium-sized, full enough, expanded, flesh pink of an incomparable shade." [JR3/26] "Double, bright crimson-pink blooms . . . 4 [ft; ca. 1.25 m]." [HRG] "Large, full, cupped, fragrant." [S] " 'Lane—Glossy blush—very beautiful.' 'Wood—bright rose—mottled—very splendid.' . . . 'Curtis—Deep pink—most beautiful form and very sweet.' . . . In some situations and in particular seasons it may not be so constant an autumnal bloomer as some of its family, but this defect has rarely come under our notice. To cause it to bloom freely in the autumn recourse must be had to summer pruning, short-ening some of the shoots to half their length; but by making it a general rule to cut long stems to all blooms, a similar result will be produced . . . vigorous habit. . . . It appears from [one] of the above descriptions that its petals are sometimes 'mottled,' but this we have never yet observed." [C] "Fresh rosy pink, very large and very double; form, cupped. Habit, erect; growth, vig-orous. . . . One of the finest of autumnal Roses, although not the freest bloomer. A good seed-bearer." [P] "Luxuriant habits and fine foliage, with flowers of the most perfect shape, and of a delicate roseate hue . . . it will not give autumnal flowers con-stantly in a moist climate, or during a wet period." [WRP] "Pale green leaves." [Hd] "This rose, known for about three years, is very interesting; its foliage is a beautiful fresh green, composed of leaves with five or seven leaflets which are finely dentate and bordered purple when young; canes big, thorny, topped by two or three flowers, which are large, quite double, and with large, notched petals of a very fresh flesh pink, paler at the nub, sta-mens showing at the center. It is the clearest [or "lightest"] color in this class; very fragrant." [An42/332–333] "Branches vigorous, stocky, green, bristling with numerous prickles of varying size, not compressed, enlarged at the base, slender. . . . Foliage fairly ample, more or less reddish in youth, pale green beneath, dark green above, composed of three to five unequal leaflets, ciliate, finely dentate, glandular along the edges. . . . Leafstalks flexuous, of a light green, caniculate above. . . . Stipules long, often very large where adjoining the leafstalk . . . flowers flesh pink, lightly shaded pale violet, very full, large to three or 3.5 in [ca. 7.5–8.75 cm], ordinarily in threes at the summit of the cane. Flower stem very short, fat, upright, very glandular-pilose. . . . Calyx an ob-long tube, contracted at the mouth, very glandular in the lower part. . . . Sepals longly narrowed, then enlarged at the summit, light green and glandular without, white-lanate within. . . . Buds rounded. Petals of the circumference large, slightly concave, up-right, regularly imbricated, those of the center narrow, more or less ruffled, mixed with the stamens. . . . Hips oblong, red . . . a worthy counterpart of 'La Reine' . . . its canes, short but vigorous, upright, and pretty nearly all of the same size, form a large rounded head, entirely covered, during the first bloom, with large and nu-merous open blossoms, perfectly full, of a very fresh color, and opening regularly. Aside from these wonderful qualities, however, it does have a little peccadillo which cannot be hidden. Around the end of each season, the flowers are no longer very full—indeed, they don't have more than two or three rows of petals. . . . The rose 'Duchesse de Sutherland' has many similarities to 'Baronne Prévost': the same deportment, the same growth. But in this lat-ter the foliage is larger and less shiny. . . . It is the product of an unknown cross between a Hybrid China and a Portland." [PIB]

DUKE OF EDINBURGH
W. Paul, 1868
Seedling of 'Général Jacqueminot' (HP).

"Rich velvety fiery crimson-shaded; flowers large and very at-tractive; the best of its line, and perhaps the finest colour." [WD] "Large, full, bright shining orange-scarlet, shaded with carmine, often shaded with maroon, large, full, and very effective . . . one of the best of my seedlings." [P1] "Vermilion crimson . . . not lasting in colour or shape." [F-M2] "Not constant in autumn . . . few [HP's] will do well under our hot [U.S.] sun." [EIC] "Of perfect form. A few blooms may be expected in autumn. Easy to grow." [OM] "Little fragrance; foliage large and attractive. Occasionally this is very fine early in the season, but the flowers lack substance and durability of color. It is more shy in the autumn than ['Général Jacqueminot']; not to be commended for general culture." [EL]

"Most beautiful and useful Rose, always to be found in exhibi-tion stands, and one of those that flower freely in autumn; should be lightly pruned." [DO] "Fair growth; very few blooms; poor fo-liage." [ARA18/115] "Strong good growth and foliage . . . rather apt to run to wood . . . should therefore be lightly pruned . . . seems to stand the extreme . . . temperatures well." [F-M2] "An erect, robust plant . . . 4 × 3 [ft; ca. 1.25 × 1 m]." [B] "A very bright red rose, certainly first-rate and grows well." [HmC] Prince Alfred, Duke of Edinburgh and Saxe-Coburg-Gotha; lived 1844–1900.

DUKE OF WELLINGTON
Listed as 'Duc de Wellington'.

DUPUY-JAMAIN
Dupuy-Jamain, 1868

"Cherry-red, with a shade of crimson; large, double, well-formed, fragrant; a good seed-bearer. Were this more full, it would be a rose of the first rank." [EL] "Brilliant carmine-crimson, colour very fine, petals large, broad, and smooth, flowers well formed, luxuriant foliage . . . vigorous." [JC] "Brilliant cerise, of fine form and substance." [P1] "Round fat smooth blooms . . . centre is weak in hot weather . . . large size but a bad one to last; very free in bloom." [F-M2] "Free-flowering and hardy; good in autumn, especially in cool seasons." [W/Hn] "Of nice fragrance . . . should be lightly pruned." [DO] "Very strong, stiff, stout growth and foliage." [F-M2] "Tidy, well foliated and healthy plant . . . 4 × 3 [ft; ca. 1.25 × 1 m]." [B] "A good Rose." [WD] "French horticulture has lost one of its most trusty servants in the death of Mons Dupuy Jamain, who died May 9 [1888] at the age of 72. He was the founder of one of the oldest horticultural establishments in Paris, and was above all distinguished in arboriculture, in which he stood in the first rank." [JR12/98]

EARL OF DUFFERIN
A. Dickson, 1887

"Velvety-crimson, shaded with maroon, large, full, and finely formed; a continuous bloomer; of vigorous growth, and bushy habit." [P1] "Very large, erect, fine form, bright velvety carmine-red, shaded with deep chestnut-brown. Flowers a long time." [Hn] "Highly-coloured blooms of semi-globular shape, sweet-scented, lasting, sometimes very fine . . . not very free-flowering. . . . I have never had a decent bloom." [F-M2] "Delicious perfume." [JR14/41] "Blossoms need to be tied; late flowering." [DO] "Long but pliable growth . . . must be staked . . . for exhibitors, but not for garden culture." [F-M2]

ÉCLAIR   PLATE 137
(trans., 'Lightning'; syn., 'Gärtendirektor Lauche')
Lacharme, 1883
Seedling of 'Général Jacqueminot' (HP).

"Handsome vermilion red; flower very large, cupped, fra-grant." [Cx] "Of the 'Charles Lefebvre' sort; flower large, well formed, full, bright fiery red; of the greatest merit." [S] "Very dark . . . almost black. Fairly vigorous, free flowering and scented . . . 4 × 2 [ft; ca. 1.25 × 6 dm]." [B] "Vigorous, nice dark green fo-liage, and quite floriferous. The blossoms are medium-sized to large . . . their fragrance is delicious." [JR13/56] "Fine habit. . . . Stems slender with many prickles." [Hn] "At its best one of the very brightest of the crimsons. The growth is good, the form the Cabbage type . . . very good autumnal . . . difficult to get form and colour really good . . . the beginner would do well to avoid it." [F-M2]

ÉLISA BOËLLE
PLATE 112

Guillot père, 1869

Seedling of 'Mme Récamier' (HP).

"White, delicately tinged with pink, medium size, full, beautiful circular form . . . a lovely rose." [EL] "Light rose-red, becoming pure white; free." [Hn] "A vigorous rose with shapely, cupped flowers having incurving petals. Whitish-pink. Highly scented . . . 3 × 3 [ft; ca. 9 × 9 dm]." [B] "Small." [TW] "Moderate vigor." [Cx] "Vigorous and branching, strong enough, smooth stems of a light green, furnished with numerous straight reddish-brown prickles of varying small sizes, which are in rows. The flowers are numerous, large, full, well formed, usually solitary at the ends of the branchlets, sometimes in a cluster of two or three at the end of a particularly strong shoot. White, lightly tinted flesh-pink, passing quickly to pure white. The petals are concave, imbricated." [JR3/8] "Petals in a cup; those in the center, smaller, are crumpled and very numerous, and fill the center of the flower; flower stem fairly long, slender, and nodding. Calyx rounded. This rose, in which the wood is tender and pith-filled, doesn't live long grafted; it is necessary to renew it every two or three years." [JF] "Leaves of 5–7 leaflets, which are oval and finely toothed." [S] "Very pretty." [P1]

EMPEREUR DU MAROC

(trans., 'Emperor of Morocco')

Guinoisseau-Flon, 1858

Seedling of 'Géant des Batailles' (HP).

"Intensely deep crimson and purple, changing to bluish-purple; petals thick, and the flowers of good form, but not large . . . free habit." [JC] "Flowers large, in a cluster of five to ten, bright red, velvety purple passing to blackish red." [JDR58/36] "Large, very full, intense red tinged dark purple." [JR1/2/8] "At a distance, the blossoms appear to be totally black globes." [VH62/98] "Not large, nor perfectly cupped . . . yet they are most beautiful, their colour is so remarkably rich." [R8] "The summits of the petals folding back with so much regularity and grace, are unique and lovely." [P2] "Flattish . . . Rather subject to mildew, and a poor autumnal." [Hn] "Fragrant; moderate vigor." [Cx] "Vigorous, flower large, full, imbricated, in clusters, very full [*again*], opening well, bright velvety red passing to blackish." [I'H58/128] "The most known of roses. . . . To my way of thinking, it burns too much in the sun in our climate [that of Tunisia], capricious growth." [JR34/171] "4 × 3 [ft; ca. 1.25 × 1 m]." [B] "To 5 [ft; ca. 1.5 m]." [HRG] "Very distinct." [P1]

ENFANT DE FRANCE

(trans., 'Child of France')

Lartay, 1860

Not to be confused with Dupont's pink Gallica of 1802, Prévost's pink Gallica of 1835, nor with Vibert's blush Alba of 1830. Somewhere along the line, however, someone *has* become confused:

"Flower large, full; color, violet red." [S] "Pink, edged white, big and full, well foliated, growth strong." [N] "Violet red." [LS] "Huge rose of silvery pink with a satin-like texture. Very full and scented. A beautiful rarity . . . 4 × 3 [ft; ca. 1.25 × 1 m]." [B]

ERINNERUNG AN BROD
PLATE 149

(trans., 'In Remembrance of Brod')

Geschwindt, 1886

From *R. rubifolia* × 'Génie de Châteaubriand' (HP).

"Flower nearly purplish- or violet-blue, most often with a dark red center, large, very full, flat; it is the only rose that approaches true blue, and surpasses 'Reine des Violettes'. . . . Very vigorous,

with pendant branches." [JR10/26] "One of the prettiest 'Hungarian Climbers'. . . . Though the canes don't grow as long as those of the Ayrshires, the Multifloras, and the Sempervirenses, it is nevertheless true that pillars of perhaps eight ft in height [ca. 2.25 m] when planted with this variety produce a superb effect during the flowering season. . . . It is a very vigorous bush covered with handsome dark green foliage, giving many fragrant blossoms in clusters, the flowers being mid-sized or large, flat, blue-maroon or violet, especially in somewhat moist soil; center, darker. . . . The name recalls a town which is in the Austrian province of Carniole." [JR31/156]

EUGENE FÜRST
PLATE 122

(trans., 'Prince Eugene'; syn., 'General Korolkow')

Soupert & Notting, 1875

Seedling of 'Baron de Bonstetten' (HP).

"Crimson-purple . . . considerable size . . . upright plant . . . 4 × 3 [ft; ca. 1.25 × 1 m]." [B] "Very vigorous, with handsome foliage; its large-petaled flowers are large, full, and spendidly colored velvety crimson, shaded glowing purple, the reverse of the petals being dark violet mingled with silvery pink. The very fragrant blossoms are cupped." [JR7/57] "Of good shape." [P1] "A very strong grower with good foliage, liable to orange fungus, and to mildew which appears even on the petals, but not much injured by rain. This is a Rose whose manner it is to waste all its strength upon the wood, and have none to spare to swell the bud. . . . This rose has small blooms on very long shoots . . . comes generally well, of a good dark velvety colour, and nice shape, lasting fairly." [F-M3]

EVEREST

Easlea, 1927

From 'Candeur Lyonnaise' (HP) × 'Mme Caristie Martel' (Pernetiana, Pernet-Ducher, 1916, yellow; parentage unknown).

"Immense blooms of creamy white, sometimes with a decided lemon cast, and they remind me more of a peony than any rose I know . . . little bloom after June." [ARA34/76] "Only a once-bloomer, but . . . well worth growing . . . plants vary from climbinglike growth to dwarfs, producing an abundance of enormous blooms which last for many days . . . likely to ball in wet weather. . . . *Middleton* divides the name in the middle and suggests that we let it Ever Rest." [ARA32/183] "Coarser than 'Frau Karl Druschki' and lacks remontant qualities . . . a little tender in winter . . . a bloom of very fine quality, especially in shape and substance." [ARA31/195]

EXPOSITION DE BRIE-COMTE-ROBERT

Listed as 'Maurice Bernardin'.

FERDINAND DE LESSEPS

Listed as 'Maurice Bernardin'.

FERDINAND PICHARD

Tanne, 1921

"Striped red and pale pink and white . . . fragrant . . . to 2 metres [ca. 6 ft] . . . recurrent." [G] "Double . . . crimson striped on pink background, free-flowering, 5 [ft; ca. 1.5 m]." [HRG] "Luscious foliage . . . 5 × 4 [ft; ca. 1.5 × 1.25 m]." [B]

FISHER HOLMES
E. Verdier, 1865
Possibly a seedling of 'Maurice Bernardin' (HP).

"Rich purplish-crimson, flowers large, cupped, double, and of fine imbricated form." [JC] "Reddish scarlet shaded with deep velvety-crimson, very brilliant, medium size, full, and of good form; growth vigorous." [P1] "Large, full, camellia-like form, brilliant scarlet with deeper shades. A good autumnal. A splendid rose." [Hn] "The blooms come well, of . . . good pointed shape . . . and the shape is lasting, though the brightness soon fades." [F-M2] "High-centred." [S] "Perhaps the prettiest rose in the reds, a color so numerous in the HP's; the blossom is large, globular, full, and imbricated, with slender petals which are a very brilliant scarlet red. The bush is vigorous and abundantly floriferous." [JR17/102] "Requires careful disbudding." [DO] "Sheer beauty. Smaller than most of the Hybrid Perpetuals, it is the brightest." [ARA29/49] "An improved 'Général Jacqueminot'; the flowers are fuller and more freely produced . . . very valuable." [EL] "Quite one of the best of the Hybrid Perpetuals. . . . This variety flowers again in autumn. Seems to thrive best as a standard. In bush form growth is often poor." [OM] "Good growth and foliage. Particularly liable to mildew." [F-M2] "Shapely bud. . . . Healthy . . . 4 × 3 [ft; ca. 1.25 × 1 m]." [B] "Excellent for pegging down." [WD] "Its beautifully shaped and exquisitely fragrant blooms of dark velvety reddish crimson are regally magnificent." [ARA34/78]

FORTUNÉ BESSON
Listed as 'Georg Arends'.

FRANÇOIS MICHELON
Levet, 1871
Seedling of 'La Reine' (HP).

"Fine deep rose, reverse of petals silvery-white, flowers large and full; habit vigorous." [JC] "Well-formed; color, very lively cerise-red with ashy shadings." [S] "Deep rose, tinged with lilac, very large, full, of fine, globular form; fragrant, free-blooming. The wood and foliage are light-green, erect habit, thorns not numerous, wood long-jointed, the foliage somewhat crimpled. A very distinct choice sort; excelling in June and July, when other kinds are past their prime, and also in the autumn." [EL] "Blooms come fairly well, but the centre though almost always well covered has seldom a defined point and is sometimes irregular. The outline is often rough and the colour is not lasting. It cannot be called a free bloomer." [F-M2] "One of the finest Roses for exhibition." [WD] "Green slender yet fairly stiff stems, and thin poor foliage . . . requires . . . a cool season, and generous treatment." [F-M2] "Little affected by mildew. Do not prune as much as the average." [Th2] "Exceedingly fine." [DO]

FRAU KARL DRUSCHKI   PLATE 169
('Schneekönigen', 'Reine des Neiges', 'Mme Charles Druschki', 'Druschki')
Lambert, 1901
From 'Merveille de Lyon' (HP) × 'Mme Caroline Testout' (HT).

"A white HP with the form and size of 'Charles Lefebvre' or 'Marie Baumann' would be a true Koh-i-noor among Roses." (1879) [JR3/170] "For a long time, rose growers have sought to develop a rose which was both remontant and completely white. Such a desirable variety has at last made its appearance. . . . It is a vigorous variety, robust and very hardy, and covered with handsome foliage; the blossoms are solitary but numerous, and what is more they are borne on long, strong stems. They are snow white, and of a firm consistency which allows them to stay

fresh for a long time, thus resisting bad weather better than any other white variety. This rose is very remontant, but the main bloom is in June–July." [JR25/20] "Snowy white, of large size, and beautiful form. Extra fine in bud; growth vigorous; thoroughly perpetual. An excellent addition to this group." [P1] "Pure white; flower large, full, cupped; very floriferous." [Cx] "Shell-shaped petals; flowers with a high pointed centre; large, free, and a good grower." [DO] "Now and then there is a flower with a faint violet perfume." [NRS12/93] "An abundant bloomer, and a good autumnal . . . will not hold their shape very long in hot weather." [F-M] "Most admired white in bloom [of all whites in Houston, Texas]." [ET] "Does well here [in Mexico] too!" [VD] "Gives freely of its symmetrical blooms." [E] "50 to 129 blooms per season." [ARA21/90] "Indispensible . . . a splendid June bloom . . . also a fine fall display." [ARA34/76] "I do not like 'Frau Karl'; she has very little scent or none; mere giganticness as such, makes no appeal to me; and her flowers are the colour of inferior type-writing paper, and make me feel chilly with the thin deadness of their white." [Fa] "Very vigorous growth, shoots running up to 5-ft. [ca. 1.5 m] and from maidens at times to 10-ft. [ca. 3 m]. Foliage dark green, but unfortunately liable to mildew . . . it is one of the most continuous bloomers among the HP's . . . this beautiful Rose is Queen of the white Roses." [NRS/10] "Foliage is large and dark . . . to 7 ft [ca. 2 m]." [W] "Beautiful light green foliage." [Th] "Upright bush . . . 6 × 4 [ft; ca. 1.75 × 1.25 m]." [B] "Finest, least troublesome, and most vigorous." [PS] "Dedicated to the wife of the general superintendent of the great Spæth nurseries in Berlin, herself a noted horticulturalist." [K] "Karl Druschki, businessman [in] Gorlitz." [JR12/109] "Still the best white rose." [OM]

GÄRTENDIREKTOR LAUCHE
Listed as 'Éclair'.

GÉANT DES BATAILLES
(trans., 'Battle-Giant')
Nérard/Guillot père, 1846

"Sparkling red, changing to dark lilac." [BJ] "Crimson, shaded with purple; form expanded; growth vigorous." [P1] "Very good fragrance." [LR] "Still one of the best and most constant flowering roses grown; habit free and good." [JC] "Deep, fiery crimson, very brilliant and rich when first opening, but quickly fades, medium or small size, full, well formed, handsome, Bourbon-like foliage, very liable to mildew . . . of delicate constitution." [EL] "Perhaps no rose among the Hybrid Perpetuals has been so famous, and so much praised . . . but we cannot fully echo the commendations . . . requires more skill and precaution for successful culture . . . more or less liable to mildew . . . by no means of . . . vigorous growth. . . . Its flowers, however, are very brilliant, and, in a favorable season, are produced in abundance. In color, they resemble those of 'Général Jacqueminot'." [FP] "Doubtless has Bourbon blood in its veins." [EIC] "Supposed . . . to be nearly related to that very brilliant Rose, 'Gloire des Rosomanes'. . . . Rivers in C.

GÉNÉRAL JACQUEMINOT
Roussel/Rousselet, 1853
Seedling of 'Gloire des Rosomanes' (B).
Not to be confused with Laffay's 1846 HCh of the same name and color.

"Crimson." [E] "Large, full, dark purple shaded bright crimson." [JR9/163] "A dark red, and a model in shape." [WHoIII] "Loose, flimsy, and often washy in colour." [P2] "Large, globular, dazzling red, velvety, very abundant." [JR1/2/7] "Of a fine crimson, and, though not perfectly double, is, nevertheless, one of the most splendid of roses. Its size, under good cultures, is immense. It is a strong grower and abundant bloomer, and glows like a firebrand among the paler hues around it. It is one of the hardier kinds, and is easily managed. Its offspring are innumerable." [FP] "Luxuriant growth and magnificent clusters of flowers . . . its large crimson flowers are not so full and perfect in shape." [R8] "Large, well-formed blooms." [OM] "Exquisite in its dazzling brightness." [Ed] "Produces here [the Riviera] flowers of great splendour, but they are very jealous of the sun, which quickly turns the lovely crimson into a false mauve, and gives the petals an appearance of being par-boiled." [B&V] "Elegant fragrance." [LR] "Very fragrant buds of scarlet-crimson, opening into moderate-sized, clear red flowers of fine shape . . . of strong, bushy growth; often blooms the second time in fall." [ARA34/78] "One of our new Roses, and most striking, from the size of its flowers, which are of rich shaded crimson. It has, however, two faults—its flowers are not sufficiently double, and its habit of growth is rather slender and delicate." [HstX:84] "A strong grower, and when in bud, one of the most beautiful of roses. Its open flower, not being perfectly double, is surpassed by others. Its color is a scarlet crimson, with a soft velvety sheen, and a few thousand of them in full bloom is a sight to be remembered." [SBP] "Very free-flowering, fragrant, and a good autumnal, but decidedly thin . . . not lasting or of the largest size." [F-M2] "Gives single flowers [in Havana]." [JR6/44] "[Very satisfactory in Brazil]." [PS] "[Does] not get wide enough awake to give us a blossom even in the spring." [ET] "[Reblooms] some in fall *if* old flowers are removed . . . 4 to 7 ft [ca. 1.25–2 m]." [W] "The flowers standing high and clear above the plant, rendering it very conspicuous." [HstXXVI:331] "Flower to four in across [ca. 1 dm], nearly full, globular, solitary or in clusters of two or three on vigorous branches . . . outer petals large and closely packed, those of the center smaller and shorter; flower stem slender, slightly nodding. Calyx rounded; sepals leaf-like." [JF] "Good but rather slender growth and fine but thin foliage; liable to mildew." [F-M2] "Rich green foliage . . . 4 × 3 [ft; ca. 1.25 × 1 m]." [B] "To 6 [ft; ca. 1.75 m]." [HRG] "For bush, pillar, or standard, it is scarcely surpassed." [WD]

"Vigorous growth, with large sparkling velvety red flowers which are nearly full, globular, large (8–10 cm [ca. 4 in]). This plant, because of the abundance of its flowers and the richness of its coloration, will ornament the most beautiful collections; it was put into commerce by Mons Rousselet, gardener at Meudon, near Paris. The jury of the Versailles Exhibition gave it First Prize." [l'H53/242–243] "This magnificent flower, known by all rosarians, is found in all the best collections. Much grown for selling the bud. . . . Growth, vigorous; the branches are slender and divergent; the bark is green, bristling with numerous prickles, which are unequal, short, and pointed; leaves are a somber green, pointed and finely toothed. Profuse flowering in the summer, with good repeat in the fall." [S] "An amateur, Mons Roussel, of Meudon, having gotten nothing from the various sowings he had made, left their result at his death to his gardener Rousselet, who the following year discovered among them this rose of the first order . . . of the most elegant bearing and the most vivid shadings." [JF] "An old Rose, but one still able to carry off medals." [DO] "A free and responsive garden rose, blooming in great splendour for six weeks in spring and early summer. No rose can altogether take its place." [Dr] "Named for a French general of the early Nineteenth Century and founder of a famous brewery of Paris still in existence today [1938]." [K]

GÉNÉRAL KOROLKOW

Listed as 'Eugene Fürst'.

GÉNÉRAL WASHINGTON

Granger, 1860

Sport of 'Triomphe de l'Exposition' (HP).

Not to be confused with Page's red Tea of 1855.

"Red, shaded with crimson, large, very full, flat form; the flowers are often malformed, greatly lessening its value. A profuse bloomer, and when in perfection, a very fine sort." [EL] "Bright rosy red flowers of large size and full . . . sometimes splendid, but uncertain." [P2] "An HP *par excellence*, covered—above all, in the fall—with magnificent blossoms of a light red inclining towards amaranth; it is a model in form." [VH62/98] "Very full, brilliant red blooms . . . very free flowering . . . 3 [ft; ca. 9 dm]." [HRG] "Loses something of its brilliant coloration before it is completely open." [JR25/103] "One of the finest of its class. It is a good grower, very full bloomer, and a general favorite." [SBP] "Fairly vigorous; branches weak; flower very large, strongly built, quite full, expanded form." [S] "It is a new rose; but there can be little doubt of its merit." [FP]

GEORG ARENDS

('Fortuné Besson')

Hinner, 1910

From 'Frau Karl Druschki' (HP) × 'La France' (HT).

"A marshmallow pink shade hinting at the slight lilac shading found in 'La France'. A splendid grower flowering with me in the shade both early and late." [RP] "Produces its flowers singly on the branches, of a handsome pink color. What is more, it also has the advantage of possessing an exquisite perfume like that of a Centifolia." [JR34/104] "The same vigor as 'Druschki'; flower, very large, pure pink, color unchanging; stem, upright. . . . Of the greatest merit." [JR34/182] "Perfect in shape, enormous in size, and sweetly fragrant." [ARA29/49] "Considered by many the most beautiful unshaded pink rose in existence. . . . It blooms quite steadily, but not freely, practically all season, on a strong-growing plant that is rather tender for this class." [ARA34/77] "[For] everywhere. . . . Foliage mildews . . . periods of no bloom but gives plenty in bursts through entire season. Used as a semi-climber it does much finer than as a bush." [Capt28] "Color and fragrance [make] up for ugly habit of growth." [PS] "Better than most as a fall bloomer." [Th2] "Vigorous, healthy plant . . . 4 × 3 [ft; ca. 1.25 × 1 m]." [B] "Originated by a French hybridist [*Mons Besson, doubtless*] but renamed by a German nurseryman, Hinner. The true name of this rose is 'Fortuné Besson'." [K]

GEORGE DICKSON

A. Dickson, 1912

"Deep velvety crimson, heavily veined." [NRS/14] "Indeed a wonderful flower, very large, full, and perfect in shape . . . flowers freely, nearly every flower being perfect . . . it hangs its head owing to the size and weight of the flower." [NRS/14] "Great, double, fragrant blooms of rich, dark, gleaming red." [ARA29/96] "Heavy fleshy petals." [ARA21/66] "The best rose we ever raised [at Dickson & Sons] . . . bears the name of the oldest member of our family, who is nearing 80. . . . It has an exquisite Tea scent . . . its color is a dark velvety red; the underside of the petals is veined blackish-red . . . For the last show, we had flowers nearly five in [ca. 1.25 dm] across!" [JR35/90] "[For the] interior with heat. . . . Not advised in seacoast climates. Does best leaning on a fence." [Capt28] "Has characteristics of Hybrid Perpetual. . . . Growth and color good; form not of best . . . lacking in number of blooms . . . mildews badly." [ARA18/116] "The plant grows well and bears fragrant, finely formed blooms of deep crimson colouring. It is apparently valuable alike for garden and exhibition." [OM] "It is acknowledged by the originators and everybody else that as a garden rose (decorative or bedding) 'George Dickson' is worthless." [K] "One perfect bloom would pay for a year's waiting." [ARA29/49]

GERMANIA
Listed as 'Gloire de Ducher'.

GLOIRE DE CHÉDANE-GUINOISSEAU
Chédane-Pajotin, 1907
Seedling of 'Gloire de Ducher' (HP).

"Beautiful bright crimson blooms of delicate fragrance, and fades less in heat than most roses . . . blooms over a long season on a healthy, vigorous plant." [ARA34/78] "Gave some fine large blooms early in July, but has not flowered since." [NRS14/159] "A deep crimson rose of real quality, has an unusually good plant." [ARA29/49] "Very vigorous, erect, thorny, ample foliage, leaves dark green; magnificent very long bud, nearly always solitary, strong flower-stem; superb flower, cupped, very large, very full, of perfect form, with large rounded petals; opens slowly and well in all conditions; color, very intense vermilion red, sometimes velvety and of very beautiful appearance. This variety in which the flowers easily attain six in [ca. 1.5 dm] or more in width is expected to be much used for pot-culture." [JR31/150] "Growth is fairly vigorous, but the blooms are not freely produced." [OM] "Floriferous." [Cx] "Good foliage, growth, and stem." [Th2]

GLOIRE DE BRUXELLES
Listed as 'Gloire de l'Exposition de Bruxelles'.

GLOIRE DE DUCHER   PLATE 107
('Germania')
Ducher, 1865

"Maroon at the center, shaded slate-violet around the edges; flower large, flat, somewhat imbricated." [Cx] "Crimson-purple, large, very full, subject to mildew. If the color were permanent, this would be a good kind." [EL] "Well formed, dull purple." [JR1/2/8] "Appeals through its handsome maroon-violet color." [JR32/34] "Red to maroon with paler reverse, double flowers on arching canes to 7 [ft; ca. 2 m]." [HRG] "Borne abundantly . . . vigorous . . . 6 × 5 [ft; ca. 1.75 × 1.5 m]." [B] "Branches strong, divergent . . . foliage ample, dark green." [S] "Calyx pear-shaped." [JF] "Its branches are quite strong, with light reddish bark. The thorns, brownish red, are unequal and slightly hooked. The blossoms of this beautiful variety, which are four or so in[ches] in diameter [ca. 1 dm+], are of the expanded form, solitary or sometimes clustered in twos or threes. The color is purplish red, 'bluing' at the edge. The petals are very large, while the stem is long and firm, holding the blossom well. It is a variety of much merit." [JR5/104]

GLOIRE DE L'EXPOSITION DE BRUXELLES
Soupert & Notting, 1889
From 'Souvenir de William Wood' (HP) × 'Lord Macaulay' (HP).

"Deep velvety purplish amaranth, almost black, base of petals fiery red; large, full, and very sweet." [P1] "Very vigorous, handsome foliage; flower . . . of good form . . . reverse of the petals wine red; very fragrant." [JR13/147] "Very large flowers of 60 or more petals of velvety crimson to purple in colour. Highly scented and upright in growth . . . 4 × 3 [ft; ca. 1.25 × 1 m]." [B]

GLOIRE D'UN ENFANT D'HIRAM   PLATE 167
Vilin, 1899
Seedling of 'Ulrich Brunner fils' (HP).

"Red, shaded." [LS] "Planted outside, in the garden, it will figure in the top rank of good roses due to its abundant bloom and resemblance to 'Ulrich Brunner fils' in all characteristics. . . . One of its great advantages is that the cupped blossom is very sturdy; when the blossom opens out, it doesn't change color. . . . The bush is vigorous, and very floriferous; the medium or large flowers, full and fragrant, are vermilion red lightly touched carmine, and shaded a velvety violet. It is dedicated to a Masonic society of Melun: *The Children of Hiram*, taking its name from the famous architect of Tyre, who constructed the first Temple of Jerusalem in 985 BC." [JR24/120]

GLOIRE LYONNAISE   PLATE 141
Guillot fils, 1884
Third generation of a cross between 'Baronne Adolphe de Rothschild' (HP) and 'Mme Falcot' (T).

"Lightly creamy white; flower large, full, cupped; floriferous." [Cx] "Tea-scented, lemon-coloured, with pretty buds." [HRH] "Medium-sized, tinted light yellow and largely bordered in white." [JR10/46] "White, tinted yellow-fawn; large, but somewhat flat; slight tea perfume; only one blooming period in the East. Never sets seed-hips, and generally has been considered sterile. Foliage remarkably fine and lasting." [Th2] "[For] seacoast districts; very hardy. . . . In California it blooms well and over a long season, but comes in bursts; foliage immune to disease." [Capt28] "Much to be recommended for its great vigor, the beauty of its foliage, and the size of its flowers." [JR30/17] "Small to medium-sized flowers." [ARA17/29] "Practically white, the yellow shade being very faint. Of very strong growth, even in poor soil, not liking clay land. . . . The buds are beautiful, but the petals are very thin, and it will not stand in hot weather. Not free-flowering if pruned hard, but capital in autumn, when fine well-shaped blooms may sometimes be gathered." [F-M3] "Very vigorous, strong and upright branches, purplish and smooth; thorns somewhat numerous, straight and strong; leaves composed of 5–7 leaflets, with prominent purplish serrations; flowers very large, full, very well formed, with large firm petals, well held, and a fragrance of Tea roses, which the blossom also resembles in shape; the color is a nice chrome yellow, with the edges of the petals pretty much gone towards icy white; the flowers are solitary." [JR8/133] "Often surpasses three ft [ca. 1 m]. . . . In June I have seen this variety to blossom exceptionally well while others were depleted by poor conditions. To be fully remontant, this plant needs to be cut long." [JR10/155] "The leaves have a distinct fragrance." [Ro] "A good grower, and evergreen; does not care for a too strong soil. Nothing in the rose world much finer than really good examples of this rose, an opinion shared alas! by the rose bugs who are greatly attracted by these beautiful flowers. Resembles a Tea Rose both in form and fragrance." [B&V] "Of queenly form and bearing." [Dr] "Good and distinct." [J]

GRAND MOGUL
Listed as 'Jean Soupert'.

HANS MACKART
E. Verdier, 1884

"Cinnabar scarlet." [JR20/5] "Vigorous with long branches, which are reddish green; numerous thorns, which are unequal, recurved, fine, and brown; leaves of 3–5 leaflets, quite rounded dark green with irregular dentation, fairly deep-set; flower stem very long; blossom of medium size, full, with fine petals; color, very bright scarlet red; very remontant." [JR8/165]

HEINRICH MÜNCH

Hinner/Münch & Haufe, 1911

From 'Frau Karl Druschki' (HP) × a seedling resulting from 'Mme Caroline Testout' (HT) × 'Mrs. W. J. Grant' (HT).

"Mons Heinrich Münch, of Münch & Haufe, at Leuben near Dresden, has discovered a pink-flowered 'Druschki'." [JR35/118] "The growth is quite as vigorous as that of 'Druschki', a little less thorny, and covered with soft green foliage. The buds are round though pointed, and are borne on long and upright stems; they come singly, and open slowly but nevertheless easily. The large full flowers are as pretty a silvery pink as one might imagine; they stay half open for a long time. . . . One of their salient qualities is that the petals, expanded around the perimeter, nevertheless clothe the heart of the blossom much in the way of 'La France', while having a softer color which is more elegant and more pleasing to the eye." [JR35/106] "The flowers are large and firm and the bud is magnificent; as it opens the petals curl over in the manner of a 'La France'. The flowers are a deep pink, with a sheen not often found." [C&Js15] "Not a good bloomer." [ARA18/116]

HEINRICH SCHULTHEIS

Bennett, 1882

From 'Mabel Morrison' (HP) × 'E.Y. Teas' (HP).

"Delicate pinkish rose, large, full, and sweet." [P1] "Well-formed, of a very clean pink." [JR11/50] "Pinkish-rose, bright in colour, but apt to go off when expanded. Very fragrant." [DO] "Early and free bloomer, and a good autumnal . . . large handsome petals . . . beautiful shape and color when young, but soon loses both." [F-M2] "Large but shapely. Fragrant. Soft pink. . . . Vigorous . . . 4 × 3 [ft; ca. 1.25 × 1 m]." [B] "Capital growth and fine foliage. . . . Not liable to mildew or injury from rain and does well in America." [F-M2] "Much appreciated in England." [JR11/2] "Excellent exhibition variety." [S]

HENRY NEVARD

F. Cant, 1924

"A deep red Rose with large, perfect blooms of old-fashioned form and exhilarating perfume, nesting in a tuft of verdant foliage. If pruned short in the spring and the blooms picked with long stems, it will be an almost continuous bloomer. Sometimes mildews in late autumn; is worth protecting." [C-Ps29] "Massive, intensely fragrant . . . gorgeous dark red, but of only fair growth and once-blooming." [ARA30/170–171] "Very fine and [blooms] quite recurrently." [ARA31/118] "The finest production in the red Hybrid Perpetual class, to date . . . very healthy . . . finely-formed, very fragrant, crimson-scarlet blooms with a greater continuity than any other red Hybrid Perpetual, being almost as free as a Hybrid Tea in this respect." [ARA34/79] "Good-sized crimson-scarlet blooms of splendid fragrance on a moderately vigorous plant. Continuous. . . . Slight mildew; bad black-spot . . . bore 36 blooms." [PP28] "Bud very large, ovoid; flower very large, very double, full, very lasting, strong fragrance . . . borne singly on a long stem. Foliage abundant, large, dark green, leathery. Many thorns. Vigorous, bushy, compact; continuous bloomer from May to December." [ARA25/184] "A good everblooming red rose on a Hybrid Perpetual plant." [ARA29/49]

HER MAJESTY

Bennett, 1885

From 'Mabel Morrison' (HP) × 'Canari' (T).

"Light pink . . . very full, enormous (six in) [ca. 1.5 dm], with thick, ponderous petals and a perfectly symmetrical form." [JR10/39] "Huge blooms of clear rose pink with deeper flecks towards the center. Not the most healthy . . . but very beautiful . . . 3 × 3 [ft; ca. 9 × 9 dm]." [B] "Pale rose; vigorous upright habit. Flowers very large . . . late-flowering . . . scentless." [J] "Without contradiction, the biggest of roses." [JR30/18] "The largest rose next to 'Paul Neyron'." [Hn] "Clear and bright satiny rose, very large and full; petals most symmetrically arranged, foliage handsome. . . . An extraordinary rose, but unfortunately very liable to mildew." [P1] "The leaves have the glossiness of those of the Teas." [S] "Very robust, having uniquely strong wood." [JR5/22] "Manners and customs are notoriously strict and exacting in royal circles, and in this remarkable Rose we certainly have some striking peculiarities. Of long, strong and yet robust growth if well fed, but by no means free: it makes extraordinary growth under favourable conditions, but a poor show if not treated regally and favoured with queen's weather [*Victorian weather had a knack of clearing up whenever Queen Victoria was to appear*]. Prune high or low you will get but few shoots to a plant, and if the single growth of a maiden shoot be stopped, instead of breaking [*i.e., branching out*] in several places like the vulgar herd, 'Her Majesty' generally shoots only from the top bud left, and continues one stem upwards as before. We may place the plants close together, for the stems of each are few in number and upright and stiff. It has fine foliage and large stems with tremendous thorns, the whole being extremely and notoriously subject to mildew, so that it is best planted by itself or among the Teas, where the infection will be less dangerous in the summer season. It is a very slow starter in growth if pruned hard, and as it is advisable to get the blooms as early as possible before the plant is crippled with the inevitable mildew, this Rose alone of all may, with possible advantage, be pruned in the Autumn, as it will still not start growth early enough to be injured by frost. Better still perhaps is to leave it so long in pruning as to get a plump and well developed bud for the coming shoot. If grown well, a large proportion of the blooms come good, and they can stand a little rain They have fine stout petals, and are wonderfully full in the centre, so much so that the Rose has quite two shapes, and the best one was not known for the first year or two: for it has in the first stage a grand regular semi-globular shape, and when expanded and overblown it is yet so perfectly full, even when flat as a pancake, as to show no eye, and to be still presentable and wonderful, though not so beautiful as a Rose. The colour is best and purest in the first of these stages: in the second it is more mixed. . . . When presented for the Gold Medal, which was granted by acclamation, it was shown by Mr. Bennett in great quantity, several large boxes of it being staged. Every bloom was fully expanded, and its true beauty remained unknown. It was then sold to America and we had to wait a year for it. When it was at last obtainable, there was a large demand for the half-guinea plants, with the result I believe that there was hardly a bloom seen in the country that year, the plants having no doubt been budded from non-flowering shoots. The following year the true form was seen, and it is not now quite so shy a bloomer as it was. In size and lasting qualities it is quite at the top of the tree: as a free bloomer and autumnal, absolutely at the bottom. A secondary or true autumnal bloom is rare: it does bloom as a maiden, otherwise its title to the term Perpetual might yet be in abeyance. It is decidedly a hot-season Rose with us, and is very highly esteemed in America, for a valued correspondent in Philadelphia calls it 'The Queen of all the Roses' and tells me he has had eleven very fine blooms from one plant. It is, however, liable to be killed outright by the very severe winters of that latitude, unless protected, and is therefore even more highly valued in southern and warmer districts of U.S.A., as Florida. A remarkable point about this Rose is its reputed parentage; for it is said, though it is generally supposed there must have been some mistake or accident [*Mendelian genetics not being perfectly understood by most rosarians of the day*], to be a seedling from the old Tea 'Canary', a yellow flimsy thing according to modern notions, and 'Mabel Morrison', a white sport from 'Baroness Rothschild', which is particularly open and deficient in the centre. If this is so, it should strictly be called a Hybrid Tea. Mr. Bennett was one of the first to practice hybridising in this country, and sent out his new issues as Pedigree Roses: but one would think that on beholding the illustrious progeny of this apparently ill assorted pair he must have been inclined to consider chance as likely to be successful as the careful choosing of seed-parents." [F-M2]

"It could be considered that this colossal flower is not only the best rose of its color, but that it is also the best introduction to this day." [JR10/148]

HIPPOLYTE JAMAIN

Lacharme, 1874

Seedling of 'Victor Verdier' (HP).

Not to be confused with the similarly colored Faudon HP of 1870, which was globular; nor with the maroon Bourbon of 1856 by Pradel; nor with the light pink 1871 HP by Garçon/Jamain '*Mme Hippolyte Jamain*'.

"Intense red; flower very large, cupped." [Cx] "Full, expanded form, well held; one of the best seedlings of the breeder, who has given rosarians a great number of roses, always appreciated and much admired. Color, bright pink, shaded carmine." [S] "Carmine-rose . . . vigorous habit . . . good strong growth . . . with fine foliage." [HstXXX:236] "Carmine-red, well-built flowers; the foliage when young has a deeper shade of red than is seen in any other sort, and is also the handsomest." [EL]

HORACE VERNET

Guillot fils, 1866

Seedling of 'Général Jacqueminot' (HP).

"Rich brilliant velvety crimson, petals large and smooth, flowers large, full, and most perfectly imbricated; a truly superb rose." [JC] "Large, fairly well-filled, half cup-shaped, velvety carmine; strong-growing, free-flowering, fragrant." [Hn] "Beautiful velvety purplish red, shaded with dark crimson . . . growth moderate." [P1] "Crimson, illumined with scarlet . . . beautiful wavy outline; nearly smooth wood, of delicate constitution. Few roses have such a lovely form as this." [EL] "A typical show Rose; grand . . . on the exhibition table . . . but to be avoided . . . for ordinary garden purposes. . . . Blooms are large . . . stoutest of petals . . . capital centre, perfect shape . . . good dark colour, and lasting. . . . Not a free bloomer." [F-M2] "Very fragrant, high centred, rich crimson. . . . Tidy, well-foliated . . . 4 × 3 [ft; ca. 1.25 × 1 m]." [B] "Growth moderate. . . . By no means an easy Rose to grow in many localities." [J] "Weak constitution . . . plant is almost sure to dwindle . . . not very liable to mildew." [F-M2] "A perfect exhibition variety, and indispensible to those who grow for show." [OM] "Hundreds of gardeners and rosarians, who would otherwise never have heard of the great French artist, have had his name 'familiar in their mouths as household words' by the help of this most noble Rose." [F-M2]

HUGH DICKSON

H. Dickson, 1905

From 'Lord Bacon' (HP) × 'Gruss an Teplitz' (B).

"A good crimson shaded scarlet . . . very fragrant." [F-M] "Large, quite full, well held, of perfect form, dark red; very beautiful." [JR31/178] "High-pointed centre." [DO] "Thoroughly satisfactory in every respect, and keeps its colour in the sun better than most crimsons do." [NRS/14] "Gives bloom off and on during the summer in southern California seacoast. Best on a leaning fence. Fair growth and foliage, with cutting value." [Capt28] "Flowers borne quite continuously on a plant almost rivaling 'Druschki' in growth." [ARA34/79] "Considered the finest autumn bloomer of all roses." [Dr] "Very vigorous, free from mildew . . . in the front rank." [F-M] "Strong, thick shoots, which are often six to eight ft long [ca. 1.75–2.25 m]." [OM] "More fitted for pillars than for growing as bushes." [NRS/17] "Young foliage is very beautiful, and carried well above the leaves. The perfume is delightful. . . . It is not mildew proof, neither is it especially troublesome in this respect. . . . The flowers stand wet well." [NRS/13] "Strong erect shoots four to five ft in height [ca. 1.25–1.5 m], which later in the season become rather straggling. . . . The foliage is good, at first red, then green with a bronze tinge becoming green in autumn, indicating a connexion with the HT's . . . not specially free-flowering. The flowers are carried erect on long stems but full flowers are inclined to droop. It has large firm rounded petals of considerable substance of a fine crimson colour slightly tinged with scarlet which never turns purple. The flowers last well when cut and are very fragrant . . . one of the most reliable of the red exhibition Roses." [NRS/10] "The finest of all the Hybrid Perpetuals, and a rose that should be in every garden in the country." [OM]

J.B. CLARK

H. Dickson, 1905

From 'Lord Bacon' (HP) × 'Gruss an Teplitz' (B).

"Dark scarlet shaded blackish crimson; flower very large, very full; very floriferous; very vigorous." [Cx] "Deep scarlet, shaded plum." [NRS/10] "In full sun the color bleaches. Averages 80 blooms." [ARA21/90] "Fragrant." [ARA17/29] "A wonderful pillar rose, growing twelve to fifteen ft [ca. 3.5–4.5 m] and producing hundreds of handsome flowers. Its color is much better in partial shade." [ARA23/64] "More fitted for pillars than for growing as bushes." [NRS/17] "Does well when left to grow at will." [NRS/14] "A positive nuisance — there is no keeping it within bounds." [NRS/12] "Has fine bold foliage and makes huge growth of stiff upright very thorny stems, eight to twelve ft long [ca. 2.25–3.5 m] when growing well. It flowers very freely and for a long time at each flowering. . . . The flowers are large and rather coarse, generally fairly well shaped and pointed, sometimes beautiful. The colour is very variable. At times it is a washed out crimson-scarlet, at others a fine shade of that colour, especially when young. Very rarely the flowers are covered with a plum coloured bloom like a bunch of grapes, and then they are a magnificent colour. . . . It is not troubled with mildew." [NRS/12] "[Among the only HP's] that pay their board bills [in Texas]." [ET] "The best red rose I ever saw." [ARA25/113]

JEAN LIABAUD   PLATE 123

Liabaud, 1875

Seedling of 'Baron de Bonstetten' (HP).

"Fiery crimson, centre rich velvety-crimson, flowers large, double, and well formed." [JC] "Crimson-maroon, illumined with scarlet, large, full; a lovely rose, but shy in the autumn." [EL] "Rich crimson, shaded violet and maroon." [WD] "Does not 'blue'.

Flower large, full, cupped, fragrant." [Cx] "Of fair growth and foliage, not liable to mildew or injury from rain. A free bloomer, but a poor autumnal, and a Rose of shocking manners. Occasionally one gets a lovely bloom, of open imbricated shape, not strong in the centre, but shaded in the most beautiful way with all sorts of tints from vermilion to the deepest crimson or maroon. But if you get one such in the course of a year from a dozen plants, you will be pretty lucky, for most of the flowers come distorted in all sorts of ways." [F-M3] "Of good stature and growth." [JR3/120] "Growth not good; poor bloomer." [ARA18/116] "Vigorous and floriferous, but not continuous." [JR10/29] "French horticulture has lost one of its most estimable veterans in the person of Mons Jean Liabaud, senior horticulturalist at La Croix-Rousse, near Lyon (Rhone), who died last January 14th [1904] at the age of 90. Mons Liabaud, officer of the Agricultural Order of Merit, vice president of the Society of Applied Horticulture of the Rhone, member of the Pomological Society of France, and member as well of the Lyon Horticultural Association, was a self-made man. It is just tribute to his intelligence, energy, and work that he was able to attain a proper renown throughout French horticulture. . . . 'Our colleague was born April 18, 1814, at Volesures, Paray-le-Monial (Seine-et-Loire). Son of a laborer and orphaned at the age of 12, he found a place at that time with a great agricultor, Mons Dujonchet . . . where he stayed until 1831. [*After learning his trade at various locations,*] he began to work as chief gardener . . . for the Marquis de Tournon, with whom he remained until 1844. . . . After this . . . he decided to go into business for himself, and it was Lyon . . . which saw him succeed Mons Mille, horticulturalist, whose operation he transformed. . . . ' All know the handsome old man, tall, patriarchal, energetic, strong, gaunt and angular, hair and beard completely framing his face, from which shone bright and perceptive eyes. Loved by all, he would animate meetings with his verve and jollity." [JR28/24−26]

JEAN ROSENKRANTZ
Portemer fils, 1864
Seedling of 'Victor Verdier' (HP).

"Very brilliant coral-red; flower large, full." [S] "Rich rosy-crimson, flowers large and globular, a beautiful rose, with fine, handsome foliage." [JC] "Large flowers neatly formed of pinkish-red petals on an upright, vigorous plant . . . 4 × 3 [ft; ca. 1.25 × 1 m]." [B]

JEAN SOUPERT   PLATE 124
('Grand Mogul'?)
Lacharme, 1875
From 'Charles Lefebvre' (HP) × 'Souvenir du Baron de Sémur' (HP).

"Plum purple, almost black, flowers good size and evenly formed; a superb dark rose." [JC] "Carmine crimson, shaded with fiery scarlet and black, large, full, expanded; very free and sweet." [P1] "Crimson-maroon, in the way of 'Jean Liabaud'; dark green foliage, with many thorns; not free in the autumn." [EL] "The foliage is fair and the growth good, but characteristic and peculiar. One or two shoots run away considerably above the others and give promise of good blooms, and when the bud forms it is of very good typical shape and seldom comes cracked or divided; but now, when you expect the plant to put all its strength into the bud, it does not do so; the stem thickens at the base, and tempting buds for budding form all up the stem, but the flower buds swell very little, although they open slowly. The bloom, though sometimes of fair average size, is smaller and weaker than one would expect from the size of the shoot, but the shape is quite first class, with a round smooth button in the centre, the petals perfectly imbricated,

and the outline regular. It is quite one of the three or four best examples of the imbricated form among H.P.'s. The bloom is not very lasting, the colour, though striking in its very deep shade, is sometimes rather dull, and it cannot be called a free bloomer or reckoned as a good autumnal. Decidedly liable to mildew, which sometimes affects the petals. A late bloomer, which is well worth growing if only for its thoroughly distinct appearance in many particulars." [F-M2] "One of the greatest rosarians in the world . . . Jean Soupert, died last July 16th [1910] at the age of 76. With him disappears one of the great figures of rosedom. . . . Born February 19, 1834, in the environs of Luxembourg, Soupert, still quite young, began work at the horticultural establishment of Mons Wilhelm, a well-known firm there, where he was well able to study all branches of horticulture. . . . It was at Wilhelm's that he got to know his future brother-in-law, later his business associate, Mons Pierre Notting. . . . It was in 1855 that the firm 'Soupert & Notting' was born. . . . All his colleagues became his friends. . . . The death of Notting hit Soupert hard, and . . . his robust health began to decline." [JR34/135−136]

JOHN HOPPER   PLATE 10
Ward, 1862
From 'Jules Margottin' (HP) × 'Mme Vidot' (HP).

"I open several catalogs, and find there the following descriptions: *Duval, rose-grower of Montmorency,* 'H.P., vig., lg., full, brilliant pink with a crimson center'; *Cochet, at Suisnes,* 'Bourbon, very lg., full, beautiful bright pink'; *Dauvesse, in Orléans,* 'H.P., lg., full, globular, brilliant pink'; *Schwartz, of Lyon,* 'H.P., lg., full, brilliant pink with a carmine center'; *Van Houtte, the Ghent rosarian,* 'H.P., extremely vigorous, giving canes a yard long, short stems, very stocky, fl. very lg., very full, cupped, very pretty carmine'." [JR1/3/4] "Centre brilliant rosy-crimson, the outer petals paler, flowers . . . well formed." [JC] "Bright rose, with carmine center . . . light red thorns, stout bushy growth. A free blooming, standard sort." [EL] "Lilac-rose, their centres rosy-crimson." [P1] "Took the Rose world by storm. A splendid grower, and equally grand as a flower — brilliant rosy-scarlet, with silvery back." [WD] "Reverse of petals purplish-lilac." [FP] "Blooms come early . . . and are fairly regular, but the shape is open . . . colour is beautifully fresh just at first, but is . . . fleeting. . . . Of fair size, a free bloomer . . . a capital garden Rose." [F-M2] "Petals of the circumference large, center ones smaller; flower stem short and strong; bud pretty. Calyx pear-shaped." [JF] "Upright and healthy. . . . Fragrant . . . 4 × 3 [ft; ca. 1.25 × 1 m]." [B] "A very strong grower, very hardy, with good constitution and foliage." [F-M2] "Extremely vigorous, it throws out canes a meter in length [ca. 1 yard], but the flower-peduncles are short, holding the blossoms quite upright; the blossoms are very large, very full, and superbly cupped." [VH62/99−100] "Much appreciated because of the prices the blossoms fetch on the market, and because of the luxuriant growth. Vigorous; very large branches, straight upright or divergent; smooth bark, green with a 'bloom,' reddish in the sun; prickles very clinging, hooked, and pointed. Leaves large, light green, in 3−5 acuminate, dentate, rounded leaflets; leafstalk pretty strong, light green though somewhat reddish at the base, armed with a few prickles. Hardy." [S] "Mr. Ward named his glorious seedling after his friend." [R1/251]

JOHN KEYNES
Simon Louis/E. Verdier, 1864

"Bright reddish-scarlet, shaded with maroon; large and full; growth vigorous." [FP] "Sparkling red." [JR8/27] "Rich dark cherry-red blooms; delightfully fragrant. Foliage sufficient to plentiful.

Tall. Averages 64–148 blooms per season." [ARA21/89] Named after neither of the economists John Neville K. nor John Maynard K., but rather: "One of the most celebrated English rosarians has died — Mr. John Keynes, of Salisbury — at the age of 72. He began his horticultural work in growing carnations, and particularly, dahlias, with which he had great success. . . . John Keynes was much esteemed in the horticultural world; the citizens of Salisbury had elected him mayor last year [1876]." [JR2/49]

JUBILEE
Walsh/F. Cant, 1897
From 'Victor Hugo' (HP) × 'Prince Camille de Rohan' (HP).

"Rich pure red, shading to deep crimson and velvety maroon." [P1] "The darkest, sweetest rose of all, every bloom perfect and each petal like a piece of dark red velvet with a blackish sheen." [ARA29] "Large, well-shaped blooms of deep velvety crimson. Foliage sufficient and healthy . . . medium to tall. . . . Averages 57 blooms per season." [ARA21/89] "Has done well in Massachusetts." [Th2] "It is a pleasure to offer this Grand New Hardy Perpetual Rose, knowing that it is one of the most beautiful and satisfactory roses for general planting ever introduced. It is a true hybrid perpetual, and blooms finely in the fall as well as in the early summer. Perfectly hardy, and needs no protection; a healthy vigorous grower, with handsome dark green foliage, blooms abundantly, three flowers on each shoot. The flowers are very large, frequently 6 in across [ca. 1.5 dm], outer petals partially reflexed, the center petals upright, giving grace and beauty without showing the center. The buds are long and rounded; the color is bright flashing red, shading to glowing velvety crimson, the fragrance is delightfully rich and lasting. It is a truly magnificent rose in every way, and cannot be recommended too highly." [C&Js99] The name commemorates Queen Victoria's Diamond Jubilee.

JULES MARGOTTIN   PLATE 91
Margottin, 1853
Seedling of 'La Reine' (HP).

"Bright carmine." [JR1/7/7] "Bright cherry-colour, large and full; form cupped." [P1] "Imbricated, perfect, very bright cerise pink." [JR1/2/8] "Brilliant glossy pink; a glowing fresh colour, flowers large, beautifully smooth and cupped . . . robust." [JC] "Large, full, of beautiful centifolia form, deep pink; free-flowering, strong-growing, and good in autumn." [Hn] "Very free bloomer and good autumnal, but a poorly shaped rough bloom. . . . Early, sweet scented." [F-M2] "Nearly without fragrance." [JR10/151] "Globular." [JR3/27] "Carmine rose, large, full, somewhat flat, slight fragrance; five to seven leaflets, foliage light green, and somewhat crimped; wood armed with dark red thorns; free flowering and hardy." [EL] "Has no superior in its way: it is of a clear, rosy-crimson color, and its half-opened buds are especially beautiful." [FP] "More often semi-double than full." [JDR56/48] "Very strong, thorny, hardy growth . . . good foliage and strong constitution." [F-M2] "Very liable to mildew." [B&V] "One of the most widely cultivated roses; very vigorous and remontant; branches olive green, somewhat glaucous, armed with numerous and very unequal thorns of a brownish red . . . the foliage is very ample, dark green above, whitish beneath . . . the flowers are large, full, rounded, regular; color, carmine-maroon with shades of pink." [S]

"Vigorous; canes of moderate size, branching; bark light green, reddish where the sun strikes, with numerous thorns which are somewhat long, fairly upright, and very sharp. Leaves very ample, smooth, somber green, divided into 5–7 oval-pointed and finely toothed leaflets; leafstalk light green, reddish above and bearing beneath several small slightly hooked prickles. Flowers nearly four in across [ca. 1 dm], full, well formed into a cup, solitary or in clusters of two or three on the strongest branches . . . outer petals concave; inner ones smaller; flower stem strong and pretty long. Calyx long, slightly pear-shaped; sepals very leaf-like. A superb variety, very remontant, and of great merit; it has the elegance, the bearing, and the color of 'Brennus'." [JF] "Quite worthy of its descriptive English name, 'Perpetual Brennus'; its very vigorous habit, and large finely-shaped light vivid crimson flowers, remind us much of that very fine old Hybrid China." [HstX:84]

"Wood large, very strong and long, yellowish-green where shaded, reddish-green in the sun; long internodes. . . . Flower-stem strong, pretty long, holding the flowers firmly, studded with little brownish bristles. . . . Buds large, nearly globular, flat at the base, eight to a dozen at the end of the cane on young plants; on older, only two to three, sometimes but one. . . . Flowers very large (more than 4.5 in [ca. 1.25 dm]), full, regular; petals very numerous, ample, substantial, swirled elegantly in the center; concave at first, making the blossom at that stage deeply goblet-shaped; next, the petals stand up, indeed becoming slightly convex, the flower, when expansion is complete, appearing to be somewhat reversed; sexual organs apparent . . . scent elegant though faint. . . . This Rose came from the nurseries of Mons Margottin of Paris, and is perhaps his most notable introduction. . . . It is a hybrid of Bourbon extraction, of energetic growth and easy remontancy." [PIB] "A most superb old Rose . . . good for beds and groups." [WD] "Of admirable quality, from which many fine seedlings have been procured." [WD] "4 × 3 [ft; ca. 1.25 × 1 m]." [B] "It is no longer necessary to sing the praises of this charming and magnificent rose." [JR4/184]

"Mons Jules Margottin, whose father's nursery was just opposite the gateway of the horse market, depicted in Rosa Bonheur's famous picture, was my [George Paul's] boy chum, and we have been friends for sixty years." [NRS17/101] "Mons Margottin, Jacques-Julien, more commonly known as Margottin père . . . died last May 13th [1892] at his home at Bourg-la-Reine in his 75th year. Born September 7, 1817, in the community of Val-Saint-Germain, Margottin became an orphan at 14, without any means of support. It was then that he commenced his profession, as an apprentice gardener with Count Molé at Marais Castle, where he stayed three years . . . in 1839, he began work at the Jardin du Luxembourg as chief gardener in the rosary, under the supervision of Mons Hardy père. In 1840, he left the Luxembourg to get married, and to establish his rose business. . . . He developed a great many good roses, 'Jules Margottin' among others . . . dedicated to his oldest son." [JR16/83]

JULIET   PLATE 171
Easlea/W. Paul, 1910
From 'Captain Hayward' (HP) × 'Soleil d'Or' (Pern., Pernet-Ducher, 1900, yellow orange; parentage: 'Antoine Ducher' [HP] × R. fœtida persiana).

"Outside of petals old gold; interior rich rosy red changing to deep rose. Very remarkable color. Fragrant. . . . Foliage, poor." [Th] "Vermilion-red, reverse of petals old gold. Very vigorous." [NRS/11] "The color of the flower is somewhat variable. When it is warm and humid, weather often found in England during the summer, the predominating color is a crimson-rose . . . the petal exterior taking on a golden color, richly and noticeably constrasting with the red shades. When cold and dry, the crimson shades are replaced by a bright pink lit by scarlet, with the exteriors still yellow, though perhaps a little more brilliant. This rose blooms during the summer and fall. . . . Of remarkable vigor, this is a good variety to choose for making shrubberies in the garden." [JR34/140–141] "Really a most incongruous mixture of colours, but at the same time nearly everyone admits that it is fascinating and very beautiful." [NRS/12] "Early bloom only." [M-P] "A very pretty novelty which blooms as well in fall as it does in summer. . . . The very large flowers have an exquisite scent." [JR34/85] "A lovely variety, and as fragrant as beautiful." [OM] "Blend of Damask and Fruit-scented [perfumes]." [NRS/17] "Does not ball . . . does not do well in extremely hot climates. . . . Prune very lightly." [Th2]

LA REINE   PLATE 90
(trans., 'The Queen')
Laffay, 1844
Possibly a seedling of 'William Jesse' (HB).

"Bright rose tinged with lilac." [HoBoIV/319] "One of the gems of the [1844] season . . . pink with a lilac hue, very glossy . . . globular in shape, large, and very sweet." [P2] "Its flowers open freely, of a pale rose colour, blooming freely all season, holding its place with 'du Roi' in every character." [Bu] "The largest and most magnificent of all the Perpetuals, often attaining the size of a double Pæony . . . a brilliant satin rose . . . very slightly tinged with lilac, of most regular and perfect cupped form, and delightfully fragrant; the growth of the plant is very strong and vigorous, and each new spring shoot is crowned with flowers." [WRP] "Often shaded with lilac, and sometimes with crimson." [P] "Has the appearance of a true perpetual Cabbage, but much larger; strong robust grower, and free bloomer." [HstVI:367] "Sometimes coarse, and its flowers are so very double that they frequently open badly." [HstX:30] "Sometimes fine, but very uncertain." [P2] "It varies very much in quality with the circumstances of soil and cultivation, and in its color is surpassed by many other roses. Its very large size when well grown, its fine form and perfect hardiness, are its points of merit." [FP] "In dry seasons, most beautiful and fragrant." [R8] "Very large, full blooms of pink with silvery rose-pink reverse, robust . . . 4 × 4 [ft; ca. 1.25 × 1.25 m]." [HRG] "Semi-globular form, somewhat fragrant; the foliage slightly crimpled, five to seven leaflets." [EL] "Suitable for dwarf groups." [Hn] "Vigorous, with branches of medium size, straight upright or branching; smooth bark, green with a 'bloom,' with occasional thorns which are reddish, unequal, and enlarged at the base; foliage pale green, 5–7 leaflets, acuminate and irregularly dentate; leafstalk the same color, with no prickles; flower about four in across [ca. 1 dm], full, well formed, cupped, solitary, or in twos or threes on strong branches . . . petals very large and concave; not very hardy." [S] "Calyx elongated, pear-shaped. 'La Reine' is worthy of the name it bears; it rivals the Centifolias in scent and color, but surpasses them in the size of the flower." [JF] "In some situations — particularly late in the autumn — delicately striped or veined with carmine; its form globular, very double and massive. The singularly stiff reflexed edges, contrasting with the glossy pale pink on the backs of the petals, give a distinct character to this rose, while the guard petals, being very stout and rigid — more so than any other rose we know — enable it to retain its perfect form to the last. In warm situations 'La Reine' blooms of an immense size, forming an almost solid mass of petals, frequently measuring fifteen in[ches] in circumference [ca. 3.75 dm] by three in[ches] in depth [ca. 7.5 cm]. . . . To induce this rose to flower luxuriantly in the autumn, two or three of the central shoots should be shortened to three or four eyes as soon as the terminal flower buds appear, and the tree be kept well watered with liquid manure." [C]

"The appearance of this magnificent rose is an event. It always seems as if we could never develop roses more beautiful than those we have already; and yet, here is one which surpasses them all, because it equals the most beautiful Centifolias by its size, its form, the abundance of its petals, and the beauty of its

coloration, as well as by its fragrance. But it surpasses them in merit because, from the beginning of the blooming season until frost, it is covered, continuously, with numerous blossoms, which always open perfectly. The bush is vigorous, the branches upright; the strong stems seem to have been made to bear the enormous flowers, which are always solitary. . . . The foliage is that of the Bourbons, slightly glaucous beneath; the wood is glaucous as well. The only thing left to be desired would be Centifolia foliage. The flower, among the biggest of the class, seems full because many of the inner petals fold back, clothing the center and hiding the stamens. The inner surface of the petals is a pretty pink when the flower is completely open, after having been a brighter pink; the underside of the petals is a whitish lilac-pink. . . . We owe this beautiful rose to the efforts of Mons Laffay, whose skills are well known; it is the product of planned breeding. The seeds were produced in 1835, and first bloomed in 1841." [R-H43] "The *Journal d'Horticulture Pratique*, which is always the first horticultural publication to note and call attention to wonderful novelties, had the first word on the 'Rose de la Reine'. Here is what we said in the issue of September 16, 1843: 'With two thousand and more varieties of Roses known, here we find the 'Rose de la Reine', which is to say the most beautiful of all Roses, the Rose of artists, the Rose which dethrones the Centifolias! It was on September 5, 1843, that Mons Laffay, amateur horticulturalist of Bellevue, near Paris, presented to the general circle of horticulture four samples of a large Rose attaining a diameter of about four in [ca. 1 dm], in which the exterior petals, very large and hollowed, form a cockade; the central petals are equally large, folded, sometimes gracefully recurved in such a way as to hide twenty-ish stamens, which a person only sees if an indiscreet hand uncovers them. This magnificent Rose, held on an iron-strong stem, is a whitish-pink on the exterior and a beautiful light lilac-pink towards the center [within], shaded delicately, lightly, a quality intensified by the satiny nature of the petals. The fragrance is that of the Centifolia, but the color of the foliage is a glaucous green; the leaves are comprised of five, or, only at the branch-ends, three leaflets which are extra long, flat, a little wavy, pretty large, and look rather like those of the Bourbons. The branches are upright, armed with some remote, feeble prickles insecurely held on the cane. The bark is glaucous green like the leaves, very smooth, and laden with the same sort of powdery substance as raisins and plums have. The shrub is very vigorous, giving many flowers which open well all the time, except on those rare occasions when three buds are found together in a cluster. What is notable is that it was nearly the only flower in Paris that 13th of September. . . . ' The following January, the *Journal* gave as lagniappe to its subscribers a beautiful double plate representing 'La Reine', of which two hundred slips were delivered into commerce, slips which had been [hurriedly] rooted in the hot-house such that they were starved and etiolated; these were sold in February, March, and April at 2, 3, 4, or 5 francs apiece depending upon the conscience of the vendors as well as the strength of the plants. It was in 1844 that 'La Reine' bloomed for the fanciers and vendors. All agree that here we have a beautiful Rose. . . . Mons. Laffay, who has bred many introductions, always dedicates them to English princes. It is perhaps due to our intervention that the name 'Reine Victoria' was not used. . . . Might one hope for something better than 'La Reine'? Yes! Though perhaps we have arrived at the apogee with Dahlias, we are still far off with Roses. . . . 'La Reine' holds the middle ground between properly-called hybrids, and the Bourbons. By the wood and foliage, it is kin to Hybrid Chinas; considering its ovary, it has something of the Portland or Centifolia. . . . We will end this article by stating that 'La Reine' perfectly justifies the name 'The Autumnal Centifolia'." [PIB]

"Has stood for a long time at the head of the HP's." [JR4/40] "Grown so much formerly, today somewhat neglected." [JR31/124] "Others have now surpassed it. It is, however, still valuable for its glossy rose color, and its large, full, semi-globular form." [SBP]

LE HAVRE
Eude, 1871

"Brilliant vermilion, large, and very double; form expanded." [P1] "Beautifully formed." [EL] "Of good substance." [DO] "Beautiful show rose . . . imbricated form but . . . not . . . in bad weather . . . not often large." [F-M2] "Good foliage: not specially liable to mildew." [F-M2] "Vigorous . . . very floriferous." [S] "Bushy plant . . . leathery foliage . . . 4 × 4 [ft; ca. 1.25 × 1.25 m]." [B] "Habit moderate." [JC] Le Havre is a seaport town in northern France.

LŒLIA
Listed as 'Louise Peyronny'.

LOUIS VAN HOUTTE   PLATE 113
Lacharme, 1869
Seedling of 'Général Jacqueminot' (HP).
Not to be confused with Granger's carmine HP of 1863.

"A new rose . . . quite remontant. . . . 'vigorous, with very large flowers, full, beautiful Centifolia form, fiery red and amaranth, bordered with blackish crimson, shaded a blue resembling that in a rainbow.' " [R-H69] "Velvety crimson; mottled and shaded with violet-purple, flowers very large, full, and cupped, a superb rose; habit vigorous." [JC] "Reddish scarlet and amaranth, the circumference blackish crimson, large, full, and of fine globular form; large foliage, fewer thorns than most other dark roses, highly perfumed. This is a tender sort, but it is very free blooming, and decidedly the finest crimson yet sent out." [EL] "Color at its most perfect in summer." [JR28/11] "Of weak growth and small foliage: not much injured by mildew, but suffers from orange fungus and rain and 'burns' in hot weather. The blooms will only come fine if strong shoots are produced . . . a fine well-built bloom when you get it, with stout petals, high centre, fine globular outline, full size and dark, sometimes rather dull, colour. The flowers being heavy and the wood weak, flowering shoots . . . should be staked when the bud is formed. The lasting powers of the blooms are particularly good . . . a respectable bloom even on strong shoots is a rarity: but many others grow it well and esteem it highly." [F-M2] "Grown mainly for show purposes, very sweet." [Wr] "Vigorous; branches dark green; thorns somewhat numerous; flower large, full . . . one of the best in commerce." [S] "Medium-sized canes, which branch; bark smooth, light green, slightly reddish, with occasional evenly-sized reddish thorns which are short and tapered. Leaves glossy, light green, 5–7 oval-acuminate, finely dentate leaflets; leafstalk slender and slightly nodding. Flowers to four in across [ca. 1 dm], full, well formed, globular, solitary on the branchlets, in clusters of two or three on vigorous canes; beautiful fiery red nuanced amaranth and bordered bluish crimson; outer petals large, center petals slightly smaller; flower stalk slender, longish. Calyx rounded. Beautiful variety, of magnificent coloration; hardy." [JF] "Houtte (Louis Van).—Well-known Belgian horticulturalist . . . his very large company propagated many plants. He published *Flore des Serres et Jardins de l'Europe*, a veritable plant museum including over 2,000 colored plates." [R-HC]

"This variety sparked an act of rare probity which we are lucky to be able to report. Last September, at the Horticultural Exhibition, the jury gave the top prize to one of Mons Guillot père's roses. That honorable breeder having heard that Mons Lacharme had one which was quite similar in color, which, upon comparison, he had recognized as the better rose, he withdrew his own rose [from the market] even though it had taken first place, and instead advertised and sold his competitor's rose — 'Louis Van Houtte'. Mons Guillot's conduct is above all praise." [I'H69/351]

"Often it is said that great men have no homeland, that all countries have an equal share in them as all have profited by their efforts. Such is the case with Louis Van Houtte. . . . Louis Van Houtte, who died at Ghent May 9, 1876, was born at Ypres on June 29, 1810 [*a footnote adds:* 'At that time, Ypres, as a consequence of the wars of the First Empire, was capital of the department of Lys. Thus, Louis Van Houtte was born in France, and, above all, was French in his heart. Further, he pursued part of his studies in France, where he lived for many years.']. Very early in life, he showed a great aptitude for Science, and, after having spent two years at l'Institut Supérieur du Commerce, in Paris . . . he went, still young, as a botanical explorer to Brazil, where he spent nearly four years; later, he explored the western coast of Africa. . . . Coming back to Belgium shortly thereafter, he was named director of the Brussels botanical garden. Meanwhile, a most distinguished Belgian naturalist, Alexandre Verschaffelt, determined the future of Louis Van Houtte by settling in Ghent, where Van Houtte was. It was then that he took up decidedly the horticultural career which he followed so brilliantly. . . .

"But Mons Van Houtte was not only a horticulturalist and savant — he was also an artist in every sense of the word. All of his doings were marked by that special cachet which showed the grandeur of his concepts. The boldness of his enterprises astonished everyone; even his friends quailed. He founded at Ghent an establishment which today is unique, not only in extent, but also in concept and direction. At the side of the horticulturalist was always found the artist, and the one sometimes got the better of the other. . . .

"Such labors were still not enough for the powerful imagination of Mons Van Houtte, who added to an already considerable establishment a lithographic and chromolithographic print-shop, where aside from the numerous catalogs which, by their appearance and editing, were models of the sort, he printed the gigantic work, the *Flore des Serres et des Jardins de l'Europe*, which, alone, would be more than sufficient to establish his reputation and immortalize his name. . . .

"In personal relationships, few men were as agreeable as Mons Van Houtte; his wide and varied knowledge, and his lively spirit, joined with his good will, made him one of the most charming storytellers. Always, with his upright nature, he detested lies, and was appalled at dissimulation and bad faith; if circumstances forced him to have anything to do with persons he could not respect, the relations were kept distant. But if he realized that he had made a mistake, he sometimes went to extremes in making it up to the person, a consequence of an extremely honest nature. . . .

" 'He was no more than ten years old when he lost his father. The considerable fortune of the family was shaken by the events of 1815. An energetic and courageous woman, the mother of Van Houtte tried nevertheless to continue the great enterprises of her husband, but poorly helped and too trusting, she had the misfortune to see all her hopes dashed; her entire fortune was soon gone. The young Louis . . . was sent to Paris, to l'École Centrale du Commerce.'

"He would get up every day at 3 or 4 A.M., and would rarely leave his desk before ten at night. . . . All in all, fatigue on the one hand, and the overstimulation native to his lively and impressionable nature on the other, joined to make the cruel illness which had long since undermined his health, and which put an end to his life. . . . 'Tuesday, the 9th of May, around 3, he felt a certain feeling of disquietude, and arose, speaking of the plants he loved so well, quite himself. Suddenly, he said with pain the name of one of his daughters—his hand clenched—his eyes closed. They thought it would pass, but, alas!, the great horticulturalist was dead.'

"All the horticultural world feels the loss of one whom we can regard as the prince of 19th Century horticulture." [R-H76]

LOUIS XIV
Guillot fils, 1859
Seedling of 'Général Jacqueminot' (HP).
Not to be confusesd with Hardy's bright pink Gallica.

"Bright red shaded maroon." [BJ] "Rich blood-color, large and full, form globular; a distinct and beautiful variety." [FP] "Intense dark crimson, velvety, medium-sized, full, very beautiful, though unfortunately the blossoms nod somewhat, weak growth." [N] "Vigorous . . . intense red, nuanced poppy-red." [S] "Many varieties that are quite second-rate in respect of habit are grown for the sake of some peculiar quality, and a good example of this is 'Louis XIV', which is so exquisitely beautiful, 'when you can catch it,' that the amateur who loves high quality will be content and happy to have its half dozen flowers, while other varieties, not altogether wanting in quality, are producing their flowers by hundred." [Hd] "Good fragrance . . . 3 × 3 [ft; ca. 9 × 9 dm]." [B]

LOUISE D'ARZENS
Listed as a Bourbon.

LOUISE PEYRONNY
('Lœlia')
Lacharme, 1844
Seedling of 'La Reine' (HP).

"Satin rose, globular, fine bold petal, a handsome rose; habit moderate." [JC] "Bright pink; finer than 'La Reine'." [HstXI:224] "Silvery rose." [EL] "Very large, full; color, deep pink shaded carmine." [S] "Brilliant rose color—globular—a very handsome variety . . . a free opener, this extremely handsome new variety will be a great acquisition to the north of England. . . . It is of a bright rose color with petals slightly incurved, of great size and substance . . . remarkably hardy, very fragrant." [C] "[Resembling] a large gown in disorder." [VH62/92] "Charming . . . opens well in all seasons." [R8] "Of great beauty, though scarcely so vigorous as 'La Reine'." [FP]

"Mons François Lacharme, the eminent rosarian of Lyon, died last November 5th [1887]. Lacharme . . . was born at Saint-Didier-sur-Chalaronne (Ain) the 23rd of January, 1817. His father was a local farmer, and wanted him to follow in that career; but, despite this, loving flowers and particularly roses in his childhood, and learning horticulture from his father, he was placed in 1836 in the nursery form of Mons Poncet. . . . He would often visit the gardens of Mons Plantier. . . . In 1840, Mons Plantier offered to sell him his establishment in Lyon. He accepted, and, aided by Plantier's counsel, began to sow rose seed." [JR11/177] "Lacharme astonished the rosarians with the splendid and enormous 'Louise Peyronny'." [JR12/52] "We have only this to add, that, while being honest and loyal, he was at the same time modest to the extreme; indeed, he did not believe that it was his place to perpetuate his name by giving it to any of his varieties. . . . Rosarians will not forget him, and are going to honor his memory by erecting on his grave a lasting token of their sympathy and friendship." [JR12/54]

MABEL MORRISON
Broughton, 1878
Sport of 'Baronne Adolphe de Rothschild' (HP).

"Flesh white, changing to pure white, in the autumn it is sometimes tinged with pink; semi-double, cup-shaped flowers . . . not so full as we would like, it is yet a very useful garden rose, and occasionally it is good enough for exhibition." [EL] "In every way, an extra fine white rose. Blooms in full clusters. Buds handsome. Foliage elegant. Delicate perfume." [Dr] "Immaculate bloom and unsurpassed foliage." [L] "Large, loosely-filled, pure white to pale pink. Growths sturdy, very prickly, erect." [Hn] "Vigorous, hardy." [S] "4 × 3 [ft; ca. 1.25 × 1 m]." [B] "This new rose was obtained by Mr. Joseph Broughton, a Leicester florist." [JR2/65]

MAGNA CHARTA   PLATE 127
W. Paul, 1876

"Bright pink, suffused with carmine, very large, full, of good form, habit erect, growth vigorous; magnificent foliage; flowers produced in more than usual abundance for so fine a variety." [P1] "Fresh rose-pink." [ARA29/96] "Imbricated." [Cx] "Globular; foliage and wood light green; numerous, dark spines. A fragrant, excellent variety." [EL] "Very big, full, and cupped; held upright; the foliage is large and a handsome glossy dark green . . . very remontant." [S] "Very large flower . . . rough and irregular, very full and showy . . . a very bad autumnal." [F-M2] "A new English rose possessing all the necessary qualifications to make a rose of the first order; it is luxuriant, robust, and very floriferous." [JR1/6/9] "Probably the hardiest pink variety . . . exceptionally fine during its blooming period." [ARA34/77] "Very fragrant . . . tall . . . 50 [blossoms] per season." [ARA21/90] "To 10 [ft; ca. 3 m] . . . some rebloom." [HRG] "This splendid variety . . . merits a place of honor in the most choice collection." [JR2/40]

MARCHIONESS OF LONDONDERRY   PLATE 157
A. Dickson, 1893
Possibly a seedling of 'Baronne Adolphe de Rothschild' (HP).

"Large, beautiful form, borne on erect stalks, ivory-white tinted with rose; strong, free, fragrant." [Hn] "Often a very unpleasant shade of white." [J] "Of great substance. Magnificent in form and size, but rather dull in colour when expanded." [P1] "Globular." [DO] "Full, cupped, fragrant; vigorous; stocky." [Cx] "Not free-flowering enough for general cultivation . . . very large and smooth and of great substance, on very stout stems, but they do not open well, and the colour, which is a greyish-white, is not pleasing . . . of no use as an autumnal." [F-M2] " 'This rose is superb' say Messers Dickson & Sons, 'and incontestably one of the most beautiful we have ever grown. It is quite certain that it takes a premier place in the world of Roses. The flowers are of an extraordinary size, of perfect form, and borne on firm and upright stems. The colour is a very pure ivory-white; the petals are large, thick, substantial, and reflexed. The vigorous bush is clothed in very thick and handsome foliage, and the flowers have their share of perfume' " [JR17/85] "The blossom is lightly perfumed." [JR23/105] "The foliage is fine and free from mildew." [F-M2] "The best white HP that we have." [JR22/106]

MARCHIONESS OF LORNE
W. Paul, 1889

"Fulgent rose colour, full, finely cupped. The blossoms are freely produced throughout the season, and they are deliciously fragrant." [P1] "Crimson." [LS] "Vivid carmine . . . large, sweet." [TW] "Rich rose-colour, cup-shaped, double and deep." [Dr] "This beautiful rose, dedicated by special permission of Her

Majesty Princess Louise . . . produces extremely bright pink flowers, which are tinted at the center with bright carmine. The flowers are large, full, and well formed; petals, large; buds, pretty. Above all, the variety is notable for its continuous bloom; each branch bears a bud." [JR13/70] "1.5 metres [ca. 4.5 ft]." [G]

MARGARET DICKSON
A. Dickson, 1891
From 'Lady Mary Fitzwilliam' (HT) × 'Merveille de Lyon' (HP).

"White, with pale flesh centres; large shell-like petals of good substance. Form good, foliage handsome." [P1] "Large, rather flat, blush-white flowers." [OM] "Long petals forming a good point . . . a poor autumnal." [F-M2] "It is full and magnificent in form; its growth is very vigorous; its stalk is replete with very strong thorns; its foliage is very large and of a handsome dark green. This rose is, without a doubt, the best introduction of the last six years." [JR15/84] "Vigorous in growth, with fine foliage sadly liable . . . to mildew." [F-M2] "Should not be too closely pruned; very large, and strong grower." [DO]

MARGUERITE GUILLARD
Chambard, 1915
Sport of 'Frau Karl Druschki' (HP).

"A sport from 'Frau Karl Druschki' and similar except that it is absolutely thornless, has superior foliage, and a mild but distinct perfume. . . . Flower lasts longer after being cut although perhaps a trifle smaller. Blooms almost the entire year in southern California and is in full bloom in December." [Capt28] "5 × 4 [ft; ca. 1.5 × 1.25 m]." [B] "Fair . . . not so good as others." [ARA18/116] "I like it very much." [ARA34/77]

MARQUISE DE BOCCELLA
Listed as a Damask Perpetual.

MARSHALL P. WILDER
Ellwanger & Barry, 1885
Seedling of 'Général Jacqueminot' (HP).

"Studied for three years [*before being released to commerce*] . . . very vigorous, handsome foliage, large flowers on the globular side, full, well-formed; cherry-carmine . . . this is a perfected 'Alfred Colomb'." [JR8/29] "A very handsome rose with extra-large, full flowers of deep dark red. Sufficient healthy foliage . . . most bloom in spring, a little in fall . . . about 71 [blossoms per season]." [ARA21/89] "Expanded form, well 'built'; color, cherry-red mixed with carmine . . . in wood, foliage, and flower-form much like 'Alfred Colomb', but superior; in flowering, it blooms much longer than do other remontant roses." [S] "Practically duplicates 'Alfred Colomb', but is a better grower generally." [ARA34/79] "Rich foliage; flowers, enormous and semi-globular, full, of a very handsome outline . . . exquisite scent. It is one of the best autumnals." [JR16/37] Marshall P. Wilder, quondam president of the Massachusetts Horticultural Society.

MARTHA
Listed as a Bourbon.

MAURICE BERNARDIN
('Souvenir de l'Exposition de Brie', 'Ferdinand de Lesseps')
Granger, 1861
Seedling of 'Général Jacqueminot' (HP).

"Bright crimson, large, moderately full; a good free-flowering sort, generally coming in clusters." [EL] "Blooms come pretty well, of good semi-globular shape and fair general qualities . . . a fair

average crimson rose." [F-M2] "Bright cherry crimson colour." [SBP] "Globular with high centre . . . sweetly fragrant." [W/Hn] "Vermilion, large, full, and of fine form; growth vigorous." [P1] "Moderate [in growth], rich crimson shaded with violet; colour superb . . . a splendid Rose in suitable localities." [WD] "Good growth and foliage, rather liable to mildew." [F-M2] "Growth very vigorous; foliage dark green; flowers large, well imbricated, in clusters, beautiful light vermilion red; very effective plant." [I'H61/166] "One of the best of its color." [S] "Quite first-rate." [P2]

MERRIE ENGLAND
Harkness, 1897
Sport of 'Heinrich Schultheis' (HP).

"Pink striped silvery." [LS] "Crimson, blush; vigorous . . . early, striped." [TW]

MERVEILLE DE LYON
Pernet père, 1882
Sport of 'Baronne Adolphe de Rothschild' (HP).

"Large, closely filled, cup-like form, white with a pink centre, becoming pink with age. Growth erect, sturdy." [Hn] "Pure white, sometimes washed with satin-rose, very large, full, and cupped." [P1] "White, center slightly peach." [ARA17/29] "Generally of a lovely pure white colour, but comes sometimes rather pink in the autumn. . . . A grand rose of the largest size . . . weak in the centre." [F-M2] "Uni-blossomed strong stems . . . a handsome white, tinted flesh pink." [JR31/105] "Practically scentless." [ARA34/76] "No scent." [JR9/41] "Monster size." [L] "Does not last. No fall bloom. . . . Prune long. Best pegged down." [Th2] "Of 'Baroness Rothschild' race . . . this race has a splendid hardy robust constitution." [F-M2] "Sadly given to mildew." [K2] "Vigorous; heavy growth; numerous thorns, not hooked; handsome light green foliage, thick on the bush; flowers very large, full, perfectly cupped, and opening very well; well held; attaining a size of about 4.5 in [ca. 1 dm+]. The blossom is a beautiful pure white with large petals which are well rounded and very fine, lightly washed satin pink at the center. The flowers are always solitary, and the plant is quite remontant." [JR6/149] "It resembles 'Mabel Morrison' too much to please me." [JR7/156]

MME ALBERT BARBIER
Barbier, 1925
From 'Frau Karl Druschki' (HP) × ?

"An almost indescribable combination of fawn-yellow, white, and pinkish tints, with colors varying in different blooms. It is of medium growth and practically as free blooming as a Hybrid Tea." [ARA34/79] "Full, double, yellow flowers, shaded soft pink." [ARA29/96] "Pearly white at the edge of the petals, blending through flesh-pink to orange-yellow at the center, fading to soft flesh-pink: of very good lasting quality and slightly fragrant . . . abundant, leathery, disease-resistant foliage. Compact habit (3 ft [ca. 9 dm]); blooms continuously . . . the thorns are vicious." [ARA27/138] "Foliage mildews." [ARA27/138] "As good color and free-flowering as any HT; very desirable [in Massachusetts] . . . delicate salmon-buff, with yellow suffusion and strong yellow at base of petals when first opening. . . . Not profuse [Massachusetts]. . . . Should be in every garden [Pennsylvania]. . . . Neat, healthy, free-blooming [Iowa]. . . . Healthy, even under adverse conditions [Missouri]. . . . Cream, pink, apricot — but wood and growth poor [Idaho]. . . . Very vigorous, upright. . . . Stands rain well [State of Washington]. . . . Does well in interior valleys [California]. . . . Only 40 blooms the first year, but each was a real event [California] . . . high quality and delicate color." [PP28] "Bud very large; flower large, double, slightly fragrant, very lasting, salmon, tinted nankeen-yellow, darker center of orange-yellow and light rose (does not fade in sunlight in France), borne singly. Foliage abundant, light green, glossy, leathery, large, resistant to disease. Very vigorous, upright, bushy; profuse, continuous bloom. Claimed to be a truly everblooming H.P. of remarkable color." [ARA26/183] "Is a gem . . . the inside of a half-opened bloom has the iridescence of a pearl . . . practically an everbloomer, but I would want it if it were not." [ARA29/49]

MME BOLL   PLATE 99
D. Boll/Boyau, 1859

Two parentages have been given: (1) An unspecified HP × 'Belle Fabert' (DP); or, (2) 'Baronne Prévost' (HP) × 'Portlandica' (DP, flesh).

"Beautiful intense pink; flower very large . . . vigorous." [Cx] "Bright pink; well formed." [BJ] "Opens well." [TW] "Foliage very good and ample, large flowers, flat, carmine-pink, very hardy, and a late bloomer." [JR4/60] "Carmine-rose . . . very stout shoots." [EL] "Flower about three in [ca. 7.5 cm] . . . it is said that this rose is descended from 'Baronne Prévost' [HP]. Such is possible, but it would have to be that variety crossed with a Portland. . . . Mme Boll is a lady rosarian of New York, originally from Switzerland." [JR10/37] "Very vigorous bush, blossom 10 cm [ca. 4 in], very full, perfect form, slightly plump [or 'hemispherical'], beautiful bright pink; very fragrant." [I'H59/138] " 'Mme Boll' was raised by Mons J. Boyau père, horticulturalist of Angers (successor of Mons Guérin), who secured the seedlings in 1856 from a cross between an HP and a Portland ('Belle Favert' [*sic*]), which latter the flowers resemble. This beautiful variety, released to commerce in 1859, was dedicated to the wife of a Swiss horticulturalist, Mons Boll, who resided for a long time in America, where he was well known. The rose 'Mme Boll' is of extraordinary growth, with large leaves carried on long stems. The usually solitary flowers are very large, full, of perfect form, and of a lively pink. The fragrance is quite penetrating." [JR6/168] "Vigorous; canes large and upright; bark light green, with numerous dark gray prickles which are unequal, small, straight, and pointed. Leaves large, light green, strongly nerved, divided into 3 or 5 oval-rounded, finely dentate leaflets; leafstalk slender, nodding, same color as the leaves. Flowers large, approaching four in across [ca. 1 dm], very full, flat, somewhat rounded, generally solitary; color, a handsome intense pink; outer petals large, those of the center very numerous, muddled, unequal, and folded; flower stem short, stout, bristly, glandular. Calyx flared-tubular; sepals leaf-like. A variety of the first order." [JF] "Most perfect in all that constitutes a fine rose." [R8]

MME CHARLES DRUSCHKI
Listed as 'Frau Karl Druschki'.

MME CHARLES WOOD
('Dinsmore')
E. Verdier, 1861

"Vinous-crimson, very large, full, and effective." [FP] "Flower very large, very full, with large petals; well held; beautiful sparkling intense red fading to bright deep pink; reverse of petals whitish; superb." [I'H61/264] "Beautiful clear rosy-crimson, petals large and of good substance, expanded, full, and beautifully formed; a distinct and magnificent rose; habit moderate." [JC] "Vigorous; flower large, very full, cupped, then flat; color, dazzling bright red." [S] "Dwarf. . . . Reddish crimson, large or very large, nearly full; one of the freest flowering kinds, but not of first quality. Occasionally, as with 'Général Washington', some first-rate blooms are produced." [EL] "A bad grower, divided and

rain will spoil them. Sometimes a strong fine Rose, with large petals, rather flat in shape, and tightly incurved in the centre. A good lasting flower, of full size, but a 'bad doer' and not to be recommended." [F-M3] "Beautiful foliage . . . the flower expands rather quickly and is soon overblown." [P2] "One of the best of its own, or of any, class of roses. Large, full, flat roses of crimson, without a dull or purplish shade throughout the hottest summer. Begins to bloom on quite young bushes and continues to bloom better as growth advances. Dwarf bush, but luxuriant, rich, dark green foliage. Very long-lived and hardy." [Dr]

[MME FERDINAND JAMIN]
(*not* ' — Jamain')
Lédéchaux, 1875
See also 'American Beauty'.

"Rosy-claret, deep petals, and large bold flower, distinct and good." [JC] "Jamin (Ferdinand). — Well-known nurseryman of Bourg-la-Reine (Seine) where he died in 1916 at the age of 89." [R-HC]

MME GABRIEL LUIZET
Liabaud, 1877
Seedling of 'Jules Margottin' (HP).
Not to be confused with the Bourbon of the same name.

"Light silvery pink; one of the most beautiful pink Roses that we have; early flowering, very free, and fragrant; should be lightly pruned." [DO] "Pale pink, a delicate and beautiful tint of colour, large and full, cupped, very sweet . . . quite first-rate." [P1] "Large, full, purple cherry red." [JR1/12/12] "The blooms are occasionally divided, but generally good . . . not . . . lasting . . . but of fair size, very smooth, with good petals and a capital pointed centre . . . delightful fragrance . . . the most attractive shade of pink among HP's. A very free bloomer, but a shocking autumnal." [F-M2] "An early bloomer; does not last; no fall bloom. Prune long." [Th2] "Long foliage; a promising kind, worthy of attention." [EL] "Strong, vigorous growth. . . . The foliage is very fine, but liable to mildew . . . quite a big bush . . . in good soil." [F-M2] "5 × 3 [ft; ca. 1.5 × 1 m]." [B] "Certainly a rose of the first merit, much surpassing 'Mrs. John Laing' in growth, rigidity of branch, and size of flower." [JR32/30] "Luizet (Gabriel). — Born in 1794, died at Ecully (Rhône) in 1872. Meritorious arboriculturalist. Developed many valuable varieties of fruits. It is to him that we owe the practice of budding fruit trees, something he popularized. Author of *Classification du Genre Pêcher*." [R-HC]

MME KNORR
('Mme de Knorr')
V. & C. Verdier, 1855

"Pink, reverse white." [LS] "Soft rose . . . fragrant." [TW] "Medium size, full, flat form, very sweet." [EL] "100 mm [ca. 4 in] across . . . rather loose." [G] "Darker in the center." [S] "HP with large, full flower which is bright pink at the center, lighter at the edge." [I'H55/246] "Semi-double . . . 4 × 3 [ft; ca. 1.25 m x 9 dm]." [B] "Flowers freely." [P2] "Very vigorous." [Cx]

MME ROSA MONNET
Monnet, 1885

"Very vigorous; flower large, full, of perfect form, superbly colored bright fresh amaranth with bluish shadings after the blossom has expanded; a delightful perfume; it opens well no matter what the weather, and is very remontant." [JR9/179]

MME SCIPION COCHET   PLATE 116

S. Cochet, 1871

Not to be confused with Bernaix's Tea of the same name.

"Purplish pink bordered delicate light pink; flower full, cupped; center petals ruffled a bit." [Cx]   "Cherry-rose." [EL]   "Vigorous, floriferous, particularly in summer; flower large, full, well-formed, forming a rosette in the center; color, cerise-pink bordered fresh white; a very pretty variety, recommended by all." [S]   "Flowers wrinkled when fully open . . . 4 × 3 [ft; ca. 1.25 × 1 m]." [B]   "Its large and strong branches . . . are complemented by husky leaves of a very pretty green. The flowers are very large and full; the numerous petals, which are imbricated and slightly ruffled, give a sort of lightness to the flower which, though bold, is nevertheless graceful. What is more, the form is perfect; the bright cerise-pink petals are silvery on the back, producing reflections which contrast prettily with the darker color of the rest of the petals. All in all, it is a top-of-the-line variety." [JR1/4/8]

MME VICTOR VERDIER   PLATE 103

E. Verdier, 1863

Seedling of 'Sénateur Vaïsse' (HP).

Not to be confused with the pale flesh HP of 1840, 'Mme Verdier', nor with the rose-red 'Victor Verdier', an important HP of 1859.

"Rich, bright rosy-cherry color, large, full, and fine formed, cupped; blooms in clusters." [FP]   "Carmine-crimson, large, full, globular form, very fragrant; a superb rose." [EL]   "Carmine-rose . . . though not new, excellent." [SBP]   "Brilliant rosy-crimson, colour very beautiful, flowers . . . very lasting; a distinct and very superb rose." [JC]   "Crimson . . . later blooms on the longest and strongest shoots are the best, and occasionally these are very fine, full, lasting, and bright. Fairly free-flowering." [F-M2]   "Somewhat resembles 'Sénateur Vaïsse'; excellent for every purpose; one of the finest rich-coloured Roses." [WD]   "An excellent old rose, strong growing, and bearing its light crimson flowers freely in summer." [OM]   "Very free flowering, and constant." [DO]   "A strong grower with fine foliage beautifully coloured in the early spring . . . large clusters of buds which should be carefully thinned . . . high cultivation is necessary for . . . really good blooms." [F-M2]   "5 × 4 [ft; ca. 1.5 × 1.25 m]." [B]   "Vigorous, of medium size, branching; bark smooth, light green, furnished with the occasional reddish thorn, which is slightly hooked; leaves large, somber green, in 3–5 crowded leaflets which are oval and rounded, terminating in a point; leafstalks pretty strong, with some prickles; flower about three in across [ca. 7.5 cm], full, cupped, solitary, or sometimes in clusters of two or three on the most vigorous branches; color, brilliant cerise-pink; outer petals large; center petals smaller; flower stalk short and slender; magnificent flower for exhibition, very remarkable by all reports . . . good autumnal." [S]   "Calyx pear-shaped, nearly round." [JF]   "A rose of the first merit." [JR25/180]   "Flowers cupped, beautiful bright cherry pink, 10–12 in a terminal cluster . . . the name which it bears will always be attached to the history of rose-culture in France; Mons Eugène Verdier could not have chosen a worthier name to emphasize the merit of this magnificent variety than that of his mother." [I'H63/224]

MONSIEUR BONÇENNE

Liabaud, 1864

From 'Général Jacqueminot' (HP) × ? 'Géant des Batailles' (HP).

"Velvety maroon which does not 'blue'; flower very large, full, cupped, fragrant." [Cx]   "Fine form, velvety deep dark carmine-red. Growth strong, erect. A beautiful rose of the first order, but only fairly good in autumn." [Hn]   "Very deep crimson, double, medium size; a good rose, but now displaced by 'Baron de Bonstetten'." [EL]   "Intensely dark crimson, colour very superb . . . one of the best dark flowers; habit vigorous." [JC]   "Nearly scentless; it can be grown own-root as well as budded; does well in a pot, forced. Good bloom in summer. It is hardy and needs to be pruned long. 'Baron de Bonstetten' and 'Baron Chaurand' are two varieties coming from 'Monsieur Bonçenne' which are very much like it. *Monsieur Bonçenne* is a judge in the Fontenay-le-Comte court, and is president of the horticultural society of that town." [JR10/58]   "A strong grower with fair foliage, but liable to mildew and orange fungus, and not liking rain. Very early; one of the first to show flower buds. A poorly shaped flat bloom at the best, only a small proportion of them coming good, but a beautiful dark colour, particularly 'velvety'. Requires a hot season, and yet is likely to be 'burnt.' Fairly free blooming and of average size, but not lasting or a good autumnal and of no use as an exhibition Rose." [F-M3]   "Vigorous; branches of medium size, divergent; bark dark green, with fairly numerous blackish-brown thorns which are unequal, slightly hooked, and sharp. Leaves somber green, composed of 3–5 leaflets which are oval-rounded, slightly acuminate, and finely dentate; leafstalks slender, dark green, somewhat reddish. Flowers around three in across [ca. 7.5 cm], full, cupped, solitary or in clusters of two or three on the stronger branches; color, dark velvety maroon, petals large; flower stem short, glabrous, slightly nodding. Calyx rounded. This is a variety of the first order, and one of the darkest." [JF]   "Mons Ernest Bonçenne, president of the Société d'Horticulture de Fonteney-le-Comte." [JR26/31]

MRS. F. W. SANFORD

('Pride of the Valley')

Curtis, Sanford, & Co., 1898

Sport of 'Mrs. John Laing' (HP).

"Pale blush pink shading to white . . . possesses all the good points of the parent." [P1]   "The form is perfect; full. This rose is an excellent exhibition variety." [JR21/164]   F. W. Sanford was the business partner of Henry Curtis (who wrote *Beauties of the Rose*) in their nursery at Torquay, England.

MRS. JOHN LAING   PLATE 19

Bennett, 1887

Seedling of 'François Michelon' (HP).

"Silvery lilac pink . . . superbly fragrant." [RP]   "Rosy pink." [J]   "Clear, bright rose, a continous bloomer, fragrant, and always to be relied on. The best of the late Mr. Bennett's seedlings." [DO]   "Lovely shell pink. Elegant in form, texture and habit of growth. Large, full and double roses. Large well-shaped buds. Tea-scented. Blooms as continuously as the best of Tea roses. No finer rose exists for the out-of-door garden, park, or cemetary. Fine for cut-roses." [Dr]   "First-rate in petal, fulness, semi-globular pointed shape, lasting qualities, size, and freedom of bloom . . . the pink colour is not very decided or bright." [F-M2]   "Bright pink, richly fragrant blooms of splendid shape." [ARA29/96]   "The prettiest pink in this class." [ARA29/100]   "Very large, well-filled, cupped, bright glossy pink colour. Free flowering, good in autumn. Stems erect, slightly prickled." [Hn]   "Long buds. . . . Strong grower; free bloomer, averaging 50 blooms [per season]." [ARA29/49]   "Almost always some flowers, and no thorns to bother." [ARA29/49]   "An excellent rose, with characteristic upright shoots, and beautiful big, clear pink blooms which are produced more or less in autumn as well as in July. A rose that all should grow." [OM]   "Longer flowering period than most of the class." [TRh2]   "One of the best half-dozen. . . . Not liable to mildew or injured by rain, and retaining its foliage well in the autumn." [F-M2]   "Holds its leaves, but capriciously." [JR37/170]   "Extremely free from mildew. It commences to flower very early, is remarkably profuse, and continues to bloom till late in Autumn; quite first-rate." [P1] "The growth is hardy and vigorous, and the habit erect, the foliage is good, light green, and retained well into autumn, but decidedly subject to mildew as far as my experience goes. . . . It flowers well again in the autumn, giving a few stray blooms in between, but it is not continuous. . . . The flowers are grand exhibition blooms, full, pointed, and globular, with a good depth of petal, soft pale pink in colour. They stand sun and rain well, but are apt to be dull when much shaded. . . . It is very sweet scented." [JRS/10] "4 × 3 [ft; ca. 1.25 × 1 m]." [B] "Although introduced as far back as 1887, 'Mrs. John Laing' has never been superseded, and looks like holding its own indefinitely." [Wr] "One of the principal English horticulturalists, Mr. John Laing, has died at the age of 77 at Forest Hill, where he had a vast and well known establishment. He was one of the most esteemed and distinguished hybridists in England because of his numerous and interesting crosses." [JR24/145]

NURIA DE RECOLONS
('Nuria de Recolona')
Dot, 1933
From 'Canigó' (HT, Dot, 1927, white; parentage: 'Antoine Rivoire' [HT] × 'Mme Ravary' [HT]) × 'Frau Karl Druschki' (HP).

"[Has the] greatest thrips resistance of any white rose . . . good form but no fragrance." [ARA39/215]

OAKMONT
May, 1893
"Deep pink." [Hÿ] "Clear light pink. Profuse and constant bloomer." [Dr] "Peach-pink, fragrant . . . of good size. Sufficient healthy foliage. Growth tall. Blooms mostly in spring . . . about 132 [blooms per season]." [ARA21/90] "Large and sweet, good bloomer, hardy and productive; always gives satisfaction." [C&Js06]

OSKAR CORDEL
Lambert, 1897
From 'Merveille de Lyon' (HP) × 'André Schwartz' (T).
"Bright rich carmine, large and full; sweetly scented. Very free and distinct." [P1] "Cup-like. Bright deep rosy-red. Flowers always solitary. Growth strong." [Hn] "Very fragrant; fairly vigorous." [Cx] "Very vigorous, bushy, stems upright, with slender and large thorns. In appearance and growth, it resembles 'Merveille de Lyon'. Each branch bears only one blossom, which is very large, rounded, cupped, and has rather large petals. Color, light bright carmine, very floriferous and remontant. Good as a garden plant. . . . Dedicated to the Editor-in-Chief of the *Voss Gazette*." [JR21/51]

PANACHÉE D'ANGERS   PLATE 132
('Commandant Beaurepaire')
Moreau-Robert, 1879
"Intense pink variegated purple and violet, and spotted white; flower large, full, cupped; moderate vigor." [Cx] "Strong bush with fresh green leaves. Large double crimson flowers striped pink and purple and marbled white . . . occasionally repeating . . . 4 × 4 [ft; ca. 1.25 × 1.25 m]." [B] "The late Mons Vibert had raised a single-flowered, striped HP seed-bearer around 1845, which later, in 1856, produced the HP 'Belle Angevine' [*now extinct; introduced by Vibert's successor Robert*], a rose with full, striped blossoms, but not very vigorous. The rose 'Commandant Beaurepaire' arose from the same seed-bearer. Sown in 1864,

the plant . . . grew with extraordinary vigor the first year. The second year, its luxuriant growth made it look like a Banksiana; its canes measured as long as nine to twelve ft [ca. 3–3.75 m]. I cut back these enormous branches the *third* year, branches which gave me some blossoms, and made sure to use only these for the budding. . . . At length, the growth having slowed down, my hope in 1872 was to coax this variety into reblooming. After three years of effort, despairing of success, and being importuned by many fanciers to bring the variety into commerce, I decided to do so. The difficulty was in classifying the thing. Doubtless, its place was among the 'unknown hybrids,' but this class having nearly disappeared from cultivation, I chose the Gallica class, having lost all hope of seeing this variety rebloom. But — voila! — in 1876, after the spring pruning, forty or fifty specimens gave me blossoms over the course of the summer, and the same thing happened in 1877 and 1878. And so it was that I recognized the necessity of reclassifying the variety among the HP's under the name 'Panachée d'Angers', noting that it was the same as 'Commandant Beaurepaire', only remontant. I earnestly wish that its HP name, 'Panachée d'Angers', be retained, as it is a name it most assuredly merits. It is very vigorous, with medium-sized flowers which are double and of a soft pink striped and marbled with purple and violet." [JR6/72]

PANACHÉE DE LYON
Listed as a Damask Perpetual.

PAUL JAMAIN
Listed as 'Charles Lefebvre'.

PAUL NEYRON   PLATE 114
Levet, 1869
From 'Victor Verdier' (HP) × 'Anna de Diesbach' (HP).
"Dark lilac-rose, of extra size, fine form and habit." [P1] "Pale soft rose, violet shade, flowers immensely large and full; habit robust." [JC] "Huge crimson flowers." [HRH] "Giant blooms, stout in petal and very full . . . wanting in delicacy and symmetry . . . colour of the peony type." [F-M2] "Outstanding . . . in size and shape . . . rich, warm pink . . . 4 × 3 [ft; ca. 1.25 × 1 m]." [B] "Deep rose, very large, very full, somewhat fragrant, free blooming; the wood is nearly smooth, the foliage tough and enduring, somewhat tender, the growth is very upright. The largest variety known, and a very desirable sort for the garden." [EL] "Liable to ball in wet." [Th2] "Unusually strong growth and foliage, almost entirely untouched by mildew and little injured by rain." [F-M2] "Very vigorous; large branches; bark with a 'bloom'; thorns somewhat numerous, blackish, unequal, a few of them big and strong. Handsome, large foliage of a light green; leaves divided into 3–4 acuminate and finely toothed leaflets; leafstalks strong, with some small prickles; flower about five in across [ca. 1.25 dm], quite full, cupped, solitary or in a cluster of 2–4 on the more vigorous branches; beautifully colored bright rose; outer petals very large, those in the center smaller and folded. This variety is notable for the size of the enormous blossoms. Hardy, and a good autumnal." [S] "Occasional bloom after spring." [ARA18/114] "Bud pretty; flower stem short and firm. Calyx pear-shaped; sepals leaf-like." [JF] "[Among the only HP's] that pay their board bills [in Texas]." [ET] "The favorite rose amongst Brazilians." [PS] "Dedicated to a medical student . . . who died in 1872 after having borne the fatigues of the 1870–1871 war [*siege of Paris by the Prussians*]." [JR34/14]

PAUL RICAULT
Listed as a Hybrid Bourbon.

PAUL VERDIER
C. Verdier, 1866

"Magnificent bright pink." [I'H66/370] "Carmine-red, large, globular flowers, well built; a splendid sort." [EL] "Bright pink double . . . medium to large . . . fragrant." [G] "Rich pink to light red. Perfumed. Good foliage . . . 4 × 3 [ft; ca. 1.25 × 1 m]." [B] "Rich rosy-crimson, flowers large, double, and of fine imbricated form; a beautiful rose, habit very vigorous, forming a good pillar rose." [JC]

PAUL'S EARLY BLUSH
G. Paul, 1893
Sport of 'Heinrich Schultheis' (HP).

"Light silvery blush." [P1] "Flesh-pink with silvery reflections; flower large; vigorous." [Cx] "Has the singular habit of bearing flowers of two different colors in the same cluster; sometimes two colors are found in the same blossom." [JR21/40] "Flowers large, full, purple-red becoming whitish; early, habit of 'Heinrich Schultheis'." [JR17/178] "Huge, very double, scented flowers of pale pink on a sturdy plant . . . 3 × 3 [ft; ca. 9 × 9 dm]." [B]

PIERRE NOTTING
Portemer, 1863
Seedling of 'Alfred Colomb' (HP).
Not to be confused with the Tea 'Souvenir de Pierre Notting'.

"Blackish red, shaded with violet, very large and full; form globular; habit good." [P1] "Deep velvety shaded crimson, a fine deep globular flower, very large; a superb rose." [JC] "A muddy maroon." [JR10/29] "Cluster-flowering . . . very fragrant." [S] "Egg-shaped bud." [WD] "Strong-growing . . . good in autumn." [Hn] "Of vigorous strong growth, good on all stocks, with extra large fine foliage rather liable to mildew. A fine-weather Rose that will rot without opening in a wet season. It comes badly as a rule, slow in opening, and often showing a great hollow in the centre down to the eye before it expands. The plants are passed by as hopeless again and again: then, with some mysterious climatic change, for fine weather alone will not do it, toward the end of the season the blooms sometimes begin to open properly when all the strongest are over, and we see what a grand flower it can be when it chooses. Though still inclined to be weak in centre and endurance, it is then excellent in shape, colour, size, fragrance, and substance. . . . It is free-flowering but late, and not a good autumnal, as the second crop is rarely of any value. The violet shade on the outer petals is one of the nearest approaches to blue that we have." [F-M3] "Upright, vigorous plant . . . 4 × 3 [ft; ca. 1.25 × 1 m]." [B] "Most beautiful." [EL] "One of the best." [FP] "Born February 11, 1825, at Bollendorf, a hamlet near la Sare on the border of Luxembourg, Mons Notting passed his youth in very modest circumstances. From his most tender years, he evinced a passion for flowers. . . . In 1845, he settled in Luxembourg, and labored as friend and worker at Mons Wilhelm's establishment, where he worked until 1855. It was then that he got to know Mons Jean Soupert, ten years younger than himself, and the two of them founded the company so well known since that time." [JR19/177]

POLAR BEAR
Nicolas, 1934
From 'Schœner's Nutkana' (HNut, Schœner, 1930, rose-pink single; parentage: *R. nutkana* × 'Paul Neyron' [HP]) × 'New Century' (HRg, Van Fleet/Conard & Jones, 1900, flesh-pink; parentage: *R. rugosa alba* × 'Clotilde Soupert' [Pol]).

"Bud large, ovoid, white with blush; flower large, very double, full, globular, extremely lasting, intensely fragrant (wild rose), white with a faint blush, becoming pure white, on long, strong stem. Foliage abundant, large, leathery, wrinkled. Vigorous, upright, bushy, like 'Radiance' [HT]; abundant, continuous bloomer." [ARA34/220] "Fragrant blooms reminiscent of the old Bourbons." [ARA37/242] "A fine, vigorous, everblooming Hybrid Tea with Hybrid Perpetual vigor and hardiness. Flowers are intensely fragrant . . . freely produced its very double, fragrant, white flowers in rather drooping clusters." [ARA35/197] "Quantities of flowers off and on all season . . . makes a good background rose." [ARA36/206] "Flowers are not outstanding but the plant is vigorous, blooms freely and requires little care, so why complain." [ARA39/217]

PRIDE OF THE VALLEY
Listed as 'Mrs. F. W. Sanford'.

PRINCE CAMILLE DE ROHAN   PLATE 100
E. Verdier, 1861
Possibly from 'Général Jacqueminot' (HP) × 'Géant des Batailles' (HP).

"Flower medium-sized or large, full, maroon crimson, very dark, velvety, nuanced blood red." [I'H61/264] "Large, well-filled, deep velvety chestnut brown with blood red; flowers freely in clusters. An old and proved rose—one of the best dark HP's." [Hn] "Intensely dark crimson colour, and deliciously sweet." [E] "Crimson and maroon highlighted with bright red." [JR1/2/7] "Intense maroon red which does not blue." [Cx] "The blooms are apt to 'burn,' but are not much injured by rain, thin and apt to show the eye, below the average size, but remarkable for colour . . . velvety in the highest degree . . . free blooming and a good autumnal . . . requires a cool season." [F-M2] "Its maroon blooms, with black shading, are fine in June, but seldom appear afterward. The plant is moderate and divergent in growth." [ARA34/78] "Moderately full, habit somewhat spreading, shy in autumn." [EL] "Hardy . . . flower of moderate size, full, cupped, imbricated . . . beautiful exhibition rose." [S] "Opens well in dampness." [Th2] "Weak neck . . . a fascinating rose . . . almost colossal . . . vigorous . . . 3 × 3 [ft; ca. 9 × 9 dm]." [B] "A poor grower." [HmC] "Of good growth and foliage . . . very liable to mildew and orange fungus." [F-M2] "Growth vigorous." [P1] "Of weak growth, and useless for garden display." [OM] "Does not care for too much sun. Blooms freely, but here [on the Riviera] is not vigorous or a good doer, dirty and a prey to many insect pests." [B&V] "This very pretty plant makes a vigorous bush, stocky, floriferous, providing round buds and large flowers . . . still among the most notable of its sort." [JR30/169] "Still prince of its hue." [WD]

PROSPER LAUGIER   PLATE 125
E. Verdier, 1883
Not to be confused with 'Mme Prosper Laugier', the rose-pink HP of 1875.

"Flower large, full, bright crimson-red." [JR9/146] "Cupped, fragrant." [Cx] "Very vigorous; branches strong and upright, reddish; numerous unequal, pointed, recurved, pink thorns; leaves comprised of five leaflets, oblong, dark green, irregularly but deeply toothed; flower large, full, of a form most perfect and regular; color very brilliant—scarlet red with very bright carmine. A superb variety." [S]

RED DRUSCHKI
Listed as 'Ruhm von Steinfurth'.

REINE DES NEIGES
Listed as 'Frau Karl Druschki'.

REINE DES VIOLETTES

Mille-Malet, 1860
Seedling of 'Pie IX' (HP).

"Light violet." [BJ] "Violet-red, a muddy color." [EL] "Vigorous, hardy; flower large, full, flat; dark violet; one of the best of its color." [S] "Foliage . . . having a greyish sheen . . . incurved petals forming a wide, flat, quartered flower with button eye." [T1] "Abundant leaves . . . velvety, violet flowers in early Summer . . . some later. Fragrant . . . 6 × 6 [ft; ca. 1.75 × 1.75 m]." [B] "Healthy, robust, long and upright canes; the flower's perfume is of the sweet-yeasty variety, not unlike that of 'Souvenir de la Malmaison'." [BCD] "Lavender-rose with a velvety violet center . . . ages to a rich purple. Large and very double, with cupped petals, it flowers freely in early summer and intermittently thereafter . . . 7–8 ft [ca. 2–2.25 m] . . . dull, smooth, green leaves . . . practically thornless." [W]

ROGER LAMBELIN   PLATE 164

Widow Schwartz, 1890
Sport of 'Fisher Holmes' (HP).

"Deep velvety red, spotted with white; distinct and curious." [P1] "Frilled petals . . . crimson maroon with unusual white and pink stripes. Needs extra care. 4 × 3 [ft; ca. 1.25 × 1 m]." [B] "Quite a free bloomer and unique in color but not of exceptionally good form." [ARA34/79] "Abundant light green foliage. Flower medium-sized, well formed; the petals are a magnificent velvety currant-red, abundantly touched and margined with white and pink. The numerous stamens are very evident." [JR14/149] "A 6- to 8-foot pillar [ca. 1.75–2.25 m] . . . beautiful and also full of scent." [W] "Wine-scented." [JR33/101] "This variety makes a bush which is vigorous and very floriferous, and having growth somewhat like its parent [*which the quoted writer considers to be 'Prince Camille de Rohan'*]. The numerous blossoms are full . . . sometimes touched but always edged with pure white and light pink. We have often seen striped blossoms as well, like our very pretty striped Gallicas." [JR19/72] "The royalist, Roger Lambelin." [JR34/8]

RUHM VON STEINFURTH

(trans., 'Glory of Steinfurth'; syn., 'Red Druschki')
Weigand, 1920
From 'Frau Karl Druschki' (HP) × 'Ulrich Brunner fils' (HP).

"Double, high centred flowers of ruby red. Very fragrant with dark green leathery foliage . . . 4 × 3 [ft; ca. 1.25 × 1 m]." [B] "Bud very large, long-pointed; flower very large, full, double, cupped, lasting; pure red, does not 'blue'; borne, singly and several together, on long, strong stems; strong fragrance. Foliage abundant, large . . . glossy . . . Few thorns. Very vigorous, upright; blooms profusely in June and July and in September and October." [ARA22/154–155] "Profuse all-season bloom . . . tall, sturdy bush with good foliage . . . cutting value." [Capt28] "Bright red . . . very healthy . . . produces fine, fragrant blooms profusely and to a less extent in fall." [ARA34/79]

SALAMANDER

W. Paul, 1891

"Bright scarlet-crimson, magnificent colour. Very free and effective." [P1] "Very bright in the summer, and a shade more brilliant and more somber in the fall . . . blooms very freely, notable foliage and bearing, vigorous growth and good constitution." [JR15/87] "Notable for the beautiful color of bright, dark red, and for the form recalling that of 'Charles Lefebvre'. The petals are large, recurved, and substantial. — Certainly a pretty exhibition

flower considering its symmetry and form." [JR14/174] "The blossom is curious in form, the outer petals being reflexed, and those of the center drawn up [*similar characteristics are noted in 'Jules Margottin'*]." [JR17/101] "The growth and foliage seem to be good, and I have had no mildew on it. The blooms are bright and almost always try to come of good pointed shape, and in a cool season on good soil they may possibly be excellent, but it seems to be rather a small and thin Rose and hardly likely to be a good laster in a general way. It is free blooming and a fair autumnal." [F-M3] Salamanders are traditionally — and wrongly — supposed to be able to live in fire, making this a curious but appropriate name for a rose which the introducer perhaps hoped would be considered flame-colored.

SCHNEEKÖNIGEN

Listed as 'Frau Karl Druschki'.

SIDONIE

Listed as a Damask Perpetual.

SOUVENIR D'ALPHONSE LAVALLÉ   PLATE 145

C. Verdier, 1884

"Large, full, imbricated, dark grenadine maroon." [JR8/164] "Lovely double . . . many shades of crimson to purple maroon. Scented. Inclined to wander if not tethered . . . 8 × 7 [ft; ca. 2.25 × 2 m]." [B] "The growth is vigorous enough, with branches which are nearly thornless, and somewhat red at the tip; the leaves are dark green, and the bloom abundant. . . . Among the dark roses, 'Souvenir d'Alphonse Lavallée' [*sic*] is one of the best; its one fault, which it shares with others of the color, is that it burns under the rays of the summer sun." [JR25/21] "Rather sparse, small foliage of mid-green." [T3] "Lavallé (Alphonse). — Amateur, well-known dendrologist, who died in 1884 at Segrez (Seine-et-Oise) at the age of 51. Created the 'Arboretum Segrezianum,' now gone, where he brought together 4,500 species. Member of the Academy of Agriculture and President of the National Horticultural Society of France." [R-HC]

SOUVENIR DE L'EXPOSITION DE BRIE

Listed as 'Maurice Bernardin'

SOUVENIR DE MME H. THURET

Texier, 1922
From 'Frau Karl Druschki' (HP) × 'Lyon Rose' (Pern., Pernet-Ducher, 1907, pink to yellow; parentage: 'Mme Mélanie Soupert' [HT, Pernet-Ducher, 1905, saffron with red; parentage unknown] × a seedling of 'Soleil d'Or' [Pern., Pernet-Ducher, 1900, yellow; parentage: 'Antoine Ducher' (HP) × *R. fœtida persiana*]).

"A new and very interesting tint in Hybrid Perpetuals. The bud is long-pointed, coppery when the sepals divide, and the bloom is semi-double and fairly recurrent. Throughout the day the color is a blend of shiny salmon, copper and pink, drawing to each one according to time of day and angle of the sun's rays. Quite perfumed. Plant vigorous and could be used as a low pillar" [C-Ps29], attributing it to "Nabonnand, 1926." "A semi-pillar Hybrid Perpetual well worth trial. Foliage a little small, but the large, fairly remontant bloom is exquisite, of deep salmon-rose with yellow at base . . . fragrant. . . . A 'Frau Karl Druschki' in habit and blooming and shape . . . superb." [PP28]

SOUVENIR DE MME JEANNE BALANDREAU
Vilin-Robichon, 1899
Sport of 'Ulrich Brunner fils' (HP).

"Madder-red, shaded with vermilion; growth moderate." [P1] "Deep pink with vermilion highlights. Shapely, large flowers on strong necks. Scented . . . 4 × 3 [ft; ca. 1.25 × 1 m]." [B]

SOUVENIR DU DR. JAMAIN
Lacharme, 1865
Seedling of 'Charles Lefebvre' (HP).
Not to be confused with the 1853 HP 'Dr. Jamain', also a dark red, by Jamain.

"Flowers full, large, bluish violet." [I'H65/340] "Deep rich plum colour, velvety and superb, petals thick and smooth, flowers moderate size; distinct and beautiful." [JC] "Shaded with deep crimson." [EL] "Of moderate vigor . . . flower large, full, ruffled; color, dark velvety black violet." [S] "Requires shade to prevent the flowers from burning . . . deep port-wine colour . . . a rich fragrance." [G] "A sumptuous rare beauty of shape, texture and bouquet . . . 9 × 7 [ft; ca. 2.75 × 2 m]." [B]

SPENSER
('Spencer')
W. Paul, 1892
Sport of 'Merveille de Lyon' (HP).

"Beautiful satin pink, outer petals reflexed with white. A magnificent and effective Rose." [P1] "Shimmering pink." [JR20/6] "Cupped; vigorous." [Cx] "Flat, fully double. . . . Good foliage . . . 4 × 3 [ft; ca. 1.25 × 1 m]." [B] "Very large, quite full, and of a compact form; of robust growth . . . opens freely; and, due to its fulness, it keeps for a long time. As a garden flower it is without rival for its color." [JR16/6] "Apparently a stouter and fuller 'Baroness Rothschild', with similar growth and habit. Likely to be very valuable, if this estimate should be maintained; but, as seen up to the present, its additional fulness makes it a bad opener in wet weather." [F-M3]

ST. INGEBERT
Lambert, 1926
From 'Frau Karl Druschki' (HP) × 'Mme Mélanie Soupert' (HT, Pernet-Ducher, 1905, saffron with red; parentage unknown).

"One of Lambert's steps towards a yellow 'Druschki' . . . a very interesting combination of colors—white outer petals as a collarette, toning to yellowish toward the center which is reddish. Well-formed bloom with a sweet fragrance. The plant is erect, the branches slender for the class and almost thornless. Foliage olive-green and glossy." [C-Ps29] "Bud long-pointed, creamy yellow; flower large, double, moderately fragrant, lasting, white with yellowish and reddish center, borne singly. Vigorous, upright growth." [ARA26/186]

SYMPHONY
Weigand, 1935
From 'Frau Karl Druschki' (HP) × 'Souvenir de Claudius Pernet' (Pern., Pernet-Ducher, 1920, sunflower yellow).

"Continuously blooming . . . a shell-pink 'Druschki' . . . good throughout the season . . . very much taken with the dainty color of the splendidly formed flowers." [ARA37/252] "Poor color in extrme heat, but superb blooms in the fall . . . moderate vigor." [ARA39/233] "A poor grower and bloomer." [ARA36/217] "Bud very large, long-pointed; flower unusually large, double, high-centered, extremely lasting; flesh-pink to Venetian pink, on long, strong stem. Foliage large, leathery, dark green. Vigorous (as tall as

'Frau Karl Druschki'), upright; free, intermittent bloomer all season." [ARA35/218]

THOMAS MILLS
E. Verdier, 1872

"Bright crimson, large and double." [P1] "Flowers extra large, full, and of fine cup shape, colour dazzling bright rosy-carmine, with whitish stripes; a very free bloomer." [JC] "Very vigorous, erect, pretty hardy; flower . . . imbricated; color, bright carmine cherry pink, bordered lighter." [S] "A good garden variety." [EL]

TRIOMPHE DE L'EXPOSITION   PLATE 95
Margottin, 1855

"Large, crimson-purple." [JR3/28] "Dark red; flower large, full, flat." [Cx] "Reddish crimson . . . rather coarse flowers, fragrant, numerous red thorns, hardy; occasionally comes very fine, but generally the quality is inferior." [EL] "This rose makes a large bush with many long, strong, and upright branches. . . . The foliage is very ample. . . . The stems are long and strong. . . . The flowers, which open well in all seasons, come at the tips of the branches in twos, threes, or fours, or sometimes solitary . . . large (four to five in [ca. 1–1.25 dm], sumptuous, regular, full, the upright petals holding out well against the sun; open; bright velvety red, tinted and spotted dark purple towards the tips of the petals; the perfume is pleasant though faint." [JR8/71–72] "Very vigorous, giving big, long canes, green with a 'bloom,' also having very unequal thorns, flattened at the edges, upright or nearly so, of a brownish red. The foliage is very ample and of a beautiful green; each leaf is composed of 5–7 oblong or oval-lanceolate leaflets, pointed, toothed, sometimes finely toothed; the flower . . . varies according to the weather or exposure: bright crimson red in the sun, darker in the shade." [S] "The upper face [of the leaves] is glabrous, and beautiful green; the lower face is pale green, and slightly downy as with the Centifolia; some rudimentary prickles may be seen on the mid-vein; the terminal leaflet is much larger than the lateral ones . . . the rachis is big, firm, and pretty straight, glandular, particularly above where it is slightly furrowed; 8–10 very unequal small prickles may be found beneath. Two very lacy stipules, adherent at the base to the petiole . . . are edged with numerous glandular hairs; the free part is linear, narrowing into an awl, much divergent, making a right angle to the petiole. At first bloom, the canes are tipped with 4 or 5 blossoms; the reblooming canes [*i.e., those which grow to bloom later in the season*] usually only have one blossom." [I'H55/217] "Canes pretty strong and branching; bark smooth, a slightly reddish dark green, thorns the same color, and big, thick, hooked, and sharp. Leaves somber green, divided into 3 or 5 leaflets which are acuminate and dentate; leafstalk pretty strong, armed with 3 or 4 little prickles. Flowers 3.5–4 in across [ca. 8 cm–1 dm], full, cupped, concave, well formed; solitary or in clusters of 3 or 4 on the strongest branches; color crimson red, dark as well as intense; outer petals large and concave, those of the center smaller; bud very pretty; flower stalk firm and long. Calyx rounded and pear-shaped; sepals leaflike. . . . This rose . . . took first prize at the Universal Exposition of 1855 at Paris." [JF]

ULRICH BRUNNER FILS   PLATE 134
(trans., 'Ulrich Brunner, the Son')
Levet, 1881
Seedling of 'Paul Neyron' (HP).

"Bright cerise red, very large and full . . . of magnificent petal, and in all respects one of the best." [P1] "Large flowers, with splendid petals, well-formed, brilliant rosy crimson with light purple tints." [JR7/157] "Rather loose blooms of rosy-carmine fading quickly. Sweetly scented and vigorous . . . 5 × 4; [ca. 1.5 × 1.25 m]." [B] "Extra-large flowers of light red, bordering on scarlet or crimson. Foliage plentiful . . . very vigorous . . . about 30 blooms per season." [ARA21/90] "Shell-petaled Rose of sweet fragrance, and a great favorite." [DO] "Blooms come well, of extra large size, with stout petals generally tightly incurved in the centre, fine regular smooth shape . . . capital lasting qualities, not much injured by rain, though the colour soon fades . . . free-blooming and capital in the autumn." [F-M2] "Beautiful in spring." [ARA18/114] "June-blooming only." [ARA34/78] "Another Hybrid Perpetual which is not very perpetual." [JR37/171] "Of moderate vigor, coming, say some rosarians, from 'Paul Neyron', or by open pollination writes the breeder — we incline towards the latter opinion. The branches are upright and strong, with few thorns, and bear large, cupped flowers which are fragrant and of a nice cherry-red when well open." [JR12/105] "Good leathery foliage, free from mildew. . . . A great Rose in many ways . . . of strong constitution and does well almost anywhere." [F-M2] "Plant is symmetrical." [ARA29/49] "A variety of the first order." [S] "Ulrich Brunner, rose-grower at Lausanne." [JR30/53]

VICK'S CAPRICE PLATE 154

Vick, 1889

Sport of 'Archiduchesse Elisabeth d'Autriche' (HP).

"Imperial pink, distinctly variegated with deep rose, unique and lovely." [Dr] "Very much like 'Hermosa' [B] in form; the color is dark scarlet with touches of white." [JR13/91] "Large, double, cupped flowers with high centres . . . pale pink and lilac with white and deep pink stripes. Attractive foliage . . . 4 × 3 [ft; ca. 1.25 × 1 m]." [B] "Flowers large with a ground color of soft satiny pink, distinctly striped and dashed with carmine. It is beautiful in bud form, being quite long and pointed also plainly showing the stripes and markings." [CA93] "Elegant buds. Constant." [Dr] "Without rival in its type; it is quite remontant and all the flowers are always distinct in their characteristic; they are light pink, a satiny carnation, bizarrely plumed and striped white and carmine. The blossoms are solitary, and develop at the ends of the erect and vigorous branches. This variety is very hardy, has plain green foliage, and is good for forcing . . . of a finesse and incontestable elegance, it is the striped rose *par excellence*." [JR22/42]

VICTOR HUGO

Schwartz, 1884

Possibly a seedling of 'Charles Lefebvre' (HP).

Not to be confused with the rosy-lilac HB of the same name.

"Brilliant crimson, shaded with purple, very striking, of medium size, almost full." [P1] "Sparkling crimson red; flower large, imbricated, fragrant; vigorous." [Cx] "When 'well done by,' the blooms are very handsome, of fine shape, fair petal and centre, glorious colour, and good size . . . fairly free-blooming . . . but the petals are rather thin, and the blooms not very lasting." [F-M2] "A bright 'Xavier Olibo'; will be, without a doubt, a valuable novelty." [JR12/21] "A great favorite with many rosarians on account of its brilliant crimson-scarlet blooms of perfect form, which always compel admiration. Growth is rather weak, and a fine display is not to be expected." [OM] "Of good growth in rich soil with very distinct foliage and habit, liable to mildew, and requiring high cultivation." [F-M2] "One of the best of its colour." [DO] Victor Marie Hugo, French *littérateur,* 1802–1885.

VICTOR VERDIER

('Monsieur Victor Verdier')

Lacharme, 1859

From 'Jules Margottin' (HP) × 'Safrano' (T).

Not to be confused with Dorisy's 1852 scarlet Bourbon of the same name.

"Bright rose, with carmine centre, a very fresh shade, but not permanent, semi-globular form, of good size, not fragrant; very free, the wood is all but smooth, the foliage lustrous. This variety is doubtless of Bourbon origin; it is a beautiful rose, but with its entire progeny is more tender than any other types in the class." [EL] "Very bright pink, with violet." [JR2/60] "Rosy carmine, purplish edges, very large and full; form cupped; growth robust." [P1] "Pink shaded with carmine, of an admirable shade." [JR3/28] "Intense red; flower large, full, globular, high-centered; very floriferous; vigorous." [Cx] "Very vigorous bush; flower very large, full, pink nuanced very intense carmine." [I'H59/138] "Deep rose, centre brilliant rose, a beautiful colour . . . an exquisite rose, free-flowering, and of good habit." [JC] "Large flowers and wondrously beautiful large petals so shell-like." [R8] "Rather small, bright crimson." [HRH] "Bounteous summer flowering, good autumnal." [S] "Beautiful foliage." [P2] "Much like ['John Hopper']; a first-rate hardy kind." [WD] "Still in favour [*in 1908*]." [K2] "Verdier (Philippe-Victor). — Horticulturalist of Ivry (Seine); died in 1878 at the age of 75. Was vice-president of the National Horticultural Society. Important breeder of Roses, Peonies, Irises, and Gladioli." [R-HC] "Born August 5, 1803, at Yerres (Seine-et-Oise), died in February, 1878. . . . He was still under-manager of cultures at Neuilly when he undertook growing roses from seed. He developed at that time, in collaboration with his uncle [*Mons Jacques*], the 'Sempervirens' line: 'Adélaïde d'Orléans', 'Félicité et Perpétue', 'Léopoldine d'Orléans', 'Mélanie de Montjoie', 'Princesse Louise', 'Princesse Marie', and finally 'Général Athalin' [*which we list as 'Athalin' among the Hybrid Bourbons*], a non-remontant variety, but one which at length stood at the head of the new race to which we have given the name of Hybrid Perpetuals — despite the fact that Mons Verdier never in the least practiced cross-breeding between the genres which he perfected! It's from 'Général Athalin' that his 'Perpétuelle de Neuilly' came in 1834, as well as so many others bred by his contemporaries Hardy, Vibert, Prévost, and Laffay, whose [*recent*] death we mourn. In 1838, the remontant roses began to take the place of the non-remontants, and Victor Verdier, who had the most complete collection of these latter, disposed of them, rebuilding a new collection with the new roses — and it indeed became one of the largest and most admired. . . . The roses of Victor Verdier remain in collections as being among the most perfect in form and color: 'Perpétuelle de Neuilly' [HP, 1834, rose-pink], 'Mme Bréon' [Ch, 1841, red], 'Mme Andry' [HP, 1850, bright pink shaded violet], 'Mme Pépin' [HP, 1847, pink with white reverse], 'Mme Hilaire' [HP, 1850, lilac-pink], 'Mme Furtado' [HP, 1860, bright rose-red], 'François Lacharme' [HP, 1861, red], 'Olivier Delhomme' ['Olivier *Bel*homme', that is; see Supplement], 'Vicomte Vigier' [HP, 1861, violet-red], 'Vulcain' [see chapter supplement], and many others. . . . The first white-striped-pink variety [*of Gladioli*], 'Mme Hérincq', was a charming obtention of Mons Verdier's. Entered into commerce by him in 1851, it was at the same time bought and sold in England by Mr. Cole, who announced it as the product of a cross between *Gladiolus gandevensis* and *G. floribundus*." [SNH78/279] "*Catalog of Species and Varieties of the genus* Rosa, *cultivated by Mons Verdier at Neuilly-sur-Seine, near Paris, available autumn 1833 and spring 1834. It is particularly in the* China, Tea, and Noisette sorts of Roses, remontant or perpetual, that Mons Verdier is rich in novelties and meritorious species, not however neglecting the best of the other sections. The moderate prices, sizes, forms, and flower-colors are indicated for each variety. The order and intelligence with which his establishment is run inspire confidence." [R-H34] "An attempt to cultivate the friendship of a rosarian, whose name is borne by my last selection, 'Victor Verdier'. I called upon him in the year 1861, and supposing that he knew a little English, and that I knew a little French, I anticipated a gush of fraternal sympathy and sweet communion of kindred spirits. The gush did not take place. We could not understand each other in the least; and I do not suppose that two large men ever looked, or felt themselves to be, so small. I fled to my wife (I was on my wedding tour). . . . It is one of the grandest and most constant of roses." [R1/251]

WALDFEE
(trans., 'Woodsprite')
Kordes, 1960
From 'Indepedence' (Flor., red) × 'Mrs. John Laing' (HP).
   "Very bright . . . large, fragrant, blood-red . . . glossy foliage, strong growth . . . recurrent." [G]

[WILLIAM JESSE]
Listed as an HB.

XAVIER OLIBO
Lacharme, 1865
Sport of 'Général Jacqueminot' (HP).
   "Velvety black, shaded with amaranth . . . 'cockscomb colour' . . . blooms come divided sometimes, but it is often a fine Rose . . . centre sometimes incurved . . . sometimes with a fine point: a good lasting bloom, of full size . . . not a free bloomer." [F-M2] "Rich, velvety crimson, often blackish-crimson, the colour of this rose is most superb, petals large and smooth, flowers finely cupped and very beautiful." [JC] "Pleasing in colour when it does not burn, but irregular in shape; pretty, but much over-praised." [P2] "Large and full; very showy . . . a moderate grower." [P1] "Very fragrant, a beautiful rose, but not full." [JR10/29] "A shy bloomer." [ARA17/29] "Has the merit of flowering well at the end of summer." [Wr] "A weak grower with poor constitution . . . liable to mildew . . . must be 'liberally treated' . . . not . . . suitable for general cultivation." [F-M2] "4 × 3 [ft; ca. 1.25 × 1 m]." [B] "Such blooms . . . magnificent in size and beautifully full; of a deep, yet brilliant velvety scarlet when first open, and gradually changing to darkest crimson. It is an exceedingly showy rose . . . beautiful when only its thick, deep green glossy leaves are to be seen, but gorgeous when mingling with its shining foliage, the darkly glowing roses are seen in the height of their beauty." [HstXXVIII:166] "A superb rose." [EL]

Supplement

A. DRAWIEL
Lévêque, 1886
   "Growth vigorous; flowers large, full, form perfect and globular, blackish poppy red, brightened with carmine; one of the most beautiful dark roses yet developed." [JR10/149] "Medium height." [Sn]

A. GEOFFREY DE ST.-HILAIRE
E. Verdier, 1878
   "Red, with a shade of crimson; medium size, full; fine, circular form, fragrant and free. Seed organs well developed; seven leaflets are common, a great rarity among dark varieties of this class." [EL] "Growth vigorous with upright, short, delicate green canes; thorns numerous, straight, pink; leaves composed of 5–7 oblong, brownish green leaflets, with irregular, deep dentation; flowers medium-sized or large, full, admirably formed into a quite regular cup-shape; color, beautiful intense cerise red, superb . . . very remontant and very fragrant." [JR2/186] "Exquisite scent." [S]

[A.-M. AMPÈRE]
Liabaud, 1881
Seedling of 'Lion des Combats' (HP).
   "Fine large flowers, borne in clusters; color, rich purplish red, tinged with violet; very showy and attractive." [CA90] "Very vigorous bush, with erect canes; flower of medium size, full, cupped; color, purplish red with bluish reflection; very pretty." [JR5/171] "Canes armed with sparse red thorns; leaves comprised of 5 leaflets; petiole slightly prickly; peduncle stiff. . . . This pretty rose may be grown own-root or grafted, but not in a pot. It can't be forced; it is hardy. Prune short. It bears the name of Mons André-Marie Ampère, a knowledgeable [physicist and] mathematician, born at Polemieux, near Lyon, who died in 1836.

ABBÉ BERLÈZE
Guillot fils, 1864
Seedling of 'Géant des Batailles' (HP).
   "Flowers varying from bright-reddish-cerise to rosy-carmine, large, full, and of fine form; growth vigorous." [FP] "Very vigorous growth, flowers large, very full, well formed, color varying from bright cherry red to carmine pink." [I'H64/328] "Canes somewhat slight and nearly thornless; flower pretty large; color, bright cerise red . . . dedicated to Mons l'Abbé Berlèze, a great fancier of Camellias." [JR10/9]

ABBÉ BRAMEREL
Guillot fils, 1871
Seedling of 'Géant des Batailles' (HP).
   "Rich velvety-crimson, intense deep colour, flowers large, full, and evenly formed; a handsome and distinct rose, habit robust." [JC] "One of the beautiful flowers admired at exhibitions; it opens easily and may be distinguished by its scent. Growth is vigorous; the irregularly toothed leaves are pilose. Mildews. Color, bright crimson red, nuanced a velvety deep blackish brown purple." [S]

ABBÉ GIRAUDIER
Levet, 1869
From 'Géant des Batailles' (HP) × 'Victor Verdier' (HP).
   "Bright rose." [EL] "The foliage of this rose is rather becoming, being olive-green; growth is vigorous, and it makes handsome bushes. On Polyantha stock [which is to say, R. multiflora 'Polyantha'] the roses attain about four in in diameter [ca. 1 dm]; its cerise-red color is very charming." [S]

ABEL GRAND

('Abel Grant')
Damaizin, 1865
Seedling of 'Jules Margottin' (HP).

"Clear silvery-pink, flowers large, full, and well formed, habit robust; a large and handsome rose, and very distinct." [JC] "Foliage very dark, irregularly dentate; flower large, full; color, delicate pink shaded with silvery streaks; one of the best exhibition roses . . . blooms early and abundantly." [S] " 'Jules Margottin' type. Glossy rose, large and full, fragrant; unreliable as to form, often the finest in autumn." [EL] "Rosy blush. . . . A fine Rose." [P1]

ABRAHAM ZIMMERMAN

Lévêque, 1879

"Growth very vigorous; foliage dark green; beautiful large, full flowers, quite regular in form; richly colored bright red shaded poppy and nuanced purple; superb and sparkling." [JR3/167] "Light scent, tall." [Sn]

ACHILLE CESBRON

Rousset, 1894
Seedling of 'Mme Eugène Frémy' (HP, E. Verdier, 1885, pink; parentage unknown).

"Sparkling poppy." [LS] "Red, very large, full, medium scent, medium height." [Sn]

ACHILLE GONOD

Gonod, 1863
Seedling of 'Jules Margottin' (HP).

"Rosy carmine." [EL] "Flower large, full, sparkling carmine; very fragrant." [S] "Brilliant scarlet crimson, shaded deep maroon, large, full and sweet." [C&Js02] "Flowers bright-reddish carmine . . . very large and full; extra fine foliage, dark green; growth vigorous." [FP]

ADÉLAÏDE DE MEYNOT

Gonod, 1882

"Vigorous; strong, upright canes, very dark green; numerous thorns; foliage of five finely dentate leaflets; strong stem; flower large, imbricated, with quite rounded petals; color, bright cerise pink; Centifolia fragrance; quite remontant." [JR6/149]

ADIANTIFOLIA

Cochet-Cochet, 1907

"Pink." [Ŷ] Probably another in the series of which Cochet's 1899 Rosa Heterophylla' (from *R. rugosa* × *R. fœtida*) was a member: "One of the most bizarre forms in the genus *Rosa*. In spring, the various leaves which come out first are normal, but later the bush is covered with a multitude of leaves composed of three pairs of leaflets, 4–5 cm long [ca. 2 in], but only 3 or 4 mm wide [ca. an eighth of an inch]." [JR23/169] — Thus, a Hybrid Rugosa rather than an HP.

ADRIEN SCHMITT

Schmitt, 1889

"Carmine." [LS] "Red, large, full, tall." [Sn]

ALBERT LA BLOTAIS

('Albert La Blottais')
Moreau-Robert, 1881
Not to be confused with Pernet's red climbing HP of 1887.

"Vigorous, beautiful light green foliage, flower medium, full, globular, perfect form, color velvety blackish nuanced flame, very floriferous." [JR5/172] "Mons Albert La Blotais, sometime cavalry officer, died May 22 [1895] after a sad and cruel illness. . . . He was a passionate fancier of roses, a man who conquered all by his affability, his modesty, his loyalty, his good heart, and by the esteem and consideration he showed to all." [JR19/98]

ALBERT PAYÉ

('Albert Pagé')
Touvais, 1873

"Growth vigorous; irregular branching; foliage light green; flower large, full; flesh pink, overlaid with darker pink." [S]

ALEXANDRE CHOMER

Liabaud, 1875

"Growth strong and vigorous; thorns irregular and reddish; flower large, full; color, velvety purple, nuanced bishop's violet." [S]

ALEXANDRE DUMAS

Margottin, 1861

"Velvety-maroon, highly scented." [FP] "Flower large, full, well formed, velvety blackish crimson, striped poppy." [l'H61/263] "Flower large, often very large, depending upon the soil; form perfect; notable for its good poise; color, velvety crimson striped deep poppy. In strong ground, the color is much blacker." [S] Alexandre Dumas, either *père* (1802–1870) or *fils* (1824–1895); in either case, French novelist and dramatist.

ALEXANDRE DUPONT

Liabaud, 1882
Seedling of 'Triomphe de l'Exposition' (HP).

"Red, shaded." [LS] "Very vigorous bush; canes with green surface; foliage ample, handsome dark green, deeply toothed, leafstalk armed with two or three white prickles; flower-stalk stiff, bristly; blossom 7–8 cm across [ca. 3 in], quite double, well formed, velvety purple-red nuanced crimson; fragrant. This pretty variety . . . is better grafted on the briar than on its own roots; good in pots and for forcing; hardy. It bears the name of a young nephew of Liabaud's. To ensure good bloom, prune long." [JR10/11] "Two pairs of leaflets. Flower very large . . . well-held." [JR6/150]

ALEXANDRE DUTITRE

Lévêque, 1878

"Bright rose." [EL] "Vigorous, flower large, full, perfectly imbricated like 'Annie Wood'. Color, handsome light bright pink; very remontant; considering the perfection of form and beautiful coloration, this is an extra good variety." [JR2/166]

ALEXIS LEPÈRE

Vigneron, 1875

"Growth vigorous; foliage velvety, very dark; flower very large, full, globular and of notable form; color, glossy light red." [S]

ALFRED LEVEAU

Listed as 'Monsieur Alfred Leveau'.

ALINE ROZEY
('Aline Rosey')
Schwartz, 1884
Sometimes called a Hybrid Noisette.
"Vigorous, flower medium-sized, full, imbicated, very perfect form, color flesh-pink fading to white. Abundantly floriferous." [JR8/133]

ALI PACHA CHÉRIFF
('Aly Pacha Chérif')
Lévêque, 1886
"Cinnabar." [JR20/5] "Very vigorous, flowers large, full, very well formed, beautiful fiery vermilion red nuanced blackish purple." [JR10/149]

ALPAÏDE DE ROTALIER
('Alphaïde de Rotallier')
Campy/C. Verdier, 1863
"Fine transparent rose-color, glossy." [FP] "Flower large, full, well-formed; color, transparent light pink; good for forcing in February." [S]

ALPHONSE DE LAMARTINE
Ducher, 1853
"Light rosy-pink." [FP] "Blossom medium-sized, full, well-formed, delicate lilac-pink. Very beautiful variety." [JDR56/48] "Very vigorous, branches upright and very thorny, foliage dark green, blossom medium or large, depending upon the season, very full, delicate pink, perfect form, well held, very fragrant." [JDR54/11] "Distinctly hooked thorns; leaves . . . rough to the touch; flower . . . globular; color, white shaded lilac-pink." [S] "Dark carmine red." [Y̆]

ALPHONSE SOUPERT   PLATE 135
Lacharme, 1883
Seedling of 'Jules Margottin' (HP).
"Bright rose-colour, large and very showy." [P1] "Very vigorous (like 'Jules Margottin'), flower, form, and size that of 'La Reine'; color, pure bright pink, blooming very early." [JR7/160] "Very thorny growth, but not strong with me . . . the blooms are rather loose and by no means first-class. They are large and may be valued where the first Roses may be esteemed, as they are quite among the earliest. The petals are rather thin, and the shape is somewhat uncertain: still it is said to be a 'showy' Rose, which in catalogue-English generally means 'showy at a distance,' i.e., that it will not bear a close inspection." [F-M3] "Sepals foliaceous; flower large, well-formed . . . dedicated by its raiser to . . . the elder son of the great Luxembourgian rosarian." [JR10/12]

ALSACE-LORRAINE
H. Duval, 1879
"Very vigorous, very remontant, flowers full, regular in form, borne majestically, particularly handsome foliage; color, deep velvety black." [JR3/182] "An extra-handsome variety." [S] Sometimes considered synonymous with 'Directeur Alphand' (HP).

AMBROGIO MAGGI
Pernet fils, 1879
Seedling of 'John Hopper' (HP).
"Bright rose." [EL] "Growth vigorous, very large wood, canes upright; beautiful light green foliage; flower very large, nearly full, globular, beautiful very intense pink, well held, quite remontant." [JR3/165] "Tall." [Sn]

AMÉDÉE PHILIBERT
Lévêque, 1879
"Very vigorous, beautiful very green foliage, flowers very large, full, beautiful very regular globular form, handsome deep violet nuanced blackish purple, a superb and rich coloring." [JR3/167]

[AMERICAN BELLE]
Burton, 1893
Sport of 'American Beauty' (HP).
"Crimson." [LS] "Pleasing shade of pink; very distinct." [CA96] "'American Belle' will be . . . an improvement on 'American Beauty', from which it sported in 1890 . . . 'American Belle' is completely lacking the violet tint which 'American Beauty' has shown for several years. Both have nearly the same growth characteristics; however, the more recent variety is not quite as vigorous as the other, its flowers are more open, and the darker green foliage is generally somewhat longer." [JR17/38]

AMI CHARMET
Dubreuil, 1900
"Flower very large, quite double, wafting an elegant and pure Gallia-rose scent; form notably beautiful, with thick petals, wider than long, gracefully recurved and waved on the upper part, regularly and elegantly imbricated like a Camellia . . . color, China pink with satiny reflections. The stems . . . are strong and robust, bearing from one to six blossoms, depending upon their vigor. The blossoms measure up to 5.5 in across [ca. 1.3 dm], open with a 'neck,' and recurve like a Medici vase." [JR24/164] "Pure China-rose colour, reflexed with satiny rose, very large and sweet; fine foliage." [P1]

AMI MARTIN
Chédane-Guinoisseau, 1906
From an unnamed seedling pollinated by 'Eugene Fürst' (HP).
"Very vigorous, with rigid canes, thorny, dark green foliage; very large flower, very full, plump, petals very thick and often reticulated; color, very intense, bright vermilion red, doesn't blue, very fragrant, very floriferous." [JR30/167]

AMIRAL COURBET   PLATE 139
Dubreuil, 1884
"Vigorous, with continuous bloom. Canes ashen with occasional thorns. Leaves large and beautiful, pale matte green, evenly colored. Buds oval. Flowers upright, cupped, perfectly held, bright carmine red with magenta reflections. Outer petals very numerous, quite concave, imbricated, inner petals shorter, muddled. Very fragrant . . . elegant and penetrating aroma which it wafts forth all season. A magnificent variety." [JR8/152]

AMIRAL GRAVINA
Robert & Moreau, 1860
"Not very vigorous; branches very flexile; leaves fall; flower blackish purple, dark amaranth around the edges. The blossom is well formed, of medium size, and full." [S] "[The blossom] humbly kisses the ground." [VH62/91] "Medium to tall." [Sn]

ANDRÉ LEROY D'ANGERS
Trouillard/Standish, 1866
"Dark violet red." [JR25/14] "Crimson, with a shade of violet; an attractive color, but very transient; often ill-formed." [EL] "Purplish-crimson, fine color, large and full." [FP] "Vigorous; foliage very dark; blossom deep violet outside and dark pink within." [S]

ANNA SCHARSACH

Geschwindt, 1890

From 'Baronne Adolphe de Rothschild' (HP) × 'Mme Lauriol de Barney' (HB).

"Blossom fresh pink, center brighter and often light purple, large, full, cupped. Bush very vigorous, hardy." [JR14/147] "Very fragrant, tall." [S]

ANNE LAFERRÈRE

P. Nabonnand, 1916

"Blood red." [Ÿ]

ANTOINE MOUTON

Levet, 1874

Seedling of 'La Reine' (HP).

"Deep rose, tinged with lilac, not unlike 'Paul Neyron'; it is more fragrant and more hardy, but in color and size is below that sort." [EL] "Fine bright rose, reverse of the petals silvery; a large flower, somewhat coarse, but often good." [JC] "Very full." [CA90] "Vigorous and hardy . . . few thorns, green canes; leaves of 3–5 leaflets which are much serrated; leafstalk bears some small white prickles; flowerstalk green, firm, pubescent, sepals appendiculate and covered with glands; blossom to four in across [ca. 1 dm], of perfect form, bright pink, reverse of petals paler; very fragrant." [JR10/20] "One of Mons Levet's best; the growth is very vigorous." [S]

ANTONIE SCHURZ

Geschwindt, 1890

"Flower flesh-white, very large, full, centifolia form and fragrance. Moderate vigor; hardy." [JR13/147]

ANTONINE VERDIER

Listed as a Hybrid Tea.

ARISTIDE DUPUY

('Aristide Dupuis')

Trouillard, 1867

Also attributed to Touvais, 1866.

"Purplish-rose, a muddy hue; double or full, fragrant; of no value." [EL] "Growth vigorous; branches grow upright; flower large, full, very remontant; slaty violet bordered bright pink." [S]

ARTHUR OGER

Oger, 1875

Seedling of 'Gloire de Ducher' (HP).

"Flower very large, well formed, full, borne singly; color, velvety purple, very dark but bright." [S] "Tall." [Sn]

ARTHUR WEIDLING

Vogel, 1932

Sport of 'Pride of Reigate' (HP).

"Dark pink, large, full, medium scent, moderately tall." [Sn]

AUGUSTE CHAPLAIN

Tanne, 1921

"Red." [Ÿ]

[AUGUSTE MIE]

('Mme Rivals')

Laffay, 1851

Seedling of 'La Reine' (HP).

"Glossy pink, a large globular flower, very full and well formed, a very vigorous grower, forms a good pillar; it does not open freely in cold damp situations." [JC] "Flower large, very double, cupped; sparkling pink; magnificent." [VH51/111] "Very vigorous plant; flowers large, full or nearly full, bright pink. A superb variety, both grafted and own-root." [l'H53/225] "A red rose of exquisite form, resembling, by more than one report, 'Coupe d'Hébé'." [R-H63] "Branches very strong, with abundant straight thorns; flower well formed, large; quite remontant, and blooms for a long time; glossy pink, silvery on the reverse." [S] "Growing very vigorously, and bearing flowers equal to those of its parent in beauty of form, and superior in delicacy of color." [FP]

AURORE BORÉALE

Oger, 1865

"Growth vigorous; flower perfectly formed, large, full, quite remontant and blooms until October; color, bright shining red." [S]

AURORE DU MATIN

Roland, 1867

"Flowers very large, full, beautiful dawn coloration, reverse of petals silvery." [l'H68/49] "Reverse of petals bright red; beautiful exhibition flower." [S] "Light red . . . very fragrant, tall." [Sn]

AVOCAT DUVIVIER

Lévêque, 1875

Seedling of 'Général Jacqueminot' (HP).

"Brilliant dark crimson, a large bold flower, like 'Maréchal Vaillant' [HP, Viennot, 1861, purple]; fine and distinct." [JC] "Flower very large, full, very well formed, very effective; color, bright purplish red with light purple; growth vigorous; floriferous." [S] "Tall." [Sn]

BARON DE WOLSELEY

E. Verdier, 1882

"Vigorous, reddish-green upright canes; thorns somewhat numerous, short, pink; leaves of five oval-rounded leaflets, with regular serration, delicate green; flowers large, full, well formed, velvety bright crimson nuanced flame." [JR6/165]

BARON ELISI DE ST.-ALBERT

Widow Schwartz, 1893

"Violet red, very large, full, medium height." [Sn] "Vigorous bush, beautiful gay green foliage; flower very large, well formed, beautiful very bright carmine red passing to lilac red; comes up to the size of 'Paul Neyron'. Very floriferous." [JR17/165]

BARON HAUSSMANN

Lévêque, 1867

Not to be confused with E. Verdier's red HP of the same year 'Baronne Haussmann'.

"Dark red, large, well-built flowers." [EL] "Clear carmine-crimson, flowers of good size, beautiful and full; habit vigorous." [JC] "Flower large, full, compact, blooming in clusters; color, very beautiful carmine red, touched from time to time with deep crimson. Much to be recommended." [S]

BARON NATHANIEL DE ROTHSCHILD   PLATE 140
Lévêque, 1882
"Very vigorous; foliage ample, handsome dark green; flower large, full, extremely well formed; beautiful uniform bright crimson red . . . regular form." [JR6/148] "A splendid variety." [S]

BARON TAYLOR
Dugat, 1879
Sport of 'John Hopper' (HP).
"Light red, large, full, tall." [Sn] "The growth and everything about the wood and foliage are the same [as with 'John Hopper']; the color of the blossom, which has the same form, is a very delicate pink; flower large, full." [S] "Does not appear to be constant [in the sported character]." [EL]

BARON T'KINT DE ROODENBEKE
('Baron T'Kind de Roodenbecke')
Lévêque, 1897
"Very vigorous bush; beautiful dark somber green foliage; flowers large, full, very well formed, deep purple, nuanced and brightened with carmine and vermilion." [JR21/163–164]

BARONNE DE MEDEM
E. Verdier, 1876
"Very vigorous, flower large, full, globular, bright carmine cerise-red." [JR1/6/10] "Has the form of the China Aster." [S]

BARONNE DE PRAILLY
V. Verdier/Liabaud, 1871
Seedling of 'Victor Verdier' (HP).
"Bright red, large, very full; often does not open well." [EL] "Bright pink." [Ÿ] "Moderate vigor . . . flower large, bright red, globular, too heavy for the stems which are rather slight and flexuose. . . . Mme la Baronne de Prailly lives in Hyères." [JR10/34]

BARONNE DE ST.-DIDIER
Lévêque, 1886
"Vigorous, flowers very large, full, crimson red or intense cerise, shaded lilac and purple, petals often edged white." [JR10/150]

BARONNE GUSTAVE DE ST.-PAUL
Glantenet/Bernaix, 1894
"Flower extra large, about 4.5 in [ca. 1.25 dm], borne on a strong stem. Beautiful pale pink color, with silvery reflections—very effective. Very floriferous." [JR18/164]

BARONNE MAURICE DE GRAVIERS
E. Verdier, 1866
"Beautiful intense cerise red, nuanced and shaded pink and carmine, reverse of petals whitish." [l'H66/370] "Growth very vigorous; canes upright and very thorny; flower medium-sized, well formed, full; color, dark crimson red." [S]

BARONNE NATHANIEL DE ROTHSCHILD
Pernet père, 1884
Seedling of 'Baronne Adolphe de Rothschild' (HP).
Not to be confused with '*Baron* Nathaniel de Rothschild' (HP).
"Vigorous bush; foliage light green, very thick, much serrated, abundant. From 'Baronne Adolphe de Rothschild', to which it bears a great resemblance in wood and foliage; flower very large, nearly full, plump; color, beautiful bright pink with silvery shadings. This rose is beautiful and much to be recommended." [S] "Canes upright . . . flower very large, nearly full, globular . . . well held; very perfect form." [JR8/151]

BARTHÉLEMY-JOUBERT
Moreau-Robert, 1877
"Very vigorous, flower large, full, very bright cerise red." [JR1/12/12]

BEAUTY OF BEESTON
Frettingham, 1882
"Growth vigorous; canes strong, but without growing very tall; flower small, full; velvety crimson." [S]

[BEAUTY OF WALTHAM]
W. Paul, 1862
Seedling of 'Général Jacqueminot' (HP).
"Bright carmine, and blooms profusely." [FP] "Cherry-crimson, petals large and well disposed, flowers cupped, large and finely formed, habit free." [JC] "Fair in growth and foliage, and not much liable to injury from fungoid pests or rain. The blooms come true and well, being seldom divided or malformed. The shape varies according to situation and cultivation . . . the petals are very closely curved inwards in the centre in a manner that proclaims the variety at once. . . . This Rose has the good custom of closing in and guarding its centre more tightly in hot weather when it is most needed than at other times. Not first class, but a free bloomer, rather late, good in lasting qualities and as an autumnal, but not very large." [F-M2] "Very remontant, blooming until winter; flower large, full, cupped; color, cerise red shaded bright carmine. Distinguished by its delicious scent." [S]

[BELLE DE NORMANDY]
(*not* 'Belle Normande', Oger, 1864, white)
California Nursery Co.?, by 1890
"Beautiful clear rose, shaded and clouded with rosy carmine and lilac; very large and sweet." [CA90] "A lovely rose with great large flowers of pure silvery pink; one of the most beautiful. Flowers especially fragrant. The plant is a strong erect grower and good every way." [C&Js09]

BELLE YVRIENNE
Lévêque, 1890
"Very vigorous, beautiful glaucous green foliage, very thick, flower very large, very full, opens perfectly, beautiful brilliant red, shaded white and carmine; very effective plant." [JR14/179]

BEN CANT   PLATE 1
B.R. Cant, 1901
From 'Suzanne-Marie Rodocanachi' (HP) × 'Victor Hugo' (HP).
"Deep clear crimson, with dark veining, and slightly darker flushes in the centre; large and finely formed, with stout rounded outer petals of good lasting power; growth strong and sturdy." [P1] "Of fine, clean, strong growth with grand foliage, and seems to be a splendid crimson Rose for exhibition when grown on good HP soil . . . only occasionally will it give a show bloom." [F-M]

BENJAMIN DROUET
E. Verdier, 1878
"Red, shaded with purple." [EL] "Very vigorous with strong reddish green canes; thorns numerous, strong, and big, brownish green; leaves composed of 5–7 large and oval leaflets, somber green, toothed deeply and irregularly; flowers large or very large, clustered, full, and well-formed; color, intense purplish red brightened with fiery red, most beautiful." [JR2/186]

BENOÎT PERNIN
('Benoist Pernin')
Myard, 1889
Sport of 'Duchess of Edinburgh' (HP).
"Bright velvety pink." [Y̌]

BERNARD VERLOT
E. Verdier, 1874
"Purplish crimson-red and violet." [JR25/14] "Crimson, centre deep velvety-crimson, flowers full and compact, very sweet." [JC] "Growth vigorous; flower very good under glass, large, full." [S]

BERTHE BARON
Baron-Veillard, 1868
Seedling of 'Jules Margottin' (HP).
"Delicate rose color." [EL] "Of moderate growth, from the 'Jules Margottin' clan; flower large, full; color, delicate pink nuanced white." [S] "Baron[-]Veillard, Orléans horticulturalist." [JR13/101]

BERTHE DU MESNIL DE MONT CHAUVEAU
Jamain, 1876
"Silvery red." [Y̌] "Silvery rose, long cup-shaped flowers, large deep petals; a distinct and very fine rose." [JC] "Flower very large, full; color, silvery pink, center lighter. This variety is very floriferous, and much to be recommended." [S] "Vigorous bush, flower medium-sized or large, full, beautiful silvery pink." [JR1/6/10] "Du Mesnil de Mont Chauveau, rose fancier at the Château Freslonières, near Ballon." [JR2/165]

BERTHE LÉVÊQUE
Listed as 'Mlle Berthe Lévêque'.

BERTI GIMPEL
Altmüller, 1913
From 'Frau Karl Druschki' (HP) × 'Fisher-Holmes' (HP).
"Pink, large, full, dwarf." [Sn]

BESSIE JOHNSON
Curtis, 1872
Sport of 'Abel Grand' (HP).
"Light blush, large, very double, and sweet; a fine Rose of good habit; growth vigorous." [P1] "Large, globular, full, light flesh pink, very fragrant." [JR3/26] "Growth vigorous, climbing; wood long, vining; flower well formed, and nearly pure white." [S]

BICOLORE
Oger, 1877
"Moderate growth; flower large, nearly flat, full, white with a light pink edge, passing to frosty pink." [S]

[BIJOU DE COUASNON]
Vigneron, 1886
Seedling of 'Charles Lefebvre' (HP).
"Growth very vigorous; wood big, upright, with few thorns; flower large, full, beautifully colored intense velvety red; well held; very floriferous; very effective plant." [JR10/147–148]

BISCHOF DR. KORUM
Lambert, 1921
From 'Frau Karl Druschki' (HP) × 'Laurent Carle' (HT).
"Bud large, ovoid, red; flower very large, full, cupped, very double, lasting; yellowish rose, with silvery shade; borne singly on strong stem; strong fragrance. Foliage sufficient, glossy, rich green, disease-resistant. Vigorous, upright, bushy; blooms freely in June, July, September and October; hardy." [ARA22/154] "Tall." [Sn]

[BLANCHE DE MÉRU]
C. Verdier, 1869
Seedling of 'Jules Margottin' (HP).
"A lightly blushing white while opening, passing to pure white, and in clusters." [I'H70/125] "Large full flowers; color pure white; a good grower and free bloomer." [C&Js98] "Vigorous bush." [S]

BOCCACE
Moreau-Robert, 1859
"Crimson." [Y̌] "Growth vigorous, canes knotty; foliage dark and very rough to the touch; flower large, full, well formed; color, bright carmine." [S] Giovanni Boccaccio, 1313–1375; Italian author.

BOILEAU
Moreau-Robert, 1883
Seedling of 'Victor Verdier' (HP).
"Flower large, full, cupped; color, beautiful bright satiny pink, nuanced. Very floriferous." [S] Nicolas Boileau-Despréaux, 1636–1711; influential French critic.

BOUQUET BLANC
Robert, 1856
"Flower medium-sized, full, plump, very floriferous; color, pure white." [S]

BOUQUET DE MARIE
Damaizin/Touvais & Fontaine, 1858
"Very vigorous, wood very thorny, thorns short; foliage light green; flowers medium-sized, in clusters; color, a lightly greenish-white fading to pure white; very floriferous." [JDR58/36] "This variety should be pruned long; it is hardy to $12°–14°$." [JR10/60]

BRADOVA LOSOSOVA DRUSCHKI
Brada, 1937
"Salmon-pink, large, full, tall." [Sn]

BUFFALO-BILL
E. Verdier, 1889
"Vigorous, canes short, erect; flowers large, full, flat, imbricated; color, very light pink." [JR13/167] Buffalo Bill, pseudonym of William F. Cody; lived 1846–1917; American frontiersman and showman.

CÆCILIE SCHARSACH
Geschwindt, 1887
Seedling of 'Jules Margottin' (HP).
"Flesh white fading to white, large, often very large, very full, fragrant, well formed." [JR11/184] "Pinkish white . . . tall." [Sn]

[CALIFORNIA]
California Nursery Co.?, by 1905
"Bright pink." [CA05] "Rosy pink." [CA10]

CAPITAINE JOUEN   PLATE 168
Boutigny, 1901
From 'Eugene Fürst' (HP) × 'Triomphe de l'Exposition' (HP).

"Bright vivid crimson, very large and full; growth very vigorous." [P1] "Sown in 1887, the original plant, preserved by its breeder Mons Boutigny . . . is trained in a palmate form, ten ft in height and six in width, and each year the show is of a rare beauty. The plant makes a very vigorous bush, perhaps even 'climbing' . . . it blooms freely." [JR27/7]

CAPITAINE LOUIS FRÈRE
Listed as 'Monsieur le Capitaine Louis Frère'.

CAPITAINE PEILLON
Liabaud, 1893
"Vigorous bush with upright canes; beautiful dark green foliage; flower large, full, perfect form, spherical; color, beautiful crimson purple red." [JR17/164] "Tall." [Sn]

CARDINAL PATRIZZI
(*not* synonymous with 'Vainqueur de Solferino')
Trouillard/E. Verdier, 1857
Seedling of 'Géant des Batailles' (HP).

"Crimson, with a tinge of purple." [EL] "Growth vigorous." [S] "A superb Rose in a temperate climate, but which, in the North, and in England in particular, doesn't bloom well except under glass." [R-H63] "A seedling of Mons Trouillard's, of 1855, released to commerce in 1857 by Mons Eugène Verdier. Of moderate vigor . . . flower medium-sized, well formed, very full, velvety purplish red tending towards black; edges a bright flame . . . more sensitive to frost than other HP's. . . . Monseigneur Constantin Patrizzi is an Italian prelate born in Siena in 1798, it seems . . . and was bishop of Portugal and Sainte-Rufine." [JR10/77]

CAROLINE D'ARDEN
A. Dickson, 1888
From 'Alfred K. Williams' (HP) × 'Marie Baumann' (HP).

"Very delicate pure pink. Its blossoms are very large, sumptuous, and perfect as to form. The scent is delicious, the petals firm, large, rounded, and very smooth. Particularly good for exhibition. It blooms profusely; the leaves are very large; the plant is robust." [JR12/105–106]

CATHERINE SOUPERT
Lacharme, 1879
Seedling of 'Jules Margottin' (HP).

"Rosy-peach; distinct." [EL] "White, shaded with rose, large and full; form and habit perfect. A beautiful Rose." [P1] "Reblooms very freely, is vigorous and hardy, and is beginning to be appreciated for the garden . . . flower large, full, imbricated, well formed, white washed pink, held on a long stem. It is dedicated to the daughter of Mons Soupert, the able rosarian of Luxembourg." [JR10/92]

CENTIFOLIA ROSEA
('Centfeuilles Roses')
Touvais, 1863
Seedling of 'La Reine' (HP).

"Rich rosy-pink, flowers large and cupped; petals smooth and even; a very distinct and beautiful rose, with abundant foliage, habit vigorous." [JC] "Bright rose, circular, shell form; light green wood, with numerous red thorns; foliage crimped." [EL]

CHARLES BONNET
Bonnet, 1884
"Pearly pink." [LS] "Large, full, medium height." [Sn] "Much liked in Switzerland and in Haute-Savoie, next to Lake Léman. . . . It's a rose with very tenacious foliage, hardy, vigorous, floriferous, and extremely remontant; its pretty and graceful fragrant blossoms are semi-double and delicate pink; the numerous buds open quite late into the fall. This variety is so vigorous that it can be used to advantage to make shrubberies. . . . 'Charles Bonnet' should be better known, and deserves to be propagated in all countries. It originated in Switzerland where it was bred a long time ago by an arboriculturist of Renens-sous-Lausanne, who gave it his own name." [JR22/50] "It was in 1873, in a garden belonging to Mons Bonnet, a horticulturalist then at Vanves (Seine), that Mons F. Jamin first saw it [*the Boursault 'Mme Sancy de Parabère', which we will examine in Volume II*], and, upon the request of Mme Bonnet, he provisionally named it 'Mme de Sancy de Parabère' [*sic*]." [JR9/124]

[CHARLES DARWIN]
Laxton/G. Paul, 1879
From 'Pierre Notting' (HP) × 'Mme Julia Daran' (HP).

"Crimson brown, very floriferous, with well-rounded blossoms." [JR3/12] "Good growth and foliage, the blooms having a color described universally as brownish-crimson. I have been unable to detect the brown shade, but must, as I have said, leave these delicate distinctions of tints to experts. Rather late, and a good autumnal. The shape is open, and the variety does not prove very satisfactory with me, though often well shown by others." [F-M3] Parent of 'Balduin' (HT). Charles Robert Darwin, English naturalist, 1809–1882.

CHARLES DICKENS
W. Paul, 1886
"Vigorous, very hardy and blooming abundantly; blossoms large, full, beautiful pink; a splendid variety for gardens and beds." [JR10/19] Charles Dickens, 1812–1870; English author.

CHARLES LAMB
W. Paul, 1883
"Bright cerise." [Y̆] "Carmine-red. Good foliage." [H] "Flower large, full, perfectly held; color light glossy red; abundant bloom in summer and autumn; magnificent garden rose and much to be recommended for cutting." [S] "Bright red, lovely clear colour, very beautiful in the bud; foliage handsome, habit hardy. This variety flowers continuously." [P1] Charles Lamb, 1775–1834; English author.

CHARLES MARTEL
Oger, 1876
Not to be confused with Parmentier's ca. 1840 Gallica, nor with Guillot's 1847 Bourbon.

"Flower very large, nearly full, well formed, very remontant, blooms late, good rose to force; color, purple red, which sometimes takes on a violet tinge." [S] "Tall." [Sn] Charles Martel, 689–741; ruler of the Franks; defeated the Moslems at Tours in 732, stopping the spread of Islam in Europe.

CHARLES TURNER
Margottin, 1869
Not to be confused with E. Verdier's pink HP of 1868.

"Very large flower opening into a cup; beautiful sparkling intense red." [I'H70/125] "Flower large, full, cupped, well held; color, bright grenadine." [S] "Crimson-vermilion, large, full flowers, flat form, resembling 'Général Washington'; wood armed with numerous dark red thorns. A shy bloomer." [EL] "Tall." [Sn]

[CHARLES WAGNER]
Van Fleet/Conard & Jones, 1907
From 'Jean Liabaud' (HP) × 'Victor Hugo' (HP).

"A vigorous growing rose with large double flowers of clear bright red (approaching scarlet). Blossoms appear in clusters of 3 to 5, of great substance and exceedingly fragrant. It has luxuriant foliage, usually composed of seven leaflets, of dark rich green and not liable to mildew. It is one of the best bloomers." [C&Js07] "Rev. Charles Wagner, Mission Chapel, Paris, France. Author of 'Simple Life' in whose honor by special permission this Rose is named." [C&Js07]

CHARLES WOOD
Portemer, 1864

"Red, reverse white." [Ÿ] "Beautiful exhibition rose." [S] "Flowers deep red, shaded with blackish-crimson, very large, full, and of fine form; growth vigorous." [FP]

CHOT PĚSTITELE
Böhm, 1932
Sport of 'Frau Karl Druschki' (HP).

"Pink, large, full, light scent, tall." [Sn]

CHRISTINA NILSSON
Listed as 'Mme Boutin'.

CHRISTOBEL
Listed as an HT.

CLARA COCHET
Lacharme, 1885
Seedling of 'Jules Margottin' (HP).

"Very vigorous; flowers very large, rather globular, full; petals very large, color beautiful light pink, center brighter pink; petal edges have the sparkle of diamonds." [JR8/165]

CLAUDE JACQUET   PLATE 156
Liabaud, 1892

"Bush very vigorous with smooth upright canes, small and rare thorns, beautiful closely-set foliage of a glaucous green; flower very large, full, plump; color, scarlet purple, light shaded. The beginning of a new race!" [JR16/152] "Medium scent, tall." [Sn]

CLAUDE MILLION
('Claude Millon')
E. Verdier, 1863

"Flower large, full, cupped, slightly flaring; color, scarlet bordered deep violet and dark grenadine." [S] "Scarlet-crimson, dashed with rose and violet, velvety, large, full, and of excellent form, habit good." [FP] "Flowers cupped, beautiful velvety carmine scarlet, highlighted with pink and violet, growing in 4–5's in a terminal cluster." [l'H63/224] "Rich velvety crimson, beautifully shaded with violet, petals smooth and even, flowers large, cupped and well formed; habit vigorous." [JC]

CLÉMENCE JOIGNEAUX
Liabaud, 1861

"Flower very large, full; color, bright sparkling red." [S] "Carmine." [Ÿ] "Red and lilac color, and grows with great vigor." [FP] "At the top level of the schools may be placed the National School of Horticulture at Versailles, created in 1873 on the initiative of Joigneaux, replacing the former kitchen-garden of the King." [Pd]

CLÉMENCE RAOUX
Granger/Lee, 1869

"Vigorous bush; canes robust, glossy deep green, thorns straight, flat; flower large, full, well formed; color, bright pink shaded silvery pink." [S] "A washed-out pink; large, fragrant flowers, quartered shape; worthless." [EL]

COLONEL DE SANSAL
Jamain, 1875

"Flower large, full, well formed; velvety carmine shaded very deep carmine." [S] "Pink." [Ÿ]

COLONEL FÉLIX BRETON   PLATE 136
Schwartz, 1883

"Vigorous, having the look of 'Charles Lefebvre', foliage ample, cheerful green; flower large, full, with regularly imbricated petals, velvety grenadine red, exterior petals aniline violet, brilliantly velvety, with a matte amaranth reverse, a totally novel coloration." [JR7/121] "Canes of medium size, branching; bark smooth, with occasional much compressed red thorns which are slightly hooked; foliage . . . of 3–5 oval-acuminate dentate leaflets; leafstalk slender, light green, armed with 4–5 prickles; flower . . . well formed, solitary or in twos or threes." [S]

COLONEL FOISSY
Margottin, 1849

"Flower large, full, well formed, very remontant; blooms till winter; color, light cerise." [S] "Flower . . . 6–8 cm [ca. 3 in] . . . very abundant bloom." [M-V50/229] "Vigorous plant; blooms in clusters; medium size, full, bright cerise." [l'H53/171] "Bush having a great resemblance to [those of] the Bourbon group. Vigorous canes, flower-clusters at the tips, dark green, bearing large very numerous reddish thorns as well as leaves composed of 3–5 medium-sized, slightly long, dark green, irregularly dentate leaflets; flowers a beautiful bright cherry red, full, from 6–8 cm in diameter [ca. 3 in], in clusters of 5–10 in a terminal panicle; peduncles long, upright; calyx-tube inflated in the middle, slightly glandular, with sepals often foliaceous." [VH49/534–534d]

COMMANDEUR JULES GRAVEREAUX
Croibier, 1908
From 'Frau Karl Druschki' (HP) × 'Liberty' (HT).

"Vermilion-red. Vigorous. Garden. Semi-double. Distinct in colour." [NRS10/99] "Growth vigorous, with strong, upright canes; medium-sized thorns; foliage ample and beautiful dark green; blossoms borne on a strong, rigid stem; buds generally solitary, well-formed, long, and pointed; blossoms large and full; petals very large and thick, scalloped at the edge, giving the opening flower a particular elegance; color, beautiful fiery red, velvety, lightly shaded maroon within; does not blue; very fragrant . . . has the growth and bloom of 'Druschki', but it a little less vigorous; very remontant." [JR32/152] "Lovely pointed buds and rather single, peony-like, velvety red, fragrant flowers . . . the large blooms, with ragged petals, are often 6 in across [ca. 1.5 dm], and make a very striking picture in a bud-vase. The bush is low and blooms all summer." [ARA29/55]

COMTE ADRIEN DE GERMINY   PLATE 133
Lévêque, 1881
Seedling of 'Jules Margottin' (HP).

"Bright rose." [EL] "Very vigorous, beautiful ample dark green foliage, flower large, full, very well formed, imbricated, handsome bright pink, very brilliant and sparkling, very remontant and beautiful." [JR5/149]

COMTE BOBRINSKY

('Bobrinski', 'Count Bawbrinzki')
Marest, 1849

"Velvety deep crimson." [LS] "Medium-sized, very full, bright carmine." [Pq] "Deep maroon." [JR2/59] "Brilliant scarlet-crimson, a most attractive colour, though the flowers are not well formed." [JC] "Full or nearly full . . . blooms continuously. . . . It does well grafted, less well own-root." [I'H53/171] "This is a Bourbon hybrid, with very vigorous branches, smooth, with long, narrow, and slightly hooked thorns which are brownish green; leaves glossy green, smooth, with 5–7 oval-oblong leaflets which are sharp at the tip, and bordered with slightly reddish teeth; flowers solitary or in twos, 3.5 to 4 in across [ca. 1 dm], resembling in form 'Sidonie' [DP], outer petals flat, somewhat erect, poppy-red above, pink beneath; center petals muddled, but the same color; flower stem about 3 in [ca. 7.5 cm], quite upright, covered with glandular bristles; calyx funnel-shaped, glabrous, in five linear segments, of which three are lacy, foliaceous at the tip. The rich color of this rose, more brilliant than that of 'Géant des Batailles', gives a very pretty effect; unfortunately, not all the blossoms open up easily, but its earliness makes up for this — its blossoms are among the first to open, and among the last to fade." [R-H49]

COMTE CHARLES D'HARCOURT

Lévêque, 1897

"Very vigorous, foliage dark green, large flowers, full, very well formed, beautiful bright carmine red, abundant bloom." [JR21/164]

COMTE DE FALLOUX

Trouillard/Standish & Noble, 1863

"Crimson-pink." [Ў] "Not very vigorous, the canes being quite weak." [S]

COMTE DE FLANDRES

Lévêque, 1881

Seedling of 'Mme Victor Verdier' (HP).

"Very vigorous, foliage brownish green, flower very large, full, very well formed, plump, handsome velvety blackish purple red shaded carmine." [JR5/150]

COMTE DE MORTEMART

('Comtesse de Mortemart')
Margottin fils, 1879

"Flesh pink." [Ў] "Light lavender rose; very large, with fine petals. A splendid early rose." [CA90] "Flower large, full, well formed; color, beautiful light pink. Very fragrant; of much merit." [S] "Rose color, very fragrant; smooth, pale-green wood." [EL]

COMTE DE NANTEUIL

Quétier, 1852

"Color, bright pink edged deep crimson." [S] "Flower plump, bright pink at the center, exterior petals lightly veined violet pink." [I'H52/172] "Growth vigorous; flowers medium-sized or large, very full, perfect 'plump' form, deep pink nuanced lilac; superb." [I'H56/199]

[COMTE DE PARIS]

('Général Hudelet')
Laffay, 1839

"Purplish pink, full, very large, cupped, superb." [LF] "Dark crimson." [HoBoIV] "Large, full, violet-red, often striped." [R-H42] "Very large." [Pq] "Growth moderate; prune long; flower very large, full, cupped; color, delicate pink." [S] "Rosy lilac, glossy, sometimes purplish, very large and very double. Habit, erect; growth, moderate. A noble Rose, and very sweet." [P] "Very remontant." [JR6/43] "Much esteemed." [M'I]

COMTE DE PARIS   PLATE 147

Lévêque, 1886

"Very vigorous; flowers large, full, very well formed, poppy red nuanced and illuminated bright purple, brown, and intense crimson. Magnificent color and form." [JR10/149] "A large full red Rose, of ordinary growth and habits, with flowers of 'reflexed' shape." [F-M3]

COMTE FLORIMUND DE BERGEYK

Soupert & Notting, 1879

"Very vigorous, flower large, very full, Centifolia form; color pink-brick distinctly nuanced orange red, very fragrant and effective." [JR3/168]

COMTE FRÉDÉRIC DE THUN-HOHENSTEIN

Lévêque, 1880

"Reddish crimson." [EL] "Blackish." [JR20/5] "Very vigorous, foliage large, dark green; flower large, full, very well formed, beautiful deep crimson nuanced brown and carmine, very distinct coloration." [JR4/164] "Canes with green bark, armed with thick, small, white thorns . . . flower to 3.5 in across [ca. 8.75 cm], fairly well formed, but showing the stamens; color, crimson red shaded brown. This variety bears the name of an enthusiastic Austrian rose fancier." [JR10/141]

COMTE HORACE DE CHOISEUL

Lévêque, 1879

"Flower large, full, well imbricated, fiery vermilion brightened with scarlet, velvety, brown nuances; color much brighter than that of 'Duc de Montpensier' [HP]." [JR3/166–167] "Deep orange-red, large, full, medium scent, tall." [Sn]

COMTE ODART

Dupuy-Jamain, 1850

"Very vigorous, but with short brown-green canes having numerous, nearly straight, deep maroon thorns; leaves ample, of 5–7 nearly round leaflets which are a beautiful dark green; flowers large, 8–9 cm [ca. 4 in], full, well formed, beautiful bright red passing to violet; the center petals are quartered. This variety is close to 'Géant des Batailles' [HP]." [I'H51/8]

COMTE RAOUL CHANDON

Lévêque, 1896

"Very vigorous bush, foliage somber green; flower large, full, very well formed, vermilion nuanced with brown; color and flower both superb." [JR20/162]

COMTESSE BERTRAND DE BLACAS

E. Verdier, 1888

"Soft bright rose colour; large, full, and globular. Very sweet; an excellent and effective variety." [P1] "Vigorous, with strong, erect, delicate green canes; thorns remote, straight, pink; leaves composed of 3–5 very large light green leaflets, elliptical with irregular, fairly deep serrations; flowers large, full, of an admirable globular form, cupped; color, the most beautiful, very fresh, most seductive bright pink; fragrance elegant and penetrating." [JR12/162]

COMTESSE BRANICKA

Lévêque, 1888

"Very vigorous; leaves ample, handsome glossy green. Flower large, full, very delicate silvery pink. . . . Very pretty." [JR12/181]

COMTESSE CAHEN D'ANVERS

Widow Lédéchaux, 1884

Seedling of 'La Reine' (HP).

"Deep pink." [Ў] "Vigorous, canes upright, leaves of 5–7 leaflets of a handsome dark green, flowers large, full, globular, beautiful bright pink." [JR8/165] "This variety sprang from 'La Reine', to which it is superior; it grows well in a pot, and is popular among florists." [S]

COMTESSE DE BRESSON

Guinoisseau-Flon, 1873

Seedling of 'Jules Margottin' (HP).

"Very vigorous bush; flower large, full within, folded into a rosette; color, bright pink, petal edges white." [S]

COMTESSE DE FALLOUX

Trouillard, 1867

"Flowers very large, very full, pink nuanced mauve." [I'H68/49] "Delicate pink shaded crimson." [S]

COMTESSE DE FLANDRES

E. Verdier, 1877

"Vigorous bush; flower large, full, very globular, beautiful light silvery pink, very delicate, very fresh, center bright pink, beautiful cupped form, well held; large petals; canes strong, upright, delicate green; thorns very rare; leaves of 3–5 very delicate green leaflets, teeth large and deep." [S] "Tall." [Sn]

COMTESSE DE FRESSINET DE BELLANGER

Lévêque, 1885

"Very vigorous, foliage light green, flower very large, full, well formed, beautiful flesh pink. Very beautiful." [JR9/148] "Tall." [Sn]

COMTESSE DE PARIS

E. Verdier, 1864

Seedling of 'Victor Verdier' (HP).

"Crimson, edges of petals tipped with silvery shade, a perfect deep reflexed flower, large and full. Very fine." [B&V] "Vigorous, flowers full, 10–12 cm [ca. 4 in], beautiful intense currant pink, lined whitish." [I'H64/327] "Vigorous bush; ample beautiful dark green foliage; flower large, full, globular, perfect form, magnificent bright pink, petal edges nuanced white; considering color, form, and its abundant bloom, it will be ranked as a top of the line variety." [S] Evidently re-released by Lévêque in 1882 after a period of obscurity.

COMTESSE DE POLIGNAC

Granger/Lévêque, 1862

"Vigorous bush; blossom medium-sized, full; color, bright crimson nuanced deep purple." [S] "Growth very vigorous; foliage glaucous green; flower medium or full, very brilliant poppy red, velvety, nuanced flame-red." [I'H62/278] "Tall." [Sn]

COMTESSE DE ROQUETTE-BUISSON

Lévêque, 1888

"Very vigorous, leaves handsome light green and very large. Flower very large, beautiful light pink nuanced or tinted both a darker and a lighter pink; form most attractive." [JR12/181]

[COMTESSE DE SERENYI]   PLATE 117

('Comtesse de Serenye')

Lacharme, 1874

Seedling of 'La Reine' (HP).

"Rosy flesh, with silvery reflexed petals; full and finely shaped." [CA90] "Very vigorous bush; canes strong, dark green, garnished with flattened, hooked thorns; foliage dark green, regularly dentate; flower very large, full, character of the Centifolia; color, delicate pink shaded carmine. Much to be recommended for forcing." [S] "Of fair growth and foliage, rather liable to mildew, and easily spoiled by rain. A very free bloomer and good autumnal. This is a Rose with awkward manners, for it has great possibilities and can be very fine when it chooses, but it is one of the 'coarse' varieties, too full in petal, in regard to which the stronger you grow them the worse they are. On a maiden growth, especially if the buds be thinned, the survivor will often be a most unsightly object, and indeed it is very seldom that a large bloom will come without distorted shape; but on the side-shoots of a cut-back in a dry autumn, flowers of a beautiful 'globular imbricated' shape may be got, of good lasting qualities." [F-M3] "Very good variety from 'La Reine', which it is much like. Max Singer calls it good for forcing; its breeder, *au contraire*, says in a note which he was so kind as to send us that it forces poorly. It can be propagated just as well by cuttings as by budding; it needs to be pruned long, and bears $15°–20°$. of frost. It is dedicated to the wife of the Count Serenyi, a great Hungarian rose fancier." [JR10/186]

COMTESSE DE TURENNE

E. Verdier, 1867

Not to be confused with Oger's flesh-colored, lilac-centered HP of 1853, nor with 'Mme Wagram, Comtesse de Turenne', Bernaix's 1895 Tea.

"Flesh pink." [Ў] "Growth vigorous; canes robust; very handsome dark green foliage; flower large, full." [S]

COMTESSE HÉLÈNE MIER

Soupert & Notting, 1876

"Vigorous, flower large, full, light satiny pink, nuanced darker." [JR1/6/10] "A superb variety; indispensible." [S]

COMTESSE HENRIETTA COMBES

Schwartz, 1881

"Vigorous, having the look of 'Marie Baumann', flower large, full, centifolia form; color, bright satiny pink with silvery reflections, reverse of petals lighter, very fragrant, and quite remontant." [JR5/149]

COMTESSE O'GORMAN

Lévêque, 1888

"Violet red, large, full, medium height." [Sn] "Growth vigorous, leaves ample, glaucous green; flower large, full, very well formed, bright red nuanced poppy and violet." [JR12/181]

COMTESSE RENÉE DE BÉARN

Lévêque, 1896

"Vigorous, leaves glaucous green, flower large, full, magnificent form, beautiful nuanced carmine, brightened with blackish purple nuanced flame. Superb." [JR20/163]

COQUETTE BORDELAISE
('Paul Neyron Panachée', 'Panachée de Bordeaux')
Duprat, 1896
Sport of 'Mme Georges Desse' (HP, Desse/Duprat, 1897; pink/red; parentage unknown).

"Clear, bright rose, richly shaded with dark velvety red and broadly striped with pure white." [C&Js02] "Deep pink striped white, very large, full, medium scent, tall." [Sn] "Buds large and flat; blossom bright pink with a large white central blotch on each petal, which, though having the form of a rose, gives it the look of a camellia. . . . As for growth, foliage, wood, etc., it is just like 'Paul Neyron'." [JR21/88]

CORNET
('Rose Cornet')
Lacharme, 1845
"Of a delicate roseate color, with imbricate petals." [WRP] "Flower large with rounded petals, of a fresh delicate pink color." [An47/209] "Vigorous bush; canes very flexile, supporting the flower with difficulty; flower very large, full, cupped. Very beautiful form. Good exhibition rose, not only because of its form, but also because of its color, grenadine nuanced pink." [S] "Flowers rose, tinted with purple, very large and double; form, cupped. Habit, branching; growth, vigorous. A very showy rose, partaking somewhat of the nature of the Provence, whose scent it bears." [P] Benoit Cornet was one of Lacharme's fellow *rosiéristes* in Lyon (see JR3/54).

[CORONATION]
H. Dickson, 1913
"The flowers are of immense size and great substance; color shading from flesh to bright shrimp-pink." [C&Js14] "Vigorously growing bush. Canes upright, smooth, with magnificent foliage, quite refined; [the flower] is enormous. . . . The largest rose known." [JR37/58] "A magnificent Rose." [C&Js16]

[COUNTESS OF ROSEBERY]
Postans/W. Paul, 1879
Seedling of 'Victor Verdier' (HP).

"Fine carmine red, large and full, finely cupped form, makes a handsome bush with few thorns." [C&Js99] "Flower large, full; color, carmine, bright pink; beautifully cupped; foliage dark green; wood smooth." [S] "Of long strong growth, with distinct smooth wood and fair foliage. A little liable to mildew but not much injured by rain. The blooms do not come very well, only a small percentage being quite regular in shape, which is somewhat open. The petals are good and very smooth, and a capital specimen may be had occasionally, though not of the largest size. Only fair in freedom of bloom, and not first-class as an autumnal." [F-M3]

CRIMSON BEDDER
('Souvenir de Louis Van Houtte')
Cranston, 1874
Not to be confused with Cooling's 1896 introduction.

"Vigorous bush; flower large, full, well formed; color, bright grenadine." [S] "Belongs to 'Giant of Battles' type. Crimson." [EL] "As a crimson bedding rose this variety surpasses every other rose for brilliancy of colour and continuous blooming; its habit of growth is moderate, and shoots short-jointed, producing a mass of flowers the whole season; colour scarlet and crimson, very effective and lasting, clean glossy foliage, and free from mildew." [JC]

CRIMSON QUEEN
W. Paul, 1890
"Velvety crimson, shaded with fiery red and maroon; very large; globular and handsome; fine foliage." [P1] "Center nuanced flame, interior petals maroon." [JR19/36]

DAMES PATRONESSES D'ORLÉANS
Vigneron, 1877
"Vigorous, flowers large, full, deep crimson red, very floriferous." [JR1/12/12]

DESGACHES
Lacharme, 1850
Not to be confused with the light pink China of 1840, nor with the light pink Hybrid China of 1850.

"Growth vigorous; canes upright, having many irregular thorns; leaves delicate green; the young growth, reddish green; flower medium-sized, full, well formed; color, bright red; exterior petals bordered crimson." [S]

DESIRÉE FONTAINE
Fontaine, 1884
"Vigorous, flower large, full, well formed, well held, cupped, 4–5 blossoms per branch; color, deep rich grenadine, illuminated with bluish violet." [JR8/164]

DEUIL DE DUNOIS
Lévêque, 1873
"Blackish-red." [Y̆]

DEUIL DE COLONEL DENFERT
('Deuil du Colonel D'Enfer')
Margottin père, 1878
"Vigorous, flower large, full. Color, velvety purplish black — one of the darkest." [JR3/10]

DEVIENNE-LAMY
('Devienne l'Ami')
Lévêque, 1868
"Deep carmine, a large full flower of imbricated form." [JC] "Flower medium-sized, full, very well formed; color, bright carmine; center cupped; globular; of moderate growth, blooms in the fall." [S] "A good sort." [EL]

DIRECTEUR ALPHAND
Lévêque, 1883
"Growth very vigorous; ample dark green foliage; flower large, full, perfect form; deep blackish purple, highlighted by velvety brown and bright fiery red." [JR7/158] "Tall." [Sn] Sometimes equated with 'Alsace-Lorraine'.

DIRECTEUR N. JENSEN
E. Verdier, 1883
"Vigorous, look of 'Charles Lefebvre', with strong branches; thorns remote, short, hooked; leaves composed of 5 beautiful rounded leaflets with slightly deep and irregular serration; flowers large, full, well formed; color, carmine red strongly nuanced and marbled velvety purplish amaranth red; very beautiful variety dedicated to the director of an impressive establishment in Sweden." [JR7/171]

DR. ANTONIN JOLY
Besson, 1886
Seedling of 'Baronne Adolphe de Rothschild' (HP).

"Vigorous plant of the 'Baronne A. de Rothschild' sort from which it came and of which it retains the characteristics and growth. Blossom about 12–15 cm across [ca. 6 in], very full, well formed, cupped; color, bright pink on a brighter ground, illumined with salmon." [JR10/149]

DR. AUGUSTE KRELL
E. Verdier, 1877

"Vigorous with upright canes, slightly reddish green; thorns numerous, unequal, straight, pink; leaves composed of 3–5 leaflets, rounded, dark green, finely dentate; flowers large, full, well-formed, with petals rounded and curled under; color, carmine cerise red shaded purple, whitish on the reverse." [JR2/29]

DR. BAILLON
Margottin père, 1878
"Vigorous, flower large, full, well-formed. Color, bright crimson red, shaded purple." [JR3/10]

DR. BRADA'S ROSA DRUSCHKI
Brada, 1934
Presumably from 'Frau Karl Druschki' (HP).
"Pink, very large, full, tall." [Sn]

DR. BRETONNEAU
Trouillard, 1858
Seedling of 'Géant des Batailles' (HP).

"Large; red passing to pink and to violet." [I'H58/198] "Vigorous bush; flower large, full; color, reddish violet." [S] "Tall." [Sn] "This variety [Prune 'Dunmore'] was also announced in the catalog of Mons André Leroy of Angers, but it is to Dr. Bretonneau, of Tours—a very distinguished amateur—that we owe its introduction into France." [I'H52/195]

DR. GEORGES MARTIN
Widow Vilin & fils, 1907
From 'Mme Prosper Laugier' (HP) × 'L'Ami E. Daumont' (HP).

"Red, pink middle, very large, very full, tall." [Sn] "Very vigorous, reblooming until frost; wood smooth, tinted antique bronze; foliage dark green; thorns recurved and fairly numerous; bud well held on strong, upright stem; flower large, very full, opening well; its very fine pink is enclosed by very intense dark madder petals, brightened by pretty Peruvian yellow reflections, which give it a superb appearance; and, oddly enough, the rose keeps its pretty coloration even when fully open." [JR31/137]

DR. HOGG
Laxton/G. Paul, 1880
Seedling of 'Pierre Notting' (HP).

"Deep violet-red, medium size." [EL] "Deep violet, the nearest approach to blue, pretty bell-shaped petals; growth vigorous." [P1] "Not very floriferous." [S] "A splendid variety, a good strong grower and free bloomer; color bright violet red; good size and substance, very sweet." [C&Js99] "Not delicate." [JR4/39] "Of good habit. The flowers are not large but of good shape." [B&V]

DR. HURTA
Geschwindt, 1867

"Lilac-pink." [Y̆] "Flower large, full, flat; color, glossy purplish pink." [S] "Rose passing to rosy-purple, a flower very similar in form and colour to 'Baronne Prévost' . . . robust." [JC]

DR. INGOMAR H. BLOHM
Lambert, 1919
"Deep red, large, full, very fragrant, tall." [Sn]

DR. JAMAIN
flag
Jamain, 1851

"From a variety derived from 'Gloire des Rosomanes' (B)." [I'H56/248] "Vigorous shrub, with glaucous canes, glabrous, armed with some thorns which are much enlarged at the base, very sharp, and slightly hooked. Leaves fairly ample, brownish red nuanced green when young, aging to beautiful green, paler beneath, glabrous on both sides; 3–7 smooth, fairly long, finely dentate, and not very thick leaflets; flower large, well formed, beautiful bright crimson fading to pink." [S] "Moderately vigorous; flowers medium-sized, full, ruffled, deep intense red, often pink; . . . it much resembles ['Gloire des Rosomanes'], but it is not worth as much as 'Comte de Bobrinsky', 'La Bedoyère', etc., etc. Best own-root." [I'H56/248] "This variety, which Mons Verdier compares to 'Comte de Bobrinsky' and 'Labedoyère' [HP, grenadine], has much in common with 'Comte d'Eu' [B, Lacharme, 1844, light carmine], going by its growth and inflorescence." [JDR56/47] "The leaves are pretty lush, brown-red nuanced red when young, then beautiful green in age; paler beneath; glabrous on both sides; composed of 3–7 leaflets which grade smaller from summit to base, and are smooth, not stiff, and fairly longly and finely dentate; the terminal one is larger, and oval-acute; the lateral ones are lanceolate and nearly sessile; the lower part of the rachis is bristly, and has long, slightly hooked, very sharp prickles beneath; the upper part is nearly glabrous, or only slightly glandular; the ciliate stipules are pretty large in the adherent portion, and subulate in the divergent part. . . . The peduncle is thick, long, very stiff, and glandular-bristly, as is the calyx tube, which gradually enlarges into a funnel which is slightly enlarged at the mouth. The sepals are long, green, glandular on the back, white-downy within; 3 are lacily acuminate towards the tip, and 2 are more or less completely foliaceous. The outer petals are concave, nearly round, obtuse or terminated in a tiny point smaller than is the case with the petals of 'Comte de Bobrinsky'; those of the center are longitudinally folded and slightly ragged as well as intermixed with the long, feeble styles and a few perfect stamens." [I'H51/171] "Branches slender, divergent, reddish; when young, bark light green, with reddish-brown thorns which are nearly straight, elongated, flattened at the base, and very sharp. Beautiful dark green foliage, glossy, divided into 3 or 5 oval, much rounded, and regularly dentate leaflets; petiole slender, nodding, with 3 or 4 little prickles which are hooked and pointed. Flowers about 3 in across [ca. 7.5 cm], full, plump, solitary on the branchlets, in groups of 4 or 5 on the most vigorous branches; color, deep red nuanced crimson, sometimes bright pink; outer petals pretty large, muddled and interfolded towards the center. Calyx rounded; sepals leaf-like. Very remontant and vigorous when grown on its own roots; contrariwise, it grows very little when grafted on the briar; hardy." [JF]

DR. MARX
('Marquis d'Ailsa')
Laffay, 1842

"Carmine, very large." [HoBoIV] "Red, tinged with violet; a bad shade." [EL] "Rich rosy crimson, glowing, very large and full; form, cupped. Habit, erect; growth, moderate. A superb Rose, and very sweet." [P] "Lacking in form." [VH62/92] "Growth very vigorous; branches very short, with cylindrical thorns; leaves rough, dark green, regularly dentate; flower large, full, cupped; color, very bright crimson shaded satiny white." [S] " 'Rivers — Rosy carmine — perfect — superb — large,' 'Lane — Crimson — large and fine,' 'Wood — Very deep red, shaded with lilac,' 'Curtis — Rich carmine — perfect — superb — and highly fragrant.' . . . Of a brilliant shaded carmine and crimson color, and remarkably fragrant perfume, of vigorous growth — though in this respect not quite equal to 'Louis Bonaparte' [HP, Laffay, 1839, carmine-pink], which fine rose it closely resembles — and of a hardy nature; it makes a fine tree, either as a standard or dwarf, and is a good autumnal bloomer." [C]

DR. MÜLLERS ROTE
(trans., 'Dr. Müller's Red')
Müller, 1920

"Purplish red." [Y̆]

DR. WILLIAM GORDON
W. Paul, 1905

"Brilliant satiny carnation pink." [Y̆] "Large satiny pink flowers." [JR29/53]

DRUSCHKA
Kordes, 1932
From 'Frau Karl Druschki' (HP) × 'Hawlmark Scarlet' (HT).

"Pink, large, full, light scent, tall." [Sn]

DRUSCHKI RUBRA
Lambert, 1929
From 'Frau Karl Druschki' (HP) × 'Luise Lilia' (HT, Lambert, 1912, dark red; parentage: 'General MacArthur' [HT] × 'Frau Peter Lambert' [HT, Welter, 1902, pink]).

"Crimson red." [Y̆] "A hybrid of 'Frau Karl Druschki' and 'American Beauty'. The bud and bloom have the same form and size as 'Frau Karl Druschki', and the color is a dull — the furniture man would say 'egg shell finish' — crimson lightening to scarlet around the edges of the petals. 'American Beauty' has also transmitted its delightful perfume. The habit of the plant is very similar to 'Frau Karl Druschki', although perhaps not quite as vigorous, but its foliage is better and less subject to mildew, and it has the same recurrence of bloom." [C-Ps29]

DUC D'ANJOU
Boyau/Lévêque, 1862

"Crimson, shaded with dark red, very large, full, and well formed." [FP] "Growth very vigorous; foliage dark green; flower very large, full, crimson red nuanced somber red." [I'H62/278] "Tall." [Sn]

DUC D'AUDIFFRET-PASQUIER
E. Verdier, 1887

"Vigorous, canes upright, delicate green; thorns very numerous, unequal, straight, thin, yellowish; leaves of 3-5 leaflets, oblong, rounded, somber green, with fine, irregular, fairly deep serration; flowers large, full, well formed; color, carmine red with bright purplish hue, center brighter, sometimes bordered white." [JR11167]

DUC D'HARCOURT
('Duc d'Arcourt')
Robert & Moreau, 1863

"Bright reddish-carmine, blooming freely and in clusters, large and full." [FP] "Very vigorous, making a bush with strong, straight thorns; foliage, somber green and very abundant; flower large, full, globular; color, carmine red; outer petals, light carmine." [S]

[DUC DE CAZES]
Touvais, 1861
Seedling of 'Général Jacqueminot' (HP).

"Purplish crimson, so deep as almost to appear black." [FP] "A very distinct variety, with purplish crimson flowers, velvety, very effective in the garden; it is a vigorous plant, and only needs moderate pruning." [R-H63] "Petals cupped . . . habit moderate." [JC] "Growth vigorous; flower large, full, recurved; color, very dark purple mixed with deep violet; reverse of petals brown. Magnificent exhibition flower." [S] Parent of 'Princesse de Béarn' (HP). "Mons le Duc Decazes [*sic*], who died suddenly in Paris October 24th [1860]. He was over 80 years old. . . . [He was] the founder and keeper of the rich nurseries of the Luxembourg, and was the person who put together the greatest collection of grape-vines in the entire world." [R-H60]

DUC DE CHARTRES
E. Verdier, 1876

"Growth very vigorous; branches amply covered with recurved thorns; leaves rough and dark green; flower large, full, very well formed, majestically held; found almost inevitably solitary high on the cane; color, violet purple red nuanced crimson and plumed flame and carmine." [S]

DUC DE MARLBOROUGH
Lévêque, 1884

"Very vigorous, ample dark green foliage, flowers large, full, very well formed, bright crimson red, sparkling, very remontant and very beautiful." [JR8/150]

DUC DE MONTPENSIER
Chédane-Guinoisseau/Lévêque, 1875

"Very vigorous; branches green, somewhat blackish; thorns hooked; very subject to mildew; blossom very large, full, of notable form, taking 1st in nearly all the votes; color, beautiful red, nuanced with crimson and enhanced with brown." [S] "Medium scent, tall." [Sn] "A good sort." [EL]

DUCHESS OF BEDFORD   PLATE 130
Postans/W. Paul, 1879
Seedling of 'Charles Lefebvre' (HP).

"Very vigorous, beautiful foliage, very floriferous; flower large, full, perfectly formed; color, a crimson red surpassing all other similarly colored roses in its sparkling scarlet color . . . globular." [S] "Belongs to the 'Victor Verdier' type. Cherry red; not very promising." [EL] "Of rather weakly growth and best as a maiden. A lovely and striking flower, beautiful in its semi-imbricated form, and bright with glorious colour, a mixture of scarlet and crimson. Not strong in constitution, free-flowering, or good as an autumnal, and often fails to come good, either in colour or shape. An exhibitor's Rose, and never very large, it seems to like a cool season, and is said to be best in the North and Midlands." [F-M2]

DUCHESS OF CONNAUGHT
Standish & Noble, 1882
Not to be confused with Bennett's pink HT of 1879.

"Flower large, full, globular; color, sparkling crimson red shaded velvety purple-black sometimes with metal-blue reflections." [S] "Medium scent, medium to tall." [Sn]

[DUCHESS OF EDINBURGH]
Bennett, 1874
Not to be confused with the red Tea 'Duchess of Edinburgh'.

"Vigorous growth; of the 'Jules Margottin' sort; flower large, full; color, delicate shaded silvery pink, center brighter." [S] Parent of 'Benoît Pernin' (HP).

DUCHESS OF FIFE
Cocker, 1892
Seedling or sport of 'Countess of Rosebery' (HP).

"Delicate silvery pink, a thoroughly new color; the flower is large and full, and beautifully cupped; beautiful foliage and satisfactory habit; very elegant scent." [JR16/19] "A lighter and beautifully coloured sport from 'Countess of Rosebery', similar in all other respects." [F-M3] "Very fragrant, tall." [Sn] "Occurred in our Morningfield nursery during autumn, 1888, and has since maintained its reputation." [JR16/19]

DUCHESSE D'AOSTE
Margottin, 1867
"Rich vivid rose, flowers large, full, and well up in the centre, beautifully formed, habit free." [JC] "Flowers very large, full, flat, beautiful frosty bright pink." [I'H68/48] "Tall." [Sn] "Vigorous, with canes which are light maroon nuanced olive green, and covered with a fine 'bloom' like that on a plum; the thorns are carmine, laterally flattened, recurved like a corbel, unequal in size, the smaller ones being upright and grading into glandular bristles which cover the upper part of the cane; the leaves, light green above and pale whitish green beneath, are of 3–5 leaflets borne on a petiole which is angled at the point where the upper leaflet is attached, creased into furrows, reddish, clothed with glandular hairs above, and armed with some rudimentary prickles beneath. The stipules are green, ciliate along the edges, enlarged in the attached section, very lacy, linear-lanceolate, and pointed in the free portion, forming a right angle to the petiole. The leaflets are of a consistency between that of the Bourbons and that of the Hybrids [HP's, that is]: the two lower leaflets, much smaller, are oblong-lanceolate and pointed; the upper two are oval-oblong, growing thinner towards the tip; all are unequally and finely dentate, glabrous above, and having glandular hairs on the mid-vein beneath. The peduncle, which is very large and stiff, is light maroon red, and bristles with numerous short glandular hairs. The blossom, held strongly on its peduncle, is large, very full, a pretty carmine currant pink, nuanced paler, exhaling a fine Centifolia perfume. The outer petals are obovate, first upright, then more or less spreading, forming a collar; [they are] pale pink veined bright pink above, and silvery pink beneath; the center petals, a beautiful bright carmine pink, are smaller or [? and ?] more or less folded, like the center of the rosette of an officer of the Legion of Honor. The calyx-tube or ovary is oblong, slightly contracted at the tip, and olive green nuanced light brown in color; the sepals or calyx-leaflets are very unequal: two are edged to their bases with appendages on both sides, thoroughly foliaceous and more or less deeply toothed to the tip; two others are entire, and terminating in a point or in a small foliate extension; the fifth is intermediate, which is to say

that it only has appendages on one side. It is indeed, this last sepal which allows us to pose the Latin enigma of the botanical poet:

Quinque sumus fratres, duo sunt sine barba
Barbatique duo, sum semi-barbis ego

— which is to say: we are five brothers; two are beardless, two are bearded along the edges; and me, I am bearded on only one side. . . . Margottin . . . was permitted to dedicate it to Mme la Princesse Dalpozzo della Cisterna, just married to one of the sons of the king of Italy, his royal highness the Duke of Aoste." [I'H68/205]

DUCHESSE D'ORLÉANS
Quétier, 1851
"Fine lavender-blush, large, full, and good." [FP] "Beautiful soft rosy-peach, back of petals glaucous white, a flower of great substance, very full, and of extra large size . . . vigorous." [JC] "A good exhibition rose, with carmine-lilac, full, large, well-formed blossoms." [R-H63] "Often opens badly, and is subject to mildew." [EL] "[This rose] is not the first [nor the last] to bear the name of her ladyship the Duchess of Orléans; the rosarium has possessed, in fact, since 1836, another very pretty rose dedicated to that princess who is one of the most generous and devoted protectresses of French horticulture. The first plant so dedicated is a Tea, and this one is attached to that section of Roses called remontant hybrids. This new obtention is evidently a seedling of 'La Reine'; it has that variety's deportment, foliage, and floral form. Its very vigorous canes generally lack large thorns in the upper reaches; they are tipped by 3, 4, or indeed 5 buds. The flowers, perfectly formed, with large, well imbricated, petals, measure perhaps 9 cm across [ca. 4 in]; they are a very noticeable hydrangea pink, giving them a certain cachet of sweetness and distinction not to be found in any other of the 'La Reine' sort." [I'H53/29–30]

DUCHESSE D'OSSUNA
Jamain, 1877
"Fine vermilion rose, large, full, well formed, blooming in clusters; growth vigorous." [JC] "Very vigorous, flower large, full, handsome and very bright vermilion pink." [JR1/6/10] "Very floriferous, and a person may gather blossoms from it up until the latter part of the season; good to force for March." [S]

DUCHESSE DE BRAGANCE   PLATE 148
E. Verdier, 1886
"Vigorous, canes upright, delicate green; thorns unequal, short, straight, brown; leaves of 3–5 oval-elongated leaflets, dark green, irregularly and not very deeply toothed; flowers extra large, full, well formed, color a beautiful and delicate satiny pink nuanced brighter pink." [JR10/170]

DUCHESSE DE CAMBACÉRÉS   PLATE 92
('Mme de Cambacérès')
Fontaine, 1854
"Blossom large, globular, pink." [JDR55/19] "Lilac rose, impure color; double." [EL] "Large flowers, full, cupped, carmine pink with distinct purplish tones; also a good autumnal, and to be recommended above all for its very beautiful foliage." [R-H63] "A most vigorous growing rose, blooming in immense clusters, giving flowers with a powerful fragrance." [R8] "This rose, according to Mons Fontaine's way of thinking, is the product of a cross involving the Centifolia 'des Peintres' or 'Quatre Saisons de Puteaux'. In any case, it is a vigorous plant, blooming abundantly . . . has large flowers, full, well formed, globular, and a beautiful bright pink." [JR5/118] "Growth very vigorous; canes pretty big,

upright or branching; bark smooth, glaucous green, slightly yellowish; thorns numerous, gray-brown, unequal, slightly hooked, and enlarged at the base. Foliage thick, large, glaucous green, slightly rugose, divided into 5 or 7 oval-rounded, strongly toothed leaflets; leafstalk pretty strong, slightly reddish at the base, armed all along its length with small, sharp, hooked prickles. Flowers about four in across [ca. 1 dm], well formed, full, globular, solitary on the branchlets, in clusters of 3–5 on the stronger branches; color, beautiful bright pink; petals large and concave, those of the center muddled and folded; flower stalk pretty long, glandular-hirsute. Ovary very long; sepals very leaf-like. This variety is very vigorous . . . in form and color it resembles the old Centifolia." [JF]

DUCHESSE DE CAYLUS

('Penelope Mayo')
C. Verdier, 1864
Seedling of 'Alfred Colomb' (HP).

"Brilliant carmine red, beautiful blossom of perfect form . . . very vigorous and truly remontant." [JR3/11] "Glowing rosy-crimson, flowers large, full, and beautifully cupped, fine outline with high centre . . . habit free." [JC] "Of moderate growth; beautiful form, though small; of the 'Alfred Colomb' type; flower large, full, globular; color, brilliant carmine pink." [S] "Foliage very rich and fine." [FP] "Vigorous, with light green canes; flower large, full, of the most perfect form, bright light carmine." [I'H64/327] "Only fair in growth with rather weak foliage, the wood and habit being very distinct in appearance. Not liable to mildew or any injury from rain. The blooms come wonderfully well, every one being alike. . . . Sweet-scented, perfect in form, good in centre and bright in colour, but decidedly below par in size. Not free-flowering or a good autumnal." [F-M3]

DUCHESSE DE DINO

Lévêque, 1889

"Very vigorous bush; beautiful ample dark green foliage; flower very large, full, perfectly imbricated and held; beautifully colored blackish crimson nuanced carmine and velvety purple." [JR13/164] "Tall." [Sn]

DUCHESSE DE GALLIERA

Portemer, 1847
Not to be confused with E. Verdier's rose-pink HP of 1887.

"Bright rose, shaded with flesh colour, large and full; form, cupped. Habit, erect; growth, moderate." [P] "Flower . . . delicate pink shaded lilac." [S] "Freely remontant Hybrid Perpetual. Canes strong and upright; thorns strong and numerous, nearly straight, very sharp, brownish-red. Leaves of three to five oval-obtuse leaflets, mostly serrated, a pretty fresh green. Peduncle and ovary like the preceding, the ovary not so big; calyx with foliaceous sepals. Flower 7–8 cm [ca. 3 in], pretty full, center petals forming several bundles, beautiful bright pink nuanced flesh; outer petals large, well imbricated, reticulated. Scent very strong and quite pleasant. The blossoms are sometimes solitary, but more often in threes or fours. The buds are round and take on, when opening, a fresh bright purple color. Bearing and hold perfect." [An47/204–205]

DUCHESSE DE MORNY

Listed as 'La Duchesse de Morny'.

DUCHESSE DE VALLOMBROSA   PLATE 121

Dunand/Schwartz, 1875
Seedling of 'Jules Margottin' (HP).

"Blush, centre delicate flesh, flowers large, full, and cupped; an exquisitely formed and beautiful rose." [JC] "Flesh, changing to white. Good and free-flowering; impatient of wet." [H] "Pink, generally opens badly; not valuable." [EL] "Very vigorous, with upright dark green canes; the foliage is perfect and ample by all reports. As for the blooms, they are large, full, and well formed, the deep pink of the central petals grading nicely through delicate pink to the blush of the outer petals. This rose reblooms freely." [JR1/8/9] "Requires good soil and generous treatment; with these it will grow strongly with distinct habit and foliage, but it will not thrive everywhere. It is not very liable to mildew, but the blooms cannot stand rain at all, and being of a light colour are subject to injury from thrips in a dry season. They have a decided tendency to come badly shaped, often with me having a gap or chasm in the outline, as though a piece had been cut out. The shape is rather too open and flat at the best, but it is of large size, free-flowering, fair in lasting qualities, and pretty good in a dry autumn." [F-M2]

DUHAMEL-DUMONCEAU

Vilin/C. Verdier, 1872

"Fiery-red, splendid colour, like the old 'Tuscany' [*Gallica*]; tolerably well shaped and full." [JC] "Large, full, bright red, very brilliant at the center, shaded and nuanced violet around the edges." [JR3/27] "Growth vigorous." [S]

DUKE OF FIFE

Cocker & Sons, 1892

"A deep crimson sport from ['Étienne Levet'], and a much worse grower. Noteworthy, as a sport generally comes of a lighter colour than the type." [F-M2] "The richest crimson-scarlet, with perfectly folded petals, large, full, and well formed." [JR16/19] "Very good in dull weather." [H]

DUKE OF TECK

G. Paul, 1880
Seedling of 'Duke of Edinburgh' (HP).

"Brilliant crimson-scarlet, a color both clear and distinct, truly an advance towards a true scarlet rose. Flowers large, very double, quite globular; plant floriferous, upright, with handsome foliage." [JR4/39] "Clear and distinct in colour, but not large." [P1] "Globular form and rather pointed centre, comes true to shape. Good growth and foliage with characteristic wood without thorns; not very liable to mildew." [B&V] "Not well tested in this country [U.S.A.]; we were much pleased with it as seen at Cheshunt." [EL] "Strong and hardy . . . not so dark in crimson and not so brilliant in vermilion as ['Duke of Edinburgh'], but, like it, should be left long in pruning, and is of good repute in America. Best on old plants, and good under glass." [F-M2]

EARL OF PEMBROKE

Bennett, 1882
From 'Marquise de Castellane' (HP) × 'Maurice Bernardin' (HP).

"Vigorous, good form, few thorns; color, velvety crimson with the petal edges bright red; very distinct, good for any sort of rose." [S] "Of fair thorny growth, late, and a distinct shade of colour; a free bloomer, rather thin in petal, and only worth classing for its value in autumn, when it is often at its best." [F-M3]

ECLAIREUR
Vigneron, 1895
Seedling of 'Duhamel-Dumonceau' (HP).

"Very vigorous, beautiful very dark green foliage, flower large, well-formed, cupped, handsome dark bright red, exterior petals velvety, stem very strong, perfectly poised, flower usually solitary, very remontant, fragrant." [JR19/147]

EDELWEISS
Dienemann, 1925
Seedling of 'Frau Karl Druschki' (HP).

"White, medium size, full, medium height." [Sn]

EDOUARD ANDRÉ LE BOTANISTE
E. Verdier, 1879

"Red, tinged with purple." [EL] "Very vigorous, having the appearance of 'Mme Victor Verdier', with delicate green, upright, firm canes; thorns somewhat numerous, irregular, pointed, pink; leaves composed of 5 light green, oblong, finely dentate leaflets; flowers large, full, well-formed, an even currant red, bright and very attractive." [JR3/181] "E. André, editor-in-chief of *Revue Horticole*." [JR17/80]

EDOUARD FONTAINE
Fontaine, 1878

"Vigorous, flower large, very well formed, full. Color, frosty pink." [JR3/10] "In color, it resembles 'Baron [G.-B.] Gonella' [Bourbon]." [S]

EDOUARD HERVÉ
E. Verdier, 1884

"Vigorous, canes reflexing, pinkish green; thorns long, unequal, very sharp; leaves composed of 3–5 leaflets, oblong, dark green, deeply toothed; flowers large, full, very well formed, dark intense currant red, very fragrant." [JR8/165]

EGERIA
Listed as 'Peach Blossom'. Not to be confused with Bennett's HT of 1878, 'Ægeria', which was bright crimson.

[ELISABETH VIGNERON]   PLATE 106
('Elise Vigneron')
Vigneron/W. Paul, 1865
Seedling of 'Duchesse de Sutherland' (HP).

"Growth very vigorous; very floriferous; branches upright, light green; thorns pretty numerous, chestnut; leaves light green, 5–6 leaflets; flower very large, very full; petals large; beautifully colored light pink, darker within; resembling in size, color, and scent, the Centifolia; buds very large, opening well; as beautiful in fall as in spring." [S] "Bright carmine, flowers very large and double; habit vigorous." [JC]

ELISE LEMAIRE
Introducer unknown, before 1886

"Vigorous bush; canes glossy dark green, nearly thornless; leaves yellowish dark green; blossom medium sized, Centifolia form; color, delicate pink. Much to be recommended. It blooms up to winter, and forces well in January." [S]

ELISKA KRÁSNOHORSKÁ
Böhm, 1932
From 'Captain Hayward' (HP) × 'Una Wallace' (HT, McGredy, 1921, cherry-red; parentage unknown).

"Rose-red, large, full, very fragrant, tall." [Sn]

EMDEN
Schmidt, 1915
From 'Frau Karl Druschki' (HP) × 'Veluwezoom' (Pern.-HT, Lourens/Pallandt, 1909; from 'Mme Caroline Testout" [HT] × 'Soleil d'Or' [Pern]).

"Deep pink, large, full, medium height." [Sn]

EMILE BARDIAUX
Lévêque, 1889
Seedling of 'Mme Isaac Pereire' (B).

"Very vigorous, leaves dark green, very large; flower very large, full, well formed; bright carmine red nuanced poppy and deep violet. From 'Mme Isaac Pereire', from which it takes its growth and flower size." [JR13/164]

EMILY LAXTON
Laxton/G. Paul, 1876
Seedling of 'Jules Margottin' (HP).

"A large full flower with globular, pointed bud, opening into a large globular flower . . . rich cherry-rose . . . strong vigorous habit." [JC] "Light pink." [Y̌] "Of the 'Jules Margottin' tribe; much like 'Monsieur Normand' [*sic*; 'Monsieur Nomann', HP, Laffay, 1866], but the color is darker and the form prettier." [S]

EMPEROR
W. Paul, 1883

"Flower small, full, beautiful form; color, very dark, nearly blackish; good growth, beautiful foliage, and abundant bloom." [S] "Hardy." [JR7/173] "Tall." [Sn]

EMPRESS OF INDIA
Laxton/G. Paul, 1876
Seedling of 'Triomphe des Beaux-Arts' (HP).

"Brownish-crimson, medium size, globular, fragrant; dark green foliage, spines light colored. Many of the buds do not open well, and it is shy in the autumn; a splendid sort when perfect." [EL] "Rich velvety crimson and purple, somewhat in form and colour like 'Louis Van Houtte'." [JC] "Very well formed . . . very easily damaged by the sun." [S] "Vigorous, flower large, full, blackish-red, of the 'Louis XIV' sort." [JR1/6/10]

ERNEST MOREL   PLATE 166
Cochet, 1898
Seedling of 'Général Jacqueminot' (HP).

"Flower large, full, well formed, light grenadine red, illumined with flame-color, reverse of petals somewhat velvety, with a 'bloom'. Bush very vigorous and extremely floriferous." [JR22/166] "Very fragrant, tall." [Sn] "Entirely hardy and excellent for garden planting." [C&Js02]

ERNEST PRINCE
Ducher Children & Successors, 1881
Seedling of 'Antoine Ducher' (HP).

"Very vigorous, with strong and upright canes, rather numerous thorns, beautiful dark green foliage, flower very large, very well formed, globular, light red, darker at the center, reverse of petals silvery, abundant bloom." [JR5/185] "Without particular merit." [JR7/157]

ETIENNE DUBOIS
Damaizin, 1873

"Vigorous bush; flower large, full; color, deep velvety crimson." [S] "Tall." [Sn]

ETIENNE LEVET
Levet, 1871
Seedling of 'Victor Verdier' (HP).

"Pinkish carmine." [Y] "Carmine, large, full, and of fine form." [P1] "Carmine-red, one of the finest in the type." [EL] "Growth robust and upright, of the 'Victor Verdier' sort. Resembles 'Hippolyte Jamain' and 'Président Thiers'; flower very large, full, globular at first, then flat." [S] "Of robust and smooth but very uncertain growth; long, strong, and stout in rich soil where it has a good hold, but otherwise quite short and stumpy. The foliage is very fine, and the blooms come early and well, with large very smooth shell-like petals; there is, or should be, a good point, but the general shape is open, the centre weak, and the form not lasting . . . of no use in hot weather. Not much injured by mildew or rain, but not good as a free bloomer or autumnal, and of no use in hot climates. It is of large, size, and its grand petals and smooth even outline make it an effective show Rose in a cool season. . . . For general cultivation or on weak soils it is not one of the best." [F-M2]

EUGÈNE APPERT   PLATE 98
Trouillard/Standish & Noble, 1859
Seedling of 'Géant des Batailles' (HP).

"Blossom medium-sized, full; color, velvety crimson scarlet. One of the best of the purple and crimson roses." [S] "Belongs to 'Giant of Battles' type. Velvety maroon, shaded with deep crimson. A rose of superb color, but with all the family failings." [EL] "Brilliant scarlet-crimson, colour superb and lasting, petals of unusual substance though rather pointed, flowers tolerably well formed, robust habit and fine foliage; a most striking and beautiful rose." [JC] "Free bloomer." [FP] "Better than its elders through the vigor of its growth, the size of its foliage, the graceful disposition and amplitude of its petals, its most brilliant tintings, etc., etc. [*sic*]." [VH61/129]

EUGÈNE DE LUXEMBOURG
Listed as 'Prince Eugène de Beauharnais'.

[EUGÈNE VERDIER]
Guillot fils, 1863
Seedling of 'Victor Verdier' (HP). Not to be confused with the 1872 Moss.

"Rich dark violet, large, full, and of perfect form; one of the best." [FP] "Of moderate growth." [S] "Very vigorous; flowers very large, full, well formed, superb deep violet." [l'H64/62] An ancestor of 'Gloire de Deventer' (T).

[E. Y. TEAS]
Seedling of 'Alfred Colomb' (HP).

"Flower very large, full, globular, fragrant; color, bright sparkling deep cerise red. From 'Alfred Colomb', and resembles 'Sénateur Vaïsse' and 'François Fontaine' [HP, Fontaine, 1867, vermilion; syns., 'Sénateur Favre', Rousseau, 1862; 'Puebla', Rousseau, 1861]." [S] "Only moderate in growth and foliage. Not much liable to mildew, and stands rain fairly. The blooms come well, very full and fragrant, of compact regular smooth globular shape, a very bright colour, and good lasting qualities, but below the average in size. Fairly free in bloom, but of little use as an autumnal, and not to be recommended for any but exhibitors." [F-M2]

FELBERGS ROSA DRUSCHKI
Felberg-Leclerc, 1925
From 'Frau Karl Druschki' (HP) × 'Farbenkönigen' (HT, Hinner, 1902, rose-red; from a cross of 'La France' [HT] × ?).

"Rich pink. . . . The plants and flowers resemble 'Frau Karl Druschki' in everything but color, which is a rich shade of pink." [C-Pf33] "Flower large, clear bright rose-pink, borne on long, strong stem." [ARA29/225] "Full, light scent, tall." [Sn]

FÉLICIEN DAVID
E. Verdier, 1872

"Deep rose, tinged with purple." [EL] "Brilliant rose, purple shaded, flowers large and very full, partakes of the Bourbon habit; a well formed and good flower." [JC] "Moderate growth; flower very large, full, plump; color, dark red nuanced carmine, magenta pink, and light violet." [S]

FÉLIX MOUSSET
E. Verdier, 1884

"Vigorous with upright canes, delicate green; thorns unequal, short, straight, pink; leaves composed of 3–5 leaflets, rounded, dark green, regularly and somewhat deeply toothed; flowers large, full, very well formed, petals curling beneath, deep intense purplish pink, very fragrant." [JR8/165]

FERDINAND CHAFFOLTE   PLATE 131
Pernet fils, 1879

"Reddish-crimson, not well formed, without fragrance; does not seem an addition of merit." [EL] "Very vigorous rose; big-wooded with upright canes, and beautiful close-set somber green leaves; flower very large, nearly full, cupped, very well formed, beautiful brilliant red, first to rows of petals nuanced superb violet; flower nearly always solitary. Good growth, top-of-the-line." [S] "Same 'hold' as 'Baronne Adolphe de Rothschild', this magnificent variety leaves nothing to be desired; good growth, very well branched, reblooms with the greatest freedom . . . dedicated to a great fancier of roses." [JR3/165]

FERDINAND JAMIN
Lévêque, 1888
Not to be confused with the HP 'Mme Ferdinand Jamin'.

"Very vigorous, foliage ample, dark glaucous green. Flower large, full, extremely well formed, rich bright vermilion red; floriferous." [JR12/181]

[FIREBRAND]
Labruyère/W. Paul, 1874
Not to be confused with A. Clark's HT of 1924.

"Flower very large, full; color, bright crimson, sometimes shaded maroon brown; robust; it is 'Baronne [Adolphe] de Rothschild' in crimson." [S]

FLORENCE PAUL
W. Paul, 1886

"Scarlet red." [JR25/13] "Scarlet-crimson, shaded with rose, large and full; form compact, petals recurved; habit good." [P1] "Very floriferous . . . good garden rose." [JR10/19]

FONTENELLE
Moreau-Robert, 1877
Not to be confused with Vibert's rose colored Moss of 1849.
"Red, spotted." [Y̌] "Vigorous, flowers large, full, carmine red." [JR1/12/12] "In clusters." [S]

FRANÇOIS I
('François Premier')
Trouillard, 1858
Seedling of 'Géant des Batailles' (HP).
"Red, shaded with crimson." [EL] "Clusters; cerise-red; well-formed." [I'H58/198] "Flower large, full, well formed; color, cherry red nuanced deep red." [S]

FRANÇOIS ARAGO
Trouillard, 1858
"Belongs to 'Giant of Battles' type. Velvety-maroon, illumined with fiery red. Resembles 'Lord Raglan' [HP]." [EL] "Moderate growth; flower medium-sized, full; color, velvety amaranth, nuanced." [S] "Extremely abundant with very beautiful amaranth blossoms clouded with black." [VH62/100]

FRANÇOIS COPPÉE   PLATE 161
Widow Lédéchaux, 1895
Seedling of 'Victor Verdier' (HP).
"Vigorous, with very erect dark green canes, numerous thorns which are short, straight, and brown; leaves of 3–5 medium, oblong, dark green leaflets, with fine, irregular dentations; flowers medium sized, full, good form, opening very well, crimson, brilliant, illuminated with velvety grenadine red, darker reverse; the bud is long and well formed . . . quite remontant." [JR19/130] "Very fragrant." [JR21/9] "One of the most beautiful roses, with a velvety crimson red hue; good vigorous plant with blossoms burning little in the sun of our clime [that of Tunisia], a merit not shared by many of the red roses which find themselves cooking under the African sun. Beautiful long buds on long and rigid stems . . . dedicated to the great poet François Coppée, who died recently in Paris." [JR34/169]

FRANÇOIS GAULAIN
Schwartz, 1878
"Violet." [Y̌] "Deep purplish crimson." [EL] "Very vigorous with upright branches, dark green foliage, wood smooth, nearly thornless, flower large, full, well formed, intense wine-dregs red, one of the darkest known." [JR2/166]

FRANÇOIS LEVET
Levet, 1880
Seedling of 'Anna de Diesbach' (HP).
"Cherry-rose, medium size; style of 'Paul Verdier'." [EL] "Vigorous and very remontant, branches firm, foliage light green, thorns short and straight, flower of medium size, beautiful China pink." [JR4/167]

FRANÇOIS OLIN
Ducher Children & Successors, 1881
"Vigorous bush with strong, upright canes; numerous thorns; beautiful dark green foliage; flower large, full, and very well formed; form of a camellia; blooms in clusters; large long buds; color, cerise red marbled with pure white, very floriferous; novel coloration." [JR5/186]

FREDERIC SCHNEIDER II
Ludovic, 1885
"Pink and red." [Y̌] "Deep pink with red, large, full, tall." [Sn]

FRÉRE MARIE PIERRE
Bernaix, 1891
"Cerise." [Y̌] "Vigor, bearing, and ample foliage of 'Baronne A. de Rothschild'. Flower usually solitary at the tip of the cane, borne horizontally on a strong, upright stem. Flower very large, about 11 cm [ca. 4.5 in] across, very double, large thick petals, symmetrically arranged in a perfect cup, very beautiful China pink, fading to blush . . . penetrating fragrance." [JR15/150]

FRIEDRICH VON SCHILLER
Mietzsch, 1881
"Blossom medium sized, very full; outer petals imbricated; color, sparkling crimson shaded with violet; very floriferous and very fragrant." [S] Johann Christoph Friedrich von Schiller, 1759–1805; influential German poet and dramatist.

FÜRST LEOPOLD IV ZU SCHAUMBURG-LIPPE
Kiese, 1918
"Deep red, large, full, medium scent, tall." [Sn]

GAËTANO GONSOLI
Listed as 'Gonsoli Gaëtano'.

[GÉNÉRAL APPERT]
Schwartz, 1884
Seedling of 'Souvenir de William Wood' (HP).
"Very vigorous, quite remontant . . . flower large, full, well formed; velvety blackish purple red." [S]

[GÉNÉRAL BARON BERGE]
Pernet père, 1891
"Large, finely formed flowers of exquisite shape. Color, brilliant currant red, shaded silvery maroon. Very fragrant and free flowering." [CA96] "Bush vigorous, shooting out upright, strong canes; foliage very closely set; flower large, nearly full, perfect hold, beautiful grenadine red, outer rows of petals nuanced violet, very fragrant, freely remontant, continuously covered with flowers during the height of the season." [JR15/163]

GÉNÉRAL BARRAL
('Général Baral')
Damaizin, 1867
"Violet red." [Y̌] "Medium-sized, full, violet pink." [S]

GÉNÉRAL BEDEAU
Margottin, 1851
"Rose red, large, full, tall." [Sn] "Flower large, full, very bright red, admirable form." [VH51/112] "Plant moderately vigorous; flowers medium-sized, full, bright red. Good variety grafted." [I'H53/225] "Very vigorous bush; canes dark green, sometimes touched violet; leaves olive green, irregularly serrated; flower large, full, form very beautiful; color, bright pink." [S]

GÉNÉRAL DE LA MARTINIÈRE
De Sansal, 1869
"Carmine pink." [Y̌] "Not very vigorous; canes unequal and weak; flower very large and full; color, wine red, center glossy crimson pink; outer petals lilac pink; beautiful exhibition rose." [S]

GÉNÉRAL DÉSAIX
Moreau-Robert, 1867
Not to be confused with Boutigny's pink Gallica.
"Growth vigorous; flower large, full; color, sparkling fiery red, shaded poppy red." [S]

GÉNÉRAL DUC D'AUMALE
E. Verdier, 1875
"Beautiful bright dark cerise red." [JR3/27] "Crimson; a good sort, not unlike 'Maurice Bernardin'." [EL] "Deep rose, good even petal, and a good second-class flower." [JC] "A superb flower, very effective; solitary at the ends of the canes; color, deep crimson shaded bright red." [S]

GENERAL STEFÁNIK
('Krásná Azurea')
Böhm, 1933
Seedling or sport of 'La Brillante' (HP).
"Violet blue." [Y]

GENERAL VON BOTHNIA-ANDREÆ
Verschuren, 1899
From 'Victor Verdier' (HP) × an unnamed seedling.
"Reddish violet, very large, full, medium height." [Sn] "The blossom is large, and very beautifully shaped; the bud, very long; color, very bright red, sometimes dark. Freely remontant. This very vigorous variety takes well to culture under glass." [JR23/150]

GÉNÉRALE MARIE RAIEWSKY
Ketten Bros., 1911
From 'Frau Karl Druschki' (HP) × 'Fisher-Holmes' (HP).
"Blossom flesh pink passing to bright pink, center nuanced yellowish salmon; vigor, habit, and size that of 'Druschki', but the flowers are fuller." [JR36/74]

[GÉNIE DE CHÂTEAUBRIAND]
Oudin, 1852
"Flower large, full, very well formed; color, bishop's violet; reverse of petals pink." [S] "Amaranth with blackish reflections." [S] "It is to be regretted that the blossoms of this variety are not better formed and, above all, that they vary in coloration, which both detract from their merit." [I'H53/172] "The growth is vigorous, the canes are upright, with smooth wood, thorns . . . which are down-hooked, reddish on the young branches and grayish on the old, sharp, easily detached, unequally distributed in the proportion of 25–30 per decimeter, mixed with . . . other smaller, less hooked, very small thorns, which are paler and which disappear on mature branches. The leaves are flat, dark green above, silvery light green beneath; nearly always comprised of 7 leaflets, occasionally 5, nearly always perfectly oval, sometimes cordiform at the base, lightly serrated, veins not very deep, always hollow and as if folded at the center. The rachis is covered with reddish pubescence, much colored carmine around the stipules, which are also pubescent, ciliated with short, purplish, glandular bristles. Altogether, the foliage is cheerful and vigorous; it takes on a brighter tint around the blossoms, about which it arches and recurves with elegance. The blossoms grow at the tips of the canes, on a very strong stem of about 4–5 cm [ca. 2 in], nearly always in groups of 2, 3, or 4; the stems of the secondary buds are about twice as long as that which bears the central flower. . . . The ovary is smooth, long, slightly inflated, rugose at the base; the sepals are velvety or rough, often bristling with purple bristles, and having small foliaceous appendages along the edges. The buds are short

and nearly spherical. . . . Each blossom is never less than 9–10 cm across (about 4 in), sometimes more; the petals are very ample, and like a rosette in arrangement; they grade smaller towards the center, where may be found petals rolled into a crown. The main color is red, or, indeed, a most beautiful bishop's violet, with scarlet reflections, and nuanced black violet, enhancing the blossom's sparkle; the reverse of the petals is a pale silvery-lilac, which neither the burin of the engraver nor the talent of the colorist can reproduce. . . . It is perfectly remontant and double." [M-V50/321]

GEORGE SAND
Roseraie de l'Haÿ, 1909
"Flesh pink." [Y] George Sand, *nom de plume* of Amandine Aurore Lucie Dupin, Baronne Dudevant; lived 1803–1876; French novelist.

GEORGES MOREAU
Moreau-Robert, 1880
Seedling of 'Paul Neyron' (HP).
"Of extraordinary vigor, very beautiful dark green wood, nearly thornless; very beautiful foliage as well, of the most attractive green possible, composed of 5–7 leaflets; flower extra large, opening very well, globular, beautiful very bright satiny red, nuanced vermilion." [JR4/165] "A useful addition to the red-flowered roses because the flowers are of good size, very full, well formed, and brightly colored." [JR7/157]

GEORGE PAUL
E. Verdier, 1863
"Bright red, velvety, blooming in clusters, large and full." [FP] "Flower 8–10 cm across [ca. 4 in], beautiful, sparkling, bright, velvety pink, 6–8 to a cluster." [I'H63/224] George Paul, eminent rosarian of Cheshunt, England. "The lamented death of his [George Paul the younger's] father, Mr. George Paul, at the early age of 57 [in the early 1870's], left him in the charge of the large nursery." [NRS20/26]

GEORGES ROUSSET
Rousset, 1893
"Satiny red." [Y]

GERBE DE ROSES
(trans., 'Spray of Roses')
Laffay, 1847
"Rosy lilac, double. An abundant bloomer." [P] "Growth very vigorous; branches short, with short thorns flattened at the base; leaves dark green, nuanced myrtle green; flowers medium-sized, full, in clusters; color, lilac-pink." [S] Also attributed to Vibert.

GIULETTA
Laurentius, 1858
"Remontant, branches upright, vigorous, and nearly thornless; blooms in panicles; white with light flesh, effective; large leaves of a handsome somber green, blossoms of the 'Souvenir de la Malmaison' sort, smaller, but opening better." [JDR58/48] "Nevertheless, far from being as pretty [as 'Souvenir de la Malmaison']." [S] Laurentius was based in Leipzig, Germany.

GLOIRE DE BOURG-LA-REINE
Margottin, 1879

"Vivid red, double." [EL] "Very vigorous, flowers large, full; color beautiful very billiant scarlet red." [JR3/181] Bourg-la-Reine was the Margottin headquarters: "Mons Jules Margottin fils is going to build up his nursery at Bourg-la-Reine (Seine), near the railway station. His nurseries, which escaped damage in the war [*Franco-Prussian War*], are composed of the very best existing varieties of Roses, the same as his father had. The name of Margottin is one which needs no recommendation: its good reputation, buttressed by the very beautiful roses sent out by Margottin père, is an established fact." [l'H70/327]

[GLOIRE DE GUÉRIN]
Guérin, 1833
Seedling of 'Malton' (HCh).

"Purple." [V4] "Deep carmine, full, medium sized." [LF] "Flower large, full, widely cupped; flesh pink." [S] "Rich deep cherry, of medium size, full; form, cupped. Habit, branching; growth, dwarf." [P] May be considered the first HP. As we learn from *Les Amis des Roses*, nº 215 (page 5), Guérin was a gardener-florist on the Paris road in Angers.

GLORY OF WALTHAM
Listed as a climber.

GOLFE-JUAN
Nabonnand, 1872
Seedling of 'Victor Verdier' (HP).

"Moderate growth; flower very large, full, imbricated; color, ruby red." [S] "Superb in form . . . of the greatest merit for the winter [florist's] trade." [R-H75] Nabonnand's headquarters was located at Golfe-Juan.

GONSOLI GAËTANO
Pernet père, 1874

"Delicate satiny white, in the way of 'Souvenir de [la] Malmaison', and very beautiful." [R7/417] "Bush vigorous, upright, blooms in clusters; flower large, nearly full, fragrant; color, satiny flesh." [S] "Pinkish white, very large, very full, very fragrant, tall." [Sn]

GRAF FRITZ METTERNICH
Soupert & Notting, 1895
From 'Sultan of Zanzibar' (HP) × 'Thomas Mills' (HP).

"Deep red, large, full, very fragrant, tall." [Sn] "Vigorous bush; flower large, full; color, velvety brownish red shaded black, the center bright cardinal red. Very fragrant." [JR19/148]

GRAND-DUC ALEXIS
Lévêque, 1892

"Very vigorous bush; large very green foliage; flowers large, full, extremely well formed, beautiful blood red nuanced purple and light vermilion and brightened with intense carmine." [JR16/167]

GRANDEUR OF CHESHUNT
G. Paul, 1883

"Flower very large, full; color, bright carmine nuanced pink. Abundant autumn bloom. Very beautiful exhibition rose. Growth vigorous, quite remontant." [S]

GRUSS AN WEIMAR
(trans., 'Greetings to Weimar')
Kiese, 1919
From 'Frau Karl Druschki' (HP) × 'Lyon Rose' (Pernetiana).

"Yellowish white, pink center, very large, full, medium to tall." [Sn] "Bud yellowish pink; flower very large, pink on yellowish ground." [ARA21/164]

GRUSS AUS PALLIEN
(trans., 'Greetings from Pallien')
Welter, 1900
From 'Baronne Adolphe de Rothschild' (HP) × 'Princesse de Béarn' (HP).

"The wood and foliage of this variety as well as the growth are all nearly identical to those of 'Baronne A. de Rothschild'. The bright fiery red with purple center coloration as well as the fragrance are much like those of 'Princesse de Béarn'. The long bud holds in a semi-open state quite a long time on the plant; in opening, the blossom takes on the cupped form of 'Baronne A. de Rothschild'. Neither high temperature nor humidity affect the pretty color. . . . According to the breeder, no other HP's bud can rival that of 'Gruss aus Pallien'." [JR24/18] Welter was located at Pallien in Prussia.

GUILLAUME GILLEMOT
Schwartz, 1880
Seedling of 'Mme Charles Wood' (HP).

"Rosy-carmine." [EL] "Vigorous, flower very large, full, globular, form and poise perfect; color, beautiful delicate carmine pink with pale silvery pink reflections . . . blooms freely." [JR4/165]

GUSTAVE PIGANEAU   PLATE 151
Pernet-Ducher, 1889
From 'Charlotte Corday' (HP, Joubert, 1864, purple-red; parentage unknown) × 'Baronne Adolphe de Rothschild' (HP).

"Bush vigorous; flowers extra large, full, cupped; color, beautiful bright carmine lake red." [JR13/167] "Very short in growth, which is nearly the only fault of this very fine Rose. The foliage is good, and the plump fat buds above it open into very large, brilliant, grandly shaped blooms, with broad stout petals, and beautiful centre. Very little liable to mildew, and not much injured by rain. It was a great disappointment when this splendid Rose proved to be a poor grower. Moreover the plant is not lasting in vigour, but often gets weaker. . . . It is very free-flowering, which seems to be a cause of its weakness of growth; it will not make wood, but is constantly forming buds. A good autumnal, capital for forcing, and a large lasting reliable exhibition Rose of the first rank." [F-M2]

GUSTAVE THIERRY
Oger, 1881

"Lilac pink." [Y̆] "Growth vigorous; flower full, globular; color, bright cherry red fading to lilac pink." [S]

HAILEYBURY
G. Paul, 1895

"Crimson cerise." [Y̆] "Red, large, very full, medium scent, tall." [Sn]

[HARMONY]
Nicolas/Conard-Pyle, 1933

"A new type of H.P. of strong growth which makes a splendid short pillar. Salmon-pink flowers with a golden center. Rare 'old rose' perfume. Beautiful Hybrid Tea flowers on Hybrid Perpetual plants. Blooms over a long period in early summer." [C-Pf33]

HELEN KELLER
A. Dickson, 1895

"Beautiful cerise color. Superb." [JR19/67] "Of striking cherry colour inclined to red, large flower and full with well defined cup. A very effective variety." [B&V] "At its best this is a very beautiful Show Rose. In a favourable season it would often be among the three or four most noteworthy H.P.'s, in the large stands of the leading nurserymen. Not of very strong growth, 'moderately vigorous' representing it fairly. The blooms are of the ordinary 'semi-globular' shape, very regular and seldom malformed, of a very bright shade of pink catalogued as 'rosy cerise,' fragrant, full-sized, with stout petals and good lasting qualities. The buds form early, with frequent fatal results. . . . It is only in exceptionally good seasons that any but the longer later shoots yield good blooms with me: but the variety is well worth growing if only a few fine specimens can be secured." [F-M2]

HENRI IV
V. & C. Verdier, 1862

"Violet maroon." [Ў] "Shaded vermilion, very good." [FP] "Flower large, full; color, bright purple red shaded violet." [S] King Henri IV of France; lived 1553–1610.

HENRI COUPÉ
Barbier, 1916
From 'Frau Karl Druschki' (HP) × 'Gruss an Teplitz' (B).

"China pink." [Ў]

HENRIETTE PETIT
Margottin père, 1879

"Very vigorous, flowers large, full, well-formed; color, beautiful red and deep amaranth." [JR3/181]

HENRY BENNETT
Lacharme, 1875
Seedling of 'Charles Lefebvre' (HP).
Not to be confused with Levet's Tea of 1872.

"Velvety fiery red." [JR25/13] "Crimson, medium size, mildews, and burns badly; shy in autumn, and of no value." [EL] "Intense violet-crimson, colour very rich, flowers cupped, good even petals, but not sufficiently full." [JC] "Flower large, full, well formed; color, red, flame, and blackish carmine; growth vigorous." [S] Henry Bennett, eminent English rose-breeder.

HENRY IRVING
Listed as a Climber in the supplement to Chapter 8.

HIPPOLYTE JAMAIN
Faudon, 1869
Seedling of 'Victor Verdier' (HP).
Not to be confused with Lacharme's similarly colored HP of 1874.

"Large, full, well formed, beautiful bright pink." [JR3/27] "Growth vigorous, with smooth wood; very remontant . . . flower very large, full, semi-globular; color, bright carmine pink; resembles 'Etienne Levet' [HP] and 'Président Thiers' [HP, Lacharme, 1871, fiery red]. The most hardy of the 'Victor Verdier' clan." [S]

HOLD SLUNCI
Blatná, 1956

"Light yellow, medium size, full, light scent, medium to tall." [Sn]

HUGH WATSON
A. Dickson, 1905

"Fiery red, shaded carmine." [Ў] "Crimson but with a good deal of carmine in its flowers. This is a good exhibition variety — fairly vigorous in growth — the bloom of medium rather than of large size but excellent in shape. Should be more grown." [F-M]

IMPÉRATRICE MARIA FEODOROWNA
Lévêque, 1892
Not to be confused with Nabonnand's Tea of 1883.

"Vigorous, foliage ample, glaucous green, flowers large, globular, perfectly formed, magnificent bright delicate pink." [JR16/167]

INGÉNIEUR MADÈLÉ
Moreau-Robert, 1874

"Currant red." [Ў] "Growth moderate; floriferous; flower very large, full, imbricated; color, currant pink." [S]

INIGO JONES
W. Paul, 1886

"Vigorous, very floriferous; flowers large, full, globular, perfectly formed, beautiful pink tinted purple. Good for exhibitions, and a good autumnal." [JR10/19] Inigo Jones, 1573–1652; English architect.

ISABEL LLORACH
Dot, 1929
From 'Frau Karl Druschki' (HP) × 'Bénédicte Seguin' (HT, Pernet-Ducher, 1918, orange; parentage unknown).

"Bud very large, long-pointed; flower very large, semi-double, open, lasting, moderately fragrant, nankeen-yellow, tinted red, borne singly on a long stem. Foliage abundant, large, dark green, glossy, disease-resistant. Few thorns. Growth very vigorous, semi-climbing; abundant, intermittent bloomer from May to July and again in October." [ARA29/229]

JACQUES LAFFITTE
Vibert, 1846

"Carmine pink." [R-H56] "Rosy-crimson." [EL] "Flower 7–8 cm [ca. 3 in], full, carmine-pink, superb. Very vigorous bush." [M-L46/272] "Bright rose, large and full; form, expanded. Habit, erect; growth, vigorous; the flowers often produced singly for some distance along the stem. The colour stands the sun well, and is clear and decided." [P] "[The blossom's width is] 7–8 cm [ca. 3 in], full, carmine pink, superb flower." [VPt48/153]

JAMES BOUGAULT   PLATE 150
Renaud-Guépet/C. Verdier, 1887
Sport of 'Auguste Mie' (HP).

"Vigorous . . . flowers medium, full, white lightly tinted pink when opening, fading to pure white." [JR11/168] "Blooms more easily than its progenitor, which, as we know, opens only with difficulty, particularly when the weather is somewhat humid. This sport of 'Auguste Mie' appeared 12–14 years ago in the nurseries of Mons Renaud-Guépet . . . who, after assuring himself that the sport would not revert, sold it to Mons Charles Verdier." [JR16/56]

JAN BÖHM
Svoboda, 1934
From 'Hugh Dickson' (HP) × 'King George V' (HP, H. Dickson, 1912, crimson; parentage unknown).

"Red, large, full, very fragrant, medium height." [Sn]

JANINE VIAUD-BRUANT

Viaud-Bruant, 1910

From 'Triomphe d'Orléans' (HP, Corbœuf, 1902, red and deep violet; itself from 'Général Jacqueminot' [HP] × 'Général de la Martinière' [HP, De Sansal/Jamain, 1869, wine-red; parentage unknown]) × 'Princesse de Béarn' (HP).

"Growth more vigorous than that of either parent, flowers large, shaped like a champagne glass. This new rose is one lovely small rose sparkling with a color of crimson purple ruby. The very brilliant color shines and glows; it is a warmer color than has 'Princesse de Béarn'. Exquisite scent." [JR34/166]

JEAN-BAPTISTE CASATI

('Duchesse d'Orléans'?)

Widow Schwartz, 1886

"Bush vigorous; flower large, well formed, cupped, very full, very delicate lilac pink, center whitish; very fragrant." [JR10/182]

JEAN CHERPIN

Liabaud, 1865

"Plum color, double, often semi-double, inclined to burn; fragrant and a fine seed parent. One of the richest shades of color yet produced." [EL] "Flower very large, full; velvety purple red with a lighter center, brightened with flame." [l'H65/339] "Rich violet-plum, a superb colour, petals smooth and well formed, flowers cupped, a good and distinct rose; habit moderate." [JC] "Growth vigorous." [P1] Jean Cherpin, rosarian, horticulturalist, editor of various mid-century horticultural periodicals.

JEAN GOUJON

Margottin, 1862

"Fresh pink." [Ÿ] "Bright red." [JR25/23] "Rich deep rose, flowers extra large and handsome, a robust growing fine rose." [JC] "Beautiful clear red, very large, full, and good." [FP] "Vigorous; color, deep pink; flower very large, full, cupped; much to be recommended for its late bloom, which lasts until winter." [S] "Nearly smooth wood; of second quality." [EL]

JEAN LELIÈVRE

Oger, 1879

"Vigorous, flowers large, very full, well formed, blooms easily; color, bright deep crimson." [JR3/181] "Very floriferous; one of the best." [S]

JEANNE MASSON

Liabaud, 1891

"White, flesh reflections." [LS] "Whitish pink, medium size, full, medium scent, medium height." [Sn]

JEANNE SURY

('Jeanne Surey')

Faudon, 1868

"Moderately vigorous; flower large, full; light crimson." [S] "Bright claret and crimson, flowers very large and full, petals smooth and well formed; a large and handsome rose." [JC]

[JEANNIE DICKSON]

A. Dickson, 1890

"Rosy pink, edged with silvery pink; very large, full, high-scented flowers, thick smooth petals." [CA93] "Apparently hybridized, though perhaps remotely, with the Teas, the shape of the foliage suggesting some such strain. A good grower, but requires generous treatment, not liable to mildew or much injured by rain, free-flowering and pretty good in the autumn. The blooms have capital long large smooth petals, with centres high and finely pointed. Not very lasting, and difficult to keep clean in trying weather, but a fine show flower if grown strong, cut young, and tied up if necessary." [F-M3]

JOACHIM DU BELLAY

Moreau-Robert, 1882

"Very vigorous, handsome dark green foliage, flower very large, full, well formed, beautiful vermilion red nuanced flame, very floriferous." [JR6/163]

JOASINE HANET

('Johasine Hanet')

Listed as a Damask Perpetual.

JOHN BRIGHT

G. Paul, 1878

"Bright crimson, medium size." [EL] "The blossom is a bright color—a sparkling and pure crimson; the form of the rose is round, globular, with large petals sometimes recurved; the interior petals are shorter." [S]

JOHN GOULD VEITCH

('John Weitch')

Lévêque, 1864

"Flower large, full; color, beautiful brilliant red." [S]

JOHN LAING

E. Verdier, 1872

"Crimson-maroon, colour of the old 'Tuscany'; flowers moderate size, rather small." [JC] "Growth moderately vigorous, blooming in clusters; flower medium sized, full; color, deep bright crimson, velvety and sparkling." [S] "One of the principal English horticulturalists, Mr. John Laing, has died at the age of 77 at Forest Hill, where he had an establishment both vast and very well known. He was a worker best known and appreciated in England for his numerous and interesting hybridizations." [JR24/145]

JOHN STUART MILL

Turner, 1874

Seedling of 'Beauty of Waltham' (HP).

"Bright clear red, large, full, and beautiful form; fine shell-like petal of good substance." [JC] "Rosy crimson, large, full, or double; does not bloom until late; shy in the autumn." [EL] "Growth vigorous; color, light red; flower large, full, imbricated, lasting; grows erect; wood smooth . . . of the 'Sénateur Vaïsse' sort." [S] "Of strong long growth, not liable to injury from mildew or rai. A late bloomer, uncertain as to quality and usefulness. In some seasons all the flowers come as mere red lumps but in others the majority come of fine imbricated shape and colour, and it is then a good show rose, of average size and fair lasting qualities, but it is not a free bloomer or a good autumnal. In my experience it comes best in a cool season." [F-M2] John Stuart Mill, 1806–1873; British utilitarian philosopher.

JOSÉPHINE DE BEAUHARNAIS
Guillot fils, 1865

"Growth vigorous, flower very large, full, well formed, cupped; beautiful delicate pink, reverse of petals silvery." [S] "Petal edges silvery." [I'H65/340] Joséphine de Beauharnais, the Empress Josephine, wife of Napoleon, superlatively important patroness of the Rose; lived 1763–1814.

JULES BARIGNY
E. Verdier, 1886

"Very vigorous, light green erect canes; thorns remote, straight, large, pink; leaves, 3–5 large oval-rounded somber green leaflets, irregularly and rather deeply toothed; flowers large, very full, beautiful plump form, firmly held; color, carmine red with a paler reverse, very fragrant." [JR10/170]

JULES CHRÉTIEN   PLATE 128
Schwartz, 1878

"Belongs to the 'Prince Camille [de Rohan]' type. Crimson, tinged with purple." [EL] "Upright canes with whitish thorns, having very large glossy green leaves . . . the form of the leaflets is oval-lanceolate acuminate, the upper leaflets most distinctly so; the stipules are linear, entire; the sepals are nothing more than little linear segments. The flower is large, well-formed, and perhaps the only one of its color. . . . It is full, bright poppy red, showing up well, the backs of the petals having a light violet tint which brings out the bright red. . . . This variety was announced . . . under the name 'André Schwartz', but . . . I have dedicated it to my friend Jules Chrétien, the able chief floral horticulturalist of the Tête d'Or park in Lyon." [JR2/167–168]

JULES SEURRE
Liabaud, 1869
Seedling of 'Victor Verdier' (HP).

"Growth vigorous; color, carmine red nuanced blue; flower large, full." [S]

JULIUS FINGER
Listed as an HT.

KAISER WILHELM I
Elze/Ruschpler, 1878

"Light purple red, large, full, medium scent, medium height." [Sn] "Vigorous bush; canes short, nearly thornless; leaves dark green, much veined; undersides of leaves grayish-green; blossom very large, full, good form; color, golden grenadine nuanced reddish violet." [S] Kaiser Wilhelm I; lived 1797–1888; king of Prussia.

KATKOFF
Moreau-Robert, 1887
Seedling of 'Charles Lefebvre' (HP).

"Growth vigorous; very handsome glossy green foliage; flower large, full, perfectly formed, imbricated like a camellia; bright cerise red sparkling with carmine, nuanced currant red, very floriferous and very fragrant; very beautiful plant." [JR11/150]

KÖNIG FRIEDRICH II VON DÄNEMARK
Introducer and date unknown

"Dark red, medium size, full, lightly scented, medium height." [Sn]

L'AMI E. DAUMONT
Vilin, 1903

"Growth of great vigor with upright canes; few thorns; foliage delicate green; bud conical, very large; flower very full; well held; color, alizarine scarlet red tempered by old-rose red, the underside of the petals becoming silvery towards the vase, the edges of the flower taking up purplish madder tones." [JR28/27]

L'AMI MAUBRAY
Mercier, 1890
Seedling of 'Xavier Olibo' (HP).

"Vigorous, making a beautiful bush. Flower solitary, sometimes in a cluster, very fragrant, very double, very remontant, light red shaded delicate violet." [JR15/164]

L'ESPERANCE
(trans., 'Hope')
Lartay/Fontaine, 1871

"Sparkling pink." [Ÿ] "Rosy-cerise, colour clear and satiny, flowers large and double, highly scented . . . habit moderate." [JC] "Growth vigorous; flower large, full, flat; color, light cherry red." [S] The privations and difficulties of the Franco-Prussian War no doubt inspired the name.

L'ÉTINCELANTE
Vigneron, 1891
Seedling of 'Bijou de Couasnon' (HP).

"Vigorous, very floriferous, flower large, full, cupped, perfectly poised, extremely bright red, somewhat velvety within." [JR15/148]

LA BRILLANTE
V. & C. Verdier, 1861

"Light clear carmine." [I'H61/264] "Bright crimson, a clear shade, large, double, fragrant; a free bloomer." [EL] "Transparent carmine, very bright and beautiful, large, and of fine form." [FP] "Growth vigorous; branches upright, very thorny; flower medium sized, full, very well formed, in clusters of 10–12 flowers." [S]

LA BRUNOYENNE
('La Brunajeune')
Bourgeois, 1908

"Very vigorous, flower large, very full, well formed, cupped, deep velvety lake towards the outside, fading to golden lake red with flame reflections; center light but very intense madder red; reverse of petals bright madder pink with bluish reflections; very fragrant. Dedicated to Mme Gutierrez de Estrada, the great philanthropist [of the French town of Brunoy]." [JR32/135]

LA DUCHESSE DE MORNY
E. Verdier, 1863

"Bright rose; erect growth; mildew." [EL] "Brilliant pleasing rose, flowers large, full, and beautifully formed . . . robust." [JC] "Bright but delicate rose-color, the reverse of the petals silvery, large and full, form globular." [FP] "Growth vigorous, very remontant, with robust canes armed with some unequal thorns on the lower part; ample foliage, dark above, pale green beneath; each leaf is comprised of 3–5 large, oval-cordate, pointed, finely dentate leaflets; the canes are all topped by a solitary blossom of the Centifolia form, perfect, globular at first, then opening into a cup, at that point not measuring less than four in across [ca. 1 dm]; its color is one of the most delicate — very fresh, tender pink, reverse of petals pale pink nuanced matte silver; beneath this 'terminal' blossom, 5 or 6 other flowers grow from the axils of the upper leaves, the opening of which blossoms prolongs the spring bloom up until the appearance of the reblooming canes; in form, size, and color, these blossoms cede nothing to the spring bloom." [I'H63/223] "Of fair growth and foliage in strong rich soil, the wood and leaves being very distinct and characteristic. Decidedly liable to mildew, and cannot stand much rain. The blooms come well shaped, with very smooth stout petals, beautifully full, of distinct and lovely colour, large size, and fair lasting qualities. This Rose is one of the very smoothest and most regular in semi-globular imbricated shape that we have; a free bloomer, but not so good in autumn, and rather dainty as to soil and treatment. The buds should be well thinned . . . the shoots often come wholly or partly fasciated." [F-M]

LA NANTAISE
Boisselot/Cochet, 1885
Seedling of 'Général Jacqueminot' (HP).

"Vigorous, stocky, erect canes bearing medium sized, hooked thorns, and foliage of good size, dark green. The large flowers, regularly cupped, borne on a strong, upright stem, are quite full with large petals, intense red darkened by deeper reflections, especially at the end of the season, when it blooms nicely. The vigorous canes bear clusters blossoms, while the branchlets bear solitary roses . . . seems to belong to the 'Jacqueminot' group." [JR8/169]

LA ROSIÈRE   PLATE 118
Damaizin, 1874

"Maroon crimson, shaded with black, of medium size, cupped, double and effective." [P1] "Vigorous, flowers large, full, fiery amaranth red, petal edges crimson. The bud is long and borne on a strong stem." [JR18/56] "Belongs to the 'Prince Camille [de Rohan]' type. Crimson, the flowers are identical in color and form with 'Prince Camille', but seems a little fuller, and are more freely produced; the habit of growth, too, seems somewhat stronger; it may usurp the place of its rival." [EL]

LA SYRÈNE
Touvais, 1874
Not to be confused with the China 'Sirene', synonymous for 'Charlotte Klemm'.

"Cherry." [LS] "Light red, large, full, medium height." [Sn]

LA TENDRESSE
Oger, 1864

"Flower large, full; color beautiful, Hydrangea pink." [S]

LA VIERZIONNAISE
André, 1893
Seedling of 'Jules Margottin' (HP).

"This pretty rose, of which the salient qualities are the fresh color, the graceful form, the perfume, the great abundance of flowers, and continuity of bloom from June till October, was raised from seed at Vierzon by Mons Charles André, a longtime horticulturalist. . . . The growth is upright, the wood cheerful green, few thorns, which are red and hooked. . . . The blossoms are borne in clusters; the buds, with foliaceous sepals, are very fresh looking." [JR16/52] "Delicate pink, or rather light lilac pink, nuanced darker pink, shaded and frosted a light carmine pink." [JR17/179]

LADY ARTHUR HILL
A. Dickson, 1889
Seedling of 'Beauty of Waltham' (HP).

"Lilac-pink, quite distinctive and charming, a shade unknown till now. The flowers are large, full, very symmetrical, and appear abundantly, each branch bearing a bud. The growth is vigorous, the foliage distinctive and very pretty. . . . This rose is unique in form." [JR13/90] "Blooms abundantly and late; flower . . . of good form." [JR22/105] "Distinct in colour but small." [F-M3]

LADY EMILY PEEL
Listed as a Bourbon.

[LADY HELEN STEWART]
A. Dickson, 1887

"Bright scarlety crimson; flowers fully rounded out, petals large and thick; highly perfumed and very beautiful." [CA93] "Large round solid flowers, very fragrant; color bright crimson, flamed with scarlet, very beautiful." [C&Js99] "The same fault [as has 'Lady Arthur Hill'], want of size, is noticeable in this Rose, which is however very bright and free blooming and a good grower." [F-M3] "Vigorous growth having strong, upright wood, and pretty thick foliage. Flower carried well on a long, thick stem; it is full, of good form and exquisite scent. Color, bright crimson scarlet; petals large, uniform, of great substance, and a very beautiful lustre. Very distinct and beautiful, blooming in profusion the whole season until late, when it is especially pretty." [JR11/93]

LADY OVERTOUN
H. Dickson, 1907

"Salmon flesh." [Y] "Much like 'Ulster' in leaf and growth, and 'La France' in color, though perhaps lighter pink." [JR31/38]

LADY STUART
Portemer, 1852
Not to be confused with 'Lady Helen Stuart'.

"Pink, changing to blush; five to seven-leaflets." [EL] "Very remontant hybrid resembling the non-remontant hybrid of the same name, which is to say: flower large, very full, regular, and prettily colored delicate flesh." [I'H52/187] "Very vigorous bush; flowers medium or large, very full, globular, very pale flesh, darker at the center; very beautiful variety, but not very remontant and doesn't always open perfectly." [I'H56/201]

LAFORCADE
Lévêque, 1889

"Vigorous, very strong upright canes, foliage ample, dark green; flower very large, cupped, beautiful carmine red . . . dedicated to the very able Chief Gardener of Paris." [JR13/164]

LAMOTTE SANGUIN
('La Motte Sanguine')
Vigneron, 1869

"Growth vigorous; canes pretty big, branching; bark somber green, reddish where the sun strikes, with numerous thorns of a reddish brown, and straight, strong, unequal, and stout. Foliage thick, quite rugose or bullate, somber green, generally of 5 acuminate, dentate, oval-rounded leaflets; petiole pretty strong, armed with 3 or 4 little prickles of the same color as those on the canes. Flower about 4 in across [ca. 1 dm], full, widely cupped, slightly plump, usually solitary, occasionally in twos or threes; color, a beautiful bright carmine red; very large petals, peduncle glandular, short, strong, Ovary pear-shaped; sepals leaf-like. Plant very vigorous and of good stature. It makes magnificent, hardy bushes." [JF]

LAURENT DE RILLÉ
Lévêque, 1884

"Vigorous bush . . . flower large, full, imbricated; color, very bright light cerise red; foliage glaucous green." [S] "Very abundant bloom; one of the breeder's best introductions." [JR8/150]

LE TRIOMPHE DE SAINTES
Derouet, 1885

"Vigorous; flower large, very full, sparkling scarlet red, very floriferous. Remarkably beautiful." [JR9/166]

LECOCQ-DUMESNIL
E. Verdier, 1882

"Very vigorous bush with upright reddish canes; thorns numerous, unequal, short, very pointed, pink; leaves comprised of five oblong leaflets with fairly deep irregular serration, dark green; flower extra large, quite full, and perfectly imbricated; unique coloration: sparkling red much marbled and shaded crimson brown and violet." [JR6/165]

LÉNA TURNER
E. Verdier, 1869

"Cerise, shaded with violet, flowers large, full, and imbricated; a good rose." [JC] "Cerise-red with slatey nuances; camellia form." [S] "The blossom is of perfect form, wonderfully imbricated except right in the center, where the petals are slightly ragged; ideally double; good size; excellently held. Its color is a rich deep carmine, brightened at the center with flame red, leaving nothing which could improve on its sparkling effect. The foliage is, above, a beautiful dark green, slightly reddish along the crenelated edges; delicate green veined darker beneath; the thorns are reddish. The bush is vigorous, very floriferous, and quite hardy." [VH80/283]

LÉON DELAVILLE
E. Verdier, 1885

"Red, shaded." [Y̆] "Very vigorous, with strong canes; foliage dark green; flowers large, full, well-formed, dark red strongly shaded carmine, illuminated with violet crimson." [JR8/178]

LÉON RENAULT
Widow Lédéchaux, 1878
Seedling of 'Général Jacqueminot' (HP).

"Cherry-red, very large, full; promises well." [EL] "Vigorous bush; flower large, well formed; color, beautiful light red with the reverse of the petals tinted carmine." [JR3/10]

LÉON ROBICHON
Robichon, 1901

"White, large, full, medium scent, tall." [Sn]

LÉON SAY
Lévêque, 1882

"Vigorous, leaves large, thick, glaucous green; flower very large, bright red shaded brown, light pink, and lilac pink shaded white; the size of the foliage and the very curious and effective coloration make this variety head the list for bedding." [JR6/148] "Centifolia scent." [S]

LEONIE LAMBERT
Lambert, 1913
From 'Frau Karl Druschki' (HP) × 'Prince de Bulgarie' (HT).

"Vigorous bush, stiff, like 'Baronne Adolphe de Rothschild'; large leaves. Flower very large, 10–14 cm across [ca. 5 in], solitary, erect on a long, stiff stem, silvery pink, with a glossy yellowish pink center; petal edges pink becoming violet. Fragrant. Height, 1.5–2 m [ca. 4.5–6 ft]; everblooming until October." [JR38/56]

LÉONIE LARTAY
Lartay, 1860

"Wine-lee." [Y̆] "Flower large, full; color, bright scarlet." [S]

[LÉOPOLD I, ROI DES BELGES]
('Léopold Premier')
Van Asche, 1863
Seedling of 'Général Jacqueminot' (HP).

"Velvety purple." [LS] "Bright dark-red, very large and full, fine form." [FP] "Flower very large, full; color, shining dark red; resembles 'Mme Victor Verdier'." [S] "Crimson, with soft tint of violet, flowers large, full, and imbricated; a good rose; habit vigorous." [JC] "A magnificent Rose . . . very full and fragrant." [C&Js12] Often called a Hybrid China.

[LION DES COMBATS]
Lartay, 1850

"Reddish-violet, often shaded with scarlet, large and full." [FP] "Hardy." [S] "Very vigorous plant; flowers large, full, dark red nuanced flame. Superb grafted or own-root. We are fortunate to be able to save the reputation of this Rose, which some have discredited. Having received it in bloom, we thought well of it at once; we only regret that, along with this variety, the same year brought us ten other varieties which should have been scrapped." [I'H53/226] Parent of 'A.-M. Ampère' (HP).

LISETTE DE BÉRANGER
F. Moreau/Guillot fils, 1867

"Vigorous, wood and foliage resembling those of 'Lord Raglan'; blossoms medium-sized, full, well formed, globular, well held, a pretty very fresh flesh pink, much like that of 'Reine des Île-Bourbons', fading later to a ground of white with petals much bordered pink, like the Tea 'Homère'; totally new coloration." [I'H67/287]

LORD BACON
W. Paul, 1883

"Deep crimson, illumined with scarlet, and shaded with velvety black, large, full, and globular. A very fine and showy Rose, blooming abundantly, and till late in the season; growth vigorous." [P1]

LORD BEACONSFIELD
Christy/Schwartz/Bennett, 1878

"Crimson, nuanced." [Y̆] "Crimson, large, well formed." [EL] "Growth vigorous; flower very large, full, globular; color, blackish crimson." [S]

LORD FREDERIC CAVENDISH
Frettingham, 1884

"Flower large, full, of unique form — globular and quite perfect; sparkling bright red; petals pointed. . . . Growth vigorous." [S]

[LORD MACAULAY]
W. Paul, 1863

"Bright crimson." [LS] "Flower large, full, perfectly held; form nearly globular; magnificent exhibition rose. Its scarlet red coloring changes depending upon the soil in which it grows; in clay soil, the blossom becomes maroon red, and may be burned by the sun." [S] A parent of 'Gloire de Bruxelles' (HP).

LORD RAGLAN
Guillot père, 1854
Seedling of 'Géant des Batailles' (HP).

"Burgundy crimson, a lovely shade; tender and shy in autumn." [EL] "Deep crimson, changing to mottled crimson, flowers large, full, and well formed, habit vigorous; a very superb rose." [JC] "Vigorous, wood reddish, nearly thornless, blossoms fiery red, brighter at the center, and violet purple at the edge." [JDR55/9] "Growth very vigorous and remontant, with robust upright canes of a delicate green armed with some reddish thorns of medium size, nearly straight, perhaps a little hooked at the base of the cane. The young foliage has a strong tint of red, which disappears bit by bit, making way for a beautiful dark green. Each leaf is comprised of 7 or sometimes 5 leaflets of varying size. The blossom is of the greatest size, very full, well formed, opens perfectly." [S] "One of the very finest flowers of this section [*i.e., progeny of 'Géant des Batailles'*]; and the plant is more vigorous, and less liable to mildew, than the rest of the group." [FP]

LOUIS CALLA
E. Verdier, 1885

"Vigorous bush with erect canes; leaves very large, rounded, dark green; blossoms large, full, plump; color, scarlet purple red nuanced poppy and marbled whitish." [JR9/178]

LOUIS DONADINE
Gonod, 1887
Seedling of 'Duhamel-Dumonceau' (HP).

"Very vigorous, canes upright, strong; leaves of five leaflets, dark green, the odd one very long, stem strong; flower large, full, well formed; color, deep velvety maroon red, nuanced flame red; very remontant, very fragrant." [JR11/163]

LOUIS LILLE
Dubreuil, 1887
From 'Baronne Adolphe de Rothschild' (HP) × 'Firebrand' (HP).

"Bush vigorous but stocky with ample beautiful dark green foliage; flower very large, full, cupped, bright red with light flame reflections." [JR11/184]

LOUIS NOISETTE
Ducher, 1865

"Flowers full, globular, beautiful carmine pink; like those of 'Baronne Prévost'." [I'H65/340] "Growth vigorous, flower large, full, in a cluster; carmine pink." [S]

LOUIS PHILIPPE ALBERT D'ORLÉANS
E. Verdier, 1884

"Vigorous with upright light green canes; thorns unequal, short and hooked, pink; leaves composed of 3–5 leaflets, large, rounded, somber green, with irregular slightly deep serrations; flowers large, full, very well formed, bright cerise red nuanced and illuminated purplish scarlet grenadine." [JR8/165]

LOUIS ROLLET
Gonod, 1886

"Extra vigorous, notable for its growth, with red wood, large thorns of the same color, leaves with five large leaflets; in spring, the foliage is as red as that of a Coleus; flower large, full, purplish red, very remontant." [JR10/148]

LOUISE CRETTÉ
Chambard, 1915
From 'Frau Karl Druschki' (HP) × 'Cl. Kaiserin Auguste Viktoria' (Cl. HT).

"Snow-white, cream center; very large, full, fine form. . . . Described . . . as being a grand exhibition rose of 'Frau Karl Druschki' type, with a slightly yellowish tint." [Th2] "Perfect form, opening well; some fragrance. Growth vigorous; almost thornless. One of the finest and largest white Roses and a decided improvement on 'Frau Karl Druschki'." [C-Ps29] "An almost continuous bloomer when once established." [C-Ps30]

LUCIEN DURANTHON
Bonnaire, 1893

"Extra vigorous bush with stiff, upright canes, thornless, beautiful foliage; flower large, full, form of 'Baronne Adolphe de Rothschild'; color, pure carmine red, very bright, a color unique in the sort; continuous bloom; very good for cutting and forcing." [JR17/147]

LYONFARBIGE DRUSCHKI
Sangerhausen, 1928
From 'Frau Karl Druschki' (HP) × 'Lyon Rose' (Pernetiana).

"Pink on yellow, large, full, light scent, medium height." [Sn]

LYONNAIS
Lacharme, 1871
Seedling of 'Victor Verdier' (HP).
Not to be confused with Lacharme's pink HP 'Belle Lyonnaise' of 1854, nor with Levet's yellow Noisette of 1870 'Belle Lyonnaise'.

"Satin rose, colour clear and beautiful, flowers cupped, very large and full; a very distinct and superb rose, habit vigorous." [JC] "Pink, with deeper centre, fades quickly; a coarse, inferior sort." [EL] "Bush vigorous; flower very large, full, Centifolia-form; color, delicate pink, center brighter." [S]

M.H. WALSH
A. Dickson, 1905

"Beautiful velvety crimson . . . especially notable during the autumn-tide." [JR29/153] "This Rose is apt to be rather too late in flowering to come in as a useful exhibition variety, but in a very early season it would be wanted. Velvety crimson in colour, it is a first-rate autumnal, fairly vigorous grower, and fragrant, needs shading as it is apt to burn." [F-M]

MAGNOLIJA
Kosteckij, 1940

"White, large, full, medium height." [Sn]

MAHARAJAH
B. R. Cant, 1904

"Rich crimson, bright golden anthers; bush." [NRS18/135] "Deep red, large, not very full, medium scent, tall." [Sn] "Deep velvety crimson. — Vigorous. — Pillar. — Semi-single." [Cat12]

MARCHIONESS OF EXETER
Laxton/G. Paul, 1877
Seedling of 'Jules Margottin' (HP).

"Cherry-rose, fragrant."[EL] "Beautiful light bright pink." [JR1/12/13] "Beautiful rose with recurved petals; color, pale pink nuanced cherry pink; very well formed, semi-globular . . . of the 'Annie Laxton' sort." [S]

MARGARET HAYWOOD
Haywood, 1890
Sport of 'Mme Clémence Joigneaux' (HP).

"Brilliant pink." [Ÿ] "Light pink, very large, full, tall." [Sn]

MARGUERITE BRASSAC
Brassac, 1874
Considered by some to be synonymous with 'Charles Lefebvre'.

"Purplish crimson. One of the best Roses grown; very fragrant."[H] "Petals very large, well rounded, deep velvety carmine."[JR3/27] "Very smooth and even in form."[JC] "Growth very vigorous; flower large, full, well formed; petals large; color, deep velvety carmine; magnificent exhibition rose." [S]

MARGUERITE DE ROMAN
Schwartz, 1882

"Vigorous bush, having the look of 'Mlle Eugénie Verdier' [HP]; canes upright and strong; foliage light green; flower very large, well formed, flesh white with flesh pink center; plant effective; freely remontant." [JR6/148]

MARGUERITE JAMAIN
Jamain, 1873

"Vigorous bush; flower large, very full; color, very fresh flesh pink." [S]

MARGUERITE LECUREAUX
('Marguerite Lectureaux')
Cherpin, 1853

"Flowers medium sized, full, bright red plumed white." [I'H54/14] "Sometimes, in the spring, striped with a single white line down the middle of each petal. Of little merit due to its inconstancy." [I'H56/250] "A striped variety of 'Géant des Batailles'. Its canes are frailer, its foliage thinner and more dentate, and its blossoms slightly less full. . . . We first saw it bloom in a little garden in 1846 or 1847. . . . We began to propagate it in 1849, as we wanted to be certain of the permanence of the stripe characteristic, which only occurs during the first bloom, up to July. We must add quickly that this variety has already given us two others . . . a very strong Provins perfume throughout the season." [JDR54/10] "Not very vigorous, and inconstant in its striping, as are all striped roses. . . . It is nevertheless one of the best varieties for bedding, as, striped or not, its flowers come all year." [JDR56/48]

MARIE BAUMANN
('Mme Alphonse Lavallée')
Baumann, 1863
From 'Général Jacqueminot' (HP) × 'Victor Verdier' (HP).

"Delicate carmine." [LS] "Rich carmine-crimson, flowers large and of exquisite form, perfectly full, and very beautiful; habit vigorous."[JC] "A Rose of great reputation. The growth as a cutback cannot be called more than fair, and the foliage is not large. The wood is weak and pliable, and the flowering shoots of dwarfs must be staked, as the stem is not stiff enough to support a heavy bloom. This habit much detracts from the appearance of the flowers while on the plant, as they generally fall over with their faces to the ground. Fragrant, not much injured by rain, but decidedly liable to mildew. It is especially noted as one of the most reliable of Roses, for the blooms nearly always come good and well shaped, semi-globular, without high centre. Free blooming and a good autumnal, fair in petal, good in centre, of large size and fair lasting qualities, and particularly excellent in smoothness and regularity. More often good than 'Alfred Colomb', which is sometimes very like it in shape and colour, though the habits of the plants are widely different. Does fairly as a standard, but not so well on the manetti[i], must be highly cultivated, and requires rich soil. Not a hardy sort of strong constitution, but it has been for many years, and appears likely to continue to be, one of the most popular of exhibition Roses, though it does not seem to succeed in the hot summers of America." [F-M2]

MARIE BOISSÉE
Oger, 1864

"Blush-white in opening, passing to pure white when expanded; flowers double and cup-shaped; habit vigorous; very free-flowering."[FP] "Flower large, full, very beautiful form." [S]

MARIE LOUISE PERNET
Pernet père, 1876
Seedling of 'Baronne Adolphe de Rothschild' (HP).

"Deep rose."[EL] "Moderate growth . . . flower large, full, cupped; color, very bright pink." [S]

MARIE MENUDEL
Barbier, 1927

"Bud and flower very large, double, full, open, lasting, moderate fragrance, rose-pink tinted salmon, borne singly on long, strong stem. Foliage sufficient, large, rich green, leathery, disease-resistant. Few thorns. Growth very vigorous, upright; free and continuous bloomer." [ARA28/239]

MARIE POCHIN
Listed as 'Mary Pochin'.

MARIE RADY
Listed as 'Mlle Marie Rady'.

MARQUISE DE CASTELLANE
Pernet père, 1869
Seedling of 'Jules Margottin' (HP).

"Clear cherry-rose. Stout, bold, and free-flowering."[H] "Carmine-rose, a bright and permanent shade, very large, very full, not fragrant but effective, does not bloom until late — a valuable sort for exhibition purposes. Does not propagate from cuttings." [EL] "Beautiful bright rose, very large and full; form perfect; blooms freely; growth robust. One of the best."[P1] "Deep cerise, colour clear and good, flowers large, circular and full; a superb rose."[JC] "Growth vigorous, hardy, floriferous . . . flower very large, full, scentless, globular, pointed center; color, bright pink; very good to force."[S] "Of robust habit; sometimes a very strong grower with thick long thorny shoots and fine foliage, but capricious in this matter, and rather difficult to please. Sometimes it will grow well in light soil, but at any rate it will be of little use if it does not make strong growth. The blooms are frequently of uneven shape, occasionally rough and coarse, but they are large, and effective when they come good with a pointed centre. Not liable to mildew or much injured by rain, early, and free-flowering if it grows well. Not very good in lasting qualities, but quite noted as an autumnal, fine large blooms being frequently produced even till quite late in the season." [F-M2]

MARQUISE DE GIBOT
De Sansal, 1868

"Pale rose, flowers large, full, and globular; a fine and distinct rose." [JC] "Growth very vigorous; foliage beautiful bright dark green, reddish beneath; flower large, full, plump; very floriferous; color, pale pink, bright pink rebloom." [S]

MARQUISE DE MORTEMART
Liabaud, 1868
Seedling of 'Jules Margottin' (HP).

"Blush, well formed. A fine rose of delicate habit." [EL] "Blush-white, centre pale flesh, colour delicate and beautiful, petals smooth and even, flowers large and cupped; an exquisite rose, and one of the best light varieties . . . vigorous." [JC] "Growth vigorous; flower large, full, very well formed, very pretty delicate pink; nice scent; reminiscent of 'Duchesse de Sutherland', and much resembles 'Souvenir de la Malmaison'." [S]

MARQUISE DE VERDUN
Oger, 1868

"Growth vigorous; flower large, full, globular; color, bright carmine pink." [S]

MARTIN LIEBAU
Kiese, 1930
"Pink, large, full, medium scent, medium height." [Sn]

MARY CORELLY
Prince, 1901
"Deep salmon, medium size, full, tall." [Sn]

MARY POCHIN
Pochin, 1881

"Of moderate vigor; color, bright red tinted velvety crimson; flower of medium size, well formed, with large smooth petals." [S]

MAURICE LEPELLETIER
Moreau-Robert, 1868
"Bright pink." [Ÿ] "Growth vigorous; flower large, full; globular; color, vermilion red." [S]

MAXIME DE LA ROCHETERIE
('Maxime de la Rochetterie')
Vigneron, 1871
Seedling of 'Victor Verdier' (HP).

"Growth vigorous; flower large, full; color, velvety blackish purple red." [S] "Mons Maxime de La Rocheterie, president of the *Société d'Horticulture d'Orléans et du Loiret*." [JR9/168]

MÈRE DE ST. LOUIS
Lacharme, 1851
Seedling of 'La Reine' (HP).

"A waxy flesh-color, and, though not very full, is distinct and beautiful." [FP] "Pink, medium size." [EL] "A beautiful and important prize; its large, nearly full, flowers pass from white to very delicate pink." [I'H51/173] "A novel coloration." [VH51/112]

MEYERBEER
E. Verdier, 1867

"Flowers very large, full; petals wavy, purple red nuanced bright flame." [I'H68/49] "Growth vigorous." [S] Giacomo Meyerbeer, German composer; lived 1791–1864.

MICHEL-ANGE
Oger, 1863

"Flower large, full; color, bright grenadine." [S] Michelangelo Buonarroti, the great Italian artist; lived 1475–1564.

MICHEL STROGOFF
Barault, 1882

"Vigorous, branches upright, thorns remote, short, brown; leaves composed of 3–5 oval leaflets, deeply toothed, flowers medium, full, well-formed, imbricated; unique color, slatey violet red, shaded crimson." [JR6/165]

MILLER-HAYES
('Millier-Hayes')
E. Verdier, 1873
Seedling of 'Charles Lefebvre' (HP).

"Moderate growth; flower large, full; color, crimson red with brighter center, nuanced poppy." [S]

MISS ANNIE CRAWFORD
Dr. Hall, 1915

"Light pink, very large, full, medium height." [Sn] "Vigorous-growing and an almost continuous bloomer in bright pink with deeper veins; sweetly perfumed. Blooms in clusters, but if dis-budded, the remaining buds will attain very large size. Has long stems, excellent for cutting. Specially adapted to form hedges, or as a mate to 'Gruss an Teplitz'." [C-Ps29]

MISS ETHEL RICHARDSON
A. Dickson, 1897

"Completely new and different from everything else we [Dickson's] have seen. Very vigorous and floriferous, with very large blossoms in a rather cone-like shape with the center extruding. Petals large, slightly folded back on themselves as if hemmed. Color, cream with a flesh center. Exhibition Rose." [JR21/68]

MISS HASSARD
Turner, 1874
Seedling of 'Marguerite de St.-Amand' (HP, De Sansal, 1864, pink; itself a seedling of 'Jules Margottin' [HP]).

"Rosy flesh, round, and full." [R7/534] "Delicate pinkish flesh, large, perhaps rather loose in shape; early to bloom and very sweet scented. Has quantities of strong thorns." [B&V] "Fine form, very sweet, free autumnal bloomer." [JC] "Many imperfect blooms." [EL] "Growth not very vigorous; canes feeble, with strong thorns; flower large, full, very beautiful form, well held; color, delicate flesh; fragrant; one of the hardiest; early bloom. . . . Resembles 'Elisabeth Vigneron' [HP] and 'Duchesse de Vallombrosa' [HP]." [S] "Of strong thorny growth, hardy, free blooming and a pretty pink colour, but weak and loose in shape. A garden Rose, worthy of note as being one of the earliest to bloom." [F-M3]

MISS HOUSE
House, 1838?

"Satiny white." [LS] One would like to know more about this cultivar and its history.

[MISTRESS ELLIOT]
Laffay, 1841

"Variable lilac, full, large, cupped." [LF] "Foliage glaucous." [R-H42] "Flower large, full, flaring; color, bright crimson; growth vigorous." [S] "Purplish rose, very large and very double; form, cupped, fine. Habit, erect; growth, vigorous. A beautiful Rose, with fine large petals, and handsome foliage." [P] "The bush re-blooms pretty freely; blossom medium-sized, cupped, showing the stamens, quite double; petals deeply notched, large, round, well arranged, a pretty purplish pink which is fresh and silky, sometimes having a tint of violet; elegant foliage; canes bearing short, pointed, reddish thorns; very fragrant; blooms in threes and fours; grown from seed by Mons Laffay, and entered into commerce in November, 1841." [An42/333]

MLLE ANNIE WOOD   PLATE 109
('Annie Wood')
C. Verdier and/or E. Verdier, 1866

"Brilliant crimson-scarlet, flowers large and full, imbricated; a first-rate rose; habit free." [JC] "Beautiful clear red, very large, full, and of excellent form; growth vigorous." [P1] "Very vigorous, having reddish canes with strong, upright thorns of the same color as the canes; foliage large and dark green; the blossom is large and sometimes measures four in [ca. 1 dm] across, very full, perfectly imbricated; color, a beautiful light red." [S] "Flower very large, full, poppy-red with velvety reflections" JR1/2/7, as a rose having certain affinities with "Général Jacqueminot' (HP). "Bright crimson with a shade of vermilion; a good autumnal rose." [EL] "Here we have a Rose with manners and customs (fortunately) peculiar to itself. It is a fine strong grower, with fair foliage, liable to mildew and orange fungus, but not much injured by rain. A great quantity of buds form on each stem: the top bud of all, which one would naturally reserve, is nearly always cracked, hollow, and distorted before it is much bigger than a thimble, and sometimes has a great green pip in the centre. You may search for the best-shaped bud, and do away with all others for its sake. Even then, nine out of ten buds will show a great eye before they are more than half expanded, and the tenth will do it soon after being cut. You make up your mind to discard the sort altogether: but, just at the close of the season, a beautiful bloom makes its appearance on a shoot you had not noticed, with brilliant colour, full size, delightful fragrance, and good imbricated shape — a lovely Rose: and the plants are spared to serve you just the same trick another season. . . . It seems impossible to avoid sooner or later bringing in the time-honoured anecdote of the traveller who, describing the 'manners and customs' of some native tribes he had been visiting, was constrained to dismiss one of them with the terse remark, 'manners none — customs disgusting.' If it be possible to say anything so bad of a Rose, I am doubtful whether a better example than 'Annie Wood' can be found." [F-M3]

MLLE BERTHE LÉVÊQUE
Cochet-Aubin/Lévêque, 1866

"Vigorous, even very vigorous, with strong upright canes; leaves very large (I have measured them at up to 6.5 in [ca. 1.65 dm]), rough to the touch, ordinarily having five leaflets, which are oval-elongate, slightly but regularly dentate; leafstalk prickly; stipules foliate and adnate-subulate; flowers about 2.5 in across [ca. 6.5 cm], flesh white changing to pink. Messers Ketten [*the nurserymen*] find that this variety resembles 'Caroline de Sansal' . . . dedicated to the daughter of Mons Lévêque, the well-known rosarian of Ivry-sur-Seine." [JR10/36]

MLLE BONNAIRE
Pernet père, 1859

"White, rosy-centre, large, full, and of exquisite form; one of the best." [FP] "Pure white, centre shaded palest flesh; flowers of medium size, full and well formed; a beautiful free blooming and distinct rose; habit free." [JC] "Closely resembles 'Mme Noman' [HP], it is difficult to see any points of difference by which one may be distinguished from the other." [EL] "Vigorous bush, flowers 10–11 cm across [ca. 4 in]." [I'H59/138] "Moderate growth; flower large, full; color, pure white, sometimes pink at the center. The first white HP." [S]

MLLE ELISABETH DE LA ROCHETERIE
Vigneron, 1881

"Flesh pink." [Ỹ] "Vigorous, canes large and upright, beautiful dark green foliage, thorns chestnut brown, somewhat numerous, flower very large, full, well-formed, beautiful delicate pink, outside of the petals silvery, well held, quite remontant." [JR5/185]

MLLE ELISE CHABRIER
('Mlle Louise Chabrier')
S. Cochet, 1867

"Growth vigorous; flower large, full, well formed; color, delicate pink; petal edged satiny blush white." [S]

MLLE EUGÉNIE VERDIER
Guillot fils, 1859
Seedling of 'Victor Verdier' (HP).
Not to be confused with Schwartz's remontant red Moss of 1872. Sometimes "Marie Finger" is considered synonymous to "Mlle Eugénie Verdier'.

"Very intense flesh." [Ỹ] "Flower medium-sized, full; color, blush-pink." [S] "Large, globular, bright flesh pink, center darker." [JR3/27] "Pearly-white with the palest flesh centre, flowers of moderate size, cupped, and finely formed; distinct and very beautiful." [JC] "Silvery-pink, tinged with fawn; a lovely shade; fine in the bud. One of the best of the type." [EL] "Bright flesh-coloured rose, the reverse of the petals silvery white, very large and full, of fine form and habit; growth robust. . . . One of the best." [P1] "Of 'Victor Verdier' race, with all the manners and customs of the family, and of moderate growth. Of large size, and beautiful and attractive colour, which might be called silvery pink, but not of very good lasting qualities, the centre being rather weak, and the form soon lost. Very free blooming, and an excellent autumnal. A great favorite in America." [F-M2] "Growth vigorous; canes pretty strong, erect; bark smooth, pale green, armed with occasional thorns, which are blackish, hooked, and sharp. Leaves light green, divided into 3 or 5 leaflets, which are oval, pointed, and dentate; petiole slender, furnished with 2 to 3 little prickles. Flowers about four in [ca. 1 dm] across, quite full, widely cupped, usually solitary; color, light pink, brighter at the center, with silvery reflections; outer petals large, inner ones smaller; flower stem short, pretty big, and glabrous. Ovary pear-shaped; sepals leaf-like. Hardy, but nevertheless suffers from frost in the coldest winters." [JF]

MLLE GABRIELLE DE PEYRONNY
Lacharme, 1863

"Vigorous bush; flowers large, full, well formed, fiery red nuanced violet towards the center." [I'H64/63]

MLLE HÉLÈNE CROISSANDEAU
Vigneron, 1882
Seedling of 'Victor Verdier' (HP).
"Velvety pink." [Ŷ] "Vigorous, big-wooded, upright, few thorns, beautiful dark green foliage, very large elongated bud, flower enormous, a beautiful delicate color, center brighter, held perfectly, quite remontant." [JR6/164] "From 'Victor Verdier', but more vigorous." [S]

MLLE HÉLÈNE MICHEL
Vigneron, 1883
"Pink." [Ŷ] "Very vigorous, upright, thorns chestnut brown, fairly numerous, foliage light green, flower large, full, well-formed, beautiful deep red, center brighter, exterior petals velvety, free bloomer." [JR7/170]

MLLE HONORINE DUBOC   PLATE 159
Duboc, 1894
"Winey pink." [Ŷ] "Vigorous, handsome brownish green foliage; the flowers are solitary, very large, full, very well formed, beautiful bright pink, and very fragrant. Reblooms freely . . . dedicated to . . . the daughter of its raiser." [JR18/120]

MLLE JULES GRÉVY
('Mlle Grévy')
Gautreau, 1879
Seedling of 'Duhamel-Dumonceau' (HP).
"Flower large, full, well formed; color, intense dark red, with velvety reflections . . . quite remontant." [S]

MLLE LÉONIE GIESSEN
Lacharme, 1876
"Growth vigorous; canes bushy, with long recurved thorns; flower large, full, Centifolia form; pink washed white." [S]

MLLE LÉONIE PERSIN
Fontaine, 1861
"Flower large; color, a frosty intense silvery pink." [S]

MLLE LOUISE CHABRIER
Listed as 'Mlle Elise Chabrier'.

MLLE MADELEINE NONIN
('Madeleine Nonin')
Ducher, 1866
"Moderate growth; flower medium-sized, full, globular; color, pink with some salmon." [S]

MLLE MARIE ACHARD
Liabaud, 1896
"Very vigorous with upright canes, ample dark green foliage; flower very large, cupped, delicate frosty pink." [JR20/147]

MLLE MARIE CHAUVET
Besson, 1881
Seedling of 'Baronne Adolphe de Rothschild' (HP).
"Deep rose." [EL] "Remontant . . . very well held." [JR5/117] "Very vigorous, canes upright, flowers very large, very full, very well formed, very fresh deep pink fading to pink, center darker." [JR5/172]

MLLE MARIE CLOSON
('Mme Marie Closon')
E. Verdier, 1882
"Vigorous; canes upright, delicate green; thorns very numerous, unequal, upright, brown; leaves composed of five elongated leaflets, with fairly regular dentations, and dark green; flowers medium-sized or large; very full and very well formed; color, very delicate and fresh pink, edged perfectly in white; very fragrant; very floriferous and remontant, nearly as much as a China." [JR6/165]

MLLE MARIE DAUVESSE
Vigneron, 1859
"Bright light pink." [LS] "Medium size, full, medium height." [Sn] "Vigorous bush, flowers large, full, beautiful light intense pink." [l'H59/138]

MLLE MARIE DE LA VILLEBOISNET
Trouillard, 1864
"Delicate pink." [Ŷ] "Growth vigorous; flower large, full, very well formed; color, bright pink." [S]

MLLE MARIE MAGAT
Liabaud, 1889
"Vigorous with upright canes, handsome dark green foliage . . . thorns pretty strong, sparse, reddish. Flower large, full, well-formed, brilliant light red, very elegant." [JR13/163]

MLLE MARIE RADY
('Marie Rady')
Fontaine, 1865
"Rich rose, flowers large and beautifully imbricated . . . vigorous." [JC] "Flower large, full; color, bright red, bordered and touched pink." [S] "Fine brilliant red, very large, full, and of perfect form, blooms freely; growth vigorous." [P1] "Vermilion-red shaded with crimson, large or very large, very full, of splendid globular form, very fragrant; it has more vermilion than 'Alfred Colomb', making it somewhat lighter and more dull; the shoots are armed with numerous red thorns, the foliage shows considerable lustre. There is no finer exhibition sort among the red roses, and were it as constant, it would be quite as valuable as 'Alfred Colomb' and 'Marie Baumann', varieties which bear it some considerable resemblance." [EL]

MLLE RENÉE DENIS
Chédane-Guinoisseau, 1906
From 'Margaret Dickson' (HP) × 'Paul Neyron' (HP).
"Very vigorous, beautiful light green foliage; bud long, nearly always solitary and borne on a long, strong stem; flowers very large, quite full, perfect form, cupped; petals very large, rounded; color, ground of white, edge of petals strongly washed delicate pink, center very salmony . . . very remontant, opens well under all circumstances, very distinct." [JR30/167]

MLLE SUZANNE-MARIE RODOCANACHI
Lévêque, 1883
Seedling of 'Victor Verdier' (HP).
"Growth vigorous; handsome ample dark green foliage; flower very large, full, globular, beautifully colored very delicate pink, clear, shaded, washed and bordered silvery white." [JR7/158] "Of 'Victor Verdier' race, and requiring therefore no description here of manners and customs. A noble Rose, the best of this family, and much esteemed in America. The colour is not only bright,

glowing, and most attractive, but also lasting, a most desirable attribute for a show Rose; it also retains its shape when cut better than any other Rose of the globular form that I know. The growth is good, it does well as a standard, is free-flowering and a good autumnal, and the blooms are very large and well formed, but nearly scentless. A Rose held in high estimation by exhibitors, and worthy of a name more suitable to British tongues and pencils." [F-M2]

MLLE THÉRÈSE LEVET   PLATE 108

('Mme Thérèse Levet')
Levet, 1866
Seedling of 'Jules Margottin' (HP).

"Light carmine-rose, flowers large and full, beautifully imbricated; a superb rose . . . vigorous." [JC] "Salmon-rose, medium size, free blooming." [EL] "Has all the vigor and hardiness of its mother. Quite remontant. The wonderful flower is large, rounded, of perfect form, and very full. Its very fine coloration is a superb and brilliant bright pink, with the reverse of petals being silvery." [S]

MME ALEXANDRE JULLIEN

Vigneron, 1882
Seedling of 'Elisabeth Vigneron' (HP).

"Satiny pink." [Y̆] "Very vigorous, upright, many thorns, beautiful light green foliage, flower large, full, beautiful very fresh light pink, bud elongated, accompanied by leaflets, quite remontant, well held, a superb plant." [JR6/164] "Big-wooded." [S]

MME ALFRED LEVEAU

Listed as 'Monsieur Alfred Leveau'.

MME ALICE DUREAU

Vigneron, 1867

"Lilac pink." [Y̆] "Belongs to 'La Reine' type. Rose color; much like the parent, but more shy in the autumn." [EL] "Flower large, full; beautiful light pink; a variety of the greatest merit. A rose which will always cause a stir at exhibitions." [S]

MME ALPHONSE SEUX

Liabaud, 1887
Seedling of 'Victor Verdier' (HP).

"Very vigorous, branches upright; foliage glaucous green, with two pairs of leaflets; flower very large, full, delicate pink, sometimes bright pink." [JR11/165]

MME AMÉLIE BALTET

E. Verdier, 1878

"Vigorous, with strong and upright delicate green canes; thorns remote, short, slightly recurved, yellowish; leaves composed of 5–7 leaflets, rounded, light green, regularly and finely toothed; flowers large, full, beautifully cupped; color, handsome satiny delicate pink of the greatest freshness, nuanced, silvery, superb." [JR2/187] "Well formed." [EL]

MME ANATOLE LEROY

Leroy, 1892
"Delicate pink." [Y̆]

MME ANDRÉ SAINT

Barbier, 1926
From 'Frau Karl Druschki' (HP) × 'Bénédicte Seguin' (HT, Pernet-Ducher, 1918, orange; parentage unknown).

"Bud large, long-pointed, cream-white; flower large, double, full, cupped, moderately fragrant, milk-white passing to pure white with creamy or clear chamois center, borne on strong stem. Foliage sufficient, beautiful. No thorns. Growth vigorous, stocky. Bushy; profuse bloomer." [ARA28/239]

MME ANTOINE RIVOIRE

Liabaud, 1894

"Very vigorous, canes erect, growth compact, leaves light green, flower extra large, cupped, very delicate frosty pink with carmine reflections." [JR18/146]

MME APOLLINE FOULON

Vigneron, 1882

"Growth very vigorous; wood upright; few thorns; flower large, full, beautifully colored light salmon; petal reflexes lilac-y; good hold; very remontant; superb plant; novel coloration." [JR6/164]

MME AUGUSTE VAN GEERT

P. Robichon, 1861

"Rosy-pink, striped white, very beautiful." [FP] "Flower medium-sized, full; color, bright deep red, striped sometimes." [S]

MME BAULOT

Lévêque, 1885

"Vigorous bush; foliage glaucous green; flower large, full, beautifully imbricated; beautiful coloration: very bright pink nuanced carmine; bloom abundant and continuous." [JR9/148]

MME BELLON

Pernet père, 1871

"Brilliant cerise, flowers very large, and well formed, full[,] high centre; a very fine rose; habit vigorous." [JC] "Moderate growth; flower very large, full, well held; color, delicate pink." [S]

MME BERNUTZ

Jamain, 1873

"Vigorous bush; flower very large, full, cupped; color, satiny pink." [S]

MME BERTHA MACKART

E. Verdier, 1883

"Very vigorous, with very long, reddish-green, upright canes; thorns long, straight, unequal, very sharp, pink; leaves composed of 5–7 leaflets, oblong, dark green, regularly and deeply toothed; flowers extra large, full, impressively formed, cupped, globular; color, the most beautiful bright carmine pink, the freshest imaginable, reverse of petals silvery . . . not perfectly remontant, though it depends; its name is that of the wife of the celebrated Viennese painter." [JR7/171] "One of the best large-flowered kinds." [S]

MME BOUTIN
('Christina Nilson')
Jamain, 1861
Seedling of 'Général Jacqueminot' (HP).
"Cherry-crimson, large and full." [FP] "Well formed, opening easily, beautiful bright cerise red, very fragrant." [l'H61/263] "Cerise, a beautiful clear colour; flowers very large and full, petals broad, even, and well disposed; an excellent rose of robust habit." [JC] "Growth vigorous; flower large, very full, cupped." [S] "A good garden rose." [EL]

MME BRUEL
Listed as 'Mme François Bruel'.

MME CÉCILE MORAND
Corbœuf-Marsault, 1890
"Moderately vigorous, flower large, very full, very well formed; color, deep carmine red, reverse of petals silvery; very floriferous." [JR14/178]

MME CÉLINE TOUVAIS
Touvais, 1859
"Flower large, full, peony-shape; color, bright pink." [S] "Very vigorous bush, flowers 12 cm across [ca. 4.25 in], full, sparkling intense pink." [l'H59/138]

MME CÉSAR BRUNIER
Bernaix, 1887
"Bush with strong, upright growth bristling with numerous unequal thorns, all mixed together; leaves, 5 relatively short leaflets which are obtuse-acuminate and keel-shaped; blossom well-formed, very double, with an elegant, strong scent; not hollowed at the center; opening well, upright, borne on a strong stem; 1, 2, or 3 at the tip of the cane; outer petals reflexed, curled at the edge; center petals more muddled, unequal, all coloured China pink, satiny and bright; bud oval, long at the moment of expansion. Very profuse, amply double, uncommon coloration, elegant Centifolia perfume." [JR11/152]

MME CHARLES CRAPELET
('Mme Hérivaux', 'Mme Charles Chapelet')
Fontaine, 1859
"Bright cerise frosted lilac and currant red." [JR3/27] "Flower large, full, very well formed; color, cerise shaded satiny pink." [S] "Rosy scarlet, often veined with lilac, large and full; form cupped; growth vigorous." [P1] "Rosy-carmine, large smooth petals, exquisitely formed and beautifully disposed . . . habit free." [JC] "Very vigorous, branches upright, flower four or so in across [ca. 1 dm], cherry red nuanced lilac." [JDR59/43] "Fragrant and good; wood armed with numerous thorns." [EL] "Canes with green bark; thorns numerous, small, unequal; leaves of three and five leaflets, large and rugose; petiole prickly; flower to three in across [ca. 7.5 cm], solitary, well formed, often cupped and showing the stamens; color, cerise red. This variety is certainly not perfect, but is nevertheless much appreciated in the garden due to its vigor and hardiness; what is more, it is very fragrant and well held, things which hardly detract from a rose! Prune to 4 to 6 buds." [JR10/139] "Very good at its best, as a smooth refined show Rose of the popular imbricated shape. Best as a maiden, being rather a weak grower, and liable to mildew, but not soon spoiled by rain, and a sort which well repays high cultivation . . . probably best in a cool season. Of capital form, very smooth, regular, and full, of good lasting quality and fair size. Not a free bloomer or a good autumnal, but though never of strong or hardy constitution . . . it cannot . . . be suspected of having deteriorated." [F-M2]

MME CHARLES MEURICE
Meurice de St.-Quentin/Lévêque, 1878
"Maroon, nuanced." [Ÿ] "Growth very vigorous; foliage glossy light green; flower large, full, well formed; color, purple red, very dark, velvety, blackish; very beautiful. This is one of the darkest roses we have seen to date." [JR2/166]

MME CHARLES TRUFFAUT
E. Verdier, 1878
"Vigorous, with short, upright canes of a delicate green; thorns straight, pointed, pink; leaves composed of five oblong, light green leaflets, regularly dentate; flowers large, full, very well formed, imbricated; color, very delicate pale satiny pink, distinctly bordered silvery, superb; a charming variety." [JR2/187]

MME CHARLES VERDIER
Lacharme, 1863
"Belongs to the 'Baronne Prévost' type. Rosy vermilion, very large, a free bloomer." [EL] "Very well proportioned in form and color." [l'H67/54] "Vigorous, with a flower which is full, large, well formed, globular, fragrant, and rosy pink. . . . It is dedicated to the wife of Mons Charles Verdier, horticulturalist of Ivry-sur-Seine." [JR10/140] "Charles-Félix Verdier, who died, at his home at Ivry-sur-Seine, August 18 [1893], at the age of 64." [JR17/129]

MME CHIRARD
Pernet père, 1867
"Velvety pink." [Ÿ] "Rose, tinged with vermilion, full, peculiar rich scent; bushy habit, shy in autumn, many malformed flowers." [EL] "Growth very vigorous; flower large, full, globular; very well formed; color, bright pink." [S]

MME CLÉMENCE JOIGNEAUX
Liabaud, 1861
"Lilac-rose. Bold and distinct in growth and foliage." [H] "Very vigorous; canes upright, heavily thorned; leaves large, beautiful dark green, regularly serrated; color, bright pink, shaded light violet. This rose should only be grown in the warmer areas; in Germany and the north of France, the blossom opens only occasionally. Much to be recommended for forcing." [S]

MME CLERT
Gonod, 1868
"Salmon rose." [EL] "Growth vigorous; flower large, full; color, salmon pink." [S]

MME CONSTANT DAVID
Boutigny, 1909
"Grenadine red illuminated with velvety vermilion, very large, about five in across [ca. 1.25 dm], full, very well held, long bud, growth very vigorous with long canes of the 'Ulrich Brunner' sort; thorns long; very handsome ample foliage, dark green, very remontant." [JR33/169]

MME CORDIER
Leroy, 1903
"Violet- and lilac-pink." [Ÿ]

MME CRESPIN
Damaizin, 1862

"Rose, shaded with dark violet, medium size, full, form good." [FP]

MME CROZY
('Mme Crosy')
Levet, 1881
Seedling of 'Souvenir de la Reine d'Angleterre' (HP).

"Rose color, very large." [EL] "Growth with very strong wood; foliage dark green; thorns very pointed; color, China pink; flower large, plump, with large petals; well formed." [S]

MME DE RIDDER
Margottin, 1871

"Beautiful bright amaranth red." [S] "Rich dark shaded crimson, large, handsome, well formed flowers; habit vigorous; a most excellent rose." [JC] "Free or vigorous. . . . Red, shaded with violet-crimson, large, full, fine globular form; green wood and thorns. A distinct sort, fragrant and beautiful, but fades easily." [EL]

MME DE SELVE
('Mme de Selves')
Bernède, 1886
Seedling of 'Monsieur Fillion' (HP).

"Very vigorous; flowers very large, well formed, beautiful bright red with lilac reflections." [JR10/171]

MME DE TROTTER
('Mme Trotter')
Granger, 1854

"Vigorous plant, flower medium-sized, bright red, reblooms with difficulty." [JDR55/9] "A free bloomer in the spring." [EL] "Very vigorous bush with canes armed with very unequal thorns; the large ones are laterally flattened, upright, or slightly back-hooked; the small ones grade down to glandular bristles. The stipules are fairly wide in the adherent part, being on the contrary long and lacy in the free part. The flowers are full, carmine pink, 'Duchesse de Sutherland' form, 7–8 cm [ca. 3.5 in] in size, clustered in 2–4's at the tip of the cane; occasionally solitary. This variety is pretty and very interesting in its origin. Born of a non-remontant variety, it is very floriferous in spring, and grows, after first bloom, vigorous canes which, for the most part, give flowers which are as pretty as the early ones. It is not freely remontant, but with age seems to become so." [l'H55/29]

MME DESIRÉE GIRAUD
Giraud-d'Haussy/Van Houtte, 1854 (but see below)

"Flower very large, full, ground white and pink, consistently plumed crimson, slate, amaranth, etc." [l'H54/15] "An HP with consistently variegated blossoms is something breeders of roses have sought for a long time. . . . This Rose was not raised from seed, but is rather a sport from the HP 'Baronne Prévost'. . . . Mons. Van Houtte bought out the entire stock of this variety from Mme L. Giraud d'Haussy of Marly, at whose establishment this sport occurred . . . a white and pink ground, plumed with crimson, violet, and amaranth." [R-H53] "Vigorous. . . . Blush-white, striped with deep rose." [EL] "Moderate growth . . . flower large, full; color, white striped pink and crimson." [S] "Branches so meager that we are unable to appreciate it; and whenever the branches are frail, they don't always give striped flowers." [JDR57/28] "Its blossoms are often deformed and small. This variety is much

inferior to 'Panachée d'Orléans'." [JR12/172] "It will be released to commerce on April 1, 1854, as winter grafts, at the price of five francs." [VH52/281] "We do not count 'Mme Desirée Giraud', [*the picture of which*] appears to such good effect in *Flore des Serres* [by Van Houtte], as Mons Van Houtte has not yet released it to commerce — because the picture is too good and the rose too bad." [l'H55/54]

MME EDMOND FABRE
E. Verdier, 1884(?)

"Pink, large, full, medium scent, medium height." [Sn]

MME EDOUARD MICHEL
E. Verdier, 1886

"A clear deep pink, flowers of beautiful shape when perfect, but in the early part of the season they are not unfrequently divided. Very smooth, good petals and a capital pointed centre, attractive colour, one of the best shades of pink among the Hybrid Perpetuals, and sweet scented. Hardy and good constitution." [B&V] "Vigorous, canes light green, upright, strong; thorns unequal, straight, pink; leaves delicate green, 3–5 leaflets, fairly deeply but irregularly toothed; flowers extra large, full, with large petals, beautiful form, very well held; color, very beautiful and fresh bright pink; Tea-scent." [JR10/170]

MME ELISA TASSON
Lévêque, 1879

"Scarlet cerise." [Ÿ] "Very vigorous, handsome ample foliage of a glossy green, flowers very large, full, beautiful globular form; petals well imbricated, handsome light cerise, intense . . . gives quantities of very large blossoms." [JR3/166]

MME ERNEST LEVAVASSEUR
Vigneron, 1900
From 'Mme Isaac Pereire' (B) × 'Ulrich Brunner' (HP).

"Soft carmine-red, in the way of 'Ulrich Brunner', but brighter in colour; very large and full, growth vigorous." [P1] "Very vigorous, beautiful very dark green foliage, flower very large, to four in in diameter [ca. 1 dm], globular, very full, opens admirably well, borne on a very rigid stem; color, bright vermilion red shaded fiery carmine; extremely floriferous, fragrant. Enormous very long bud, well formed . . . Surpasses 'Ulrich Brunner' in form and beauty." [JR24/146]

MME EUGÈNE VERDIER
E. Verdier, 1878
Not to be confused with 'Mme Eugène Verdier fils aîne', Guillot fils' bright pink HP of 1869, nor with Levet's 1882 Noisette.

"Delicate pink." [Ÿ] "Belongs to 'La Reine' type. Mottled rose, very large, full, globular; a promising kind." [EL] "Silvery rose, large and full; form, globular; growth vigorous. One of the best." [P1] "A fine large-petaled Rose." [H] "Vigorous with strong, upright, and short light green canes; thorns numerous, unequal, slightly recurved, pink; leaves composed of 2–5 oval-elongate leaflets, deeply toothed with large teeth; flowers extra large, full, satiny pink, strongly nuanced and shaded silver; a splendid vigorous variety, quite remontant." [JR2/187] "Grows well as a maiden, but the first growths of cutbacks are sometimes very short: still the blooms come just as well, and the foliage is fine. The constitution is delicate in some localities and the plants often gradually die. . . . It is not very liable to mildew, but a slight shower will stain the colour, and much rain will cause the petals to . . . stick together, and rot. The blooms are likely to be coarse and are not often of refined shape or appearance; but they are very large with wonderfully fine petals and well-filled centres. Fairly free in bloom and a pretty good autumnal; the shape is globular, but delicacy and regularity of outline are often wanting, and really it is sometimes almost like a prize cabbage, for it is quite one of the largest Roses." [F-M2] "One of the most able breeders of roses has left us — Mons Louis-Eugène-Jules Verdier, who died March 11, 1902, at his home, 37 Rue Clisson, Paris, at the age of 75. He was the last survivor of the Verdier family which played a very great role in French rosiculture in the last century. . . . For many years, Mons Verdier hadn't left his home; having been struck down by blindness, and it being a struggle to go out, he was reduced to complete inaction." [JR26/82–83] "Madame Eugène Verdier . . . has died at the age of 64 after a long illness. The obsequies will take place the 17th of October [1893]." [JR17/163]

MME EUGÉNIE FRÉMY   PLATE 142

E. Verdier, 1884

"Very vigorous bush; canes strong and upright, delicate green; thorns unequal, straight, brown; leaves composed of 5 rounded leaflets, thick and glossy, dark green, with fine and irregular serration; flower very large, very full, uniquely convex form; color, very bright fresh pink with silvery reverse." [JR8/166]

MME FILLION

Gonod, 1865

Seedling of 'Mme Domage' (HP, Margottin, 1853, crimson; parentage unknown).

"Fresh rosy pink, flowers large, full, and of good form, a very distinct and beautiful rose, very fragrant; habit moderate." [JC] "Growth vigorous; canes strong, covered with thick blackish green foliage; flower large, full; color, bright salmon pink, center deep salmon; magnificent exhibition rose." [S]

MME FORTUNÉ BESSON

Besson/Liabaud, 1881

Seedling of 'Jules Margottin' (HP).

"Very vigorous, abundantly floriferous up to frost; flowers very fragrant, very large, very full, very delicate flesh." [JR5/117] "Branches upright, perfect deportment, flowers fragrant, very large, very full, very delicate flesh, blooming abundantly until frost . . . should be considered as being in the first rank." [JR5/172]

MME FRANCIS BUCHNER

Lévêque, 1884

"Very vigorous, foliage shiny green, flowers large, full, beautiful very light pink nuanced darker pink towards the center, beautiful shading, a plant of the first order, quite remontant." [JR8/150]

MME FRANÇOIS BRUEL

('Mme Bruel')

Levet, 1882

From 'Victor Verdier' (HP) × ? 'Comtesse d'Oxford' (HP).

"Carmine-rose." [EL] "Vigorous, foliage light green; flower large, carmine pink, few thorns, very remontant; a quite beautiful variety." [S]

MME FRANÇOIS PITTET

Listed as a Bourbon.

MME GEORGES SCHWARTZ

Schwartz, 1871

"Glossy rose with soft lavender shade, flowers large, full, and cupped, a very deep well formed flower, and a fine rose; habit vigorous." [JC] "Very large, very well-formed, full, beautiful Hydrangea pink fading to frosty pink." [JR3/27] "Belongs to the 'Victor Verdier' type. Silvery-rose, fades badly and is coarse." [EL] "Growth very vigorous; magnificent first-rate flower." [S]

MME GEORGES VIBERT

Moreau-Robert, 1879

"Veined bright pink, attractive on its ground color of fresh pink." [JR12/172] "Very vigorous, flower very large, full, opens well, very delicate pink, center carmine, blooms a great deal, and in clusters, handsome dark green foliage." [JR3/167]

MME GRANDIN-MONVILLE

('—Montville')

E. Verdier, 1875

"Flower large, full, well formed, growing in a cluster; color, bright sparkling crimson, edged bright pink; vigorous." [S]

MME HENRI PEREIRE

Vilin, 1886

"Bright red with flame reflections." [Y̌] "A crimson rose of pretty good growth that is generally well spoken of, but it is very liable to mildew and proves of little value with me." [F-M3]

MME HENRI PERRIN

Widow Schwartz, 1892

"Lilac carmine." [Y̌] "Vigorous, foliage abundant, bullate. Flower large, perfect form, bright carmine lilac pink, exterior petals large and concave, inner petals ragged, sometimes striped pure white; always bordered and brightened with delicate pink, with silvery reflections; nubs yellowish." [JR16/154]

MME HERSILIE ORTGIES

Soupert & Notting, 1868

Not to be confused with Moreau-Robert's salmon-white Bourbon of 1868.

"Growth vigorous; flower medium-sized, full, very well formed; color, delicate pink and pinkish lilac." [S]

MME HIPPOLYTE JAMAIN

Garçon/Jamain, 1871

"Blush, flowers globular, large, and full; habit moderate." [JC] "White, tinged with rose, very large, full." [EL] "Of good growth and foliage, not very liable to mildew, but rain will injure the blooms. A coarse Rose, generally rough and irregular if grown strong, but occasionally of even globular shape in hot dry weather and then valuable for exhibition as it is very large, full, and lasting. A free bloomer in the season, but not much of an autumnal." [F-M3] "Growth vigorous; canes of medium size, branching; bark a glaucescent green with numerous slender reddish thorns. Leaves light green, slightly glaucous, 5–9 oval-acuminate, finely dentate leaflets; leafstalk slim, light green. Flowers about 4.5 in across [ca. 1.25 dm], very full, cupped, often solitary, sometimes in clusters of three or four on the strongest branches; color, lightly blushing white; outer petals large and thick, central petals smaller, numerous, muddled; very pretty bud, shaded carmine; flower stalk pretty long, and has glandular bristles. Calyx tubular; sepals leaf-like. A plant of the first order; hardy." [JF]

MME JEAN EVERAERTS
('Improved Princesse de Béarn')
Geduldig, 1907
From 'Eugene Fürst' (HP) × a seedling which was the result of 'Mme Eugène Verdier' (HP) × 'Johannes Wesselhöft' (HT, Welter & Hinner, 1899, yellow; from 'Kaiserin Auguste Viktoria' [HT] × an unnamed seedling which was the result of 'William Francis Bennett' [HT] × 'Comtesse de Frigneuse' [T]).

"Dark flame red." [Y̆] "Deep red, large, full, medium scent, tall." [Sn]

MME JOSEPH BONNAIRE
Listed as an HT.

MME JULES GRÉVY
Listed as an HT.

[MME JULIA DARAN]
Touvais, 1861
"Purplish-vermilion, glossy, very large and full; one of the best." [FP] "Flower large, full, globular, very fragrant; color, bright scarlet." [S] "Violet-crimson, flowers cupped and beautifully formed, having large smooth petals of good quality; a rose of vigorous habit." [JC] Ancestor of 'Balduin' (HT).

MME LA GÉNÉRALE DECAEN
Gautreau, 1869
"Flower large, full, very well formed; color, bright pink with a flesh pink center." [S]

MME LACHARME
Listed as an HT.

[MME LAFFAY]
Laffay, 1839
Seedling of 'Général Allard' (HCh).
"Carmine pink, full, large, cupped, superb." [LF] "Rich purplish rose, large and very double; form, cupped. Habit, erect, fine; growth, vigorous. Too well known to need recommending. An excellent seed-bearer, and very sweet." [P] "Light red." [R-H56] "Rosy-crimson." [FP] "Rose color, large, double, cupped form, red spines; surpassed by many others of the same shade." [EL] "Growth very vigorous; flower medium-sized, full, widely cupped; very fragrant; good seed-bearer; bright crimson." [S]

MME LEFEBVRE
('Mme Lefèvre')
Moreau-Robert, 1885
"Vigorous; handsome glossy green foliage; flower large, full, cupped, very delicate satiny pink, center brighter; blooms in clusters; very floriferous; very beautiful." [JR8/149]

MME LEMESLE
('Mme Lemelles', 'Mme Lemerle')
Moreau-Robert, 1890
"Very vigorous, big-wooded and robust, with recurved thorns, beautiful dark green foliage, large flowers, full, globular, velvety purplish red nuanced violet." [JR14/148]

MME LÉON HALKIN
Lévêque, 1886
"Vigorous, flowers large, full, perfect form, globular, beautiful bright crimson red nuanced sparkling purple." [JR10/149–150]

MME LIERVAL
Fontaine, 1868
"Flower large, full; very well formed, and distinctive in form; color, delicate pink mixed with bright crimson." [S]

[MME LOEBEN DE SELS]
Soupert & Notting, 1878
Not to be confused with Soupert & Notting's HT of 1879, 'Mme de Loeben-Sels', which was silvery white.
"Vigorous, flowers medium sized, full, flat, beautifully rosette-formed; color, deep red nuanced velvety crimson passing to bishop's violet." [JR3/12]

MME LOUIS LÉVÊQUE
Lévêque, 1873
Seedling of 'Jules Margottin' (HP).
"Cerise, colour brilliant and distinct, flowers very large, full, and expanded; a good rose." [JC] "Moderate growth; flower very large, full, globular; color, flesh pink, brighter center." [S] "Belongs to the 'Jules Margottin' type, large, very full, somewhat flat form, slightly fragrant; blooms late in the season, but is shy in the autumn." [EL]

MME LOUIS RICART   PLATE 160
('Mme Louis Ricard')
Duboc, 1892
Possibly a seedling of 'Baron G.-B. Gonella' (B).
"Dedicated to the wife of our sympatico deputé . . . freely remontant . . . vigorous, with somewhat lengthy canes, few thorns, which are nearly straight, and pink; leaves of 5 oval leaflets, somewhat contracted at the tip, pale green, no stipule; large bud, solitary; stem strong and short; ovary medium-sized. Flower large and quite full; petals large, thick and reflexed, pale pink, brighter around the center; adequately fragrant . . . easy to propagate." [JR16/34]

MME LOUISE PIRON
Piron-Medard, 1903
From 'La Reine' (HP) × 'Ulrich Brunner fils' (HP).
"This plant bears strong blossoms of beautiful light pink." [JR27/100] "Light pink, large, full, medium height." [Sn]

MME LOUISE VIGNERON
Vigneron, 1882
Seedling of 'Elisabeth Vigneron' (HP).
"Very vigorous, upright, thorns fairly numerous, brown, foliage light green, flower large, full, well-formed, beautiful light pink, center darker, beautiful elongated bud, well held, quite remontant, a magnificent plant." [JR6/164]

MME LUCIEN CHAURÉ
Vigneron, 1884
Seedling of 'Souvenir de la Reine d'Angleterre' (HP).
"Very vigorous, upright, thorns chestnut, slightly numerous, foliage dark green, beautiful very large bud which always opens well, flower very large, about five in across [ca. 1.25 dm], very full, globular, well formed, handsome bright cerise red, flower generally solitary; quite remontant." [JR8/134]

MME LUREAU-ESCALAÏS
Maindion/E. Verdier, 1886
Seedling of 'Victor Verdier' (HP).

"Vigorous . . . flowers large, full, well formed, very beautifully held; color, beautiful smooth delicate pink." [JR10/183]

MME MARCEL FAUNEAU
Vigneron, 1886
Seedling of 'Alexis Lepère' (HP).

"Vigorous bush, heavy wood, upright, few thorns, foliage light green; bud very large, conical; flower very large, full, globular form, beautifully colored lilac pink, darker within, perfect hold, very floriferous." [JR10/147]

MME MARGUERITE MARSAULT
Corbœuf-Marsault, 1894

"Bush of moderate vigor, well-branched; flowers large, full, well formed, plump; color, bright red with violet reflections, petal exteriors bluish at full expansion. Extremely floriferous." [JR18/162]

MME MARIE LEGRANGE
Liabaud, 1882
Seedling of 'Sénateur Vaïsse' (HP).

"Very vigorous, flower large or very large, nearly full, well-formed, handsome brilliant carmine lake, stalk firm, hold perfect. Blooms freely. Very beautiful." [JR6/150]

MME MARIE VAN HOUTTE
Margottin, 1857
Not to be confused with the yellow/pink Tea 'Marie Van Houtte'.

"Delicate pink." [JDR57/37] "Flower large, full; satiny pink." [S]

MME MARTHE D'HALLOY
Lévêque, 1881
Seedling of 'Mme Boutin' (HP).

"Cherry-red." [EL] "Vigorous, foliage glaucous green, flower large, full, very well formed, beautiful carmine cerise pink, very remontant, constantly in bloom, very beautiful." [JR5/150]

[MME MASSON]
('Gloire de Châtillon')
Masson/Marest, 1854

"Fine dark crimson, large well filled flowers; a most constant and profuse bloomer, highly prized for bedding." [C&Js98] "Very vigorous variety, giving blossoms of an immense size — 12–15 cm [ca. 5–6 in] — color, purple crimson brightened with intense red, passing to violet." [I'H55/30] "Foliage ample and a beautiful green, the perfect accompaniment to the very large and quite full magnificent blossoms." [S] "For some reason we cannot explain, this splendid constant blooming hybrid perpetual rose has never had the attention it deserves; it blooms the first season and all the time, the flowers are large, full and delightfully perfumed, the color is bright rich crimson, it is a robust sturdy grower, continues loaded with flowers almost the whole season. Entirely different from the ever-blooming roses, and a real floral treasure." [C&Js00]

MME MAURICE RIVOIRE
Gonod, 1876

"Fine deep flesh colour, moderate size, compact and full." [JC] "Vigorous, flower large, full, well-formed . . . exterior petals white." [JR1/6/10] "Branches strong, dark green, sometimes touched violet on the sunny side." [S]

MME MONTEL
('Mme Montet', 'Mme Mantel')
Liabaud, 1880
Seedling of 'La Reine' (HP).

"Light pink, large petals." [EL] "Delicate rose colour, large petals, almost full." [P1] "Very vigorous, branches strong, erect, ample foliage of a cheerful green; flower very large, nearly full, beautiful delicate pink, with large petals, beautiful form, well held, a superb variety." [JR4/167] "Disappoints us; the flowers are a pretty pink, with a beautiful petal, but they are thin and lack refinement." [JR7/157]

MME NOMAN
('Mme Norman', 'Mme Nomann')
Guillot père, 1867
Seedling of 'Mlle Bonnaire' (HP).

"Moderate growth; floriferous; flower medium-sized, full; color, pure white." [S] "Another pure white H.P., but a weak bad grower with small foliage. The blooms also are quite small but of exquisite form and the purest colour. This Rose and 'Boule de Neige' are much better shaped than 'Mme Lacharme' or 'Merveille de Lyon', but are so very small in comparison as to be completely out of it." [F-M3] "White, sometimes with shaded centre, medium size, full, globular; foliage somewhat crimped, wood armed with quite numerous, small spines. A rose of exquisite beauty." [EL]

MME PETIT
Corbœuf, 1900
From 'Charles Lefebvre' (HP) × 'Pride of Reigate' (HP).

"Vigorous, big-wooded, well branched, very floriferous, cluster-flowered; color, velvety carmine shaded purple; petals striped with one pure white line . . . very fragrant." [JR24/164]

MME PIERRE MARGERY
Liabaud, 1881
Seedling of 'Jules Margottin' (HP).

"Vigorous, freely remontant, flower large, full, very fresh pink with a luminous center; very beautiful." [JR5/171] "Very beautiful rose of a charming cerise color." [JR7/157]

MME PROSPER LAUGIER
E. Verdier, 1875
Seedling of 'John Hopper' (HP).

"Velvety pink." [Ÿ] "Rich clear rose, flowers extra large size, flowers somewhat expanded, petals even and well formed." [JC] "Red, quartered shape, not fragrant, numerous red thorns; of second quality." [EL] "Of good strong stiff growth with characteristic appearance and habit. Distinct also in colour, but unreliable and not to be recommended, of irreproachable form, very full, distinctly fringed; color, bright clear pink; growth very vigorous; canes strong and upright, handsome reddish green; thorns numerous, compressed, brown; leaves of 3–5 leaflets which are somber green and oblong with unequal, deep dentations; bud very well formed and very beautiful." [S]

MME RAMBAUX
('Mme Rambaud')
Widow Rambaux, 1881

"Very vigorous, with leaves which are dark green above and glaucescent beneath. Flowers very large, very full, the same in the Fall, petals concave and imbricated in the outer rows, beautiful nuanced carmine pink, paler amaranth on the reverse. Perfectly shaped conical buds." [JR5/186] "Very good rose to force." [S]

[MME RÉCAMIER]
Lacharme, 1853

"Plant forming a cute small bush of the 'Aimée Vibert' sort; flower medium-sized, well-formed, a pretty flesh white while opening, passing to pure white." [l'H53/244–245] "Bush pretty vigorous; flowers medium-sized, full or nearly full, in clusters, light flesh white fading to pure white. Rather pretty Noisette cross; very floriferous." [l'H56/250] Jane Frances Julia Adélaïde Récamier, French beauty; 1777–1849; see her portrait by David.

MME RENAHY
Guillot & fils/E. Verdier, 1889

"Vigorous, flowers large, full, well formed, globular; color, carmine pink with a brighter center, reverse of petals delicate pink." [JR13/181]

MME RENARD
Moreau-Robert, 1871
Seedling of 'Jules Margottin' (HP).

"Moderate growth; blooms in clusters; flower large, full, globular; color, icy salmon pink." [S]

MME ROGER
Moreau-Robert, 1877

"Bluish purple pink." [Ў] "Vigorous, flower large, full, very delicate pink, nearly white." [JR1/12/12]

MME ROSE CARON
Lévêque, 1898

"Vigorous, foliage light green, flower large, well imbricated, monotone pink, nuanced carmine pink at the center, very beautiful." [JR22/147]

MME ROUDILLON
Vigneron, 1903
From 'Mme Isaac Pereire' (B) × 'Mme Ernest Levavasseur' (HP).

"Very vigorous bush, very beautiful dark green foliage; enormous flower, very full, beautiful form, beautiful slightly carmine bright red; very fragrant, extremely floriferous. The blossom is borne on a very stiff stem. A magnificent plant." [JR27/131]

MME SCHMITT
('Mme Schmidt')
Schmitt, 1854

"Shaded rosy-pink, large and beautiful." [FP] "Flowers full, 12–15 cm in size [ca. 4–4.5 in], in a cluster, beautiful pink, shaded carmine, reverse silvery white." [l'H55/34] "Of Bourbon ancestry, with upright branches, vigorous, occasional thorns; leaves somber; blossoms big and globular or large and with petals slightly ruffled at the center." [JDR56/32]

MME SOPHIE STERN
Lévêque, 1887

"Very vigorous bush; very ample blackish green foliage; flowers very large, very well formed, globular, with large petals, magnificently colored very brilliant light bright rose, lit by metallic reflections, whitish at the center. A plant which is very effective. Superb." [JR11/162]

MME SOPHIE TROPOT
('—Fropot', '—Froppot')
Levet, 1876
Seedling of 'Victor Verdier' (HP).

"Pale satin rose, broad, smooth, even petals, flowers cupped; a beautiful rose." [JC] "Bright rose, nearly smooth wood; a shy autumnal and not of first quality." [EL] "Very vigorous, nearly thornless, flower large, full, well-formed, centifolia-form; color, handsome bright pink to good effect." [JR1/1/7–8]

MME SOUBEYRAN
Gonod, 1872

"Growth vigorous; flower small, full, very well formed, very fragrant; bright pink." [S]

MME THÉOBALD SERNIN
Brassac, 1877

"Vigorous, having a flower which is large, full, and well-formed, with a currant-red color nuanced carmine." [JR1/2/14]

MME THÉODORE VERNES
Lévêque, 1891

"Vigorous, foliage ample, dark green; flower large, full, very well formed, bright pink with lighter edges, very beautiful." [JR15/167]

MME THÉVENOT
Jamain, 1877

"Moderate growth; very floriferous; flower large, very full; color, bright red, nuanced." [S]

MME THIBAUT
Lévêque, 1889

"Vigorous bush, foliage bright green, flower large, full, imbricated in the camellia way; beautiful delicate satiny pink nuanced carmine pink; very pretty variety dedicated to the wife of our simpatico colleague Mons Thibaut of Thibaut & Ketleer." [JR13/164]

MME VERLOT
E. Verdier, 1876

"Bright velvety pink." [Ў] "Flower extra large, slightly cupped, very full, very fragrant." [S] "Vigorous; flower very large, sufficiently full, cupped, well-formed, beautiful very fresh bright pink." [JR1/6/10]

MME VERRIER CACHET   PLATE 162
(*not* '—Cochet')
Chédane-Guinoisseau, 1895

"Very vigorous, canes green, very large light green foliage of five leaflets, thorns red, flower very large, very full, globular; color very fresh, pink nuanced vermilion with slatey reflections, very fragrant." [JR19/131] "Very pronounced and pleasing fragrance." [JR25/104]

MME VEUVE ALEXANDRE POMMERY
Lévêque, 1882

"Very vigorous; leaves large, dark green; flower very large, well formed, delicate pink nuanced bright pink within; petal edges very light pink." [JR6/148]

MME VIDOT
PLATE 93

Couturier fils/E. Verdier, 1854

"A model in form; its blossom is large and full . . . clear flesh shaded pink." [R-H63] "This rose . . . is very vigorous and produces charming flowers of a delicate satiny pink, most perfectly formed." [I'H55/30] "Much to be recommended; hardy." [S] "Canes stocky, light green, covered with a fine layer of 'bloom'; armed with very unequal thorns, not laterally flattened, nearly straight or slightly back-hooked; the larger ones no longer than 5 mm in length and 2 mm in diameter [ca. .25 × .125 inch] at their thickened base, very sharp at the tip; the smaller ones grade down into glandular-stipitation, and are more numerous than the [large] thorns in the upper reaches of the canes. Leaves ordinarily composed of 5 slightly stiff leaflets, which are pretty smooth, beautiful light green above, paler beneath, oval-elliptical, pointed, and cordate at the base; the lateral leaflets are nearly sessile and gradually smaller; the mid-vein bristles with rudimentary prickles; the rachis is completely glandulose and is furrowed into a groove above, armed with several small hooked prickles beneath; the stipules are very lacy and short, divergent, ciliate along the edges, adherent for a third of their length to the petiole, at the base of which they form two very lacy flanges hardly larger than a millimeter. The flowers are above the median in size, perfect in form, and admirable in color, which is delicate clear flesh-pink-white, nuanced brighter pink. The peduncle is large, short, very glandular, widening gradually into the funnel-shaped calyx-tube, which is not contracted at the mouth; the sepals are five in number, long, acuminate for the most part, glandulose on the back, downy within and at the edges; in three of the segments, the tip is more or less enlarged and foliaceous, and the edges have one or two small linear ciliate processes. The petals are very numerous, obovate straightened out, a little spoon-shaped, admirably and very regularly imbricated in the outer rows, the central petals being more or less folded and a little muddled, making a veritable Legion of Honor's officer's medal. No stamens. Styles salient, free, numerous, topping off the ovaries enclosed in the calyx." [I'H55/101–102]

MME YORKE
('Mme York')

Moreau-Robert, 1881

"Vigorous bush; beautiful dark green foliage; flower large, full; color, vermilion red shaded carmine and nuanced blackish purple; extraordinary coloration." [JR5/172]

MONSEIGNEUR FOURNIER
Lalande/Lévêque, 1876

"Flower very large, full, very well formed; color, beautiful very brilliant light red." [S]

MONSIEUR ALFRED LEVEAU
('Alfred Leveau', 'Mme Alfred Leveau')

Vigneron, 1880

"Carmine-rose." [EL] "Flower large, bright carmine pink." [JR5/42] "Growth vigorous, canes upright, stocky; flower large, full, well formed, solitary; bright carmine pink; later, delicate pink; handsome dark green foliage; thorns chestnut brown, not very numerous." [S]

MONSIEUR CORDIER
Gonod, 1871

Seedling of 'Géant des Batailles' (HP).

"Flower very large, full, flat, camellia-form; scarlet." [S]

MONSIEUR DE MONTIGNY
Paillet, 1855

"Lilac pink." [Ў] "Rosy-carmine, large and full." [FP] "Brilliant rose colour, fresh and beautiful, flowers very large and well formed; a handsome robust growing rose." [JC] "Growth vigorous; flower large; color, intense pink." [S] "Strong canes armed with large dark slightly hooked purple-red thorns; leaves lush, light green above, whitish beneath; leaflets deeply toothed; flowers fairly large, to 8–10 cm [ca. 4 in], purplish pink passing to slatey violet, solitary or in twos at the tip of the cane." [I'H56/49]

MONSIEUR DE MORAND
Widow Schwartz, 1891

Seedling of 'Général Jacqueminot' (HP).

"Vigorous bush; graceful foliage, quite denticulate; flower large, of good hold, full, opening easily; color, bright crimson cerise nuanced bluish lilac purple; center petals imbricated in such a way as to give the blossom the form of a camellia; margined pinkish white." [JR15/149]

MONSIEUR EDOUARD DETAILLE
Gouchault, 1893

"Flower very full, opens well, deep purple red shaded black, center vermilion red, very fragrant and very floriferous. The habit of this plant makes it good for pot culture." [JR17/165–166]

MONSIEUR ERNEST DUPRÉ
Boutigny, 1904

"Flower large, full, very bright carmine red nuanced deep carmine, velvety; beautiful camellia form; well held, long bud, very vigorous. Dedicated to the former vice-president of the Horticultural Society of Seine-Inférieure." [JR28/89]

MONSIEUR ÉTIENNE DUPUY
('—Dupuis')

Levet, 1873

From 'Victor Verdier' (HP) × 'Anna de Diesbach' (HP).

"Pale satin and rosy pink, colour beautifully clear and fresh, cupped, large, and full; a distinct and very fine rose; habit vigorous." [JC] "Flower large, full; color, delicate pink; reverse of petals silvery pink." [S]

MONSIEUR EUGÈNE DELAIRE
Vigneron, 1879

"Very vigorous bush, with upright canes; beautiful green foliage, thorns chestnut brown; flower large, full, in a cluster or solitary; color, velvety red illuminated with bright flame-color; freely remontant, very floriferous." [JR3/167]

MONSIEUR FILLION
Gonod/Lévêque, 1876

"Vigorous, flower large, carmine pink, center brighter." [JR1/6/11] "Belongs to the 'Victor Verdier' type. Carmine-rose, not of first quality." [EL] "Flower very large, full, imbricated; color, magenta pink, brighter at the center." [S] "Fine rose, striking in the centre, very large, full and well formed, good bloomer, a first-class variety; growth vigorous." [JC]

MONSIEUR FOURNIER
Listed as 'Monseigneur Fournier'.

MONSIEUR FRANCISQUE RIVE
Schwartz, 1883
　"Poppy." [Y̆] "Very vigorous, having the look of 'Marie Baumann', foliage light, flower very large, full, well formed, bright cerise red nuanced carmine, petals concave, reverse glaucescent, producing a charming contrast, very fragrant, quite remontant." [JR7/122]

MONSIEUR HOSTE   PLATE 143
Liabaud, 1884
Seedling of 'Baron de Bonstetten' (HP).
　"Bush very vigorous; flower large, full, beautiful velvety crimson red. Magnificent thick, dark green foliage." [S]

MONSIEUR JOSEPH CHAPPAZ
Schmitt, 1882
Seedling of 'Jules Margottin' (HP).
　"Very vigorous bush; flower very large, full, perfectly globular, beautiful lilac pink. Has the look of 'Jules Margottin'." [JR6/164]

MONSIEUR JOURNAIX
Marest, 1868
　"Vigorous . . . brilliant red." [EL] "Weak growth; flower large, full; very remontant; scarlet, nuanced dark red." [S]

MONSIEUR JULES DEROUDILHE
Liabaud, 1886
　"Very vigorous bush with stocky, upright canes; beautiful light green foliage with two pairs of leaflets; flower medium sized or large, crimson purple red, perfectly cupped. Blooms constantly." [JR10/171]

MONSIEUR JULES LEMAÎTRE   PLATE 155
Vigneron, 1890
Seedling of 'Mme Isaac Pereire' (B).
　"Very vigorous with stiff, upright canes; dark green foliage; flower very large, full, globular, very beautifully colored bright carmine red. Perfect hold; very remontant and floriferous; the blossoms have the most charming scent . . . dedicated to Monsieur Jules Lemaître, well-known writer." [JR14/148–149]

MONSIEUR JULES MAQUINANT
Vigneron, 1882
Seedling of 'Jules Margottin' (HP).
　"Very vigorous, flower large, full, well formed, beautiful light red, center brighter, perfectly held." [JR6/164]

MONSIEUR JULES MONGES
Guillot fils, 1881
Seedling of 'Souvenir de la Reine d'Angleterre' (HP).
　"Cerise pink." [Y̆] "Carmine-rose, cupped." [EL] "Superbly poised." [JR5/147] "Very vigorous; canes upright, light green; leaves light green, composed of 5–7 leaflets; flowers very large, full, well formed, cupped; superbly colored a very sparkling carmine pink; stalk firm, holding the flower well." [JR5/116]

MONSIEUR LAURIOL DE BARNEY
Trouillard, 1866
　"Purple, nuanced." [Y̆] "Growth vigorous; flower large, full, imbricated; color, currant red." [S]

MONSIEUR LE CAPITAINE LOUIS FRÈRE
Vigneron, 1883
　"Velvety crimson." [Y̆] "Very vigorous, upright, thorns small, chestnut brown, fairly numerous, foliage beautiful green, flower very large, full, well formed, handsome bright light red, freely remontant." [JR7/170]

MONSIEUR LE PRÉFET LIMBOURG
Margottin fils, 1878
Seedling of 'Pierre Notting' (HP).
　"Crimson, tinged with violet, double, or full; a rose of fine color." [EL] "Vigorous bush; flower large, full, well formed; color, beautiful nuanced light red; very beautiful, very floriferous." [S]

MONSIEUR LOUIS RICART   PLATE 160
('Monsieur Louis Ricard')
Boutigny, 1901
From 'Simon de St.-Jean' (HP) × 'Abel Carrière' (HP).
　"A large and showy Pæony-like flower; deep velvety crimson shaded with vermilion and black; does not burn; growth very vigorous and good habit." [P1] "Vigorous growth, with more or less somber green canes, thorns sharp and recurved, leaves of five oblong leaflets, light green beneath, darker above. Bloom is continuous, producing enormous rounded buds, borne on long, strong stems, beautiful blackish purple, very velvety, brightened by brilliant vermilion. The flowers, sometimes solitary, are very large, to five in [ca. 1.25 dm], full, globular, Peony-shaped, excellently held, with very long petals, large and thick, bullate, lighter at the nub, sometimes striped white on the reverse, fragrant." [JR16/119] Originally bred in 1894.

MONSIEUR MATHIEU BARON
('Monsieur M. Baron')
Widow Schwartz, 1886
　"Vigorous bush; flower large, full, red with deep violet; fragrant." [JR10/182]

MONTEBELLO
Fontaine, 1859
　"Red, medium size, full, tall." [Sn] "—Not big enough." [VH62/92]

MRS. BAKER
Turner/Laxton, 1876
Seedling of 'Victor Verdier' (HP).
　"Red lake." [JR20/5] "A smooth-petaled rosy-crimson flower of good substance, the older flowers abeing tinted with purple." [R7/534] "Of moderate size." [JC] "Of 'Victor Verdier' race, with the usual habits of the family. The brightest of them all in colour, with a beautiful pointed shape, one of the earliest of H.P.'s, of large size, but not very lasting in colour or form." [F-M3] "Vigorous, flower large, pretty form, handsome delicate pink." [JR1/6/11] "Moderate growth, with smooth wood; has the look of 'Comtesse d'Oxford'; flower very large, full, globular, pointed center; color, bright carmine shaded crimson." [S]

MRS. COCKER
Cocker, 1899
From 'Mrs. John Laing' (HP) × 'Mabel Morrison' (HP).

"A seedling, I believe, from 'Mme Gabriel Luizet' [HP], this Rose is like it in wood, foliage, and habit, often not blooming as a maiden, and of not much use in autumn. The blooms are a lovely shade of pink, large and very full but not pointed, with fine petals and good lasting qualities. It is a fine Exhibition Rose, but, as a new Rose of which we have had but short experience, it would hardly seem to be among the best for general cultivation." [F-M2]

MRS. GEORGE DICKSON
Bennett, 1884
From 'Mme Clémence Joigneaux' (HP) × ?

"Very vigorous and . . . robust . . . blooming early, persistently, and late . . . the flowers are large, not very full, opening well. A new color, brilliant satiny pink." [JR8/54] "Vigorous, rather like 'Clémence Joigneaux'; flower large, full, double, opens well; brilliant satiny pink. Blooms early and abundantly to the end of the season. No fungal problems." [S]

MRS. HARKNESS
Harkness, 1894
Sport of 'Heinrich Schultheis' (HP).

"White striped pink." [JR20/6] "Lighter than ['Heinrich Schultheis']." [F-M2]

MRS. J. F. REDLY
('Mrs. V. F. Redly')
Introducer and date unknown.
Flesh pink. No further information!

[MRS. JOHN MCLAREN]
California Nursery Co.?, by 1905
"Deep pink." [CA05] "Silvery pink." [CA10]

MRS. LAING
E. Verdier, 1872
"Growth vigorous; flower medium-sized, full, very fragrant; color, bright carmine pink." [S] Not to be confused with 'Mrs. John Laing'.

MRS. R. G. SHARMAN-CRAWFORD
A. Dickson, 1894
"Rosy-pink." [H] "Beautiful deep pink, magnificent in bud." [JR19/38] "A very valuable introduction, and has gained much popularity both here and in America, where it is one of the few H.P.'s which bloom in the autumn. It is of fair growth and not much liable to mildew, very free-flowering, and a capital autumnal: in fact it is almost a continuous bloomer. The flowers are a lovely shade of pink, and quite large enough; they seldom come malformed, though the shape is not of the highest class. It has a high reputation as being easy to grow, and not exacting in its requirements." [F-M2]

MRS. RUMSEY
Rumsey, 1899
Sport of 'Mrs. George Dickson' (HP).

"Rosy pink, very freely produced, and the growth is quite proof against mildew." [P1]

NAPOLÉON III
E. Verdier, 1866
Not to be confused with Granger's deep crimson HP of 1855, 'Empereur Napoléon III'.

"Two distinct colors: very bright scarlet and deep slatey violet." [I'H66/370] "Bush vigorous; flower large, full, imbricated." [S]

NOTAIRE BONNEFOND
Liabaud, 1868
"Flower very large, full; color, velvety purple; vigorous." [S]

ORDERIC VITAL
('Oderic Vital')
Oger, 1858
"Large, full, delicate pink; sport of 'Baronne Prévost'." [JR3/27] "Silvery-rose, large and full, good form." [FP] "Vigorous. . . . A little lighter in color than the parent, the habit is the same." [EL] "Very distinct and very constant. The bush is quite vigorous; flower large, very full, rosette in the center, delicate pink nuanced and shaded." [JDR58/36]

OLGA MARIX
Listed as a Bourbon.

OLIVIER BELHOMME
('Olivier Delhomme')
V. & C. Verdier, 1861
"Flower medium-sized, full, bright intense red." [I'H61/264] "Brilliant purplish-red, large, and perfect shape, foliage handsome." [FP] "Brilliant rosy-carmine, flowers well formed, of good depth and high centre, fine petal and good outline; a superb rose." [JC] "Vigorous bush; flower medium-sized, full, very well formed; color, fiery red." [S]

OLIVIER MÉTRA
E. Verdier, 1884
"Vigorous with upright delicate green canes; thorns pink, somewhat numerous, very long and recurved; leaves composed of 5 large, elliptical, dark green leaflets with irregular very deep dentations; flowers large, quite full, of a very beautiful globular form, brilliant bright cerise red." [JR8/166]

ORGEUIL DE LYON
(trans., 'Pride of Lyon')
Besson, 1886
"Plant vigorous; flower medium-sized, well-formed, pretty full; color, velvety poppy crimson brightened with vermilion and flame reflections; petals waffled at expansion; abundant bloom; wood upright and pretty thornless." [JR10/149]

ORIFLAMME DE ST. LOUIS
(trans., 'St. Louis' Banner')
Baudry & Hamel, 1858
Seedling of 'Général Jacqueminot' (HP).
"A very brilliant rose." [FP] "Brilliant crimson; resembles the parent, but is inferior to it." [EL] "Very vigorous and very remontant; from 'Général Jacqueminot'; flower fuller, brighter; very large, sparkling carmine red." [I'H58/98]

ORNEMENT DU LUXEMBOURG
Hardy, 1840
"Violet red, small, full, very fragrant, medium height." [Sn]

OSCAR II, ROI DE SUÉDE   PLATE 152
('King of Sweden')
Soupert & Notting, 1889
    "Vigorous bush; flower large, full, well formed; buds long and beautifully formed; color, carmine-vermilion with silvery reflections. Very fragrant." [JR12/147] "Very dark, rich and handsome, a splendid rose." [C&Js99]

PÆONIA
('Plonia', 'Pœonia')
Lacharme, 1855
    "Growth vigorous; flower large, full, crimson red." [l'H56/2] "Moderate vigor, hardy, floriferous, of the 'Jules Margottin' tribe; . . . much to be recommended." [S] "Grows strong and erect, flowers very large, regular, full form, perfectly double, deep flashing crimson, very fragrant, a grand rose in every way." [C&Js02]

PÆONIA
Geduldig, 1914
From 'Frau Karl Druschki' (HP) × an unnamed seedling which was the result of 'Ulrich Brunner fils' (HP) × 'Mrs. John Laing' (HP).
Not to be confused with Lacharme's HP, above.
    "Pink, large, full, medium height." [Sn]

PANACHÉE D'ORLÉANS
Dauvesse/Wilhelm, 1854
Sport of 'Duchesse d'Orléans' (HP).
    "A white and rose color striped." [HstXV:252] "A freely remontant perpetual, with a pink blossom striped lilac." [JDR55/10] "Flesh striped lilac-red; constant." [l'H57/62] "Vigorous bush; canes strong, olive green, nearly thornless; flower large, full, in a cluster of 5 or 7 blossoms at the end of the branch; color, delicate pink striped purple . . . one of the more striped." [S] "Identical with the parent sort, except that the flowers are striped with rosy-white. It is not constant, soon running back to the original." [EL] "This variety comes from 'Duchesse d'Orléans' and not 'Baronne Prévost' as we sometimes see mentioned." [JR12/172] Introduced by Wilhelm's in the year prior to that in which his two workers Soupert & Notting left to start their own business.

PANACHÉE DE BORDEAUX
Listed as 'Coquette Bordelaise'.

PANACHÉE LANGROISE
Rimancourt, 1873
Sport of 'Jules Margottin' (HP).
    "Reticulated carmine pink." [JR12/172] "Growth vigorous; flower large, full; color, bright cherry red, plumed deep carmine." [S]

PAUL DE LA MEILLERAYE
Guillot fils, 1863
    "Very vigorous; flowers very large, full, well formed, with large petals, beautiful purple cerise." [l'H64/62]

PAUL NEYRON PANACHÉE
Listed as 'Coquette Bordelaise'.

PAULA CLEGG
Kiese, 1912
From 'Kaiserin Auguste Viktoria' (HT) × 'Jaune Bicolore' (an *R. fœtida* hybrid of unknown origin).
    "This introduction is very hardy. The blossom has the same form and color as that of 'Richmond'—which is to say bright scarlet red—but is fuller, and has a very pleasant scent. It always opens very well. It is one of the most fragrant roses." [JR37/57]

PAULINE LANSEZEUR
('Pauline Lancézeur')
Lansezeur/E. Verdier. 1855
    "Red, shaded with violet-crimson, medium size, free blooming." [EL] "Bright crimson when opening, passing later to violet-pink." [l'H55/246] "Growth very vigorous, very remontant, giving flowers until the end of fall; flower medium-sized, full; color, brilliant violet, and pink." [S]

PEACH BLOSSOM   PLATE 119
('Egeria', 'Ægeria')
W. Paul, 1874
Seedling of 'Jules Margottin' (HP).
    "Flesh." [Y̆] "Bush vigorous; its large, full flowers are a delicate pink nuanced carmine and washed with white." [VH75/81] "Salmon-pink, a very lovely shade; medium size, full, semi-globular; not of good constitution. For experienced cultivators this is a superb sort." [EL] "Fairly hardy; profuse summer bloom." [S] As 'Ægeria," sold by Schwartz to Bennett in 1878.

PENELOPE MAYO
Listed as 'Duchesse de Caylus'.

[PERPÉTUELLE DE NEUILLY]
V. Verdier, 1834
Seedling of 'Athalin' (HB).
    "Lilac-pink, full, cupped, medium-sized, superb." [LF] "Flowers rose-colour, large and full; form, globular. Habit erect, fine; growth, moderate. A superb forcing Rose, and very sweet. Rarely flowers well out of doors." [P] "A variety of great excellence, having all the peculiar beauty of the Bourbon Rose, one of its parents [*say, rather, 'grandparents'*], with the fragrance of the Damask. It is a most abundant autumnal bloomer, and ought to be extensively cultivated." [WRP] One of the first Hybrid Perpetuals.

PETER LAWSON
Thomas, 1862
    "Brilliant red, shaded with carmine, large and double." [FP] "Vigorous; flower very large, full, poppy red, very intense, shaded with carmine." [l'H62/278]

PFAFFSTÄDT
Herzogin Elsa von Württemberg, 1929
From 'Frau Karl Druschki' (HP) × 'Lyon Rose' (Pernetiana).
    "Yellowish white, large, full, medium scent, tall." [Sn]

PHILIPP PAULIG
('Philippe Paulig')
Lambert, 1908
From 'Captain Hayward' (HP) × 'Baronne Adolphe de Rothschild' (HP).
    "Deep red, large, full, medium scent, tall." [Sn]

PHILIPPE BARDET
('—Barbet')
Moreau-Robert, 1874

"Growth vigorous; blooms in clusters; flower very large, full; color, bright sparkling red nuanced carmine." [S]

[PIE IX]
('Pius IX')
Vibert, 1848

"Large, full, crimson." [Pq] "Deep rose, tinged with crimson," [FP] who places it in the "La Reine" tribe. "9–10 cm [ca. 4 in], full, incarnate pink going to crimson, flat, nearly thornless, very vigorous. This rose is among the most beautiful." [M-L48/427–428] "Branches vigorous; brown at first, bristling with numerous little stickers and some fairly large, though remote, thorns, hooked, brownish red; foliage ample, a handsome light green, shiny above, pale and slightly glaucous beneath; composed of 3–7 unequal, nearly smooth, leaflets, upturned at the edge, irregularly dentate; the flowers are fragrant, large, full, a handsome bright crimson red, usually in threes at the end of the cane." [S] "Does as well grafted as own-root." [I'H53/172] "Large, double, full and of deep red colour. The bush is tree-like in habit. Unless cut regularly, it will preempt more space than an ordinary garden allows for one rose-bush . . . bold, dark green foliage, free from diseases, the constitutional strength and healthful growth overbalancing any harm to foliage or flowers done by insects. The immense red roses and large buds are in evidence from early spring to late autumn. The only 'Pius IX' I can recall stands in an old garden where it was planted fifty years ago. It is as vigorous and prolific now as it was when planted." [Dr]

"Horticulturalists place the rose 'Pie IX' in the category of those hybrids which resemble *Hybrid Chinas* in wood and foliage, but *Portlands* in the ovary. All of such hybrids have wood of a delicate green, sometimes more or less brown in youth, clothed with numerous very unequal prickles, sharp and slightly hooked; some are small, like a large bristle enlarged at the base; others are longer and look quite completely like thorns. The leaves are perfectly glabrous, smooth in youth; in age, however, they become slightly thicker, stiff, and somewhat rugose; it is this which distinguishes these hybrids from the *true* Portlands, which have soft leaves, which are slender and downy. The ovary is oblong or elongated, or funnel-shaped. The rose 'Pie IX' is a charming introduction of Mons Vibert's . . . The canes . . . are vigorous, brown when young, bristling with numerous small sharp points as well as with some pretty big hooked reddish-brown thorns. The leaves are lush, beautiful light green, glossy above, paler and slightly glaucous beneath; they are composed of 3–7 unequal leaflets which are nearly smooth, rolled at the edges, irregularly dentate and ciliate; the odd leaflet is shortly acuminate, with a mid-vein bristling with small prickles; the side-leaflets grade smaller, are nearly sessile, and are, in form, quite variable—oval, elliptical, oblong—with a slightly bristly midvein. The petiole is flexuose, glandulose, supplied with several prickles beneath, and marked with a shallow furrow; red-brown above. The stipules are very lacey, ciliate, longly adherent to the petiole, with the free part linear and subulate. The flowers are fragrant, large, full, beautiful bright crimson red, usually in threes, at the tip of the cane, and borne on fairly strong, upright peduncles which are 2–3 cm long [ca. 1 inch] and covered with glandular hairs. The calyx-tube (ovary), an extension of the peduncle, gradually enlarges into funnel-form, and is not constricted at the summit; it is a very delicate green, glabrous, or only glandular at the base. The calyx-leaflets (sepals) are long, gradually and lacily narrowing towards the tip, glandular and green on the back, slightly cottony within; 2 are quite entire; 2 others have, on both sides, small, lacy, glandular processes; the fifth has these processes only on the edges. The many petals which constitute the corolla are all a beautiful bright crimson above, paler and somewhat violet beneath, and white at the base; the outer petals are large, mostly obovate—somewhat spoon-like—rather spreading out than upright; the central petals are unequal, slightly ragged, quite serrate, sometimes reflexed on the interior, and covering some occasional stamens which one finds within the bundle which clothes the much dilated, glabrous mouth of the ovary. Inside the tube, which is bristling with silky white bristles in the lower part, one finds many ovules which are usually sterile, each one tipped with a silky style, fleshed out and tipped with enlarged, greenish stigmata." [I'H51/121–122]

PIERRE CARO
('—Carot')
Levet, 1878
Seedling of 'Victor Verdier' (HP).

"Bush vigorous; canes upright; foliage dark green; blossom medium-sized or large, full, perfect form; color, dark red, fading to a beautiful, superb light red." [JR2/166]

PIRON-MÉDARD
Piron-Médard, 1906

"Very vigorous, canes upright, nearly thornless, handsome foliage. Bud well formed and long, flower full. Color, beautiful satin pink." [JR31/7]

PLONIA
Listed as 'Pæonia'.

PRÉFET LIMBOURG
Listed as 'Monsieur le Préfet Limbourg'.

PRÉSIDENT BRIAND
M. Guillot/Mallerin, 1929
From a cross of two unnamed seedlings: Seedling A (from another unnamed seedling which came from 'Frau Karl Druschki' [HP] and which was crossed with 'Lyon Rose' [Pernetiana]) × Seedling B (from 'Frau Karl Druschki' [HP] × 'Willowmere' [Pernetiana]).

"Light pink, tinted mauve." [Ÿ] "Bud and bloom very large, double, high-centered, globular, very lasting, moderately fragrant, pink with salmon suffusion, borne singly on strong stem. Foliage abundant, large, rich green, wrinkled, mildews. Growth vigorous (about 3 ft), upright, compact; profuse, intermittent bloomer. Very hardy." [ARA30/224] "Named for Aristide Briand, President of the French Republic, to commemorate the Kellogg Peace Pact, of which Briand was the instigator. 'President Briand' is 'Perpetual' in the full meaning of the word, sending out in quick succession crop after crop of mammoth 'peony' Roses. The bud is globular and for a long while the open flower retains the globular form of a peony of the bomb type and bears a delicious fragrance. In color it is a bright clear pink with a salmon suffusion, and the bloom is long-lasting, either on the plant or cut. The plant is vigorous, extremely hardy, and, when once established, will make a large bush seldom out of bloom throughout the season. Its wood is very thorny and the foliage interestingly goffered. A splendid example of the new strain of Hybrid Perpetuals." [C-Ps29]

PRÉSIDENT CARNOT
Degressy, 1891

"Bright red nuanced carmine." [Ÿ] "Vigorous, nearly thornless, bullate beautiful dark green foliage; flower large, full, well formed, well held, bright pink nuanced carmine with flame reflections. Very remontant." [JR15/164]

PRÉSIDENT LINCOLN
Granger/Lévêque, 1862

"Wine-red." [Y̆] "Vigorous . . . flower large, full; cerise-red." [S] "Vermilion-red, tinged with crimson, the flowers are much like 'Général Washington', but inferior in quality to that variety, the habit of growth is stronger." [EL] "Very vigorous; foliage dark green; flower very large, full, imbricated, beautiful cerise pink nuanced superb brown; from 'Lord Raglan' [HP]." [l'H62/278]

PRÉSIDENT SCHLACHTER
E. Verdier, 1877

"Reddish crimson, tinged with violet." [EL] "Vigorous bush; flower large, full, well formed, velvety crimson red shaded purple, flame, and violet; canes strong and upright, reddish green; thorns rare, thick, short and straight, pink; leaves composed of 5 close-set oblong leaflets, dark green with irregular, shallow serration." [S]

PRÉSIDENT SÉNÉLAR
Schwartz, 1883

"Very vigorous and with a look all its own, foliage brownish green, flower large, full, petals rounded, imbricated, mucronate, deep cerise red, brilliantly velvety, illuminated by some flame-color, fading to purple nuanced cinnabar. A magnificent variety." [JR7/122]

PRÉSIDENT WILLERMOZ
Ducher, 1867

"Flower very large, full; bright pink." [S] "Rich brilliant carmine, with a very soft and pleasing violet tint, color new and distinct, fine petal and very beautiful; habit vigorous." [JC]

PRIDE OF REIGATE
J. Brown/G. Paul, 1884
Sport of 'Comtesse d'Oxford' (HP).

"Light crimson plumed and splotched white and pink." [JR25/24] "All the manners and customs of the 'Victor Verdier' race. This Rose has at least the merit of being the most distinct in colour of all H.P.'s, so that the merest tyro could pick it out anywhere, for it has the dark ground shade of the original striped and splashed with white." [F-M3]

PRIDE OF WALTHAM
W. Paul, 1881
Sport of 'Comtesse d'Oxford' (HP).

"Light salmon-pink, shaded violet. Similar in growth and foliage to 'Comtesse d'Oxford'." [H] "Delicate flesh-colour richly shaded with bright rose, very clear and distinct. The flowers are very large and full, with petals of great substance. Habit and constitution good. One of the best." [P1] "A sport from ['Comtesse d'Oxford'], with all the manners and customs of the family . . . as good a grower as any of them, with large blooms opening well to good shape with stout petals and fine colour . . . popular in Australia." [F-M2] "Vigorous; foliage and wood perfect." [S]

[PRINCE ALBERT]
Laffay, 1837
From 'Gloire des Rosomanes' (B) × a Damask Perpetual.
Not to be confused with A. Paul's Bourbon of 1852, which is crimson.

"Color changing from pink to pansy purple and crimson, superb." [LF] "Medium or large, very full, color varying from pink to dark violet." [R-H42] "Rich crimson purple, large and full; form, compact. Habit, branching; growth, moderate. Uncertain out of

doors, but a good forcing Rose, and very sweet." [P] "Very vigorous; flower large, full, very dense, unique scent; color, deep purple shaded carmine; cold changes color to a shade of carmine which is rather towards violet." [S] "In full bloom in December [in Havana], its best season; it is much liked because it has four bloom-periods during the year." [JR8/41] "Vigorous bush; leaves of three or five glaucous green leaflets. Thorns rare, but long; flowers cupped, very full, 5–6 cm across [ca. 2–2.5 in]. Their color is variable; while some are fresh pink, others are a more or less dark purple, sometimes with a crimson tint, or indeed an intense, velvety violet, more so than that of a Pansy. Each blossom is uniform in coloration, but these differing shades can be found on different flowers from the same specimen. What is more, they have the advantage of wafting a fairly strong, pleasant scent, more pronounced than that of the 'Quatre-Saison'." [An40/89] Prince Albert of Saxe-Coburg-Gotha, 1819-1861; husband of Queen Victoria of England.

PRINCE ALBERT
('Mme Fontaine')
Listed as a Bourbon.

PRINCE ARTHUR
B. R. Cant, 1875

"Shaded crimson; vigorous. A good exhibition and garden Rose." [J] "Belongs to the 'Général Jacqueminot' type. Deep crimson, smaller but better formed than 'Jacqueminot'." [EL] "Vigorous; flower medium-sized, full; intense crimson." [S] "Of good vigorous growth, but the wood is not quite stiff enough to support the blooms . . . liable to mildew and orange-fungus, but not much injured by rain. The blooms come generally well, in a capital characteristic form, and though the petals are thin and the flowers look fragile, they last well. I gathered from the last Mr. B. R. Cant that the origin of this fine rose is rather obscure, but the general appearance points to 'Général Jacqueminot' as an ancestor. It is however much darker in colour, larger, and does better with me in every way. It is very free blooming and fairly good in autumn, but requires good treatment to be seen in perfection, though it is hardy and healthy in most soils and appreciated in America." [F-M2] "The best dark red rose. A hybrid, and therefore, of course, it gets red rust and loses its leaves." [HmC] Prince Arthur, son of Queen Victoria.

PRINCE DE JOINVILLE
W. Paul, 1867

"Flowers light crimson; a fine, large, showy rose, of vigorous and hardy habit." [FP] "Flower medium sized, quite full, very robust; color, very bright carmine red." [S]

PRINCE DE PORTIA
('Prince de Porcia', 'Prince de Parcia')
E. Verdier, 1865

"Flowers about 10 cm [ca. 4 in], full, a most beautiful deep vermilion." [l'H65/340] "Vermilion, large, full, well formed, one of the most fragrant, somewhat subject to mildew. A splendid variety." [EL] "Bush vigorous; flower large, full; color, deep scarlet." [S]

PRINCE EUGÈNE DE BEAUHARNAIS
Moreau-Robert, 1864

"Brilliant reddish-scarlet, shaded with purple." [FP] "Bush vigorous; flower large, full, plump; color, sparkling fiery red; beautiful exhibition rose." [S]

PRINCE HENRI D'ORLÉANS
E. Verdier, 1886

"Brilliant pink." [Ў] "Vigorous, big erect light green canes; thorns very numerous, unequal, usually thin and sharp, slightly hooked, greenish pink; leaves of 5 elliptical dark green leaflets, deeply serrated with large teeth; flowers large, full, very well formed, cupped, charming when half open; color, light carmine cerise red." [JR10/170]

PRINCE NOIR
Boyau, 1854
Not to be confused with 'Black Prince' (HP).

"Deep crimson shaded with almost black. Large and globular, with high centre. Nice rose of good shape." [B&V] "Bush of moderate vigor; flower medium-sized, nearly full; color, blackish purple; exterior petals deep velvety carmine." [S] "Very dark maroon, good climber." [FP]

PRINCE STIRBEY
Schwartz, 1871

"Bush of moderate vigor; flower large, full; color, flesh pink." [S]

PRINCE WALDEMAR
E. Verdier, 1885

"Very vigorous, canes strong, look of 'Dr. Andry'; leaves large, delicate green; flowers large, full, very well formed, cupped, a most beautiful bright carmine cerise red bordered whitish." [JR8/179]

PRINCESS LOUISE
Laxton/W. Paul, 1869
From 'Mme Vidot' (HP) × 'Virginale' (HP).

"White, sometimes bluish [*sic*; 'blush,' perhaps?] -white, pretty, but wanting in substance." [JC] "Flower medium-sized, full, well-formed, white, sometimes flesh." [S]

PRINCESS OF WALES
W. Paul, 1864
Not to be confused with Laxton's pink HP of 1871, nor with Bennett's Tea of 1882.

"Bright crimson, with thick and firm petals." [FP] "Double." [EL] "Carmine, colour bright and beautiful, flowers good size, cupped, and well formed; a fine rose, habit vigorous." [JC]

PRINCESSE AMEDÉE DE BROGLIE
Lévêque, 1885

"Very vigorous, beautiful large dark green foliage; flower very large, full, globular, perfectly imbricated, beautiful bright light pink, silvery towards the center, reverse of the petals blush, very remontant." [JR8/148]

PRINCESSE CHARLES D'AREMBERG
Soupert & Notting, 1876
From 'Dupuy Jamain' (HP) × 'Mme de Sévigné' (HP).

"Flower large, full; petals large; Centifolia form; outer petals very delicate silvery lilac; center, bright carmine; much to be recommended; quite remontant; blooms until the end of the season." [S] "Vigorous." [JR1/6/11]

PRINCESSE DE BÉARN
Lévêque, 1885
Seedling of 'Duc de Cazes' (HP).

PLATE 144

"Very vigorous, dark green leaves, flowers very large, globular, full, extremely well formed, rich blackish poppy red, nuanced and brightened with brilliant vermilion . . . abundant bloom." [JR8/150] "Strong stems, excellently held . . . very pretty foliage . . . dedicated to Mme la Princesse de Béarn, a great fancier of roses, who died, alas, in the bloom of life." [JR16/152]

PRINCESSE DE JOINVILLE
Poncet/V. Verdier, 1840
Not to be confused with the 1840 Tea.

"Medium-sized, full, bright pink [and listed as a 'remontant hybrid']." [Pq]

PRINCESSE DE NAPLES
Gaëtano, Bonfiglioli & Figlio , 1897

"Silvery pink on a ground of cream." [Ў] "In the deportment of the plant and form of the flower, very much like 'Captain Christy' [HT]. The fragrance would seem to be superior to that of 'La France' [HT]. The growth is vigorous, compact, and regular; the foliage ample and beautiful brilliant light green. Flower, very large, imbricated, silvery flesh pink, very fresh, reverse of petals bright lilac pink; very fragrant. The plant blooms abundantly, and is quite remontant." [JR21/82]

[PRINCESSE HÉLÈNE]
Laffay, 1837

"Pink and crimson, nuanced, large, full, superb." [LF] "Lilacrose." [HoBoIV] "Rosy purple, of medium size, very double; form globular. Habit, erect; growth, moderate. A most abundant bloomer, when in full vigour." [P] "It was in 1837 that Mons Laffay . . . sent to Mr. William Paul, his friend, the first cross-bred hybrid from the old Damasks, then so much in fashion . . . a superb purple Rose. . . . This hybrid was, fortunately, fertile, and gave seed abundantly. Not four years had passed before Mr. William Paul and other rosarians had grown more than twenty varieties." [R-H 63]

PRINCESSE HÉLÈNE D'ORLÉANS
E. Verdier, 1886

"Brilliant pink." [Ў] "Vigorous, canes unbranched and erect, light green; thorns somewhat numerous, strong, fairly straight, yellowish pink; leaves composed of five oval undulate dark green leaflets, with irregular shallow denatations; flowers large, full, of very beautiful rounded form, cupped, firmly held; color, beautiful very fresh brilliant pink, very fragrant." [JR10/170]

PRINCESSE LISE TROUBETZKOÏ
Lévêque, 1877

"Vigorous, flower medium-sized or large, full, very well formed, imbricated, handsome delicate pink, petals bordered white; very fetching, most attractive." [JR1/12/11]

PRINCESSE MARIE DOLGOROUKY
Gonod, 1878
Seedling of 'Anna de Diesbach' (HP).

"Bush very vigorous, with stiff, upright canes; foliage of 5 leaflets, very dark green; peduncle strong; flower very large, cupped, very well formed, magnificent coloration — satiny bright pink, very frequently striped with carmine to good effect." [JR2/167]

PLATE 2. 'Sydonie'

PLATE 3. 'Président Dutailly'

PLATE 4. 'Le Vésuve'

PLATE 5. 'Cramoisi Supérieur'

PLATE 6. 'Louis-Philippe'

PLATE 7. 'Ducher'

PLATE 8. 'Princesse de Sagan'

PLATE 9. 'Mme Eugène Résal'

PLATE 10. 'Irène Watts'

PLATE 11. 'Souvenir de Catherine Guillot'

PLATE 12. 'Beauty of Rosemawr', 'Viridiflora'

Journal des Roses (Suisnes près Brie Comte Robert (S et M.) France Juillet 1882.

Rose thé Safrano.

Chromo-lith. De Tavernere Bruxelles.

PLATE 13. 'Safrano'

PLATE 14. 'Mme Falcot'

PLATE 15. 'Mme Pauline Labonté'

PLATE 16. 'Mme Azélie Imbert'

PLATE 17. 'Ma Capucine'

PLATE 18. 'Marie Van Houtte'

PLATE 19. 'Perle des Jardins', 'Sunset', 'Mrs John Laing'

PLATE 20. 'Comtesse Riza du Parc'

PLATE 21. 'Mlle Franziska Krüger'

PLATE 22. 'Mme Joseph Schwartz'

PLATE 23. 'Étoile de Lyon'

PLATE 24. 'Mme Cusin'

PLATE 25. 'Papa Gontier'

PLATE 26. 'Souvenir du Rosiériste Rambaux'

PLATE 27. 'Sunset'

PLATE 28. 'Charles de Legrady'

PLATE 29. 'Souvenir de Gabrielle Drevet'

PLATE 30. 'Marquise de Vivens'

PLATE 31. 'Mme David'

PLATE 32. 'Souvenir de Victor Hugo'

PLATE 33. 'Dr Grill'

PLATE 34. 'Luciole'

PLATE 35. 'Mlle Claudine Perreau'

PLATE 36. 'Mme Scipion Cochet'

PLATE 37. 'Mme Honoré Defresne'

PLATE 38. 'Vicomtesse de Wauthier'

PLATE 39. 'Mme Claire Jaubert'

PLATE 40. 'Mme Hoste'

PLATE 41. 'Mme Philémon Cochet'

PLATE 42. 'V. Viviand-Morel'

PLATE 43. 'Comtesse Julie Hunyadi'

PLATE 44. 'Edmond Sablayrolles'

PLATE 45. 'G. Nabonnand'

PLATE 46. 'Mlle Jeanne Guillaumez'

PLATE 47. 'Mme Philippe Kuntz'

PLATE 48. 'Elisa Fugier'

PLATE 49. 'Miss Marston'

PLATE 50. 'Mme la Princesse de Bessaraba de Brancovan'

PLATE 51. 'Professeur Ganiviat'

PLATE 52. 'Souvenir de Mme Sablayrolles'

PLATE 53. 'Dr Grandvilliers'

PLATE 54. 'Monsieur Tillier'

PLATE 55. 'Archiduc Joseph'

PLATE 56. 'Madeleine Guillaumez'

PLATE 57. 'Maman Cochet'

PLATE 58. 'Jean André'

PLATE 59. 'Erzherzog Franz Ferdinand'/syn. 'Louis Lévêque'

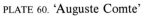

PLATE 60. 'Auguste Comte'   PLATE 61. 'Grand-Duc Pierre de Russie'   PLATE 62. 'Mme Emilie Charrin'

PLATE 63. 'White Maman Cochet'   PLATE 64. 'Dr Pouleur'

Madame C. P. Strassheim (Thé)

PLATE 65. 'Mme C. P. Strassheim'

PLATE 66. 'Mme Jacques Charreton', 'Mme Badin'

PLATE 67. 'Mlle Jeanne Philippe', 'Alister Stella Gray'

PLATE 68. 'Princesse Étienne de Croy'

PLATE 69. 'Comte Amédé de Foras'

PLATE 70. 'Mme Antoine Mari'

PLATE 71. 'Souvenir de Pierre Notting'

PLATE 72. 'Mlle Blanche Martignat'

PLATE 73. 'Hugo Roller'

PLATE 74. 'Recuerdo de Antonio Peluffo'

Rose Souvenir de la Malmaison.

PLATE 75. 'Souvenir de la Malmaison'

PLATE 76. 'Louise Odier'

PLATE 77. 'Comtesse de Barbantanne'

PLATE 78. 'Coquette des Blanches'

PLATE 79. 'Boule de Neige'

PLATE 80. 'Mme Pierre Oger'

PLATE 81. 'Mme Isaac Pereire'

PLATE 82. 'Bardou Job'

PLATE 83. 'Mme Nobécourt'

PLATE 84. 'Philémon Cochet'

PLATE 85. 'Gruss an Teplitz'

PLATE 86. 'Malton'

PLATE 87. 'Cardinal de Richelieu'

PLATE 88. 'Impératrice Eugénie'

PLATE 89. 'Baronne Prévost'

PLATE 90. 'La Reine'

PLATE 91. 'Jules Margottin'

PLATE 92. 'Duchesse de Cambacérès'

PLATE 93. 'Mme Vidot'

PLATE 94. 'Souvenir de la Reine d'Angleterre'

PLATE 95. 'Triomphe de l'Exposition'

PLATE 96. 'Anna Alexieff'

PLATE 97. 'Anna de Diesbach'

PLATE 98. 'Eugène Appert'

PLATE 99. 'Mme Boll'

PLATE 100. 'Prince Camille de Rohan'

PLATE 101. 'John Hopper'

PLATE 102. 'Charles Margottin'

PLATE 103. 'Mme Victor Verdier'

PLATE 104. 'Alfred Colomb'

PLATE 105. 'Camille Bernardin'

PLATE 106. 'Elisabeth Vigneron'

PLATE 107. 'Gloire de Ducher'

PLATE 108. 'Mlle Thérèse Levet'

PLATE 109. 'Mlle Annie Wood'

PLATE 110. 'Baronne Adolphe de Rothschild'

PLATE 111. 'Comtesse d'Oxford'

PLATE 112. 'Elisa Boëlle'

PLATE 113. 'Louis Van Houtte'

PLATE 114. 'Paul Neyron'

PLATE 115. 'Baron de Bonstetten'

PLATE 116. 'Mme Scipion Cochet'

PLATE 117. 'Comtesse de Serenye'

PLATE 118. 'La Rosière'

PLATE 119. 'Peach Blossom'

PLATE 120. 'Abel Carrière'

PLATE 121. 'Duchesse de Vallombrosa'

PLATE 122. 'Eugene Fürst'

PLATE 123. 'Jean Liabaud'

PLATE 124. 'Jean Soupert'

PLATE 125. 'Mme Prosper Laugier'

PLATE 126. 'Star of Waltham'

PLATE 127. 'Magna Charta'

PLATE 128. 'Jules Chrétien'

PLATE 129. 'Rosy Morn'

PLATE 130. 'Duchess of Bedford'

PLATE 131. 'Ferdinand Chaffolte'

PLATE 132. 'Panachée d'Angers'/syn. 'Commandant Beaurepaire'

PLATE 133. 'Comte Adrien de Germiny'

PLATE 134. 'Ulrich Brunner fils'

PLATE 135. 'Alphonse Soupert'

PLATE 136. 'Colonel Félix Breton'

PLATE 137. 'Éclair'

PLATE 138. 'Secrétaire J. Nicolas'

PLATE 139. 'Amiral Courbet'

PLATE 140. 'Baronne Nathaniel de Rothschild'

PLATE 141. 'Gloire Lyonnaise'

PLATE 142. 'Mme Eugénie Frémy'

PLATE 143. 'Monsieur Hoste'

PLATE 144. 'Princesse de Béarn'

PLATE 145. 'Souvenir d'Alphonse Lavallée'

PLATE 146. 'Princesse Marie d'Orléans'

PLATE 147. 'Comte de Paris'

PLATE 148. 'Duchesse de Bragance'

PLATE 149. 'Erinnerung an Brod'

PLATE 150. 'James Bougault'

PLATE 151. 'Gustave Piganeau'

PLATE 152. 'Oscar II, Roi de Suède'

PLATE 153. 'Souvenir du Rosiériste Gonod'

PLATE 154. 'Vick's Caprice'

PLATE 155. 'Monsieur Jules Lemaître'

PLATE 156. 'Claude Jacquet'

PLATE 157. 'Marchioness of Londonderry'

PLATE 158. 'Clio'

PLATE 159. 'Mlle Honorine Duboc'

PLATE 160. 'Monsieur Louis Ricart'

PLATE 161. 'François Coppée'

PLATE 162. 'Mme Verrier-Cachet'

PLATE 163. 'Baron Girod de l'Ain'

PLATE 164. 'Roger Lambelin'

PLATE 165. 'Mme Louis Ricart'

PLATE 166. 'Ernest Morel'

PLATE 167. 'Gloire d'un Enfant d'Hiram'

PLATE 168. 'Capitaine Jouen'

Frau Karl Druschki.
P. Lambert 1901.

(Remontant.)

PLATE 169. 'Frau Karl Druschki'

PLATE 170. 'Rouge Angevine'

PLATE 171. 'Juliet'

PLATE 172. 'Aimée Vibert'

PLATE 173. 'Lamarque'

PLATE 174. 'Céline Forestier'

PLATE 175. 'Gloire de Dijon'

PLATE 176. 'Maréchal Niel'

PLATE 177. 'Rêve d'Or'

PLATE 178. 'Mme Bérard'

PLATE 179. 'Mme Emilie Dupuy'

PLATE 180. 'Belle Lyonnaise'

PLATE 181. 'Beauty of Glazenwood'

PLATE 182. 'Reine Marie Henriette'

PLATE 183. 'William Allen Richardson'

PLATE 184. 'Duarte de Oliveira'

PLATE 185. 'Mme Alfred Carrière'

PLATE 186. 'Beauté de l'Europe'

PLATE 187. 'Caroline Schmitt'

PLATE 188. 'Étendard de Jeanne d'Arc'

PLATE 189. 'Mme Eugène Verdier'

PLATE 190. 'Mme Chauvry'

PLATE 191. 'Elie Beauvilain'

PLATE 192. 'L'Idéal'

PLATE 193. 'Mme la Duchesse d'Auerstädt'

PLATE 194. 'Souvenir de Mme Joseph Métral'

PLATE 195. 'Nardy'

PLATE 196. 'Kaiserin Friedrich'

PLATE 197. 'La France de 89'

PLATE 198. 'Pink Rover'

PLATE 199. 'Mme Pierre Cochet'

PLATE 200. 'Beauté Inconstante'

PLATE 201. 'Comtesse de Galard-Béarn'

PLATE 202. 'Marie Robert'

PLATE 203. 'E. Veyrat Hermanos'

PLATE 204. 'Belle Vichysoise'

PLATE 205. 'Ards Rover'

PLATE 206. 'Mme Jules Gravereaux'

PLATE 207. 'Aimée Vibert à Fleur Jaune'

PLATE 208. 'Tausendschön'

PLATE 209. 'Indiana'

PLATE 210. 'Pâquerette', 'Parvula', 'Pompon de Bourgogne'

PLATE 211. 'Mlle Cécile Brunner'

PLATE 212. 'Mignonette', 'Miss Kate Schultheis'

PLATE 213. 'Perle d'Or'

PLATE 214. 'Polyantha Grandiflora'

PLATE 215. 'Georges Pernet', 'Étoile de Mai'

PLATE 216. 'Gloire des Polyantha'

PLATE 217. 'Mlle Blanche Rebatel'

PLATE 218. 'Clotilde Soupert'

PLATE 219. 'Petite Léonie', 'Filius Strassheim'

PLATE 220. 'Mme Norbert Levavasseur'

PLATE 221. 'Ännchen Müller', 'Frau Elise Kreis'

PLATE 222. 'Mrs W. H. Cutbush'

PLATE 223. 'Jeanne d'Arc', 'Mme Norbert Levavasseur', 'Orléans-Rose', 'Mme Taft'

PLATE 224. 'Erna Teschendorff'

PLATE 225. *R. multiflora* form showing Polyant characteristics.

PLATE 226. 'La France'

PLATE 227. 'Captain Christy'

PLATE 228. 'Mme Étienne Levet'

PLATE 229. 'Julius Finger'

PLATE 230. 'Camoëns'

PLATE 231. 'Lady Mary Fitzwilliam'

PLATE 232. 'Mme Joseph Desbois'

PLATE 233. 'Viscountess Folkestone'

PLATE 234. 'William Francis Bennett'

PLATE 235. 'Mlle Germaine Caillot'

PLATE 236. 'Comte Henri Rignon'

PLATE 237. 'Mlle Augustine Guinoisseau'

PLATE 238. 'Danmark'

PLATE 239. 'Gustave Regis'

JOURNAL DES ROSES.(Suisnes près Brie-Comte-Robert) (S.et M) France. *Septembre 1896*

PLATE 240. 'Mme Caroline Testout'

PLATE 241. 'Baronne G. de Noirmont'

PLATE 242. 'Grand-Duc Adolphe de Luxembourg'

PLATE 243. 'Kaiserin Auguste Viktoria'

PLATE 244. 'Mme Joseph Bonnaire'

PLATE 245. 'Mme Veuve Menier'

PLATE 246. 'Lady Henry Grosvenor'

PLATE 247. 'Marquise Litta de Breteuil'

PLATE 248. 'Mme Joseph Combet'

PLATE 249. 'Joséphine Marot'

PLATE 250. 'Mme Abel Chatenay'

PLATE 251. 'Souvenir de Mme Eugène Verdier'

PLATE 252. 'Souvenir du Président Carnot'

PLATE 253. 'Mme Wagram, Comtesse de Turenne'

PLATE 254. 'Mrs W. J. Grant'/syn. 'Belle Siebrecht'

PLATE 255. 'Mme Jules Grolez'

PLATE 256. 'Gardenia'

PLATE 257. 'Mrs Robert Garrett'

PLATE 258. 'Papa Lambert'

PLATE 259. 'Rosomane Gravereaux'

PLATE 260. 'Bessie Brown'

PLATE 261. 'Mme Viger'

PLATE 262. 'Prince de Bulgarie'

PLATE 263. 'Paul Meunier'

önigin Carola, (Hybride de thé)
R. Tuerke 1903.

PLATE 264. 'Reine Carola de Saxe'

PLATE 265. 'Gustav Grünerwald'

PLATE 266. 'Dean Hole'

PLATE 267. 'Mme Maurice de Luze'

PLATE 268. 'Mme Segond-Weber'

PLATE 269. 'Château de Clos-Vougeot'

PLATE 270. 'Radiance'

PLATE 271. 'Gruss an Aachen'

PLATE 272. 'His Majesty'

PLATE 273. 'Jonkheer J. L. Mock'

Général-supérior Arnold Janssen. (H. DE THÉ)

Jos. Kohren

PLATE 274. 'General-Superior Arnold Janssen'

PRINCESSE MARIE D'ORLÉANS   PLATE 146
E. Verdier, 1885

"Very vigorous with upright canes; foliage large, rounded, and very glossy, light green; flowers large, full, well-formed, a most beautiful bright cerise pink shaded silvery." [JR8/179]

PRINCESSE RADZIWILL
Lévêque, 1883

"China pink." [Y̆] "Very vigorous, foliage bright light green, flower large, full, perfect form, perfectly imbricated, beautiful light pink or bright carmine pink shaded bright crimson; superb." [JR7/158] "The Radziwill grounds would also present a specimen of a taste more than genteel: to cross a 20-foot water course, it would be necessary to board a boat moored at the side of a sphinx, that emblem of the perils of navigation, with an altar to Hope on the other side. Debarking would take place in a sacred grove filled with other altars, where a shady footpath led to a Gothic shelter, sanctuary of Melancholy. The visitor would then pass a Greek temple where vestal figures were grouped around statues of Love and Silence, and then a knight's tent, an Oriental salon with mahogany doors, a museum of ersatz antiquities, and, as the crowning touch, the funeral monument erected, before need, by the Princess Radziwill, no doubt to cheer up the visitor." [Pd]

PRINZ MAX ZU SCHAUMBURG-LIPPE
Herzogin Elsa von Württemberg, 1934
From 'Frau Karl Druschki' (HP) × 'Lyon Rose' (Pernetiana).
"Salmon pink, large, full, medium scent, tall." [Sn]

PRINZESSIN ELSA ZU SCHAUMBURG-LIPPE
Herzogin Elsa von Württemberg, 1929
"Yellowish white, very large, full, medium scent, tall." [Sn]

PROFESSEUR CHARGUEREAUD
Lévêque, 1890

"Vigorous, foliage ample, dark green, flower large, full, well formed, deep red marbled brown and poppy, very distinct and effective." [JR14/179]

PROFESSEUR MAXIME CORNU
Lévêque, 1885

"Very vigorous; foliage ample, lanceolate, glaucous green; flower very large, full, well formed, beautiful bright cerise red; color very scintillating . . . blooms abundantly." [JR8/148]

PRUDENCE BESSON
Lacharme, 1865

"Cerise pink." [Y̆] "Growth vigorous; flower very large, semi-full, flat, very effective; color, carmine red." [S] "Much like 'Souvenir de la Reine d'Angleterre'." [I'H65/340]

[QUEEN OF EDGELY]
('Pink American Beauty')
Florist's Exchange, 1901
Sport of 'American Beauty' (HP).

"Color a bright pink; flowers large and deep cup shaped; very fragrant, like its parent." [CA02] "This famous New Rose originated near Philadelphia, and is a sport from the well-known 'American Beauty', of which it is an exact counterpart in every particular except color. It has the same vigorous growth and beautiful foliage, and the same exquisite fragrance. The color is a lovely shade of bright, clear pink, very beautiful. The flowers are large and very deep, averaging over five in across, and are borne on long stiff stems." [C&Js02]

QUEEN OF QUEENS
('Reine des Reines')
W. Paul, 1882
From 'Victor Verdier' (HP) × a seedling which was the result of 'La Reine' (HP) × 'Maiden's Blush' (Alba).

"Pink, with blush edges, large and full; growth vigorous." [P1] "Of perfect form; grows and flowers freely." [EL] "Of 'Victor Verdier' race with the usual habit, but not quite so strong in growth as most of them. Hardly full-sized, but of nice globular form." [F-M3] "Good both as a garden rose and as an exhibition variety; one of the best modern introductions." [S]

REINE DE CASTILLE
Lartay, 1852

"Flowers large, full, globular, deep carmine red." [I'H56/199] "Whitish-rose, large and full, of good habit, and blooms freely." [FP] "Bush very vigorous; flower large, very full, imbricated, very well formed; color, velvety flame red." [S]

REINE DE DANEMARK
Granger, 1857

"Flesh-lilac flowers, large, full, admirably clear, fairly often a rose of the first merit, but not a dependable bloomer." [R-H63] "Growth vigorous; canes short, nearly thornless; leaves small, pointed, very serrate; flower large, full, well formed, opening with difficulty; color, pinkish lilac tending towards flesh pink." [S]

REINE DES REINES
Listed as 'Queen of Queens'.

[REMBRANDT]
Van Rossem, 1914
From 'Frau Karl Druschki' (HP) × 'Lyon Rose' (Pern).
Not to be confused with the Damask Perpetual of the same name.

"A fair representative of the new type of Hybrid Perpetual, the product of a renaissance of this once-neglected class. The blooms are creamy pink, with a tawny center, and are enormous, with leathery, long-lasting petals, full to the center. Growth and habit of 'Frau Karl Druschki', but with better foliage, and almost thornless. Can be used as a pillar or trained on a fence." [C-Ps29]

RÉVEIL DU PRINTEMPS
(trans., 'Spring's Awakening')
Oger, 1883

"Growth very vigorous; flower large, very full, well formed; very delicate flesh white; of the 'Mme Vidot' sort." [S]

REVEREND ALAN CHEALES
G. Paul, 1897

"This variety is very different from previously known roses; the flower is very big, in a very original peony form; color, pale lake pink, petal reverse shaded darker. The very floriferous plant is extremely decorative; its foliage appears very early in the spring, and does not fall until the heavy frosts. It is dedicated to the sectretary of the Brockham Rose Society." [JR21/66] "A pretty good grower which does not require close pruning. It flowers freely and is a 'good doer'. The blooms are of a nice fresh colour — pure lake with reverse of petals silvery white' — but not very lasting. The shape is rather loose, and the raiser calls it a 'peony-like Rose' but I do not think it is quite as bad as that, and I have seen it with a good point, and shown well. Still, it should not be relied on as an Exhibition Rose, and would be better for garden purposes if its growth was stronger." [F-M2]

RICCORDO DI FERNANDO SCARLATTI
Italy?, ca. 1925

"Dark red, large, full, very fragrant, tall." [Sn]

ROBERT DE BRIE
Granger, 1860

"Salmon pink." [LS] "Flower large, full; color, lilac-pink marbled white." [S] "Outer petals of a gray leaden pink, inner petals lighter pink, where they form a belt around the reproductive organs. . . . And, when it rains, all the blossoms become little reservoirs of water of a very picturesque metallic appearance." [VH62/93]

ROBERT DUNCAN
A. Dickson, 1897

"Plant very vigorous and floriferous; flowers large, well-formed, with large and markedly concave petals. Color, light pinkish lake. Garden and exhibition variety." [JR21/68]

ROSA VERSCHUREN
Verschuren, 1905
Seedling of 'Souvenir de la Reine d'Angleterre' (HP).

"Very fresh pink." [Ý] "Pink, large, full, medium scent, medium height." [Sn]

ROSE CORNET
Listed as 'Cornet'.

ROSE DE FRANCE
E. Verdier, 1893

"Vigorous with erect canes; flowers medium or large, full, of admirable form and exquisite freshness; color, beautiful bright carmine pink with reverse of petals silvery; fragrance notably Centifolia-like. Superb." [JR17/178]

ROSIÉRISTE HARMS
E. Verdier, 1879

"Bush vigorous, having the look of 'Mme Victor Verdier'; canes stiff and upright, light green; thorns fairly numerous, very fine and pointed, yellowish; leaves composed of 3–5 delicate green leaflets; deep serration; flower large, full, extremely well formed; color, beautiful velvety scarlet red." [JR3/181]

[ROSSLYN]
A. Dickson, 1900
Sport of 'Mlle Suzanne-Marie Rodocanachi' (HP).

"Large full flowers and very sweet, color exquisite rosy flesh, very fragrant and attractive, free bloomer and entirely hardy." [C&Js02]

ROSY MORN   PLATE 129
W. Paul, 1878
Seedling of 'Victor Verdier' (HP).

"Delicate peach color, richly shaded salmon pink; they are very large with thin petals; the fragrance is delicate, and the form perfect. Its foliage is abundant and pretty, while the growth is very vigorous, the wood strong and lightly spiny." [JR2/7] "Belongs to the 'Victor Verdier' type. Salmon-pink, a deeper shade than '[Mlle] Eugénie Verdier' [HP]; peculiar wood and foliage more like 'Captain Christy' [HT] than any other variety. A good rose, but with too many imperfect blooms." [EL]

ROUGE ANGEVINE   PLATE 170
Chédane-Guinoisseau, 1907

"Vigorous, canes upright, wood light green, very smooth, nearly thornless, foliage very beautiful green; bud long, with spiraled petals; flower opens very well; nearly full, large, with very large rounded petals; color, the most beautiful madder red, resembling the color of the prettiest red geraniums, never bluing, early, continuous till frost." [JR31/149]

ROYAT MONDAIN
Veysset, 1901

"Crimson red nuanced light red, petals pointed, some edges lined white to a sixteenth of an inch. The blossom is large, full, fragrant, and held on a strong stem. The growth is vigorous and very floriferous." [JR25/147] "Distinct." [P1]

RUBENS
Laffay, 1852
Not to be confused with Robert's Tea of 1859.

"Amaranth." [LS] "Bright red, a fine color, flowers loose." [EL]

RUSHTON-RADCLYFFE
E. Verdier, 1864

"Flowers beautiful clear bright red; large, full, and of perfect form; growth vigorous." [FP] "Vigorous, flowers full, from 10–12 cm [ca. 4 in], beautiful light bright cherry red." [I'H64/327] "Mr. Radclyffe, a clergyman, a horticulturalist, an excellent amateur of the rose, and a very amusing contributor to the *Florist*." [FP]

[SA MAJESTÉ GUSTAVE V]
Nabonnand, 1922
From 'Frau Karl Druschki' (HP) × 'Avoca' (HT).

"His Majesty, Gustave, King of Sweden by birth but rosarian by choice, offered a cash premium for an everblooming Rose that would resist the bleak winters of the land of the midnight sun. Such an offer caused a flurry among European hybridizers and started a Renaissance of the Hybrid Perpetual. The winner was Nabonnand, the French Master of the Tea Rose (irony of fate!) from the Riviera that knows not the meaning of the word 'winter'. The bud is ovoid, the bloom large size and double, beautifully imbricated, solid 'Paul Neyron' pink and sweetly perfumed. One of the most finished Roses of the Hybrid Perpetual class. Blooms recurrently at brief intervals until fall when it makes a wonderful display. Plant extra vigorous with beautiful, healthy foliage." [C-Pf29]

SCHÖN INGEBORG
Kiese, 1921
From 'Frau Karl Druschki' (HP) × 'Natalie Böttner' (HT, Böttner, 1909, cream; from 'Frau Karl Druschki' [HP] × 'Goldelse' [HT, Hinner, 1902, yellow; seedling of 'Kaiserin Auguste Viktoria' (HT)]).
Not to be confused with 'St. Ingebert' (HP).

"Light pink, large, full, medium height." [Sn]

SECRÉTAIRE J. NICOLAS   PLATE 138
('Secrétaire Jean Nicolas')
Schwartz, 1883

"Very vigorous bush; canes upright with thin thorns; foliage light green; flower fragrant, large, full, well formed, cupped, globular; petals concave, exterior ones imbricated, gracefully reflexed;

color, beautiful somber red with intense velvety purple, matte reflections; reverse of petals amaranth, pale, pruinose; plant of good 'posture' and very effective; the blossom is solitary on strong canes and in a cluster of 2 or 3 on the even more vigorous ones; freely remontant; well held and effective." [S]

[SÉNATEUR VAÏSSE]
Guillot père, 1859
Seedling of 'Général Jacqueminot' (HP).

"Vigorous, flower large, full, some stamens in the center, bright red." [JDR59/28] "Intense glowing scarlet, fine petal, flower full, with high centre, large and perfectly formed, free growing, handsome foliage, and one of the very best roses in cultivation." [JC] "A very effective variety; deep velvety crimson; wood smooth; hardy . . . continuous bloom; good rose to force; excellent exhibition flower." [S] "Bright flashing crimson, flamed with scarlet; very large, full and double. 15 cts. each." [C&Js01] "Senator Vaïsse, in charge of the administration of the Département du Rhône." [R-H 63]

SILVER QUEEN
W. Paul, 1887
Sport of 'Queen of Queens' (HP).

"Silvery pink." [Ÿ] "Silvery red." [JR20/5] "Flowers extra large, full and deep, with broad thick petals and delightful fragrance; color exquisite silvery rose, passing to delicate rosy pink; beautiful cupped form, very handsome and an abundant bloomer." [C&Js02] "Silvery blush, shaded in the centre with very delicate rosy pink, distinct and lovely, large and full, of beautifully cupped form, and produced in great abundance, every shoot being crowned with a flower bud, the latter characteristic rendering it a fine autumnal bloomer." [P1] "Of 'Victor Verdier' race, of the same class as 'Queen of Queens', from which it appears to be a lighter coloured sport. Very free flowering, a good autumnal, fragrant, of fine form and attractive colour." [F-M3] "Medium height." [Sn] "A Hybrid Perpetual with smooth wood, whose flowers are a pure silvery pink of great beauty and perfect form." [JR12/107]

SIMON DE ST.-JEAN
Liabaud, 1861

"Velvety purple." [LS] "Flower large, nearly full; purple nuanced velvety deep grenadine." [S]

SIR GARNET WOLSELEY
Cranston, 1875
Seedling of 'Prince Camille de Rohan' (HP).

"Rich vermilion shaded with bright carmine, and the colour well maintained throughout, flowers very large, full, and perfectly formed, standing out bold and erect; habit strong and vigorous, producing flowers most freely." [JC] "Branches with coppery brown thorns; each branch bears a rose at the tip; flower large, very well formed, plump; color, vermilion red nuanced brilliant carmine." [S]

SIR ROWLAND HILL
Mack, 1887
Sport of 'Charles Lefebvre' (HP).

"Violet red." [JR25/13] "Very large and full, with petals of great substance; sweet." [P1] "Vigorous, covered with beautiful foliage; flower large, full, and of good form, delicate perfume. Port-wine color, nuanced blackish maroon when opening, changing to brilliant Bordeaux-wine color. Very floriferous." [JR11/166] " 'Deep velvety plum' is the general description, and, when seen at its best,

it certainly has a very deep, almost dark blue, shade. But it must be grown very strong to show its colour to perfection, and more often comes of a dark claret or maroon, or even simply crimson . . . It seems decidedly less hardy and strong, and not so good a grower as the type from which it sprang: in other respects it has the same habit. A Rose of unique colour, but tender, liable to orange fungus and requiring high cultivation: not to be recommended for general culture." [F-M2]

[SISLEY]
Sisley, 1835

"Light carmine, full, flat, medium size." [LF] (listed among the Damask Perpetuals). "Rosy crimson, of medium size, full. A shy grower." [P] "Growth vigorous; flower large, full; color, violet amaranth." [S] "Medium or large, full, bright cherry-violet." [R-H42] "French horticulture has lost one of its oldest and most intelligent adepts in the person of Jean Sisley, who died last January 12 [1891], at Montplaisir-Lyon, at the age of 87. . . . Born at Flessingue, Holland, in 1804, Jean Sisley later became a naturalized Frenchman; he was the nephew of the famous painter Jean Van Dael. . . . Mons Sisley was one of the creators of the Lyon Horticultural Circle, of which he was General Secretary, and which has since become the Lyon Horticultural Association." [JR15/17] "Sisley, who developed at Lyon the first double white zonale pelargonium." [JR22/160] Sisley, sometimes called Sisley-Vandael or Sisley-Van Dael, who introduced among other varieties "Desprez à Fleur Jaune' (N), should be noted as an early (if unheeded) advocate of systematic cross-breeding, at length reaffirming Henry Bennett's own determinations on the subject.

SOUVENIR D'ADOLPHE THIERS
Moreau-Robert, 1877
Seedling of 'Comtesse d'Oxford' (HP).

"Red, tinged with vermilion, very large." [EL] "Bush vigorous; flower very large, full; color, vermilion red. . . . Very floriferous. This rose gets as big as those of 'Paul Neyron'." [S]

SOUVENIR D'ALEXANDRE HARDY
Lévêque, 1898

"Very vigorous bush; ample foliage, bright dark green; flower large, full, very well formed; richly colored maroon red lit with carmine and bright vermilion, superb shades." [JR22/147]

SOUVENIR D'ALINE FONTAINE
Fontaine, 1879

"Beautiful, well-formed flowers, opening from tight buds, cupped, reflexed, quartered, well filled with crinkled petals of flesh pink, becoming paler with age. The pale colour of the foliage makes a pleasing complement. Perhaps 4 ft [ca. 1.25 m]." [T3] "Bush very vigorous; flower large, very full; color, light salmon pink within, purplish carmine red towards the edge. Beautiful form; blooms in panicles." [S]

SOUVENIR D'ANDRÉ RAFFY
Vigneron, 1899

"Vigorous, erect bush; foliage dark; flower large, full, globular, borne on strong stem; beautifully colored vermilion red, with light velvety touches. Blossom doesn't burn in the sun. Extremely floriferous." [JR23/149]

SOUVENIR D'ARTHUR DE SANSAL

Guénoux/Jamain, 1875

Seedling of 'Jules Margottin' (HP).

"Beautiful clear rose, colour of 'Jules Margottin' [HP], but brighter; flowers large and well formed; a fine exhibition rose." [JC] "Flower large, full, perfect Centifolia form; color, bright pink, sometimes silvery; very fragrant. Growth vigorous." [S]

SOUVENIR D'AUGUSTE RIVIÈRE

E. Verdier, 1877

"Belongs to the 'Prince Camille [de Rohan]' type. Velvety crimson." [EL] "Vigorous, flower very well formed, rich crimson red, purple and scarlet reflections." [JR1/12/13] "Very vigorous with strong reddish brown canes; thorns numerous, unequal, very sharp, reddish; leaves composed of 5 elongated leaflets, delicate green, irregularly and deeply toothed; flowers large, full, well formed; color, crimson red, bright, velvety, and sparkling, brilliant poppy-scarlet reflections, strongly shaded deep maroon." [JR2/30]

SOUVENIR DE BÉRANGER

Bruant, 1857

"Light rose, very large and double." [FP] "Pink, medium size, full, tall." [Sn]

SOUVENIR DE BERTRAND GUINOISSEAU

Chédane-Guinoisseau, 1895

"Bush vigorous; foliage dark green; thorns yellowish, numerous; flower large, very full, purple red nuanced crimson; very fragrant and very floriferous." [JR19/130–131]

SOUVENIR DE CAILLAT

E. Verdier, 1867

"Flowers large, full, in clusters, purple and flame." [I'H68/50] "Moderate growth." [S]

SOUVENIR DE CHARLES MONTAULT

('—Montant', '—Montaut')

Robert & Moreau, 1862

"Brilliant red, cupped." [FP] "Velvety purple suffused with crimson, large and double; free blooming and pretty; habit free." [JC] "Growth vigorous; flower large, full, cupped; color, sparkling fiery red." [S]

SOUVENIR DE GRÉGOIRE BORDILLON

Moreau-Robert, 1889

"Very vigorous, wood big and strong, with sharp and dense thorns; handsome dark green foliage; flower very large and full, globular, perfect form, beautiful sparkling bright red nuanced vermilion, very floriferous. This variety is dedicated to the late Grégoire Bordillon, former prefect of Maine-et-Loire." [JR13/146]

SOUVENIR DE HENRI LÉVÊQUE DE VILMORIN

Lévêque, 1899

"Very vigorous, beautiful dark green foliage, flower large, full, extremely well formed, handsome deep velvety crimson red with brown." [JR23/178]

SOUVENIR DE JOHN GOULD VEITCH

E. Verdier, 1872

"Deep crimson, shaded with violet-purple, flowers imbricated." [JC] "Growth vigorous; flower large, full; color, deep velvety carmine." [S]

SOUVENIR DE L'AMI LABRUYÈRE

Gonod, 1884

"Growth very vigorous, upright; buds with bracts; outer petals China pink; central petals darker." [S]

SOUVENIR DE LA PRINCESSE AMÉLIE DES PAYS-BAS

Liabaud, 1873

"Moderate growth; flower large, full, globular; color, grenadine red shaded purple. Good forcing variety; very good exhibition rose." [S]

SOUVENIR DE LA REINE D'ANGLETERRE   PLATE 94

Cochet Bros., 1855

Seedling of 'La Reine' (HP).

"Bright silvery pink." [Ў] "Bright rose, very large, double, shy in autumn." [EL] "This charming variety is extra hardy and extremely vigorous; it makes, in three or four years, a bush which is three to four ft high [ca. 1–1.25 m] and six to ten ft around [ca. 2–3 m]. Reblooms freely; until the end of good weather it is covered with its foliage of a beautiful green and bears beautiful large bright pink blossoms . . . doesn't blue." [JR3/60] "Foliage large, beautiful green; flowers measure up to 15 cm across [ca. 6 in], full, cupped, bright pink, held upright on its stem." [I'H55/246] "Vigorous, perhaps even 'climbing,' excellent for covering walls or trellises, recommended for its very large, full flowers of beautiful crimson pink." [R-H63] Commemorates a visit to Paris undertaken by Queen Victoria in 1855: " 'Souvenir de Sa Majesté la reine d'Angleterre' is large, colored centifolia pink; corolla effective, petals free, sexual organs visible—much like 'Mme Domage'. Its name seems to us to be rather on the laconic side; we would rather call it 'Souvenir du voyage en France de Sa Majesté la reine du Royaume-Uni: Angleterre, Écosse et Irlande; accompagnée de son Altesse royale la princesse Adélaïde Victoria sa fille,' etc., etc. This name would perhaps take a little more room in the catalogs, but what sacrifice of paper should *not* be made for horticulturalists in order to thus simplify and render more harmonious the nomenclature of plants!" [I'H55/207]

SOUVENIR DE LAFFAY

E. Verdier, 1878

"Violet-crimson." [EL] "Very vigorous, with short, upright, delicate green canes; thorns large, short, and upright, pink; leaves composed of 5–7 leaflets which are oblong and dark green, also being regularly and fairly deeply toothed; flowers medium or large, very full, admirably shaped, in clusters; color, crimson red, bright, center fiery red, nuanced and shaded poppy, purple, and violet; superb." [JR2/187]

SOUVENIR DE LÉON GAMBETTA

Gonod, 1883

Seedling of 'Victor Verdier' (HP).

"Flesh." [Ў] "Very vigorous, canes upright, flower stem very strong, thorns large, recurved, foliage of 3–5 bright green leaflets, flower very large, about five in across [ca. 1.25 dm], very well formed, beautiful nuanced carmine red, very floriferous." [JR7/160]

SOUVENIR DE LÉON ROUDILLON

Vigneron, 1908

From 'Général Appert' (HP) × 'Louis Van Houtte' (HP).

"Vigorous, beautiful dark green foliage; flower large, full, very beautiful deep velvety red with a fiery red nub. Borne on a strong, rigid stem." [JR32/134]

SOUVENIR DE LEVESON-GOWER
('Souvenir de Leweson Gower')
Guillot père, 1852

"Fiery red." [Ÿ] "Effective plant; blossoms deep ruby red fading to light ruby." [I'H52/148] "Fine dark red, changing to ruby, very large and full." [FP] "Deep-rose, very large, double, or full, fine flowers; quite tender, and subject to mildew." [EL] "Very vigorous bush; flowers very large, full, very intense deep ruby red; brilliant, magnificent color." [I'H56/200]

SOUVENIR DE LOUIS VAN HOUTTE
Listed as 'Crimson Bedder' (HP).

SOUVENIR DE MAMAN CORBŒUF
Bénard/Corbœuf-Marsault, 1899
Seedling of 'Her Majesty' (HP).

"Pink, medium size, full, medium height." [Sn]

SOUVENIR DE MCKINLEY
Godard, 1902
From 'Magna Charta' (HP) × 'Captain Christy' (HT).

"Delicate pink." [Ÿ] Has been called a "Portland"!

SOUVENIR DE MME ALFRED VY
Jamain, 1880

"Growth vigorous; very floriferous; flower large, full; color, deep currant red, intense; well formed; well held. A variety of the first merit." [S]

SOUVENIR DE MME BERTHIER
Berthier/Liabaud, 1881
From 'Victor Verdier' (HP) × 'Jules Margottin' (HP).

"Velvety red." [Ÿ] "Very vigorous, very profuse, and above all very remontant . . . well-held, with large imbricated petals of a bright red sometimes streaked white; lit from behind, the blossom has violet reflections. Sown in 1872, this plant bloomed for the first time in 1876. In spring, when the leaves begin to develop, they are a handsome nuanced purple, changing thereafter to dark green." [JR5/171]

SOUVENIR DE MME CHÉDANE-GUINOISSEAU
Chédane-Guinoisseau, 1900

"Bush vigorous; canes upright; foliage ample, deep green; bud long; flower very large, very full, well formed, flat, with very large petals, very bright red, sparkling; very floriferous; novel coloration; of the greatest merit for pot culture." [JR24/147]

SOUVENIR DE MME DE CORVAL
Gonod, 1867

"Flower medium-sized, semi-full, saffron [*'aurore'*]." [S]

SOUVENIR DE MME HENNECOURT
('—Hennecart')
S. Cochet, 1869

"Bush vigorous; flower large, full; color, glossy pink fading to icy pink." [S]

SOUVENIR DE MME ROBERT
Moreau-Robert, 1878
Seedling of 'Jules Margottin' (HP).

"Very vigorous bush; flower large, full, opens well, cupped; color, delicate icy salmon-pink, center brighter; very floriferous." [S]

SOUVENIR DE MME SADI CARNOT
Lévêque, 1898
Seedling of 'Mme Victor Verdier' (HP).

"Very vigorous, very ample beautiful glaucous green foliage, flowers very large, perfect form . . . vigor, continuous bloom . . . beautiful deep carmine red nuanced purple and velvety brown." [JR22/147]

SOUVENIR DE MONSIEUR BOLL
Boyau, 1866

"Cerise tinted saffron." [Ÿ] "Cherry-red, large, very full." [EL] "Bright shaded red, very large, full, and well formed, habit very robust." [JC] "A strong hardy grower, with very large full red blooms, very sweet, and occasionally good enough to show, making a useful garden Rose." [F-M3]

SOUVENIR DE MONSIEUR DROCHE
Pernet père, 1881

"Carmine-rose, double." [EL] "Growth vigorous; flower large, nearly full; globular while opening, later a flat cup; color, carmine pink." [S]

SOUVENIR DE MONSIEUR FAIVRE
Levet, 1879

"Very vigorous, with branches strong and upright; handsome brilliant green foliage; flower very large, full, well formed; color, beautiful poppy red with slate reflections; very pretty." [JR3/165]

SOUVENIR DE MONSIEUR ROUSSEAU
('—Mme—')
Fargeton, 1861

"Scarlet, changing to crimson, shaded with maroon, very rich and velvety, large and very double." [FP] "Bloom medium-sized, full; color, bright red nuanced carmine." [S] "Bush vigorous; foliage light green; flowers large, full, imbricated; form and hold perfect; bright red nuanced carmine, center sometimes brightened with white; beautiful plant." [I'H61/166] In introducing the variety, Mons Fargeton specifies that the name refers to Mons Rousseau of *Angers*, evidently lest we think he have any affection for *Jean-Jacques Rousseau* of Geneva, Ermenonville, etc., or perhaps *Pierre Etienne Théodore Rousseau* of Fontainebleau.

SOUVENIR DE PAUL DUPUY
Listed as a Hybrid China.

SOUVENIR DE SPA
Gautreau, 1873
Seedling of 'Mme Victor Verdier' (HP).

"Very beautiful dark red pink with flame reflections." [JR22/23] "Bright red, shaded with crimson, well formed." [EL] "Deep red with scarlet reflex, large, full, and globular, and very well formed . . . vigorous habit." [JC]

SOUVENIR DE VICTOR HUGO
Pernet père, 1885
Seedling of 'Ambrogio Maggi' (HP).
Not to be confused with Bonnaire's pink Tea of 1885.

"Vigorous bush with canes upright, thick; beautiful thick light green foliage; flower very large, nearly full, globular, beautiful and very bright satiny pink; very well held, freely remontant." [JR9/148]

SOUVENIR DE VICTOR VERDIER

E. Verdier, 1878

"Red, shaded with violet crimson, a well-formed, good rose." [EL] "Vigorous with upright branches, which are reddish green; thorns fairly numerous, recurved, sharp, pink; leaves composed of 5–7 leaflets which are oval, delicate green, and regularly and deeply toothed; flowers large, full, well formed; color, brilliant scarlet poppy-red nuanced purple crimson, flame, and violet; splendid, very remontant, and most effective." [JR2/187] "Much to be recommended for exhibitions." [S]

SOUVENIR DE WILLIAM WOOD

E. Verdier, 1864

Seedling of 'Général Jacqueminot' (HP).

"Flowers dark blackish-purple, shaded with scarlet; darker than 'Prince Camille de Rohan'; large, full, and very effective; growth vigorous." [FP] "A bright flower and sweet." [B&V] "Vigorous, floriferous; flower large, full, cupped; color, very deep black-purple nuanced flame." [S] "Belongs to the 'Prince Camille [de Rohan]' type. A fine, very dark crimson, not equalling 'Prince Camille'." [EL] "Centre deep violet-purple, outer petals rich velvety crimson, colour superb, though somewhat inclined to burn, flowers good size, compact and full, habit free." [JC] "Vigorous, flowers full, 9–10 cm [ca. 4 in], very dark purplish black nuanced flame, much like 'Prince Camille de Rohan', but darker." [I'H64/327]

[SOUVENIR DU BARON DE SÉMUR]

Lacharme, 1874

Seedling of 'Charles Lefebvre' (HP).

"Growth vigorous; flower large, full; color, very dark purplish red nuanced flame red and shaded black; beautiful exhibition variety." [S] A parent of 'Jean Soupert' (HP).

SOUVENIR DU COMTE DE CAVOUR

Margottin, 1861

"Growth very vigorous; flower large, full, very well formed; of much merit; color, bright velvety crimson shaded darker crimson." [S]

SOUVENIR DU PRÉSIDENT PORCHER

Granger/Vigneron, 1880

Seedling of 'Victor Verdier' (HP).

"Deep rose." [EL] "Vigorous, with upright canes, big-wooded, few thorns, handsome light green foliage, flower large, full, beautiful dark pink, outside of the petals lighter, blooms freely, beautiful plant." [JR4/166]

SOUVENIR DU ROSIÉRISTE GONOD   PLATE 153

Ducher fils, 1889

"Very vigorous; flowers very large, full, well formed; color, cerise red veined bright pink." [JR13/167] This cultivar was found by Ducher the younger in Gonod's garden.

STÄMMLER

Tantau/Conard-Pyle, 1933

From 'Victor Verdier' (HP) × 'Arabella' (HT, Schilling/Tantau, 1917, crimson-pink; sport of 'Mme Caroline Testout' [HT]).

"Strong pink." [Y̆] "A new, pink, everblooming Hybrid Perpetual with slightly cupped, fully double pink flowers. Pleasing perfume. Plants make about 4-foot canes, literally hidden behind the first mass of bloom in June." [C-Ps33]

STAR OF WALTHAM   PLATE 126

W. Paul, 1875

"Deep crimson, colour very rich and effective, very large, double, and of fine form, smooth petals and fine substance, said to be a very fine rose." [JC] "A full, globular-shaped, rosy-lilac, Hybrid Perpetual kind, suffused with crimson, the petals wax-like in substance and smooth." [R8/17] "Carmine-crimson, medium size, semi-globular, full, fragrant; very large foliage, smooth green wood, with occasional red thorns. A good rose but not reliable." [EL] "Vigorous bush; branches very thorny; leaves dark and velvety, with irregular serration; flower large, full, well formed, very effective. The color changes, depending upon the soil, from carmine pink to deep crimson. Rain makes the color violet red." [S] "Of strong growth with fine foliage; not very liable to mildew but requiring fine weather. This Rose cannot be depended upon to come good, but it is a splendid bloom when seen at its best, in petal, shape, colour, smoothness, size, and lasting qualities. Not one of the best as a free bloomer or autumnal; it requires the best of weather to show its qualities to perfection, and should be left long in pruning and the buds not thinned too much, as it is extra full and often fails to open properly." [F-M2]

SULTAN OF ZANZIBAR

G. Paul, 1876

Seedling of 'Duke of Edinburgh' (HP).

"Blackish-maroon, shaded with crimson, flowers globular." [JC] "Crimson-maroon, in the style of 'S. Reynolds Hole' [HP, G. Paul, 1874, maroon red], but a weaker grower with a very bad constitution. This is one of the very few Roses I cannot keep alive at all, and I do not think I have once succeeded in getting even a decent bloom. A magnificent dark colour, and a splendid flower as sometimes shown, but a Rose to be avoided as more than likely to give absolutely no return." [F-M3]

SUZANNE CARROL OF CARROLTON

P. Nabonnand, 1924

From 'Frau Karl Druschki' (HP) × 'Mme Gabriel Luizet' (HP).

"Light salmon pink, large, semidouble, moderate scent, tall." [Sn]

SUZANNE-MARIE RODOCANACHI

Listed as 'Mlle Suzanne-Marie Rodocanachi'.

SUZANNE WOOD

E. Verdier, 1869

"Flower large, full; very floriferous; color, beautiful pink." [S]

SYMMETRY

G. Paul, 1910

Seedling of 'Mrs. John Laing' (HP).

"Crimson red." [Y̆]

TANCRÈDE

Oger, 1876

"Flower medium-sized, full, globular; color, very bright red. Moderate vigor." [S] Tancred, Norman leader of the First Crusade; lived 1078–1112.

TARTARUS

Geschwindt, 1887

From 'Erinnerung an Brod' (HP) × 'Souvenir du Dr. Jamain' (HP).

"Violet purple." [Y̆] Tartarus, a.k.a. Hades.

TATIK BRADA
Brada, 1933
From 'Frau Karl Druschki' (HP) × 'Louise Catherine Breslau' (Pern).
"Orange-pink, large, full, tall." [Sn]

TENDRESSE
Listed as 'La Tendresse'.

THÉODORE LIBERTON
Soupert & Notting, 1886
"Vigorous bush; flower large, full, Centifolia form; color, sparkling carmine red nuanced madder pink fading to deep pink; reverse of petals light purple. Scent one of the best." [JR10/148]

THORIN
Lacharme, 1866
"Growth very vigorous; flower large, nearly full, widely cupped; color, brilliant carmine pink." [S]

THYRA HAMMERICH
Vilin/C. Verdier, 1868
Seedling of 'Duchesse de Sutherland' (HP).
"Rosy-flesh, large, well formed; distinct and good." [EL] "Delicate clear flesh changing to paler flesh, colour beautiful and even throughout, flowers erect, very large, full and cupped; a superb rose, and one of the best of its colour." [JC] "Growth very vigorous, with heavy wood armed with some small hooked thorns; its very ample and light violet leaves are usually of 3–5 leaflets; its very large and full blossoms, cupped at first, then outspread, are white slightly tinted flesh pink, more intense at the base of the petals. This variety sprang from 'Duchesse de Sutherland', the growth and floriferousness of which it inherited; good rose to force." [S]

TOM WOOD
A. Dickson, 1896
"Cerise red." [Y̆] "Deep red, very large, full, tall." [Sn] "Large, cherry-red flowers; shell shaped petals." [C&Js06] "A very useful Rose, of vigorous hardy growth, with good foliage, not much liable to mildew. The blooms are well-shaped and seldom deformed, of average size and with stout petals, but the colour is rather a dull shade of red. It is a good autumnal, and the plants seem to have a good constitution, growing and doing well where others fail." [F-M2]

TRIOMPHE D'ALENÇON
Chauvel/Touvais, 1859
"Vigorous bush; flower very large, very full, form of 'Baronne Prévost'; sparkling intense red." [I'H59/138] "Much to be recommended because of its good habit and perfume." [S]

TRIOMPHE DE CAEN
Oger, 1861
"Purplish currant-red." [Y̆] "Crimson, tinged with purple, a non-permanent shade, not desirable." [EL] "Deep velvety-purple, shaded with scarlet-crimson, large and full." [FP] "Flower large, full, globular; deep velvety grenadine nuanced flame red." [S] "Brilliant scarlet, shaded with purple; large and full; growth vigorous." [P1]

TRIOMPHE DE FRANCE
Garçon, 1875
"Bright carmine rose, colour beautiful, a very large full expanded flower, but too coarse for exhibition." [JC] "Flower very large, full, of very beautiful form; blooms abundantly from June to October; color, beautiful bright carmine pink; very beautiful exhibition rose." [S]

TRIOMPHE DE LA TERRE DES ROSES
Guillot père, 1864
"Flower 14–15 cm [ca. 5.5 in], full, beautiful violet pink, very fragrant, freely remontant." [I'H64/328] "Moderate vigor; flower very large, full, violet pink." [S] "La Terre des Roses" was the name of Guillot père's establishment. "Mons Guillot père has decided, after so many years of fatigue and stubborn work during which he has given us such good and beautiful roses, to take some rest, which is both well merited and honorably achieved. He has sold his firm [in 1870] to Mons Joseph Schwartz, who has indeed for six years run the nursery." [I'H70/327]

TRIOMPHE DE SAINTES
Listed as 'Le Triomphe de Saintes'.

TRIOMPHE DE TOULOUSE
Brassac, 1873
"Red, shaded with violet-crimson." [EL] "Vigorous; flower large, full; color, velvety wine red, bluing." [S]

TURENNE
V. & C. Verdier, 1861
Not to be confused with Laffay's violet China.
"Brilliant red, large, handsome petals, very effective." [FP] "Vigorous bush; flower medium-sized, full, with large petals; color, sparkling red; blossom often imperfect." [S]

TURNVATER JAHN
Müller-Almrich, 1927
From 'Frau Karl Druschki' (HP) × an unnamed seedling which was the result of 'Mme Abel Chatenay' (HT) × 'General MacArthur' (HT).
"White, pink center, very large, full, tall." [Sn]

ULSTER
A. Dickson, 1900
"Salmon pink, deep petaled, large and full." [H] "Large, salmon-pink in colour, full, and of great substance. A poor grower." [P1] "The flower, as seen in a show stand, is magnificent, very large, and very finely and regularly formed, with beautiful bright colour and good fragrance. But as to its growth I can say nothing, simply because I have not succeeded in getting it to grow . . . more than a very few in[ches]. What little growth it does make is robust, and it is plainly a Rose for exhibitors only, and for those only of them who can give it the most 'liberal treatment.' " [F-M2]

URDH
Tantau/Conard-Pyle, 1933
From 'Victor Verdier' (HP) × 'Papa Lambert' (HT).
"Strong pink." [Y̆] "Pink, very large, very full, very fragrant, tall." [Sn] "Very double, medium-sized blooms of lovely old-rose are freely produced throughout the season. The rich, old-time perfume is unforgettable." [C-Pf33]

VAINQUEUR DE GOLIATH

F. Moreau, 1862

"Brilliant crimson-scarlet, very large and double."[FP] "Growth vigorous; flower large, full; color, bright sparkling red; very fragrant. Magnificent exhibition rose." [S]

VELOURS POURPRE

(trans., 'Purple Velvet')

E. Verdier, 1866

"Velvety bright crimson illuminated with deep brown, scarlet, and violet." [I'H66/370] "Bush very vigorous; flower large, full; color, bright velvety carmine with violet reflections." [S]

VELOUTÉ D'ORLÉANS

Listed as a Bourbon.

VENUS

Kiese/Schmidt, 1895

From 'Général Jacqueminot' (HP) × 'Princesse de Béarn' (HP).

"Purple-red, large, full, very fragrant, tall." [Sn]

VICOMTE DE LAUZIÈRES

Liabaud, 1889

"Purple." [Ÿ] "Very vigorous with erect canes, beautiful dark green foliage. . . . Flower very large, well formed, full, plump, handsome purplish red without other tints." [JR13/163]

VICOMTE MAISON

Fontaine, 1868

"Cherry-red, double, fades quickly, straggling habit." [EL] "Growth very vigorous; flower large, full; color, cerise red nuanced white." [S]

VICOMTESSE DE VEZINS

Gautreau, 1867

"Velvety pink." [Ÿ] "Growth vigorous; flower very large, full, center in a rosette formation; color, fresh bright pink." [S]

VICOMTESSE LAURE DE GIRONDE

Pradel, 1852

"Moderately vigorous bush; flowers medium-sized, full, imbricated, clear delicate pink." [I'H56/200]

VICTOR-EMMANUEL

Guillot père, 1859

"Purple and purplish-maroon, large and double, good and distinct." [FP] "Medium or large, full, red, varies to purple, very beautiful." [JDR59/28] "Richly-coloured and finely-shaped flowers." [R8] "Admirable in color and form, velvety black carmine." [JR3/29] "Moderate vigor." [S] Victor Emmanuel II, 1st king of Italy (2nd of that name of Sardinia); lived 1820–1878.

VICTOR LE BIHAN

Guillot père, 1868

"Beautiful bright carmine pink." [JR3/28] "Flower very large, full; well-formed." [S]

VICTOR LEMOINE

Lévêque, 1888

"Very vigorous bush; large dark green leaves. Blossom large, very well formed, dark red nuanced purple, brown, and violet. Very beautiful." [JR12/181]

VICTORY ROSE

Dingee-Conard, 1901

"Pink." [Ÿ]

VILLE DE LYON

Ducher, 1866

"Metallic rose and silvery-white, flowers large, full and of fine form; habit vigorous." [JC] "Very vigorous hybrid; flowers upright, very large, globular, full, and very well formed; deep pink. Good for forcing." [RJC66/209]

VILLE DE SAINT-DENIS

Thomas, 1853

Sport or seedling of 'La Reine' (HP).

"Flowers large, full, beautiful pink nuanced brighter." [I'H54/15] "Carmine pink . . . inferior, however, to ['Louise Peyronny' (HP)]." [R-H63] "Bright crimson." [S] "Rosy-carmine, flowers large and globular, exquisitely formed; a free growing, constant, and excellent rose." [JC] "Vigorous bush from 'La Reine', the characteristics of which are retained in this variety; flowers large, very full, beautiful red. Good variety." [I'H56/251]

VINCENT-HIPPOLYTE DUVAL

H. Duval, 1879

"Dedicated to Mons Duval père . . . very vigorous, with very large, full, and well-formed flowers; color, beautiful bright carmine pink." [JR3/182]

VINCENTE PELUFFO

Lévêque, 1902

"Very vigorous bush, beautiful glaucous green foliage; flowers very large, full, well formed, light cerise pink nuanced darker. Very remontant." [JR26/149]

VIOLET QUEEN

G. Paul, 1892

"Violet red, medium size, full, tall." [Sn]

VIOLETTE BOUYER

(' — Bowyer')

Lacharme, 1881

From 'Jules Margottin' (HP) × 'Mlle de Sombreuil' (Cl. T).

"Very vigorous, large flowers, well formed, white nuanced very delicate flesh. Of the 'Jules Margottin' sort." [JR5/172] "Globular form, later a flaring cup, fragrant." [S] "A good grower, very distinct in habit. This is perhaps the earliest to bloom of all the H.P.'s mentioned here, and one of the few which at its best is of true globular shape. It is practically white, though tinted sometimes on the outer petals, and is only good in dry weather, being easily spoiled by rain. A free bloomer, but not of much use as an autumnal." [F-M2] "Lacharme had announced some new roses, and I [Mons Bouyer] asked him to give one of his newborns the name of my second granddaughter Violette Bouyer." [JR26/123]

VIRGINALE

Lacharme, 1858

"Pearly white, with the palest flesh centre, flowers of moderate size and well formed, though not full; an exquisite rose, but a delicate and unsatisfactory grower." [JC] "Moderate vigor; flower medium-sized, full, well formed, pure white." [I'H58/127] "A pure white rose raised from seed at Lyons, with petals rather too thin and unequal . . . still a very interesting variety, and quite worthy of culture." [R8]

VULCAIN
('Vulcan')
V. & C. Verdier, 1861

"Bright purplish-violet, shaded with black, good and distinct." [FP] "Rich crimson, double, well formed; a rose of splendid color." [EL] "Flower large, nearly full, deep intense violet purple, nuanced blackish, in clusters of 8–15." [l'H61/264] "Dwarf habit . . . small flowers of a deep purplish maroon colour." [R8] "Moderate vigor." [S] Vulcan, Roman god of fire.

VYSLANEC KALINA
Böhm, 1935

"Red, large, full, very fragrant, tall." [Sn]

WALTHAM STANDARD
W. Paul, 1897

"Violet crimson." [Ў] "Rich carmine color, shaded scarlet and violet; the slightly opened bud has a very bright color, with the very firm petals holding well to the end; flower and petals like those of 'A. K. Williams'. . . . Handsome foliage." [JR21/50] "Vigorous." [JR21/66] "Of fair growth and foliage, this variety produces moderately sized flowers of good shape and of beautiful colour with capital fragrance: but I am doubtful if it will survive many seasons among choice selections." [F-M2]

WHITE BARONESS
G. Paul, 1883
Sport of 'Baronne Adolphe de Rothschild' (HP).

"More double than 'Mabel Morrison'; color, pure white; vigorous." [S] "Flowers large and full." [P1] "Was studied for three years in the Cheshunt nurseries [*prior to release to commerce*]." [JR8/130]

WILLIAM GRIFFITH
Portemer, 1850

"Glossy pink changing to light satin-rose, petals curiously curved; a very beautiful and free growing rose." [JC] "An old and excellent rose, of a peculiar light satin rose-color." [FP] "Remarkable for the elegance and profusion of its flowers." [R8] "Pink, much resembling 'Comtesse Cécile de Chabrillant', but the flowers are somewhat smaller, the wood smoother, and in habit it is more vigorous, but also much more liable to injury from the cold." [EL] "A fine distinct variety, of robust and upright growth; the flowers are of a rosy lilac, with petals very stout and leathery, and with foliage luxuriant and Bourbon-like." [C] "Very remontant hybrid . . . large, slightly hooked, reddish thorns. The leaves are composed of 5–7 lush leaflets, reddish in youth, then dark green above, pale beneath, oval-cordate, slightly rugose; petiole glandular-bristly, with some prickles beneath. Flowers fragrant, deep pink with frosty reflections, very full, cupped, rather like those of the Centifolia, opening perfectly, solitary or in twos or threes at the tip of the cane." [l'H51/8] "This rose is, without a doubt, one of the best introductions of this decade; its habit is vigorous, its canes strong and light green, clothed in a fine coating of 'bloom' or glaucous dust, often tinted brown; thorns reddish, very large at the base; foliage dark green, glaucescent beneath. The blossoms have the form of our old well-beloved Centifolia, and are a very fresh carmine pink. This beautiful rose is for sale for 15 francs at the breeder's, Mons Portemer's, nurseryman at Gentilly." [M-V50/192] "In this beautiful plate [picturing William Griffith] in which the calm and reflective expression is animated by an elegant and melancholy frown, we have the whole story of a strong intelligence pausing in its wonderful dreams of the future. William Griffith is one of that phalanx of botanists who, having chosen to devote themselves to Science . . . work on the yoked disciplines of organic anatomy and physiology, the morphological ramifications of their structure, and the study of plants considered as members of floras and natural groups. Born March 4, 1810, at Ham Common, near Kingston-on-the-Thames in Surrey, he undertook, when it came time to choose a career, to study medicine. His taste for Botany brought him to the attention of Lindley. In 1832, we find him debuting as an author, and becoming an assistant surgeon in the service of the East India Company. Due to this position . . . W. Griffith was able to explore, as a naturalist, the most wide-ranging possessions of the Company." [VH49/535b]

WILLIAM WARDEN
Mitchell, 1878
Sport of 'Mme Clémence Joigneaux' (HP).

"Light pink." [Ў] "Salmon-pink." [H] "Fine shape." [P1] "Vigorous growth . . . flower very large, full; carmine red nuanced pink." [S] "The habit, etc., is the same as that of the parent." [EL]

Chapter Eight
NOISETTES AND CLIMBERS

"The Noisettes originated during John Champneys' time in Charleston, South Carolina. From *R. moschata* pollinated by the pink *R. bengalensis* [*presumed to be 'Parsons' Pink China'*], he obtained a variety which he named 'Champneys' Pink Cluster'. The date of this development is not certain, and could be any time between 1802 and 1805. Philippe Noisette, who lived in Charleston and who was related to Champneys, sowed the seeds of this rose, which gave a remontant variety with flesh-white flowers [*'Blush Noisette'*]. Much contented, he took it to his brother Louis, who was a Parisian horticulturalist. These [*cuttings?*] would propagate the new race." [JR25/152]

"It [*the first Noisette*] was raised by a gentleman on Long Island; a plant was brought from there by Mons Landonne [*or 'Lendormi'; see below*], an intimate acquaintance of the raiser, to Rouen, where it was cultivated in large quantities. Pailland, a gardener at Rouen [*was growing it already*], when Noisette of Paris received a plant from his brother in America. . . . [*Noisette*] grew it under an iron cage in one of his houses for protection, while it was being commonly sold in Rouen at a moderate price! Prévost, the well-known nurseryman at Rouen, can attest to these facts." [Hstl:46–47]

"A note from John D. Legare, Esq., of Charleston, S.C. . . . informs us that the account . . . of its having been originated on Long Island . . . is entirely a fabrication. Its true history, he says, is that it was raised from seed by Mr. Philip [*sic*] Noisette, of Charleston. Mr. L. informs us that he was for many years acquainted with Mr. Noisette, who owned a small farm on Charleston neck. From his own lips Mr. Legare heard the account of the origin of this rose more than once. . . . Mr. Noisette frequently spoke of the attempts of the nurserymen in Europe to rob him of the honor of originating the first of this beautiful class of Roses. . . . Mr. Noisette mentioned to Mr. Legare the sorts of roses between which the original Noisette was a hybrid—but the latter does not recollect which were the varieties. 'Certain it is, however,' says Mr. Legare, 'no one in the neighborhood of Charleston but knows as to its originating here and by the hands of Mr. Philip Noisette.' " [Hstl:145]

"These [*the Noisettes*] are from the seeds of the rose found by John Champney[s] and sown by Philippe Noisette, florist, also of Charleston, which [seeds] gave rise to that [rose] which bears the name of a distinguished family of horticulturalists [*=the Noisette family*], a rose which the American nurseryman [*P. Noisette*] sent to his brother Louis in 1814, who possessed at that time at 51 rue du faubourg St.-Jacques, Paris, an immense horticultural establishment well-known throughout the world. Independently of this parcel sent to his brother, Philippe Noisette, two years later, sent two specimens of his rose to Mons Jacques Durand, a Rouen businessman, who took delivery in March of 1816, and put them under the care of Mons Prévost fils, able horticulturalist on the rue du Champ-des-Oiseaux of that city. In 1829, one could see at the home of the fancier Mons Lendormi [*or 'Landonne'; see above*], *also* of Rouen, one of those two plants sent by the Philippe Noisette establishment thirteen years before." [JR6/13]

"*Noisette Rose. Rosa Noisettiana, Bosc.* —Taken from America by Philippe Noisette, my brother, in 1814." [No] "One sees that Louis Noisette is very cautious in his *Manual* about speaking of the origin of the Rose which bears his name. . . . Without the Noisette Rose, who today would know Noisette?" [JR34/81]

"The first Noisette rose, as all good rosarians know, was produced in Charleston, S.C., by a horticulturalist heretofore known as John Champney. It is pleasant to have the interesting contact with his memory provided by the following letter from Julia R. Tunno, of Atlanta, Ga.: 'I would be glad if you will correct the name of my great-great-grandfather which was Champneys, and not Champney. His daughter, Sarah Champneys, was the last of the name, and when she married my great grandfather William Tunno, the name of Champneys ended. John Champneys was a rice planter, but a great lover of flowers, especially roses, and he had a wonderful flower-garden. In an old family Bible is this record, "John Champneys, son of John and Sarah Champneys (whose maiden name was Saunders), born December 28th , 1743, in Charleston, S.C., and baptized by Rev. Mr. Gay at Ashley River"; and on another page is this, "John Champneys died Wednesday, July 26th, 1820." ' " [ARA29/214]

"More than 25 varieties of Noisettes are comprised in that quantity [*of selections in Vibert's 1824 collection*] . . . which are mostly full-flowered. . . . [They are] destined to exercise a great influence on the cultivation — and the pleasure — of this beautiful family. . . . The deportment, the foliage, the form of the flowers and of the petals in these roses present more variety than is to be found in the Chinas. . . . Nature has given the Noisettes a liberality without precedent; scarcely born, already they have happily supplied us with all the colors from the most delicate to the darkest. The whites, the flesh, the pink, the rosy-pink, and the crimson have already shown up, the first three particularly, in a number of varieties; the white, so rare in the Chinas, leaves little to be desired. As for the perfume, lacking up till now in these, it has yielded to these essays, and I believe that I am able to assure you that we now possess one or two fragrant sorts." [V2] "Ten years after the introduction into France of the Noisette, the horticulturalists had raised a hundred and two varieties!" [PIB] "As the Champney [*sic*] rose produces seeds far more abundantly than the 'Blush Noisette', it has doubtless been the parent of much the greatest number." [WRP]

"Since that time [*that of the original introduction of the Noisette into France in 1814*], Mons Robert, director of the Toulon botanical garden, has raised an identical rose from a Musk Rose seed." [JF] "What do I receive from Mons Robert, director of the marine garden at Toulon, but a rose pretty nearly just like the [*original*] Noisette in all ways, except that the flowers, instead of being white with a light touch of pink on the outer petals, are entirely the latter color. Hm! This new rose of Mons Robert's came from a seed which he himself gathered from the Musk Rose in a garden in Hyères in Provence. Thus, it is evident that the Noisette Rose and that of Mons Robert can't be considered as otherwise than as having come from the Musk Rose." [L-D] "At Coubert, a small town in Brie, Mons Cochet the elder [*i.e., Pierre Cochet*], in 1862 or 1863, obtained from seeds of an ordinary *R. semperflorens*, usually called the Bengal Rose, which had been naturally pollinated by a Moschata hybrid — 'Princesse de Nassau' — which was close by, a seedling which was quite identical with *R. Noisettiana* [*sic*; ='Blush Noisette'], save that the flowers were single, and more carminey than the type." [JR6/12]

"There was a time when the Noisettes, complex hybrids though they were, preserved their characteristics to some degree, and were easy to recognize in the garden. But not for long. When the Tea roses were, naturally or artificially, crossed with the Noisettes or their hybrids, it suddenly brought into being a whole new series of Roses which the rosarians were at their wits' ends to classify." [JR34/96] "We believe that the first Hybrid Noisette was 'Prudence Rœser', developed around 1840 by Mons Rœser at Crécy [*"Prudence Rœser. Noisette. Growth very vigorous; flower medium-sized, very full, cupped; color, bright pink, fawn at the center."* [S].*" [Cx]

Those wishing to survey all the climbers listed in this book should check among the Bourbons, Hybrid Bourbons, and Hybrid Chinas, several of which are "climberish," and among the Teas, most of which will "climb" under the right conditions. Some Hybrid Perpetuals and Hybrid Teas of extra-vigorous growth may serve as pillar-type climbers.

"With so many climbing roses to choose from . . . monotony should not exist. It can only be blamed upon a lack of knowledge that different kinds of roses can be obtained and to a certain sheep-like tendency in many humans to follow where their neighbors lead." [GAS]

AIMÉE VIBERT   PLATE 172
('Repens')
Vibert, 1828
Noisette
From 'Champneys' Pink Cluster' (N) × *R. sempervirens* 'Plena'.

"Flowers pure white, medium size, full, freely borne in umbel-like clusters. Buds tinted with red. Foliage shining, deep green. Branches springing up from the base, hence this rose is particularly suitable for planting on graves." [Hn] "Cup., pure white, in clusters, beautiful." [CC] "White, blushing." [JR2/60] "Pure white, produced in large clusters, of medium size, full; form compact; growth vigorous . . . foliage of a dark green and shining." [P1] "Flowers mid-sized, full, well-formed, erect when opening, nodding in maturity, milk-white, musk-scent very marked, in clusters of many flowers on big canes, giving a charming appearance of a well-made bouquet, and bearing simultaneously both the milky flowers and the many attractive buds which are often shaded carmine — all in all a very pretty sight." [JR5/24] "Branches covered with very rich and brilliant foliage, and when it blooms it produces veritable garlands of snowy white to very charming effect." [JR18/136] "Very free-flowering." [H] "Of beautiful form; the foliage is a dark lustrous green; growth vigorous." [EL] "A very delicate grower." [HstXI:225] "Very vigorous." [J] "Not among the most vigorous in growth of the Noisettes." [FP] "Rather lax climber or shrub." [Hk] "Good for pillars." [F-M] "Perfect in form, a profuse bloomer . . . exquisite." [Bu] "Heavy everblooming groundcover with fine foliage and horizontal growth." [Capt28] "Growth: 10–15 [ft; ca. 3–4.5 m]. Lovely, delicate light-green foliage. Good repeat bloom." [Lg] "12 × 10 [ft; ca. 3.5 × 3 m]." [B] "Branches of moderate size, more or less long depending upon the vigor of the particular specimen; bark green, smooth, nearly thornless; thorns sparse, small, short, and somewhat reflexed. Leaves a handsome green, divided into 5 or 7 leaflets, or 3 with those subtending the inflorescence; the leaflets are oval-elongate, pointed, and finely toothed; leafstalk green, weak, often curled, having a number of small light green prickles beneath. Flower, about two in across [ca. 5 cm], very full, rounded, blooming in clusters of 3–20 and sometimes more, depending upon the vigor of the branch; color, pure white; outer petals concave; those of the center, small and rumpled; bud washed carmine; flower stem slender, green, a little

reddish where the sun hits. Calyx medium-sized, rounded; sepals leaf-like. Lightly fragrant, this variety is notable for its vigor." [JF] "One of the introductions of Mons Vibert, who raised it at his breeding-grounds at Longjumeau, near Paris, in 1828. Though 18 years separate us from the day this Rose bloomed for the first time, and despite the more than four thousand introductions which have been paraded before our eyes since 1828, of which nearly 500 have been Noisettes, not one of these conquerors has been able to dethrone 'Aimée Vibert'. As the Rose of the King [*unexplained*], it is popular in the markets, well-liked by both proud lady and trullion; its white splashes appear in both royal garden and doorstep plot. Some people believe that this rose was a sport of *R. semperflorens* perpetuated by grafting. — This is of little importance. Let us admire the flower without caring whether it be seedling or sport. In either case, all we would have to show for our trouble would be to be able to say ' . . . which was sown . . . ' or ' . . . which was grafted. . . . ' 'Aimée Vibert' is the sort of Noisette that has short branches, all or nearly all flower-bearing, in the way of the Chinas. . . . The flower . . . is composed of numerous small petals which unite in a veritable rosette. In all regards, this is a charming rose." [PIB] *Curtis* evidently introduced a 'Climbing Aimée Vibert' in 1841: "It's an excellent rose for fences, giving canes of 4–5 meters [ca. 13–16 ft], and is pretty robust. I prune it back to 15 to 20 eyes [*buds*], and I get wonderful bloom." [JR10/10] "This very exquisite variety was grown from seed of a rose that blooms only once in the season (Sempervirens Pleno) by J. P. Vibert, of Lonjeameaux [*sic*], near Paris. When I visited him, in 1839, whilst discoursing upon roses, he directed my attention with great enthusiasm to this plant, and said, 'Celle ci est si belle, que Je lui ai donné le nom de ma fille chérie — Aimée Vibert' [*sic; 'It's so pretty that I gave it the name of my dear daughter — Aimée Vibert'*]. This enthusiasm can be easily understood by those who, like myself, have been so fortunate as to see the two 'Aimée Viberts' — the rose and the young girl — both in their full bloom, and both as lovely as their sweet name." [Bu] "Aimée Vibert" was also the name of Vibert's mother.

We find the following for the synonym 'Repens': "*Rosa Noisettiana Repens*. Obtained by Mons Marie Noisette, nurseryman at Brie-Comte-Robert. Rampant stems, 10 to 12 ft long, double flowers of a sparkling white in large bouquets, all of which sufficiently distinguish this rose from all others, and shows its proper use, as an 'own-root' for covering rocks; or, grafted on the briar at eight to ten ft, it will 'weep' all the way to the ground." [R-H 29/114]

[AIMÉE VIBERT JAUNE]
Listed as 'Mme Brunner'.

ALISTER STELLA GRAY   PLATE 67
A. H. Gray/G. Paul, 1894
Noisette
"Pale yellow with orange center, changing to white as flowers expand; small, and produced in fine clusters. A continuous bloomer." [P1] "Yolk-yellow . . . flower 3 in across [ca. 7.5 cm]." [T2] "Pale yellow." [J] "Buff." [J] "Deep yellow with lighter edges; flowers in clusters." [Th] "Pale and rather dull yellow." [F-M2] "Self yellow clusters summer and autumn." [E] "Buff-yellow buds . . . flowers that fade to ivory-white . . . 15 [ft; ca. 4.5 m]." [HRG] "Flowers beautifully formed." [Hk] "Shapely. . . . Rich tea scent . . . long flowering season . . . 15 × 10 [ft; ca. 4.5 × 3 m]." [B] "Free-flowering miniature." [H] "Growth: 10–12 [ft; ca. 3–3.5 m]. Repeats bloom well." [Lg] "Very vigorous. The buds are quite pretty and seem made to be painted." [JR23/42] "Short zigzag shoots, horizontally poised glossy leaves, few thorns." [T2] "Good in South." [ARA18/119] "A slow starter." [Hk] "Of vigorous growth and upright rather branching habit; it throws up good strong branches to about 8-ft. high [ca. 2.25 m], which arch if left untrained, and have smooth green bark bronzing in autumn to a nice russet tint on the sunny side. . . . The flowering period is long. . . . The flowers are about a couple of in across, semi-double, sometimes full, and are carried in fair trusses or rather sprays. They possess a fragrance that is not strong, but quite distinct [suggesting] the musk rose. . . . The buds are pretty and lasting and of a deep buff yellow and the expanded flowers are pale yellow with a centre of light orange yellow . . . it often takes some time to 'get started.' . . . The strong point of this Rose is its early autumn flowering. . . . Its weak points are that though a pretty little Rose, in neither colour nor shape is it very striking, and the early flowers are poor." [NRS/11] "Throughout the whole Summer and Autumn it was a solid mass of blossom, every little new brown shoot from the ground upward being tipped with flower buds." [K1] "The best of all Roses for stumps." [Wr]

AMERICAN BEAUTY, CL.
Hoopes Bros. & Thomas, 1909
From an unnamed seedling (parentage: *R. wichuraiana* × 'Marion Dingee' [T]) × 'American Beauty' (HP).
"Carmine to rich imperial pink — blues in heat, fades quickly; fine buds; large, double flowers. . . . Gives one large burst of bloom only. Vigorous, foliage usually lost early." [Th2] "Cerise flowers blue with age. Very large, cupped. . . . Vigorous to 12 to 15 ft [ca. 3.5–4.5 m]. Best grown in semishade to slow up fading . . . sweet and heady damask fragrance." [W] "Rich rosy crimson . . . remarkable amount of spring bloom . . . practically no summer or fall bloom. Loses foliage early." [ARA17/26] "Flower red nuanced vermilion as in its mother, and similarly perfumed as well. Grows very strongly, and annually gives scions of 9 to 12 ft [ca. 2.75–3.5 m], durable as an oak; flower large; blooms profusely and early, over four weeks, then less abundantly up to fall. A good variety for pillars and columns." [JR38/88–89] "Very useful and very glorious in spring." [ET] "The '[Climbing] American Beauty' reposed in luxury less than a foot above the body of a finally useful cat that had been run over on the highway." [ARA25/23]

ANNIE VIBERT
Vibert?, pre-1871
Noisette
"Double, medium-sized and pink on opening, then white . . . fragrant . . . vigorous . . . 4 metres or more [ca. 12 ft or so] . . . glossy green foliage and long arching young growths." [G] Listed as a "standard blooming" rose in HstXXV:262. We know of no one in Vibert's family named "Annie". . . .

ARCHDUCHESS CHARLOTTE
Earing/Kern Rose Nurs., 1975
Sport of 'Archiduc Charles' (Ch).
Rose-pink climbing China.

ARDS ROVER   PLATE 205
A. Dickson, 1898
Hybrid Perpetual
"Crimson, shaded maroon; a good pillar rose, and moderate climber." [P1] "Flowers globular, deep crimson." [W/Hn] "Good-sized flowers with stiff petals." [F-M2] "Medium size; good form . . . spring only . . . very fragrant." [ARA17/26] "Shapely . . . strong scent . . . occasionally recurrent . . . 15 × 10 [ft; ca. 4.5 × 3 m]." [B] "Fine growth." [ARA18/119] "Handsome foliage . . . best as a Pillar Rose." [F-M2] "[Excellent in Norway]." [ARA20/46] "For a low wall, say 4-ft. to 6-ft. [ca. 1.25–1.75 m] high, is a gem, flowering very profusely quite early in the season." [NRS/17] "For a rose planted for a grand effect during its bloom, considering the color, size, and its vigorous growth, it easily surpasses those varieties for which one searches either because of their renown, or because of the magniloquent descriptions with which catalogs try to woo amateurs. . . . The word 'Rover' means 'Rambler' . . . the Ards Peninsula, where the introducer resides. It is very vigorous, climbing, quite floriferous, giving large blossoms, full, well-formed, crimson shaded maroon-brown. The graceful bud is supported by a long and rigid stem." [JR28/43] "Carries its foliage late into the autumn . . . flowers freely and well in early summer, the blooms being fairly large, nicely shaped in the bud, and of a fine crimson colour, which looks well in the garden. The autumn flowering is sparse and, particularly in wet weather, the colour is not so bright as in summer, but in favourable weather they look well. The sparseness of the autumn flowers, and a slight tendency at that time of year to mildew, are its worst defects as a Pillar Rose; its good qualities are its ready and rapid growth, the ease with which it adapts itself to life on a Pillar, and its bright handsome colour and fragrance." [NRS/14]

AUGUSTA
Listed as 'Solfatare'.

AUTUMNALIS
Noisette?, 1812
Noisette
"White flushed pink and red . . . in many flowered corymbs . . . 8 × 6 [ft; ca. 2.25 × 1.75 m]." [B] Jg calls it an English Hybrid Musk of unknown date. Conceivably a sibling or near relative of 'Blush Noisette'. Phillips & Rix equate it with 'Princesse de Nassau', Laffay's ca. 1835 Musk hybrid.

BEAUTY OF GLAZENWOOD
Listed as 'Fortune's Double Yellow'.

BELLE BLANCA
Introducer and date unknown
Hybrid Gigantea
Presumably a sport of 'Belle Portugaise' (HGig).
"Large climbing shrub, large semi-double white flowers." [HRG87]

BELLE LYONNAISE   PLATE 180
Levet, 1870
Noisette
Seedling of 'Gloire de Dijon' (N).
Not to be confused with Lacharme's pink 1854 HP of the same name.
"Deep lemon." [H] "Well-shaped, fragrant, yellow." [ARA29/98] "Dark canary passing to salmon shades." [JR8/26] "Deep canary-yellow, changing to white, slightly tinted with salmon, large, full, and of fine form." [P1] "Large or very large, very full, cup-shaped, canary-yellow. Very vigorous. . . . A beautiful sweet-scented rose." [Hn] "Large yellow blooms, which are not very freely produced." [OM] "One is always sure of some of its huge, solid blossoms till November." [K1] "Very vigorous grower." [FRB] "One of the most remarkable and best. . . . The occupation of a part of France by the German army in 1870–1871 restricted the distribution of this beautiful rose to its source. . . . This rose, of the highest merit . . . is a very vigorous plant . . . its flower is large, full, and well-formed . . . with a very satisfying fragrance . . . very floriferous." [JR1/1/14] "Very handsome foliage, ample." [JR3/142] "Leaves . . . strongly toothed . . . very floriferous and vigorous, but only for the first two or three years." [JR10/36]

BELLE MARSEILLAISE
Listed as 'Fellemberg'.

BELLE PORTUGAISE
('Belle of Portugal')
Cayeux, ca. 1905
Hybrid Gigantea
From *R. gigantea* × ? 'Reine Marie Henriette' (Cl. HT).
"Flesh-pink, spring only, but very profuse." [W] "Loosely double flower . . . composed of silky quilled petals, rolled at the edges, creamy salmon with deeper reverse." [T2] "Vigorous . . . beautiful pointed buds." [HRG] "Profuse foliage . . . 20 × 10 [ft; ca. 6 × 3 m]." [B] "He [*Dr. Franchesci Fenzi*] imported 'Belle of Portugal' from the Lisbon Botanical Garden. . . . From Dr. [Fenzi's] garden in Santa Barbara [California], 'Belle of Portugal' gradually found its way over California and into other Southern states." [ARA32/92]

BELLE VICHYSOISE   PLATE 204
('Cornélie'?)
Lévêque, 1895
Noisette
"A climbing perpetual variety with pale pink flowers, produced in clusters." [P1] "Extra vigorous, handsome slightly glaucous foliage, blooms in clusters of 20–30 of medium or small size, pinkish white or light pink, the two colors appearing simultaneously in the same panicle. Very pretty; superb." [JR19/164] "A vigorous bush or pillar 8 ft [ca. 2.25 m] or more high with recurrent clusters of 30 to 50 white or pinkish flowers." [GAS] "Taking the cure at Vichy, Mons Lévêque noticed the pretty flowers of a rose climbing on the orangery wall. . . . Struck by its astonishing vigor as well as by the abundant bloom of the variety, resembling nothing he had [heretofore] seen in cultivation, this rosarian took a cutting to his friend Mons Eugène Verdier. . . . The plant . . . is of extraordinary growth, producing very long branches covered with quite numerous clusters of a pretty blush white, sometimes deeper in

color. . . . For two years, we have scrutinized this Noisette in full bloom, and, compared with the variety 'Cornélie', of Moreau-Robert, 1858, there seems to be no difference." [JR27/88]

BLACK BOY
A. Clark, 1919
From 'Étoile de France' (HT) × 'Bardou Job' (B).
"Dark red satin petals shaded with black velvet." [ARA32/120] "Semi-double." [Th2] "Deep crimson, shaded with blackish maroon, overlaying scarlet . . . good mildew-proof foliage and fine climbing habit . . . opens quickly, retains its rich color." [TS] "Without a peer . . . in formation of flower, richness of color, and freedom of bloom." [PP28] "Excellent growth the first season, giving a few superb, dark red flowers, which blackened agreeably instead of fading." [ARA27/129] "Lustrous, mildew-free leaves." [ARA23/119] "Highly resistant to mildew and an intermittent bloomer until midsummer but sparingly thereafter." [ARA35/171] "15 ft tall [ca. 4.5 m] in a season." [ARA31/186] "Dark crimson blooms of medium size. A vigorous climber which comes into bloom early. It makes a fine splash of color." [ARA30/153]

BLAIRII Nº1
Blair, 1845
Hybrid China
Two parentages given: (1) 'Parks' Yellow' (T) × 'Hardy Rose'; (2) "A China Rose" × 'Tuscany' (Gallica, maroon).
"Brilliant roseate, splendid, very fragrant." [WRP] "Flowers bright rose, sometimes tinged with lake, large and semi-double; form, cupped. Raised at Stamford Hill, near London, a few years since, by Mr. Blair . . . habit, branching; growth, vigorous." [P] "Very double." [JR9/162] "Large, blowsy, scented . . . soft blush pink . . . good climber . . . 8 × 6 [ft; ca. 2.25 × 1.75 m]." [B]

BLAIRII Nº2
Blair, 1845
Hybrid China
Same parentage as 'Blairii Nº 1'.
"Blush, rose center." [HoBoIV/318] "Delicate flesh." [H] "Large, flattish blooms of pale pink. Fragrant. Very double and free flowering." [B] "Flower rosy blush, very large and double. Habit, branching; growth, vigorous; foliage, fine. One of the largest of Roses, and one of the freest growers, often attaining to ten or twelve ft [ca. 3–3.5 m] in one season." [P] "There is no rose tree more generally useful. If its luxuriant shoots are only reduced one fourth of their length in pruning (the weakly wood being altogether excised), it produces its blushing beauties in abundance, amid foliage large and glossy." [R1/159] "Much esteemed in England as a Pillar rose. We do not value it highly for this climate [*that of New York*]." [EL] "A very distinct and unique variety, so impatient of the knife, that if pruned at all severely, it will scarcely put forth a flower: it is perhaps better as a pillar rose than grown in any other mode, as it shoots ten or twelve ft [ca. 3–3.5 m] in one season, and its pendulous clusters of flowers, which are produced from these long shoots unshortened, have a beautiful effect on a pillar." [R8] "A rare charm." [J]

[BLAIRII Nº3]
Blair, 1845
Hybrid China
Same parentage as 'Blairii Nº 1'.
"Pink." [LS]

BLANC PUR
(trans., 'Pure White')
Mauget, 1827
Noisette

"White, exterior greenish shades, large-flowered, double; growth very strong, to . . . 13.2 ft [=4 m]." [Kr] "Extremely vigorous and has large lush leaves, big thorns and enormous pure white full flowers which are fragrant." [G]

BLUSH NOISETTE
('Flesh-Coloured Noisette')
Noisette, 1814
Noisette
Seedling of 'Champneys' Pink Cluster' (N).

"Pinkish-white . . . good repeat bloom. Attractive light green foliage . . . 8–10 [ft; ca. 2.25 × 3 m]." [Lg] "5 × 4 [ft; ca. 1.5 × 1.25 m]." [B] "Flesh-white; flower small; very vigorous; climbing." [Cx] "More double than its parent, and of much more dwarf and compact growth; the flowers in very large dense panicles." [WRP] "Shrub, very vigorous. Branches, glossy and flexile, armed with large strong thorns. Leaflets, oval, near together, pointed or acuminated; of a delicate green. Tube of calyx, oval-fusiform. Flowers, middle-sized, regular, very double, flesh-coloured." [Go] See the headnote to this chapter for the original distribution of 'Blush Noisette'. "Noisette (Louis). — Born in 1772, died at Paris in 1849. Renowned horticulturalist; built one of the first winter gardens. Introduced the Tree Peony, the Noisette Rose, and the American strawberry, and improved the Dahlia. Responsible for *Manuel Complet du Jardinier, Jardin fruitier,* etc." [R-HC]

BOUQUET D'OR
Ducher, 1872
Noisette
Seedling of 'Gloire de Dijon' (N).

"Dark coppery yellow, a beautiful variety; a good climber." [FRB] "A handsome bright yellow with touches of orange, a semi-climber." [JR10/46] "Dark yellow. An improved 'Gloire de Dijon'." [H] "Buff and orange . . . very vigorous." [J] "A lot of pink." [Hk] "Very double, yellow with coppery salmon center. Good repeat bloom . . . 15–20 [ft; ca. 4.5–6 m]." [Lg] "Coppery-salmon with yellow centre. Slightly scented. Vigorous . . . 10 × 6 [ft; ca. 3 × 1.75 m]." [B] "Large, finely formed, lemon-yellow, fragrant . . . shaded rose." [ARA29/98] "Buff yellow. — Vigorous pillar." [JP] "Pale yellow, centres coppery, large and full, and of good form; growth vigorous. One of the best." [P1] "Somewhat similar to 'Gloire de Dijon'; the blooms, which are of fairly good shape in the bud, are creamy yellow with deeper centre." [OM] "Exquisite when half open." [Hn] "Very vigorous; flower large, full, fragrant, cupped." [S] "Vigorous branches, green on one side, brownish on the other; foliage of 5–7 leaflets, shiny, thick, reddish in youth." [JR10/59–60] "Superior to 'Gloire de Dijon' . . . in form . . . color and freedom from mildew . . . [but] not so prolific." [Capt28] "A capital rose." [HRH]

BOUQUET TOUT FAIT
(trans., 'Perfect Bouquet')
Laffay, pre-1836
Noisette

"Creamy white, produced in large handsome clusters, of medium size, very double; form, expanded. Growth, vigorous. Very sweet." [P] "Middle-sized, full; of a nankin-tinted white, bearing numerous flowers." [Go] "Very fragrant." [S] "A pillar noisette . . . a most vigorous grower, forming immense corymbs; this may be

taken for the original Noisette at first sight, but it is more fragrant, and its flowers buff towards their center." [WRP] "Repeats bloom well . . . 5–10 [ft; ca. 1.5–3 m]." [Lg]

CAPTAIN CHRISTY, CL.
Ducher Children and Successors, 1881
Hybrid Tea
Sport of 'Captain Christy' (HT).

"Blush and pink." [J] "Large, full double blooms of soft pink with darker center, vigorous . . . to 8 [ft; ca. 2.25 m]." [HRG] "Globular flowers are generously produced and fragrant . . . 12 × 10 [ft; ca. 3.5 × 3 m]." [B] "Delicate flesh colour, deeper in the centre, large." [P1] "Seldom gives fall blooms." [Th2] "Same as 'Captain Christy', except more floriferous, and of a climbing habit." [JR5/186] "Poor grower; shy bloomer." [ARA18/121] "Even more delightful [than the bush form], because more vigorous and abundant in blossoms. . . . With me it certainly does better than its dwarf original; and nothing could exceed the perfection of its blossoms outside a south window on a day in early June; while as I write these words on almost the last day of October, a great six-inch flower [ca. 1.5 dm] as well as many half-open buds look in at that same window on the Chrysanthemums that fill the vases within. In a neighbour's sheltered garden a much older plant than mine climbs over a wide wooden arch, and when in full bloom it is worth a journey to behold its huge blossoms, borne so freely on long stalks, and set off by the singularly fine foliage." [K1]

CÉCILE BRUNNER, CL.
Listed as 'Mlle Cécile Brunner, Cl'.

CÉLINE FORESTIER   PLATE 174
('Lusiadas', 'Liésis')
Trouillard, 1842
Noisette
Affiliated with 'Lamarque' (N).

"Pale yellow, deepening toward the centre." [EL] "A pretty canary-yellow." [BJ] "Large very full delicate flowers of white shading to lemon-yellow, blushing delicate pink . . . to 6 [ft; ca. 1.75 m]." [HRG] "Fairly free flowering; old-gold." [ARA17/26] "Medium-sized, full, well-formed, light yellow." [JR1/2/8] "Free bloomer, fair autumnal . . . prettily colored buds add much to the beauty of the truss." [F-M2] "Pale primrose to white . . . abundant, healthy, light green foliage. Well scented . . . 6 × 4 [ft; ca. 1.75 × 1.25 m]." [B] "Vigorous, large-flowered, blossoms full, well-formed, of a handsome and magnificent golden yellow." [JR4/153] "Not, I think, a very quick grower . . . though, perhaps, it is never showy, I find the nicely shaped and pointed flowers of sulphur-yellow with a deeper centre very homely and attractive. When a situation suits it and it is doing well, it flowers fairly freely and continuously." [NRS/14] "Large and full; form cupped." [P1] "Medium-sized, flat." [JR3/29] "A pleasant scent." [JR18/136] "Spicy fragrance." [G] "Flowers freely in clusters." [Hn] "Of good growth, but not sufficiently lengthy to make a climber." [F-M2] "An old variety, but an excellent climber." [FRB] "Good growth; wood and foliage very distinct, latter nearly evergreen and glazed, a proof against mildew." [B&V] "Vigorous, somewhat 'climbing,' with divergent branches with green bark, brown flat thorns, sparse and small and towards the extremities of the branches . . . flower about 2.5 in across [ca. 6.25 cm], fragrant, flat, cupped, either in a cluster or solitary; pale yellow, darker at the center, often washed pink, outer petals pointed red. . . . It bears the name of a close friend of Mons Trouillard." [JR10/93]

CHAMPNEYS' PINK CLUSTER
('Champneyana', 'Chamnagagna', etc.)
Champneys, ca. 1802
Noisette
From *R. moschata* × *R. chinensis* 'Parsons' Pink'.

"Light pink, a rampant grower, profuse bloomer, quite hardy . . . it is universally cultivated." [Bu] "Flower small, loose, large clusters; light pink. Delicate light green foliage. Repeats bloom well with good watering and fertilizing . . . 8–12 [ft; ca. 2.25–3.5 m]." [Lg] "Small blush pink double blooms in clusters." [HRG] "Rosy white." [Sx] "Very pale pink and heavily clustering." [ARA36/17] "Semi-double." [JR4/60] "Although not full double, is still quite a favorite for its rapid growth, its appropriateness for pillars and other climbing positions, and for the profusion of its flowers which are in very large panicles much more diffuse than [those of 'Blush Noisette'] . . . produces seed far more abundantly than the 'Blush Noisette'." [WRP] "Shrub, having a purple bark. Leaflets, five or seven; oval, pointed, notched; green on the upper surface, whitish underneath. . . . Flowers, large; deep flesh-coloured, slightly fragrant." [Go] "A rose long well known and very widely diffused. It was raised from seed by the late John Champney[s], Esq., of Charleston, S.C., an eminent and most liberal votary of Flora, from the seed of the White Musk Rose, or *Rosa Moschata*, fertilized by the old Blush China, and as he had been for a long period in constant correspondence with the late William Prince, he most kindly presented him with two tubs, each containing six plants, grown from cuttings of the original plant. From these an immense number were propagated and sent to England and France." [WRP]

CHÂTEAU DE CLOS-VOUGEOT, CL.
Morse, 1920
Hybrid Tea
Sport of 'Château de Clos-Vougeot' (HT).

"Deep velvety red . . . highly scented. Glossy foliage but of sprawly habit . . . 15 × 8 [ft; ca. 4.5 × 2.25 m]." [B] "Superb, everblooming, blackish red rose, turning darker with age. . . . Fine growth (8 ft [ca. 2.25 m]) . . . holds foliage better than dwarf." [PP28] "Bud very large; flower very large, full, open form, very double, borne singly and together on long stems; very lasting; strong fragrance. . . . Foliage abundant, medium size, leathery, rich green; disease resistant. Very vigorous and free blooming, producing its blooms from June to September. Very hardy." [ARA20/126] "Though a shy bloomer, is well worth growing." [ARA18/79] "Foliage is lost early." [Th2] "Growth usually poor . . . distinct. Valuable." [Capt28]

CHINA DOLL, CL.
Weeks, 1977
Polyantha
Sport of 'China Doll' (Pol).

Light pink; semi-double; in clusters.

CHROMATELLA
('Cloth of Gold')
Coquereau/Vibert, 1843
Noisette
Seedling of 'Lamarque' (N).

"Sulphur-yellow, deeper center; large." [ARA17/26] "Large; double, deep golden yellow, fragrant." [ARA29/98] "Flowers creamy white, their centre yellow, varies as to colour and fulness, usually very large and very double; form, globular. Growth, vigorous.

A beautiful Rose, and sweet, but a shy bloomer . . . when thoroughly established it will flower." [P] "Quartered centers and stiff petals. . . . Continuous bloom . . . 8–12 [ft; ca. 2.25–3.5 m] . . . outstanding." [Lg] "Has charms of colour which . . . make it very desirable. It is described as . . . 'large double yellow, of as bright a shade as our old yellow rose [*R.* × *hemispherica*]; colour as yet unique in the group of Noisettes.' The English advertise it under the name of 'Cloth of Gold Noisette, with very large flowers and fine bold stiff petals, withstanding the effects of the sun, retaining its colour, a perfect yellow, equal to the Yellow Harrison Rose.' . . . It is very rare, and sells at twenty-five francs in France." [Bu] "Its flowers were like large golden bells . . . each flower was pendulous so that their bright yellow centres were most conspicuous . . . no yellow rose has approached in beauty this grand and remarkable variety." [R8] "A magnificent yellow rose, but opens with difficulty, and late." [S] "Large, unique, splendid." [CC] "Well formed, of a weakish color." [JR10/44–45] "A noble rose, of exquisite odor, and strong growth." [HstXI:225] "I have never seen a strong plant." [Hk] "Buds bruise . . . easily. . . . Special prey to mildew." [J] "A grand rose, but difficult to grow well." [EL] "The original plant still [*in 1857*] exists in Angers at Coquereau's ." [VH57/77]

"This new rose . . . upon which so many praises have been lavished . . . will, I fear, prove a downright disappointment. I have had six plants in my possession for eighteen months, and have never seen but two flowers." [Hstl:145] "Is, when in perfection, the most beautiful of all the yellow roses; but it is shy of bloom, and difficult of culture." [FP] "The wood requires roasting on a south wall to bring it to sufficient maturity to enable it to produce a full crop of blossoms." [NRS/17] "Flowers are borne February to May. Dormant in hot season, rampant in autumn—September to Christmas, if no frost." [ARA40/36–37] "This plant, with two others, budded . . . on seedling Noisette stocks, had last autumn made shoots from eight to ten ft high [ca. 2.25–3 m]. . . . These plants, in November and October, produced from ten to fifteen flowers each—the color, at this season, nearly equal to ['Harison's Yellow'], or one shade deeper than what they are." [Hstl:35] "Vigorous, very 'climbing,' giving magnificent and numerous flowers of a straw yellow." [JR10/140] "I have just seen several specimens . . . in full bloom. The flowers were very full, of a rather deep creamy yellow, yellowest in the center, and of a handsome cup shape. When compared with its twin sister, the 'Solfaterre' . . . the 'Cloth of Gold' was seen to be much superior in size and shape. . . . It quite answers the description of it as given by Rivers himself. . . . Near Natchez, I have seen it really blooming well, but never at the North." [Hstl:196]

"Outer petals pale yellow, with golden centre—globular—large and magnificent—sometimes a shy bloomer, of the most luxuriant growth. . . . There can be but little doubt that this is the finest of yellow autumnal Roses. . . . 'In the month of July, 1842, I [Rivers] was at Angers, and looking over the gardens of Mons Vibert, when his foreman brought me a bouquet of yellow Roses, some in bud and some about half expanded. I had never in my life seen anything so beautiful, and I warmly expressed my admiration . . . it had been raised from the seed of Noisette "Lamarque," by an amateur, living in the neighbourhood.' . . . Most beautiful foliage . . . blossoms, distinctly Tea scented, are of the most beautiful globular-shape, petals of great substance, with centres of the richest golden yellow. In spring the flowers are more frequently produced singly of a great size, but in the autumn it assumes its Noisette habit, blooming in clusters." [C] "Foliage large and spreading . . . of a dark green tint . . . flowers large, three in[ches] in diameter [7.5 cm], (I have often seen them four,) very double, petals firm, particularly the two outer rows, which are of a round form, guarding the interior ones well; these are smaller, more pointed, a little reflexed at the apex, becoming more irregular in their arrangement towards the centre of the flower, lasting long; not so fugacious as Noisette 'Solfaterre' [*sic*] . . . blooms freely in early summer, and late autumn; frequently transient flowers between these periods." [HstII:36] "The finest of climbing roses is the 'Cloth of Gold'. The finest of yellow roses is the 'Cloth of Gold'. The finest of Noisettes is the 'Cloth of Gold'. And yet how few know it except as a dwarf, grown in a pot or border, and bearing there a scanty supply of its noble blossoms. Nevertheless, it yields to none in the power of flowering, producing, if well managed, enormous quantities of golden balls. . . . To bloom it in perfection, it should never be pruned; and we add, that the plant must have some age to insure a profuse bloom." [HstXII:94] "It is indeed the queen of roses. In the bud, and until it is half expanded, it is impossible to conceive of an object more exquisite. . . . Nor indeed is it less perfect when fully blown." [HstII:47] "Queen Victoria carried the 'Cloth of Gold' rose when, with Albert, her consort, she opened the Crystal Palace in 1847." [ARA40/36] "Still, for its purpose, without equal as a mild-climate climber." [ARA31/30]

CLAIRE JACQUIER

Listed as 'Mlle Claire Jacquier'.

CLOTH OF GOLD

Listed as 'Chromatella'.

COLCESTRIA

B. R. Cant, 1916
Hybrid Tea

"Satin pink." [Cw] "Fair growth and bloom. A pillar rose." [ARA18/118] "Strong Pillar in habit of growth, with good stout foliage of a light green shade, and retained well in winter. The blooms are large and full; satin-rose in the centre, shading off to silver-pink in the outer petals, which are beautifully reflexed. It possesses a most delightful perfume. . . . Very free in flowering when established." [NRS/17]

CONDESA DA FOZ

Listed as 'Rêve d'Or'.

CORNÉLIE

See 'Belle Vichysoise'.

COOPER'S BURMESE ROSE

Cooper?, 1927
Hybrid Gigantea?
Possibly *R. lævigata* × *R. gigantea.*

"Fantastic, creamy-white rose . . . large, glossy foliage . . . large, single, scented flowers of immense attraction. Very vigorous . . . 35 × 20 [ft; ca. 11.25 × 6 m]." [B] "Very strong climber . . . 8 to 10 metres [ca. 30 ft or so] . . . single white flowers up to 50 mm [ca. 2 in]." [G]

CRAMOISI SUPÉRIEUR, CL.

Could be either of two varieties: 'Mme Couturier-Mention', listed in this chapter, or 'James Sprunt', listed in the chapter supplement.

CRÉPUSCULE

(trans., 'Twilight')
Dubreuil, 1904
Noisette

"Copper, yellow and pink shades." [OM] "Double, shapely . . . orange and apricot. Light green, plentiful foliage . . . 8 × 5 [ft; ca. 2.25 × 1.5 m]." [B] "In color and simple beauty its coppery fawn flower of exquisite grace, borne all season long, and its handsome foliage, are without a superior in my garden." [ARA34/44] "Of good vigor, bushy, elongated bud of perfect form and of pretty chamois yellow, the exterior petals striped nasturtium red. Flower, medium-sized, full, salmon-chamois, in clusters of 3–5, fragrant." [JR28/157] "Copper orange fading to apricot. . . . Continuous bloom . . . 5–8 [ft; ca. 1.5–2.25 m] . . . outstanding." [Lg] "Eager bloomer . . . to 12 [ft; ca. 3.5 m]." [HRG] "A climbing Noisette resembling 'Ma Capucine' [T; *listed in the Chapter 4 Supplement*]." [JR31/73]

CRIMSON CONQUEST

Chaplin Bros., 1931
Hybrid Tea
Sport of 'Red Letter Day' (HT).

"Medium-sized, semi-double, rich crimson . . . healthy plant with dark green, glossy foliage . . . 15 × 8 [ft; ca. 4.5 × 2.25 m]." [B1]

CUPID

B. R. Cant, 1915
Hybrid Tea

"Blush-colour." [OM] "Superbly formed. . . . Large, single, peachy . . . tawny gold anthers. Sparse bloom . . . 12 × 12 [ft; ca. 3.5 × 3.5 m]." [B] "Small growth; single blooms; attractive color, fading quickly." [ARA18/120] "A pillar Rose of strong growth . . . of good habit and abundant foliage. The flowers are single, four to five in across [ca. 1–1.25 dm], sometimes larger, and the colour in the half-developed stage is a glowing flesh, with a touch of peach, softening to delicate flesh and opal when fully expanded. In the Autumn it produces pretty rose-coloured seed pods." [NRS/15]

DAINTY BESS, CL.

VanBarneveld, 1935
Hybrid Tea
Sport of 'Dainty Bess' (HT).

Single pink. "Pointed buds . . . 3.5 to 4 inch [ca. 7.75 cm–1 dm] flowers with wine-colored stamens. . . . Heavy resistant foliage . . . vigorous . . . 8 to 10 ft [ca. 2.25–3 m]." [W] "An ideal Climber with flowers larger than the bush form . . . a few flowers all season." [ARA39/182–183] "Perfect foliage." [ARA38/181] "Grew well . . . should be in every garden." [ARA37/213]

DESCHAMPS

Deschamps, 1877
Noisette
'Longworth Rambler' is an 1880 climber by Liabaud which might — or might not — be synonymous.

"Cerise red fading to pink." [JR32/173] "Bright carmine, of medium size, but produced in great profusion. Grand in Autumn, and almost evergreen." [P1] "Cerise . . . cupped . . . very vigorous." [Cx] "An old rose that is free flowering, though the blooms are small and not very shapely. The colour is light crimson." [OM] "One of the best autumnal climbers that we have. The cerise-pink flowers are very pretty." [JR22/74]

DESPREZ À FLEUR JAUNE

('Jaune Desprez', 'Jean Desprez', 'Desprez', 'Noisette Desprez', 'Desprez à Fleurs Jaunes', etc., etc.)
Desprez/Sisley, 1830
Noisette
I am regarding 'Desprez' as being the same entity as 'Desprez à Fleur Jaune'. All authorities listing the 'Desprez' cognomen find *yellow* in the blossom, and authorities of the 'à Fleur Jaune' persuasion tend to find there some shade of *pink*.
From 'Blush Noisette' (N) × 'Parks' Yellow' (T).

"Rosy yellow." [Sx] "Red, buff, and sulphur." [WD] "Double, flat, strongly fragrant; very light yellow with apricot tints, fading to white. Repeats . . . 15–20 [ft; ca. 4.5–6 m]." [Lg] "Style of 'Gloire de Dijon'. Yellow shaded orange with buff tints . . . 20 × 10 [ft; ca. 6 × 3 m]." [B] "Reddish yellow." [HoBoIV/319] "Pink; saffron." [LS] "Buff or Fawn, deliciously fragrant, blooms freely in autumn . . . beautiful foliage." [H] "Double flowers fairly large, give the impression of soaking up the sun's warmth and paying it back in a sleepy scent . . . said to be shaded peach and apricot . . . rather white when I visited it." [Hk] "Pale yellow overshot with pink blush . . . to 20 [ft; ca. 6 m]." [HRG] "Rose, blended with coppery yellow, highly scented." [EL] "Cup., bright fawn color, large, very fragrant." [CC] "Sulphur-color tinged with red, very large and fragrant." [FP] "Large, full, very well formed, cupped; copper yellow mixed with sulphur yellow." [S] "Bud, bright pink. — Flower, semi-double and cupped, or full and more or less flat. — Color, pink; reverse washed salmon yellow." [JR23/151] "Reddish, buff-coloured flowers. It is a vigorous grower, retaining its foliage during the greater part of the winter." [OM] "Red, buff, flesh, and sulphur, very large and full; form cupped; growth vigorous; the flowers forming in clusters, the foliage large and fine; very sweet. A most desirable kind for a wall." [P1] "Grown against a west wall here, it covered a space some 20 × 20 ft [ca. 6 × 6 m] in three years, throwing laterals five ft [ca. 1.5 m] and more every summer; and from the ends of these in late autumn the great heads of bloom hang down, filling the whole air with fragrance; in one cluster alone I have counted seventy-two blossoms, soft sulphur, salmon, and red." [K2] "Flowers of a ravishing beauty. Though the form may be irregular, the general effect is most agreeable to the eye." [JR22/74] "Apricot scented." [JR33/101] "Flower stem stiff, short, somewhat slender. Calyx oblong; sepals leaf-like; scent agreeable." [JF] "A well-known and much esteemed rose, of rapid growth and quite hardy . . . its fragrance is also very remarkable. This was originated by Mons Desprez about eighteen years since, and is still, and will be for some time to come, a very popular rose. . . . Its rosy copper-colored flowers are very singular, and so powerfully fragrant that one plant will perfume a large garden in the cool weather of autumn." [WRP] "It has been cultivated about Philadelphia these ten years past . . . when well established, [produces a] profusion of flowers . . . in large clusters. The colour is a rosy-buff inclining to orange, and perfectly double. It should always be planted where it will be under the eye, as its colour does not make it a remarkable object from a distance." [Bu] "At one time highly esteemed, and even now its fawn-coloured and very fragrant flowers are often, in autumn, very beautiful." [R8] "Rapidity of its growth and the magnificence of its foliage." [P2] "The lovely and fragrant old Noisette . . . has in these few years spread over a space 18 by 20 ft [ca. 5.5 × 6 m] and more, with its light green, graceful foliage and great clusters of sweet-scented flowers . . . sometimes ten or twelve ft long [ca. 3–3.5 m] in a year." [K1]

"Mons Pirolle described this rose in the August and September 1831 numbers of the *Annals of the Society of Practical Agriculture*. . . . The bearing and vigor of the plant resemble those of a Bourbon. . . . Noisette 'Desprez' is a vigorous bush, well supported, and its thorns are purplish and sparse; its foliage is large, outspread, leathery, of a nice shiny green, with 5 oval-acuminate leaflets bordered with numerous blunt teeth. The leafstalk has prickles beneath, and often the base of the terminal leaflet's vein has a prickle as well when the leaves are large. Flowers terminal, 3–5 on each cane, borne on stems which are fairly long and flexible enough so that they don't interfere with each other; the peduncles are purplish and slightly pubescent, as are the ovaries and calyces, which stay green. The ovaries are oval-oblong, and the sepals somewhat lacinated. The blossom is full, large to 4 in [ca. 1 dm], with large exterior petals which are concave and saucer-shaped like those of the Centifolia; inner petals muddled; color, nankeen yellow or fawn washed pink towards the edge. The scent is elegant; many people say that it resembles that of a ripe banana. No one can confuse this rose with any other." [R-H33] "Grown from seed around 1828 by Mons Desprez . . . who sold it for the exorbitant sum of 3,000 francs to Mons Sisley-Vandael with the proviso that he would not give it to anyone else for several years. . . . This rose is not one to be victimized by changing fashions; it will stand always in the forefront of the Noisettes." [R-H 34] "Shrub, very vigorous. Thorns, purplish, scattered. Leaves, coriaceous, glossy, large, of a dark green. Flowers, usually in a cluster of three; three in wide [ca. 7.5 cm]; yellow in the centre, pale at the circumference." [Go] "Large branches, which are very long and flexile; bark, yellowish-green, somewhat reddish where exposed to the sun; thorns not numerous, short, hooked, of the same green as that of the bark, but tinged red; leaves, handsome green, paler beneath, pointed and finely toothed; leafstalks green, slender, armed beneath with five or six little prickles which are hooked and sharp; flower, about 2.5 in across [ca. 7 cm], full, expanded, in clusters at the ends of the branches; color, flesh-colored saffron yellow, going to light pinkish yellow, outer petals concave, obovate, and rounded, while those of the center are narrower." [S]

"Such was [Mons] Desprez that, after being so often inclined while on this Earth to admire one of these most perfect works of creation [*referring to rose blossoms*], this fancier/enthusiast had brought to him, on his death-bed, one of these beloved roses, the one which bears his name, to take one last look before sinking into the peace of death." [JF]

DEVONIENSIS, CL.

('Magnolia Rose')
Pavitt/Curtis, 1858
Tea
Sport of 'Devoniensis' (T).

"Very pale creamy white . . . centres sometimes buff, sometimes yellowish; very large and full; form cupped." [P1] "Pink-tinged white, recurrent." [W] "Blush centre. Fragrant." [H] "Large, full, handsome white with some sulphur-yellow." [Sx] "Very large flowers of cream/white with an occasional blush of pink . . . 10 × 6 [ft; ca. 3 × 1.75 m]." [B] Often come divided . . . deficient in size." [F-M2] "Richly perfumed." [ARA29/98] "The strongest, most untidy, and irregular grower of all Tea Roses. Growing is its strong point." [F-M2] "The early, strong, sappy wood should be pinched or stopped when about a foot in length [ca. 3 dm], in order to cause it to break into several shoots . . . which almost invariably flower at each point the first season." [R1/278] "Vigorous; branches very 'climbing,' of a dark green, not very spiny; foliage brilliant green, regularly toothed; flower large, quite full; the inner petals are curled and artistically arranged, giving the appearance of a smaller rose placed within a larger; color, white, yellower towards the center of the petal, flesh towards the base." [S] "When established, very vigorous, and bearing its small cream-coloured flowers freely." [OM]

DORIS DOWNES
A. Clark, 1932
Hybrid Gigantea
> Pink, semi-double Gigantea hybrid.

DR. W. VAN FLEET
Van Fleet/Henderson, 1910
From an unnamed seedling (parentage: *R. wichuraiana* × 'Safrano' [T]) × 'Souvenir du Président Carnot' (HT).
> "Soft flesh, shading to delicate peach-pink." [ARA21/93] "Pale pink fading to blush . . . to 20 [ft; ca. 6 m]." [HRG] "Vigorous, robust, covered with handsome shiny bronze foliage. The flowers are cupped, about four in across [ca. 1 dm]; petals are wavy, flesh-pink at the base, more of a delicate pink towards the edges. The flowers are full, on strong stems, and are very fragrant." [JR33/135] "Beautiful flowers of good form; blooms well in spring, an occasional bloom thereafter." [ARA18/120] "Bloom free last three weeks of June." [ARA18/130] "A grand show if there is enough cold weather to render dormant in winter." [ET] "Foliage very good." [ARA17/27] "Well-foliated . . . flesh-pink to white of soft delicate texture . . . 15 × 10 [ft; ca. 4.5 × 3 m]." [B]

DUCHESSE D'AUERSTÄDT
Listed as 'Mme la Duchesse d'Auerstädt'.

DUCHESSE DE GRAMMONT
Laffay?, pre-1838 (ca. 1825?)
Noisette
Not to be confused with Cels' 1825 pink Damask of the same name, nor with Laffay's pinkish-lilac Tea of 1825, 'Duc de Grammont'.
> "Flowers, small, full; flesh-coloured." [Go] "To about 2 metres [ca. 6 ft] . . . fragrant small double pink flowers which appear in clusters." [G]

E. VEYRAT HERMANOS   PLATE 203
('Pillar of Gold')
Bernaix, 1894
Tea
> "The flower is ravishing with a beautiful color of sulphur enhanced by apricot pink and washed with a light tint of carmine, marvelous when the blossom is half open. The plant is very vigorous, but should not be pruned much." [JR23/42] "Another lovely rose, though not generally very free [with] its flowers, which are of apricot-yellow and rose." [OM] "Flower very large, full, cupped, very fragrant; very vigorous." [Cx] "Very sweet, distinct, and good, but rather a shy bloomer." [P1] "Best in heated zones. . . . Good strong growth; foliage only fair; blooms well but balls in damp; some blooms very fine. Well worth growing even with its fault. Color varies from light yellow to apricot red, and bronze." [Capt28] "Branches strong and big, foliage thick and bright, flowers large, nicely double, very fragrant, bud of pretty form, flower bi-colored, with petals of apricot yellow and delicate carmine-pink with amaranth pink reflections. The contrast produced by these two noticeable shades, its great vigor, its intense and pleasant scent, all make it an elite variety of great merit." [JR18/163]

ELIE BEAUVILAIN   PLATE 191
Beauvilain, 1887
Noisette
From 'Gloire de Dijon' (N) × 'Ophirie' (N).
> "Two-toned pink and yellow, recurrent, very showy." [W] "Very floriferous. Very vigorous. Flowers large, full, copper-pink." [Lc] "Climbing, vigorous, growing shoots nine or ten ft in length [ca. 2.75–3 m]; foliage very large and of a nice brilliant green; very numerous and strong thorns; flower large, full, imbricated; prettily colored silvery blush, copper-veined with a ground of red, the reverse of the petals pink; all in all, a quite novel coloration for this sort; very floriferous, quite remontant." [JR11/163–164]

ÉTENDARD DE JEANNE D'ARC   PLATE 188
('Jeanne d'Arc', 'Comtesse Eva Starkemberg')
Garçon/Margottin, 1882
Noisette
Seedling of 'Gloire de Dijon' (N).
Not to be confused with the 1818 Alba, the 1847 HP, nor with the 1909 Polyantha, all going by the name "Jeanne d'Arc".
> "Creamy white changing to pure white; very large and full, opening well . . . very free." [P1] "Opens quickly, free, fragrant." [Hn] "Very good scent." [JR5/106] "An inferior 'Lamarque'." [EL] "Reminds one a little of 'Souvenir de la Malmaison'." [JR9/146] "This new Tea rose . . . is a very vigorous variety, but is nevertheless not so vigorous as its parent 'Gloire de Dijon'; its flowers are very large, very full, and open well; they are of good form, having much in common with 'Gloire de Dijon'." [JR7/153] "Repeats . . . 8–12 [ft; ca. 2.25–3.5 m]." [Lg] "To 15 [ft; ca. 4.5 m]." [HRG]

ÉTOILE DE HOLLANDE, CL.
Leenders, 1931
Hybrid Tea
Sport of 'Étoile de Hollande' (HT).
> "Bright red, double . . . very large, cupped. . . . Color is quite sun-resistant. Recurrent . . . soft foliage . . . to 8 ft [ca. 2.25 m]. . . . Beautiful buds. . . . Marvelous old-rose fragrance." [W] "Highly scented . . . rich velvet crimson . . . 12 × 10 [ft; ca. 3.5 × 3 m]." [B] "During the spring blooming period the flowers completely cover the plant, with some recurrence on old wood." [ARA36/178] "One of the finest red climbers. . . . Large blooms all season." [ARA37/213]

ÉTOILE DE PORTUGAL
Cayeux/Chénault & fils, 1909
Hybrid Gigantea
From *R. gigantea* × ? 'Reine Marie Henriette' (Cl. HT).
> "Most notable as being the first Gigantea hybrid. The ample foliage is light green. The large, well-formed blossoms, with regular petals, are a nice salmon shrimp pink, yellow at the nub; the bud is of perfect form and long duration. The color is superb and a novelty among Climbers." [JR33/152] "Vigorous . . . to . . . 12 [ft; ca. 3.5 m]. Large, loose, double rose-red blooms." [HRG] "Of astonishing vigor, as with 'Reine Marie Henriette', a very great quantity of flowers of a handsome silvery carmine-pink, shaded yellow at the base. The fragrant blossom is large, full, and becomes slightly lighter when fully open. Mons Cayeux doesn't yet know if it will be remontant; such is to be hoped." [JR29/120] "Once-blooming only." [GAS] "The first of these [Gigantea] hybrids bloomed here after two years. . . . Luxuriantly vigorous, the

plant would seem to have borrowed [from 'Reine Marie Henriette'] its great floriferousness. The buds are elongated, often in twos or threes, of a pretty silvery carmine-pink, shaded yellow at the base. The flower is large, full, and fragrant, and fades lighter after opening." [JR29/77–78] Evidently developed around 1905.

FELLEMBERG

('Fellenberg')
Fellemberg, 1835
Noisette

"Light carmine, double, cupped, beautiful." [LF] "Bright red." [V4] "Rosy crimson, very free bloomer." [FP] "Maroon." [R-H35] "Bright crimson, strong, very free." [H] "Bright pink to crimson . . . attractive cascading habit if grown free . . . 7 × 4 [ft; ca. 2 × 1.25 m]." [B] "Has no equal for brilliancy of colour, during the autumnal months; in the early part of the season, it is of a pale red, but in the fall its colour approaches a scarlet, with large flowers produced in clusters of thirty to fifty. It is perfectly hardy . . . the foliage, when young, has also a peculiar red colour." [Bu] "Pretty crimson." [R8] "Delightfully fragrant." [NRS/13] "Medium size, double, cupped; bright crimson. Slightly fragrant . . . continuous . . . 6–10 [ft; ca. 1.75–3 m]." [Lg] "Flowers in random scattered array." [Hk] "Never seems out of bloom, very vigorous." [E] "Clusters . . . double crimson-pink blooms . . . 6 [ft; ca. 1.75 m]." [HRG] "Of medium size, double, form cupped; growth vigorous. An abundant bloomer . . . dark foliage, showy, but rather loose . . . fine late in the year." [P1] "Medium size, carmine-pink, well-filled, vigorous growth; flowers free till late autumn." [Hn] "Flowering from the end of June to the end of November . . . bright crimson, flowers double and small, joints short as the crimson china [either 'Slater's Crimson China' or 'Cramoisi Supérieur']." [HstV:46] "The pretty little 'Fellemberg', poorest in quality of any, but flowering the most profusely, in colour and habit indicates a near relationship to the semperflorens type ['Slater's Crimson China']." [Hd] "Believed by some authorities to be a cross of China with Multiflora." [ARA38/13] "Good in damp climates . . . does not last well." [Capt28] "Good growth. Very fine foliage. Blooms over long period. . . . Specially recommended in the Southern Zones." [Th2] "Beautiful." [CC]

FLYING COLOURS

A. Clark, 1922
Hybrid Gigantea
Not to be confused with 'Flying Colors', a Miniature.

"Striking, bright purplish red, single flowers about five in across [ca. 1.25 dm]." [GAS] "Very large, single, lasting; light red; slight fragrance. Foliage disease-resistant. Very vigorous climber; abundant bloomer in spring only." [ARA24/175] "Large, single, rich cerise-pink. . . . If grown on a sheltered wall or trellis facing the morning sun, it comes into bloom three weeks before the flush, simply covering itself with bloom and making a glorious sight. It is spring-blooming only, but well worth having." [ARA30/153] "Lustrous, mildew-free leaves." [ARA23/119]

FORTUNE'S DOUBLE YELLOW   PLATE 181

('Beauty of Glazenwood', 'Wang-Jang-Ve')
Fortune, 1845
Hybrid Gigantea?

There seems to have been a measure of doubt as to whether or not 'Beauty of Glazenwood' and 'Fortune's Double Yellow' were synonymous. As JR has it, the London Royal Horticultural Society declared that 'Beauty of Glazenwood', lately introduced by Mr. Woodthorpe, seemed much of a piece with *"la vielle rose*

Jaune de Fortune." Mr. Woodthorpe, *"rosiériste à Glazenwood"* and putative raiser of the rose, points to very pronounced striping as differentiating the two—striping certainly very evident in an accompanying illustration—adding that the rootstock used affects the appearance of the flowers, and to come see for yourself next summer. The Royal Society remains adamant, as meantime crowds of amateur rosarians clamor to buy a rose which is striped and plumed like a tulip. See JR1/5/8, JR3/1–2, and JR6/173–175 for *l'histoire*.

"Bronzed yellow." [EL] "Of a bright fawn-color, with a tinge of copper." [FP] "Rich salmon and pink." [K1] "A dull buff, with a tinge of purple; flowers small, semi-double, and loose . . . at its best, it falls far below expectation." [HstVIII:380] "The flecked flowers, semi-double, washed carmine-pink, of changing color . . . the buds are superb and much liked. . . . It is a plant of the first merit." [JR18/135] "Very vigorous; flower of medium size, fairly full; color, yellow shaded rosy-red. Do not prune." [S] "Large golden blooms washed with pink and apricot, sometimes splashed with red . . . early . . . to 15 [ft; ca. 4.5 m]." [HRG] "Semi-double, shapely . . . loosely formed clusters. Glossy foliage . . . 8 × 5 [ft; ca. 2.25 × 1.5 m]." [B] "In a cold spring the flowers are vivid; in a warm spring they pale." [ARA40/37] "One of the roses which thrive best in Madeira, bearing its burden of yellow and pink-tipped blossoms in the spring." [DuC] "A source of pride and delight to its happy possessor . . . vivid recollections of its exquisite effect tumbling over a high grey stone wall by the dusty roadside from Genoa to Pegli. . . . And each year from the ground to the roof it is showered over with scores of lovely blossoms . . . it is without exception the most cruelly prickly, thorny Rose I know—every dainty twig, every shiny leaf being armed with ferocious fish-hooks. The flowers are borne singly on the well-ripened branchlets of last year's growth." [K1] "Must be treated [*in pruning, etc.*] similar to the Banksian [*i.e., summer pruning only*] . . . it is a rapid grower, and quite hardy, excellent for covering a wall or trellis, or grown as a pillar rose." [WHoIII] "Small grower." [ARA18/120] "40, 50 and even 60 ft high [ca. 1.25–2 dkm]." [ARA19/133] "The best example I have seen is in Nabonnand's garden at Golfe Juan; an old plant which grows in a Pergola covered with other creepers, so much shaded that neither its stem nor roots can feel the sun's influence, has forced its head through this ceiling of other growths, and extending its arms on every side produces a mass of flowers innumerable and beautiful. It requires shading in burning weather, or the striking tints of the flowers are soon reduced to a yellowish white." [B&V] "Discovered in the garden of a rich mandarin at Ningpo. It completely covered an old wall in the garden, and was in full bloom at the time of my visit; masses of glowing yellowish and salmon colored flowers hung down in the greatest profusion. . . . It is called by the Chinese the 'Wang-jang-ve,' or 'Yellow Rose.' They vary, however, a good deal in color; a circumstance which, in my opinion, adds not a little to the beauty and character of the plant." [Mr] [Fortune, being quoted secondhand in WHoIII.]

FRAU KARL DRUSCHKI, CL.

Lawrenson, 1906
Hybrid Perpetual
Sport of 'Frau Karl Druschki' (HP).

White. "A little inferior, however, to its mother; the flowers are smaller, and the buds pinker." [JR30/69] "It grows as vigorously as the Tea and Hybrid Tea climbers." [ET] "It frequently reverts to the type . . . [it has an] inveterate desire to grow from the top and leave the base bare . . . the long straggling shoots are difficult to control in autumn . . . it is worth a good deal of care, for a well grown Pillar of 'Frau Karl Druschki' is most decorative, its glistening white flowers showing up from distant parts of the garden, while it blooms more or less all summer and autumn, and Mr. Courtney Page adds, 'I think I might add winter too.' " [NRS14] "12 × 8 [ft; ca. 3.5 × 2.25 m]." [B]

FUN JWAN LO

('Indica Major', 'Odorata 22449')
Unknown (Chinese), pre-1811
Tea

"[Discovered] in a garden at Pautung Fu, Chihli Province. . . . It produces small, double white flowers with pale pink centers; its canes are slender, smooth and of very rapid growth." [ARA23/92] "Plant has branches which are thin and 'climbing'; the foliage is very shiny, lasting well on the plant; styles, free; flower, of medium size, very double, flesh-colored with tints of pink." [S] "With slender, scandent branches, more or less 'climbing,' is the most appropriate subject for warm climates with prolonged summers, arid terrain, desert-like conditions, stony, or quite humid." [JR21/141] "[Nowhere] does it bear the slightest resemblance to the Tea roses which comprise the true species *R. odorata*." [ARA32/45] Vibert's 'Belmont', which we list as a Hybrid China — though it might merely be a *China hybrid* — has also been associated with this cultivar, as has, particularly, Baumann with his 'Triomphe de Bollwiller'. Other associated entities: 'Rosier de la Chine à Feuilles Longues', 'Sempervirens of Italy', and a dubious *R. fraxinifolia*.

GÉNÉRAL LAMARQUE

Listed as 'Lamarque'.

GENERAL MACARTHUR, CL.

H. Dickson, 1923
Hybrid Tea
Sport of 'General MacArthur' (HT).

"Large, loosely formed, scented, deep rosy-red. . . . Very free flowering and vigorous . . . 15 × 10 [ft; ca. 4.5 × 3 m]." [B] "About 5 ft high [ca. 1.5 m] the first year." [ARA25/183] "Best near coast. Wonderful as a decorative rose; continuous bloomer, and fine in every way, though fails somewhat in cutting value." [Capt28] "The best tender climber of its color [*red*]." [PP28]

GLOIRE DE DIJON   PLATE 175

(trans., 'Dijon's Glory')
Jacotot, 1853
Noisette
From 'Desprez à Fleur Jaune' (N) × 'Souvenir de la Malmaison' (B).

"After two weeks in the steerage of an army transport, and two weeks of quarantine in a bitterly cold French camp, the last Sunday of December, 1917, found us in the railroad station of Dijon, with five hours between trains. As soon as our eyes lighted upon the sign 'Dijon,' one of my friends and I made up our minds to visit the home of the rose which I had grown and admired for so many years, but when we started out I was dismayed to find that I had forgotten the originator's name. It did not occur to us, however, that we would have any trouble finding such a famous place, until we had, in our very bad French, asked the way of several shopkeepers. They were very polite — 'Yes, there were nurseries in Dijon; which one did we want to see? Roses? Yes, they all grew roses!' After getting these answers in four or five places, we gave it up and began to search blindly. Luck was with us, for after walking about an hour, we turned a corner, and beheld, painted in large letters on the brick wall of the house

opposite, *'Jacotot, Horticulteur.'* Like a flash, the name I had been trying to remember came back to me, and we crossed the street, entered the little gate, and walked toward the house. The brick walk leading from the gate to the house divided the little enclosure in half. On the right was a formal rose-garden, 60 or 80 ft wide [ca. 2 dkm or 2.5 dkm], and perhaps a hundred long [ca. 3 dkm], with little rectangular beds, having standard (tree) roses marking their corners, and with ocasional arches or posts for climbers, these two types of roses standing out boldly while the dwarfer roses were mostly hidden with snow. On the left were three greenhouses, about 18 by 50 each [ca. 5.5 m × 1.5 dkm], and between them and beyond them, roses and other plants in nursery rows. Entering the little office, we announced that we were American soldiers, interested in roses, and that we would like to see the original vine of 'Gloire de Dijon', which we knew well in America. A woman, who told us that she was Jacotot's daughter, greeted us, and took us outside and showed us an old climbing rose, which, however, hardly seemed old enough to be the original vine, unless it had been pruned back so severely as to leave no trace of old wood. Then she took us into the greenhouses, which were indeed a pitiable sight. They were of the steep-roof type, with small glass, houses such as are now but seldom seen in this country [U.S.A.]. The framework, and even the doors and benches were of steel. Owing to fuel restrictions, there was no heat, and the houses were covered with straw mats, so that they were as dark as a cellar, getting light from the ends only. . . . We came away marveling that from this little place could have come a rose so fine that, after more than sixty years' trial in nearly every civilized country in the world, it is still so grown and loved that it has made a place for itself which but few other roses have ever attained." [ARA20/20–22]

"Cream and salmon yellow; climber or bush." [WD] "Buff and orange." [J] "Amber-flushed, pale pink." [W] "In color a combination of rose, salmon and yellow; flowers very large, very full, good globular form, the outer petals inclined to fade. A very useful rose." [EL] "Soft pink, suffused yellow; fragrant." [ARA29/98] "Yellow shaded with salmon, very large and full; a superb variety for wall or pillar." [P1] "Buff, very vigorous and hardy climber; still one of the best." [FRB] "Magnificent . . . cream-coloured blooms, tinted with fawn and blush." [Ed] "Almost an exact resemblance of the Bourbon Rose 'Souvenir de la Malmaison', and, like that fine Rose, it requires dry warm weather to open its flowers in perfection. Its perfume is Tea-like and powerful, and in color it is quite unique, being tinted with fawn, salmon, and rose, and difficult to describe." [HstX:85] "Certainly the colour, an ochraceous yellow, the size, as large as 'Jaune Desprez', and the Tea scent, make it a great acquisition." [HstX:398] "In Southern California, the blossoms range in color from being predominantly buff-yellow in the winter to being predominantly light pink in the summer, always with hints of burnt orange, gold, and rose." [BCD] "Luscious shades of pink, buff, apricot and peach . . . to 15 [ft; ca. 4.5 m]." [HRG] "Little beauty of colour or form . . . except perhaps quite in the bud . . . and even these are comparatively fat and squat." [F-M2] "Beautiful, old fashioned flowers, delicious Tea fragrance . . . never out of bloom until the frost stops it." [ARA29/50] "Will supply more good roses in a season than any other variety, for it is first in spring and last in winter to produce its abundant flowers, exquisite in colour, form, and fragrance." [R1/159] "It has one defect — a crumpled appearance of the central petals, which gives them a somewhat withered look, even when just open." [FP] "Gives more flowers than any Hybrid Tea sport, being a continuous bloomer;

growth is good." [ARA18/120] "Large, very full, the cupped buds becoming flatter with age. Salmon-yellow with fiery copper-red towards center. Growth very vigorous; should not be pruned severely. The flowering period is extended by bending down the shoots. . . . Flowers from June till November. Very fragrant." [Hn]

"We [*at Jacotot's*] have grown it since 1850; we wanted, before releasing it to commerce, to assure ourselves of its true merit. . . . Since 1852, we have been propagating it *en masse*; we now have a very great quantity in 'heads' of one, two, and three years, on wonderful briar stock in all sizes [*as tree roses, we see*]; we have noted with pleasure that it bears with ease the cold of the worst winters. Exhibited at Dijon in June, 1852, the Société d'Horticulture de la Côte-d'Or awarded it First Prize; it was at this meeting that the jury gave it the name 'Gloire de Dijon'." [VH53/39] "A new variety, exhibited in 1853, in Paris, raised at Dijon . . . is a great acquisition; its flowers are as large and as durable as those of the Bourbon 'Souvenir de la Malmaison', which they much resemble in shape; but their colour, nearly as deep as the buds of 'Safrano', is most striking; its foliage is as thick and large, and its habit as robust, as those of the above well-known Bourbon Rose, and as it opens freely in our climate it is highly popular . . . near Aberdeen it has bloomed beautifully." [R8] "It is a hybrid of Tea and Bourbon, with a large, full flower which resembles in form and delicate flesh tint 'Malmaison', from which it differs in the icy saffron-salmon tint which brightens at the base of the corolla." [I'H53/242] "We saw this beautiful rose at the Paris exposition in June, 1853, where it received a gold medal. The flowers exhibited were of a beautiful clear yellow with a light salmon tint. In a picture which Mons Jacotot sent his correspondents, the color was slightly exaggerated; instead of light salmon reflections, the artist added pink tints which were not quite to be found in the blossom." [I'H54/55] "Admirable. . . . This variety appeared in [Jacotot's] acreage of Teas, and, by its elegant bearing, its handsome foliage, its remontant qualities, its perfect form, its beautiful coloration, and its delicious scent, it has not been surpassed to this day. . . . Very vigorous; its branches are upright, reddish when young, aging to ashy-green; the stem is smooth and furnished with reddish prickles which are hooked and of differing sizes; the leaves are of five to seven leaflets, an attractive brilliant green on top, and, on the bottom, reddish when young, aging to a glaucous green. The general foliation is vigorous and quite characteristic; it is easy to recognize among the group's varieties. The foliage of 'Souvenir de la Malmaison' would be quite the same were it larger and more rounded; it is nearly of the same character. The flowers develop at the ends of the branches, supported by a large and firm stem, and nearly always supported by two or three large, expanding buds—inevitably opening, however, with the greatest of ease. The flower, of good form and full, attains a breadth of about 4.5 to 5 in [ca. 1–1.25 dm]; the petals are large at the outer edge of the blossom, reflexing a little, and diminishing in size towards the center, which itself is formed of rolled petals, and is 'quartered.' The color of the rose is a yellow strongly suffused with salmon." [JR1/10/5–6] "The foliage is very large, thick, and lustrous; thorns comparatively few." [EL]

"Very vigorous, and the canes, generally big and limber, develop leafy branchlets at the nodes which terminate in blossoms; bark, light green, reddish where the sun hits, with homogeneously reddish thorns which are large, hooked, sharp, and thick. Foliage shiny, light green, divided into 3–5 leaflets which are oval-rounded, slightly acuminate, and dentate; leafstalk strongly nod-ding, slightly reddish, with several little prickles beneath. Flowers about 3.5 in across [ca. 8.75 cm], very full, globular, sometimes solitary, or in clusters of 2 or 3 on the branchlets, but always in bouquets of 5–10 or more on the vigorous canes. Color, salmon yellow; petals large and concave, those of the center smaller and inter-folded; flower stem pretty long, nodding under the weight of the blossom. Calyx rounded pear-shape; sepals unroll onto the calyx at expansion . . . one of the most beautiful varieties of its section." [JF] "Equal to any demands that can be made upon a wall, pole, or pillar Rose. This splendid variety is first-rate for all purposes . . . further a most prolific parent." [WD] "[For] climates without extremes of damp or heat. Fine strong climber, with prolific bloom . . . mildews badly at times, and requires equable conditions for best results." [Capt28] "Not liable to mildew." [F-M2] "Liable, oddly, to both mildew and rust, though more as a host than a victim." [BCD] "[Excellent in Norway]." [ARA20/46] "The best and hardiest of all the Teas." [HRH]

An unintroduced gold-leafed sport is recorded: "All the leaves are golden, with veins and blotches of green . . . the flower is perfectly similar to 'Gloire de Dijon'." [JR3/172]

"I decided to investigate the 'Gloire de Dijon' pedigree when in Dijon, France, in July, 1925. From the originator Jacotot's grand-daughter I heard that while no written record was in existence it was the oral tradition in the family that 'Souvenir de la Malmaison' was the pollen parent and a vigorous unnamed climbing yellow Tea the seed bearer." [K] "At a recent sitting of the Central Horticultural Society of France Mons Andry, in alluding to the death of the late Mons Lucy, remarked that the latter was the first to recognize the peculiar merits of the 'Gloire de Dijon' Rose, after it had been obtained from seed by Mons Jacotot, who scarcely noticed it amongst many others. Mons Lucy advised him to propagate and send it out, which was done." [R7/378] "Mons de Lucy, former president of the Dijon [*Horticultural?*] Society, now in Marseille." [I'H57/61] "The famous old 'Gloire de Dijon' at Toulon, France, is described as being seventy-five ft in height [ca. 2.25 dkm], producing fifty thousand roses at a time." [Dr] "On the occasion of this meeting of rose-men at Dijon, a special fête was organized in honor of the Rose, and, naturally, 'Gloire de Dijon', that variety so well known and esteemed, took the place of honor." [JR32/101]

"On June 27 [1922], I stopped off at Dijon to visit again the home of the famed rose 'Gloire de Dijon', which was originated . . . in a little garden near the center of the city. The nursery is now kept up by the grandson, but roses are no longer the chief specialty. The original plant, which grew for many years in the corner of the property, is now dead." [ARA23/129]

"This, to me, is the rose par excellence." [ARA24/184] "Stands unrivalled and alone." [P2] "If ever, for some heinous crime, I were miserably sentenced, for the rest of my life, to possess but a single Rose-tree, I should desire to be supplied, on leaving the dock, with a strong plant of 'Gloire de Dijon'." [H]

GRUSS AN AACHEN, CL.

Kordes, 1937

Hybrid Tea

Sport of 'Gruss an Aachen' (HT).

"Ivory-white . . . enriched with apricot pink . . . rich fragrance." [T2] "Very vigorous." [ARA38/239]

HADLEY, CL.
Heizmann, 1927
Hybrid Tea
Sport of 'Hadley' (HT).

"Large, double, very fragrant blooms of deep, dark crimson, vigorous climber to 10 [ft; ca. 3 m]." [HRG] "Too thin for great heat. The best red climber for cutting, and certainly the best dark red; fine grower and better foliage than the dwarf, with long stems and fine perfume . . . a splendid bloomer, and better all around than 'Climbing Château de Clos Vougeot', which varies in growth and loses foliage." [Capt28] "I wish that someone would suggest a red climbing rose that would take the place of our splendid old 'Hadley'. It blooms in the spring with long stems and there is always a rose to be had, if it is given half a chance; but oh, the mildew!" [CaRoIII/6/6]

HERMOSA, CL.
Listed as 'Setina'.

INDICA MAJOR
Listed as 'Fun Jwan Lo'.

IRISH FIREFLAME, CL.
A. Dickson, 1916
Hybrid Tea
Sport of 'Irish Fireflame' (HT).

"Large, single . . . quiet orange-yellow and peach. Healthy and vigorous . . . 10 × 6 [ft; ca. 3 × 1.75 m]." [B] "A grand introduction . . . not a tall climber, but bushy, and must be left to grow quite freely." [ARA18/47] "Foliage good." [Capt28]

[ISABELLA GRAY]
Gray/Buist, 1857
Noisette
Seedling of 'Chromatella' (N).

"Of a most beautiful bright yellow . . . its buds are, however, so hard that they open very rarely. It should be planted against a wall with a warm aspect." [R8] "Vigorous; flower very large, full, of very good form; color, golden yellow. Very sensitive to dampness." [S] "Reputedly the parent of 'Maréchal Niel'. It has large, full, globular blooms of deep colouring." [OM] "Mons Andrea Gray, long-time chief gardener to Mons Buist . . . settled in Charleston, South Carolina. On his property, he flowered and obtained seed from . . . 'Chromatella' . . . and grew from this seed two specimens; one he dedicated to his elder daughter Isabelle, and the other to his wife Jane Hardy. The first of these two bloomed well in America, but without the felicities of 'Chromatella'. . . . 'Isabella' was sent to England by Mons Buist, who gave us these details; he had not, however, seen a blossom up to that time [1857]." [JR13/107–108] Introduced into France by Portemer.

JAUNE DESPREZ
Listed as 'Desprez à Fleur Jaune'.

JEANNE D'ARC
Listed as 'Étendard de Jeanne d'Arc'.

KAISERIN AUGUSTE VIKTORIA, CL.
('Mrs. Robert Peary')
A. Dickson, 1897
Hybrid Tea
Sport of 'Kaiserin Auguste Viktoria' (HT).

"Primrose." [Th] "Very large, double; cream-white. Excellent repeat bloom . . . 8–10 [ft; ca. 2.25–3 m] . . . one of the best." [Lg] "Only gives scattering blooms throughout the season." [ARA17/26] "Constantly in bloom from the earliest to the latest of the season. Elegant climbing habit. Rich, luxuriant, clean, healthy foliage. The climbing white rose for everybody." [Dr] "The buds are very beautiful, of good form, and creamy-yellow." [OM] "[For] everywhere. Better than the dwarf; good to very good grower; nice foliage; not a very free bloomer, but yields some exceptionally fine cut flowers, and gives them through a long season; distinct in color." [Capt28] "A person needn't hesitate to compare its vigor . . . to that of specimens of 'Gloire de Dijon'." [JR25/36] "[Of white climbers in Houston, Texas,] we favor 'Cl. Kaiserin Auguste Viktoria' most." [ET] "Reliable in every way." [Th2] Also attributed to the Americans De Voecht & De Wilde, 1897, whence comes 'Mrs. Robert Peary'.

KITTY KININMONTH
('Kitty Kinnonmouth', etc.)
A. Clark, 1922
Hybrid Gigantea

"Bud large, globular; flower very large, semi-double, cupped, very lasting; pink — almost fadeless — with many golden stamens; slight fragrance. Very vigorous climber; moderate bloomer in spring." [ARA24/176] "[For] everywhere. A wonderful decorative rose with a specially clear, brisk color; flower very large; growth fine; foliage fair and will hold." [Capt28] "To 12 ft [ca. 3.5 m]. Dark wrinkled foliage, few thorns. Heavy June bloom . . . sparingly repeated. Slight fragrance." [W] "Will repeat . . . if dead blooms are removed." [Lg] "It does especially well in southern California, with mildew-proof foliage and very large, semi-double, rose-pink flowers . . . to 15 ft or more [ca. 4.5 m+] . . . very nearly the same vivid carmine-pink . . . as the old favorite 'Zéphirine Drouhin'." [ARA31/186] "It is my idea of a perfect rose; the heavy waxy petals of brilliant pink form a shapely flower that lasts for three days outdoors in our [Georgian] hot southern sunshine." [ARA32/120]

LA BICHE
(trans., 'The Doe')
Toullier, 1832
Noisette

"White with a pink heart." [R-H35] "Flesh-white, large and full." [FP] "Pale rose and white." [HoBoIV/319] "Cup., deep blush, extra large [*and marked as being* 'particularly fragrant']." [CC] "Yellowish flesh." [LS] "White . . . centres flesh-colour, very large and very double; form cupped; growth vigorous. A fine Pillar Rose." [P1] "Globular." [LF] "Still a good rose when first open, of a pale flesh colour, though almost instantly changing to pure white, rather large and double . . . of free growth." [Bu] "Inclining to fawn color at the center . . . a very fragrant, beautiful, and distinct variety." [WRP] "Large, flat; pure striking white. Continuous . . . 6–8 [ft; ca. 1.75–2.25 m] . . . unexpected beauty." [Lg] "Very dainty." [OM] "Stem purple; bushy, very vigorous; alternate leaves, petiole sharp, usually seven bright green leaflets, serrated, prickles beneath on the mid-vein; thorns big, pointed, pretty numerous. Blossoms well formed, full, flesh-white, wafting the characteristic tea scent, well-held; borne on a moderately long stem accompanied by a purplish bract. This very remontant, beautiful rose blooms from the end of May until heavy frost. . . . It is not very delicate, and does well in all areas and exposures. It's just the thing for arbors and beds because of its rapid growth making canes from six to seven ft long [ca. 1–1.3 m]; and, above all, because of the persistence of its leaves, which hold for a long time." [An32/26] "Vigorous; branches large or of medium size, elongated and fairly 'climbing'; bark is smooth, olive-green, armed with brown, longish thorns which are very sharp and clinging; leaves are smooth, divided into 5 or 7 leaflets which are rounded and somewhat pointed, and with very small teeth; the stalks are weak and thin, with 2 or 3 small, sharp, and pointed prickles; the flower is 2.5 to 3 in[ches] in diameter [to 7.5 cm], pretty full, cupped, somewhat muddled, rarely solitary, usually in fairly full clusters, depending upon the strength of the branch; color, flesh-white, lightly yellowish at the center; outer petals are concave, with smaller ones towards the center; flower stems bend under the weight of the blossom; calyx green, smooth, ovoid; a very pretty variety, thoroughly remontant; best for fences; hardy." [S]

"It was a defender of his country turned gardener—retired Lieutenant-Colonel Toullier, who rests on his laurels in the cozy community of Rueil, near Paris—who captured the beautiful Noisette 'La Biche'. . . . Branches of a brownish or purplish green, long thorns which are very thick and pointed, light red in youth and brown in age, sometimes recurved, looking like the beak of a parakeet. Foliage of seven leaflets which are curled, glabrous, rounded, very slightly dentate and feebly petiolate; leafstalk bristling with small hairs, short, remote, stiff, and furnished beneath with two or three small, thin prickles. Stipules long and narrow, glabrous, finely ciliate with glandular hairs; flowers large, to about 3 in [ca. 7.5 cm], handsome flesh white on a yellowish ground by way of contrast. The rose's scent is like that of the Teas. . . . What charm and what grace in those long and vigorous canes, which fountain majestically to the ground!" [PIB] "This variety is absolutely unknown in our region. . . . Nevertheless, it is one of the most noteworthy." [JR20/60]

L'ABONDANCE
Moreau-Robert, 1887
Noisette
"Flesh-pink, double flowers on well spaced clusters, moderate climber to 8 [ft; ca. 2.25 m]." [HRG] "Flower medium-sized, full, pure white lightly tinted pink while opening." [LR] "10 × 6 [ft; ca. 3 × 1.75 m]." [B] "Extremely vigorous, semi-climbing; foliage handsome shiny green; flower of medium size, of pretty form, pure white, lightly blushing upon opening, blooming abundantly and in clusters of 50–100 flowers; the plant is a sight to see." [JR11/150]

LAFOLLETTE
Busby, 1910
Hybrid Gigantea
"Salmon-pink." [ARA35/98] "Beautiful . . . loose, long-pointed shape." [T2]

LA FRANCE, CL.
Henderson, 1893
Hybrid Tea
Sport of 'La France' (HT).
"Rich peach pink, delicious perfume, same beautiful buds as 'La France', but a vigorous climber and abundant bloomer, and quite hardy." [C&Js98] "Flowers equal to the old variety, but growth very vigorous." [P1] "It seems that the roses are enormous and abundant." [JR17/81] "Not of much use." [F-M2] "Individual

charms." [ET] "Often a tendency to revert to the dwarf type. . . . It is quite likely not to flower much for the first two or three years; Mr. Frank Cant notices it is most important to secure free root action, and Mr. Easlea lays stress on the fact that it must become well established before it will flower well. When this is attained, however, it often flowers better, if not more profusely, than do the dwarf plants, the flowers expanding more readily; and it is stated that on heavy soils some have discarded the dwarf plants in its favour. It is slightly subject to mildew and readily infected by black spot. . . . There are few more fragrant Roses than 'La France'." [NRS/14] "An elegant standby in any garden." [ARA40/37]

LADY HILLINGDON, CL.
Hicks, 1917
Tea
Sport of 'Lady Hillingdon' (T).
"Outstanding . . . shapely, apricot-yellow . . . healthy plum-coloured shoots and gray-green leaves. Scented . . . 12 × 6 [ft; ca. 3.5 × 1.75 m]." [B] "Rampant growth to 20 [ft; ca. 6 m]. Excellent repeat bloom . . . excellent low-maintenance hedge, if watered." [Lg] "A wonderful plant for sunny walls." [T2] "[Liked in Texas]." [ET] "Takes time to become established." [GAS]

LADY SYLVIA, CL.
Stevens/Low, 1933
Hybrid Tea
Sport of 'Lady Sylvia' (HT).
Pink, cream, and apricot. "Superb . . . rich pink . . . fine perfume. Outstanding as a climber . . . 10 × 10 [ft; ca. 3 × 3 m]." [B] "Its 'Ophelia'-like flowers are of a little darker color and of the finest quality, produced throughout the entire season." [ARA36/178]

LADY WATERLOW
Nabonnand, 1902
Hybrid Tea
From 'La France de 89' (Cl. HT) × 'Mme Marie Lavalley' (N).
"Light salmon pink, saffron nub; flower large, semi-double; very vigorous." [Cx] "Soft pink salmon with deeper edges . . . healthy and robust . . . 12 × 6 [ft; ca. 3.5 × 1.75 m]." [B] "Salmon-rose, golden centres." [P1] "Very beautiful semi-double . . . clear salmon-pink petals edged with crimson; and when gathered in large bunches its effect is most striking." [K1] "Should become more popular not only for its intrinsic beauty, but it flowers freely in late autumn. . . . There is an alluring charm in the large half-double flowers with petals of softest pink and white." [NRS/12] "Lovely light green foliage, which is not only distinct . . . but . . . immune from disease [excepting blackspot] . . . carries twice, and often three times in the year quantities of most lovely pale salmon pink flowers, nearly single, with large petals held well up above the foliage. The bright cherry-coloured buds are very pleasing." [NRS/13] "Bud well formed; very large and handsome foliage; plant very vigorous, very floriferous." [JR26/149] "The hardihood of the growth is superlative, the foliage wonderful. I have had leaves 5 in long by 4 wide [ca. 1.25 × 1 dm]. . . . It is exempt from disease, both mildew and rust; it is one of the first to leaf out, and one of the last to shed in the fall; it climbs quite as high as 'Mme Alfred Carrière', while remaining clothed to the ground. . . . The best climber I know." [JR36/106] "Extremely 'climbing,' with strong, thorny wood. . . . Three-year-olds have attained 18 ft in height [ca. 5.25 m]. . . . Pruned specimens make very pretty shrubs." [JR36/123] "A very charming rose." [OM]

LAMARQUE
PLATE 173

('Général Lamarque', 'Thé Maréchal')
Maréchal, 1830
Noisette
From 'Blush Noisette' (N) × 'Parks' Yellow' (T).

"Outer petals soft white; inner, pale straw." [H] "Sulphur yellow." [HoBoIV/319] "White, with sulphur centre, sometimes pure white, very large, full, somewhat fragrant, generally seven leaflets. A superb climbing rose, quite too much neglected." [EL] "Cup., large straw col'd, lemon centre, sup'rb." [CC] "White . . . centres deep straw colour, very large and full; form cupped; growth vigorous. A splendid kind for a wall with a sunny aspect, producing its elegant flowers in large clusters. Raised by Mons Maréchal, a shoemaker, from his window-garden at Angers." [P1] We learn from *Les Amis des Roses* n° 215 (page 4) that Mons Maréchal was gardener at la Croix Montaillé. "Magnificent, large, perfectly double, yellowish-white, pendulous flowers, which it produces in clusters of three to ten in each. In good dry rich soils it will grow twenty ft in a season." [Bu] "A continuous bloomer with white, violet-scented flowers." [ARA31/30] "Lemon-centred and lemon-scented." [J] "Blend of Musk and Tea [perfumes]." [NRS/17] "Approaching to the Tea-scented rose in the size and fragrance of its flowers. It is of most vigorous growth but not quite as hardy as 'Jaune Desprez'. . . . Its large pale sulphur-colored or nearly white flowers are pendant from their weight, and have a fine effect. . . . In a rich warm soil, it will grow fifteen to twenty ft in one season, and produce from May to December a profusion of its drooping clusters, comprised of five to ten flowers each. In the Southern States it attains a magnificent development, extending its branches in some cases for fifty ft in length and above twenty ft in height." [WRP] "Continuous." [Capt28] "Bud is high-centred, delicate. Lovely healthy gray-green foliage . . . 8–12 [ft; ca. 2.25–3.5 m]. Good repeat bloom." [Lg] "To 15 [ft; ca. 4.5 m]." [HRG] "10 × 6 [ft; ca. 3 × 1.75 m]." [B] "Tremendous grower." [W] "Flower . . . widely cupped." [S] "Unfortunately little known today . . . its cupped flowers are very pretty and of long duration." [JR18/135]

"Around 1830, Mons Maréchal, cobbler—so it is said—at Angers, raised this variety from seedlings grown in a pot in his window. It had, at that time, the name 'Thé Maréchal' because of its tea-like features." [PIB] "Here is the description given by Mons Maréchal himself, who wasn't a professional, but rather a very distinguished amateur: 'Shrub very vigorous, branches flexile and big, with light green bark, sometimes smooth, with numerous reddish prickles which are somewhat flattened and hooked, enlarged at the base, and very sharp. The foliage is smooth, shiny, and a nice green, with 5–7 leaflets which are oval-lanceolate, pointed, and finely toothed; the leafstalk is slender, slightly reddish green, armed with five or six little prickles of the same color, unequal, hooked, and very sharp. The flower is three or so in[ches] in diameter [ca. 7.5 cm], very full, flat, blooming in clusters of 3–6 roses at the ends of the branches. Color, a yellowish white; outer petals large, those of the center a little smaller and muddled with the stamens. Flower stalk big enough, somewhat glandular and nodding, calyx nearly globular, light green, sepals long, narrow, and downy. Slight tea-scent." [JR20/43] "It has always been a great favorite with me, and when in its full beauty I think it almost the most beautiful of white roses. . . . It has the reputation of being rather tender, which I very much doubt, my plant having been in the same place for certainly over fifty years, during which it must have passed through many a severe winter with little injury. Its numerous trusses of pure white sweet-scented roses are most beautiful, especially in dry seasons." [GG] "A superior old white rose . . . it retains the clustering tendency . . . and produces

an immense quantity of flowers during the season. It is a noble rose." [EL]

[LE VÉSUVE, CL.]
P. Guillot, 1904
China
Sport of 'Le Vésuve' (Ch).

"Blood red, sometimes red with a white center; flower large, full; very floriferous; very vigorous." [Cx] "Climbing, bushy, robust . . . flower large, full, color variable, bearing on the same bush blossoms of dark red, bright red, delicate pink, and red-edged pink." [JR28/154]

LIÉSIS
Listed as 'Céline Forestier'.

LONGWORTH RAMBLER
See 'Deschamps'.

LORRAINE LEE, CL.
McKay, 1932
Hybrid Gigantea
Sport of 'Lorraine Lee' (HGig).

"Golden apricot-pink, recurrent, fragrant." [W] "Very vigorous." [G]

LOUISE D'ARZENS
Listed as an HP.

[LOUIS-PHILIPPE, CL.]
Introducer and date unknown
China
Sport of 'Louis-Philippe' (Ch).

"Deep-red, recurrent." [W]

LUSIADAS
Listed as 'Céline Forestier'.

MAGNOLIA ROSE, CL.
Listed as 'Devoniensis, Cl'.

MAMAN COCHET, CL.
Upton, 1909
Tea
Sport of 'Maman Cochet' (T).

Shades of pink and cream. "Less fine in cool dampness. Wonderful in every way except strength of stem . . . tendency to ball in dampness." [Capt28] "Recurrent." [W] "Vigorous . . . to 12 [ft; ca. 3.5 m]." [HRG] "Individual charms." [ET]

MANETTII
('Manetti', '*R. × noisettiana manettii*')
Manetti/Crivelli/Rivers, 1835
Noisette

"Violet-rose, small size, single, not productive . . . dark, brownish wood, and always seven leaflets, sometimes nine." [EL] "Vig. shrub with red shoots and pink fl. 2-in diam." [MR8] "I am rejoiced to have it; for its charming foliage and bunches of delicate pink blossoms make it well worth growing for its own sake." [K1] "A variety of great vigor, coming I believe from *R. fraxinifolia*, and which was developed in 1820 by Messer Manetti, director of the gardens at Monza in Lombardy. It is pretty hardy, and takes easily to budding, but it is being abandoned as a stock because of certain faults. These faults are, firstly, overly continuous growth which hinders the harvesting of the plants; also, it forms numerous suckers, which exhaust the plant." [JF] "The *Rosa Manetti* [*sic*] is a rose I [Rivers] received some thirty years since, from Como, from Signor Crivelli, who recommended it as the very best of all roses for a stock. It was raised from seed by Signor Manetti, of the Botanic Garden at Monza." [R8] "Bred in 1832 from the seed of a Bourbon — I cannot say which." [JR7/79] "Considered as a hybrid of *R. semperflorens* ['Slater's Crimson China'] and *R. moschata*." [JR25/138] "It was the late Mons Granger who was the first to recommend 'Manettii' as a stock on which to graft." [JR27/64] "It was found so vigorous, so easy to propagate from cuttings, and the bark ran so readily, that it soon became a general favorite [as a stock]. . . . There was one class of Roses, however, which it did not suit — Teas; its growth was too strong, and overpowered the more delicate growth of the [Tea] Rose, and consequently for these the Briar still held its own." [DO]

MARÉCHAL NIEL   PLATE 176
Pradel, 1864
Noisette
Seedling of 'Isabella Gray' (N).

"Deep yellow, very large, very full, globular form, delightfully fragrant, the finest of all yellow roses . . . of delicate constitution . . . requires very careful treatment to produce satisfactory results." [EL] "Deep golden yellow, the yellow of all the yellows, its only fault for exhibition being that it flowers rather too early, and is not sufficiently perpetual. . . . It must be very slightly pruned, and not allowed to flower too freely, as this probably exhausts the plant and hastens on canker, which seems inevitable to this variety." [FRB] "A vigorous growing rose, more free blooming than 'Chromatella'. Its color is yellow, deepening at the center to a rich golden yellow. It is, perhaps, the largest and most beautiful yellow rose known, and very fragrant." [SBP] "Strongly Tea-scented . . . magnificent foliage . . . very liable to mildew . . . blooms . . . lose colour when exposed to the sun . . . fine in petal, centre, shape, colour, fragrance and size: of fair lasting qualities if kept dry and fairly cool." [F-M2] "Large, full, fine form." [ARA17/26] "Shapely, pointed buds . . . 10 × 6 [ft; ca. 3 × 1.75 m]." [B] "Perfectly shaped buds and flowers of soft deep yellow, with richer fragrance than any other rose." [ARA29/98] "Blend of Musk and Tea [perfumes]." [NRS/17] "Raspberry-scented." [JR33/101] "Very tender, and mildews and balls easily." [Capt28] "Truly yellow and a real climber [in Brazil]." [PS] "Rich-green foliage . . . 12–15 ft. [ca. 3.5–4.5 m]." [W] "The most aristocratic [foliage] of any climbing rose — like smooth kid in texture; with its tender, reddish tips." [ARA29/101] "Shoots well clothed with large shining leaves." [FP] "A most rampant growing kind." [P1] "A rapid climber, which requires time before it blooms. Patience is of primary importance to get this into order." [WD]

"The circular which announced its release to commerce in 1864 gives the following description: 'Vigorous plant, with large, long branches producing slender branchlets. Bark smooth, of a glabrous green, or perhaps a little yellowish, numerous hooked, very dark and sharp thorns. Foliage plain green, brilliant, wavy, divided into 5 or 6 pointed oval leaflets; the leafstalk, which is pretty long, is furnished beneath with 3 or 4 hooked and very sharp prickles. The superb flower is 3–4 in[ches] in diameter [ca. 7.5 cm–1 dm], full, globular, borne singly on the branches, but usually in a cluster on the stronger limbs. Its color is a beautiful golden yellow which is quite dark indeed; petals, large. The flower-stalk is slender and somewhat too weak for the blossom, which consequently nods. Calyx flared.'" [JR20/43] "By its vigor

and bloom, the Rose 'Maréchal Niel' surpasses 'Chromatella', 'Solfatare', 'Isabella Gray', etc., other varieties with yellow flowers. Its wood is deep olive green nuanced brownish red where the sun strikes; it is armed with dark red thorns which are laterally flattened, and hooked like the beak of a parakeet. The ample leaves are composed of 3–5 leaflets of a beautiful glossy green above, pale green beneath, finely dentate — the lateral leaves, slightly petiolate, are obovate, pointed, or shortly acuminate; the terminal leaflet is larger, longly petiolate, and acuminate; the rachis is glandular-hirsute above, and armed beneath with very fine hooked prickles; it is slightly winged at the base due to its stipules which, where free, are subulate, and at a right angle to the petiole. The blossoms are very beautiful, full, globular at first, then opening out, large to 12–14 cm [ca. 4.5–6 in], beautiful deep yellow, and very fragrant. This beautiful Tea comes from the South [*of France*], raised a few years ago by a horticulturalist in *le Midi*; it is not [otherwise] known to commerce." [l'H64/327] "Branches large, elongated, and limber, producing equally both slender and strong branchlets. . . . Calyx rounded." [JF] "The *Canada Farmer* mentions the fact that this new and splendid rose has been exposed to a temperature of eighteen degrees below zero [*F*] without injury. . . . We have some doubts of the general hardiness of this variety." [HstXXIV:91] "When budding it is advisable to use only buds from those shoots that are seen to produce flowers freely." [Hn] "As a variety, 'Maréchal Niel' seems to be suffering from old age." [ARA37/152]

"Mons Pradel responded that the rose came from a sowing made by himself, and was one which he had grafted on many stocks; that the previous year he had planted one of these stocks in the garden of Mons Château in the place of a 'Chromatella' which he had lost. . . . It was [*continues correspondent G. T.*] in 1858 that Mons Géraud Pradel the younger sowed a certain quantity of seed gathered from his collections, there being among others the seed of 'Chromatella'. He had the satisfaction of seeing born one plant which attracted his attention. It repaid his efforts. The following year, a yellow rose appeared; it was grafted by him on the Briar; it became magnificent. Instead of taking advantage of this great find . . . Mons Pradel became jealous about it. He hid it mysteriously. In 1860, the wife of one of his clients having lost a very pretty 'Chromatella' which had grown on one of her garden walls . . . she said to him 'Never will you be able to replace it!'; 'Yes, madame,' responded Pradel, 'I will replace it for you with another even prettier which you will hold dear, because *my* yellow rose is a veritable marvel.' He gave it to her. The Rose was well looked after, and grew wonderfully. Some time later, Mons R—, a great fancier, went to pay a visit to the woman, and saw the rose [— *the rest being History*]." [JR19/85–87] "This magnificent rose, always held in esteem and sought out, has given rise to a little horticultural fraud at its place of origin, 'Isabella Gray' being supplied in place of what everyone wanted to have, 'Maréchal Niel', commerce not being able to supply enough. This did not last long." [JR1/3/12] "The marks of resemblance to 'Isabella Gray', particularly the birthmark of indented petals, are unmistakeable." [Dr]

"Outside of commerce commonly and justly called the Queen of Roses, one is not able to confuse it with 'Lamarque' or 'Isabella Gray'; neither the one nor the other has the pleasurable perfume of 'Maréchal Niel'. . . . Though every year we see novelties, it must be said that not one of them is the equal of 'Maréchal Niel' in form or the freshness of its color." [S] "The 'Maréchal Niel' Rose . . . is, like the 'Général Jacqueminot', most extensively forced under glass for its buds; probably three acres of glass surface are used for it in the vicinity of New York City, but it is now [*1889*] superseded by some of the yellow 'Teas' which, though not quite equal to it in quality, flower continuously." [pH] "It used to abound in the southern states, but nowadays it is rarely met with, although its fame abides." [GAS] "By the unreversed judgment of over forty years, 'Maréchal Niel' is the most remarkable rose of the nineteenth century. It is a proud triumph of nature that exceeds all expectation and defies criticism." [Dr] "Named after a French general, Minister of War of Napoleon III." [K]

MARGO KOSTER, CL.

Golie, 1962
Polyantha
Sport of 'Margo Koster' (Pol).

Coral-orange, and different from the dwarf only in its "climbing" growth. I have seen some very nice weeping standards made from it.

MARIE-JEANNE

Listed as a bush Polyantha.

[MARIE VAN HOUTTE, CL.]

Hjort, ca. 1940
Tea
Sport of 'Marie Van Houtte' (T).

"Creamy, pink-tinged yellow, recurrent." [W] "It was a sport discovered here [at the Thomasville Nurseries, Georgia] in 1936. It appeared in our catalogs in the early '40's for several years and there is no further reference to it. We have no stock now." [Hj]

MERVEILLE

Listed as 'Tausendschoen'.

MILKMAID

A. Clark/Brundrett, 1925
Noisette
From 'Crépuscule' (N) × ?

"A strong-growing Noisette with large sprays of rather small white or creamy yellow, single flowers. Recommended as a fragrant spring-blooming climber for the South." [GAS]

MLLE CÉCILE BRUNNER, CL.

Hosp, 1894 and Kerschaw, 1905
Polyantha
Sport of 'Mlle Cécile Brunner' (Pol).

"[For] everywhere. A good, large-growing decorative pink with perfect, well-held foliage and a most prolific bloomer. Flower . . . fades in sun. Plant stands shade or sun." [Capt28] "Flowers . . . are sparsely distributed . . . 25 × 20 [ft; ca. 7.5 × 6 m]." [B] "Always blooming, with large foliage which doesn't drop until December." [JR36/188] "In clusters. . . . Sparse, soft, light foliage." [W] "Black-spots somewhat; bloom abundant in May and June, free in July, moderate later, almost continuous." [ARA18/129] "Graceful vine, with uncommonly beautiful foliage." [Dr]

MLLE CLAIRE JACQUIER

('Claire Jacquier')
Bernaix, 1887
Noisette

"Buff-yellow." [J] "Deep orange . . . and thornless." [BSA] "Finishes pale." [Hk] "Medium size, double, yellow fading to white . . . blooms once yearly . . . 10–12 [ft; ca. 3–3.5 m]." [Lg] "Flowers nankeen-yellow, small, but produced in very large clusters;

exceedingly pretty and distinct, and remarkably vigorous." [P1] "Well foliated . . . shapely . . . pleasing perfume. . . . Recurrent. 25 × 10 [ft; ca. 7.5 × 3 m]." [B] "Flowers very numerous, at the ends of the branches, in clusters; small (an inch or so in diameter [ca. 2.5 cm+]), of perfect form, erect, very double; petals self-colored, nankeen-yellow, not fading more than a little upon opening . . . climbing, of great vigor, in one season growing to 15 ft [ca. 4.5 m] . . . large leaves, glossy green on top, purplish beneath." [JR11/151] "20 [ft; ca. 6 m]." [HRG] We read in *Les Amis des Roses* (nº 245) of the Lyonnais nurseryman Claude Jacquier . . .

MLLE DE SOMBREUIL

('Mme de Sombreuil', 'Sombreuil')
Robert, 1851
Tea

Reputed to be a seedling of 'Parks' Yellow' (T). Also has been associated with 'Adam'.

"White, tinged with rose, very large and full; form cupped; growth vigorous. A good hardy free flowering sort." [P1] "A fine large blush with a yellowish tint, of the right form." [WHoIII] "Flower from 8–9 cm [nearly 4 in], quite double, lightly blushing, beautiful form, strong peduncles." [VH51/112] "Flat . . . fragrant; creamy-white, center tinted pinkish in cooler weather. Profuse, continuous bloom . . . 8–10 [ft; ca. 2.25–3 m] . . . one of the most beautiful." [Lg] "Classically formed flowers . . . 8 × 4 [ft; ca. 2.25 × 1.25 m]." [B] "White with some salmon." [JR1/2/8] "Flowers of a pale straw color." [SBP] "Vigorous plant; flowers large, nearly full, white touched salmon." [I'H53/223] "Vigorous, hardy . . . blooms in panicles." [S] "Evidently of Bourbon parentage on one side . . . the hardiest and most vigorous of the white Teas, and free from mildew. A valuable sort for the open air." [EL] "Short, ovoid bud, opening quickly to a double flower of large size, but somewhat flat. Plant of strong growth. . . . Foliage holds well and is usually free from disease. Discolors in damp winds." [Th2] "This rose is dedicated to Mlle de Sombreuil, the heroine who, during the Terror, locked herself up with her father, the Count Sombreuil, governor of Les Invalides, prisoner of the Abbaye, in Paris, and who stopped the September assassins' arms by her supplications; and, according to legend, who drank a glass of human blood, a glass which she then offered to the assailants!" [JR34/15] "Or note old Mons de Sombreuil, who also had a Daughter:—My Father is not an aristocrat: O good gentlemen, I will swear it, and testify it, and in all ways prove it; we are not; we hate aristocrats! 'Wilt thou drink Aristocrats' blood?' The man lifts blood (if universal Rumour can be credited); the poor maiden does drink. 'This Sombreuil is innocent then!' Yes, indeed,—and now note, most of all, how the bloody pikes, at this news, do rattle to the ground." [Cy] "Mons Robert, Mons Vibert's gardener [in 1846]." [M-L46/273]

MME ABEL CHATENAY, CL.

Page/Easlea, 1917
Hybrid Tea
Sport of 'Mme Abel Chatenay' (HT).

Pink shades. *The* climbing rose for autumn . . . most beautiful flowers." [RATS] "Larger flowers than the dwarf." [Th2] "[For] everywhere. Very fine grower . . . well-held foliage; flower medium size; lasts well; slight perfume; continuous bloomer in occasional bursts." [Capt28] "Semi-vigorous . . . 10 × 6 [ft; ca. 3 × 1.75 m]." [B]

MME ALFRED CARRIÈRE   PLATE 185
Schwartz, 1879
Noisette

"White, yellowish base. Large, fragrant, very perpetual." [H] "Pure white, very free; a good pillar rose." [Th] "Pearly-white, with long stems . . . good foliage . . . one of the most constant." [BSA] "Pinky-white to white clusters . . . globular flowers. Vigorous . . . 12 × 10 [ft; ca.   3.5 × 3 m]." [B] "White, not free blooming, undesirable." [EL] "Free-blooming." [F-M] "Its white blossoms, which some liken to the porcelain roses manufactured abroad, are borne singly on the stalks, and last long in water, while it is never out of flower from June to November." [K2] "One of the earliest climbing roses to open its blossoms, which are produced profusely." [NRS/17] "Large pale leaves of the tea-rose character, and large loose flowers of a low-toned warm white." [E] "Very big grower; good foliage; double, flat flowers with blush at center." [Capt28] "One of the most beautiful climbing roses we possess . . . flesh white shaded with salmon; large and full. Sweet-scented, growth extra vigorous." [P1] "Ample foliage of a handsome brilliant green." [JR3/165] "Foliage mildews in shade or extreme damp, but [the variety] is indispensible in Southern Zones." [Th2] "Fine upright growths, branching in the second season . . . quite free from mildew. So continuously does this beautiful Rose flower that its flowering period may almost be said to be the whole season. . . . The flowers are large, almost full, and carried singly or in small loose clusters. They are very sweetly scented . . . the wood of the previous year must be retained." [NRS/11] "Most artistic flower. It suffers from mildew occasionally, but not badly." [NRS/13] "It requires thinning out freely every year. . . . The foliage is of a lightish green and very good, lasting long on the plant . . . it is liable to make a dense growth which hides the flowers." [NRS/14] "Very vigorous . . . 20 ft [ca. 6 m]." [W] "[Excellent in Norway]." [ARA20/46] "Dedicated to the wife of a great lover of roses from our province of Dauphiné." [JR10/57] "The best white climbing Rose." [J]

[MME BRUNNER]   PLATE 207
('Aimée Vibert Jaune')
Brunner/Frœbel, 1890
Noisette
Sport of 'Aimée Vibert' (N).

"Pale yellow." [LS] "A rampant, rambling shrub of evergreen, everblooming habit, very like Yellow Banksia, but of deeper color." [ARA31/28] There was also an 'Aimée Vibert à Fleur Jaune' by Perny/Cochet, 1904: "A seedling from the rose 'Aimée Vibert' in which the flowers are salmon yellow and not white. . . . All the characteristics are those of 'Aimée Vibert', except for the differing color." [JR28/185]

MME BUTTERFLY, CL.
Smith, 1926
Hybrid Tea
Sport of 'Mme Butterfly' (HT).

Pale pink. "[As compared with 'Mme Butterfly', bush form:] Flower longer, outer petals cleaner, more fragrant, and altogether superior . . . vigorous . . . to 7 ft [ca. 2 m]." [ARA26/181] "10 × 10 [ft; ca. 3 × 3 m]." [B]

MME CAROLINE TESTOUT, CL.
Chauvry, 1901
Hybrid Tea
Sport of 'Mme Caroline Testout' (HT).

"Satin pink with a deeper centre. . . . Huge blooms . . . strongly scented . . . strong stems . . . 15 × 8 [ft; ca.   4.5 × 2.25 m]." [B]

"Good blooms when you get them; not one of the best growers; susceptible to mildew." [ARA18/122] "Good grower, fair foliage, good bloomer but balls in dampness. Best in Pacific Northwest." [Capt28] "[Favorite in Houston, Texas]." [ET] "[Splendid in Norway]." [ARA20/46] "A gorgeous show in early June but seldom another bloom the rest of the season." [K] "Vigorous growth characterises this Rose, and an upright but branching habit . . . more or less constantly in flower. . . . Its strong points are its vigor, reliability, and bold big blossoms, and continuity of flowering. Its weakness that it is apt to become bare at the base unless carefully treated, and from its stiff growth bending the shoots down to prevent this is often difficult." [NRS/11] "Branches 'climbing,' excellent variety for pyramids." [JR25/163]

MME COUTURIER-MENTION
('Cl. Cramoisi Supérieur')
Couturier/Moser, 1885
China
Seedling of 'Cramoisi Supérieur' (Ch).

"Shining crimson; flower medium-sized, cupped, semi-double; floriferous; vigorous." [Cx] "Full, crimson red. Continuous flowering." [LR] "Dark scarlet. Fine foliage and continuous bloom; not a tall grower; train on a fence or pillar; does well in shade." [Th2] "Rather large, double, purplish red flowers, borne more or less continuously." [GAS] "A fine climber, though it is not very free flowering until well established." [OM] "Fair everywhere . . . only slight perfume." [Capt28] "12 × 10 [ft; ca. 3.5 × 3 m]." [B] "Will climb to fully twenty ft high, and cover itself with its rich crimson flowers." [J] "We have the pleasure of making known to fanciers of pretty roses that the China roses have been enriched by a new variety which will certainly not be considered the least attractive of that race. This new offering was raised from seed by Mons Couturier-Mention. . . . Contrary to the type, known to be naturally weak in all its parts, this variety is vigorous, and is able to attain — after a few years — seven ft or so [ca. 2 m+] on a pillar, nearly always covered with flowers. The flowers, borne on long stems, nod, and are cupped and regularly formed, with large, concave petals, rather large for the sort, bright crimson-maroon, and showing that distinctive mark of this race, a certain number of central petals marked longitudinally down the middle with a white, readily-apparent, stripe. Its foliage, of a green rather darker than lighter, has leaflets deeply toothed, and more oval than those of 'Bengale cerise' and 'Bengale sanguin' The thorns are not a problem, being rather sparse. Its raiser, Mons Couturier-Mention, considers it the hardiest of the Chinas, assuring us that it weathers the frosts of central France without much trouble. Last September, the young plants we saw were quite as full of blossoms as their brother 'Cramoisi Supérieur'." [JR9/167] "Bears a great resemblance to 'James Sprunt' " [*for which see chapter supplement*]. [JR22/21]

MME DRIOUT
('Mme Dréout')
Bolut & Thiriat, 1902
Hybrid Tea
Sport of 'Reine Marie Henriette' (Cl. HT).

"Pink striped cerise." [LS] "The flower is a delicate shaded satin-pink, plumed and striped bright carmine, making a most agreeable contrast. The striping is constant, and pretty regular on all the flowers, though at times a very large and distinct splotch might be formed, or perhaps one big stripe." [JR28/27] "Admirably plumed, flamed, striped bright carmine on pale pink. . . . Its vigor and floriferousness are not inferior to those of 'Reine Marie Henriette'. The striping varies with the flower: sometimes the red predominates . . . other times, the pink, at which times the blossom gains in freshness, I think." [JR27/153] "Deep red. This rose resembles the shape of 'Gloire de Dijon' . . . 10 × 8 [ft; ca. 3 × 2.25 m]." [B] "This novelty was noted by Messers Bolut and Thiriat when on a visit to the gardens at Saint-Dizier at the home of Mons Driout, mayor of that community. The striping is sharper in spring, and less pronounced in fall. The characteristics of the variety are exactly the same as those of the mother, except that it is of a little less vigor." [JR26/113]

MME JULES GRAVEREUX   PLATE 206
Soupert & Notting, 1900
Hybrid Tea
From 'Rêve d'Or' (N) × 'Viscountess Folkestone' (HT).
"Buff-white, shaded peach . . . free and good." [P1] "Flesh, shaded yellow." [NRS/10] "Pink undertones . . . slight scent. Good foliage . . . 12 × 8 [ft; ca. 3.5 × 2.25 m]." [B] "Very vigorous and 'climbing,' magnificent foliage; bud, very long and pointed; flower extremely large, very full; color, chamois yellow, with a peach-pink center and dawn-gold reflections. Of the best, very floriferous and fragrant." [JR24/148] "This variety has big, well-formed blooms of buff-white with rose and yellow shading, and is often grown for exhibition. It is disappointing as a garden rose." [OM] "Flowers of great size and beautiful form. Mildews badly . . . does not develop well in dampness." [Capt28] "Exquisite buds." [ARA18/79] "Very double blooms . . . vigorous to 12 [ft; ca. 3.5 m]." [HRG] "Tall, compact, vigorous, hardy; foliage plentiful, blackspots slightly; bloom free, continuous." [ARA18/126] "It resembles, in the form of the plant as well as in its abundant autumnal flowering, 'Gloire de Dijon'." [JR32/34] "Gravereux (Jules). — Former administrator of 'Bon Marché,' died in 1916 at the age of 71. Great rose fancier. He created in 1899 a magnificent rosarium at his estate at L'Haÿ (Seine)." [R-HC]

MME LA DUCHESSE D'AUERSTÄDT   PLATE 193
('Duchesse d'Auerstädt')
Bernaix, 1887
Noisette
Seedling of 'Rêve d'Or' (N).
"Golden yellow; flower very large, very full, imbricated, cupped, fragrant; vigorous." [Cx] "Deep buff, very double . . . to 10 [ft; ca. 3 m]." [HRG] "Bright yellow, shaded with nankeen at the centre. Very vigorous." [P1] "More intense colouring [than has 'Gloire de Dijon']. Good foliage . . . 10 × 6 [ft; ca. 3 × 1.75 m]." [B] "A lovely rose, but shy flowering. It is of good growth on a warm wall, but the shapely flowers . . . are usually sparsely produced." [OM] "Remarkably vigorous growth. Blooms constantly in Southern Zones . . . does not open well in dampness." [Th2] "The bush grows somewhat larger than medium size; great big leaves, thick, leathery, shiny, in stiff stalks; flowers large, of perfect form, most often solitary at the end of the branch, very double and opening well; large concave petals, thick, firm, imbricated in the outer rows." [JR11/151] "Wonderful . . . equal to 'Maréchal Niel' and a better grower." [ARA25/113] "Excellent in every way." [J]

MONSIEUR PAUL LÉDÉ, CL.
('Paul Lédé')
Low, 1913
Hybrid Tea
Sport of 'Monsieur Paul Lédé' (HT).
"Carmine pink and dawn yellow." [JR38/109] "Yellow and apricot. Graceful in vigor and color, 'Climbing Paul Lédé' is a

precious enrichment in yellow climbers." [JR38/72] "[For] everywhere. Not pure yellow, but otherwise very fine, with splendid growth, good foliage, and cutting value. A prolific and constant bloomer." [Capt28] "Large shapely pink flowers with apricot overtones, sweetly fragrant and very free flowering, 12 [ft; ca. 3.5 m]." [HRG] "A sight to remember . . . 12 × 8 [ft; ca. 3.5 × 2.25 m]." [B]

MONTECITO
Franceschi-Fenzi, 1930
Hybrid Gigantea
From *R. gigantea* × *R. brunonii*.
White to blush? "Grown to some extent in California." [GAS] Also, of the same provenance, MONTARIOSO ('Montariosa'), concerning which we have no reports.

[MRS. B. R. CANT, CL.]
Hjort, 1960
Tea
Sport of 'Mrs. B. R. Cant' (T).
Rose-red to silvery-pink. "A very vigorous climber, reaching . . . ten to twelve ft [ca. 3–3.5 m] . . . the same good foliage and bloom of the bush 'Mrs. B. R. Cant' . . . a good spring bloom and intermittent bloom the rest of the . . . season. . . . We doubt that it is still growing anywhere now." [Hj]

MRS. HERBERT STEVENS, CL.
Pernet-Ducher, 1922
Hybrid Tea
Sport of 'Mrs. Herbert Stevens' (HT).
"Lovely white . . . stamina. Fragrant and vigorous . . . 12 × 16 [ca. 3.5 × 4.75 m]." [B] "Semi-double and delightfully fragrant . . . a rampant grower." [GAS] "[For] everywhere. Fine grower; good foliage; a rose for cutting and far ahead of 'Niphetos' and 'Devoniensis'. Blooms through a long season. Prefer this to 'Cl. Frau Karl Druschki'." [Capt28]

MRS. ROBERT PEARY
Listed as 'Kaiserin Auguste Viktoria, Cl'.

MULTIFLORE DE VAUMARCUS
Menet, 1875
Noisette
"Soft pink, very double, medium large, in large trusses, continuous bloom; growth bushy, medium, foliage healthy." [Kr]

NANCY HAYWARD
A. Clark, 1937
Hybrid Gigantea
From 'Jessy Clark' (HGig, A. Clark, 1924, rose-pink single; parentage: *R. gigantea* × 'Mme Martignier' [Cl. T]) × ?
Cherry red, single. No doubt a "once-bloomer," like most Hybrid Giganteas.

NEW DAWN
Dreer, 1930
Sport of 'Dr. W. Van Fleet' (Cl.)
Light pink. "Outstanding. . . . Shapely and perfumed . . . 10 × 8 [ft; ca. 3 × 2.25 m]." [B] "Bloomed continuously all summer . . . smaller [flowers] than 'Dr. W. Van Fleet' but otherwise similar. . . . Vigor is equal to 'Dr. W. Van Fleet' . . . bloomed continuously until late in November." [ARA32/199] "Never disappointed anyone! . . . tremendous display . . . slightly fragrant." [W] "Of no value in Texas." [ARA34/204]

NIPHETOS, CL.

('Paul Krüger')
Keynes, Williams & Co., 1889
Tea
Sport of 'Niphetos' (T).

"Pure white, a good climber." [FRB] "The flowers are long and shapely and pure white, but the stalks are weak." [OM] "Lovely, creamy bud. . . . Highly scented . . . 10 × 6 [ft; ca. 3 × 1.75 m]." [B] "[As compared to the bush form,] the flowers are larger, whiter, and considerably more fragrant." [JR17/35] "Does not ball, but discolored by rain. Medium foliage. Better as a climber than a dwarf. . . . The flowering is continuous." [Th2] "Another example of a luxuriant climber, exceeding the parent rose in the substance of the flowers." [Dr] "Constant supply of fine pure white flowers . . . much appreciated in hot climates." [F-M2] "A bit stingy with its flowers." [Hk] "Very vigorous." [DO] "Sometimes a little difficulty in getting it to commence 'running.' " [F-M2] "Habit thoroughly climbing." [P1]

NOËLLA NABONNAND

Nabonnand, 1900
From 'Reine Marie Henriette' (Cl. HT) × 'Bardou Job' (B).

"Velvety crimson red, white nub." [Cx] "Velvet crimson and carmine." [RR] "A gorgeous semi-double velvety crimson Rose with extra large petals . . . extra vigorous in growth." [P1] "Flower very large, even enormous, semi-double; color, velvety crimson-red; very large petals; elongated bud, well-formed, well-held; very large and handsome foliage; growth very vigorous, very floriferous. Fragrant. More vigorous than 'Reine Marie Henriette'." [JR25/4] "Sweet scented and of good shape and size . . . crimson having a bluish tinge." [F-M] "Fair growth . . . color good, tending to blue somewhat." [ARA18/121] "A most magnificent rose, still classed as a Tea, though it seems more closely allied to the Hybrid Teas. It grows vigorously, and bears very long, fragrant buds of the most vivid velvety-crimson shade; they soon become full-blown, but in the bud are splendid. It flowers freely." [OM] "Rich old-rose fragrance. Canes to 10 [ft; ca. 3 m]." [HRG] "Foliage well retained." [Th2] "Foliage perfectly healthy; heavy spring bloom; light subsequently." [BCD] "A really good winter-blooming deep red Rose." [J]

ODORATA 22449

Listed as 'Fun Jwan Lo'.

OLD BLUSH, CL.

('Cl. Parsons' Pink China')
Introducer and date unknown
China
Sport of *R. chinensis* 'Parsons' Pink'.

"Medium size, double, loose spray; bright to medium pink. Repeats . . . builds up to 15–20 [ft; ca. 4.5–6 m]." [Lg]

OPHELIA, CL.

A. Dickson, 1920
Hybrid Tea
Sport of 'Ophelia' (HT).

"Large, double, flat, fragrant; soft salmon pink. Repeats . . . 8–10 [ft; ca. 2.25–3 m]." [Lg] "Very valuable. In great heat, this rose opens flat. If possible, should be given partial shade in Southern Zones." [Th2] "Vigorous, healthy plant. Outstanding

. . . 12 × 8 [ft; ca. 3.5 × 2.25 m]." [B] "Will become exceedingly popular . . . superior flowers to the dwarf variety." [NRS22/159]

[OPHIRIE]

Goubault, 1841
Noisette

"Reddish copper, the outer petals rosy and fawn, of medium size, very double; form cupped; growth vigorous; distinct and sweet; foliage handsome." [P1] "Nasturtium-yellow, suffused with coppery-red, medium-size, double; a very distinct sort, but very shy." [EL] "Queerly coloured and queerly shaped, as they are nearly always quartered, flowers abundantly in clusters. Except as a curiosity, hardly worth growing." [B&V]

PAPA GONTIER, CL.

Hosp, 1898
Tea
Sport of 'Papa Gontier' (T).

"Intense pink, shaded yellow towards the center; reverse of petals purplish-red." [JR32/173] "The buds are long and shapely, of rose-red colour, but they are thin and soon become full-blown." [OM] "Very fine foliage; does not mildew in shade." [Th2] The same sport also occurred for Vigneron/Chevrier in 1904 and for Chase & Co. in 1905.

PAPILLON

Nabonnand, 1878
Tea

"Pink and white, with coppery shading. Fine pillar rose." [H] "Coppery salmon-rose, of medium size, semi-double; very free in blooming." [P1] "Quite a curious rose in the form of its flower and the disposition of its petals." [JR14/132] "Very vigorous, climbing, flowers of medium size, and semi-double. Color is the coppery-pink of dawn, the underside of the petals being bright pink; bloom is profuse, and the blossoms look, in their form and arrangement, like a flock of butterflies perched on the bush. This variety of such originality is one of the best of the climbing sort." [JR3/9] "Foliage deep green and coppery." [B1] "Rather tender." [OM] "4 × 3 [ft; ca. 1.25 × 1 m]." [B] "[One of the] Hybrids of Tea and Noisette." [JR24/44] "This Rose is quite easy to grow on an 8-ft. or 9-ft. Pillar [ca. 2.25–2.75 m]. I incline to think I should call it the best Tea Rose we possess for this purpose. It so readily clothes itself right up from the base and allows . . . much latitude in pruning. . . . The first plant I had of this variety absolutely refused to grow more than about three ft [ca. 9 dm], and it still remains about that height, though I have had it undisturbed for some ten years. . . . On getting a strong plant, however, I found it would readily make a 15-ft. Pillar [ca. 4.5 m]. . . . It is extremely free flowering all the season through, and the flowers, which are borne in large trusses, are very fresh and decorative, particularly if picked young. . . . They are wanting in form it is true, but I think this is the only bad quality my friends have been able to find in this Rose as a Pillar." [NRS/14]

PAUL KRÜGER

Listed as 'Niphetos, Cl'.

PAUL LÉDÉ, CL.

Listed as 'Monsieur Paul Lédé, Cl'.

PAUL'S LEMON PILLAR
G. Paul, 1915
Hybrid Tea
From 'Frau Karl Druschki' (HP) × 'Maréchal Niel' (N).

"Exquisite large pale yellow double blooms with Tea fragrance . . . 10 [ft; ca. 3 m]." [HRG] "Probably this is the most beautiful white of any class." [GAS] "Massive blooms, off-white suffused with lemon. . . . Scented . . . vigorous . . . very thick branches and large leaves . . . 15 × 10 [ft; ca. 4.5 × 3 m]." [B] "Wonderful blooms—large and of fine form; fair growth; rather shy bloomer." [ARA18/120] "Best in Pacific Northwest. Balls in dampness; mildews." [Capt28]

PENNANT
A. Clark, 1941
Hybrid Gigantea
Pink; non-remontant. No further information!

PERLE DES JARDINS, CL.
J. Henderson, 1890
Tea
Sport of 'Perle des Jardins' (T).

"Golden-yellow, recurrent, fragrant." [W] "Intense yellow fading to very light yellow." [JR32/139] "Pure yellow . . . a fine addition to the climbing kinds." [P1] "Intense straw yellow; flower very large, very full, cupped; very floriferous; very vigorous." [Cx] "Richly fragrant." [ARA29/98] "The buds of this rose . . . are very pretty though small." [OM] "Better than the dwarf. Easier to grow than 'Maréchal Niel', and of much the same color. Balls in ocean climates early and late." [Th2]

[PERLE D'OR, CL.]
('Yellow Cécile Brunner, Cl'.)
Introducer and date unknown
Polyantha
Sport of 'Perle d'Or' (Pol).

"Deep yellow, opening lemon-yellow, outer edges yellow-cream. Foliage slightly different from the pink climber ['Climbing Cécile Brunner']. . . . Does not flower as continuously as the pink, and is not as strong a grower." [Th2] "Great clusters of small double flowers even more abundantly than in bush form." [SHj]

PHYLLIS BIDE
Bide, 1923
Polyantha
From 'Perle d'Or' (Pol) × 'Gloire de Dijon' (N).

"Golden yellow shaded pinkish carmine." [Cw] "Pink, salmon and gold. Slight scent. Medium growth . . . 10 × 6 [ft; ca. 3 × 1.75 m]." [B] "Small, double blooms of pale gold, shaded pink, borne in clusters, vigorous to 6 [ft; ca. 1.75 m]." [HRG] "Long, loose clusters in June . . . old blooms stay too long, turning green . . . to 6 ft [ca. 1.75 m]." [W] "Very pretty perpetual-flowering Polyantha variety of fairly vigorous habit, the plants growing to a height of about 6 ft [ca. 1.75 m]. The blooms, which are produced in loose sprays, are almost double, the color pale gold, tipped with pale pink. The foliage is handsome." [ARA24/166] "Not very high-climbing, with clusters of few flowers, neither large nor small, mostly yellow in the bud, but pink in age . . . some scented bloom . . . pretty buds have a delicious color." [ARA30/172]

PINK PET, CL.
Introducer and date unknown
Polyantha
Sport of 'Pink Pet' (Pol).

"Mid-sized, double bright pink blooms in clusters . . . to 10 [ft; ca. 3 m]." [HRG]

PINKIE, CL.
Dering, 1952
Polyantha
Sport of 'Pinkie' (Pol).

"Large clusters of semidouble, 1.75 to 2.5 in [ca. 3.75–6.25 cm], rose-colored, cupped flowers in . . . constant profusion. . . . Soft, glossy foliage. Vigorous to 8 to 9 ft [ca. 2.25–3 m] . . . slightly fragrant." [W] "Not a typically huge-growing climbing Polyantha . . . 3–5 [ft; ca. 1–1.5 m]. Repeats bloom well." [Lg]

POMPON DE PARIS, CL.
Introducer and date unknown
Miniature China

"Vigorous . . . small, greyish-green foliage and twiggy growth. Flowers small and button-like, produced profusely in small clusters." [B1]

PRINCES VAN ORANJE
Sliedrecht & Co., 1933
Polyantha
Sport of 'Gloria Mundi' (Pol).

"Huge clusters of blazing red and orange flowers produced more or less continuously throughout the season." [GAS] "6 ft [ca. 1.75 m] and is literally covered with masses of blazing red flowers in trusses." [ARA33/179] "Very strong growth . . . the color burns less than that of the dwarf form ['Gloria Mundi']." [ARA34/208]

PURITY
Hoopes Bros. & Thomas Co., 1917
Hybrid Tea
From an unnamed seedling × 'Mme Caroline Testout' (HT).

"Big, cup-shaped, pure white flowers borne with remarkable freedom. Plant is excessively thorny and extremely vigorous." [GAS] "Semi-double." [ARA18/91] "One blooming season. Vigorous growth, varying sometimes. . . . Foliage good and well held. Very fine when well grown." [Th2] "Rather low, bushy growth; good foliage; blooms attractive." [ARA18/121] "Foliage black-spots in midsummer, very slightly in late summer, slightly mildews in midsummer; bloom sparse in June." [ARA18/131] "A sturdy trellis or pillar Rose." [McF]

REINE MARIE HENRIETTE   PLATE 182
Levet, 1878
Hybrid Tea
From 'Mme Bérard' (N) × 'Général Jacqueminot' (HP).

"Rosy-red." [J] "Fulgent crimson, large and full; magnificent and effective." [P1] "Cherry-carmine, another hybrid tea; an excellent climber." [FRB] "Brilliant red clusters . . . the foliage is sparse and shabby in color." [BSA] "Vigorous, very floriferous, nice foliage, flower cupped, of good form, cherry-red." [JR3/142] "Cherry-red, a pure shade, large, double, somewhat fragrant; a beautiful, but rather unproductive sort." [EL] "Free-flowering and vigorous . . . 12 × 8 [ft; ca. 3.5 × 2.25 m]." [B] "Blooms prolifically in the spring . . . good form and petalage . . . fragrant; it occasionally gives blooms in summer and autumn." [ARA17/27] "The most constant of autumnals." [F-M2] "A new rose, and on being entered into commerce it was put out as being a red 'Gloire de Dijon'. I can hardly see why it should be thus compared with that old favorite. The shoots are different, being more wiry; the buds are more pointed; and, once open, the blossoms are poorly held and have no perfume; it isn't as floriferous, though it certainly grows vigorously enough." [JR6/110] "Large, three-parts full, globular to cup-shaped, of a distinct fiery cherry-red . . . should not be severely pruned . . . very fragrant." [Hn] "Scent of plums in marmalade." [JR33/101] "Peculiar sweet vinous odour." [Dr] "It has shapely buds, of fair size and red colouring. . . . I always expected (and rarely was disappointed) to gather the first blossoms late in May and the last in November or December. . . . This variety has a fault, but it is only that of most red roses, which on fading take on a depressing purplish tint. This, however, soon ensures their being cut off, so the evil is not a very great one." [OM] "Vigorous with heavy wood, green, strong, and slightly thorny, foliage dark green." [JR2/153] "Mildews; foliage lost early." [Th2] "[Excellent in Norway]." [ARA20/46] "Dedicated to Queen Marie-Henriette of Belgium." [JR34/15]

REPENS
Listed as 'Aimée Vibert'.

RÊVE D'OR
PLATE 177

(trans., 'Golden Dream'; syn., 'Condesa da Foz')
Ducher, 1869
Noisette
Seedling of 'Mme Schultz' (N).

"Buff-yellow . . . free-flowering." [H] "Deep rich yellow; fragrant." [ARA29/98] "Buff yellow flowers partly lighter, and going over paler." [Hk] "Sometimes, a hint of pink . . . 10 × 6 [ft; ca. 3 × 1.75 m]." [B] "Deep yellow, sometimes coppery yellow, large and full; growth vigorous. A good wall Rose. One of the best." [P1] "Large, double, fragrant; buff-yellow with pinkish center. Repeats bloom well . . . 10 to 15 [ft; ca. 3–4.5 m]. A healthy plant, lovely foliage and blooms; graceful. One of the best Noisettes. Easy." [Lg] "Lovely, tea-rose shaped blooms . . . to 12 [ft; ca. 3.5 m]." [HRG] "Usually gives semi-double flowers of a salmon-yellow, sometimes golden yellow." [JR10/47] "Flower large, full, chamois yellow. Very fragrant." [LR] "Seldom bears a cluster of more than three flowers. . . . One of the mosts useful and hardy of the race, a rampant grower, with buff-yellow blossoms borne in immense numbers both in summer and autumn, while its rich red shoots and reddish-green foliage make it a beautiful object before and after it blooms. It strongly resents any pruning beyond shortening its vigorous summer shoots." [K2] "One of the best climbers and nearly evergreen." [FRB] "Its foliage is one of its chief attractions, clothing the plant to its base, coming very early and continuing late . . . I, and most of my friends, have found it free from mildew. . . . During its flowering periods the blossoms are very freely produced and cover the plant well. . . . The flowers have a Tea scent, their colour generally resembles 'Mme Falcot' and the rose has, in fact, been called a climbing 'Mme Falcot', but when more closely examined the opened flowers will be found to have two colours, a buff yellow and a coppery yellow tint. They are borne in clusters and are fairly shapely, but not good enough for exhibition . . . requires some time to get established before it is at its best." [NRS/11] "A charming Rose, with its copper-tinted foliage, which associates well with the yellow apricot-tinted blooms, which are produced in huge clusters." [NRS/17] "The most prolific climber of medium size . . . very vigorous growth; resistant, restrained foliage . . . better than '[Mme la] Duchesse d'Auerstädt'." [Capt28] "Foliage well retained." [Th2]

"The original of this beautiful rose . . . exists still . . . and each year, in June, it is covered with flowers to the great admiration of visitors. This variety . . . is one of the most vigorous of climbing roses. As compared to others, it grows with astonishing rapidity. Its branches are slender and its foliage large and shiny dark green, and is composed of 5 or perhaps 7 leaflets. The beautiful flowers are large, full, well-formed, and of a nice dark yellow, light at the edges, coppery towards the center. At the first bloom, the blossoms come in clusters of 8–10; afterwards they come one at a time." [JR6/185] "Though in point of perfection and size the flowers are not to be compared with many other roses, it is to my mind one of the most delightful of all climbers; for even when out of bloom its handsome foliage and reddish shoots are highly decorative." [K1] "[Especially good in Florida]." [ARA24/85]

ROULETII, CL.
Introducer and date unknown
Miniature China
Pink miniature climber. No further information!

SÉNATEUR AMIC
P. Nabonnand, 1924
Hybrid Gigantea
From *R. gigantea* × 'General MacArthur' (HT).

"Bud large . . . Nilson red; flower large . . . cupped, brilliant cochineal-carmine with cochineal reflex. Foliage rich green. many thorns. Very vigorous; makes 32-ft. shoots [ca. 1 dkm] in a season." [ARA25/188] "A striking, single-flowered Gigantea, with beautiful warm red, single flowers. Enormously vigorous." [GAS] "Light green foliage with seven leaflets. Flower rather large, cupped, almost single, borne gracefully, very large petals, coloring superb." [ARA26/174] "Bright carmine . . . superb perfume. Healthy and vigorous . . . 10 × 8 [ft; ca. 3 × 2.25 m]." [B]

SETINA
('Climbing Hermosa')
Henderson, 1879
Bourbon
Sport of 'Hermosa' (B).

"A beautiful new introduction from the U.S., bearing many well-formed blossoms of a beautiful silvery-rose." [JR3/114] "Sometimes bright pink." [JR3/166] "Very fragrant." [CA93] "A deeper shade of pink than the bush 'Hermosa', and the roses are larger." [Dr] "Flower medium-sized, full, globular; very vigorous." [Cx] "A strong grower and a free bloomer." [CA96] Introduced in France by Schwartz.

SNOWBIRD, CL.
Weeks, 1949
Hybrid Tea
Sport of 'Snowbird' (HT).

"Exquisite buds, large, very double, high-centered white flowers, tinged lemon-yellow. Leathery foliage and very vigorous. Blooms dependably all season. . . . Heavy tea fragrance." [W]

SOLFATARE
('Solfaterre', 'Augusta')
Boyau, 1843
Noisette
Seedling of 'Lamarque' (N).

"Cup., sulphur, large, double, splendid." [CC] "Creamy white . . . centres bright sulphur, very large and full; form cupped; growth vigorous. A fine Rose, with handsome foliage and very sweet." [P1] "The most useful yellow [as compared to 'Maréchal Niel' and 'Chromatella']; . . . hardier, of better habit, and more certain to flower . . . and the blooms are but little inferior." [EL] "The flowers are not so globular as [those of 'Chromatella'], but rather flat like those of 'Jaune Desprez', very large, of a deeper saffron yellow than ['Chromatella'], and retaining its color more permanently. It is a splendid rose, universally esteemed . . . vigorous." [WRP] "Bright lemon. When half opened, the buds are superb . . . its growth is very luxuriant." [SBP] "Bright straw, with a deeper sulphur centre . . . though not so fine in either color or form as the 'Cloth of Gold' ['Chromatella'], is a truly superb variety, ever repays high cultivation by constantly producing fine clusters of sulphur flowers at the points of every shoot. . . . Care should be taken to stop all *very strong* young shoots when about eighteen in long [ca. 4.5 dm], to induce a more branching growth and greater number of flowers." [C] "Sent to me, by its grower, two years ago [=*1842*], as a 'superb Yellow Tea Rose, not equalled,' and when it first bloomed it fully maintained its Tea character, but as soon as I grew it on its own roots, it directly assumed the habit of our favorite 'Lamarque' . . . an agreeable fragrance. . . . When fully established it flowers freely, and grows rapidly. . . . An eastern or northern aspect, where it will have a portion of sun, will suit it best, and fully preserve its beautiful colour." [Bu] "Fugacious." [HstII:36] "Foliage very good." [Th2] "Apt to cast its leaves." [P2] "10 × 8 [ft; ca.   3 × 2.25 m]." [B] "[Liked in Texas]." [ET] "An excellent climbing rose, and valuable as a stock on which to bud Teas." [EL] As for the name:

A Solfatare's a sulphur spring;
A Solfaterre's not anything.

SOMBREUIL

Listed as 'Mlle de Sombreuil'.

SOUVENIR DE CLAUDIUS DENOYEL

Chambard, 1920
Hybrid Tea
From 'Château de Clos Vougeot' (HT) × 'Commandeur Jules Gravereaux' (HP).

"A magnificent, perfectly formed flower of glistening crimson with shadings of vermilion. It will grow 7 to 8 ft high and is the most desirable Red *Pillar Rose* we know. The fall blooms are exceptionally fine." [C-Ps28] "Large, double, cupped, intensely fragrant; bright crimson red. Pillar type climber; repeats . . . well with good fertilizing and water." [Lg] "Good in all districts. A peculiar color, verging on dark brown; very large grower with particularly fine foliage. Opens a trifle flat, but with clothed center and good stems and perfume. A continuous but not prolific bloomer." [Capt28] "One of the best red climbers. It has the happy faculty of blooming all the way up the stalk. It is very fragrant and is of good color." [CaRol/5/7] "Does not blue nor pale, it is of a vigorous habit and is very sweet scented." [CaRolI/1/8] "Shapely, double, cupped . . . rich red to scarlet. Fragrant. Vigorous, angular growth . . . 12 × 8 [ft; ca. 3.5 × 2.25 m]." [B]

SOUVENIR DE LA MALMAISON, CL.

Bennett, 1893
Bourbon
Sport of 'Souvenir de la Malmaison' (B).

"Blush white; flower very large, very full, flat, fragrant; floriferous; very vigorous." [Cx]   "Well formed, flesh-white." [JR26/56] "Among the very choicest. . . . Huge, double, pale-pink . . . cupped and quartered . . . a great spring mass . . . to 20 ft [ca. 6 m] . . . fine fragrance." [W] "Does not repeat bloom well

when established . . . 10–12 [ft; ca. 3–3.5 m]." [Lg] "Has no superior. It is luxuriant, profuse, strong and vigorous, and the large, double roses are light pink low down on the vines, but higher up, appear white, with charming effect." [Dr] "Foliage sparse and poor; growth fair." [ARA18/122]

SOUVENIR DE MME LÉONIE VIENNOT

Bernaix fils, 1898
Noisette
From 'Gloire de Dijon' (N) × ?

"Jonquil yellow, shading to China rose. Distinct." [H] "Light rose-pink with yellow shading." [Capt28] "Fully double, sometimes quartered blooms of deep primrose yellow with coppery tints, fragrant and free flowering . . . 10 [ft; ca. 3 m]." [HRG] "Tremendous amount of bloom . . . little fall bloom. . . . Foliage only fair." [Capt28] "Climbing, sumptuous foliage, purple-green in the shoots, shiny and somber when older. Flower-stalk hirsute, stiff, holding the blossom erect. Flower very large, of exquisite form, very double, and lasts well. Handsomely colored jonquil yellow shading to amber yellow at the nub, aging subtly to China rose tinted cochineal of a very fresh tone, with azalea red; and, on the reverse, a silvery grayish-white with reddish tinge. Center petals numerous, chamois at the heart, illumined with pink." [JR21/149] "Vigorous . . . 10 × 8 [ft; ca. 3 × 2.25 m]." [B] "One of the main booths [at the 1890 exhibition at Dijon] — the best, perhaps — was that of Messers Viennot & fils, Dijon rose-men. . . . This magnificent booth . . . gained for Messers Viennot the Exhibition's grand prize." [JR15/4–5]

SPRAY CÉCILE BRUNNER

Eventually "climbs," but listed as a Polyantha.

SUNDAY BEST

A. Clark, 1924
Hybrid Perpetual
From 'Frau Karl Druschki' (HP) × an unnamed seedling.

"Its gorgeous, single red flowers have conspicuous white centers and are borne very freely early in the season. Autumn blooms scarce." [GAS] "Long, pointed bud; 3-inch [ca. 7.5 cm], semi-double, ruffled flowers, vivid crimson to carmine with a white eye, richer coloring in partial shade. Starts to bloom early and goes right on even past a first light frost. Wrinkled foliage, not too attractive. . . . It appears to me . . . it should branch more, great long canes springing from base are garlanded the entire length with bloom. Grows to 8 to 10 ft [ca. 2.25–3 m]." [W]

TEA RAMBLER

G. Paul, 1903
From 'Turner's Crimson Rambler' (Mult. Rambler, Turner, 1894) × 'a climbing Tea.'

"Beautiful . . . deep coppery pink in the bud, changing to soft pink in the older flowers." [F-M] "Clusters of mid-sized double flowers . . . salmon-pink, fragrant, one profuse bloom, vig. to 12 [ft; ca. 3.5 m]." [HRG] "Very vigorous upright stems. . . . The foliage is particularly good and persistent; the leaves are moderately dark green in colour, surrounded with a faint red edge, with a fine glossy surface, while the young undeveloped leaves at the end of the shoots are delicate and fern-like. It is particularly free from mildew . . . only one flowering period . . . large clusters . . . tea-scented. The individual blossoms are rather large for a rambling rose, a little fuller than semi-double, and somewhat loosely put together. The colour of the buds is cherry-carmine, that of the open flowers coppery pink, fading to 'La France' pink . . . more form than most ramblers." [NRS/11] "Among the novelties of autumn, 1902, it was also mentioned that Messers Paul & Sons . . . announced one of their originations, The Tea Rambler, which made quite a stir. . . . The bush is very vigorous, developing numerous and large leaves, and bearing quantities of petite blossoms of 'La France' coloration." [JR26/161] "Growth not of best; profuse bloomer; most attractive." [ARA18/121] "The leaves are unusually handsome, and persist on the stems until midwinter." [OM] "12 × 8 [ft; ca. 3.5 × 2.25 m]." [B] "Unsuitable for northern gardens." [NRS/14]

THÉ MARÉCHAL
Listed as 'Lamarque'.

TRIOMPHE DE BOLLWILLER
Listed as 'Fun Jwan Lo'.

VICOMTESSE PIERRE DE FOU
Sauvageot, 1921
Noisette
From 'L'Ideal' (N) × 'Joseph Hill' (HT, salmon).
"Deep pink to magenta-red, with a tip of yellow. Foliage large, dark green." [ARA24/173] "Large, quartered bloom . . . to 15 [ft; ca. 4.5 m]." [HRG] "Bud medium size, ovoid; flower large, very double and lasting; red passing to deep pink . . . short stem; strong fragrance. Foliage . . . glossy dark green, disease-resistant. Few thorns. Climbing, bushy habit; profuse bloomer; all season; very hardy." [ARA22/151] "Luxuriant, glossy foliage of coppery, dark green . . . fragrant . . . flowers . . . are coppery-pink . . . 15 × 10 [ft; ca. 4.5 × 3 m]." [B] "The finest climber in the garden. An immense grower, it produces a constant succession of large double blooms of a wonderfully brilliant shrimp pink with gold shadings. By disbudding, excellent flowers for cutting may be secured. It made twenty-foot canes the second year from budding, and has handsome, glossy, disease-resistant foliage." [CaRol/6/6]

WHITE MAMAN COCHET, CL.
Knight, 1907 — or Needle & Co., 1911
Tea
Sport of 'White Maman Cochet' (T).
"Very large, double; white streaked pink. Repeats . . . 8–12 [ft; ca. 2.25–3.5 m]." [Lg] "Best in reasonable heat. The best light-colored climber — a light yellow 'Maman Cochet'." [Capt28] "Small grower; blooms attractive, but shy." [ARA18/119] "Vigorous canes to 12 [ft; ca. 3.5 m]." [HRG]

WHITE PET, CL.
Corbœuf-Marsault, 1894
Polyantha
Sport of 'White Pet' (Pol).
"This is a superb new variety that will please and delight everyone who wishes a pure white constant blooming Climbing Rose. It is a true ever bloomer, and bears great clusters of snowy white blossoms continually all through the season. The flowers are deliciously fragrant. It blooms the first year, and is a most rapid and graceful climber, surpassing nearly all others, in quick growth, early and constant bloom, and the astonishing number of flowers

produced." [C&Js98] "This variety will be able, it would seem, to rival 'Turner's Crimson Rambler'; it 'creeps' the same way, and is also vigorous. It is not remontant, but gives flowers just like those of 'White Pet'." [JR18/162]

WILLIAM ALLEN RICHARDSON   PLATE 183
Ducher, 1878
Noisette
Sport of 'Rêve d'Or' (N).
"Colour of a cut apricot." [E] "A real orange . . . quite small." [F-M] "Very deep orange yellow, sometimes pale straw, with beautiful foliage; one of the best noisette varieties for button-holes." [FRB] "Medium size, fairly well filled, fiery orange-yellow, usually white at the edges. Very strong-growing and free-flowering, continuing into the autumn. Exquisite when half-expanded, but flatter and rather irregular with age." [Hn] "It stands alone as regards depth of yellow." [DO] "Buff to apricot. Free-flowering and vigorous . . . 12 × 8 [ft; ca. 3.5 × 2.25 m]." [B] "Deep orange, with white edges. A most distinct and valuable climbing Rose. Early in the season the flowers often come almost white." [J] "Striking . . . fragrant." [ARA29/98] "Easy to grow, particularly where there is some shelter . . . sadly wanting in form of flower." [NRS/14] "Very showy and distinct; growth vigorous." [P1] "Long branches, 'climbing,' of a dark green, well branched; the blossoms are borne in clusters at the ends of the branches, and are of a nice shade of orange and saffron yellow." [S] "Not, it is true, a model rose, as the blossoms are too small, but these flowers are nevertheless charming and of use in bouquets." [JR7/178] "At first of quite modest appearance, parsimonious with its flowers . . . with age . . . the bloom becomes more generous, the rebloom is greater, and the color gains intensity. . . . It was dedicated to a rich American fancier. . . . 'Vigorous as a bush or climber, with branches both flexible and divergent, wood a lightly browned green, furnished with short, recurved thorns, somewhat numerous; the leaves are composed of 5–7 leaflets of a handsome though somber brilliant green; flowers in clusters on the large branches, singly on the branchlets, varying from pretty orange-yellow tinted with saffron to a very fresh nankeen-yellow.' " [JR10/40] "Suffers somewhat from mildew, but this is easily kept in check on this plant." [NRS/13] "It is a Rose of singularly dirty habits, attracting every vile form of blight and caterpillar." [K1] "The writer, Mr. W. R. Belknap, roundly states himself to be William Allen Richardson's nephew. He continues: — 'William Allen Richardson was born in New Orleans, La., on Feb. 20, 1819. When he was but two years old his father moved to Lexington, Ky., where he resided until his death, in October, 1892 . . . much interested in the cultivation and propagation of Roses. He imported a good many, and in this way became acquainted by correspondence with Madame Ducher." [NRS/10] "Indefinable individuality." [Hk] "Popular all over the world." [H]

YELLOW CÉCILE BRUNNER, CL.
Listed as 'Perle d'Or, Cl'.

ZÉPHIRINE DROUHIN
Listed with the Bourbons.

Supplement

ADELE FREY
Walter, 1911
Hybrid Tea
  "Deep pink, large, very full, light scent, tall." [Sn]

[ADRIENNE CHRISTOPHLE]
('Adrienne Christophe')
Guillot fils, 1868
Noisette
  "The flowers attain a diameter of up to 4 in [ca. 1 dm] . . . borne on a flower-stem which frequently is feeble, and bends under the weight of the blossom as do the branches which bear the clusters of flowers. The growth is of moderate vigor, fairly floriferous; the drooping branches are not unpleasant in effect. The only fault I can find with this rose . . . is that sometimes its petals are clustered in three or four entirely separate groups, giving the impression of a blossom which has been broken apart." [JR9/54–55] "Thorns hooked and remote; leaves of five leaflets, sometimes seven, but the uppermost pair always very small, often abortive and represented by a simple foliole; petiole prickly; flowers in a cluster of 10–12, usually nodding under their weight . . . coppery apricot yellow, shaded peach pink, sometimes deep yellow . . . planted in the north, it blooms little or not at all." [JR10/10] "Growth vigorous; branches slender and nodding, with reddish-green bark, and long, sharp, brown thorns. Foliage smooth, pale green; leaves composed of 3–5 oval-acuminate, finely dentate, red-bordered leaflets; leafstalk slender, of the same color as the branches and armed with some small thorns. Flowers about three in across [ca. 7.5 cm], nearly full, slightly globular, cupped, solitary on the little branchlets, clustered on vigorous branches; color, coppery pink-yellow, apricot, shaded pink; petals large, central petals smaller; stem slender, nodding under the weight of the blossom. Calyx rounded. Because of the variety of its colors, this rose is very beautiful. Hardy, and proof against winter's cold." [JF] "Distinct and beautiful." [JC] A parent of 'Erzherzog Franz Ferdinand' (T).

ANNE-MARIE CÔTE
('Anna-Marie Côte')
Guillot fils, 1875
Noisette
  "Blush, medium size, full, tall." [Sn] "Well-formed . . . pure white, very often nuanced lilac pink." [S] "Appeared in 1871 among Mons Guillot fils' seedlings, and entered into commerce by him in 1875. Growth vigorous with upright canes armed with long and straight thorns; beautiful dark green foliage, leafstalk green or purplish; blossom medium-sized, full, globular, pure white, sometimes tinted pink; blooms in clusters. Grows poorly in pots, and can't be forced. Freezes at 12°. Prune to 4–6 eyes." [JR10/19]

ALBERT LA BLOTAIS, [CL.]
Pernet père, 1887
Hybrid Tea
From 'Gloire de Dijon' (N) × 'Général Jacqueminot' (HP).
  "Bush vigorous; flower very large, nearly full, globular, stem upright and strong, very good 'hold'; beautiful bright red, sometimes darker, passing to crimson. . . . Reblooms freely; of the first merit." [JR11/163] "Red, large, very full, tall." [Sn] Not a sport of

the Moreau-Robert HP 'Albert La Blotais', Pernet's cultivar was introduced without the *Climbing* in its name; it seems practical and appropriate to retain the *Climbing* for purposes of differentiation.

ANNA OLIVIER, CL.
Introducer and date unknown
Tea
  "Golden pink, large, full, medium scent, medium height" [Sn], which also speculates that it came from England. Presumably, of course, it is a sport of 'Anna Olivier' (T).

APELES MESTRES
Dot, 1926
Hybrid Perpetual
From 'Frau Karl Druschki' (HP) × 'Souvenir de Claudius Pernet' (Pern. HT, Pernet-Duch_r, 1920, sunflower-yellow).
  "Sunflower-yellow, full, globular flowers which are very lasting and fragrant. Vigorous growth, with abundant May, and June bloom." [C-Ps31] "Remarkable for gigantic, very double, bright yellow flowers, which, alas, are only sparingly produced. The plant is a mean grower but well worth coddling." [GAS]

APOTHEKER GEORG HÖFER, CL.
Vogel, 1941
Hybrid Tea
Sport of 'Apotheker Georg Höfer' (HT).
  "Red, very large, full, very fragrant, tall." [Sn]

ARDS RAMBLER
A. Dickson, 1908
Hybrid Tea
  "Orange-red, large, full, very fragrant, tall." [Sn]

[BARONNE CHARLES DE GARGAN]
Soupert & Notting, 1893
Tea
From 'Mme Barthélemy Levet' (T) × 'Socrate' (T).
  "Climbing, flower large, full, beautiful form, outer petals light daffodil yellow, inner ones shining Naples yellow. Fragrant." [JR17/147] "A climber of good growth, very fine retained foliage, and double, sulphur-yellow bloom of medium size." [ARA28/101]

BEAUTÉ DE L'EUROPE   PLATE 186
Gonod, 1881
Noisette
Seedling of 'Gloire de Dijon' (N).
  "Flowers, which are globular and full, of dark yellow to salmon-colour. Has vigorous growth, free-flowering and pretty." [B&V] "Very vigorous, of good bearing, heavy wood and nearly thornless reddish canes. The foliage is comprised of 5–7 rounded, dark green, serrated leaflets. The flower stem is strong, and the large flowers ve--- full and well formed, of the Centifolia shape. Color, dark yellow, with a reverse of coppery yellow. This variety . . . is very floriferous, and the most notable yellow to date of this sort." [JR5/136] "Small growth; attractive blooms scattered throughout season; requires winter protection." [ARA18/119]

BEAUTÉ INCONSTANTE   PLATE 200
('Beauté de Lyon')
Pernet-Ducher, 1892
Noisette

"Metallic red shaded yellow; vigorous. Distinct and charming in colour, but variable in this respect, as its name implies." [J] "Even more brilliant orange-scarlet tones than any hybrid China . . . free and hardy, as well as solid in petal. coppery red, shaded with carmine and yellow . . . variable . . . of irregular shape. Distinct and beautiful. Very fragrant." [P1] "A red-orange rose. Oh! such a colour . . . sometimes. . . . Rather a weak grower, but one bloom will repay the growth." [HmC] "Carmine shaded to yellow, very variable in colour, large, full and of good form, in every respect an acquisition; has a more free habit, but in many ways reminds one of 'L'Idéal' [N]." [B&V] "Very vigorous, making a rather tall bush; thorns protrusive and somewhat numerous; foliage bronze-green; flower large, full or semi-double, nasturtium red with yellow-tinted carmine reflections . . . sometimes bears paler colored blossoms." [JR16/166] "Extremely 'climbing' branches . . . probably from the Noisette 'Earl of Eldon'." [JR21/99] "Very pretty buttonhole variety." [H]

[BELLE D'ORLÉANS]
Conard & Jones, 1902
Noisette?

"A new constant blooming Cluster Rose, flowering continuously through the whole season; pure white flowers in grape form clusters, sometimes tinted rose; semi-climbing habit, best for low trellises and beds, from which roses can be picked from June to December." [C&Js02]

BELLE DE BORDEAUX
Listed as 'Gloire de Bordeaux'.

BILLARD ET BARRÉ
Pernet-Ducher, 1898
Noisette
From 'Mlle Alice Furon' (HT, Pernet-Ducher, 1896, cream; parentage: 'Lady Mary Fitzwilliam' [HT] × 'Mme Chédane-Guinoisseau' [T]) × 'Mme la Duchesse d'Auerstädt' (N).

"Climbing Tea with double, sweet-scented, golden yellow flowers." [GAS] "Dependable grower . . . bright yellow." [ARA28/99] "Semi-climbing, canes strong and erect; large leaves of a lustrous somber green; bud superb when half open; flower large, nearly full, globular." [JR22/163]

BOUGAINVILLE
Pierre Cochet/Vibert, 1822
Noisette

"Here is the description which Mons Prévost fils, of Rouen, gives this rose . . . 'Canes very thorny. Leaflets lacy, wavy, ovary obconical or oblong, and glabrous. Buds red. Flower medium-sized, full, pink, paler and more lilac at the edge.' . . . This variety prefers open ground. . . . It is dedicated to Admiral Bougainville, owner of the château of Suisnes." [JR10/59] "Vigorous; canes with magnificent lustrous dark green foliage; flower medium-sized, well formed, cupped; color, peachy lilac-red." [S]

[BRIDESMAID, CL.]
Dingee & Conard, 1897
Tea
Sport of 'Bridesmaid' (T).

"Pink." [CA06] "'Bridesmaid' is well known as one of the grandest Ever-blooming Roses we have, and is more extensively grown for cut-flowers than any other variety except 'American Beauty'. The 'Climbing Bridesmaid' is exactly like the other, except that the plant is a strong vigorous climber, sometimes growing 8 to 10 ft in a season, and producing a constant succession of the most lovely roses imaginable. The color is clear rose-pink, with crimson shading, and both buds and flowers are exquisitely beautiful and deliciously sweet — not entirely hardy, but will usually stand the winter with moderate protection." [C&Js02]

CAMÉLIA ROSE
Prévost, ca. 1830
Noisette

"Flowers bright rosy pink, double; form, cupped." [P] "Growth vigorous with very flexuose canes, pretty 'climbing,' dark green leaves, thick on the plant; flower medium-sized, full, well formed, bright pink shaded lilac." [S]

CAPITAINE SISOLET
Listed as a Bourbon.

CAPITAINE SOUPA, CL.
Vogel, 1938
Hybrid Tea
Sport of 'Capitaine Soupa' (HT, Laperrière, 1902; from 'Mme Caroline Testout' [HT] × 'Victor Verdier' [HP]).

"Rose-red, large, full, tall." [Sn]

CAPTAIN HAYWARD, CL.
W. Paul, 1906
Hybrid Perpetual
Sport of 'Captain Hayward' (HP).

"Healthy disposition. . . . Pinkish-crimson flowers large and cupped until fully open . . . 8 × 4 [ft; ca. 2.5 × 3.5 m]." [B1]

CAROLINE MARNIESSE
Rœser, 1848
Noisette

"An old cluster-flowering Noisette, nearly hardy in the North, with small, globular flowers of pale flesh-pink, almost white. Blooms continuously, and should be a good rose in the South." [GAS] "Creamy white, small and full; seven leaflets, nearly hardy." [EL] "This rose, by its stature, foliage, and the placement of its white, clustered flowers, bears a great resemblance to the Sempervirens rose 'Félicité et Perpetué' [*sic*], but is not a climber. It blooms continuously up to frost; its blossoms are medium-sized, very full, globular, and of a light flesh white. It is hardy, and in growth is like 'Aimée Vibert'." [R-H48]

[CAROLINE SCHMITT]   PLATE 187
('Mme Caroline Schmitt')
Schmitt/Schwartz, 1881
Noisette

"Blooms in large clusters; flowers full and regular; color coppery rose, passing to buff and white; very pretty and fragrant." [CA90] "Vigorous bush with branching, climbing canes; foliage somber green; flowers medium-sized or large, full, well-formed, salmon yellow fading to yellowish white. This variety is freely remontant; its manner of blooming is the same as that of the Noisette 'Narcisse', but with much larger flowers." [JR5/148]

CATALUNYA

Nonin, 1917

Bourbon

Sport of 'Gruss an Teplitz' (B).

"Bright maroon." [Ÿ] "Brilliant red flowers more or less continuously." [GAS]

CHERUBIM

A. Clark, 1923

Polyantha

Seedling of 'Mlle Claire Jacquier' (Pol).

"Small, pointed, yellow-and-salmon-pink buds; semidouble flowers in huge, clear-pink clusters, May into June. This looks like the Sweetheart Rose, '[Mlle] Cécile Brunner'. . . . The foliage is small, wrinkled, glossy, and rich green; the canes almost thornless. Very vigorous where it is hardy." [W] "Clusters of exquisitely formed little pale yellow flowers, flushed with salmon-pink. Charming, and somewhat like 'Phyllis Bide'." [GAS]

CHESHUNT HYBRID

G. Paul, 1872

Hybrid Tea

From 'Mme de Tartas' (T) ? × 'Prince Camille de Rohan' (HP).

"Cherry-carmine, large, full, open flower, very hardy, free, and distinct." [JC] "Maroon-crimson, changing to slatey red, large and full; a useful climbing Rose, its principal defect being the dull hue of the expanded flowers." [P1] "Cherry-carmine, shaded violet. A good early and very free-flowering variety." [H] "Dark brown leaves, and reddish brown stems reveal the Tea ancestor, while the color of the flower and growth of the plant proclaim its descent from Bourbons or HP's." [JR8/157–158] "Shows the Tea blood in its veins in its foliage more than in any other way; what fragrance it has is more like that of 'Alfred Colomb' or 'Prince Camille [de Rohan]' than like a Tea; it seldom shows a flower after the first of August." [EL] "A tall, straight, gawky plant, fit to be tied to a clothes post. It was the first red Hybrid Tea, but was virtually sterile." [Hk] "The first Rose to be known and recognized as a Hybrid Tea. Very vigorous in growth, hardy and free flowering, it will do well for a pillar or paling. An early bloomer and good autumnal, with large flowers, but the shape is open and the colour wanting in brightness." [F-M2] "A glorious rose." [HRH]

CINDERELLA

Page, 1859

Noisette

Not to be confused with Walsh's Wichuriana of 1909.

"Salmon." [I'H59/137] "Carmine pink." [JR4/60]

[CLAIRE CARNOT]

Guillot fils, 1873

Noisette

Seedling of 'Ophirie' (N).

"Yellow, bordered with white and carmine rose; medium size; full and well formed; growth vigorous." [CA88] "Bush very vigorous and climbing; flower medium-sized, full; beautiful bright coppery yellow, sparkling, edged white and carmine pink; flower cupped, fragrant, opening easily, in clusters. Resembles 'Céline Forestier', but is more fragrant." [S]

CLAUDIA AUGUSTA

('Claudie Augustin')

Damaizin, 1856

Noisette

"Vigorous; canes dark green; leaves brilliant dark green; flower large, full; color, white with a cream center." [S]

CLOTILDE SOUPERT, CL.

Dingee & Conard, 1902

Polyantha

Sport of 'Clotilde Soupert' (Pol).

"One of the very finest varieties, unequalled for quick and abundant bloom and healthy, vigorous growth. The flowers are 2.5 to 3 in across, and perfectly double; rich creamy white, sometimes tinted with blush. Not subject to insects or disease, and is altogether one of the most beautiful and satisfactory hardy ever-blooming climbing roses for porch or trellis yet produced." [C&Js10] "Poor growth; blooms not of good form." [ARA18/122]

COLUMBIA, CL.

Lens, 1929

Hybrid Tea

Sport of 'Columbia' (HT).

"Pink changing to brighter pink." [Ÿ] "Best in cool dampness. One of the best of the pink Hybrid Tea climbers, with the fault of discoloration in heat, but fine growth and foliage, long stems and lovely perfume; not a prolific bloomer, yet always furnishes a few fine blooms for cutting." [Capt28]

COMTE DE TORRES

A. Schwartz, 1905

Hybrid Tea

From 'Kaiserin Auguste Viktoria' (HT) × 'Mme Bérard' (N).

"Light salmon Hybrid Tea with pink center." [GAS] "Growth very vigorous; foliage somber green; flower large, full, well formed, opening well; outer petals salmony white, those of the center coppery salmon yellow lightly tinted pink; climbing." [JR29/150]

COMTESSE DE GALARD-BÉARN　　　　　PLATE 201

Bernaix, 1893

Noisette

"Long bud, the flower is pretty large, flesh-white, and it [the plant] seems to be very floriferous." [JR17/84] "Very vigorous and very floriferous, with climbing canes having thick, beautiful, bright green foliage. Blossom of large size, beautifully double, with large and numerous petals which spread out and recurve; light canary yellow which fades upon expansion to chrome, brightened with incarnadine towards the center. Remarkable due to the delicate tint of its large blossoms, the beautiful form of its buds, its vigor, and its abundant bloom." [JR17/164]

COMTESSE GEORGES DE ROQUETTE-BUISSON

Nabonnand, 1885

Noisette

"Very vigorous, climbing, big-wooded; flower medium-sized, perfect, very full, globular, imbricated, erect; color, a novel bright yellow." [JR8/166]

CRACKER, CL.

A. Clark, 1927

Hybrid Gigantea

"Red with white, large, single, very fragrant, tall." [Sn]

DAME EDITH HELEN, CL.
Howard & Smith, 1930
Hybrid Tea
Sport of 'Dame Edith Helen' (HT).
"Dark pink, very large, very full, very fragrant, tall." [Sn]

DAWN
G. Paul, 1898
Hybrid Tea
From 'Mme Caroline Testout' (HT) × 'Mrs. Paul' (HP).
"Semi-double, rosy pink Hybrid Tea." [GAS] "Light pink, large, lightly full, tall." [Sn] "Silvery pink, shaded rose. — Very vigorous. — Bush, pillar." [Cat12/22] "Quite easy to grow. . . . If tied in too closely it may often refuse to break from the bottom, and then becomes woefully leggy, and when this state of affairs becomes established nothing seems to avail but digging it up and starting afresh with a new plant. . . . Its beautiful shiny pink flowers come freely in summer and fairly continuously, though more sparingly, later. . . . Very little pruning is required, and that should be directed to the encouragement of young growths. Consequently thinning will be freely practised. It is somewhat, though not very, liable to mildew, but suffers badly from black spot if that is anywhere near. . . . Only semi-double, or nearly single." [NRS14/70]

DÉPUTÉ DEBUSSY
Buatois, 1902
Hybrid Tea
"Flesh white, yellow nub." [Ў]

DISTINCTION, CL.
Lens, 1935
Polyantha
Sport of 'Distinction' (Pol).
"Pink, medium size, semi-double, tall." [Sn]

DR. DOMINGOS PEREIRA
De Magalhaes, 1925
Tea
"Big, fragrant flowers of lilac-pink and yellow. A vigorous Tea reported to be very floriferous." [GAS]

DR. LANDE
('Dr. Laude')
Berger/Chauvry, 1901
Tea
"Very vigorous, semi-climbing; foliage deep bronze green, buds medium, very long; flower large, semi-double; color, deep salmon pink in spring, coppery brick red nuanced salmon on a ground of golden bronze in fall. Petals recurved and ruffled; fragrant and very floriferous. Dedicated to Mons Dr. Lande, mayor of Bordeaux." [JR25/163]

DR. ROUGES
Widow Schwartz, 1893
Tea
"China pink." [LS] "Deep coppery-red, with orange shading. Very free-flowering." [H] "The most intensely brilliant shade of orange-red that I know. . . . The rich claret-red shoots in January are almost as brilliant as any flower could be." [J] "Red, with yellowish centres . . . [flowers] of good effect on the plant." [P1] "Vigorous, foliage beautiful green with purplish leafstalks. Flower irregular in form, like that of a cactus Dahlia; petals rolled into a horn, China red on a dawn-gold ground." [JR17/165] "Needs

coolness and dryness for best results. Another distinct color, much like wine; good growth; lots of bloom; some liability to mildew; and little perfume or cutting value." [ARA28/95] "A fine Tea. . . . Good as a shrub." [GAS]

DUARTE DE OLIVEIRA   PLATE 184
Brassac, 1879
Noisette
From 'Ophirie' (N) × 'Rêve d'Or' (N).
"Salmon-rose, coppery at base, medium size, full." [EL] "Dedicated to our brother the editor of the *Portuguese Horticultural Review*. . . . Very vigorous, flower of medium size, full, well-formed, coppery salmon-pink; climbing." [JR2/167] "Mons Brassac . . . delivers into commerce this year a new rose ['Duarte de Oliveira'] which he had intended to release *last* year, a rose whose entry into the world of flowers was delayed due to an accident in propagation." [JR3/167]

EARL OF ELDON
Eldon/Coppin/G. Paul, 1872
Noisette
"Coppery gold." [Ў] "Copper-orange." [LS] "Bud yellow. Flower semi-full or full, large, flat; color, chamois yellow, orange yellow." [JR23/154] "Orange buff, a loose semi-double flower, very attractive, and highly fragrant; a good climbing rose." [JC] "Flesh and copper-coloured, handsome large regular flowers, and sweet scented. Well worth growing; a large successfully cultivated plant is a splendid feature in any collection." [B&V] "Growth vigorous." [S]

EFFECTIVE
Hobbies, 1913
Hybrid Tea
From an unnamed seedling (parentage: 'General MacArthur' [HT]) × 'Paul's Carmine Pillar' [HMult, G. Paul, 1896, carmine; parentage: 'Gloire de Margottin' (HP) × ?]).
"Brilliant scarlet red." [Ў] "Continuous bloom. We hope to have found [in this] the best autumnal climber . . . pretty color [of 'General MacArthur'] and [from 'Paul's Carmine Pillar'] its early blooming and climbing habit. The long buds are much prized." [JR37/26]

EMILIA PLANTIER
Schwartz, 1878
Noisette
"A vigorous Noisette with semi-double, yellowish white flowers. There is a dwarf Bourbon of the same name ['Emilie Plantier', Plantier, ca. 1845, pink]." [GAS] "Semi-double, sometimes double, ill formed; utterly worthless." [EL] "Medium scent." [Sn] "Very vigorous, beautiful distinctive foliage, purplish green becoming glossy green; blossom medium to large, full, light coppery yellow, developing a yellowish-white tint — new in the Noisettes." [S]

EMILIE DUPUY
Listed as 'Mme Emilie Dupuy'.

EMMANUELLA DE MOUCHY
P. Nabonnand, 1922
Hybrid Gigantea
R. gigantea × 'Lady Waterlow' (HT).
"A vigorous Gigantea hybrid with medium-sized, globular flowers of pale flesh-pink." [GAS]

EMPRESS OF CHINA

Jackson/Elizabeth Nursery Co., 1896

China

"Bright red." [Ỹ] "Resembles a beautiful Tea Rose; blooms the first year and all through the season. The color is soft dark red passing to light pink or apple blossom; the flowers are medium size and quite fragrant, and borne in long stems, nice for cutting. It is a rapid grower, of slender twining habit, bearing few thorns and valuable for having over porches and arches. It is entirely hardy—needs no protection, and will thrive in any locality." [C&Js99] "Widely distributed everblooming Bengal or China rose of little value, with reddish pink, semi-double flowers." [GAS]

[EUGENE JARDINE]

Conard & Jones, 1898

Noisette?

"A hardy, everblooming climber, fully tested and highly recommended for its rapid, vigorous growth, and constant and abundant bloom. The flowers are pure white, large, full and fragrant, and borne in solid wreaths and clusters all over the vine; entirely hardy and sure to please." [C&Js98]

EVA TESCHENDORFF, CL.

Opdebeek, 1926

Polyantha

Sport of 'Eva Teschendorff' (Pol).

"Creamy white, small, full, light scent, moderately tall." [Sn]

FLORENCE HASWELL VEITCH

W. Paul, 1911

Hybrid Tea

From 'Mme Emile Metz' (HT, Soupert & Notting, 1893, blush; itself from 'Mme de Loeben-Sels' [HT] × 'La Tulipe' [T, Ducher, 1868, white/pink]—parentage of both unknown) × 'Victor Hugo' (HP).

"Blossom bright scarlet, shaded black, large, moderately full, perfect form, stiff petals. Bush very vigorous, nearly climbing. Wonderful scent, continuous bloom; excellent as a large bush, or for clothing walls of medium height." [JR35/101] "One of the best rich crimsons." [NRS20/69] "Rich blackish crimson colour. It is not a fast grower, but with a little patience one is rewarded with a fine plant that yields its blossoms until quite late in the year." [NRS22/162] "Many of the qualities of 'Sarah Bernhardt' [cl. HT], but it is a far better shaped flower, and seems to me most promising." [NRS14/63–64]

FRANÇOIS CROUSSE

P. Guillot, 1900

Tea

"Cherry crimson, shaded dark." [RR] "Large, globular, crimson flowers, both double and fragrant." [GAS] "Vigorous and hardy, climbing, flower large, full, well-formed, cupped, fragrant, bright crimson red, sometimes fiery red." [JR24/146] "One of the best crimson pillar roses, rather late flowering, hardy and perpetual." [F-M] "Small growth; fair foliage; color attractive, tending to fade quickly; an occasional bloom during season; needs winter protection." [ARA18/120] "A real acquisition." [P1]

FRAU GEHEIMRAT DR. STAUB

Lambert, 1908

Hybrid Tea

From 'Mrs. W. J. Grant' × 'Duke of Edinburgh' (HP).

"Deep red, large, full, very fragrant, tall." [Sn]

FÜRST BISMARCK

Drögemüller/Schultheis, 1887

Noisette

Seedling of 'Gloire de Dijon' (N).

"Growth, foliage, and bearing like that of ['Gloire de Dijon']; color, brilliant golden yellow, darker than 'Belle Lyonnaise' [N]. This rose has all the good qualities of its mother, adding to them the advantage of being more floriferous; hardy; good for forcing." [JR11/93]

FÜRSTIN BISMARCK

Drögemüller/Schultheis, 1887

Hybrid Tea

From 'Gloire de Dijon' (N) × 'Comtesse d'Oxford' (HP).

"Cherry." [LS] "Large, very full, imbricated, and well-held; color changes from China pink to cerise pink, but is very pretty despite the changes; reblooms freely. Growth very vigorous . . . foliage large, bright green." [JR11/92]

GAINESBOROUGH

('Cl. Viscountess Folkestone')

Good & Reese, 1903

Hybrid Tea

Sport of 'Viscountess Folkestone' (HT).

"Pinkish white, very large, full, medium scent, tall." [Sn] "A lovely Hybrid Tea with well-shaped, delicate shell-pink flowers flushed rose. Relatively hardy, but a shy summer bloomer." [GAS] Thomas Gainesborough, English painter; lived 1727–1788.

GASTON CHANDON

Schwartz, 1884

Noisette

Seedling of 'Gloire de Dijon' (N).

"Very vigorous . . . flower large or of medium size, full, well-formed, cherry-pink, shaded delicate pink, on a ground of coppery yellow." [JR8/133]

GENERAL-SUPERIOR ARNOLD JANSSEN, CL.

Böhm, 1931

Hybrid Tea

Sport of 'General-Superior Arnold Janssen' (HT).

"Deep rose-red, large, full, moderate scent, tall." [Sn]

GEORGE DICKSON, CL.

Woodward, 1949

Hybrid Perpetual

Sport of 'George Dickson' (HP).

Red.

GESCHWINDT'S GORGEOUS

Geschwindt, 1916

Hybrid Tea

"Light red, medium size, not very full, light scent, tall." [Sn]

GIGANTEA BLANC

(*R. gigantea*)
Colett, 1889
Gigantea

"The principal attraction of *R. gigantea* is the exceptional size of the blossoms, which attain six in [ca. 1.5 dm] across, and have been compared to those of the Clematis. Their color is an undecided one, fading from pale primrose yellow to ivory white. The bud is long, pointed. . . . The leaves have from five to seven large oval leaflets. . . . The branches are lengthily 'climbing.'" [JR29/30] "Imported from Upper Burmah at an altitude of 4,000 to 5,000 ft, and also found in Manypore 2,000 ft higher. It is said never to have produced blooms in Europe till we had the good fortune to flower it in this garden last month. A splendid plant, making growths of forty ft or more, with rambling branches armed with irregular prickles of moderate size, often in pairs at base of leaves, which are about three in long and glabrous. The flowers are solitary, about six in[ches] in diameter [ca. 1.5 dm], which size will not unlikely be increased when the plant is older and stronger, of a golden white with yellow centre, containing an unusual quantity of pollen. Petals large, broad, imbricated, disk large, styles much exserted, free, villous, stamens long. The most desirable and by far the finest single rose I have ever seen. It does not seem to be very hardy, and is subject to mildew. The bud is long, larger, but very closely resembles that of 'Mme Marie Lavallée' [*sic;* 'Mme Marie Lavalley', N] and of pure gold colour. This rose when in flower should obviously be shaded, as the sun soon extracts the gold from the blooms, leaving behind a substitute of dirty white. At a short distance the flowers bear a close resemblance to a Clematis." [B&V]

GLOIRE DE BORDEAUX

('Belle de Bordeaux')
Lartay, 1861
Noisette
Seedling of 'Gloire de Dijon' (N).

"Large, bright pink flowers silvered with white." [GAS] "Rose color, tinged with fawn." [EL] "Silvery-rose, the back of the petals rosy, very large and full" [of 'Gloire']. [FP] "Pink, large and full, habit and growth of 'Gloire de Dijon'" [of 'Belle']. [FP] "Vigorous habit of the Bourbon 'Sir Joseph Paxton', to which it bears some resemblance; its large, coarse rose-coloured flowers are however very fragrant, and the variety is well calculated for training to walls." [R8]

GLORY OF CALIFORNIA

A. Clark, 1935
Hybrid Gigantea

"Light pink, large, full, moderate fragrance, tall." [Sn]

GLORY OF WALTHAM

Vigneron/W. Paul, 1865
Hybrid Perpetual
Seedling of 'Souvenir de Leveson-Gower' (HP).

"Purplish-carmine." [Ÿ] "Rich crimson, very large and full . . . larger, brighter, darker, and of better form, than the parent; a superb rose, of hardy, vigorous growth." [FP] "Very floriferous; color, crimson nuanced carmine." [S] "Very large, very double, and very sweet; growth vigorous. One of the best Climbing or Pillar roses." [P1]

GRIBALDO NICOLA

Soupert & Notting, 1890
Noisette
From 'Bouquet d'Or' (N) × 'La Sylphide' (T).

"Very vigorous growth; 'climbing'; foliage large and glossy; flower very large, fairly full, form of 'Souvenir de la Malmaison' [B]; color, silvery white on a ground of blush pink; center tinted nankeen yellow, reverse of petals isabelle pink. Fragrant . . . blooms little on new growth, but the two year old canes are covered with flowers." [JR14/147]

GRUSS AN FRIEDBURG

Rogmans/Metz, 1902
Noisette
Sport of 'Duarte de Oliveira' (N).

"Vigorous, flowers medium or large, full, pale yellow with a golden center. The bloom lasts from July to frost." [JR26/114]

GRUSS AN TEPLITZ, CL.

Storrs & Harrison Co., 1911
Bourbon
Sport of 'Gruss an Teplitz' (B).

Red. "Blooms with great freedom in June but seldom thereafter. Its delightful fragrance and brilliant color make this a most popular climber." [C-Ps27] "For interior districts without dampness. Fine growth; little bloom on some plants unless root-pruned; foliage mildews; no cutting value but fine perfume." [ARA28/95]

HENRY IRVING

Conard & Jones, 1907
From a cross of an unnamed HP with an unnamed Multiflora.

"Light orange red, medium size, not very full, tall." [Sn] "New, fine large full flowers; deep rich crimson, an early and abundant bloomer, fragrant and good every way." [C&Js03] Henry Irving, English actor; lived 1838–1905.

INDIANA   PLATE 209

E. G. Hill, 1907
Hybrid Tea
From 'Rosalind Orr English' (HT, E. G. Hill, 1905, cerise; from 'Mme Abel Chatenay' [HT] × 'Papa Gontier' [T]) × 'Frau Karl Druschki' (HP).

"The bloom is pretty abundant; the blossoms, medium to large, are a beautiful light silvery pink, with light violet reflections. We have seen it used to great advantage in many roseries." [JR33/125]

IRÈNE BONNET

P. Nabonnand, 1920
Hybrid Tea

"Salmon pink, medium size, full, medium scent, tall." [Sn]

IRISH BEAUTY

A. Dickson, 1900
Hybrid Tea

"Produces blossoms 7–8 cm across [ca. 3 in] resembling those of *R. lævigata* [that is, they are single and white]." [JR26/86]

ISIS

Robert, 1853
Noisette

"Flowers medium-sized, full, well-formed, pure white, in corymbs of 8 to 10." [I'H54/12] "Growth vigorous; branches short, clothed with sturdy thorns which are hooked and flat; leaves bright dark green; flower large, full, very well formed, in a cluster; color, virginal white." [S] Isis, Egyptian goddess of fertility.

JACQUES AMYOT
Listed as a Damask Perpetual.

JAMES SPRUNT
Sprunt, 1858
China
Sport of 'Cramoisi Supérieur' (Ch).

"Carmine-red, just the same as its parent, but fuller and larger. Couldn't be better for exhibitions in le Midi [*in France*]." [JR16/36] "Deep cherry red flowers, rich and velvety, medium size, full, very double and sweet. A strong quick grower and good bloomer." [C&Js05] "Medium-sized, double, bright red flowers. Not notably valuable." [GAS] "Advise against its use. So bad it is mentioned only to be avoided." [Capt28] "Rev. James M. Sprunt, D.D., a Presbyterian clergyman of Kenansville, North Carolina, divided some strong plants of 'Agrippina' ['Cramoisi Supérieur']. Afterwards he observed a *single* shoot from one of these plants growing vigorously without flowers or branches; it grew over *fifteen* ft [ca. 5 m] before it showed any flower buds, the rest of the plant retaining its normal characteristics. This shoot branched out very freely the following year, and cuttings taken from it invariably retained the same climbing habit. The flowers . . . are somewhat larger and fuller than 'Agrippina', but are, of course, not produced till the plant has made considerable growth. It is a valuable greenhouse climber." [EL]

JEANNE CORBŒUF
Corbœuf-Marsault, 1901
Hybrid Tea
From 'Mme la Duchesse d'Auerstädt' (N) × 'Mme Jules Grolez' (HT).

"Growth very vigorous, climbing, floriferous, flower very large, very full, cupped, long bud; color, satiny pink with carmine reflections on a yellow ground, fragrant." [JR26/2]

JONKHEER J. L. MOCK, CL.
Timmermans, 1923
Hybrid Tea
Sport of 'Jonkheer J. L. Mock' (HT).

"Whitish pink, large, full, very fragrant, tall." [Sn] "Best for interior with some alititude giving dry heat. A fine grower with good stem and fragrance, but balls easily in damp and mildews." [Capt28]

JULES MARGOTTIN, CL.
Cranston, 1874
Hybrid Perpetual
Sport of 'Jules Margottin' (HP).

"Light purplish crimson." [Ÿ] "Flower large, full, very well formed; color, brilliant carmine. Magnificent exhibition rose." [S] "Vigorous. . . . Flowers are the same as in the old sort, except being a little smaller, and for this reason it is finer in the bud state. The best of all the climbing sports; highly commended as a useful pillar rose." [EL] "Free and vigorous habit; not in a robust form, but branching as freely as an evergreen climbing rose [*presumably referring to a Sempervirens rose*]; a great acquisition as a free growing perpetual climbing rose." [JC]

KAISER WILHELM DER SIEGREICHE
Drögemüller/Schultheis, 1887
Noisette
From 'Mme Bérard' (N) × 'Perle des Jardins' (T).

"Flower large, very full, opens well, of good form and well held; exterior of petals yellowish-white, interior brilliant deep yellow with carmine-pink reflections; very fragrant. Vigorous, good bright green foliage. More floriferous and hardy than 'Mme Bérard' [N]." [JR11/92]

KAISERIN FRIEDRICH   PLATE 196
Drögemüller/Schultheis, 1889
Noisette
From 'Gloire de Dijon' (N) × 'Perle des Jardins' (T).

"This rose resembles 'Marie Van Houtte' [T] in color, and 'Gloire de Dijon' [N] in form." [JR13/20] "A good autumn-flowering Tea, with large, very fragrant, pale pink flowers tinged with yellow." [GAS] "Flowers shaded with red when dying off; good and hardy." [P1] "Dedicated to the late Empress of Germany . . . very vigorous and floriferous. The blossoms, most often solitary, are large, and despite their size always open well. . . . As for the coloration, it varies quite a bit. At expansion, the rose is an overall brilliant intense yellow; then the petals develop carmine pink." [JR25/120] "Growth vigorous, foliage shiny, young growths reddish; thorns thinner and sharper than those of 'Gloire de Dijon'. Flowers large, solitary, well held on the long branches, very full, and opening well. Held perfectly, and also perfect is the bright yellow blossom. The petals are large, carmine-red, lighter in the interior, and, on the reverse, shading gradually to white. Very fragrant." [JR13/20]

KÖNIG FRIEDRICH II VON DÄNEMARK, CL.
Vogel, 1940
Hybrid Perpetual
Sport of 'König Friedrich II von Dänemark' (HP).

"Deep red, medium size, full, light scent, tall." [Sn]

L'ARIOSTE
Moreau-Robert, 1859
Noisette

"Delicate pink." [Ÿ] Lodovico Ariosto, 1474–1533; Italian poet.

[L'IDÉAL]   PLATE 192
('L'Idéale')
Nabonnand, 1887
Noisette

"Lovely old Noisette, with big, coppery pink and golden yellow flowers. Extremely tender." [GAS] "Extremely vigorous climbing bush; flower large, semi-full, pretty form; color, yellow and metallic red, shaded, washed indefineably with sparkling golden tints. Thoroughly distinct from all other shadings found till now. This delectable variety is without a doubt the *ne plus ultra*, being, of all colorations, the most beautiful and striking. It's ideal! Very fragrant, very floriferous, extraordinary." [JR11/165] "That's the trouble with 'L'Idéale' [*sic*]—wonderful as to color, but to be faulted for a too-single blossom which is only beautiful in the bud." [JR19/66] "In 'L'Idéal' we find together both a ravishing color and an exquisite perfume, but it is far from being as vigorous as is believed. . . . [JR22/75] Parent of 'Vicomtesse Pierre de Fou' (N).]

LA FRANCE DE 89   PLATE 197
Moreau-Robert, 1889
Hybrid Tea
From 'Reine Marie Henriette' (Cl. HT) × 'La France' (HT).

"Large, dark red flowers occasionally marked with white." [GAS] "A bright large showy red Rose, sometimes pretty good." [F-M3] "Dedicated to the memory of the Revolution of 1789. It is still one of the most beautiful roses known, its blossoms in our climate [that of Tunisia] attaining the size of Peonies. Color superb and variable, bright red, scarlet, and sometimes deep pink; the long bud opens very well, and is borne on a short but erect and strong stem. Very fragrant. . . . Its fall bloom is not so good as that of 'La France' [HT], but it is nevertheless of the first merit, considering its vigor and bloom." [JR34/14] "Very large, fragrant, and deep rose-red flower of great beauty, which makes prodigious shoots in autumn, and flowers by degrees, beginning at the top in December and continuing to do so down the long shoots throughout the season. It is of the very largest size, fragrant, and double, but I think it is capricious in some gardens." [J] "Extra-vigorous, always growing, wood strong and robust, with slightly recurved thorns; beautiful light green foliage . . . bud very long, big as an egg and always opening well; flower enormous, well formed, sparkling bright red, sometimes lined white, in effect quite a Peony, extra-floriferous . . . needs several years to develop its growth." [JR13/99]

LA SYLPHIDE
Listed as a Tea.

LADY CLONBROCK
Introducer and date unknown
Noisette
"Light pink, medium size, full, tall." [Sn] From Ireland?

LEMON QUEEN
Hobbies, 1912
Hybrid Tea
From 'Frau Karl Druschki' (HP) × 'Mme Ravary' (HT).

"Large, very fragrant, pale lemon-yellow flowers tinted deeper. A pillar rose." [GAS] "As for the form of the blossom, one can't do much better than to say it is the same as that of 'Druschki', but much prettier, with a yellow tint to each petal — very pretty. It is excellent for decoration, and is a semi-climber with nearly continuous bloom." [JR37/26]

[LES FIANÇAILLES DE LA PRINCESSE STÉPHANIE ET DE L'ARCHIDUC RODOLPHE]
('Stéphanie et Rodolphe', 'Princesse Stéphanie," etc., etc.)
Levet, 1880
Noisette
Seedling of 'Gloire de Dijon' (N).

"Climbing; foliage dark green; thorns long and hooked; flower medium-sized; color, orange salmon yellow." [JR4/167] "Vigorous; strong growth; the flowers are borne several to a cluster at the tip of the cane, which is long and tendentially nodding; flower quite full, petals all the same length, making it neither cupped nor globular; the later it is in the year, the smaller the blossom." [S]

LIBERTY, CL.
H. B. May, 1908
Hybrid Tea
Sport of 'Liberty' (HT).
"Dark red." [Ў] "Velvety crimson; good bloomer." [Th2]

LILLIPUT
G. Paul, 1897
Polyantha
"Red, small, full, tall." [Sn]

LILY METSCHERSKY
('Lily Mestchersky', 'Lily Mertschersky')
Nabonnand, 1877
Noisette
"Blossom medium-sized, very full, well formed, very remontant, violet red, the only one of its color among the Noisettes; wood dark, climbing, very thorny, and very vigorous." [JR1/12/14]

LUCY THOMAS
P. Nabonnand, 1924
Hybrid Perpetual
From 'Ulrich Brunner fils' (HP) × 'Georg Arends' (HP).
"Pink, large, semi-double, tall." [Sn]

MARGUERITE CARELS
P. Nabonnand, 1922
Hybrid Tea
From 'Frau Karl Druschki' (HP) × 'General MacArthur' (HT).
"Pink, large, full, tall." [Sn]

MARGUERITE DESRAYAUX
P. & C. Nabonnand, 1906
Noisette
From 'Mme Alfred Carrière' (N) × 'Mme Marie Lavalley' (HN).
"Pink, large, semi-double, tall." [Sn]

MARIE ACCARY
Guillot fils, 1872
Noisette
"White tinted pink and yellow." [JR8/26] "Creamy-blush, changing to nearly white, somewhat similar to 'Acidalie' [B], flowers small, full, and compact." [JC] "Very vigorous and 'climbing'; flower medium-sized, full, well formed; white lightly tinted salmon pink at the center. For forcing." [S]

[MARIE BÜLOW]
Welter, 1903
Noisette
From 'Maréchal Niel' (N) × 'Luciole' (T)
"This is a very promising climber of the 'Maréchal Niel' type. It has long pointed buds that open into large full flowers. Color, china rose, changing to carmine and pure yellow." [C&Js08]

[MARIE GUILLOT, CL.]
Dingee & Conard, 1898
Tea
Sport of 'Marie Guillot' (T).
"Yellowish white." [LS] — Among White Roses, this splendid variety stands at the head, the flowers are extra large, full and fragrant, the petals are thick and durable, lasting a long time when cut; color pure snowy white; it is a most constant and abundant bloomer, covered with beautiful buds and flowers the whole season; one of the best for garden planting, always in bloom and always satsisfactory." [C&Js04]

233

MARIE ROBERT   PLATE 202
Cochet, 1893
Noisette
Seedling of 'Isabella Gray' (N).
Not to be confused with the Damask Perpetual of the same name.
"Bright rose marbled with salmon and apricot, outer petals paler; a free and continuous bloomer." [P1] "Of the color of 'Blairii Nº 2'." [JR22/74] "Good Noisette with large, dark pink flowers flushed salmon and apricot." [GAS] "Extremely vigorous, 'climbing,' extremely abundant bloom. Flower large, full, center bright pink marbled light apricot salmon, outermost petals paler. A child of 'Isabella Gray' from which it takes its growth and beautiful, distinctive foliage. An excellent climber, blooming from spring to fall." [JR17/163–164] "Dedicated to Mlle Marie Robert, the well-known innkeeper at Antony (Seine)." [JR17/180]

MARIE THÉRÈSE DUBOURG
Godard, 1888
Noisette
"Deep coppery golden yellow." [P1]

[MÉLANIE SOUPERT]
Nabonnand, 1881
Noisette
Seedling of 'Gloire de Dijon' (N).
"Very vigorous bush, the same as 'Gloire de Dijon' . . . flower large, very full, pure white." [JR5/148]

METEOR
('Climbing Meteor')
Geschwindt, 1887
Noisette
"Crimson, shaded." [LS] "A beautiful brilliant red color nuanced fiery red, very vigorous." [JR34/17] "Requires a warm, sunshiny location to get the best buds out." [BSA] "Fair growth; bloom not of best form; requires winter protection." [ARA18/121] "One of the finest yet introduced, makes exquisite buds and large, beautifully shaped flowers of the true 'Jacqueminot' color. A vigorous grower and most constant and profuse bloomer, produces immense numbers of magnificent roses all through the season." [C&Js98]

MIKADO
Kiese, 1913
Hybrid Tea
Not to be confused with the modern bush HT.
"Red, large, not very full, tall." [Sn]

MINIATURE, CL.
('Rankende Miniature')
Lambert, 1908
Polyantha
"Whitish pink, very small, very full, medium scent, tall." [Sn]

MISS G. MESMAN
('Cl. Baby Rambler')
Mesman, 1910
Polyantha
Sport of 'Mme Norbert Levavasseur' (Pol).
"Clusters of purplish red flowers throughout the season." [GAS] "Foliage very plentiful, black-spots badly in midsummer, slightly in late summer, leaves held on; bloom moderate early and late, profuse in July, almost continuous into November." [ARA18/130] "Rather low, bushy growth; fair bloomer—occasionally some fall bloom; needs winter protection." [ARA18/121]

MISS MARION MANIFOLD
Adamson/Brundrett, 1913
Hybrid Tea
"A vigorous climbing rose with full, large, well-formed flowers of rich, velvety crimson, and a free and continuous bloomer, opening well in all weathers. It has a slight Bourbon scent. In this country [Australia] it sends out strong, vigorous canes each year up to, and sometimes exceeding, nine ft [ca. 3 m], and when covered with bloom is a glorious sight. One of our growers recently counted 150 blooms on his bush, and experts here consider it the finest climbing rose in the world." [ARA28/112]

[MLLE ADÈLE JOUGANT]
('—Jourgant')
Lédéchaux/C. Verdier, 1862
Tea
Seedling of 'Mlle de Sombreuil' (Cl. T).
"Clear yellow, medium size." [FP] "Leaves beautiful light green; flower medium-sized, nearly full, light yellow." [I'H62/277] "Very vigorous; branches 'climbing'; leaves small, much serrated, yellowish green; flower medium-sized, nearly full; sulphur yellow." [S] A parent of 'Erzherzog Franz Ferdinand' (T) and 'Mme C. P. Strassheim' (T).

MLLE GENEVIÈVE GODARD
Godard, 1889
Tea
"Growth vigorous, flowers large, very full; color, handsome carmine red." [JR13/181]

MLLE MADELEINE DELAROCHE
Corbœuf, 1890
Noisette
Seedling of 'Mlle Mathilde Lenaerts' (N).
"'Climbing,' flower large, very full, well formed, flesh pink, very floriferous, superb plant." [JR14/178]

MLLE MARIE GAZE
Godard, 1892
Noisette
"Yellow." [Ỹ]

MLLE MATHILDE LENAERTS
Levet, 1879
Noisette
Seedling of 'Gloire de Dijon' (N).
"Large, double, bright pink flowers silvered white." [GAS] "Rose colour." [EL] "Very vigorous, 'climbing,' leaves large, composed of seven leaflets which are a beautiful intense pink, distinctly bordered white, making a most charming appearance, a new coloration in the 'Gloire de Dijon' clan." [JR3/165] "[One of the] hybrids of Tea and Bourbon." [JR24/44] Daughter of B. Lenaerts, president of the Antwerp Circle of Rosarians.

MME AUGUSTE CHOUTET
Godard, 1901
Hybrid Tea
From 'William Allen Richardson' (N) × 'Kaiserin Auguste Viktoria' (HT).

"Yellow nuanced dawn gold." [LS] "Golden yellow, semiclimbing." [JR32/140] "Large, semi-double, dark orange-yellow, fragrant flowers." [GAS] "Grows 6 ft [ca. 2 m] the first year. Foliage dark green, without disease; flower very large, double, deep saffron-yellow, lasting well. Somewhat shy but so beautiful it is most valuable . . . much superior in lasting quality to 'Cl. Lady Hillingdon'." [ARA28/103] "This is a most charming, continuous-flowering, yellow pillar Rose which appears to be so little known that I venture to direct special attention to it. I was myself not impressed with it in the first two or three seasons of its life with me; but now that it is established it is charming. It forms a compact, evergreen pillar clothed from the base; it has small glossy leaves, apparently mildew and vermin proof, and is covered with perfectly formed but smallish yellow flowers, the colour of 'Mme Pierre Cochet', not so vivid as 'William Allen Richardson', and which does not fade. It is a perfect companion for 'Lady Waterlow', and with that and 'Johanna Sebus' [Cl. HT, Müller, 1894, cerise] makes a lovely trio." [NRS13/148] "None other than that old favorite 'Crépuscule'." [NRS18/148]

MME AUGUSTE PERRIN
Schwartz, 1878
Noisette

"Mottled pink, small or medium size, well formed; a new color in this class. We are most favorably impressed with it." [EL] "Vigorous, beautiful olive green foliage; blossom medium sized, full, well formed; very fine coloration: beautiful pearly pink; reverse of petals whitish; very fetching." [JR2/166]

MME BÉRARD   PLATE 178
Levet, 1870
Noisette
From 'Mme Falcot' (T) × 'Gloire de Dijon' (N).

"Bright buff or fawn colour with slight salmon tint, flowers very large, full, and well formed; a very distinct and superb rose . . . vigorous." [JC] "Large, semi-double, salmon-yellow flowers edged with pink; fragrant." [GAS] "Without perfume." [JR3/62] "Very similar to ['Gloire de Dijon']; the flowers are somewhat less full, of a fresher shade, and are better in the bud state." [EL] "From 'Gloire de Dijon', its flowers are better formed, its colors darker (light pink with salmon), and it has a darker yellow heart. It is more vigorous than 'Gloire', but not so floriferous. This variety is good for breeding." [JR10/47] "Foliage a very handsome dark green, blooms profusely; flower medium-sized to large; very prettily colored coppery yellow at the center; outer petals a beautiful salmon pink. Coppery yellow in the shade." [S] "One of the best in shape and colour, very pretty at times, but not as hardy or free-flowering as ['Gloire de Dijon']." [F-M2]

MME CAROLINE KÜSTER
Listed as a Tea.

MME CHABANNE
Liabaud, 1896
Tea

"Very vigorous and very floriferous, metallic foliage, flower medium or large, full, opening into a cup, center petals numerous, canary yellow, outermost petals cream white." [JR20/147]

[MME CHAUVRY]   PLATE 190
Bonnaire, 1886
Noisette
From 'Mme Bérard' (N) × 'William Allen Richardson' (N).

"Nankeen shaded with rose, reverse of petals coppery, distinct and handsome; one of the best." [P1] "Very large, full, fragrant flowers of deep nankeen-yellow, shaded with copper and pink." [GAS] "Very vigorous, with long, 'climbing,' branches, very floriferous and remontant. Foliage very handsome, large, glossy dark green above, glaucous and often reddish beneath. Flower very large, measuring about 4.5 in across [ca. 1.25 dm], good form, numerous concave petals, imbricated, nankeen yellow upon opening, nuanced China pink on the backs of the petals, and copper yellow towards the tips." [JR10/137] "Dedicated to Mme Chauvry, wife of a well-known rosarian of the Bordelais region." [JR10/184] A parent of 'Mme la Général Paul de Benoist' (Cl. T.).

MME CREUX
Godard, 1890
Tea

"Fine rose colour to salmon, reverse of petals having a tint of bronze." [B&V] "First class certificate." [JR16/20]

MME E. SOUFFRAIN
Chauvry, 1897
Noisette
From 'Rêve d'Or' (N) × 'Duarte de Oliveira' (N).

"Large, richly fragrant, golden yellow flowers tinged with salmon and marked pink." [GAS] "Smooth reddish canes, thornless; very 'climbing'; foliage glossy green; buds large, ovoid; flower large, very full, imbricated; ground color golden yellow, shading to salmon yellow at the center, touched white at the edge of the petals; lined and bordered pink and very light violet; very fragrant." [JR21/149]

MME EDMÉE COCTEAU
('Edmée Cocteau')
Margottin fils, 1903
Hybrid Tea
Seedling of 'Captain Christy' (HT).

" 'Climbing,' very vigorous; foliage resistant, dark; flower enormous, beautiful delicate pink; long stem." [JR28/27]

MME EMILIE DUPUY   PLATE 179
Levet, 1870
Noisette
From 'Mme Falcot' (T) × 'Gloire de Dijon' (N).

"Large, full, globular flowers of creamy yellow, suffused salmon." [GAS] "Pale fawn, buds long and handsome, flowers large, full, and tolerably well formed." [JC] "Climbing, blossom well formed, large and full, coppery yellow." [JR6/136] "Magnificent exhibition rose." [S]

[MME EUGÈNE VERDIER]   PLATE 189

Levet, 1882

Noisette

From 'Gloire de Dijon' (N) × 'Mme Barthélemy Levet' (T).

"A very pretty rose, with large shell-shaped petals of a pleasant pink." [JR4/97] "Rich golden yellow. Requires a warm wall." [H] "'Climbing,' with heavy wood and occasional thorns; its foliage is a beautiful dark green. . . . Its blossoms vary in color depending upon the season: sometimes canary yellow, one may also encounter deep yellow in the center with the reverse of the petals straw yellow, and, later in the season, when flowers are abundant, one can find the most beautiful deep chamois color imaginable." [JR14/39] "Canes strong, very handsome shiny green foliage; flower large and well formed, surpassing all the other 'Gloire de Dijon' brood in this respect, thorns upright and light . . . very fragrant." [JR6/149] "Vigorous with strong canes, which are upright and short, and light green; numerous thorns of varying size, slightly hooked, pink; leaves comprised of 2–5 oval-elongate leaflets with large petals which are well held; color, the most beautiful satiny bright pink, much nuanced and shaded silver; a splendid, vigorous variety, very remontant." [JR2/187] A parent of 'Princesse Étienne de Croy' (T).

MME FOUREAU

Viaud-Bruant, 1913

Noisette

Seedling of 'Rêve d'Or' (N).

"Yellowish salmon, medium size, full, medium height." [Sn] "Extremely vigorous, with beautiful foliage, and strong-growing canes; flower well-formed, light salmon pink with pale Indian yellow; very good and hardy variety." [JR37/26]

MME GASTON ANNOUILH

Chauvry, 1899

Noisette

"'Climbing,' with slender, bronze green canes, nearly thornless; foliage purplish passing to ashy delicate green; buds medium long, canary yellow; flower semi-double, fairly large; white tinted canary with greenish reflections; very floriferous and fragrant." [JR24/2]

MME HECTOR LEUILLIOT

('—Leuillot')

Pernet-Ducher, 1903

Hybrid Tea

"Golden yellow Hybrid Tea tinged pink." [GAS] "Tinted with carmine in the center; large; full; gives scattering blooms throughout the entire season; most attractive color." [ARA17/27] "Growth semi-climbing, beautiful bright bronzy green foliage; flower large, globular, quite full, superbly colored golden yellow on a red ground. This magnificent variety has a hardiness equal to that of the HP's, and may be grown as either a climber or a bush, as with 'William Allen Richardson.'" [JR27/131] "Hard to establish in southern climates but worth extra effort. Produces in its second year distinct and lovely double blooms of orange-yellow, sometimes splashed with crimson; good cutting value; exquisite perfume." [ARA28/103] "Practically no disbudding. . . . Tops winter kill badly. Splendid in South without cutting back." [Th]

MME JULES BOUCHÉ, CL.

California Roses, 1938

Hybrid Tea

Sport of 'Mme Jules Bouché' (HT).

White, flesh center.

MME JULES FRANKE

('Mme Jules Francke')

Nabonnand, 1887

Noisette

"Extremely vigorous, climbing; flower medium-sized, very full, imbricated, a paragon in form; pure white, finally yellowish. Floriferous." [JR11/165]

MME JULIE LASSEN

Nabonnand, 1881

Noisette

"Very vigorous, wood short and big, flower large, very full, perfectly cupped . . . deep pink." [JR5/148]

MME LA GÉNÉRAL PAUL DE BENOIST

Berland/Chauvry, 1901

Noisette

Seedling of 'Mme Chauvry' (N).

"Climbing, buds very large, rounded, nuanced light violet, opening well; flower very large and full, salmon on a dawn-gold ground, petal edges reflexed creamy white; fragrant." [JR25/163]

MME LÉON CONSTANTIN

Bonnaire, 1907

Tea

"Free-flowering Tea, producing large, fragrant, full flowers of rosy white." [GAS] "Very vigorous with strong branches . . . ornamented with handsome foliage. Beautiful long bud, flower extra-large, very full, always opens well, beautiful satiny pink with a light salmon interior. Very distinct and floriferous. Climbing." [JR31/135]

MME LOUIS BLANCHET

Godard, 1894

Noisette

"Lilac pink, marbled." [Ÿ]

MME LOUIS HENRY

Widow Ducher, 1879

Noisette

"Pale yellow, fragrant; in the way of 'Solfaterre' [sic]." [EL] "Very vigorous, with branches 'climbing,' thorns somewhat numerous, short and reddish, handsome light green foliage composed of seven leaflets, flower medium or large, full, very well formed; color white, slightly yellowish in the center, reblooms freely." [JR3/164]

MME LOUIS RICART, CL.

Boutigny, 1904

Hybrid Perpetual

Sport of 'Mme Louis Ricart' (HP).

"Flower large, bright pink, beautiful form, blooming in a cluster, very vigorous." [JR28/89]

[MME MARIE BERTON]

Levet, 1875

Noisette

Seedling of 'Gloire de Dijon' (N).

"Flower very large, full; color, straw yellow fading to cream." [S] "Particularly good in autumn." [GAS]

[MME MARIE LAVALLEY]

Nabonnand, 1881

Noisette Hybrid

"Growth extra vigorous, big-wooded, few thorns; flower very large, nearly single, well formed, bright pink, shaded, lined white in an indefinite reflection; very floriferous; a superb effect, from the ample supply of flowers." [S] "Not a long-lived sort. The flowers from young plants being greatly superior to those of say four years or more. The petals are delicate and easily injured by wind or sun; answers very well under glass." [B&V]

MME MARTIGNIER

Dubreuil, 1903

A Tea × Noisette hybrid.

"Vigorous Tea with medium-sized, bright red flowers tinged purple and flushed with gold." [GAS] "Climbing, extremely floriferous, with medium-sized blossoms, leaves bronzy, glossy green. Buds ovoid-elongate, 3–4 at the ends of the canes. Flower cupped . . . brilliantly colored intense cochineal nuanced mauve-aniline with amaranth reflections when fully open. Petals neatly and abruptly acuminate-mucronate with a fawn-yellow nub; very fragrant." [JR27/163]

MME PIERRE COCHET   PLATE 198

Cochet, 1891

Noisette

Seedling of 'Rêve d'Or' (N).

"Yellow, striped." [Ÿ] "First-rate Noisette with beautiful, fragrant, chrome-yellow flowers, tinged pink and apricot." [GAS] "Climbing, strong canes, nearly thornless, leaves and wood greenish brown. Flowers medium-sized, full, basically golden yellow fading to yellowish white, reverse dark coppery yellow. Long buds. This variety . . . is 'William Allen Richardson' perfected." [JR15/164]

MME ROSE ROMARIN

Nabonnand, 1888

Tea

From 'Papillon' (Cl. T) × 'Chromatella' (N).

"Extremely vigorous, climbing; wood red; leaves thick, of a handsome glossy green resembling those of 'Chromatella' very much; bud long and of perfect form; flower large, semi-double, very erect; color, bright red, shaded, center coppery . . . very floriferous. Extraordinary by all reports." [JR12/148] "[For] everywhere. Not a solid red, but with sufficiently dark marking to be so classed, although much of the center is lighter; very prolific, fine foliage, some fragrance, and although of only fair form, lasts; valuable for cutting." [ARA28/95] "Small growth; winterkilled." [ARA18/122]

[MME SCHULTZ]

Béluze, 1856

Noisette

Related to 'Lamarque' (N).

"Primrose, shaded with carmine, very sweet." [FP] "Medium-sized, yellow or yellowish." [JDR56/53] "Canary yellow." [S] "Another new yellow rose . . . it is the most vigorous grower of all, but appears to be very chary in giving its flowers." [R8] "Centre pale yellow, outer petals straw, flowers full, of moderate size and good substance; a fine rose of vigorous habit." [JC] Parent of 'Rêve d'Or' (N).

MME SEGOND-WEBER, CL.

Reymond, 1929

Hybrid Tea

Sport of 'Mme Segond Weber' (HT).

"Salmon pink, very large, full, medium scent, tall." [Sn] "[For] everywhere. A new introduction which gives very large, blooms with fine stems for cutting. Seems most promising; strongly recommended." [Capt28]

[MME THERESE ROSWELL]

Listed as a non-climbing Tea.

MME TRIFLE

Levet, 1869

Noisette

Seedling of 'Gloire de Dijon' (N).

"Pale fawn changing to cream, shape of the flower and habit like 'Gloire de Dijon', flowers somewhat paler, a good rose; habit vigorous." [JC] "Without perfume." [JR3/62] "Inferior to ['Gloire de Dijon'] in value." [EL] "Stands out because of its large and handsome foliage, and because of its large, very full, cupped flowers which are nearly upright; deep yellow; sometimes the center of the blossom is salmon yellow with coppery reflections. Like 'Gloire de Dijon', it blooms freely up till frost." [S]

MONSIEUR DÉSIR

Pernet père, 1888

Noisette

From 'Gloire de Dijon' (N) × ?

"Growth vigorous, climbing, foliage reddish green; flower very large, pretty full, perfect form, well held, of a handsome crimson red often much darkened with violet." [JR12/165] "Fine in dry heat. Very fine in spring; only fault, foliage mildews in dampness; good cutting value; fine fragrance; good lasting." [ARA28/95] "Good form and habit. One of the best dark colored climbers." [P1] I would speculate, on the basis of 'Climbing Albert La Blotais,' Pernet's release of the previous year, that this is another seedling from 'Gloire de Dijon' × 'Général Jacqueminot'.

MONSIEUR GEORGES DE CADOUDAL

('Georges de Cadondal')

Schwartz, 1904

Tea

"Vigorous, foliage purplish green; flower large, very full, globular; color bright pink nuanced carmine on a coppery ground. Fragrant." [JR28/154]

MONSIEUR ROSIER

Nabonnand, 1887

Noisette

Seedling of 'Mlle Mathilde Lenaerts' (N).

"Vigorous; flower large, full, well formed, cupped; color, bright pink on a ground of translucent yellowish white . . . very floriferous." [JR11/165]

[MOSELLA, CL.]

Conard & Jones, 1909

Polyantha

Sport of 'Mosella' (Pol)

"The flower is precisely like the golden yellow, cream colored blossoms of the Bush Rose by the same name; a healthy vigorous climber that continues producing its lovely clusters almost without interruption from Spring till frost." [C&Js10]

MRS. AARON WARD, CL.

A. Dickson, 1922

Hybrid Tea

Sport of 'Mrs. Aaron Ward' (HT, Pernet-Ducher, 1907; parentage unknown).

"Yellow, very large, full, medium scent, tall." [Sn]

MRS. HENRY MORSE, CL.

Chaplin Bros., 1929

Hybrid Tea

Sport of 'Mrs. Henry Morse' (HT).

"Yellowish pink, very large, full, medium scent, tall." [Sn]

MRS. ROSALIE WRINCH

W. & J. Brown, 1915

Hybrid Perpetual

From 'Frau Karl Druschki' (HP) × 'Hugh Dickson' (HP).

"A fine climbing single H.T. . . . The flowers are a delightful shade of pink, and withstand all weathers." [NRS18/140] "A vigorous Hybrid Tea with stout stems and very large, single pink flowers. Fine pillar." [GAS] "Has . . . become very popular, and deservedly so. There is a brilliancy and charm about its rose-coloured flowers, and they are excellent for decorative purposes." [NRS18/148]

MRS. W. H. CUTBUSH, CL.

Paling, 1911

Polyantha

Sport of 'Mrs. W. H. Cutbush' (Pol).

"Flowers and leaves of this novelty are similar to those of its mother. . . . Its deportment is strong and upright . . . blooms without interruption; the blossoms are erect rather than nodding. Having grown to four ft [ca. 1.25 m], it begins to bloom at the base; it will grow that same year to perhaps six ft [ca. 2 m]. In fall, the rose is covered with pale pink blossoms, and is ornamented with pretty light green foliage resistant to all diseases." [JR35/118]

MRS. W. J. GRANT, CL.

('Cl. Belle Siebrecht')

E. G. Hill Co., 1899

Hybrid Tea

Sport of 'Mrs. W. J. Grant' (HT).

"Light pink, large, full, medium scent, tall." [Sn] "Fair to good growth; not a good bloomer." [ARA18/121]

NARDY   PLATE 195

Nabonnand, 1888

Noisette

Seedling of 'Gloire de Dijon' (N).

"Very large, fragrant, globular flowers of coppery yellow." [GAS] "Growth extremely vigorous, climbing; heavy-wooded; foliage bronzy green; bud like that of 'Gloire de Dijon', but larger; flower very large, very full, globular, stout; color, coppery salmon yellow; very floriferous. More vigorous than 'Gloire de Dijon'." [JR12/148] "The foliage . . . is very ornamental." [JR22/9] "Nardy (Sébastien). — Landscape gardener from Hyères, where he died in 1909 at the age of 79. Following a trip to America, he introduced, around 1876, the peach 'Amsde' into cultivation." [R-HC]

NEERVELT

Verschuren, 1910

Hybrid Tea

From 'Gloire de Dijon' (N) × 'Princesse de Béarn' (HP).

"Fiery red." [Jg] "Red, large, full, tall." [Sn]

NOISETTE DE L'INDE

Noisette, 1814

Noisette

"Blush white." [Ÿ]

NOISETTE MOSCHATA

Schwartz, 1873

Noisette Hybrid

"Blush white." [LS]

NYMPHE

Türke, 1910

From 'Mignonette' (Pol) × 'Maréchal Niel' (N).

"White, center yellow, medium size, full, medium scent, tall." [Sn]

ORANGE TRIUMPH, CL.

Koopmann, 1948

Polyantha

Sport of 'Orange Triumph' (Pol).

"Salmon orange red, small, semi-double, light scent, tall." [Sn]

OSCAR CHAUVRY

Chauvry, 1900

Noisette

Seedling of 'Elise Heymann' (T).

"Canes fluxuose and very climbing; bud pretty large, full, beautiful deep China pink with metallic reflections on a golden yellow ground; central petals touched and lined white, purple reverse. Reblooms fairly freely; fragrant." [JR24/165]

PALE PINK CHINA, CL.

Introducer and date unknown

China

Sport of 'Pale Pink China' (Ch).

"Light pink, medium size, semi-double, tall." [Sn]

PAUL'S SINGLE WHITE PERPETUAL

G. Paul, 1883

Hybrid Perpetual

"Hybrid Perpetual with large, single white flowers, sometimes freely produced in autumn." [GAS] "Growth vigorous; flower medium-sized, single; remontant; color, pure white." [S] "There can be no question that this is an easy Rose to grow. Mr. Dickson calls it of extraordinary vigour and hardiness, requiring abundant room, the most vigorous Rose he knows . . . long, rather straggling growth. . . . It flowers well and freely summer and autumn, and its pure white flowers are very pleasing. Moreover, it opens freely in any weather, and in a wet year is particularly useful. It has good rather light green foliage which is practically free from mildew, but sometimes touched by black spot, and the plant makes long lax laterals, which flower late into autumn, and altogether the growth is clean and satisfactory. There is generally a good deal of thinning to be done at pruning time, and laterals that have flowered may be closely but back. Almost its only fault is that it is rather too vigorous, a fault at least on the right side." [NRS14/75] Phillips & Rix report *R. moschata* ancestry.

PAVILLON DE PRÉGNY

Guillot père, 1863

Noisette

"Purplish pink, medium size, full, medium scent, moderate height." [Sn] "Growth vigorous, floriferous; flower medium-sized, full; color, wine pink; reverse of petals white." [S]

PHILOMÈLE

Vibert, 1844

Noisette

"Flesh." [Ў] Philomel is a poetic name for the nightingale.

PINK ROVER   **PLATE 198**

W. Paul, 1890

Hybrid Tea

"Very pale pink, deeper in the centre, buds long, clean, and handsome . . . growth semi-climbing." [P1] "Very fragrant." [GAS] "Appeared in a row of HT's, but, considering its principal characteristics, it seems more of a Bourbon, looking a lot like 'Souvenir de la Malmaison', only darker pink and somewhat more vigorous . . . beautiful green, persistent foliage, an abundance of flowers from spring to very late fall, pale pink in summer, darker at the end of the season . . . flowers fragrant, nearly always solitary, strong stem." [JR31/42]

POMPON DE PARIS, CL.

Introducer and date unknown

Miniature China

Sport of 'Pompon de Paris' (Miniature Ch).

"Blush." [Ў] "Pink, small, full, moderately tall." [Sn]

PRIDE OF REIGATE, CL.

Vogel, 1941

Hybrid Perpetual

Sport of 'Pride of Reigate' (HP).

"Red, striped white, large, full, moderate scent, tall." [Sn]

PRINCESS MAY   **PLATE 1**

W. Paul, 1893

Noisette

Seedling of 'Gloire de Dijon' (N).

"From 'Gloire de Dijon', this new variety is however somewhat less vigorous than its mother, and in color differs much from its siblings. The blossoms are an opaque pink which is very light and sweet, large, full, and globular. It forces well, and under those conditions produces very pretty foliage." [JR17/85–86]

PUMILA ALBA

Hardy/Margottin, 1847

Noisette

"Flower very small, full, pure white." [JR4/21] "Form, cupped. A free bloomer of small growth." [P] "Origin and raiser unknown. Salmon-rose, seeming to have 'Safrano' blood, very free." [EL] "I have also seen — at Mons Margottin's — an interesting dwarf rose; it is 'Pumila Alba' (Hardy), a type of Noisette. Small bushy plant with dark green foliage and medium-sized pure white flowers; should be used in borders, where it is very decorative." [An47/210]

PURPLE EAST

G. Paul, 1901

From 'Turner's Crimson Rambler' (Multiflora Rambler, Turner, 1894, crimson) × 'Beauté Inconstante' (N).

"Deep carmine purple." [Ў] "Huge clusters of rather large, semi-double, brilliant purple flowers. It is a strange and rather violent color, bound to attract attention. An outstanding characteristic is its earliness." [GAS]

QUEEN OF HEARTS

A. Clark, 1919

Hybrid Tea

From 'Gustav Grünerwald' (HT) × 'Rosy Morn' (HP).

"Orange pink, large, semi-double, very fragrant, tall." [Sn] "An easy-growing tall climber of Hybrid Tea appearance, although its everblooming qualities are slight in this country [U.S.A.]. Flowers are large, semi-double, bright reddish pink, sometimes tending toward crimson." [GAS]

[QUEEN OF QUEENS, CL.]

W. Paul, 1892

Hybrid Perpetual

Sport of 'Queen of Queens' (HP).

"Of strong climbing habit producing pink flowers of extra size and fine form." [CA96]

RADIANCE, CL.

Griffing, 1926

Hybrid Tea

Sport of 'Radiance' (HT).

"Salmon pink with yellow, large, full, very fragrant, tall." [Sn]

[RATHSWELL]

Listed as 'Mme Therese Roswell' among the non-climbing Teas.

REINE MARIA PIA

Schwartz, 1880

Noisette

Seedling of 'Gloire de Dijon' (N).

"Deep rose-colored flowers stained red in the center." [GAS] "Very vigorous, flower·large, full, deep pink with a crimson center. . . . A very beautiful variety." [JR4/165]

REINE OLGA DE WURTEMBERG

Nabonnand, 1881

Noisette

"Crimson, almost a summer-flowering climbing Rose, as it yields so few blooms in the autumn. There is no red climber to equal it in colour." [J] "Flower very large, well-formed, semi-double, sparkling red — as brilliant a color as it is possible to see. Luxuriant growth." [JR5/147] "Fragrant flowers of reddish scarlet." [GAS] "Bright light crimson. A fine climber, with magnificent foliage." [H] "Though so good in England is here [*on the French Riviera*] so fleeting and ugly in colour that I regret to see it." [J] "Vivid cherry red, which exposure to the sun converts to a false crimson . . . semi-double, but very graceful and perfect in shape before it is too full blown. A climber, and most free-flowering. A wall covered with this rose in full bloom before the sun has sucked the flowers, is a truly beautiful sight." [B&V] "Vigorous, almost evergreen, foliage handsome." [P1] "[For the] interior South. Reported fine in Texas. I have discarded it on Southern California seacoast." [Capt28] "Nice growth and foliage; large attractive blooms; needs winter protection." [ARA18/121]

RICHMOND, CL.
A. Dickson, 1912
Hybrid Tea
Sport of 'Richmond' (HT).

"Bright red." [Ў] "Pure red scarlet . . . of fair form only and blooming less freely in the autumn and summer." [Th] "A grand colour, rather stiff perhaps in growth. . . . The flowers seem to have more substance than the dwarf form." [NRS22/160] "Many basal shoots attained a length of from 6-ft. to 10-ft. These I carefully trained in, merely 'tipping' the ends. . . . The result was largely a thicket of flowerless laterals and only about a half-dozen blooms." [NRS22/173] "Best near coast. The best of the lighter reds, and a very prolific bloomer. Has fair cutting value; superior to 'Liberty'." [Capt28] "Very vigorous . . . the best addition to the climbers for many years." [JR36/92]

ROSABELLE
Bruant, 1900
Tea
From 'Fortune's Double Yellow' (HGig) × 'Mme de Tartas' (T).

"Pale rose reflexed with salmon." [P1] "Brownish pink." [LS] "Great vigor . . . 'climbing,' canes purplish, ample and superb foliage, which is glossy, bronze, and purplish when young. Blooms in clusters, large or very large, of elegant form; petal edges crinkled, reflexed; light pink with salmon reflections, contrasting China pink on the back; very pretty long bud; elegant and pronounced scent. In this variety, the influence of the pollen parent, the Tea rose, comes to the fore . . . reblooms in fall." [JR23/167] "Producing in one season canes more than six ft long [ca. 2 m], covered beginning to end with pretty clusters of flowers." [JR27/99–100]

ROSEMARY, CL.
Dingee & Conard, 1920
Hybrid Tea
Sport of 'Rosemary' (HT, E.G. Hill, 1907; parentage unknown).
"Light pink, very large, full, tall." [Sn]

SARAH BERNHARDT
Dubreuil, 1906
Hybrid Tea

"Rosy scarlet flowers shaded velvety red, semi-double and fragrant." [GAS] "Deep red, large, semi-double, moderate scent, tall." [Sn] "Growth very hardy, very vigorous and floriferous, with upright semi-climbing canes. Blossom full, very large, with large incarnadine petals, bright scarlet crimson red nuanced velvety purple. The blossom is very fragrant with a scent of violets, and does not burn in the sun." [JR30/150] "Non-remontant." [JR33/185] "Has a fine crimson colour and good perfume, and gets up to the top of an 8-ft. [ca. 2.5 m] bamboo without difficulty. The flowers are perhaps a little thin and sometimes apt to be rather ragged, but it is a Rose that has been rather overlooked, and seems to me quite useful for our purpose [*of making Pillars*]." [NRS14/63] Sarah Bernhardt, 1844–1923; French actress.

SCORCHER
A. Clark, 1922
Hybrid Tea
Seedling of 'Mme Abel Chatenay' (HT).

"Early. Scarlet. Four-inch [ca. 1 dm], semi-double, ruffled flowers of crimson-scarlet. The September bloom of 'Scorcher' in our test-garden was very striking last fall. It is fragrant, too." [C-Ps34] "Stunning Australian variety of most vigorous growth, with very large, ruffled, semi-double flowers of blazing rosy-scarlet, a different 'Paul's Scarlet Climber' and even brighter. It is evidently a throw-back to the Bourbon type, as its parent was a Hybrid Tea. Occasional blooms are produced in midsummer and autumn. One of the finest modern climbers." [GAS]

[SMITH'S YELLOW CHINA]
Listed as a Tea.

SOUVENIR D'EMILE ZOLA
Begault-Pigné, 1907
Hybrid Tea
Seedling of 'La France de 89' (Cl. HT).

"Bright pink in bud, delicate silvery pink upon opening, very large, full, very fragrant, distinctive fragrance; vigor and bearing of 'La France de 89'." [JR31/166]

SOUVENIR DE LUCIE
Widow Schwartz, 1893
Noisette Hybrid
From 'Fellemberg' (N) × 'Ernestine de Barante' (HP, Lacharme, 1843, pink; parentage unknown).

"Very vigorous, climbing, leaves glaucous green washed purple. Flower medium-sized, well formed, in a cluster; color varies from ruby red to pale carmine pink; center blush white; reverse whitish. The mid-vein of the petal is often white." [JR17/165]

SOUVENIR DE MÈRE FONTAINE
Listed as a Hybrid China.

SOUVENIR DE MME JOSEPH MÉTRAL   PLATE 194
Bernaix, 1887
Hybrid Tea
From 'Mme Bérard' (N) × 'Eugene Fürst' (HP).

"Bright cerise, illumined with crimson and vermilion; very large, full, and of splendid shape and substance." [P1] "Cherry-red Tea with very large, fragrant, double flowers." [GAS] " 'Climbing' canes; of the 'Gloire de Dijon' class; vigorous and hardy; leaves very large with oval leaflets, rather long, of a brilliant and handsome green; flower very large, very double, with many petals, regularly imbricated. . . . This variety, by its abundance and the brightness of its flowers, enriches the climbing Teas with its distinct and novel characteristics." [JR11/150–151]

SOUVENIR DE MME LADVOCAT
Veysset, 1899
Noisette
Sport of 'Duarte de Oliveira' (N).

"Salmon pink on a light copper ground, medium size, full, fragrant. Vigorous growth, foliage striped." [JR23/178]

SOUVENIR OF WOOTTON, CL.
Butler/Craig, ca. 1897
Hybrid Tea
Sport of 'Souvenir of Wootton' (HT).

"Bright magenta red." [CA97] "Flower rosy crimson, full, cup-shaped, fair to good form; strong, enduring fragrance. The medium to large flowers come singly and in small clusters and last three to four days. Fine foliage. Very vigorous grower. Averages 300 to 500 blooms per season; most in spring, a few in summer and autumn. Suitable for arches and pillars. Very hardy." [ARA21/93] "I have a plant in my garden which has stood the test of fifteen winters and a very changeable climate without loss of any kind. It is situated in an open spot subject to all the elements except a direct northern wind. It is a strong, vigorous climber, on an arch eight ft high [ca. 2.5 m] with a span of four ft [ca. 1.25 m], growing way beyond this distance if allowed. The strong canes are produced annually from the base right through the season, these branching at different distancs from the bottom. The canes bountifully produce fragrant, large, fine looking buds, opening into double, cup-shaped flowers of fair to good form, coming singly and in clusters of two to eight, on stems, some short but most from long to extra long, making them fine for cutting as well as garden decoration. In the spring of 1917 and 1918 the plant showed by actual count over 500 buds and flowers. There is a heavy crop in spring always, and almost as many flowers in the fall (but at this time variable), with a scattering of blooms through the summer. The color ranges from deep pink to a rosy crimson, deeper in cool weather and the fall, the lighter flowers being produced in the shade of the foliage, which is large, luxuriant, healthy and lasting, remaining on the plant till heavy frosts appear." [ARA19/126] "Entirely new [1898] and believed one of the best and most beautiful ever-blooming climbing roses yet produced. Pure, rich velvety red, fully equal to 'Jacqueminot' in color; delightfully sweet, and a most constant and profuse bloomer, every shoot producing a bud; extra large fully double flowers, frequently over 6 in across [ca. 1.5 dm]. A vigorous grower and quite hardy; a real treasure; for partially sheltered places." [C&Js98] "One of the best of the climbing Hybrid Tea sports." [Th]

SUMMER SNOW, CL.
Couteau, 1936
Polyantha
Sport of 'Summer Snow' (Pol).
"White." [Ÿ]

TRIOMPHE DES NOISETTES
Pernet père, 1887
Noisette
From 'Général Jacqueminot' (HP) × 'Ophirie' (N).

"Bright rose colour; large, full and vigorous. Gives an abundance of sweet-scented flowers. A good thing." [B&V] "Vigorous, 'climbing'; foliage very dark; thorns protrusive and numerous; flower very large, nearly full; blooming in clusters; beautiful intense pink; very fragrant; quite remontant . . . a variety of the first order." [JR11/163]

VICOMTESSE D'AVESNES
Rœser, 1848
Noisette

"Light salmon-rose, large, full, and distinct." [FP] "A very neat rose-coloured rose, blooming most abundantly." [R8] "Growth vigorous; flower medium sized, full; color, delicate pink." [S] "Very vigorous plant; flowers medium-sized, full, well-formed, lilac pink. Very good variety, good for bedding, arbors, etc., pretty freely remontant, as vigorous grafted as own-root." [I'H53/155]

VISCOUNTESS FOLKESTONE, CL.
Listed as 'Gainesborough'.

WALTHAM CLIMBER I
W. Paul, 1885
Noisette Hybrid

"Bright rosy-crimson, shaped like a Camellia when expanded; growth extra vigorous." [P1] "['Waltham Climbers I, II, and III'] are seedlings of 'Gloire de Dijon', possessing all the best qualities of that variety, but of better form, and of brighter color than other 'Gloire' seedlings. . . . They bloom abundantly in autumn, and have very pretty foliage. The flowers last a long time, and are bright until the end. . . . The color of these three novelties is crimson red, but different for each . . . 'I' is the brightest, 'III' the darkest, and 'II' the most 'climbing.'" [JR10/19]

WALTHAM CLIMBER II
W. Paul, 1885
Noisette Hybrid

"Bright pink." [Ÿ] "Large, flame-red flowers tinged with crimson." [GAS] See also under 'Waltham Climber I'.

[WALTHAM CLIMBER III]
W. Paul, 1885
Noisette Hybrid

"Vigorous . . . with large, bright rosy-crimson flowers." [GAS] See also under 'Waltham Climber I'.

[WEISSER MARÉCHAL NIEL]
('White Maréchal Niel')
Deegan, 1896
Noisette

"Identical in every way with 'Maréchal Niel' except in color, which is pure creamy-white; splendid large roses, full and deep and deliciously tea-scented." [C&Js02] "This rose is a veritable treasure for hothouse culture or indeed under glass, what is more leaving nothing to be desired as an outdoor plant. . . . It is a seedling of our old favorite 'Maréchal Niel' [*An editor's note adds:* 'It is a sport. As for the rest, it is more often yellow than white.'] . . . It is equally good in warm-house or cool. Its flowers are splendid." [JR23/42]

WENZEL GESCHWINDT, CL.
Vogel, 1940
Hybrid Tea
Sport of 'Wenzel Geschwindt' (HT, Geschwindt, 1902; from 'Princesse de Sagan' [Ch] × 'Comte Bobrinsky' [HP]).
"Deep purple, large, full, medium scent, tall." [Sn]

Chapter Nine
POLYANTHAS

"In February 1869, I [Guillot fils] sowed a great quantity of seed which I had harvested from the variety 'Polyantha', a Multiflora variety originating in Japan which was very much a climber, and non-remontant, having a quite small single white blossom much like that of a bramble or strawberry, and blooming in panicles. Among the many seedlings, there were many which resembled in their wood and foliage multifloras and Noisettes. Quite a few bore flowers of moderate quality, singles, semi-doubles, and full blossoms, with petals as large as the roses of our gardens, and with a variety of colors: yellow, white, bright pink, etc. I didn't have so many as two which resembled their mother! Among the seedlings which didn't bloom until the second or third year there was found one which had blossoms with two rows of petals, an inch to an inch and a half across, not remontant as the others were, but which gave me wonderful seeds which I sowed in February, 1872. Out of this came my dear little 'Pâquerette', which I put into commerce in November, 1875." [JR2/137-138]

One sees a certain amount of speculation that China cultivars said to be in the proximity of Guillot's *R. multiflora* 'Polyantha' played a paternal role in the generation of these first Polyanthas. The nature and range of variation evident in the "many seedlings" mentioned in Guillot's account would certainly lend an air of plausibility to this speculation — *but* seedlings of a similar nature and range of variation were produced by another specimen of *R. multiflora* 'Polyantha' owned by Guillot's fellow Lyonnais breeder Rambaux (see Appendix Nine). It thus seems probable that the similar *R. chinensis* characteristics manifested in these two separate crops of seedlings from different specimens — seedlings which in the aggregate seem to be of the nature of an F^2 generation rather than an F^1 — were due to *R. chinensis* genes inherent in *R. multiflora* 'Polyantha'.

We learn from *Les Amis des Roses* (nº 243) that the Polyanthas did not really surpass 'Hermosa' and the Chinas as most-favored bedding roses until Ernest Levavasseur had released 'Mme Norbert Levavasseur', 'Maman Levavasseur' (1910, carmine), 'Triomphe Orléanais', and 'Orléans Rose', which, with their progeny, also in large part replaced the older Polyanthas.

"The growth on most varieties is quite compact, but the foliage varies greatly, some kinds being extremely susceptible to mildew. The flowers usually come in sprays, trusses, or corymbs, each individual blossom being of small to very small size. With a few exceptions, the class may be divided into two distinct types, one of which is either semi-double or double, with short, flat buds that open into shallow, cupped flowers, generally coming in large clusters. The other division produces a perfect miniature rose, beautifully formed, with a long, spiral bud and a lovely half-open flower, which is very attractive even when fully matured, this type being usually produced in small sprays, but occasionally singly. Neither of these types balls, but the flat forms often discolor very badly." [Th2]

"The little Polyanthas rise to the occasion. The little tree-like bushes are well-clothed with delicate foliage, and the way they bloom is to send up stiff, straight stems with panicles of tiny roses by dozens, each tall stem holding up its ready-made bouquet. The fascination of the true Polyantha roses is very much that each perfectly formed double rose is not beyond the circumference of a silver dime, and the little buds seem like something Nature might have made for fun." [Dr]

Polyanthas only require the removal of crossed, dead, or dying branches, resenting the heavy-handed approach with the shears. Occasionally unusually vigorous canes shoot up which destroy the symmetry of the bush. These should be pruned back just beneath the inflorescence *after* they have bloomed, as it is senseless to sacrifice the immense clusters to which such shoots give rise simply to maintain a strict — and unnatural — neatness.

Further information on the parent of this class, *R. multiflora* 'Polyantha', may be found in Appendix Nine.

Combining this chapter with its supplement, we list *all* Polyanthas expected to be in commerce — though only glancing at the more modern varieties — as well as all other extant or otherwise important varieties introduced prior to 1920.

ALBERICH
('Happy')
De Ruiter, 1954
Red. As with the others in the "7 Dwarfs" series ('Bashful'/'Giesebrecht', 'Doc'/'Degenhard', 'Grumpy'/'Burkhard', 'Sleepy'/'Balduin', 'Sneezy'/'Bertram'; see also 'Dopey'), we give preference to the European name of the European introduction.

ANNE MARIE DE MONTRAVEL
('Anna Maria de Montravel')
Widow Rambaux/Dubreuil, 1879
From 'Polyantha alba plena' × 'Mme de Tartas' (T).
"Pure white, small, full and imbricated; produced in clusters and in extraordinary quantities. One of the best." [P1] "Dwarf, to

about 12 or 15 in [ca. 3–4 dm], well-branched, and the greater number of the branches bear flower clusters, distinctive in that the flower stems carry the blossoms well above the foliage, bearing a great quantity of blooms. I have counted 65 on the same stem, which seems quite extraordinary to me. The blossoms are pure white, and last well. They are about an inch and a quarter [ca. 3 cm] in diameter, very full, and of the 'expanded' form — a worthy relative of the pretty 'Pâquerette'." [JR3/153] "Gives a particular scent of rose and lily-of-the-valley." [JR3/166] "Foliage very plentiful, holds well, black-spots slightly; bloom profuse last two and a half weeks in June, few in July." [ARA18/129] "The flowers are very large, but quite irregular in form, sometimes open, but when only half open much more beautiful." [JR7/15] "Flowers flat, very well formed, large to 2 in [ca. 5 cm], pure white, large petals, imbricated, spread out, sometimes showing a few stamens. Very

remontant and ornamental." [JR9/7] "Best of the white Pompons."
[J] "Lovely 'Cécile Brunner' form. Very small growth. Not
as continuous as rest of class." [Th2] "Slightly sprawly plant but
fairly dense . . . globular flowers . . . in profusion . . . 2 × 3 [ft;
ca. 6 × 9 dm]." [B]

BABY ALBERIC
Chaplin, 1932
"Bud yellow; flower double, creamy white. Vigorous; perpetual bloomer." [ARA33/171]

BABY FAURAX
Lille, 1924
"Violet-purple with slate tones . . . to 2 [ft; ca. 6 dm]." [HRG]
"Baby small; flower small, double, sweet fragrance, violet-blue,
borne in large clusters. Growth dwarf (12 to 15 in [ca. 3–3.75
dm])." [ARA27/222] "Dark amethyst . . . small, very double, and
fragrant. . . . The plant . . . stumpy and rather ugly . . . an interesting curiosity." [Hk]

BABY TAUSENDSCHÖN
Listed as 'Echo'.

BALDUIN
('Sleepy')
De Ruiter, 1955
From an unnamed seedling (parentage: 'Orange Triumph' [Pol]
× 'Golden Rapture' [Pern. HT]) × "A Polyantha Seedling."
Not to be confused with the red HT 'Balduin'.
Pink.

BASHFUL
Listed as 'Giesebrecht'.

BERTRAM
('Sneezy')
De Ruiter, 1955
Deep pink.

BLOOMFIELD ABUNDANCE
G. C. Thomas, 1920
From 'Sylvia' (Rambler, W. Paul, 1912, pale yellow; parentage
unknown) × 'Dorothy Page-Roberts ' (HT, A. Dickson, 1906,
coppery pink; parentage unknown).
"A dwarf Wichuriana, 'Sylvia', crossed with the Hybrid Tea,
'Dorothy Page-Roberts', gave 'Bloomfield Abundance' . . . the
stem, the flower-form, and the number of blooms on the stem were
those of 'Sylvia'; the color, fragrance, and blooming continuity
were the same as those of 'Dorothy Page-Roberts'." [ARA31/34]
"Flowers double, salmon-pink, produced singly and in sprays.
Foliage glossy, dark green, not susceptible to mildew. Grows 3 to
6 ft high [ca. 1–2 m], bushy. Similar to 'Cécile Brunner', with
flowers larger and more full in bud, and darker in color." [ARA24/94]
"A failure [in Massachusetts], producing very few flowers and giving no second crop." [ARA22/43] "Blooms constantly from June to
heavy frost." [ARA20/36] "Lacks substance." [ARA25/105] "Vigorous." [B] "A low hedge rose, or, if not cut back, a five to six foot
[ca. 1.75–2 m] pillar rose . . . blooms in sprays . . . it is double
and lasting . . . foliage nearly perfect, dark green varnished. A
dainty little rose." [Th]

BORDER KING
De Ruiter, 1952
Red.

BURKHARD
('Grumpy')
De Ruiter, 1956
Pink.

CAID
Delforge, 1971
Orange.

CAMEO
De Ruiter, 1932
Sport of 'Orléans Rose' (Pol).
"Bud ovoid, salmon-pink; flower small, semi-double, cupped,
very lasting; slightly fragrant . . . turning to shell-pink, in cluster . . . 15 to 18 in high [ca. 3.75–4.25 dm]; profuse bloomer."
[ARA32/220–221] "A peculiar mixture of salmon, coral, and orange." [ARA35/134] "Its much softer color makes it easier to handle
in the garden than either 'Paul Crampel' or 'Golden Salmon'."
[ARA35/174] "[One gardener] likes the way it drops its dead petals."
[ARA36/176] "Very worth-while." [ARA37/210]

CASQUE D'OR
Delbard, 1979
Gold.

CÉCILE BRUNNER
Listed as 'Mlle Cécile Brunner'.

CHATILLON ROSE
Nonin, 1923
From 'Orléans Rose' (Pol) × unnamed seedling.
"A light cerise-pink with white center, semi-double and very
lasting." [ARA25/102] "Silvery crimson, shading to white . . . grows
in large bunches. Very attractive." [ARA25/121] "The prettiest
truly pink of its class, providing, without stopping, enormous
thyrses of flowers, semi-double, large, and of long duration."
[ARA26/175] "Large clusters of sparkling pink . . . tinged with
bronze." [ARA29/97] "Bud small, long-pointed; flower medium-size, semi-double . . . very lasting . . . slight fragrance. Foliage
disease-resistant. Very vigorous, bushy, 1 to 2 ft high [ca. 3–6
dm]; profuse and continuous bloomer." [ARA24/172] "Never out
of bloom all summer, never had black-spot." [ARA31/118] "Fades
brown in great heat; ten to twelve petals; comes in corymbs, about
a hundred blooms in a corymb; does not shatter easily. . . . Stems
strong. Vigorous grower; continuous bloomer. A remarkable
novelty." [Th2]

CHINA DOLL
Lammerts, 1946
From 'Mrs. Dudley Fulton' (Pol, Thomas, 1929, single white;
parentage: 'Dorothy Howarth' [Pol, Bees, 1921, coral; parentage:
'Léonie Lamesch' (Pol) × 'Annchen Müller' (Pol)] × 'Perle
d'Or' [Pol]) × 'Tom Thumb' (or 'Peon', Min, de Vink, 1935;
parentage: 'Rouletii' [Min Ch, red] × 'Gloria Mundi' [Pol]).
"Light pink, yellow base, small . . . 1.2–2 in [3–5 cm], double, some scent, many in clusters together, abundant; growth
strong, dwarf . . . 14 in [ca. 3.5 dm], branched; foliage coarse."
[Kr] A 'WEEPING CHINA DOLL' is also to be found.

CLOTILDE SOUPERT   PLATE 218
('Mme Hardy du Thé', 'Mme Melon du Thé')
Soupert & Notting, 1889
From 'Mignonette' (Pol) × 'Mme Damaizin' (T).

"Vigorous, upright, about 1.5 ft high [ca. 4.5 dm], handsome mid-green foliage, healthy. Flower large, very full, magnificently imbricated . . . exterior of petals, pearly white; center, lake-pink tinted soft Paris red . . . bears on the same plant both pink and white blossoms . . . very floriferous and fragrant." [JR12/147] "The flower is held upright, slightly inclined when fully open . . . blooms pretty continuously." [JR13/41] "Fairly good in autumn." [Hn] "Too lazy to . . . open her buds properly . . . dropsical yet constricted blossoms that blighted instead of bloomed." [ARA20/16] "Flowers large for its class, but of perfect shape; outer petals white, centres rosy; full and imbricated. Liable to vary, but at all times a most beautiful kind." [P1] "Too unsightly after blooming." [ARA25/105] "Continuous bloom. Shiny light green foliage." [Lg] "The flower changes color beautifully depending upon its exposure to the air, going from a darker pink to pure white. . . . In humidity, the flowers open with difficulty if at all, and in rainy areas it is certainly better to cultivate it under glass." [JR23/38] "The petals are lovely little shells, closely compacted together, forming an indescribably beautiful rose." [Dr]

CORAL CLUSTER
Murrell, 1920
Sport of 'Orléans Rose' (Pol).

"An entrancing soft coral." [ARA25/103] "Pale coral-pink, rather a new color, and comes in fairly large trusses; fades in great heat. More susceptible to black-spot than most. . . . Vigorous grower." [Th2] "It resembles ['Orléans Rose'] in every way except color." [ARA21/153] "Semi-double . . . slight fragrance . . . bushy . . . 2 × 2 [ft; ca. 6 × 6 dm]." [B]

DEGENHARD
('Doc')
De Ruiter, 1954
From 'Robin Hood' (HMk, Pemberton, 1927, red; parentage: ? × 'Miss Edith Cavell' [Pol]) × "Polyantha seedling."
Pink.

DICK KOSTER
Koster, 1929
Sport of 'Anneke Koster' (Pol), the lineage at length tracing back to 'Tausendschön' (Rambler; see Chapter Eight).

"Orange-red, dwarf, and compact, suitable for low hedges and for forcing in pots." [ARA37/196] "Flower large, bright salmon-rose to orange, in cluster. Vigorous; free-flowering all season." [ARA37/268]

DOC
Listed as 'Degenhard'.

[DOPEY]
The only of the "7 Dwarfs" who did *not* have his name applied to a previously-named cultivar, though we should think 'Dopey' much preferable to 'Sneezy' for a flower. We should like to dedicate the name 'Dopey', therefore, to the idea of introducing any cultivar under more than one name.

ÉBLOUISSANT
(trans., 'Dazzling')
Turbat, 1918
From 'Bengale Rose' (?) × 'Cramoisi Supérieur' (Ch).

"The best red dwarf perpetual Polyantha. Flowers of good size, in bouquets of ten to twenty, in color similar to 'Cramoisi Supérieur' and 'Fabvier', with the advantage that they are produced on a true dwarf perpetual Polyantha. They last a long time without fading or turning violet, and when fully open take a cactus form. Wood and foliage purplish green. Erect grower . . . shapely bud." [ARA19/101] "Quilled flowers of gleaming dark crimson." [ARA29/97] "Brilliant deep velvety red—holds color well; small clusters. Bushy growth. Very good foliage." [Th2] Were this not "the best red dwarf perpetual Polyantha," it would be more appropriate, considering its ancestry, to place 'Éblouissant' among the Chinas.

ECHO
('Baby Tausendschön')
Ludorf/Lambert, 1914
Sport of 'Tausendschön' (Multiflora Rambler; see Plate 208).

"Dwarf, or nearly so—about two ft high [ca. 6 dm]—vigorous, hardy, erect thornless branches, handsome foliage. Blooms in bouquets which are quite large and fairly flat—perhaps a foot [ca. 3 dm] in diameter—on firm and upright stems. The blossoms are fairly large, full, pink and white mottled, much like 'Tausendschön'. Blooms June to November . . . the flower lasts eight days in water." [JR38/75] "Fairly wide blooms with the outer petals curving up to make a bowl-shaped flower." [Hk] "A free bloomer, remaining in flower throughout the season." [ARA18/133] "Foliage mildews. Continuous bloomer. Vigorous grower for this class. Discolors badly in California." [Th2]

ELLEN POULSEN
Poulsen, 1911
From 'Mme Norbert Levavasseur' (Pol) × 'Dorothy Perkins' (Rambler).

"Dark brilliant pink." [ARA16/20] "Large, full; sweet-scented; vigorous, bushy habit, most floriferous; very fine." [C&Js16] "Medium height, moderate [growth]; foliage very plentiful till midsummer, then sufficient, black-spots somewhat; bloom moderate, continuous." [ARA18/128] "Sweet-scented." [Bk] "Doesn't grow more than perhaps two ft high [ca. 6 dm]; it blooms all summer, giving large bouquets of quite full blossoms . . . of a pretty carnation pink with light yellow at the base of the petal. The growth is vigorous; the leaves are dark green and shiny, resembling those of the Wichuraianas." [JR36/40] "Mildew and black-spot resistant . . . always so fresh and clean." [ARA24/94]

ÉTOILE DE MAI   PLATE 215
(trans., 'May Star')
Gamon, 1892
"Blooms in fine yellow buds, clusters quite full and double, orange passing to pale canary yellow when open." [C&Js02] "Dwarf, vigorous, blooming abundantly, producing a seductive effect as the pretty buds expand, starting as they do nankeen yellow, and finishing up yellowish white. The blossoms always open well, are small, but very fragrant." [JR26/88–89] "Flowers large for this class." [JR17/166] "Sulphury white, flower small, full, very fragrant, very floriferous, vigorous." [Cx] "Unusually profuse." [Dr]

EVA TESCHENDORFF
Grunewald/Teschendorff, 1923
Sport of 'Echo' (Pol).
 "The best [white Polyantha] we have today . . . a greenish white color. The blooms are not spoiled by rain . . . the plant is healthy and blooms freely." [ARA25/137] "Bud small, long-pointed; flower medium size, double, very lasting, slight fragrance, greenish white (like 'Kaiserin Auguste Viktoria'), borne in clusters on long, strong stems. Foliage small, abundant, light green, glossy, disease-resistant. Thornless. Very vigorous, bushy habit (15 to 20 in [ca. 4–5 dm]; abundant; intermittent bloomer in June and July and September and October. Tips freeze." [ARA25/190]

FAIRY CHANGELING
Harkness, 1979
From 'The Fairy' (Pol) × 'Yesterday' (Floribunda, pink).
 Pink.

FAIRY DAMSEL
Harkness, 1981
 "Dense, spreading, well-foliaged shoots . . . deep red, semi-double flowers . . . 2 × 5 [ft; ca. 6 × 15 dm]." [B]

FAIRY MAID
Harkness, 1979
From 'The Fairy' (Pol) × 'Yesterday' (Floribunda, pink).
 Pink.

FAIRY PRINCE
Harkness, 1979
From 'The Fairy' (Pol) × 'Yesterday' (Floribunda, pink).
 Red.

FAIRY RING
Harkness, ca. 1980
From 'The Fairy' (Pol) × 'Yesterday' (Floribunda, pink).
 Rose-pink.

FAIRYLAND
Harkness, 1979
From 'The Fairy' (Pol) × 'Yesterday' (Floribunda, pink).
 Pink. "2 × 5 [ft,] 60 cm × 1.5 m." [B1]

FIREGLOW
Wezelenburg, 1929
Sport of 'Orange King' (Pol).
 "Bud small, ovoid; flower medium size, single, open, very lasting, slightly fragrant, brilliant vermilion-red, shaded orange, borne in cluster on short stem. Foliage sufficient, medium size, rich green, glossy. Growth moderate (15 in [ca. 4 dm]), dwarf, compact; abundant bloomer all season. Very hardy." [ARA31/239]

FLAMBOYANT
Turbat, 1931
 "Flower large, double, bright scarlet, passing to crimson-carmine which does not blue, in cluster of 10 to 20. Foliage glossy, serrated. Dwarf." [ARA]

GABRIELLE PRIVAT
Barthélemy-Privat, 1931
 "Brilliant carmine-pink." [ARA33/174]

GEORGE ELGER
Turbat, 1912
 "A dainty yellow." [ARA24/94] "Deepest and most lasting yellow of the class; lovely '[Mlle] Cécile Brunner' form. Very continuous bloomer. Medium growth." [Th2] "[Listed as giving between 100 and 200 blossoms annually]." [ARA20/84] "Singly and in small sprays, double, fine form, small, Tea fragrance . . . fine foliage, plentiful." [ARA23/162] "Very floriferous, growth erect, wood smooth, reddish green, foliage dark green, glossy above, reddish brown beneath, blooms in large clusters, coppery golden yellow changing to light yellow at expansion, buds golden yellow. The yellowest reblooming Polyantha. Could be called a dwarf 'W. A. Richardson'." [JR36/183]

GIESEBRECHT
('Bashful')
De Ruiter, 1955
 "Single, red with a white eye." [Hk]

GLOIRE DU MIDI
De Ruiter, 1932
Sport of 'Gloria Mundi' (Pol).
 Orange-red. "Like 'Gloria Mundi', but keeps color outside." [ARA33/178]

GLORIA MUNDI
Sliedrecht/De Ruiter, 1929
Sport of 'Superb' (Pol, De Ruiter, 1927, crimson; parentage unknown; called 'Improved Eblouissant').
 "Neat, full, well-formed flowers of the most brilliant scarlet-orange color imaginable, said to be unfading." [ARA29/227] "Flower large for the class, fully double, very lasting . . . orange-scarlet, borne in clusters. Foliage abundant, medium size, light green, glossy. Growth vigorous, upright, bushy; free, intermittent bloomer for ten weeks, from July to September." [ARA30/228] "Has a more double flower than 'Golden Salmon', and a faster color." [ARA32/128] "It is good but nothing to rave about . . . the color is harsh and ugly at its best and it turns just as blue as any of them." [ARA32/185] "It is oak-hardy." [C-Pf33] "2 × 2 [ft; ca. 6 × 6 dm]." [B]

GOLDEN SALMON
Cutbush/De Ruiter, 1926
Sport of 'Superb' (Pol; see 'Gloria Mundi' above).
 "Vivid orange." [RATS] "Shows up." [ARA29/50] "Healthy plant about 15 in high [ca. 3.75 dm], with a fair amount of bloom of striking color, which becomes rather tiresome. . . . Blooms more persistently than any other Polyantha. . . . Fascinating when it opens, the blooms soon turn a peculiar slatey blue-purple which is exceedingly painful to look at." [ARA30/182] "Strong growth and prolific bloom." [ARA32/186] "Large clusters of small, semi-double, rich bright salmon . . . 2 × 2 [ft; ca. 6 × 6 dm]." [B]

GOLDEN SALMON SUPERIOR
De Ruiter, 1929
Sport of 'Golden Salmon' (Pol).
 "Color almost like 'Golden Salmon', perhaps a little more yellow-salmon, and stands weather conditions better and does not fade." [ARA32/221] "Bud small, globular; flower small, cupped, semi-double, very lasting, golden salmon that does not fade or burn, in cluster on long stem. Foliage wrinkled, light green. Vigorous (30 in [ca. 7.5 dm]), upright; profuse bloomer (1000 blooms in a season)." [ARA33/178]

GRETA KLUIS
Kluis & Koning, 1916
Sport of 'Echo' (Pol).

"Deep crimson-pink. Very free." [ARA25/121] "Medium-sized, globular blooms of deep pink, passing to carmine-red. A continuous, even bloomer." [C-Ps28]

GRUMPY
Listed as 'Burkhard'.

HAPPY
Listed as 'Alberich'.

IDEAL
Spek, 1920
Sport of 'Miss Edith Cavell' (Pol).

"Small, brilliant red blooms in compact clusters." [ARA29/97] "Very dark garnet, in large clusters; grows quite dwarf; vigorous." [ARA25/121] "The darkest of all." [ARA29/50] "The flowers are semi-double, come in great heads of thirty or more, and the color is retained remarkably well until they drop. A neat and compact grower. Has everything a Polyantha of this type needs, except fragrance." [C-Ps25] "Bud globular; flower medium size, double, full open, globular . . . very lasting . . . slight fragrance. Growth moderate; bushy; blooms abundantly all season. Hardy." [ARA21/165]

JEAN MERMOZ
Chenault, 1937
From *R. wichuraiana* × "A Hybrid Tea."
Pink.

JULIE DELBARD
Delbard, 1976
Apricot.

KATHARINA ZEIMET
Lambert, 1901
Two parentages given: Either from (1) 'Étoile de Mai' (Pol) × 'Marie Pavič' (Pol); or (2) 'Euphrosyne' (HMk, Schmitt/Lambert, 1896; parentage *R. multiflora* × 'Mignonette' [Pol]) × 'Marie Pavič' (Pol).

"Very small, double, fragrant, pure white . . . large clusters. Free, continuous bloom. Compact . . . 1–2 [ft; ca. 3–6 dm]. Shiny, healthy foliage . . . perhaps the best white Polyantha." [Lg] "Bright green glossy foliage." [HRG] "Stocky plant, twiggy growth . . . 2 × 2 [ft; ca. 6 × 6 dm]." [B] "Fine for massing." [P1] "Moderate vigor." [Cx] "Low-growing, vigorous; foliage very plentiful till late summer, then plentiful, black-spots somewhat; bloom free, continuous." [ARA18/128] "One of the most remarkable among white varieties. It is more floriferous than 'Marie Pavie' [*sic*], its parent." [JR28/128] "Fades to brown in heat; double, flat flowers, in clusters . . . shows black open center in California . . . reported better in East [U.S.]. . . . Strong growth." [Th2] "A record-breaker for bloom and hardiness." [MLS] "A little plant of great refinement." [Hk]

KERSBERGEN
Oosthoek/Kersbergen, 1927
Sport of 'Miss Edith Cavell' (Pol).
Red.

LADY READING
Van Kleef? Van Herk?, 1921
Sport of 'Ellen Poulsen' (Pol).

"Bright red, semi-double flowers in clusters; holds color well. Very attractive. Black spots. Fine [*Rhode Island, U.S.A.*]/ . . . of good growth . . . not an attractive color . . . [*Massachusetts*]/ . . . one of the finest Polyanthas [*Ontario, Canada*]/ . . . washed-out, pale pink [*Iowa*]/ . . . muddy color . . . profuse . . . for forcing." [PP28]

LA MARNE
Barbier, 1915
From 'Mme Norbert Levavasseur' (Pol) × 'Comtesse du Caÿla' (Ch).

"Semi-double flowers, bright salmon-rose at the edges, rosy blush inside . . . glossy and mildew-proof foliage." [ARA24/94] "Apple-blossom-pink clusters." [ARA29/97] "Clusters of double flowers of rich pink with creamy centers . . . to 4 [ft; ca. 1.25 m]." [HRG] "The growth is uniform and the bluish-green foliage very distinctive. . . . Its foliage is retained until well into the winter." [C-Ps27] "Very handsome." [ARA31/118]

LEGION D'HONNEUR
Delbard, 1974
Orange-red.

LÉONIE LAMESCH
Lambert, 1899
From 'Aglaia' (Multiflora Rambler; Lambert, 1896, straw; parentage: *R. multiflora* × 'Rêve d'Or' [N]) × 'Kleiner Alfred' (Pol).

"A quaint but novel variety, producing flowers of a coppery red colour with terra-cotta edges . . . rather imperfect in shape, but . . . valuable . . . vigorous." [P1] "The blooms are medium size and very durable and ten distinctly colored flowers are frequently shown on the bush at one time, varying from cochineal red in the bud to glowing coppery red tinged with orange when the flower opens." [C&Js10] "Shrub bushy, vigorous, and hardy; upright branches, height about two ft [ca. 6 dm]; wood brownish, with red prickles, which are very large and not very numerous. Foliage medium-sized, dark green, new foliage reddish-brown. . . . The flowers often come singly, and often 25 to the cluster; they are small or medium-sized, well-formed, globular, and quite full; the color is distinct and unique in its group . . . deep copper-red, darker beneath, and the edges are shaded, bordered, and striped copper-red . . . the semi-open bud is deep blood-red. Strong perfume." [JR23/171] "Medium height, moderate [vigor], foliage plentiful, healthy; bloom moderate, continuous." [ARA18/128] "Perfect foliage. Large grower." [Th2] "A most charming little rose." [Wr]

LILLAN
De Vink, 1958
From 'Ellen Poulsen' (Pol) × 'Tom Thumb' (Min, De Vink, 1935, crimson; parentage, 'Rouletii' [Min Ch] × 'Gloria Mundi' [Pol]).
Deep red.

LITTLE DORRIT
Reeves, 1930
Sport of 'Coral Cluster' (Pol).

"Bud and flower large, semi-double, full, open, very lasting, slightly fragrant, coral-salmon, borne in large cluster on long stem. Foliage abundant, medium size, glossy. Growth vigorous, bushy, dwarf; profuse, continuous bloomer. Very hardy." [ARA31/232]

LITTLE WHITE PET
Listed as 'White Pet'.

LULLABY
Shepherd, 1953
From an unnamed seedling (parentage: *R. soulieana* × 'Mrs. Joseph Heiss' [Pol, pink]) × 'Mlle Cécile Brunner' (Pol).
   White, center blush.

MA PÂQUERETTE
Listed as 'Pâquerette'.

MARGO KOSTER
Koster, 1931
Sport of 'Dick Koster' (Pol); lineage at length commences with 'Tausendschön' (Rambler; see Chapter Eight).
   "Flower large, orange-red, in cluster. Fine forcer." [ARA37/269] "Varies from intense orange salmon (in cool weather) to light pinkish salmon (in warm weather). No scent. Twiggy. May lose leaves during the summer, but compensates for this by blooming straight through winter, just when one needs some cheerful-looking flowers. Mildews; no rust. My thirty-year-old plants, unpruned for fifteen years, have never exceeded the dimensions they attained their first season — 2.5 × 2.5 ft (ca. 7.5 × 7.5 dm)." [BCD]

MARGO'S SISTER
Ratcliffe, 1954
Sport of 'Margo Koster' (Pol).
   Light pink.

MARIE-JEANNE
Turbat, 1913
   "Very vigorous, with handsome shiny green foliage; wood without thorns; enormous clusters of 40–60 blossoms, large for the type, of long duration and pure white, sometimes shaded very light salmon as it opens. Quite remontant, all in all producing a very decorative effect by its white masses of flowers at first bloom." [*Listed as "climbing," a quality not cited in "modern" descriptions*] [JR37/137] "Pale blush-cream in clusters. Almost thornless . . . 2 × 2 [ft; ca. 6 × 6 dm]." [B]

MARIE PAVIČ
('Marie Pavié', 'Marie Parvie')
Alégatière, 1888
   "Thornless, extra floriferous, handsome green foliage of 5–7 leaflets; flower large for a Polyantha; principally blush-white to the center, the same as 'Souvenir de la Malmaison', and much more floriferous." [JR12/165] "Fragrant . . . very vigorous." [Cx] "Rosy white." [P1] "Flower medium sized, full, flesh-white, center tinted pink." [LR] "Medium height, vigorous; foliage very plentiful, black-spots slightly; bloom free, continuous." [ARA18/129] "Holds its foliage among the best." [ARA20/58] "Very lasting. . . . Foliage large, abundant, rich green, soft, disease-resistant. Vigorous grower, reaching 15 to 20 in [ca. 3.75–5 dm], very bushy. Blooms profusely in June and at intervals the remainder of the season." [Th2] "A good scent." [Hk] "Large cluster. Continuous . . . 1–3 [ft; ca. 3–9 dm]." [Lg] "Upright . . . 4 × 3 [ft; ca. 1.25 × 1 m]." [B] The hacek is conjectural.

MARTHA
Lambert, 1905
From 'Thalia' (Multiflora Rambler, Schmitt/Lambert, 1895, white; parentage, *R. multiflora* × 'Pâquerette' [Pol]) × 'Mme Laurette Messimy' (Ch).
Not to be confused with the 1912 Bourbon of the same name.
   "Copper red, flowers in large corymbs." [K2] "A 'Bengale Multiflora' rose . . . blooms in profusion over a great part of the season, developing corymbs of small, full blossoms." [JR29/179] "Shrub dwarf, bushy, very floriferous; flower small, coppery pink." [JR30/25]

MARYTJE CAZANT
Van Nes, 1927
Sport of 'Jessie' (Pol).
   "Buds salmon-pink on white ground, globular, lasting." [ARA29/227] "A charming flesh-colored Polyantha." [ARA33/155]

MEVROUW NATHALIE NYPELS
Leenders, 1919
From 'Orléans Rose' (Pol) × an unnamed seedling (parentage: 'Comtesse du Caÿla' [Ch] × 'Jaune Bicolore' [*R. fœtida* relative; yellow streaked red]).
   "Bud large; flower large, open form, double, borne in clusters; very lasting; strong fragrance. Color, hydrangea-pink. Foliage abundant, small, leathery bronze-green. A vigorous grower of bushy habit and a profuse bloomer." [ARA20/135] "Reddish orange, changing to hydrangea pink — a striking color." [ARA25/102]

MIGNONETTE   PLATE 212
Guillot fils, 1881
Seedling of a seedling of *R. multiflora* 'Polyantha'. Evidently of the same parentage and generation as 'Pâquerette'.
   "In February, 1869, I sowed a great quantity of seed which I had harvested from the variety 'Polyantha', a multiflora variety originating in Japan which was very much a climber, and non-remontant, having a quite small single white blossom much like that of a bramble or strawberry, and blooming in panicles. Among the many seedlings, there were many which resembled in their wood and foliage multifloras and Noisettes. Quite a few bore flowers of moderate quality, singles, semi-doubles, and full blossoms, with petals as large as the roses of our gardens, with a variety of colors: yellow, white, bright pink, etc. I didn't have so many as two which resembled their mother! Among the seedlings which didn't bloom until the second or third year, there was found one which had blossoms with two rows of petals, an inch to an inch and a half across, not remontant as the others were, but which gave me wonderful seeds which I sowed in February, 1872. [*I suspect that this two-rowed seedling which gave wonderful seeds is the non-remontant 'Polyantha alba plena sarmentosa' which appears here and there in the literature, notably in the parentage of 'Anne Marie de Montravel', 'Mlle Cécile Brunner', and 'Perle d'Or'; good breeding material was uncommon, and to be valued and used when found. We might also note that all of the breeders responsible for these varieties — Rambaux, Dubreuil, Ducher, Guillot fils — were from the Lyon area, which had and has a very active horticultural association.* BCD]] Out of this came my dear little 'Pâquerette', which I put into commerce in November, 1875. From these seedlings I further got many varieties equally dwarf and very remontant, one giving yellowish-white double flowers, more petite than those of 'Pâquerette' and keeping the form and character of the climbing 'Polyantha', as well as another similarly remontant dwarf, of the same sort as 'Pâquerette', but with soft

pink flowers which were full and well-formed though small [*this, presumably, is 'Mignonette'*]; I am going to propagate a quantity sufficient to deliver them into commerce in November 1880." [JR2/137–138]

"Dwarf, of the Lawrenciana sort, very vigorous, with small flowers in the shape of full tulips, well formed, ruffled. The color is flesh-pink, brighter at the center." [JR3/9] "Vigorous, quite remontant, with very small flowers of about an inch [ca. 2.5 cm], well formed and held well, colored pale pink fading to white, in clusters of 30–40 making a single stem into a pretty bouquet." [JR5/147] "Very beautiful, full regular flowers about the size of a twenty-five cent piece, perfectly double, deliciously perfumed; bright rosy pink; immense bloomer." [C&Js98] "Very dwarf, bushy, floriferous. Stature of China roses. Branches compact, short, with dark reddish-brown bark, twiggy, bearing strong hooked prickles of a reddish color. Leaves glabrous, of 5–7 leaflets, narrowly oval, slender, smooth, dark green on top, reddish below. The young foliage is reddish-brown edged, and finely serrated. The inflorescence is a short panicle, compact, like that of the Chinas. The flowers are full, pink, sometimes flesh, bordered or blotched with rose." [JR9/6–7] "Weak in growth." [Hn] "Foliage very plentiful till late summer, then sufficient, some black-spot . . . mildew . . . bloom free, continuous." [ARA18/129] "One of the best." [P1]

MILROSE
Delbard-Chabert, 1965
From 'Orléans Rose' (Pol) × a seedling of 'Français' (Floribunda, pink) × 'Lafayette' (Floribunda, crimson).
Light pink.

MISS EDITH CAVELL
Meiderwyk/Spek, 1917
Sport of 'Orléans Rose' (Pol).
Not to be confused with the single white HT 'Edith Cavell' of 1918.

"Brilliant dark red." [Cw] "Color brilliant scarlet, overlaid with deep, velvety crimson or maroon. The blooms come in great open clusters all season. The most attractive red Polyantha Rose in existence." [C&Js22] "Very floriferous." [Lc] "Little flowers . . . close in the large trusses." [Hk] "Semi-double, scarlet-crimson flowers amid dark green foliage . . . 3 × 2 [ft; ca. 9 × 6 dm]." [B] "Foliage disease-resistant." [ARA21/165] There is also another Polyantha 'Miss Edith Cavell', of the same color, attributed to De Ruiter, 1932.

MLLE CÉCILE BRUNNER   PLATE 211
Widow Ducher, 1880
'Polyantha alba plena' × 'Mme de Tartas' (T).

"Dwarf, very vigorous and suitable for bedding . . . blooms in clusters; pretty, bright pink on a yellowish ground, outside petals light pink; very fragrant." [JR4/167] "Spreading branches, diverging, looking like a Tea rose, thornless, or here and there a thorn or two; bark smooth, glossy, of a rusty green; leaves of 3–5 fairly oval leaflets . . . flowers numerous, small, very full, delicately scented; an exquisite miniature." [EL] "Perfect pink buds, diffused with yellow." [ARA29/97] "I have never found it set seed." [Hk] "Low-growing, weak; foliage barely sufficient, black-spots slightly; bloom moderate, but continuous." [ARA18/128] "Practically free from mildew . . . graceful habit." [NRS/12] "Blooms of HT shape. Continuous . . . 3 × 2 [ft; ca. 9 × 6 dm]." [B] "Vigorous to 4 [ft; ca. 1.25 m]." [HRG] "Dedicated to the charming daughter of the late Ulrich Brunner, rose-grower at Lausanne." [JR30/53]

'Mlle Cécile Brunner' has not lost any of her charms over the years. Recently, I was strolling meditatively down an aisle of modern roses at a local nursery when I heard a housewife in the neighboring aisle call out to her husband, "Oh, *look!*" as if she had found the dearest jewel in all the world. I peeked through some intervening canes of 'Peace' to find that she was gazing at an unfurling bud of 'Mlle Cécile Brunner', holding its own easily against the heavy artillery of more recent times.

MME HARDY DU THÉ
Listed as 'Clotilde Soupert'.

MME JULES THIBAUD
Introducer and date unknown
Sport of 'Mlle Cécile Brunner' (Pol).
"A deeper peachy-pink [than 'Mlle Cécile Brunner']. Young foliage is deep bronze . . . rolled centre with a button eye." [G]

MME MELON DU THÉ
Listed as 'Clotilde Soupert'.

MRS. R. M. FINCH
Finch, 1923
Seedling of 'Orléans Rose' (Pol).
"Flowers of bright rose-pink come in branching fragrant clusters." [C-Pf33] "Medium . . . double, cupped, cluster; rosy pink, fading lighter. Repeats . . . 2–3 [ft; ca. 6–9 dm]." [Lg]

MRS. W. H. CUTBUSH   PLATE 222
Levavasseur, 1907
Sport or seedling of 'Mme Norbert Levavasseur' (Pol).
"Very light pink." [JR32/161] "More vigorous than 'Mme Norbert Levavasseur', from which it however takes its stature and mode of flowering. . . . A pretty, delicate pink, sometimes washed slightly with a light salmon . . . blooms throughout the winter under glass, and furthermore is very hardy." [JR33/12] "Flower large, full; moderate vigor; for borders." [Cx] "Coral pink. . . . Clean, healthy growth." [Dr] "The foliage is rather small but sufficiently dense, light green in colour, as also are the stems of the current year's growth. The habit of the plant is dwarf, bushy and compact, very suitable for bedding purposes . . . almost continuously in flower until November. The flowers are small and slightly cup-shaped; they are produced in large compact trusses and are bright clear pink in colour. These trusses are carried on strong stems well above the foliage and the flowers stand wet weather very well for a Rose of this class . . . little affected by mildew. . . . Its weakness lies in its want of perfume and the absence of any pronounced form in the flowers." [NRS/12] "Medium height, vigorous; foliage very plentiful till late summer, then sparse, black-spots badly; bloom abundant till late summer, then moderate, continuous." [ARA18/129] "This rose was sold in 1904 to Messers Cutbush and Son of London, who bought 10,000 slips and propagated it the following year." [JR33/25]

MUTTERTAG.
(trans., 'Mother's Day')
Grootendorst, 1949
Sport of 'Dick Koster' (Pol).
Deep red.

NEIGES D'ÉTÉ
(trans., 'Snows of Summer')
Gailloux, 1984
White.

NYPELS PERFECTION
Leenders, 1930
Sport of 'Mevrouw Nathalie Nypels' (Pol).

"Bud ovoid; flower large, semi-double, open, lasting, hydrangea pink, shaded rose-neyron-red, borne in a cluster on medium-strength stem. Foliage sufficient, medium size, rich green. Growth vigorous, bushy; profuse bloomer." [ARA31/240]

ORANGE KOSTER
Introducer and date unknown
Presumably a sport from 'Margo Koster' or 'Dick Koster'.
Orange.

ORANGE MORSDAG
(trans., 'Orange Mother's Day')
Grootendorst, 1956
Sport of 'Muttertag' (Pol).
Orange.

ORANGE TRIUMPH
Kordes, 1937
From 'Eva' (HMk, Kordes, 1933, red) × 'Solarium' (Wichuraiana Rambler, Turbat, 1925, single red; parentage unknown).

"Bud small, ovoid; flower small, semi-double, cupped, very lasting, slightly fragrant, salmon-red, with orange shadings, in cluster. Foliage abundant, glossy. Very vigorous (2 ft. [ca. 6 dm]), compact, bushy; profuse, continuous bloomer." [ARA37/270] "Orange only under special conditions; usually the color is coral . . . is really a triumph . . . 1.5-foot [ca. 4.5 dm] plants with enormous clusters of deep salmon-pink bloom. It is a good Polyantha, but apparently wrongly named." [ARA39/215] "No fragrance . . . free from mildew, constant in bloom, and holds its color well in heat." [ARA40/215]

ORLÉANS-ROSE
PLATE 223
Levavasseur, 1909
From 'Mme Norbert Levavasseur' (Pol) × an unnamed seedling.

"Very floriferous . . . has the advantage of innumerable buds on one upright stem on which the flower-stems have small, rigid brown bristles . . . geranium red, tinted Neyron pink, whitish at the center, with carmine petals, very decorative, keeping its color until completely open. Very vigorous, attaining perhaps 2.5 to 3 ft [ca. 7.5–9 dm]; foliage a handsome shiny light green, quite hardy, and healthy." [JR33/169] "Foliage dark." [JR34/24] "Flower medium-sized, full." [Cx] "Small, bright red blooms with white center." [ARA29/97] "Nearer pink . . . to call it rose-red is generous enough." [Hk] "Medium height, vigorous; foliage very plentiful till late summer, then sparse, black-spots some . . . bloom profuse in June, grading to moderate in October and November, continuous." [ARA18/129] "Said to be the best Polyantha Rose ever raised." [C&Js12]

PACIFIC TRIUMPH
Heers, 1949
Sport of 'Orange Triumph' (Pol).
Salmon.

PAPA HÉMERAY
Hémeray-Aubert, 1912
From 'Hiawatha' (Mult) × 'Parsons' Pink' (Ch).

"Scarlet crimson." [NRS/15] "Single red with white centre, produced in clusters. Vigorous . . . 4 × 3 [ft; ca. 1.25 × 1 m]." [B] "Foliage dark green." [B1] "Single flowers of a very intense vermilion red around the edges, with a white center. This dwarf continuously reblooming variety is only a copy of the climber 'Hiawatha' with a very abundant flowering; it blooms in clusters which are very full, and has the same blossoms as 'Hiawatha'. This rose, which is very vigorous, blooms very well until frost. . . . Its brilliant color is not 'washed out' by rain, nor does it 'blue' in the sun." [JR36/12/184] "It is a China hybrid. . . . One is able to say that it is, at one and the same time, a China and a dwarf 'Hiawatha'; but it is remontant and always blooms up to the autumn frosts. . . . Very vigorous, could be used for bedding where, because of the nature of its flowers, it would produce a grand sight." [JR37/9/145]

PÂQUERETTE
PLATE 210
(trans., 'Daisy'; syn., 'Ma Pâquerette')
Guillot fils, 1875
Seedling of a seedling of *R. multiflora* 'Polyantha'.

"Pure white, about one inch [ca. 2.5 cm] in diameter, full, prettily formed, recalling blossoms of the double flowering cherry; there are five to seven leaflets, the growth is slender." [EL] " 'Pâquerette' . . . attains a height of one foot to fifteen in [ca. 3–3.8 dm]." [JR2/138] "Moderately vigorous; a variety of many merits, well-branched, blooms abundantly and constantly; the plant is dwarf and bushy; has branches of shiny green bark, fairly thornless; leaves of three to five smooth leaflets, which are glossy." [S] "Has the general aspect of a Noisette." [JR9/6] "Continuous . . . excellent." [Lg] For the history of this, the first Polyantha, see the headnote to this chapter.

PARIS
De Ruiter, 1929
"Flower bright red, unfading. Vigorous." [ARA32/221] "Crimson . . . with some tendency to fade and blue." [ARA35/196]

PAUL CRAMPEL
('Paul Grampel')
Kersbergen, 1930
"Flower deep orange-scarlet (does not burn), in large cluster; brighter than 'Gloria Mundi' — not as double, but larger." [ARA32/221] "Moderately vigorous . . . with clean foliage . . . orange-scarlet flowers which scarcely fade or blue." [ARA35/196] "Its orange color is not as hard as that of some others." [ARA34/205] "A vigorous erect plant with light green foliage . . . 2 × 2 [ft; ca. 6 × 6 dm]." [B] "Still-glorious." [ARA35/143]

PERLE D'OR
PLATE 213
(trans., 'Golden Pearl')
Rambaux/Dubreuil, 1883
From 'Polyantha alba plena' × 'Mme Falcot' (T).

"Apricot, pink and cream tones . . . to 3 [ft; ca. 9 dm]." [HRG] "A golden copper." [ARA24/94] "Clusters of buff-yellow . . . with pink shadings . . . shapely . . . rich green foliage . . . 4 × 3 [ft; ca. 1.23 × 1 m]." [B] "Double, small, fragrant; light golden yellow, center pinkish. Continuous." [Lg] "Fragrant . . . vigorous." [Cx] "[As compared to other early Polyanthas,] more blossoms, better shaped and larger, plant dwarfer, with handsome foliage of a bright green. The flowers are in a tight cluster of 20–30, buds long-oval, stems strong and upright, flowers large for the type, well formed, expanding well, of nankeen-yellow with an orange center and elongated elliptical petals which are imbricated and recurved. Surpasses all others of this sort by reason of its bearing and coloration." [JR7/169] "Developed by P. Rambaux in 1875 and released to commerce in 1883 by F. Dubreuil." [JR24/5]

[PINK CÉCILE BRUNNER]
Western Rose Co., 1918
Presumably a sport from 'Mlle Cécile Brunner'.

"Rose-pink, darker than 'Cécile Brunner', with darker colored foliage, and not quite as large a grower. Continuous. Tested only in California." [Th2]

PINK PET
Lilley, 1928
"Flower double, bright pink, borne in large clusters. Growth upright; early bloomer." [ARA29/222] "Small stocky plant . . . deep green foliage, plant 2 [ft; ca. 6 dm]." [HRG] "Small, double, flat; bright soft pink. Continuous . . . 1–3 [ft; ca. 3–9 dm]. Healthy, shiny green foliage . . . outstanding." [Lg]

PINK POSY
Cocker, 1983
Pink.

PINKIE
Swim, 1947
Sport of 'China Doll' (Pol).
"Small, double; deep rose pink. Profuse . . . 1 [ft; ca. 3 dm] . . . excellent border plant." [Lg]

PREVUE
James, 1978
White.

RED TRIUMPH
Morse, 1956
Sport of 'Orange Triumph' (Pol).
Very dark red.

SLEEPY
Listed as 'Balduin'.

SNEEZY
Listed as 'Bertram'.

SNEPRINSESSE
('Snow White')
Grootendorst, 1946
Sport of 'Dick Koster' (Pol).
White.

SNOW WHITE
Listed as 'Sneprinsesse'.

SPARKLER
De Ruiter, 1929
Sport of 'Golden Salmon' (Pol).
"Sparkling brilliant red." [ARA32/222] "Bud small, globular; flower small, cupped, semi-double, very lasting, red, burning in the sun, in cluster on long stem. Foliage light green. Growth moderate (1.5 ft [ca. 4.5 dm]), upright; profuse bloomer (1000 blooms in season)." [ARA22/179]

SPRAY CÉCILE BRUNNER
Howard Rose Co., 1941
Sport of 'Mlle Cécile Brunner' (Pol).

"Small, double, very fragrant; light to medium pink. Excellent repeat . . . when established . . . 10–15 [ft; ca. 3–4.5 m] . . . shorter, and repeats bloom much better than 'Cl. Cécile Brunner'." [Lg] Said to be much confused in commerce with 'Bloomfield Abundance'.

SUMMER DAWN
Proctor, 1950
Sport of 'Margo Koster' (Pol).
Dawn pink to light rose.

SUNSHINE
Robichon, 1927
Not to be confused with Cutbush's similarly named Polyantha of the same color and year.

"Charming . . . best yellow of the race. . . . While the plants are only moderate in vigor, and the pale orange flowers fade almost white in hot weather, the light scarlet buds are most attractive and it is decidedly worth having if you like Polyanthas." [ARA34/213] "Fades too quickly but is really worth keeping because of the yellow shades of the newly opened buds." [ARA35/204]

THE ALLIES
Heers, 1930
"Bud small, globular; flower small, double, full, open, lasting, slightly fragrant, white suffused pale pink, in cluster. Foliage small, glossy. Growth dwarf (16 in [ca. 4 dm]), bushy; free bloomer in May, June, and November." [ARA33/178]

THE FAIRY
Bentall, 1932
Two parentages given: (1) from 'Paul Crampel' (Pol) × 'Lady Gay' (Wichuraiana Rambler, Walsh, 1903, pink; parentage: *R. wichuraiana* × 'Bardou Job' [B]); or (2) sport of 'Lady Godiva' (Wichuraiana Rambler, G. Paul, 1907, pink; sport of 'Dorothy Perkins' [Rambler]).

"Flower salmon-pink, in cluster. Beautiful foliage." [ARA33/173] "Ideal for massed, groundcover planting. Clusters of bead-like buds open to globular, pink flowers . . . flowering almost continuously. . . . Good foliage . . . 2 × 4 [ft; ca. 6 × 12 dm]." [B]

TIP-TOP
('Baby Doll')
Lambert, 1909
From 'Trier' (Lambertiana, Lambert, 1904, rosy white) × a seedling of *R. fœtida bicolor*.

"Coppery, orange towards the center, edges pink and white; flower very large, full, very floriferous, moderate vigor; good for bedding." [Cx] "Low-growing . . . foliage plentiful until midsummer, then barely sufficient, black-spots very little . . . mildews some . . . bloom moderate, continuous." [ARA18/129] "Its blooms are rather large, the petals beautifully crimped and white, with a broad margin of clear pink . . . not as floriferous as many others . . . growth relatively weak . . . eighteen in [ca. 4.5 dm]. The foliage is also small, which helps to give the plant an undernourished appearance." [ARA20/59] "The open flowers look like balls of pink and white pop-corn." [ARA29/50] "Lovely little blossoms of rose and copper." [ARA29/97] "Lovely bud, opening with high but loose center, petals often reflexed, lasting. Continuous bloomer. Vigorous. Small to medium growth. Fine foliage. A distinct and desirable rose." [Th2]

TOPAZ
Tantau/Conard-Pyle, 1937
From 'Johanna Tantau' (Pol, Tantau, 1928, white) × a unnamed seedling (parentage: 'Professor Gnau' [HT, Tantau, 1928, cream; parentage: 'Oskar Cordel' (HP) × ?] × 'Julien Potin' [Pern. HT, Pernet-Ducher, 1927, primrose]).

"Small blooms like tiny H.T. blooms, light golden yellow on petite twiggy plant, 12" [ca. 3 dm]." [HRG]

TRIOMPHE ORLÉANAISE
Peauger, 1912
"Growth vigorous, foliage a handsome glossy green, with erect branches. Flowers large for the sort, in clusters, a pretty and intense cherry-red, lasting well and long without bluing, and weather-resistant. . . . Superior to and distinct from the beautiful variety 'Mme Norbert Levavasseur'. In color, this novelty resembles 'Jessie' and 'Eva Teschendorff', but it is more vigorous, more disease-resistant, and the flower clusters are larger." [JR36/184] "The best red-colored, as well as the most vigorous growing, Polyantha. Flower-clusters very large; holds its color well over a long period." [ARA18/134] "Of the clearest and brightest red, borne in abundance." [ARA20/59] "Tall, vigorous; foliage very plentiful till late summer, then barely sparse, black-spot increasing from midsummer, mildew in late summer; bloom profuse till late summer, then decreasing to moderate in October and November, continuous." [ARA18/129]

VATERTAG
(trans., 'Father's Day')
Tantau, 1959
Sport of 'Muttertag' (Pol).
Coral-orange.

VERDUN
Barbier, 1918
"Purplish carmine-red." [Cw] "Flowers are borne in pyramidal trusses of twenty-five to fifty, and are rather large, well-formed, globular, of a splendid carmine-purple, brighter than 'Crimson Rambler'. Do not fade or turn violet. Dwarf, branching shrub; exceedingly floriferous." [ARA19/101] A 'VERDUN SUPERIOR', of which we have no further reports and which is of unknown provenance, is also to be found.

WAVERLY TRIUMPH
Poulter, 1951
Sport of 'Orange Triumph' (Pol).
Pink, yellow at the nub.

WHITE CÉCILE BRUNNER
Fauque & fils/Vigneron, 1909
Sport of 'Mlle Cécile Brunner' (Pol).

"Cream-yellow to white, light yellow or fawn center, bleaches when fully open to white cream. Foliage lighter in color than 'Cécile Brunner'. Continuous bloomer. The smallest grower of the 'Cécile Brunner' type." [Th2] "Maintains all of the good qualities of 'Cécile Brunner' . . . flowers of pure white, sulphur yellow, and chamois may be found on the same plant." [JR33/152] "Not a white." [ARA25/105]

WHITE KOSTER
Introducer and date unknown
Presumably a sport from 'Margo Koster' or 'Dick Koster'.
White.

WHITE PET
('Little White Pet', 'Little Pet')
Henderson, 1879
Sport of 'Félicité et Perpétue' (HSempervirens, Jacques, 1827, white).

"White, small, and double; a pretty miniature Rose, and exceedingly free in flowering." [P1] "Double, flat, fragrant; white sometimes tinged pink on the edges . . . 2 [ft; ca. 6 dm] . . . outstanding . . . healthy." [Lg] "Huge trusses of pure white pompon-like blooms throughout the Summer . . . 3 × 2 [ft; ca. 9 × 6 dm]." [B] "Vigorous." [J] "Much to be admired for its charm . . . graceful." [JR4/111] "A beautiful rose to own." [Hk]

YVONNE RABIER
Turbat, 1910
R. wichuraiana cultivar × a Polyantha cultivar.
"Double, flat; pure white, center tinted soft yellow. Continuous . . . compact, vigorous . . . 1–2 [ft; ca. 3–6 dm]." [Lg] "Very free and perpetual flowering." [NRS/13] "Clusters of small double white flowers . . . hints of lemon in the base. . . . Glossy rich green foliage . . . 2 × 2 [ft; ca. 6 × 6 dm]." [B] "Very hardy, foliage ample and abundant, brilliant green, persistent, very decorative. Its numerous, sturdy scapes bear great clusters of good-sized flowers, pure white with a very light touch of sulphur. The buds are white with a light tinge of green, open easily, and are well poised." [JR34/167] "Medium height, vigorous; foliage very plentiful, black-spots slightly . . . bloom abundant and moderate by turns, but continuous." [ARA18/129] "Discolors badly in heat. . . . Very strong grower." [Th2]

Supplement

ABONDANT
Turbat, 1914
"Pink, medium-sized, full, dwarf." [Sn]

ÄNNCHEN MÜLLER   PLATE 221
('Anny Muller')
Schmidt, 1906
From 'Turner's Crimson Rambler' (Multiflora Rambler, Turner, 1894, crimson) × 'Georges Pernet' (Pol).

"Dark pink." [Ÿ] "The blossoms are a fascinating shade of deep rose with petals curled and twisted, producing a fluffy effect.

Its hardiness, vigorous habit of growth, with healthy, rich green foliage, all commend it to the careful buyer. 'A magnificent bedding variety, and very persistent in holding its flowers.' " [C&Js10] "Rigid branches to a meter [yard] in height, growth much like that of 'Mme Norbert Levavasseur' [Pol]. Very abundant bloom, particularly in June when it gives pretty and effective red blossoms." [JR30/182–183]

APFELBLÜTE
Wirtz & Eicke, 1907
Seedling of 'Mme Norbert Levavasseur' (Pol).

"Light pink, small, full, medium scent, dwarf." [Sn]

BAPTISTE LAFAYE
Puyravaud, 1909

"Flower pale currant red, lined white, fading to pink, well formed, like a daisy, large for the sort, full, abundant bloom, in a cluster; very vigorous bush for the center of the bed with 'Mme Norbert Levavasseur', good for pot culture, very vigorous on its own roots, foliage dark green, thorns large and not very numerous. Dedicated to a horticulturalist from Coutras (Gironde)." [JR33/152]

BETSY VAN NES
Van Ryn, 1914
Sport of 'Mrs. W. H. Cutbush' (Pol).

"Pure bright red; flowers unusually large and double for this class. Does not fade or mildew." [C&Js15] "Small, semi-double, in clusters, short stems. Foliage fair, sparse. Growth weak; hardy. Light red which fades badly." [ARA23/156]

BORDURE
Barbier, 1911
Seedling of 'Universal Favorite' (Wichuraiana, Manda, 1899, lilac and white; itself from *R. wichuraiana* × 'American Beauty' [HP]).

"Completely dwarf, not above 3 dm high [ca. 1 foot], with stocky growth. Covered all season long with cascades of blossoms to the point of obscuring the foliage. Flowers 3–5 cm across [ca. 1–2 in], double, well formed, pure carmine. Bud bright carmine. The color doesn't fade in the sun, and in the clusters of 25–50 flowers, a person can't make out any difference between old blossoms and those newly opened. Magnificent plant for borders and pot culture. Dwarfer than 'Mme Norbert Levavasseur'." [JR36/10] "Low-growing, moderate; foliage very plentiful till late summer, when it black-spots, causing it to become sparse; bloom abundant till September then moderate, continuous." [ARA18/128]

BOUQUET BLANC
Corrard, 1914

"Dwarf bush, pretty vigorous, early blooming. Blossom medium-sized, full, very fragrant; color, pure white with some sulphur towards the middle. Good for pot culture." [JR38/72]

BOUQUET DE NEIGE
(trans., 'Bouquet of Snow')
Vilin, 1899

"Growth dwarf, very hardy, handsome foliage, flower very bright white, medium size for the sort, pretty double, very pretty form; blooms abundantly in clusters of 20–30 blossoms on each stem. Very pretty." [JR24/2]

CHARLES MÉTROZ
Schwartz, 1900

"Delicate pink bordered light pink." [Ÿ] "Foliage bright green, as if varnished; flower small, well formed, China pink tinted salmon pink and carmine." [JR24/164]

CINERARIA
Lambert, 1909
Not to be confused with Leenders' semidouble Polyantha of 1934.

"Light red, white in the center, small, single, dwarf." [Sn]

COLIBRI
Lille, 1898

"Buds coppery yellow; flowers medium, full, well formed, white tinted coppery yellow fading to pure white. Growth vigorous; blooms in clusters, producing a most charming effect by the contrast of the yellow buds and white blossoms." [JR22/166]

CORONET
W. Paul, 1912
Not to be confused with the Dingee-Conard HT of 1897, which was silvery carnation pink.

"Yellow tinted pink . . . very beautiful. Very floriferous, quite distinct." [JR36/103]

CORRIE KOSTER
W. Paul, 1923
Sport of the pale salmon 'Juliana-Roos' introduced by den Ouden in 1921, which was itself a sport of 'Orléans Rose' (Pol).

"Coral red and salmon yellow." [Ÿ]

CYCLOPE
Dubreuil, 1909
Seedling of 'Mme Norbert Levavasseur' (Pol).

"Dwarf, blooming in clusters of ten to twenty flowers, which are small, and of a bizarre coloration: velvety carmine purple, lined white, with pale yellow stamens forming an eye in the center of the blossom, giving it the look of a garden primrose. Very hardy and remontant; does not lose its leaves." [JR33/169]

DENISE CASSEGRAIN
Grandes Roseraies, 1922
"White." [Ÿ]

DIAMANT
Robichon, 1908
Seedling of 'Marie Pavič' (Pol).

"Bush vigorous, foliage small, flowers fringed and ruffled like a carnation, clusters of 6–12, large for the sort, very full; petals lustrous sulphur white, water-green reflections; bud conical; almond scent." [JR32/152–153]

DR. RICAUD
Corbœuf-Marsault, 1907
Seedling of 'White Pet' (Pol).

"Salmony flesh on a ground of copper." [Ÿ] "Vigorous, bushy, 12–15 in[ches] in height [ca. 3–4 dm]. Blooms profusely from May to October . . . blooms in clusters, large blossoms for the class, well formed, fragrant. Color, light pink on a light sulphur ground, center nuanced coppery, fading after opening." [JR31/38]

EILEEN LOOW
('Eileen Low')
Levavasseur, 1910
From 'Mme Norbert Levavasseur' (Pol) × 'Orléans Rose' (Pol).

"Vigorous bush, foliage glossy green, as abundant as that of 'Orléans Rose'; color, China pink, grading to cream at the base of the petals." [JR34/167]

ELISE KREIS
Listed as 'Frau Elise Kreis'.

ERNA TESCHENDORFF   PLATE 224
Teschendorff, 1911
Sport of 'Mme Norbert Levavasseur' (Pol).

"Deep red flowers in clusters. Medium growth." [Th2] "Low-growing, vigorous; foliage very abundant till late summer, mildews most of season, black-spots in late summer; bloom free, continuous." [ARA18/128] "Born three years ago as a sport of 'Mme Norbert Levavasseur', [it] has been watched all this time with much attention, and I am able to state that it has all the growth, bloom, and hardiness of its mother. The umbel of flowers is much the same as that of 'Levavasseur'; the blossoms, too, are much the same size, but they are fuller and the incurved petals, which are an intense, deep carmine red, closely resemble those of 'Gruss an Teplitz'. The great benefit of this variety is that the flowers last a very long time, and without fading. Cut stems have lasted, still fresh, for more than eight days, without showing even the least change in color." [JR34/140]

ÉTOILE LUISANTE
(trans., 'Shining Star'; syn., 'Baby Herriot')
Turbat, 1918

"Long, pointed, vermilion-red buds; flowers in long, pyramidal corymbs of forty to fifty, scarlet-red and bright shrimp-rose, with coppery red reflexes; golden yellow aiglets [*what we would call 'nubs'*]. Wood and leaves clear green. Dwarf; vigorous grower." [ARA19/101] "Orange-red bud, opening coral and carmine, base golden yellow, much on the order of 'Mme Edouard Herriot'. '[Mlle] Cécile Brunner' form. Doing well in California and well worthy of trial." [Th2]

[EUGÉNIE LAMESCH]
Lambert, 1899
From 'Aglaia' (Lambertiana) × 'William Allen Richardson' (N).

"An exquisite Rose, orange-yellow, passing to clear yellow, heavily shaded with rose." [C&Js21] "Dwarf bushy plant, very vigorous and hardy; foliage bright green, medium sized; thorns rare but strong. The medium-sized flowers appear in a bunch of 5–30 in large but closely-placed corymbs; the dormant buds open very easily. . . . Color, pure bright ochre yellow passing to light yellow shaded pink. Beautiful, very regular form, cupped. Bud coppery yellow/red; quite full. Very fine perfume, smelling like a Pippin." [JR23/171]

EVELYN THORNTON
Bees, 1919
From 'Léonie Lamesch' (Pol) × 'Mrs. W. H. Cutbush' (Pol).

"Bud medium size; flower medium size, full, double, open form, borne in clusters on medium-length stems; very lasting; fragrant. Color shell-pink, deepening to salmon and lemon with orange shading. Foliage abundant, large, leathery, glossy, dark, bronzy green; disease-resistant. Vigorous grower of bushy habit; blooms profusely all season." [ARA20/127] "A free growing little Polyantha Rose, of dwarf and bushy habit. The blooms are of a soft pink colour, with a golden glow at the base of the petals, the golden stamens making the blooms very attractive. Perpetual flowering." [NRS20/150]

EXCELLENS
('Excelsior')
Levavasseur, 1913

"Bush vigorous, hardy, blooming in clusters; the wood in nearly thornless. Color, Nilson pink washed white, petals'

edges cochineal carmine; considered altogether, making a blossom which appears delicate pink washed white when fully open." [JR37/119]

EXCELSIOR
Listed as 'Excellens'.

FLOCON DE NEIGE
(trans., 'Snowflake')
Lille, 1897
Not to be confused with the Knapper/Blanc Polyantha 'Snowflake' of 1900.

"Flowers small, full, very well formed, pure white. Bush dwarf, bearing clusters of flowers, and very floriferous." [JR22/166]

FLORIBUNDA
Dubreuil, 1885

"Flowers pale rose color, medium size, very double and fragrant, and borne in large clusters; constant bloomer." [CA90] "Growth bushy with vigorous shoots topped by large clusters of 30–50 blossoms; buds ovoid; flowers very double, expanding well; petals striped with very fresh pink and lilac. This variety has the stature and bloom of the charming variety 'Anna Maria de Montravel', from which it differs only in the shading of the blossoms." [JR9/167]

FRAU ALEXANDER WEISS
Lambert, 1909
From 'Petite Léonie' (Pol) × 'Lutea Bicolore' (*R. fœtida* hybrid).

"Yellowish pink, small, full, dwarf." [Sn]

FRAU ANNA PASQUAY
Walter, 1909
From 'Trier' (Lambertiana, Lambert, 1904, creamy) × 'Mme Norbert Levavasseur' (Pol).

"Deep pink, small, full, dwarf." [Sn]

FRAU CECILIE WALTER
Lambert, 1904
From 'Aglaia' (Multiflora, Schmidt, 1895, white) × 'Kleiner Alfred' (Pol).

"Light yellow, small, full, very fragrant, dwarf." [Sn]

FRAU ELISE KREIS   PLATE 221
Kreis, 1913
Seedling or sport of 'Ännchen Müller' (Pol).

"The form of the blossom is the same [as that of 'Ännchen Müller'], but the color is bright carmine, which it holds throughout bloom. 'Frau Elise Kreis' grows 4–5 dm high [ca. 20 in], is elegantly branched, and blooms without interruption from June till fall. The blossoms are about 5 cm across [ca. 2 in], and grow in large clusters. Due to its great floriferousness, this introduction may be used alone or in a group." [JR38/30]

FRAU OBERHOFGÄRTNER SCHULTZE
Lambert, 1909
From 'Euphrosyne' (Multiflora, Schmidt/Lambert, 1896, pink) × 'Mrs. W. J. Grant' (HT).

"Deep pink, small, full, dwarf." [Sn]

FRAU RUDOLF SCHMIDT
Schmidt, 1919
Sport of 'Jessie' (Pol).

"Dark red, small, not very full, dwarf." [Sn]

253

GEORGES PERNET   PLATE 215

Pernet-Ducher, 1887

Seedling of 'Mignonette' (Pol).

"Flowers bright rosy pink, medium size with petals beautifully rayed and reflexed; very fragrant and beautiful." [C&Js98] "Growth very dwarf, making a compact bush, good for border work or pots, blooming constantly and abundantly; blossom large for the class, graceful in form, very bright pink nuanced yellow, fading to peach pink nuanced white." [JR11/164]

GLOIRE D'ORLÉANS

Levavasseur, 1912

"Vigorous bush, with strong, erect canes. Foliage dark green; blooms in terminal panicles which are numerous; color, very dark red. It is, when all is said and done, 'Mme Norbert Levavasseur', but with a much redder blossom having the great advantage of not bluing." [JR36/153]

GLOIRE DE CHARPENNES

Lille, 1897

"Blossoms small, full, well-formed, varying from purplish pink to bluish purple-red. Growth dwarf, blooming in tight clusters, very floriferous, the plant looking like a ball of bloom." [JR22/166]

[GLOIRE DES POLYANTHA]   PLATE 216

Guillot & fils, 1887

Seedling of 'Mignonette' (Pol).

"Growth dwarf; flower small, from 2–3 cm in diameter [ca. 1 inch], full, very well formed, petals imbricated; color, bright pink on a white ground; the middle of each petal is often striped deep pink or red; bloom very abundant, in a panicle of 60–80 blossoms, forming a striking bouquet." [JR11/149] "Lovely little roses, somewhat cup-shaped, color salmon rose flamed with carmine, blooms in clusters." [C&Js02]

GRETE SCHREIBER

Altmüller, 1916

"Pink, medium size, full, dwarf." [Sn]

GUSTEL MAYER

Lambert, 1909

From 'Turner's Crimson Rambler' (Multiflora, Turner, 1894) × an unnamed seedling which was the result of 'Mme Pierre Cochet' (N) × 'Dunkelrote Hermosa' (B).

"Light red, middle yellow, small, full, dwarf." [Sn]

HERMINE MADÈLE

Soupert & Notting, 1888

From 'Mignonette' (Pol) × 'Marquise de Vivens' (T).

"Dwarf, flower small, full, very well formed; color, creamy white with yellowish reflections. Center darker." [JR12/55]

HERZBLÄTTCHENS

Geschwindt, 1889

"Pink, small, full, medium height." [Sn]

INDÉFECTIBLE

Turbat, 1919

Sport of a seedling of 'Ännchen Müller' (Pol).

"Buds medium size, long-pointed; flowers medium-size, cupped, semi-double, borne in clusters of 15 to 20 on long stems; very lasting; slight fragrance. Color bright, clear red. Foliage abundant, medium size, bronzy green; disease resistant. A very vigorous grower of bushy habit, reaching a height of 2 to 3 ft, and blooming continuously the whole season." [ARA20/131]

IVAN MISSON

Soupert & Notting, 1912

From 'Jeanny Soupert' (Pol) × 'Katharina Zeimet' (Pol).

"Pink, then white." [Ÿ]

JACQUES PROUST

Robichon, 1904

"Stocky bush, with dark green foliage; flower large for the sort; color, velvety grenadine red tinted amaranth when fully open. Very floriferous and fragrant." [JR28/155]

JEANNE D'ARC   PLATE 223

Levavasseur, 1909

"A seedling of 'Mme Norbert Levavasseur', from which it takes its abundance, having however smaller leaves and magnificent pure milk-white blossoms." [JR33/169]

JEANNE DRIVON

Schwartz, 1883

"A lovely rose; perfect, full form; very double and sweet; color, pure white, faintly tinged with crimson." [CA90] "Growth dwarf, very remontant, foliage glossy; blooms in terminal clusters, amply furnished with numerous buds; flowers very double, looking like those of the camellia-flowered balsam, rather large for the sort, white bordered and shaded pink, reverse of petals white. Unique coloration. Distinct from other Polyanthas in commerce." [JR7/121]

JEANNY SOUPERT

Soupert & Notting, 1912

From 'Mme Norbert Levavasseur' (Pol) × 'Petite Léonie' (Pol).

"Very delicate light flesh pink. Flower small, very regular in form, produced in large, tight bouquets. It blooms constantly. For bedding and borders, it is just the thing. It is a wonderful child of 'Levavasseur', from which it takes all the other's well known qualities." [JR37/19]

JESSIE

Merryweather, 1909

Sport of 'Phyllis' (Pol).

"Brilliant red shaded pink." [Ÿ] "A fine Rose for massing as it flowers profusely. The color is glowing crimson, which does not fade until the blooms are ready to fall. If you have anywhere in your garden that needs a touch of bright red all summer you should try this excellent, continuous-flowering variety." [C&Js23] "Very small, cerise red, and single. Of feeble growth, it nevertheless grows more vigorously than 'Maman Levavasseur' [Pol, Levavasseur, 1908, 'bright pink of the 'Dorothy Perkins' shade." [C&Js08]].' [JR24/140]

JOSÉPHINE MOREL

Alégatière, 1891

"Shrub to 35–40 cm [ca. 15 in], same deportment as 'Miniature', and blooming continuously; flowers small, very full, bright intense pink." [JR15/148] "Pink, small, full, dwarf." [Sn]

KLEINER ALFRED
Lambert, 1903
From 'Anne Marie de Montravel' (Pol) × 'Shirley Hibberd' (T).
   "Red-yellow with nasturtium red." [Ў] "Colors grade from orange yellow to pale yellow . . . buds prettily tinted grenadine." [JR28/128]

[KLEINER LIEBLING]
('Little Darling')
J. C. Schmidt/Kiese, 1895
From 'Polyantha Grandiflora' (Mult) × 'Fellemberg' (N).
   "An entirely new and very handsome variety; blooms in beautiful clusters, frequently 100 roses in a bunch; the flowers are medium size, somewhat cupped form; lovely carmine rose; very constant and free bloomer." [C&Js98]

LA ROSÉE
Turbat, 1920
   "Sulphur-white fading to pure white." [Ў]

LINDBERGH
Croibier, 1927
Sport of 'Orléans Rose' (Pol).
   "Very brilliant geranium-red — does not burn in sun and retains color until petals fall. Foliage mildew-resistant; growth vigorous, upright; very free-flowering." [ARA28/239]

LITTLE DOT
Bennett, 1889
   "Pale pink, very pretty but apt to be too small." [JR17/9]

[LITTLE GEM]
Conard & Jones, 1898
   "Loaded with perfectly double little roses all season; pure white and very sweet." [C&Js98]

LORELEY
Kiese, 1913
   "From a cross involving 'Tausendschön'; it gained from its mother a very fresh pink color. The flowers grow in big clusters, and have the great advantage of lasting a very long time. The flowers are quite full, which however doesn't keep the buds from opening easily. Blooming lasts far into autumn, up to frost. The foliage is glossy and similar to that of 'Mme Norbert Levavasseur'. In coloring, it can't be beaten by any other Polyantha. Its small stature — 3–4 dm [ca. 12–16 in] — recommends it for bedding." [JR38/40]

LOUISE WALTER
Walter, 1909
From 'Tausendschön' (Cl) × 'Rösel Dach' (Pol).
   "Pink, changing to rosy carmine. Resembles considerably the standard 'Tausendschön'." [Th2] "Medium size, in clusters, double, fair form, delicate fragrance, medium stems. Good foliage, sufficient. Medium dwarf growth; hardy. Blush pink to white." [ARA23/165–166] "Very like new Rose 'Echo'!" [C&Js16]

[MA PETITE ANDRÉE]
('Red Soupert')
Chauvry, 1898
Seedling of 'Étoile de Mai' (Pol).
   "Flower pretty large, a beautiful deep carmine red (of the 'Blanche Rebatel' sort, but darker); more vigorous, very floriferous." [JR22/165] "Vigorous growth and dwarf bushy habit, mostly covered with bright crimson buds, fully double flowers, the whole season. It is a very useful rose and quite hardy." [C&Js06] "Dedicated to the grand-daughter of the breeder." [JR22/165]

MADELEINE OROSDY
Gravereaux, 1912
   "Fresh pink." [Ў]

MAGENTA
Barbier, 1916
   "Flowers semi-double, cup-shaped, of medium size, in long spikes of twenty to forty; violet-red, the middle of petal magenta-violet — a new shade in the dwarf Polyanthas — sometimes turns reddish violet. Dwarf grower; very floriferous." [ARA19/100]

MAMAN TURBAT
Turbat, 1911
From 'Mme Norbert Levavasseur' (Pol) × 'Katharina Zeimet' (Pol).
   "Very vigorous, very hardy; growth erect; wood very smooth and thornless; persistent glossy green foliage. Strong panicles of 30–40 blossoms, very long-lasting, delicate China pink nuanced light peachblossom pink and dawn gold as well as delicate flesh white." [JR36/10]

MARÉCHAL FOCH
Levavasseur, 1918
Sport of 'Orléans Rose' (Pol).
   "Cerise red." [Ў] "Bud medium size; flower medium size, open form, semi-double, borne in clusters on medium length stems; very lasting; strong fragrance. Color deep red." [ARA20/131] Also attributed to a cross between "Orléans Rose" and "Jessie" (Pol). Marshal Ferdinand Foch, 1851–1929; French general in World War I.

MARIE BRISSONET
Turbat, 1913
   "Plant dwarf, with delicate green foliage which disappears completely under the abundant bloom. Large pyramidal clusters, with 75–100 medium-sized blossoms, delicate flesh pink in color, with petal tips light carmine. This variety, of such abundance, will be very useful for bedding and borders." [JR37/137]

MARTHA KELLER
Walter, 1912
   "Yellowish white, medium size, very full, medium height." [Sn]

MARY BRUNI
Gratama, 1914
   "Pink, small, full, dwarf." [Sn]

MAUVE
Turbat, 1915
   "Mauve pink." [Ў]

MELLE FISCHER
Pfitzer, 1914
"Pink, small, full, dwarf." [Sn]

MERVEILLE DES POLYANTHAS
Mermet, 1909
"Very vigorous, flowers pure white passing to lilac pink upon opening; very fragrant and floriferous; foliage light green." [JR32/153]

MERVEILLE DES ROUGES
Dubreuil, 1911
"Very bright red." [Ў] "Dwarf, much branched, continuous bloom. Branches strong and robust, bearing clusters of 7–15 little blossoms of a color as bright as that of 'Général Jacqueminot' [HP]. Thick foliage, 5–7 beautiful somber green leaflets; buds turbinate, with crested sepals. Blooms in elegant clusters, small, cupped, intense velvety crimson with a small white halo at the center which only adds to the sparkle. The plant is extra floriferous, does not lose its leaves, and surpasses in abundance and color all Polyanthas previously developed." [JR35/167]

MIGNON
Mille-Toussaint, 1904
From 'Mme Laurette Messimy' (Ch) × 'Marie Pavič' (Pol).
"Flesh yellow fading to white." [Ў]

MIMI PINSON
Barbier, 1919
"Flower clear crimson, passing to purplish rose and then to 'Paul Neyron' pink." [ARA21/161] "Rose-red, medium size, full, dwarf." [Sn]

MINIATURE
Alégatière, 1884
"Pink, then yellowish white." [Ў] "Bushy, vigorous, extra remontant; to a foot in height [ca. 3 dm], stout, with thick foliage. . . . The buds are in a cluster and are of a deep pink tint; they always open well. The flowers are very fragrant, small, hardly larger than a double violet, very full, well formed, blush white fading to white." [JR8/178] "This is the smallest of all roses, but perfect full regular flowers, borne in wreaths and clusters, cover the plant with a mass of fairy roses; rosy blush, delightfully perfumed and very pretty. 10 cts." [C&Js98]

MLLE ALICE ROUSSEAU
Vilin, 1903
"Bush vigorous, canes VanDyck red, foliage emerald green, bud golden pink, which opens into the form of a small cactus Dahlia, taking on the tints of an Italian fresco of pretty vivid color; at full expansion, the blossom becomes a delicate flesh pink. Very pretty variety." [JR28/27]

MLLE BLANCHE REBATEL   PLATE 217
('Blanche Rebatel')
Bernaix, 1888
"Stocky, vigorous, small growth, extraordinarily floriferous. Inflorescence nearly a thyrse before expansion, then a large corymb of 40–50 buds. Often all blossoms open at once, small, charming. Color uniformly bright carmine red nuanced pink on the reverse, with a white nub. A new coloration." [JR12/164] "Purplish crimson, shaded rose; a somewhat dull colour, but prettily shaped." [P1]

MLLE FERNANDE DUPUY
Vigneron, 1899
"Dwarf, compact, and vigorous, bearing clusters of flowers; blossom small and full, zinnia-formed, beautifully colored currant pink, sometimes a little darker. Good for pot and border work." [JR23/149] "Penetrating scent." [JR25/11]

MLLE JOSÉPHINE BURLAND
Bernaix, 1886
"Much branched, moderate vigor, continuously covered with flowers throughout the whole season. Flower large for the class, very double, petals longly acuminate, upright in the center, inclining in the middle, and reflexing in the outer rows. Pure white upon opening, taking on nuances of carmine pink. Distinguished from others in this class by having solitary blossoms." [JR10/172]

MLLE MARCELLE GAUGIN
Corbœuf, 1910
"Light salmon pink, small, full, dwarf." [Sn]

MLLE MARTHE CAHUZAC
Ketten Bros., 1901
From 'Mignonette' (Pol) × 'Safrano' (T).
"Flower yellowish white, center silky yellow passing to whitish pink, medium sized, full, flat, bud long and pointed, opening well. Bush dwarf, vigorous, hardy, blooming in clusters." [JR25/146]

MLLE SUZANNE BIDARD
Vigneron, 1913
From 'Georges Pernet' (Pol) × 'Perle d'Or' (Pol).
"Bush vigorous, compact; flowers medium-sized, full, in clusters; very pretty coloration, light coppery salmon, petal bases lighter yet, stamens golden yellow; buds very long, salmon, superb. Very beautiful variety which will be much sought out for pot culture." [JR38/71]

MME ALÉGATIÈRE
Alégatière, 1888
From 'Polyantha Alba Plena' (Mult) × 'Jules Margottin' (HP).
"Always in bloom, branches upright, numerous thorns of a fawn-green; foliage small, of 3–5 leaflets; blossom of moderate size, beautiful bright pink, full, and staying in good form for a long time." [JR12/165]

MME ARTHUR ROBICHON
Robichon, 1912
From 'Mme Norbert Levavasseur' (Pol) × 'Mrs. W. H. Cutbush' (Pol).
"Color, beautiful and very fresh purplish pink, previously unknown among Polyanthas; blooms in very compact panicles; wood smooth, few thorns, foliage reddish green; plant dwarf." [JR36/153]

MME E. A. NOLTE
Bernaix, 1892
"Nankeen yellow, passing to white." [H] "Buds chamois-yellow, changing to rosy white as they expand; very free. A lovely variety." [P1] "Dwarf, very floriferous. Corymbs profuse, buds very unique in form and color, stocky, flattened, wider than high when opening; chamois yellow paling with age to blush white. Flowers of perfect form, making, with their differing nuances, a delightful contrast between flower and bud." [JR16/165]

MME JULES GOUCHAULT
Turbat, 1912

From 'Maman Turbat' (Pol) × 'George Elger' (Pol).

"In large and in small sprays, double, good form, medium size, medium stems. Good foliage, sufficient. Growth strong; hardy. Vermilion-pink shaded orange, passing to brilliant pink." [ARA23/169] "Light green wood and foliage; blooms in large erect panicles of 25–50 blossoms, well held, long lasting. Bud bright vermilion red nuanced orange vermilion, fading to bright pink, then to light pink when open." [JR37/137]

[MME NORBERT LEVAVASSEUR]   PLATES 220, 223
('Dwarf Crimson Rambler')
Levavasseur, 1903

"This Rose is in many ways one of the most remarkable that has been introduced in many years. It is a cross between 'Crimson Rambler' and 'Glory of Polyanthas' [*sic*], retaining the color of the former with the exceeding free flowering and dwarf growing habit of the latter. The plants are very vigorous and grow to 18 or 24 in. The foliage is dark, glossy green and remarkably free from insects and fungus. The flowers are borne in clusters of 20, 30 or more to the cluster." [C&Js06] "Growth vigorous, dwarf, very handsome foliage, glossy green; flower large for the sort, very double, magnificent very bright carmine red, extremely floriferous and remontant. Resembles in its floribundity 'Crimson Rambler', whence it sprang [*that is, 'Crimson Rambler' × 'Gloire des Polyantha'*]." [JR27/131]

MME TAFT   PLATE 223
Levavasseur, 1909

From 'Turner's Crimson Rambler' (Multiflora Rambler, Turner, 1894, crimson) × 'Mme Norbert Levavasseur' (Pol).

"Red." [Y̌] "Color is rosy crimson. Habit is similar to 'Baby Red Rambler'. Splendid for massing or for borders." [C&Js11] "Lighter than ['Mme Norbert Levavasseur']. The foliage is identical to that of 'Levavasseur', as is the blossom. Blooms continuously in large panicles all summer." [JR33/169]

[MOSELLA]
Lambert & Reiter, 1895

From 'Mignonette' × [a seedling of 'Mme Falcot' (T) × 'Shirley Hibberd' (T)].

"Large flowers of a pretty cream white. This variety is, according to my experience, pretty hardy." [JR23/42] "Makes a neat handsome bush, loaded with flowers all the time . . . medium size, finely formed flowers borne in large clusters and quite fragrant; color, pretty buff or peachy-yellow; fine for bedding and house culture." [C&Js98]

MRS. WILLIAM G. KONING
('—Konig')
Kluis & Koning, 1917
Sport of 'Louise Walter' (Pol).

"White, medium size, full, moderate scent, dwarf." [Sn]

MULTIFLORA NANA PERPÉTUELLE
('Multiflore Nain Remontant')
Lille, 1893

"This variety is so floriferous that I have seen bloom on seedlings having no more foliage than their cotyledons. . . . In their fourth year, they make little spreading bushes varying from 3–4 dm [ca. 12–16 in]. The foliage is of two sorts: small,

oval-rounded or shortly lanceolate on the regular branches, somewhat more lengthily lanceolate on the young canes. The stipules, which are pretty large, are elegantly lacinated. In the inflorescence, which is in the form of a thyrse or irregular cyme, the multiplex floral axes give rise to caducous bracts. The peduncle, which is obscurely segmented, bristles with glandular hairs, and grades into a fusiform calyx. The sepals do not extend beyond the conical bud, and the outer lobes have one or two pairs of lanceolate auricles. The blossom is usually white, small, full or semi-double, sometimes nearly single. The styles adhere into a column, and the stigmata are capitate. The hips are red and turbinate. The calyx-lobes [sepals] are deciduous. In this sort, the dwarfness is only relative; the bushes which provide the seed [of this strain] have grown, in their fourth year, over 8 dm tall [ca. 30 in]." [JR24/4] "Floriferous . . . makes a very pretty border and a superb potted plant." [JR18/105]

PERLE
Kiese, 1913

"Considering stature, this introduction bears much resemblance to 'Katharina Zeimet'. The light pink color is very delicate, but the blossoms aren't fragile. Each inflorescence is composed of forty blossoms, and indeed forms a perfect bouquet." [JR38/40]

PERLE DES ROUGES
Dubreuil, 1896

"Deep velvety crimson, produced in clusters, and blooming abundantly and late in the season." [P1] "Dwarf, very floriferous, blooms in clusters, blooming until frost, as sparkling as those of 'Cramoisi Supérieur' [Ch], shallowly cupped, numerous petals, thick, regularly imbricated, stiff, looking like a pompon when opening, superb velvety crimson red with bright cerise reflections." [JR21/3] "The best of the red Pompons." [J]

PERLE ORLÉANAISE
Duveau, 1912

From 'Mme Norbert Levavasseur' (Pol) × 'Frau Cecilie Walter' (Pol).

"Bush vigorous, canes strong, erect, red-tinted; foliage brilliant dark green, glossy, tinted purple-red, very hardy, healthy; thorns rare. Flowers in terminal panicles, quite erect, profuse, medium-sized, rosette-form, quite double, of a pretty coloration: bright salmon pink nuanced saffron, particularly at the base of the petals, making a most charming effect with the bronzy-green foliage; bloom continuous." [JR37/9]

PETITE FRANÇOISE
Gravereaux, 1915
"Delicate pink." [Y̌]

PETITE LÉONIE   PLATE 219
Soupert & Notting, 1892

From 'Mignonette' (Pol) × 'Duke of Connaught' (HT).
The "Floribunda" ancestry is perhaps worth noting.

"Dwarf, bushy, flower small, full, imbricated, outer petals porcelain white tinted light pink, the center shining carmine lake." [JR16/139]

PETITE MARCELLE
Dubreuil, 1910

"Bush of small dimensions, much branched, always in bloom, clothed in beautiful dark green leaves. Inflorescence a cluster of 5 to 10 small flowers, the buds when opening looking much like those of 'Rose du Roi' [DP] in miniature, making a very pretty rosette. Flowers very double, snow white, opening well, numerous muddled petals, imbricated like those of a big daisy." [JR34/168]

[PHYLLIS]
Merryweather, 1908

"Beautiful cerise pink. Flowers are borne in great clusters on a little bush from a foot to eighteen in high [ca. 3–4.5 dm] and very symmetrical in shape. As a bedding variety it is splendid." [C&Js11]

[PINK SOUPERT]
Dingee & Conard, 1896
From 'Clotilde Soupert' (Pol) × 'Lucullus' (Ch).

"Perfectly full and double, very sweet, blooms all the time; fine rose pink, sometimes striped with white." [C&Jf97] "A seedling from 'Clotilde Soupert', with rosette-shaped flowers varying from pale pink to red." [CA97] "Very low-growing, weak; foliage barely sufficient, black-spots very slightly in midsummer, mildews in late summer; bloom hardly more than sparse, continuous." [ARA18/129]

PRIMULA
Soupert & Notting, 1900
From 'Mignonette' (Pol) × an unnamed seedling.

"Carmine pink with a white eye." [Ÿ] "Vigorous and stocky; graceful bud; flower small, fullish; color, bright China pink, center snow white. Distinctive coloration, like that of *Primula chinensis*." [JR24/148]

PRINCESS ENA
H. B. May, 1906
Sport of 'Mme Nobert Levavasseur' (Pol).

"Pink." [Ÿ] "Pretty little flowers which are very effective, quite another 'Mrs. W. H. Cutbush' of the 'Gloire des Polyantha' type, only slightly paler." [JR31/74]

PRINCESSE JOSÉPHINE DE FLANDRES
Soupert & Notting, 1888
From 'Mignonette' (Pol) × 'Marquise de Vivens' (T).

"Dwarf, flower small, full; color, blush pink on a ground of salmon; very fragrant." [JR12/55]

PRINCESSE MARIE ADÉLAÏDE DE LUXEMBOURG
Soupert & Notting, 1895
Seedling of 'Mignonette' (Pol).

"Bushy, blooming in corymbs; flower small, very full, magnificently imbricated; color, ivory white nuanced flesh pink, center bright pink. Very attractive fragrance." [JR19/148] "Neat compact grower . . . flowers medium size with over-lapping petals, very double; color rosy flesh with carmine centre; very sweet." [C&Js98]

RADIUM
Grandes Roseraies/Houry, 1913

"Dwarf, very vigorous and hardy bush, with erect canes, well-held, foliage persistent. Blooms in profuse panicles of 15–20 buds opening successively; color, very delicate pink, pearly gold at the center, a very pretty look for beds and the open border." [JR38/25]

RENONCULE
Barbier, 1913

"Dwarf; foliage cheerful green, glossy. Continuous bloom, abundant, clusters of 15–50 blossoms. Flowers of medium size, double, in the form of a Ranunculus, very prettily colored bright salmon pink, very fresh, quite different from other varieties." [JR37/167]

[RÖSEL DACH]
Walter, 1906

"Cherry-red, edge lighter, very full." [Jg]

ROTTKÄPPCHEN
Geschwindt, 1887

"Bright red." [JR17/9] "Red, large, full, dwarf." [Sn]

[SCHNEEKOPF]
Lambert, 1903
From 'Mignonette' (Pol) × 'Souvenir de Mme Sablayrolles' (T).

"Shell pink." [CA07] "Yellow, turning white." [CA10] "Has the same vigorous habit of growth as Clotilde Soupert — a bush thick with branches and usually quite full of bloom; the blossoms open perfectly, showing beautiful cup-shaped petals, waxy white and sometimes tinged flesh pink." [C&Js08]

SCHNEEWITCHEN
Lambert, 1901
From 'Aglaia' (Multiflora, Lambert, 1896, creamy; from *R. multiflora* × 'Rêve d'Or' [N]) × an unnamed seedling which was the result of 'Pâquerette' (Pol) × 'Souvenir de Mme Levet' (T).

"Yellowish white, small, moderately full, moderate scent, dwarf." [Sn] "Bushes candelabra shaped and each branch bearing from 15 to 50 little flowers, creamy-white passing to snow-white." [C&Js07]

SCHÖNE VON HOLSTEIN
(trans., 'Beauty of Holstein')
Tantau, 1919
Seedling of 'Orléans Rose' (Pol).

"Pink, medium size, full, dwarf." [Sn] "Flower full, pure 'Hermosa'-pink, better than 'Mrs. W. H. Cutbush'. A free bloomer." [ARA21/164]

SIEGESPERLE
Kiese, 1915
Seedling of 'Tausendschön' (Cl).

"Yellowish white, small, not very full, dwarf." [Sn]

SISI KETTEN
Ketten Bros., 1900
From 'Mignonette' (Pol) × 'Safrano' (T).

"Blossom peach pink veined carmine on a ground of yellowish white, large for the sort, full, starry [*astrée*], opening well. Growth dwarf, vigorous, erect, very floriferous. . . . Dedicated to a daughter of the breeders. Excellent for borders and pots." [JR24/147]

[SNOWBALL]
('Snow Ball')
Walsh, 1901

"A most charming little rose, everyone wants it, blooms in large clusters, completely covering the plant — pure snow white and delightfully perfumed." [C&Js02] Also attributed to Henderson, 1899.

STADTRAT MEYN
Tantau, 1919
Seedling of 'Orléans Rose' (Pol).

"Light orange red, medium size, full, dwarf." [Sn] "Large, full flowers in very large clusters; luminous brick-red. Vigorous." [ARA21/164]

SUSANNA
Weigand, 1914
Seedling of 'Tausendschön' (Cl).

"The plant maintains a bearing which is both very dwarf and compact, without shooting out the long stems produced by the likes of 'Mme Norbert Levavasseur'. The coloration is that of 'Tausendschön' [*i.e., pink fading to blush or white, the differing colors evident in each cluster*]. The blossoms are small, quite full, with petals slightly folded back like those of 'Ännchen Müller'; they are produced in large clusters which cover the whole plant and last a very long time. The flower clusters strike one as those expected of a climber rather than of a dwarf Polyantha, and are indeed much like those of 'Tausendschön'. The good keeping qualities of the cut flowers have impressed those who have seen it for themselves." [JR38/75]

Chapter Ten
HYBRID TEAS

"The Hybrid Tea Rose (*Rosa Indica odorata hybrida*) is a group produced from crossing Teas with Hybrid Perpetuals." [pH] The cultivar often named as the "first Hybrid Tea," 'La France', is, of course, not this at all, being rather a Tea seedling exhibiting some ancestral Bourbon characteristics—while some Bourbons—particularly 'Souvenir de la Malmaison'—could be designated Hybrid Teas quite as easily as the later 'La France'. Many early Tea/Hybrid Perpetual crosses, such as 'Victor Verdier', were put into the *Hybrid Perpetual* class: "These, like the Hybrid China roses, are usually classed with the Hybrid Perpetuals; indeed, there is practically very little difference between them . . . [they] possess the delicacy of color and fragrance of the Teas, and the vigor of those Hybrid Perpetuals owing their parentage to the Damask Rose." [TW] "They have all the qualities of the tea-rose but their color is not so rich." [G&B]

"In hardiness it excels the Teas as a class, and in blooming it is more constant than the Hybrid Perpetuals, but, *per contra*, it is seldom as hardy as the best of the Hybrid Perpetuals and flowers less continuously than the Teas. . . . In the North it is much smaller than the Hybrid Perpetual, and in the Southwest and South it is rivaled or excelled by the Tea in vigor. The foliage is more resistant to mildew than most Hybrid Perpetuals, yet generally inferior to the Tea in this respect. Loss of foliage varies also between the easily-lost leaves of the Hybrid Perpetual to the long-lived Tea foliage. . . . Altogether, the Hybrid Teas combine everything and anything!" [Th2]

Though Lacharme, working in Lyon, had already made important contributions to the HT's by the time Henry Bennett's introductions were released, Bennett was the first to systematically develop this class. "For quite a long time, I had been a rose propagator, and, over forty years, had gotten to know many introductions. In 1865, I began to make roses the object of my study, and indeed found that during all this time no one had made great progress; I thought at that point that one should be able to get good results from intelligent cross breeding. I had had a great deal of experience in breeding domestic animals, and the wonderful results I had obtained encouraged me to continue my experimentation on flowers. In 1870, I visited the nurseries of the various rosarians at Lyon, but nowhere saw any progress being made in breeding roses by scientific methods. Jean Sisley lamented continually that he had brought artificial pollination to the attention of his comrades in vain. Looking closer, I saw that raising seedlings in France was comparable to raising livestock on the Mexican prairies—everything was left to itself; a person would simply choose the best of what nature had to offer. This made me certain that before me lay an open, unexplored field. I made my first attempts, and found that there were many difficulties to surmount before I would be able to gather the first seeds from the crosses; it was necessary to know which of the different types differed from one another in their individual characteristics. Tea roses were often crossed with the remontants, and vice-versa; I have found that Moss Roses, and Chinas, etc., are equally easy to cross. For my main tries, I ordinarily use 'Alba Rosea' ['Mme Bravy'] and 'President' ['Adam'] as the seed-bearer, crossing them with 'Louis Van Houtte', 'Victor Verdier', and so forth.

"My purpose was to raise remontant roses of pure white and of yellow, as well as purplish-red Tea roses of a color both intense and dark. In token of my progress, I offer the first six Hybrid Teas to be released to commerce." [JR10/23] The six are: 'Beauty of Stapleford', 'Duchess of Connaught', 'Duchess of Westminster', 'Duke of Connaught', 'Jean Sisley', and 'Michael Saunders'.

"In the year 1879, when Bennett came out in Stapleford for the first time with the so-called Hybrid Tea Roses, most of his fellow countrymen shook their heads in disbelief about his undertaking, particularly since he was no gardener, denying him any success at it because his roses produced no firm stems, and what was more were good only for greenhouse culture! I am still amused by the recollection of William Paul showing me Bennett's first six Hybrid Teas in his greenhouse at Waltham, and saying 'These are good for nothing but the greenhouse.'—What successes he has had with his seedlings since then!" [RZ86/5–6]

We primarily cover in this chapter the non-Pernetiana Hybrid Teas of the early period, exception being made for various singles, which hold a special fascination for many lovers of "old" roses, and for a few other interesting varieties. The later Hybrid Teas as well as the Pernetianas and their descendants are no less interesting, but exist in such overwhelming battalions that they are best left alone for now lest they swamp the book.

Perhaps because "Hybrid Tea" is not so exotic a name as "Bourbon" or "Hybrid Perpetual," the original Hybrid Teas are very much neglected today, a most unfortunate situation.

"So what shall remain of that whole riot of fine, gloriously colored and gracefully shaped Hybrid Teas? They will disappear like the old Hybrid Perpetuals." [ARA37/197]

ANTOINE RIVOIRE
Pernet-Ducher, 1895
From 'Dr. Grill' (T) × 'Lady Mary Fitzwilliam' (HT).

"In the soft shell pink or cream-tinted pinks, the beautiful old 'Antoine Rivoire', a clean-foliaged plant, is the sturdiest and best." [ARA40/42] "A charming rose of rose-pink colouring, shaded with yellow. The flowers are rather flat, and borne moderately freely. Its growth is fairly vigorous and erect, displaying the blossoms perfectly." [OM] "Cream, touched with salmon rose." [E] "Cream with orange centre. Camellia-like flower; very free." [H] "Fresh pink and white." [J] "Rosy flesh shaded and bordered carmine, base of petals yellow . . . large, full, and imbricated. A splendid Rose for all purposes." [P1] "Pale creamy buff." [Hk] "It grows with vigor, giving very pretty flowers which are large, well-formed, flesh-pink and even salmon-pink, the edges of the petals shaded carmine." [JR21/98] "Frequently five in[ches] in diameter [ca. 1.25 dm]. Full and double." [Dr] "Flesh to cream-yellow-peach center, sometimes with lilac shading; perfume mild . . . growth high and strong but lacking in bushiness." [ARA17/22–23] "Lacks perfume." [ARA25/99] "Holds center in heat; slight fragrance. Best in spring, not only in bloom, but in strength of stem. Owing to loss of foliage, cannot be recommended for [the warmest zones], but being almost immune from mildew is splendid in damp climates. Form seldom beautiful enough for exhibition." [Th2] "Early, and good in autumn. — (Prune medium)." [JP] "Vigorous free bloomer." [HRG] "The flowers, cupped, are the prettiest color one could desire: flesh pink with a yellow center. . . . It has a quantity of good qualities not possessed by other varieties — the very delicate tone of the blossoms, and their pretty form, their upright bearing, its dark foliage, and the longevity of the flowers. This last is not a worthless quality because, even while lasting so long as eight days, the flower doesn't change at all." [JR23/42] "Bud not of the best; opens flat but attractive and pleasing. . . . Foliage, leathery, and of great substance; seldom affected by mildew, but sometimes lost by [black-] spot. . . . Its worst fault is that in most seasons there is very little August bloom." [Th] "While not rampant, this Rose is vigorous in growth and of a rather branching habit; it is capable of making a good shaped plant, but does not always do so when grown as a dwarf. . . . The foliage is fine, large, and leathery, of a dark green color with a bronzy tint, while the upper surface of the leaves is rather shiny. It is not subject to mildew, but rather liable to black spot. It flowers freely both early (mid-June) and late, the early blooms being the largest. The flowers are carried on erect stems and are of good shape and fairly full, pale cream in colour with a deeper centre, sometimes almost approaching very light orange at the base of the petals, which are of good substance, stout, and clean-cut, large for the size of the flower, deep and shell-shaped. . . . Though best in fair weather, they will stand a fair amount of wet. They are fragrant, but not very sweet-scented." [NRS/10] "Branches slightly divergent; handsome foliage of a light green." [JR19/148] "Dark green foliage . . . 3 × 3 [ft; ca. 9 × 9 dm]." [B] "Good blooms [in Madeira]." [DuC] "Blooms abundantly, nearly continuously in Tunisia . . . very vigorous, hardy . . . dedicated to a well-known horticulturalist of Lyon." [JR34/170] Mons Antoine Rivoire was a president of the Lyon Horticulturalists' Association.

AUGUSTINE GUINOISSEAU

Listed as 'Mlle Augustine Guinoisseau'.

AUGUSTINE HALEM

Guillot & fils, 1891

"Carmine rose shaded with purple; medium size and good form; free flowering and sweet." [P1] "Bright pink deepening to deep rose colour." [Dr] "Copper overlaid with pink, with deeper reverse . . . 3 × 3 [ft; ca. 9 × 9 dm]." [B] "Vigorous, robust, very floriferous, flower large, globular, full, very well formed, well-held; color, carmine-purplish-pink; fragrant; a very pretty variety." [JR15/148] "Of good habit and sweet." [CA95]

BALDUIN

('Helen Gould')
Lambert, 1898
From 'Charles Darwin' (HP) × 'Marie Van Houtte' (T).

"Pure carmine; flower large, very full, globular, Camellia form; very floriferous; vigorous." [Cx] "Bright watermelon-red. Extensively used throughout the South." [Th2] "This novelty of 1898 is a ravishing variety for planting in any bed one wishes to have constantly in bloom. It is one of the best introductions of P. Lambert of Trèves who has carefully tested this rose over several years before releasing it to commerce. . . . This new rose should be placed, considering its quality, in the first rank with such varieties as 'La France' or 'K. A. Viktoria'. The flower is large, very full, and of a crimson pink; the buds are long and usually in threes or fives at the ends of the vigorous branches; this variety is very remontant, and the flower buds keep developing without interruption until late in the season; the foliage of a nice shiny green is very ornamental . . . perfectly hardy. . . . [In Trèves there was] a charming bed around the statue of the celebrated archbishop Balduin, to whom this rose was dedicated." [JR23/34–35]

CAPTAIN CHRISTY   PLATE 227

Lacharme, 1873
From 'Victor Verdier' (HP) × 'Safrano' (T).

"Light salmon, petals edged in white, a new and fine distinct habited kind." [HstXXVIII:350] "Fine, fragrant soft pink." [ARA29/96] "Delicate flesh, deeper in center . . . flowers well in Autumn." [H] "Tea-scented, a most charming and delicate white, very large and fine." [HRH] "Peach-blow, deepening to rose-colour." [Dr] "Medium-size, sometimes large, full; the foliage when young somewhat resembles Mahonia leaves. Ill-shaped flowers are not uncommon, but it is a most lovely sort when in perfection." [EL] "Open." [F-M2] "[Occasional ideal flowers with minimum care]." [L] "Very large and very full, short-jointed, erect, delicate pink, with deeper centre; cup-shaped, becomes flatter." [Hn] "Has never given me seeds." [JR26/101] "Robust . . . handsome foliage, beautifully colored in Spring, coming well up under the flowers." [F-M2] "Ample foliage of a handsome lustrous green on top, paler beneath. . . . As for the flower, it is the simple expression of grace and freshness — it is large, full, cupped, well-formed, well held, and, in color, tender flesh-white with tints of pink. Unfortunately, it has little scent, and has difficulty opening in unfavorable weather. The bud is very pretty." [JR10/77] "Plant is rather dwarf but sturdy. It is a dependable autumn bloomer." [ARA34/77] "[Very satisfactory in Brazil]." [PS] "In the breeding of 1869, [Lacharme] created a new rose of the first order which he dedicated to Capt. Christy of London, one of the great amateur rosarians of England. . . . The buds are much sought-after by florists." [JR2/25] "Talking of judging at the Lyons Exhibition, he [George Paul] tells me he well remembers suggesting Captain Christy's name being attached to Lacharme's new Rose of the year." [NRS20/27] "The flowers produced in the South of France are certainly more delicate and beautiful than those we are accustomed to in England. . . . Foliage when young somewhat resembles Mahonia leaves." [B&V] "I can find no fault as to colour, shape, foliage, or anything else, save that I cannot have enough of his glorious blossoms set in the midst of their strong, handsome leaves, as if each one intended to be placed in a glass alone." [K1]

CAROLINE TESTOUT

Listed as 'Mme Caroline Testout'.

CECIL

B. R. Cant, 1926
"Rich, deep golden yellow . . . in clusters, but each flower has a ten-inch stem [ca. 2.25 dm]." [ARA34/81] "The growth and vitality of the plant is all that can be asked of any rose. . . . Free-flowering

. . . [but] at Breeze Hill it is one of the stingiest bloomers we know." [ARA32/178] "A very attractive yellow single rose, freely borne on a rather reluctant plant until the end of June and very sparingly afterward. . . . It is most attractive." [ARA31/186] "Succession of large, single buttercups." [ARA28/150] "Pretty golden stamens." [ARA28/150]

CHÂTEAU DE CLOS-VOUGEOT

Pernet-Ducher, 1908

"Velvety maroon red nuanced and shaded dark maroon." [Riv] "Keeps its brilliant coloration despite the temperature." [JR32/85] "The darkest red, black as night, to be stroked with the eyes, velvet and voluptuous . . . spindly, sprawling growth." [Hk] "Growth above average; wonderful color; good fragrance; fair bloomer." [ARA18/110] "Good vigor, branching; foliage somber green; thorns occasional and slightly protrusive; flower large, globular, full, richly colored crimson scarlet nuanced fiery red passing to blackish velvety purple." [JR32/25] "Delicious perfume." [JR32/124]

COLUMBIA

E. G. Hill Co., 1916

From 'Ophelia' (HT) × 'Mrs. George Shawyer' (HT, Lowe & Shawyer, 1911, rose-pink; parentage: 'Mme Hoste' [T] × 'Joseph Lowe' [HT, Lowe, 1907, salmon-pink; sport of 'Mrs. W. J. Grant' (HT)]).

"Hydrangea pink." [Cw] "Light pink, with full petalage; opens somewhat flat in heat; deliciously fragrant. Good but not strong grower. . . . Of exceptional value in cool conditions; must be given careful protection. Good in early and late seasons in southern California. Scorches in heat." [Th2] "Perfume is its best point, although its keeping quality and form make it valuable as a cut-flower. . . . The color does not spot in partial shade. It blooms freely." [ARA31/99] "Beautiful foliage and fine, healthy growth." [ARA18/96]

DAINTY BESS

Archer, 1925

From 'Ophelia' (HT) × 'K. of K'. (HT).

"Very lovely and attractive, single, sweet-scented blooms in clusters on strong, upright stems . . . a delightful shade of salmon-pink, the daintiness of which is greatly increased by prominent red stamens and somewhat frilled petals. . . . Its growth is robust and its foliage free of mildew. Considered the finest single rose introduced for some years." [ARA26/178] "Flower 3.5 to 4 in across [ca. 7.5–8.5 cm], single, broad petaled, fimbriated petals, rose color, borne several together." [ARA26/181] "Very little autumn bloom . . . the notched petals form a flower more nearly square than round . . . exceedingly lovely." [ARA30/174] "Has won friends everywhere. All reports are favorable . . . it is more or less stingy, giving very few flowers throughout the summer and in autumn." [ARA31/187] "There seems to be no halting the flow of enthusiastic adjectives concerning this rose. . . . We still stick to our opinion, expressed last year, that, in spite of her beauty, Bess is a stingy and ungrateful girl." [ARA32/180] "The most delicately beautiful single rose, in both form and color . . . two tones of either light rose or rose-pink . . . from three to four in[ches] in diameter [ca. 7.5 cm–1 dm] . . . in clusters." [ARA34/81] "Very free bloom . . . 3–4 [ft; ca. 1–1.25 m]." [Lg] "Exquisitely beautiful." [ARA40/43]

DAME EDITH HELEN

A. Dickson, 1926

From 'Mrs. John Laing' (HP) × ? a Pernetiana.

"A large, finely shaped, clear pink bloom, with plenty of substance, freely produced on long, stiff stems; sweetly scented. Vigorous; foliage free of mildew; good for garden purposes." [ARA26/181] "Beautiful, but not vigorous . . . shy after the first blooming . . . plants grow little, and seem to get smaller every year . . . leaves fall off early . . . very beautiful, fragrant blooms. . . . Throughout the South, it seems to do well." [ARA30/175] "Did wonderfully the first year but has done nothing since." [ARA31/97] "Its long-pointed buds develop into perfect, double pink flowers which do not fade and whose fragrance is also pleasing." [ARA] "Very lazy bloomer." [Kr]

DEAN HOLE

PLATE 266

A. Dickson, 1904

Sport of 'Mme Caroline Testout' (HT).

"Silvery carmine tinted salmon; flower very large, full, high-centered; very floriferous, very vigorous." [Cx] "Pretty form; petals thick and strong." [JR31/177] "Occasionally comes split . . . impatient of too much wet . . . very free-flowering." [F-M] "Blooms of excellent form, long and pointed, though the colour is rather unattractive — silvery rose and salmon." [OM] "Subject, but not badly, to mildew. . . . Good grower." [F-M] "Fair growth; color not of best; mildews." [ARA18/115] "Low, weak grower; foliage sufficient; bloom sparse, well scattered through season." [ARA18/124] "Often not a clear color. In autumn, usually muddy." [Th] "The variety 'Dean Hole' is one of the best of today's roses, and indeed one of the best roses of any time. The growth is very vigorous, branching, and very floriferous. The bud is long and pointed, and of pretty shape; the flower is very large, very full, with a high center. The color is superb and very fresh, and is silvery carmine with salmon-tinted reflections." [JR37/30] "Pale silvery rose, with deep shading, sometimes muddy; nice shape; substance varies; above average size and cuts well; fragrant. Very nice growth and stem. Foliage mildews badly." [Th2] "Plenty of buds, some of which failed to open on account of the wet. It requires shading to get the best out of this Rose." [NRS14/159] "It was a singular coincidence that the last letter the Dean wrote on Roses had as its subject matter this Rose that had been named after him. He saw a flower of it, but never saw the plant growing." [F-M]

DUCHESS OF ALBANY

('Red La France')

W. Paul, 1888

Sport of 'La France' (HT).

Not to be confused with Lévêque's Tea of 1903, 'Duchesse d'Albe', which was red with yellow tints.

"Fine deep pink, in the way of 'La France', but darker in colour; quite first-rate; growth vigorous." [P1] "Clear red, broad petals of silky texture." [Dr] "Vigorous; flower very large, full, globular, a nice rose color, very fragrant . . . maintains all the characteristics of 'La France', from which it differs only by its rosy color." [JR30/17] "Dark pink." [LS] "Low moderate growth, hardy; foliage sufficient to plentiful, healthy; bloom moderate, continuous." [ARA18/125] "Bright pinkish-red . . . shapely . . . well proportioned bush with good foliage . . . 3 × 2 [ft; ca. 9 × 6 dm]." [B]

ELLEN WILMOTT
Archer, 1936
From 'Dainty Bess' (HT) × 'Lady Hillingdon' (T).
Not to be confused with Bernaix's 1898 HT, similarly colored, but double.

"Fair growth with beautiful single flowers of cerise, with red calyx." [ARA40/197] "Flower large, lasting, creamy lemon, flushed rosy pink with pink at edges of petals, on long stem. Foliage leathery, dark green. Vigorous, upright; abundant, continuous bloomer all season." [ARA37/264] "Golden anthers framed by wavy petals of cream and pink. Upright growth. Foliage and stems tinted purple . . . 3 × 3 [ft; ca. 9 × 9 dm]." [B] "Glossy foliage . . . superb." [G]

ÉTOILE DE HOLLANDE
Verschuren, 1919
From 'General MacArthur' (HT) × 'Hadley' (HT).
"Large, semi-double flowers of a very beautiful scarlet-red." [ARA21/148] "Medium-sized, ovoid buds and medium to small, cupped, deep bright red, double flowers of good lasting quality and strong fragrance, borne singly or several together on long, strong stems. Soft, disease-resistant foliage. Moderate, upright growth." [ARA27/132] "The rose of roses to me; a great, big, loose fellow of velvety crimson." [ARA29/48] "Large; rich, deep red, gleaming with color." [ARA29/96] "Buds opened too quickly." [Hk]

FRANCES ASHTON
DuPuy/Stocking, 1937
From 'Lady Battersea' (HT, G. Paul, 1901, cherry; parentage: 'Liberty' [HT] × 'Mme Abel Chatenay' [HT]) × 'Hawlmark Crimson' (HT, A. Dickson, 1920, crimson; parentage unknown).

"Bud large, long-pointed; flower large, single, lasting, slightly fragrant, carmine, no variations, wine-colored stamens, on long stems. Foliage leathery. Vigorous, upright; profuse bloomer." [ARA38/232] "Good growth and good foliage and . . . the flowers beautiful." [ARA40/199] "Continuous . . . 3–4 [ft; ca. 9 dm–1.25 m] . . . outstanding." [Lg] "One of the best of the singles . . . no serious faults after two years of observation." [ARA39/193]

GENERAL MACARTHUR
E. G. Hill Co., 1905
One worker speculates descent from 'Gruss an Teplitz'.

"Vivid scarlet, almost vermilion. Dazzling, with the effect of scarlet geraniums." [Dr] "Flower large, full, flat, fragrant." [JR30/25] "Bright crimson; perfume good . . . of all-round worth." [ARA17/24] "Tending to blue; fragrance strong and enduring; buds attractive . . . about 35 flowers in season." [ARA21/90] "Lacks substance." [ARA25/105] "One of the very best of the Hybrid Teas. It is of strong growth, and bears bright red flowers, which, if somewhat thin, are very freely produced. A splendid rose for the garden." [OM] "Always good, but too pinkish a red . . . fragrance, form, fine foliage . . . free-flowering." [RATS] "Color tends to blue . . . small [blossoms] in hot weather . . . almost immune from mildew; slightly susceptible to [black-] spot." [Th] "Cherry red . . . thin, open quickly, and possess no great charm in form. . . . Healthy, it grew well, and flowered freely." [Hk] "Scarlet-crimson; tall, bushy." [ARA17/31] "Low, spreading, compact, weak; foliage plentiful, healthy; bloom moderate, intermittent." [ARA18/125] "Very vigorous, floriferous and remontant . . . develops solitary blossoms on stems up to eighteen in long [ca. 4.5 dm]! The flowers are a dark crimson of a very brilliant shade, and are deliciously fragrant." [JR28/80] "[Does] only passably well [in Houston, Texas, in comparison to 'Red Radiance']." [ET] "Growth above average."

[ARA18/110] "Very vigorous." [M] "It was a failure on my light soil till I took it down to the wettest and heaviest part of my garden, where it receives a half shade. . . . [Its] foliage . . . is noteworthy. It has a blackish tinge in the green, joined with a bluish black shade, which pervades the whole plant. . . . The carriage of the flowers is excellent . . . the open flowers rather soon lose their shape. . . . Very free flowering and continuous and not to suffer from mildew." [NRS/13] "Blend of Musk and Damask [perfumes]." [NRS/17] "Perfectly magnificent in flower." [Fa]

GEORGE DICKSON
Listed as an HP.

GOLDEN OPHELIA
B. R. Cant, 1918
From 'Ophelia' (HT) × 'Mrs. Aaron Ward' (HT, Pernet-Ducher, 1907, salmon; parentage unknown).

"A seedling from 'Ophelia', possessing many of its characteristics. Flower of fair size, very compact, opening in perfect symmetrical form, golden yellow in center, and paling to almost white at outer petals." [ARA19/102] "Odor slight; fine shape, rather small but exquisite; lasts well when cut. Bush slim but strong." [ARA26/94] "Shorter bud than 'Ophelia', but holding center better; smaller and less pointed; slight fragrance; petals have less substance than its parent, but lasts. Nice grower, with very fine and retained foliage; stems not so stout as 'Ophelia'. Does well in Pacific South-West and very well in winter in Southern zones. Much to be preferred to most yellows for general garden cultivation and ordinary cut-flowers." [Th2] "Shapely flowers of delicate texture with good fragrance. More yellow than golden . . . 3 × 2 [ft; ca. 9 × 6 dm]." [B] "Popular [in Houston, Texas]." [ET]

GRACE DARLING
Bennett, 1884
"It is necessary that the kingdom of flowers fairly teem with quite amiable creatures since we inevitably turn to it when we want to symbolize joy, happiness, amity, gratitude, and other such warm, heart-felt sentiments. When we feel the need of catharsis by some gesture, we charge Flowers with the responsibility of being our intermediators, our interpretors. Thus it can be believed, then, that no one would ever have dreamed of dedicating a Rose to the daughter of an English lighthouse keeper, to Grace Darling, if, one stormy night, she had not, alone, saved the crew of a shipwrecked vessel. That heroic act was sung by the English poets, but the poems were quickly forgotten. . . . In seeing the beautiful [Hybrid] Tea rose 'Grace Darling', we remember her act of courage and devotion. . . . The blossom is large, very full, and of a beautiful coloration: fundamentally cream-white, strongly tinted peach-pink; the flower opens well, and is adequately fragrant. The bush is vigorous, and blooms abundantly on each branch; it begins to flower early, and blooms late as well." [JR15/43–44] "The blossoms are large, very full, and open well in greenhouse or garden. The color is novel." [JR8/54] "Very pretty sometimes when half open. . . . Colour rather confused. . . . Of good growth." [F-M2] "Cupped." [Hn] "Moderate vigor." [Cx] "3 × 3 [ft; ca. 9 × 9 dm]." [B] "One of the newest and best." [JR11/50] Grace Horsley Darling, 1815–1842; rescued, with her father, nine survivors of the ship *Forfarshire* in 1838 during a storm sweeping over the Farne Islands off Bamburgh in Northumberland, England. It was thought that the fame and celebrity proceeding from this feat contributed to her early death.

GRUSS AN AACHEN   PLATE 271

(trans., 'Greetings to Aachen')
Geduldig, 1909
From 'Frau Karl Druschki' (HP) × 'Franz Deegen' (HT, Hinner, 1901, yellow; seedling of 'Kaiserin Auguste Viktoria' [HT]).

"Large, very double blooms of warm pink with peach tones, low growing, 2 [ft; ca. 6 dm]." [HRG] "Superb . . . very tidy habit. Flesh-pink changing to cream . . . shapely. . . . Slightly fragrant. Good, glossy foliage . . . 2 × 2 [ft; ca. 6 × 6 dm]." [B] "Low growing . . . flowers open flat . . . creamy pink, richly fragrant and recurrent." [G] "Color fades quickly in hot weather, becoming almost white; perfume mild . . . growth fair." [ARA17/22] "Buds gold and red." [ARA29/97] "Of good vigor; the branches are strong, rigid, fairly erect. Continuous-flowering. . . . The bud is long and of attractive form; color, orange red strongly tinted yellow. The color of the rose is quite difficult to describe . . . truly very beautiful. One gathers that the blossom will attain perhaps six in across [ca. 1.5 dm] — but I have never seen it that large." [JR36/124] "Tall, vigorous; foliage very plentiful till late summer, then plentiful, black-spots . . . mildews . . . bloom moderate, continuous, size and quality compensate for lack of quantity." [ARA18/128] Aachen, or Aix-la-Chapelle, was Charlemagne's capital city. Those partial to "Gruss an Aachen" may wish to know of its extant sports (all but the climber in our supplement): 'Climbing Gruss an Aachen', 'Gruss an Aachen Superior', 'Jean Muraour', 'Minna', 'Rosa Gruss an Aachen'.

GRUSS AN TEPLITZ

Listed as a Bourbon.

GUSTAV GRÜNERWALD   PLATE 265

Lambert, 1903
From 'Safrano' (T) × 'Mme Caroline Testout' (HT).

"Carmine pink with a radiant center of yellow; flower large, full, fragrant; floriferous; very vigorous." [Cx] "Flowers . . . cupped, with a high centre . . . buds yellowish red, long and pointed." [W/Hn] "A beautiful flower . . . of a very distinct shade of bright carmine pink with pale orange shading at the base of the petal which lights up the flower well. It has a delicious perfume, being one of the best of the pink Roses in this respect. The flowers are not badly affected by either sun or rain, but in hot weather, especially in mid season, they are apt to get loose and lose their shape. . . . The autumnal blooming is generally good and free." [NRS/12] "Free vigorous growth of an upright yet branching habit, and good though rather sparse dark green bold leathery foliage but little liable to mildew. It flowers fairly continuously and freely from early July till late autumn. The flowers are carried erect singly and on good stems, though full flowers will droop at times. The petals are strong and of good substance, bright carmine pink in colour, rather paler in hot weather . . . sweetly fragrant." [NRS/10] "Good autumnal." [JP] "A good early variety . . . must be disbudded freely." [F-M] "Not the most floriferous, despite being very vigorous." [JR32/33] "Pretty vigorous, floriferous, having buds which are elongated, pointed, and good for vases. The flowers are large, cupped, of a pretty and fresh pink, the interior of the petals being saffron yellow. Were it not for this last color, it would very much resemble the charming 'Mme Caroline Testout', with which it shares many other characteristics, notably form, wood, and thorns." [JR29/92] "Moderate height, compact, vigorous, hardy; foliage plentiful, black-spots slightly; bloom almost free, continuous." [ARA18/125] "3 × 3 [ft; ca. 9 × 9 dm]." [B] "Everyone should grow this variety if only for the sake of the bright rose-pink colour of the flowers. There are many pink

roses, but this is distinct from them all. It grows well and flowers freely." [OM] "Good . . . not one of the best." [ARA18/111]

HADLEY

Pierson/Montgomery Co., 1914
From an unnamed seedling (parentage: 'Liberty' [HT] × 'Richmond' [HT]) × 'General MacArthur' (HT).

"A rich crimson-red flower with velvety texture, lovely form, and perfume. Moderate in growth and bloom. Splendid color which blues very little. Flowers small in summer; superb in fall." [ARA26/110] "Velvety crimson to darkest black-purple — blues in extreme heat more than 'Hoosier Beauty'; double and attractive in form; fine fragrance. Foliage good. Stem usually long and strong. Weak grower in Central zone; satisfactory in cool, moist climates of Pacific North-West and Pacific South-West. Reported by Miss Creighton, of western Florida, as continuous." [Th2] "In the summer-time and all the time, 'Hadley' yields wonderfully fine blooms for cutting." [ARA29/106] "Free and constant flowerer." [Au] "The pre-disposition to blind wood . . . is the weak spot in 'Hadley'." [ARA16/116] "Produces so few flowers that it is hardly worth growing [in the florist trade]." [ARA22/140] "With its wonderful color and quality, is considered ideal by the buyer [of cut flowers], but not by the grower." [ARA23/108] "Has been almost entirely discarded [by commercial growers of cut flowers]." [ARA26/158] " 'Hadley' certainly is not [easy to grow]." [ARA25/170] "The plant grows well, but is of a rather straggling habit, and the carriage of the flowers is not good." [NRS21/51] "Mildews easily." [BCD] "Of our dark red roses 'Hadley' is the favorite." [ARA21/142] "Superior to the reds I previously had." [ARA25/98] "Color distinct; growth and blooming fair; foliage quite good; best in the spring." [ARA18/111] "A grand rose." [ARA25/144] "In 1916 there was a flower show at Philadelphia. . . . Basing my opinion on the opinion of those with whom I talked after the show, it seems that 'Hadley' is 'some rose.' Those who saw this finest of the crimson roses at Philadelphia have something to remember. . . . Growers have decided that 'Hadley' is worth all the extra care which a good variety needs. It has come into its own. 'Montgomery's mistake' was the nickname tacked onto 'Hadley' by those who thought they knew more about roses than the originator of 'Hadley'." [ARA17/110] "Alexander W. Montgomery, Jr., of Hadley, Mass." [ARA16/44]

HELEN GOULD

Listed as 'Balduin'

INNOCENCE

Chaplin, 1921
Supposedly R. ×hibernica × "a hybrid tea."

"A lovely, large . . . single-flowering white rose that opens well. The delicate wave of the petals, coupled with the golden stamens, makes it a very attractive variety. . . . The perfume is not pronounced." [ARA23/145] "Pure white, five-inch [ca. 1.25 dm] beauty with yellow stamens . . . both in clusters and singly on long, thick, thorny stems." [ARA34/81] "Very lovely . . . of twelve petals, with unusual stamens." [ARA40/43] "Tapering buds, and fine, large, white, single blooms of great beauty. . . . Very vigorous. Free from mildew; some black-spot . . . lovely. . . . Bore 57 blooms [Rhode Island]. . . . Odorless [Indiana]. . . . No special merit [California]." [PP28]

IRISH ELEGANCE
A. Dickson, 1905
Supposedly *R.* ×*hibernica* × "a hybrid tea."

"Single flowers of a bronze and orange color, from which the roses turn completely to a shade of apricot at maturity." [JR29/153] "A medley of apricot, pink and orange-red." [Hk] "A variegated rose with a lot of pink in the combination; it is beautiful but nothing to get excited about." [ARA34/81] "Buds are orange-scarlet. Vigorous . . . 4 × 3 [ft; ca. 1.25 × 1 m]." [B] "A delightful fragrance of cloves." [ARA24/95] "A wonderfully free bloomer." [ARA20/149] "Fades in heat . . . opens quickly. Very good foliage. Very fine growth in Pacific North-West." [Th2] "The foliage is specially beautiful and harmonises well with the flowers, particularly in autumn, when it turns a ruddy green. The early foliage is also most beautiful, of a rich red tint. The habit is good and branching . . . free flowering and fairly continuous. . . . The colour of the single flower is unique, the buds are a fine orange scarlet, and the petals of the open flower coppery fawn with a pink shade running through it. It has a sweet but not very strong fragrance, and good lasting flowers for a single Rose. . . . Its charm lies not merely in the flowers, lovely as they are, but in their delightful harmony with the foliage and in the good and healthy habit of the plants . . . Decidedly liable to mildew." [NRS/12] "A very beautiful rose." [K2]

IRISH FIREFLAME
A. Dickson, 1913
Supposedly *R.* ×*hibernica* × "a hybrid tea."

"The sumptuous color of 'Irish Fireflame' immediately conveys the notion of a flame; its color is dark Madeira orange, veneered with maroon which changes to crimson orange; when the buds are developing, they are a pure delicate orange which changes, when the blossoms expand, to a rich, satiny old gold, deliciously veined and mottled as if a beam of sunlight had tinted the crimson and the lemon yellow shading the crimson, which makes, considering the large size of the flowers (which reach 5.25 in [ca. 1.25 dm]), the prettiest contrast and the most delicious coloration. The buds have a special feature: the oval receptacles are chocolate-color, and the base, hidden from the sun, is apple-green; the foliage is oval. Strongly and deliciously perfumed with a Persian-Tea scent. The vigorous branches are never without flowers." [JR37/105–106] "Orange yellow and red." [OM] "Fiery crimson at the base, shading to orange-salmon . . . in the bud state they are very attractive." [ARA16/117] "Deep madder-orange . . . blossoms all season." [ARA25/121] "A reddish bronze yellow . . . brilliant and very pleasing in the sunshine. A feature is the contrast in the varying shades of colour in the bud, half open and fully expanded flower; it is very striking and, combined with the deep bronze-green foliage, the whole makes a very fine decorative garden plant." [NRS/13] "Perfumed. Foliage good. Stem weak; growth good in Southern zones; does well in shade in Pacific South-West, but flower and stem wilt in heat." [Th2] "Dependable." [Capt28]

ISOBEL
McGredy, 1916
Supposedly *R.* ×*hibernica* × "a hybrid tea."

"Flame, copper, and gold . . . ['Isobel'] is my favorite among the singles of these blended shades." [ARA24/95] "Although single, the enormous petals, with their mingled shades of carmine, red, and orange, make a plant of 'Isobel', in bloom, a beautiful sight, and the manner in which the petals fold up after sundown is also delightful." [ARA29/48] "A large flower on a large bush . . . light rose-pink, with apricot shadings." [ARA34/80–81] "Said to be good." [ARA18/47] "Of remarkable color. Fair growth." [ARA18/118]

"Growth rather small, not bushy. Wonderful decorative rose where well grown." [Th2] "Huge, warm, pink, five petaled, fragrant flowers . . . an enchanting rose by any standards." [DP]

JEAN SISLEY
Bennett, 1879
From 'Adam' (T) × 'Emilie Hausbourg' (HP, Lévêque, 1868, lilac-rose; parentage unknown).

"Large flowers, very full, beautifully formed petals, lilac-pink around the perimeter, bright pink in the center; flowering perfect and of long duration." [JR3/114] "Moderate vigor, floriferousness; no scent. Opens with difficulty." [S] "[Has a tendency to] fade very quickly . . . difficult to open . . . rather a muddy shade . . . very subject to mildew. The color is bad, and the buds rarely open well; it is entirely worthless." [EL] "2 × 2 [ft; ca. 6 × 6 dm]." [B]

KAISERIN AUGUSTE VIKTORIA   PLATE 243
('K. A. Viktoria', 'Reine Augusta Victoria', 'Grande Duchesse Olga')
Lambert & Reiter, 1891
Two parentages given: either (1) 'Perle des Jardins' (T) × 'Belle Lyonnaise' (N); or (2) 'Coquette de Lyon' (T) × 'Lady Mary Fitzwilliam' (HT).

"Pure white with an orange-yellow center; flower large, very full, globular; very floriferous; vigorous." [Cx] "Cream . . . one of the best. . . . Vigorous." [J] "A dainty, creamy-white rose of moderately vigorous growth. The flowers are of perfect form." [OM] "Primrose. Very beautiful glossy leathery foliage . . . unique in color and must be included in any large collection." [Th] "Splendid large buds and full flowers like camellias." [BSA] "Pure white with yellow centre, outer petals reflexed; a very free and effective decorative Rose; also fine for exhibition; growth vigorous." [P1] "This variety was obtained by crossing 'Perle des Jardins' and 'Belle Lyonnaise'; it has preserved a slight resemblance to this latter." [JR22/56] "Vigorous, with strong and upright branches; thorns sparse but big; foliage large, brownish red, shiny when young, brilliant dark green with age; flower, large or very large, very full, well-held . . . imbricated, opening easily, and of long duration. Exterior petals, pure white; those of the interior, Naples yellow; center of the flower, orange yellow . . . very fragrant. The blossoms are usually solitary, rarely 2 or 3 on the long stalks, which are erect and strong. Bloom is very abundant up to frost . . . resists cold well." [JR15/5] "Semi-globular . . . stands hot weather well. . . . Fair growth and foliage, requiring 'liberal treatment.' " [F-M2] "Bushy, tall, moderately compact . . . foliage plentiful, black-spots; bloom free most of the time, almost continuous." [ARA18/125] "Does not discolor under rain, wind, or heat." [Th2] "Another superb rose, particularly as a bud or half-open. . . . White, or often with some orange, globular . . . dedicated to [the German] Empress. . . . Blooms in fall and winter; very nice under the north African skies." [JR34/170] "Most planted [of white roses in Houston, Texas]." [ET] "3 [ft; ca. 9 dm]." [HRG] "Its majestic bearing, its graceful form, its fine coloration — all these place it in the first range of beautiful roses." [JR30/18] "No white rose has yet surpassed old 'Kaiserin Auguste Viktoria', at least in shape." [ARA35/92] "A true aristocrat in rosedom." [ARA29/102]

KATHLEEN MILLS
Le Grice, 1934
"Bud large, long-pointed, carmine; flower large, semi-double, open, intense briar fragrance, pale pink, washed silvery sheen, reverse deep pink, on a long stem. Foliage leathery. Vigorous (3 ft [ca. 9 dm]), upright, open; profuse, continuous bloomer all

season." [ARA37/264] "Iridescent pink petals and stamens shining like particles of gold . . . truly beautiful. Of all the roses I know it is the most prolific . . . the display is continuous . . . not a lusty plant." [DP] "3–5 [ft; ca. 9 dm–1.5 m] . . . striking, unique." [Lg]

KILLARNEY DOUBLE WHITE
Budlong, 1913
Sport of 'Killarney White' (HT).

"[Liked in Houston, Texas] . . . beautiful in the bud in early spring, but . . . not a good summer boarder." [ET] "The only good, first-class white rose that we have available today, commercially." [ARA21/138] Much used as a florist's rose in the Teens.

KILLARNEY QUEEN
Budlong, 1912
Sport of 'Killarney' (HT).

"Bright pink . . . vigorous . . . 30 to 40 blooms per season." [ARA21/91] "The best of the Killarneys for outdoor planting. Flowers larger, color deeper and more lasting than 'Pink Killarney'; growth more vigorous." [ARA18/133] "Extremely heavy foliage . . . lesser production in bloom." [ARA18/99] "Tall, compact, free-growing, hardy; foliage sufficient, black-spots; bloom free, almost continuous." [ARA18/125] "For decoration or hedges in Interior South districts with dry conditions." [Th2]

K. OF K.
('Kitchener of Khartoum')
A. Dickson, 1917

"Bright crimson . . . half double, with large petals. Seems to be extremely floriferous." [ARA20/123] "Each petal resembling a piece of fine scarlet velvet." [ARA29/49] "A Rose of vigorous free-branching habit, with dark green foliage. The blooms, which are freely produced and sweetly scented, are carried on fairly stiff stems. The colour is a brilliant scarlet crimson, which does not burn." [NRS/17] "Beautiful but somewhat weak-necked." [ARA26/21] "3 × 3 [ft; ca. 9 × 9 dm]." [B] "Does well in California. . . . Continuous bloomer." [Th2] "Quite took our fancy." [ARA18/47]

KOOTENAY
('Mary Greer')
A. Dickson, 1917

"Almost white, faint blush, tinged yellow; large; odor slight to good. Bush tall and strong." [ARA26/94] "Yellowish white with pink, large, full, medium scent, medium height." [Sn] "Of vigorous growth and branching habit; the blooms are freely produced on long rigid stalks. They are large and full and of perfect form, of primrose yellow colour, and strongly perfumed. The Rose is described as an improved 'Kaiserin Auguste Viktoria'." [NRS16/141] "Obtained some triumphs in America." [NRS21/57]

LA FRANCE   PLATE 226
Guillot fils, 1867
Seedling of 'Mme Falcot' (T).

"Silvery-rose, with pale lilac shading . . . most abundant . . . highly fragrant." [H] "Now, upon examination, 'La France' corresponds exactly in its details to the Bourbon: its spination, with pretty numerous thorns intermingled with stickers, bristly and glandular on the young canes, and especially around the flower-stems before the blossom opens . . . it was declared by the introducer himself, Mons Guillot fils [to be a] Hybrid Bourbon." [JR31/126] "Pronounced somewhat suddenly by the National Rose

Society to be a Hybrid Tea. There does not seem to be sufficient evidence or authority for this distinction, and opinions on the matter are divided; but some signs of affinity to the China race are to be seen in the habit and freedom of bloom." [F-M3] "An invaluable rose for its hardiness, and its constant blooming qualities. Its color is pale peach, with rosy center; its form is globular, full, and very large." [SBP] "Silvery-rose, changing to pink . . . the sweetest of all roses. If the buds remain firm, by gently pressing the point and blowing into the center, the flowers will, almost invariably, expand. An invaluable sort." [EL] "Beautiful shining lilac-rose on the interior." [JR1/2/8] "Blush, shaded peach; a superb Rose, one of the best for all purposes, except for walls." [WD] "It blooms perpetually, the end of each shoot always carrying a flower-bud, and these shoots constantly pushing forth." [EIC] "Globular, with pointed centre; free and very sweet." [DO] "Tight with petals, of attractive form . . . flowers . . . float gracefully above the foliage." [Hk] "Monster size." [L] "The most odiferous of roses." [JR1/11/2] "Tea-scented . . . and generally satisfactory . . . should not be too closely pruned." [HRH] "Fragrance just like that of Centifolias." [JR1/3/4] "Blend of Musk and Damask [perfumes]." [NRS/17] "A good hot weather rose." [L] "Not a good laster in very hot weather . . . scent distinct and exquisite." [F-M2] "Best on own root in Southern zones." [Th2] "Practically worthless in this section [Texas]." [ARA18/79] "Of great beauty, except in wet weather . . . 3 × 3 [ft; ca. 9 × 9 dm]." [B] "Often 'balls' in our 'liquid summers' . . . a charm and silvery subtlety." [RP] "Bright pink . . . blues slightly . . . bud is not long and tends to ball . . . susceptible to mildew and [black-] spot . . . if not properly grown has bad faults which are especially noticeable in wet seasons. If planted in poor ground in a bed which drains readily and not fed, it is well worth cultivating." [Th]

"Growth very vigorous; flowers very large, full, beautiful form and well held, with large petals; the center of the flower is a silvery white, the exterior a beautiful shining lilac pink; its scent surpasses that of the Centifolia; this introduction will be of great merit for bedding." [I'H67/286, classified as a "freely remontant Bourbon hybrid."] "Grows better in soil that is not too rich." [M-P] "[Liberal treatment encourages balling]." [F-M2] "Growth well above the average . . . worthy of cultivation if planted in poor ground." [ARA17/23] "Medium height, compact, moderate in growth and hardiness; foliage sufficient to plentiful, black-spots slightly; bloom moderate, almost continuous." [ARA18/125] "Vigorous; canes pretty large, and, when so, straight and upright; smaller ones branch; bark, pale green, reddish on the sunny side; thorns short, very large and clinging, terminating in sharp points; foliage large, light green, slightly bullate, divided into 3–5 rounded leaflets, which are pointed and toothed; leafstalks are strong, reflexed, furnished with numerous small prickles; flower, between 3 and 4 in across [ca. 7.5 cm–1 dm], full, globular, solitary on the small branches and in a bouquet of 3–5 on vigorous branches; color, light pink, silvery on the interior, and lilac on the exterior; outer petals tight, large, and reflexed, those of the center more petite; flower stalks slender, nodding under the weight of the flower. A very pretty variety, by all reports, and quite hardy." [S]

"The growth is free and vigorous, making a bush from 3–4 ft high [ca. 9 dm–1.25 m], the habit branching; the foliage is thick and good, seldom affected by mildew, and the flowering period continuous from late June to early Autumn. The flowers are produced freely and borne on fairly stiff stems, but full blossoms are apt to droop. . . . At its best it is a beautiful flower and still one of the sweetest, free-flowering and most fragrant Roses we have . . . a good bedding rose . . . plants on their own roots being, I suppose, less vigorous will often give excellent flowers of this beautiful Rose in a wet season, when those on the briar have become nothing but melancholy sopping balls. It has the advantage, too, of rooting from autumn cuttings more readily than most garden Roses." [NRS/10]

"Calyx tubular, only slightly apparent." [JF] "Always blooming, but never sets seeds." [JR12/47] "I have made use of 'La France' often enough in my hybridizing, but I have never been able to get any seeds from it." [JR26/100–101] "It seems that this rose has decided to become productive, and that it bore seeds at the home of Herr Dienemann, of Klein-Furra, in Thuringia. From three hips gathered, Dienemann obtained one rose which was single, another a lot like 'Mme Julie Weidmann' [HT, Soupert & Notting, 1881, pink; parent, 'Antonine Verdier', (HT, Jamain, 1872, light carmine; parentage unknown)], but paler. Finally, a third seedling, a climber, absolutely refused to bloom. Much as the results have heretofore been negative, we nevertheless believe that it will be good to try to breed with 'La France' in hopes of better success." [JR27/17–18]

Sports of 'La France': 'Danmark', 'Duchess of Albany', 'Mlle Augustine Guinoisseau', 'Mme Angelique Veysset', 'Becker's Ideal' (HT, Becker, 1903, pink; "this new obtention differs from ['La France'] by way of its own unique configuration, which is that of a perfect cup with the petals incurving rather than spreading out" [JR27/17]), and of course 'Climbing La France'.

" 'La France' blooms itself to death. *Mea culpa*, if others do not find it a short-lived rose. It is remarkably free in growth, almost immune from diseases and blemishes. In all nature, I know nothing to surpass 'La France' in full bloom." [Dr]

LADY ALICE STANLEY
McGredy, 1909

"Deep coral-rose on outside . . . inside pale flesh; perfume mild to fair . . . growth fair." [ARA17/23] "Silvery pink; moderate [height], spare [in leafage]." [ARA17/32] "The arrangement of petals, gently curved back just a trifle, even in the center, so gracefully overlapping and supporting one another, like the studied folds of a lovely frock, all so uniform, so well-proportioned, so regular, so strongly placed on its stem, and the whole so well guarded by its outer rows of petals — this it is which gives us the essence of ladyhood, the two tones of softer and deeper rose, together with a bountiful fragrance, that give it its lovableness." [ARA30/36] "Good form." [OM] "Bloom lasts well; fair grower; moderately good bloomer." [ARA18/111] "Growth is vigorous and the flowers large and of good shape and distinct colour." [F-M] "Good foliage. Medium grower. Averages 34 blooms per season." [ARA21/92] "Open flower very attractive . . . very little affected by mildew, but susceptible to [black-] spot . . . growth fair." [Th] "Height and compactness medium, vigorous, hardy; foliage plentiful, blackspots slightly; bloom free, almost continuous." [ARA18/125] "[Very satisfactory in Brazil]." [PS]

LADY MARY FITZWILLIAM   PLATE 231
Bennett, 1882
From 'Devoniensis' (T) × 'Victor Verdier' (HP).

"Robust, well-branched, enormous flowers, globular, very full, pale delicate flesh, of the 'Captain Christy' sort; excellent for exhibition." [JR6/69] "Blooms in abundance on short branches, giving blossoms of 3 in [ca. 7.5 cm] at the height of bloom." [JR7/136] "Flowers which would be difficult to surpass in beauty." [JR8/156] "Of moderate vigor, giving enormous globular blossoms which are full and of a light flesh-white. The large bud is well-formed, and has the advantage of lasting a long time before opening . . . lightly fragrant." [JR14/84] "Of a delicate rosy flesh-colour, very large globular well-formed flowers with long and fine petals, dwarf growth, hardy and robust, but its growth seems to be checked by

the habit of producing too many of these large and exhausting flowers." [B&V] "One of the best . . . dwarf, but robust and very floriferous." [JR7/83]

LADY SYLVIA
Stevens, 1926
Sport of 'Ophelia' (HT).

"A clear fresh pink, as pleasing a pink Hybrid Tea, I think, as there has ever been." [Hk] "Lovely, shapely buds opening to full flowers of flesh-pink with deeper undertones . . . bushy and fairly vigorous. Superb scent . . . 3 × 2 [ft; ca. 9 × 6 dm]." [B]

LIBERTY
A. Dickson, 1900
From 'Mrs. W. J. Grant' (HT) × 'Charles J. Graham' (HT).

"Rich velvety crimson, fine stiff petals. . . . Growth fairly vigorous." [P1] "Very floriferous, producing deliciously perfumed blossoms like those of 'American Beauty'; they are perhaps paler in summer, but in autumn their tint is much the same deep crimson as that of 'Gruss an Teplitz'." [JR24/21] "Fairly mediocre by the end of September. Its color has a lilac tint." [JR28/10–11] "It seems to be a fairly good grower, with well-formed flowers not large enough for exhibition, but of a colour — bright crimson — which is much wanted in this section [HT's]." [F-M2] "The *ne plus ultra* of red roses . . . very floriferous, remontant, and irreproachably held; the growth is vigorous, stocky, and furnished with handsome glossy foliage." [JR25/20]

LULU
Easlea, 1919

"Orange-salmon and pink." [ARA25/102] "Pretty buds; opens too quick; too thin; fades quickly. Foliage crinkly; no [black-] spot." [ARA26/117] "Foliage mildews. Growth good." [Th2] "Bud very long-pointed; flower orange, salmon, and pink. Vigorous grower of bushy habit . . . abundance of bloom all season." [ARA] "This is said to hold the record for the longest bud yet produced." [ARA20/120] "A tall, eight petaled, very slender orange bud which was eye-catching . . . a charmer." [DP]

MARCHIONESS OF SALISBURY
Pernet père, 1890
Not to be confused with Lévêque's 1888 'Marquise de Salisbury', flesh, nor with G. Paul's 1880 'Marquis de Salisbury', a crimson-red HP.

"Handsome very velvety intense red; flower medium-sized, fairly full, imbricated; very floriferous; vigorous." [Cx] "Glowing crimson flowers and deep green leaves." [Ro] "Velvety bright red." [LS] "Brilliant crimson, sometimes sparkling scarlet; very abundant bloom, semi-double, a good garden rose." [JR22/106] "Vigorous, branches upright and strong, thorns prominent and numerous, foliage very thick and conspicuous, of a handsome somber green bordered reddish, flowers of moderate size or large, fairly full, of a handsome and very velvety bright red; bud, elongated and in the form of a **T**; bloom, continuous and abundant; this wonderful variety will be much sought out for bedding . . . of the highest merit." [JR14/164] "Moderately bushy; flower large, pretty full; very floriferous." [JR30/32] "A good bright rose for bedding. I am persuaded that the best results with this variety are secured by cutting the branches very short." [JR28/10] "Gorgeous and thorny." [K2] "Dark red to maroon. Fragrant and free-flowering . . . 3 × 3 [ft; ca. 9 × 9 dm]." [B]

MLLE AUGUSTINE GUINOISSEAU PLATE 237

('Augustine Guinnoisseau', 'White La France')
Guinoisseau fils, 1889
Sport of 'La France' (HT).

"A nearly white sport, tinted blush.... As a bedding Rose, 'Augustine Guinoisseau' is one of the very best; it is thinner than 'La France', and therefore better for this purpose, and if possible even freer in flowering. Having less substance, it seldom balls ... it has all the delightful 'La France' perfume."[NRS/10] "Rosy white ... produced in great profusion.... Deliciously fragrant and vigorous."[P1] "Flowers large, full, beautiful light pink, erect; growth moderately vigorous. Branches slender, buds small."[Hn] "White with some flesh; flower large, full, imbricated; floriferous, vigorous."[Cx] "As good a white garden rose as a heart can desire."[K2] "Not white—a poor thing."[ARA25/105] "Nearly white, very free and late in flowering."[E] "Especially fine in the autumn."[Ro] "A fair degree of perfection [in cool seasons]."[L] "Good in heat."[Th2] "Oh, no! The rose is rather disheveled, wilts quickly, the petals don't hold well, the blossom is skimpy, the hardiness precarious."[JR37/170] "A branch-sport of 'La France', known to advantage for its abundant bloom and vigor, the only difference being in its color, lightly-fleshed white.... Cultivated for over eight years, it has always been of good behavior. Thoroughly of the first order."[JR13/166] "Flowers very inferior in size, color, and shape [to those of 'La France']."[F-M2] "We know all of 'La France's' advantages—abundant bloom, vigor, the shape of the bud, the fragrance, etc.—there is nothing lacking in these. And her child 'Mlle Augustine Guinoisseau' is no different—except in color."[JR21/56] "Somewhat less vigorous than ['La France']. It blooms remarkably freely, and the recurving petals give it a quaintly attractive appearance. A rose for the beginner."[OM] "Most of my friends agree in describing the foliage as good; it is, I think, slightly lighter in colour than that of its parent.... The stems are smooth and a nice light green colour ... delightfully fragrant, the scent being that described as sweet or honeyed in character ... this scent resembles that of no other Rose excepting 'La France'.... Perhaps not mildew proof, it is very little affected by this, or indeed, any other fungus pests.... Free-flowering and continuous."[NRS/12] "Medium height, compact, winterkills somewhat; foliage plentiful, black-spots somewhat; bloom free, continuous."[ARA18/128] "Very strong in growth, and highly scented; perhaps a little stiff and artificial looking, but a fine variety."[Wr]

MME ABEL CHATENAY PLATES 1, 250

Pernet-Ducher, 1894
From 'Dr. Grill' (T) × 'Victor Verdier' (HP).

"Carmine pink shaded vermilion, tinted pale salmon; flower large, very full, cupped; vigorous."[Cx] "Salmon pink, very free."[H] "Carmine-rose-buff mixture ... distinctive."[Hk] "Light pink deepening towards the centre."[T2] "Carmine rose, shaded with salmon. Very popular in England."[Th] "One of the best roses of recent introduction, not so much as a show bloom as for its excellent decorative qualities and attractive colour ... rosy carmine shaded with vermilion rose and tinged with salmon; base of petals deeper. Flowers of exquisite shape, not large, but full and fragrant; growth vigorous."[P1] "The finest decorative Rose in the world."[NRS/12] "One of the prettiest Hybrid Teas. The growth is vigorous, hardy, with branching canes armed with strong, sparse thorns. The foliage is a pretty bronze green; bloom is continuous. The bud is very elegant, opening in a spiral. The blossom is large and full; the petals recurve on themselves in the most graceful fashion, giving the variety a particular distinction and an unequaled elegance. The magnificent color is carmine pink shaded pale vermilion pink and touched with salmon; the tone is very intense and

warm around the petals' nub."[JR37/93] "Utterly distinct in color and form with a sharp, penetrating fragrance, carmine shading on salmon with wonderful reflexing. The flower is medium sized and the growth rather straggling."[RP] "Good blooms [in Madiera]."[DuC] "Tall, moderately compact, fairly hardy; foliage sufficient, black-spots slightly; bloom free, almost continuous."[ARA18/126] "Subject to mildew and the blooms decrease in size as the season advances, but its long season, great productiveness, beautifully formed buds, and fine color make it desirable."[ARA25/99] "Both in bud and when fully open an exquisite Rose of lovely shape and colour, it grows freely and flowers freely, and is quite hardy."[NRS/14]

"This beautiful Rose has free, vigorous, if somewhat erratic growth and a branching habit rather apt when closely pruned to push up single strong flower shoots in panicles, and if not closely pruned to become 'leggy.' The foliage is strong and good, but scattered, not disposed well on the plant, and not enough of it ... rather liable to mildew.... It flowers very freely and continuously from the third week of June till late autumn. The flowers, carried on long erect stems, come as long-pointed buds opening to beautifully shaped flowers of moderate size. The petals are of good substance, the centre and outside of a deep salmon pink, the inner side much lighter towards the edges, giving the effect of blended shades of colour in sunshine or rain; they last long in water (four days) and on the plant, and their fragrance, though not strong, is very sweet.... One of the very best all-round Roses."[NRS/10] "Certainly a short-lived Rose ... decidedly liable to mildew, and I have found it suffer from black-spot."[NRS/12] "Very vigorous."[M] "Poor grower."[NRS/14] "One of the most beautiful."[E] "Opens easily.... Dedicated to the wife of the secretary-general of the Société National d'Horticulture."[JR34/171] "3 × 3 [ft; ca. 9 × 9 dm]."[B] "Fair; good in color and growth, but superseded by better roses of the same type."[ARA18/116] "A general perfection all round which I should imagine that it would be very long before any Rose could rival—much less out-do."[Fa]

MME BUTTERFLY

E. G. Hill Co., 1918
Sport of 'Ophelia' (HT).

"Soft flesh, shaded rose; beautiful spiral bud; attractive open flower of good size; lasts quite well; very fragrant. Stem very good. Foliage good.... Should be planted in partial shade in hot climates. In California coast areas does not discolor as quickly as its parent, and must be given the preference."[Th2] "Rather more salmon to apricot [than 'Ophelia']."[RP] "Very feminine ... shades of pale pink to blush with lemon centre. Very fragrant."[B] "A glorified 'Ophelia'. Much larger in flower ... more vigorous ... and more prolific."[ARA20/xiii] "Similar to 'Ophelia' in all characteristics, except that the color is greatly intensified."[ARA19/159] "Very free-flowering."[ARA29/48] "A hot weather rose."[ARA24/95] "Many admirers [in Houston, Texas]."[ET] We note early references to "*Madam* Butterfly," under which pronunciation, we find, both the rose and the opera are usually cited.

MME CAROLINE TESTOUT PLATE 240

Pernet-Ducher, 1890
From 'Mme de Tartas' (T) × 'Lady Mary Fitzwilliam' (HT).

"Satin rose with brighter center ... color, most beautiful; fragrance, very distinct ... slightly susceptible to mildew and [black-] spot ... sometimes tends to have a weak neck ... a universal favorite."[Th] "Very large, deep pink ... showing the eye ... sweet scented also, like a wild Rose."[HRH] "Bright pink ... well-formed."[Hk] "A light salmon-pink. This magnificent variety makes a fine bush, has the longest flowering season of all the roses, except 'Frau Karl Druschki', and is suitable for both the garden and exhibition." [JP] "Very large, well-filled, cupped, centifolia form, beautiful rosy-red like 'La France', but the petals are stronger and less tinted with silvery white. A magnificent rose of recent years, with vigorous growth." [Hn] "Opens quickly." [Th2] "The bud is of a pretty form, quite elongated; the blossom, which opens easily, bears something of a resemblance to a variety which one would have thought inimitable — 'La France' — in its satiny flesh-pink color, though a little brighter at the center; it wafts a fragrance which is very agreeable, though a little less strong than that of 'La France'." [JR16/99] "Good decided self-pink . . . very free bloomer. . . . Fair foliage and thorny growth." [F-M2] "Splendid . . . strong leafy stems . . . pink colouring is clear and pretty." [E] "Notable in color and fragrance; good bloomer; not of the best in form or growth." [ARA18/112] "Growth good." [ARA17/23] "One of the most beautiful introductions of recent years. In many respects it resembles 'La France', but differs in form, and the growth is more vigorous. Petals large and shell-shaped. Abundant bloomer." [P1] "The flowers for the most part are too coarse and loose for close inspection." [NRS/12] "Carnation-scented." [JR33/101] "A good hot weather rose." [L]

"Of free, vigorous growth and branching habit, armed with many and strong thorns. The foliage is thick, large, and green, and free from mildew till August . . . stems, which are erect with young flowers . . . apt to bend over with a full bloom. [The blossoms are] rather round in shape, large, full, and of great substance, bright, full, pink in colour, but rather lighter in hot weather. . . . They fade rather quickly on the plant when open, but this is of less importance, as they open slowly so that the plants generally seem to have plenty of bloom. It stands rain well, and is perhaps at its best in dull weather or where it will get shade part of the day, but it is apt somewhat to 'ball' in bad weather. . . . It is fairly fragrant, and the perfume is clean and pleasing. . . . Its special characteristic is its regular branching habit and freedom of flowering. . . . One of the most reliable . . . it fails to inspire me with that personal affection which is quite inexplicable, and yet often arises in respect of some far less satisfactory Rose." [NRS/10] "Tall, rather upright, hardy; foliage sufficient, black-spots somewhat; bloom moderate, continuous." [ARA18/126] "It has no serious fault other perhaps than that of being very spiny." [JR23/39] "Can hardly be beaten in all-round good qualities." [ARA20/46] "Indeed a treasure." [K1] "A generation old and still in the front rank." [McF] "The rose-advance of the past dozen years has, in a sense, outmoded 'Testout'." [ARA36/23] "Dedicated to a lady of Grenoble, a flower fancier." [JR34/14]

MME ELISA DE VILMORIN
Lévêque, 1864

"Carmine-rose." [JR8/27] "Flower large, full; color, scarlet red with tints of brown." [S] "Blood red." [LS] "Very large, handsome dark vermilion red, shaded brown." [BJ] "Like an amaranth peony." [I'H67/54] "Vigorous; branches short, furnished with stickers that are both short and hooked; leaves, dark green, often touched with yellow; flower, of medium size, full; color, crimson." [S] "Double, deep carmine, fragrant with upright growth . . . 3 × 3 [ft; ca. 9 × 9 dm]." [B] Also called a Hybrid Perpetual. "Vilmorin (Mme Elisa). — wife of Louis Lévêque de Vilmorin, née Bailly, associated with Maison Vilmorin [*French seedsmen*] from 1860 to 1866. A woman of great culture and intelligence. Produced a notable book *Les Fraisiers*." [R-HC]

MME LÉON PAIN
P. Guillot, 1904
From 'Mme Caroline Testout' (HT) × 'Souvenir de Catherine Guillot' (Ch).

"Flesh, center vermilion." [LS] "Vigorous, robust, numerous somewhat branching canes, occasional thorns, handsome purplish foliage; flower very large, quite full, very well formed, fragrant, silvery flesh white, center brightened by orange yellow, petals' reverse salmon tinted vermilion and chamois yellow; very beautiful." [JR28/154] "A good rose. Color most attractive; satisfactory in form, growth, and blooming qualities." [ARA18/112]

MME RAVARY
Pernet-Ducher, 1899

"The blossoms . . . are large, cupped, and beautiful orange-yellow; its fairly long bud is golden yellow. The growth is excellent and the blooming abundant." [JR34/69–70] "A kind of light chamois pink." [Hk] "Good vigor, well-branched, strong thorns, handsome brownish green foliage, bud conical, beautiful golden yellow; flower very large, globular, nearly full, orange yellow." [JR23/149] "Color very pretty; good growth, foliage, and bloom; bud attractive." [ARA18/112]

MME WAGRAM, COMTESSE DE TURENNE   PLATE 253
Bernaix, 1895
Please note: "Comtesse de Turenne" is not a synonym of this cultivar, but is rather, as above, part of the complete name.

"Bright satin-rose in opening, changing to carnation; extra large bud and flower. A very fine Rose; growth vigorous." [P1] "Rosy red with yellow base. . . . Full blooms . . . healthy bush . . . 4 × 3 [ft; ca. 1.25 × 1 m]." [B] "Buds very large, ovoid; flower very large, of admirable form (like 'Merveille de Lyon'), surpassing 4.5 in[ches] in diameter [ca. 1.1 dm]. Beautiful color, satiny pink and flesh-pink upon opening, with a sulphur nub to the petal, fading to intense incarnadine with deep rose reflections when the flower is open. One of the biggest Tea roses, having the form of a hybrid." [JR18/163] [*I take it to be a hybrid — BCD*] "One of the most vigorous Tea roses. The beautiful coloration of sulphur yellow tinted pink makes this flower one of the prettiest you could hope to see. It is, in my opinion, one of the best introductions of these last few years." [JR23/42] "Rather shy; might be better in a dry summer." [NRS/14] "Sometimes muddy. Fine rose in heat." [Th2] "Very vigorous, covered with superb foliage, and blooming abundantly from June until frost." [JR23/71–72]

MRS. CHARLES J. BELL
Mrs. C. J. Bell/Pierson, 1917
Sport of 'Red Radiance' (HT).

"Color light or shell-pink on a salmon-shaded background. Superior in growth to 'Radiance', being equally vigorous but more robust in habit." [ARA17/140] "Of an unusual color. . . . Very fine." [ARA24/90] "Described . . . as a constant and steady bloomer." [Th2]

MRS. HENRY MORSE
McGredy, 1919
From 'Mme Abel Chatenay' (HT) × 'Lady Pirrie' (HT, H. Dickson, 1910, apricot; parentage unknown).

"Brilliant pink shaded vermilion red." [Riv] "Bright rose, darker shadings; beautiful spiral bud, holding high center when open; good size; lasting; very free; thirty petals; fragrant. Tall but somewhat spindly growth, with good stem. Foliage mildews . . . would seem to mildew in moist heat rather than damp coolness, but would do better still in dry climates. A rose well worth test, particularly adapted to Central Zone conditions with altitude." [Th2] "We have never raised or sent out a Rose with a feeling of greater pride than we do in offering this wonderful novelty to the Rose-loving world." [NRS19/163]

MRS. HERBERT STEVENS

McGredy, 1910

From 'Frau Karl Druschki' (HP) × 'Niphetos' (T).

"White, slim, prone to weather damage." [Hk] "Grows strongly, has perfectly formed flowers, white tinged with a faint pink." [OM] "Nearly pure white, with a fawn and peach base to the petal. Habit, free and vigorous for a Tea [*mainly because it is a Hybrid Tea—BCD*], of excellent bedding type. The flowers are remarkable for their 'pointed' character, with good length of petal and excellent shape." [NRS/10] "Growth and color good; foliage inclined to mildew; fairly good bloomer." [ARA18/113] "The best bloomer in whites in my garden." [ARA24/96] "Beautiful buds of rather thin petalage, and balls slightly, although frequently of exhibition value." [Th2] "Tall, compact, hardy; foliage very plentiful, black-spots and mildews somewhat; bloom free, continuous." [ARA18/127] "Very branching growth. . . . To myself and some of my friends the foliage appears rather small and scanty, but others have referred to it as good dark foliage. It is always in flower throughout the season, and the blossoms are a nearly pure white (some notice a fawn and peach shading which I have not observed), and are a very beautiful shape, usually rather thin, and particularly elegant. . . . One of the most beautiful decorative Roses we have had for a long time . . . rather bad in respect to mildew." [NRS/13] "I prefer this to any other white, for its shapely buds, its delicately toned color, and its healthy foliage. Not a rampant grower, but a very constant bloomer." [ARA29/52] "I asked him [McGredy] if it was not from 'Niphetos'. He said, No! but it had some of that blood in it, but only indirectly. It was the result of no less than 6 different crossings with his own seedlings." [NRS22/26]

MRS. OAKLEY FISHER

B. R. Cant, 1921

"A single tinted salmon-copper." [ARA23/125] "A uniform egg-yellow. It seems to be a good keeper, and the blooms appear in masses." [ARA23/140] "A very large, single-flowering rose, somewhat after the style of 'Irish Fireflame' . . . dark red stems . . . of good form, [the blossoms are] not apt to crinkle with age . . . pale golden buff, with deeper-colored stamens." [ARA22/145] "Orange and yellow without . . . harshness. . . . Highly scented . . . 3 × 3 [ft; ca. 9 × 9 dm]." [B] "In constant flower . . . deliciously fragrant." [T3]

MRS. WAKEFIELD CHRISTIE-MILLER

McGredy, 1909

"Soft pearly blush, shaded salmon; outside of petal clear vermilion rose; loosely built with petals of good size." [Th] "Silvery pink shaded salmon; exterior light vermilion pink; flower very large, full, peony-shaped; very floriferous; very vigorous." [Cx] "Blush, shaded salmon. The flowers open out like a big tree Pæony, and are most decorative. They are produced on erect, strong growths." [OM] "The deeper colour being on the outside of the petal and the lighter shade inside, respectively clear vermilion rose and soft blush shaded salmon—a very striking combination. Habit, very vigorous, branching and with good foliage. Flowers of an enormous size, as large as any of the Hybrid Teas, quite full, and retaining their colour well in the hottest sun. A remarkable decorative Rose." [NRS/10] "28 to 57 blooms per season." [ARA21/92] "Growth, fairly good; lacks in blooming; color and form not of best." [ARA18/117] "Tall, bushy, vigorous, hardy; foliage very plentiful, black-spots very much, bloom abundant, continuous." [ARA18/127] "Does exceedingly well here [Denver, Colorado], especially in hot weather." [ARA24/95]

OLD GOLD

McGredy, 1913

"Orange red, very beautiful in the bud." [OM] "Reddish orange, semi-double. — Moderately vigorous." [JP] "Strong growth . . . a deep coppery old gold." [NRS/13] "Best in the bud. While it is orange at first, the color fades to light buff as the flower opens." [ARA34/81] "Great beauty of colour, which the raisers call reddish rouge, with rich coppery red and apricot shadings . . . a very beautiful and a striking decorative plant . . . spreading and not too tall. It has very dark coppery foliage, which appeared quite mildew proof . . . very free-flowering. It is sweetly scented and lasts well when cut." [NRS/13] "Does not last; especially fragrant. . . . Foliage good." [Th2] "Without a doubt the most beautiful decorative existing, its color never having been equaled by another rose; the color is orange-red tinted apricot-red. It is a gem for vases, as the roses last a very long time in the best condition. The foliage is a somber coppery green, making a delicious contrast. The blossom is pleasantly perfumed; this variety is continuously in bloom and grows vigorously; the roses are always borne singly at the ends of the long stems." [JR37/89]

OPHELIA

W. Paul, 1912

Seedling of 'Antoine Rivoire' (HT).

"Salmon color, with pink reflections, perfect form, well-held — upright at the end of a long stem. Excellent for forcing and the garden." [JR36/103] "Delicate touches of blush pink, a suggestion of yellow at the petal's foot . . . clean, trim shape of the petals around a simple and upright heart. . . . Its growth is free." [Hk] "Salmon-flesh shaded rose . . . with a flush of pale apricot whilst in the opening stage . . . honey scent." [RP] "Shapely buds . . . rich, flesh pink with deeper shadings. Slight lemon tints in the centre. . . . Good foliage and highly fragrant . . . 3 × 2 [ft; ca. 9 × 6 dm]." [B] "One unfurling bud on the desk fills one with awe and happiness. It is one of the most dependable bloomers and seldom has blackspot. In the early morning these creamy, pink-toned flowers with their high, deeper pink centers are lovely." [ARA31/99] "Fragrance quite marked for light-colored rose." [ARA18/114] "Brighter in autumn." [ARA26/95] "Growth good; fine foliage, stem good; perfect form, lasts well; color beautiful." [ARA16/20] "30 blooms a season." [ARA21/92] "Fragrance, fair, very delicate; shape, very good in bud and open flower." [Th] "Foliage mildews slightly and may be lost by black-spot. . . . In extreme heat, 'Ophelia' blasts in the bud." [Th2] "Blooms perfectly in our cool [Norwegian] summers." [ARA20/47] "Many admirers [in Houston, Texas]." [ET] "I cannot but feel that 'Antoine Rivoire' must have been very close to the place in the nursery from which that pod [containing the seed originating 'Ophelia'] was gathered." [ARA31/146]

PHARISÄER

Hinner, 1901

Seedling of 'Mrs. W. J. Grant' (HT).

"Pinkish yellow." [LS] "Large, full, whitish-pink with salmon-pink; fairly long-stalked, free-flowering." [Hn] "Buds long on stiff stems, of splendid texture, flower very large, rose colour shading to silver, with centre of salmon; very free." [P1] "The most perfect Rose in the garden; the blooms open in any weather; a good size, and when disbudded are very large." [NRS/14] "Opens somewhat loose but holds its center. . . . Only fair foliage, but holds in long seasons. Fine, tall, fairly bushy growth . . . continuous bloomer." [Th2] "Perfume mild . . . growth well above the average." [ARA17/22] "Low-growing, compact, hardy; foliage sufficient, black-spots somewhat; blooms free, continuous."

[ARA18/127] "A very pretty variety; its salient features are the vigor of its canes, and the abundance of its bloom." [JR32/33] "The flowers are carried erect and well above the foliage, and are sweet scented. Its strong points are the beautiful shape of its flowers and elongated buds, its good constitution and its autumnal blooming and erect habit. Its weak ones are not many, but it is too tall for an ideal bedder, and the substance of petal is rather thin." [NRS/12] "Vigorous and rather tall (4-ft. [ca. 1.25 m]) with a branching but erect habit. The young foliage is a beautiful red, getting greener with age, and it is not subject to mildew. . . . It flowers very freely and continuously from the end of June till October . . . the flower, though nicely pointed, is not very full. The colour is somewhat difficult to describe. 'Rosy white, shaded pale salmon' . . . the centre is somewhat deeper. . . . The buds are long and specially beautiful. . . . It is a very beautiful garden Rose . . . though a fair-sized (often large) Rose, it never looks heavy. . . . It has moderate fragrance. This is not perhaps everybody's Rose, but it is one of my chief favorites. . . . The shade of colouring of the flowers is very delicate and they harmonise well with the foliage." [NRS/10] "Bronzy foliage . . . 3 × 3 [ft; ca. 9 × 9 dm]." [B]

PINK RADIANCE
Listed as 'Radiance'.

RADIANCE   PLATE 270
('Pink Radiance')
J. Cook/Henderson, 1908
From 'Enchanter' (HT, J. Cook, 1904, deep pink; parentage: 'Mme Caroline Testout' [HT] × 'Mlle Alice Furon' [HT, Pernet-Ducher, 1895, yellowish-white; parentage: 'Lady Mary Fitzwilliam' (HT) × 'Mme Chédane-Guinoisseau' (T)]) × 'Cardinal' (HT).

"Light silver flesh to salmon pink . . . tends to blue slightly . . . shape, only fair . . . growth, very strong . . . splendid constitution . . . the best pink rose in cultivation today [1920]." [Th] "Carmine-rose; tall, bushy." [ARA17/31] "Brilliant rosy-carmine displaying beaiutiful opaline pink tints in the open flower." [C&Js11] "Blooms medium to large. . . . Lasts well . . . slightly subject to mildew and [black-] spot . . . average of 51 blooms per season." [ARA21/91] "A hot weather rose." [ARA24/95] "We can depend on it for blossoms at all times. While the form is not always good, nevertheless it is never so poor that it doesn't add to a bouquet . . . strong, disease-resisting plant." [ARA31/99] "Foliage very abundant, blackspots slightly; bloom free, continuous all season." [ARA18/127] "A beauty both novel and remarkable. Its foliage is luxuriant; the plant, bushy, with voluptuous foliage, freely bearing buds emerging above the plant, everblooming. . . . The blossoms have large rounded petals and long stems, are upright, and are of a brilliant carmine-lake, resembling a pretty 'Mme Abel Chatenay'; the coppery shadings and gradations of red and yellow contrast strongly. These remarkable characteristics are accompanied by a sweet fragrance and lengthy bloom . . . beautiful and productive in fall, and, up till now, healthy." [JR34/76] "Valuable because of its all-round worth and wonderful constitution. Particularly notable for fragrance, strong growth, and very good blooming qualities." [ARA18/114]

RED RADIANCE
Gude, 1915
Sport from 'Radiance', above. *Pierson Co.* also introduced its *own* 'Red Radiance' in 1916.

"Dark, rich red . . . quite fragrant; fine form; lasting about five days. . . . Growth vigorous . . . average [in one season] 45

blooms." [ARA21/91] "Red; tall, bushy." [ARA17/32] "Lighter in heat." [Th2] "Moderate height, compact, hardy; foliage very abundant, black-spots very slightly; bloom free, continuous." [ARA18/127]

RICHMOND
E. G. Hill Co., 1905
From 'Lady Battersea' (HT, G. Paul, 1901, cherry; parentage: 'Mme Abel Chatenay' [HT] × 'Liberty' [HT]) × 'Liberty' (HT). 'Général Jacqueminot' (HP) is mentioned in place of 'Liberty' in NRS/10.

"Pure red scarlet. At times varies greatly. Fragrant." [Th] "Scarlet crimson; flower large, full, fragrant; blooms continuously; very vigorous." [Cx] "Very small in heat and its form is flat; fragrant." [Th2] "Too single (many better reds)." [ARA25/105] "Continuous bloom . . . gorgeous in the spring and fall, although they fade and blue in the sun, and the midsummer blooms are not very attractive." [ARA29/70] "Brilliant color; fairly good growth; blooming qualities good on Multiflora [stock]; not dependable; varies greatly; seldom grown well." [ARA18/118] "The roses are generally solitary and . . . develop on long, firm, and erect stems. The foliage . . . is a dark green . . . the color of this variety, which is delicately perfumed, is a bright scarlet crimson." [JR28/182] "Another florist's rose, like 'Mme Abel Chatenay'." [JR37/171] "Long slim buds . . . colour burned in hot sun." [Hk] "Moderately high, compact, and hardy; foliage abundant, black-spots some; bloom moderate, continuous spring and fall, almost continuous in midsummer." [ARA18/127] "Delightful . . . more continuously produced with me than those of any other Rose in my garden . . . a most grateful and refreshing perfume." [NRS/12] "This Rose makes but moderate growth with stems rather twiggy and thin, in habit rather a poor bush, not very hardy. The foliage is nice when young and only of fair substance, but clean and little affected by mildew. The flowers are carried splendidly erect and well above the foliage in a way that is quite remarkable considering their thin stems. The flowers are produced most freely . . . the bud and half opened flowers are very beautiful, and the summer flowers come an almost perfect shape . . . bright crimson without any trace of purple. . . . It flowers so much that it seems almost to flower itself to death, and the plants are apt to dwindle away. . . . I was inclined to think it a weakly edition of 'Liberty'." [NRS/10]

SNOWBIRD
Hatton, 1936
From 'Chastity' (Cl. HT, F. Cant, 1924, white; parentage unknown) × 'Louise Cretté' (HP).

"Large, very double, fragrant; white with creamy center. Profuse, continuous bloom . . . 2–3 [ft; ca. 6–9 dm]." [Lg] "Production is incessant on a practically disease-proof plant . . . exquisite white flowers." [ARA37/250] "Bud long-pointed; flower double, high centered, very sweetly fragrant, white, creamy white center. Foliage abundant, leathery. Vigorous (2.5–3 ft. [ca. 7.5–9 dm]), compact, bushy; profuse, continuous bloomer." [ARA36/225] "Apparently a lasting addition to our very few worth-while and dependable white roses. Plants are vigorous, with intensely fragrant white flowers with a cream center." [ARA36/212] I have grown "Snowbird" for about twenty years, and, having had the opportunity to scrutinize it under all conditions afforded by my Southern Californian climate, have little but praise for it. Chubby yet graceful urn-shaped buds, ivory sometimes spattered with rose-red, open into large, flat, very fragrant blossoms with the "old" look to them, reminding me of a 'Souvenir de la Malmaison' in which the pink tints are changed to yellow—rather like 'Kronprinzessin Viktoria'. This book includes 'Snowbird' mainly because it is frequently mistaken for a Tea. It does indeed look very Tea-like, and has certain Tea characteristics: the blossoms will ball in extreme dampness; the dark green foliage is Tea-like in appearance, and is held in a characteristically stiff Tea manner; in shady conditions, the bush form does not grow tall and spindly, as do most HT's — it "climbs," as Teas frequently will; lastly, the fragrance is, to a great degree, that associated with the Teas. Unlike Teas, however, 'Snowbird' will host a certain amount of mildew and rust, both of which are fortunately easily controlled on this variety. The plant itself is as handsome and bushy a *rosier* as can be desired, producing blossoms in spurts year-round (BCD). "The most satisfactory of all white roses . . . dainty blossoms on a shapely plant . . . an indispensible white rose." [ARA39/230]

SOUVENIR DU PRÉSIDENT CARNOT   PLATE 252
Pernet-Ducher, 1894
Seedling of 'Lady Mary Fitzwilliam' (HT).

"Light pink, very delicate at the center; flesh white around the edges; flower very large, full, imbricated; bud elongated; floriferous; vigorous." [Cx] "White, vigorous . . . very free-flowering." [J] "Flesh shaded white. With us, flesh to shell pink center. . . . Fragrance, mild; shape, very good in bud and open flower . . . foliage, very good . . . tall, but not uniform." [Th] "Rosy flesh shaded with white, fine long buds on stiff and long stems, quite first-rate; growth vigorous." [P1] "Clear, bright rose colour on ivory-white ground. Large, full buds of 'Niphetos' shape. . . . Experts of the world concede this to be one of the finest roses in existence. Exquisitely lovely." [Dr] "It is a strong, healthy grower and profuse bloomer, and so wonderfully beautiful that it has already [1897] taken more medals and certificates of merit than any other rose. It is elegantly formed, very large, full and double, and deliciously sweet. Color, lovely sea-shell pink, delicately tinted with golden fawn on rich creamery white." [C&Jf97] "Large, well-filled, white, with a delicate fleshy-pink centre. Free-flowering, strong-growing, erect, with sturdy stems. Beautiful tulip-like form when expanding, becoming flatter with age." [Hn] "Clear and attractive color, good form and foliage; growth tall . . . blooming qualities fair." [ARA18/114] "Very low-growing, slender, winterkills some; foliage sufficient, black-spots in midsummer; bloom free, intermittent during warm months." [ARA18/128] "Very vigorous with lightly bronzed branches; very floriferous; bud as long as that of 'Niphetos', admirably poised on a firm and long stem; flower very large, full, with large petals throughout. . . . A magnificent variety, very floriferous and perfectly hardy, and will be much sought out for its prettily-shaped blossoms." [JR18/149] "This pretty rose, dedicated to the unfortunate president of the Republic who fell under the dagger of the miserable Caserio, was raised in 1890." [JR19/132]

VESUVIUS
McGredy, 1923

"Six petals . . . soft dark crimson flowers of good form." [ARA34/81] "Long buds, opening to beautiful single blooms of a deep velvety crimson; slightly fragrant. Moderate growth and both mildews and black-spots [*Rhode Island*]. A poor harsh shade. Strong grower but unattractive in habit and form [*California*]. A five-petal rose that is a winner. Growth, vigorous and upright . . . I am very partial to it [*California*]. Pretty, single, dark red flower, shaped like California poppies, but . . . very shy-blooming." [ARA28/193]

VISCOUNTESS FOLKESTONE   PLATE 233
Bennett, 1886

"Creamy pink, centre salmon-pink, large and sweet. Very distinct and attractive. One of the best for garden decoration and massing; growth vigorous." [P1] "Very large, full, delicate pink, centre deep salmon-pink. Strong-growing, free-flowering." [Hn] "Beautiful . . . creamy white, shaded flesh. . . . The most charming white, or nearly white, garden rose." [J] "As free-flowering a rose as I know, even till late into the Autumn . . . flowers very distinct, sweetly scented, and of quiet but taking colour, but they open quickly." [F-M2] "A good hot weather rose." [L] "Great petallage; bloom heavy, stem usually drooping. An old favorite. Very fragrant. Foliage, fair." [Th] "Of exquisite shape." [DO] "Strong but not long growth . . . much like the Chinas." [F-M2] "Good growth and color; fragrant; large flowers, generally too heavy for stems; good bloomer." [ARA18/114] "Low-growing, moderately compact, not entirely hardy; foliage plentiful, black-spots somewhat; bloom moderate, occasional." [ARA18/128] "An old favorite, still worth growing. The blooms are large, though not of good form, and the colour is cream-pink. It grows vigorously . . . liable to mildew." [OM] "Growth fairly vigorous but not tall, habit rather spreading and bushy, foliage a fair size and good, but I fear (though all do not agree) rather subject to mildew. The flowers are borne on somewhat thin stems generally drooping, but sometimes erect, and are produced freely and continuously . . . always seems to be in flower, and it is at its best in early autumn . . . large heavy-shaped blooms with petals of good substance, the colour creamy white, shaded salmon flesh. The flowers . . . open quickly, becoming loose and shapeless. They will stand some bad weather, and are quite fragrant. . . . 'Viscountess Folkestone' is a highly artistic Rose. . . . I should be very sorry to be without it." [NRS/10] "A lovely flower." [E]

W. E. LIPPIAT
A. Dickson, 1907

"Probably the best dark HT in cultivation — the colour is deep crimson shaded maroon. Rather late flowering, but particularly good in autumn . . . a good grower, free from mildew, fragrant, and the flowers are of good size and shape." [F-M] "The flowers are large, full, symmetrically formed center." [C&Js09] "Tall, bushy, hardy; foliage very plentiful, black-spots somewhat; bloom moderate and intermittent first half of season." [ARA18/128] "Very deep, velvety crimson with sweet scent. Shapely with mid green foliage . . . 3 × 3 [ft; ca. 9 × 9 dm]." [B] W. E. Lippiat, rosarian; introduced, among other varieties, the China 'Primrose Queen'.

WESTFIELD STAR
Morse, 1920
Sport of 'Ophelia' (HT).

"Dwarf; stems short; disease-resistant; very little bloom. Buds good shape but blooms open flat, lemon-yellow which soon fades to creamy white [*Ontario, Canada*]. Yellowish buds, opening to nearly perfect glistening white blooms of delightful fragrance, the same lovely shape as 'Ophelia'. Foliage large, free from disease; blooms singly on strong stems . . . the best white rose we have [*Rhode Island*]." [ARA28/194–195]

WHITE WINGS
Krebs, 1947
From 'Dainty Bess' (HT) × an unnamed seedling.

Single. "Papery white with pronounced, chocolate anthers. Foliage is leathery and dark green . . . 4 × 3 [ft; ca. 1.25 m × 9 dm]." [B]

Supplement

ABBÉ ANDRÉ REITTER
Welter, 1901
  "Delicate flesh." [LS] "Light pink, large, full, light fragrance, medium height." [Sn]

ABBÉ MILLOT
Bénard/Corbœuf-Marsault, 1899
  "Silvery pink." [LS] "Large, full, medium height." [Sn]

ADAM RACKLES
Rommel, 1905
Sport of 'Mme Caroline Testout' (HT).
  "Pink on a white ground." [LS] "Light pink, very large, full, light fragrance, moderately tall." [Sn]

ADMIRAL DEWEY
Taylor, 1899
Sport of 'Mme Caroline Testout' (HT).
  "A splendid new Constant-Blooming Rose; flowers large and beautifully formed, quite full and double, with broad, shell-shaped petals, delightfully tea-scented; color, rich creamy rose, delicately shaded with fine golden-yellow and peach blossom tints. A clean, healthy grower and abundant bloomer, very handsome." [C&Js02] "A light-coloured sport of ['Mme Caroline Testout'] from America." [F-M2] "Velvety cinnabar." [LS] "Red, large, full, medium height." [Sn] "Color a beautiful light blush pink, clear and distinct; free bloomer and very fragrant." [CA01] There is obviously long-standing confusion between a red and a blush 'Admiral Dewey'!

AMATEUR ANDRÉ FOURCAUD
Puyravaud, 1903
Seedling of 'Mme Caroline Testout' (HT).
  "Light pink, reverse darker." [Ў] "Flower handsome pink, reverse of petals very bright pink, very large, high-centered, bud very long, semi-double, fragrant, borne on a firm stem, very well branched, very floriferous, very beautiful." [JR27/149]

ANDENKEN AN MORITZ VON FRÖLICH
(trans., 'In Memory of Moritz von Frölich')
Hinner, 1905
From 'Mme Caroline Testout' (HT) × ? 'Princesse de Béarn'(HP).
  "Dark red, large, full, light scent, tall." [Sn]

ANTONINE VERDIER
Jamain, 1872
  "Flower large, full, light carmine." [S] Parent of the HT's 'Mlle Brigitte Viollet', 'Camoëns', and 'Mme Etienne Levet'.

ARCHIDUCHESSE MARIE-DOROTHÉE AMÉLIE
Listed as 'Erzherzogin Marie Dorothea'.

ARGENTINE CRAMON
Listed as 'Mlle Argentine Cramon'.

ASTRA
Geschwindt/Ketten Bros., 1890
  "Flower flesh pink, petals sometimes edged lighter, large, full, cupped, solitary. Moderate vigor, very floriferous. 'Astra' is probably 'Astrée', goddess of Justice." [JR14/146] "Light pink, large, full, tall." [Sn]

ATTRACTION
Dubreuil, 1886
  "Of good vigor, very floriferous and extra-remontant, with somber green foliage, matte above, glaucescent beneath. Inflorescence an erect corymb of 3–5 upright blossoms with strong stems. Buds ovoid. Petals numerous, concave, mucronate, imbricated in the outer rows, light carmine, nuanced China pink, with a paler edging, yellowish nub; in appearance and scent intermediate between Centifolias and Teas." [JR10/149]

AUGUSTUS HARTMANN
B. R. Cant, 1914
  "Light red, large, full, medium scent, tall." [Sn]

[AURORA]
W. Paul, 1898
  "Pretty vigorous bush with beautiful dark green foliage, and abundant bloom; flower large, full, petals ragged; very fragrant and long lasting; color, salmon towards the center, paler at the petal edges. The very long buds and beautiful form make it easy to use for making bouquets." [JR22/58]

AUSTRALIA FELIX
A. Clark, 1919
From 'Jersey Beauty' (Tea-Rambler hybrid, Manda, 1899, cream; itself from *R. wichuraiana* × 'Perle des Jardins' [T]) × 'La France' (HT).
  "Pink, medium size, moderately full, moderate fragrance, medium height." [Sn]

AUSTRALIE
Kerslake, 1907
  "Dark pink, large, full, tall." [Sn]

AVIATEUR MICHEL MAHIEU
Soupert & Notting, 1912
From 'Mme Mélanie Soupert' (HT, Pernet-Ducher, 1905, salmon; parentage unknown) × 'Lady Ashtown' (HT).
  "Coral red with a bright center. Flower large, perfect form, held upright above the ample and rich foliage. Petals thick. Splendid rose for bedding. . . . Blooms without interruption until the first frosts. Very fragrant. Of the greatest value for all purposes." [JR37/10]

AVOCA
A. Dickson, 1907

"Crimson scarlet, buds very long and pointed, flowers large and sweetly perfumed, foliage large and very dark green." [C&Js09] "A beautiful shaped flower, of medium size, only useful for the late shows, as it is produced on the ends of long shoots which take time to grow. . . . Not very free flowering. Fragrant." [H] "Very vigorous, semi-climbing; flower scarlet-red." [JR35/14] "Another crimson Rose I grow as a pillar is 'Avoca'. Grown in this way it is far more free flowering than as a cutback, and has given me some fine flowers. . . . It is somewhat difficult to keep furnished at the base as a pillar, and . . . it is hardly sufficiently decorative in the garden, and is perhaps best grown pegged down." [NRS14/64]

BARONNE G. DE NOIRMONT   PLATE 241
Cochet, 1891

"Vigorous, with upright branches; strong and reddish thorns which are remote; wood and leaves light green. Buds rounded; flowers large and full, having the form of the rose 'La France', globular, large petals, flesh pink with some salmon fading to blush white. The flowers open well, the stem is strong, the poise is good, and the shrub is very floriferous." [JR15/163]

BEATRIX, COMTESSE DE BUISSERET
Soupert & Notting, 1899
From an unnamed seedling × 'Mme Caroline Testout' (HT).

"In the way of '[Mme] Caroline Testout'; . . . lovely silver rose passing to rosy carmine red." [C&Js02] "Bush vigorous with magnificent foliage; bud of extraordinary beauty; flower very large, full, of beautiful form and well-held; outer petals large and thick, those of the middle smaller and pointed. Color, silvery pink with carmine pink. Very floriferous and fragrant. Excellent for forcing and cutting." [JR23/170]

BEAUTY OF STAPLEFORD
Bennett, 1879
From 'Mme Bravy' (T) × 'Comtesse d'Oxford' (HP).

"Foliage like that of 'Alba Rosea' [='Mme Bravy' (T)], but more rounded; flowers large; petals large and well placed. Beautiful form; color, pale pink, darker towards the center. Beautiful exhibition rose." [JR3/114] "No particular merit, having flowers of pale rose colour, with darker centre." [B&V]

BEDFORD BELLE
Laxton, 1884
From 'Gloire de Dijon' (N) × 'Souvenir du Comte de Cavour' (HP).

"Light red." [Y̆] "Flower large, very full, cupped, always opens easily; reddish white; of the 'La France' tribe; sometimes redder towards the outside. This variety, one of the most vigorous Hybrid Teas known so far, blooms from May until October. . . . Very beautiful exhibition rose." [S] "Very vigorous . . . Flower very double, well formed, opens well, marbled pink, somewhat resembles 'La France'. Abundant bloom early to late. The bluish-green foliage is very distinct." [JR8/179]

BELLE SIEBRECHT
Listed as 'Mrs. W. J. Grant'.

BERYL
Listed as a Tea.

BESSIE BROWN   PLATE 260
A. Dickson, 1900

"Creamy white; immense flowers of perfect shape and great substance; free blooming and vigorous. The flowers are impatient of wet, and they also droop." [P1] "Fine form, full, large to extra large, fine fragrance, medium long stems. Good foliage, sufficient. Growth strong; hardy. Soft ivory-white, very lightly blushed in cool weather." [ARA23/156] "Lovely peachy pink, delicately shaded with rose and fawn." [C&Js02] "For exhibition, it is quite one of the best. . . . The growth and foliage are strong, stout, and stiff; the blooms come exceedingly well, being rarely divided, and if there is any malformation it is usually of a slight nature. They are very large, sweet-scented, of perfect pointed semi-globular shape, and the fine petals open just as they should do, neither too stiffly nor too easily. The colour is a good true creamy white unstained; but it does not display the beauty of the flowers well upon the plant, for the stalk, though stout, is pliable, and the heavy blooms hang their heads. . . . I have not found it affected by mildew; and though rain will harm it as it will all white Roses, its pendant position protects the centre. It is not so good in autumn, and I fear it will be rather an exhibitor's Rose." [F-M2]

BETTY
A. Dickson, 1905

"A coppery rose overspread with golden yellow. Its flowers are extremely large, flowers all season and is deliciously perfumed." [C&Js08] "A superb novelty with marvelous coloration . . . its coppery salmon color is difficult to describe." [JR29/153] "Strong and upright growth; beautiful color; good bloomer, attractive bud." [ARA18/110] "Opens well in wet; rather thin." [NRS14/159]

BONA WEILLSCHOTT
Soupert & Notting, 1889
From 'Bon Silène' (T) × 'Marie Baumann' (HP).

"Growth vigorous, flower large, full, centifolia-form; color, vermilion pink, center orange red; fragrant." [JR13/147]

BRITISH QUEEN
McGredy, 1912

"The most beautiful white rose existing, surpassing, in perfection of form, all other white roses. . . . The floriferousness is notable; it blooms from June to winter. The blossom type is between 'Maman Cochet' [T] and 'Frau Karl Druschki' [HP] with a Tea rose form. The petals are large, and well arranged; we often note in the bud a light pink tint which disappears when the flower opens, and is transformed into immaculate white." [JR36/171] "Small growth; shy bloomer." [ARA18/115]

[CAMOËNS]   PLATE 230
Schwartz, 1881
Seedling of 'Antonine Verdier' (HT).

"Red on a yellow ground." [LS] "Extra large, full flowers; color China rose, suffused with pale yellow, passing to white, flushed with carmine; fragrant and fine." [CA90] "The flowers, in a thick cluster, are of normal size, long, beautifully colored China pink striped white; the long pedicel is very bristly; the slightly glossy leaves are somewhat bronze; the wood is of moderate strength, with strong, widely-spaced thorns." [JR5/117] "Moderate growth, very floriferous, very fragrant." [S] "Plant regular in form and very upright." [JR20/58] "One of Schwartz's best. Found in 1877, it didn't make its horticultural debut until November 1, 1881. . . . Canes delicate green with some purple . . . the blossoms are about 9 cm [ca. 4 in] across, well held, with central petals both short and long of a bright China pink which is very often striped white;

not much scent; bud long, pointed. Blooms abundantly, and in clusters. . . . Dedicated by its breeder to the author of 'The Lusiad', who died in 1579. . . . Prune to 5 or 6 eyes." [JR10/76] Luiz Vaz de Camoëns (or Camões), 1524–1580; Portuguese poet.

CAPTAIN CHRISTY PANACHÉ

Letellier, 1896

Sport of 'Captain Christy' (HT).

"Striped white and pink." [Y̆]

[CARDINAL]

Cook, 1904

From 'Liberty' (HT) × an unnamed red seedling.

"Cardinal-red; medium size, full, but opens flat and blues in heat. Stems strong. Foliage lasts." [Th2] "Excels in perfume and blooming qualities." [ARA18/110] "Growth strong." [ARA23/157] "Form fair; fragrance good and enduring. Foliage susceptible to mildew and spot. Growth bushy but not tall; average stem. Averages 48 blooms per season. Prune to 5 eyes. Hardy." [ARA21/90]

CARMEN SYLVA

Heydecker/Dubreuil, 1891

From 'Baronne Adolphe de Rothschild' (HP) × 'Mme Barthélemy Levet' (T).

"Cream and carmine." [LS] "Seems to have sprung from 'Captain Christy' [HT]. The deportment and form of the rose are those of 'Captain Christy'. The only difference is in the yellowish color of the blossom. This variety is extremely floriferous." [JR23/39]

[CHARLES J. GRAHAM]

A. Dickson, 1906

"Thoroughly remarkable HT; its enormous flowers . . . are a superb orange crimson." [JR29/153] "Vigorous, flower large, full, sparkling crimson orange." [JR22/190]

CHRISTOBEL

Croibier, 1937

From 'Frau Karl Druschki' (HP) × 'Mme Butterfly' (HT).

"Yellowish orange salmon, very large, full, tall." [Sn]

[CLARA BARTON]

Van Fleet/Conard & Jones, 1898

"A cross between the splendid 'American Beauty' [HP] Rose and the beautiful 'Clotilde Soupert' [Pol]. The color is a rare and exquisite shade of delicate amber pink, entirely different from any other rose with which we are acquainted. The flowers are quite large, three to three and one-half in[ches] in diameter [ca. 7.5–8 cm], and double to the center; they are delightfully fragrant, and each one is set in a lovely rosette of leaves, completely encircling the flower and making it an elegant bouquet in itself. It is a most constant and abundant bloomer, continuously loaded with flowers during the whole growing season. . . . It is an exquisite Rose in every way." [C&Js99]

[CLARA WATSON]

Prince, 1894

"Silvery flesh with deep pink center." [CA17] "A very pretty hybrid tea, of a slightly fawn pink which everybody likes." [JR23/42] "Fair growth and foliage; pretty color." [ARA18/118] "It has pretty pink flowers which last a long time, and when it is still a bud, it is particularly pretty. . . . It seems superior to 'Souvenir du Président Carnot'." [JR24/129] "The flowers are very graceful, resembling 'Bridesmaid' in form, and are produced in remarkable profusion. The buds are very beautiful and are supported on long stems, making it desirable for cutting. The color is salmon pink, very difficult to describe." [C&Js07]

COMMANDANT LETOURNEUX

Bahaud/Ketten Bros., 1903

Sport of 'Joséphine Marot' (HT).

"Bright, soft pink." [Y̆]

[COMTE HENRI RIGNON]   PLATE 236

Pernet-Ducher, 1888

From 'Baronne Adolphe de Rothschild' (HP) × 'Ma Capucine' (T).

"For many years, I [Mons Pernet-Ducher] have doggedly pursued creating a hybrid tea which was not only yellow but which also had all the good qualities for which one might hope. In 1882, I fertilized some blossoms of the HP 'Baronne Adolphe de Rothschild' with pollen from 'Mme Falcot' [T], from which I got several seeds, among which was the one which gave me, the following year, 'Mlle Germaine Caillot'. . . . Since then, I have crossed Teas with 'Rothschild' on a grand scale, and have gotten very curious and diverse results. From one of these crosses came, in 1885, the Hybrid Tea 'Comte Henri Rignon'." [JR12/136] "Dwarf, very hardy, strong growth, bloom abundant and constant; beautifully colored coppery yellow with a salmon pink center nuanced dawn gold, fading to salmon flesh white." [JR12/166] "Large, to very large, full, cupped, but flattish afterwards, delicate creamy-yellow, with a salmon-colored rose-red centre, unique. A magnificent rose, but owing to its short-jointed growth and very prickly stems, is not very suitable for cutting." [Hn] Joseph Pernet, born in Lyon in November of 1859, died in November of 1928; took the name "Pernet-*Ducher*" upon his marriage to Marie Ducher, daughter of the rose-breeders, in 1882; their two sons Claudius and Georges were killed early in the First World War. Mons Pernet-Ducher's "dogged pursuit" was the initial step in the creation of the *modern* Hybrid Tea. Not finding his ideal yellow Hybrid Tea by crossing Teas with Hybrid Perpetuals — results not yellow enough — he turned to crossing *R. fœtida* with Hybrid Perpetuals. We do not know how many of the crosses took, but that with the old HP 'Antoine Ducher' resulted in the Pernetiana class, also called "Lutea Hybrids," which, subsequently crossed and recrossed with the "true" or "old" Hybrid Teas, produced the initial members of our present race of Hybrid Teas.

COMTESSE ICY HARDEGG

Soupert & Notting, 1907

From 'Mrs. W. J. Grant' (HT) × 'Liberty' (HT).

"Shining pure carmine, always constant. . . . The blossoms are larger and fuller than are those of 'Belle Siebrecht' [i.e., 'Mrs. W. J. Grant'], with larger petals of better consistency; the perfect bud is longer than that of its mother." [JR31/137]

[CORONET]
Dingee & Conard, 1897
From 'Paul Neyron' (HP) × 'Bon Silène' (T).

"The flowers are very large, full and round; the color is clear pink, petals beautifully edged with reddish violet; they have a delicious tea fragrance, and are produced in great profusion." [C&Js99] "Like a continuous-blooming 'Paul Neyron'. The blossom is as large as that of 'Paul Neyron', but the bloom is much more abundant. The perfume is as delicious as that of the Damask, and the flower as beautiful as that of a Peony. The breeders kept it under study for four years, and have scrutinized its various characteristics. . . . The plant begins to bloom early, and all season produces long, large, beautiful, and quite full flowers. The bud is deep carmine and the expanded blossom is carnation pink with a silvery tone. The bush has the form and 'cut' of that of 'Paul Neyron', and takes the same culture as 'Bon Silène'. Very pretty plant." [JR21/68]

DANMARK   PLATE 238
Zeiner-Lassen & Dithmer, 1890
Sport of 'La France' (HT); or from 'La France' × either 'Safrano' (T) or 'Isabella Sprunt' (T).

"Pink, large, full, very fragrant, medium height." [Sn] "Not so good [as 'La France'] in growth and very apt to ball." [F-M2] "Large, cupped, silvery rose-red, like 'La France', but darker outside. Flowers erect, and not so drooping as in 'La France'. Free, vigorous, bushy." [Hn]

DIRECTEUR CONSTANT BERNARD
Soupert & Notting, 1886
From 'Abel Grand' (HP) × 'Mlle Adèle Jougant' (T).

"Vigorous, floriferous, flower large, very full, well imbricated; color, very delicate magenta pink on a silvery ground; edge of outer petals often light violet; very fragrant." [JR10/148]

[DISTINCTION]
Bennett, 1882
Two parentages given: (1) 'Mme de St.-Joseph' (T) × 'Eugène Verdier' (HP); or, (2)'Mabel Morrison' (HP) × 'Devoniensis' (T).

"Growth very vigorous; flower not very full but well formed; color tinted with peach, difficult to describe; opens easily; magnificent exhibition rose; cupped; Centifolia scent." [S] "Flowers of shaded peach. No particular merit." [B&V]

DR. CAZENEUVE
Dubreuil, 1899

"Extra large flowers of beautiful form and texture, color rich dark velvety crimson, somewhat resembling 'Jean Liabaud'; almost black, and one of the finest dark hybrid tea roses yet produced. Very beautiful." [C&Js02] "Bush with dark brilliant foliage; branches with true vigor, blooming all year. Blossom of the color and form of that of 'Géant des Batailles' [HP]; bud purple, so deep when opening that it seems black. The open rose bears comparison to the splendid HP's 'Jean Liabaud', 'Louis Van Houtte', and 'Charles Lefebvre', as far as color goes, by the intensity and depth of its velvety crimson. This will be one of the best deep-colored HT's." [JR23/167–168]

[DR. PASTEUR]
Moreau-Robert, 1887

"A strong, vigorous-growing variety, with very dark, rich foliage; flowers finely formed, globular, but becoming reflexed when over half open; color, a very pleasing soft rosy crimson with satiny shading." [CA93] "Vigorous bush; magnificent dark green foliage; flower large, full, opening well, bud very long, form globular, beautiful intense carminy pink nuanced currant red, extremely floriferous." [JR11/150]

DR. SCHNITZLER
Listed as 'Emin Pascha'.

DUCHESS OF CONNAUGHT
Bennett, 1879
From 'Adam' (T) × 'Duchesse de Vallombrosa' (HP).

"Large, cupped, silvery-pink; free-flowering; fragrant, similar to 'La France'." [Hn] "At first glance, might readily be mistaken for 'La France', having much the same shade of color, but the flowers are somewhat smaller and of rounder form; it is the only variety which resembles 'La France' in perfume." [EL] "Foliage and flowers very distinct, well-formed, delicate silvery-pink, center salmon, very fragrant, a charming rose." [JR3/114] "Foliage larger and better [than that of 'La France'] . . . petals recurving to a less extent." [EL]

DUCHESS OF WESTMINSTER
Bennett, 1879
From 'Adam' (T) × 'Marquise de Castellane' (HP).

"Flowers quite large without seeming 'gross'; well formed; bright cerise." [JR3/114] "Growth and foliage above average; color and form good; variably hardy; shy in blooming." [ARA18/110]

DUKE OF CONNAUGHT
Bennett, 1879
From 'Adam' (T) × 'Louis Van Houtte' (HP).
Not to be confused with G. Paul's HP.

"Rosy-crimson, large, full, well formed, good in bud, almost without fragrance; the buds do not always open. A fine rose when well grown, but it will never be useful for ordinary cultivators." [EL] "Beautiful foliage, flowers very large, of very beautiful form, dark velvety crimson bordered brilliant red." [JR3/114] "A free autumnal bloomer; rather small; very hardy." [H] "Buds large and of good form . . . dwarf in growth." [S] "Its foliage is that of the Tea, it has an elongated bud as in that class . . . bloom is . . . continuous." [JR3/171] "Almost without fragrance." [CA88]

EDMÉE ET ROGER
Ketten Bros., 1902
From 'Safrano' (T) × 'Mme Caroline Testout' (HT).

"Flesh white, center salmon flesh pink, darker ground, large or very large, long bud, opens well, stem long and firm. Vigorous, floriferous. . . . Dedicated to Dr. Dumas of Faverny and his wife." [JR26/163]

EMIN PASCHA
('Dr. Schnitzler')
Drögemüller, 1894
From 'Gloire de Dijon' (N) × 'Louis Van Houtte' (HP).

"Deep pink, large, full, tall." [Sn] "A very bold and handsome rose borne well up on strong stiff stems, the flowers are extra large and massive, with broad thick petals — very double full and sweet and a profuse bloomer. Color, deep carmine, rose shaded crimson." [C&Js98]

ERINNERUNG AN SCHLOSS SCHARFENSTEIN
Geschwindt, 1892

"Purplish red, large, full, very fragrant, medium height." [Sn]

ERZHERZOGIN MARIE DOROTHEA

('Archiduchesse Marie-Dorothée Amelié')
Balogh, 1892
From 'Mme Falcot' (T) × 'Général Jacqueminot' (HP).

"Yellowish rose-red, large, very full, very fragrant, tall." [Sn] "Very vigorous. Its blossoms are a yellowish pink which is most agreeable to the eye. They are only barely full, but the plant is so floriferous that this alone makes it valuable." [JR23/39]

EXQUISITE

W. Paul, 1899

"Very bright crimson shaded magenta, large, full, globular; the buds are large and long; the expanded blossom is very open and quite regular; this variety blooms continuously and profusely. . . . Its fragrance is that of 'La France' . . . very vigorous." [JR23/81]

FERDINAND BATEL

Pernet-Ducher, 1896

"Variable from rosy flesh on a yellow ground to nankeen orange; remarkable for the contrasts of its colour." [P1] "Vigorous, well-branched; foliage somber green; flower fairly full, oval; bi-colored, varying from very delicate flesh to a ground of orange nankeen yellow . . . blooms abundantly." [JR20/164]

FERDINAND JAMIN

Pernet-Ducher, 1896

"Growth very vigorous; canes branching; foliage bronzy green; flower large, full, globular; color, carmine pink nuanced salmon. The coloration of this variety much resembles that of 'Mme Abel Chatenay' [HT], except the flowers are larger and fuller, and will be much appreciated for cutting purposes." [JR20/164]

FRAU J. REITER

Welter, 1904
From 'Mlle Augustine Guinoisseau' (HT) × an unnamed seedling which was the result of a cross between 'Viscountess Folkestone' (HT) and 'Kaiserin Auguste Viktoria' (HT).

"Pure white, or slightly coppery." [Y̆] "Flower very large, very full, cupped, very delicate flesh pink, or pure white." [JR31/178]

GARDENIA   PLATE 256

Soupert & Notting, 1898
From 'Comtesse Dusy' (T) × 'Mlle Hélène Cambier' (HT).

"Vigorous, handsome foliage, long pure white bud sometimes tinted virginal blush; flower large, full, imbricated like a camellia; color, gardenia white. . . . Very floriferous and fragrant." [JR22/148]

GENERAL-SUPERIOR ARNOLD JANSSEN   PLATE 274

Leenders, 1912
From 'Farbenkönigen' (HT, Hinner, 1902, red; parentage, 'Grand-Duc Adolphe de Luxembourg' [HT] × 'La France' [HT]) × 'General MacArthur' (HT).

"Fiery red." [Y̆] "Excellent in color and lasting qualities; nice growth; fairly good bloomer." [ARA18/110] "Particularly intense deep carmine . . . large, full, and very fragrant flowers. The perfectly formed buds are very distinctive. The plant is vigorous, compact, and continuous." [JR36/74]

GERTRUDE

A. Dickson, 1903
Sport of 'Countess of Caledon' (HT, A. Dickson, 1897, pale pink with darker center).

"Flesh pink." [Y̆]

GLADYS HARKNESS

A. Dickson, 1901

"Deep salmon pink, silvery pink reflections; cupped." [JR30/16] "Very large, good constitution and fragrant. A fine Rose." [P1] "Inclining to the H.P. side of the class, this variety is sturdy and hardy in growth and foliage, and the pink blooms, though not of the most refined shape, are large, with fine petals, sweet-scented, and good in the autumn." [F-M] "Growth very erect and vigorous; large and beautifully formed buds and flowers, resembling the famous 'American Beauty' in size and fullness; color, bright rich salmon pink; very fragrant and first-class in every way." [C&Js02]

GRAND-DUC ADOLPHE DE LUXEMBOURG   PLATE 242

Soupert & Notting, 1891
From 'Triomphe de la Terre des Roses' (HP, Guillot père, 1864, lilac-pink; parentage unknown) × 'Mme Loeben de Sels' (HP).

"Vigorous, floriferous, giving well-formed buds. . . . The flower is very large, nearly full, with large petals, light brick pink within, bright geranium lake without." [JR23/154]

[GROSSHERZOG ERNST LUDWIG VON HESSE]

('Red Maréchal Niel')
Müller/Lambert, 1898
From 'Pierre Notting' (HP) × 'Maréchal Niel' (N); Jg replaces 'Notting' with 'Général Jacqueminot' (HP).

"Bright pink." [LS] "Bright rosy red." [CA11] "Flower very large, well formed, quite full, flower and bud like those of 'Maréchal Niel', and held similarly [i.e., nodding]. Color, carmine red, very fragrant; very floriferous on last season's canes; foliage ample, glossy. Very vigorous bush, nearly climbing." [JR22/20] "Though climbing, [it] is not as vigorous as 'Maréchal Niel'. . . . It is, what is more, not very abundant, and doesn't rebloom. . . . *Further*, we have noted that this rose is very susceptible to mildew. . . . It's a fraud that this novelty is described in rosarian's catalogs as 'Red Maréchal Niel'! . . . we have found on the flowers we have seen *not one trace* of what might *properly* be called Red . . . they are simply a more or less bright pink which one could compare to the coloration of common pink China [i.e., 'Parsons' Pink'], or 'Hermosa'." [JR25/84]

[GROSSHERZOGIN VIKTORIA MELITTA VON HESSEN]

('Grand Duchess Victoria Melita')
Lambert, 1897
From 'Safrano' (T) × 'Mme Caroline Testout' (HT).

"Very vigorous plant, one of the most floriferous, freely remontant. The wood is reddish brown and the leaves are large. The flower is very large, quite full, of a nearly closed form, usually solitary on the stem, and drying there without shedding its petals. The buds are long and open easily; the color is cream with a yellow center, resembling 'K.A. Viktoria' somewhat, though being more vigorous. The plant is bushy and takes to all sorts of fantastical pruning. The perfume is sweet but penetrating. Dedicated to her highness the Grand Duchess of Hesse." [JR21/50–51]

GRUSS AN AACHEN SUPERIOR

Leenders, 1942
Presumably a "superior" sport of 'Gruss an Aachen' (HT).

"Blush white, large, full, moderate height." [Sn]

GRUSS AN PALLIEN

Listed as an HP.

GUSTAVE REGIS   PLATE 239
Pernet-Ducher, 1890
Possibly a seedling of 'Mlle Blanche Durrschmidt' (T).

"Pale yellow." [Y̆] "Large, semi-double, canary yellow with saffron-yellow centre; erect growing, free-flowering." [Hn] "Distinct and beautiful in bud." [H] "A very vigorous Hybrid Tea pillar with semi-double, nankeen-yellow flowers." [GAS] "Tall growth; very good bloomer. Useful mainly as a decorative rose." [ARA18/111] "Another strong growing garden Rose which should not be closely pruned. The blooms are quite thin, and fall abroad as soon as expanded, though even then the clean petals give the idea of a Rose of good quality. It is in the very early bud stage that this Rose is at its best, for the shape is long and pointed, and the three colours, red, yellow, and white, are present together in a more charming combination than I am aware of in any other Rose." [F-M2] "The best and most vigorous of the yellow garden Roses." [J]

HENRI BRICHARD
Bonnaire, 1890

"Bush of great vigor, with upright canes; beautiful large leaves, bronzy somber green; flower large, very full, on a very strong stem; color, pure white outside; within, very bright carmine red shaded salmon pink; abundant, continuous bloom; distinct among HT's." [JR14/146] "A splendid grower, producing quantities of buds which are large and quite double; nearly white, shading into a bright rosy carmine center." [CA96]

HIS MAJESTY   PLATE 272
McGredy, 1909

"Large growth without being 'climbing'; the quite upright blossoms are large, of good substance . . . beautiful deep crimson shaded blackish vermilion. One might call it the 'Red Frau Karl Druschki' due to its resemblance to that variety in form and growth. . . . Wafts the most elegant fragrance." [JR33/10]

HOFGARTENDIREKTOR GRAEBENER
Lambert/Ketten Bros., 1899
From 'Mme Caroline Testout' (HT) × 'Antoinette Durieu' (T).

"Graebener, director of the court gardens. . . . Blossom pinkish yellow or coppery orange yellow, medium sized, full, opens well. Vigorous, erect, abundant bloom." [JR23/171]

[HON. GEORGE BANCROFT]
From 'Mme de St.-Joseph' (T) × 'Lord Macaulay' (HP).
Bennett, 1880

"Red, shaded with violet crimson; large, full flowers, and good pointed buds." [CA88] "Large flower the same form as that of 'Lord Macaulay'; color, beautiful crimson pink shaded purple; very beautiful; semi-globular; very fragrant; medium growth; very good rose to force." [S] "[Flowers] fade very quickly . . . if grown so that the original color is retained, [it] will generally give satisfaction, though many more malformed blooms are produced than we expect to see in a variety put down as desirable." [EL]

IRISH BRIGHTNESS
A. Dickson, 1904

"Light orange red, medium size, single, moderate height." [Sn]

IRISH GLORY
A. Dickson, 1900

"Light pink, large, single, moderate scent, tall." [Sn]

IRISH MODESTY
A. Dickson, 1900

"Light orange pink, large, single, tall." [Sn]

JEAN LORTHOIS
Widow Ducher, 1879
Seedling of 'Gloire de Dijon' (N).

"Splendid large flowers, very full and double, and exceedingly sweet; color, bright glossy pink, deepening at center to intense carmine; reverse of petals silver rose." [CA90] "Growth very vigorous with short, upright canes; thorns occasional, upright, and brown; beautiful dark green foliage composed of 5 leaflets; flower large, full, very well formed; color, China pink, darker at the center, passing to lilac; reverse of petals whitish; very beutiful plant." [JR3/164]

JEAN MURAOUR
Vogel, 1935
Sport of 'Gruss an Aachen' (HT).

"White, large, full, medium height." [Sn]

[JOHANNES WESSELHÖFT]
Welter & Hinner/Ketten Bros., 1899
From the cross of a seedling of 'K.A. Viktoria' (HT) and 'William Francis Bennett' (HT) with 'Comtesse de Frigneuse' (T).

"Flower sulphur yellow passing to light yellow, large, full, very fragrant; long bud; long stem. Bush vigorous, branching . . . Dedicated to a rosarian from Langensalza." [JR23/171] "A strong growing, free blooming Hybrid Tea Rose, valuable for garden planting, as it is quite hardy and a great bloomer; soft pale sulphur yellow, passing to ivory-white; bears beautiful buds and fine handsome flowers in great profusion." [C&Js09]

JONKHEER J.L. MOCK   PLATE 273
Leenders, 1909
From an unnamed seedling (parentage: 'Mme Caroline Testout' [HT] × 'Mme Abel Chatenay' [HT]) × 'Farbenkönigen' (HT, Hinner, 1902, red; parentage: 'Grand-Duc Alexis de Luxembourg' [HT] × 'La France' [HT]).

"Mixture of ochre and light red." [Y̆] "Large to extra large, full, fine form, tea fragrance, medium to long stem. Foliage good, sufficient. Growth vigorous, hardy. Inside of petals silvery pink, outside bright cherry-rose — very thick and leathery." [ARA23/164] "Distinct; notable for color, size, stem, and lasting qualities; tall growth, lacking in bushiness; fairly good bloomer." [ARA18/111] "In growth resembles 'Mme Caroline Testout' to some degree. Its blossoms are borne on upright and rigid stems, and are held well above the foliage; they are large, full, very fragrant, pink and light red with dawn-gold reflections, resembling 'Farbenkönigen' (HT) a little. The long bud opens well, and the form of the blossom much resembles that of 'La France'. Dedicated to Mons J.L. Mock, president of the Dutch rosarian's society." [JR33/102]

JOSÉPHINE MAROT   PLATE 249
Bonnaire, 1894

"Very vigorous bush with erect canes; somber green foliage; flower large, full, beautiful muslin white; bud lightly washed pink." [JR18/131]

JULES TOUSSAINT
Bonnaire, 1899

"Brownish red, base of petals citron yellow, and reverse of petals slightly silvery; growth vigorous." [P1] "Very vigorous, foliage . . . somber glossy green. Flower very large, quite full, always opening well . . . notable variety." [JR23/168]

JULIUS FINGER   PLATE 229
Lacharme, 1879
From 'Victor Verdier' (HP) × 'Mlle de Sombreuil' (Cl. T).
Not to be confused with the "red" Tea 'Jules Finger', nor with the creamy white HT 'Mme Jules Finger' by Pierre Guillot.

"Salmon pink, in the style of 'Captain Christy' [HT]; a promising sort." [EL] " 'Captain Christy' perfected." [S] "Very vigorous, flower stem long, flowers large, full, form and poise the most perfect; color, pure white, center pink, towards the end of bloom, the pink predominates." [JR3/164] "[Julius Finger] died December 19, 1894, at Millstatt, Austria [now in Czechoslovakia]. Despite his high duties with the Imperial Court [of Austria], he was much occupied with roses." [JR19/18]

[KAISERIN GOLDIFOLIA]
Conard & Jones, 1909
A sport of 'Kaiserin Auguste Viktoria' (HT).

"The flower of this variety is identical with [that of] 'Kaiserin Auguste Viktoria' but the distinction between the two Roses is the bright, golden yellow foliage of 'Kaiserin Goldifolia'. It is a decided novelty, beautifully attractive in leaf and flower." [C&Js09]

KATHLEEN
A. Dickson, 1895
Not to be confused with W. Paul's single, cluster-flowered, pale pink Multiflora-Sempervirens hybrid 'Kathleen' of 1908, nor with Pemberton's Hybrid Musk 'Kathleen' of 1922, which has single white flowers.

"Coral pink." [Y̆] Single.

KILLARNEY
A. Dickson, 1899
From 'Mrs. W. J. Grant' (HT) × 'Charles J. Graham' (HT).

"Flesh colour shaded with white and suffused with pale pink. A showy flower with large petals and fine long buds; growth vigorous. A splendid Rose." [P1] "Large, good to fine form, semi-double, quite fragrant, medium to long stem. Sufficient foliage, slight [black-] spot and mildew. Growth poor; hardy. Clear bright pink." [ARA23/164] "Several marked faults. Growth and blooming qualities good; color beautiful; attractive in bud form but not in open flower; foliage mildews." [ARA18/111] "A fairly good grower, flowering freely in summer and autumn. The blooms are very large, of quite first-class pointed shape, and the colour a lovely shade of pale pink. The petals are long and stout, but there are not enough of them, the centre being badly filled." [F-M2]

KILLARNEY BRILLIANT
A. Dickson, 1914
Sport of 'Killarney' (HT).

"Large to very large, double, good to fine form, very fragrant, medium to long stem. Fine foliage, sufficient. Growth strong; hardy. Clear rosy crimson." [ARA23/164] "Fair, having the faults of [its] parent, but not so good growers or bloomers." [ARA18/111]

[L'INNOCENCE]
Pernet-Ducher, 1897
From a cross between an unnamed seedling and 'Mme Caroline Testout' (HT).

"Very vigorous well-branched bush, thorns small and occasional, foliage bronze green; flower large, full, globular; color, sparkling white. The blossoms are nicely double without being full, and [thus] are light [enough to be] well-held on their erect stems." [JR21/146] "Most lovely buds and flowers of beautiful form and delightful fragrance." [C&Js01]

LA TOSCA
Schwartz, 1900
From 'Joséphine Marot' (HT, Bonnaire, 1895, blush; parentage unknown) × 'Luciole' (T).

"Soft pink tinted with rosy white and yellow, large and full; very free flowering." [P1] "Medium to medium-large, double, good to fine form, very fragrant, medium to long stems. Fine foliage, sufficient, slight [black-] spot. Growth very vigorous, tall, bushy; hardy. Silvery pink with deeper center." [ARA23/165] "Vigorous, growth well disposed, branched tinted purple, terminating in a solitary blossom which is large, well formed, borne on a strong stem, beautiful delicate pink nuanced blush white, nubs yellowish." [JR24/163] "Splendid for garden decoraton. Noteworthy in growth, blooming, and hardiness; color good; bud fair in shape, but opens loose." [ARA18/112]

LADY ASHTOWN
A. Dickson, 1904
Seedling of 'Mrs. W. J. Grant' (HT).

"Flower very large, full, well held, pale pink shaded yellow with silvery reflections." [JR31/178] "Medium large, fine form, double, faint fragrance, medium stem. Fine foliage, sufficient. Growth medium strong; hardy. Light rose with silvery reflex, bases light yellow." [ARA23/165] "Distinct and attrtactive in color and form; good growth and foliage; blooming qualities fairly good." [ARA18/111]

[LADY CLANMORRIS]
A. Dickson, 1900

"Distinct and different from all others; flowers very large and graceful, petals large and of excellent substance, color rich creamy-white with pale rose centre, edge of petals beautifully bordered with deep rose; altogether a rose of unusual excellence." [C&Js02]

[LADY HENRY GROSVENOR]   PLATE 246
Bennett, 1892

"Pale pink." [LS] "Flowers flesh color; large, full, and globular; an exceedingly free and effective variety; also a fine young forcing rose." [CA96]

LINA SCHMIDT-MICHEL
Lambert, 1905
From 'Mme Abel Chatenay' (HT) × 'Kleiner Alfred' (Pol).

"A novelty dedicated to the artist whose watercolors . . . have appeared these last several years in the *Journal des Roses*. It is a vigorous rose . . . it grows to six to ten ft in height [ca. 1.75–3 m], and blooms profusely in season. Its flowers are semi-double, bright pink nuanced carmine, staying fresh and open a long time." [JR29/179] The floribunda-formula parentage is perhaps worth noting.

MA TULIPE
Bonnaire, 1899

"Extremely vigorous, though without being 'climbing'; blossom semi-full, with large, very firm petals, beautiful dark crimson red. This variety, noticeable because of its long buds which resemble tulips, will serve well for cutting." [JR23/168]

MADELEINE GAILLARD

Bernaix fils, 1908

"Fresh pink." [Ў] "Vigorous, well held, quite special blooming qualities, flower large, beautifully formed, cupped, thick concave petals, beautiful pure white slightly nuanced pale cream. Beautiful and floriferous." [JR32/135]

[MAGNAFRANO]

Van Fleet/Conard & Jones, 1900

From 'Magna Charta' (HP) × 'Safrano' (T).

"It combines the hardiness and vigor of the 'Magna Charta' with the free-blooming habit and delightful fragrance of the Tea Roses. The flowers are extra large, frequently four to five in across [ca. 1–1.25 dm]; very regular, full and double, and deliciously sweet. The color is deep, bright, shining rose, very rich and handsome. The bush is a strong, upright grower and a constant and most abundant bloomer." [C&Js02] "Low-growing, compact, reasonably hardy; foliage plentiful, healthy; bloom moderate, intermittent." [ARA18/126]

MAMIE

('Mrs. Conway Jones')

A. Dickson, 1902

"Rosy carmine, with yellow base. Beautiful shape; growth vigorous." [P1] "Vigorous, well-spaced branches, very floriferous. It blooms early and continuously. The blossoms are fragrant, beautifully colored carmine pink with a splotch of yellow very evident at the base of the petals, which are large, smooth, and very sturdy. The blossom lasts a long time." [JR25/100] "A well-formed flower of good pointed shape, but rather undecided in colour." [F-M2] "Of strong healthy growth with good foliage. The buds are large and open slowly into very full flowers having fine petals and globular shape with high centre. A fine Rose for exhibition." [F-M]

MARIE GIRARD

Buatois, 1898

"Vigorous and bushy; leaves large, beautiful dark green; flowers very large, with large petals, cupped; full; color, flesh white nuanced yellowish salmon; fragrant. Strong stem, good for cutting." [JR22/164]

MARIE ZAHN

Müller/Lambert, 1897

From a cross of two unnamed seedlings: Seedling A (from a seedling of 'Reine des Île-Bourbons' [B] × 'Maréchal Niel' [N]) × Seedling B (from 'Pierre Notting' [HP] × 'Safrano' [T]).

"Light pink, yellow at the center, large, full, medium height." [Sn] "Hybrid of Tea and Bourbon. . . . The bush is of vigorous growth, with thick foliage, light green in color. The flower is large, full, cupped; the buds are long and pointed. The color is silvery pink shaded carmine on a yellowish ground; very floriferous and hardy." [JR21/68]

MARJORIE

A. Dickson, 1895

"White with a pink center. Magnificent." [JR19/67] "White, suffused with salmon-pink; of medium size and exquisite form; growth robust." [P1] "Very free-flowering." [H] "Growth and blooming fair; flower not distinctive." [ARA18/117]

MARQUISE DE SALISBURY

Pernet père, 1891

"Bright velvety pink." [Ў] "Bright crimson. A semi-double bedding Rose." [H] "Brilliant velvety red, almost full, buds long . . . growth vigorous." [P1] "Strong and upright branches, protrusive and numerous thorns, foliage very thick and noticeable, handsome dark green, edge reddish; flowers medium or large, nearly full, beautiful very velvety red, long **T**-shaped bud, continuously and abundantly blooming." [JR14/164]

MARQUISE LITTA DE BRETEUIL PLATE 247

Pernet-Ducher, 1893

"A splendid carmine-rose colour, and very large blooms. It grows on a strong upright stalk, and is proud of its beauty. Every one asks its name, as a matter of course, on entering the rosary. Mine grows in the shade, and is apt to lose its leaves in the autumn." [HmC] "Elegantly formed large full flowers with broad thick petals of good substance, delightfully sweet-scented." [C&Js05] "Growth very vigorous, handsome foliage, flower very large, to five in [ca. 1.25 dm], very full, cupped, carmine pink, center vermilion red." [JR17/165] "This very soon became a well-known and popular variety, as being practically the only dark-red Show Rose among the H.T.s. It is of stout stiff thorny growth, with foliage and general appearance of a H.P. character; and the flowers are very dsitinct, there being something characteristic in the arrangement of the inner petals which is often very regular and pleasing. They are large, very bright and fairly lasting. Free-flowering, and a good autumnal even in hot climates, it is a Rose to be much recommended as a short Standard for any purposes or situation." [F-M2]

MAVOURNEEN

A. Dickson, 1895

Sport from 'Killarney' (HT).

"Pale pink. A strong grower." [P1] "Silvery flesh. Unrivalled." [JR19/67]

[MICHAEL SAUNDERS]

Bennett, 1879

From 'Adam' (T) × 'Victor Verdier' (HP).

"A superb rose; flowers extra large, finely formed, very double and full; petals of good substance and beautifully reflexed; color deep rich crimson; very brilliant." [CA93] "It is large, of good form, of a curious pink color, with a very distinct Tea fragrance." [JR3/171] "Quite full. . . . Growth moderate." [S]

MILDRED GRANT

A. Dickson, 1901

From 'Niphetos' (T) × 'Mme Mélanie Willermoz' (T).

"Blush white, large, full, medium height." [Sn] "The flowers . . . grow up to 12–15 cm across [ca. 6 in]. . . . The roses are a silvery white tinted crimson pink towards the center, and deliciously perfumed. It is very floriferous. . . . This variety is dedicated to a charming Miss, the daughter of one of the principal English rosarians." [JR27/20] "The blossoms are quite large, have a high center, and keep a long time. The petals, which are very long, are very well formed, and, what is more, are enormous. The bush is vigorous, with the branches well placed and separate, each crowned by a flower, which is borne on an absolutely upright and very strong stem. The wood and foliage are very attractive, the latter being light green." [JR25/100] "Small growth; attractive blooms." [ARA18/113] "It appears to be the largest Rose of good pointed shape yet issued . . . Very fine indeed in form, petal and substance, but unfortunately undecided and whitish in colour." [F-M2]

MINNA
Kordes, 1930
Sport of 'Gruss an Aachen' (HT).

"Pink, medium size, very full, light scent, dwarf." [Sn] "Bloom not so full [as that of 'Gruss an Aachen']. Bud medium size, ovoid, deeper in color than the flower; flower large, double, full, high-centered, very lasting, slightly fragrant, fine rosy pink, borne in cluster on medium-length, strong stem. Foliage sufficient, medium size, rich green, leathery, disease-resistant. Growth moderate, bushy, dwarf; profuse, intermittent bloomer all season. Tips freeze." [ARA31/243]

[MLLE ALICE FURON]
Pernet-Ducher, 1895
From 'Lady Mary Fitzwilliam' (HT) × 'Mme Chédane-Guinoisseau' (T).

"Vigorous, with strong and upright branches, foliage ample, somber green; flower large, globular, full, yellowish white, resembling 'Gloire Lyonnaise'. Very floriferous, and has the deportment of 'Lady Mary Fitzwilliant', being however more vigorous." [JR19/149] A parent of 'Billard et Barré' (Cl. T).

MLLE ARGENTINE CRAMON
('Argentine Cramon', 'Mlle Argentine Gramon')
Chambard, 1915

"A very double white Rose carried on rigid stems." [NRS18/155] "White, very large, full, medium height." [Sn] "Fair growth; color clear and attractive." [ARA18/118]

MLLE BRIGITTE VIOLLET
Levet, 1878
Seedling of 'Antonine Verdier' (HT).

"Silvery-rose, slightly tinged with violet; not highly scented, but quite a pleasing sort." [EL] "Vigorous, flower large, full, well-formed, blooms in clusters; color, bright pink with some violet, petals edged salmon; a plant of the first order." [JR2/165–166]

[MLLE GERMAINE CAILLOT]   PLATE 235
Pernet-Ducher, 1887
From 'Baronne Adolphe de Rothschild' (HP) × 'Mme Falcot' (T).

"The shrub is vigorous, with strong and upright canes; foliage, beautiful dark green; thorns, remote, nearly straight; flower stalk strong; long bud; flower very large, quite full, very well formed; color, salmon flesh pink, brighter at the center, creamy white at the edge of the petals; the open flower has recurving petals. The plant blooms abundantly, and the blossoms are solitary." [JR11/99] "Vigorous, dwarf . . . flower very large (12 to 14 cm across [ca. 5 in])." [JR11/164] See also 'Comte Henri Rignon' (HT).

MLLE HÉLÈNE CAMBIER
(' — Gambier')
Pernet-Ducher, 1895

"Very pretty and desirable, makes a neat handsome bush, bears abundantly, large, very double Roses. Color, lovely canary yellow, with deep peachy red centre, becoming lighter as the flowers open. Very sweet and handsome." [C&Js99] "Very vigorous, bushy, erect, beautiful bronzy green foliage; flower medium-sized or large, very full, color varying from salmon flesh-pink to coppery pink, often having a beautiful dawn gold tint which fades at full expansion of the blossom. Very abundant bloom." [JR19/149]

[MME A. SCHWALLER]
Bernaix, 1886

"The flowers are large and globular and of excellent substance. Color fine, soft coral pink, delicately edged with violet rose and richly perfumed. A strong healthy grower and constant bloomer, fine in every way." [C&Js02] "Thick, bushy plant with non-climbing canes; flower large, full, very well formed; color uniformly incarnate pink to the base of the petals, and fading towards the tip. Plant extremely floriferous." [JR10/172]

[MME ADOLPHE LOISEAU]
Buatois, 1897
From 'Merveille de Lyon' (HP) × 'Kaiserin Auguste Viktoria' (HT).

"Elegantly formed and deliciously sweet; color, fine rosy flesh, passing to rich creamy white, delicately tinged with blush." [C&Js99] "Vigorous bush with thornless smooth wood; foliage shining yellowish green; flower very full, sometimes as large as that of 'Paul Neyron'." [JR21/148]

MME ALFRED SABATIER
Bernaix fils, 1904

"Sturdy handsome dark green foliage, plant of good vigor. Bud of pretty form, blossom fairly large, with thick petals, wavy, gracefully intermingled at the center and delicately pleated towards the outside, bright satiny peach red, fading when open." [JR28/155]

[MME ANDRÉ DURON]
Bonnaire, 1887

"Clear red." [CA97] "Growth very vigorous, with strong, upright canes; beautiful foliage; flower very large, sometimes attaining the size of 'Paul Neyron'; beautiful fresh light red; continuous bloom; very good for cutting." [JR11/149]

MME ANGÈLE FAVRE
Perny, 1888
"Pink and salmon." [Ÿ]

MME ANGELIQUE VEYSSET
('Striped La France')
Veysset, 1890
Sport of 'La France' (HT).

"Pink, striped and plumed bright red; more floriferous than 'La France'." [JR14/149] "Distinctly striped with pearl-white and satin rose; a most pleasing combination." [C&Js99] "A magnificent new rose, identical in every respect with its parent 'La France', except it is much stronger in growth, and the flowers are beautifully striped and shaded with a delicate white. The coloring is exquisite. It forces freely, and produces magnificent large buds and flowers." [CA96]

MME AUGUSTINE HAMONT
(' — Hammond')
Vigneron, 1897

"Clear satin-rose, very large and sweet; vigorous." [P1] "Blossom very large, full, globular, satiny flesh pink, lighter at the petal edges. The growth is vigorous, with handsome light green foliage; very strong stem." [JR21/147]

[MME BESSEMER]
Conard & Jones, 1898
  "A beautiful new rose, producing flowers of elegant form and substance. Color, beautiful peachy-pink, delicately shaded and clouded. Large, very full, sweet and handsome." [C&Js98]

MME BLONDEL
Veysset, 1899
Seedling of 'La France de 89' (HT).
  "Blossom bright pink; petals very thick, with a silvery edge; very large, full; opens well; fragrant. Growth, very vigorous; floriferous." [JR23/178]

MME C. CHAMBARD
Chambard, 1911
From 'Frau Karl Druschki' (HP) × 'Prince de Bulgarie' (HT).
  "Very vigorous with erect canes; beautiful light green resistant foliage; solitary, long bud, borne on a long rigid stem, silvery flesh pink with some salmon; flowers very large, opening well, flesh pink, salmon nuanced dawn gold, nub deep yellow, fragrant and floriferous.... It takes from 'Druschki' its great vigor, and from 'Prince de Bulgarie' its beautiful foliage and floriferousness." [JR35/156]

MME CHARLES BOUTMY
Vigneron, 1892
  "Very vigorous, very beautiful light green foliage, flower very large, full, cupped, perfect form, well held, beautifully colored flesh pink, becoming, when fully open, beautiful light pink." [JR16/153]

MME CHARLES DÉTRAUX
Vigneron, 1895
  "Velvety red." [Y̆] "Very vigorous, beautiful glaucous green foliage, flower very large, quite full, globular, bright red with some carmine. Very fragrant . . . extremely floriferous." [JR19/147]

MME CUNISSET-CARNOT
Buatois, 1899
  "Vigorous, medium-sized blossom, bud very long, solitary; color, salmony carnation pink." [JR23/169]

MME DAILLEUX
Buatois, 1900
From 'Victor Verdier' (HP) × 'Dr. Grill' (T).
  "Salmon pink, outer petals somewhat imbricated; center brighter pink on a coppery yellow ground; large, full, central petals muddled and for the most part folded at an angle for the greater part of their length; very fragrant; conical bud opens well. Very vigorous growth." [JR24/163]

[MME DE LOEBEN-SELS]
Soupert & Notting, 1879
Not to be confused with 'Mme Loeben de Sels' (HP).
  "Flower large, very full. Flat form like that of 'Souvenir de la Malmaison'. Color, silvery white nuanced salmon/dawn-gold, reverse of petals flesh lake; very abundant bloom." [JR3/168]

MME EMILIE LAFON
Morainville, 1905
Seedling of 'La France de 89' (Cl. HT).
  "Light red, large, full, medium height." [Sn]

MME ERNEST PIARD
Bonnaire, 1887
  "Bright silvery pink." [Y̆] "Handsome bright red, with a kind of silver polish." [B&V] "Extra-vigorous, with upright, very firm branches; foliage large, to eight in [ca. 2 dm], a handsome blackish dark green; flower very large, cupped, beautiful bright red with a silvery edging. Reblooms freely." [JR11/149]

MME ÉTIENNE LEVET   PLATE 228
Levet, 1878
Seedling of 'Antonine Verdier' (HT).
  "Vigorous; flower large, full, well formed; color, beautiful cerise red with superb coppery yellow nubs. This beautiful plant is one of the most remontant." [JR2/166]

[MME EUGÉNIE BOULLET]
Pernet-Ducher, 1897
  "Magnificent flowers and buds; extra large; fine cup form, well filled and delightfully fragrant; color, fine buff pink, shading to yellow and rich carmine. Very handsome." [C&Js99] "Vigorous bush with upright reddish canes, rare thorns, beautiful bright bronze green foliage; bud of elegant form, superb half open; flower large, cupped, nearly full; color, china pink nuanced yellow and bright carmine. Very beautiful variety." [JR21/146]

MME GUSTAVE METZ
Lamesch, 1905
Seedling of 'Mme Caroline Testout' (HT).
  "Vigorous, large and handsome bright foliage. Flower very large, large petals, magnificent form, quite full, nearly always solitary.... Color, creamy white, going to pink. The bloom is very abundant, and lasts until autumn." [JR29/22]

MME JEAN FAVRE
Godard, 1900
From 'La France de 89' (Cl. HT) × 'Xavier Olibo' (HP).
  "White, pink reverse." [Y̆] "Compact, foliage light green, bud long, deep carmine, flower large, well formed; when fully open, light carmine with bluish reflections." [JR25/6]

MME JOSEPH BONNAIRE   PLATE 244
('Mme J. Bonnaire-Pierre')
Bonnaire, 1891
From 'Adam' (T) × 'Paul Neyron' (HP).
  "Bright China rose, reverse of petals silvery, extra large; in the way of 'Paul Neyron', but paler . . . a very handsome and show Rose." [P1] "Supported by a strong stem, its enormous bud, beautifully colored bright China pink with the reverse of the petals silvery, will most certainly be a delicacy much prized by florists. It is a 'Paul Neyron' of much more delicate color, but of equal vigor." [JR19/146] "Vigorous, with upright branches.... Flower very large, very full, opening very well, growing to seven in [ca. 1.75 dm] across.... Handsome foliage, thorns rare. Very remontant, blooming until frost." [JR15/164] "Mons Joseph Bonnaire, dead at the age of 68. Born at Saint-Chef (Isère) in 1842, Bonnaire went while still quite young to Lyon where he worked at the establishments of Damaizin and Ducher, going then to Paris.... [At length, he returned to Lyon] where he ultimately set up shop in 1878." [JR34/136]

MME JOSEPH COMBET   PLATE 248
Bonnaire, 1893

"A continuation of the type of which 'Gloire Lyonnaise' was the inception. Its flowers are very large and full, and the petals well arranged; the colour is creamy white. A beautiful Rose, but does not always open well; growth almost climbing, with bold and massive foliage." [P1] "Beautifully cup-shaped." [Hn] "Extremely vigorous, branches upright, handsome somber green foliage, nearly thornless, flower large, very full, perfectly imbricated, always opens well, beautiful creamy white shaded pink, interior dawn-gold, very fragrant, very remontant, blooming until frost." [JR17/147]

[MME JOSEPH DESBOIS]   PLATE 232
Guillot & fils, 1886

From 'Baronne Adolphe de Rothschild' (HP) × 'Mme Falcot' (T).

"Very vigorous bush; flower very big, measuring 14–16 cm across [ca. 6 in], quite full, very well formed; color, flesh white with a very delicate salmon pink center." [JR10/147]

MME JULES BOUCHÉ
Croibier, 1910

"Vigorous, branches slender and strong, bud very long, flower large, full, well formed, petals of great substance, folding back at expansion. Color, salmon-white, center nuanced virginal pink, stem very strong. Good for all purposes." [JR24/169] "Best light-colored rose; useful both for cutting and decorative purposes; growth and blooming qualities splendid; color clear, beautiful." [ARA18/112]

MME JULES FINGER
P. Guillot, 1893

"Creamy white changing to almost pure white, fine globular form, full; growth moderate." [P1] "Vigorous bush; flower very large, quite full, very well formed, globular and of good 'hold'; color, beautiful creamy white nuanced salmon pink at the center passing to pure white; very floriferous, nicely perfumed." [JR17/131] "Extra large, handsome buds and flowers . . . delicately tinted with rose and salmon." [C&Jf97] "Free bloomer. A distinct and novel variety, in all respects very desirable." [B&V]

MME JULES GROLEZ   PLATE 255
P. Guillot, 1896

From 'Triomphe de l'Exposition' (HP) × 'Mme Falcot' (T).

"Bright silvery rose. — Vigorous. — Garden, standard, bedding. — A good and distinct garden rose. Fragrant." [Cat12/40] "Very floriferous; numerous branches; flower large, full, very well formed, beautiful frosty China pink, very bright." [JR20/147] "It is a colour which does not harmonise with some other Roses, especially with those of pink, or pink and copper shades." [NRS12/73] "Growth and color not of best; good bloomer, but superseded by better roses of same type." [ARA18/116] "Disbud." [Th] "Moderate height, bushy, hardy; foliage very plentiful, healthy; bloom free first half of season, moderate last half, continuous." [ARA18/126] "Growth rather dwarf, but fairly vigorous habit, bushy, making a good shaped plant. Foliage distinct, dark bronze when young and effective, but decidedly liable to mildew. Flowers from the end of June to October, good early and late. The flowers are freely produced, and carried erect on short, moderately thick stems. The petals are of a very silky texture, and a clear deep rosy pink. The flowers last well in water (four days) and stand wet well, if there be not too much of it, but they become paler in damp weather. . . . It flowers well on light soil and, I am told, also on

the clay." [NRS10/33] "Bright China rose, not always clear — blues in heat; nice bud; center held quite well; fair size only; lasting; fragrant. Foliage practically perfect, and holds. Bushy but not tall growth in Central and Northern Zones; stem long with fair strength. Shows distinct Tea characteristics, especially in its retention of foliage, while its hardiness makes it useful where late frosts are encountered. Fair for cutting and requires little attention . . . very fine and continuous." [Th2] "Messers Grolez brothers, of Ronchin [*were among the exhibitors at the 1881 general meeting of the members of the Société Regionale du Nord de la France in Lille, where,*] in their 600 roses exhibited, there was not even one which could be regarded as anything but first-choice." [JR5/150]

MME JULES GRÉVY
Schwartz, 1881

From 'Triomphe de l'Exposition' (HP) × 'Mme Falcot' (T).

"Dark red shaded grenadine." [Ÿ] "Salmon-pink." [EL] "Growth very vigorous . . . foliage purple at first, like Tea foliage; flower medium-sized or large, full, salmon-white within, bright carmine-pink without. Not very floriferous, and subject to mildew." [S] "Large, full, very fragrant and, in form, campanulate; its novel color is salmon white inside and salmon pink outside. The pedicel is short, with numerous fine prickles; the wood is strong; the foliage is bright and purplish." [JR5/117]

MME LACHARME
Lacharme, 1872

From 'Jules Margottin' (HP) × 'Mlle de Sombreuil' (T).

"White, the centre the palest blush colour, beautifully clear and wax-like, a large circular cupped shaped flower, and highly scented; requires fine dry weather to open." [JC] "Vigorous; flower large, full, Centifolia form, opens with difficulty, white lightly blushing, fades to white." [S] "Shy in the autumn. Of bushy growth, and quite hardy." [EL] "Of fair growth and foliage, with characteristic habit. The shoots themselves require to be severely thinned, and then they must be looked over from top to bottom several times during the growing season, as it is such a free bloomer that every wood bud will break and try to form a flower bud before the top one has begun to swell. Very liable to mildew, and absolutely spoilt by any rain even at quite an early stage. Even a heavy dew will sometimes soil the blooms. These are of a pure white, and for years this was the best HP of its colour [*we call it an HT*], a row of it in full bloom looking most charming just as the dusk of a July evening comes on. . . . The shape is good and lasting, globular with the centre well filled, but the size is not up to the average. It will come again well in the autumn, if it should be particularly dry and fine." [F-M3] "The most beautiful white hybrid known till now." [I'H72/261]

MME MARIE CROIBIER
Croibier, 1901

Seedling of 'Mme Caroline Testout' (HT).

"Very vigorous, foliage deep maroon green, thorns upright and numerous, flower full, very large, deep China pink, long bud, strong stem, very floriferous. This superb rose comes from 'Mme Caroline Testout', from which it takes its vigor, and the main characteristics of its growth; its bud is longer, making the blossom more graceful; its color doesn't blue, and keeps until the petals fall." [JR25/147]

MME MAURICE DE LUZE   PLATE 267
Pernet-Ducher, 1907
From 'Mme Abel Chatenay' (HT) × 'Eugene Fürst' (HP).

"Of good vigor, with upright canes, cheerful green foliage, superb buds borne on long and strong stems; flower very large, with large petals, in the form of a full cup. Color, Nilsson pink, center cochineal carmine, reverse of petals lighter." [JR31/103]

MME MÉHA SABATIER
Pernet-Ducher, 1916
From an unnamed seedling × 'Château de Clos Vougeot' (HT).

"Deep crimson." [Y̆] "Red, large, full, medium height." [Sn]

MME MOSER
Vigneron, 1889

"Growth very vigorous, with strong and upright canes, handsome dark green foliage, numerous brown thorns, large and beautiful buds, strong flower-stems; flower very large, full, globular, beautifully colored silvery white and lilac-pink in the interior, well held. Quite remontant; very fragrant . . . dedicated to the wife of Mons Moser, a well known horticulturalist of Versailles." [JR13/165]

MME PAUL LACOUTIÈRE
Buatois, 1897
From 'Ma Capucine'(T) × 'Baronne Adolphe de Rothschild'(HP).

"Bud very long; flower large, semi-full, coppery saffron yellow, center golden yellow, petal edges slightly touched carmine; very fragrant; growth vigorous with upright canes; foliage bright dark green. The blossoms are sometimes solitary and sometimes in clusters of three to six." [JR21/148] The *R. fœtida* heritage of 'Ma Capucine' makes 'Mme Paul Lacoutière' very close to being able to be considered as the first commercial Pernetiana.

MME PERNET-DUCHER
Pernet-Ducher, 1891
From an unnanmed Tea × 'Victor Verdier' (HP).

"Vigorous, making a compact, erect bush; flower medium-sized or large, nearly full, bud conical, nicely colored canary yellow, outer petals washed carmine, fading to creamy white by the time the petals fall. . . . The plant has handsome foliage, blooms continually and abundantly, and, what is more, is very hardy." [JR15/166]

MME P. EULER
P. Guillot, 1907
From 'Antoine Rivoire' (HT) × 'Killarney' (HT).

"Vermilion silvery pink; extra-fine for cut-flowers." [C&Js12] "Vigorous, flower very large, supported on a long, strong stem, very full, long duration, very beautifully colored . . . fragrant." [JR31/139]

MME SEGOND-WEBER   PLATE 268
Soupert & Notting, 1907
From 'Antoine Rivoire' (HT) × 'Souvenir de Victor Hugo' (T).

"Pure salmon pink, very delicate, new among HT's, bright center. The enormous blossom, with its large and strong petals, lasts a very long time; it is cupped, quite regular, and faultless in form . . . blooms without interruption from spring to November." [JR31/136–137] "Beautiful color; almost perfect form; growth fair; blooming qualities very good; lasts well; splendid cut-flower." [ARA18/112] "Very large, fragrant, long stem. Fine foliage, sufficient. Growth poor; fairly hardy." [ARA23/167]

MME TONY BABOUD
Godard, 1895

"Very vigorous without being a climber, somewhat branching, thorns strong and somewhat numerous, foliage beautiful light green, flower large, semi-double, pretty fawn nankeen yellow fading to canary, deliciously perfumed; bud always solitary, borne on a long and strong stem." [JR19/163] "Baboud, of Thoissey, the nursery-maker of l'Ain." [JR22/160]

[MME VEUVE MÉNIER]   PLATE 245
Widow Schwartz, 1891
Seedling of 'Camoëns' (HT).

"Pale light rose." [CA97] "Vigorous bush; canes tinted purple; foliage glaucous green; flower large, very full, perfect form, ruffled; color, pale pink on a blush white ground nuanced dawn gold and a very delicate carmine; petals nubs yellowish. From 'Camoëns', and showing all the characteristics of that precious variety." [JR15/149]

MME VIGER   PLATE 261
Jupeau, 1901
From 'Heinrich Schultheis' (HP) × 'G. Nabonnand' (T).

"Vigorous, upright branches, wood glaucous green, thorns rare, handsome foliage, very long and graceful buds, well held; borne on a long, strong stem, goes well with the foliage, nearly always solitary; flower very large, imbricated form, opens well; the most beautiful delicate pink, edges and reverse silvery pink touched carmine; nearly white in fall. . . . Extra floriferous, always blooming." [JR24/146]

MONSIEUR BUNEL
Pernet-Ducher, 1899

"Rosy peach, shaded with yellow and edged with bright rose; very full and compact; somewhat flat, but a fine Rose; growth vigorous." [P1] "Erect branches, beautiful cheerful green foliage, flower very large, quite full, imbricated, peachblossom pink, ground yellow, petals edged bright pink." [JR23/149]

MONSIEUR CHARLES DE LAPISSE
Laroulandie, 1909
Sport of 'Mme Caroline Testout' (HT).

"Vigorous, well-branched, pretty buds, virginal pink upon opening; flower very large, full, pearly white, sometimes blush white fading to creamy white, very pretty coloration." [JR23/153]

MONSIEUR FRAISSENON
Gamon, 1911
Seedling of 'Lady Ashtown' (HT).

"Vigorous, long bud, flower large, full, deep frosty pink." [JR35/167]

[MONSIEUR PAUL LÉDÉ]
Pernet-Ducher, 1902
Not to be confused with its own climbing sport, 'Climbing Monsieur Paul Lédé', often called simply, and confusingly, 'Paul Lédé'.

"Very vigorous, bushy; beautiful dark green foliage; flower very large, full, cupped, superbly colored carmine pink nuanced and shaded yellow; very fragrant; continuous bloom." [JR26/131]

MRS. CONWAY JONES
Listed as 'Mamie'.

MRS. CYNTHIA FORDE

A. Dickson, 1910

"The flowers, large, numerous, and always opening well, are borne upright on very rigid stems; they have a unique form: the center juts out, and the petals fall back gracefully around it. The perfectly formed blossom is of a splendid color . . . delicate carmine red nuanced pink; it has a chrome yellow zone at the base of each petal. The branches are particularly strong and robust; the plant is much branched; the foliage is lime-green; each branch is crowned with a bud . . . a very strong, delicious Tea scent." [JR36/91–92]

MRS. ROBERT GARRETT   PLATE 257

J. Cook, 1898

Several parentages have been given: (1) From 'Mlle de Sombreuil' (Cl. T) × 'Mme Caroline Testout' (HT); (2) from 'Mlle de Sombreuil' (Cl. T) × a seedling of 'Mme la Comtesse de Caserta' (T) × 'Mme Eugène Verdier' (HP); or (3) from 'Mme la Comtesse de Caserta' (T) × 'Mme Eugène Verdier' (HP).

"Shell pink with deeper center." [CA10] "Pink, medium size, full, medium scent, medium height." [Sn] "Both flowers and buds are of grand size and perfect full form. The flowers are of remarkable depth and sweetness. The petals are broad and of excellent substance. The color is exquisite shell pink, passing to soft glowing rose, delicately tinged with creamy yellow. . . . The bush is a strong, vigorous grower, with handsome foliage and quite hardy. It is a constant and abundant bloomer, and can not be recommended too highly." [C&Js99] "A variety of really vigorous growth, appearing to be thoroughly hardy and healthy. The flowers are large and rather inclined to hang their heads, the colour being somewhat similar to '[Mme] Caroline Testout' [HT]. I was somewhat disappointed on finding that the flowers came rather 'balled' in the season, but I have had one or two very long blooms of fine pointed shape late in the autumn. This looks rather as if it would prefer not being closely pruned, which I think is likely. Being very free flowering and a good autumnal, it seems to be a variety of considerable promise for all purposes." [F-M2]

[MRS. W. C. WHITNEY]

May, 1894

From 'Mme Ferdinand Jamin' (HP) × 'Souvenir d'Un Ami' (T).

"Clear, deep pink color, and very fragrant; flowers large, coming with long buds. A very free bloomer." [CA96]

MRS. W. J. GRANT   PLATE 254

('Belle Siebrecht')

A. Dickson, 1895

From 'Lady Mary Fitzwilliam' (HT) × 'La France' (HT).

"Brilliant intense pink with large petals." [JR22/107] "Large camellia-like flowers, bright pink. Beautiful long buds." [Hn] "The plant is unfortunately not strong in growth, and is best as a maiden . . . it is excessively free-flowering until quite late in the autumn, and the blooms at their best are very large, of a bright deep pink colour, very fragrant, and may be taken, I think, as a type of the finest and best pointed form with pointed petals known among Roses. The flowers generally come good, if the plant can be grown strongly enough, for it requires 'liberal treatment': and a good specimen is indeed something for a Rosarian to feast his eyes upon. The weak growth is an unfortunate drawback." [F-M2]

PAPA LAMBERT   PLATE 258

Lambert, 1898

From an unnamed seedling (parentage: 'White Lady' [HT, W. Paul, 1889, white; sport of 'Lady Mary Fitzwilliam' (HT)] × 'Marie Baumann' [HP]) × 'Oskar Cordel' (HP).

"Large, full, beautifully cupped form. Vivid pink, darker inside. Growth erect, straight, flowers solitary with a strong centifolia fragrance." [Hn] "Very floriferous, remontant, and extremely fragrant. The vigorous branches are erect and amply covered with attractive glossy leaves; the solitary buds come at the ends of the very long stems. They are more or less oval, and delicate pink, being slightly darker without; the half opened blossom is regularly formed and quite full; its petals are large and slightly recurved. . . . This rose is very hardy . . . As for appearance, we unhesitatingly compare it to 'Baronne Adolphe de Rothschild', being however darker and, above all, deliciously perfumed." [JR22/180]

PAUL MEUNIER   PLATE 263

Buatois, 1902

"Very vigorous with heavy, upright wood, and handsome bronzy green foliage. Flower large, full, long bud. Color, straw yellow, strongly tinted salmon." [JR26/178] "Strong stem, held on heavy wood, upright and strong . . . hardy and floriferous." [JR29/184]

[PEARL]

Bennett, 1879

From 'Adam' (T) × 'Comtesse de Serenye' (HP).

"Flesh pink, well formed, large." [JR3/114] "Soft rosy pink, or pale flesh-color, shaded carmine, passing to white; medium size, very full, perfect form; delightfully scented; a constant and very free bloomer." [CA90]

PIERRE GUILLOT

Guillot fils, 1879

From 'Mme Falcot' (T) × an unnamed HP.

"Vigorous, flower large to very large, full, well formed, and well held; color, bright sparkling red, petals bordered white, very floriferous, extra pretty." [JR3/164] "Very sweet." [B&V] "Moderately vigorous . . . canes upright, purplish green; leaves dark green; 5–7 leaflets; very good for forcing." [S]

PIERRE WATTINNE

Soupert & Notting, 1901

From 'Papa Gontier' (T) × an unnamed seedling.

"Vigorous, handsome foliage; long bud; flower large, full, of a beautiful form; color, glossy cherry pink nuanced salmon yellow. Floriferous and fragrant." [JR25/162]

PRINCE DE BULGARIE   PLATE 262

Pernet-Ducher, 1901

"Very vigorous; leaves large, bright green; bud long, very graceful; flower very large, quite full, in the form of an elongated cup; outer petals large; coloration superb, difficult to describe; silvery flesh pink, very delicately nuanced or shaded salmon and dawn-gold . . . form resembles that of 'Souvenir du Président Carnot'. Like it, 'Bulgarie' holds its blossom on a strong and quite erect stem." [JR25/131]

RED MARÉCHAL NIEL

Listed as 'Grossherzog Ernst Ludwig von Hesse'.

REINE CAROLA DE SAXE PLATE 264
(trans., 'Queen Carola of Saxony')
Gamon, 1902

"Vigorous, flower large, full, very well formed, flower solitary, beautiful delicate silvery pink on a deep salmony pink ground, fragrant. . . . Dedicated to the memory of the great care exercised by Her Majesty on behalf of an ill, restless gentleman of Lyon at the town of Strehlen in Saxony, 1870–1871 [*during, one should note, the Franco-Prussian War*]." [JR26/147]

REINE MARGUERITE D'ITALIE
Soupert & Notting, 1904
From 'Baron Nathaniel de Rothschild' (HP) × 'Mme la Princesse de Bessaraba de Brancovan' (T).

"Vigorous, handsome dark green foliage; the bud is magnificently formed, and held proudly above the foliage. Flower very large, very full, of great beauty, and excellently held. Color, shining carmine red, the center brightened with vermilion red . . . literally covered with blossoms and buds throughout the season. Centifolia fragrance." [JR28/153]

ROSA GRUSS AN AACHEN
(trans., 'Pink Gruss an Aachen')
Spek, 1930
A pink sport, presumably, of 'Gruss an Aachen' (HT).

"Yellowish pink, large, full, moderate height." [Sn]

ROSETTE DE LA LEGION D'HONNEUR
Bonnaire, 1895

"Carnation red, veined yellow. — Semi-climber. — Garden, pillar. — A pretty and distinct variety. A good buttonhole rose. Fragrant." [Cat12/53] "Extra vigorous, semi-climbing, continuous blooming, canes numerous, growing to 1.5 m [ca. 4.5 ft]; leaves glossy, thick; buds small, well formed, ovoid, red nuanced cerise at the tip, and colored vermilion-grenadine; petals salmon-carmine, with a yellow line in the center. The bud looks singularly like the medal of an officer of the Legion of Honor." [JR19/147]

ROSOMANE GRAVEREAUX PLATE 259
Soupert & Notting, 1899

"Growth bushy, of great vigor, magnificent foliage; enormous long bud of the 'Souvenir du Président Carnot' sort; blossom very large, very full, borne on a long, strong stem; beautiful form, perfectly held, petals large and thick; color, silvery white, exterior tinted very lightly with a very delicate flesh pink. . . . Very fragrant and floriferous." [JR23/170] "Blooms well." [JR25/11]

RUHM DER GARTENWELT
(trans., 'Glory of the Garden-World')
Jacobs, 1905
From 'American Beauty' (HP) × 'Francis Dubreuil' (T).

"Brilliant fiery red." [Ÿ] "Very vigorous, blooms profusely, giving globular blossoms, a non-bluing blood red." [JR28/166]

SACHSENGRUSS
(trans., 'Saxon Greeting')
Neubert/Hoyer & Klemm, 1913
From 'Frau Karl Druschki' (HP) × 'Mme Jules Gravereaux' (Cl).

"Delicate flesh on a white ground. Center blush with China pink reflections. Form and placement of the blossoms just like 'Frau Karl Druschki'." [JR37/10]

SHANDON
A. Dickson, 1899

"Growth vigorous, flower large, full, deep carmine. Fragrant and beautiful." [JR25/11] "Center light red." [JR32/140] "Very fragrant, medium height." [Sn]

SHEILA
A. Dickson, 1895
"Bright pink." [Ÿ]

[SOUVENIR D'AUGUSTE MÉTRAL]
P. Guillot, 1895

"Pure deep red, large full flowers of good form and substance, delightfully fragrant." [C&Js98] "Vigorous bush, very floriferous, canes numerous and thick, bud crimson red. Flower large, full, very well formed, varying from purple red to crimson red; fragrant; very beautiful." [JR19/147]

[SOUVENIR DE MME ERNEST CAUVIN]
('Souvenir de Mme Ernest Corvin')
Pernet-Ducher, 1898

"Bush of good vigor with not very thorny upright canes; foliage shiny; flower large, very full, well formed, imbricated; color, delicate flesh, petals bordered a brighter pink, center light yellow, very often beautiful orange yellow. Very beautiful variety with abundant bloom. From an unreleased variety." [JR22/163]

[SOUVENIR DE MME EUGÈNE VERDIER] PLATE 251
Pernet-Ducher, 1894
From 'Lady Mary Fitzwilliam' (HT) × 'Mme Chédane-Guinoisseau' (T).

"Very vigorous with upright canes branching somewhat; foliage finely serrated, and handsome green; the blossom is borne on a strong stem and is large, very full, oval, with the petals gracefully recurving beneath; beautiful coloration, electric white on a ground of saffron yellow, sometimes shaded darker yellow." [JR19/25] A parent of 'Frau Dr. Schricker' (B).

SOUVENIR DE MONSIEUR FRÉDÉRIC VERCELLONE
Schwartz, 1906
From 'Antoine Rivoire' (HT) × 'André Schwartz' (T).

"Vigorous, flower large, full, very well formed, good poise, opens well, fragrant; carmine pink, lightly coppery, nuanced blush white tinted bright carmine." [JR30/136]

SOUVENIR OF WOOTTON
J. Cook/Strauss & Co., 1888
From 'Bon Silène' (T) × 'Louis Van Houtte' (HP).

"Pure rich, velvety red, delightfully sweet and constant bloomer; extra large fully double flowers. A vigorous grower and quite hardy." [C&Js06] "Cup-shaped, double flowers of a rosy crimson; very fragrant. Fine healthy foliage. Strong grower. Gives 34 blooms per season. Hardy." [ARA21/91] "Its coloration is a very beautiful display of crimson carmine, being meanwhile very fragrant and of strong growth. Whenever it appears, it attracts attention, but its manner of bloom makes it inappropriate for the frame, where it produces many blossoms wanting in form and color. For this reason, it isn't very popular; it is, nevertheless, a quite notable introduction." [JR16/37] "Medium height, compact, winterkills some; foliage sufficient, some black-spot in July; bloom abundant in July, free rest of season." [ARA18/128] "Take for example 'Souvenir of Wootton', which does very well in pots, blooming well enough, as long as it is not placed on the north side." [JR26/118] "Said to be the first Hybrid Tea rose raised in the United States." [ARA22/187]

SUNNY SOUTH
A. Clark, 1918
From 'Gustav Grünerwald' (HT) × 'Betty Berkeley' (T).

"The color is pink, flushed with carmine on a yellow base — a most distinct and charming combination. It possesses a strong constitution and good habit, growing naturally five to six ft high, sometimes very much taller, and flowering practically throughout the year." [ARA28/112] "An Australian introduction of highest value for decorative purposes and as a cut-flower. Very bushy up to 10 ft [ca. 3 m]. Flowers continuously and freely; soft pink with yellow shadings. Foliage remarkably resistant to disease. Almost in a class by itself for hedge or massing." [Capt28] "Not a strong climber, but makes a fine pillar or is good trained fan-wise on a lattice wall. The blooms are large, fairly double, and of a lovely deep shell pink shading to white in the center. It is a very constant bloomer." [CaRol/6/6]

THE DANDY
G. Paul, 1905
Seedling of 'Bardou Job' (B).

"Fiery maroon crimson." [Y̆] "Flower small, sparkling blackish crimson." [JR30/25]

THE METEOR
Evans, 1887

"Rich velvety crimson, exceedingly bright and striking; buds and flowers are large, and elegantly formed, and borne on nice long stems. It is a vigorous, strong grower, and free bloomer." [CA93] "Dark red, medium size, not very full, medium scent, dwarf." [Sn] "'Meteor' and 'Liberty', having such beautiful coloration, grow too feebly, and the [*short*?] length of the stem makes for poor lasting qualities." [JR26/118] "One of the best for all purposes." [C&Jf97]

[THE PURITAN]
Bennett, 1886
From 'Mabel Morrison' (HP) × 'Devoniensis' (T).

"In size and shape resembles 'Mabel Morrison'; flowers large, pure white, sweet; fine foliage." [CA90] "[It] caused a veritable sensation when exhibited at South Kensington, coming from America [*that is, the blossoms*]. It is indeed a precious rose for forcing, evidently being able to bear any rise in temperature. Its white flowers are tinged light yellow at the base, are lush, and retain for a long time their freshness." [JR12/107]

TRIOMPHE DE PERNET PÈRE
Pernet père, 1890
From 'Monsieur Désir' (N) × 'Général Jacqueminot' (HP).

"Vigorous, good growth, growing upright and strongly; wood and foliage very dark; flowers large, nearly full, beautiful bright red, very well held; bud very long, in the form of a **T**, opening very well, continuously and abundantly blooming . . . as vigorous as 'Souvenir de la Malmaison', and reblooms freely." [JR14/164] "A magnificent rose. . . . The flowers are extra large, full and double and deliciously tea scented. Color brilliant carmine lake, with rich crimson shading, exquisitely beautiful. The plant is a neat compact grower, quite hardy and a free bloomer." [C&Js02] "Jean Pernet, who died last March 31st [1896] at Charpennes, near Lyon,

at the age of 64. . . . Born October 15, 1832, at Passin . . . of a family of modest gardeners, Jean Pernet early devoted himself to horticulture, and worked at Lyon at the establishment of Guillot père from 1853 to 1855, when he left for Paris, staying first with Portemer père at Gentilly, then with Victor Verdier père at Paris, returning to Lyon in 1856 to complete his horticultural education at the establishment of J.-B. Guillot fils. . . . We hear the happy news that the business of the late Jean Pernet will not fall into the hands of strangers, but will be united with that of his son, Mons J. Pernet-Ducher." [JR20/65–66]

VIOLETTE BOUYER
Listed as an HP.

VIOLINISTE EMILE LÉVÊQUE
Pernet-Ducher, 1897

"Growth vigorous and bushy; foliage purplish green; long buds; blossom medium or large, full, and very well formed; color, bright flesh pink nuanced yellow with orange reflections within Very floriferous." [JR21/146]

[VISCOUNTESS FALMOUTH]
Bennett, 1879
From 'Adam' (T) × 'Soupert & Notting' (Mossy Remontant, Pernet père, 1874, pink and carmine).

"A very extraordinary plant, the color of the blossom is very distinct, being pale pink with the reverse of the petals darker, very fragrant." [JR3/171] "Wood nearly as thorny as that of Moss Roses, though the bud isn't. Blossom very large, well formed; color, delicate pink, with a darker reverse; globular; scent like that of the Moss." [S]

[WILLIAM FRANCIS BENNETT]   PLATE 234
Bennett/Evans, 1886
From 'Adam' (T) × 'Xavier Olibo' (HP).

"Velvety crimson." [LS] "Large, loosely filled, glossy carmine-red, becoming violet with age; flowers continuously. Highly prized as a good forcing rose, but not much favored as a standard, as it is not full enough." [Hn] "A fine Tea Rose, in profusion [of] bloom unsurpassed by any of the monthly roses. It produces extra fine buds of the most brilliant crimson, with a delicious fragrance." [CA88] "The buds of 'William Francis Bennett' resemble those of the well-known 'Niphetos', up to but excluding the color — we think that we are seeing a rich fiery carmine-red 'Niphetos' before our eyes — that is 'William Francis Bennett'." [RZ86/6] "Moderate, bushy growth, with very dark leaves; long buds; color, carmine red like 'Général Jacqueminot' [HP]." [JR10/24] "In 1884, Bennett exhibited these ['pedigree'] roses at several English rose shows, and frequently they took first place because of the perfection of their blossoms. But he never released them to commerce. One day, Mrs. Evans, a dealer in flowers, was visiting Bennett at Shepperton with her young son. They were so struck by the beauty of the new rose, particularly as a cutting variety, that she acquired from Bennett all rights to the variety, paying $5,000. Such a sum for one variety is unique in rose history!" [JR10/23] "Everyone remembers the fuss made about the sale of the rose 'William Francis Bennett' for $5,000 . . . it was a good rose." [JR19/55]

287

Appendix One

ROSE IDENTIFICATION

For many involved with "old" roses, the greatest delight of all is to find a gnarled old rose bush in some out-of-the-way cemetery or abandoned dooryard garden, and then, all the meanwhile dreaming heady reveries of the fabled — and frequently fabulous — past, to make an attempt to identify the plant. The following will perhaps assist the ambitious rosarian in his or her brave endeavor.

Methodology of Identification

Identification of roses old or new is an intricate and demanding affair, and one should begin any attempt with the clear understanding that success is unlikely. Disenheartening words! But let us consider:

Even in their purest form, many of the most significant roses are such a complex brew of species that Science despairs of sorting out *what crossed with what and when.* The Damask Perpetual may derive from *Rosa gallica, R. phœnicea,* and/or *R. moschata* — not to mention *R. damascena* — all bred, interbred, and re-bred together as well as — who knows? — with other species or hybrids. The other groups are no less complex, and consequently every cultivar may be considered not so much a representative of a particular "family," but rather a citizen of the world. It is best, perhaps, to regard divisions of cultivars as indicating not species derivations so much as horticultural concepts. The pragmatic French breeders would, for instance, regard as a "China" not something demonstrably free of non-*chinensis* characters — whatever *R. chinensis* might be; rather, if the entity bloomed repeatedly (ruling out the old European roses and their primary hybrids), was well-branched (ruling out Damask Perpetuals), was restrained in growth (ruling out Hybrid Perpetuals and Noisettes), had fairly regular broad-based thorns rather than bristles and broad-based thorns all mixed together (ruling out Bourbons), and had a blossom which was less than impeccable in form and/or doubleness (ruling out Teas), they would probably — but not necessarily — have considered it a *"China,"* be its parentage China, Bourbon, "pure" Tea, Noisette × Tea, China × Tea, or whatever.

We must therefore scrutinize every fact or attribute very closely indeed all the while doing just the opposite and guarding against setting too much store by any single fact or attribute!

Distribution

It is important that such foundlings not be allowed to merely languish in the study-gardens of specialists, awaiting rediscovery of their official names. The mystery of their past does not obscure their beauty — to some it enhances it! — and there is thus no reason to "punish" them for the fact that insouciant horticulturists have let their names fade along with their flowers. And things happen. A "hundred-year" storm could wipe out both parent plant and newly-rooted cuttings, or the caring rosarian him- or herself could expire or lose interest, the end result perhaps extinguishing the remaining earthly stock of some most desirable cultivar. The plants must be made available and *distributed* for the delight of the horticulturist and the richness of Horticulture.

But — how to do this without having the same cultivar being shipped around the world by 16 different nurseries under 16 different names?

First, the discoverer assigns a provisional name composed of the word "unknown" followed by an appropriate word or two such as the name of the town, street, or person involved in the discovery (for example, "Avalon"), and finally an honest guess at the classification of the cultivar ("Tea," perhaps). Those wishing to vend this discovery would thus do so under the name 'Unknown Avalon Tea,' which would accomplish making it available while making it patently obvious that it is an *unknown;* provisional names not including "unknown" run the risk of having their names taken as the "real thing," leading to unnecessary confusion and frustration on all sides.

Second, let us hope that at some point a wise rosarian will stand up and venture to opine that the 'Unknown Avalon Tea' is very possibly 'Egine', Vibert's 1852 Tea. As likely as this identification might be, prudence would seem to dictate that we not immediately shout "Hurrah! Yes, this is it!" carve this opinion in stone, and start celebrating a solemn but joy-filled *Te Deum.* Rather, let these and any other sincere and earnest attempts at indentification be gathered under a name which — as "unknown" did in the first instance — allows us to offer the cultivar while being perfectly straightforward with the customers who venture to buy the offering. It would thus be appropriate to offer this example not as 'Egine,' but rather as *'Possible* Egine' for a set period of 5 years or 10 to give *other* wise rosarians a chance to assess the identification.

After these 5 or 10 years, if no substantive objections are raised, let the *third* and final incarnation stand as long as it can stand; let 'Possible Egine' become, for once and for all, simply 'Egine.'

Documentation

When a subject for identification is first chosen, it would be wise to complete and keep on file a form with the following information:

Provisional name [_not_ a suggested identification, but rather a random appellation for use until an i.d. has been made]:_____

_____

Seemingly in which group:_____

Main flower color:_____

Other colors or tintings, with locations (i.e., "lower third of petal yellow," "reverse of petals striped pink," etc.):_____

Doubleness:_____

Form of blossom:_____

Stamens & pistils hidden or evident:_____

Size of average blossom:_____

Strength and type of fragrance:_____

Other remarks on the blossom:_____

_____

Form of bud:_____

Form & characteristics of ovary:_____

Flower-stem stiff or bending:_____

Flower-stem smooth or prickly:_____

Describe the thorniness, color, and tendency to branch of the canes:_____

_____

Describe the growth (heavy, feeble, etc.):_____

Describe the thorns:_____

Describe the color (above and beneath), **size, serration, rachis-color, and prickles of the leaves:**_____

_____

Describe the stipules:_____

Foliation of plant (light, medium, heavy):_____

Characteristics of roots:_____

Does this cultivar remind you of any other? If so, which one, why, and why do you think it is _not_ that other cultivar?:_____

_____

_____

Geographical location specimen found:_____

Estimated age of property or garden or community where found:_____

_____

Identifiable roses and/or other significant plants in the same garden:_____

_____

_____

Other observations or remarks:_____

_____

_____

Classification

The first question to ask in attempting identification is "What does this entity *look* like?" and the second, "How does it behave?" If the identifier's experience with "old" roses is well-rounded, and the plant looks or acts like a Bourbon, very likely the breeder who classed it and named it felt the same way.

Here is a rough attempt at a key to identification, in the use of which one must remember that other characteristics may take precedence in certain cases over those mentioned, and that the characteristics specified may in some cases be suppressed in the cultivar without prejudicing that cultivar's placement in a particular group—*and* that personal quirks or market conditions may have induced a breeder to place a cultivar in what we would now consider to be an inappropriate class!

I. Once-blooming, or feeble remontancy.
   A. Growth more compact; foliage rough, dull; spination bristly or needle-like; flowers open radially. **Old European Roses**.
   B. Growth more diffuse; foliage smooth, glossy; spination unequal, both bristly and with heavy, often hooked, thorns; flowers open spirally.
      1. Inflorescence a large cluster of flowers; individual blossoms smallish. **Hybrid Noisette**.
      2. Inflorescence few or uni-flowered; individual blossoms largish.
         a. Foliage slender, leaflets more acuminate; petals of heavier substance, usually opaque. **Hybrid China**.
         b. Foliage broad, stout, leaflets more obtuse; petals of a more delicate substance, often quasi-translucent. **Hybrid Bourbon**.
II. Markedly remontant.
   A. Leaves, blossoms medium to tiny in size; secondary growths twiggy, though bush may grow to 1 m (ca. 3 ft) or more.
      1. Flowers in large terminal panicles or clusters on primary canes; fragrance faint or lacking; *R. multiflora* characters frequently present. **Polyanthas**.
      2. Flowers not in large clusters on primary canes; fragrance moderate to strong; *R. multiflora* characters lacking.
         a. Plant, leaves, and flowers markedly reduced in size. **Lawrencianas**.
         b. Plant of average size, though in many cases scandent or "climbing"; flowers usually 5–7 cm in diameter [ca. 2–2.5 in], frequently "nodding." **Teas**, old type.
   B. Leaves, growths of average or large size; flowers usually in smaller clusters or solitary; fragrance generally strong.
      1. Leaves soft, slender, downy; not stiff or rugose in age; spination bristly, often unequal, but all spines tendentially needle-like, narrow or only slightly enlarged at the base; spines straight or in a shallow arc; inflorescence multi-flowered, terminal or quasi-terminal on the cane; calyx narrow to narrowly funnel-shaped, grading into the stem; sepals tendentially foliaceous; flower buds round or squat; flowers open radially, not spirally. **Damask Perpetuals**.
      2. Spination occasional, sometimes remote, usually including at least some large, laterally flattened thorns, enlarged at the base, often strongly hooked; inflorescence often few- or uni-flowered, though in large clusters in certain climbers; ovary more oval to spherical, often much enlarged, usually distinct from stem; sepals tendentially entire; flower buds more conical; flowers open spirally, not radially.
         a. Canes of plant much elongated, quasi-climbing.
            i. Inflorescence composed of many-flowered clusters; leaves more or less narrowly oval-acuminate, tendentially matte-green, not undulate; flower medium-sized or small.
               AA. Leaves, stems reduced in size; scent generally faint. **Climbing Polyanthas**.
               BB. Leaves, stems of average size; scent generally strong. **Noisettes**, old type.
            ii. Inflorescence few-flowered, or flowers solitary; leaves moderately or broadly oval, tendentially glossy green, often undulate; flower average to large in size. **Tea-type Noisettes** and miscellaneous **Climbers**.
         b. Canes of plant moderately or not much elongated; plant bushy or quasi-bushy.
            i. Plant stocky, well ramified.
               AA. Plant glabrous, often glaucous, green; flowers large, well-formed, often pendant; ovary usually large, spherical. **Teas**.
               BB. Plant minutely hirsutulous; ovary medium-sized, oval to elongated.
                  aa. Petals of heavy substance; flowers shallow, convex; petals often quilled in age. **Chinas**.
                  bb. Petals delicate; flowers deeper, concave, rounded when fully open; petals not quilled in age. **China-type Bourbons**.
            ii. Plant open, moderately or poorly ramified.
               AA. Plants usually more restrained in growth, flowers usually in few-flowered clusters or solitary; bud urn-shaped in early stages of expansion; spination tendentially equal, not mixed; thorns usually broad-based, laterally flattened. **Hybrid Teas**.
               BB. Plants usually more robust in growth; flowers frequently in few- to many-flowered clusters; opening bud often not urn-shaped; spination tendentially mixed, both bristly and broad-based.
                  aa. Petals of heavy substance; flowers usually large, more or less erect; growth usually robust, stout. **Hybrid Perpetuals**.
                  bb. Petals delicate; flower usually nodding, medium-sized; growth more slender, long. **Bourbons**.

Having come this far, some groups may be whittled down further—remembering meantime that each group has a large, unspecified, miscellaneous contingent of entities which do not fit neatly into any of the various types and clans: Hybrid Tea–like Teas; Pernetiana Hybrid Perpetuals; undecided entities hovering between China, Tea, and Bourbon; Polyanthas that are actually dwarf Sempervirenses; cluster-flowered Hybrid Teas; recessive Hybrid Perpetuals more like Damask Perpetuals or Bourbons; progressive Bourbons more like Hybrid Teas; and so on! But let us try:

Teas

I. Thorns sparse, strong; flower with fairly faint scent; petals large and rounded; pedicel upright and strong. **Tea/China** hybrids.
II. Thorns abundant; flowers tendentially with medium to strong scent; petals, particularly inner ones, tendentially narrow and acuminate; pedicel weak, often bending under weight of flower.
    A. Color of flower predominantly light pink to white; ovary globular, much inflated at maturity; flower bud rounded, slightly pointed; leaves leathery. **'Adam'** clan.
    B. Color of flower predominantly intense pink, coppery pink, coppery rose-red, to ivory, yellow, or buff.
        1. Growth bushy, spreading; leaflets ovalish, light green; tendency towards blooming in clusters; bud short; pedicel short and weak; ovary small, widening towards the top. **'Caroline'** clan.
            a. Secondary branches tendentially upright.
                i. Foliage ample, flowers large, fragrant, salmon-pink. **'Mme Damaizin'** group.
                ii. Foliage scant to moderate; flowers medium-sized or smallish, not or only lightly fragrant, bright pink, coppery at the nub. **'Comtesse de Labarthe'** group.
            b. Secondary branches tendentially pendant; flower bright red to deep crimson to wine-lee. **'Souvenir de David d'Angers'** group.
        2. Growth upright; leaflets elongate, dentate, purplish at first, then dark green; tendentially uni- to few-flowered inflorescence; bud long, pointed; pedicel relatively long, moderately strong; ovary large, spherical or often pyriform, much enlarged at maturity.
            a. Flowers ivory, primrose, yellow, buff, or apricot in color. **'Safrano'** clan.
            b. Flowers intense pink to coppery red shades, with yellow reflections and yellow nub. **'Red Safrano'** clan.

Hybrid Perpetuals

I. Leaflets small, crowded on rachis; leaves somewhat sparse on bush; flowers relatively small, flat or cupped, red. **'Géant des Batailles'** type.
II. Leaflets large, not markedly crowded on rachis; leaves fairly to very ample on bush; flowers medium to large.
    A. Canes spreading, long, and slender.
        1. Flower flat. **'Baronne Prévost'** type.
        2. Flower cupped to imbricated.
            a. Canes brownish; thorns large. **'Charles Lefebvre'** type.
            b. Canes greenish; thorns medium to small.
                i. Flowers white to blush. **'Mme Récamier'** type.
                ii. Flowers pink, red, or maroon.
                    AA. Thorns numerous, hooked; canes rough. **'Général Jacqueminot'** type.
                    BB. Thorns rare; canes smooth. **'Mme Victor Verdier'** type.
    B. Canes upright, strong, medium to thick.
        1. Canes rigid, stiff.
            a. Internodes short; thorns large. **'Souvenir de la Reine d'Angleterre'** type.
            b. Internodes average length; thorns small. **'La Reine'** type.
        2. Canes not markedly rigid.
            a. Canes short, stocky, smooth; leaves glossy. **'Victor Verdier'** type.
            b. Canes more slender, elongate to "climbing"; leaves not markedly glossy.
                i. Internodes long; flowers medium to dark red, flat; ovary round. **'Triomphe de l'Exposition'** type.
                ii. Internodes not markedly long; flowers light pink to light red, imbricated; ovary elongate. **'Jules Margottin'** type.

Polyanthas

I. Bush dwarf; primary inflorescence on main canes a tendentially leafless, much ramified cluster of many small, usually semi-double, cupped or Ranunculus-form flowers; petals short, rarely or never reflexing; petal-nubs usually white; pedicel strong, upright; little or no scent in flower. **Multiflora-type Polyanthas**.
II. Bush medium to tall; primary inflorescence on main canes a few- to moderately-branched cluster of a moderate number of medium-sized double or full, pointed or often quilled or "cactus-form" flowers of tendentially Tea- or China-rose form; petals long, outer ones usually reflexing in age; petal nubs usually yellowish; pedicel tendentially weak; flower often nodding; flower with moderate scent. **Tea-type Polyanthas**.

To leap from "'Safrano' clan" or "'Général Jacqueminot' type" and land — correctly — on a specific cultivar name takes more than a little intuition combined with just less than infinite luck. If one is very lucky indeed, one, having noticed "deep, irregular serrations in the leaf, purple at the edge," or "scent of plums in marmalade," will recall from one's studies references to such, and a name will come to mind. Otherwise — woe! — more whittling, more tedious sifting — often to no end at all, many if not most cultivars being very hazily defined even in the best old sources, and *wrongly* defined in modern sources. One may very easily be left with half a dozen or more candidates jostling for precedence, all undifferentiated and perhaps undifferentiatable! Still, there are other factors to consider:

Certain flower formations are more typical of some decades than of others. For instance, the "flat" form of 'Souvenir de la Malmaison' or 'Baronne Prévost' was not much favored after perhaps 1860. A truly "full" flower — showing no stamens or pistils — is a rarity among cultivars introduced after about 1910 or 1915, but is to be expected, particularly in "exhibition-class" cultivars, prior to 1895 or 1900. An often unexpected variable would be just what is meant in the literature by the citing of certain color names. A "white" from the pre-'Druschki' era can look rather pinkish or primrose to us; "red" usually means what we would call "deep rose." Depending upon the climate in which the blossom as described was seen, equally veracious authors could describe the same rose as being anything from white or blush with yellow or salmon to being "deep pink." Worse, one must consider what stage of the flower the era was interested in, was describing — a "red" Tea might be one that is only "deep rose" when the bud is first expanding, then quite pink when fully open; the definitive "yellow" Tea, 'Safrano', was nevertheless known as early as 1844 for turning *whitish* by the end of its first day open. Study of the development of the cultivars, knowledge of the stated or inferential goals of the breeders of each era, and familiarity with the "manners and customs" of the breeding-stock to which breeders had recourse can give important hints.

Some cultivars had very wide distribution and thus by sheer force of numbers would be more likely to have survived here and there than would an introduction which never "caught on." Particularly in those areas most remote from France, England, and Germany, the survivors are often cultivars which were "old favorites" even when originally planted. Even when novelty-minded outlanders would manage to get rare, new introductions, they would be precisely the ones most likely to *discard* last year's novelties to make way for *this* year's novelties, thus constantly renewing their collections, and indeed tending to retain only those which performed the best — which would usually turn out to be, at length, the same "old favorites" we should have considered to begin with! Thus, "likelihood" is something to be figured into the calculations. Every factor is worthy of careful consideration. The very fact that a cultivar is rather ambiguous may be significant; look in the literature for cultivars that are listed under different groups by different "authorities" — ambiguity is not erased by the passage of time!

But if, after these extended and profound lucubrations, one is still left with an unidentified red Hybrid Perpetual, light yellow Tea, or pink China, so be it! That is the stage at which we may finally enjoy the plant not because it was introduced in such-and-such a year by so-and-so, and not because one celebrity or another lavished perfumed praises on it — no; we may finally cast aside these spurs towards faddish attraction and genuinely enjoy the rose for what it really is: Nature's simple gift of quiet and most pure beauty.

Appendix Two
DISTINGUISHED SEED BEARERS

"Distinguished seed-bearers which have exercised, and still exercise, such a predominant influence upon Rose advancement." [WD] Origins and a short description are included for each cultivar not otherwise mentioned in this book.

1848

Compiled from *The Rose Garden,* by William Paul:

Hybrid Chinas
'Aurora' [Laffay, pre-1836, light crimson, sometimes with a white line at the center of the petal]
'Chénédolé'
'Duke of Devonshire' [Laffay, pre-1841, rosy lilac striped with white]
'Fulgens' ['Malton']
'Général Allard'
'Jenny' [Duval, pre-1846, rosy lilac]
'Magna Rosea' [Breeder unknown, pre-1848, light rose, very large and very double]
'Maréchal Soult' [light vermilion; "raised at Brenchley, in Kent,"or by Laffay, 1838]
'Petit Pierre' [Breeder unknown, pre-1841, purplish red, very large and very double]
'Riégo' [Vibert, 1831, carmine, "forming an immense bush or tree with fine dark foliage. A little hybridized with the sweet-brier, but retains more of the features of this group (Hybrid Chinas) than of any other seed-bearer"].

Hybrid Bourbons
'Athalin'
'Capitaine Sisolet' [*which we list as a Bourbon*]
'Céline'
'Charles Duval'
'Coupe d'Hébé'
'Daphné' [V. Verdier, 1835, light carmine]
'Dombrowskii'
'Great Western'
'Henri Barbet' [Breeder unknown, pre-1846, light carmine, large and double]
'La Majesteuse' [Breeder unknown, pre-1841, bright rose, large and full]
'Legouvé' [Vibert, 1828, bright carmine]
'Lord John Russell' [Laffay, 1835, brilliant rose, fading; very abundant]
'Paul Perras'

Damask Perpetuals
'D'Esquermes' [Miellez, pre-1836, lively rose, large and full]
'Louis-Philippe I'
'Saint Fiacre' [Mauget, 1844, violet and crimson]

Hybrid Perpetuals
'Comtesse Duchâtel' [Laffay, 1844, rose sometimes tinged with purple]
'Duc d'Alençon' [Breeder unknown, pre-1845, crimson, pale in summer]
'Duc d'Isly' [Lacharme, 1845, "an autumnal Tuscany"]
'Duchesse de Sutherland'
'Edouard Jesse' [*which we call a Hybrid Bourbon*]
'La Bouquetière' [Laffay, 1843, pale rose]
'Lady Elphinstone' [Laffay, 1842, rosy crimson]
'Mme Laffay'
'William Jesse' [*which we call a Hybrid Bourbon*]

Bourbons
'Amarantine' [Breeder unknown, pre-1846, rosy pink]
'Augustine Lelieur' [Breeder unknown, pre-1836, rose-colored, large and double]
'Bouquet de Flore'

'Célimène' [Breeder unknown, pre-1841, silvery blush]
'Cérès' [Breeder unknown, 1841, pale glossy rose]
'Comice de Seine et Marne' [Desprez, 1842, crimson-scarlet to rosy-purple]
'Comte de Rambuteau' [Rolland, 1843, dark rose, tinted with lilac]
'Duc de Chartres' [Breeder unknown, pre-1848, rosy crimson]
'Emile Courtier'
'Gloire des Rosomanes'
'Mme Nérard' [Nérard, 1838, pink]
'Malvina' [Vibert, 1829, rosy pink]
'Marianne' [Laffay, 1845, rosy pink]
'Pierre de St.-Cyr'
'Proserpine'
'Thérèse Margat' [Breeder unknown, pre-1844, rose-pink, edges lighter].

1877

According to *Cultural Directions for the Rose*, [JC] the following may be taken as good seed-bearers:

Hybrid Chinas
'Blairii Nº 2'
'Brennus'
'Chénédolé'
'Fulgens' ['Malton']
'Général Allard'
'Magna Rosea.

Hybrid Bourbons
'Charles Lawson'
'Coupe d'Hébé'
'Paul Ricault'
'Paul Perras'

Damask Perpetuals
'[Rose] Du Roi'

Hybrid Perpetuals
'[Mlle] Annie Wood'
'Baronne Prévost'
'Black Prince'
'Centifolia Rosea'
'Charles Lefebvre'
'Dr. Andry'
'Duchess of Sutherland'
'Duc de Cazes'
'Duc de Rohan' [Lévêque, 1861, red]
'François Lacharme' [V. Verdier, 1861, carmine]
'Géant des Batailles'
'Général Jacqueminot'
'Gloire de Santenay' [Ducher, 1859, purple]
'John Hopper'
'Jules Margottin'
'King's Acre' [Cranston, 1864, rose]
'La Reine'
'Le Rhône' [Guillot fils, 1862, vermilion]
'Lord Clyde' [W. Paul, 1862, crimson]
'Lord Raglan'
'Mme Charles Crapelet'
'Mme Hector Jacquin'
'Pierre Notting'
'Peter Lawson'

'Prince Léon' ['Prince Léon Kotschoubey'? Marest, 1852, flesh]
'Sénateur Vaisse'
'Souvenir de Leveson-Gower'
'Thorin'
'William Jesse'

Bourbons

'Bouquet de Flore'
'Louise Odier'
'Pierre de St.-Cyr'
'Sir Joseph Paxton'

Chinas

'Mrs. Bosanquet'
'Fabvier'
'Old White' [? ='Alba' of William Paul? — or ='Mme Desprez' (Ch)?]

1882

Cited in *The Rose*, by Henry B. Ellwanger:

'Baron Chaurand' [HP, Liabaud, 1869, velvety scarlet]
'Jean Cherpin' [HP]
'Dr. de Chalus' [HP, Touvais, 1871, scarlet]
'Thomas Mills' [HP]
'Adam' [T]
'Alba Rosea' ['Mme Bravy', T]
'Anna de Diesbach' [HP]
'[Mlle] Annie Wood' [HP]
'Antoine Ducher' [HP]
'Baronne Adolphe de Rothschild' [HP]
'Baron de Bonstetten' [HP]
'Beauty of Waltham' [HP]
'Catherine Mermet' [T]
'Charles Lefebvre' [HP]
'Chromatella' [N]
'Comtesse de Labarthe' [T]
'Comtesse d'Oxford' [HP]
'Devoniensis' [T]
'Duchesse de Sutherland' [HP]
'Duchesse d'Edinburgh' [T]
'Duke of Edinburgh' [HP]
'Général Jacqueminot' [HP]
'Géant des Batailles' [HP]
'Gloire de Dijon' [N]
'John Hopper' [HP]
'Jules Margottin' [HP]
'La Reine' [HP]
'Lamarque' [N]
'Lion des Combats' [HP]
'Louise Odier' [B]
'Mme Boutin' [HP]
'Mme Charles Wood' [HP]
'Mme de Tartas' [T]
'Mme de St.-Joseph' [T]
'Mme Falcot' [T]
'Mme Julia Daran' [HP]
'Mme Laffay' [HP]
'Mme Récamier' [HP]

'Mme Victor Verdier' [HP]
'Mme Vidot' [HP]
'Marguerite de St.-Amande' [HP, De Sansal, 1864, light pink]
'Mlle Marie Rady' [HP]
'Ophirie' [N]
'Paul Neyron' [HP]
'Safrano' [T]
'Sénateur Vaisse' [HP]
'Solfatare' [N]
'Souvenir de la Reine d'Angleterre' [HP]
'Souvenir de la Reine des Belges' [HP, De Fauw, 1850, carmine]
'Triomphe des Beaux Arts' [HP]
'Triomphe de l'Exposition' [HP]
'Victor Verdier' [HP]
'Parks' Yellow' [T]

1910

"A few good seed-bearing kinds . . . " listed in *The Rose Annual* [NRS10/55–56]:

'Antoine Rivoire'
'Mme Abel Chatenay'
'Pharisäer'
'Joseph Hill' [HT, Pernet-Ducher, 1903, salmon-pink]
'Frau Karl Druschki'
'Mme Edmée Metz' [? 'Edmée Metz', HT, Soupert & Notting, 1900, rose]
'Mme Ravary'
'[Monsieur] Paul Lédé'
'Le Progrès' [Pernetiana, Pernet-Ducher, 1903, yellow]
'Gustav Grünerwald'
'Laurent Carle'
'Killarney'
'Earl of Warwick' [HT, W. Paul, 1904, salmon-pink]
'[Mme] Caroline Testout'
'White Lady' [HT, W. Paul, 1889, white]
'K.A. Viktoria'
'Mme Lambard'
'Souvenir de William Robinson' [T, Bernaix, 1900, pink]
'Richmond'
'Mme Mélanie Soupert' [HT, Pernet-Ducher, 1905, dawn-pink on yellow]
'Warrior' [HT, W. Paul, 1906, scarlet]
'Mme Gamon'
'Captain Hayward'
'Mrs. John Laing'
'Mme Jean Dupuy'
'Betty'
'General MacArthur'
'G. Nabonnand'
'Farbenkönigen' [HT, Hinner, 1902, rose-red]
'Lady Battersea' [HT, G. Paul, 1901, pink]
'Étoile de France' [HT, Pernet-Ducher, 1905, red]
'Mme Hoste'
'Corallina'
'White Lady' [*again*]
'Lady Roberts'
'Lady Mary Fitzwilliam'
'Prince de Bulgarie'
'Instituteur Sirdey' [HT, Pernet-Ducher, 1905, yellow]

'Marie Van Houtte'
'Countess of Caledon' [HT, A. Dickson, 1897, pink]
'Mme Segond-Weber' [HT, Soupert & Notting, 1908, salmon-pink]
'Dr. Grill'
'Marquise Litta de Breteuil'
'Mme Berkeley'
'President'
'Souvenir d'Un Ami'
'Beryl'
'Souvenir de Pierre Notting'

Appendix Three
SINGLE AND NEARLY SINGLE ROSES

Damask Perpetuals
'Portland Rose'

Chinas
'Beauty of Glenhurst'
'Miss Lowe's Variety'
'Mutabilis'
'Papa Hémeray'
'Pourpre'
'Rose de Bengale'

Teas
— None —

Bourbons
'Bardou Job'

Hybrid Bourbons, Hybrid Chinas,
and Hybrid Noisettes
'L'Admiration'

Hybrid Perpetuals
'Maharajah'

Noisettes and Climbers
'Cooper's Burmese Rose'
'Climbing Dainty Bess'
'Climbing Irish Fireflame'
'Crimson Conquest'
'Cupid'
'Dawn'
'Flying Colours'
'Gigantea Blanc'
'Irish Beauty'

'Lady Waterlow'
'Manettii'
'Milkmaid'
'Mrs. Rosalie Wrinch'
'Nancy Hayward'
'Noëlla Nabonnand'
'Paul's Single White Perpetual'
'Sénateur Amic'
'Sunday Best'

Polyanthas
'Cineraria'
'Cyclope'
'Fireglow'
'Jessie'

Hybrid Teas
'Cecil'
'Dainty Bess'
'Ellen Wilmott'
'Frances Ashton'
'Innocence'
'Irish Brightness'
'Irish Elegance'
'Irish Fireflame'
'Irish Glory'
'Irish Modesty'
'Isobel'
'Kathleen'
'Kathleen Mills'
'K. of K.'
'Lulu'
'Old Gold'
'Sheila'
'Vesuvius'
'White Wings'

Appendix Four
R. multiflora 'POLYANTHA'

A note on the parent of the Polyantha roses:

"This species originated in Japan, whence it was introduced into France for the first time, as far as we know, around 1862. It was the Fleuriste de Paris which received the first slip, which still exists, and which, planted in the nursery of Longchamps, grew into a strong shrub which, each year, is covered with thousands of blossoms of a very beautiful white. Here are the characteristics of the type: Shrub extremely bushy, very vigorous; non-blooming branches nearly 'climbing,' growing to nearly two meters [ca. 6 ft] in the case of young plants on their own roots; strong thorns, enlarged at the base, slightly hooked; 5–7 leaflets, sometimes even nine pairs of oval-elliptical leaflets, which are soft, gentle to the touch, villose, and thoroughly but shallowly dentate; rachis rust-colored, with short prickles similarly colored, enlarged at the base and sharply barbed on each side; blooming branches comparatively slender, with smaller leaflets which are more rounded and more obviously dentate than those of the sterile branches; inflorescence in long, pyramidal, subconical panicles, quite upright, much branched; buds very small, solitary, or most often clustered, on a shortly-villose flower stalk; blossoms lightly and pleasantly fragrant, the scent somewhat resembling that of Tea roses, pure white, or slightly sulphurous; 5 wedge-shaped petals, very large at the summit, which, in the middle, exhibits a large notch, giving it the appearance of the 5-armed Maltese Cross . . . ; hips . . . very small, with deciduous sepals, beautiful glossy red, as if varnished, at maturity, with many long and narrow seeds.

"It blooms around the end of May, and is very ornamental. If perhaps this species originated in Japan, it is also, we are told, found in China. . . . It is from this latter country that Mons A. Leroy's firm has received it with no other name than that of 'new rose.'

"It is evidently quite variable, and the small number of seedlings it has given us have sometimes differed from the type so much that none of the characteristics of the original are preserved. Along the same lines, Mons Jean Sisley tells us, in a letter written September 8, 1873, 'This single 'Polyantha' . . . produced, *without artificial pollination*, very distinct and notable varieties. Guillot fils has obtained double blossoms, yellow as those of the Banksia, and double reds, as well as one he calls remontant, and one with foliage like that of *R. microphylla*; but *none* of these varieties has that characteristic which distinguishes the type: blooming in a panicle, which, to my way of thinking, makes it distinct from all other roses — as well as more meritorious.'

"June 30 of that same year, Mons Sisley wrote to us, ' 'Polyantha' is very hardy. . . . It seeds easily, producing many varieties, which however are not out yet — single pinks, double pinks, single and double yellows, and a very double white. This last is going to be released to commerce. [A footnote adds: *This very double white-blossomed plant looks like a miniature Noisette; it seems to be the equivalent of the Pompon Chinas, and could be used, like them, in borders. . . . It was to be seen at the last exposition at the Palais de l'Industrie, in the booth of Messers Lévêque and Son . . . under the name 'Pâquerette', in allusion to the small size of all its parts, and the elegance of its flower.*] . . . Ph. Rambaux has shown some seedlings which he calls Noisettes, because they have that look — but they are from 'Polyantha'. '

"We have had a chance to see and study the growth and bloom of Monsieur Rambaux's plants, and cannot hesitate to say that they have the appearance of Teas and Noisettes, and that their flowers have, in color, fragrance, and general character, the look of these of these two groups. All the plants are freely remontant, blooming until frost stops them. The hips are nearly all subspherical, smooth, and glossy, varying from 7 to 10 millimeters [ca. .25–.45 in], and in color varying from orange red to brownish violet; one exceptional variety has longly oval-acuminate sepals which are persistant, while all the others are deciduous.

"In a letter of October 25, 1875, on the same subject, Mons Sisley adds, 'I forgot to tell you that the seeds of my children of 'Polyantha' are three or four times larger than those of their mother.' " [R-H76]

Appendix Five
THE ROSE IN CALIFORNIA

The Rose has played a role as garden *conquistador* or colonialist throughout history, accompanying mankind as it has forged into and beyond the frontiers of traditional civilization. Historians have rarely picked up their chisels, styluses, quills, or fountain pens to record the traveling companionship of what is surely Man's best *horticultural* friend as societies migrated and matured. Perhaps the following words on the Rose in California can stand as a representative of the role the Rose has played in all such treks through the millenia, and will also be of interest as showing the speed with which new introductions were embraced by gardeners thousands of miles away from the place of origin of most of the cultivars.

"It is fit to tell the children how those cuttings crossed the plains, cherished and kept moist all the weary way that the pioneer women might have a reminder of home in a new, strange land. And how those pioneer roses reveled in the warm, red soil of the foothills, and cheered many lives which were full of loneliness and longing and often of deep disappointment! With what affection the roses spread a mantle of beauty and fragrance over the forsaken ruins of solitary camps, and how they grow to this day in such solitary places until their stems look like the trunks of old grape vines, but are still full of sap to push out new wood and new bloom aloft. . . . There are few, if any, places in the world where the rose enters more fully into daily life than it does in California. . . . It is . . . as an arbor plant that the rose comes most fully into California life. To live under the rose is literally a possibility in California. Under the shade of the rose the hammock can be drawn and the table spread for *al fresco* refreshment. Many a rural table is spread for months on a rose fringed veranda or in a simple arbor made of poles to support the masses of rose bloom and foliage in which the birds build their nests and from which their songs break forth to greet the dawn or dismiss the evening twilight. California open air life is delightful and the rose is its charming priestess." [EJW]

Roses Preferred in Southern California, May, 1886 (from JR10/66):

'William Allen Richardson' (N)
'Marie Van Houtte' (T)
'Alfred Colomb' (HP)
'Comtesse d'Oxford' (HP)
'Elisa Boëlle' (HP)
'La France' (HT)

'Paul Neyron' (HP)
'Rosy Morn' (HP)
'Julius Finger' (HT)
'William Francis Bennett' (HT)
'American Beauty' (HP)

Recommended for Southern California, 1904 (from L):

White
  'Mabel Morrison' (HP)
  'Niphetos' (T)
  'Lamarque' (N)
  'Aimée Vibert' (N)
  'The Bride' (T)
  'Devoniensis' (T)
  'Kaiserin Auguste Viktoria' (HT)

Flesh Color to Blush
  'Mme Laurette Messimy' (Ch)
  '[Mlle] Augustine Guinoisseau' (HT)
  'Duchesse de Brabant' [='Comtesse de Labarthe'] (T)
  'Viscountess Folkestone' (HT)
  'Captain Christy' (HT)
  'Souvenir de la Malmaison' (B)

Pink to Rose
  'Hermosa' (B)
  'Mme Caroline Testout' (HT)
  'Paul Neyron' (HP)

  'Maman Cochet' (T)
  'Comtesse Riza du Parc' (T)
  'Triomphe du Luxembourg' (T)
  'Catherine Mermet' (T)
  'Mrs. John Laing' (HP)
  'Magna Charta' (HP)

Rose to Red or Carmine
  'Papa Gontier' (T)
  'Duchess of Albany' (HT)
  'Reine Marie Henriette' (Cl)
  'Mme Lambard' (T)
  'Bon Silène' (T)

Scarlet to Deep Red
  'Gloire des Rosomanes' (B)
  'Cramoisi Supérieur' (Ch)
  'Général Washington' (HP)
  'Ulrich Brunner fils' (HP)
  'Général Jacqueminot' (HP)

Dark Crimson
'Black Prince' (HP)
'Prince Camille de Rohan' (HP)
'Empereur du Maroc' (HP)
'Xavier Olibo' (HP)

Sulphur to Light Yellow
'Céline Forestier' (N)
'Chromatella' (N)
'Isabella Sprunt' (T)

Deep Yellow to Apricot
'Safrano' (T)
'Perle des Jardins' (T)
'Rêve d'Or' (N)
'Maréchal Niel' (N)

'Mlle Franziska Krüger' (T)
'Mme Falcot' (T)
'William Allen Richardson' (N)

Various
'Marie Van Houtte' (T)
'Rainbow' (T)
'Archiduc Charles' (Ch)
'Homère' (T)
'Mme de Watteville' (T)
'Fortune's Double Yellow' (Cl)
'Gloire de Dijon' (N)
'Dr. Grill' (T)
'Grace Darling' (HT)
'[Mlle] Cécile Brunner' (Pol)

Southern California, The Rosarian's Carbonek _(or veritable site of the Holy Grail):_

"California is 'different' and eastern experience is oftentimes deceiving." [ARA19/133] "In this favored section not only is it possible and easy to produce outdoor roses the year round, but it is also practicable to grow all the different classes and types." [ARA21/58]

"Only after an exhaustive search from Canada to Mexico did he [Capt. George C. Thomas Jr.] conclude his prospecting for a spot in America best suited for rose-perfection. Later I called at this spot, near Beverly Hills, Calif., where his dreams for finer roses began to be realized." [ARA33/111]

Appendix Six
CULTIVARS BY YEAR

Damask Perpetuals

Ancient
  'Bifera'
Circa 1680
  'Tous les Mois'
Circa 1780
  'Portland Rose'
Pre-1814
  'Venusta'
1815
  'Jeune Henry'
  'Quatre Saisons d'Italie' (circa 1815)
1817
  'Palmyre'
1819
  'Rose du Roi'
Pre-1825
  'Belle Fabert'
Pre-1826
  'Belle de Trianon'
Circa 1831
  'Félicité Hardy'
1832
  'Louis-Philippe I'
Circa 1835
  'Quatre Saisons Blanc Mousseux'
1836
  'Bernard'
1840
  'Marquise de Boccella'
1843
  'Yolande d'Aragon'
1844
  'Jacques Amyot'
  'Mogador'
1847
  'Adèle Mauzé'
  'Blanche-Vibert'
  'Duchesse de Rohan'
  'Joasine Hanet'
  'Julie de Krudner'
  'Sapho'
  'Sydonie'
1849
  'Celina Dubos'
1856
  'Robert Perpétuel'
1858
  'Marbrée'
1859
  'Laurent Heister'
  'Comte de Chambord'
1860
  'Pergolèse'
  'Marie Robert'
1863
  'Delambre'
1868
  'Jacques Cartier'
1869
  'Marie de St.Jean
  'Miranda'
1874
  'Mme Souveton'
1883
  'Rembrandt'
1888
  'Président Dutailly'
1895
  'Panachée de Lyon'

Chinas

Circa 1780
  'Parsons' Pink China'
Circa 1790
  'Slater's Crimson China'
1804
  'Bengale Centfeuilles'
1806
  'Pumila'
1815
  'Rouletii'
Circa 1820
  'Bengale Pompon'
1825
  'Archiduc Charles'
  'Belle de Monza'
  'Bengale d'Automne'
  'Laffay'
  'Le Vésuve'
Circa 1826
  'Papillon'
1827
  'Darius'
  'Pourpre'
1831
  'Fimbriata à Petales Frangés'
1832
  'Catherine II'
  'Bengale Animée'
  'Cramoisi Supérieur'
  'Fabvier'
1834
  'Louis-Philippe'
1835
  'Mme Desprez'
  'Napoléon'

1836
'Némésis'
1837
'Eugène de Beauharnais'
1838
'Bengale Sanguinaire'
'St. Priest de Breuze'
1839
'Pompon de Paris'
1840
'Duchesse de Kent'
1848
'Douglas'
1852
'Elyse Flory'
1854
'Lucullus'
1855
'Viridiflora'
1869
'Ducher'
1872
'Marquisette'
1873
'Sanglant'
1886
'Bengale Nabonnand'
1887
'Miss Lowe's Variety'
'Mme Laurette Messimy'
'Princesse de Sagan'
1888
'Red Pet'
1893
'Institutrice Moulins'
Circa 1894?
'Mutabilis'
1894
'Duke of York'
'Mme Eugène Résal'
1895
'Irène Watts'
'Souvenir de Catherine Guillot'
1896
'Queen Mab'
1897
'Alice Hoffmann'
'Antoinette Cuillerat'
'Aurore'
'Souvenir d'Aimée Terrel des Chênes'
'Souvenir de J. B. Guillot'
1898
'Jean Bach Sisley'
1901
'L'Ouche'
'Maddalena Scalarandis'
1902
'Comtesse du Caÿla'
1903
'Alice Hamilton'
'Arethusa'
1904
'Beauty of Rosemawr'
'Unermüdliche'

1905
'Charlotte Klemm'
1906
'Bébé Fleuri'
1910
'Laure de Broglie'
1913
'Bengali'
1922
'Primrose Queen'
1930
'Purpurea'
1948
'Granate'
1950
'Rosada'

Teas

1810
'Hume's Blush Tea-Scented China'
1824
'Parks' Yellow Tea-Scented China'
1825
'Roi de Siam'
1832
'Bougère'
1834
'Smith's Yellow China'
1835
'Bon Silène'
'Caroline'
'Gigantesque'
'Triomphe du Luxembourg'
1836
'Cels Multiflore'
1838
'Adam'
'Devoniensis'
'Elise Sauvage'
1839
'Safrano'
1841
'Le Pactole' (ca. 1841)
'Niphetos'
'Rival de Pæstum'
1842
'La Sylphide'
1843
'Abricotée'
1845
'Mme Bravy'
'Mme Mélanie Willermoz'
1846
'Mme de St.-Joseph'
'Souvenir d'Un Ami'
1851
'David Pradel'
1852
'Canari'
'Mme Pauline Labonté'
1854
'Louise de Savoie'
'Souvenir d'Elisa Vardon'

1855
'Cornelia Cook'
'Mme de Vatry'
1856
'Souvenir de David d'Angers'
1857
'Comtesse de Labarthe'
1858
'Enfant de Lyon'
'Homère'
'Mme Damaizin'
'Mme Falcot'
'Socrate'
1859
'Duc de Magenta'
'Mme de Tartas'
'Narcisse'
'Rubens'
1860
'Esther Pradel'
'Général Tartas'
'Regulus'
1864
'Mme Charles'
1865
'Isabella Sprunt'
1866
'Mme Margottin'
1867
'Safrano à Fleurs Rouges'
1868
'La Tulipe'
'Marie Sisley'
'Mme Céline Noirey'
1869
'Catherine Mermet'
'Chamoïs'
'Grossherzogin Mathilde'
1870
'Hortensia'
'Mme Azélie Imbert'
'Victor Pulliat'
1871
'Coquette de Lyon'
'La Nankeen'
'Ma Capucine'
'Marie Van Houtte'
'Mme Camille'
'Perfection de Monplaisir'
'Souvenir de Paul Neyron'
1872
'Amazone'
'Anna Olivier'
'Henry Bennett'
'Mme Caroline Küster'
'Mme Dr. Jütté'
'Vallée de Chamonix'
1873
'A. Bouquet'
'Aureus'
'Helvetia'
'Isabelle Nabonnand'
'Mont Rosa'

1874
'Aline Sisley'
'Duchess of Edinburgh'
'Jean Ducher'
'Lutea Flora'
'Marie Guillot'
'Mme Devoucoux'
'Perle des Jardins'
'Shirley Hibberd'
1875
'Maréchal Robert'
1876
'Charles Rovolli'
'Comtesse Riza du Parc'
'Letty Coles'
'Mlle Lazarine Poizeau'
'Mme Welche'
'Souvenir de George Sand'
1877
'American Banner'
'La Princesse Vera'
'Louis Richard'
'Mme la Comtesse de Caserta'
'Mme Maurice Kuppenheim'
'Mme Nabonnand'
'Mystère'
'Paul Nabonnand'
'Triomphe de Milan'
1878
'Alphonse Karr'
'Général Schablikine'
'Innocente Pirola'
'Mlle Blanche Durrschmidt'
'Mlle la Comtesse de Leusse'
'Mme Lambard'
1879
'Duchesse de Vallombrosa'
'Jules Finger'
'Mlle Franziska Krüger'
'Mlle Marie Moreau'
'Mme Barthélemy Levet'
'Mme Pierre Perny'
'Reine Emma des Pays-Bas'
1880
'Mme Caro'
'Mme Chédane-Guinoisseau'
'Mme Joseph Schwartz'
1881
'Comtesse Alban de Villeneuve'
'Étoile de Lyon'
'Mme Cusin'
1882
'André Schwartz'
'Baron de St.-Triviers'
'Blanche Nabonnand'
'Hermance Louisa de La Rive'
'Honourable Edith Gifford'
'Mme Crombez'
'Mme Dubroca'
'Mme Eugène Verdier'
'Mme Léon Février'
'Mme Remond'
'Papa Gontier'
'Princess of Wales'

'Rose Nabonnand'
'Souvenir de Germain de St.-Pierre'
'Souvenir de Thérèse Levet'
1883
'Edouard Gautier'
'Impératrice Maria Féodorowna de Russie'
'Marie d'Orléans'
'Mme de Watteville'
'Mme F. Brassac'
'Souvenir du Rosiériste Rambaux'
'Sunset'
'Vicomtesse de Bernis'
1884
'Charles de Legrady'
'Mme Fanny Pauwels'
'Rosalie'
'Souvenir de Gabrielle Drevet'
'White Bon Silène'
1885
'Camille Roux'
'Comtesse de Frigneuse'
'Edmond de Biauzat'
'Exadelphé'
'Flavien Budillon'
'Marquise de Vivens'
'Mlle Suzanne Blanchet'
'Mme David'
'Reine Olga'
'Souvenir de l'Amiral Courbet'
'Souvenir de Victor Hugo'
'The Bride'
1886
'Château des Bergeries'
'Claudius Levet'
'Dr. Grill'
'Lady Stanley'
'Lady Zoë Brougham'
'Luciole'
'Marie Lambert'
'Mlle Claudine Perreau'
'Mme A. Étienne'
'Mme Agathe Nabonnand'
'Mme Honoré Defresne'
'Mme Scipion Cochet'
'Namenlose Schöne'
'S.A.R. Mme la Princesse de Hohenzollern,
    Infante de Portugal'
'Vicomtesse de Wauthier'
1887
'Comtesse Anna Thun'
'Ethel Brownlow'
'Mme Claire Jaubert'
'Mme Hoste'
'Mme Philémon Cochet'
'Thérèse Lambert'
'V. Viviand Morel'
1888
'Adèle de Bellabre'
'Annie Cook'
'Baronne Henriette de Loew'
'Capitaine Lefort'
'Comtesse Julie Hunyady'
'Edmond Sablayrolles'
'Ernest Metz'

'Francisca Pries'
'G. Nabonnand'
'Joseph Métral'
'Lady Castlereagh'
'Mme Jules Cambon'
'Mme Pierre Guillot'
'Mme Thérèse Deschamps'
'Monsieur Charles de Thézillat'
'Souvenir d'Espagne'
1889
'Duchesse Marie Salviati'
'Georges Farber'
'J.-B. Varonne'
'Marion Dingee'
'Mlle Jeanne Guillaumez'
'Mme Marthe du Bourg'
'Mme Olga'
'Mme Philippe Kuntz'
'Mrs. James Wilson'
'Rainbow'
'Sappho'
'Souvenir d'Auguste Legros'
'Souvenir de François Gaulain'
'Souvenir du Dr. Passot'
'The Queen'
'White Pearl'
1890
'Antoinette Durieu'
'Bella'
'Charles de Franciosi'
'Comtesse de Vitzthum'
'Comtesse Eva Starhemberg'
'Elisa Fugier'
'Général D. Mertschansky'
'Maurice Rouvier'
'Medea'
'Miss Marston'
'Miss Wenn'
'Mlle Christine de Noué'
'Mme Elie Lambert'
'Mme la Princesse de Bessaraba
    de Brancovan'
'Pearl Rivers'
'Professeur Ganiviat'
'Souvenir de Clairvaux'
'Souvenir de Lady Ashburton'
'Souvenir de Mme Lambard'
'Souvenir de Mme Sablayrolles'
1891
'Dr. Grandvilliers'
'Elise Heymann'
'Henry M. Stanley'
'Maud Little'
'Mme Pelisson'
'Mme Victor Caillet'
'Monsieur Edouard Littaye'
'Monsieur Tillier'
'Mrs. Jessie Fremont'
'Sénateur Loubet'
'Souvenir de Mme Levet'
'Waban'
1892
'Archiduc Joseph'
'Comtesse Festetics Hamilton'

'Golden Gate'
'H. Plantagenet Comte d'Anjou'
'Léon XIII'
'Léonie Osterrieth'
'Madeleine Guillaumez'
'Maman Cochet'
'Mme la Baronne Berge'
'Winnie Davis'

1893
'Bridesmaid'
'Comtesse Dusy'
'Corinna'
'Erzherzog Franz Ferdinand'
'Graziella'
'Perle de Feu'
'Princesse Alice de Monaco'
'Souvenir de Geneviève Godard'

1894
'Comte Chandon'
'Francis Dubreuil'
'Jean André'
'Mme Ernestine Verdier'
'Mme Laurent Simons'
'Rose d'Evian'
'Souvenir de Laurent Guillot'
'V. Vivo é Hijos'
'Virginia'

1895
'Auguste Comte'
'Comtesse Bardi'
'Comtesse Lily Kinsky'
'Grand-Duc Pierre de Russie'
'Léon de Bruyn'
'Marie Soleau'
'Mlle Marie-Louise Oger'
'Mme Emilie Charrin'
'Mme Henri Graire'
'Mme Von Siemens'
'Mrs. J. Pierpont Morgan'
'Princesse de Venosa'
'Senator McNaughton'
'Sylph'
'Zephyr'

1896
'Émilie Gonin'
'Enchantress'
'General Robert E. Lee'
'Gloire de Deventer'
'Improved Rainbow'
'Mlle Anna Charron'
'Princess Bonnie'
'Souvenir de Jeanne Cabaud'
'White Maman Cochet'

1897
'Baronne Ada'
'Baronne Henriette Snoy'
'Dr. Pouleur'
'Empress Alexandra of Russia'
'Marguerite Ketten'
'Mme C. P. Strassheim'
'Mme Derepas-Matrat'
'Mme Jacques Charreton'
'The Sweet Little Queen of Holland'

1898
'Albert Stopford'
'Beryl'
'F. L. Segers'
'Frau Geheimrat Von Boch'
'Fürstin Infantin de Hohenzollern'
'Lucie Faure'
'Margherita di Simone'
'Meta'
'Mlle Jeanne Philippe'
'Mme Ada Carmody'
'Mme Berkeley'
'Mrs. Oliver Ames'
'Muriel Grahame'
'Palo Alto'
'Peach Blossom'
'Princesse Etienne de Croy'
'Principessa di Napoli'
'Reichsgraf E. von Kesselstatt'
'Rosa Mundi'
'Winter Gem'

1899
'Alliance Franco-Russe'
'Antoine Weber'
'Captain Philip Green'
'Frances E. Willard'
'Général Gallieni'
'Georges Schwartz'
'Hovyn de Tronchère'
'Maid of Honour'
'Mme Clémence Marchix'
'Mme C. Liger'
'Mme Errera'
'Mme Gustave Henry'
'Mrs. Edward Mawley'
'Santa Rosa'
'Souvenir de William Robinson'
'Sunrise'

1900
'Burbank'
'Comte Amédé de Foras'
'Corallina'
'Lady Mary Corry'
'Mme Adolphe Dohair'
'Mme Antoine Rébé'
'Mme Ernest Perrin'
'Mrs. Reynolds Hole'
'Sulphurea'
'The Alexandra'

1901
'Boadicea'
'Capitaine Millet'
'Dr. Félix Guyon'
'Ivory'
'Marquise de Querhoënt'
'Miss Agnes C. Sherman'
'Mlle Emma Vercellone'
'Mme Antoine Mari'
'Mme Jean Dupuy'
'Mme Vermorel'
'Mrs. B. R. Cant'

1902
'Abbé Garroute'
'Comtesse de Noghera'

'Comtesse Sophie Torby'
'Fortuna'
'Julius Fabianics de Misefa'
'Lady Roberts'
'Marguerite Gigandet'
'Marie Segond'
'Morning Glow'
'Souvenir de Pierre Notting'
1903
'Anna Jung'
'Betty Berkeley'
'Comtesse Emmeline de Guigné'
'Empereur Nicolas II'
'Freiherr von Marschall'
'Mlle Blanche Martignat'
'Mme Achille Fould'
'Perle des Jaunes'
1904
'Albert Hoffmann'
'Koningin Wilhelmina'
'Mme Albert Bernardin'
'Uncle John'
1905
'Blumenschmidt'
'Golden Oriole'
'Joseph Paquet'
'Minnie Francis'
'Mme Constant Soupert'
'Mme Gamon'
'True Friend'
1906
'Helen Good'
'Lena'
'Mme Paul Varin-Bernier'
'Mme Therese Roswell'
'Mrs. Myles Kennedy'
'Nelly Johnstone'
'Pénélope'
1907
'Canadian Belle'
'Harry Kirk'
'Hugo Roller'
'Mrs. Dudley Cross'
'Souvenir of Stella Gray'
1908
'Alix Roussel'
'Molly Sharman-Crawford'
'Nita Weldon'
'Primrose'
'Rhodologue Jules Gravereaux'
'Rosomane Narcisse Thomas'
'William R. Smith'
1910
'Lady Hillingdon'
'Miss Alice de Rothschild'
'Mrs. Alice Broomhall'
'Mrs. Foley-Hobbs'
'Mrs. Hubert Taylor'
'Recuerdo di Antonio Peluffo'
1911
'Alexander Hill Gray'
'Niles Cochet'
1912
'Madison'

'Mrs. Herbert Hawksworth'
1913
'Clementina Carbonieri'
'Maria Star'
1914
'Lady Plymouth'
'Mrs. Campbell-Hall'
'Mrs. S. T. Wright'
1916
'Mme Charles Singer'
1918
'Mevrouw Boreel van Hogelander'
1920
'Souvenir de Gilbert Nabonnand'
1922
'Rosette Delizy'
1924
'Lorraine Lee'
Circa 1927
'Simone Thomas'
1929
'Susan Louise'
Circa 1936?
'Baxter Beauty'

Bourbons

1820
'Rosier de Bourbon'
1821
'Rose Edouard'
1825
'Gloire des Rosomanes'
1831
'Mme Desprez'
1832
'Mrs. Bosanquet'
1834
'Hermosa'
'Reine des Île-Bourbons'
1837
'Emile Courtier'
1838
'Acidalie'
'Mme Nérard'
'Pierre de St.-Cyr'
1839
'Bouquet de Flore'
1841
'Proserpine'
1842
'Georges Cuvier'
'Souchet'
1843
'Souvenir de la Malmaison'
1844
'Reine des Vierges'
Circa 1845
'Capitaine Sisolet'
1845
'Deuil de Duc d'Orléans'
'Vicomte Fritz de Cussy'
1846
'Leveson-Gower'

'Maréchal du Palais'
'Triomphe de la Duchère'
1847
'Duchesse de Thuringe'
1848
'Apolline'
1849
'Toussaint-Louverture'
1850
'Scipion Cochet'
1851
'Louise Odier'
'Mlle Blanche Laffitte'
'Souvenir de l'Exposition de Londres'
1852
'Comice de Tarn et Garonne'
'Dr. Leprestre'
'Prince Albert'
'Reveil'
'Velouté d'Orléans'
1854
'Omer-Pacha'
1855
'Marquis de Balbiano'
1856
'Mme Massot'
1858
'Comtesse de Barbantane'
'Edith de Murat'
1859
'Baron G.-B. Gonella'
'Gourdault'
1860
'Dr. Brière'
'Duc de Crillon'
'Garibaldi'
'Michel Bonnet'
1861
'Baronne de Noirmont'
'Loúise D'Arzens'
'Mme Adélaïde Ristori'
1862
'Deuil du Dr. Reynaud'
'Emotion'
'Lady Emily Peel'
'Mme Alfred de Rougemont'
'Président Gausen'
'Reynolds Hole'
1863
'Heroïne de Vaucluse'
'Mlle Joséphine Guyet'
'Mme Doré'
'Reverend H. d'Ombrain'
1864
'Adrienne de Cardoville'
'Monsieur Dubost'
'Prince Napoléon'
'Souvenir de Louis Gaudin'
1865
'Baronne de Maynard'
'Béatrix'
'Coquette des Blanches'
'Mme Charles Baltet'
'Mme Cornélissen'

'Souvenir du Président Lincoln'
1866
'Souvenir de Mme August Charles'
1867
'Boule de Neige'
'Coquette des Alpes'
'Mme Gabriel Luizet'
1868
'Le Roitelet'
'Zéphirine Drouhin'
1869
'Mlle Favart'
1872
'Amédée de Langlois'
'Belle Nanon'
'Perle des Blanches'
'Reine Victoria'
'Souvenir d'Adèle Launay'
1873
'Olga Marix'
1874
'Comtesse de Rocquigny'
'Mme de Sévigny'
'Mme Thiers'
1876
'Queen of Bedders'
1877
'Mme François Pittet'
'Robusta'
1878
'Mme Pierre Oger'
1879
'Alexandre Pelletier'
'Perle d'Angers'
1880
'Mme Isaac Pereire'
1881
'Mlle Madeleine de Vauzelles'
1882
'Malmaison Rouge'
'Mme Fanny de Forest'
'Mme Olympe Térestchenko'
1884
'Mlle Berger'
1886
'Gloire d'Olivet'
'Mme Chevalier'
1887
'Bardou Job'
'Mlle Claire Truffaut'
'Mlle Marie Drivon'
'Mme Létuvée de Colnet'
1888
'Kronprinzessin Viktoria von Preussen'
'Mme Ernst Calvat'
1889
'Marie Dermar'
'Monsieur A. Maillé'
'Souvenir de Monsieur Bruel'
'Zigeunerblut'
1890
'Mlle Andrée Worth'
'Mme Dubost'
'Souvenir de Victor Landeau'

1891
    'Bijou de Royat-les-Bains'
    'Mlle Alice Marchand'
    'Mrs. Paul'
    'Président de la Rocheterie'
    'Souvenir du Lieutenant Bujon'
1892
    'Monsieur Cordeau'
1893
    'Mme Edmond Laporte'
    'Mme Nobécourt'
1894
    'Champion of the World'
1895
    'Philemon Cochet'
1897
    'Gruss an Teplitz'
1899
    'Dunkelrote Hermosa'
    'Mme Arthur Oger'
1900
    'J. B. M. Camm'
    'Mme Eugène E. Marlitt'
1904
    'Mme d'Enfert'
1905
    'Capitaine Dyel, de Graville'
1909
    'Frau O. Plegg'
    'Variegata di Bologna'
1912
    'Martha'
1913
    'Hofgärtner Kalb'
1918
    'Jean Rameau'
1919
    'Kathleen Harrop'
1920
    'Adam Messerich'
1927
    'Frau Dr. Schricker'
1950
    'Souvenir de St. Anne's'

Hybrid Bourbons, Hybrid Chinas, and Hybrid Noisettes

1820
    'George IV'
Circa 1825
    'Chévrier'
    'Roxelane'
1825
    'La Nubienne'
1828
    'Las-Cases'
1829
    'Belle de Crécy'
    'Malton'
By 1829
    'Duchesse de Montebello'
Circa 1830
    'Triomphe de Laffay'

1830
    'Athalin'
    'Brennus'
1831
    'Riégo'
1835
    'Mme Plantier'
Circa 1835
    'Céline'
    'Général Allard'
Circa 1836
    'Le Vingt-Neuf Juillet'
1838
    'Great Western'
    'William Jesse'
1840
    'Cardinal de Richelieu'
    'Charles Duval'
    'Charles Louis Nº 1'
    'Charles Louis Nº 2'
    'Chénédolé'
    'Coupe d'Hébé'
    'Comtesse de Lacépède'
    'Dembrowski'
    'Edward Jesse'
1842
    'Prince Charles'
1845
    'Paul Ricault'
    'Richelieu'
1846
    'Belmont'
1847
    'Frédéric II de Prusse'
1851
    'Joseph Gourdon'
1852
    'Sir Joseph Paxton'
1853
    'Charles Lawson'
    'Vivid'
1855
    'Impératrice Eugénie'
1856
    'L'Admiration'
1859
    'Souvenir de Némours'
1866
    'Paul Verdier'
1868
    'Mme Lauriol de Barney'
1870
    'Paul Perras'
1873
    'Catherine Bonnard'
1874
    'Souvenir de Mère Fontaine'
1876
    'Mme Galli-Marie'
    'Souvenir de Paul Dupuy'
1877
    'Mme Jeannine Joubert'
1879
    'Jules Jürgensen'

1885
'Mrs. Degraw'
1892
'Frances Bloxam'
'Francis B. Hayes'
1897
'Mme Auguste Rodrigues'
1899
'Purity'
1909
'Parkzierde'
'Zigeunerknabe'

Hybrid Perpetuals

1833
'Gloire de Guérin'
1834
'Perpétuelle de Neuilly'
1835
'Sisley'
1837
'Prince Albert'
'Princesse Hélène'
1838
'Miss House'
1839
'Comte de Paris'
'Duchesse de Sutherland'
'Mme Laffay'
1840
'Ornement du Luxembourg'
'Princesse de Joinville'
1841
'Mistress Elliot'
1842
'Baronne Prévost'
'Dr. Marx'
1844
'La Reine'
'Louise Peyronny'
1845
'Cornet'
'Jacques Laffitte'
1846
'Géant des Batailles'
1847
'Duchesse de Galliera'
'Gerbe de Roses'
1848
'Pie IX'
1849
'Caroline De Sansal'
'Colonel Foissy'
'Comte Bobrinsky'
1850
'Comte Odart'
'Desgaches'
'Lion des Combats'
'William Griffith'
1851
'Auguste Mie'
'Dr. Jamain'
'Duchesse d'Orléans'

'Général Bedeau'
'Mère de St. Louis'
1852
'Comte de Nanteuil'
'Génie de Châteaubriand'
'Lady Stuart'
'Reine de Castille'
'Rubens'
'Souvenir de Leveson-Gower'
'Vicomtesse Laure de Gironde'
1853
'Alphonse de Lamartine'
'Général Jacqueminot'
'Jules Margottin'
'Marguerite Lecureaux'
'Mme Récamier'
'Ville de St.-Denis'
1854
'Duchesse de Cambacèrès'
'Lord Raglan'
'Mme de Trotter'
'Mme Desirée Giraud'
'Mme Masson'
'Mme Schmitt'
'Mme Vidot'
'Panachée d'Orléans'
'Prince Noir'
1855
'Arthur De Sansal'
'Mme Knorr'
'Monsieur de Montigny'
'Pæonia'
'Pauline Lansezeur'
'Souvenir de la Reine d'Angleterre'
'Triomphe de l'Exposition'
1856
'Bouquet Blanc'
1857
'Cardinal Patrizzi'
'Mme Marie Van Houtte'
'Reine de Danemark'
'Souvenir de Béranger'
1858
'Anna Alexieff'
'Anna de Diesbach'
'Ardoisée de Lyon'
'Bouquet de Marie'
'Comtesse Cécile de Chabrillant'
'Dr. Bretonneau'
'Empereur du Maroc'
'François I'
'François Arago'
'Giuletta'
'Orderic Vital'
'Oriflamme de St.-Louis'
'Virginale'
1859
'Boccace '
'Eugène Appert'
'Louis XIV'
'Mlle Bonnaire'
'Mlle Eugénie Verdier'
'Mlle Marie Dauvesse'
'Mme Boll'

'Mme Céline Touvais'
'Mme Charles Crapelet'
'Montebello'
'Sénateur Vaïsse'
'Triomphe d'Alençon'
'Victor-Emmanuel'
'Victor Verdier'
1860
'Amiral Gravina'
'Enfant de France'
'Général Washington'
'Léonie Lartay'
'Reine des Violettes'
'Robert de Brie'
1861
'Alexandre Dumas'
'Charles Lefebvre'
'Clémence Joigneaux'
'Duc de Cazes'
'La Brillante'
'Maurice Bernardin'
'Mlle Léonie Persin'
'Mme Auguste van Geert'
'Mme Boutin'
'Mme Charles Wood'
'Mme Clémence Joigneaux'
'Mme Julia Daran'
'Olivier Belhomme'
'Prince Camille de Rohan'
'Simon de St.-Jean'
'Souvenir de Monsieur Rousseau'
'Souvenir du Comte de Cavour'
'Triomphe de Caen'
'Turenne'
'Vulcain'
1862
'Beauty of Waltham'
'Comtesse de Polignac'
'Duc d'Anjou'
'Henri IV'
'Jean Goujon'
'John Hopper'
'Mme Crespin'
'Peter Lawson'
'Président Lincoln'
'Souvenir de Charles Montault'
'Vainqueur de Goliath'
1863
'Alpaïde de Rotalier'
'Centifolia Rosea'
'Charles Margottin'
'Claude Million'
'Comte de Falloux'
'Duc d'Harcourt'
'Eugène Verdier'
'George Paul'
'La Duchesse de Morny'
'Léopold I, Roi des Belges'
'Lord Macaulay'
'Marie Baumann'
'Michel-Ange'
'Mlle Gabrielle de Peyronny'
'Mme Charles Verdier'
'Mme Victor Verdier'

'Paul de la Meilleraye'
'Pierre Notting'
1864
'Abbé Berlèze'
'Achille Gonod'
'Charles Wood'
'Comtesse de Paris'
'Dr. Andry'
'Duc de Wellington'
'Duchesse de Caylus'
'Jean Rosenkrantz'
'John Gould Veitch'
'John Keynes'
'La Tendresse'
'Marie Boissée'
'Mlle Marie de la Villeboisnet'
'Monsieur Bonçenne'
'Prince Eugène de la Beauharnais'
'Princess of Wales'
'Rushton-Radclyffe'
'Souvenir de William Wood'
'Triomphe de la Terre des Roses'
1865
'Abel Grand'
'Alfred Colomb'
'Aurore Boréale'
'Camille Bernardin'
'Denis Hélye'
'Elisabeth Vigneron'
'Fisher-Holmes'
'Gloire de Ducher'
'Jean Cherpin'
'Joséphine de Beauharnais'
'Louis Noisette'
'Mlle Marie Rady'
'Mme Fillion'
'Prince de Portia'
'Prudence Besson'
'Souvenir du Dr. Jamain'
'Xavier Olibo'
1866
'André Leroy d'Angers'
'Antoine Ducher'
'Baronne Maurice de Graviers'
'Black Prince'
'Horace Vernet'
'Mlle Annie Wood'
'Mlle Berthe Lévêque'
'Mlle Madeleine Nonin'
'Mlle Thérèse Levet'
'Monsieur Lauriol de Barney'
'Napoléon III'
'Paul Verdier'
'Souvenir de Monsieur Boll'
'Thorin'
'Velours Pourpre'
'Ville de Lyon'
1867
'Aristide Dupuy'
'Aurore du Matin'
'Baron Haussmann'
'Comtesse de Falloux'
'Comtesse de Turenne'
'Dr. Hurta'

'Duchesse d'Aoste'
'Général Barral'
'Général Désaix'
'Lisette de Béranger'
'Meyerbeer'
'Mlle Elise Chabrier'
'Mme Alice Dureau'
'Mme Chirard'
'Mme Noman'
'Président Willermoz'
'Prince de Joinville'
'Souvenir de Caillat'
'Souvenir de Mme de Corval'
'Vicomtesse de Vezins'

1868
'Baronne Adolphe de Rothschild'
'Berthe Baron'
'Devienne-Lamy'
'Duke of Edinburgh'
'Dupuy-Jamain'
'Jeanne Sury'
'Marquise de Gibot'
'Marquise de Mortemart'
'Marquise de Verdun'
'Maurice Lepelletier'
'Mme Clert'
'Mme Hersilie Ortgies'
'Mme Lierval'
'Monsieur Journaux'
'Notaire Bonnefond'
'Thyra Hammerich'
'Vicomte Maison'
'Victor Le Bihan'

1869
'Abbé Giraudier'
'Blanche de Méru'
'Charles Turner'
'Clémence Raoux'
'Comtesse d'Oxford'
'Elisa Boëlle'
'Ferdinand de Lesseps'
'Général de la Martinière'
'Hippolyte Jamain'
'Jules Seurre'
'La Motte Sanguin'
'Lena Turner'
'Louis Van Houtte'
'Marquise de Castellane'
'Mme la Générale Decaen'
'Paul Neyron'
'Princesse Louise'
'Souvenir de Mme Hennecourt'
'Suzanne Wood'

1871
'Abbé Bramerel'
'Baron de Bonstetten'
'Baronne de Prailly'
'François Michelon'
'L'Espérance'
'Le Havre'
'Lyonnais'
'Maxime de la Rocheterie'
'Mme Bellon'
'Mme de Ridder'

'Mme Georges Schwartz'
'Mme Hippolyte Jamain'
'Mme Renard'
'Mme Scipion Cochet'
'Monsieur Cordier'
'Prince Stirbey'

1872
'Bessie Johnson'
'Duhamel-Dumonceau'
'Etienne Levet'
'Félicien David'
'Golfe-Juan'
'John Laing'
'Mme Soubeyran'
'Mrs. Laing'
'Souvenir de John Gould Veitch'
'Souvenir de Spa'

1873
'Albert Payé'
'Comtesse de Bresson'
'Deuil de Dunois'
'Etienne Dubois'
'Marguerite Jamain'
'Miller-Hayes'
'Mme Bernutz'
'Mme Louis Lévêque'
'Monsieur Etienne Dupuy'
'Panachée Langroise'
'Souvenir de la Princesse Amélie
      des Pays-Bas'
'Thomas Mills'
'Triomphe de Toulouse'

1874
'Antoine Mouton'
'Bernard Verlot'
'Comtesse de Serenyi'
'Crimson Bedder'
'Duchess of Edinburgh'
'E. Y. Teas'
'Firebrand'
'Gonsoli Gaëtano'
'Hippolyte Jamain'
'Ingénieur Madèlé'
'John Stuart Mill'
'La Rosière'
'La Syrène'
'Marguerite Brassac'
'Miss Hassard'
'Peach Blossom'
'Philippe Bardet'
'Souvenir du Baron de Semur'

1875
'Abel Carrière'
'Alexandre Chomer'
'Alexis Lepère'
'Arthur Oger'
'Avocat Duvivier'
'Colonel De Sansal'
'Duc de Montpensier'
'Duchesse de Vallombrosa'
'Eugene Fürst'
'Général Duc d'Aumale'
'Henry Bennett'
'Jean Liabaud'

'Jean Soupert'
'Mme Ferdinand Jamin'
'Mme Grandin-Monville'
'Prince Arthur'
'Sir Garnet Wolseley'
'Souvenir d'Arthur De Sansal'
'Star of Waltham'
'Triomphe de France'

1876
'Baronne de Medem'
'Berthe Du Mesnil de Mont Chauveau'
'Charles Martel'
'Comtesse Hélène Mier'
'Duc de Chartres'
'Emily Laxton'
'Empress of India'
'Magna Charta'
'Marchioness of Exeter'
'Marie Louise Pernet'
'Mlle Léonie Giessen'
'Mme Maurice Rivoire'
'Mme Sophie Tropot'
'Mme Verlot'
'Monseigneur Fournier'
'Monsieur Fillion'
'Mrs. Baker'
'Princesse Charles d'Aremberg'
'Sultan of Zanzibar'
'Tancrède'
'Alfred K. Williams'
'Barthélemy-Joubert'
'Bicolore'
'Comtesse de Flandres'
'Dames Patronesses d'Orléans'
'Dr. Auguste Krell'
'Duchesse d'Ossuna'
'Fontenelle'
'Mme Gabriel Luizet'
'Mme Roger'
'Mme Théobald Sernin'
'Mme Thévenot'
'Président Schlachter'
'Princesse Lise Troubetzkoï'
'Souvenir d'Adolphe Thiers'
'Souvenir d'Auguste Rivière'

1878
'A. Geoffrey de St.-Hilaire'
'Alexandre Dutitre'
'Benjamin Drouet'
'Deuil de Colonel Denfert'
'Dr. Baillon'
'Edouard Fontaine'
'François Gaulain'
'John Bright'
'Jules Chrétien'
'Kaiser Wilhelm I'
'Léon Renault'
'Lord Beaconsfield'
'Mabel Morrison'
'Mme Amélie Baltet'
'Mme Charles Meurice'
'Mme Charles Truffaut'
'Mme Eugène Verdier'
'Mme Loeben de Sels'

'Monsieur le Préfet Limbourg'
'Pierre Caro'
'Princesse Marie Dolgorouky'
'Rosy Morn'
'Souvenir de Laffay'
'Souvenir de Mme Robert'
'Souvenir de Victor Verdier'
'William Warden'

1879
'Abraham Zimmermann'
'Alsace-Lorraine'
'Ambrogio Maggi'
'Amedée Philibert'
'Baron Taylor'
'Catherine Soupert'
'Charles Darwin'
'Comte de Mortemart'
'Comte Florimund de Bergeyck'
'Comte Horace de Choiseul'
'Countess of Rosebery'
'Duchess of Bedford'
'Édouard André le Botaniste'
'Ferdinand Chaffolte'
'Gloire de Bourg-la-Reine'
'Henriette Petit'
'Jean Lelièvre'
'Mlle Jules Grévy'
'Mme Elisa Tasson'
'Mme Georges Vibert'
'Monsieur Eugène Delaire'
'Panachée d'Angers'
'Rosièriste Harms'
'Souvenir d'Aline Fontaine'
'Souvenir de Monsieur Faivre'
'Vincent-Hippolyte Duval'

1880
'Comte Frédéric de Thun de Hohenstein'
'Crown Prince'
'Dr. Hogg'
'Duke of Teck'
'François Levet'
'Georges Moreau'
'Guillaume Gillemot'
'Mme Montel'
'Monsieur Alfred Leveau'
'Souvenir de Mme Alfred Vy'
'Souvenir du Président Porcher'

1881
'A.-M. Ampère'
'Albert La Blotais'
'Archidechesse Elizabeth d'Autriche'
'Comte Adrien de Germiny'
'Comte de Flandres'
'Comtesse Henriette Combes'
'Ernest Prince'
'François Olin'
'Friedrich von Schiller'
'Gustave Thierry'
'Mary Pochin'
'Mlle Elisabeth de la Rocheterie'
'Mlle Marie Chauvet'
'Mme Crozy'
'Mme Fortuné Besson'
'Mme Marie Lavalley'

'Mme Marthe d'Halloy'
'Mme Pierre Margery'
'Mme Rambaux'
'Mme Yorke'
'Monsieur Jules Monges'
'Pride of Waltham'
'Souvenir de Mme Berthier'
'Souvenir de Monsieur Droche'
'Ulrich Brunner fils'
'Violette Bouyer'

1882

'Adélaïde de Meynot'
'Alexandre Dupont'
'Baron de Wolseley'
'Baron Nathaniel de Rothschild'
'Beauty of Beeston'
'Duchess of Connaught'
'Earl of Pembroke'
'Heinrich Schultheis'
'Joachim du Bellay'
'Lecocq-Dumesnil'
'Léon Say'
'Marguerite de Roman'
'Merveille de Lyon'
'Michel Strogoff'
'Mlle Hélène Croissandeau'
'Mlle Marie Closon'
'Mme Alexandre Jullien'
'Mme Apolline Foulon'
'Mme François Bruel'
'Mme Louise Vigneron'
'Mme Marie Lagrange'
'Mme Veuve Alexandre Pommery'
'Monsieur Joseph Chappaz'
'Monsieur Jules Maquinant'

1883

'Alphonse Soupert'
'Boileau'
'Charles Lamb'
'Colonel Félix Breton'
'Directeur Alphand'
'Directeur N. Jensen'
'Eclair'
'Emperor'
'Grandeur of Cheshunt'
'Lord Bacon'
'Mlle Hélène Michel'
'Mlle Suzanne-Marie Rodocanachi'
'Mme Bertha Mackart'
'Monsieur Francisque Rive'
'Monsieur le Capitaine Louis Frère'
'Président Sénélar'
'Princesse Radziwill'
'Prosper Laugier'
'Reveil du Primtemps'
'Secrétaire J. Nicolas'
'Souvenir de Léon Gambetta'
'White Baroness'

1884

'Aline Rozey'
'Amiral Courbet'
'Baronne Nathaniel de Rothschild'
'Charles Bonnet'
'Comtesse Cahen d'Anvers'

'Desirée Fontaine'
'Duc de Marlborough'
'Edouard Hervé'
'Félix Mousset'
'Général Appert'
'Mans Mackart'
'Laurent de Rillé'
'Lord Frederic Cavendish'
'Louis Philippe Albert d'Orléans'
'Mme Edmond Fabre'
'Mme Eugénie Frémy'
'Mme Francis Buchner'
'Mme Lucien Chauré'
'Monsieur Hoste'
'Mrs. George Dickson'
'Olivier Métra'
'Pride of Reigate'
'Queen of Queens'
'Souvenir d'Alphonse Lavallée'
'Souvenir de l'Ami Labruyère'
'Victor Hugo'

1885

'Clara Cochet'
'Comtesse de Fressinet de Bellanger'
'Frédéric Schneider II'
'Gloire Lyonnaise'
'Her Majesty'
'La Nantaise'
'Le Triomphe de Saintes'
'Léon Delaville'
'Louis Calla'
'Marshall P. Wilder'
'Mme Baulot'
'Mme Lefebvre'
'Mme Rosa Monnet'
'Prince Waldemar'
'Princesse Amedée de Broglie'
'Princesse de Béarn'
'Princesse Marie d'Orléans'
'Professeur Maxime Cornu'
'Souvenir de Victor Hugo'

1886

'A. Drawiel'
'Ali Pacha Cheriff'
'American Beauty'
'Baronne de St. Didier'
'Bijou de Couasnon'
'Charles Dickens'
'Comte de Paris'
'Dr. Antonin Joly'
'Duchesse de Bragance'
'Elise Lemaire'
'Erinnerung an Brod'
'Florence Paul'
'Inigo Jones'
'Jean-Baptiste Casati'
'Jules Barigny'
'Louis Rolet'
'Mme de Selve'
'Mme Edouard Michel'
'Mme Henri Pereire'
'Mme Léon Halkin'
'Mme Lureau Escalaïs'
'Mme Marcel Fauneau'

'Monsieur Jules Deroudilhe'
'Monsieur Mathieu Baron'
'Orgeuil de Lyon'
'Prince Henri d'Orléans'
'Princesse Hélène d'Orléans'
'Théodore Liberton'
1887
'Cæcilie Scharsach'
'Duc d'Audiffret-Pasquier'
'Earl of Dufferin'
'James Bougault'
'Katkoff'
'Lady Helen Stewart'
'Louis Donadine'
'Louis Lille'
'Mme Alphonse Seux'
'Mme César Brunier'
'Mme Sophie Stern'
'Mrs. John Laing'
'Silver Queen'
'Sir Rowland Hill'
'Tartarus'
1888
'Caroline d'Arden'
'Comtesse Bertrand de Blacas'
'Comtesse Branicka'
'Comtesse de Roquette-Buisson'
'Comtesse O'Gorman'
'Ferdinand Jamin'
'Victor Lemoine'
1889
'Adrien Schmitt'
'Benoît Pernin'
'Buffalo-Bill'
'Duchesse de Dino'
'Emile Bardiaux'
'Gloire de l'Exposition de Bruxelles'
'Gustave Piganeau'
'Lady Arthur Hill'
'Marchioness of Lorne'
'Mlle Marie Magat'
'Mme Renahy'
'Mme Thibaud'
'Oscar II, Roi de Suède'
'Souvenir de Grégoire Bordillon'
'Souvenir de Rosièriste Gonod'
'Vick's Caprice'
'Vicomte de Lauzières'
1890
'Anna Scharsach'
'Antonie Schurz'
'Belle de Normandy'
'Belle Yvrienne'
'Crimson Queen'
'Jeannie Dickson'
'L'Ami Maubray'
'Margaret Haywood'
'Mme Cécile Morand'
'Mme Lemesle'
'Monsieur Jules Lemaître'
'Professeur Charguereaud'
'Roger Lambelin'
1891
'Frère Marie Pierre'

'Général Baron Berge'
'Jeanne Masson'
'L'Etincelante'
'Margaret Dickson'
'Mme Théodore Vernes'
'Monsieur de Morand'
'Président Carnot'
'Salamander'
1892
'Claude Jacquet'
'Duchess of Fife'
'Duke of Fife'
'Grand-Duc Alexis'
'Impératrice Maria Feodorowna'
'Mme Anatole Leroy'
'Mme Henri Perrin'
'Mme Louis Ricart'
'Spenser'
'Violet Queen'
1893
'American Belle'
'Baron Elisi de St.-Albert'
'Capitaine Peillon'
'Captain Hayward'
'Charles Gater'
'Georges Rousset'
'La Vierzonnaise'
'Lucien Duranthon'
'Marchioness of Londonderry'
'Monsieur Edouard Detaille'
'Oakmont'
'Paul's Early Blush'
'Rose de France'
1894
'Achille Cesbron'
'Baronne Gustave de St. Paul'
'Mme Marguerite Marsault'
'Mrs. Harkness'
'Mrs. R. G. Sharman-Crawford'
1895
'Eclaireur'
'François Coppée'
'Graf Fritz Metternich'
'Haileybury'
'Helen Keller'
'Mme Verrier Cachet'
'Souvenir de Bertrand Guinoisseau'
'Venus'
1896
'Comte Raoul Chandon'
'Comtesse Renée de Béarn'
'Coquette Bordelaise'
'Mlle Marie Achard'
'Tom Wood'
1897
'Baron Girod de l'Ain'
'Baron T'Kint de Roodenbeke'
'Comte Charles d'Harcourt'
'Jubilee'
'Merrie England'
'Miss Ethel Richardson'
'Oskar Cordel'
'Princesse de Naples'
'Reverend Alan Cheales'

'Robert Duncan'
'Waltham Standard'
1898
'Ernest Morel'
'Mme Rose Caron'
'Mrs. F. W. Sanford'
'Souvenir d'Alexandre Hardy'
'Souvenir de Mme Sadi Carnot'
1899
'General von Bothnia-Andreæ'
'Gloire d'Un Enfant d'Hiram'
'Mrs. Cocker'
'Mrs. Rumsey'
'Souvenir d'André Raffy'
'Souvenir de Henri Lévêque de Vilmorin'
'Souvenir de Maman Corbœuf'
'Souvenir de Mme Jeanne Balandreau'
1900
'Ami Charmet'
'Gruss aus Pallien'
'Mme Ernest Levavasseur'
'Mme Petit'
'Rosslyn'
'Souvenir de Mme Chédane-Guinoisseau'
'Ulster'
1901
'Ben Cant'
'Capitaine Jouen'
'Frau Karl Druschki'
'Léon Robichon'
'May Corelly'
'Monsieur Louis Ricart'
'Queen of Edgely'
'Royat Mondain'
'Victory Rose'
1902
'Souvenir de McKinley'
'Vincente Peluffo'
1903
'L'Ami E. Daumont'
'Mme Cordier'
'Mme Louise Piron'
'Mme Roudillon'
1904
'Maharajah'
'Monsieur Ernest Dupré'
1905
'California'
'Dr. William Gordon'
'Hugh Dickson'
'Hugh Watson'
'J.B. Clark'
'M. H. Walsh'
'Mrs. John McLaren'
'Rosa Verschuren'
1906
'Ami Martin'
'Barbarossa'
'Mlle Renée Denis'
'Piron-Medard'
1907
'Adiantifolia'
'Charles Wagner'
'Dr. Georges Martin'

'Gloire de Chédane-Guinoisseau'
'Lady Overtoun'
'Mme Jean Everaerts'
'Philipp Paulig'
'Rouge Angevin'
1908
'Commandeur Jules Gravereaux'
'La Brunoyenne'
'Souvenir de Léon Roudillon'
1909
'George Sand'
'Mme Constant David'
1910
'Georg Arends'
'Janine Viaud-Bruant'
'Juliet'
'Symmetry'
1911
'Générale Marie Raiewesky'
'Heinrich Münch'
1912
'George Dickson'
'Paula Clegg'
1913
'Berti Gimpel'
'Candeur Lyonnaise'
'Coronation'
'Leonie Lambert'
1914
'Pæonia'
'Rembrandt'
1915
'Emden'
'Louise Cretté'
'Marguerite Guillard'
'Miss Annie Crawford'
1916
'Anne Laferrère'
'Henri Coupé'
1918
'Fürst Leopold IV zu Schaumburg-Lippe'
1919
'Dr. Ingomar H. Blohm'
'Gruss an Weimar'
1920
'Dr. Müllers Rote'
'Ruhm von Steinfurth'
1921
'Auguste Chaplain'
'Bischof Dr. Korum'
'Ferdinand Pichard'
'Schön Ingeborg'
1922
'Sa Majesté Gustave V'
'Souvenir de Mme H. Thuret'
1924
'Henry Nevard'
'Suzanne Carrol of Carrolton'
Circa 1925
'Riccordo di Fernando Scarlatti'
1925
'Edelweiss'
'Felbergs Rosa Druschki'
'Mme Albert Barbier'

1926
'Mme André Saint'
'St. Ingebert'
1927
'Everest'
'Marie Menudel'
'Turnvater Jahn'
1928
'Lyonfarbige Druschki'
1929
'Arrillaga'
'Druschki Rubra'
'Isabel Llorach'
'Pfaffstädt'
'Président Briand'
'Prinzessin Elsa zu Schaumburg-Lippe'
1930
'Martin Liebau'
1932
'Arthur Weidling'
'Chot Pĕstitele'
'Druschka'
'Eliska Krásnohorská'
1933
'General Stefanik'
'Harmony'
'Nuria de Recolons'
'Stämmler'
'Tatik Brada'
'Urdh'
1934
'Dr. Bradas Rosa Druschki'
'Jan Böhm'
'Polar Bear'
'Prinz Max zu Schaumburg-Lippe'
1935
'Symphony'
'Vyslanec Kalina'
1937
'Bradova Lososova Druschki'
1940
'Magnolija'
1956
'Hold Slunci'
1960
'Waldfee'

Noisettes and Climbers

1811
'Champneys' Pink Cluster'
'Fun Jwan Lo' (pre-1811)
1812
'Autumnalis'
1814
'Blush Noisette'
'Noisette de l'Inde'
1822
'Bougainville'
Circa 1825
'Duchesse de Grammont'
1827
'Blanc Pur'

1828
'Aimée Vibert'
1830
'Camélia Rose'
'Desprez à Fleur Jaune'
'Général Lamarque'
1832
'La Biche'
1835
'Bouquet Tout Fait'
'Fellemberg'
'Manettii'
1842
'Céline Forestier'
1843
'Chromatella'
'Solfatare'
1844
'Ophirie'
'Philomèle'
1845
'Blairii N° 1
'Blairii N° 2
'Blairii N° 3
'Fortune's Double Yellow'
1847
'Pumila Alba'
1848
'Caroline Marniesse'
'Vicomtesse d'Avesnes'
1851
'Mlle de Sombreuil'
1853
'Gloire de Dijon'
'Isis'
1856
'Claudia Augusta'
'Mme Schultz'
1857
'Isabella Gray'
1858
'Climbing Devoniensis'
'James Sprunt'
1859
'Cinderella'
'L'Arioste'
1861
'Gloire de Bordeaux'
1862
'Mlle Adèle Jougant'
1863
'Pavillon de Pregny'
1864
'Maréchal Niel'
1865
'Glory of Waltham'
1868
'Adrienne Christophle'
1869
'Mme Trifle'
'Rêve d'Or'
1870
'Belle Lyonnaise'
'Mme Bérard'
'Mme Emilie Dupuy'

Circa 1871
    'Annie Vibert'
1872
    'Bouquet d'Or'
    'Cheshunt Hybrid'
    'Earl of Eldon'
    'Marie Accary'
1873
    'Claire Carnot'
    'Noisette Moschata'
1874
    'Climbing Jules Margottin'
1875
    'Anne-Marie Côte'
    'Mme Marie Berton'
    'Multiflore de Vaumarcus'
1877
    'Deschamps'
    'Lily Metschersky'
1878
    'Emilia Plantier'
    'Mme Auguste Perrin'
    'Papillon'
    'Reine Marie Henriette'
    'William Allen Richardson'
1879
    'Duarte de Oliveira'
    'Mlle Mathilde Lenaerts'
    'Mme Alfred Carrière'
    'Mme Louis Henry'
    'Setina'
1880
    'Les Fiançailles de la Princesse Stéphanie
        et de l'Archiduc Rodolphe'
    'Reine Maria Pia'
1881
    'Beauté de l'Europe'
    'Caroline Schmitt'
    'Climbing Captain Christy'
    'Mélanie Soupert'
    'Mme Julie Lassen'
    'Reine Olga de Wurtemberg'
1882
    'Étendard de Jeanne d'Arc'
    'Mme Eugène Verdier'
1883
    'Paul's Single White Perpetual'
1884
    'Gaston Chandon'
1885
    'Comtesse Georges de Roquette-Buisson'
    'Mme Couturier-Mention'
    'Waltham Climber I'
    'Waltham Climber II'
    'Waltham Climber III'
1886
    'Mme Chauvry'
1887
    'Climbing Albert La Blotais'
    'Elie Beauvilain'
    'Fürst Bismarck'
    'Fürstin Bismarck'
    'Kaiser Wilhelm der Seigreiche'
    'L'Abondance'

    'L'Idéal'
    'Meteor'
    'Mlle Claire Jacquier'
    'Mme Jules Franke'
    'Mme la Duchesse d'Auerstädt'
    'Monsieur Rosier'
    'Souvenir de Mme Joseph Métral'
    'Triomphe des Noisettes'
1888
    'Marie Thérèse Dubourg'
    'Mme Rose Romarin'
    'Monsieur Désir'
    'Nardy'
1889
    'Climbing Niphetos'
    'Gigantea Blanc'
    'Kaiserin Friedrich'
    'La France de 89'
    'Mlle Geneviève Godard'
1890
    'Climbing Perle des Jardins'
    'Gribaldo Nicola'
    'Mlle Madeleine Delaroche'
    'Mme Brunner'
    'Mme Creux'
    'Pink Rover'
1891
    'Mme Pierre Cochet'
1892
    'Beauté Inconstante'
    'Mlle Marie Gaze'
    'Climbing Queen of Queens'
1893
    'Alister Stella Gray'
    'Baronne Charles de Gargan'
    'Climbing La France'
    'Climbing Souvenir de la Malmaison'
    'Comtesse de Galard-Béarn'
    'Dr. Rouges'
    'Marie Robert'
    'Princess May'
    'Souvenir de Lucie'
1894
    'Climbing Cécile Brunner'
    'Climbing White Pet'
    'E. Veyrat Hermanos'
    'Mme Louis Blanchet'
1895
    'Belle Vichysoise'
1896
    'Empress of China'
    'Mme Chabanne'
    'Weisser Maréchal Niel'
1897
    'Climbing Bridesmaid'
    'Climbing Kaiserin Auguste Viktoria'
    'Climbing Souvenir of Wootton'
    'Lilliput'
    'Mme E. Souffrain'
1898
    'Ards Rover'
    'Billard et Barré'
    'Climbing Marie Guillot'
    'Climbing Papa Gontier'

'Dawn'
'Eugene Jardine'
'Souvenir de Mme Léonie Viennot'
1899
'Climbing Mrs. W. J. Grant'
'Mme Gaston Annouilh'
'Souvenir de Mme Ladvocat'
1900
'François Crousse'
'Irish Beauty'
'Mme Jules Gravereaux'
'Noella Nabonnand'
'Oscar Chauvry'
'Rosabelle'
1901
'Climbing Mme Caroline Testout'
'Dr. Lande'
'Jeanne Corbœuf'
'Mme Auguste Choutet'
'Mme la Général Paul de Benoist'
'Purple East'
1902
'Belle d'Orléans'
'Climbing Clotilde Soupert'
'Deputé Debussy'
'Gruss an Friedberg'
'Lady Waterlow'
'Mme Driout'
1903
'Gainesborough'
'Marie Bülow'
'Mme Edmée Cocteau'
'Mme Hector Leuilliot'
'Mme Martignier'
'Tea Rambler'
1904
'Climbing Le Vésuve'
'Climbing Mme Louis Ricart'
'Crepuscule'
'Monsieur Georges de Cadoudal'
1905
'Comte de Torres'
Circa 1905
'Belle Portugaise'
1906
'Climbing Captain Hayward'
'Climbing Frau Karl Druschki'
'Marguerite Desrayaux'
'Sarah Bernhardt'
'Tausendschön'
1907
'Climbing White Maman Cochet'
'Henry Irving'
'Indiana'
'Mme Léon Constantin'
'Souvenir d'Emile Zola'
1908
'Ards Rambler'
'Climbing Liberty'
'Climbing Miniature'
'Frau Geheimrat Dr. Staub'
1909
'Climbing American Beauty'
'Climbing Maman Cochet'

'Climbing Mosella'
'Etoile de Portugal'
1910
'Dr. W. Van Fleet'
'Lafollette'
'Miss G. Mesman'
'Neervelt'
'Nymphe'
1911
'Adele Frey'
'Climbing Gruss an Teplitz'
'Climbing Mrs. W. H. Cutbush'
'Florence Haswell Veitch'
1912
'Climbing Richmond'
'Lemon Queen'
1913
'Climbing Monsieur Paul Lédé'
'Effective'
'Mikado'
'Miss Marion Manifold'
'Mme Foureau'
1915
'Cupid'
'Mrs. Rosalie Wrinch'
'Paul's Lemon Pillar'
1916
'Climbing Irish Fireflame'
'Colcestria'
'Geschwindts Gorgeous'
1917
'Catalunya'
'Climbing Lady Hillingdon'
'Climbing Mme Abel Chatenay'
'Purity'
1919
'Black Boy'
1920
'Climbing Château de Clos-Vougeot'
'Climbing Ophelia'
'Climbing Rosemary'
'Irène Bonnet'
'Souvenir de Claudius Denoyel'
1921
'Vicomtesse Pierre de Fou'
1922
'Climbing Mrs. Aaron Ward'
'Climbing Mrs. Herbert Stevens'
'Emmanuella de Mouchy'
'Flying Colours'
'Kitty Kininmonth'
'Marguerite Carels'
'Scorcher'
1923
'Cherubim'
'Climbing General MacArthur'
'Climbing Jonkheer J. L. Mock'
'Phyllis Bide'
1924
'Lucy Thomas'
'Sénateur Amic'
'Sunday Best'
1925
'Dr. Domingos Pereira'
'Milkmaid'

1926
'Apeles Mestres'
'Climbing Eva Tescendorff'
'Climbing Mme Butterfly'
'Climbing Radiance'
'Queen of Hearts'
1927
'Climbing Cracker'
'Climbing Hadley'
'Cooper's Burmese Rose'
1929
'Climbing Columbia'
'Climbing Mme Segond-Weber'
'Climbing Mrs. Henry Morse'
1930
'Climbing Dame Edith Helen'
'Montarioso'
'Montecito'
'New Dawn'
1931
'Climbing Étoile de Hollande'
'Climbing General Superior Arnold Janssen'
'Crimson Conquest'
1932
'Climbing Lorraine Lee'
'Doris Downes'
1933
'Climbing Lady Sylvia'
'Princes van Oranje'
1935
'Climbing Dainty Bess'
'Climbing Distinction'
'Glory of California'
1936
'Climbing Summer Snow'
1937
'Climbing Gruss an Aachen'
'Nancy Hayward'
1938
'Climbing Capitaine Soupa'
'Climbing Mme Jules Bouché'
1940
'Climbing König Friedrich II von Danemark'
'Climbing Marie Van Houtte'
'Climbing Wenzel Geschwindt'
1941
'Climbing Apotheker Georg Höfer'
'Climbing Pride of Reigate'
'Pennant'
1948
'Climbing Orange Triumph'
1949
'Climbing George Dickson'
'Climbing Snowbird'
1952
'Climbing Pinkie'
1960
'Climbing Mrs. B. R. Cant'
1962
'Climbing Margo Koster'
1975
'Archduchess Charlotte'
1977
'Climbing China Doll'

Polyanthas

1875
'Pâquerette'
1879
'Anne-Marie de Montravel'
'White Pet'
1880
'Mlle Cécile Brunner'
1881
'Mignonette'
1883
'Jeanne Drivon'
'Perle d'Or'
1884
'Miniature'
1885
'Floribunda'
1886
'Mlle Joséphine Burland'
1887
'Georges Pernet'
'Gloire des Polyantha'
'Rotkäppchen'
1888
'Hérmine Madèlé'
'Marie Pavič'
'Mlle Blanche Rebatel'
'Mme Alégatière'
'Princesse Joséphine de Flandres'
1889
'Clotilde Soupert'
'Herzblättchens'
'Joséphine Morel'
'Little Dot'
1892
'Étoile de Mai'
'Mme E. A. Nolte'
'Petite Léonie'
1893
'Multiflora Nana Perpétuelle'
1895
'Kleiner Liebling'
'Mosella'
'Princesse Marie Adélaïde de Luxembourg'
1896
'Perle des Rouges'
'Pink Soupert'
1897
'Flocon de Neige'
'Gloire de Charpennes'
1898
'Colibri'
'Little Gem'
'Ma Petite Andrée'
1899
'Bouquet de Neige'
'Eugénie Lamesch'
'Leonie Lamesch'
'Mlle Fernande Dupuy'
1900
'Charles Metroz'
'Primula'
'Sisi Ketten'

1901
'Katharina Zeimet'
'Mlle Marthe Cahuzac'
'Schneewittchen'
'Snowball'
1903
'Kleiner Alfred'
'Mlle Alice Rousseau'
'Mme Norbert Levavasseur'
'Schneekopf'
1904
'Frau Cecilie Walter'
'Jacques Proust'
'Mignon'
1905
'Martha'
1906
'Ännchen Müller'
'Princess Ena'
'Rösel Dach'
1907
'Apfelblüte'
'Dr. Ricaud'
'Mrs. W. H. Cutbush'
1908
'Diamant'
'Phyllis'
1909
'Baptiste Lafaye'
'Cineraria'
'Cyclope'
'Frau Alexander Weiss'
'Frau Anna Pasquay'
'Frau Oberhofgärtner Schultze'
'Gustel Mayer'
'Jeanne d'Arc'
'Jessie'
'Louise Walter'
'Merveille des Polyanthas'
'Mme Taft'
'Orléans-Rose'
'Tip-Top'
'White Cécile Brunner'
1910
'Eileen Loow'
'Mlle Marcelle Gaugin'
'Petite Marcelle'
'Yvonne Rabier'
1911
'Bordure'
'Ellen Poulsen'
'Erna Teschendorff'
'Maman Turbat'
'Merveille des Rouges'
1912
'Coronet'
'George Elger'
'Gloire d'Orléans'
'Ivan Misson'
'Jeanny Soupert'
'Madeleine Orosdy'
'Martha Keller'
'Mme Arthur Robichon'
'Mme Jules Gouchault'

'Papa Hémeray'
'Perle Orléanaise'
'Triomphe Orléanaise'
1913
'Excellens'
'Frau Elise Kreis'
'Loreley'
'Marie Brissonet'
'Marie-Jeanne'
'Mlle Suzanne Bidard'
'Perle'
'Radium'
'Renoncule'
1914
'Abondant'
'Betsy van Nes'
'Bouquet Blanc'
'Echo'
'Mary Bruni'
'Melle Fischer'
'Susanna'
1915
'La Marne'
'Mauve'
'Petite Françoise'
'Siegesperle'
1916
'Greta Kluis'
'Grete Schreiber'
'Magenta'
1917
'Miss Edith Cavell'
'Mrs. William G. Koning'
1918
'Eblouissant'
'Étoile Luisante'
'Maréchal Foch'
'Pink Cécile Brunner'
'Verdun'
1919
'Evelyn Thornton'
'Frau Rudolf Schmidt'
'Indéfectible'
'Mevrouw Nathalie Nypels'
'Mimi Pinson'
'Schöne von Holstein'
'Stadtrat Meyn'
1920
'Bloomfield Abundance'
'Coral Cluster'
'Ideal'
'La Rosée'
1921
'Lady Reading'
1922
'Denise Cassegrain'
1923
'Chatillon Rose'
'Corrie Koster'
'Eva Teschendorff'
'Mrs. R. M. Finch'
1924
'Baby Faurax'

1926
'Golden Salmon'
1927
'Kersbergen'
'Lindbergh'
'Marytje Cazant'
'Sunshine'
1928
'Pink Pet'
1929
'Dick Koster'
'Fireglow'
'Gloria Mundi'
'Paris'
'Sparkler'
1930
'Little Dorrit'
'Nypels Perfection'
'Paul Crampel'
'The Allies'
1931
'Flamboyant'
'Gabrielle Privat'
'Margo Koster'
1932
'Baby Alberic'
'Cameo'
'Gloire du Midi'
'The Fairy'
1937
'Jean Mermoz'
'Orange Triumph'
'Topaz'
1941
'Spray Cécile Brunner'
1946
'China Doll'
'Sneprinsesse'
1947
'Pinkie'
1949
'Muttertag'
'Pacific Triumph'
1950
'Summer Dawn'
1951
'Waverly Triumph'
1952
'Border King'
1953
'Lullaby'
1954
'Alberich'
'Degenhard'
'Margo's Sister'
1955
'Balduin'
'Bertram'
'Giesebrecht'
1956
'Burkhard'
'Orange Morsdag'
'Red Triumph'
1958
'Lillan'

1959
'Vatertag'
1965
'Milrose'
1971
'Caid'
1974
'Legion d'Honneur'
1976
'Julie Delbard'
1978
'Prevue'
1979
'Casque d'Or'
'Fairy Changeling'
'Fairy Maid'
'Fairy Prince'
'Fairyland'
Circa 1980
'Fairy Ring'
1982
'Fairy Damsel'
1983
'Pink Posy'
1984
'Neiges d'Été'

Hybrid Teas

1864
'Mme Elisa de Vilmorin'
1867
'La France'
1872
'Antonine Verdier'
'Mme Lacharme'
1873
'Captain Christy'
1878
'Mlle Brigitte Viollet'
'Mme Etienne Levet'
1879
'Beauty of Stapleford'
'Duchess of Connaught'
'Duchess of Westminster'
'Duke of Connaught'
'Jean Lorthois'
'Jean Sisley'
'Julius Finger'
'Michael Saunders'
'Mme de Loeben-Sels'
'Pearl'
'Pierre Guillot'
1880
'Hon. George Bancroft'
1881
'Camoëns'
'Mme Jules Grévy'
1882
'Distinction'
'Lady Mary Fitzwilliam'
1884
'Bedford Belle'
'Grace Darling'

1886
'Attraction'
'Directeur Constant Bernard'
'Mme A. Schwaller'
'Mme Joseph Desbois'
'The Puritan'
'Viscountess Folkestone'
'William Francis Bennett'
1887
'Dr. Pasteur'
'Mlle Germaine Caillot'
'Mme André Duron'
'Mme Ernest Piard'
'The Meteor'
1888
'Comte Henri Rignon'
'Duchess of Albany'
'Mme Angèle Favre'
'Souvenir of Wootton'
1889
'Mlle Augustine Guinoisseau'
'Bona Weilschott'
'Mme Moser'
1890
'Astra'
'Danmark'
'Gustave Regis'
'Henri Brichard'
'Marchioness of Salisbury'
'Mme Angelique Veysset'
'Mme Caroline Testout'
'Triomphe de Pernet père'
1891
'Augustine Halem'
'Baronne G. de Noirmont'
'Carmen Sylva'
'Grand-Duc Adolphe de Luxembourg'
'Kaiserin Auguste Viktoria'
'Mme Joseph Bonnaire'
'Mme Pernet-Ducher'
'Mme Veuve Ménier'
1892
'Erinnerung an Schloss Scharfenstein'
'Erzherzogin Marie Dorothea'
'Lady Henry Grosvenor'
'Mme Charles Boutmy'
1893
'Marquise Litta de Breteuil'
'Mme Joseph Combet'
'Mme Jules Finger'
1894
'Clara Watson'
'Emin Pascha'
'Joséphine Marot'
'Mrs. W. C. Whitney'
'Mme Abel Chatenay'
'Souvenir de Mme Eugène Verdier'
'Souvenir du Président Carnot'
1895
'Antoine Rivoire'
'Kathleen'
'Marjorie'
'Mavourneen'
'Mlle Alice Furon'
'Mlle Hélène Cambier'

'Mme Charles Détraux'
'Mme Tony Baboud'
'Mme Wagram, Comtesse de Turenne'
'Mrs. W. J. Grant'
'Rosette de la Legion d'Honneur'
'Sheila'
'Souvenir d'Auguste Métral'
1896
'Captain Christy Panaché'
'Ferdinand Batel'
'Ferdinand Jamin'
'Mme Jules Grolez'
1897
'Coronet'
'Grossherzogin Viktoria Melitta von Hessen'
'L'Innocence'
'Marie Zahn'
'Mme Adolphe Loiseau'
'Mme Augustine Hamont'
'Mme Eugénie Boullet'
'Mme Paul Lacoutière'
'Violiniste Emile Lévêque'
1898
'Aurore'
'Balduin'
'Gardenia'
'Grossherzog Ernst Ludwig von Hesse'
'Marie Girard'
'Mme Bessemer'
'Mrs. Robert Garrett'
'Papa Lambert'
'Souvenir de Mme Ernest Cauvin'
1899
'Abbé Millot'
'Admiral Dewey'
'Beatrix, Comtesse de Buisseret'
'Clara Barton'
'Dr. Cazeneuve'
'Exquisite'
'Hofgärtendirektor Graebener'
'Johannes Wesselhöft'
'Jules Toussaint'
'Killarney'
'Ma Tulipe'
'Mme Blondel'
'Mme Cunisset-Carnot'
'Mme Ravary'
'Monsieur Bunel'
'Rosomane Gravereaux'
'Shandon'
1900
'Bessie Brown'
'Irish Glory'
'Irish Modesty'
'La Tosca'
'Lady Clanmorris'
'Liberty'
'Magnafrano'
'Mme Dailleux'
'Mme Jean Favre'
1901
'Abbé André Reitter'
'Gladys Harkness'
'Mildred Grant'
'Mme Marie Croibier'

'Mme Viger'
'Pharisäer'
'Pierre Wattinne'
'Prince de Bulgarie'
1902
'Edmée et Roger'
'Mamie'
'Monsieur Paul Lédé'
'Paul Meunier'
'Reine Carola de Saxe'
1903
'Amateur André Fourcaud'
'Commandant Letourneux'
'Gertrude'
'Gustav Grünerwald'
1904
'Cardinal'
'Frau J. Reiter'
'Irish Brightness'
'Lady Ashtown'
'Mme Alfred Sabatier'
'Mme Léon Pain'
'Reine Marguerite d'Italie'
1905
'Adam Rackles'
'Andenken an Moritz von Frohlich'
'Betty'
'General MacArthur'
'Irish Elegance'
'Lina Schmidt-Michel'
'Mme Emilie Lafon'
'Mme Gustav Metz'
'Richmond'
'Ruhm der Gartenwelt'
'The Dandy'
1906
'Charles J. Graham'
'Souvenir de Monsieur Frédéric Vercellone'
1907
'Australie'
'Avoca'
'Comtesse Icy Hardegg'
'Mme Maurice de Luze'
'Mme P. Euler'
'Mme Segond-Weber'
'W. E. Lippiat'
1908
'Château de Clos-Vougeot'
'Madeleine Gaillard'
'Radiance'
1909
'Gruss an Aachen'
'His Majesty'
'Jonkheer J. L. Mock'
'Kaiserin Goldifolia'
'Lady Alice Stanley'
'Monsieur Charles de Lapisse'
'Mrs. Wakefield Christie-Miller'
1910
'Mme Jules Bouché'
'Mrs. Cynthia Forde'
'Mrs. Herbert Stevens'
1911
'Mme C. Chambard'
'Monsieur Fraissenon'

1912
'Aviateur Michel Mahieu'
'British Queen'
'General-Superior Arnold Janssen'
'Killarney Queen'
'Ophelia'
1913
'Irish Fireflame'
'Killarney Double White'
'Old Gold'
'Sachsengruss'
1914
'Augustus Hartmann'
'Hadley'
'Killarney Brilliant'
1915
'Mlle Argentine Cramon'
'Red Radiance'
1916
'Columbia'
'Isobel'
'Mme Méha Sabatier'
1917
'K. of K.'
'Kootenay'
'Mrs. Charles J. Bell'
1918
'Golden Ophelia'
'Mme Butterfly'
'Sunny South'
1919
'Australia Felix'
'Étoile de Hollande'
'Lulu'
'Mrs. Henry Morse'
1920
'Westfield Star'
1921
'Innocence'
'Mrs. Oakley Fisher'
1923
'Vesuvius'
1925
'Dainty Bess'
1926
'Cecil'
'Dame Edith Helen'
'Lady Sylvia'
1930
'Minna'
'Rosa Gruss an Aachen'
1934
'Kathleen Mills'
1935
'Jean Muraour'
1936
'Ellen Wilmott'
'Snowbird'
1937
'Christobel'
'Frances Ashton'
1942
'Gruss an Aachen Superior'
1947
'White Wings'

CULTIVARS BY BREEDER OR INTRODUCER

Only breeders or family groups with two or more introductions included in this book are listed. When breeder and introducer are different, the variety is listed under the breeder's name. Family groups (Guillot, Ducher, etc.) are listed with the elder generation preceding the younger. Arrangement under each heading is chronological. Those varieties which are of unknown provenance are listed alphabetically at the end. In a number of cases, the breeder's company continued to release new offerings under his name after his decease. Close study of the listings for those breeders who undertook their crossings in a "scientific" manner will provide many insights.

Alégatière, Alphonse
Lyon, France

'Miniature' (Pol)	1884
'Marie Pavič' (Pol)	1888
'Mme Alégatière' (Pol)	1888
'Joséphine Morel' (Pol)	1891

Altmüller, Johann
Schwerin, Mecklenbourg, Germany

'Berti Gimpel' (HP)	1913
'Grete Schreiber' (Pol)	1916

Archer, W. E. B.
Sellindge, England

'Dainty Bess' (HT)	1925
'Ellen Wilmott' (HT)	1936

Avoux & Crozy
La Guillotière, Lyon, France

'Enfant de Lyon' (T)	1858
'Narcisse' (T)	1859

Barbier Brothers & Company
Orléans, France

'Bordure' (Pol)	1911
'Renoncule' (Pol)	1913
'La Marne' (Pol)	1915
'Henri Coupé' (HP)	1916
'Magenta' (Pol)	1916
'Verdun' (Pol)	1918
'Mimi Pinson' (Pol)	1919
'Mme Albert Barbier' (HP)	1925
'Mme André Saint' (HP)	1926
'Marie Menudel' (HP)	1927

Béluze, Jean
Lyon, France

'Rival de Pæstum' (T)	1841
'Souvenir de la Malmaison' (B)	1843
'Reine des Vierges' (B)	1844
'Leveson-Gower' (B)	1846
'Maréchal du Palais' (B)	1846
'Triomphe de la Duchère' (B)	1846
'Impératrice Eugénie' (HB)	1855
'Mme Schultz' (N)	1856

Bénard, G.
Orléans, France

'Abbé Millot' (HT)	1899
'Souvenir de Maman Corbœuf' (HP)	1899

Bennett, Henry
Manor Farm Nursery
Shepperton/Stapleford, England

'Duchess of Edinburgh' (HP)	1874
'Beauty of Stapleford' (HT)	1879
'Duchess of Connaught' (HT)	1879
'Duchess of Westminster' (HT)	1879
'Duke of Connaught' (HT)	1879
'Jean Sisley' (HT)	1879
'Michael Saunders' (HT)	1879
'Pearl' (HT)	1879
'Viscountess Falmouth' (HT)	1879
'Hon. George Bancroft' (HT)	1880
'Distinction' (HT)	1882
'Earl of Pembroke' (HP)	1882
'Heinrich Schultheis' (HP)	1882
'Lady Mary Fitzwilliam' (HT)	1882
'Princess of Wales' (T)	1882
'Grace Darling' (HT)	1884
'Mrs. George Dickson' (HP)	1884
'Her Majesty' (HP)	1885
'The Puritan' (HT)	1886
'Viscountess Folkestone' (HT)	1886
'William Francis Bennett' (HT)	1886
'Mrs. John Laing' (HP)	1887
'Little Dot' (Pol)	1889
'Lady Henry Grosvenor' (HT)	1892
'Captain Hayward' (HP)	1893
'Climbing Souvenir de la Malmaison' (B)	1893

Berland
Bordeaux?, France

'Mme C. Liger' (T)	1899
'Mme la Général Paul de Benoist' (Cl. T)	1901

Bernaix, Alexandre
Villeurbanne-Lyon, France

'Mlle Joséphine Burland' (Pol)	1886
'Mme A. Schwaller' (HT)	1886
'Mme A. Étienne' (T)	1886
'Mme Scipion Cochet' (T)	1886
'Vicomtesse de Wauthier' (T)	1886
'Mlle Claire Jacquier' (Cl. Pol)	1887
'Mme César Brunier' (HP)	1887
'Mme la Duchesse d'Auerstädt' (N)	1887
'Souvenir de Mme Joseph Métral' (Cl. HT)	1887
'V. Viviand-Morel' (T)	1887
'Joseph Métral' (T)	1888
'Mlle Blanche Rebatel' (Pol)	1888
'Mme Jules Cambon' (T)	1888

'Georges Farber' (T) 1889
'Mme Marthe du Bourg' (T) 1889
'Mme Philippe Kuntz' (T) 1889
'Mme la Princesse de Bessaraba de Brancovan' (T) 1890
'Frère Marie Pierre' (HP) 1891
'Mme Victor Caillet' (T) 1891
'Monsieur Edouard Littaye' (T) 1891
'Monsieur Tillier' (T) 1891
'Mme E. A. Nolte' (Pol) 1892
'Comtesse de Galard-Béarn' (N) 1893
'E. Veyrat Hermanos' (N) 1894
'Rose d'Evian' (T) 1894
'V. Vivo é Hijos' (T) 1894
'Mme Wagram, Comtesse de Turenne' (HT) 1895
'Baronne Henriette Snoy' (T) 1897

Bernaix fils (Pierre)
Villeurbanne, France
'Mme Berkeley' (T) 1898
'Souvenir de Mme Léonie Viennot' (Cl. T) 1898
'Mme Clémence Marchix' (T) 1899
'Souvenir de William Robinson' (T) 1899
'Betty Berkeley' (T) 1903
'Mme Alfred Sabatier' (HT) 1904
'Madeleine Gaillard' (HT) 1908
'Rosomane Narcisse Thomas' (T) 1908

Bernède, H. B.
Bordeaux, France
'Comtesse de Labarthe' (T) 1857
'Mme de Tartas' (T) 1859
'Général Tartas' (T) 1860
'Mme de Selve' (HP) 1886

Besson, Antoine
Monplaisir, Lyon, France
'Mlle Marie Chauvet' (HP) 1881
'Dr. Antonin Joly' (HP) 1886
'Orgeuil de Lyon' (HP) 1886

Bizard
Angers, France
'Némésis' (Ch) 1836
'Bouquet de Flore' (B) 1839

Blair
Stamford Hill, England
'Blairii Nº 1' (HCh) 1845
'Blairii Nº 2' (HCh) 1845
'Blairii Nº 3' (HCh) 1845

Böhm, Jan
Blatná-Cechy, Czechoslovakia
'Climbing General-Superior Arnold Janssen' (HT) 1931
'Chot Pěstitele' (HP) 1932
'Eliska Krásnohorská' (HP) 1932
'General Stefanik' (HP) 1933
'Vyslanec Kalina' (HP) 1935

Bonfiglioli, A., & Son
Bologna, Italy
'Principessa di Napoli' (T) 1898
'Clementina Carbonieri' (T) 1913

Bonnaire, Joseph
Lyon, France
'Souvenir de Victor Hugo' (T) 1885
'Dr. Grill' (T) 1886
'Mme Chauvry' (Cl. T) 1886
'Mme André Duron' (HT) 1887
'Mme Ernest Piard' (HT) 1887
'Capitaine Lefort' (T) 1888
'Edmond Sablayrolles' (T) 1888
'Mlle Jeanne Guillaumez' (T) 1889
'Souvenir d'Auguste Legros' (T) 1889
'Elisa Fugier' (T) 1890
'Henri Brichard' (HT) 1890
'Souvenir de Mme Sablayrolles' (T) 1890
'Mme Joseph Bonnaire' (HT) 1891
'Madeleine Guillaumez' (T) 1892
'Lucien Duranthon' (HP) 1893
'Mme Joseph Combet' (HT) 1893
'Joséphine Marot' (HT) 1894
'Souvenir de Laurent Guillot' (T) 1894
'Rosette de la Legion d'Honneur' (HT) 1895
'Mme Jacques Charreton' (T) 1897
'Jules Toussaint' (HT) 1899
'Ma Tulipe' (HT) 1899
'Abbé Garroute' (T) 1902
'Mme Léon Constantin' (Cl. T) 1907

Bougère (or Bougère-Breton)
Angers, France
'Bougère' (T) 1832
'Niphetos' (T) by 1841

Boutigny, Jules-Philibert
Rouen, France
'Mme Edmond Laporte' (B) 1893
'Capitaine Jouen' (HP) 1901
'Monsieur Louis Ricart' (HP) 1901
'Climbing Monsieur Louis Ricart' (HP) 1904
'Monsieur Ernest Dupré' (HP) 1904
'Capitaine Dyel, de Graville' (B) 1905
'Mme Constant David' (HP) 1909

Boyau, Joseph
Angers, France
'La Sylphide' (T) 1842
'Solfatare' (N) 1843
'Prince Noir' (HP) 1854
'Duc d'Anjou' (HP) 1862
'Souvenir de Monsieur Boll' (HP) 1866

Brada, Dr. Gustav
Czechoslovakia
'Tatik Brada' (HP) 1933
'Dr. Bradas Rosa Druschki' (HP) 1934
'Bradova Lososova Druschki' (HP) 1937

Brassac, François
Toulouse, France
'Triomphe de Toulouse' (HP) 1873
'Marguerite Brassac' (HP) 1874
'Mme Théobald Sernin' (HP) 1877
'Duarte de Oliveira' (N) 1879

Bruant, Georges
Poitiers, France

'Souvenir de Béranger' (HP)	1857

Buatois, Emmanuel
Dijon, France

'Antoinette Cuillerat' (Ch)	1897
'Mme Adolphe Loiseau' (HT)	1897
'Mme Derepas-Matrat' (T)	1897
'Mme Paul Lacoutière' (HT)	1897
'Marie Girard' (HT)	1898
'Mme Cunisset-Carnot' (HT)	1899
'Mme Gustave Henry' (T)	1899
'Mme Dailleux' (HT)	1900
'L'Ouche' (Ch)	1901
'Deputé Debussy' (Cl. HT)	1902
'Paul Meunier' (HT)	1902

Budlong & Son Co.
Auburn, Rhode Island, U.S.A.

'Killarney Queen' (HT)	1912
'Killarney Double White' (HT)	1913

Burbank, Luther
Santa Rosa, California, U.S.A.

'Improved Rainbow' (T)	1896
'Santa Rosa' (T)	1899
'Burbank' (T)	1900

California Nursery Company
Niles, California, U.S.A.

'Bella' (T)	1890
'Belle de Normandy' (HP)	1890
'Souvenir de Mme Lambard' (T)	1890
'Senator McNaughton' (T)	1895
'California' (HP)	1905
'Mrs. John McLaren' (HP)	1905
'True Friend' (T)	1905
'Mme Therese Roswell' (T)	1906
'Niles Cochet' (T)	1911

Cant, Benjamin R.
Colchester, England

'Prince Arthur' (HP)	1875
'Ben Cant' (HP)	1901
'Mrs. B. R. Cant' (T)	1901
'Maharajah' (HP)	1904
'Augustus Hartmann' (HT)	1914
'Cupid' (Cl. HT)	1915
'Colcestria' (Cl. HT)	1916
'Golden Ophelia' (HT)	1918
'Mrs. Oakley Fisher' (HT)	1921
'Cecil' (HT)	1926

Cant, Frank
Colchester, England

'Lady Roberts' (T)	1902
'Henry Nevard' (HP)	1924

Cayeux, Henri
Lisbon, Portugal

'Belle Portugaise' (HGig)	ca.1905
'Étoile de Portugal' (HGig)	1909

Chambard, C.
Lyon, France

'Mme C. Chambard' (HT)	1911
'Louise Cretté' (HP)	1915
'Marguerite Guillard' (HP)	1915
'Mlle Argentine Cramon' (HT)	1915
'Souvenir de Claudius Denoyel' (Cl. HT)	1920

Chaplin Bros.
Waltham Cross, England

'Innocence' (HT)	1921
'Climbing Mrs. Henry Morse' (HT)	1929
'Crimson Conquest' (Cl. HT)	1931
'Baby Alberic' (Pol)	1932

Chauvry, J.-B.
Bordeaux, France

'Mme Auguste Rodrigues' (HB)	1897
'Mme E. Souffrain' (N)	1897
'Ma Petite Andrée' (Pol)	1898
'Mme Gaston Annouilh' (N)	1899
'Oscar Chauvry' (N)	1900
'Climbing Mme Caroline Testout' (HT)	1901

Chédane-Guinoisseau
Angers, France

'Duc de Montpensier' (HP)	1875
'Mme Chédane-Guinoisseau' (T)	1880
'Mme Verrier-Cachet' (HP)	1895
'Souvenir de Bertrand Guinoisseau' (HP)	1895
'Souvenir de Mme Chédane-Guinoisseau' (HP)	1900
'Ami Martin' (HP)	1906
'Mlle Renée Denis' (HP)	1906
'Gloire de Chédane-Guinoisseau' (HP)	1907
'Rouge Angevin' (HP)	1907

Chenault, R.
Orléans, France

'Purpurea' (Ch)	1930
'Jean Mermoz' (Pol)	1937

Cherpin, Jean
Lyon, France

'Marguerite Lecureaux' (HP)	1853
'Béatrix' (B)	1865
'Sanglant' (Ch)	1873

Clark, Alister
Bulla, Australia

'Sunny South' (HT)	1918
'Australia Felix' (HT)	1919
'Black Boy' (Cl)	1919
'Queen of Hearts' (Cl. HT)	1919
'Flying Colours' (HGig)	1922
'Kitty Kininmonth' (HGig)	1922
'Scorcher' (Cl)	1922
'Cherubim' (Cl)	1923
'Lorraine Lee' (HGig)	1924
'Sunday Best' (Cl. HP)	1924
'Milkmaid' (N)	1925
'Climbing Cracker' (HGig)	1927
'Doris Downes' (HGig)	1932

'Glory of California' (HGig)   1935
'Baxter Beauty' (T)   ca. 1936?
'Nancy Hayward' (HGig)   1937
'Pennant' (HGig)   1941

Cochet père (Pierre)
Grisy-Suisnes, France
'Bougainville' (N)   1822
'Scipion Cochet' (B)   1850
'Arthur De Sansal' (HP)   1855

Cochet Brothers (Scipion & Pierre fils)
Grisy-Suisnes, France
'Souvenir de la Reine d'Angleterre' (HP)   1855

Cochet-Aubin
Grisy-Suisnes, France
'Mlle Berthe Lévêque' (HP)   1866

Cochet, Scipion
Grisy-Suisnes, France
'Mlle Elise Chabrier' (HP)   1867
'Souvenir de Mme Hennecourt' (HP)   1869
'Mme Scipion Cochet' (HP)   1871
'Mme Philémon Cochet' (T)   1887
'Baronne G. de Noirmont' (HT)   1891
'Mme Pierre Cochet' (N)   1891
'Maman Cochet' (T)   1892
'Marie Robert' (N)   1893

Cochet, Pierre (fils)
Grisy-Suisnes, France
'Philémon Cochet' (B)   1895
'Ernest Morel' (HP)   1898

Cocker, James (& Sons)
Aberdeen, Scotland
'Duchess of Fife' (HP)   1892
'Mrs. Cocker' (HP)   1899

Conard & Jones Co.
West Grove, Pennsylvania, U.S.A.
'Eugene Jardine' (N)   1898
'Little Gem' (Pol)   1898
'Mme Bessemer' (HT)   1898
'Palo Alto' (T)   1898
'Peach Blossom' (T)   1898
'Rosa Mundi' (T)   1898
'Belle d'Orléans' (N)   1902
'Henry Irving' (HP)   1903
'Canadian Belle' (T)   1907
'Climbing Mosella' (Pol)   1909
'Kaiserin Goldifolia' (HT)   1909

Cook, Anthony
Baltimore, Maryland, U.S.A.
'Cornelia Cook' (T)   1855

Cook, John (& Son)
Baltimore, Maryland, U.S.A.
'American Beauty' (HP)   1886
'Annie Cook' (T)   1888

'Souvenir of Wootton' (HT)   1888
'Marion Dingee' (T)   1889
'White Maman Cochet' (T)   1896
'Mrs. Robert Garrett' (HT)   1898
'Cardinal' (HT)   1904
'Radiance' (HT)   1908

Coquereau
Maître-École, Angers, France
'Cramoisi Supérieur' (Ch)   1832
'Chromatella' (N)   1843

Corbœuf-Marsault
Orléans, France
'Mlle Madeleine Delaroche' (N)   1890
'Mme Marguerite Marsault' (HP)   1894
'Climbing White Pet' (Pol)   1894
'Mme Petit' (HP)   1900
'Jeanne Corbœuf' (Cl. HT)   1901
'Dr. Ricaud' (Pol)   1907
'Mlle Marcelle Gaugin' (Pol)   1910

Couturier fils/Couturier-Mention
Paris?, France
'Mme Vidot' (HP)   1854
'Mme Couturier-Mention' (Cl. Ch)   1885

Cranston, John
King's Acre, England
'Climbing Jules Margottin' (HP)   1874
'Crimson Bedder' (HP)   1874
'Sir Garnet Wolseley' (HP)   1875

Croibier, Jean (& Son)
Lyon, France
'Mme Marie Croibier' (HT)   1901
'Commandeur Jules Gravereaux' (HP)   1908
'Mme Jules Bouché' (HT)   1910
'Candeur Lyonnaise' (HP)   1913
'Lindbergh' (Pol)   1927
'Christobel' (HT)   1937

Curtis, Sanford, & Co.
Torquay, England
'Bessie Johnson' (HP)   1872
'Mrs. F. W. Sanford' (HP)   1898

Damaizin, Frédéric
Lyon, France
'Claudia Augusta' (N)   1856
'Mme Damaizin' (T)   1858
'Bouquet de Marie' (HP)   1858
'Mme Crespin' (HP)   1862
'Mme Charles' (T)   1864
'Abel Grand' (HP)   1865
'Général Barral' (HP)   1867
'Marie de St.-Jean' (DP)   1869
'Etienne Dubois' (HP)   1873
'La Rosière' (HP)   1874

Dauvesse, D.
Orléans, France

'Velouté d'Orléans' (B)	1852
'Panachée d'Orléans' (HP)	1854

De Ruiter, G.
Hazerswoude, The Netherlands

'Gloria Mundi' (Pol)	1929
'Paris' (Pol)	1929
'Sparkler' (Pol)	1929
'Cameo' (Pol)	1932
'Gloire du Midi' (Pol)	1932
'Border King' (Pol)	1952
'Degenhard' (Pol)	1954
'Alberich' (Pol)	1954
'Giesebrecht' (Pol)	1955
'Balduin' (Pol)	1955
'Bertram' (Pol)	1955
'Burkhard' (Pol)	1956

De Sansal, Arthur
Farcy-les-Lys, France

'Marquise de Gibot' (HP)	1868
'Général de la Martinière' (HP)	1869
'Miranda' (DP)	1869

Delbard-Chabert
Paris, France

'Milrose' (Pol)	1965
'Legion d'Honneur' (Pol)	1974
'Julie Delbard' (Pol)	1976
'Casque d'Or' (Pol)	1979

Descemet
St.-Denis, France

'Venusta' (DP)	pre-1814
'Jeune Henry' (DP)	pre-1815

Desprez
Yèbles, France

'Desprez à Fleur Jaune' (N)	1830
'Mme Desprez' (B)	1831
'Bengale Sanguinaire' (Ch)	1838
'St. Priest de Breuze' (Ch)	1838
'Marquise de Boccella' (DP)	1840
'Baronne Prévost' (HP)	1842
'Caroline De Sansal' (HP)	1849

Dickson, Alexander
Hawlmark, Newtownards, Northern Ireland

'Earl of Dufferin' (HP)	1887
'Ethel Brownlow' (T)	1887
'Lady Helen Stewart' (HP)	1887
'Caroline d'Arden' (HP)	1888
'Lady Castlereagh' (T)	1888
'Lady Arthur Hill' (HP)	1889
'Mrs. James Wilson' (T)	1889
'Jeannie Dickson' (HP)	1890
'Margaret Dickson' (HP)	1891
'Marchioness of Londonderry' (HP)	1893
'Mrs. R. G. Sharman-Crawford' (HP)	1894
'Helen Keller' (HP)	1895
'Kathleen' (HT)	1895
'Marjorie' (HT)	1895
'Mavourneen' (HT)	1895
'Mrs. W. J. Grant' (HT)	1895
'Sheila' (HT)	1895
'Tom Wood' (HP)	1896
'Climbing Kaiserin Auguste Viktoria' (HT)	1897
'Miss Ethel Richardson' (HP)	1897
'Robert Duncan' (HP)	1897
'Ards Rover' (Cl. HP)	1898
'Beryl' (T)	1898
'Meta' (T)	1898
'Muriel Grahame' (T)	1898
'Killarney' (HT)	1899
'Mrs. Edward Mawley' (T)	1899
'Shandon' (HT)	1899
'Bessie Brown' (HT)	1900
'Irish Beauty' (Cl. HT)	1900
'Irish Glory' (HT)	1900
'Irish Modesty' (HT)	1900
'Lady Clanmorris' (HT)	1900
'Lady Mary Corry' (T)	1900
'Liberty' (HT)	1900
'Rosslyn' (HP)	1900
'Ulster' (HP)	1900
'Gladys Harkness' (HT)	1901
'Mildred Grant' (HT)	1901
'Mamie' (HT)	1902
'Gertrude' (HT)	1903
'Dean Hole' (HT)	1904
'Irish Brightness' (HT)	1904
'Lady Ashtown' (HT)	1904
'Betty' (HT)	1905
'Hugh Watson' (HP)	1905
'Irish Elegance' (HT)	1905
'M. H. Walsh' (HP)	1905
'Charles J. Graham' (HT)	1906
'Lena' (T)	1906
'Mrs. Myles Kennedy' (T)	1906
'Avoca' (HT)	1907
'Harry Kirk' (T)	1907
'Souvenir of Stella Gray' (T)	1907
'W. E. Lippiat' (HT)	1907
'Ards Rambler' (Cl. HT)	1908
'Molly Sharman-Crawford' (T)	1908
'Nita Weldon' (T)	1908
'Miss Alice de Rothschild' (T)	1910
'Mrs. Cynthia Forde' (HT)	1910
'Mrs. Foley-Hobbs' (T)	1910
'Mrs. Hubert Taylor' (T)	1910
'Alexander Hill Gray' (T)	1911
'George Dickson' (HP)	1912
'Climbing Richmond' (HT)	1912
'Mrs. Herbert Hawksworth' (T)	1912
'Irish Fireflame' (HT)	1913
'Killarney Brilliant' (HT)	1914
'Lady Plymouth' (T)	1914
'Mrs. S. T. Wright' (T)	1914
'Climbing Irish Fireflame' (HT)	1916
'K. of K.' (HT)	1917
'Kootenay' (HT)	1917
'Kathleen Harrop' (B)	1919
'Climbing Ophelia' (HT)	1920
'Climbing Mrs. Aaron Ward' (HT)	1922
'Dame Edith Helen' (HT)	1926

Dickson, Hugh
Belfast, Northern Ireland
'Hugh Dickson' (HP)	1905
'J. B. Clark' (HP)	1905
'Lady Overtoun' (HP)	1907
'Coronation' (HP)	1913
'Climbing General MacArthur' (HT)	1923

Dingee-Conard
West Grove, Pennsylvania, U.S.A.
'The Queen' (T)	1889
'Pearl Rivers' (T)	1890
'Henry M. Stanley' (T)	1891
'Maud Little' (T)	1891
'Mrs. Jessie Fremont' (T)	1891
'Virginia' (T)	1894
'Pink Soupert' (Pol)	1896
'Princess Bonnie' (T)	1896
'Climbing Bridesmaid' (T)	1897
'Coronet' (HT)	1897
'Climbing Marie Guillot' (T)	1898
'Victory Rose' (HP)	1901
'Climbing Clotilde Soupert' (Pol)	1902
'Primrose' (T)	1908
'Climbing Rosemary' (HT)	1920

Dot, Pedro
Barcelona, Spain
'Apeles Mestres' (Cl. HP)	1926
'Isabel Llorach' (HP)	1929
'Nuria de Recolons' (HP)	1933
'Granate' (Ch)	1948
'Rosada' (Ch)	1950

Drögemüller, Heinrich
Neuhauss, Hanover, Germany
'Fürst Bismarck' (N)	1887
'Fürstin Bismarck' (Cl. HT)	1887
'Kaiser Wilhelm der Siegreiche' (Cl. T)	1887
'Kaiserin Friedrich' (Cl. T)	1889
'Emin Pascha' (HT)	1894

Duboc fils
Rouen, France
'Mme Louis Ricart' (HP)	1892
'Mlle Honorine Duboc' (HP)	1894

Dubreuil, Francis
Lyon, France
'Amiral Courbet' (HP)	1884
'Floribunda' (Pol)	1885
'Marquise de Vivens' (T)	1885
'Attraction' (HT)	1886
'Louis Lille' (HP)	1887
'Princesse de Sagan' (Ch)	1887
'Président Dutailly' (DP)	1888
'Graziella' (T)	1893
'Perle de Feu' (T)	1893
'Francis Dubreuil' (T)	1894
'Panachée de Lyon' (HP)	1895
'Princesse de Venosa' (T)	1895
'Perle des Rouges' (Pol)	1896
'Jean Bach Sisley' (Ch)	1898

'Dr. Cazeneuve' (HT)	1899
'Ami Charmet' (HP)	1900
'Mme Martignier' (Cl. T)	1903
'Crepuscule' (N)	1904
'Bébé Fleuri' (Ch)	1906
'Sarah Bernhardt' (Cl. HT)	1906
'Cyclope' (Pol)	1909
'Laure de Broglie' (Ch)	1910
'Petite Marcelle' (Pol)	1910
'Merveille des Rouges' (Pol)	1911

Ducher, Jean-Claude
Lyon, France
'Alphonse de Lamartine' (HP)	1853
'Louise de Savoie' (T)	1854
'Edith de Murat' (B)	1858
'Gloire de Ducher' (HP)	1865
'Louis Noisette' (HP)	1865
'Antoine Ducher' (HP)	1866
'Mlle Madeleine Nonin' (HP)	1866
'Ville de Lyon' (HP)	1866
'Président Willermoz' (HP)	1867
'La Tulipe' (T)	1868
'Chamoïs' (T)	1869
'Ducher' (Ch)	1869
'Rêve d'Or' (N)	1869
'Coquette de Lyon' (T)	1870
'Hortensia' (T)	1870
'Victor Pulliat' (T)	1870
'La Nankeen' (T)	1871
'Marie Van Houtte' (T)	1871
'Amazone' (T)	1872
'Anna Olivier' (T)	1872
'Bouquet d'Or' (N)	1872
'Marquisette' (Ch)	1872
'Vallée de Chamonix' (T)	1872
'Aureus' (T)	1873
'Helvetia' (T)	1873
'Mont Rosa' (T)	1873

Widow Ducher
Lyon, France
'Jean Ducher' (T)	1874
'Mme Devoucoux' (T)	1874
'Maréchal Robert' (T)	1875
'Mme Welche' (T)	1876
'Souvenir de George Sand' (T)	1876
'Louis Richard' (T)	1877
'Mme Maurice Kuppenheim' (T)	1877
'Triomphe de Milan' (T)	1877
'Innocente Pirola' (T)	1878
'William Allen Richardson' (N)	1878
'Jean Lorthois' (HT)	1879
'Jules Finger' (T)	1879
'Mme Louis Henry' (N)	1879
'Mlle Cécile Brunner' (Pol)	1880

Ducher "Children & Successors"
Lyon, France
'Climbing Captain Christy' (HT)	1881
'Ernest Prince' (HP)	1881
'François Olin' (HP)	1881

Ducher fils (Antoine)
Lyon, France

'Adèle de Bellabre' (T)	1888
'Souvenir du Rosiériste Gonod' (HP)	1889

Dupuy-Jamain
Paris, France

'Comte Odart' (HP)	1850
'Dupuy-Jamain' (HP)	1868

Duval, Charles
Montmorency, France

'Louis-Philippe I' (DP)	1832
'Comtesse de Lacépède' (HCh)	1840
'Charles Duval' (HB)	1841

Duval, Hippolyte *(Evidently grandson of the above)*
Montmorency, France

'Alsace-Lorraine' (HP)	1879
'Monsieur Alexandre Pelletier' (B)	1879
'Vincent-Hippolyte Duval' (HP)	1879

Easlea, Walter
Leigh-On-Sea, England

'Lulu' (HT)	1919
'Everest' (HP)	1927

Ellwanger (Henry B.) & Barry
Rochester, New York, U.S.A.

'Rosalie' (T)	1884
'Marshall P. Wilder' (HP)	1885

Elsa von Württemberg, Herzogin
Württemberg, Germany

'Pfaffstädt' (HP)	1929
'Prinzessin Elsa zu Schaumburg-Lippe' (HP)	1929
'Prinz Max zu Schaumburg-Lippe' (HP)	1934

Faudon
St.-Didier-au-Mont-d'Or, France

'Jeanne Sury' (HP)	1868
'Hippolyte Jamain' (HP)	1869

Felberg-Leclerc, Walter
Trier, Germany

'Hofgärtner Kalb' (B)	1913
'Felbergs Rosa Druschki' (HP)	1925
'Frau Dr. Schricker' (B)	1927

Fontaine, François
Clamart, France

'Prince Albert' (B)	1852
'Duchesse de Cambacérès' (HP)	1854
'Mme Charles Crapelet' (HP)	1859
'Montebello' (HP)	1859
'Mlle Léonie Persin' (HP)	1861
'Mme Doré' (B)	1863
'Mlle Marie Rady' (HP)	1865
'Mme Lierval' (HP)	1868
'Vicomte Maison' (HP)	1868
'Souvenir de Mère Fontaine' (N)	1874
'Edouard Fontaine' (HP)	1878

'Souvenir d'Aline Fontaine' (HP)	1879
'Desirée Fontaine' (HP)	1884

Franceschi-Fenzi, Dr.
Santa Barbara, California, U.S.A.

'Montarioso' (HGig)	1930
'Montecito' (HGig)	1930

Frettingham
Beeston?, England

'Beauty of Beeston' (HP)	1882
'Lord Frederic Cavendish' (HP)	1884

Gamon, André
Lyon, France

'Étoile de Mai' (Pol)	1892
'Comte Amédé de Foras' (T)	1900
'Reine Carola de Saxe' (HT)	1902
'Mlle Blanche Martignat' (T)	1903
'Mme Gamon' (T)	1905
'Alix Roussel' (T)	1908
'Monsieur Fraissenon' (HT)	1911

Garçon
Rouen, France

'Mme Hippolyte Jamain' (HP)	1871
'Triomphe de France' (HP)	1875
'Mme Isaac Pereire' (B)	1880
'Etendard de Jeanne d'Arc' (N)	1882

Gautreau, Victor
Brie-Comte-Robert, France

'Camille Bernardin' (HP)	1865
'Denis Hélye' (HP)	1865
'Vicomtesse de Vezins' (HP)	1867
'Mme la Générale Decaen' (HP)	1869
'Souvenir de Spa' (HP)	1873
'Mlle Jules Grévy' (HP)	1879

Geduldig, Philipp
Aachen, Germany

'Mme Jean Everaerts' (HP)	1907
'Gruss an Aachen' (HT)	1909
'Pæonia' (HP)	1914

Geschwindt, Rudolf
Karpona, Hungary

'Dr. Hurta' (HP)	1867
'Erinnerung an Brod' (HP)	1886
'Cæcilie Scharsach' (HP)	1887
'Meteor' (N)	1887
'Rotkäppchen' (Pol)	1887
'Tartarus' (HP)	1887
'Herzblättchens' (Pol)	1889
'Marie Dermar' (B)	1889
'Zigeunerblut' (B)	1889
'Anna Scharsach' (HP)	1890
'Antonie Schurz' (HP)	1890
'Astra' (HT)	1890
'Erinnerung an Schloss Scharfenstein' (HT)	1892
'Gruss an Teplitz' (B)	1897
'Mme Eugene E. Marlitt' (B)	1900
'Julius Fabianics de Misefa' (T)	1902
'Parkzierde' (B)	1909
'Geschwindt's Gorgeous' (Cl. HT)	1916

Godard, Antoine
Lyon, France

'Marie Thérèse Dubourg' (N)	1888
'Mlle Geneviève Godard' (Cl. T)	1889
'Souvenir du Dr. Passot' (T)	1889
'Antoinette Durieu' (T)	1890
'Mme Creux' (Cl. T)	1890
'Mlle Marie Gaze' (N)	1892
'Souvenir de Geneviève Godard' (T)	1893
'Mme Louis Blanchet' (N)	1894
'Mme Tony Baboud' (HT)	1895
'Mlle Jeanne Philippe' (T)	1898
'Mme Jean Favre' (HT)	1900
'Marquise de Querhoënt' (T)	1901
'Mme Auguste Choutet' (Cl. HT)	1901
'Souvenir de McKinley' (HP)	1902

Gonod, J.-M.
Lyon, France

'Achille Gonod' (HP)	1864
'Mme Fillion' (HP)	1865
'Souvenir de Mme de Corval' (HP)	1867
'Mme Clert' (HP)	1868
'Monsieur Cordier' (HP)	1871
'Mme Soubeyran' (HP)	1872
'Mme Maurice Rivoire' (HP)	1876
'Monsieur Fillion' (HP)	1876
'Princesse Marie Dolgorouky' (HP)	1878
'Beauté de l'Europe' (N)	1881
'Adélaïde de Meynot' (HP)	1882
'Malmaison Rouge' (B)	1882
'Souvenir de Léon Gambetta' (HP)	1883
'Souvenir de l'Ami Labruyère' (HP)	1884
'Louis Rollet' (HP)	1886
'Louis Donadine' (HP)	1887

Good & Reese Co.
Springfield, Ohio, U.S.A.

'General Robert E. Lee' (T)	1896
'Frances E. Willard' (T)	1899
'Gainesborough' (Cl. HT)	1903
'Helen Good' (T)	1906

Grandes Roseraies du Val de la Loire
Orléans, France

'Radium' (Pol)	1913
'Denise Cassegrain' (Pol)	1922

Granger, Théophile
Grisy-Suisnes, France

'Mme de Trotter' (HP)	1854
'Reine de Danemark' (HP)	1857
'Général Washington' (HP)	1860
'Robert de Brie' (HP)	1860
'Baronne de Noirmont' (B)	1861
'Maurice Bernardin' (HP)	1861
'Comtesse de Polignac' (HP)	1862
'Président Lincoln' (HP)	1862
'Duc de Wellington' (HP)	1864
'Clémence Raoux' (HP)	1869
'Souvenir du Président Porcher' (HP)	1880

Gravereaux, Jules
Roseraie de l'Haÿ, l'Haÿ, France

'Madeleine Orosdy' (Pol)	1912
'Maria Star' (T)	1913
'Petite Françoise' (Pol)	1915

Grootendorst, F. J. (& Sons)
Boskoop, The Netherlands

'Sneprinsesse' (Pol)	1946
'Muttertag' (Pol)	1949
'Orange Morsdag' (Pol)	1956

Guérin, Modeste
Angers, France

'Malton' (HCh)	1829
'Gloire de Guérin' (HP)	1833
'Louis-Philippe' (Ch)	1834
'Caroline' (T)	1835
'Mme de Vatry' (T)	1855

Guillot père (Laurent)
Lyon, France

'Mme Bravy' (T)	1845
'Duchesse de Thuringe' (B)	1847
'Souvenir de l'Exposition de Londres' (B)	1851
'Canari' (T)	1852
'Elyse Flory' (Ch)	1852
'Reveil' (B)	1852
'Souvenir de Leveson-Gower' (HP)	1852
'Lord Raglan' (HP)	1854
'Comtesse de Barbantane' (B)	1858
'Baron G.-B. Gonella' (B)	1859
'Gourdault' (B)	1859
'Sénateur Vaïsse' (HP)	1859
'Victor-Emmanuel' (HP)	1859
'Emotion' (B)	1862
'Pavillon de Pregny' (N)	1863
'Adrienne de Cardoville' (B)	1864
'Triomphe de la Terre des Roses' (HP)	1864
'Mme Noman' (HP)	1867
'Victor le Bihan' (HP)	1868
'Comtesse d'Oxford' (HP)	1869
'Elisa Boëlle' (HP)	1869

Guillot fils (Jean-Baptiste)
Lyon, France

'Mme Falcot' (T)	1858
'Louis XIV' (HP)	1859
'Mlle Eugénie Verdier' (HP)	1859
'Catherine Guillot' (B)	1860
'Eugène Verdier' (HP)	1863
'Paul de la Meilleraye' (HP)	1863
'Abbé Berlèze' (HP)	1864
'Joséphine de Beauharnais' (HP)	1865
'Horace Vernet' (HP)	1866
'Mme Margottin' (T)	1866
'La France' (HT)	1867
'Adrienne Christophle' (Cl. T)	1868
'Marie Sisley' (T)	1868
'Mme Céline Noirey' (T)	1868
'Catherine Mermet' (T)	1869
'Abbé Bramerel' (HP)	1871
'Catherine Bonnard' (HCh)	1871

'Mme Camille' (T)	1871
'Marie Accary' (N)	1872
'Claire Carnot' (N)	1873
'Aline Sisley' (T)	1874
'Marie Guillot' (T)	1874
'Anne-Marie Côte' (N)	1875
'Pâquerette' (Pol)	1875
'Mlle Blanche Durrschmidt' (T)	1878
'Pierre Guillot' (HT)	1879
'Étoile de Lyon' (T)	1881
'Mignonette' (Pol)	1881
'Mme Cusin' (T)	1881
'Monsieur Jules Monges' (HP)	1881
'Honourable Edith Gifford' (T)	1882
'Mme de Watteville' (T)	1883
'Gloire Lyonnaise' (HP)	1884

Guillot & fils
Lyon, France

'Souvenir de Gabrielle Drevet' (T)	1884
'Comtesse de Frigneuse' (T)	1885
'Luciole' (T)	1886
'Mme Joseph Desbois' (HT)	1886
'Gloire des Polyantha' (Pol)	1887
'Mme Hoste' (T)	1887
'Mme Laurette Messimy' (Ch)	1887
'Ernest Metz' (T)	1888
'Mme Pierre Guillot' (T)	1888
'J.-B. Varonne' (T)	1889
'Mme Renahy' (HP)	1889
'Souvenir de François Gaulain' (T)	1889
'Miss Wenn' (T)	1890
'Mlle Christine de Noué' (T)	1890
'Augustine Halem' (HT)	1891

Guillot, Pierre
Lyon, France

'Mme Jules Finger' (HT)	1893
'Mme Eugène Résal' (Ch)	1894
'Irène Watts' (Ch)	1895
'Souvenir d'Auguste Métral' (HT)	1895
'Souvenir de Catherine Guillot' (Ch)	1895
'Émilie Gonin' (T)	1896
'Mme Jules Grolez' (HT)	1896
'Souvenir de Jeanne Cabaud' (T)	1896
'Souvenir de J.-B. Guillot' (Ch)	1897
'Margherita di Simone' (T)	1898
'François Crousse' (Cl. T)	1900
'Comtesse du Caÿla' (Ch)	1902
'Climbing Le Vésuve' (Ch)	1904
'Mme Léon Pain' (HT)	1904
'Mme P. Euler' (HT)	1907

Guillot, Marc
Saint-Priest, Isère, France

'Président Briand' (HP)	1929

Guinoisseau (Bertrand)-Flon
Angers, France

'Lucullus' (Ch)	1854
'Empereur du Maroc' (HP)	1858
'Comtesse de Bresson' (HP)	1873

Guinoisseau fils
Angers, France

'Mlle Augustine Guinoisseau' (HT)	1889

Hall, Dr. J. Campbell
England

'Mrs. Campbell Hall' (T)	1914
'Miss Annie Crawford' (HP)	1915

Hardy, Alexandre
Paris, France

'Belle de Crécy' (HCh)	1829
'Félicité Hardy' (DP)	ca. 1831
'Bon Silène' (T)	1835
'Gigantesque' (T)	1835
'Triomphe de Luxembourg' (T)	1835
'Cels Multiflore' (T)	1836
'Eugène de Beauharnais' (Ch)	1837
'Ornement du Luxembourg' (HP)	1840
'Prince Charles' (HB)	1842
'Pumila Alba' (N)	1847

Harkness & Company
Hitchin, England

'Mrs. Harkness' (HP)	1894
'Merrie England' (HP)	1897
'Fairy Changeling' (Pol)	1979
'Fairy Maid' (Pol)	1979
'Fairy Prince' (Pol)	1979
'Fairyland' (Pol)	1979
'Fairy Ring' (Pol)	ca. 1980
'Fairy Damsel' (Pol)	1982

Heers, C. W.
Manly, Australia

'The Allies' (Pol)	1930
'Pacific Triumph' (Pol)	1949

Henderson, Peter
New York City, New York, U.S.A.

'Setina' (Cl. B)	1879
'White Pet' (Pol)	1879
'Sunset' (T)	1883
'Climbing La France' (HT)	1893

Hill, E.G.
Richmond, Indiana, U.S.A.

'Climbing Mrs. W. J. Grant' (HT)	1899
'General MacArthur' (HT)	1905
'Richmond' (HT)	1905
'Indiana' (Cl. HT)	1907
'Columbia' (HT)	1916
'Mme Butterfly' (HT)	1918

Hinner, Wilhelm
Trier, Germany

'Pharisäer' (HT)	1901
'Andenken an Moritz von Frohlich' (HT)	1905
'Georg Arends' (HP)	1910
'Heinrich Münch' (HP)	1911

Hjort, Samuel
Thomasville, Georgia, U.S.A.
'Climbing Marie Van Houtte' (T)	ca. 1940
'Climbing Mrs. B. R. Cant' (T)	1960

Hobbies Ltd.
Dereham, England
'Lemon Queen' (Cl. HT)	1912
'Effective' (Cl. HT)	1913

Hoopes Bros. & Thomas Co.
West Chester, Pennsylvania, U.S.A.
'Climbing American Beauty' (Cl)	1909
'Purity' (Cl)	1917

Hosp, F. P.
Riverside, California, U.S.A.
'Climbing Mlle Cécile Brunner' (Pol)	1894
'Climbing Papa Gontier' (T)	1898

Jacques, Antoine A. *(Uncle of Victor Verdier)*
Neuilly, France
'Rosier de Bourbon' (B)	1821
'Athalin' (HB)	1830
'Fimbriata à Pétales Frangés' (Ch)	1831

Jamain, Hippolyte
Paris, France
'Dr. Jamain' (HP)	1851
'Mme Boutin' (HP)	1861
'Antonine Verdier' (HT)	1872
'Marguerite Jamain' (HP)	1873
'Mme Bernutz' (HP)	1873
'Colonel De Sansal' (HP)	1875
'Berthe Du Mesnil de Mont Chauveau' (HP)	1876
'Duchesse d'Ossuna' (HP)	1877
'Mme Thévenot' (HP)	1877
'Souvenir de Mme Alfred Vy' (HP)	1880

Kersbergen
Boskoop, The Netherlands
'Kersbergen' (Pol)	1927
'Paul Crampel' (Pol)	1930

Ketten Bros.
Luxembourg
'Dr. Pouleur' (T)	1897
'Marguerite Ketten' (T)	1897
'F. L. Segers' (T)	1898
'Princesse Etienne de Croy' (T)	1898
'Sisi Ketten' (Pol)	1900
'Capitaine Millet' (T)	1901
'Mlle Marthe Cahuzac' (Pol)	1901
'Edmée et Roger' (HT)	1902
'Joseph Paquet' (T)	1905
'Générale Marie Raiewsky' (HP)	1911

Kiese, Hermann (& Company)
Wieselbach-Erfurt, Germany
'Venus' (HP)	1895
'Paula Clegg' (HP)	1912
'Loreley' (Pol)	1913
'Mikado' (Cl. HT)	1913

'Perle' (Pol)	1913
'Siegesperle' (Pol)	1915
'Fürst Leopold zu Schaumburg-Lippe' (HP)	1918
'Gruss an Weimar' (HP)	1919
'Schön Ingeborg' (HP)	1921
'Martin Liebau' (HP)	1930

Kluis & Koning
Boskoop, The Netherlands
'Greta Kluis' (Pol)	1916
'Mrs. William G. Koning' (Pol)	1917

Kordes, Wilhelm
Sparrieshoop, Germany
'Minna' (HT)	1930
'Druschka' (HP)	1932
'Climbing Gruss an Aachen' (HT)	1937
'Orange Triumph' (Pol)	1937
'Waldfee' (HP)	1960

Koster & Sons
Boskoop, The Netherlands
'Dick Koster' (Pol)	1929
'Margo Koster' (Pol)	1931

Labruyère, Eugène
Lyon, France
'Reine Victoria' (B)	1872
'Firebrand' (HP)	1874

Lacharme, François
Lyon, France
'Louise Peyronny' (HP)	1844
'Cornet' (HP)	1845
'Deuil de Duc d'Orléans' (B)	1845
'Mme Mélanie Willermoz' (T)	1845
'Desgaches' (HP)	1850
'Mère de St. Louis' (HP)	1851
'Mme Récamier' (HP)	1853
'Marquis de Balbiano' (B)	1855
'Pæonia' (HP)	1855
'Mme Massot' (B)	1856
'Anna de Diesbach' (HP)	1858
'Virginale' (HP)	1858
'Victor Verdier' (HP)	1859
'Charles Lefebvre' (HP)	1861
'Louise d'Arzens' (B)	1861
'Lady Emily Peel' (B)	1862
'Mme Alfred de Rougemont' (B)	1862
'Mlle Gabrielle de Peyronny' (HP)	1863
'Mme Charles Verdier' (HP)	1863
'Alfred Colomb' (HP)	1865
'Baronne de Maynard' (B)	1865
'Coquette des Blanches' (B)	1865
'Prudence Besson' (HP)	1865
'Souvenir du Dr. Jamain' (HP)	1865
'Xavier Olibo' (HP)	1865
'Thorin' (HP)	1866
'Boule de Neige' (B)	1867
'Coquette des Alpes' (B)	1867
'Louis Van Houtte' (HP)	1869
'Lyonnais' (HP)	1871
'Mme Lacharme' (HT)	1872
'Perle des Blanches' (B)	1872

'Captain Christy' (HT) — 1873
'Comtesse de Serenyi' (HP) — 1874
'Hippolyte Jamain' (HP) — 1874
'Souvenir du Baron de Semur' (HP) — 1874
'Henry Bennett' (HP) — 1875
'Jean Soupert' (HP) — 1875
'Mlle Léonie Giessen' (HP) — 1876
'Mme François Pittet' (B) — 1877
'Mme Lambard' (T) — 1878
'Catherine Soupert' (HP) — 1879
'Julius Finger' (HT) — 1879
'Violette Bouyer' (HP) — 1881
'Alphonse Soupert' (HP) — 1883
'Eclair' (HP) — 1883
'Clara Cochet' (HP) — 1885

Laffay, Jean
Bellevue-Meudon, France

'Archiduc Charles' (Ch) — ca. 1825
'Bengale d'Automne' (Ch) — 1825
'Chévrier' (HCh) — ca. 1825
'Laffay' (Ch) — 1825
'Le Vésuve' (Ch) — 1825
'La Nubienne' (HCh) — 1825
'Roi de Siam' (T) — 1825
'Darius' (Ch) — 1827
'Duchesse de Montebello' (HCh) — by 1829
'Brennus' (HB) — 1830
'Triomphe de Laffay' (HCh) — ca. 1830
'Catherine II' (Ch) — 1832
'Fabvier' (Ch) — 1832
'Mistress Bosanquet' (B) — 1832
'Bouquet Tout Fait' (N) — 1835
'Céline' (HB) — 1835
'Général Allard' (HCh) — ca. 1835
'Mme Desprez' (Ch) — by 1835
'Napoléon' (Ch) — ca. 1835
'Quatre Saisons Blanc Mousseux' (DP) — ca. 1835
'Prince Albert' (HP) — 1837
'Princesse Hélène' (HP) — 1837
'Great Western' (HB) — 1838
'William Jesse' (HB) — 1838
'Comte de Paris' (HP) — 1839
'Duchesse de Sutherland' (HP) — 1839
'Mme Laffay' (HP) — 1839
'Cardinal de Richelieu' (HCh) — 1840
'Coupe d'Hébé' (HB) — 1840
'Duchesse de Kent' (Ch) — 1840
'Edward Jesse' (HB) — ca. 1840
'Mistress Elliot' (HP) — 1841
'Dr. Marx' (HP) — 1842
'La Reine' (HP) — 1844
'Gerbe de Roses' (HP) — 1847
'Julie de Krudner' (DP) — 1847
'Auguste Mie' (HP) — 1851
'Rubens' (HP) — 1852
'Sir Joseph Paxton' (HB) — 1852

Lambert, Elie
Lyon, France

'Marie Remond' (T) — 1882
'Marie Lambert' (T) — 1886
'Mlle Claudine Perreau' (T) — 1886
'Mme Elie Lambert' (T) — 1890

Lambert, Peter
Trier, Germany

'Kaiserin Auguste Viktoria' (HT) — 1891
'Mosella' (Pol) — 1895
'Grossherzogin Vikoria Melitta von Hessen' (HT) — 1897
'Oskar Cordel' (HP) — 1897
'Balduin' (HT) — 1898
'Frau Geheimrat Von Boch' (T) — 1898
'Papa Lambert' (HT) — 1898
'Reichsgraf E. von Kesselstatt' (T) — 1898
'Eugénie Lamesch' (Pol) — 1899
'Hofgärtendirektor Graebener' (HT) — 1899
'Leonie Lamesch' (Pol) — 1899
'Frau Karl Druschki' (HP) — 1901
'Katharina Zeimet' (Pol) — 1901
'Mme Jean Dupuy' (T) — 1901
'Schneewittchen' (Pol) — 1901
'Freiherr von Marschall' (T) — 1903
'Gustav Grünerwald' (HT) — 1903
'Kleiner Alfred' (Pol) — 1903
'Schneekopf' (Pol) — 1903
'Frau Cecilie Walter' (Pol) — 1904
'Unermüdliche' (Ch) — 1904
'Lina Schmidt-Michel' (HT) — 1905
'Martha' (Pol) — 1905
'Frau Geheimrat Dr. Staub' (Cl. HT) — 1908
'Climbing Miniature' (Pol) — 1908
'Philipp Paulig' (HP) — 1908
'Cineraria' (Pol) — 1909
'Frau Alexander Weiss' (Pol) — 1909
'Frau Oberhofgärtner Schultze' (Pol) — 1909
'Gustel Mayer' (Pol) — 1909
'Tip-Top' (Pol) — 1909
'Zigeunerknabe' (HB) — 1909
'Leonie Lambert' (HP) — 1913
'Echo' (Pol) — 1914
'Dr. Ingomar H. Blohm' (HP) — 1919
'Adam Messerich' (B) — 1920
'Bischof Dr. Korum' (HP) — 1921
'St. Ingebert' (HP) — 1926
'Druschki Rubra' (HP) — 1929

Lartay, Clém. (?)
Bordeaux, France

'Lion des Combats' (HP) — 1850
'Reine de Castille' (HP) — 1852
'Enfant de France' (HP) — 1860
'Léonie Lartay' (HP) — 1860
'Gloire de Bordeaux' (N) — 1861
'L'Espérance' (HP) — 1871
'Belle Nanon' (B) — 1872

Laxton Bros. (Philip & Thomas)
Bedford, England

'Princess Louise' (HP) — 1869
'Emily Laxton' (HP) — 1876
'Empress of India' (HP) — 1876
'Marchioness of Exeter' (HP) — 1876
'Charles Darwin' (HP) — 1879
'Dr. Hogg' (HP) — 1880
'Bedford Belle' (HT) — 1884

Lédéchaux, Henri
Villecresne, France

'Mlle Adèle Jougant' (Cl. T)	1862
'Mme Ferdinand Jamin' (HP)	1875

Widow Lédéchaux
Villecresne, France

'Léon Renault' (HP)	1878
'Comtesse Cahen d'Anvers' (HP)	1884
'Château des Bergeries' (T)	1886
'François Coppée' (HP)	1895

Leenders Bros.
Tegelen, The Netherlands

'Jonkheer J. L. Mock' (HT)	1909
'General-Superior Arnold Janssen' (HT)	1912
'Mevrouw Boreel van Hogelander' (T)	1918
'Mevrouw Nathalie Nypels' (Pol)	1919
'Nypels Perfection' (Pol)	1930
'Climbing Étoile de Hollande' (HT)	1931
'Gruss an Aachen Superior' (HT)	1942

Lens, Louis
Wavre-Notre-Dame, Belgium

'Climbing Columbia' (HT)	1929
'Climbing Distinction' (Pol)	1935

Leroy, Anatole
Angers, France

'Mme Anatole Leroy' (HP)	1892
'Mme Cordier' (HP)	1903

Levavasseur & Sons
Orléans, France

'Mme Norbert Levavasseur' (Pol)	1903
'Mrs. W. H. Cutbush' (Pol)	1907
'Jeanne d'Arc' (Pol)	1909
'Mme Taft' (Pol)	1909
'Orléans-Rose' (Pol)	1909
'Eileen Loow' (Pol)	1910
'Gloire d'Orléans' (Pol)	1912
'Excellens' (Pol)	1913
'Maréchal Foch' (Pol)	1918

Lévêque, René
Ivry-sur-Seine, France

'Duchesse de Rohan' (DP)	1847

Lévêque, Louis
Ivry-sur-Seine, France

'John Gould Veitch' (HP)	1864
'Mme Elisa de Vilmorin' (HT)	1864
'Baron Haussmann' (HP)	1867
'Devienne-Lamy' (HP)	1868
'Mlle Favart' (B)	1869
'Deuil de Dunois' (HP)	1873
'Mme Louis Lévêque' (HP)	1873
'Avocat Duvivier' (HP)	1875
'Princesse Lise Troubetzkoï' (HP)	1877
'Alexandre Dutitre' (HP)	1878
'Abraham Zimmermann' (HP)	1879
'Amedée Philibert' (HP)	1879
'Comte Horace de Choiseul' (HP)	1879

'Mme Elisa Tasson' (HP)	1879
'Comte Frédéric de Thun de Hohenstein' (HP)	1880
'Comte Adrien de Germiny' (HP)	1881
'Comte de Flandres' (HP)	1881
'Mme Marthe d'Halloy' (HP)	1881
'Baron Nathaniel de Rothschild' (HP)	1882
'Léon Say' (HP)	1882
'Mme Olympe Térestchenko' (B)	1882
'Mme Veuve Alexandre Pommery' (HP)	1882
'Directeur Alphand' (HP)	1883
'Mlle Suzanne-Marie Rodocanachi' (HP)	1883
'Princesse Radziwill' (HP)	1883
'Duc de Marlborough' (HP)	1884
'Laurent de Rillé' (HP)	1884
'Mme Francis Buchner' (HP)	1884
'Comtesse de Fressinet de Bellanger' (HP)	1885
'Mme Baulot' (HP)	1885
'Princesse Amedée de Broglie' (HP)	1885
'Professeur Maxime Cornu' (HP)	1885
'A. Drawiel' (HP)	1886
'Ali Pacha Cherif' (HP)	1886
'Baronne de St. Didier' (HP)	1886
'Comte de Paris' (HP)	1886
'Mme Léon Halkin' (HP)	1886
'Mme Sophie Stern' (HP)	1887
'Comtesse Branicka' (HP)	1888
'Comtesse de Roquette-Buisson' (HP)	1888
'Comtesse O'Gorman' (HP)	1888
'Ferdinand Jamin' (HP)	1888
'Victor Lemoine' (HP)	1888
'Duchesse de Dino' (HP)	1889
'Emile Bardiaux' (HP)	1889
'Laforcade' (HP)	1889
'Mme Olga' (T)	1889
'Mme Thibaut' (HP)	1889
'Belle Yvrienne' (HP)	1890
'Mlle Andrée Worth' (B)	1890
'Professeur Charguereaud' (HP)	1890
'Mme Théodore Vernes' (HP)	1891
'Grand-Duc Alexis' (HP)	1892
'Impératrice Maria Feodorowna' (HP)	1892
'Mme Laurent Simons' (T)	1894
'Belle Vichysoise' (N)	1895
'Mlle Marie-Louise Oger' (T)	1895
'Mme Henri Graire' (T)	1895
'Comte Raoul Chandon' (HP)	1896
'Comtesse Renée de Béarn' (HP)	1896
'Baron T'Kint de Roodenbeke' (HP)	1897
'Comte Charles d'Harcourt' (HP)	1897
'Mme Rose Caron' (HP)	1898
'Souvenir d'Alexandre Hardy' (HP)	1898
'Souvenir de Mme Sadi Carnot' (HP)	1898
'Souvenir de Henri Lévêque de Vilmorin' (HP)	1899
'Vincente Peluffo' (HP)	1902
'Empereur Nicolas II' (T)	1903
'Mme Achille Fould' (T)	1903

Levet, Antoine
Lyon, France

'Mlle Thérèse Levet' (HP)	1866
'Abbé Giraudier' (HP)	1869
'Mme Trifle' (N)	1869
'Paul Neyron' (HP)	1869
'Belle Lyonnaise' (N)	1870

'Mme Azélie Imbert' (T) 1870
'Mme Bérard' (N) 1870
'Mme Emilie Dupuy' (Cl. T) 1870
'Paul Perras' (HB) 1870
'François Michelon' (HP) 1871
'Ma Capucine' (T) 1871
'Perfection de Monplaisir' (T) 1871
'Souvenir de Paul Neyron' (T) 1871
'Étienne Levet' (HP) 1872
'Henry Bennett' (T) 1872
'Mme Dr. Jütté' (T) 1872
'Monsieur Etienne Dupuy' (HP) 1873
'Antoine Mouton' (HP) 1874
'Perle des Jardins' (T) 1874
'Shirley Hibberd' (T) 1874
'Mme Marie Berton' (N) 1875
'Mlle Lazarine Poizeau' (T) 1876
'Mme Sophie Tropot' (HP) 1876
'Souvenir de Paul Dupuy' (HCh) 1876
'Mlle Brigitte Viollet' (HT) 1878
'Mme Etienne Levet' (HT) 1878
'Pierre Carot' (HP) 1878
'Reine Marie Henriette' (Cl. HT) 1878
'Mlle Mathilde Lenaerts' (N) 1879
'Mme Barthélemy Levet' (T) 1879
'Souvenir de Monsieur Faivre' (HP) 1879
'François Levet' (HP) 1880
'Les Fiançailles de la Princesse Stéphanie
   et de l'Archiduc Rodolphe' (N) 1880
'Mme Caro' (T) 1880
'Mme Crozy' (HP) 1881
'Ulrich Brunner fils' (HP) 1881
'Mme Eugène Verdier' (Cl. T) 1882
'Mme François Bruel' (HP) 1882
'Souvenir de Thérèse Levet' (T) 1882
'Edmond de Biauzat' (T) 1885
'Claudius Levet' (T) 1886
'Mme Honoré Defresne' (T) 1886
'Souvenir de Monsieur Bruel' (B) 1889

Levet, Étienne
Lyon, France
'Souvenir de Mme Levet' (T) 1891

Liabaud, Jean
Lyon, France
'Clémence Joigneux' (HP) 1861
'Mme Clémence Joigneux' (HP) 1861
'Simon de St.-Jean' (HP) 1861
'Monsieur Bonçenne' (HP) 1864
'Jean Cherpin' (HP) 1865
'Mme Gabriel Luizet' (B) 1867
'Marquise de Mortemart' (HP) 1868
'Notaire Bonnefond' (HP) 1868
'Jules Seurre' (HP) 1869
'Baron de Bonstetten' (HP) 1871
'A. Bouquet' (T) 1873
'Souvenir de la Princesse Amélie des Pays-Bas' (HP) 1873
'Alexandre Chomer' (HP) 1875
'Jean Liabaud' (HP) 1875
'Mme Gabriel Luizet' (HP) 1877
'Mme Montel' (HP) 1880
'A.-M. Ampère' (HP) 1881

'Mme Pierre Margery' (HP) 1881
'Alexandre Dupont' (HP) 1882
'Mme Marie Legrange' (HP) 1882
'Monsieur Hoste' (HP) 1884
'Monsieur Jules Deroudilhe' (HP) 1886
'Mme Alphonse Seux' (HP) 1887
'Mlle Marie Magat' (HP) 1889
'Vicomte de Lauzières' (HP) 1889
'Jeanne Masson' (HP) 1891
'Claude Jacquet' (HP) 1892
'Capitaine Peillon' (HP) 1893
'Mme Antoine Rivoire' (HP) 1894
'Mme Chabanne' (HP) 1896
'Mlle Marie Achard' (HP) 1896

Lille, Léon
Lyon-Villeurbanne, France
'Multiflora Nana Perpétuelle' (Pol) 1893
'Flocon de Neige' (Pol) 1897
'Gloire de Charpennes' (Pol) 1897
'Colibri' (Pol) 1898
'Baby Faurax' (Pol) 1924

Marest
Paris, France
'Comte Bobrinsky' (HP) 1849
'Souvenir d'Elisa Vardon' (T) 1855
'Comtesse Cécile de Chabrillant' (HP) 1858
'Monsieur Journaux' (HP) 1868

Margottin père (Jacques-Julien)
Bourg-la-Reine, France
'Vicomte Fritz de Cussy' (B) 1845
'Colonel Foissy' (HP) 1849
'Général Bedeau' (HP) 1851
'Louise Odier' (B) 1851
'Jules Margottin' (HP) 1853
'Triomphe de l'Exposition' (HP) 1855
'Mme Marie Van Houtte' (HP) 1857
'Anna Alexieff' (HP) 1858
'Duc de Magenta' (T) 1859
'Alexandre Dumas' (HP) 1861
'Souvenir du Comte de Cavour' (HP) 1861
'Jean Goujon' (HP) 1862
'Charles Margottin' (HP) 1863
'Rev. H. d'Ombrain' (B) 1863
'Duchesse d'Aoste' (HP) 1867
'Charles Turner' (HP) 1869
'Mme de Ridder' (HP) 1871
'Deuil du Colonel Denfert' (HP) 1878
'Dr. Baillon' (HP) 1878
'Comte de Mortemart' (HP) 1879
'Gloire de Bourg-la-Reine' (HP) 1879
'Henriette Petit' (HP) 1879

Margottin fils (Jules)
Pierrefitte, France
'Mme Jeannine Joubert' (HB) 1877
'Monsieur le Préfet Limbourg' (HP) 1878
'Mme Edmée Cocteau' (Cl. HT) 1903

Mari, Antoine
Nice, France

'Dr. Félix Guyon' (T)	1901
'Mme Antoine Mari' (T)	1901
'Mme Vermorel' (T)	1901
'Mme Albert Bernardin' (T)	1904

Mauget
Orléans, France

'Blanc Pur' (N)	1827
'Reine des Île-Bourbons' (B)	1834

May, John M.
Summit, New Jersey, U.S.A.

'The Bride' (T)	1885
'Francis B. Hayes' (HB)	1892
'Oakmont' (HP)	1893
'Mrs. W. C. Whitney' (HT)	1894
'Mrs. J. Pierpont Morgan' (T)	1895

May, H.B.
Summit, New Jersey, U.S.A.

'Princess Ena' (Pol)	1906
'Climbing Liberty' (Cl. HT)	1908

McGredy, Samuel (& Son)
Portadown, Ireland

'His Majesty' (HT)	1909
'Lady Alice Stanley' (HT)	1909
'Mrs. Wakefield Christie-Miller' (HT)	1909
'Mrs. Herbert Stevens' (HT)	1910
'British Queen' (HT)	1912
'Old Gold' (HT)	1913
'Isobel' (HT)	1916
'Mrs. Henry Morse' (HT)	1919
'Vesuvius' (HT)	1923

Merryweather (H.) & Sons
Southwell, Nottinghamshire, England

'Phyllis' (Pol)	1908
'Jessie' (Pol)	1909

Miellez
Esquermes, France

'Elise Sauvage' (T)	1838
'Le Pactole' (T)	pre-1841
'Toussaint-Louverture' (B)	1849

Moreau, F. (called "Louis")
Fontenay-aux-Roses, France

'Vainqueur de Goliath' (HP)	1862
'Lisette de Béranger' (HP)	1867

Moreau-Robert
Angers, France

'Prince Eugène de Beauharnais' (HP)	1864
'Souvenir du Président Lincoln' (B)	1865
'Souvenir de Mme Auguste Charles' (B)	1866
'Général Désaix' (HP)	1867
'Jacques Cartier' (DP)	1868
'Maurice Lepelletier' (HP)	1868
'Mme Renard' (HP)	1871
'Souvenir d'Adèle Launay' (B)	1872

'Ingénieur Madèlé' (HP)	1874
'Mme de Sevigné' (B)	1874
'Philippe Bardet' (HP)	1874
'Barthélemy-Joubert' (HP)	1877
'Fontenelle' (HP)	1877
'Mme Roger' (HP)	1877
'Souvenir d'Adolphe Thiers' (HP)	1877
'Souvenir de Mme Robert' (HP)	1878
'Mme Georges Vibert' (HP)	1879
'Panachée d'Angers' (HP)	1879
'Perle d'Angers' (B)	1879
'Georges Moreau' (HP)	1880
'Albert La Blotais' (HP)	1881
'Archiduchesse Elizabeth d'Autriche' (HP)	1881
'Mme Yorke' (HP)	1881
'Joachim du Bellay' (HP)	1882
'Boileau' (HP)	1883
'Rembrandt' (DP)	1883
'Mme Lefebvre' (HP)	1885
'Dr. Pasteur' (HT)	1887
'Katkoff' (HP)	1887
'L'Abondance' (N)	1887
'La France de 89' (Cl. HT)	1889
'Monsieur A. Maillé' (B)	1889
'Souvenir de Grégoire Bordillon' (HP)	1889
'Mme Lemesle' (HP)	1890
'Souvenir de Victor Landeau' (B)	1890
'Souvenir du Lieutenant Bujon' (B)	1891
'Monsieur Cordeau' (B)	1892
'Mme Nobécourt' (B)	1893

Morse, Henry
Norwich, England

'Climbing Château de Clos Vougeot' (HT)	1920
'Westfield Star' (HT)	1920

Müller, Dr. F.
Weingarten, Bavaria, Germany

'Marie Zahn' (HT)	1897
'Grossherzog Ernst Ludwig von Hesse' (HT)	1898
'Dr. Müllers Rote' (HP)	1920
'Turnvater Jahn' (HP)	1927

Nabonnand, Gilbert
Golfe Juan, France

'Golfe-Juan' (HP)	1872
'Isabelle Nabonnand' (T)	1873
'Duchess of Edinburgh' (T)	1874
'La Princesse Vera' (T)	1877
'Lily Metschersky' (N)	1877
'Mme la Comtesse de Caserta' (T)	1877
'Mme Nabonnand' (T)	1877
'Mystère' (T)	1877
'Paul Nabonnand' (T)	1877
'Alphonse Karr' (T)	1878
'Général Schablikine' (T)	1878
'Papillon' (Cl. T)	1878
'Duchesse de Vallombrosa' (T)	1879
'Mlle Franziska Krüger' (T)	1879
'Mlle Marie Moreau' (T)	1879
'Mme Pierre Perny' (T)	1879
'Reine Emma des Pays-Bas' (T)	1879
'Comtesse Alban de Villeneuve' (T)	1881
'Mélanie Soupert' (N)	1881

'Mme Julie Lassen' (N)	1881
'Mme Marie Lavalley' (N)	1881
'Reine Olga de Wurtemberg' (N)	1881
'Baronne de St.-Triviers' (T)	1882
'Blanche Nabonnand' (T)	1882
'Souvenir de Germain de St.-Pierre' (T)	1882
'Hermance Louisa de La Rive' (T)	1882
'Mme Crombez' (T)	1882
'Mme Dubroca' (T)	1882
'Mme Léon Février' (T)	1882
'Papa Gontier' (T)	1882
'Rose Nabonnand' (T)	1882
'Impératrice Marie Féodorowna de Russie' (T)	1883
'Marie d'Orléans' (T)	1883
'Mme F. Brassac' (T)	1883
'Vicomtesse de Bernis' (T)	1883
'Camille Roux' (T)	1885
'Comtesse Georges de Roquette-Buisson' (N)	1885
'Exadelphé' (T)	1885
'Flavien Budillon' (T)	1885
'Mlle Suzanne Blanchet' (T)	1885
'Reine Olga' (T)	1885
'Bengale Nabonnand' (Ch)	1886
'Lady Zoë Brougham' (T)	1886
'Lord Stanley' (T)	1886
'Mme Agathe Nabonnand' (T)	1886
'S.A.R. Mme la Princesse de Hohenzollern, Infante de Portugal' (T)	1886
'Bardou Job' (B)	1887
'L'Idéal' (N)	1887
'Mme Claire Jaubert' (T)	1887
'Mme Jules Franke' (N)	1887
'Monsieur Rosier' (Cl. T)	1887
'Baronne Henriette de Loew' (T)	1888
'G. Nabonnand' (T)	1888
'Mme Rose Romarin' (Cl. T)	1888
'Mme Thérèse Deschamps' (T)	1888
'Monsieur Charles de Thézillat' (T)	1888
'Nardy' (N)	1888
'Général D. Mertchansky' (T)	1890
'Maurice Rouvier' (T)	1890
'Archiduc Joseph' (T)	1892
'Comtesse Festetics Hamilton' (T)	1892
'Marie Soleau' (T)	1895
'Mme Von Siemens' (T)	1895
'Albert Stopford' (T)	1898
'Lucie Faure' (T)	1898
'Général Gallieni' (T)	1899
'Captain Philip Green' (T)	1899
'Mrs. Reynolds Hole' (T)	1900
'Noella Nabonnand' (Cl. HT)	1900
'Miss Agnes C. Sherman' (T)	1901
'Comtesse de Noghera' (T)	1902
'Comtesse Sophie Torby' (T)	1902
'Lady Waterlow' (Cl. HT)	1902
'Marguerite Gigandet' (T)	1902
'Marie Segond' (T)	1902
'Alice Hamilton' (Ch)	1903
'Anna Jung' (T)	1903
'Comtesse Emmeline de Guigné' (T)	1903

Nabonnand, Paul & Clément
Golfe-Juan, France

'Marguerite Desrayaux' (N)	1906

Nabonnand, Paul
Golfe-Juan, France

'Frau O. Plegg' (B)	1909
'Anne Laferrère' (HP)	1916
'Mme Charles Singer' (T)	1916
'Irène Bonnet' (Cl. HT)	1920
'Souvenir de Gilbert Nabonnand' (T)	1920
'Emmanuella de Mouchy' (HGig)	1922
'Marguerite Carels' (Cl. HT)	1922
'Rosette Delizy' (T)	1922
'Sa Majesté Gustave V' (HP)	1922
'Lucy Thomas' (Cl. HP)	1924
'Sénateur Amic' (HGig)	1924
'Suzanne Carrol of Carrolton' (HP)	1924

Nérard
Vaise, France

'Mme Nérard' (B)	1838
'Géant des Batailles' (HP)	1846

Nicolas, J. H.
Newark, New York, U.S.A.

'Harmony' (HP)	1933
'Polar Bear' (HP)	1934

Noisette, Louis (& Philippe)
Paris, France (and Charleston, South Carolina, U.S.A.)

'Bengale Centfeuilles' (Ch)	1804
'Blush Noisette' (N)	1814
'Noisette de l'Inde' (N)	1814
'Minnie Francis' (T)	1905

Nonin, Auguste
Chatillon, France

'Bengali' (Ch)	1913
'Catalunya' (B)	1917
'Chatillon Rose' (Pol)	1923

Oger, Pierre
Caen, France

'Dr. Leprestre' (B)	1852
'Orderic Vital' (HP)	1858
'Triomphe de Caen' (HP)	1861
'Michel-Ange' (HP)	1863
'La Tendresse' (HP)	1864
'Marie Boissée' (HP)	1864
'Safrano à Fleurs Rouges' (T)	1867
'Marquise de Verdun' (HP)	1868
'Arthur Oger' (HP)	1875
'Charles Martel' (HP)	1876
'Tancrède' (HP)	1876
'Bicolore' (HP)	1877
'Mme Pierre Oger' (B)	1878
'Jean Lelièvre' (HP)	1879
'Gustave Thierry' (HP)	1881
'Réveil du Printemps' (HP)	1883
'Mme Arthur Oger' (B)	1899

Paul, A[rthur William? Adam?]
Cheshunt, England

'Vivid' (HB)	1853

Paul, George (*Cousin of William Paul*)
Cheshunt, England

'Cheshunt Hybrid' (Cl. HT)	1872
'Sultan of Zanzibar' (HP)	1876
'John Bright' (HP)	1878
'Duke of Teck' (HP)	1880
'Grandeur of Cheshunt' (HP)	1883
'Paul's Single White Perpetual' (Cl)	1883
'White Baroness' (HP)	1883
'Mrs. Paul' (B)	1891
'Frances Bloxam' (HCh)	1892
'Violet Queen' (HP)	1892
'Charles Gater' (HP)	1893
'Paul's Early Blush' (HP)	1893
'Haileybury' (HP)	1895
'Lilliput' (Cl. Pol)	1897
'Reverend Alan Cheales' (HP)	1897
'Dawn' (Cl. HT)	1898
'J. B. M. Camm' (B)	1900
'Purple East' (Cl)	1901
'Tea Rambler' (Cl)	1903
'The Dandy' (HT)	1905
'Nelly Johnstone' (T)	1906
'Symmetry' (HP)	1910

Paul, William (*Cousin of George Paul*)
Waltham Cross, England

'Beauty of Waltham' (HP)	1862
'Lord Macaulay' (HP)	1863
'Princess of Wales' (HP)	1864
'Black Prince' (HP)	1866
'Prince de Joinville' (HP)	1867
'Duke of Edinburgh' (HP)	1868
'Peach Blossom' (HP)	1874
'Star of Waltham' (HP)	1875
'Magna Charta' (HP)	1876
'Rosy Morn' (HP)	1878
'Crown Prince' (HP)	1880
'Pride of Waltham' (HP)	1881
'Queen of Queens' (HP)	1882
'Charles Lamb' (HP)	1883
'Emperor' (HP)	1883
'Lord Bacon' (HP)	1883
'Waltham Climber I' (Cl. HT)	1885
'Waltham Climber II' (Cl. HT)	1885
'Waltham Climber III' (Cl. HT)	1885
'Charles Dickens' (HP)	1886
'Florence Paul' (HP)	1886
'Inigo Jones' (HP)	1886
'Silver Queen' (HP)	1887
'Duchess of Albany' (HT)	1888
'Marchioness of Lorne' (HP)	1889
'Sappho' (T)	1889
'Crimson Queen' (HP)	1890
'Medea' (T)	1890
'Pink Rover' (Cl. HT)	1890
'Salamander' (HP)	1891
'Climbing Queen of Queens' (Cl. HP)	1892
'Spenser' (HP)	1892
'Corinna' (T)	1893

'Princess May' (N)	1893
'Clio' (HP)	1894
'Duke of York' (Ch)	1894
'Sylph' (T)	1895
'Zephyr' (T)	1895
'Enchantress' (T)	1896
'Queen Mab' (Ch)	1896
'Empress Alexandra of Russia' (T)	1897
'Waltham Standard' (HP)	1897
'Aurora' (HT)	1898
'Mme Ada Carmody' (T)	1898
'Exquisite' (HT)	1899
'Corallina' (T)	1900
'Sulphurea' (T)	1900
'The Alexandra' (T)	1900
'Boadicea' (T)	1901
'Fortuna' (T)	1902
'Morning Glow' (T)	1902
'Arethusa' (Ch)	1903
'Dr. William Gordon' (HP)	1905
'Climbing Captain Hayward' (HP)	1906
'Hugo Roller' (T)	1907
'Mrs. Dudley Cross' (T)	1907
'Juliet' (HP)	1910
'Florence Haswell Veitch' (Cl. HT)	1911
'Coronet' (Pol)	1912
'Ophelia' (HT)	1912
'Paul's Lemon Pillar' (Cl)	1915
'Corrie Koster' (Pol)	1923

Pernet pére (Jean)
Lyon, France

'Mlle Bonnaire' (HP)	1859
'Prince Napoléon' (B)	1864
'Mme Chirard' (HP)	1867
'Baronne Adolphe de Rothschild' (HP)	1868
'Marquise de Castellane' (HP)	1869
'Mme Bellon' (HP)	1871
'Mme Caroline Küster' (N)	1872
'Gonsoli Gaëtano' (HP)	1874
'Charles Rovolli' (T)	1876
'Marie Louise Pernet' (HP)	1876
'Souvenir de Monsieur Droche' (HP)	1881
'Merveille de Lyon' (HP)	1882
'Baronne Nathaniel de Rothschild' (HP)	1884
'Mlle Berger' (B)	1884
'Mme David' (T)	1885
'Souvenir de l'Amiral Courbet' (T)	1885
'Souvenir de Victor Hugo' (HP)	1885
'Mme Chevalier' (B)	1886
'Climbing Albert La Blotais' (Cl)	1887
'Triomphe des Noisettes' (N)	1887
'Monsieur Désir' (Cl. T)	1888
'Marchioness of Salisbury' (HT)	1890
'Mme Dubost' (B)	1890
'Triomphe de Pernet Père' (HT)	1890
'Général Baron Berge' (HP)	1891
'Mme la Baronne Berge' (T)	1892

Pernet-Ducher, Joseph (= "*Pernet fils*")
Lyon, France

'Ambrogio Maggi' (HP)	1879
'Ferdinand Chaffolte' (HP)	1879

'Edouard Gauthier' (T)	1883
'Charles de Legrady' (T)	1884
'Georges Pernet' (Pol)	1887
'Mlle Germaine Caillot' (HT)	1887
'Comte Henri Rignon' (HT)	1888
'Gustave Piganeau' (HP)	1889
'Gustav Regis' (HT)	1890
'Mme Pernet-Ducher' (HT)	1891
'Beauté Inconstante' (Cl. T)	1892
'Marquise Litta de Breteuil' (HT)	1893
'Mme Abel Chatenay' (HT)	1894
'Souvenir de Mme Eugène Verdier' (HT)	1894
'Souvenir du Président Carnot' (HT)	1894
'Antoine Rivoire' (HT)	1895
'Mlle Alice Furon' (HT)	1895
'Mlle Hélène Cambier' (HT)	1895
'Ferdinand Batel' (HT)	1896
'Ferdinand Jamin' (HT)	1896
'L'Innocence' (HT)	1897
'Mme Eugénie Boullet' (HT)	1897
'Violiniste Emile Lévêque' (HT)	1897
'Billard et Barré' (N)	1898
'Souvenir de Mme Ernest Cauvin' (HT)	1898
'Mme Ravary' (HT)	1899
'Monsieur Bunel' (HT)	1899
'Prince de Bulgarie' (HT)	1901
'Monsieur Paul Lédé' (HT)	1902
'Mme Hector Leuilliot' (Cl. HT)	1903
'Mme Maurice de Luze' (HT)	1907
'Château de Clos-Vougeot' (HT)	1908
'Mme Méha Sabatier' (HT)	1916
'Climbing Mrs. Herbert Stevens' (HT)	1922

Perny, Pierre
Nice, France

'Mme Angèle Favre' (HT)	1888
'Dr. Grandvilliers' (T)	1891
'Mme Ernestine Verdier' (T)	1894
'Grand-Duc Pierre de Russie' (T)	1895

Perrier, Jean
Rivières, France

'Professeur Ganiviat' (T)	1890
'Mme Emilie Charrin' (T)	1895

Plantier
La Guillotière, Lyon, France

'Gloire des Rosomanes' (B)	1825
'Mme Plantier' (HN)	1835
'Ardoisée de Lyon' (HP)	1858

Portemer (père)
Gentilly, France

'Emile Courtier' (B)	1837
'Paul Ricault' (HCh)	1845
'Duchesse de Galliera' (HP)	1847
'William Griffith' (HP)	1850
'Lady Stuart' (HP)	1852
'Pierre Notting' (HP)	1863
'Charles Wood' (HP)	1864
'Jean Rosenkrantz' (HP)	1864

Postans, R.B.
England

'Countess of Rosebery' (HP)	1879
'Duchess of Bedford' (HP)	1879

Pradel, Henri
Montauban, France

'David Pradel' (T)	1851
'Mlle Blanche Laffitte' (B)	1851
'Comice de Tarn et Garonne' (B)	1852
'Vicomtesse Laure de Gironde' (HP)	1852
'Mme Pauline Labonté' (T)	1852
'Omer-Pacha' (B)	1854
'Esther Pradel' (T)	1860
'Garibaldi' (B)	1860
'Mme Adélaïde Ristori' (B)	1861
'Deuil du Dr. Raunaud' (B)	1862
'Président Gausen' (B)	1862
'Maréchal Niel' (N)	1864
'Mme Thiers' (B)	1874

Prévost fils
Rouen, France

'Roxelane' (HCh)	ca. 1825
'Belle de Trianon' (DP)	pre-1826
'Camélia Rose' (N)	ca. 1830

Pries
Malaga, Spain

'Francisca Pries' (T)	1888
'Souvenir d'Espagne' (T)	1888
'Miss Marston' (T)	1890

Prince, George
Oxford, England

'Clara Watson' (HT)	1894
'Mary Corelly' (HP)	1901

Puyravaud, Jouannem
Roseraie de Goubière
Sainte-Foy-la-Grande, France

'Hovyn de Tronchère' (T)	1899
'Mme Adolphe Dohair' (T)	1900
'Amateur Andre Fourcaud' (HT)	1903
'Baptiste Lafaye' (Pol)	1909

Quétier
Meux, France

'Duchesse d'Orléans' (HP)	1851
'Comte de Nanteuil' (HP)	1852

Rambaux, Widow (*Mother-in-law of Dubreuil*)
Lyon, France

'Anne Marie de Montravel' (Pol)	1879
'Mme Rambaux' (HP)	1881
'Souvenir du Rosiériste Rambaux' (T)	1883
'Perle d'Or' (Pol)	1884

Reymond, Louis
Lyon-Villeurbanne, France

'Perle des Jaunes' (T)	1903
'Climbing Mme Segond-Weber' (HT)	1929

Robert
Angers, France

'Mlle de Sombreuil' (Cl. T)	1851
'Joseph Gourdon' (HB)	1851
'Isis' (N)	1853
'Bouquet Blanc' (HP)	1856
'Robert Perpétuel' (DP)	1856
'L'Admiration' (HCh)	1856
'Souvenir de David d'Angers' (T)	1856

Robert & Moreau
Angers, France

'Homère' (T)	1858
'Marbrée' (DP)	1858
'Socrate' (T)	1858
'Boccace' (HP)	1859
'L'Arioste' (N)	1859
'Laurent Heister' (DP)	1859
'Rubens' (T)	1859
'Amiral Gravina' (HP)	1860
'Comte de Chambord' (DP)	ca.1860
'Duc de Crillon' (B)	1860
'Marie Robert' (HP)	ca.1860
'Pergolèse' (DP)	1860
'Regulus' (T)	1860
'Souvenir de Charles Montault' (HP)	1862
'Delambre' (DP)	1863
'Duc d'Harcourt' (HP)	1863
'Heroïne de Vaucluse' (B)	1863

Robichon, Altin
Orléans, France

'Léon Robichon' (HP)	1901
'Jacques Proust' (Pol)	1904
'Diamant' (Pol)	1908
'Mme Arthur Robichon' (Pol)	1912
'Sunshine' (Pol)	1927

Rœser
Crécy-en-Brie, France

'Caroline Marniesse' (N)	1848
'Vicomtesse d'Avesnes' (N)	1848

Rousset, Georges
France

'Georges Rousset' (HP)	1893
'Achille Cesbron' (HP)	1894

Schmidt, J.-C.
Erfurt, Germany

'Kleiner Liebling' (Pol)	1895
'Blumenschmidt' (T)	1905
'Ännchen Müller' (Pol)	1906
'Tausendschön' (Cl)	1906
'Emden' (HP)	1915
'Frau Rudolf Schmidt' (Pol)	1919

Schmitt
Lyon, France

'Mme Schmitt' (HP)	1854
'Caroline Schmitt' (N)	1881
'Monsieur Joseph Chappaz' (HP)	1882
'Adrien Schmitt' (HP)	1889

Schwartz, Joseph
Lyon, France

'Mme Georges Schwartz' (HP)	1871
'Prince Stirbey' (HP)	1871
'Noisette Moschata' (N)	1873
'Olga Marix' (B)	1873
'Comtesse Riza du Parc' (T)	1876
'Alfred K. Williams' (HP)	1877
'Emilia Plantier' (N)	1878
'François Gaulain' (HP)	1878
'Jules Chrétien' (HP)	1878
'Mme Auguste Perrin' (N)	1878
'Jules Jürgensen' (HB)	1879
'Mme Alfred Carrière' (N)	1879
'Guillaume Gillemot' (HP)	1880
'Mme Joseph Schwartz' (T)	1880
'Reine Maria Pia' (Cl. T)	1880
'Camoëns' (HT)	1881
'Comtesse Henriette Combes' (HP)	1881
'Mme Jules Grévy' (HT)	1881
'André Schwartz' (T)	1882
'Mme Fanny de Forest' (B)	1882
'Colonel Félix Breton' (HP)	1883
'Jeanne Drivon' (Pol)	1883
'Monsieur Francisque Rive' (HP)	1883
'Président Sénélar' (HP)	1883
'Secrétaire J. Nicolas' (HP)	1883
'Aline Rozey' (HP)	1884
'Gaston Chandon' (Cl. HT)	1884
'Général Appert' (HP)	1884
'Victor Hugo' (HP)	1884

Widow Schwartz
Lyon, France

'Monsieur Mathieu Baron' (HP)	1886
'Jean-Baptiste Casati' (HP)	1886
'Mlle Marie Drivon' (B)	1887
'Mme Ernst Calvat' (B)	1888
'Roger Lambelin' (HP)	1890
'Mme Veuve Ménier' (HT)	1891
'Monsieur de Morand' (HP)	1891
'Mme Henri Perrin' (HP)	1892
'Baron Elisi de St.-Albert' (HP)	1893
'Dr. Rouges' (Cl. T)	1893
'Souvenir de Lucie' (Cl)	1893
'Mlle Anna Charron' (T)	1896
'Aurore' (Ch)	1897
'Souvenir d'Aimée Terrel des Chênes' (Ch)	1897
'Georges Schwartz' (T)	1899
'Charles Metroz' (Pol)	1900
'La Tosca' (HT)	1900
'Mme Ernest Perrin' (T)	1900

Schwartz, André
Lyon, France

'Mlle Emma Vercellone' (T)	1901
'Monsieur Georges de Cadoudal' (Cl. T)	1904
'Comte de Torres' (Cl. HT)	1905
'Souvenir de Monsieur Frédéric Vercellone' (HT)	1906
'Mrs. Alice Broomhall' (T)	1910

Souchet, Charles
Bagnolet, France

'Georges Cuvier' (B)	1842
'Souchet' (B)	1842

Soupert (Jean) & Notting (Pierre)
Luxembourg

'Le Roitelet' (B)	1868
'Mme Hersilie Ortgies' (HP)	1868
'Eugene Fürst' (HP)	1875
'Comtesse Hélène Mier' (HP)	1876
'Princesse Charles d'Aremberg' (HP)	1876
'Robusta' (B)	1877
'Mme Loeben de Sels' (HP)	1878
'Comte Florimund de Bergeyck' (HP)	1879
'Mme de Loeben-Sels' (HT)	1879
'Mme Fanny Pauwels' (T)	1884
'Directeur Constant Bernard' (HT)	1886
'Théodore Liberton' (HP)	1886
'Comtesse Anna Thun' (T)	1887
'Thérèse Lambert' (T)	1887
'Comtesse Julie Hunyadi' (T)	1888
'Hermine Madèlé' (Pol)	1888
'Princesse Joséphine de Flandres' (Pol)	1888
'Bona Weillschott' (HT)	1889
'Clotilde Soupert' (Pol)	1889
'Duchesse Marie Salviati' (T)	1889
'Gloire de l'Exposition de Bruxelles' (HP)	1889
'Oscar II, Roi de Suède' (HP)	1889
'Charles de Franciosi' (T)	1890
'Comtesse de Vitzthum' (T)	1890
'Comtesse Eva Starhemberg' (T)	1890
'Gribaldo Nicola' (N)	1890
'Grand-Duc Adolphe de Luxembourg' (HT)	1891
'Erzherzog Franz Ferdinand' (T)	1892
'Léon XIII' (T)	1892
'Léonie Osterrieth' (T)	1892
'Petite Léonie' (Pol)	1892
'Baronne Charles de Gargan' (Cl. T)	1893
'Comtesse Dusy' (T)	1893
'Comte Chandon' (T)	1894
'Pincesse Marie Adélaïde de Luxembourg' (Pol)	1895
'Auguste Comte' (T)	1895
'Comtesse Bardi' (T)	1895
'Comtesse Lily Kinsky' (T)	1895
'Graf Fritz Metternich' (HP)	1895
'Léon de Bruyn' (T)	1895
'Gloire de Deventer' (T)	1896
'Baronne Ada' (T)	1897
'Mme C. P. Strassheim' (T)	1897
'The Sweet Little Queen of Holland' (T)	1897
'Gardenia' (HT)	1898
'Beatrix, Comtesse de Buisseret' (HT)	1899
'Mme Errera' (T)	1899
'Rosomane Gravereaux (HT)	1899
'Mme Jules Gravereaux' (Cl. T)	1900
'Primula' (Pol)	1900
'Pierre Wattinne' (HT)	1901
'Souvenir de Pierre Notting' (T)	1902
'Reine Marguerite d'Italie' (HT)	1904
'Mme Constant Soupert' (T)	1905
'Mme Paul Varin-Bernier' (T)	1906
'Comtesse Icy Hardegg' (HT)	1907
'Mme Segond-Weber' (HT)	1907

'Recuerdo di Antonio Peluffo' (T)	1910
'Aviateur Michel Mahieu' (HT)	1912
'Ivan Misson' (Pol)	1912
'Jeanny Soupert' (Pol)	1912

Spek, Jan
Boskoop, The Netherlands

'Ideal' (Pol)	1920
'Rosa Gruss an Aachen' (HT)	1930

Sprunt, Rev. James
Kenansville, North Carolina, U.S.A.

'Isabella Sprunt' (T)	1855
'James Sprunt' (Cl. Ch)	1858

Standish & Noble
Bagshot, England

'Reynolds Hole' (B)	1862
'Queen of Bedders' (B)	1877
'Duchess of Connaught' (HP)	1882

Stevens, Walter
Hoddesdon, England

'Lady Sylvia' (HT)	1926
'Climbing Lady Sylvia' (HT)	1933

Tanne, Remi
Rouen, France

'Auguste Chaplain' (HP)	1921
'Ferdinand Pichard' (HP)	1921

Tantau, M.
Ütersen, Germany

'Schöne von Holstein' (Pol)	1919
'Stadtrat Meyn' (Pol)	1919
'Stämmler' (HP)	1933
'Urdh' (HP)	1933
'Topaz' (Pol)	1937
'Vatertag' (Pol)	1959

Thomas (Desiré?)
St.-Denis, France

'Ville de St.-Denis' (HP)	1853
'Peter Lawson' (HP)	1862

Touvais, Jean
Petit-Montrouge, France

'Mme Céline Touvais' (HP)	1859
'Duc de Cazes' (HP)	1861
'Mme Julia Daran' (HP)	1861
'Centifolia Rosea' (HP)	1863
'Mlle Joséphine Guyet' (B)	1863
'Albert Payé' (HP)	1873
'La Syrène' (HP)	1874
'Lutea Flora' (T)	1874

Trouillard, Victor
Angers, France

'Céline Forestier' (N)	1842
'Cardinal Patrizzi' (HP)	1857
'Dr. Bretonneau' (HP)	1858
'François I' (HP)	1858
'François Arago' (HP)	1858

'Eugène Appert' (HP) 1859
'Comte de Falloux' (HP) 1863
'Mlle Marie de la Villeboisnet' (HP) 1864
'Souvenir de Louis Gaudin' (B) 1864
'André Leroy d'Angers' (HP) 1866
'Monsieur Lauriol de Barney' (HP) 1866
'Aristide Dupuy' (HP) 1867
'Comtesse de Falloux' (HP) 1867
'Mme Lauriol de Barney' (B) 1868

Turbat, (Eugène) & Co.
Orléans, France
'Yvonne Rabier' (Pol) 1910
'Maman Turbat' (Pol) 1911
'George Elger' (Pol) 1912
'Mme Jules Gouchault' (Pol) 1912
'Marie Brissonet' (Pol) 1913
'Marie-Jeanne' (Pol) 1913
'Abondant' (Pol) 1914
'Mauve' (Pol) 1915
'Eblouissant' (Pol) 1918
'Étoile Luisante' (Pol) 1918
'Indéfectible' (Pol) 1919
'La Rosée' (Pol) 1920
'Flamboyant' (Pol) 1931

Türke, Robert
Meissen, Germany
'Charlotte Klemm' (Ch) 1905
'Nymphe' (Cl) 1910

Turner, Charles
Slough, England
'John Stuart Mill' (HP) 1874
'Miss Hassard' (HP) 1874
'Mrs. Baker' (HP) 1876

Van Fleet, Walter
Glenn Dale, Maryland, U.S.A.
'Clara Barton' (HT) 1898
'Magnafrano' (HT) 1900
'Beauty of Rosemawr' (Ch) 1904
'Charles Wagner' (HP) 1907
'Dr. W. Van Fleet' (Cl) 1910

Varangot, Victor
Melun, France
'Jacques Amyot' (DP) 1844
'Mogador' (DP) 1844

Verdier, Victor (*Nephew of A. Jacques*)
Paris, France
'Perpétuelle de Neuilly' (HP) 1834
'Richelieu' (HCh) 1845
'Frédéric II de Prusse' (HB) 1847
'Apolline' (B) 1848
'Douglas' (Ch) 1848
'Baronne de Prailly' (HP) 1871

Verdier, Victor & Charles
Paris, France
'Mme Knorr' (HP) 1855
'La Brillante' (HP) 1861

'Olivier Belhomme' (HP) 1861
'Turenne' (HP) 1861
'Vulcain' (HP) 1861
'Henri IV' (HP) 1862

Verdier, Charles
Paris, France
'Duchesse de Caylus' (HP) 1864
'Paul Verdier' (HP) 1866
'Blanche de Méru' (HP) 1869
'Souvenir d'Alphonse Lavallée' (HP) 1884
'Souvenir de Lady Ashburton' (T) 1890

Verdier, Eugène
Paris, France
'Mme Charles Wood' (HP) 1861
'Prince Camille de Rohan' (HP) 1861
'Claude Million' (HP) 1863
'Mme Victor Verdier' (HP) 1863
'La Duchesse de Morny' (HP) 1863
'George Paul' (HP) 1863
'Comtesse de Paris' (HP) 1864
'Dr. Andry' (HP) 1864
'Rushton-Radclyffe' (HP) 1864
'Souvenir de William Wood' (HP) 1864
'Fisher-Holmes' (HP) 1865
'Mme Charles Baltet' (B) 1865
'Prince de Portia' (HP) 1865
'Baronne Maurice de Graviers' (HP) 1866
'Mlle Annie Wood' (HP) 1866
'Napoléon III' (HP) 1866
'Velours Pourpre' (HP) 1866
'Comtesse de Turenne' (HP) 1867
'Meyerbeer' (HP) 1867
'Souvenir de Caillat' (HP) 1867
'Lena Turner' (HP) 1869
'Suzanne Wood' (HP) 1869
'Félicien David' (HP) 1872
'John Laing' (HP) 1872
'Mrs. Laing' (HP) 1872
'Souvenir de John Gould Veitch' (HP) 1872
'Miller-Hayes' (HP) 1873
'Thomas Mills' (HP) 1873
'Bernard Verlot' (HP) 1874
'E. Y. Teas' (HP) 1874
'Abel Carrière' (HP) 1875
'Général Duc d'Aumale' (HP) 1875
'Mme Grandin-Monville' (HP) 1875
'Mme Prosper Laugier' (HP) 1875
'Baronne de Medem' (HP) 1876
'Duc de Chartres' (HP) 1876
'Mme Galli-Marie' (HCh) 1876
'Mme Verlot' (HP) 1876
'Comtesse de Flandres' (HP) 1877
'Dr. Auguste Krell' (HP) 1877
'Président Schlachter' (HP) 1877
'Souvenir d'Auguste Rivière' (HP) 1877
'A. Geoffrey de St.-Hilaire' (HP) 1878
'Benjamin Drouet' (HP) 1878
'Mme Amélie Baltet' (HP) 1878
'Mme Charles Truffaut' (HP) 1878
'Mme Eugène Verdier' (HP) 1878
'Souvenir de Laffay' (HP) 1878
'Souvenir de Victor Verdier' (HP) 1878

'Édouard André le Botaniste' (HP)	1879
'Rosiériste Harms' (HP)	1879
'Baron de Wolseley' (HP)	1882
'Lecocq-Dumesnil' (HP)	1882
'Mlle Marie Closon' (HP)	1882
'Directeur N. Jensen' (HP)	1883
'Mme Bertha Mackart' (HP)	1883
'Prosper Laugier' (HP)	1883
'Edouard Hervé' (HP)	1884
'Félix Mousset' (HP)	1884
'Hans Mackart' (HP)	1884
'Louis Philippe d'Orléans' (HP)	1884
'Mme Edmond Fabre' (HP)	1884
'Mme Eugénie Frémy' (HP)	1884
'Olivier Métra' (HP)	1884
'Léon Delaville' (HP)	1885
'Louis Calla' (HP)	1885
'Prince Waldemar' (HP)	1885
'Princesse Marie d'Orléans' (HP)	1885
'Duchesse de Bragance' (HP)	1886
'Jules Barigny' (HP)	1886
'Mme Edouard Michel' (HP)	1886
'Prince Henri d'Orléans' (HP)	1886
'Princesse Hélène d'Orléans' (HP)	1886
'Duc d'Audiffret-Pasquier' (HP)	1887
'Mlle Claire Truffaut' (B)	1887
'Comtesse Bertrand de Blacas' (HP)	1888
'Buffalo-Bill' (HP)	1889
'Souvenir de Clairvaux' (T)	1890
'Rose de France' (HP)	1893

Verschuren (H.A.) & Sons
Haps, The Netherlands

'General von Bothnia-Andreæ' (HP)	1899
'Koningin Wilhelmina' (T)	1904
'Rosa Verschuren' (HP)	1905
'Neervelt' (Cl. HT)	1910
'Étoile de Hollande' (HT)	1919

Veysset
Royat-les-Bains, France

'Mme Angelique Veysset' (HT)	1890
'Bijou de Royat-les-Bains' (B)	1891
'Mme Blondel' (HT)	1899
'Souvenir de Mme Ladvocat' (N)	1899
'Royat Mondain' (HP)	1901

Viaud-Bruant
Poitiers, France

'Janine Viaud-Bruant' (HP)	1910
'Mme Foureau' (N)	1913

Vibert, Jean-Pierre
Chennevières-sur-Marne, etc., later Angers, France

'Palmyre' (DP)	1817
'Gloire des Rosomanes' (B)	1825
'Pourpre' (Ch)	1827
'Aimée Vibert' (N)	1828
'Las-Cases' (HB)	1828
'Riégo' (HCh)	1831
'Dembrowski' (HB)	1840
'Yolande d'Aragon' (DP)	1843
'Philomèle' (N)	1844

'Belmont' (HCh)	1846
'Jacques Laffitte' (HP)	1846
'Adèle Mauzé' (DP)	1847
'Blanche-Vibert' (DP)	1847
'Joasine Hanet' (DP)	1847
'Sapho' (DP)	1847
'Sydonie' (DP)	1847
'Pie IX' (HP)	1848

Vigneron, Jacques
Olivet, France

'Mlle Marie Dauvesse' (HP)	1859
'Dr. Brière' (B)	1860
'Monsieur Dubost' (B)	1864
'Elisabeth Vigneron' (HP)	1865
'Glory of Waltham' (Cl. HP)	1865
'Mme Alice Dureau' (HP)	1867
'La Motte Sanguin' (HP)	1869
'Maxime de la Rocheterie' (HP)	1871
'Amédée de Langlois' (B)	1872
'Alexis Lepère' (HP)	1875
'Dames Patronesses d'Orléans' (HP)	1877
'Monsieur Eugène Delaire' (HP)	1879
'Monsieur Alfred Leveau' (HP)	1880
'Mlle Elisabeth de la Rocheterie' (HP)	1881
'Mlle Madeleine de Vauzelles' (B)	1881
'Mlle Hélène Croissandeau' (HP)	1882
'Mme Alexandre Jullien' (HP)	1882
'Mme Apolline Foulon' (HP)	1882
'Mme Louise Vigneron' (HP)	1882
'Monsieur Jules Maquinant' (HP)	1882
'Mlle Hélène Michel' (HP)	1883
'Monsieur le Capitaine Louis Frère' (HP)	1883
'Mme Lucien Chauré' (HP)	1884
'Bijou de Couasnon' (HP)	1886
'Gloire d'Olivet' (B)	1886
'Mme Marcel Fauneau' (HP)	1886
'Mme Létuvée de Colnet' (B)	1887
'Mme Moser' (HT)	1889
'Monsieur Jules Lemaître' (HP)	1890
'L'Etincelante' (HP)	1891
'Mlle Alice Marchand' (B)	1891
'Président de la Rocheterie' (B)	1891
'Mme Charles Boutmy' (HT)	1892
'Eclaireur' (HP)	1895
'Mme Charles Détraux' (HT)	1895
'Mme Augustine Hamont' (HT)	1897
'Mlle Fernande Dupuy' (Pol)	1899
'Souvenir d'André Raffy' (HP)	1899
'Mme Ernest Levavasseur' (HP)	1900
'Mme Roudillon' (HP)	1903
'Souvenir de Léon Roudillon' (HP)	1908
'Mlle Suzanne Bidard' (Pol)	1913

Vilin, Rose
Grisy-Suisnes, France

'Thyra Hammerich' (HP)	1868
'Duhamel-Dumonceau' (HP)	1872
'Mme Henri Pereire' (HP)	1886
'Bouquet de Neige' (Pol)	1899
'Gloire d'Un Enfant de Hiram' (HP)	1899
'Souvenir de Mme Jeanne Balandreau' (HP)	1899
'L'Ami E. Daumont' (HP)	1901
'Mlle Alice Rousseau' (Pol)	1903

Widow Vilin & fils
Grisy-Suisnes, France

'Mme d'Enfert' (B)	1904
'Dr. Georges Martin' (HP)	1907

Vogel, Max
Sangerhausen, Germany

'Arthur Weidling' (HP)	1932
'Jean Muraour' (HT)	1935
'Climbing Capitaine Soupa' (HT)	1938
'Climbing König Friedrich II von Dänemark' (HP)	1940
'Climbing Wenzel Geschwindt' (HT)	1940
'Climbing Apotheker Georg Höfer' (HT)	1941
'Climbing Pride of Reigate' (HP)	1941

Walsh, M.H.
Woods Hole, Massachusetts, U.S.A.

'Jubilee' (HP)	1897
'Snowball' (Pol)	1901

Walter, Louis
Saverne, France

'Rösel Dach' (Pol)	1906
'Frau Anna Pasquay' (Pol)	1909
'Louise Walter' (Pol)	1909
'Adele Frey' (Cl. HT)	1911
'Martha Keller' (Pol)	1912

Weber, Antoine (?)
Dijon, France

'Princesse Alice de Monaco' (T)	1893
'Antoine Weber' (T)	1899

Weeks (O. L.) Wholesale Rose Grower
Chino and Ontario, California, U.S.A.

'Climbing Snowbird' (HT)	1949
'Climbing China Doll' (Pol)	1977

Weigand, Christoph
Bad Sonen a Taunus, Germany

'Susanna' (Pol)	1914
'Ruhm von Steinfurth' (HP)	1920
'Symphony' (HP)	1935

Welter, Nicola
Trier, Germany

'Johannes Wesselhöft' (HT)	1899
'Gruss aus Pallien' (HP)	1900
'Abbé André Reitter' (HT)	1901
'Marie Bülow' (N)	1903
'Albert Hoffmann' (T)	1904
'Frau J. Reiter' (HT)	1904
'Barbarossa' (HP)	1906

Of Unknown Provenance

'Anaïse' (HB)
'Anna Olivier, Climbing' (T)
'Annie Vibert' (N)
'Belle Blanca' (Gig)
'Capitaine Sisolet' (B)
'Elise Lemaire' (HP)
'Fun Jwan Lo' (Cl)
'Honorine de Brabant' (B)
'König Friedrich II von Dänemark' (HP)
'Lady Clonbrock' (N)
'Le Vingt-Neuf Juillet' (HCh)
'Louis-Philippe, Climbing' (Ch)
'Mme Jules Thibaud' (Pol)
'Mrs. J. F. Redly' (HP)
'Old Blush, Climbing' (Ch)

'Orange Koster' (Pol)
'Pale Pink China' (Ch)
'Pale Pink China, Climbing' (Ch)
'Perle d'Or, Climbing' (Pol)
'Pink Pet, Climbing' (Pol)
'Pompon de Paris' (Ch)
'Pompon de Paris, Climbing' (Ch)
'Riccordo di Fernando Scarlatti' (HP)
'Rouge Marbrée' (B)
'Rouletii, Climbing' (Ch)
'Simone Thomas' (T)
'Sophie's Perpetual' (B)
'Souvenir d'Anselme' (HB)
'Verdun Superior' (Pol)
'White Koster' (Pol)

CULTIVARS LISTED BY COLOR

White to Near-White

Damask Perpetuals
'Blanche-Vibert'
'Celina Dubos'
'Félicité Hardy'
'Marie de St.-Jean'
'Quatre Saisons Blanc Mousseux'
'Sapho'

Chinas
'Duchesse de Kent'
'Mme Desprez'
'Pumila'

Teas
'Bella'
'Blanche Nabonnand'
'Comtesse Dusy'
'Cornelia Cook'
'Elisa Fugier'
'Enchantress'
'Frances E. Willard'
'Grossherzogin Mathilde'
'Innocente Pirola'
'Ivory'
'Lady Plymouth'
'Léon XIII'
'Léonie Osterrieth'
'Madison'
'Marie Guillot'
'Marie Lambert'
'Mlle Marie-Louise Oger'
'Mme Adolphe Dohair'
'Mme Joseph Schwartz'
'Molly Sharman-Crawford'
'Mrs. Herbert Hawksworth'
'Niphetos'
'Rival de Pæstum'
'Senator McNaughton'
'The Bride'
'The Queen'
'White Bon Silène'
'White Maman Cochet'
'White Pearl'
'William R. Smith'

Bourbons
'Acidalie'
'Baronne de Maynard'
'Boule de Neige'
'Comtesse de Rocquigny'
'Coquette des Alpes'
'Coquette des Blanches'
'Duchesse de Thuringe'
'Lady Emily Peel'

'Louise D'Arzens'
'Mme Fanny de Forest'
'Mme François Pittet'
'Mme Massot'
'Perle des Blanches'

Hybrid Bourbons, Hybrid Chinas, and Hybrid Noisettes
'Purity'
'Mme Plantier'
'Triomphe de Laffay'

Hybrid Perpetuals
'Blanche de Méru'
'Bouquet Blanc'
'Bouquet de Marie'
'Candeur Lyonnaise'
'Edelweiss'
'Everest'
'Frau Karl Druschki'
'Gloire Lyonnaise'
'James Bougault'
'Léon Robichon'
'Louise Cretté'
'Mabel Morrison'
'Magnolija'
'Margaret Dickson'
'Marguerite Guillard'
'Miss House'
'Mlle Bonnaire'
'Mme André Saint'
'Mme Noman'
'Nuria de Recolons'
'Polar Bear'
'Princess Louise'
'Virginale'
'White Baroness'

Noisettes & Climbers
'Aimée Vibert' (N)
'Autumnalis' (N)
'Belle d'Orléans' (N)
'Blanc Pur' (N)
'Claudia Augusta' (N)
'Clotilde Soupert, Cl.' (Pol)
'Devoniensis, Cl.' (T)
'Étendard de Jeanne d'Arc' (N)
'Eugene Jardine' (N)
'Eva Teschendorff, Cl.' (Pol)
'Frau Karl Druschki, Cl.' (HP)
'Gigantea Blanc' (Gig)
'Irish Beauty' (HT)
'Isis' (N)
'Kaiserin Auguste Viktoria, Cl.' (HT)

'Marie Guillot, Cl.' (T)
'Marie Accary' (N)
'Mélanie Soupert' (N)
'Milkmaid' (N)
'Mme Alfred Carrière' (N)
'Mme Jules Bouché, Cl.' (HT)
'Mme Jules Franke' (N)
'Montecito' (HGig)
'Mrs. Herbert Stevens, Cl.' (HT)
'Niphetos, Cl.' (T)
'Nymphe' (Cl.)
'Paul's Single White Perpetual' (Cl.)
'Pumila Alba' (N)
'Purity' (Cl.)
'Snowbird, Cl.' (HT)
'Mlle de Sombreuil' (T)
'Summer Snow, Cl.' (Pol)
'Weisser Maréchal Niel' (N)
'White Maman Cochet, Cl.' (T)
'White Pet, Cl.' (Pol)

Polyanthas
'Anne Marie de Montravel'
'Baby Alberic'
'Bouquet Blanc'
'Bouquet de Neige'
'Clotilde Soupert'
'Colibri'
'Denise Cassegrain'
'Eva Teschendorff'
'Flocon de Neige'
'Hermine Madèlé'
'Jeanne d'Arc'

'Katharina Zeimet'
'Little Gem'
'Lullaby'
'Mrs. William G. Koning'
'Multiflora Nana Perpétuelle'
'Neiges d'Été'
'Pâquerette'
'Petite Marcelle'
'Prevue'
'Sneprinsesse'
'Snowball'
'White Cécile Brunner'
'White Koster'
'White Pet'
'Yvonne Rabier'

Hybrid Teas
'British Queen'
'Gardenia'
'Innocence'
'Jean Muraour'
'Joséphine Marot'
'Kaiserin Auguste Viktoria'
'Kaiserin Goldifolia'
'Killarney Double White'
'L'Innocence'
'Mlle Argentine Cramon'
'Mlle Augustine Guinoisseau'
'Mme Jules Finger'
'Mrs. Herbert Stevens'
'Snowbird'
'The Puritan'
'White Wings'

Cream to Flesh and Blush

Damask Perpetuals
'Jacques Cartier'
'Julie de Krudner'
'Mme Souveton'
'Palmyre'

Chinas
'Catherine II'
'Ducher'
'Pompon de Paris'

Teas
'A. Bouquet'
'Annie Cook'
'Baron de St.-Triviers'
'Baronne Ada'
'Baronne Henriette de Loew'
'Catherine Mermet'
'Cels Multiflore'
'Comtesse Lily Kinsky'
'Comtesse Emmeline de Guigné'
'Devoniensis'
'Francisca Pries'
'Frau Geheimrat Von Boch'
'G. Nabonannand'
'Gigantesque'

'Gloire de Deventer'
'Graziella'
'Hermance Louisa de La Rive'
'Homère'
'Honourable Edith Gifford'
'Hume's Blush Tea-Scented China'
'Isabelle Nabonnand'
'La Princesse Vera'
'La Sylphide'
'La Tulipe'
'Lucie Faure'
'Marie Sisley'
'Mlle Blanche Durrschmidt'
'Mlle Suzanne Blanchet'
'Mme Ada Carmody'
'Mme Antoine Mari'
'Mme Bravy'
'Mme Damaizin'
'Mme Elie Lambert'
'Mme Hoste'
'Mme Léon Février'
'Mme Mélanie Willermoz'
'Mme Nabonnand'
'Mme Olga'
'Mrs. Foley-Hobbs'
'Mrs. Hubert Taylor'

'Mrs. Myles Kennedy'
'Nita Weldon'
'Pearl Rivers'
'Princesse Alice de Monaco'
'Princesse de Venosa'
'Rubens'
'Souvenir d'Elisa Vardon'
'Winnie Davis'

Bourbons

'Edith de Murat'
'Emotion'
'Gloire d'Olived'
'Maréchal du Palais'
'Marie Dermar'
'Mlle Berger'
'Mlle Blanche Laffitte'
'Mme Alfred de Rougemont'
'Mme Cornélissen'
'Mme d'Enfert'
'Mme Nérard'
'Mme Olympe Térestchenko'
'Mrs. Paul'
'Olga Marix'
'Perle d'Angers'
'Reine des Vierges'
'Souvenir de la Malmaison'
'Souvenir de St. Anne's'
'Triomphe de la Duchère'

Hybrid Bourbons, Hybrid Chinas, and Hybrid Noisettes

'Belmont'
'Comtesse de Lacépède'

Hybrid Perpetuals

'Aline Rozey'
'Andonie Schurz'
'Bessie Johnson'
'Bicolore'
'Cæcilie Scharsach'
'Comtesse de Turenne'
'Elisa Boëlle'
'George Sand'
'Giuletta'
'Générale Marie Raiewesky'
'Gloire de Guérin'
'Gonsoli Gaëtano'
'Jeanne Masson'
'Lady Overtoun'
'Lady Stuart'
'Lisette de Béranger'
'Marguerite de Roman'
'Marguerite Jamain'
'Marie Boisée'
'Marquise de Mortemart'
'Mère de St. Louis'
'Merveille de Lyon'
'Miss Ethel Richardson'
'Mlle Eugénie Verdier'
'Mme Fortuné Besson'
'Mme Hippolyte Jamain'
'Mme Louis Léveque'

'Mme Maurice Rivoire'
'Mme Récamier'
'Mme Vidot'
'Mrs. F. W. Sanford'
'Paul's Early Blush'
'Prince Stirbey'
'Reveil du Printemps'
'Thyra Hammerich'
'Violette Bouyer'

Noisettes & Climbers

'Anne-Marie Côte' (N)
'Annie Vibert' (N)
'Belle Blanca' (Gig)
'Blush Noisette' (N)
'Bouquet Tout Fait' (N)
'Caroline Marniesse' (N)
'Comtesse de Galard-Béarn' (N)
'Cooper's Burmese Rose' (Gig)
'Cupid' (HT)
'Deputé Debussy' (HT)
'Dr. W. Van Fleet' (Cl.)
'Emmanuella de Mouchy' (Gig)
'Fun Jwan Lo' (T)
'Gribaldo Nicola' (N)
'Gruss an Aachen, Cl.' (HT)
'L'Arioste' (N)
'La Biche' (N)
'Mlle Madeliene Delaroche' (N)
'New Dawn' (Cl.)
'Noisette de l'Inde' (N)
'Noisette Moschata' (HN)
'Ophelia, Cl.' (HT)
'Philomèle' (N)
'Pale Pink China, Cl.' (Ch)
'Pompon de Paris, Cl.' (Ch)
'Souvenir de la Malmaison, Cl.' (B)

Polyanthas

'Ivan Misson'
'Jeanny Soupert'
'Little Dot'
'Louise Walter'
'Marie Brissonet'
'Marie-Jeanne'
'Marie Pavič'
'Merveille des Polyanthas'
'Mignon'
'Mignonette'
'Mlle Alice Rousseau'
'Mlle Joséphine Burland'
'Perle'
'Princesse Joséphine de Flandres'
'Princesse Marie Adélaïde de Luxembourg'

Hybrid Teas

'Abbé André Reitter'
'Adam Rackles'
'Admiral Dewey'
'Antoine Rivoire'
'Baronne G. de Noirmont'
'Bessie Brown'
'Carmen Sylva'
'Clara Watson'

'Edmée et Roger'
'Frau J. Reiter'
'Gertrude'
'Grace Darling'
'Grossherzogin Viktoria Melitta von Hessen'
'Gruss an Aachen'
'Gruss an Aachen Superior'
'Killarney'
'La Tosca'
'Lady Clanmorris'
'Lady Henry Grosvenor'
'Marie Girard'
'Marjorie'
'Mavourneen'
'Mildred Grant'
'Mme Adolphe Loiseau'
'Mme Augustine Hamont'
'Mme C. Chambard'
'Mme de Loeben-Sels'

'Mme Gustave Metz'
'Mme Joseph Combet'
'Mme Joseph Desbois'
'Mme Jules Bouché'
'Mme Lacharme'
'Mme Léon Pain'
'Mme Moser'
'Mme Veuve Ménier'
'Monsieur Charles de Lapisse'
'Ophelia'
'Pearl'
'Prince de Bulgarie'
'Rosomane Gravereaux'
'Sachsengruss'
'Souvenir de Mme Ernest Cauvin'
'Souvenir du Président Carnot'
'Violiniste Émile Lévêque'
'Westfield Star'

Shades of Pink

Damask Perpetuals
'Adèle Mauzé'
'Belle de Trianon'
'Bifera'
'Comte de Chambord'
'Duchesse de Rohan'
'Marie Robert'
'Marquise de Boccella'
'Miranda'
'Robert Perpétuel'
'Sydonie'
'Venusta'

Chinas
'Alice Hoffmann'
'Beauty of Glenhurst'
'Elyse Flory'
'Général Labutère'
'Hébé'
'Irène Watts'
'Jean Bach Sisley'
'L'Ouche'
'Marquisette'
'Napoléon'
'Parsons' Pink China'
'Rosada'
'Rouletii'

Teas
'Anna Jung'
'Boadicea'
'Bridesmaid'
'Burbank'
'Caroline'
'Charles Rovolli'
'Comte Amédé de Foras'
'Comtesse de Labarthe'
'Comtesse de Noghera'
'Corinna'
'David Pradel'

'Flavien Budillon'
'Grand-Duc Pierre de Russie'
'Helvetia'
'Henry Bennett'
'Hortensia'
'J.-B Varonne'
'Lady Castlereagh'
'Lady Stanley'
'Letty Coles'
'Maid of Honour'
'Maman Cochet'
'Marie d'Orléans'
'Marie Soleau'
'Maud Little'
'Maurice Rouvier'
'Miss Wenn'
'Mlle Claudine Perreau'
'Mlle la Comtesse de Leusse'
'Mlle Marie Moreau'
'Mme Berkeley'
'Mme C. Liger'
'Mme Camille'
'Mme David'
'Mme de Tartas'
'Mme de Vatry'
'Mme Dubroca'
'Mme Émilie Charrin'
'Mme Philémon Cochet'
'Mme Pauline Labonté'
'Mme Scipion Cochet'
'Mme Von Siemens'
'Monte Rosa'
'Mrs. Campbell Hall'
'Mrs. Edward Mawley'
'Mrs. Jessie Fremont'
'Mrs. Oliver Ames'
'Principessa di Napoli'
'Roi de Siam'
'Rosabelle'
'Rosalie'

'Rose d'Evian'
'Rose Nabonnand'
'Santa Rosa'
'Socrate'
'Souvenir de Gabrielle Drevet'
'Souvenir de Geneviève Godard'
'Souvenir de George Sand'
'Souvenir d'Un Ami'
'Susan Louise'
'Sylph'
'Vicomtesse de Bernis'
'Vicomtesse de Wauthier'
'Winter Gem'

Bourbons
'Adrienne de Cardoville'
'Apolline'
'Baron G.-B. Gonella'
'Baronne de Noirmont'
'Capitaine Dyel, de Graville'
'Champion of the World'
'Comtesse de Barbantane'
'Hermosa'
'Hofgärtner Kalb'
'J. B. M. Camm'
'Kathleen Harrop'
'Le Roitelet'
'Louise Odier'
'Mistress Bosanquet'
'Mlle Alice Marchand'
'Mlle Andrée Worth'
'Mlle Claire Truffaut'
'Mlle Favart'
'Mlle Marie Drivon'
'Mlle Madeleine de Vauzelles'
'Mme Charles Baltet'
'Mme Chevalier'
'Mme de Sevigny'
'Mme Doré'
'Mme Dubost'
'Mme Ernst Calvat'
'Mme Létuvée de Colnet'
'Mme Nobécourt'
'Mme Thiers'
'Monsieur Alexandre Pelletier'
'Monsieur Dubost'
'Philémon Cochet'
'Pierre de St.-Cyr'
'Reine des Île-Bourbons'
'Rev. H. d'Ombrain'
'Reynolds Hole'
'Rosier de Bourbon'
'Scipion Cochet'
'Sophie's Perpetual'
'Souvenir de Mme Auguste Charlet'

Hybrid Bourbons, Hybrid Chinas, and Hybrid Noisettes
'Anaïse'
'Blairii Nº 1'
'Blairii Nº 2'
'Blairii Nº 3'
'Céline'

'Charles Louis Nº 1'
'Coupe d'Hébé'
'Duchesse de Montebello'
'Frances Bloxam'
'Impératrice Eugénie'
'L'Admiration'
'Mme Auguste Rodrigues'
'Mme Galli-Marie'
'Mme Lauriol de Barney'
'Mrs. Degraw'
'Paul Perras'
'Roxelane'
'Souvenir de Némours'

Hybrid Perpetuals
'Abel Grand'
'Adiantifolia'
'Albert Payé'
'Alexandre Dutitre'
'Anna Scharsach'
'Archiduchesse Elizabeth d'Autriche'
'Arrillaga'
'Arthur Weidling'
'Auguste Mie'
'Aurore du Matin'
'Baron Taylor'
'Baronne Adolphe de Rothschild'
'Baronne Nathaniel de Rothschild'
'Baronne de Prailly'
'Baronne Gustave de St.-Paul'
'Berthe Baron'
'Berthe Du Mesnil de Mont Chauveau'
'Berti Gimpel'
'Boileau'
'Buffalo-Bill'
'California'
'Caroline d'Arden'
'Caroline De Sansal'
'Charles Bonnet'
'Chot Pěstitele'
'Clara Cochet'
'Clémence Raoux'
'Clio'
'Colonel De Sansal'
'Comte Adrien de Germiny'
'Comte de Mortemart'
'Comtesse Branicka'
'Comtesse Cécile de Chabrillant'
'Comtesse de Bresson'
'Comtesse de Flandres'
'Comtesse de Fressinet de Bellanger'
'Comtesse de Roquette-Buisson'
'Comtesse de Serenyi'
'Comtesse Hélène Mier'
'Comtesse Henriette Combes'
'Coronation'
'Dr. Antonin Joly'
'Dr. Bradas Rosa Druschki'
'Dr. Georges Martin'
'Dr. William Gordon'
'Druschka'
'Duchess of Edinburgh'
'Duchess of Fife'
'Duchesse de Bragance'

'Duchesse de Galliera'
'Duchesse de Sutherland'
'Duchesse d'Orléans'
'Edouard Fontaine'
'Elise Lemaire'
'Emden'
'Emily Laxton'
'Enfant de France'
'François Levet'
'Général Bedeau'
'Georg Arends'
'Gustave Thierry'
'Harmony'
'Heinrich Münch'
'Heinrich Schultheis'
'Henri Coupé'
'Her Majesty'
'Impératrice Maria Feodorowna'
'Jean-Baptiste Casati'
'Joséphine de Beauharnais'
'La Reine'
'La Tendresse'
'La Vierzonnaise'
'Lady Arthur Hill'
'Leonie Lambert'
'Marchioness of Exeter'
'Marchioness of Londonderry'
'Margaret Haywood'
'Marquise de Gibot'
'Martin Liebau'
'Mary Corely'
'Miss Annie Crawford'
'Miss Hassard'
'Mlle Berthe Lévêque'
'Mlle Elisabeth de la Rocheterie'
'Mlle Elise Chabrier'
'Mlle Honorine Duboc'
'Mlle Léonie Giessen'
'Mlle Léonie Persin'
'Mlle Madeleine Nonin'
'Mlle Marie Achard'
'Mlle Marie Chauvet'
'Mlle Marie de la Villboisnet'
'Mlle Marie Closon'
'Mlle Marie Rady'
'Mlle Renée Davis'
'Mlle Suzanne-Marie Rodocanachi'
'Mme Alexandre Jullien'
'Mme Alice Dureau'
'Mme Alphonse Seux'
'Mme Amélie Baltet'
'Mme Anatole Leroy'
'Mme Antoine Rivoire'
'Mme Apolline Foulon'
'Mme Bernutz'
'Mme Boll'
'Mme Céline Touvais'
'Mme César Brunier'
'Mme Charles Truffaut'
'Mme Clert'
'Mme Crozy'
'Mme Edmond Fabre'
'Mme Edouard Michel'
'Mme Eugène Verdier'

'Mme Eugénie Frémy'
'Mme Francis Buchner'
'Mme Gabriel Luizet'
'Mme Georges Schwartz'
'Mme Georges Vibert'
'Mme Hersilie Ortgies'
'Mme Knorr'
'Mme la Générale Decaen'
'Mme Lefebvre'
'Mme Louis Ricart'
'Mme Louise Piron'
'Mme Louise Vigneron'
'Mme Lureau-Escalaïs'
'Mme Marcel Fauneau'
'Mme Marie Van Houtte'
'Mme Montel'
'Mme Pierre Margery'
'Mme Renard'
'Mme Rose Caron'
'Mme Scipion Cochet'
'Mme Soubeyran'
'Mme Théodore Vernes'
'Mme Verlot'
'Mme Verrier Cachet'
'Mme Veuve Alexandre Pommery'
'Monsieur Etienne Dupuy'
'Monsieur Joseph Chappaz'
'Mrs. Cocker'
'Mrs. George Dickson'
'Mrs. J. F. Redly'
'Mrs. John Laing'
'Mrs. John McLaren'
'Mrs. R. G. Sharman-Crawford'
'Oakmont'
'Orderic Vital'
'Pæonia'
'Peach Blossom'
'Perpétuelle de Neuilly'
'Piron-Medard'
'Président Briand'
'Prince Henri d'Orléans'
'Princesse Amedée de Broglie'
'Princesse de Joinville'
'Princesse de Naples'
'Princesse Hélène d'Orléans'
'Princesse Lise Troubetzkoï'
'Princesse Radziwill'
'Queen of Edgely'
'Queen of Queens'
'Reine de Danemark'
'Rembrandt'
'Rosa Verschuren'
'Rosslyn'
'Rosy Morn'
'Sa Majesté Gustave V'
'Schön Ingeborg'
'Silver Queen'
'Souvenir d'Arthur De Sansal'
'Souvenir de la Reine d'Angleterre'
'Souvenir de McKinley'
'Souvenir de Mme Corbœuf'
'Souvenir de Mme de Corval'
'Souvenir de Mme H. Thuret'
'Souvenir de Mme Hennecourt'

'Souvenir de Mme Robert'
'Souvenir de Victor Hugo'
'Spenser'
'Stämmler'
'Suzanne Carrol of Carrolton'
'Suzanne Wood'
'Symphony'
'Ulster'
'Urdh'
'Vicomtesse Laure de Gironde'
'Victory Rose'
'William Griffith'
'William Warden'

Noisettes & Climbers

'Adele Frey' (HT)
'Belle Portugaise' (HGig)
'Belle Vichysoise' (N)
'Bougainville' (N)
'Bridesmaid, Cl.' (T)
'Camélia Rose' (N)
'Captain Christy, Cl.' (HT)
'Cécile Brunner, Cl.' (Pol)
'Champneys' Pink Cluster' (N)
'China Doll, Cl.' (Pol)
'Cinderella' (N)
'Colcestria' (HT)
'Columbia, Cl.' (HT)
'Dainty Bess, Cl.' (HT)
'Dawn' (HT)
'Doris Downes' (HGig)
'Dr. Domingos Pereira' (T)
'Dr. Rouges' (T)
'Distinction, Cl.' (Pol)
'Duchesse de Grammont' (N)
'Gainesborough' (HT)
'Gaston Chandon' (HT)
'Glory of California' (HGig)
'Indiana' (HT)
'Irène Bonnet' (HT)
'Jeanne Corbœuf' (HT)
'Jonkheer J. L. Mock, Cl.' (HT)
'Kitty Kininmonth' (HGig)
'L'Abondance' (N)
'La Follette' (HGig)
'La France, Cl.' (HT)
'Lady Clonbrock' (N)
'Lady Sylvia, Cl.' (HT)
'Lucy Thomas' (HP)
'Maman Cochet, Cl.' (T)
'Manettii' (N)
'Marguerite Carels' (HT)
'Marguerite Desrayaux' (N)
'Marie Robert' (N)
'Miniature, Cl.' (Pol)
'Mlle Mathilde Lenaerts' (N)
'Mme Abel Chatenay, Cl.' (HT)
'Mme Auguste Perrin' (N)
'Mme Butterfly, Cl.' (HT)
'Mme Caroline Testout, Cl.' (HT)
'Mme Edmée Cocteau' (HT)
'Mme la Général Paul de Benoît' (T)
'Mme Léon Constantin' (T)
'Mme Marie Lavalley' (N)

'Mme Segond-Weber, Cl.' (HT)
'Mrs. Henry Morse, Cl.' (HT)
'Mrs. W. H. Cutbush, Cl.' (Pol)
'Multiflore de Vaumarcus' (N)
'Old Blush, Cl.' (Ch)
'Papillon' (T)
'Pennant' (HGig)
'Pink Pet, Cl.' (Pol)
'Pink Rover' (HT)
'Pinkie, Cl.' (Pol)
'Pompon de Paris, Cl.' (Ch)
'Princess May' (N)
'Queen of Queens, Cl.' (HP)
'Radiance, Cl.' (HT)
'Rosemary, Cl.' (HT)
'Rouletii, Cl.' (Ch)
'Setina' (B)
'Souvenir de Mme Ladvocat' (N)
'Tausendschön' (Cl.)
'Tea Rambler' (Cl.)
'Triomphe des Noisettes' (N)

Polyanthas

'Abondant'
'Apfelblüte'
'Balduin'
'Bertram'
'Bloomfield Abundance'
'Burkhard'
'Charles Metroz'
'China Doll'
'Degenhard'
'Echo'
'Eileen Loow'
'Ellen Poulsen'
'Evelyn Thornton'
'Fairy Changeling'
'Fairy Maid'
'Fairyland'
'Georges Pernet'
'Giesebrecht'
'Gloire des Polyantha'
'Grete Schreiber'
'Herzblättchens'
'Joséphine Morel'
'La Marne'
'Little Dorrit'
'Loreley'
'Madeleine Orosdy'
'Maman Turbat'
'Margo's Sister'
'Mary Bruni'
'Melle Fischer'
'Mevrouw Nathalie Nypels'
'Milrose'
'Miniature'
'Mlle Cécile Brunner'
'Mlle Fernande Dupuy'
'Mlle Marcelle Gaugin'
'Mme Alégatière'
'Mme Jules Gouchault'
'Mrs. R. M. Finch'
'Mrs. W. H. Cutbush'
'Nypels Perfection'

'Petite François'
'Phyllis'
'Pink Cécile Brunner'
'Pink Pet'
'Pink Posy'
'Pink Soupert'
'Pinkie'
'Princess Ena'
'Radium'
'Renoncule'
'Schöne von Holstein'
'Sisi Ketten'
'Spray Cécile Brunner'
'Summer Dawn'
'Susanna'
'The Allies'
'The Fairy'
'Waverly Triumph'

Hybrid Teas
'Abbé Millot'
'Amateur André Fourcaud'
'Astra'
'Aurora'
'Australia Felix'
'Beatrix, Comtesse de Buisseret'
'Beauty of Stapleford'
'Camoëns'
'Captain Christy'
'Charles Dickens'
'Clara Barton'
'Columbia'
'Commandant Letourneux'
'Coronet'
'Dainty Bess'
'Dame Edith Helen'
'Distinction'
'Duchess of Connaught'
'Emin Pascha'
'Gladys Harkness'
'Irish Glory'
'Isobel'
'Jean Sisley'

'Jonkheer J. L. Mock'
'Kathleen'
'Kathleen Mills'
'Killarney Queen'
'La France'
'Lady Alice Stanley'
'Lady Ashtown'
'Lady Mary Fitzwilliam'
'Lady Sylvia'
'Lina Schmidt-Michel'
'Madeleine Gaillard'
'Marie Zahn'
'Minna'
'Mlle Germaine Caillot'
'Mme A. Schwaller'
'Mme Abel Chatenay'
'Mme Angèle Favre'
'Mme Bessemer'
'Mme Blondel'
'Mme Butterfly'
'Mme Caroline Testout'
'Mme Charles Boutmy'
'Mme Cunisset-Carnot'
'Mme Dailleux'
'Mme Ernest Piard'
'Mme Eugénie Boullet'
'Mme Joseph Bonnaire'
'Mme Marie Croibier'
'Mme Maurice de Luze'
'Mme Segond-Weber'
'Mme Viger'
'Monsieur Fraissenon'
'Mrs. Charles J. Bell'
'Mrs. Henry Morse'
'Mrs. Robert Garrett'
'Mrs. Wakefield Christie-Miller'
'Mrs. W.C. Whitney'
'Papa Lambert'
'Pharisäer'
'Reine Carola de Saxe'
'Rosa Gruss an Aachen'
'Sheila'
'Sunny South'
'Viscountess Folkestone'

Deep Pink to Rose and Rose-Red

Damask Perpetuals
'Belle Fabert'
'Bernard'
'Delambre'
'Portland Rose'
'Quatre Saisons d'Italie'
'Rose de Rescht'
'Rose de Trianon'
'Tous-les-Mois'
'Yolande d'Aragon'

Chinas
'Beauty of Rosemawr'
'Bébé Fleuri'

'Bengale Animée'
'Bengale Centfeuilles'
'Bengali'
'Douglas'
'Fimbriata á Petales Frangés'
'Institutrice Moulins'
'Le Vésuve'
'Rose de l'Inde'

Teas
'Adam'
'Albert Stopford'
'Archiduc Joseph'
'Auguste Comte'

'Bon Silène'
'Bougère'
'Camille Roux'
'Captain Philip Green'
'Charles de Legrady'
'Claudius Levet'
'Ernest Metz'
'Ethel Brownlow'
'F. L. Segers'
'Freiherr von Marschall'
'Général D. Mertchansky'
'H. Plantagenet Comte d'Anjou'
'Joseph Paquet'
'Marquise de Vivens'
'Mevrouw Boreel van Hogelander'
'Minnie Francis'
'Miss Agnes C. Sherman'
'Mme A. Etienne'
'Mme Céline Noirey'
'Mme Ernestine Verdier'
'Mme P. Kuntz'
'Mme Victor Caillet'
'Monsieur Tillier'
'Morning Glow'
'Mrs. B. R. Cant'
'Mrs. J. Pierpont Morgan'
'Mrs. Reynolds Hole'
'Nelly Johnstone'
'Niles Cochet'
'Papa Gontier'
'Paul Nabonnand'
'Regulus'
'Reichsgraf E. von Kesselstatt'
'Reine Olga'
'Safrano à Fleurs Rouges'
'Sénateur Loubet'
'Souvenir de Clairvaux'
'Souvenir de David d'Angers'
'Triomphe du Luxembourg'
'V. Vivo é Hijos'
'Waban'

Bourbons

'Adam Messerich'
'Béatrix'
'Capitaine Sisolet'
'Catherine Guillot'
'Emile Courtier'
'Georges Cuvier'
'Heroïne de Vaucluse'
'Jean Rameau'
'Leveson-Gower'
'Martha'
'Mme Arthur Oger'
'Mme Desprez'
'Mme Isaac Pereire'
'Monsieur Cordeau'
'Prince Napoléon'
'Reine Victoria'
'Reveil'
'Rose Edouard'
'Souvenir d'Adèle Launay'
'Zéphirine Drouhin'

Hybrid Bourbons, Hybrid Chinas, and Hybrid Noisettes

'Athalin'
'Charles Duval'
'Charles Lawson'
'Général Allard'
'Las-Cases'
'Marguerite Lartay'
'Paul Ricault'
'Paul Verdier'
'Richelieu'
'Riégo'
'Sir Joseph Paxton'
'Vivid'

Hybrid Perpetuals

'Abbé Giraudier'
'Adélaïde de Meynot'
'Alfred Colomb'
'Alpaïde de Rotalier'
'Alphonse Soupert'
'Ambrogio Maggi'
'American Beauty'
'American Belle'
'Ami Charmet'
'Anna Alexieff'
'Anna de Diesbach'
'Antoine Mouton'
'Aristide Dupuy'
'Baronne Prévost'
'Belle de Normandy'
'Benoist Pernin'
'Captain Hayward'
'Centifolia Rosea'
'Colonel Foissy'
'Comte de Falloux'
'Comte de Paris'
'Comte Florimund de Bergeyck'
'Comtesse Bertrand de Blacas'
'Comtesse Cahen d'Anvers'
'Comtesse de Falloux'
'Cornet'
'Countess of Rosebery'
'Dr. Hurta'
'Dr. Marx'
'Duchesse d'Aoste'
'Duchesse de Cambacérès'
'Duchesse de Caylus'
'Duchesse de Vallombrosa'
'Eliska Krásnohorská'
'Etienne Levet'
'Felbergs Rosa Druschki'
'Felicien David'
'François Michelon'
'Général de la Martinière'
'George Paul'
'Gerbe de Roses'
'Grandeur of Cheshunt'
'Guillaume Gillemot'
'Helen Keller'
'Hippolyte Jamain' (Faudon)
'Hippolyte Jamain' (Lacharme)

'Inigo Jones'
'Jacques Laffitte'
'Jean Goujon'
'Jean Rosenkrantz'
'Jeannie Dickson'
'John Hopper'
'Jules Margottin'
'L'Ami E. Daumont'
'L'Espérance'
'La Duchesse de Morny'
'Lena Turner'
'Louis Noisette'
'Louise Peyronny'
'Lyonnais'
'Magna Charta'
'Marchioness of Lorne'
'Marie Louise Pernet'
'Marie Menudel'
'Marquise de Castellane'
'Marquise de Verdun'
'Maurice Lepelletier'
'Mlle Hélène Croissandeau'
'Mlle Thérèse Levet'
'Mme Baulot'
'Mme Bellon'
'Mme Bertha Mackart'
'Mme Charles Verdier'
'Mme Chirard'
'Mme Clémence Joigneaux'
'Mme Cordier'
'Mme Crespin'
'Mme Ferdinand Jamin'
'Mme Fillion'
'Mme Henri Perrin'
'Mme Laffay'
'Mme Lierval'
'Mme Rambaux'
'Mme Renahy'
'Mme Roger'
'Mme Schmitt'
'Mme Scipion Cochet'
'Mme Sophie Stern'
'Mme Sophie Tropot'
'Mme Thibaut '
'Monsieur Alfred Leveau'
'Monsieur de Montigny'
'Monsieur Fillion'
'Monsieur Jules Monges'
'Mrs. Laing'
'Mrs. Rumsey'
'Olivier Belhomme'
'Paul Neyron'
'Paul Verdier'
'Pride of Waltham'
'Princesse Hélène'
'Princesse Marie d'Orléans'
'Princesse Marie Dolgorouky'
'Prudence Besson'
'Reine de Castille'
'Reverend Alan Cheales'
'Robert Duncan'
'Rose de France'
'Sisley'
'Souvenir de Béranger'

'Souvenir de l'Ami Labruyère'
'Souvenir de Leveson-Gower'
'Souvenir de Mme Jeanne Balandreau'
'Souvenir de Monsieur Droche'
'Souvenir du Président Porcher'
'Théodore Liberton'
'Thomas Mills'
'Thorin'
'Triomphe de France'
'Triomphe de la Terre des Roses'
'Ulrich Brunner fils'
'Vicomtesse de Vezins'
'Ville de Lyon'
'Ville de St.-Denis'
'Vincent-Hippolyte Duval'
'Vincente Peluffo'
'Victor le Bihan'
'Victor Verdier'

Noisettes & Climbers

'American Beauty, Cl.' (Cl.)
'Archduchess Charlotte' (Ch)
'Capitaine Soupa, Cl.' (HT)
'Captain Hayward, Cl.' (HP)
'Dame Edith Helen, Cl.' (HT)
'Étoile de Portugal' (HGig)
'Flying Colours' (HGig)
'General-Superior Arnold Janssen, Cl.' (HT)
'Gloire de Bordeaux' (N)
'La France de 89' (HT)
'Le Vésuve, Cl.' (Ch)
'Marie Bülow' (N)
'Mme Julie Lassen' (N)
'Monsieur Rosier' (T)
'Mrs. B. R. Cant, Cl.' (T)
'Mrs. Rosalie Wrinch' (HP)
'Mrs. W. J. Grant, Cl.' (HT)
'Papa Gontier, Cl.' (T)
'Queen of Hearts' (HT)
'Reine Maria Pia' (T)
'Scorcher' (Cl.)
'Souvenir de Lucie' (HN)
'Souvenir of Wootton, Cl.' (HT)
'Vicomtesse d'Avesnes' (N)
'Vicomtesse Pierre de Fou' (N)

Polyanthas

'Ännchen Müller'
'Baptiste Lafaye'
'Fairy Ring'
'Frau Anna Pasquay'
'Frau Oberhofgärtner Singer'
'Gabrielle Privat'
'Greta Kluis'
'Jean Mermoz'
'Kleiner Liebling'
'Mauve'
'Mimi Pinson'
'Mme Arthur Robichon'
'Primula'
'Rösel Dach'

Hybrid Teas

'Australie'
'Bona Weillschott'
'Danmark'
'Dean Hole'
'Directeur Constant Bernard'
'Dr. Pasteur'
'Duchess of Albany'
'Duchess of Westminster'
'Ferdinand Jamin'
'General-Superior Arnold Janssen'
'Grand-Duc Adolphe de Luxembourg'
'Grossherzog Ernst Ludwig von Hesse'
'Gustav Grünerwald'
'Jean Lorthois'

'Killarney Brilliant'
'Magnafrano'
'Mamie'
'Marquise Litta de Breteuil'
'Mlle Brigitte Viollet'
'Mme Jules Grolez'
'Mme P. Euler'
'Mme Wagram, Comtesse de Turenne'
'Mrs. W. J. Grant'
'Pierre Wattinne'
'Radiance'
'Red Radiance'
'Souvenir de Monsieur Frédéric Vercellone'
'Souvenir of Wootton'

Medium Red

Damask Perpetuals

'Jeune Henry'
'Laurent Heister'
'Rembrandt'
'Rose du Roi'

Chinas

'Bengale d'Automne'
'Charlotte Klemm'
'Cramoisi Supérieur'
'Fabvier'
'Granate'
'Laffay'
'Miss Lowe's Variety'
'Red Pet'
'Rose de Bengale'
'Sanglant'
'Slater's Crimson China'
'St. Priest de Breuze'

Teas

'Betty Berkeley'
'Corallina'
'Duchess of Edinburgh'
'Empereur Nicolas II'
'Général Tartas'
'Georges Farber'
'Jules Finger'
'Julius Fabianics de Misefa'
'Margherita di Simone'
'Marion Dingee'
'Marquise de Querhoënt'
'Meta'
'Mme Antoine Rébé'
'Mme Clémence Marchix'
'Mme F. Brassac'
'Mme Jules Cambon'
'Mme Thérèse Deschamps'
'Monsieur Edouard Littaye'
'Princess Bonnie'
'Professeur Ganiviat'
'Rosa Mundi'
'S.A.R. Mme la Princesse de Hohenzollern,
    Infante de Portugal'

'Simone Thomas'
'Souvenir d'Auguste Legros'
'Souvenir de l'Amiral Courbet'
'Souvenir de Lady Ashburton'
'Souvenir du Dr. Passot'
'V. Viviand-Morel'

Bourbons

'Belle Nanon'
'Bouquet de Flore'
'Comice de Tarn et Garonne'
'Dr. Brière'
'Duc de Crillon'
'Dunkelrote Hermosa'
'Fellemberg'
'Frau Dr. Schricker'
'Garibaldi'
'Gloire des Rosomanes'
'Gruss an Teplitz'
'Marquis de Balbiano'
'Mme Adélaïde Ristori'
'Mme Eugène E. Marlitt'
'Mme Gabriel Luizet'
'Monsieur A. Maillé'
'Omer-Pacha'
'Président de la Rocheterie'
'Président Gausen'
'Queen of Bedders'
'Souvenir de l'Exposition de Londres'
'Souvenir de Monsieur Bruel'
'Souvenir de Victor Landeau'
'Souvenir de Lieutenant Bujon'
'Vicomte Fritz de Cussy'

Hybrid Bourbons, Hybrid Chinas, and Hybrid Noisettes

'Brennus'
'Catherine Bonnard'
'Chénédolé'
'Francis B. Hayes'
'Joseph Gourdon'
'Le Vingt-Neuf Juillet'
'Malton'
'Mme Jeannine Joubert'

'Souvenir d'Anselme'
'Souvenir de Paul Dupuy'
'William Jesse'

Hybrid Perpetuals

'A. Geoffrey de St.-Hilaire'
'Abbé Bérlèze'
'Abraham Zimmermann'
'Achille Cesbron'
'Achille Gonod'
'Adrien Schmitt'
'Alexandre Dupont'
'Alexis Lepère'
'Alfred K. Williams'
'Ami Martin'
'Amiral Courbet'
'Auguste Chaplain'
'Aurore Boréale'
'Baron de Wolseley'
'Baron Nathaniel de Rothschild'
'Baronne de Medem'
'Bathélemy-Joubert'
'Beauty of Beeston'
'Beauty of Waltham'
'Belle Yvrienne'
'Ben Cant'
'Bijou de Couasnon'
'Boccace'
'Camille Bernardin'
'Capitaine Jouen'
'Charles Lamb'
'Charles Margottin'
'Charles Turner'
'Charles Wagner'
'Clémence Joigneaux'
'Commandeur Jules Gravereaux'
'Comte Charles d'Harcourt'
'Comte de Paris'
'Comte Horance de Choiseul'
'Comte Odart'
'Comte Raoul Chandon'
'Comtesse d'Oxford'
'Comtesse Renée de Béarn'
'Crimson Bedder'
'Crimson Queen'
'Denis Hélye'
'Desgaches'
'Desirée Fontaine'
'Dr. Andry'
'Dr. Auguste Krell'
'Druschki Rubra'
'Duc d'Anjou'
'Duc d'Audiffret-Pasquier'
'Duc d'Harcourt'
'Duc de Marlborough'
'Duc de Montpensier'
'Duchess of Bedford'
'Duchesse d'Ossuna'
'Duhamel-Dumonceau'
'Duke of Fife'
'Duke of Teck'
'Dupuy-Jamain'
'E. Y. Teas'
'Earl of Pembroke'

'Eclaireur'
'Edouard André le Botaniste'
'Edouard Hervé'
'Elisabeth Vigneron'
'Emile Bardiaux'
'Ernest Morel'
'Ernest Prince'
'Etienne Dubois'
'Ferdinand Chaffolte'
'Ferdinand Jamin'
'Firebrand'
'Florence Paul'
'François I'
'François Coppée'
'Général Baron Berge'
'Général Désaix'
'Général Duc d'Aumale'
'General von Bothnia-Andreæ'
'George Dickson'
'Georges Moreau'
'Georges Rousset'
'Gloire d'Un Enfant d'Hiram'
'Gloire de Bourg-la-Reine'
'Gloire de Chédane-Guinoisseau'
'Golfe-Juan'
'Gustave Piganeau'
'Haileybury'
'Hans Mackart'
'Henry Bennett'
'Hugh Dickson'
'Ingénieur Madèlé'
'Jan Böhm'
'Jean Lelièvre'
'Jeanne Sury'
'Joachim du Bellay'
'John Bright'
'John Gould Veitch'
'John Stuart Mill'
'Jules Barigny'
'Jules Seurre'
'Katkoff'
'L'Ami Maubry'
'L'Etincelante'
'La Brillante'
'La Motte Sanguin'
'La Nantaise'
'La Syrène'
'Lady Helen Stewart'
'Laforcade'
'Laurent de Rillé'
'Le Havre'
'Le Triomphe de Saintes'
'Léon Renault'
'Léon Say'
'Léonie Lartay'
'Léopold I, Roi des Belges'
'Lord Frederic Cavendish'
'Lord Raglan'
'Lord Macaulay'
'Louis Lille'
'Louis Philippe Albert d'Orléans'
'Lucien Duranthon'
'Marie Baumann'
'Mary Pochin'

'Maurice Bernardin'
'Michel-Ange'
'Miller-Hayes'
'Mistress Elliot'
'Mlle Annie Wood'
'Mlle Gabrielle de Peyronny'
'Mlle Hélène Michel'
'Mlle Marie Magat'
'Mme Boutin'
'Mme Cécile Morand'
'Mme Charles Crapelet'
'Mme Charles Wood'
'Mme Constant David'
'Mme de Selve'
'Mme de Trotter'
'Mme Elisa Tasson'
'Mme Ernest Levavasseur'
'Mme François Bruel'
'Mme Grandin-Monville'
'Mme Henri Pereire'
'Mme Jean Everaerts'
'Mme Lucien Chauré'
'Mme Marie Grange'
'Mme Marthe d'Halloy'
'Mme Prosper Laugier'
'Mme Roudillon'
'Mme Théobald Sernin'
'Mme Thévenot'
'Mme Victor Verdier'
'Monsieur Cordier'
'Monsieur de Morand'
'Monsieur Francisque Rive'
'Monsieur Hoste'
'Monsieur Journaux'
'Monsieur Jules Lemaître'
'Monsieur le Capitaine Louis Frère'
'Monseigneur Fournier'
'Montebello'
'Mrs. Baker'
'Olivier Métra'
'Orgeuil de Lyon'
'Oriflamme de St. Louis'
'Oscar II, Roi de Suède'
'Oskar Cordel'
'Pæonia'
'Paul de la Meilleraye'
'Paula Clegg'
'Peter Lawson'
'Philipp Paulig'
'Philippe Bardet'
'Pierre Carot'
'Président Carnot'
'Président Sénélar'
'Président Willermoz'
'Prince de Joinville'
'Prince de Portia'
'Prince Waldemar'
'Princess of Wales'
'Princesse Charles d'Aremberg'
'Princesse de Béarn'
'Professeur Maxime Cornu'
'Prosper Laugier'
'Rouge Angevine'
'Rubens'

'Ruhm von Steinfurth'
'Rushton-Radclyffe'
'Sir Garnet Wolseley'
'Souvenir d'Adolphe Thiers'
'Souvenir d'André Raffy'
'Souvenir de Grégoire Bordillon'
'Souvenir de Laffay'
'Souvenir de Léon Gambetta'
'Souvenir de Léon Roudillon'
'Souvenir de Mme Alfred Vy'
'Souvenir de Mme Berthier'
'Souvenir de Mme Chédane-Guinoisseau'
'Souvenir de Monsieur Boll'
'Souvenir de Monsieur Faivre'
'Souvenir de Monsieur Rousseau'
'Souvenir de Victor Verdier'
'Souvenir du Rosiériste Gonod'
'Star of Waltham'
'Tancrède'
'Tom Wood'
'Triomphe d'Alencon'
'Triomphe de l'Exposition'
'Turenne'
'Vainqueur de Goliath'
'Vicomte Maison'
'Vyslanec Kalina'
'Waldfee'

Noisettes & Climbers

'Albert La Blotais, Cl.' (HP)
'Apotheker Georg Höfer, Cl.' (HT)
'Ards Rambler' (HT)
'Cracker, Cl.' (HGig)
'Crimson Conquest' (HT)
'Deschamps' (N)
'Effective' (HT)
'Empress of China' (Ch)
'François Crousse' (T)
'Fürstin Bismarck' (HT)
'General MacArthur, Cl.' (HT)
'George Dickson, Cl.' (HP)
'Geschwindts Gorgeous' (HT)
'Glory of Waltham' (HP)
'Gruss an Teplitz, Cl.' (B)
'Henry Irving' (Cl)
'James Sprunt' (Ch)
'Jules Margottin, Cl.' (HP)
'Lilliput' (Pol)
'Meteor' (N)
'Mikado' (HT)
'Miss Marion Manifold' (HT)
'Mlle Geneviève Godard' (T)
'Mme Couturier-Mention' (Ch)
'Mme Rose Romarin' (T)
'Nancy Hayward' (HGig)
'Neervelt' (HT)
'Noëlla Nabonnand' (HT)
'Reine Marie Henriette' (HT)
'Reine Olga de Wurtemberg' (N)
'Richmond, Cl.' (HT)
'Sénateur Amic' (HGig)
'Souvenir de Mère Fontaine' (N)
'Souvenir de Mme Joseph Métral' (HT)
'Sunday Best' (HP)

'Waltham Climber I' (HT)
'Waltham Climber II' (HT)
'Waltham Climber III' (HT)

Polyanthas
'Alberich'
'Betsy van Nes'
'Border King'
'Bordure'
'Chatillon Rose'
'Cineraria'
'Fairy Damsel'
'Fairy Prince'
'Flamboyant'
'Frau Elise Kreis'
'Gloire de Charpennes'
'Gustel Mayer'
'Indéfectible'
'Jessie'
'Kersbergen'
'Lady Reading'
'Lillan'
'Lindbergh'
'Ma Petite Andrée'
'Maréchal Foch'
'Merveille des Rouges'
'Mlle Blanche Rebatel'
'Mme Norbert Levavasseur'
'Mme Taft'
'Orléans-Rose'
'Papa Hémeray'
'Paris'
'Perle des Rouges'
'Rotkäppchen'

'Sparkler'
'Stadtrat Meyn'
'Triomphe Orléanais'
'Verdun Superior'

Hybrid Teas
'Admiral Dewey'
'Antonine Verdier'
'Attraction'
'Augustus Hartmann'
'Aviateur Michel Mahieu'
'Avoca'
'Balduin'
'Bedford Belle'
'Cardinal'
'Comtesse Icy Hardegg'
'Exquisite'
'Frances Ashton'
'General MacArthur'
'Henri Brichard'
'K. of K.'
'Mme André Duron'
'Mme Alfred Sabatier'
'Mme Charles Détraux'
'Mme Emilie Lafon'
'Mme Etienne Levet'
'Mrs. Cynthia Forde'
'Pierre Guillot'
'Reine Marguerite d'Italie'
'Richmond'
'Rosette de la Legion d'Honneur'
'Ruhm der Gartenwelt'
'Triomphe de Pernet Père'
'Vesuvius'

Deep Red, Maroon, Purple, and Violet

Damask Perpetuals
'Jacques Amyot'
'Joasine Hanet'
'Louis-Philippe I'
'Mogador'
'Pergolèse'
'Président Dutailly'

Chinas
'Alice Hamilton'
'Belle de Monza'
'Bengale Nabonnand'
'Bengale Sanguinaire'
'Darius'
'Eugène de Beauharnais'
'Louis-Philippe'
'Lucullus'
'Maréchal de Villars'
'Némésis'
'Papillon'
'Pourpre'
'Princesse de Sagan'
'Purpurea'
'Unermüdliche'

Teas
'Aline Sisley'
'Alphonse Karr'
'André Schwartz'
'Capitaine Lefort'
'Empress Alexandra of Russia'
'Francis Dubreuil'
'Joseph Métral'
'Mlle Christine de Noué'
'Mme Agathe Nabonnand'
'Mme Cusin'
'Pénélope'
'Souvenir de François Gaulain'
'Souvenir de Germain de Saint-Pierre'
'Souvenir de Thérèse Levet'

Bourbons
'Amedée de Langlois'
'Bardou Job'
'Catalunya'
'Deuil du Dr. Raynaud'
'Deuil du Duc d'Orléans'
'Dr. Leprestre'
'Frau O. Plegg'

'Gourdault'
'Malmaison Rouge'
'Mlle Joséphine Guyet'
'Prince Albert'
'Prosérpine'
'Robusta'
'Souchet'
'Souvenir de Louis Gaudin'
'Souvenir du Président Lincoln'
'Toussaint-Louverture'
'Velouté d'Orléans'
'Zigeunerblut'

Hybrid Bourbons, Hybrid Chinas, and Hybrid Noisettes

'Belle de Crécy'
'Cardinal de Richelieu'
'Chevrier'
'Dembrowski'
'Edward Jesse'
'George IV'
'Great Western'
'Jules Jürgensen'
'Nubienne'
'Parkzierde'
'Prince Charles'
'Souvenir de Pierre Dupuy'
'Zigeunerknabe'

Hybrid Perpetuals

'A. Drawiel'
'A.-M. Ampère'
'Abbé Bramerel'
'Abel Carrière'
'Albert La Blotais'
'Alexandre Chomer'
'Alexandre Dumas'
'Ali Pacha Cheriff'
'Alphonse de Lamartine'
'Alsace-Lorraine'
'Amedée Philibert'
'Amiral Gravina'
'André Leroy d'Angers'
'Anne Laferrère'
'Antoine Ducher'
'Ardoisée de Lyon'
'Arthur De Sansal'
'Arthur Oger'
'Avocat Duvivier'
'Barbarossa'
'Baron de Bonstetten'
'Baron Elisi de St.-Albert'
'Baron Haussmann'
'Baron T'Kint de Roodenbeke'
'Baronne de St.-Didier'
'Baronne Maurice de Graviers'
'Benjamin Drouet'
'Bernard Verlot'
'Black Prince'
'Capitaine Peillon'
'Cardinal Patrizzi'
'Charles Darwin'
'Charles Gater'

'Charles Lefebvre'
'Charles Martel'
'Charles Wood'
'Claude Jacquet'
'Claude Million'
'Colonel Félix Breton'
'Comte de Bobrinsky'
'Comte de Flandres'
'Comte Frédéric de Thun de Hohenstein'
'Comtesse de Polignac'
'Comtesse O'Gorman'
'Crown Prince'
'Dames Patronesses d'Orléans'
'Deuil de Dunois'
'Deuil du Colonel Denfert'
'Devienne-Lamy'
'Directeur Alphand'
'Directeur N. Jensen'
'Dr. Baillon'
'Dr. Bretonneau'
'Dr. Hogg'
'Dr. Ingomar H. Blohm'
'Dr. Jamain'
'Dr. Müllers Rote'
'Duc de Cazes'
'Duc de Chartres'
'Duc de Wellington'
'Duchess of Connaught'
'Duchesse de Dino'
'Duke of Edinburgh'
'Earl of Dufferin'
'Eclair'
'Empereur du Maroc'
'Emperor'
'Empress of India'
'Erinnerung an Brod'
'Eugène Appert'
'Eugene Fürst'
'Eugène Verdier'
'Félix Mousset'
'Fisher-Holmes'
'François Arago'
'François Gaulain'
'Frédéric II de Prusse'
'Friedrich von Schiller'
'Fürst Leopold zu Schaumburg-Lippe'
'Géant des Batailles'
'Général Appert'
'Général Barral'
'Général Jacqueminot'
'General Stefanik'
'Général Washington'
'Génie de Châteaubriand'
'Gloire de Ducher'
'Gloire de l'Exposition de Bruxelles'
'Graf Fritz Metternich'
'Grand-Duc Alexis'
'Gruss aus Pallien'
'Henri IV'
'Henriette Petit'
'Henry Nevard'
'Horace Vernet'
'J. B. Clark'
'Janine Viaud-Bruant'

'Jean Cherpin'
'Jean Liabaud'
'Jean Soupert'
'John Keynes'
'John Laing'
'Jubilee'
'Jules Chrétien'
'Kaiser Wilhelm I'
'König Friedrich II von Dänemark'
'La Brunoyenne'
'La Rosière'
'Lecocq-Dumesnil'
'Léon Delaville'
'Lion des Combats'
'Lord Bacon'
'Lord Beaconsfield'
'Louis XIV'
'Louis Donadine'
'Louis Rollet'
'Louis Van Houtte'
'M. H. Walsh'
'Maharajah'
'Marguerite Brassac'
'Marshall P. Wilder'
'Maxime de la Rocheterie'
'Meyerbeer'
'Michel Strogoff'
'Mlle Jules Grévy'
'Mlle Marie Dauvesse'
'Mme Charles Meurice'
'Mme de Ridder'
'Mme Julia Daran'
'Mme Lemesle'
'Mme Léon Halkin'
'Mme Loeben de Sels'
'Mme Marguerite Marsault'
'Mme Masson'
'Mme Rosa Monnet'
'Mme Yorke'
'Monsieur Bonçenne'
'Monsieur Edouard Détaille'
'Monsieur Ernest Dupré'
'Monsieur Eugène Delaire'
'Monsieur Jules Deroudilhe'
'Monsieur Lauriol de Barney'
'Monsieur le Préfet Limbourg'
'Monsieur Louis Ricart'
'Monsieur Mathieu Baron'
'Napoléon III'
'Notaire Bonnefond'
'Ornement du Luxembourg'
'Pauline Lansezeur'
'Pie IX'
'Pierre Notting'
'Président Lincoln'
'Président Schlachter'
'Prince Albert '
'Prince Arthur'
'Prince Camille de Rohan'
'Prince Eugène de Beauharnais'
'Prince Noir'
'Professeur Charguereaud'
'Reine des Violettes'
'Riccordo di Fernando Scarlatti'

'Rosiériste Harms'
'Salamander'
'Secrétaire J. Nicolas'
'Sénateur Vaïsse'
'Simon de St.-Jean'
'Sir Rowland Hill'
'Souvenir d'Alexandre Hardy'
'Souvenir d'Aline Fontaine'
'Souvenir d'Alphonse Lavallée'
'Souvenir d'Auguste Rivière'
'Souvenir de Bertrand Guinoisseau'
'Souvenir de Caillat'
'Souvenir de Charles Montault'
'Souvenir de Henry Lévêque de Vilmorin'
'Souvenir de John Gould Veitch'
'Souvenir de la Princesse Amélie des
  Pays-Bas'
'Souvenir de Mme Sadi Carnot'
'Souvenir de William Wood'
'Souvenir de Baron de Semur'
'Souvenir du Comte de Cavour'
'Souvenir du Docteur Jamain'
'Sultan of Zanzibar'
'Symmetry'
'Tartarus'
'Triomphe de Caen'
'Triomphe de Toulouse'
'Velours Poupre'
'Venus'
'Vicomte de Lauzières'
'Victor-Emmanuel'
'Victor Hugo'
'Victor Lemoine'
'Violet Queen'
'Vulcain'
'Waltham Standard'
'Xavier Olibo'

Noisettes & Climbers
'Ards Rover' (HP)
'Black Boy' (Cl)
'Château de Clos-Vougeot, Cl.' (HT)
'Cheshunt Hybrid' (HT)
'Étoile de Hollande, Cl.' (HT)
'Florence Haswell Veitch' (HT)
'Frau Geheimrat Dr. Staub' (HT)
'Hadley, Cl.' (HT)
'König Friedrich II von Danemark, Cl.' (HP)
'Liberty, Cl.' (HT)
'Lily Metschersky' (N)
'Miss G. Mesman' (Pol)
'Mme Martignier' (T)
'Monsieur Désir' (T)
'Louis Philippe, Cl.' (Ch)
'Mme Louis Ricart, Cl.' (HP)
'Purple East' (Cl)
'Sarah Bernhardt' (HT)
'Souvenir de Claudius Denoyel' (HT)
'Wenzel Geschwindt, Cl.' (HT)

Polyanthas
'Baby Faurax'
'Eblouissant'
'Erna Teschendorff'

'Frau Rudolf Schmidt'
'Gloire d'Orléans'
'Ideal'
'Jacques Proust'
'Magenta'
'Miss Edith Cavell'
'Muttertag'
'Red Triumph'
'Verdun'

Hybrid Teas
'Andenken an Moritz von Frohlich'
'Château de Clos-Vougeot'
'Dr. Cazeneuve'
'Duke of Connaught'
'Erinnerung an Schloss Scharfenstein'

'Étoile de Hollande'
'Hadley'
'His Majesty'
'Hon. George Bancroft'
'Jules Toussaint'
'Liberty'
'Ma Tulipe'
'Marchioness of Salisbury'
'Mme Elisa de Vilmorin'
'Mme Jules Grévy'
'Mme Méha Sabatier'
'Shandon'
'Souvenir d'Auguste Métral'
'The Dandy'
'The Meteor'
'W.E. Lippiat'
'William Francis Bennett'

Sulphur to Light Yellow and Paler Buff

Damask Perpetuals
— None —

Chinas
'Primrose Queen'

Teas
'Alexander Hill Gray'
'Alix Roussel'
'Canari'
'Château des Bergeries'
'Comtesse de Frigneuse'
'Comtesse de Vitzthum'
'Comtesse Eva Starhemberg'
'Coquette de Lyon'
'Elise Sauvage'
'Enfant de Lyon'
'Étoile de Lyon'
'Exadelphé'
'Golden Gate'
'Harry Kirk'
'Isabella Sprunt'
'Le Pactole'
'Léon de Bruyn'
'Louise de Savoie'
'Lutea Flora'
'Maréchal Robert'
'Medea'
'Miss Alice de Rothschild'
'Mme Azélie Imbert'
'Mme Albert Bernardin'
'Mme Barthélemy Levet'
'Mme C. P. Strassheim'
'Mme Chédane-Guinoisseau'
'Mme Derepas-Matrat'
'Mme Devoucoux'
'Mme Fanny Pauwels'
'Mme Marthe du Bourg'
'Mme Paul Varin-Bernier'
'Mme Pelisson'
'Mme Pierre Perny'

'Monsieur Charles de Thézillat'
'Mrs. Dudley Cross'
'Muriel Grahame'
'Namenlose Schöne'
'Narcisse'
'Parks' Yellow Tea-Scented China'
'Perfection de Monplaisir'
'Perle des Jardins'
'Primrose'
'Safrano'
'Shirley Hibberd'
'Smith's Yellow China'
'Sulphurea'
'Triomphe de Milan'
'True Friend'
'Uncle John'
'Victor Pulliat'
'Zephyr'

Bourbons
'Kronprinzessin Viktoria von Preussen'

Hybrid Bourbons, Hybrid Chinas, and Hybrid Noisettes
— None —

Hybrid Perpetuals
'Hold Slunci'
'Pfaffstädt'
'Prinzessin Elsa zu Schaumburg-Lippe'
'St. Ingebert'

Noisettes & Climbers
'Alister Stella Gray' (N)
'Baronne Charles de Gargan' (T)
'Belle Lyonnaise' (N)
'Céline Forestier' (N)
'Chromatella' (N)
'Climbing Mosella' (Pol)
'Comtesse Georges de Roquette-Buisson' (N)
'Desprez à Fleur Jaune' (N)
'Emilia Plantier' (N)

'Général Lamarque' (N)
'Gruss an Friedberg' (N)
'Isabella Gray' (N)
'Lemon Queen' (HT)
'Maréchal Niel' (N)
'Mlle Adèle Jougant' (T)
'Mlle Marie Gaze' (N)
'Mme Chabanne' (T)
'Mme Gaston Annouilh' (N)
'Mme Jules Gravereaux' (Cl)
'Mme Louis Henry' (N)
'Mme Schultz' (N)
'Paul's Lemon Pillar' (HT)
'Perle des Jardins, Cl.' (T)
'Rêve d'Or' (N)
'Solfatare' (N)

Polyanthas
'Coronet'
'Diamant'
'Étoile de Mai'

'Frau Cecilie Walter'
'George Elger'
'La Rosée'
'Martha Keller'
'Mlle Marthe Cahuzac'
'Mme E.A. Nolte'
'Schneewittchen'
'Siegesperle'
'Topaz'

Hybrid Teas
'Golden Ophelia'
'Gustav Regis'
'Johannes Wesselhöft'
'Kootenay'
'Mlle Alice Furon'
'Mme Pernet-Ducher'
'Mme Tony Baboud'
'Paul Meunier'
'Souvenir de Mme Eugène Verdier'

Deep Yellow to Deeper Buff and Fawn, Bronze, Apricot, Copper, Coral, Coral-Pink, Salmon, Orange, Nasturtium, Coppery-Red, and Orange-Red.

Damask Perpetuals
— None —

Chinas
'Arethusa'
'Comtesse du Caÿla'
'Mme Eugène Résal'
'Queen Mab'

Teas
'Abricotée'
'Alliance Franco-Russe'
'Anna Olivier'
'Antoine Weber'
'Antoinette Durieu'
'Aureus'
'Baxter Beauty'
'Beryl'
'Canadian Belle'
'Chamoïs'
'Charles de Franciosi'
'Comte Chandon'
'Comtesse Anna Thun'
'Comtesse Festetics Hamilton'
'Comtesse Sophie Torby'
'Dr. Félix Guyon'
'Dr. Grandvilliers'
'Duchesse de Vallombrosa'
'Edmond de Biauzat'
'Elise Heymann'
'Esther Pradel'
'Fortuna'
'Fürstin Infantin von Hohenzollern'
'Général Galliéni'
'General Robert E. Lee'
'Général Schablikine'
'Georges Schwartz'

'Golden Oriole'
'Henry M. Stanley'
'Jean André'
'Jean Ducher'
'Koningen Wilhelmina'
'La Nankeen'
'Lady Hillingdon'
'Lady Mary Corry'
'Lady Roberts'
'Lady Zoë Brougham'
'Lena'
'Lorraine Lee'
'Louis Richard'
'Luciole'
'Ma Capucine'
'Madeleine Guillaumez'
'Marguerite Gigandet'
'Marguerite Ketten'
'Maria Star'
'Marie Segond'
'Mlle Blanche Martignat'
'Mlle Franziska Krüger'
'Mlle Lazarine Poizeau'
'Mme Achille Fould'
'Mme Carot'
'Mme Charles'
'Mme Constant Soupert'
'Mme Crombez'
'Mme Dr. Jütté'
'Mme Ernest Perrin'
'Mme Errera'
'Mme Eugène Verdier'
'Mme Falcot'
'Mme Gamon'
'Mme Gustave Henry'
'Mme Henri Graire'
'Mme Honoré Dufresne'

'Mme Jean Dupuy'
'Mme la Comtesse de Caserta'
'Mme Laurent Simons'
'Mme Margottin'
'Mme Maurice Kuppenheim'
'Mme Pierre Guillot'
'Mme Remond'
'Mme Vermorel'
'Mme Welche'
'Mrs. Alice Broomhall'
'Mrs. S. T. Wright'
'Palo Alto'
'Peach Blossom'
'Perle de Feu'
'Perle des Jaunes'
'Reine Emma des Pays-Bas'
'Rhodologue Jules Gravereaux'
'Sappho'
'Souvenir d'Espagne'
'Souvenir de Jeanne Cabaud'
'Souvenir de Laurent Guillot'
'Souvenir de Mme Levet'
'Souvenir de Mme Sablayrolles'
'Souvenir de Pierre Notting'
'Souvenir of Stella Gray'
'Sunrise'
'Sunset'
'The Sweet Little Queen of Holland'
'Vallée de Chamonix'
'Virginia'

Bourbons
— None —

**Hybrid Bourbons, Hybrid Chinas,
and Hybrid Noisettes**
— None —

Hybrid Perpetuals
'Bischof Dr. Korum'
'Bradova Lososova Druschki'
'Gruss an Weimar'
'Isabel Llorach'
'Juliet'
'Lyonfarbige Druschki'
'Mme Albert Barbier'
'Prinz Max zu Schaumburg-Lippe'
'Tatik Brada'

Noisettes & Climbers
'Adrienne Christophle' (N)
'Anna Olivier, Cl.' (T)
'Apeles Mestres' (HP)
'Beauté de l'Europe' (N)
'Billard et Barré' (N)
'Bouquet d'Or' (N)
'Cherubim' (Cl)
'Crepuscule' (N)
'Duarte de Oliveira' (N)
'E. Veyrat Hermanos' (T)
'Earl of Eldon' (N)
'Fürst Bismarck' (N)
'Irish Fireflame, Cl.' (HT)

'Kaiser Wilhelm der Siegreiche' (N)
'Kaiserin Friedrich' (N)
'Les Fiançailles de la Princesse Stéphanie
    et de l'Archiduc Rodolphe' (N)
'Lorraine Lee, Cl.' (HGig)
'Margo Koster, Cl.' (Pol)
'Marie Thérèse Dubourg' (N)
'Mlle Claire Jacquier' (Pol)
'Mme Auguste Choutet' (HT)
'Mme Bérard' (N)
'Mme Brunner' (N)
'Mme Caroline Küster'
'Mme Chauvry' (N)
'Mme Creux' (T)
'Mme E. Souffrain' (N)
'Mme Emilie Dupuy' (N)
'Mme Eugénie Verdier' (N)
'Mme Foureau' (N)
'Mme la Duchesse d'Auerstädt' (N)
'Mme Pierre Cochet' (N)
'Mme Trifle' (N)
'Monsieur Paul Lédé, Cl.' (HT)
'Mrs. Aaron Ward, Cl.' (HT)
'Nardy' (N)
'Ophirie' (N)
'Orange Triumph, Cl.' (Pol)
'Oscar Chauvry' (N)
'Prinses van Oranje' (Pol)
'William Allen Richardson' (N)

Polyanthas
'Caid'
'Cameo'
'Casque d'Or'
'Coral Cluster'
'Corrie Koster'
'Dick Koster'
'Dr. Ricaud'
'Étoile Luisante'
'Eugénie Lamesch'
'Frau Alexander Weiss'
'Gloire du Midi'
'Gloria Mundi'
'Golden Salmon'
'Julie Delbard'
'Kleiner Alfred'
'Legion d'Honneur'
'Leonie Lamesch'
'Margo Koster'
'Martha'
'Marytje Cazant'
'Mlle Suzanne Bidard'
'Mme Jules Thibaud'
'Mosella'
'Orange Koster'
'Orange Morsdag'
'Orange Triumph'
'Pacific Triumph'
'Paul Crampel'
'Sunshine'
'Vatertag'

Hybrid Teas
'Augustine Halem'
'Betty'
'Cecil'
'Charles J. Graham'
'Christobel'
'Erzherzogin Marie Dorothea'
'Hofgärtendirektor Graebener'
'Irish Brightness'
'Irish Elegance'
'Irish Fireflame'
'Irish Modesty'
'Lulu'
'Mlle Hélène Cambier'
'Mme Paul Lacoutière'
'Mme Ravary'
'Monsieur Paul Lédé'
'Mrs. Oakley Fisher'
'Old Gold'

Mixed Coloration

Damask Perpetual
— None —

Chinas
'Antoinette Cuillerat'
'Archiduc Charles'
'Aurore'
'Duke of York'
'Laure de Broglie'
'Maddalena Scalarandis'
'Mme Laurette Messimy'
'Mutabilis'
'Viridiflora'

Teas
'Abbé Garroute'
'Adèle de Bellabre'
'Albert Hoffmann'
'Amazone'
'Baronne Henriette Snoy'
'Blumenschmidt'
'Capitaine Millet'
'Clementina Carbonieri'
'Comtesse Alban de Villeneuve'
'Comtesse Bardi'
'Comtesse Julie Hunyady'
'Comtesse Riza du Parc'
'Dr. Grill'
'Dr. Pouleur'
'Duc de Magenta'
'Duchesse Marie Salviati'
'Edmond Sablayrolles'
'Edouard Gautier'
'Émilie Gonin'
'Erzherzog Franz Ferdinand'
'Helen Good'
'Hovyn de Tronchère'
'Hugo Roller'
'Impératrice Maria Féodorowna de Russie'
'Marie Van Houtte'
'Miss Marston'
'Mlle Anna Charron'
'Mlle Emma Vercellone'
'Mlle Jeanne Guillaumez'
'Mlle Jeanne Philippe'
'Mme Claire Jaubert'
'Mme de St.-Joseph'
'Mme de Watteville'
'Mme Jacques Charreton'
'Mme la Baronne Berge'
'Mme la Princesse de Bessaraba
    de Brancovan'
'Mme Lambard'
'Mrs. James Wilson'
'Princess of Wales'
'Princesse Étienne de Croy'
'Recuerdo di Antonio Peluffo'
'Rosette Delizy'
'Rosomane Narcisse Thomas'
'Souvenir de Gilbert Nabonnand'
'Souvenir de Mme Lambard'
'Souvenir de Paul Neyron'
'Souvenir de Victor Hugo'
'Souvenir de William Robinson'
'Souvenir du Rosiériste Rambaux'
'The Alexandra'
'Thérèse Lambert'

Bourbons
'Mme Edmond Laporte'
'Mme Pierre Oger'

Hybrid Bourbons, Hybrid Chinas, and Hybrid Noisettes
— None —

Hybrid Perpetuals
'Catherine Soupert'
'Comte de Nanteuil'
'Frédéric Schneider II'
'Frère Marie Pierre'
'Turnvater Jahn'

Noisettes & Climbers
'Beauté Inconstante' (N)
'Caroline Schmitt'
'Claire Carnot'
'Comte de Torres' (HT)
'Dr. Lande' (T)
'Elie Beauvilain' (N)
'Fortune's Double Yellow' (Cl)
'Gloire de Dijon' (N)
'L'Idéal' (N)
'Lady Waterlow' (HT)
'Marie Van Houtte, Cl.' (T)
'Mme Hector Leuilliot' (HT)
'Monsieur Georges de Cadoudal' (T)

'Pavillon de Pregny' (N)
'Perle d'Or, Cl.' (Pol)
'Phyllis Bide' (Pol)
'Souvenir d'Emile Zola' (HT)
'Souvenir de Mme Léonie Viennot' (N)

Polyanthas
'Excellens'
'Fireglow'
'Jeanne Drivon'
'Perle d'Or'
'Perle Orléanaise'

'Petite Léonie'
'Schneekopf'
'Tip-Top'

Hybrid Teas
'Comte Henri Rignon'
'Ellen Wilmott'
'Ferdinand Batel'
'Julius Finger'
'Mme Jean Favre'
'Monsieur Bunel'

Striped or Mottled

Damask Perpetuals
'Marbrée'
'Panachée de Lyon'

Chinas
— None —

Teas
'American Banner'
'Improved Rainbow'
'Mystère'
'Rainbow'

Bourbons
'Bijou de Royat-les-Bains'
'Honorine de Brabant'
'Rouge Marbrée'
'Variegata di Bologna'

Hybrid Bourbons, Hybrid Chinas, and Hybrid Noisettes
— None —

Hybrid Perpetuals
'Baron Girod de l'Ain'
'Coquette Bordelaise'
'Ferdinand Pichard'
'Fontenelle'
'François Olin'

'Louis Calla'
'Marguerite Lecureaux'
'Merrie England'
'Mme Auguste van Geert'
'Mme Desirée Giraud'
'Mme Petit'
'Mrs. Harkness'
'Panachée d'Angers'
'Panachée d'Orléans'
'Panachée Langroise'
'Pride of Reigate'
'Robert de Brie'
'Roger Lambelin'
'Royat Mondain'
'Souvenir de Mme Jeanne Balandreau'
'Thomas Mills'
'Vick's Caprice'

Noisettes & Climbers
'Mme Driout' (N)
'Mme Louis Blanchet' (N)
'Pride of Reigate, Cl.' (HP)

Polyanthas
'Cyclope'
'Floribunda'

Hybrid Teas
'Captain Christy Panaché'
'Mme Angelique Veysset'

Leaves Striped or Mottled

Only — 'Souvenir de Mme Ladvocat' (N)

Appendix Nine
GIGANTEA HYBRIDS

The following group, though usually listed as "Teas" or "Climbers," without further clarification, are derived from *R. gigantea*. As such, they may be of particular interest to collectors who wish to specialize.

Listed with the Teas:
'Baxter Beauty'
'Lorraine Lee'
'Susan Louise'

Listed with the Climbers:
'Belle Blanca'
'Belle Portugaise'
'Climbing Cracker'
'Climbing Lorraine Lee'
'Cooper's Burmese Rose'
'Doris Downes'
'Emmanuella de Mouchy'
'Étoile de Portugal'
'Flying Colours'
'Fortune's Double Yellow' (?)
'Gigantea Blanc'
'Glory of California'
'Kitty Kininmonth'
'Lafollette'
'Montecito'
'Montarioso'
'Nancy Hayward'
'Pennant'
'Sénateur Amic'

Appendix Ten
A STATEMENT, A LETTER, A SALUTATION

"A statement I saw some time ago in a gardening paper made me a little sad. It was a letter from a head gardener, who said—I cannot remember the exact words—that the improvement of late years in Tea and Hybrid Tea Roses had been so great that he was planting nothing else, and was doing away entirely with all Hybrid Perpetuals. Now this is one of those wholesale and wanton followings of fashion that, I confess, exasperate me not a little. Why discard one beautiful thing because another is as, or even more, beautiful? Why turn our backs on the old and faithful friend, because forsooth the new acquaintance pleases us? Are our hearts so small and mean that we have not room in them for more than one liking at a time? Moreover in all things the slavish following of a fashion because it is a fashion, whatever its intrinsic merits, is odious and unworthy, reducing sentient human beings to the level of a flock of sheep hurrying blindly and foolishly through a gap. . . . I am sick of that word 'fashion'; and now, that it should be imported into our gardens, into the culture of God's loveliest gifts to poor man, into the purest, sweetest, most sane and wholesome of recreations, is indeed too much. But so it is, alas! and we hear on all sides, from morning till night, not that Hybrid Teas are beautiful, but that they 'are all the fashion.' . . . I would as soon drown one of my homely tabby cats because it was not a pale lavender Persian, as destroy my Hybrid Perpetuals because they were not Tea Roses; and though I should be charmed to possess a lavender Persian as well as the humble tabby, I can thoroughly appreciate the delights and merits of the very newest Tea Rose without abating one jot of my love for 'Ulrich Brunner [fils]', 'Duke of Edinburgh', 'Mrs. John Laing', . . . the dear old 'Général Jacqueminot', or the new and superb 'Frau Karl Druschki'. For without blindly following the fashion of the moment, it is singularly foolish to despise what is new, if at the same time it is worthy of admiration." [K1]

— ✳ —

From R-H43:

"Bellevue, November 20, 1843.

"In our discussion concerning roses yesterday at my nursery, you told me that you did not believe that I could develop any rose more beautiful than 'La Reine'. I told you that, in my opinion, roses still haven't reached their apogee. Indeed, the more a person advances with his seedlings, the more he merely advances in a botanical labyrinth. The more I sow, the more I see the immensity of what lies before me! . . . You see, Monsieur, all a person needs is faith. . . .

Laffay"

— ✳ —

" 'Goodbye, summer. Good-bye, good-bye!'

"As the leaves fall, our hearts are heavy. We feel the cold of winter as the roses feel it, but we cannot slumber in the earth till spring wakens us . . . at least not yet.

"But away with sentiment! let us think only of next year's roses, and of the sun which is shining behind the clouds."
[HmC]

BIBLIOGRAPHY

Key to Citations

ADE: Departmental Archives of Essonne at Corbeil, France.
ADVDM: Departmental Archives of Val-de-Marne at Creteil, France.
ADY: Departmental Archives of Yvelines at Versailles, France.
An: *Annales de Flore et de Pomone.* 1832–1848.
ARA16 (*et seq.*): *American Rose Annual.* 1916–1940. Quoted by kind permission of the American Rose Society.
Au: *The Australasian Rose Book,* by R. G. Elliott, ca. 1925.
B: *Peter Beales Roses* catalog, 1985. Quoted by kind permission of Peter Beales.
B1:   *Classic Roses,* by Peter Beales, 1985. Quoted by kind permission of Peter Beales.
BCD: Interpolated comments by Brent C. Dickerson.
BJ: *Le Bon Jardinier,* 1869 edition.
Bk: *Roses and How to Grow Them,* by Edwin Beckett, 1918.
Br: *A Year in a Lancashire Garden,* by Henry Bright, 1879.
BSA: *The Garden Book of California,* by Belle Sumner Angier, 1906.
Bu: *The Rose Manual,* by Robert Buist, 1844.
B&V: *List of Roses Now in Cultivation at Chateau Eléonore, Cannes . . . ,* by Henry Charles Brougham,
                     3rd Baron Brougham and Vaux, 1898.
C: *Beauties of the Rose,* by Henry Curtis, 1850–1853. Facsimile reprint, 1980, by Sweetbriar Press;
                     additional material by Léonie Bell.
CaRoI (*et seq.*): *The California Rosarian,* published by the California Rose Society 1930–1932.
CA88 (*et seq.*): *Descriptive Catalogue,* California Nursery Company, 1888 *et sequitur.*
Capt27:   Article "Tea Roses for Southern Climates" by Capt. George C. Thomas, in ARA27.
Capt28:   Article "Climbing Roses for Southern Climates" by Capt. George C. Thomas in ARA28.
Cat12:   *Official Catalogue of Roses,* by the [British] National Rose Society, 1912 edition.
CC: *Catalogue* for the Wasamequia Nurseries, New Bedford, Mass., U.S.A., by Henry H. Crapo, 1848. In ARA26.
C'H: *Dictionnaire Universel des Plantes . . . ,* by Pierre-Joseph Buc'hoz, 1770.
C&Jf: *Fall Catalog,* The Conard & Jones Co., 1897–1924. Quoted by kind permission of the Conard-Pyle Co.
C&Js: *Spring Catalog,* The Conard & Jones Co., 1897–1924. Quoted by kind permission of the Conard-Pyle Co.
C-Pf: *Fall Catalog,* The Conard-Pyle Co., 1925–1934. Quoted by kind permission of the Conard-Pyle Co.
C-Ps: *Spring Catalog,* The Conard-Pyle Co., 1925–1934. Quoted by kind permission of the Conard-Pyle Co.
C-T: *Almanach des Roses,* by Claude-Thomas Guerrapain, 1811.
Cw: *La Rose Historique,* by Edm. Van Cauwenberghe, 1927.
Cx: *Les Plus Belles Roses au Debut du XX e Siècle,* by the Société Nationale d'Horticulture de France, 1912.
Cy: *The French Revolution. A History,* by Thomas Carlyle, 1837.
Cy2:   *Oliver Cromwell's Letters and Speeches,* 3rd Edition, by Thomas Carlyle, 1849.
D: *A General History and Collection of Voyages and Travels,* by Robert Kerr, 1824.
dH: *Journal d'Horticulture Pratique et de Jardinage,* 1844-1847, edited by Martin-Victor Paquet.
DO: *Roses for Amateurs,* by Rev. H. Honywood D'Ombrain, 1908.
DP: Article "My Favorites . . . " by D. Bruce Phillips in *Pacific Horticulture,* vol. 43, no. 3, 1982.
                     Quoted by kind permission of *Pacific Horticulture.*
Dr: *Everblooming Roses,* by Georgia Torrey Drennan, 1912.
DuC: *The Flowers and Gardens of Madeira,* by Florence DuCane, 1909.
E: *Gardens of England,* by E.T. Cook, 1911.
ECS: City Archives of Soisy-sous-Etioles, France.
Ed: *The Amateur's Rosarium,* by R. Wodrow Thomson, 1862.
EER: Article "A Short History of the Tea Rose" by E. E. Robinson, in *The Rose,* vol. 17, no. 3, 1969.
EER2:   Article "The Early Hybrid Perpetuals" by E. E. Robinson, in *The Rose,* vol. 13, no. 3, 1965.
EJW: *California Garden-Flowers,* by E. J. Wickson, 1915.
EL: *The Rose,* by Henry B. Ellwanger, 1882.
ElC: Article "Old Roses and New Roses" by Henry B. Ellwanger, in *Century Magazine,* vol. 4, 1883.
ET: Article "Help Wanted in Texas?" by Edward Teas, from ARA28.
ExRé: *Guide pour servir à la visite de notre Exposition Rétrospective de la Rose . . . ,* by Roseraie de l'Haÿ, 1910.
F: *Les Roses,* by Louis Fumierre, 1910.
Fa: *In A Yorkshire Garden,* by Reginald Farrer, 1909.
Fl: *The Florist,* vol. I, 1848.
F-M: *The Book of the Rose,* 4th edition, by Andrew Foster-Melliar, 1910.
F-M2:   *The Book of the Rose,* 2nd edition, by Andrew Foster-Melliar, 1902.
F-M3:   *The Book of the Rose,* 1st edition, by Andrew Foster-Melliar, 1894.
F-M4:   *The Book of the Rose,* 3rd edition, by Andrew Foster-Melliar, 1905.

FP: *The Book of Roses,* by Francis Parkman, 1871.

Fr: *Dictionnaire du Jardinier Français,* by Monsieur Fillassier, 1791.

FRB: *Tea Roses,* by F. R. Burnside, 1893.

G: *Book of Old Roses,* by Trevor Griffiths, 1984. Quoted by kind permission of the publishers, Michael Joseph, Ltd.

GAS: *Climbing Roses,* by G.A. Stevens, 1933. Quoted by kind permission of the copyright holder, The McFarland Co.

G&B: *Roses,* by Gemen & Bourg, ca. 1908.

GG: *In A Gloucestershire Garden,* by Henry N. Ellacombe, 1896.

Gl: *The Culture of Flowers and Plants,* by George Glenny, 1861.

Go: *The Rose Fancier's Manual,* by Mrs. Gore, 1838.

Gx: *"La Malmaison" Les Roses de l'Impératrice Joséphine,* by Jules Gravereaux, 1912.

H: *A Book About Roses,* by S. Reynolds Hole, 1906.

Hd: *The Amateur's Rose Book,* by Shirley Hibberd, 1874.

Hj: Unpublished correspondence with Thomasville Nurseries, Inc. Quoted by kind permission of Thomasville Nurseries, Inc.

Hk: *Roses,* by Jack Harkness, 1978. Quoted by kind permission of Jack Harkness.

HmC: *My Roses and How I Grew Them,* by Helen (Crofton) Milman, 1899.

Hn: *The Amateur Gardener's Rose Book,* by Julius Hoffmann, English translation by John Weathers, 1905.

HoBoIV: *The Horticultural Review and Botanical Magazine,* 1854.

HRG: *Catalog,* 1985, and unpublished correspondence, Heritage Rose Gardens. Quoted by kind permission of Heritage Rose Gardens.

HRH: *A Gardener's Year,* by H. Rider Haggard, 1905.

HstI (*et seq.*):   *The Horticulturist,* 1846–1875.

Ht: *Le Livre d'Or des Roses,* by Paul Hariot, 1904.

Hÿ: *Les Roses Cultivées à l'Haÿ en 1902,* by André Theuriet, 1902.

J: *Roses for English Gardens,* by Gertrude Jekyll, 1902.

JC: *Cultural Directions for the Rose,* 6th edition, by John Cranston, 1877.

JDR54 (*et seq.*):   *Journal des Roses,* 1854–1859, edited by Jean Cherpin.

JF: *Les Roses,* by Hippolyte Jamain and Eugène Forney, 1873.

Jg: *Rosenlexicon,* by August Jäger, 1970.

JP: *Roses: Their History, Development, and Cultivation,* by Rev. Joseph H. Pemberton, 1920.

JR1 (*et seq.*):   *Journal des Roses,* 1877–1914, edited by Cochet & Bernardin.

K: *The Rose Manual,* by J.H. Nicolas, 1938. Quoted by kind permission of the publishers, Doubleday & Co., Inc.

K1:   *Eversley Gardens and Others,* by Rose G. Kingsley, 1907.

K2:   *Roses and Rose-Growing,* by Rose G. Kingsley, 1908.

Kr: *The Complete Book of Roses,* by Gerd Krüssmann, 1981. Quoted by permission of the publisher, Timber Press.

L: *Gardening in California,* 3rd revised edition, by William S. Lyon, 1904.

LaQ: *Instruction Pour les Jardins Frutiers et Potagiers . . . ,* by Jean De La Quintinye, 1695.

Lc: *Les Rosiers,* by Jean Lachaume, revised by Georges Bellair, ca. 1921.

L-D: *La Rose . . . ,* by Jean Louis Augustine Loiseleur-Deslongchamps, 1844.

LF: *Prix Courant des Espèces et Variétés de Roses,* by Jean Laffay, 1841.

LF1:   Death Certificate of Jean Laffay, Town Records of the Municipality of Cannes, France, 1878.

Lg: *Catalog,* 1985, Liggett's Rose Nursery. Quoted by kind permission of Tom and Christine Liggett.

l'H: *L'Horticulteur Français,* 1851–1872.

LR: *La Rose,* by J. Bel, 1892.

LS: *Nomenclature de Tous les Noms de Roses,* 2nd edition, by Léon Simon, 1906.

Lu: *Luther Burbank. His Methods and Discoveries,* vol. IX, by Luther Burbank, 1914.

M: *Gardening in California,* by Sidney B. Mitchell, 1923. Quoted by kind permission of the publishers, Doubleday & Co., Inc.

MCN: *Minutier Centrale des Notaires* at the French National Archives in Paris, France.

M'I: *The Book of the Garden,* by Charles M'Intosh, 1855.

M-L: *Travaux du Comice Horticole de Maine et Loire.* I have been able to examine fragments by Mons Millet from the years 1843, 1846, 1847, 1848, and 1849.

MLS: Article "Roses in Kansas City" by Minnie Long Sloan in ARA28.

M-P: *The Culture of Perennials,* by Dorothy M-P. Cloud, 1925. Quoted by kind permission of the publishers, Dodd, Mead & Company, Inc.

MR8:   *Modern Roses 8,* published by The McFarland Company, 1980. Quoted by kind permission of The American Rose Society and The McFarland Company.

M-V: *L'Instructeur Jardinier,* 1848–1851, edited by Martin-Victor Paquet.

N: *Die Rose,* by Thomas Nietner, 1880.

No: *Manuel Complet du Jardinier,* by Louis Noisette, 1825.

NRS10 (*et seq.*):   *Rose Annual,* 1910–1930, by the (British) National Rose Society. Quoted by kind permission of the Royal National Rose Society.

OM: *The Rose Book,* by H. H. Thomas, 1916.

P: *The Rose Garden,* 1st edition, by William Paul, 1848.

P1:	*The Rose Garden,* 10th edition, by William Paul, 1903.
P2:	*Contributions to Horticultural Literature, 1843–1892,* 1892.
Pd:	*Le Bilan d'Un Siècle,* by Alfred Picard, tome 3, 1906.
pH:	*Henderson's Handbook of Plants and General Horticulture,* "New Edition" (*i.e.,* 2nd), by Peter Henderson, 1889.
PlB:	*Choix des Plus Belles Roses,* by Martin-Victor Paquet *et al.,* 1845–1854.
PP28:	Article "Proof of the Pudding" in ARA28.
Pq:	*Le Jardinier Pratique,* by Jacquin and Rousselon, 1852.
PS:	Article "Roses in Brazil," by Mrs. Paul C. Schilling in ARA28.
R1 (*et seq.*):	*The Garden,* vols. I–VII, "founded and conducted by William Robinson," 1872–1875
R8:	*The Rose-Amateur's Guide,* 8th edition, by Thomas Rivers, 1863.
RATS:	Article "Roses Across the Sea" in ARA28.
R-H29 (*et seq.*):	*Revue Horticole,* issues 1829–1877. Quoted by kind permission of the publishers.
R-HC:	*Revue Horticole,* centenary number, 1929. Quoted by kind permission of the publishers.
Riv:	*Roses et Rosiers,* by Rivoire père & fils, with Marcel Ebel, 1933.
RJC60 (*et seq.*):	*Revue des Jardins et des Champs,* 1860–1871, edited by Jean Cherpin.
Ro:	*The English Flower-Garden,* 8th edition, by William Robinson, 1903.
RP:	Article "Roses — The Ophelia Strain and Kindred Spirits" by Reginald Parker in *The Rose,* vol. 13, no. 3, 1965.
RR:	Article "Check List of Red Tea Roses" by R. Robinson, in *The Rose,* vol. 13, no. 1, 1964.
RZ86:	*Rosen-Zeitung,* vol. I, 1886.
S:	*Dictionnaire des Roses,* by Max Singer, 1885.
SBP:	*Parsons on the Rose,* by Samuel B. Parsons, 1888.
SHj:	Article "Old Roses for the South," 1949, and Address "Tea Roses for Florida,' 1951, by Samuel J. Hjort. Quoted by kind permission of Sarah L. Hjort of Thomasville Nurseries, Inc.
SHP:	*Annales de la Société d'Horticulture de Paris.*
Sn:	*Rosenverzeichnis,* 3rd edition, Rosarium Sangerhausen, 1976.
SNH:	*Journal de la Société Nationale d'Horticulture.*
Sx:	*The American Rose Culturalist,* by C.M. Saxton, 1860.
T1:	*The Old Shrub Roses,* by Graham S. Thomas, 1956. Quoted by kind permission of the author and of the publishers J. M. Dent & Sons, Ltd.
T1H:	Writings of Dr. Hurst in *The Old Shrub Roses* by Graham S. Thomas.
T2:	*Climbing Roses Old and New,* by Graham S. Thomas, 1983. Quoted by kind permission of the author and of the publishers J. M. Dent & Sons, Ltd.
T3:	*Shrub Roses of Today,* by Graham S. Thomas, 1980. Quoted by kind permission of the author and of the publishers J. M. Dent & Sons, Ltd.
Th:	*The Practical Book of Outdoor Rose Growing,* by Captain George C. Thomas, 1920. Quoted by very kind permission of the Thomas family.
Th2:	*Roses for All American Climates,* by Captain George C. Thomas, 1924. Quoted by very kind permission of the Thomas family.
TS:	Article "Roses of Australia" by T. A. Stewart in ARA28.
TW:	*Cultivated Roses,* by T. W. Sanders, 1899.
UB28:	Article "Unfinished Business" in ARA28.
V1:	*Observations sur la Nomenclature et le Classement des Roses,* by Jean-Pierre Vibert, 1820.
V2:	*Essai sur les Roses,* by Jean-Pierre Vibert, 1824–1830.
V3:	*Catalogue,* by Jean-Pierre Vibert, 1826.
V4:	*Catalogue,* by Jean-Pierre Vibert, 1836.
V5:	Page from town records of Montfort l'Amaury containing *l'Acte de décès* concerning the death of Jean-Pierre Vibert, 1866.
V6:	*Le Movement Horticole,* 1866.
V7:	Minutes of the February 8, 1866, meeting of the *conseil d'administration de la Société Nationale d'Horticulture.*
V8:	*Catalogue,* by Jean-Pierre Vibert, 1844.
VD:	Article "Roses on the Mexican Coast" by V. E. Dillon in ARA28.
V-H:	*Flore des Serres et des Jardins de l'Europe,* by Louis Van Houtte, 1845–1880.
VPt:	*Almanach Horticole,* 1844–1848, edited by Martin-Victor Paquet.
W:	*Climbing Roses,* by Helen Van Pelt Wilson, 1955. Quoted by kind permission of Helen Van Pelt Wilson.
WD:	*Roses and Their Culture,* 3rd edition, by W. D. Prior, 1892.
W/Hn:	Interpolations by translator John Weathers in *The Amateur Gardener's Rose Book,* by Julius Hoffmann, 1905.
WHoI (*et seq.*):	*The Western Horticultural Review,* 1850–1853.
Wr:	*Roses and Rose Gardens,* by Walter P. Wright, 1911.
WRP:	*Manual of Roses,* by William R. Prince, 1846.
Ÿ:	*Inventaire de la Collection,* 1984, Roseraie de l'Haÿ-les- Roses. Quoted by kind permission of the *Service des Espaces Vertes* of the government of the Republic of France.

Works Consulted

Almanach Horticole. 1844–1848. Ed. Martin-Victor Paquet. Paris: Cousin.

American Rose Annual. 1916–1940. Published by the American Rose Society.

Les Amis des Roses. 1946–1961. Published by the Société Française des Rosiéristes.

Anderson, Frank J. 1979. *An Illustrated Treasury of Redouté Roses.* NY: Abbeville Press.

Annales de Flore et de Pomone. 1832–1848. Paris: Rousselon.

Angier, Belle Sumner. 1906. *The Garden Book of California.* San Francisco: P. Elder & Co.

Barron, Leonard. 1905. *Roses and How to Grow Them.* New York: Doubleday.

Beales, Peter. 1985. *Classic Roses.* London: Collins Harville.

Beales, Peter. 1979. *Edwardian Roses.* Norwich, England: Jarrold.

Beales, Peter. 1979. *Late Victorian Roses.* Norwich, England: Jarrold.

Beales, Peter. 1985. Peter Beales Roses *Catalogue, 1985.* Attleborough, England: Beales.

Bean, W. J. 1980. *Trees and Shrubs Hardy in the British Isles,* 8th edition. London: St. Martin's.

Beckett, Edwin 1918. *Roses and How to Grow Them.* London: C. A. Pearson.

Bel, J. 1892. *La Rose.* Paris: Baillière.

Le Bon Jardinier, 2 vols., 1869 edition. Paris: Maison Rustique.

Breon, Nicolas. 1825. *Catalogue des Plantes Cultivées aux Jardins Botanique et de Naturalisation de l'Ile Bourbon.* St.-Denis, Île-Bourbon: Impr. du Gouv.

Bright, Henry. 1879. *A Year in a Lancashire Garden.* London: Macmillan.

Brougham, Henry Charles, 3rd Baron Brougham & Vaux. 1898. *List of Roses Now in Cultivation at Chateau Eléonore, Cannes . . .* London: Bumpus.

Buc'hoz, Pierre-Joseph. 1770. *Dictionnaire Universel des Plantes . . .* Paris: Lacombe.

Buist, Robert. 1844. *The Rose Manual.* Philadelphia: Buist.

Bunyard, Edward A. 1936. *Old Garden Roses.* London: Country Life.

Burbank, Luther. 1914. *Luther Burbank. His Methods and Discoveries.* New York & London: Luther Burbank Press.

Burnside, F. R. 1893. *Tea Roses.* Hereford, England: Jakeman & Carver.

California Nursery Company. 1888 *et sequitur. Catalogue.* Niles, California: California Nursery Company.

The California Rosarian. 1930–1932. Point Loma, California: California Rose Society.

Cannes, France. Town Records.

Carlyle, Thomas. 1837. *The French Revolution. A History.* Rpt. New York: Modern Library, no date.

Carlyle, Thomas. 1849. *Oliver Cromwell's Letters and Speeches,* 3rd edition. Chicago: Belford, Clark & Co.

Cauwenberghe, Edm. Van. 1927. *La Rose Historique . . .* Brussels: Féd. des Soc. Hort.

Cloud, Dorothy M.-P. 1925. *The Culture of Perennials.* New York: Dodd, Mead & Co.

Comice Horticole de Maine et Loire. 1843, 1846–1849. *Travaux du Comice Horticole de Maine et Loire.*

The Conard & Jones Co. 1897–1924. *Catalog.* West Grove, Pennsylvania: Conard & Jones.

The Conard-Pyle Co. 1925–1934. *Catalog.* West Grove, Pennsulvania: Conard-Pyle.

Cook, E. T. 1911. *Gardens of England.* London: Black.

Cranston, John. 1877. *Cultural Directions for the Rose,* 6th edition. Liverpool, England: Blake & Mackenzie.

Crapo, Henry H. 1848. *Catalogue for the Wasamequia Nurseries, New Bedford, Mass.* Rpt. American Rose Annual 1926.

Curtis, Henry. 1850–1853. *Beauties of the Rose.* Bristol, England: Lavars.

Descemet, Jean. 1741. *Catalogue de Plantes du Jardin de M^{rs} les Apoticaires de Paris.* Paris: no impr.

Dickerson, Brent C. 1982–1983. Education of a Gardener. *Pacific Horticulture* (Winter): 8–10.

Dickerson, Brent C. 1990. Handbook of Old Roses. In manuscript.

Dickerson, Brent C. 1990. Notes Towards an Understanding of 19th Century Rose-Breeding. *The Yellow Rose* (March): 2–6.

Dickerson, Brent C. 1986. Review of the book *Classic Roses* by Peter Beales. *Pacific Horticulture* (Summer): 57.

Dickerson, Brent C. (*inter alia*). 1987. Roses, a Symposium. *Pacific Horticulture* (Spring): 28–31.

Dickerson, Brent C. 1989. The Portland Rose. *The Garden/Journal of the Royal Horticultural Society* (January): 9–14.

Dobson, Beverly. 1985. *Combined Rose List 1985.* Irvington, New York: Dobson.

Dobson, Beverly. 1987. *Combined Rose List 1987.* Irvington, New York: Dobson.

D'Ombrain, Rev. H. Honywood. 1908. *Roses for Amateurs.* London: L. Upcott Gill

Drennan, Georgia Torrey. 1912. *Everblooming Roses.* New York: Duffield.

DuCane, Florence. 1909. *The Flowers and Gardens of Madeira.* London: Black.

Elliott, R.G. No date (ca. 1925). *The Australasian Rose Book.* Melbourne: Whitcombe & Tombs.

Ellacombe, Henry N. 1896. *In a Gloucestershire Garden.* London: Arnold.

Ellwanger, Henry B. 1882. *The Rose.* New York: Dodd, Mead & Co.

Ellwanger, Henry B. 1883. "Old and New Roses." *Century Magazine* 26:350–358.

Farrer, Reginald. 1909. *In A Yorkshire Garden.* London: Arnold.

Festing, Sally. 1986. The Second Duchess of Portland and Her Rose. *Garden History* 14:194–200.

Fillassier, Monsieur. 1791. *Dictionnaire du Jardinier Français.* Paris: Desoer.

Fillery, J.W. 1960. *Old Fashioned Roses in New Zealand.* Ilfracombe, NZ: Stockwell.

Foster-Melliar, Andrew. 1894. *The Book of the Rose,* 1st edition. London: Macmillan.

Foster-Melliar, Andrew. 1902. *The Book of the Rose,* 2nd edition. London: Macmillan.

Foster-Melliar, Andrew. 1905. *The Book of the Rose,* 3rd edition. London: Macmillan.

Foster-Melliar, Andrew. 1910. *The Book of the Rose,* 4th edition. London: Macmillan.

Fumierre, Louis. 1910. *Les Roses.* Rouen: Cagniard.

Gemen & Bourg. No date (ca. 1908). *Roses.* Luxembourg: Impr. Victor Buck.

Glenny, George. 1861. *The Culture of Flowers and Plants.* London: Houlston.

Gore, Mrs. Catherine Grace Francis. 1838. *The Rose Fancier's Manual.* London: Colburn.

Gravereaux, Jules. 1912. *"La Malmaison" Les Roses de l'Impératrice Joséphine.* Paris: Ed. d'Art.

Griffiths, Trevor. 1987. *The Book of Classic Old Roses.* London: Michael Joseph.

Griffiths, Trevor. 1984. *The Book of Old Roses.* London: Michael Joseph.

Guerrapain, Claude-Thomas. 1811. *Almanach des Roses.* Troyes: Gobelet.

Haggard, H. Rider. 1905. *A Gardener's Year.* London: Longmans Green

Harkness, Jack. 1978. *Roses.* London: Dent.

Hariot, Paul. 1904. *Le Livre d'Or des Roses.* Paris: Laveur.

Henderson, Peter. 1889. *Henderson's Handbook of Plants and General Horticulture.* New York: Henderson.

Heritage Rose Gardens. 1985. *Catalog.* Branscomb, California: Heritage Rose Gardens.

Hibberd, Shirley. 1874. *The Amateur's Rose Book.* London: Groomsbridge.

Hjort, Samuel C. 1949. Old Roses for the South. In unknown periodical.

Hjort, Samuel C. 1951. Tea Roses for Florida. Lecture.

Hoffmann, Julius. 1905. *The Amateur's Rose Book,* trans. John Weathers. London: Longmans Green.

Hole, S. Reynolds. 1906. *A Book About Roses.* London: E. Arnold.

The Horticultural Review and Botanical Magazine. 1854. Cincinnati.

The Horticulturist. 1846–1875. Ed. A.J. Downing *et al.* New York.

How to Grow Roses. 1980. Ed. Sunset Books. Menlo Park, California: Lane.

Jacquin, P.-J., and Rousselon, H. 1852. *Le Jardinier Pratique.* Paris: Lefèvre & Guérin

Jäger, August. 1970. *Rosenlexicon.* Leipzig: Zentralantiquariat.

Jamain, Hippolyte, and Forney, Eugène. 1873. *Les Roses.* Paris: Rothschild.

Jekyll, Gertrude. 1902. *Roses for English Gardens.* London: Country Life.

Journal de la Société Nationale d'Horticulture, 1863, 1865, 1879.

Journal d'Horticulture Pratique et de Jardinage. 1844–1847. Paris: Cousin

Journal des Roses. 1854–1859. Lyon: Cherpin

Journal des Roses. 1877–1914. Melun: Cochet.

Keays, Ethelyn Emery. 1936. *Old Roses.* New York: Macmillan.

Kerr, Robert. 1824. *A General History and Collection of Voyages and Travels.* Edinburgh: Blackwood.

Kingsley, Rose G. 1907. *Eversley Gardens and Others.* London: Allen.

Kingsley, Rose G. 1908. *Roses and Rose-Growing.* New York: Macmillan.

Krüssmann, Gerd. 1981. *The Complete Book of Roses.* Portland, Oregon: Timber Press/American Horticultural Society.

La Quintinye, Jean De. 1693. *The Complete Gard'ner,* trans. John Evelyn. London: Gillyflower.

La Quintinye, Jean De. 1695. *Instruction pour les Jardins Fruitiers et Potagers . . .* Geneva: Ritter.

Lachaume, Jean. No date (ca. 1921). *Les Rosiers,* revised by Georges Bellair. Paris: Maison Rustique.

Laffay, Jean. 1841. *Prix Courant des Espèces et Variétés de Roses . . .* Bellevue-Meudon: Laffay.

Le Movement Horticole. 1866.

Leproux, Dominique. 1986. Les Roses Anciennes, un marché en expansion. Revue-Horticole. 40-41.

L'Horticulteur Français. 1851–1872. Paris: Hérincq.

Liggett's Rose Nursery. 1985. *Catalog.* San Jose, California: Liggett.

L'Instructeur Jardinier. 1848–1851. Paris: Paquet.

Loiseleur-Deslongchamps, Jean Louis Augustine. 1844. *La Rose . . .* Paris: Audot.

Lyon, William S. *Gardening in California.* 3rd revised edition, 1904. Los Angeles: G. Rice.

M'Intosh, Charles. 1855. *The Book of the Garden.* Edinburgh: Blackwood.

McFarland, J. Horace. 1928. *Roses and How to Grow Them.* Garden City, NY: Doubleday.

Milman, Helen (Crofton). 1899. *My Roses and How I Grew Them.* London: Lane.

Mitchell, Sydney B. 1923. *Gardening in California.* New York: Doubleday.

Modern Roses 8. 1980. Harrisburg, Pennsylvania: The McFarland Company.

Montaigne, Michel Eyquem de. 1962. *Œuvres Complètes.* Stanford, California: Stanford.

Montfort l'Amaury, France. Town records.

National [British] Rose Society. 1912. *Official Catalogue of Roses.* Croyden, England: National Rose Society.

Nicolas, J. H. 1938. *The Rose Manual.* New York: Doubleday.

Nietner, Thomas. 1880. *Die Rose.* Berlin: Hempel & Parey.

Noisette, Louis. 1825. *Manuel Complet du Jardinier.* Paris: Rousselon.

Nottle, Trevor. 1983. *Growing Old-Fashioned Roses.* Kangaroo Press.

Paquet, Martin-Victor (*inter alia*). 1845–1854. *Choix des Plus Belles Roses,* plates by A. Bricogne, text by M.-V. Paquet, P. C. Ruoillard, and others, edited by M.-V. Paquet. Paris: Dusacq.

Parker, Reginald. 1965. Roses, the Ophelia Strain and Kindred Spirits. *The Rose* 13:3:173–180.

Parkman, Francis. 1871. *The Book of Roses.* Boston: Tilton.

Parsons, Samuel B. 1888. *Parsons on the Rose.* New York: Orange Judd.

Paul, William. 1892. *Contributions to Horticultural Literature, 1843–1892*. Waltham Cross: Paul.

Paul, William. 1848. *The Rose Garden,* 1st edition. London: Sherwood, Gilbert, & Piper.

Paul, William. 1903. *The Rose Garden,* 10th edition. London: Simpkin.

Pemberton, Rev. Joseph J. 1920. *Roses: Their History, Development, and Cultivation*. London: Longmans Green.

Phillips, D. Bruce. 1982. My Favorites . . . *Pacific Horticulture* 43:3:28–32.

Phillips, Roger, and Rix, Martyn. 1988. *Roses*. New York: Random House.

Picard, Alfred. 1906. *Le Bilan d'Un Siècle*. Paris: Impr. Nationale.

Prince, William R. 1846. *Prince's Manual of Roses*. New York: Clark & Austin

Prior, W. D. 1892. *Roses and their Culture,* 3rd edition. London: Routledge.

Redouté, P. J. 1978. *P.J. Redouté Roses*. Location unknown: Miller Graphics.

Revue des Jardins et des Champs. 1860–1862. Paris: Cherpin

Revue Horticole. 1829–1877. Paris: Librarie Agricole.

Revue Horticole. 1929. Special centenary number. Paris: Maison Rustique.

Rivers, Thomas. 1863. *The Rose-Amateur's Guide,* 8th edition. London: Longmans Green.

Rivoire père et fils, and Ebel, Marcel. 1933. *Roses et Rosiers*. Paris: Baillière.

Robinson, E. E. 1969. A Short History of the Tea Rose. *The Rose* 17:3:178–183.

Robinson, E. E. 1964. The Early Hybrid Perpetuals. *The Rose* 13:3:195–201.

Robinson, R. 1964. Check List of Red Tea Roses. *The Rose* 13:1:62–67.

Robinson, William. 1903. *The English Flower-Garden,* 8th edition. London: Murray.

Rosarium Sangerhausen. No date (ca. 1980). *Der Welt Bedeutendster Rosengarten*. Sangerhausen, Germany: Rosarium Sangerhausen.

Rosarium Sangerhausen. 1976. *Rosenverzeichnis,* 3rd edition. Sangerhausen, Germany: Rosarium Sangerhausen.

Rosen-Zeitung. 1886. Frankfurt: Fey.

Roseraie de l'Haÿ. 1910. *Guide pour servir à la visite de notre Exposition Rétrospective de la Rose*. Paris: Exp. Int. d'Hort. de Paris.

Roseraie de l'Haÿ-les-Roses. 1984. *Inventaire de la Collection*. L'Haÿ, France: Conseil Gén. du Val de Marne.

Rose Annual. 1910–1930. Croyden, England: National [British] Rose Society.

Sanders, Thomas William. 1899. *Cultivated Roses*. London: Collingridge.

Saxton, C. M. 1860. *The American Rose Culturist*. New York: Saxton.

Simon, Léon. 1906. *Nomenclature de Tous les Noms de Roses,* 2nd edition. Paris: Libr. Hort.

Singer, Max. 1885. *Dictionnaire des Roses*. Tournai: Singer.

Société Nationale d'Horticulture de France. 1866. Minutes of the February 8, 1866 meeting of the *conseil d'administration*. Paris: Soc. Nat. d'Hort.

Société Nationale d'Horticulture de France. 1912. *Les Plus Belles Roses au Debut du XXᵉ Siècle*. Paris: Société Nationale d'Horticulture.

Stevens, G.A. 1933. *Climbing Roses*. New York: Macmillan.

Testu, Charlotte. 1984. *Les Roses Anciennes*. Paris: Flammarion.

The Florist & Pomologist. 1848. London.

The Florist & Horticultural Journal. 1852. Philadelphia.

The Garden. 1872–1875. London.

The Garden. 1987. London.

The Southern Horticulturalist. 1869. Tangipahoa, Louisiana.

The Western Horticultural Review. 1850–1853. Cincinnati.

Theuriet, André. 1902. *Les Roses Cultivées à l'Haÿ en 1902*. Grisy-Suisnes, France: Cochet.

Thomas, Capt. George C. 1920. *The Practical Book of Outdoor Rose Growing*. Philadelphia: J. B. Lippincott & Co.

Thomas, Capt. George C. 1924. *Roses for All American Climates*. New York: Macmillan.

Thomas, Graham S. 1983. *Climbing Roses Old and New*. London: Dent.

Thomas, Graham S. 1956. *The Old Shrub Roses*. London: Dent.

Thomas, Graham S. 1980. *Shrub Roses of Today*. London: Dent.

Thomas, Harry H. 1916. *The Rose Book*. London: Cassell.

Thomasville Nurseries, Inc. Unpublished correspondence. Thomasville, Georgia.

Thomson, R. Wodrow. 1862. *The Amateur's Rosarium*. Edinburgh: Paton & Ritchie.

Thomson, Richard. 1959. *Old Roses for Modern Gardens*. Princeton: Van Nostrand.

Van Houtte, Louis. 1845–1880. *Flore des Serres et des Jardins de l'Europe*. Ghent: Van Houtte.

Vibert, Jean-Pierre. 1824–1830. *Essai sur les Roses*. Paris: Mme Huzard.

Vibert, Jean-Pierre. 1820. *Observations sur la Nomenclature et le Classement des Roses*. Paris: Mme Huzard.

Vibert, Jean-Pierre. 1826. *Catalogue*. Paris: Mme Huzard.

Vibert, Jean-Pierre. 1831. *Catalogue*. Paris: Mme Huzard.

Vibert, Jean-Pierre. 1836. *Catalogue*. Paris: Mme Huzard.

Vibert, Jean-Pierre. 1844. *Catalogue*. Angers, France: Vibert.

Weston, Richard. 1775. *The English Flora* . . . London: Weston.

Weston, Richard. 1770. *The Universal Botanist and Nurseryman* . . . London: Bell.

Wickson, E. J. 1915. *California Garden-Flowers*. San Francisco: Pacific Rural.

Wilson, Helen Van Pelt. 1955. *Climbing Roses*. New York: Barrows.

Wright, Walter P. 1911. *Roses and Rose Gardens*. London: Headley.

Young, Norman. 1971. *The Complete Rosarian*. New York: St. Martin's.

Works Not Consulted

Not consulted due, in most cases, to unavailability, and, in a few cases, to prospects of very lean pickings. Occasionally, the neglected work was subsumed by another to which I was able to devote the requisite attention. To *point the way* is no less a valuable favor in fields of enquiry than to *conclude*; indeed, to toss a weighty tome down onto the desk of Public View meanwhile giving the world to understand that *this is it — there's nothing more to find out* is unfair to both subject and student. In the present case, not only is there much more to find out, there is also much more to review. Information about and from the *Orient* is sorely missed: "When we count over the numerous varieties of splendid flowering plants already received from China and Japan, it seems almost incredible to what an extent we are already indebted to those two countries, which have been hitherto so completely closed to us, that we have been kept in utter ignorance as to the extent of their Floral productions, except as regards those that have been obtained almost by stealth from their prolific shores."[WRP] The *German* side of matters has never been adequately treated. *Italian, Portuguese,* and *Spanish* rosarians and editors have doubtless made many important contributions which have been neglected, not to mention whole continents'-worth of experience existing in — but not emanating from—*Africa, South America,* and *Australia. Periodicals,* in their thirst for copy, publish many facts which never appear in books, facts which are particularly pertinent because they often reflect local conditions which would be of interest to horticulturalists gardening under similar conditions. Nurserymen's *Catalogs* have much value, and in some cases contain interesting short essays by or about breeders. The *Bulletins, Minutes, Proceedings, Annals* and other such effusions of horticultural societies, associations, and the like — especially those of rose-breeding areas — were written by specialists for specialists, and consequently contain obscure or minute facts of great interest to the specialists of the *present* day, though completely forgotten in the intervening "dark ages." In short, in this case it seems that to "point the way" is merely to point in all directions while sternly admonishing those who make it this far *not to stop here!* Some suggestions:

American Rose Annual, editions 1941–present. Harrisburg, Pennsylvania: American Rose Society.
Annales de la Société d'Horticulture de Paris. Paris: Mme Huzard.
Andrews, Henry C. 1805–1828. *Roses, or a Monograph . . .* London: Andrews.
Les Amis des Roses. 1897–ca. 1942, 1962–present. Lyon, France: Les Amis des Roses.
Belmont, Abel. 1896. *Dictionnaire Historique et Artistique de la Rose.* Melun: No impr.
Bessa, Pancrace. 1836. *Flore de Jardiniers . . .* Paris: Audot.
Biedenfeld, Freiherr Ferdinand L.C. von. 1847. *Das Buch der Rosen.* Weimar: No impr.
Boitard, Pierre. 1836. *Manuel Complet de l'Amateur des Roses . . .* Paris: Roret.
Bosanquet, Arthur Henry (as A. H. B.). 1845. *The Tree Rose.* London: No impr.
Brassac, François. *Annuaire Méridionale,* various years ca. 1880.
Buc'hoz, Pierre-Joseph. 1786. *Dissertation sur les Roses.* Paris: No impr.
Buc'hoz, Pierre-Joseph. 1804 & 1807. *Monographie de la Rose et de la Violette.* Paris: No impr.
Buist, Robert. 1855. *R. Buist's Catalogue . . .* Philadelphia: T.K. & P.G. Collins.
Le Censeur de Lyon. Ca. 1848.
Claxton, Écroyde. 1879. *Tea Roses and How to Grow Them.* Liverpool: William Potter.
De Pronville, Auguste. 1818. *Nomenclature Raisonée des Espèces, Variétés et Sous-Variétés du Genre Rosier . . .* Paris: Mme Huzard.
Desportes, Narcisse Henri François. 1829. *Roses Cultivées en France . . .* Paris: No impr.
Desportes, Narcisse Henri François. 1828. *Rosetum Gallicum.* Le Mans, France: Pesc.
Drapiez, Pierre A.J. 1828–1835. *Herbier de l'Amateur de Fleurs.* Brussels: de Mat.
Dupuis, Aristide. 1865. Une Visite aux Pépinières de M. André Leroy à Angers (from periodical *La Patrie*).
Dupuis, Aristide, & Hérincq, François. 1871. *Horticulture . . .* Paris: Guérin
The Florist & Pomologist. Issues of 1849 and later. London.
Forney, Eugène. 1875. *La Taille du Rosier.* Paris: Goin
The Garden. Issues 1876 and later. London.
Geschwindt, Rudolf. 1864–1885. *Die Hybridization und Sämlingszücht der Rosen.* Vienna: Zamarski & Dittmarsch.
Geschwindt, Rudolf. 1884. *Die Theerose und Ihre Bastarde.* Leipzig: Voight.
Godefroy. *Catalogue des Rosiers . . .* 1823.
Hérincq, François, & Jacques, Antoine. 1845–1857. *Flore des Jardins de l'Europe.* Paris: Libr. Agr.
L'Horticulteur Belge 1833. Brussels.
L'Horticulteur Chalonnais. Ca. 1840? Chalon-sur-Saône.
L'Horticulteur Provençal. Ca. 1850?
L'Horticulteur Universel. 1839–1847. Paris: Cousin.
Hy, Abbé F. 1904. *Sur les Roses Hybrides de l'Anjou.* Angers: No impr.
Jacques, Antoine A. & Hérincq, François. 1847. *Manuel des Plantes.* Paris: Libr. Agr.
Jullien, Th. P. 1863. *La Rose; étude Historique . . .* Rheims: No impr.
Kannegiesser, Friedrich-August. 1804. *Die Gattung der Rosen.* Freiburg, Germany: No impr.
Komlosy, Franz. 1868–1872. *Rosenalbum.* Vienna: Sommer.
Lachaume, Jean. 1874. *Le Rosier . . .* Paris: Bibl. du Jardinier.
Lelieur, M. J.-B. 1811. *De la Culture du Rosier.* Paris: Didot.

Lyon-Horticole. Lyon, France.

Malo, Charles. 1818. _Histoire des Roses._ Paris: Didot.

Maxwell (T. C.) & Bros. 1860. _Descriptive Catalogue_ . . .

McIntosh, Charles. 1829–1832. _Flora & Pomona._ London: Kelly.

Nestel, H. 1866–1879. _Nestels Rosengarten._ Stuttgart: No impr.

Nouveau Jardinier Illustré. No date. Paris: Libr. Cent. d'Agr.

Paul, William. Various dates. _The Rose Garden,_ editions 2–9. London.

Perrault, Pierre. 1894. _La Rose-Thé._ Paris: Charpentier & Fasquelle.

Pirolle. 1824–1825. _L'Horticulteur Français._ Paris: Roret.

Prévost fils. 1829–1830. _Catalogue descriptif, méthodique et raisoné_ . . . Rouen: Periaux.

Prince, William. 1822. _Catalogue._ . . . New York: T&J Swords.

Proceedings of the IX All India Rose Convention. 1988. Lucknow, India.

Revue Horticole. Issues 1878–present. Paris, etc.

Rivers, Thomas. 1837. _A Descriptive Catalogue of Roses_ . . . London: Rivers.

Rivers, Thomas. Various dates. _The Rose-Amateur's Guide,_ editions other than nᵒ 8. London.

Rosen-Zeitung. 1886–1933.

Shaw, Henry. 1879–1882. _The Rose_ . . . St. Louis, Missouri: Studley.

Sulzberger, Robert. 1888. _La Rose_ . . . Namur, Belgium: No impr.

Theunen, Auguste. 1893. _Guide à Usage des Amateurs de Roses._ Antwerp: No Impr.

Travaux du Comice Horticole de Maine et Loire, fl. 1840's.

Ungarische Rosen-Zeitung, fl. ca. 1890?

Vallot, Antoine. 1862. _Journal de la Santé du Roi Louis XIV._ Paris: Durand.

Ventenat, Etienne Pierre. 1803. _Choix des Plantes, dont la Plupart Sont Cultivées dans le Jardin de Cels._ Paris: Crapelet.

Welcome, Mrs. M. D. 1881. _An Essay_ . . . Yarmouth, Maine: No impr.

Beverly Dobson's yearly _Combined Rose List_ is the indispensible guide advising where one may obtain one's chosen varieties, old or new. Information on buying the booklet may be obtained by sending a stamped, self-addressed envelope to:

Beverly R. Dobson
215 Harriman Road
Irvington, New York 10533

INDEX

Items which are *not* cultivar names—names of breeders or such special subjects—are listed in **boldface**. Vignettes on breeders or related topics will usually be found in the notes on the cultivars named after them, or those of most significance in the breeder's output or most connected with the topic. Should a cultivar not seem to be listed, check under 'Mme —', 'Mlle —', 'Mons —', 'La —', 'Le —', 'Les —', 'Général —', 'Duchesse —', 'Mme la Duchesse —', etc., etc.; another thing to keep in mind is what might be called "foreign subversion" of names: *e.g.*, 'Kornelie Köch' for 'Cornelia Cook', 'Grand Duchess Hilda' for 'Grossherzogin Mathilde', or, as we often see, 'Duck of Fife' for 'Duke of Fife', and the like. Needless to say, we urge *all*—professional and amateur alike—to use the full name of the cultivar *always*, be it in writing or conversation, in the cause of clarity and *against* the cause of ambiguity.

A

'A. Bouquet', 60
'A. Drawiel', 149
'A. Geoffrey de St.-Hilaire', 149
'A.-M. Ampère', 149
'Abbé André Reitter', 273
'Abbé Berlèze', 149
'Abbé Bramerel', 149
'Abbé Garroute', 60
'Abbé Giraudier', 149
'Abbé Millot', 273
'Abel Carrière', 122
'Abel Grand', 150
'Abondant', 251
'Abraham Zimmermann', 150
'Abricotée', 60
'Achille Cesbron', 150
'Achille Gonod', 150
'Acidalie', 104
'Adam', 42
'Adam Messerich', 95
'Adam Rackles', 273
'Adélaïde de Meynot', 150
'Adèle de Bellabre', 60
'Adele Frey', 226
'Adèle Jougant', 234
'Adèle Pradel', 42
'Adèle Mauzé', 23
'Adiantifolia', 150
'Admiral Dewey', 273
'Adrien Schmitt', 150
'Adrienne Christophle', 226
'Adrienne de Cardoville', 104
'Aimé Plantier', 56
'Aimée Vibert', 203
'Aimée Vibert, Cl.', 203
'Aimée Vibert Jaune', 219
'Alba Rosea', 42
'Alberich', 242
'Albert Hoffmann', 61
'Albert La Blotais', 150
'Albert La Blotais, Cl.', 226
'Albert Payé', 150
'Albert Stopford', 61
'Alexandra', 91
'Alexander Hill Gray', 42
'Alexandre Chomer', 150
'Alexandre Dumas', 150
'Alexandre Dupont', 150
'Alexandre Dutitre', 150

'Alexandre Pelletier', 109
'Alexis Lapère', 150
'Alfred Colomb', 122
'Alfred K. Williams', 123
'Alfred Leveau', 186
'Ali Pacha Chériff', 151
'Alice Hamilton', 35
'Alice Hoffmann', 35
'Aline Rozey', 151
'Aline Sisley', 61
'Alister Stella Gray', 204
'Alix Roussel', 61
'Alliance Franco-Russe', 61
'Alpaïde de Rotallier', 151
'Alphonse Soupert', 151
'Alphonse de Lamartine', 151
'Alphonse Karr', 61
'Alsace-Lorraine', 151
'Amateur André Fourcaud', 273
'Amazone', 61
'Ambrogio Maggi', 151
'Amédée de Langlois', 104
'Amédée Philibert', 151
'American Banner', 61
'American Beauty', 123
'American Beauty, Cl.', 204
'American Belle', 151
'Ami Charmet', 151
'Ami Martin', 151
'Amiral Courbet', 151
'Amiral Gravina', 151
'Anaïse', 116
'Andenken an Moritz von Frohlich', 273
'André Leroy d'Angers', 151
'André Schwartz', 61
Andry (Monsieur), 213
'Anna Alexieff', 123
'Anna de Diesbach', 123
'Anna Jung', 62
'Anna Olivier', 42
'Anna Olivier, Cl.', 226
'Anna Scharsach', 152
'Ännchen Müller', 251
'Anne Laferrère', 152
'Anne-Marie Côte', 226
'Anne Marie de Montravel', 242
'Annie Cook', 62
'Annie Vibert', 204
'Antoine Ducher', 124
'Antoine Mouton', 152

—*Some Numbers*—

Of *Damask Perpetuals* in this book, there are entries for 42
Of *Chinas,* 75
Of *Teas,* 424
Of *Bourbons,* 143
Of *Hybrid Bourbons, Hybrid Chinas,* and *Hybrid Noisettes,* 55
Of *Hybrid Perpetuals,* 831
Of *Noisettes* and *Climbers,* 307
Of *Polyanthas,* 213
Of *Hybrid Teas,* 242
Making a **Total** of **2,332** entries.

"Vive l'Horticulture! Vive la Rose!" [P2]

———✳———